The New Millennium Reader

Third Edition

Stuart Hirschberg
Rutgers University

Terry Hirschberg

Prentice
Hall

Upper Saddle River, New Jersey 07458

Hirschberg, Stuart.
   The new millennium reader / [compiled by] Stuart Hirschberg, Terry Hirschberg.—3rd ed.
      p. cm.
   ISBN 0-13-097991-0
   1. College readers. 2. English language—Rhetoric—Problems, exercises, etc. 3. Report writing—
Problems, exercises, etc. I. Hirschberg, Terry. II. Title.

   PE1417.H53 2002
   808'.0427—dc21

                                                                    2001044799

For Tony English

VP, Editor-in-Chief: Leah Jewell
Senior Acquisitions Editor: Corey Good
Editorial Assistant: John Ragozzine
VP, Director of Production and Manufacturing: Barbara Kittle
Senior Managing Editor: Mary Rottino
Production Editor: Randy Pettit
Prepress and Manufacturing Manager: Nick Sklitsis
Prepress and Manufacturing Buyer: Sherry Lewis
Director of Marketing: Beth Mejia
Senior Marketing Manager: Brandy Dawson
Marketing Assistant: Chrissy Moodie
Cover Design Director: Jayne Conte
Cover Art: Vincent McIndoe, Stock Illustration Source, Inc.
Director, Image Resource Center: Melinda Reo
Interior Image Specialist: Beth Boyd-Brenzel
Photo Researcher: Debra Hewitson
Manager, Rights and Permissions: Kay Dellosa

For permission to use copyrighted material, grateful
acknowledgment is made to the copyright holders listed
on page 709–711, which is considered an extension of this
copyright page.

This book was set in 10/12 Bembo by Lithokraft II
and was printed and bound by Courier Companies, Inc.
The cover was printed by The Lehigh Press, Inc.

ISBN: 0-13-097991-0

Pearson Education LTD., London
Pearson Education Australia PTY, Limited, Sydney
Pearson Education Singapore, Pte. Ltd
Pearson Education North Asia Ltd, Hong Kong
Pearson Education Canada, Ltd., Toronto
Pearson Educación de Mexico, S.A. de C.V.
Pearson Education - Japan, Tokyo
Pearson Education Malaysia, Pte. Ltd
Pearson Education, Upper Saddle River, New Jersey

CONTENTS

2   INFLUENTIAL PEOPLE AND MEMORABLE PLACES   85

Nonfiction

Fiction

Poetry

Connections for Chapter 2: Influential People and Memorable Places   145

3   THE VALUE OF EDUCATION   147

Nonfiction

5   ISSUES IN POPULAR CULTURE   252

Nonfiction

Fiction

Poetry

Drama

Connections for Chapter 5: Issues in Popular Culture   314

6   OUR PLACE IN NATURE   316

Nonfiction

Fiction

Poetry

7   HISTORY IN THE MAKING   372

Nonfiction

Fiction

Poetry

11 MATTERS OF ETHICS, PHILOSOPHY, AND RELIGION 614

Nonfiction

Fiction

Parables

Poetry

Connections for Chapter 11: Matters of Ethics, Philosophy, and Religion 706

RHETORICAL CONTENTS

NARRATION

Personal Narration

Observation and Reporting

DESCRIPTION

ILLUSTRATION AND EXAMPLE

COMPARISON AND CONTRAST

PROCESS ANALYSIS

CLASSIFICATION

ANALOGY

CAUSE AND EFFECT

DEFINITION

PROBLEM SOLVING

ARGUMENTATION AND PERSUASION

AUTOBIOGRAPHY

BIOGRAPHY

IRONY, HUMOR, AND SATIRE

SPEECHES

PREFACE

The third edition of *The New Millennium Reader* is intended for freshman composition, intermediate and advanced composition course, and courses that consider the essay as a form of literature.

The book introduces students to major traditions in essay writing and explores the relationship between the writer's voice and stylistic features that express the writer's attitude toward his or her personal experiences. The text also provides guidance for students in developing skills in critical reading and writing.

The New Millennium Reader, Third Edition, provides thought-provoking and engaging models of writing by major scholars, researchers, and scientists that show writing is essential to learning in all academic fields of study.

The eighty-two nonfiction selections (thirty-three of which are new to this edition) have been chosen for their interest, reading level, and length and include a broad range of topics, authors, disciplines, and cross-cultural perspectives.

Besides the number and diversity of the selections and the wide range of topics and styles represented, quite a few of the longer readings are included because of the value that more extensive readings have in allowing students to observe the development of ideas and to enhance their own skills in reading comprehension and writing their own essays.

These readings shed light on myriad subjects, from Tutankhamen's tomb to genetic engineering, from the sinking of the *Titanic* to Mick Jagger on tour and the Internet, from the American Civil War to the Cultural Revolution in China, from Niagara Falls to the eruption of Mt. St. Helens, from autism to advertising, from popular culture to the environment, and other significant topics.

The book is thematically organized in order to bridge the gap between the expressive essays students traditionally read and their own life experiences. Selections draw from memoirs, scholarly essays, and biographies illustrate how writers move through, and beyond, personal experiences and adapt what they write to different audiences.

The book includes 134 selections by classical, modern, and contemporary authors whose work, in many cases, provides the foundation of the broader intellectual heritage of a college education.

Chapters are organized by themes that have traditionally elicited compelling expressive essays and thoughtful arguments and include accounts of personal growth, nature writing, prison literature, and narratives of religious and philosophical exploration. *The New Millennium Reader* is rich in a variety of perspectives by African American, Native American, Asian American, and Hispanic writers and offers cross-cultural and regional works as well as a core of selections by authors, of which 44 percent are women.

The eighteen short stories (six of which are new to this edition), twenty-nine poems (eight of which are new), and three dramas, including one new play, amplify the themes in each chapter in ways that introduce students to techniques and forms that writers have traditionally used in the fields of fiction, poetry, and drama.

NEW TO THIS EDITION

In addition to the thirty-two new essays, six new short stories, eight new poems, and one new drama, we have created new chapters that emphasize popular culture (Chapter 5) and the environment (Chapter 6).

We have added questions ("Connections") following each of the eleven chapters that challenge readers to make connections and comparisons between selections within the chapter and throughout the book. These "connections" can be thought of as a kind of conversation between the authors and their readers. These questions provide opportunities to consider additional perspectives on a single theme or to explore a particular issue or topic in depth.

We have strengthened the representation of argument by increasing the number and type of argumentative pieces throughout the text, and we have enlarged the discussion of argumentation and persuasion in the Introduction.

CHAPTER DESCRIPTIONS

The eleven chapters move from the sphere of reflections on personal experience, family life, influential people and memorable places, the value of education and perspectives on language, to consider issues in popular culture, our place in nature, history in the making, the pursuit of justice, the impact of technology, the artistic impulse, and matters of ethics, philosophy, and religion.

Chapter 1, "Reflections on Experience," introduces candid, introspective reminiscences by writers who want to understand the meaning of important personal events that proved to be decisive turning points in their lives.

Chapter 2, "Influential People and Memorable Places," introduces portraits of people important to the writers, presents an invaluable opportunity to study the methods biographers use, and explores the role that landscapes and natural and architectural wonders have played in the lives of the writers.

Chapter 3, "The Value of Education," attests to the value of literacy and looks at the role education plays in different settings as a vehicle for self-discovery and at questions raised by censorship and the Internet.

Chapter 4, "Perspectives on Language," explores the social impact of language, the importance of being able to communicate, and the dangers of language used to manipulate attitudes, beliefs, and emotions, whether in propaganda, in advertising, or in pornography.

Chapter 5, "Issues in Popular Culture," touches on broad issues of contemporary concern, including child abuse, consumerism here and abroad, television news, eating disorders, the significance of urban legends, the treatment of the elderly, AIDS and the Hispanic community, racism, and the national inability to solve problems without resorting to "quick fixes."

Chapter 6, "Our Place in Nature," looks at the tradition of nature writing; offers investigations of animal behavior and the ecosystems of oceans, mountains, and tropical forests, and explores the complex interactions of living things.

Chapter 7, "History in the Making," brings to life important social, economic, and political events of the past and addresses the question of how historians shape our perceptions of the past in ways that influence the present.

Chapter 8, "The Pursuit of Justice," draws on firsthand testimonies by writers whose accounts combine eyewitness reports, literary texts, and historical records in the continuing debate over the allegiance that individuals owe their government and the protection of individual rights that citizens expect in return.

Chapter 9, "The Impact of Technology," examines the extent of our culture's dependence on technology and the mixed blessings that scientific innovations, including cyberspace and genetic engineering, will bequeath to future generations.

Chapter 10, "The Artistic Impulse," considers how artists deepen and enrich our knowledge of human nature and experience and how art changes from age to age and culture to culture.

Chapter 11, "Matters of Ethics, Philosophy, and Religion," focuses on universal questions of faith and good and evil, and on basic questions about the meaning and value of life as applied to specific contemporary issues of animal research, Eastern and Western methods of punishment, religious tenets and taboos, ethics and personal choice, and the allocation of environmental resources.

EDITORIAL APPARATUS

An introduction, "Reading in the Various Genres," discusses the crucial skills of reading for ideas and organization and introduces students to the basic rhetorical techniques writers use in developing their essays. This introduction also shows students how to approach important elements in appreciating and analyzing short fiction, poetry, and drama.

Chapter introductions discuss the theme of each chapter and its relation to the individual selections. Biographical sketches preceding each selection give background information on the writer's life and identify the personal and literary context in which the selection was written.

Questions for discussion and writing at the end of each selection are designed to encourage readers to discover relationships between their own experiences and those described by the writers in the text, to explore points of agreement in areas of conflict sparked by the viewpoint of the authors, and to provide ideas for further inquiry and writing. These questions ask students to think critically about the content, meaning, and purpose of the selections, and to evaluate the authors' rhetorical strategy, the voice projected in relationship to the author's audience, the evidence cited, and the underlying assumptions. These writing suggestions afford opportunities for personal and expressive writing as well as expository and persuasive writing.

A new set of connection questions at the end of each chapter links each selection with other readings in that chapter and with readings throughout the book to afford students the opportunity to explore multiple perspectives on the same topic.

A rhetorical contents is included to enhance the usefulness of the text by permitting students to study the form (the rhetorical mode employed) of the selections as well as their content and themes.

INSTRUCTOR'S MANUAL

An accompanying Instructor's Manual provides (1) guidance for teaching fiction and nonfiction, (2) sample syllabi and suggestions for organizing courses with different kinds of focus (argumentation, cultural studies, writing across the curriculum, etc.), (3) background information about each essay and definitions of terms that may be unfamiliar to students, (4) detailed answers to the discussion and writing questions, (5) additional essay topics for writing and research, (6) supplemental resources (bibliographies, websites, etc.) for students who wish to pursue further any of the authors or issues, (7) filmography for instructors who wish to use films and videos connected to particular selections, (8) additional writing assignments that connect selections within the chapter and throughout the book, and (9) alternative tables of contents by secondary themes, disciplines, and subjects.

ACKNOWLEDGMENTS

No expression of thanks can adequately convey our gratitude to all those teachers of composition who offered thoughtful comments and suggestions on changes for this edition: Jason Horn, Gordon College; Robert Eddy, Fayetteville State University; Anna Riehl, University of Illinois at Chicago; Cornelia E. V. Wells, William Paterson University; Lynn West, Spokane Community College; Deborah Kirkman, University of Kentucky.

We thank Corey Good, who did not miss a beat in taking on this project, and whose enthusiasm made it a pleasure to work on this third edition.

For their dedication and skill, we owe much to the able staff at Prentice Hall, especially to Randy Pettit for his usual outstanding work as Production Editor, and for his patience and unfailing sense of humor. We would also like to thank Fred T. Courtright, Permissions Editor, for obtaining the rights to reprint selections in this text.

Stuart Hirschberg
Terry Hirschberg

INTRODUCTION: READING IN THE VARIOUS GENRES

READING ESSAYS

As a literary genre, the essay harks back to the form invented four hundred years ago by the French writer Michel Montaigne, who called his writings *essais* (attempts) because they were intended less as accounts of objective truth than as personal disclosures of a mind exploring its own attitudes, values, and assumptions on a diverse range of subjects. The essayist speaks directly without the mediation of imagined characters and events.

Essayists invite us to share the dramatic excitement of an observant and sensitive mind struggling to understand and clarify an issue that is of great importance to the writer. We feel the writer trying to reconcile opposing impulses to evolve a viewpoint that takes into account known facts as well as personal values.

Reading for Ideas and Organization

One of the most important skills to have is the ability to survey unfamiliar articles, essays, or excerpts and come away with an accurate understanding of what the author wanted to communicate and of how the material is organized. On the first and in subsequent readings of any of the selections in this text, especially the longer ones, pay particular attention to the title, look closely at the introductory and concluding paragraphs (with special emphasis on the author's statement or restatement of central ideas), identify the headings and subheadings (and determine the relationship between these and the title), and locate any unusual terms necessary to fully understand the author's concepts.

As you first read through an essay, you might look for cues that enable you to recognize the main parts or help you to perceive its overall organization. Once you find the main thesis, underline it. Then work your way through fairly rapidly, identifying the main ideas and the sequence in which they are presented. As you identify an important idea, ask yourself how this idea relates to the thesis statement you underlined or to the idea expressed in the title.

Finding a Thesis

Finding a thesis involves discovering the idea that serves as the focus of the essay. The thesis is often stated in the form of a single sentence that asserts the author's response to an issue that others might respond to in different ways. For example, in "The Lowest Animal" (Ch. 6), Mark Twain presents his assessment of human nature:

1

> In the course of my experiments I convinced myself that among the animals man is the only one that harbors insults and injuries, broods over them, waits till a chance offers, then takes revenge. The passion of revenge is unknown to the higher animals.

The thesis represents the writer's view of a subject or topic from a certain perspective. Here Twain states a view that serves as a focus for his essay.

Writers often place the thesis in the first paragraph or group of paragraphs so that the readers will be able to perceive the relationship between the supporting evidence and this main idea.

As you read, you might wish to underline the topic sentence or main idea of each paragraph or section (since key ideas are often developed over the course of several paragraphs). Jot it down in your own words in the margins, identify supporting statements and evidence (such as examples, statistics, and the testimony of authorities), and try to discover how the author organizes the material to support the development of important ideas. To identify supporting material, look for any ideas more specific than the main idea that is used to support it.

Pay particular attention to important transitional words, phrases, or paragraphs to better see the relationships among major sections of the selection. Noticing how certain words or phrases act as transitions to link paragraphs or sections together will dramatically improve your reading comprehension. Also look for section summaries, where the author draws together several preceding ideas.

Writers use certain words to signal the starting point of a chain of reasoning. If you detect any of the following terms, look for the main idea they introduce:

since	as shown by	for the reason that
because	inasmuch as	may be inferred from
for	otherwise	may be derived from
as	as indicated by	may be deduced from
follows from	the reason is that	in view of the fact that

An especially important category of words includes signals that the author will be stating a conclusion. Words to look for are the following:

therefore	in summary
hence	which shows that
thus	which means that
so	and which entails
accordingly	consequently
in consequence	proves that
it follows that	as a result
we may infer	which implies that
I conclude that	which allows us to infer
in conclusion	points to the conclusion that

You may find it helpful to create a running dialogue with the author in the margins, posing and then trying to answer the basic questions *who, what, where, when*, and *why*, and to note your observations on how the main idea of the article is related to the title. You can later use these notes to evaluate how effectively any specific section contributes to the overall line of thought.

Organization of the Essay   Writers use a variety of means to attract readers' interest, at the same time explicitly stating or at least implying the probable thesis. Some writers find that a brief story or anecdote is an ideal way to focus the audience's attention on the subject, as does Jill Nelson in "Number One!" (Ch. 1):

> That night I dream about my father, but it is really more a memory than a dream. "Number one! Not two! Number one!" my father intones from the head of the breakfast table. The four of us sit at attention, two on each side of the ten-foot teak expanse, our brown faces rigid. At the foot, my mother looks up at my father, the expression on her face a mixture of pride, anxiety and could it be, boredom? I am twelve. It is 1965.

Other writers use the strategy of opening with an especially telling or apt quotation. Writers may also choose to introduce their essays in many other ways, by defining key terms, offering a prediction, posing a thoughtful question, or providing a touch of humor.

Even though the introductory paragraph is the most logical place to state the thesis, one can also expect to find the central assertion of the essay in the title, as, for example, in William A. Henry III's argument, "In Defense of Elitism" (Ch. 3), which decries what he perceives to be a lowering of national educational standards in the interest of encouraging everyone to attend college.

The main portion of the essay presents and develops the main points the writer wishes to communicate. A wide range of strategies may be used, depending on the kind of point the writer is making and the form the supporting evidence takes to demonstrate the likelihood of the writer's thesis.

The conclusion of an essay may serve a variety of purposes. The writer may restate the thesis after reviewing the most convincing points or close with an appeal to the needs and values of the specific audience. This sense of closure can be achieved in many different ways. For instance, the conclusion can echo the ideas stated in the opening paragraph, or it can present a compelling image. Other writers choose to end on a note of reaffirmation and challenge or with irony or a striking paradox. The most traditional ending sums up points raised in the essay, although usually not in as impressive a fashion, as does David Rothenberg's ending in "How the Web Destroys the Quality of Students' Research Papers" (Ch. 3):

> Knowledge does not emerge in a vacuum, but we do need silence and space for sustained thought. Next semester, I'm going to urge my students to turn off their glowing boxes and think, if only once in a while.

Supporting Evidence   An important part of critical reading depends on your ability to identify and evaluate how the writer develops the essay in order to support the thesis. The most common patterns of thinking are known as the *rhetorical modes*. For example, writers might describe how something looks, narrate an experience, analyze how something works, provide examples, define important terms, create a classification, compare and contrast, create an analogy, or explore what caused something. To clarify and support the thesis, writers also use a wide variety of evidence, including examples drawn from personal experience, the testimony of experts, statistical data, and case histories.

Describing   Writers use descriptions for a variety of purposes, ranging from portraying the appearance of people, objects, events, or scenes to revealing the writer's feelings and reactions to those people, objects, events, or scenes. Gayle Pemberton (in "Antidisestablishmentarianism," Ch. 2) accomplishes this in her description of her grandmother, an intimidating woman who taught Pemberton to be independent and think for herself:

> She disliked white people, black people in the aggregate and pretty much individually too, children—particularly female children—her daughter, her husband, my mother, Episcopalianism, Catholicism, Judaism and Dinah Shore. She had a hot temper and a mean streak. . . . Grandma scared the daylights out of me.

We learn that her grandmother's curmudgeon-like attitude proved invaluable in helping Pemberton deal with the white society in which she grew up.

Perhaps the most useful method of arranging details within a description is the technique of focusing on an impression that dominates the entire scene. This main impression can center on a prominent physical feature, a tower or church steeple, or a significant psychological trait, such as Pemberton's grandmother's "take no shit" attitude. A skillful writer will often arrange a description around this central impression, in much the same way a good photographer will locate a focal point for pictures. Jack London, who was a journalist and novelist, uses this technique in his description of how San Francisco residents reacted to the devastating earthquake of 1906 in "The San Francisco Earthquake" (Ch. 7).

> Before the flames, throughout the night, fled tens of thousands of homeless ones. Some were wrapped in blankets. Others carried bundles of bedding and dear household treasures. Sometimes a whole family was harnessed to a carriage or delivery wagon that was weighted down with their possessions. Baby buggies, toy wagons, and go-carts were used as trucks, while every other person was dragging a trunk. Yet everybody was gracious. The most perfect courtesy obtained. Never, in all San Francisco's history, were her people so kind and courteous as on this night of terror.

A wealth of specific descriptive details re-creates the sights and sounds of the conflagration. Yet, the primary impression London communicates is that the citizens of San Francisco displayed forbearance and rare courtesy toward one another in the most trying of circumstances.

Description is more effective when the writer arranges details to produce a certain effect, such as suspense, empathy, or surprise.

The archaeologist Howard Carter uses this technique in "Finding the Tomb" (Ch. 7) to re-create the tension he and his crew felt at the actual moment when, after many years of research and excavations, the long-sought tomb of Tutankhamen was finally unearthed:

> At first I could see nothing, the hot air escaping from the chamber causing the candle flame to flicker, but presently, as my eyes grew accustomed to the light, details of the room within emerged slowly from the mist, strange animals, statues, and gold—everywhere the glint of gold. For the moment—an eternity it must have seemed to the others standing by—I was struck dumb with amazement, and when Lord Carnarvon, unable to stand the suspense any longer, inquired anxiously, "Can you see anything?" it was all I could do to get out the words. "Yes, wonderful things."

Carter introduces one detail after another to heighten suspense about whether the tomb was still intact or had been previously ransacked by robbers. The description is arranged to transport the readers into the scene so that they see what Carter saw on that day—concealed treasures gradually emerging out of the darkness.

Narrating Another essential technique often used by writers is narration. Narrative relates a series of events or a significant experience by telling about it in chronological order. The events related through narrative can entertain, inform, or dramatize an important moment. For example, in "West with the Night" (Ch. 1), Beryl Markham tells us of the moment on her epic cross-Atlantic flight when she faced a life-and-death decision. By relating the events of the flight as they led to this crucial moment, Markham provides her readers with a coherent framework in which to interpret the events of her story.

Effective narration focuses on a single significant action that dramatically changes the relationship of the writer (or main character) to family, friends, or environment. A significant experience may be defined as a situation in which something important to the writer or to the people he is writing about is at stake.

Narratives are usually written from the first-person point of view, as in the case of Beryl Markham:

> It is dark already and I am over the south of Ireland. There are the lights of Cork and the lights are wet; they are drenched in Irish rain, and I am above them and dry.

Events can also be related through a second-person point of view ("you") or through a more objective third-person ("he," "she," "they") point of view.

Narration can take the form of an anecdote (such as Markham's) or as a historical account synthesized from journals, logs, diaries, and even interviews, such as that compiled by Hanson W. Baldwin (in "R.M.S. *Titanic,*" Ch. 7). Baldwin's account of the events leading up to and after the moment when the *Titanic* struck an iceberg is shaped to emphasize the poignancy and irony of this catastrophe. For example, Baldwin recounts the following event:

> 12:45 A.M. Murdock, in charge on the starboard side, eyes tragic, but calm and cool, orders boat No. 7 lowered. The women hang back: they want no boat ride on an

ice-strewn sea; the *Titanic* is unsinkable. The men encourage them, explain that this is just a precautionary measure: "We'll see you again at breakfast."

We notice how skillfully Baldwin creates a composite that includes the actions of those who were there along with what was actually said at the time. Baldwin uses narration to summarize, explain, interpret, and dramatize an important moment in history.

Narratives offer writers means by which they can discover the meaning of experiences through the process of writing about them. For Mikhal Gilmore (in "My Brother, Gary Gilmore," Ch. 2), the need to understand his family history became an overpowering motivation that led him to write his autobiography:

> Over the years, many people have judged me by my brother's actions as if in coming from a family that yielded a murderer I must be formed by the same causes, the same sins, must by my brother's actions be responsible for the violence that resulted, and bear the mark of a frightening and shameful heritage. It's as if there is guilt in the fact of the blood-line itself. Maybe there is.

In these more personal, autobiographical narratives (see, for example, Fritz Peters, Jill Nelson, Richard Rhodes, Raymond Carver, Annie Dillard, and Mikhal Gilmore), the need to clarify and interpret one's past requires the writer to reconstruct the meaning and significance of experiences *whose importance may not have been appreciated at the time they occurred.*

Just as individuals can discover the meaning of past experiences through the process of writing about them, so writers use narration to focus on important moments of collective self-revelation. Golda Meir, former prime minister of Israel, employs a full spectrum of narrative techniques in "We Have Our State" (Ch. 8) to re-create the moment when Israel became a state on May 14, 1948. Meir draws on records and eyewitness accounts (including her own memories) from this moment in 1948 for specific, important details to re-create the scene for her readers, and she summarizes the necessary background information in order to set the stage for this historic moment.

Illustrating with Examples   Providing good examples is an essential part of effective writing. A single well-chosen example or a range of illustrations can provide clear cases that illustrate, document, and substantiate a writer's thesis. The report of a memorable incident, an account drawn from records, eyewitness reports, and a personal narrative account of a crucial incident are all important ways examples can document the authenticity of the writer's thesis.

One extremely effective way of substantiating a claim is by using a case history, that is, an in-depth account of the experiences of one person that typifies the experience of many people in the same situation.

John Hersey, a journalist, uses this technique in his historic account of six survivors of Hiroshima, "A Noiseless Flash from Hiroshima" (Ch. 7). The experiences of these six people stand for the experiences of untold thousands who were in Hiroshima the day the atomic bomb was dropped. In each case, Hersey begins by identifying the person and then tells us about the events that occurred in that person's life a few minutes before the bomb exploded:

> At exactly fifteen minutes past eight in the morning, on August 6, 1945, Japanese time, at the moment when the atomic bomb flashed above Hiroshima, Miss Toshiko Sasaki, a clerk in the personnel department of the East Asia Tin Works, had just sat down at her place in the plant office and was turning her head to speak to the girl at the next desk. At that same moment, Dr. Masakazu Fujii was settling down cross-legged to read the Osaka *Asahi* on the porch of his private hospital. . . . Mrs. Hatsuyo Nakamura, a tailor's widow, stood by the window of her kitchen. Father Wilhelm Kleinsorge, a German priest of the Society of Jesus, reclined in his underwear on a cot. . . . Dr. Terufumi Sasaki, a young member of the surgical staff . . . walked along one of the hospital corridors . . . and the Reverend Mr. Kiyoshi Tanimoto . . . paused at the door of a rich man's house in Koi. . . . A hundred thousand people were killed by the atomic bomb, and these six were among the survivors.

By selecting six people to represent the thousands who survived Hiroshima, Hersey brings into human terms an event that otherwise would be beyond the reader's comprehension. Exemplification is extremely effective in allowing Hersey's readers to generalize from what these six individuals experienced to what all the people in Hiroshima suffered that day.

Defining   Yet another rhetorical pattern often used by writers is definition. Definition is a useful way of specifying the basic nature of any phenomenon, idea, or thing. Definition is the method of clarifying the meaning of key terms, either in the thesis or elsewhere in the essay. For example, as part of her analysis of current research in genetic engineering ("Monsters of the Brave New World," Ch. 9), Carol Grunewald writes:

> Experiments have already produced a few animal monstrosities. "Geeps," part goat, part sheep, have been engineered through the process of cell-fusion—mixing cells of goat and sheep embryos.

In some cases, writers may need to develop an entire essay to explore all the connotations and meanings accrued by an unusual or controversial term or to challenge preconceptions attached to a familiar term, as Haunani-Kay Trask does for the term *aloha* in "From a Native Daughter" (Ch 7.):

> Social connections between our people are through *aloha,* simply translated as "love" but carrying with it a profoundly Hawaiian sense that is . . . familial and genealogical.

Besides eliminating ambiguity or defining a term important to the development of the essay, definitions can be used persuasively to influence the perceptions or stir the emotions of the reader about a particular issue. Definition of controversial terms not only characterizes the terms but effectively shapes how people perceive the issue (see, for example, Alison Lurie's broadening of the meaning of the term *language* in her article "The Language of Clothes," Ch. 4).

Dividing and Classifying   Writers also divide and classify a subject on the basis of important similarities. Classification is used to sort, group, and collect things into categories, or classes, that are based on one or more criteria. The criteria are features that members of the group all have in common. The purposes of the classifier determine which specific features are selected as the basis of the classification. Thus, classification is, first and foremost, an intellectual activity based on discovering generic characteristics shared by members of a group, according to the interests of the writer. Effective classifications shed light on the nature of what is being classified by identifying significant features, using these features as criteria in a systematic way, dividing phenomena into at least two different classes on the basis of these criteria, and presenting the results logically and consistently. For example, in "The Rhetoric of Advertising" (Ch. 4), Stuart Hirschberg classifies the techniques advertisers use according to the traditional rhetorical strategies identified by Artistotle:

> Seen in this way, ads appear as mini-arguments whose strategies and techniques of persuasion can be analyzed just like a written argument. We can discover which elements are designed to appeal to the audience's emotions (*pathos* according to Aristotle), which elements make their appeal in terms of reasons, evidence, or logic *(logos),* and how the advertiser goes about winning credibility . . . in terms of the spokesperson employed to speak on behalf of the product (the *ethos* dimension).

By being able to identify the specific techniques advertisers use, the author believes, we will be less likely to be manipulated into buying things we don't need.

Comparing and Contrasting   Another way of arranging a discussion of similarities and differences relies on the rhetorical method of comparison and contrast. Using this method, the writer compares and contrasts relevant points about one subject with corresponding aspects of another. Stephen Chapman uses this subject-by-subject method in "The Prisoner's Dilemma" (Ch. 12) in order to analyze and evaluate the differences in methods of punishment used in Eastern and Western societies. He first describes the typical forms of punishment for offenses in several Muslim countries:

> Flogging, or *ta'zir,* is the general punishment prescribed for offenses that don't carry an explicit Koranic penalty. Some crimes carry automatic *hadd* punishments—stoning or scourging (a severe whipping) for illicit sex, scourging for drinking alcoholic beverages, amputation of the hands for theft. Other crimes—as varied as murder and abandoning Islam—carry the death penalty (usually carried out in public).

Following his discussion of these Eastern methods of punishment, Chapman describes Western methods of punishment for similar crimes:

> Our custom is to confine criminals in prison for varying lengths of time. In Illinois, a reasonably typical state, grand theft involves a punishment of three to five years; armed robbery can get you from one to six. The lowest form of felony theft is punishable by one to three years in prison. Most states impose longer sentences on habitual offenders.

The comparative method serves Chapman well as a way of getting his audience to perceive basic differences between the two cultures and prepares his audience to confront the ultimate question "Would you rather lose a hand or spend ten years or more in a typical state prison?"

Comparisons may be arranged structurally in one of two ways. In one method, the writer discusses all the relevant points of one subject and then covers the same ground for the second. Writers may use transitional words like *although, however, but, on the other hand, instead of, different from,* and *as opposed to* to indicate contrast. Words used to show comparisons include *similarly, likewise,* and *in the same way.* Comparisons may also be arranged point by point to create a continual contrast from sentence to sentence between relevant aspects of two subjects. Comparisons may also evaluate two subjects. The writer contrasts sets of qualities and decides between the two on the basis of some stipulated criteria.

Dramatic contrast is a favorite device of satirists, who expose hypocrisy by reminding people of what they really do, as opposed to what they profess. In "The Lowest Animal" (Ch. 6), Mark Twain contrasts the behavior of humans with that of animals in comparable situations in order to deflate the high opinion the human species has of itself. Each of Twain's "experiments" is meant to show the preponderance in humans of such traits as greed and cruelty, and to parody Darwin's theory (then currently popular) that humans were the apex of all living species.

Although Twain's "experiments" are hypothetical and meant to underscore ironic insights, the comparative technique is indispensable as a way of structuring real scientific experiments. Such is the case in a fascinating study reported by Constance Holden in "Identical Twins Reared Apart" (Ch. 9), which followed nine sets of identical twins who had been separated at birth, raised in different environments, and then reunited. Holden reports about when one of the sets of twins, Oskar and Jack, first saw each other:

> Similarities started cropping up as soon as Oskar arrived at the airport. Both were wearing wire-rimmed glasses and mustaches, both sported two-pocket shirts with epaulets. They shared idiosyncrasies galore: they like spicy foods and sweet liqueurs, are absentminded, have a habit of falling asleep in front of the television, think it's funny to sneeze in a crowd of strangers, flush the toilet before using it, store rubber bands on their wrists, read magazines from back to front, dip buttered toast in their coffee.

Holden's analysis of different characteristics and traits is developed through a point-by-point comparison of striking similarities in behavior between each of the nine sets of twins. For Holden, the number and range of similarities shared by each set of twins argues for the overwhelming importance of heredity, rather than environment, in shaping human behavior.

Figurative Comparisons and Analogies Figurative rather than literal comparisons reveal the writer's feelings about the subject. Figurative comparisons can take the form of metaphors that identify two different things with each other, as in Annie Dillard's description in "So, This Was Adolescence" (Ch. 1) ("I was what they called a live wire"), or through similes that use the words *like* or *as* to relate two seemingly unrelated things (for example, "ornament within ornament, and again in every ornament still another ornament, almost *like* jeweler's work," in P. D. Ouspensky's "The Taj Mahal," Ch. 2).

The ability to create compelling images in picturesque language is an important element in communicating a writer's thoughts, feelings, and experiences. Creating a vivid picture or image in an audience's mind requires writers to use metaphors, similes, and other figures of speech. Imagery works by evoking a vivid picture in the audience's imagination. A simile compares one object or experience to another by using *like* or *as*. A metaphor applies a word or phrase to an object it does not literally denote in order to suggest the comparison. To be effective, metaphors must look at things in a fresh light to let the reader see a familiar subject in a new way.

Analogy, which is a comparison between two basically different things that have some points in common, is an extraordinarily useful tool that writers use to clarify subjects that otherwise might prove to be difficult to understand, unfamiliar, or hard to visualize. The greater the numbers of similarities that the writer is able to draw between what the audience finds familiar and the newer complex idea the writer is trying to clarify, the more successful the analogy. For example, Garrett Hardin in "Lifeboat Ethics" (Ch. 11) compares an affluent country to a lifeboat that is already almost full of people and the immigrants of poor countries to people in the water who desperately wish to get into the lifeboat: "Since the boat has an unused excess capacity of ten more passengers, we could admit just ten more to it. But which ten do we let in?"

Hardin's tactics are based on getting his audience to agree that a country has a limited capacity to support a population, just as there are only so many sears in a lifeboat, and that if those begging for admission are taken into "our boat," the boat will swamp and everyone will drown.

In addition to clarifying abstract concepts and processes, analogies are ideally suited to transmit religious truths in the form of parables and metaphors. An aptly chosen metaphor can create a memorable image capable of conveying truth in a way that is permanent and vivid.

An effective analogy provides a way to shed new light on hidden, difficult, or complex ideas by relating them to everyday human experience. One of the most famous analogies ever conceived, Plato's "Allegory of the Cave" (Ch. 11), uses a series of comparisons to explore how lifelong conditioning deludes people into mistaking illusions for reality.

> Behold! Human beings living in an underground den, which had a mouth open toward the light and reaching all along the den; here they have been from their childhood, and have their legs and necks chained so that they cannot move, and can only see before them, being prevented by the chains from turning around their heads. Above and behind them is a fire blazing at a distance.

Plato explains that in this den the prisoners, who have never seen anything outside the cave, mistake shadows cast on the wall by reflected firelight for realities. If some were free to leave the cave, they would be dazzled by the sunlight. It is ironic, says Plato, that once their eyes had adjusted to the light, they would be unable, if they then returned to the cave, to see as well as the others. Moreover, if they persisted in trying to lead their fellow prisoners out of the cave into the light, the others would find their claim of greater light outside the cave ridiculous. Thus, each element in the analogy—the fire, the prisoners, the shadows, the dazzling light—offers an unparalleled means for grasping the Platonic ideal of truth as a greater reality beyond the illusory shadows of what we mistake as the "real" world.

Thus, analogies are extraordinarily useful to natural and social scientists, poets, and philosophers as an intellectual strategy and rhetorical technique for clarifying difficult subjects, explaining unfamiliar terms and processes, transmitting religious truths through parables, and spurring creativity in problem solving by opening the mind to new ways of looking at things.

Process Analysis   One of the most effective ways to clarify the nature of something is to explain how it works. Process analysis divides a complex procedure into separate and easy-to-understand steps in order to explain how something works, how something happened, or how an action should be performed. Process analysis requires the writer to include all necessary steps in the procedure and to demonstrate how each step is related to preceding and subsequent steps in the overall sequence. To be effective, process analysis should emphasize the significance of each step in the overall sequence and help the reader understand how each step emerges from the preceding stage and flows into the next.

For example, in "To Make Them Stand in Fear" (Ch. 7), Kenneth M. Stampp, a noted historian, investigates a past era in our country's history when blacks were brought to America as slaves. Stampp analyzes the instructions given by manuals that told slaveowners, step-by-step, how to break the spirit of newly transported blacks in order to change them into "proper" slaves:

> Here, then, was the way to produce the perfect slave: accustom him to rigid discipline, demand from him unconditional submission, impress upon him his innate inferiority, develop in him a paralyzing fear of white men, train him to adopt the master's code of good behavior, and instill in him a sense of complete dependence. This, at least, was the goal.

Stampp's analysis of source documents reveals that slaveowners used behavior modification techniques to produce "respectful" and "docile" slaves. The process began with a series of measures designed to enforce external discipline. Later on, attention shifted to measures designed to encourage psychological conditioning so that, in theory at least, the slave would control himself or herself through internalized perceptions of inferiority.

Causal Analysis   Whereas process analysis explains *how* something works, causal analysis seeks to discover *why* something happened, or why it will happen, by dividing an ongoing stream of events into causes and effects. Writers may proceed from a given effect and seek to discover what cause or chain of causes could have produced the observed effect, or to show how further effects will flow from a known cause.

Causal analysis is an invaluable analytical technique used in many fields of study. Because of the complexity of causal relationships, writers try to identify, as precisely as possible, the contributory factors in any causal sequence. The direct or immediate causes of the event are those most likely to have triggered the actual event. Yet, behind direct causes may lie indirect or remote causes that set the stage or create the framework in which the event could occur. By the same token, long-term future effects are much more difficult to identify than are immediate, short-term effects.

This technique of distinguishing between predisposing and triggering causes is used by Aldous Huxley, political essayist and author of *Brave New World* (1932), to answer the question of why one particular segment of the German population was so easily swayed by Hitler's rhetoric:

> Hitler made his strongest appeal to those members of the lower middle classes who had been ruined by the inflation of 1923, and then ruined all over again by the depression of 1929 and the following years. "The masses" of whom he speaks were these bewildered, frustrated and chronically anxious millions.

In this passage from "Propaganda under a Dictatorship" (Ch. 4), Huxley uses causal analyis to emphasize that the people most likely to yield to propaganda were those whose security had been destroyed by previous financial disasters. That is, previous cycles of financial instability (the disastrous inflation of 1923 and the depression of 1929) played a crucial role in predisposing the lower middle classes, those whose security was most affected by the financial turmoil, to become receptive to Hitler's propaganda. Hitler, says Huxley, used techniques of propaganda—mass marches, repetition of slogans, scapegoating—to manipulate the segment of the population that was the least secure and the most fearful.

It is most important that causal analysis demonstrate the means (sometimes called the *agency*) by which an effect could have been produced. Writers are obligated to show how the specific causes they identify could have produced the effects in question.

Solving a Problem   Although not a rhetorical strategy as such, the problem-solving techniques that writers use to identify problems, apply theoretical models, define constraints, employ various search techniques, and check solutions against relevant criteria are an important part of all academic and professional research.

The process by which problems are solved in many academic areas usually involves recognizing and defining the problem, using various search techniques to discover a solution, verifying the solution, and communicating it to a particular audience, who might need to know the history of the problem, the success or failure of previous attempts to solve it, and other relevant information.

Recognizing the Existence and Nature of the Problem   The first step in solving a problem is recognizing that a problem exists. Often, the magnitude of the problem is obvious from serious effects that the problem is causing. For example, in his analysis of the dangers posed by pollution, Thor Heyerdahl in "How to Kill an Ocean" (Ch. 6) describes the disastrous effects that already have beset the Great Lakes and alerts us to how vulnerable the ocean is, a concept that most people would find hard to believe:

> In the long run the ocean can be affected by the continued discharge of all modern man's toxic waste. One generation ago no one would have thought that the great lakes of America could be polluted. Today they are, like the largest lakes of Europe. A few years ago the public was amazed to learn that industrial and urban refuse had killed the fish in Lake Erie. The enormous lake was dead.

Heyerdahl uses this dramatic evidence to persuade his readers to relinquish their concept of the ocean as a body of water so immense that it is immune to pollution.

Defining the Problem   When the problem has been clearly perceived, it is often helpful to present it as a single, clear-cut example. William A. Henry III in "In Defense of Elitism" (Ch. 3) uses the following situation to define the need for a more realistic view of who should go to college:

> U.S. colleges go on blithely "educating" many more prospective managers and professionals than the country is likely to need. In my own field, there are typically more students majoring in journalism at any given moment than there are journalists employed at all the daily newspapers in the U.S.

The way Henry frames this problem provides a context in which to understand the problem and a way to identify the most important criterion—efficiency in education—by which to evaluate solutions.

Verifying the Solution   When at last a solution is found after researchers have used various search techniques, it must meet all the tests specific to the problem and take into account all pertinent data uncovered during the search. For example, Gina Kolata reports in "A Clone Is Born" (Ch. 9) that the possibility of cloning had long been regarded as the "stuff of science fiction" and describes how Dolly, the first clone, was produced:

> She was created not out of the union of a sperm and an egg, but out of the genetic material from an udder cell of a six-year old sheep. Wilmut fused the udder cell with an egg from another sheep, after first removing all genetic material from the egg. The udder cell's genes took up residence in the egg and directed it to grow and develop.

The result was Dolly, the identical twin of the original sheep that provided the udder cells, but an identical twin born six years later.

In her article, Kolata describes how the researchers (1) analyzed the nature of the problem, (2) created a set of procedures to solve it, (3) allocated resources for the most productive investigations, and (4) verified the result of their experiment, according to scientific criteria.

Argumentation and Persuasion   Some of the most interesting and effective writing you will read takes the form of arguments that seek to persuade a specific audience (colleagues, fellow researchers, or the general public) of the validity of a proposition or claim through logical reasoning supported by facts, examples, data, or other kinds of evidence.

The purpose of argument is to persuade an audience to accept the validity or probability of an idea, proposition, or claim. Essentially, a claim is an assertion that would be met with skepticism if it were not supported with sound evidence and persuasive reasoning. Formal arguments differ from assertions based on likes and dislikes or personal opinion. Unlike questions of personal taste, arguments rest on evidence, whether in the form of facts, examples, the testimony of experts, or statistics, which can be brought forward to objectively prove or disprove the thesis in question.

Readers expect that evidence cited to substantiate or refute assertions will be sound, accurate, and relevant, and that conclusions will be drawn from this evidence according to the guidelines of logic. Readers also expect that the writer arguing in support of a proposition will acknowledge and answer objections put forth by the opposing side and will provide compelling evidence to support the writer's own position.

Although arguments explore important issues and espouse specific theories, the forms in which arguments appear vary according to the style and format of individual disciplines. Evidence in different fields of study can appear in a variety of formats, including laws, precedents, the interpretation of statistics, or the citation of authorities. The means used in constructing arguments depend on the audience within the discipline being addressed, the nature of the thesis being proposed, and the accepted methodology for that particular area of study.

In the liberal arts, critics evaluate and interpret works of fine art; review music, dance, drama, and film; and write literary analyses (for example, see Margaret Atwood's "Pornography" in Ch. 4). Philosophers probe the moral and ethical implications of people's actions and advocate specific ways of meeting the ethical challenges posed by new technologies, as in Gina Kolata's "A Clone Is Born" (Ch. 9). Historians interpret political, military, and constitutional events; analyze their causes; and theorize about how the past influences the present; for example, see Linda Simon's "The Naked Source" (Ch. 7).

In the political and social sciences, lawyers and constitutional scholars argue for specific ways of applying legal and constitutional theory to everyday problems (for example, see Jonathan Kozol's "The Human Cost of an Illiterate Society," Ch. 3).

Economists debate issues related to changes wrought by technology, distribution of income, unemployment, and commerce (as in Juliet B. Schor's "The Culture of Consumerism," in Ch. 5).

Political scientists look into how effectively governments initiate and manage social change, and they ask basic questions about the limits of governmental intrusion into individual rights (see Thomas Paine's "Rights of Man," Ch. 8). Sociologists analyze statistics and trends to evaluate how successfully institutions accommodate social change (see William A. Henry III's "In Defense of Elitism," Ch. 3).

In the sciences, biologists, as well as biochemists, zoologists, botanists, and other natural scientists, propose theories to explain the interdependence of living things with their natural environment (see Joseph K. Skinner's "Big Mac and the Tropical Forests," Ch. 6). Psychologists champion hypotheses based on physiological, experimental, social, and clinical research to explain various aspects of human behavior. Physicists, as well as mathematicians, astronomers, engineers, and computer scientists, put forward and defend hypotheses about the basic laws underlying manifestations of the physical world, from the microscopic to the cosmic (for example, see Bill Gates's "From the Road Ahead," Ch. 9).

Evaluating Tone   An important ability to develop in critical reading is making inferences about the writer from clues in the text. Looking beyond the facts to see what those facts imply requires readers to look carefully at writers' word choices, their level of knowledge, their use of personal experience, and the skill with which various elements of an essay are arranged. Inferences about a writer's frame of reference and values go beyond what is on the page and can help us get a sense of what the writer is like as a person.

Tone, or "voice," is a crucial element in establishing a writer's credibility. Tone is produced by the combined effect of word choice, sentence structure, and the writer's success in adapting his or her particular "voice" to the subject, the audience, and the occasion. When we try to identify and analyze the tone of a work, we are seeking to hear the actual "voice" of the author in order to understand how the writer intended the work to be perceived. It is important for writers to know what image of themselves they project. Writers should consciously decide on the particular style and tone that best suit the audience, the occasion, and the specific subject matter of the argument.

For example, Martin Luther King, Jr.'s speech "I Have a Dream" (Ch. 8) was delivered when King led a march of 250,000 people through Washington, D.C., to the Lincoln Memorial on the centennial of Lincoln's Emancipation Proclamation. The persuasive techniques that King uses are well suited to adapt his message of nonviolent protest to both his audience and the occasion.

King reminds his audience that the civil rights movement puts into action basic ideas contained in the Constitution. King reaffirms minority rights as a way of renewing aspirations put forward by America's founding fathers and uses figurative language drawn from the Emancipation Proclamation and the Bible to reinforce his audience's emotional resolve to continue in their quest for equal rights:

> I say to you today, my friends, even though we face the difficulties of today and to-
> morrow, I still have a dream. It is a dream deeply rooted in the American dream. I
> have a dream that one day this nation will rise up and live out the true meaning of its
> creed: "We hold these truths to be self-evident, that all men are created equal." I have
> a dream that one day, on the red hills of Georgia, sons of former slaves and the sons of
> former slaveowners will be able to sit down together at the table of brotherhood.

The effectiveness of this speech depends in large part on the audience's sense of
King as a man of high moral character. In arguments that appeal to the emotions as
well as to the intellect, the audience's perception of the speaker as a person of the
highest ethics, good character, and sound reason amplifies the logic of the discourse.

Irony, Humor, and Satire   A particular kind of tone encountered in many
essays is called *irony*. Writers adopt this rhetorical strategy to express a discrepancy
between opposites, between the ideal and the real, between the literal and the implied, and most often between the way things are and the way the writer thinks
things ought to be.

Sometimes it is difficult to pick up the fact that not everything the writer says
is intended to be taken literally. Authors occasionally say the opposite of what they
mean to catch the attention of the reader. If your first response to an ironic statement
is "Can the writer really be serious?" look for signals that the writer means the opposite of what is being said. One clear signal that the author is being ironic is a noticeable
disparity between the tone and the subject. For example, P. J. O'Rourke opens his
essay "The Greenhouse Affect" (Ch. 6) by asking, "If the great outdoors is so swell,
how come the homeless aren't more fond of it?"

Satire is an enduring form of argument that uses parody, irony, and caricature
to poke fun at a subject, an idea, or a person. Tone is especially important in satire.
The satirist frequently creates a mask, or *persona,* that is very different from the author's real self in order to shock the audience into a new awareness about an established institution or custom. Satirical works by Mark Twain (Ch. 6), and Umberto
Eco (Ch. 9), assail folly, greed, corruption, pride, self-righteous complacency, cultural
pretensions, hypocrisy, and other permanent targets of the satirist's pen.

Responding to What You Read

When reading an essay that seems to embody a certain value system, try to
examine any assumptions or beliefs the writer expects the audience to share. How
are these assumptions related to the author's purpose? If you do not agree with
these assumptions, has the writer provided sound reasons and evidence to persuade
you to change your mind?

You might describe the author's tone or voice and try to assess how much it
contributed to the essay. How effectively does the writer use authorities, statistics,
or examples to support the claim? Does the author identify the assumptions or values on which his or her views are based? Are they ones with which you would
agree or disagree? To what extent does the author use the emotional connotations

of language to try to persuade the reader? Do you see anything unworkable or disadvantageous about the solutions offered as an answer to the problem the essay addresses? All these and many other ways of analyzing someone else's essay can be used to create your own. Here are some specific guidelines to help you.

When evaluating an essay, consider what the author's purpose is in writing it. Was it to inform, explain, solve a problem, make a recommendation, amuse, enlighten, or achieve some combination of these goals? How is the tone, or voice, the author projects related to the purpose in writing the essay?

You may find it helpful to write short summaries after each major section to determine whether you understand what the writer is trying to communicate. These summaries can then serve as a basis for an analysis of how successfully the author employs reasons, examples, statistics, and expert testimony to support and develop main points.

For example, if the essay you are analyzing cites authorities to support a claim, assess whether the authorities bring the most timely opinions to bear on the subject or display any obvious biases, and determine whether they are experts in that particular field. Watch for experts described as "often quoted" or "highly placed reliable sources" without accompanying names, credentials, or appropriate documentation. If the experts cited offer what purports to be a reliable interpretation of facts, consider whether the writer also quotes equally trustworthy experts who hold opposing views.

If statistics are cited to support a point, judge whether they derive from verifiable and trustworthy sources. Also, evaluate whether the author has interpreted them in ways that are beneficial to the case, whereas someone who held an opposing view could interpret them quite differently. If real-life examples are presented to support the author's opinions, determine whether they are representative or whether they are too atypical to be used as evidence. If the author relies on hypothetical examples or analogies to dramatize ideas that otherwise would be hard to grasp, judge whether these examples are too far-fetched to back up the claims being made. If the essay depends on the stipulated definition of a term that might be defined in different ways, check whether the author provides clear reasons to indicate why one definition rather than another is preferable.

As you list observations about the various elements of the article you are analyzing, take a closer look at the underlying assumptions and see whether you can locate and distinguish between those assumptions that are explicitly stated and those that are implicit. Once the author's assump- tions are identified, you can compare them with your own beliefs about the subject, determine whether these assumptions are commonly held, and make a judgment as to their validity. Would you readily agree with these assumptions? If not, has the author provided sound reasons and supporting evidence to persuade you to change your mind?

Marking as You Read

The most effective way to think about what you read is to make notes as you read. Making notes as you read forces you to go slowly and think carefully about each sentence. This process is sometimes called *annotating the text,* and all you need is a pen or a pencil. There are as many styles of annotating as there are readers, and you will discover your own favorite technique once you have done it a few times. Some readers prefer to underline major points or statements and jot down their reactions to them in the margin. Others prefer to summarize each paragraph or section to help them follow the author's line of thinking. Other readers circle key words or phrases necessary to understand the main ideas. Feel free to use your notes as a kind of conversation with the text. Ask questions. Express doubts. Mark unfamiliar words or phrases to look up later. If the paragraphs are not already numbered, you might wish to number them as you go to help you keep track of your responses. Try to distinguish the main ideas from supporting points and examples. Most important, go slowly and think about what you are reading. Try to discover whether the author makes a credible case for the conclusions reached. One last point: Take a close look at the idea expressed in the title before and after you read the essay to see how it relates to the main idea.

Keeping a Reading Journal

The most effective way to keep track of your thoughts and impressions and to review what you have learned is to start a reading journal. The comments you record in your journal may express your reflections, observations, questions, and reactions to the essays you read. Normally, your journal would not contain lecture notes from class. A reading journal will allow you to keep a record of your progress during the term and can also reflect insights you gain during class discussions and questions you may want to ask, as well as unfamiliar words you intend to look up. Keeping a reading journal becomes a necessity if your composition course requires you to write a research paper that will be due at the end of the semester. Keep in mind that your journal is not something that will be corrected or graded, although some instructors may wish you to share your entries with the class.

Turning Annotations Into Journal Entries   Although there is no set form for what a journal should look like, reading journals are most useful for converting your brief annotations into more complete entries that explore in depth your reactions to what you have read. Interestingly, the process of turning your annotations into journal entries will often produce surprising insights that will give you a new perspective.

Summarizing   Reading journals may also be used to record summaries of the essays you read. The value of summarizing is that it requires you to pay close attention to the reading in order to distinguish the main points from the supporting details. Summarizing tests your understanding of the material by requiring you to restate concisely the author's main ideas in your own words. First, create a list composed of sentences that express in your own words the essential idea of each paragraph or of each group of related paragraphs. Your previous underlining of topic sentences, main ideas, and key terms (as part of the process of critical reading) will help you follow the author's line of thought. Next, whittle down this list still further by eliminating repetitive ideas. Then formulate a thesis statement that expresses the main idea in the article. Start your summary with this thesis statement, and combine your notes so that the summary flows together and reads easily.

Remember that summaries should be much shorter (usually no longer than half a page) than the original text (whether the original is one page or twenty pages long) and should accurately reflect the central ideas of the article in as few words as possible. Try not to intrude your own opinions or critical evaluations into the summary. Besides requiring you to read the original piece more closely, summaries are necessary first steps in developing papers that synthesize materials from different sources. The test for a good summary, of course, is whether a person reading it without having read the original article would get an accurate, balanced, and complete account of the original material.

Using Your Reading Journal to Generate Ideas for Writing   You can use all the material in your reading journal (annotations converted to journal entries, reflections, observations, questions, rough and final summaries) to relate your own ideas to the ideas of the person who wrote the essay you are reading. Here are several different kinds of strategies you can use as you analyze an essay in order to generate material for your own:

1. What is missing in the essay? Information that is not mentioned is often just as significant as information the writer chose to include. First, you must already have summarized the main points in the article. Then, make up another list of points that are not discussed, that is, missing information that you would have expected an article of this kind to cover or touch on. Write down the possible reasons why this missing material has been omitted, censored, or downplayed. What possible purpose could the author have had? Look for vested interests or biases that could explain why information of a certain kind is missing.

2. You might analyze an essay in terms of what you already knew and what you didn't know about the issue. To do this, simply make a list of what concepts were already familiar to you and a second list of information or concepts that were new to you. Then write down three to five questions you would like answered about this new information and make a list of possible sources you might consult.

3. You might consider whether the author presents a solution to a problem. List the short-term and long-term effects or consequences of the action the writer recommends. You might wish to evaluate the solution to see whether positive short-term benefits would be offset by possible negative long-term consequences not mentioned by the author. This evaluation might provide you with a starting point for your own essay.

4. After clearly stating what the author's position on an issue is, try to imagine other people in that society or culture who would view the same issue from a different perspective. How would the concerns of these people be different from those of the writer? Try to think of as many different people, representing as many different perspectives, as you can. Now, try to think of a solution

that would satisfy both the author and at least one other person who holds a different viewpoint. Try to imagine that you are an arbitrator negotiating an agreement. How would your recommendation require both parties to compromise and reach an agreement?

READING FICTION

Works of fiction communicate intense, complex, deeply felt responses to human experiences that speak to the heart, mind, body, and imagination.

Although the range of situations that stories can offer is limitless, what makes any particular story enjoyable is the writer's capacity to present an interesting plot, believable characters, and convincing dialogue. The nature of the original events matters less than the writer's ability to make us feel the impact of this experience intellectually, physically, and emotionally. The writer who uses language in skillful and precise ways allows us to share the perceptions and feelings of people different from ourselves. Works of fiction not only can take us to parts of the world we may never have the opportunity to visit but can deepen our emotional capacity to understand what life is like for others in conditions very different from our own. We become more conscious of ourselves as individual human beings when our imaginations and emotions are fully involved. We value a story when through it we touch the aspirations, motives, and feelings of other people in diverse personal and cultural situations.

Works of fiction, as distinct from biographies and historical accounts, are imaginative works that tell a story. Fiction writers use language to re-create the emotional flavor of experiences and are free to restructure their accounts in ways that will create suspense and even build conflict. They can add to or take away from the known facts, expand or compress time, invent additional imaginative details, or even invent new characters or a narrator through whose eyes the story is told.

The oldest works of fiction took the form of myths and legends that described the exploits of heroes and heroines, gods and goddesses, and supernatural beings. Other ancient forms of literature included fables (stating explicit lessons using animal characters) and parables (using analogies to suggest rather than state moral points or complex philosophical concepts) of the kind related by Jesus in the New Testament.

The modern short story differs from earlier narrative forms in emphasizing life as most people know it. The short story originated in the nineteenth century as a brief fictional prose narrative that was designed to be read in a single sitting. In a short story, all the literary elements of plot, character, setting, and the author's distinctive use of language work together to create a single effect. Short stories usually describe the experiences of one or two characters over the course of a series of related events. Realistic stories present sharply etched pictures of characters in real settings reacting to kinds of crises with which readers can identify. The emotions, reactions, perceptions, and motivations of the characters are explored in great detail. We can see these realistic elements in short stories ranging from Guy de Maupassant's "An Old Man" (Ch. 5), written in the nineteenth century, through John Cheever's "Reunion" (Ch. 2) to, most recently, Lin Sutherland's "A River Ran over Me" (Ch. 6).

Other writers, reacting against the prevailing conventions of realistic fiction, create a kind of story in which everyday reality is not presented directly but is filtered through the perceptions, associations, and emotions of the main character. In these *nonrealistic* stories, the normal chronology of events is displaced by a psychological narrative that reflects the ebb and flow of the characters' feelings and associations. Nonrealistic stories may include fantastic, bizarre, or supernatural elements as well. We can see this alternative to the realistic story in H. G. Wells's "The Country of the Blind" (Ch. 11), John Cheever's "The Enormous Radio" (Ch. 9), and Donald Barthelme's "The School" (Ch. 3).

Although it is something we have done most of our lives, when we look at it closely reading is a rather mysterious activity. The individual interpretations readers bring to characters and events in the text make every story mean something slightly different to every reader. There are, however, some strategies all readers use: We instinctively draw on our own knowledge of human relationships in interpreting characters and incidents, we simultaneously draw on clues in the text to anticipate what will happen next, and we continuously revise our past impressions as we encounter new information.

At what points in the work were you required to imagine or anticipate what would happen next? How did you make use of the information the author gave you to generate a hypothesis about what lay ahead? To what extent do your own circumstances—gender, age, race, class, and culture—differ from those of the characters in the story, poem, or play? How might your reading of the text differ from that of other readers? Has the writer explored all the possibilities raised within the work? Has the writer missed any opportunities that you as the writer would have explored?

The New Millennium Reader offers works drawn from many cultural contexts reflecting diverse styles and perspectives. Fiction produced in the second half of the twentieth century differs in a number of important ways from that produced before World War II. Writers in this postmodern period avoid seeing events as having only one meaning and produce works that represent reality in unique, complex, and highly individual ways.

Contemporary writers have a great deal to say about the forces that shape ethnic, sexual, and racial identity in various cultural contexts. Unlike traditional works that presented social dilemmas in order to resolve them, postmodernist works underscore the difficulty of integrating competing ethnic, sexual, and racial identities within a single culture. This is especially apparent in Irene Zabytko's "Home Soil" (Ch. 7) and Albert Camus's "The Guest" (Ch. 8). Other writers address the ways different cultures define gender roles and class relationships in terms of power and powerlessness. These issues are explored in Kate Chopin's "Désirée's Baby" (Ch. 5) and Raymond Carver's "What We Talk About When We Talk About Love" (Ch. 4).

READING POETRY

Poetry differs from other genres in that it achieves its effects with fewer words, compressing details into carefully organized forms in which sounds, words, and images work together to create a single intense experience. Poetry uses language in ways that communicate experience rather than simply give information.

The difference between prose and poetry emerges quite clearly when you compare a stanza from Grace Caroline Bridges's poem "Lisa's Ritual, Age 10" (Ch. 5) with the same words punctuated as a sentence in prose:

> The wall is steady while she falls away: first the hands lost arms dissolving feet gone the legs disjointed body cracking down the center like a fault she falls inside slides down like dust like kitchen dirt slips off the dustpan into noplace a place where nothing happens, nothing ever happened.

Notice how in a stanza from the poem the arrangement of the words and lines creates an entirely different relationship:

> The wall is steady
> while she falls   away:
>   first the hands   lost
> arms dissolving   feet gone
> the legs   dis- jointed
>   body cracking down
>   the center like a fault
>   she falls inside
>   slides down like
> dust   like kitchen dirt
>   slips off
>   the dustpan into
>   noplace
>   a place where
> nothing happens,
> nothing ever happened.

The way the words are arranged communicates the experience of the child's detachment, alienation, and sense of shock, whereas the same words in prose merely describe it.

Because it communicates an extraordinarily compressed moment of thought, feeling, or experience, poetry relies on figurative language, connotation, imagery, sound, and rhythm. Poetry evokes emotional associations through images whose importance is underscored by a rhythmic beat or pulse.

Patterns of sounds and images emphasize and underscore distinct thoughts and emotions, appealing simultaneously to the heart, mind, and imagination. The rhythmic beat provides the sensuous element coupled with imagery that appeals to the senses and touches the heart. At the same time, the imagination is stimulated through unexpected combinations and perceptions and figurative language (similes, metaphors, personification) that allow the reader to see things in new ways. Because these effects work simultaneously, the experience of a poem is concentrated and intense.

Like fiction, poems may have a narrator (called a speaker), a particular point of view, and a distinctive tone and style.

Learning to enjoy what poetry has to offer requires the reader to pay close attention to specific linguistic details of sound and rhythm, connotations of words, and the sensations, feelings, memories, and associations that these words evoke. After reading a poem, preferably aloud, try to determine who the speaker is. What situation does the poem describe? How might the title provide insight into the speaker's predicament? What attitude does the poet project toward the events described in the poem? Observe the language used by the speaker. What emotional state of mind is depicted? You might look for recurrent references to a particular subject and see whether these references illuminate some psychological truth.

Although it has a public use, poetry mainly unfolds private joys, tragedies, and challenges common to all people, such as the power of friendship, value of self-discovery, bondage of outworn traditions, delight in nature's beauty, devastation of war, achievement of self-respect, and despair over failed dreams. The universal elements in poetry bridge gaps in time and space and tie people together in expressing emotions shared by all people in different times, places, and cultures.

READING DRAMA

Drama, unlike fiction and poetry, is meant to be performed on a stage. The text of a play includes dialogue (conversation between two or more characters)—or a monologue (lines spoken by a single character to the audience)—and the playwright's stage directions.

Although the dramatist makes use of plot, characters, setting, and language, the nature of drama limits the playwright to presenting the events from an objective point of view. There are other important differences between short stories, novels, and drama as well. The dramatist must restrict the action in the play to what can be shown on the stage in two or three hours. Since plays must hold the attention of an audience, playwrights prefer obvious rather than subtle conflicts, clearly defined sequences of action, and fast-paced exposition that is not weighed down by long descriptive or narrative passages. Everything in drama has to be shown directly, concretely, through vivid images of human behavior.

The structure of most plays begins with an exposition or introduction that introduces the characters, shows their relationship to one another, and provides the background information necessary for the audience or reader to understand the main conflict of the play. The essence of drama is *conflict*. Conflict is produced when an individual pursuing an objective meets with resistance either from another person, from society, from nature, or from an internal aspect of that individual's own personality. In the most effective plays, the audience can see the central conflict through the eyes of each character in the play. As the play proceeds, complications make the problem more difficult to solve and increase suspense as to whether the *protagonist,* or main character, or the opposing force (referred to as the *antagonist*) will triumph. In the climax of the play, the conflict reaches the height of emotional intensity, and one side achieves a decisive advantage over the other. This is often the moment of truth, when characters see themselves and the situation clearly for the first time. The end of the play, or conclusion, explores the implications of the nature of the truth that has been realized and what the consequences will be.

Reading the script of a play is a very different kind of experience from seeing it performed on the stage. From a script containing dialogue and brief descriptions, you must visualize what the characters look like and sound like and imagine how they relate to one another. For example, try to imagine the following scene from *Protest* by the Czech playwright Václav Havel (Ch. 8). It dramatizes a confrontation between two old friends, a dissident writer, Vaněk, whose experiences reflect those of Havel himself, and Staněk, an intellectual who has sold out to the system but now needs Vaněk's help.

STANĚK: Why don't you level with me! Don't you realize that your benevolent hypocrisy is actually far more insulting than if you gave it to me straight?! Or do you mean I'm not even worthy of your comment?!

VANĚK: But I told you, didn't I, I respect your reasoning—

STANĚK: I'm not an idiot, Vaněk!

VANĚK: Of course not—

STANĚK: I know precisely what's behind your "respect"!

VANĚK: What is?

STANĚK: A feeling of moral superiority!

VANĚK: You're wrong—

STANĚK: Only, I'm not quite sure if you—you of all people—have any right to feel so superior!

VANĚK: What do you mean?

STANĚK: You know very well what I mean!

VANĚK: I don't—

STANĚK: Shall I tell you?

VANĚK: Please do—

STANĚK: Well! As far as I know, in prison you talked more than you should have!

(Vaněk jumps up, wildly staring at Staněk, who smiles triumphantly. Short tense pause. The phone rings. Vaněk, broken, sinks back into his chair. Staněk crosses to the telephone and lifts the receiver.)

How do you stage this scene in your mind? What do Vaněk and Staněk look like? What are they wearing? For example, are both or either wearing eyeglasses? Keep in mind, Staněk is employed and well-to-do while Vaněk has been in prison and cannot find a job. What do their voices sound like? How do you imagine the interior of Staněk's house where the scene takes place? What emotions are reflected in the faces of each at various points in the scene? In all of these and countless other details the reader must play a vital role in bringing the scene to life by making the kinds of decisions that would be delegated to the director, the set designer, the costume designer, and the actors in a stage production.

LITERARY WORKS IN CONTEXT

Since no short story, poem, drama, or essay is written in a vacuum, a particularly useful way of studying works of literature entails discovering the extent to which a work reflects or incorporates the historical, cultural, literary, and personal contexts in which it was written. Although works vary in what they require readers to know already, in most cases knowing more about the context in which the work was written will enhance the reader's understanding and enjoyment. For this reason, the information contained in the biographical sketches that precede each selection can be quite useful.

Investigating the biographical or psychological contexts in which the work was written assumes that the facts of an author's life are particularly relevant to a full understanding of the work. For example, the predicament confronting the speaker in Sara Teasdale's poem "The Solitary" (Ch. 1) articulates a problem the poet confronted in her own life. Similarly, we can assume that Charlotte Perkins Gilman's account of the narrator's decline into madness in her story "Yellow Wallpaper" (Ch. 1) grew out of the author's own experiences. So too, Luisa Valenzuela had to contend with the government spying on citizens in Argentina, as she dramatizes her story "The Censors" (Ch. 8). Yet, a cautionary note is in order. Notwithstanding the presumed relevance of an author's life, especially if the work seems highly autobiographical, we should remember that literature does not simply report events; it imaginatively re-creates experience.

The information that precedes each selection can be useful in a number of ways. For example, the reader can better understand a single story, poem, or play by comparing how an author has treated similar subjects and concerns in other works. Speeches, interviews, lectures, and essays by authors often provide important insights into the contexts in which a particular literary work was created. For example, the importance Raymond Carver places on being able to communicate our feelings to those we love, as he expresses it in his nonfiction work "My Father's Life" (Ch. 2), enters significantly into his classic short story "What We Talk About When We Talk About Love" (Ch. 4).

Placing individual works within the author's total repertoire is another way of studying works in their context. You can compare different works by the same author or compare different stages in the composition of the same work by studying subsequent revisions in different published versions of a story, poem, or play. Authors often address themselves to the important political and social issues of their time. For example, Bruce Springsteen's song "Streets of Philadelphia" (Ch. 5) can be understood as a protest against society's treatment of those with AIDS in its poignant depiction of the consequences in the lives of those afflicted with this disease.

In studying the social context of a work, ask yourself what dominant social values the work dramatizes, and try to determine if the author approves or disapproves of particular social values by the way in which the characters are portrayed. Or you might analyze how the author describes or draws upon the manners, mores, customs, rituals, or codes of conduct of a specific society at a particular time, as does Kate Chopin in "Désirée's Baby" (Ch. 5), a story that dramatizes the human consequences of racism in the South at the turn of the nineteenth century.

Studying the historical context in which a work is written means identifying how features of the work reveal important historical, political, economic, social, intellectual, or religious currents and problems of the time. Think how useful it would be, for example, to know what issues were at stake between France and Algeria and how they are reflected in Albert Camus's treatment of them in his story "The Guest" (Ch. 8).

In an analysis of any work, the title, names of characters, references to places and events, or topical allusions may provide important clues to the work's original sources. For example, has the writer chosen to interweave historical incidents and figures with characters and events of his or her own creation and, if so, to what effect? In any case, simply knowing more about the circumstances under which a work was written will add to your enjoyment and give you a broader understanding of the essay, short story, poem, or play.

1

REFLECTIONS ON EXPERIENCE

The authors of the essays in this chapter describe crucial moments in their lives. They are motivated by the desire to understand these life experiences and to share them with others. In each case, the writers reconstruct the meaning of important personal events, the full significance of which was not obvious at the time the events occurred. The advantage of these reminiscences is that they offer a means by which the authors can define themselves as individuals, distinct from the images fostered by societal or cultural stereotyping. The qualities of candor, honesty, and self-analysis these narratives display stem from the assumption that one's own life is an appropriate object of scrutiny. For example, the essays by Fritz Peters and Douchan Gersi explore moments that proved to be decisive turning points in the authors' lives. Jill Nelson, Annie Dillard, and Judith Ortiz Cofer recover pivotal memories that illuminate the directions their lives have taken. The essays by Beryl Markham and Lesley Hazleton provide engaging and informative reflections on experiences that draw us into the private worlds of an aviator and an auto mechanic.

Stories differ from essays in important ways. A writer of fiction can add to the known facts, expand or compress the sequence of events, build suspense, and even invent characters and create a narrator to tell the story. For example, when Charlotte Perkins Gilman creates a story that parallels her own experiences as a young woman who suffered postpartum depression, she is using the latitude allowed by fiction to more fully explore the meanings of her own life. Jerzy Kosinki's penetrating story of jealousy and revenge dramatizes a permanent theme in human nature.

The poems in this chapter are first and foremost personal reminiscences. In them we can hear the feelings and perceptions that allow us to identify with the speaker's reactions. T. S. Eliot takes us into the mind of one who is imprisoned by his own timidity. In a sonnet, William Shakespeare discovers that the memory of someone he loved gives his life meaning. Sara Teasdale realizes that being independent and self-sufficient are the values she has cherished most, and Anna Kamieńska explores the fleeting nature of human existence.

Nonfiction

JILL NELSON

Jill Nelson, born in 1952, is a native New Yorker and a graduate of the City College of New York and Columbia University's School of Journalism. A journalist for fifteen years, she is a frequent contributor to Essence, U.S.A. Weekend, *the* Village Voice, *and* Ms. *In 1986 she went to work for the* Washington Post's *new Sunday magazine as the only black woman reporter in a bastion of elite journalism, an experience she described in* Volunteer Slavery: My Authentic Negro Experience *(1993). Her latest book is* Straight, No Chaser: How I Became a Grown-Up Black Woman *(1997). In "Number One!" she reflects on the importance of her father's influence on her life.*

Number One!

That night I dream about my father, but it is really more a memory than a dream.

"Number one! Not two! Number one!" my father intones from the head of the breakfast table. The four of us sit at attention, two on each side of the ten-foot teak expanse, our brown faces rigid. At the foot, my mother looks up at my father, the expression on her face a mixture of pride, anxiety, and, could it be, boredom? I am twelve. It is 1965.

"You kids have got to be, not number two," he roars, his dark face turning darker from the effort to communicate. He holds up his index and middle fingers. "But number—" here, he pauses dramatically, a preacher going for revelation, his four children a rapt congregation, my mother a smitten church sister. "Number one!"

These last words he shouts while lowering his index finger. My father has great, big black hands, long, perfectly shaped fingers with oval nails so vast they seem landscapes all their own. The half moons leading to the cuticle take up most of the nail and seem ever encroaching, threatening to swallow up first his fingertips, then his whole hand. I always wondered if he became a dentist just to mess with people by putting those enormous fingers in their mouths, each day surprising his patients and himself by the delicacy of the work he did.

Years later my father told me that when a woman came to him with an infant 5
she asserted was his, he simply looked at the baby's hands. If they lacked the size, enormous nails, and half-moon cuticles like an ocean eroding the shore of the fingers, he dismissed them.

Early on, what I remember of my father were Sunday morning breakfasts and those hands, index finger coyly lowering, leaving the middle finger standing alone.

When he shouted "Number one!" that finger seemed to grow, thicken and harden, thrust up and at us, a phallic symbol to spur us, my sister Lynn, fifteen, brothers Stanley and Ralph, thirteen and nine, on to greatness, to number oneness.

My father's rich, heavy voice rolled down the length of the table, breaking and washing over our four trembling bodies.

When I wake up I am trembling again, but it's because the air conditioner, a luxury in New York but a necessity in D.C., is set too high. I turn it down, check on Misu,[1] light a cigarette, and think about the dream.

It wasn't until my parents had separated and Sunday breakfasts were no more that I faced the fact that my father's symbol for number one was the world's sign language for "fuck you." I know my father knew this, but I still haven't figured out what he meant by it. Were we to become number one and go out and fuck the world? If we didn't, would life fuck us? Was he intentionally sending his children a mixed message? If so, what was he trying to say?

I never went to church with my family. While other black middle-class families journeyed to Baptist church on Sundays, both to thank the Lord for their prosperity and donate a few dollars to the less fortunate brethren they'd left behind, we had what was reverentially known as "Sunday breakfast." That was our church.   10

In the dining room of the eleven-room apartment we lived in, the only black family in a building my father had threatened to file a discrimination suit to get into, my father delivered the gospel according to him. The recurring theme was the necessity that each of us be "number one," but my father preached about whatever was on his mind: current events, great black heroes, lousy black sell-outs, our responsibility as privileged children, his personal family history.

His requirements were the same as those at church: that we be on time, not fidget, hear and heed the gospel, and give generously. But Daddy's church boasted no collection plate; dropping a few nickels into a bowl would have been too easy. Instead, my father asked that we absorb his lessons and become what he wanted us to be, number one. He never told us what that meant or how to get there. It was years before I was able to forgive my father for not being more specific. It was even longer before I understood and accepted that he couldn't be.

Like most preachers, my father was stronger on imagery, oratory, and instilling fear than he was on process. I came away from fifteen years of Sunday breakfasts knowing that to be number two was not enough, and having no idea what number one was or how to become it, only that it was better.

When I was a kid, I just listened, kept a sober face, and tried to understand what was going on. Thanks to my father, my older sister Lynn and I, usually at odds, found spiritual communion. The family dishwashers, our spirits met wordlessly as my father talked. We shared each other's anguish as we watched egg yolk harden on plates, sausage fat congeal, chicken livers separate silently from gravy.

We all had our favorite sermons. Mine was the "Rockefeller wouldn't let his   15
dog shit in our dining room" sermon.

"You think we're doing well?" my father would begin, looking into each of our four faces. We knew better than to venture a response. For my father, even now, conversations are lectures. Please save your applause—and questions—until the end.

---

[1] *Misu:* Nelson's daughter.

"And we are," he'd answer his own query. "We live on West End Avenue, I'm a professional, your mother doesn't have to work, you all go to private school, we go to Martha's Vineyard in the summer. But what we have, we have because 100,000 other black people haven't made it. Have nothing! Live like dogs!"

My father has a wonderfully expressive voice. When he said dogs, you could almost hear them whimpering. In my head, I saw an uncountable mass of black faces attached to the bodies of mutts, scrambling to elevate themselves to a better life. For some reason, they were always on 125th Street, under the Apollo Theatre marquee. Years later, when I got political and decided to be the number-one black nationalist, I was thrilled by the notion that my father might have been inspired by Claude McKay's[2] poem that begins, "If we must die, let it not be like dogs."

"There is a quota system in this country for black folks, and your mother and me were allowed to make it," my father went on. It was hard to imagine anyone allowing my six-foot-three, suave, smart, take-no-shit father to do anything. Maybe his use of the word was a rhetorical device.

"Look around you," he continued. With the long arm that supported his   20
heavy hand he indicated the dining room. I looked around. At the eight-foot china cabinet gleaming from the weekly oiling administered by Margie, our housekeeper, filled to bursting with my maternal grandmother's china and silver. At the lush green carpeting, the sideboard that on holidays sagged from the weight of cakes, pies, and cookies, at the paintings on the walls. We were living kind of good, I thought. That notion lasted only an instant.

My father's arm slashed left. It was as though he had stripped the room bare. I could almost hear the china crashing to the floor, all that teak splintering, silver clanging.

"Nelson Rockefeller wouldn't let his dog shit in here!" my father roared. "What we have, compared to what Rockefeller and the people who rule the world have, is nothing. Nothing! Not even good enough for his dog. You four have to remember that and do better than I have. Not just for yourselves, but for our people, black people. You have to be number one."

My father went on, but right about there was where my mind usually started drifting. I was entranced by the image of Rockefeller's dog—which I imagined to be a Corgi or Afghan or Scottish Terrier—bladder and rectum full to bursting, sniffing around the green carpet of our dining room, refusing to relieve himself.

The possible reasons for this fascinated me. Didn't he like green carpets? Was he used to defecating on rare Persian rugs and our 100 percent wool carpeting wasn't good enough? Was it because we were black? But weren't dogs colorblind?

I've spent a good part of my life trying to figure out what my father meant by   25
number one. Born poor and dark in Washington, I think he was trying, in his own way, to protect us from the crushing assumptions of failure that he and his generation grew up with. I like to think he was simply saying, like the army, "Be all that you can be," but I'm still not sure. For years, I was haunted by the specter of

---

[2] *Claude McKay (1889–1948):* African-American poet.

number two gaining on me, of never having a house nice enough for Rockefeller dog shit, of my father's middle finger admonishing me. It's hard to move forward when you're looking over your shoulder.

When I was younger, I didn't ask my father what he meant. By the time I was confident enough to ask, my father had been through so many transformations—from dentist to hippie to lay guru—that he'd managed to forget, or convince himself he'd forgotten, those Sunday morning sermons. When I brought them up he'd look blank, his eyes would glaze over, and he'd say something like, "Jill, what are you talking about? With your dramatic imagination you should have been an actress."

But I'm not an actress. I'm a journalist, my father's daughter. I've spent a good portion of my life trying to be a good race woman and number one at the same time. Tomorrow, I go to work at the *Washington Post* magazine, a first. Falling asleep, I wonder if that's the same as being number one.

Questions for Discussion and Writing

1. What message did Jill Nelson's father wish to instill during their Sunday breakfasts?
2. How has Nelson's life been influenced by her attempt to understand and act on her father's advice?
3. Is there a member of your family who has been particularly influential in shaping your attitudes and expectations? Describe this person, and give some examples of how your life has been changed because of the expectations.

FRITZ PETERS

Fritz Peters's (1916–1979) association with the philosopher and mystic George Gurdjieff began when Peters attended a school founded by Gurdjieff in Fontainebleau, France, where he spent four and a half years between 1924 and 1929. His experiences with Gurdjieff were always unpredictable and often enigmatic and rewarding. Peters wrote two books about his experiences, Boyhood with Gurdjieff *(1964) and* Gurdjieff Remembered *(1965). In the following essay, Peters reveals the highly unconventional methods Gurdjieff used to compel his protégé to develop compassion.*

Boyhood with Gurdjieff

The Saturday evening after Gurdjieff's return from America, which had been in the middle of the week, was the first general "assembly" of everyone at the Prieuré,[1] in the study-house. The study-house was a separate building, originally

---

[1] *Prieuré:* a priory; a large chateau in Fountainebleau, France, where G. I. Gurdjieff conducted his school.

an airplane hangar. There was a linoleum-covered raised stage at one end. Directly in front of the stage there was a small, hexagonal fountain, equipped electrically so that various coloured lights played on the water. The fountain was generally used only during the playing of music on the piano which was to the left of the stage as one faced it.

The main part of the building, from the stage to the entrance at the opposite end, was carpeted with oriental rugs of various sizes, surrounded by a small fence which made a large, rectangular open space. Cushions, covered by fur rugs, surrounded the sides of this rectangle in front of the fence, and it was here that most of the students would normally sit. Behind the fence, at a higher level, were built-up benches, also covered with Oriental rugs, for spectators. Near the entrance of the building there was a small cubicle, raised a few feet from the floor, in which Gurdjieff habitually sat, and above this there was a balcony which was rarely used and then only for "important" guests. The cross-wise beams of the ceiling had painted material nailed to them, and the material hung down in billows, creating a cloud-like effect. It was an impressive interior—with a church-like feeling about it. One had the impression that it would be improper, even when it was empty, to speak above a whisper inside the building.

On that particular Saturday evening, Gurdjieff sat in his accustomed cubicle, Miss Madison sat near him on the floor with her little black book on her lap, and most of the students sat around, inside the fence, on the fur rugs. New arrivals and "spectators" or guests were on the higher benches behind the fence. Mr. Gurdjieff announced that Miss Madison would go over all the "offences" of all the students and that proper "punishments" would be meted out to the offenders. All of the children, and perhaps I, especially, waited with bated breath as Miss Madison read from her book, which seemed to have been arranged, not alphabetically, but according to the number of offences committed. As Miss Madison had warned me, I led the list, and the recitation of my crimes and offences was a lengthy one.

Gurdjieff listened impassively, occasionally glancing at one or another of the offenders, sometimes smiling at the recital of a particular misdemeanour, and interrupting Miss Madison only to take down, personally, the actual number of individual black marks. When she had completed her reading, there was a solemn, breathless silence in the room and Gurdjieff said, with a heavy sigh, that we had all created a great burden for him. He said then that he would give out punishments according to the number of offences committed. Naturally, I was the first one to be called. He motioned to me to sit on the floor before him and then had Miss Madison re-read my offences in detail. When she had finished, he asked me if I admitted all of them. I was tempted to refute some of them, at least in part, and to argue extenuating circumstances, but the solemnity of the proceedings and the silence in the room prevented me from doing so. Every word that had been uttered had dropped on the assemblage with the clarity of a bell. I did not have the courage to voice any weak defence that might have come to my mind, and I admitted that the list was accurate.

With another sigh, and shaking his head at me as if he was very much put upon, he reached into his pocket and pulled out an enormous roll of bills. Once

5

again, he enumerated the number of my crimes, and then laboriously peeled off an equal number of notes. I do not remember exactly how much he gave me—I think it was ten francs for each offence—but when he had finished counting, he handed me a sizeable roll of francs. During this process, the entire room practically screamed with silence. There was not a murmur from anyone in the entire group, and I did not even dare to glance in Miss Madison's direction.

When my money had been handed to me, he dismissed me and called up the next offender and went through the same process. As there were a great many of us, and there was not one individual who had not done something, violated some rule during his absence, the process took a long time. When he had gone through the list, he turned to Miss Madison and handed her some small sum—perhaps ten francs, or the equivalent of one "crime" payment—for her, as he put it, "conscientious fulfilment of her obligations as director of the Prieuré."

We were all aghast; we had been taken completely by surprise, of course. But the main thing we all felt was a tremendous compassion for Miss Madison. It seemed to me a senselessly cruel, heartless act against her. I have never known Miss Madison's feelings about this performance; except for blushing furiously when I was paid, she showed no obvious reaction to anything at all, and even thanked him for the pittance he had given her.

The money that I had received amazed me. It was, literally, more money than I had ever had at one time in my life. But it also repelled me. I could not bring myself to do anything with it. It was not until a few days later, one evening when I had been summoned to bring coffee to Gurdjieff's room, that the subject came up again. I had had no private, personal contact with him—in the sense of actually talking to him, for instance—since his return. That evening—he was alone—when I had served him his coffee, he asked me how I was getting along; how I felt. I blurted out my feelings about Miss Madison and about the money that I felt unable to spend.

He laughed at me and said cheerfully that there was no reason why I should not spend the money any way I chose. It was my money, and it was a reward for my activity of the past winter. I said I could not understand why I should have been rewarded for having been dilatory about my jobs and having created only trouble.

Gurdjieff laughed again and told me that I had much to learn.

"What you not understand," he said, "is that not everyone can be trouble-maker, like you. This important in life—is ingredient, like yeast for making bread. Without trouble, conflict, life become dead. People live in status-quo, live only by habit, automatically, and without conscience. You good for Miss Madison. You irritate Miss Madison all time—more than anyone else, which is why you get most reward. Without you, possibility for Miss Madison's conscience fall asleep. This money should really be reward from Miss Madison, not from me. You help keep Miss Madison alive."

I understood the actual, serious sense in which he meant what he was saying, but I said that I felt sorry for Miss Madison, that it must have been a terrible experience for her when she saw us all receiving those rewards.

10

He shook his head at me, still laughing. "You not see or understand important thing that happen to Miss Madison when give money. How you feel at time? You feel pity for Miss Madison, no? All other people also feel pity for Miss Madison, too."

I agreed that this was so.

"People not understand about learning," he went on. "Think necessary talk all time, that learn through mind, through words. Not so. Many things can only learn with feeling, even from sensation. But because man talk all time—use only formulatory centre—people not understand this. What you not see other night in study-house is that Miss Madison have new experience for her. Is poor woman, people not like, people think she funny—they laugh at. But other night, people not laugh. True, Miss Madison feel uncomfortable, feel embarrassed when I give money, feel shame perhaps. But when many people also feel for her sympathy, pity, compassion, even love, she understand this but not right away with mind. She feel, for first time in life, sympathy from many people. She not even know then that she feel this, but her life change; with you, I use you like example, last summer you hate Miss Madison. Now you not hate, you not think funny, you feel sorry. You even like Miss Madison. This good for her even if she not know right away—you will show; you cannot hide this from her, even if wish, cannot hide. So she now have friend, when used to be enemy. This good thing which I do for Miss Madison. I not concerned she understand this now—someday she understand and make her feel warm in heart. This unusual experience—this warm feeling—for such personality as Miss Madison who not have charm, who not friendly in self. Someday, perhaps even soon, she have good feeling because many people feel sorry, feel compassion for her. Someday she even understand what I do and even like me for this. But this kind learning take long time."

I understood him completely and was very moved by his words. But he had not finished.

"Also good thing for you in this," he said. "You young, only boy still, you not care about other people, care for self. I do this to Miss Madison and you think I do bad thing. You feel sorry, you not forget, you think I do bad thing to her. But now you understand not so. Also, good for you, because you feel about other person—you identify with Miss Madison, put self in her place, also regret what you do. Is necessary put self in place of other person if wish understand and help. This good for your conscience, this way is possibility for you learn not hate Miss Madison. All people same—stupid, blind, human. If I do bad thing, this make you learn love other people, not just self."

Questions for Discussion and Writing

1. How did Gurdjieff's allotment of rewards violate conventional expectations? What consequences did this have in changing Peters's view of Miss Madison?
2. What knowledge of human nature is implied in Gurdjieff's ability to create such an emotionally challenging event?
3. Write about a personal experience that forced you to completely reevaluate your attitude toward another person or group.

BERYL MARKHAM

Beryl Markham (1902–1986) achieved renown when she became the first person to fly solo across the Atlantic from England to America (a journey of over twenty-one hours). Hemingway said of her, "She can write rings around all of us who consider ourselves as writers." In this final chapter of West with the Night *(1942), Markham describes the harrowing conditions of this flight.*

West with the Night

I have seldom dreamed a dream worth dreaming again, or at least none worth recording. Mine are not enigmatic dreams; they are peopled with characters who are plausible and who do plausible things, and I am the most plausible amongst them. All the characters in my dreams have quiet voices like the voice of the man who telephoned me at Elstree one morning in September of nineteen-thirty-six and told me that there was rain and strong head winds over the west of England and over the Irish Sea, and that there were variable winds and clear skies in mid-Atlantic and fog off the coast of Newfoundland.

"If you are still determined to fly the Atlantic this late in the year," the voice said, "the Air Ministry suggests that the weather it is able to forecast for tonight, and for tomorrow morning, will be about the best you can expect."

The voice had a few others things to say, but not many, and then it was gone, and I lay in bed half-suspecting that the telephone call and the man who made it were only parts of the mediocre dream I had been dreaming. I felt that if I closed my eyes the unreal quality of the message would be re-established, and that, when I opened them again, this would be another ordinary day with its usual beginning and its usual routine.

But of course I could not close my eyes, nor my mind, nor my memory. I could lie there for a few moments—remembering how it had begun, and telling myself, with senseless repetition, that by tomorrow morning I should either have flown the Atlantic to America—or I should not have flown it. In either case this was the day I would try.

I could stare up at the ceiling of my bedroom in Aldenham House, which was   5
a ceiling undistinguished as ceilings go, and feel less resolute than anxious, much less brave than foolhardy. I could say to myself, "You needn't do it, of course," knowing at the same time that nothing is so inexorable as a promise to your pride.

I could ask, "Why risk it?" as I have been asked since, and I could answer, "Each to his element." By his nature a sailor must sail, by his nature a flyer must fly. I could compute that I had flown a quarter of a million miles; and I could foresee that, so long as I had a plane and the sky was there, I should go on flying more miles.

There was nothing extraordinary in this. I had learned a craft and had worked hard learning it. My hands had been taught to seek the controls of a plane. Usage had taught them. They were at ease clinging to a stick, as a cobbler's fingers are in repose grasping an awl. No human pursuit achieves dignity until it can be called work, and when you can experience a physical loneliness for the tools of your trade, you see that the other things—the experiments, the irrelevant vocations, the vanities you used to hold—were false to you.

Record flights had actually never interested me very much for myself. There were people who thought that such flights were done for admiration and publicity, and worse. But of all the records—from Louis Blériot's first crossing of the English Channel in nineteen hundred and nine, through and beyond Kingsford Smith's flight from San Francisco to Sydney, Australia—none had been made by amateurs, nor by novices, nor by men or women less than hardened to failure, or less than masters of their trade. None of these was false. They were a company that simple respect and simple ambition made it worth more than an effort to follow.

The Carberrys (of Seramai) were in London and I could remember everything about their dinner party—even the menu. I could remember June Carberry and all her guests, and the man named McCarthy, who lived in Zanzibar,[1] leaning across the table and saying, "J. C., why don't you finance Beryl for a record flight?"

I could lie there staring lazily at the ceiling and recall J. C.'s dry answer: "A number of pilots have flown the North Atlantic, west to east. Only Jim Mollison has done it alone the other way—from Ireland. Nobody has done it alone from England—man or woman. I'd be interested in that, but nothing else. If you want to try it, Burl, I'll back you. I think Edgar Percival could build a plane that would do it, provided you can fly it. Want to chance it?" 10

"Yes."

I could remember saying that better than I could remember anything—except J. C.'s almost ghoulish grin, and her remark that sealed the agreement: "It's a deal, Burl. I'll furnish the plane and you fly the Atlantic—but, gee, I wouldn't tackle it for a million. Think of all that black water! Think how cold it is!"

And I had thought of both.

I had thought of both for a while, and then there had been other things to think about. I had moved to Elstree, half-hour's flight from the Percival Aircraft Works at Gravesend, and almost daily for three months now I had flown down to the factory in a hired plane and watched the Vega Gull they were making for me. I had watched her birth and watched her growth. I had watched her wings take shape, and seen wood and fabric moulded to her ribs to form her long, sleek belly, and I had seen her engine cradled into her frame, and made fast.

The Gull had a turquoise-blue body and silver wings. Edgar Percival had made her with care, with skill, and with worry—the care of a veteran flyer, the skill of a master designer, and the worry of a friend. Actually the plane was a standard sport model with a range of only six hundred and sixty miles. But she had a special undercarriage built to carry the weight of her extra oil and petrol tanks. The tanks were fixed into the wings, into the centre section, and into the cabin itself. In the 15

---

[1] *Zanzibar:* an island off the east coast of Africa.

cabin they formed a wall around my seat, and each tank had a petcock of its own. The petcocks were important.

"If you open one," said Percival, "without shutting the other first, you may get an airlock. You know the tanks in the cabin have no gauges, so it may be best to let one run completely dry before opening the next. Your motor might go dead in the interval—but she'll start again. She's a De Havilland Gipsy—and Gipsys never stop."

I had talked to Tom. We had spent hours going over the Atlantic chart, and I had realized that the tinker of Molo, now one of England's great pilots, had traded his dreams and had got in return a better thing. Tom had grown older too; he had jettisoned a deadweight of irrelevant hopes and wonders, and had left himself a re-alistic code that had no room for temporizing or easy sentiment.

"I'm glad you're going to do it, Beryl. It won't be simple. If you can get off the ground in the first place, with such an immense load of fuel, you'll be alone in that plane about a night and a day—mostly night. Doing it east to west, the wind's against you. In September, so is the weather. You won't have a radio. If you misjudge your course only a few degrees, you'll end up in Labrador or in the sea—so don't misjudge anything."

Tom could still grin. He had grinned; he had said: "Anyway, it ought to amuse you to think that your financial backer lives on a farm called 'Place of Death' and your plane is being built at 'Gravesend.' If you were consistent, you'd christen the Gull 'The Flying Tombstone.'"

I hadn't been that consistent. I had watched the building of the plane and   20
I had trained for the flight like an athlete. And now, as I lay in bed, fully awake, I could still hear the quiet voice of the man from the Air Ministry intoning, like the voice of a dispassionate court clerk: ". . . the weather for tonight and tomorrow . . . will be about the best you can expect." I should have liked to discuss the flight once more with Tom before I took off, but he was on a special job up north. I got out of bed and bathed and put on my flying clothes and took some cold chicken packed in a cardboard box and flew over to the military field at Abingdon, where the Vega Gull waited for me under the care of the R.A.F. I remember that the weather was clear and still.

Jim Mollison lent me his watch. He said: "This is not a gift. I wouldn't part with it for anything. It got me across the North Atlantic and the South Atlantic too. Don't lose it—and, for God's sake, don't get it wet. Salt water would ruin the works."

Brian Lewis gave me a life-saving jacket. Brian owned the plane I had been using between Elstree and Gravesend, and he had thought a long time about a farewell gift. What could be more practical than a pneumatic jacket that could be inflated through a rubber tube?

"You could float around in it for days," said Brian. But I had to decide be-tween the life-saver and warm clothes. I couldn't have both, because of their bulk, and I hate the cold, so I left the jacket.

And Jock Cameron, Brian's mechanic, gave me a sprig of heather. If it had been a whole bush of heather, complete with roots growing in an earthen jar, I think I should have taken it, bulky or not. The blessing of Scotland, bestowed by a Scotsman, is not to be dismissed. Nor is the well-wishing of a ground mechanic to be taken lightly, for these men are the pilot's contact with reality.

It is too much that with all those pedestrian centuries behind us we should, in   25
a few decades, have learned to fly; it is too heady a thought, too proud a boast. Only the dirt on a mechanic's hands, the straining vise, the splintered bolt of steel underfoot on the hanger floor—only these and such anxiety as the face of a Jock Cameron can hold for a pilot and his plane before a flight, serve to remind us that, not unlike the heather, we too are earthbound. We fly, but we have not "conquered" the air. Nature presides in all her dignity, permitting us the study and the use of such of her forces as we may understand. It is when we presume to intimacy, having been granted only tolerance, that the harsh stick falls across our impudent knuckles and we rub the pain, staring upward, startled by our ignorance.

"Here is a sprig of heather," said Jock, and I took it and pinned it into a pocket of my flying jacket.

There were press cars parked outside the field at Abingdon, and several press planes and photographers, but the R.A.F. kept everyone away from the grounds except technicians and a few of my friends.

The Carberrys had sailed for New York a month ago to wait for me there. Tom was still out of reach with no knowledge of my decision to leave, but that didn't matter so much, I thought. It didn't matter because Tom was unchanging— neither a fairweather pilot nor a fairweather friend. If for a month, or a year, or two years we sometimes had not seen each other, it still hadn't mattered. Nor did this. Tom would never say, "You should have let me know." He assumed that I had learned all that he had tried to teach me, and for my part, I thought of him, even then, as the merest student must think of his mentor. I could sit in a cabin overcrowded with petrol tanks and set my course for North America, but the knowledge of my hands on the controls would be Tom's knowledge. His words of caution and words of guidance, spoken so long ago, so many times, on bright mornings over the veldt or over a forest, or with a far mountain visible at the tip of our wing, would be spoken again, if I asked.

So it didn't matter, I thought. It was silly to think about.

You can live a lifetime and, at the end of it, know more about other people   30
than you know about yourself. You learn to watch other people, but you never watch yourself because you strive against loneliness. If you read a book, or shuffle a deck of cards, or care for a dog, you are avoiding yourself. The abhorrence of loneliness is as natural as wanting to live at all. If it were otherwise, men would never have bothered to make an alphabet, nor to have fashioned words out of what were only animal sounds, nor to have crossed continents—each man to see what the other looked like.

Being alone in an aeroplane for even so short a time as a night and a day, irrevocably alone, with nothing to observe but your instruments and your own hands in semi-darkness, nothing to contemplate but the size of your small courage, nothing to wonder about but the beliefs, the faces, and the hopes rooted in your mind—such an experience can be as startling as the first awareness of a stranger walking by your side at night. You are the stranger.

It is dark already and I am over the south of Ireland. There are the lights of Cork and the lights are wet; they are drenched in Irish rain, and I am above them and dry. I am above them and the plane roars in a sobbing world, but it imparts no sadness to me. I feel the security of solitude, the exhilaration of escape. So long as I can see the lights and imagine the people walking under them, I feel selfishly triumphant, as if I have eluded care and left even the small sorrow of rain in other hands.

It is a little over an hour now since I left Abingdon. England, Wales, and the Irish Sea are behind me like so much time used up. On a long flight distance and time are the same. But there had been a moment when Time stopped—and Distance too. It was the moment I lifted the blue-and-silver Gull from the aerodrome, the moment the photographers aimed their cameras, the moment I felt the craft refuse its burden and strain toward the earth in sullen rebellion, only to listen at last to the persuasion of stick and elevators, the dogmatic argument of blueprints that said she *had* to fly because the figures proved it.

So she had flown, and once airborne, once she had yielded to the sophistry of a draughtsman's board, she had said, "There: I have lifted the weight. Now, where are we bound?"—and the question had frightened me.

"We are bound for a place thirty-six hundred miles from here—two thousand miles of it unbroken ocean. Most of the way it will be night. We are flying west with the night." 35

So there behind me is Cork; and ahead of me is Berehaven Lighthouse. It is the last light, standing on the last land. I watch it, counting the frequency of its flashes—so many to the minute. Then I pass it and fly out to sea.

The fear is gone now—not overcome nor reasoned away. It is gone because something else has taken its place; the confidence and the trust, the inherent belief in the security of land underfoot—now this faith is transferred to my plane, because the land has vanished and there is no other tangible thing to fix faith upon. Flight is but momentary escape from the eternal custody of earth.

Rain continues to fall, and outside the cabin it is totally dark. My altimeter says that the Atlantic is two thousand feet below me, my Sperry Artificial Horizon says that I am flying level. I judge my drift at three degrees more than my weather chart suggests, and fly accordingly. I am flying blind. A beam to follow would help. So would a radio—but then, so would clear weather. The voice of the man at the Air Ministry had not promised storm.

I feel the wind rising and the rain falls hard. The smell of petrol in the cabin is so strong and the roar of the plane so loud that my senses are almost deadened. Gradually it becomes unthinkable that existence was ever otherwise.

At ten o'clock P.M. I am flying along the Great Circle Course for Harbour 40 Grace, Newfoundland, into a forty-mile headwind at a speed of one hundred and thirty miles an hour. Because of the weather, I cannot be sure of how many more hours I have to fly, but I think it must be between sixteen and eighteen.

At ten-thirty I am still flying on the large cabin tank of petrol, hoping to use it up and put an end to the liquid swirl that has rocked the plane since my take-off.

The tank has no gauge, but written on its side is the assurance: "This tank is good for four hours."

There is nothing ambiguous about such a guaranty. I believe it, but at twenty-five minutes to eleven, my motor coughs and dies, and the Gull is powerless above the sea.

I realize that the heavy drone of the plane has been, until this moment, complete and comforting silence. It is the actual silence following the last splutter of the engine that stuns me. I can't feel any fear; I can't feel anything. I can only observe with a kind of stupid disinterest that my hands are violently active and know that, while they move, I am being hypnotized by the needle of my altimeter.

I suppose that the denial of natural impulse is what is meant by "keeping calm," but impulse has reason in it. If it is night and you are sitting in an aeroplane with a stalled motor, and there are two thousand feet between you and the sea, nothing can be more reasonable than the impulse to pull back your stick in the hope of adding to that two thousand, if only by a little. The thought, the knowledge, the law that tells you that your hope lies not in this, but in a contrary act— the act of directing your impotent craft toward the water—seems a terrifying abandonment, not only of reason, but of sanity. Your mind and your heart reject it. It is your hands—your stranger's hands—that follow with unfeeling precision the letter of the law.

I sit there and watch my hands push forward on the stick and feel the Gull respond and begin its dive to the sea. Of course it is a simple thing; surely the cabin tank has run dry too soon. I need only to turn another petcock . . .   45

But it is dark in the cabin. It is easy to see the luminous dial of the altimeter and to note that my height is now eleven hundred feet, but it is not easy to see a petcock that is somewhere near the floor of the plane. A hand gropes and reappears with an electric torch, and fingers, moving with agonizing composure, find the petcock and turn it; and I wait.

At three hundred feet the motor is still dead, and I am conscious that the needle of my altimeter seems to whirl like the spoke of a spindle winding up the remaining distance between the plane and the water. There is some lightning, but the quick flash only serves to emphasize the darkness. How high can waves reach— twenty feet, perhaps? Thirty?

It is impossible to avoid the thought that this is the end of my flight, but my reactions are not orthodox; the various incidents of my entire life do not run through my mind like a motion-picture film gone mad. I only feel that all this has happened before—and it has. It has all happened a hundred times in my mind, in my sleep, so that now I am not really caught in terror; I recognize a familiar scene, a familiar story with its climax dulled by too much telling.

I do not know how close to the waves I am when the motor explodes to life again. But the sound is almost meaningless. I see my hand easing back on the stick, and I feel the Gull climb up into the storm, and I see the altimeter whirl like a spindle again, paying out the distance between myself and the sea.

The storm is strong. It is comforting. It is like a friend shaking me and saying,   50 "Wake up! You were only dreaming."

But soon I am thinking. By simple calculation I find that my motor had been silent for perhaps an instant more than thirty seconds.

I ought to thank God—and I do, though indirectly. I thank Geoffrey De Havilland who designed the indomitable Gipsy, and who, after all, must have been designed by God in the first place.

A lighted ship—the daybreak—some steep cliffs standing in the sea. The meaning of these will never change for pilots. If one day an ocean can be flown within an hour, if men can build a plane that so masters time, the sight of land will be no less welcome to the steersman of that fantastic craft. He will have cheated laws that the cunning of science has taught him how to cheat, and he will feel his guilt and be eager for the sanctuary of the soil.

I saw the ship and the daybreak, and then I saw the cliffs of Newfoundland wound in ribbons of fog. I felt the elation I had so long imagined, and I felt the happy guilt of having circumvented the stern authority of the weather and the sea. But mine was a minor triumph; my swift Gull was not so swift as to have escaped unnoticed. The night and the storm had caught her and we had flown blind for nineteen hours.

I was tired now, and cold. Ice began to film the glass of the cabin windows and the fog played a magician's game with the land. But the land was there. I could not see it, but I had seen it. I could not afford to believe that it was any land but the land I wanted. I could not afford to believe that my navigation was at fault, because there was no time for doubt.

South to Cape Race, west to Sydney on Cape Breton Island. With my protractor, my map, and my compass, I set my new course, humming the ditty that Tom had taught me: "Variation West—magnetic best. Variation East—magnetic least." A silly rhyme, but it served to placate, for the moment, two warring poles—the magnetic and the true. I flew south and found the lighthouse of Cape Race protruding from the fog like a warning finger. I circled twice and went on over the Gulf of Saint Lawrence.

After a while there would be New Brunswick, and then Maine—and then New York. I could anticipate. I could almost say, "Well, if you stay awake, you'll find it's only a matter of time now"—but there was no question of staying awake. I was tired and I had not moved an inch since that uncertain moment at Abingdon when the Gull had elected to rise with her load and fly, but I could not have closed my eyes. I could sit there in the cabin, walled in glass and petrol tanks, and be grateful for the sun and the light, and the fact that I could see the water under me. They were almost the last waves I had to pass. Four hundred miles of water, and then the land again—Cape Breton. I would stop at Sydney to refuel and go on. It was easy now. It would be like stopping at Kisumu and going on.

Success breeds confidence. But who has a right to confidence except the Gods? I had a following wind, my last tank of petrol was more than three-quarters full, and the world was as bright to me as if it were a new world, never touched. If I had been wiser, I might have known that such moments are, like innocence, short-lived. My engine began to shudder before I saw the land. It died, it spluttered, it started again and limped along. It coughed and spat black exhaust toward the sea.

There are words for everything. There was a word for this—airlock, I thought. This had to be an airlock because there was petrol enough. I thought I might clear it by turning on and turning off all the empty tanks, and so I did that. The handles of the petcocks were sharp little pins of metal, and when I had opened and closed them a dozen times, I saw that my hands were bleeding and that the blood was dropping on my maps and on my clothes, but the effort wasn't any good. I coasted along on a sick and halting engine. The oil pressure and the oil temperature gauges were normal, the magnetos working, and yet I lost altitude slowly while the realization of failure seeped into my heart. If I made the land, I should have been the first to fly the North Atlantic from England, but from my point of view, from a pilot's point of view, a forced landing was failure because New York was my goal. If only I could land and then take off, I would make it still . . . if only, if only . . .

The engine cuts again, and then catches, and each time it spurts to life I climb   60
as high as I can get, and then it splutters and stops and I glide once more toward the water, to rise again and descend again, like a hunting sea bird.

I find the land. Visibility is perfect now and I see land forty or fifty miles ahead. If I am on my course, that will be Cape Breton. Minute after minute goes by. The minutes almost materialize; they pass before my eyes like links in a long slow-moving chain, and each time the engine cuts, I see a broken link in the chain and catch my breath until it passes.

The land is under me. I snatch my map and stare at it to confirm my whereabouts. I am, even at my present crippled speed, only twelve minutes from Sydney Airport, where I can land for repairs and then go on.

The engine cuts once more and I begin to glide, but now I am not worried; she will start again, as she has done, and I will gain altitude and fly into Sydney.

But she doesn't start. This time she's dead as death; the Gull settles earthward and it isn't any earth I know. It is black earth stuck with boulders and I hang above it, on hope and on a motionless propeller. Only I cannot hang above it long. The earth hurries to meet me, I bank, turn, and side-slip to dodge the boulders, my wheels touch, and I feel them submerge. The nose of the plane is engulfed in mud, and I go forward striking my head on the glass of the cabin front, hearing it shatter, feeling blood pour over my face.

I stumble out of the plane and sink to my knees in muck and stand there fool-   65
ishly staring, not at the lifeless land, but at my watch.

Twenty-one hours and twenty-five minutes.

Atlantic flight, Abingdon, England, to a nameless swamp—nonstop.

A Cape Breton Islander found me—a fisherman trudging over the bog saw the Gull with her tail in the air and her nose buried, and then he saw me floundering in the embracing soil of his native land. I had been wandering for an hour and the black mud had got up to my waist and the blood from the cut in my head had met the mud halfway.

From a distance, the fisherman directed me with his arms and with shouts toward the firm places in the bog, and for another hour I walked on them and came toward him like a citizen of Hades blinded by the sun, but it wasn't the sun; I hadn't slept for forty hours.

He took me to his hut on the edge of the coast and I found that built upon   70
the rocks there was a little cubicle that housed an ancient telephone—put there in case of shipwrecks.

I telephoned to Sydney Airport to say that I was safe and to prevent a needless search being made. On the following morning I did step out of a plane at Floyd Bennett Field and there was a crowd of people still waiting there to greet me, but the plane I stepped from was not the Gull, and for days while I was in New York I kept thinking about that and wishing over and over again that it had been the Gull, until the wish lost its significance, and time moved on, overcoming many things it met on the way.

Questions for Discussion and Writing

1. What motivates Markham and explains her compulsion to succeed?
2. How would you characterize Markham's personality as it emerges in her account? What sort of relationship did she have with her fellow pilots?
3. Do you consider Markham a workaholic? What distinguishes workaholics from other hard workers? Would you consider yourself one? Why or why not?

DOUCHAN GERSI

Douchan Gersi is the producer of the National Geographic *television series called* Discovery. *He has traveled extensively throughout the Philippines, New Zealand, the Polynesian Islands, the Melanesian Islands, the Sahara, Africa, New Guinea, and Peru. "Initiated into an Iban Tribe of Headhunters," from his book* Explorer *(1987), tells of the harrowing initiation process he underwent to become a member of the Iban tribe in Borneo. He subsequently wrote* Out of Africa *with Maroussia Gersi (1989). His latest work is* Faces in the Smoke: An Eyewitness Experience of Voodoo *(1991).*

Initiated into an Iban Tribe of Headhunters

The hopeful man sees success where others see shadows and storm.

—O. S. Marden

Against Tawa's excellent advice I asked the chief if I could become a member of their clan. It took him a while before he could give me an answer, for he had to question the spirits of their ancestors and wait for their reply to appear through different omens: the flight of a blackbird, the auguries of a chick they sacrificed. A few days after the question, the answer came:

"Yes . . . but!"

The "but" was that I would have to undergo their initiation. Without know-ing exactly what physical ordeal was in store, I accepted. I knew I had been through worse and survived. It was to begin in one week.

Late at night I was awakened by a girl slipping into my bed. She was sweet and already had a great knowledge of man's morphology. Like all the others who came and "visited" me this way every night, she was highly skilled in the arts of love. Among the Iban, only unmarried women offer sexual hospitality, and no one obliged these women to offer me their favors. Sexual freedom ends at marriage. Unfaithfulness—except during yearly fertility celebrations when everything, even incest at times, is permitted—is punished as an offense against their matrimonial laws.

As a sign of respect to family and the elders, sexual hospitality is not openly   5
practiced. The girls always came when my roommates were asleep and left before they awoke. They were free to return or give their place to their girlfriends.

The contrast between the violence of some Iban rituals and the beauty of their art, their sociability, their kindness, and their personal warmth has always fas-cinated me. I also witnessed that contrast among a tribe of Papuans (who, besides being headhunters, practice cannibalism) and among some African tribes. In fact, tribes devoted to cannibalism and other human sacrifices are often among the most sociable of people, and their art, industry, and trading systems are more advanced than other tribes that don't have these practices.

For my initiation, they had me lie down naked in a four-foot-deep pit filled with giant carnivorous ants. Nothing held me there. At any point I could easily have escaped, but the meaning of this rite of passage was not to kill me. The ritual was intended to test my courage and my will, to symbolically kill me by the pain in order for me to be reborn as a man of courage. I am not sure what their reactions would have been if I had tried to get out of the pit before their signal, but it oc-curred to me that although the ants might eat a little of my flesh, the Iban offered more dramatic potentials.

Since I wore, as Iban do, a long piece of cloth around my waist and nothing more, I had the ants running all over my body. They were everywhere. The pain of the ants' bites was intense, so I tried to relax to decrease the speed of my circulation and therefore the effects of the poison. But I couldn't help trying to get them away from my face where they were exploring every inch of my skin. I kept my eyes closed, inhaling through my almost closed lips and exhaling through my nose to chase them away from there.

I don't know how long I stayed in the pit, waiting with anguish for the signal which would end my ordeal. As I tried to concentrate on my relaxing, the sound of the beaten gongs and murmurs of the assistants watching me from all around the pit started to disappear into a chaos of pain and loud heartbeat.

Then suddenly I heard Tawa and the chief calling my name. I removed once   10
more the ants wandering on my eyelids before opening my eyes and seeing my friends smiling to indicate that it was over. I got out of the pit on my own, but I needed help to rid myself of the ants, which were determined to eat all my skin.

After the men washed my body, the shaman applied an herbal mixture to ease the pain and reduce the swellings. I would have quit and left the village then had I known that the "pit" experience was just the hors d'oeuvre.

The second part of the physical test started early the next morning. The chief explained the "game" to me. It was Hide and Go Seek Iban-style. I had to run without any supplies, weapons, or food, and for three days and three nights escape a group of young warriors who would leave the village a few hours after my departure and try to find me. If I were caught, my head would be used in a ceremony. The Iban would have done so without hate. It was simply the rule of their life. Birth and death. A death that always engenders new life.

When I asked, "What would happen if someone refused this part of the initiation?" the chief replied that such an idea wasn't possible. Once one had begun, there was no turning back. I knew the rules governing initiations among the cultures of tradition but never thought they would be applied to me. Whether or not I survived the initiation, I would be symbolically killed in order to be reborn among them. I had to die from my present time and identity into another life. I was aware that, among some cultures, initiatory ordeals are so arduous that young initiates sometimes really die. These are the risks if one wishes to enter into another world.

I was given time to get ready and the game began. I ran like hell without a plan or, it seemed to me, a prayer of surviving. Running along a path I had never taken, going I knew not where, I thought about every possible way I could escape from the young warriors. To hide somewhere. But where? Climb a tree and hide in it? Find a hole and squeeze in it? Bury myself under rocks and mud? But all of these seemed impossible. I had a presentiment they would find me anyway. So I ran straight ahead, my head going crazy by dint of searching for a way to safely survive the headhunters.

I would prefer staying longer with ants, I thought breathlessly. It was safer to stay among them for a whole day since they were just simple pain and fear compared to what I am about to undergo. I don't want to die.

For the first time I realized the real possibility of death—no longer in a romantic way, but rather at the hands of butchers.

Ten minutes after leaving the long house, I suddenly heard a call coming from somewhere around me. Still running, I looked all around trying to locate who was calling, and why. At the second call I stopped, cast my gaze about, and saw a woman's head peering out from the bushes. I recognized her as one of my pretty lovers. I hesitated, not knowing if she were part of the hunting party or a goddess come to save me. She called again. I thought, God, what to do? How will I escape from the warriors? As I stood there truly coming into contact with my impossible situation, I began to panic. She called again. With her fingers she showed me what the others would do if they caught me. Her forefinger traced an invisible line from one side of her throat to the other. If someone was going to kill me, why not her? I joined her and found out she was in a lair. I realized I had entered the place where the tribe's women go to hide during their menstruation. This area is taboo for men. Each woman has her own refuge. Some have shelters made of branches, others deep covered holes hidden behind bushes with enough space to eat and sleep and wait until their time is past.

She invited me to make myself comfortable. That was quite difficult since it was just large enough for one person. But I had no choice. And after all, it was a paradise compared to what I would have undergone had I not by luck crossed this special ground.

Nervously and physically exhausted by my run and fear and despair, I soon fell asleep. Around midnight I woke. She gave me rice and meat. We exchanged a few words. Then it was her turn to sleep.

The time I spent in the lair with my savior went fast. I tried to sleep all day long, an escape from the concerns of my having broken a taboo. And I wondered what would happen to me if the headhunters were to learn where I spent the time of my physical initiation.

Then, when it was safe, I snuck back to the village . . . in triumph. I arrived be- 20
fore the warriors, who congratulated and embraced me when they returned. I was a headhunter at last.

I spent the next two weeks quietly looking at the Iban through new eyes. But strangely enough, instead of the initiation putting me closer to them, it had the opposite effect. I watched them more and more from an anthropological distance: my Iban brothers became an interesting clan whose life I witnessed but did not really share. And then suddenly I was bored and yearned for my own tribe. When Tawa had to go to an outpost to exchange pepper grains for other goods, I took a place aboard his canoe. Two days later I was in a small taxi-boat heading toward Sibu, the first leg in civilization on my voyage home.

I think of them often. I wonder about the man I tried to cure. I think about Tawa and the girl who saved my life, and all the others sitting on the veranda. How long will my adopted village survive before being destroyed like all the others in the way of civilization? And what has become of those who marked my flesh with the joy of their lives and offered me the best of their souls? If they are slowly vanishing from my memories, I know that I am part of the stories they tell. I know that my life among them will be perpetuated until the farthest tomorrow. Now I am a story caught in a living legend of a timeless people.

Questions for Discussion and Writing

1. What do the unusual sexual customs and hospitality bestowed on outsiders suggest about the different cultural values of the Iban? Do these customs suggest that the initiation would be harsher or milder than Gersi expected?

2. At what point did Gersi realize that his former ideas about being accepted by the tribe were unrealistic and that his present situation was truly life-endangering? How is the narrative shaped to put the reader through the same suspenseful moments that Gersi experienced? Speculate about why Gersi's life-and-death initiation, rather than bringing him closer to the Iban, as he expected, actually made him more distant from them?

3. Have you ever gone through an initiation ritual to become part of an organization, club, fraternity, or sorority? Describe your experiences and how you felt before, during, and after this initiation.

LESLEY HAZLETON

Lesley Hazleton was born in England in 1945 and emigrated to the United States in 1979. She has worked as a feature writer and reporter and since 1989 has written about cars and driving for The New York Times, Lear's *magazine,* Newsday, *and, currently, for the* Detroit Free Press. *Her books include the award-winning* Jerusalem, Jerusalem *(1986) and* Confessions of a Fast Woman *(1992), from which the following chapter is drawn. She has also written* Everything Women Always Wanted to Know about Cars: But Didn't Know Who to Ask *(1995). Most recently, she has written* Driving to Detroit: An Automotive Odyssey *(1998).*

Confessions of a Fast Woman

I loved working at the sink. Harvey thought this was perverse of me. He was probably right. It was one of the dirtiest jobs in the shop.

The sink was a neatly self-enclosed system: a steel tub set atop a barrel containing parts cleaner, a small pump sucking the cleaner up from the barrel into a tube with a thick steel brush at the end, and a filter to clean the used fluid before it drained back into the barrel to be used again.

Working there, I'd stand with my back to everything else in the shop, concentrated entirely on the mass of gunked parts before me. The gunk was thick, black. The parts were so filthy they seemed almost anonymous, just so many interchangeable relics of the mechanical age. Even thinking of cleaning them at first seemed pointless.

But leave something to soak in that sink for a while, then come back to it and start scrubbing, and a kind of magic happened. What had been anonymous began to reveal form and personality. Vague shapes achieved particularity.

Black paled, gleamed here and there, turned slowly to silver. An ancient   5
alchemy took place right under my hands as I hosed and scrubbed. Years of baked grease and oil and road dirt gave way to the corrosiveness of the parts cleaner, and as I worked, it seemed that here, under my very hands, I was rediscovering the original form, the bright gleaming essence of each part. Old melted gaskets disappeared under the brush. Flywheel teeth became sharp and effective. Clutch plates became intricate pieces of sculpture. I had a distinct sense of creating each part anew, of restoring its form and function.

And all the time, of course, I was breathing in the fumes of the parts cleaner, so that I am still not sure if the work itself was really that satisfying, or if I was simply so high that it seemed that way.

All the cleaners began to smell good—a seductive, chemical smell that seemed to enter my head, clear my sinuses, clean up all the synapses of my brain. There was the 5-56, so much like dry-cleaning fluid that I sometimes thought if I just stood in the path of its fumes, it would clean the clothes right on me. Oddly, I'd always hated that smell before. Then there was the Carb Clean, for gummed-up carbs; the Brakleen brakes cleaner, each can with a thin red straw laid horizontally across its black cap like the headgear of a Japanese geisha; and the Gunk—a registered trademark name for heavy-duty engine cleaner.

I had no idea just how addictive the fumes were until a few weeks into my apprenticeship, on our Monday off. I was driving past another repair shop that was open on Mondays. The windows of my car were wide open, and as I went by, I recognized the smells of parts cleaner, gasoline, lubricants—all the acids and oils with which I now worked five days a week. I slowed way down, breathed in deep, and was suffused with an immense sense of well-being.

After a month, the shop and the smells and the work were in my dreams. They were good dreams, but I'd wake with the fumes still in my nostrils, wondering how smells from a dream could spill over into the first moments of waking. Was the sense of smell independent of reality? Was my brain so addicted that it could create the smell by itself, without any external stimulus?

No matter how seductive the fumes, however, there was no doubt as to the corrosiveness of the parts cleaner: it turned my tanned hands a whitish hue and made the skin parchment dry. I began to use rubber gloves when working at the sink, but even then the chemicals seemed to work their way through the rubber, and my hands still paled.   10

Meanwhile, the blackened asbestos dust from the brake pads was just plain hazardous. It was caked onto the calipers and the whole of the brake assembly. Cleaning it out demanded a screwdriver and a rag and copious amounts of Brakleen. It was close-up work, so that however careful I was, I still inhaled the dust.

You take all the precautions you can in a repair shop. You keep as many doors and windows open as possible. You keeps fans going. You back out cars and bikes to start them up, or if you have to start them inside, you attach a hose to the exhaust pipe and run the fumes outside. You could, of course, wear a mask, but few mechanics do. Most know they should, but the masks are hot and stuffy and they get in the way. And besides, the truth is that most mechanics do not worry about fumes. They have bigger things to worry about: a jack or a hoist giving way, a fire, a loose part spinning off. Auto mechanics is not a safe profession.

Despite all the protestations of writers and researchers that intellectual work is hard and exhausting, physical work is harder. Like anyone who's done it day in and day out, I now know this in my bones.

For years, I argued that intellectual work was exhausting, as indeed it can be. After a few hours at the typewriter, there is little I can do for a while. All my energy has been consumed, poured onto the page. Sometimes I do some physical work for a change—scythe an overgrown garden, for instance, or clean the oven. In such circumstances, physical work seems a pleasure and a relief, something that produces a healthy kind of exhaustion instead of the enervating overload of the mind that I am escaping.

This kind of short-term excursion into physical work can indeed make it   15 seem attractive. But when you do it for a living, it exacts a heavy toll. The long-term effects of fumes and asbestos dust working their way into the body's cells are one thing, but the short term can be riskier still. With all due respect to the physical strain on hands, eyes, back, and brain from working at a keyboard all day, in physical work you can literally break your back.

I was lucky. I only sprained mine.

The culprit was a Datsun 240Z. It arrived on a truck with a note that read, "It went to Woodstock, and while there, the gears went." Just that, and a signature.

It hadn't been cruising the idyllic scenery of Woodstock. It had been drag racing. The owners had put a six-cylinder 260 engine into it, with triple carbs and a psi gauge. There'd been a big pop, it seemed, and then—nothing. No motion.

"We'll have to pull out the transmission and replace it," said Carl.

I was delighted. The heavier the work—the more it got down to the basics,   20 into the actual drive mechanisms—the happier I was because the more I'd learn. Better still, if we had to replace the transmission, I could take the broken one apart. I already knew from the exploded diagrams in my textbook that there's nothing like taking things apart to understand how they work. Putting them back together again, I had still to discover, is yet another level of understanding.

The Z-car rode so low to the ground that we had to jack it up just to get the arms of the hydraulic lift underneath it. Harvey removed the bolt at the bottom of the transmission case so we could drain the transmission fluid—foul-smelling stuff—and found a small chunk of metal sitting on top of the bolt. "Bad sign," he said. "Something's come loose and ripped through the gears."

The next stage was to get the exhaust system off. That should have been simple enough, but there was so much gunk and rust that even after we'd loosened all the bolts, nothing moved. So Harvey stood up front and yanked, and I stood toward the back, pulling and yanking at the pipe above my head.

I felt something go inside me. Somewhere in my abdomen, it seemed. But I was focused on that exhaust pipe, eyes half-closed against flecks of grit and rust, and paid no attention. Harvey finally managed to loosen the front end, then we swapped places, me steadying as he pulled, and finally, lo and behold, the pipe slid off. We disconnected the fuel and oil lines, and then faced the really tough part.

When you're deeply involved in hard work, you simply don't notice pain. By the time we got the transmission case down from its mountings and into the yard, and then dismantled the clutch, it was late afternoon, and it was clear that this was going to be a long, drawn-out job. The drive plate and flywheel were so badly worn that they too would have to be replaced.

I went home that night exhausted. That was nothing unusual. Most evenings   25 I'd flop down in an armchair with a beer in one hand, and find myself unable to move. It was the kind of deep exhaustion that comes only from hard physical work, the kind that you can feel in every muscle of your body, that seems to reach into your bones and sit there, making them feel both incredibly heavy and weightless at the same time. There is a strange kind of floating feeling to this exhaustion, yet at the same time you are convinced that you must weigh twice what you usually weigh.

If someone had shouted, "Fire!" right then, I'd have nodded, said "Fine," and not moved an inch.

This stage of exhaustion would usually last a good half hour or so, and in that half hour, I'd hold my hands up in front of my face and wonder where all those cuts and burns and scrapes had come from. From the repair shop, obviously, but what car, what movement, what moment? I never knew. Cuts and burns and scrapes and other minor injuries were just part of the job, so much so that I never noticed them at the time. Only later, in another place and time, in a comfortable armchair as the sun was setting, did they begin to seem remarkable. And then I'd feel an odd pride in them. They were proof of my work, small badges of my apprenticeship.

That Z-car had been a tougher job than most. We'd been working on it nearly the whole of the ten-hour day, and now, as I sat still, I realized my abdomen was really hurting, and that the pain was spreading to my back. A pulled muscle, I thought. We had three days off now for the Fourth of July weekend, and I was glad: my body needed it.

The next morning, I picked up a loaded wheelbarrow of split wood, turned it to the right and could almost swear that I heard something go pop in my lower back, just like the gears of that Z-car. For the first time in my life, I understood what crippling pain was. By the time I got to a chiropractor in Barre, the only one around who'd see me on a holiday weekend, I couldn't walk without a crutch.

Half an hour later, I walked out carrying the crutch—still in pain, but mobile.   30
The chiro, young and gentle, merely smiled tolerantly when I compared him to Christ.

"This back has forty-eight hours to heal," I told him.

"It will probably take four or five weeks," he said.

I shook my head. "It can't," I said. "I've got to go to work."

He studied my face. "Come on in tomorrow and the next day," he said, "and we'll see what we can do."

That included the Fourth of July itself. Rob Borowske became more and   35
more Christ-like in my mind. Forty-eight hours of cold compresses, gentle stretching, electrical stimulation, aspirin, and chiropractic adjustments did not make for the happiest of weekends, but on the morning of July 5, I was there at Just Imports, a compress strapped to my lower back, cautiously mobile.

It wasn't macho that made me so determined. Partly it was the awareness that if I lay in bed and played invalid, my back would "freeze" and take far longer to heal. But more than that, it was the knowledge that Harvey and Bud would have to literally break their backs before they'd stay away from work. A mere "subluxation" simply did not rank. Not alongside what Harvey had been through.

The back healed quickly. Between Rob's four or five weeks and my forty-eight hours, it compromised on two weeks, although by the middle of the first week I was working as I had been. Being on my feet all day helped. Besides, I had to take apart that transmission case, discovering in the process that Harvey had been right: ball bearings had come loose and torn through the gears. No wonder nothing would move.

Harvey asked after the back a couple of times, but after that it was business as usual. Neither he nor Bud nor Carl thought it at all odd that I should turn up for work. Injuries were just part of the job. My back, the left foot I bruised badly when I moved a motorcycle the wrong way, the concussion I'd get a couple of weeks later when I'd stand up and hit my head on the strut of the hydraulic lift ("Every apprentice has to do it at least once," said Harvey)—these were just par for the course. As one injury healed and another replaced it, I began to think of them as rites of passage: stages in my evolution as an apprentice.

Questions for Discussion and Writing

1. What does being an apprentice in an automobile repair shop mean to Hazleton?
2. In what ways does Hazleton try harder because she has to prove herself in a male-dominated profession?
3. Which kind of work do you find more demanding: physical labor or hard intellectual work? Explain your answer.

ANNIE DILLARD

Annie Dillard was born in 1945 in Pittsburgh. She is the author of nine books, including An American Childhood *(1987), where this essay originally appeared;* The Writing Life *(1989), and* Holy the Firm *(1977). In 1975,* Pilgrim at Tinker Creek *was awarded the Pulitzer Prize in nonfiction. Dillard's writing appears in* Atlantic, Harper's, The New York Times Magazine, *the* Yale Review, American Heritage, *and many anthologies. She has received numerous grants and awards, including grants from the Guggenheim Foundation and the National Endowment for the Arts. Dillard's latest book is* For the Time Being *(1999). She currently lives in Connecticut with her husband, Robert D. Richardson, Jr., who is a biographer of Thoreau and Emerson, and her daughter, Rosie.*

So, This Was Adolescence

When I was fifteen, I felt it coming; now I was sixteen, and it hit. My feet had imperceptibly been set on a new path, a fast path into a long tunnel like those many turnpike tunnels near Pittsburgh, turnpike tunnels whose entrances bear on brass plaques a roll call of those men who died blasting them. I wandered witlessly forward and found myself going down, and saw the light dimming; I adjusted to the slant and dimness, traveled further down, adjusted to greater dimness, and so on. There wasn't a whole lot I could do about it, or about anything. I was going to hell on a handcart, that was all, and I knew it and everyone around me knew it, and there it was.

I was growing and thinning, as if pulled. I was getting angry, as if pushed. I morally disapproved most things in North America, and blamed my innocent parents for them. My feelings deepened and lingered. The swift moods of early childhood—each formed by and suited to its occasion—vanished. Now feelings lasted so long they left stains. They arose from nowhere, like winds or waves, and battered at me or engulfed me.

When I was angry, I felt myself coiled and longing to kill someone or bomb something big. Trying to appease myself, during one winter I whipped my bed every afternoon with my uniform belt. I despised the spectacle I made in my own eyes—whipping the bed with a belt, like a creature demented—and I often began halfheartedly, but I did it daily after school as a desperate discipline, trying to rid myself and the innocent world of my wildness. It was like trying to beat back the ocean.

Sometimes in class I couldn't stop laughing; things were too funny to be borne. It began then, my surprise that no one else saw what was so funny.

I read some few books with such reverence I didn't close them at the finish,   5
but only moved the pile of pages back to the start, without breathing, and began again. I read one such book, an enormous novel, six times that way—closing the binding between sessions, but not between readings.

On the piano in the basement I played the maniacal "Poet and Peasant Overture"[1] so loudly, for so many hours, night after night, I damaged the piano's keys and strings. When I wasn't playing this crashing overture, I played boogie-woogie, or something else, anything else in octaves—otherwise, it wasn't loud enough. My fingers were so strong I could do push-ups with them. I played one piece with my fists. I banged on a steel-stringed guitar till I bled, and once on a particularly piercing rock-and-roll downbeat I broke straight through one of Father's snare drums.

I loved my boyfriend so tenderly, I thought I must transmogrify into vapor. It would take spectroscopic analysis to locate my molecules in thin air. No possible way of holding him was close enough. Nothing could cure this bad case of gentleness except, perhaps, violence: maybe if he swung me by the legs and split my skull on a tree? Would that ease this insane wish to kiss too much his eyelids' outer corners and his temples, as if I could love up his brain?

I envied people in books who swooned. For two years I felt myself continuously swooning and continuously unable to swoon; the blood drained from my face and eyes and flooded my heart; my hands emptied, my knees unstrung, I bit at the air for something worth breathing—but I failed to fall, and I couldn't find the way to black out. I had to live on the lip of a waterfall, exhausted.

When I was bored I was first hungry, then nauseated, then furious and weak. "Calm yourself," people had been saying to me all my life. Since early childhood I had tried one thing and then another to calm myself, on those few occasions when I truly wanted to. Eating helped; singing helped. Now sometimes I truly wanted to

---

[1] "*Poet and Peasant Overture*": written (1846) by the Austrian composer Franz von Suppé for *Dichter un Bauer,* a comedy with song.

calm myself. I couldn't lower my shoulders; they seemed to wrap around my ears. I couldn't lower my voice although I could see the people around me flinch. I waved my arm in class till the very teachers wanted to kill me.

I was what they called a live wire. I was shooting out sparks that were digging a pit around me, and I was sinking into that pit. Laughing with Ellin at school recess, or driving around after school with Judy in her jeep, exultant, or dancing with my boyfriend to Louis Armstrong[2] across a polished dining-room floor, I got so excited I looked around wildly for aid; I didn't know where I should go or what I should do with myself. People in books split wood.

10

When rage or boredom reappeared, each seemed never to have left. Each so filled me with so many years' intolerable accumulation it jammed the space behind my eyes, so I couldn't see. There was no room left even on my surface to live. My rib cage was so taut I couldn't breathe. Every cubic centimeter of atmosphere above my shoulders and head was heaped with last straws. Black hatred clogged my very blood. I couldn't peep, I couldn't wiggle or blink; my blood was too mad to flow.

For as long as I could remember, I had been transparent to myself, unselfconscious, learning, doing, most of every day. Now I was in my own way; I myself was a dark object I could not ignore. I couldn't remember how to forget myself. I didn't want to think about myself, to reckon myself in, to deal with myself every livelong minute on top of everything else—but swerve as I might, I couldn't avoid it. I was a boulder blocking my own path. I was a dog barking between my own ears, a barking dog who wouldn't hush.

So this was adolescence. Is this how the people around me had died on their feet—inevitably, helplessly? Perhaps their own selves eclipsed the sun for so many years the world shriveled around them, and when at last their inescapable orbits had passed through these dark egoistic years it was too late, they had adjusted.

Must I then lose the world forever, that I had so loved? Was it all, the whole bright and various planet, where I had been so ardent about finding myself alive, only a passion peculiar to children, that I would outgrow even against my will?

Questions for Discussion and Writing

1. How does Dillard understand the nature of the crisis she experienced during her adolescence?
2. What images are especially effective in communicating her perception of this crisis? Does her attitude change over the course of the essay?
3. Compare Dillard's experience of adolescence with your own. How were they different, and in what ways were they similar?

---

[2] *Louis "Satchmo" Armstrong (1900–1971):* black American jazz trumpeter, singer, and band leader known for his improvisational genius.

JUDITH ORTIZ COFER

Judith Ortiz Cofer, a poet and novelist, was born in 1952 in Hormigueros, Puerto Rico, and was educated at Augusta College, Florida Atlantic University, and Oxford University. Her published work includes the collections of poetry Peregrina *(1985),* Terms of Survival *(1987), and* Reaching for the Mainland and Selected New Poems *(1996) and a novel,* The Line of the Sun *(1989). She also wrote* An Island Like You: Stories of the Barrio *(1995);* Year of Our Revolution: New and Selected Stories and Poems *(1998); and* Woman in Front of the Sun: On Becoming a Writer *(2001). "The Myth of the Latin Woman: I Just Met a Girl Named Maria," which first appeared in* The Latin Deli: Prose and Poetry *(1993), explores the destructive effects of the Latina stereotype.*

The Myth of The Latin Woman: I Just Met a Girl Named Maria

On a bus trip to London from Oxford University where I was earning some graduate credits one summer, a young man, obviously fresh from a pub, spotted me and as if struck by inspiration went down on his knees in the aisle. With both hands over his heart he broke into an Irish tenor's rendition of "Maria" from *West Side Story*.[1] My politely amused fellow passengers gave his lovely voice the round of gentle applause it deserved. Though I was not quite as amused, I managed my version of an English smile: no show of teeth, no extreme contortions of the facial muscles—I was at this time of my life practicing reserve and cool. Oh, that British control, how I coveted it. But "Maria" had followed me to London, reminding me of a prime fact of my life: you can leave the island, master the English language, and travel as far as you can, but if you are a Latina, especially one like me who so obviously belongs to Rita Moreno's gene pool, the island travels with you.

This is sometimes a very good thing—it may win you that extra minute of someone's attention. But with some people, the same things can make *you* an island—not a tropical paradise but an Alcatraz, a place nobody wants to visit. As a Puerto Rican girl living in the United States and wanting like most children to "belong," I resented the stereotype that my Hispanic appearance called forth from many people I met.

Growing up in a large urban center in New Jersey during the 1960s, I suffered from what I think of as "cultural schizophrenia." Our life was designed by my parents as a microcosm of their *casas* on the island. We spoke in Spanish, ate Puerto Rican food bought at the *bodega,* and practiced strict Catholicism at a church that allotted us a one-hour slot each week for mass, performed in Spanish by a Chinese priest trained as a missionary for Latin America.

---

[1] *West Side Story:* a musical (1957) by Leonard Bernstein and Arthur Laurents, which featured the song "I Just Met a Girl Named Maria."

As a girl I was kept under strict surveillance by my parents, since my virtue and modesty were, by their cultural equation, the same as their honor. As a teenager I was lectured constantly on how to behave as a proper *señorita*. But it was a conflicting message I received, since the Puerto Rican mothers also encouraged their daughters to look and act like women and to dress in clothes our Anglo friends and their mothers found too "mature" and flashy. The difference was, and is, cultural; yet I often felt humiliated when I appeared at an American friend's party wearing a dress more suitable to a semi-formal than to a playroom birthday celebration. At Puerto Rican festivities, neither the music nor the colors we wore could be too loud.

I remember Career Day in our high school, when teachers told us to come dressed as if for a job interview. It quickly became obvious that to the Puerto Rican girls "dressing up" meant wearing their mother's ornate jewelry and clothing, more appropriate (by mainstream standards) for the company Christmas party than as daily office attire. That morning I had agonized in front of my closet, trying to figure out what a "career girl" would wear. I knew how to dress for school (at the Catholic school I attended, we all wore uniforms), I knew how to dress for Sunday mass, and I knew what dresses to wear for parties at my relatives' homes. Though I do not recall the precise details of my Career Day outfit, it must have been a composite of these choices. But I remember a comment my friend (an Italian American) made in later years that coalesced my impressions of that day. She said that at the business school she was attending, the Puerto Rican girls always stood out for wearing "everything at once." She meant, of course, too much jewelry, too many accessories. On that day at school we were simply made the negative models by the nuns, who were themselves not credible fashion experts to any of us. But it was painfully obvious to me that to the others, in their tailored skirts and silk blouses, we must have seemed "hopeless" and "vulgar." Though I now know that most adolescents feel out of step much of the time, I also know that for the Puerto Rican girls of my generation that sense was intensified. The way our teachers and classmates looked at us that day in school was just a taste of the cultural clash that awaited us in the real world, where prospective employers and men on the street would often misinterpret our tight skirts and jingling bracelets as a "come-on."

Mixed cultural signals have perpetuated certain stereotypes—for example, that of the Hispanic woman as the "hot tamale" or sexual firebrand. It is a one-dimensional view that the media have found easy to promote. In their special vocabulary, advertisers have designated "sizzling" and "smoldering" as the adjectives of choice for describing not only the foods but also the women of Latin America. From conversations in my house I recall hearing about the harassment that Puerto Rican women endured in factories where the "boss-men" talked to them as if sexual innuendo was all they understood, and worse, often gave them the choice of submitting to their advances or being fired.

It is custom, however, not chromosomes, that leads us to choose scarlet over pale pink. As young girls, it was our mothers who influenced our decisions about clothes and colors—mothers who had grown up on a tropical island where the natural environment was a riot of primary colors, where showing your skin was

5

one way to keep cool as well as to look sexy. Most important of all, on the island, women perhaps felt freer to dress and move more provocatively since, in most cases, they were protected by the traditions, mores, and laws of a Spanish/Catholic system of morality and machismo whose main rule was: *You may look at my sister, but if you touch her I will kill you.* The extended family and church structure could provide a young woman with a circle of safety in her small pueblo on the island; if a man "wronged" a girl, everyone would close in to save her family honor.

My mother has told me about dressing in her best party clothes on Saturday nights and going to the town's plaza to promenade with her girlfriends in front of the boys they liked. The males were thus given an opportunity to admire the women and to express their admiration in the form of *piropos:* erotically charged street poems they composed on the spot. (I have myself been subjected to a few *piropos* while visiting the island, and they can be outrageous, although custom dictates that they must never cross into obscenity.) This ritual, as I understand it, also entails a show of studied indifference on the woman's part; if she is "decent," she must not acknowledge the man's impassioned words. So I do understand how things can be lost in translation. When a Puerto Rican girl dressed in her idea of what is attractive meets a man from the mainstream culture who has been trained to react to certain types of clothing as a sexual signal, a clash is likely to take place. I remember the boy who took me to my first formal dance leaning over to plant a sloppy, over-eager kiss painfully on my mouth; when I didn't respond with sufficient passion, he remarked resentfully: "I thought you Latin girls were supposed to mature early," as if I were expected to *ripen* like a fruit or vegetable, not just grow into womanhood like other girls.

It is surprising to my professional friends that even today some people, including those who should know better, still put others "in their place." It happened to me most recently during a stay at a classy metropolitan hotel favored by young professional couples for weddings. Late one evening after the theater, as I walked toward my room with a colleague (a woman with whom I was coordinating an arts program), a middle-aged man in a tuxedo, with a young girl in satin and lace on his arm, stepped directly into our path. With his champagne glass extended toward me, he exclaimed "Evita!"[2]

Our way blocked, my companion and I listened as the man half-recited, half-bellowed "Don't Cry for Me, Argentina." When he finished, the young girl said: "How about a round of applause for my daddy?" We complied, hoping this would bring the silly spectacle to a close. I was becoming aware that our little group was attracting the attention of the other guests. "Daddy" must have perceived this too, and he once more barred the way as we tried to walk past him. He began to shout-sing a ditty to the tune of "La Bamba"—except the lyrics were about a girl named Maria whose exploits rhymed with her name and gonorrhea. The girl kept saying "Oh, Daddy" and looking at me with pleading eyes. She wanted me to laugh along

10

────────────

[2] *Evita:* a musical about Eva Duarte de Perón, the former first lady of Argentina, opened on Broadway in 1979; "Don't Cry for Me, Argentina" is a song from the musical.

with the others. My companion and I stood silently waiting for the man to end his offensive song. When he finished, I looked not at him but at his daughter. I advised her calmly never to ask her father what he had done in the army. Then I walked between them and to my room. My friend complimented me on my cool handling of the situation, but I confessed that I had really wanted to push the jerk into the swimming pool. This same man—probably a corporate executive, well-educated, even worldly by most standards—would not have been likely to regale an Anglo woman with a dirty song in public. He might have checked his impulse by assuming that she could be somebody's wife or mother, or at least *somebody* who might take offense. But, to him, I was just an Evita or a Maria: merely a character in his cartoon-populated universe.

Another facet of the myth of the Latin woman in the United States is the menial, the domestic—Maria the housemaid or countergirl. It's true that work as domestics, as waitresses, and in factories is all that's available to women with little English and few skills. But the myth of the Hispanic menial—the funny maid, mispronouncing words and cooking up a spicy storm in a shiny California kitchen—has been perpetuated by the media in the same way that "Mammy" from *Gone with the Wind* became America's idea of the black woman for generations. Since I do not wear my diplomas around my neck for all to see, I have on occasion been sent to that "kitchen" where some think I obviously belong.

One incident has stayed with me, though I recognize it as a minor offense. My first public poetry reading took place in Miami, at a restaurant where a luncheon was being held before the event. I was nervous and excited as I walked in with notebook in hand. An older woman motioned me to her table, and thinking (foolish me) that she wanted me to autograph a copy of my newly published slender volume of verse, I went over. She ordered a cup of coffee from me, assuming that I was the waitress. (Easy enough to mistake my poems for menus, I suppose.) I know it wasn't an intentional act of cruelty. Yet of all the good things that happened later, I remember that scene most clearly, because it reminded me of what I had to overcome before anyone would take me seriously. In retrospect I understand that my anger gave my reading fire. In fact, I have almost always taken any doubt in my abilities as a challenge, the result most often being the satisfaction of winning a convert, of seeing the cold, appraising eyes warm to my words, the body language change, the smile that indicates I have opened some avenue for communication. So that day as I read, I looked directly at that woman. Her lowered eyes told me she was embarrassed at her faux pas, and when I willed her to look up at me, she graciously allowed me to punish her with my full attention. We shook hands at the end of the reading and I never saw her again. She has probably forgotten the entire incident, but maybe not.

Yet I am one of the lucky ones. There are thousands of Latinas without the privilege of an education or the entrees into society that I have. For them life is a constant struggle against the misconceptions perpetuated by the myth of the Latina. My goal is to try to replace the old stereotypes with a much more interesting set of realities. Every time I give a reading, I hope the stories I tell, the dreams and fears I examine in my work, can achieve some universal truth that will get my audience past the particulars of my skin color, my accent, or my clothes.

I once wrote a poem in which I called all Latinas "God's brown daughters." This poem is really a prayer of sorts, offered upward, but also, through the human-to-human channel of art, outward. It is a prayer for communication and for respect. In it, Latin women pray "in Spanish to an Anglo God/with a Jewish heritage," and they are "fervently hoping/that if not omnipotent,/at least He be bilingual."

Questions for Discussion and Writing

1. What characteristics define, from Cofer's perspective, the "Maria" stereotype? How has this stereotype been a source of discomfort for Cofer personally? What use does she make of her personal experience to support her thesis?
2. Have you ever been perceived in stereotyped ways? What steps, if any, did you take to correct this misimpression?
3. At different points in her narrative Cofer enters the minds of others to see things from their perspective. Try choosing a person you know whose point of view differs from yours, and write a first-person narrative describing the way the world looks to them.

Fiction

CHARLOTTE PERKINS GILMAN

Charlotte Perkins Gilman (1860–1935) was born in Hartford, Connecticut, into a family that, despite their poverty, made every attempt to give her the advantages of an education. She married an artist, Charles Stetson, in 1884, and after the birth of their daughter the following year, she suffered a nervous breakdown. Her struggle with depression brought her to the attention of an eminent neurologist, whose prescription for a "rest cure" had disastrous consequences (parallel to those experienced by the narrator in "The Yellow Wallpaper"). In later life, she became an advocate for social and political reform. Her book Women and Economics *(1898) anticipated the work of such feminists as Simone de Beauvoir, a half-century later. She promoted her views through public lectures and in her magazine,* The Forerunner, *which she edited from 1909 to 1916.*

The Yellow Wallpaper

It is very seldom that mere ordinary people like John and myself secure ancestral halls for the summer.

A colonial mansion, a hereditary estate, I would say a haunted house and reach the height of romantic felicity—but that would be asking too much of fate!

Still I will proudly declare that there is something queer about it.

Else, why should it be let so cheaply? And why have stood so long untenanted?

John laughs at me, of course, but one expects that. 5

John is practical in the extreme. He has no patience with faith, an intense horror of superstition, and he scoffs openly at any talk of things not to be felt and seen and put down in figures.

John is a physician, and *perhaps*—(I would not say it to a living soul, of course, but this is dead paper and a great relief to my mind)—*perhaps* that is one reason I do not get well faster.

You see, he does not believe I am sick! And what can one do?

If a physician of high standing, and one's own husband, assures friends and relatives that there is really nothing the matter with one but temporary nervous depression—a slight hysterical tendency—what is one to do?

My brother is also a physician, and also of high standing, and he says the same 10 thing.

So I take phosphates or phosphites—whichever it is—and tonics, and air and exercise, and journeys, and am absolutely forbidden to "work" until I am well again.

Personally, I disagree with their ideas.

Personally, I believe that congenial work, with excitement and change, would do me good.

But what is one to do?

I did write for a while in spite of them; but it *does* exhaust me a good deal— 15 having to be so sly about it, or else meet with heavy opposition.

I sometimes fancy that in my condition, if I had less opposition and more society and stimulus—but John says the very worst thing I can do is to think about my condition, and I confess it always makes me feel bad.

So I will let it alone and talk about the house.

The most beautiful place! It is quite alone, standing well back from the road, quite three miles from the village. It makes me think of English places that you read about, for there are hedges and walls and gates that lock, and lots of separate little houses for the gardeners and people.

There is a *delicious* garden! I never saw such a garden—large and shady, full of box-bordered paths, and lined with long grape-covered arbors with seats under them.

There were greenhouses, too, but they are all broken now. 20

There was some legal trouble, I believe, something about the heirs and coheirs; anyhow, the place has been empty for years.

That spoils my ghostliness, I am afraid, but I don't care—there is something strange about the house—I can feel it.

I even said so to John one moonlight evening, but he said what I felt was a draught, and shut the window.

I get unreasonably angry with John sometimes. I'm sure I never used to be so sensitive. I think it is due to this nervous condition.

But John says if I feel so I shall neglect proper self-control; so I take pains to 25 control myself—before him at least, and that makes me very tired.

I don't like our room a bit. I wanted one downstairs that opened on the piazza and had roses all over the window, and such pretty old-fashioned chintz hangings! But John would not hear of it.

He said there was only one window and not room for two beds, and no near room for him if he took another.

He is very careful and loving, and hardly lets me stir without special direction.

I have a schedule prescription for each hour in the day; he takes all care from me, and so I feel basely ungrateful not to value it more.

He said he came here solely on my account, that I was to have perfect rest and all the air I could get. "Your exercise depends on your strength, my dear," said he, "and your food somewhat on your appetite; but air you can absorb all the time." So we took the nursery at the top of the house.   30

It is a big, airy room, the whole floor nearly, with windows that look all ways, and air and sunshine galore. It was nursery first and then playroom and gymnasium, I should judge; for the windows are barred for little children, and there are rings and things in the walls.

The paint and paper look as if a boys' school had used it. It is stripped off— the paper—in great patches all around the head of my bed, about as far as I can reach, and in a great place on the other side of the room low down. I never saw a worse paper in my life. One of those sprawling flamboyant patterns committing every artistic sin.

It is dull enough to confuse the eye in following, pronounced enough to constantly irritate and provoke study, and when you follow the lame uncertain curves for a little distance they suddenly commit suicide—plunge off at outrageous angles, destroy themselves in unheard-of contradictions.

The color is repellent, almost revolting: a smouldering unclean yellow, strangely faded by the slow-turning sunlight. It is a dull yet lurid orange in some places, a sickly sulphur tint in others.

No wonder the children hated it! I should hate it myself if I had to live in this room long.   35

There comes John, and I must put this away—he hates to have me write a word.

We have been here two weeks, and I haven't felt like writing before, since that first day.

I am sitting by the window now, up in this atrocious nursery, and there is nothing to hinder my writing as much as I please, save lack of strength.

John is away all day, and even some nights when his cases are serious.

I am glad my case is not serious!

But these nervous troubles are dreadfully depressing.   40

John does not know how much I really suffer. He knows there is no reason to suffer, and that satisfies him.

Of course it is only nervousness. It does weigh on me so not to do my duty in any way!

I meant to be such a help to John, such a real rest and comfort, and here I am a comparative burden already!

Nobody would believe what an effort it is to do what little I am able—to 45
dress and entertain, and order things.

It is fortunate Mary is so good with the baby. Such a dear baby!

And yet I *cannot* be with him, it makes me so nervous.

I suppose John never was nervous in his life. He laughs at me so about this
wallpaper!

At first he meant to repaper the room, but afterward he said that I was letting
it get the better of me, and that nothing was worse for a nervous patient than to
give way to such fancies.

He said that after the wallpaper was changed it would be the heavy bedstead, 50
and then the barred windows, and then that gate at the head of the stairs, and so on.

"You know the place is doing you good," he said, "and really, dear, I don't care
to renovate the house just for a three months' rental."

"Then do let us go downstairs," I said. "There are such pretty rooms there."

Then he took me in his arms and called me a blessed little goose, and said he
would go down cellar, if I wished, and have it whitewashed into the bargain.

But he is right enough about the beds and windows and things.

It is as airy and comfortable room as any one need wish, and, of course, I 55
would not be so silly as to make him uncomfortable just for a whim.

I'm really getting quite fond of the big room, all but that horrid paper.

Out of one window I can see the garden—those mysterious deep-shaded arbors, the riotous old-fashioned flowers, and bushes and gnarly trees.

Out of another I get a lovely view of the bay and a little private wharf belonging to the estate. There is a beautiful shaded lane that runs down there from
the house. I always fancy I see people walking in these numerous paths and arbors,
but John has cautioned me not to give way to fancy in the least. He says that with
my imaginative power and habit of story-making, a nervous weakness like mine is
sure to lead to all manner of excited fancies, and that I ought to use my will and
good sense to check the tendency. So I try.

I think sometimes that if I were only well enough to write a little it would relieve the press of ideas and rest me.

But I find I get pretty tired when I try. 60

It is so discouraging not to have any advice and companionship about my
work. When I get really well, John says we will ask Cousin Henry and Julia down
for a long visit; but he says he would as soon put fireworks in my pillow-case as to
let me have those stimulating people about now.

I wish I could get well faster.

But I must not think about that. This paper looks to me as if it *knew* what a vicious influence it had!

There is a recurrent spot where the pattern lolls like a broken neck and two
bulbous eyes stare at you upside down.

I get positively angry with the impertinence of it and the everlastingness. Up 65
and down and sideways they crawl, and those absurd unblinking eyes are everywhere. There is one place where two breadths didn't match, and the eyes go all up
and down the line, one a little higher than the other.

I never saw so much expression in an inanimate thing before, and we all know how much expression they have! I used to lie awake as a child and get more entertainment and terror out of blank walls and plain furniture than most children could find in a toy-store.

I remember what a kindly wink the knobs of our big old bureau used to have, and there was one chair that always seemed like a strong friend.

I used to feel that if any of the other things looked too fierce I could always hop into that chair and be safe.

The furniture in this room is no worse than inharmonious, however, for we had to bring it all from downstairs. I suppose when this was used as a playroom they had to take the nursery things out, and no wonder! I never saw such ravages as the children have made here.

The wallpaper, as I said before, is torn off in spots, and it sticketh closer than a   70
brother—they must have had perseverance as well as hatred.

Then the floor is scratched and gouged and splintered, the plaster itself is dug out here and there, and this great heavy bed, which is all we found in the room, looks as if it had been through the wars.

But I don't mind it a bit—only the paper.

There comes John's sister. Such a dear girl as she is, and so careful of me! I must not let her find me writing.

She is a perfect and enthusiastic housekeeper, and hopes for no better profession. I verily believe she thinks it is the writing which made me sick!

But I can write when she is out, and see her a long way off from these   75
windows.

There is one that commands the road, a lovely shaded winding road, and one that just looks off over the country. A lovely country, too, full of great elms and velvet meadows.

This wallpaper has a kind of sub-pattern in a different shade, a particularly irritating one, for you can only see it in certain lights, and not clearly then.

But in the places where it isn't faded and where the sun is just so—I can see a strange, provoking, formless sort of figure that seems to skulk about behind that silly and conspicuous front design.

There's sister on the stairs!

Well, the Fourth of July is over! The people are all gone, and I am tired out.   80
John thought it might do me good to see a little company, so we just had mother and Nellie and the children down for a week.

Of course I didn't do a thing. Jennie sees to everything now.

But it tired me all the same.

John says if I don't pick up faster he shall send me to Weir Mitchell[1] in the fall.

---

[1] *Dr. Silas Weir Mitchell:* 19th-century physician known for his treatment of psychosomatic illnesses.

But I don't want to go there at all. I had a friend who was in his hands once, and she says he is just like John and my brother, only more so!

Besides, it is such an undertaking to go so far.

I don't feel as if it was worth while to turn my hand over for anything, and I'm getting dreadfully fretful and querulous.

I cry at nothing, and cry most of the time.

Of course I don't when John is here, or anybody else, but when I am alone.

And I am alone a good deal just now. John is kept in town very often by serious cases, and Jennie is good and lets me alone when I want her to.

So I walk a little in the garden or down that lovely lane, sit on the porch under the roses, and lie down up here a good deal.

I'm getting really fond of the room in spite of the wallpaper. Perhaps *because* of the wallpaper.

It dwells in my mind so!

I lie here on this great immovable bed—it is nailed down, I believe—and follow that pattern about by the hour. It is as good as gymnastics, I assure you. I start, we'll say, at the bottom, down in the corner over there where it has not been touched, and I determine for the thousandth time that I *will* follow that pointless pattern to some sort of a conclusion.

I know a little of the principle of design, and I know this thing was not arranged on any laws of radiation, or alternation, or repetition, or symmetry, or anything else that I ever heard of.

It is repeated, of course, by the breadths, but not otherwise.

Looked at in one way each breadth stands alone; the bloated curves and flourishes—a kind of "debased Romanesque"[2] with delirium tremens go waddling up and down in isolated columns of fatuity.

But, on the other hand, they connect diagonally, and the sprawling outlines run off in great slanting waves of optic horror, like a lot of wallowing sea-weeds in full chase.

The whole thing goes horizontally, too, at least it seems so, and I exhaust myself in trying to distinguish the order of its going in that direction.

They have used a horizontal breadth for a frieze, and that adds wonderfully to the confusion.

There is one end of the room where it is almost intact, and there, when the crosslights fade and the low sun shines directly upon it, I can almost fancy radiation after all—the interminable grotesque seems to form around a common center and rush off in headlong plunges of equal distraction.

It makes me tired to follow it. I will take a nap, I guess.

I don't know why I should write this.

---

[2] *Romanesque:* a style of art and architecture that prevailed throughout Europe from the mid-11th to the mid-12th centuries and that made use of Roman architectural features such as the rounded arch and the barrel vault.

I don't want to.

I don't feel able.

And I know John would think it absurd. But I *must* say what I feel and think   105
in some way—it is such a relief!

But the effort is getting to be greater than the relief.

Half the time now I am awfully lazy, and lie down ever so much. John says I
mustn't lose my strength, and has me take cod liver oil and lots of tonics and things,
to say nothing of ale and wine and rare meat.

Dear John! He loves me very dearly, and hates to have me sick. I tried to have
a real earnest reasonable talk with him the other day, and tell him how I wish he
would let me go and make a visit to Cousin Henry and Julia.

But he said I wasn't able to go, nor able to stand it after I got there; and I did
not make out a very good case for myself, for I was crying before I had finished.

It is getting to be a great effort for me to think straight. Just this nervous   110
weakness, I suppose.

And dear John gathered me up in his arms, and just carried me upstairs and
laid me on the bed, and sat by me and read to me till it tired my head.

He said I was his darling and his comfort and all he had, and that I must take
care of myself for his sake, and keep well.

He says no one but myself can help me out of it, that I must use my will and
self-control and not let any silly fancies run away with me.

There's one comfort—the baby is well and happy, and does not have to occupy this nursery with the horrid wallpaper.

If we had not used it, that blessed child would have! What a fortunate escape!   115
Why, I wouldn't have a child of mine, an impressionable little thing, live in such a
room for worlds.

I never thought of it before, but it is lucky that John kept me here after all; I
can stand it so much easier than a baby, you see.

Of course I never mention it to them any more—I am too wise—but I keep
watch for it all the same.

There are things in that paper that nobody knows but me, or ever will.

Behind that outside pattern the dim shapes get clearer every day.

It is always the same shape, only very numerous.   120

And it is like a woman stooping down and creeping about behind that pattern. I don't like it a bit. I wonder—I begin to think—I wish John would take me
away from here!

It is so hard to talk with John about my case, because he is so wise, and because he loves me so.

But I tried it last night.

It was moonlight. The moon shines in all around just as the sun does.

I hate to see it sometimes, it creeps so slowly, and always comes in by one win-   125
dow or another.

John was asleep and I hated to waken him, so I kept still and watched the
moonlight on that undulating wallpaper till I felt creepy.

The faint figure behind seemed to shake the pattern, just as if she wanted to get out.

I got up softly and went to feel and see if the paper *did* move, and when I came back John was awake.

"What is it, little girl?" he said. "Don't go walking about like that—you'll get cold."

I thought it was a good time to talk, so I told him that I really was not gain-   130
ing here, and that I wished he would take me away.

"Why, darling!" said he, "our lease will be up in three weeks, and I can't see how to leave before.

"The repairs are not done at home, and I cannot possibly leave town just now. Of course if you were in any danger, I could and would, but you really are better, dear, whether you can see it or not. I am a doctor, dear, and I know. You are gain-ing flesh and color, your appetite is better, I feel really much easier about you."

"I don't weigh a bit more," said I, "nor as much; and my appetite may be bet-ter in the evening when you are here, but it is worse in the morning when you are away!"

"Bless her little heart!" said he with a big hug. "She shall be as sick as she pleases! But now let's improve the shining hours by going to sleep, and talk about it in the morning!"

"And you won't go away?" I asked gloomily.   135

"Why, how can I, dear? It is only three weeks more and then we will take a nice little trip of a few days while Jennie is getting the house ready. Really, dear, you are better!"

"Better in body perhaps—" I began, and stopped short, for he sat up straight and looked at me with such a stern, reproachful look that I could not say another word.

"My darling," said he, "I beg of you, for my sake and for our child's sake, as well as for your own, that you will never for one instant let that idea enter your mind! There is nothing so dangerous, so fascinating, to a temperament like yours. It is a false and foolish fancy. Can you not trust me as a physician when I tell you so?"

So of course I said no more on that score, and we went to sleep before long. He thought I was asleep first, but I wasn't, and lay there for hours trying to de-cide whether that front pattern and the back pattern really did move together or separately.

On a pattern like this, by daylight, there is a lack of sequence, a defiance of   140
law, that is a constant irritant to a normal mind.

The color is hideous enough, and unreliable enough, and infuriating enough, but the pattern is torturing.

You think you have mastered it, but just as you get well under way in follow-ing, it turns a back-somersault and there you are. It slaps you in the face, knocks you down, and tramples upon you. It is like a bad dream.

The outside pattern is a florid arabesque, reminding one of a fungus. If you can imagine a toadstool in joints, an interminable string of toadstools, budding and sprouting in endless convolutions—why, that is something like it.

That is, sometimes!

There is one marked peculiarity about this paper, a thing nobody seems to   145
notice but myself, and that is that it changes as the light changes.

When the sun shoots in through the east window—I always watch for that
first long, straight ray—it changes so quickly that I never can quite believe it.

That is why I watch it always.

By moonlight—the moon shines in all night when there is a moon—I
wouldn't know it was the same paper.

At night in any kind of light, in twilight, candlelight, lamplight, and worst of
all by moonlight, it becomes bars! The outside pattern, I mean, and the woman behind it is as plain as can be.

I didn't realize for a long time what the thing was that showed behind, that   150
dim sub-pattern, but now I am quite sure it is a woman.

By daylight she is subdued, quiet. I fancy it is the pattern that keeps her so
still. It is so puzzling. It keeps me quiet by the hour.

I lie down ever so much now. John says it is good for me, and to sleep all I can.

Indeed he started the habit by making me lie down for an hour after each
meal.

It is a very bad habit I am convinced, for you see I don't sleep.

And that cultivates deceit, for I don't tell them I'm awake—oh, no!   155

The fact is I am getting a little afraid of John.

He seems very queer sometimes, and even Jennie has an inexplicable look.

It strikes me occasionally, just as a scientific hypothesis, that perhaps it is the
paper!

I have watched John when he did not know I was looking, and come into the
room suddenly on the most innocent excuses, and I've caught him several times
looking at the paper! And Jennie too. I caught Jennie with her hand on it once.

She didn't know I was in the room, and when I asked her in a quiet, a very   160
quiet voice, with the most restrained manner possible, what she was doing with the
paper, she turned around as if she had been caught stealing, and looked quite
angry—asked me why I should frighten her so!

Then she said that the paper stained everything it touched, that she had found
yellow smooches on all my clothes and John's and she wished we would be more
careful!

Did not that sound innocent? But I know she was studying that pattern, and I
am determined that nobody shall find it out but myself!

Life is very much more exciting now than it used to be. You see, I have something more to expect, to look forward to, to watch. I really do eat better, and am
more quiet than I was.

John is so pleased to see me improve! He laughed a little the other day, and
said I seemed to be flourishing in spite of my wallpaper.

I turned it off with a laugh. I had no intention of telling him it was *because* of   165
the wallpaper—he would make fun of me. He might even want to take me away.

I don't want to leave now until I have found it out. There is a week more, and
I think that will be enough.

I'm feeling ever so much better!

I don't sleep much at night, for it is so interesting to watch developments; but I sleep a good deal in the daytime.

In the daytime it is tiresome and perplexing.

There are always new shoots on the fungus, and new shades of yellow all over it. I cannot keep count of them, though I have tried conscientiously.

It is the strangest yellow, that wallpaper! It makes me think of all the yellow things I ever saw—not beautiful ones like buttercups, but old, foul, bad yellow things.

But there is something else about that paper—the smell! I noticed it the moment we came into the room, but with so much air and sun it was not bad. Now we have had a week of fog and rain, and whether the windows are open or not, the smell is here.

It creeps all over the house.

I find it hovering in the dining-room, skulking in the parlor, hiding in the hall, lying in wait for me on the stairs.

It gets into my hair.

Even when I go to ride, if I turn my head suddenly and surprise it—there is that smell!

Such a peculiar odor, too! I have spent hours in trying to analyze it, to find what it smelled like.

It is not bad—at first—and very gentle, but quite the subtlest, most enduring odor I ever met.

In this damp weather it is awful, I wake up in the night and find it hanging over me.

It used to disturb me at first. I thought seriously of burning the house—to reach the smell.

But now I am used to it. The only thing I can think of that it is like is the *color* of the paper! A yellow smell.

There is a very funny mark on this wall, low down, near the mopboard. A streak that runs round the room. It goes behind every piece of furniture, except the bed, a long, straight, even *smooch,* as if it had been rubbed over and over.

I wonder how it was done and who did it, and what they did it for. Round and round and round—round and round and round—it makes me dizzy!

I really have discovered something at last.

Through watching so much at night, when it changes so, I have finally found out.

The front pattern *does* move—and no wonder! The woman behind shakes it!

Sometimes I think there are a great many women behind, and sometimes only one, and she crawls around fast, and her crawling shakes it all over.

Then in the very bright spots she keeps still, and in the very shady spots she just takes hold of the bars and shakes them hard.

And she is all the time trying to climb through. But nobody could climb through that pattern—it strangles so; I think that is why it has so many heads.

They get through and then the pattern strangles them off and turns them upside down, and makes their eyes white!

If those heads were covered or taken off it would not be half so bad.

I think that woman gets out in the daytime!

And I'll tell you why—privately—I've seen her!

I can see her out of every one of my windows!

It is the same woman, I know, for she is always creeping, and most women do not creep by daylight.

I see her in that long shaded lane, creeping up and down. I see her in those dark grape arbors, creeping all around the garden.

I see her on that long road under the trees, creeping along, and when a carriage comes she hides under the blackberry vines.

I don't blame her a bit. It must be very humiliating to be caught creeping by daylight!

I always lock the door when I creep by daylight. I can't do it at night, for I know John would suspect something at once.

And John is so queer now that I don't want to irritate him. I wish he would take another room! Besides, I don't want anybody to get that woman out at night but myself.

I often wonder if I could see her out of all the windows at once.

But, turn as fast as I can, I can only see out of one at one time.

And though I always see her, she *may* be able to creep faster than I can turn! I have watched her sometimes away off in the open country, creeping as fast as a cloud shadow in a wind.

If only that top pattern could be gotten off from the under one! I mean to try it, little by little.

I have found out another funny thing, but I shan't tell it this time! It does not do to trust people too much.

There are only two more days to get this paper off, and I believe John is beginning to notice. I don't like the look in his eyes.

And I heard him ask Jennie a lot of professional questions about me. She had a very good report to give.

She said I slept a good deal in the daytime.

John knows I don't sleep very well at night, for all I'm so quiet!

He asked me all sorts of questions, too, and pretended to be very loving and kind.

As if I couldn't see through him!

Still, I don't wonder he acts so, sleeping under this paper for three months.

It only interests me, but I feel sure John and Jennie are affected by it.

Hurrah! This is the last day, but it is enough. John is to stay in town over night, and won't be out until this evening.

Jennie wanted to sleep with me—the sly thing; but I told her I should undoubtedly rest better for a night all alone.

That was clever, for really I wasn't alone a bit! As soon as it was moonlight and that poor thing began to crawl and shake the pattern, I got up and ran to help her.

I pulled and she shook, I shook and she pulled, and before morning we had peeled off yards of that paper.

A strip about as high as my head and half around the room.

And then when the sun came and that awful pattern began to laugh at me, I declared I would finish it today!

We go away tomorrow, and they are moving all my furniture down again to leave things as they were before.

Jennie looked at the wall in amazement, but I told her merrily that I did it out of pure spite at the vicious thing.

She laughed and said she wouldn't mind doing it herself, but I must not get tired.

How she betrayed herself that time!

But I am here, and no person touches this paper but Me—not *alive!*

She tried to get me out of the room—it was too patent! But I said it was so quiet and empty and clean now that I believed I would lie down again and sleep all I could, and not to wake me even for dinner—I would call when I woke.

So now she is gone, and the servants are gone, and the things are gone, and there is nothing left but that great bedstead nailed down, with the canvas mattress we found on it.

We shall sleep downstairs tonight, and take the boat home tomorrow.

I quite enjoy the room, now it is bare again.

How those children did tear about here!

This bedstead is fairly gnawed!

But I must get to work.

I have locked the door and thrown the key down into the front path.

I don't want to go out, and I don't want to have anybody come in, till John comes.

I want to astonish him.

I've got a rope up here that even Jennie did not find. If that woman does get out, and tries to get away, I can tie her!

But I forgot I could not reach far without anything to stand on!

This bed will *not* move!

I tried to lift and push it until I was lame, and then I got so angry I bit off a little piece at one corner—but it hurt my teeth.

Then I peeled off all the paper I could reach standing on the floor. It sticks horribly and the pattern just enjoys it! All those strangled heads and bulbous eyes and waddling fungus growths just shriek with derision!

I am getting angry enough to do something desperate. To jump out of the window would be admirable exercise, but the bars are too strong even to try.

Besides I wouldn't do it. Of course not. I know well enough that a step like that is improper and might be misconstrued.

I don't like to *look* out of the windows even—there are so many of those creeping women, and they creep so fast.

I wonder if they all come out of that wallpaper as I did?

But I am securely fastened now by my well-hidden rope—you don't get *me* out in the road there!

I suppose I shall have to get back behind the pattern when it comes night, and that is hard!

It is so pleasant to be out in this great room and creep around as I please!

I don't want to go outside. I won't, even if Jennie asks me to.

For outside you have to creep on the ground, and everything is green instead of yellow.

But here I can creep smoothly on the floor, and my shoulder just fits in that long smooch around the wall, so I cannot lose my way.

Why there's John at the door!   250

It is no use, young man, you can't open it!

How he does call and pound!

Now he's crying to Jennie for an axe.

It would be a shame to break down that beautiful door!

"John, dear!" said I in the gentlest voice. "The key is down by the front steps,   255
under a plantain leaf!"

That silenced him for a few moments.

Then he said, very quietly indeed, "Open the door, my darling!"

"I can't," said I. "The key is down by the front door under a plantain leaf!"
And then I said it again, several times, very gently and slowly, and said it so often
that he had to go and see, and he got it of course, and came in. He stopped short by
the door.

"What is the matter?" he cried. "For God's sake, what are you doing!"

I kept on creeping just the same, but I looked at him over my shoulder.   260

"I've got out at last," said I, "in spite of you and Jennie! And I've pulled off
most of the paper, so you can't put me back!"

Now why should that man have fainted? But he did, and right across my path
by the wall, so that I had to creep over him every time!

Questions for Discussion and Writing

1. What role does the narrator's husband (who is also her physician) play in her psychological deterioration?

2. How does the yellow wallpaper in the story and the narrator's attitude toward it reflect her decline into madness?

3. Does the narrator in the story elicit your sympathy? Why or why not? In what respects is the story still a timely one, even though it was written in 1892?

JERZY KOSINSKI

*Jerzy Kosinski (1933–1991) was born in Lodz, Poland. When the Nazis occupied Poland in
1939, he was sent by his parents to live in the countryside, where his nightmarish experiences
later formed the basis for his classic of Holocaust fiction,* The Painted Bird *(1965). After receiving degrees in sociology and history, he emigrated to the United States and published two
nonfiction books—*The Future Is Ours, Comrade *(1960) and* No Third Path *(1962)—
under the pseudonym Joseph Novak. In 1973, he was elected president of the American Center
of PEN, an international writer's association. A prolific writer, Kosinski's second novel,* Steps
(1968), received the National Book Award. In 1970, he received the American Academy of Arts

and Letters for Literature. Other novels include The Devil Tree *(1973),* Cockpit *(1975),*
Pinball *(1982), and* The Hermit of 69th Street *(1988). His 1971 novel,* Being There,
*was made into the Academy Award–winning 1979 film. Burdened by an increasingly serious
heart condition, Kosinski committed suicide in 1991. Chapter 4 of* The Painted Bird, *"The
Miller's Tale," depicts how a boy known only as "the gypsy" reacts to his first experience of seeing the effects of jealousy and revenge in the lives of the East European peasants with whom
he has found temporary shelter.*

The Miller's Tale

I was now living at the miller's, whom the villagers had nicknamed Jealous.
He was more taciturn than was usual in the area. Even when neighbors came to
pay him a visit, he would just sit, taking an occasional sip of vodka, and drawling
out a word once in a while, lost in thought or staring at a dried-up fly stuck to the
wall.

He abandoned his reverie only when his wife entered the room. Equally quiet
and reticent, she would always sit down behind her husband, modestly dropping
her gaze when men entered the room and furtively glanced at her.

I slept in the attic directly above their bedroom. At night I was awakened by
their quarrels. The miller suspected his wife of flirting and lasciviously displaying
her body in the fields and in the mill before a young plowboy. His wife did not
deny this, but sat passive and still. Sometimes the quarrel did not end. The enraged
miller lit candles in the room, put on his boots, and beat his wife. I would cling to
a crack in the floorboards and watch the miller lashing his naked wife with a horse-
whip. The woman cowered behind a feather quilt tugged off the bed, but the man
pulled it away, flung it on the floor, and standing over her with his legs spread wide
continued to lash her plump body with the whip. After every stroke, red blood-
swollen lines would appear on her tender skin.

The miller was merciless. With a grand sweep of the arm he looped the
leather thong of the whip over her buttocks and thighs, slashed her breasts and
neck, scourged her shoulders and shins. The woman weakened and lay whining like
a puppy. Then she crawled toward her husband's legs, begging forgiveness.

Finally the miller threw down the whip and, after blowing out the candle,   5
went to bed. The woman remained groaning. The following day she would cover
her wounds, move with difficulty, and wipe away her tears with bruised, cut palms.

There was another inhabitant of the hut: a well-fed tabby cat. One day she
was seized by a frenzy. Instead of mewing she emitted half-smothered squeals. She
slid along the walls as sinuously as a snake, swung her pulsating flanks, and clawed
at the skirts of the miller's wife. She growled in a strange voice and moaned, her
raucous shrieks making everyone restless. At dusk the tabby whined insanely, her
tail beating her flanks, her nose thrusting.

The miller locked the inflamed female in the cellar and went to his mill,
telling his wife that he would bring the plowboy home for supper. Without a word
the woman set about preparing the food and table.

The plowboy was an orphan. It was his first season of work at the miller's
farm. He was a tall, placid youth with flaxen hair which he habitually pushed back

from his sweating brow. The miller knew that the villagers gossiped about his wife and the boy. It was said that she changed when she gazed into the boy's blue eyes. Heedless of the risk of being noticed by her husband, she impulsively hiked her skirt high above her knees with one hand, and with the other pushed down the bodice of her dress to display her breasts, all the time staring into the boy's eyes.

The miller returned with the young man, carrying in a sack slung over his shoulder, a tomcat borrowed from a neighbor. The tomcat had a head as large as a turnip and a long, strong tail. The tabby was howling lustingly in the cellar. When the miller released her, she sprang to the center of the room. The two cats began to circle one another mistrustfully, panting, coming nearer and nearer.

The miller's wife served supper. They ate silently. The miller sat at the middle   10
of the table, his wife on one side and the plowboy on the other. I ate my portion squatting by the oven. I admired the appetites of the two men: huge chunks of meat and bread, washed down with gulps of vodka, disappeared in their throats like hazelnuts.

The woman was the only one who chewed her food slowly. When she bowed her head low over the bowl the plowboy would dàrt a glance faster than lightning at her bulging bodice.

In the center of the room the tabby suddenly arched her body, bared her teeth and claws, and pounced on the tomcat. He halted, stretched his back, and sputtered saliva straight into her inflamed eyes. The female circled him, leaped toward him, recoiled, and then struck him in the muzzle. Now the tomcat stalked around her cautiously, sniffing her intoxicating odor. He arched his tail and tried to come at her from the rear. But the female would not let him; she flattened her body on the floor and turned like a millstone, striking his nose with her stiff, outstretched paws.

Fascinated, the miller and the other two stared silently while eating. The woman sat with a flushed face; even her neck was reddening. The plowboy raised his eyes, only to drop them at once. Sweat ran down through his short hair and he continually pushed it away from his hot brow. Only the miller sat calmly eating, watching the cats, and glancing casually at his wife and guest.

The tomcat suddenly came to a decision. His movements became lighter. He advanced. She moved playfully as if to draw back, but the male leapt high and flopped onto her with all fours. He sank his teeth in her neck and intently, tautly, plunged directly into her without any squirming. When satiated and exhausted, he relaxed. The tabby, nailed to the floor, screamed shrilly and sprang out from under him. She jumped onto the cooled oven and tossed about on it like a fish, looping her paws over her neck, rubbing her head against the warm wall.

The miller's wife and the plowboy ceased eating. They stared at each other,   15
gaping over their food-filled mouths. The woman breathed heavily, placed her hands under her breasts and squeezed them, clearly unaware of herself. The plowboy looked alternately at the cats and at her, licked his dry lips, and got down his food with difficulty.

The miller swallowed the last of his meal, leaned his head back, and abruptly gulped down his glass of vodka. Though drunk, he got up, and grasping his iron spoon and tapping it, he approached the plowboy. The youth sat bewildered. The woman hitched up her skirt and began puttering at the fire.

The miller bent over the plowboy and whispered something in his reddened ear. The youth jumped up as if pricked with a knife and began to deny something. The miller asked loudly now whether the boy lusted after his wife. The plowboy blushed but did not answer. The miller's wife turned away and continued to clean the pots.

The miller pointed at the strolling tomcat and again whispered something to the youth. The latter, with an effort, rose from the table, intending to leave the room. The miller came forward overturning his stool and, before the youth realized it, suddenly pushed him against the wall, pressed one arm against his throat, and drove a knee into his stomach. The boy could not move. Terror stricken, panting loudly, he babbled something.

The woman dashed toward her husband, imploring and wailing. The awakened tabby cat lying on the oven looked down on the spectacle, while the frightened tomcat leapt onto the table.

With a single kick the miller got the woman out of his way. And with a rapid movement such as women use to gouge out the rotten spots while peeling potatoes, he plunged the spoon into one of the boy's eyes and twisted it. 20

The eye sprang out of his face like a yolk from a broken egg and rolled down the miller's hand onto the floor. The plowboy howled and shrieked, but the miller's hold kept him pinned against the wall. Then the blood-covered spoon plunged into the other eye, which sprang out even faster. For a moment the eye rested on the boy's cheek as if uncertain what to do next; then it finally tumbled down his shirt onto the floor.

It all had happened in a moment. I could not believe what I had seen. Something like a glimmer of hope crossed my mind that the gouged eyes could be put back where they belonged. The miller's wife was screaming wildly. She rushed to the adjoining room and woke up her children, who also started crying in terror. The plowboy screamed and then grew silent covering his face with his hands. Rivulets of blood seeped through his fingers down his arms, dripping slowly on his shirt and trousers.

The miller, still enraged, pushed him toward the window as though unaware that the youth was blind. The boy stumbled, cried out, and nearly knocked over a table. The miller grabbed him by the shoulders, opened the door with his foot, and kicked him out. The boy yelled again, stumbled through the doorway, and fell down in the yard. The dogs started barking, though they did not know what had happened.

The eyeballs lay on the floor. I walked around them, catching their steady stare. The cats timidly moved out into the middle of the room and began to play with the eyes as if they were balls of thread. Their own pupils narrowed to slits from the light of the oil lamp. The cats rolled the eyes around, sniffed them, licked them, and passed them to one another gently with their padded paws. Now it seemed that the eyes were staring at me from every corner of the room, as though they had acquired a new life and motion of their own.

I watched them with fascination. If the miller had not been there I myself 25 would have taken them. Surely they could still see. I would keep them in my pocket and take them out when needed, placing them over my own. Then I would see twice as much, maybe even more. Perhaps I could attach them to the back of my head and they would tell me, though I was not quite certain how, what went on behind me. Better still, I could leave the eyes somewhere and they would tell me later what happened during my absence.

Maybe the eyes had no intention of serving anyone. They could easily escape from the cats and roll out of the door. They could wander over the fields, lakes, and woods, viewing everything about them, free as birds released from a trap. They would no longer die, since they were free, and being small they could easily hide in various places and watch people in secret. Excited, I decided to close the door quietly and capture the eyes.

The miller, evidently annoyed by the cats' play, kicked the animals away and squashed the eyeballs with his heavy boots. Something popped under his thick sole. A marvelous mirror, which could reflect the whole world, was broken. There remained on the floor only a crushed bit of jelly. I felt a terrible sense of loss.

The miller, paying no attention to me, seated himself on the bench and swayed slowly as he fell asleep. I stood up cautiously, lifted the bloodied spoon from the floor and began to gather the dishes. It was my duty to keep the room neat and the floor swept. As I cleaned I kept away from the crushed eyes, uncertain what to do with them. Finally I looked away and quickly swept the ooze into the pail and threw it in the oven.

In the morning I awoke early. Underneath me I heard the miller and his wife snoring. Carefully I packed a sack of food, loaded the comet[1] with hot embers and, bribing the dog in the yard with a piece of sausage, fled from the hut.

At the mill wall, next to the barn, lay the plowboy. At first I meant to pass him by quickly, but I stopped when I realized that he was sightless. He was still stunned. He covered his face with his hands, he moaned and sobbed. There was caked blood on his face, hands, and shirt. I wanted to say something, but I was afraid that he would ask me about his eyes and then I would have to tell him to forget about them, since the miller had stamped them into pulp. I was terribly sorry for him.

I wondered whether the loss of one's sight would deprive a person also of the memory of everything that he had seen before. If so, the man would no longer be able to see even in his dreams. If not, if only the eyeless could still see through their memory, it would not be too bad. The world seemed to be pretty much the same everywhere, and even though people differed from one another, just as animals and trees did, one should know fairly well what they looked like after seeing them for years. I had lived only seven years, but I remembered a lot of things. When I closed my eyes, many details came back still more vividly. Who knows, perhaps without his eyes the plowboy would start seeing an entirely new, more fascinating world.

30

---

[1] *Comet:* a small portable stove consisting of a one-quart preserve can opened at one end with a lot of small nail holes punched in the sides attached to a three-foot loop of wire hooked to the top as a handle, served as a source of heat and as a weapon when filled with tinder. (described in Ch. 3 of *The Painted Bird*)

I heard some sound from the village. Afraid that the miller might wake up, I went on my way, touching my eyes from time to time. I walked more cautiously now, for I knew that eyeballs did not have strong roots. When one bent down they hung like apples from a tree and could easily drop out. I resolved to jump across fences with my head held up; but on my first try I stumbled and fell down. I lifted my fingers fearfully to my eyes to see whether they were still there. After carefully checking that they opened and closed properly, I noticed with delight the partridges and thrushes in flight. They flew very fast but my sight could follow them and even overtake them as they soared under the clouds, becoming smaller than raindrops. I made a promise to myself to remember everything I saw; if someone should pluck out my eyes, then I would retain the memory of all that I had seen for as long as I lived.

Questions for Discussion and Writing

1. What effect do the youth and innocence of the narrator have on the account he gives?
2. In what way does seeing the detached eyes of the plowboy lead the narrator to conclude that the ability to remember events and experiences is all-important?
3. How would the same events in this story appear from the perspective of one of the other characters? Rewrite this narrative as seen through the eyes of anyone of the other characters, including the cat.

Poetry

T. S. ELIOT

Thomas Stearns Eliot (1888–1965) was born into a distinguished family in St. Louis, Missouri. He took his B.A. and M.A. degrees at Harvard in 1909 and 1910, during which time he wrote "The Love Song of J. Alfred Prufrock." He did graduate work at Harvard, the Sorbonne in Paris, and Oxford University and then settled in London, becoming a British subject in 1917. He taught school, worked as a clerk for Lloyd's Bank, and in 1925 joined the publishing firm of Faber and Faber. His first book was Prufrock and Other Observations *(1917), and in 1920 his first book of criticism,* The Sacred Wood, *appeared. When* The Wasteland *was published in 1922, it established Eliot as a foremost writer of a new kind of poetry. He founded the influential literary journal,* The Criterion, *in 1922 and became a director at Faber and Faber, where he introduced the work of W. H. Auden and Louis MacNiece. In 1927 he became a convert to the Anglo-Catholic wing of The Church of England and addressed spiritual themes in both his poetry* Ash Wednesday *(1930) and* Four Quartets *(1933) and in his play* Murder in the Cathedral *(1935). In 1948 he was awarded the Nobel Prize for Literature, the only time a poet born in the United States has received this honor. "The Love Song of J. Alfred*

Prufrock" was published in Poetry *solely as a result of the efforts of Ezra Pound, who worked zealously to advance Eliot's career. Rather than telling a story, this poem uses a highly suggestive series of images to evoke associations from the reader that tap into deeply felt experiences.*

The Love Song of J. Alfred Prufrock[1]

*S'io credessi che mia risposta fosse
a persona che mai tomasse al mondo,
questa fiamma staria senza più scosse.
Ma per ciò che giammai di questo fondo
non tornò vivo alcun, s'i'odo il vero,
senza tema d'infamia ti rispondo.*[2]

Let us go then, you and I,
When the evening is spread out against the sky
Like a patient etherized upon a table;
Let us go, through certain half-deserted streets,
The muttering retreats   5
Of restless nights in one-night cheap hotels
And sawdust restaurants with oyster-shells:
Streets that follow like a tedious argument
Of insidious intent
To lead you to an overwhelming question...   10
Oh, do not ask, "What is it?"
Let us go and make our visit.

In the room the women come and go
Talking of Michelangelo.[3]

The yellow fog that rubs its back upon the window-panes   15
The yellow smoke that rubs its muzzle on the window-panes
Licked its tongue into the corners of the evening,
Lingered upon the pools that stand in drains,
Let fall upon its back the soot that falls from chimneys,

---

[1] The combination of the uptight "J. Alfred Prufrock" with a "love song" is ludicrous and pathetic.
[2] A speech from Dante's *Inferno,* XXVII.61–66, by Guido da Montefeltro, burning in hell. Literally: "If I thought that my reply would be to anyone who might go back to the world, this flame would cease any longer to tremble. But since never from this deep place did anyone return alive, if I hear truth, without fear of infamy I respond to you." This is an ironic epigraph.   [3] *Michelangelo Buonarroti (1495–1564):* Italian sculptor, painter, poet. Renowned for his panoramic painting of the ceiling of the Sistine Chapel in the Vatican.

Slipped by the terrace, made a sudden leap,   20
And seeing that it was a soft October night,
Curled once about the house, and fell asleep.

And indeed there will be time
For the yellow smoke that slides along the street
Rubbing its back upon the window-panes;   25
There will be time, there will be time
To prepare a face to meet the faces that you meet;
There will be time to murder and create,
And time for all the works and days of hands
That lift and drop a question on your plate;   30
Time for you and time for me,
And time yet for a hundred indecisions,
And for a hundred visions and revisions,
Before the taking of a toast and tea.

In the room the women come and go   35
Talking of Michelangelo.

And indeed there will be time
To wonder, "Do I dare?" and, "Do I dare?"
Time to turn back and descend the stair,
With a bald spot in the middle of my hair—   40
(They will say: "How his hair is growing thin!")
My morning coat, my collar mounting firmly to the chin,
My necktie rich and modest, but asserted by a simple pin—
(They will say: "But how his arms and legs are thin!")
Do I dare   45
Disturb the universe?
In a minute there is time
For decisions and revisions which a minute will reverse.

For I have known them all already, known them all—
Have known the evenings, mornings, afternoons,   50
I have measured out my life with coffee spoons;
I know the voices dying with a dying fall
Beneath the music from a farther room.
    So how should I presume?

And I have known the eyes already, known them all—   55
The eyes that fix you in a formulated phrase,
And when I am formulated, sprawling on a pin,
When I am pinned and wriggling on the wall,
Then how should I begin
To spit out all the butt-ends of my days and ways?   60
    And how should I presume?

And I have known the arms already, known them all—
Arms that are braceleted and white and bare
(But in the lamplight, downed with light brown hair!)
Is it perfume from a dress   65
That makes me so digress?
Arms that lie along a table, or wrap about a shawl.
   And should I then presume?
   And how should I begin?

Shall I say, I have gone at dusk through narrow streets   70
And watched the smoke that rises from the pipes
Of lonely men in shirt-sleeves, leaning out of windows? . . .

I should have been a pair of ragged claws
Scuttling across the floors of silent seas.
And the afternoon, the evening, sleeps so peacefully!   75
Smoothed by long fingers,
Asleep . . .tired . . .or it malingers,
Stretched on the floor, here beside you and me.
Should I, after tea and cakes and ices,
Have the strength to force the moment to its crisis?   80
But though I have wept and fasted, wept and prayed,
Though I have seen my head (grown slightly bald) brought in upon a
   platter,[4]
I am no prophet—and here's no great matter;
I have seen the moment of my greatness flicker,
And I have seen the eternal Footman hold my coat, and snicker,   85
And in short, I was afraid.

And would it have been worth it, after all,
After the cups, the marmalade, the tea,
Among the porcelain, among some talk of you and me,
Would it have been worth while,   90
To have bitten off the matter with a smile,
To have squeezed the universe into a ball
To roll it toward some overwhelming question,
To say: "I am Lazarus, come from the dead,[5]
Come back to tell you all, I shall tell you all"—   95
If one, settling a pillow by her head,

---

[4] l. 82 John the Baptist, the prophet who was the forerunner of Jesus and baptized him, was beheaded at Herod's command.   [5] l. 94 One of Jesus's miracles was to raise Lazarus from the dead. Prufrock feels like one of the living dead.

Should say: "That is not what I meant at all.
    That is not it, at all."

And would it have been worth it, after all,
Would it have been worth while,   100
After the sunsets and the dooryards and the sprinkled streets,
After the novels, after the teacups, after the skirts that trail along the floor—
And this, and so much more?—
It is impossible to say just what I mean!
But as if a magic lantern threw the nerves in patterns on a screen: 105
Would it have been worth while
If one, settling a pillow or throwing off a shawl,
And turning toward the window, should say:
    "That is not it at all,
      That is not what I meant, at all."   110

No! I am not Prince Hamlet, nor was meant to be;
Am an attendant lord, one that will do
To swell a progress, start a scene or two,
Advise the prince; no doubt, an easy tool,
Deferential, glad to be of use,   115
Politic, cautious, and meticulous;
Full of high sentence, but a bit obtuse;
At times, indeed, almost ridiculous—
Almost, at times, the Fool.[6]

I grow old . . . I grow old . . .   120
I shall wear the bottoms of my trousers rolled.

Shall I part my hair behind? Do I dare to eat a peach?
I shall wear white flannel trousers, and walk upon the beach.
I have heard the mermaids singing, each to each.

I do not think that they will sing to me.   125

I have seen them riding seaward on the waves
Combining the white hair of the waves blown back
When the wind blows the water white and black.

We have lingered in the chambers of the sea
By sea-girls wreathed with seaweed red and brown   130
Till human voices wake us, and we drown.[7]

---

[6] ll. 112–120 Prufrock notes rather bitterly that he hardly has the romantic stature of a Hamlet: The character in Shakespeare's play he most resembles is Polonius.   [7] ll. 125–131 These closing lines offer a purely lyrical song that expresses the tone of wistful regret that pervades the whole poem.

Questions for Discussion and Writing

1. What is the dramatic situation that frames the psychological conflict of the speaker? Who is speaking? Where is he? What time of year is it?
2. How is the psychological conflict of Prufrock reflected in the unusual sequence of images that offer insight into his state of mind? How do these images indirectly imply Prufrock's personality, social circle, life up to this point, and possible future?
3. What features of the poem mark the growing intensity of Prufrock's psychological struggle? Have you ever felt imprisoned by the way other people see you? What images would you choose to express your situation?

WILLIAM SHAKESPEARE

William Shakespeare (1564–1616) was born in Stratford-upon-Avon, the son of a prosperous merchant, and received his early education at Stratford Grammar School. In 1582, he married Anne Hathaway and over the next twenty years established himself as a professional actor and playwright in London. Shakespeare's sonnets, of which there are 154, were probably written in the 1590s but were first published in 1609. The fourteen lines of the Shakespearean sonnet fall into three quatrains and a couplet rhyming abab cdcd efef gg. They hint at a story involving a young man, a "dark lady," and the poet himself, together with a "rival poet." Sonnet 30 expresses a variation on a familiar theme: the encroachment of time, loss, and death, and the undying power of love and friendship to resist these devastations.

Sonnet 30

When to the sessions[1] of sweet silent thought
I summon up remembrance of things past,
I sigh the lack of many a thing I sought,
And with old woes new wail my dear time's waste.
Then can I drown an eye, unused to flow,   5
For precious friends hid in death's dateless[2] night,
And weep afresh love's long since cancelled[3] woe,
And moan th' expense of many a vanished sight.
Then can I grieve at grievances forgone,
And heavily from woe to woe tell o'er   10
The sad account of fore-bemoanèd moan,

---

[1] *Sessions:* as in a court of law.   [2] *Dateless:* endless.   [3] ll. 7–14: The financial metaphor, as in a court case, continues through *cancelled, expense* (loss), *tell* (count), *account, pay, losses,* etc.

Which I new pay as if not paid before.
   But if the while I think on thee, dear friend,
   All losses are restored, and sorrows end.

Questions for Discussion and Writing

1. What power does Shakespeare attribute to the person who is the object of love and friendship in this sonnet?
2. What does this sonnet imply about the importance of love to withstand the destructive effects of time and physical and emotional changes?
3. Do you feel the same way Shakespeare does, that is, that love has the power to obliterate the destructive effects of time and loss? Describe an experience that made you realize this.

SARA TEASDALE

Sara Teasdale (1884–1933) was raised and educated in St. Louis and traveled to Europe and the Near East. After returning to the United States, she settled in New York and lived a life very similar to the independent "solitary" she describes in this poem. Her published works include Rivers to the Sea *(1915) and* Love Songs *(1917).* Love Songs *went through five editions in one year and won Teasdale a special Pulitzer award, the first given to a book of poetry.*

The Solitary

My heart has grown rich with the passing of years,
   I have less need now than when I was young

To share myself with every comer
   Or shape my thoughts into words with my tongue.

It is one to me that they come or go   5
   If I have myself and the drive of my will,
And strength to climb on a summer night
   And watch the stars swarm over the hill.

Let them think I love them more than I do,
   Let them think I care, though I go alone;   10
If it lifts their pride, what is it to me
   Who am self-complete as a flower or a stone.

Questions for Discussion and Writing

1. In what way has the speaker changed from when she was young?
2. How does the speaker feel toward the way others perceive her?
3. Do you believe it is possible or desirable for someone to become as "self-complete as a flower or a stone"? Why, or why not? Alternatively, you might consider whether one becomes more self-sufficient as one grows older.

ANNA KAMIEŃSKA

Anna Kamieńska (1920–1986), a Polish poet, translator, critic, essayist, and editor, was the author of numerous collections of original and translated poetry (from Russian and other Slavic languages) as well as of anthologies, books for children, and collections of interpretations of poems. Initially, a poet of peasant themes and moral concerns, she underwent a spiritual metamorphosis in the early 1970s, becoming an important poet of religious experience. A posthumous collection of her poetry is Two Darknesses, *translated by Tomasz P. Krzeszowski and Desmond Graham (1994). "Funny" (1973), translated by Mieczyslaw Jastrun, offers a wryly thought-provoking view of the human condition.*

Funny

What's it like to be a human
the bird asked

I myself don't know
it's being held prisoner by your skin
while reaching infinity
being a captive of your scrap of time   5
while touching eternity
being hopelessly uncertain
and helplessly hopeful
being a needle of frost
and a handful of heat   10
breathing in the air
and choking wordlessly
it's being on fire
with a nest made of ashes
eating bread   15
while filling up on hunger
it's dying without love
it's loving through death

That's funny said the bird   20
and flew effortlessly up into the air

Questions for Discussion and Writing

1. How is the poem developed between a set of opposing values represented by the condition of the bird and the condition of humanity?

2. If the bird side of the equation is represented through the image of effortlessness, what details suggest the difficulties, uncertainties, and precariousness of the human condition? How does Kamieńska use irony to suggest the enormous gap between the bird and the human, especially in relationship to the title? Why would the human condition be "funny" from the bird's point of view?

3. How would you go about explaining to someone who didn't possess a particular sense (sight, hearing) or was color-blind what it is like to see, to hear, to see colors? What analogies or metaphors would you choose to use in your explanation?

Connections for Chapter 1:
Reflections on Experience

1. **Jill Nelson,** *Number One!*
   In what ways do both Nelson and Judith Ortiz Cofer strive to transcend socially restrictive expectations linked to race and ethnicity?

2. **Fritz Peters,** *Boyhood with Gurdjieff*
   Compare Gurdjieff's seemingly unfair method of teaching compassion with Jesus' teaching parable of "The Laborers in the Vineyard," in Chapter 11.

3. **Beryl Markham,** *West with the Night*
   Compare the reasons why Markham and Douchan Gersi subject themselves to life-endangering challenges that most people would not choose to encounter.

4. **Douchan Gersi,** *Initiated into an Iban Tribe of Headhunters*
   Compare the experiences, expectations, and outcomes in Gersi's account with those of the main character, Nunez, in H. G. Wells's story, "The Country of the Blind" (Chapter 11).

5. **Lesley Hazleton,** *Confessions of a Fast Woman*
   In what ways do Hazleton and Beryl Markham step outside the traditional roles of women to discover their own talents?

6. **Annie Dillard,** *So, This Was Adolescence*
   Compare the reflections of Dillard on the uncertainties of adolescence with the sense of self gained by Sara Teasdale as expressed in her poem.

7. **Judith Ortiz Cofer,** *The Myth of the Latin Woman*
   In what respects are the narrator in Charlotte Perkins Gilman's story and Cofer in this account encouraged to think less of themselves because of prevailing social and cultural stereotypes?

8. **Charlotte Perkins Gilman,** *The Yellow Wallpaper*
   Compare the very different expectations the narrators set for themselves in Gilman's story and in Beryl Markham's account.

9. **Jerry Kosinski,** *The Miller's Tale*
   In what sense do both the narrator in Kosinski's story and Douchan Gersi lose their naive illusions about the nature of violence?

10. **T. S. Eliot,** *The Love Song of J. Alfred Prufrock*
    In what ways do both Eliot and Charlotte Perkins Gilman take us on psychological journeys into the minds of their narrators and provide striking images that mirror their distress?

11. **William Shakespeare,** *Sonnet 30, When to the Sessions of Sweet Silent Thought*
    What contrasting perspectives do Shakespeare and T. S. Eliot bring to the theme of being capable of love?

12. **Sara Teasdale,** *The Solitary*
    How is the theme of self-reliance developed in Teasdale's poem and Nasreddin Hodja's folk story "Do as You Please" in Chapter 11?

13. **Anna Kamieńska,** *Funny*
    In what way do both Kamieńska and Natsume Soseki (see "I Am a Cat" in Chapter 6) use animals to express an ironic perspective on the human condition?

2

INFLUENTIAL PEOPLE AND MEMORABLE PLACES

The authors in this chapter reflect on the influence of parents, friends, teachers, and others in shaping their lives. As you read the accounts by Maya Angelou, Raymond Carver, Gayle Pemberton, Mikhal Gilmore, and Fatima Mernissi, you might ask yourself how much of your personality, outlook, and expectations is the direct result of knowing someone who was important to you.

The writers of the essays identify defining qualities and character traits, and they also relate important incidents that enable us to understand why each of the people they describe had such an impact on their lives. In other essays, places, not people, play a decisive role in eliciting unique responses. The landscapes and natural and architectural wonders described by P. D. Ouspensky, William Zinsser, and Joseph Addison transport us to the Taj Mahal, Niagara Falls, and Westminster Abbey.

A story by John Cheever dramatizes a son's disappointment in a much anticipated reunion with his father, and a story by Bessie Head reveals the impact of a seven-year drought on a family in Botswana.

The poems in this chapter deepen our emotional capacity to understand the often inexpressible dimensions of human relationships. The poems by Cathy Song and Robert Hayden give intimate portraits of a daughter and her mother and a son and his father. The influence of an important place can be observed in William Wordsworth's deeply felt tribute to the city of London.

Nonfiction

MAYA ANGELOU

Maya Angelou was born in 1928 in St. Louis, Missouri, and attended public schools in Arkansas and California. In her widely varied career, she has been a streetcar conductor, a successful singer, an actress, and a teacher. She is the author of several volumes of poetry and ten plays for stage, screen, and television, but she is best known for her autobiography, a work still in progress (five volumes of which have been published). "Liked for Myself" originally appeared in the first volume of this autobiography, I Know Why the Caged Bird Sings *(1970). Her most recent works are* Even the Stars Look Lonesome *(1997) and* Heart of a Woman *(1997).*

Liked for Myself

For nearly a year, I sopped around the house, the Store, the school and the church, like an old biscuit, dirty and inedible. Then I met, or rather got to know, the lady who threw me my first life line.

Mrs. Bertha Flowers was the aristocrat of Black Stamps. She had the grace of control to appear warm in the coldest weather, and on the Arkansas summer days it seemed she had a private breeze which swirled around, cooling her. She was thin without the taut look of wiry people, and her printed voile dresses and flowered hats were as right for her as denim overalls for a farmer. She was our side's answer to the richest white woman in town.

Her skin was a rich black that would have peeled like a plum if snagged, but then no one would have thought of getting close enough to Mrs. Flowers to ruffle her dress, let alone snag her skin. She didn't encourage familiarity. She wore gloves too.

I don't think I ever saw Mrs. Flowers laugh, but she smiled often. A slow widening of her thin black lips to show even, small white teeth, then the slow effortless closing. When she chose to smile on me, I always wanted to thank her. The action was so graceful and inclusively benign.

She was one of the few gentlewomen I have ever known, and has remained   5
throughout my life the measure of what a human being can be. . . .

One summer afternoon, sweet-milk fresh in my memory, she stopped at the Store to buy provisions. Another Negro woman of her health and age would have been expected to carry the paper sacks home in one hand, but Momma said, "Sister Flowers, I'll send Bailey up to your house with these things."

She smiled that slow dragging smile, "Thank you, Mrs. Henderson. I'd prefer Marguerite, though." My name was beautiful when she said it. "I've been meaning to talk to her, anyway." They gave each other age-group looks. . . .

There was a little path beside the rocky road, and Mrs. Flowers walked in front swinging her arms and picking her way over the stones.

She said, without turning her head, to me, "I hear you're doing very good school work, Marguerite, but that it's all written. The teachers report that they have trouble getting you to talk in class." We passed the triangular farm on our left and the path widened to allow us to walk together. I hung back in the separate unasked and unanswerable questions.

"Come and walk along with me, Marguerite." I couldn't have refused even if   10
I wanted to. She pronounced my name so nicely. Or more correctly, she spoke each word with such clarity that I was certain a foreigner who didn't understand English could have understood her.

"Now no one is going to make you talk—possibly no one can. But bear in mind, language is man's way of communicating with his fellow man and it is language alone which separates him from the lower animals." That was a totally new idea to me, and I would need time to think about it.

"Your grandmother says you read a lot. Every chance you get. That's good, but not good enough. Words mean more than what is set down on paper. It takes the human voice to infuse them with the shades of deeper meaning."

I memorized the part about the human voice infusing words. It seemed so valid and poetic.

She said she was going to give me some books and that I not only must read them, I must read them aloud. She suggested that I try to make a sentence sound in as many different ways as possible.

"I'll accept no excuse if you return a book to me that has been badly handled." My imagination boggled at the punishment I would deserve if in fact I did abuse a book of Mrs. Flowers'. Death would be too kind and brief.   15

The odors in the house surprised me. Somehow I had never connected Mrs. Flowers with food or eating or any other common experience of common people. There must have been an outhouse, too, but my mind never recorded it.

The sweet scent of vanilla had met us as she opened the door.

"I made tea cookies this morning. You see, I had planned to invite you for cookies and lemonade so we could have this little chat. The lemonade is in the icebox."

It followed that Mrs. Flowers would have ice on an ordinary day, when most families in our town bought ice late on Saturdays only a few times during the summer to be used in the wooden ice-cream freezers.

She took the bags from me and disappeared through the kitchen door. I   20
looked around the room that I had never in my wildest fantasies imagined I would see. Browned photographs leered or threatened from the walls and the white, freshly done curtains pushed against themselves and against the wind. I wanted to gobble up the room entire and take it to Bailey, who would help me analyze and enjoy it.

"Have a seat, Marguerite. Over there by the table." She carried a platter covered with a tea towel. Although she warned that she hadn't tried her hand at baking sweets for some time, I was certain that like everything else about her the cookies would be perfect.

They were flat round wafers, slightly browned on the edges and butter-yellow in the center. With the cold lemonade they were sufficient for childhood's lifelong diet. Remembering my manners, I took nice little lady-like bites off the edges. She said she had made them expressly for me and that she had a few in the kitchen that I could take home to my brother. So I jammed one whole cake in my mouth and the rough crumbs scratched the insides of my jaws, and if I hadn't had to swallow, it would have been a dream come true.

As I ate she began the first of what we later called "my lessons in living." She said that I must always be intolerant of ignorance but understanding of illiteracy. That some people, unable to go to school, were more educated and even more intelligent than college professors. She encouraged me to listen carefully to what country people called mother wit. That in those homely sayings was couched the collective wisdom of generations.

When I finished the cookies she brushed off the table and brought a thick, small book from the bookcase. I had read *A Tale of Two Cities*[1] and found it up to my standards as a romantic novel. She opened the first page and I heard poetry for the first time in my life.

"It was the best of times and the worst of times . . ." Her voice slid in and curved down through and over the words. She was nearly singing. I wanted to look at the pages. Were they the same that I had read? Or were there notes, music, lined on the pages, as in a hymn book? Her sounds began cascading gently. I knew from listening to a thousand preachers that she was nearing the end of her reading, and I hadn't really heard, heard to understand, a single word.

"How do you like that?"

It occurred to me that she expected a response. The sweet vanilla flavor was still on my tongue and her reading was a wonder in my ears. I had to speak.

I said, "Yes, ma'am." It was the least I could do, but it was the most also.

"There's one more thing. Take this book of poems and memorize one for me. Next time you pay me a visit, I want you to recite."

I have tried often to search behind the sophistication of years for the enchantment I so easily found in those gifts. The essence escapes but its aura remains. To be allowed, no, invited, into the private lives of strangers, and to share their joys and fears, was a chance to exchange the Southern bitter wormwood for a cup of mead with Beowulf[2] or a hot cup of tea and milk with Oliver Twist[3]. When I said aloud, "It is a far, far better thing that I do, than I have ever done . . ." tears of love filled my eyes at my selfishness.

On that first day, I ran down the hill and into the road (few cars ever came along it) and had the good sense to stop running before I reached the Store.

I was liked, and what a difference it made. I was respected not as Mrs. Henderson's grandchild or Bailey's sister but for just being Marguerite Johnson.

Childhood's logic never asks to be proved (all conclusions are absolute). I didn't question why Mrs. Flowers had singled me out for attention, nor did it occur to me that Momma might have asked her to give me a little talking to. All I cared about was that she had made tea cookies for *me* and read to *me* from her favorite book. It was enough to prove that she liked me.

---

[1] *A Tale of Two Cities (1859):* written by Charles Dickens (1812–1870), one of the great English writers of fiction: begins with the familiar lines "It was the best of times, it was the worst of times"; set against the background of the French Revolution, which Dickens researched with the aid of his friend Thomas Carlyle's *History of the French Revolution* (1837).   [2] *Beowulf:* the oldest English epic, in alliterative verse, probably composed in the early eighth century; drawn from Scandinavian history.   [3] *Oliver Twist (1838):* Dickens's second novel, which tells the story of an orphan living in the seamy underside of London's criminal world.

Questions for Discussion and Writing

1. What insights about attitudes toward race at that time does Angelou's account provide, as revealed in the conversations between Marguerite and Mrs. Flowers?
2. What do you think Angelou means by "mother wit"? How does it differ from formal education?
3. How did the way Bertha Flowers treated Marguerite help her gain self-esteem?

RAYMOND CARVER

Raymond Carver (1938–1988) grew up in a logging town in Oregon and was educated at Humboldt State College (B.A., 1963) and at the University of Iowa, where he studied creative writing. He first received recognition in the 1970s with the publication of stories in the New Yorker, Esquire, *and the* Atlantic Monthly. *His first collection of short stories,* Will You Please Be Quiet, Please? *(1976), was nominated for the National Book Award. Subsequent collections include* What We Talk About When We Talk About Love *(1981),* Cathedral *(1983), and* Where I'm Calling From *(1988). A posthumous book of Carver's poetry,* All of Us, *was published in 1998. "My Father's Life," which first appeared in* Esquire *(1984), displays Carver's conversational style and unique gift for getting to the heart of human relationships.*

My Father's Life

My dad's name was Clevie Raymond Carver. His family called him Raymond and friends called him C. R. I was named Raymond Clevie Carver Jr. I hated the "Junior" part. When I was little my dad called me Frog, which was okay. But later, like everybody else in the family, he began calling me Junior. He went on calling me this until I was thirteen or fourteen and announced that I wouldn't answer to that name any longer. So he began calling me Doc. From then until his death, on June 17, 1967, he called me Doc, or else Son.

When he died, my mother telephoned my wife with the news. I was away from my family at the time, between lives, trying to enroll in the School of Library Science at the University of Iowa. When my wife answered the phone, my mother blurted out, "Raymond's dead!" For a moment, my wife thought my mother was telling her that I was dead. Then my mother made it clear *which* Raymond she was talking about and my wife said, "Thank God. I thought you meant *my* Raymond."

My dad walked, hitched rides, and rode in empty boxcars when he went from Arkansas to Washington State in 1934, looking for work. I don't know whether he was pursuing a dream when he went out to Washington. I doubt it. I don't think he dreamed much. I believe he was simply looking for steady work at decent pay. Steady work was meaningful work. He picked apples for a time and then landed a construction laborer's job on the Grand Coulee Dam.[1] After he'd put aside a little money, he bought a car and drove back to Arkansas to help his folks, my grandparents, pack up for the move west. He said later that they were about to starve down there, and this wasn't meant as a figure of speech. It was during that short while in Arkansas, in a town called Leola, that my mother met my dad on the sidewalk as he came out of a tavern.

"He was drunk," she said. "I don't know why I let him talk to me. His eyes were glittery. I wish I'd had a crystal ball." They'd met once, a year or so before, at a dance. He'd had girlfriends before her, my mother told me. "Your dad always had a girlfriend, even after we married. He was my first and last. I never had another man. But I didn't miss anything."

They were married by a justice of the peace on the day they left for Washington, this big, tall country girl and a farmhand-turned-construction worker. My mother spent her wedding night with my dad and his folks, all of them camped beside the road in Arkansas.

In Omak, Washington, my dad and mother lived in a little place not much bigger than a cabin. My grandparents lived next door. My dad was still working on the dam, and later, with the huge turbines producing electricity and the water backed up for a hundred miles into Canada, he stood in the crowd and heard Franklin D. Roosevelt when he spoke at the construction site. "He never mentioned those guys who died building that dam," my dad said. Some of his friends had died there, men from Arkansas, Oklahoma, and Missouri.

He then took a job in a sawmill in Clatskanie, Oregon, a little town alongside the Columbia River. I was born there, and my mother has a picture of my dad standing in front of the gate to the mill, proudly holding me up to face the camera. My bonnet is on crooked and about to come untied. His hat is pushed back on his forehead, and he's wearing a big grin. Was he going in to work or just finishing his shift? It doesn't matter. In either case, he had a job and a family. These were his salad days.

In 1941 we moved to Yakima, Washington, where my dad went to work as a saw filer, a skilled trade he'd learned in Clatskanie. When war broke out, he was given a deferment because his work was considered necessary to the war effort. Finished lumber was in demand by the armed services, and he kept his saws so sharp they could shave the hair off your arm.

After my dad had moved us to Yakima, he moved his folks into the same neighborhood. By the mid-1940s the rest of my dad's family—his brother, his sister, and her husband, as well as uncles, cousins, nephews, and most of their extended family and friends—had come out from Arkansas. All because my dad came out first. The men went to work at Boise Cascade, where my dad worked, and the

---

[1] *Grand Coulee Dam:* on the Columbia River in central Washington. This dam is one of the largest concrete dams in the world, 550 feet high.

women packed apples in the canneries. And in just a little while, it seemed—according to my mother—everybody was better off than my dad. "Your dad couldn't keep money," my mother said. "Money burned a hole in his pocket. He was always doing for others."

The first house I clearly remember living in, at 1515 South Fifteenth Street, in Yakima, had an outdoor toilet. On Halloween night, or just any night, for the hell of it, neighbor kids, kids in their early teens, would carry our toilet away and leave it next to the road. My dad would have to get somebody to help him bring it home. Or these kids would take the toilet and stand it in somebody else's backyard. Once they actually set it on fire, but ours wasn't the only house that had an outdoor toilet. When I was old enough to know what I was doing, I threw rocks at the other toilets when I'd see someone go inside. This was called bombing the toilets. After a while, though, everyone went to indoor plumbing until, suddenly, our toilet was the last outdoor one in the neighborhood. I remember the shame I felt when my third-grade teacher, Mr. Wise, drove me home from school one day. I asked him to stop at the house just before ours, claiming I lived there. 10

I can recall what happened one night when my dad came home late to find that my mother had locked all the doors on him from the inside. He was drunk, and we could feel the house shudder as he rattled the door. When he'd managed to force open a window, she hit him between the eyes with a colander and knocked him out. We could see him down there on the grass. For years afterward, I used to pick up this colander—it was as heavy as a rolling pin—and imagine what it would feel like to be hit in the head with something like that.

It was during this period that I remember my dad taking me into the bedroom, sitting me down on the bed, and telling me that I might have to go live with my Aunt LaVon for a while. I couldn't understand what I'd done that meant I'd have to go away from home to live. But this, too—whatever prompted it—must have blown over, more or less, anyway, because we stayed together, and I didn't have to go live with her or anyone else.

I remember my mother pouring his whiskey down the sink. Sometimes she'd pour it all out and sometimes, if she was afraid of getting caught, she'd only pour half of it out and then add water to the rest. I tasted some of his whiskey once myself. It was terrible stuff, and I don't see how anybody could drink it.

After a long time without one, we finally got a car, in 1949 or 1950, a 1938 Ford. But it threw a rod the first week we had it, and my dad had to have the motor rebuilt.

"We drove the oldest car in town," my mother said. "We could have had a Cadillac for all he spent on car repairs." One time she found someone else's tube of lipstick on the floorboard, along with a lacy handkerchief. "See this?" she said to me. "Some floozy left this in the car." 15

Once I saw her take a pan of warm water into the bedroom where my dad was sleeping. She took his hand from under the covers and held it in the water. I stood in the doorway and watched. I wanted to know what was going on. This would make him talk in his sleep, she told me. There were things she needed to know, things she was sure he was keeping from her.

Every year or so, when I was little, we would take the North Coast Limited across the Cascade Range from Yakima to Seattle and stay in the Vance Hotel and eat, I remember, at a place called the Dinner Bell Cafe. Once we went to Ivar's Acres of Clams and drank glasses of warm clam broth.

In 1956, the year I was to graduate from high school, my dad quit his job at the mill in Yakima and took a job in Chester, a little sawmill town in northern California. The reasons given at the time for his taking the job had to do with a higher hourly wage and the vague promise that he might, in a few years' time, succeed to the job of head filer in this new mill. But I think, in the main, that my dad had grown restless and simply wanted to try his luck elsewhere. Things had gotten a little too predictable for him in Yakima. Also, the year before, there had been the deaths, within six months of each other, of both his parents.

But just a few days after graduation, when my mother and I were packed to move to Chester, my dad penciled a letter to say he'd been sick for a while. He didn't want us to worry, he said, but he'd cut himself on a saw. Maybe he'd got a tiny sliver of steel in his blood. Anyway, something had happened and he'd had to miss work, he said. In the same mail was an unsigned postcard from somebody down there telling my mother that my dad was about to die and that he was drinking "raw whiskey."

When we arrived in Chester, my dad was living in a trailer that belonged to   20
the company. I didn't recognize him immediately. I guess for a moment I didn't want to recognize him. He was skinny and pale and looked bewildered. His pants wouldn't stay up. He didn't look like my dad. My mother began to cry. My dad put his arm around her and patted her shoulder vaguely, like he didn't know what this was all about, either. The three of us took up life together in the trailer, and we looked after him as best we could. But my dad was sick, and he couldn't get any better. I worked with him in the mill that summer and part of the fall. We'd get up in the mornings and eat eggs and toast while we listened to the radio, and then go out the door with our lunch pails. We'd pass through the gate together at eight in the morning, and I wouldn't see him again until quitting time. In November I went back to Yakima to be closer to my girlfriend, the girl I'd made up my mind I was going to marry.

He worked at the mill in Chester until the following February, when he collapsed on the job and was taken to the hospital. My mother asked if I would come down there and help. I caught a bus from Yakima to Chester, intending to drive them back to Yakima. But now, in addition to being physically sick, my dad was in the midst of a nervous breakdown, though none of us knew to call it that at the time. During the entire trip back to Yakima, he didn't speak, not even when asked a direct question. ("How do you feel, Raymond?" "You okay, Dad?") He'd communicate if he communicated at all, by moving his head or by turning his palms up as if to say he didn't know or care. The only time he said anything on the trip, and for nearly a month afterward, was when I was speeding down a gravel road in Oregon and the car muffler came loose. "You were going too fast," he said.

Back in Yakima a doctor saw to it that my dad went to a psychiatrist. My mother and dad had to go on relief, as it was called, and the county paid for the psychiatrist. The psychiatrist asked my dad, "Who is the President?" He'd had a question put to him that he could answer. "Ike," my dad said. Nevertheless, they put him on the fifth floor of Valley Memorial Hospital and began giving him electro-shock treatments. I was married by then and about to start my own family. My dad was still locked up when my wife went into this same hospital, just one floor down, to have our first baby. After she had delivered, I went upstairs to give my dad the news. They let me in through a steel door and showed me where I could find him. He was sitting on a couch with a blanket over his lap. *Hey,* I thought. *What in hell is happening to my dad?* I sat down next to him and told him he was a grandfather. He waited a minute and then said, "I feel like a grandfather." That's all he said. He didn't smile or move. He was in a big room with a lot of other people. Then I hugged him, and he began to cry.

Somehow he got out of there. But now came the years when he couldn't work and just sat around the house trying to figure what next and what he'd done wrong in his life that he'd wound up like this. My mother went from job to crummy job. Much later she referred to that time he was in the hospital, and those years just afterward, as "when Raymond was sick." The word *sick* was never the same for me again.

In 1964, through the help of a friend, he was lucky enough to be hired on at a mill in Klamath, California. He moved down there by himself to see if he could hack it. He lived not far from the mill, in a one-room cabin not much different from the place he and my mother had started out living in when they went west. He scrawled letters to my mother, and if I called she'd read them aloud to me over the phone. In the letters, he said it was touch and go. Every day that he went to work, he felt like it was the most important day of his life. But every day, he told her, made the next day that much easier. He said for her to tell me he said hello. If he couldn't sleep at night, he said, he thought about me and the good times we used to have. Finally, after a couple of months, he regained some of his confidence. He could do the work and didn't think he had to worry that he'd let anybody down ever again. When he was sure, he sent for my mother.

He'd been off from work for six years and had lost everything in that time—home, car, furniture, and appliances, including the big freezer that had been my mother's pride and joy. He'd lost his good name too—Raymond Carver was someone who couldn't pay his bills—and his self-respect was gone. He'd even lost his virility. My mother told my wife, "All during that time Raymond was sick we slept together in the same bed, but we didn't have relations. He wanted to a few times, but nothing happened. I didn't miss it, but I think he wanted to, you know."

During those years I was trying to raise my own family and earn a living. But, one thing and another, we found ourselves having to move a lot. I couldn't keep track of what was going down in my dad's life. But I did have a chance one Christmas to tell him I wanted to be a writer. I might as well have told him I wanted to become a plastic surgeon. "What are you going to write about?" he wanted to know. Then, as if to help me out, he said, "Write about stuff you know about. Write about some of those fishing trips we took." I said I would, but I knew I wouldn't.

"Send me what you write," he said. I said I'd do that, but then I didn't. I wasn't writing anything about fishing, and I didn't think he'd particularly care about, or even necessarily understand, what I was writing in those days. Besides, he wasn't a reader. Not the sort, anyway, I imagined I was writing for.

Then he died. I was a long way off, in Iowa City, with things still to say to him. I didn't have the chance to tell him goodbye, or that I thought he was doing great at his new job. That I was proud of him for making a comeback.

My mother said he came in from work that night and ate a big supper. Then he sat at the table by himself and finished what was left of a bottle of whiskey, a bottle she found hidden in the bottom of the garbage under some coffee grounds a day or so later. Then he got up and went to bed, where my mother joined him a little later. But in the night she had to get up and make a bed for herself on the couch. "He was snoring so loud I couldn't sleep," she said. The next morning when she looked in on him, he was on his back with his mouth open, his cheeks caved in. *Graylooking,* she said. She knew he was dead—she didn't need a doctor to tell her that. But she called one anyway, and then she called my wife.

Among the pictures my mother kept of my dad and herself during those early days in Washington was a photograph of him standing in front of a car, holding a beer and a stringer of fish. In the photograph he is wearing his hat back on his forehead and has this awkward grin on his face. I asked her for it and she gave it to me, along with some others. I put it up on my wall, and each time we moved, I took the picture along and put it up on another wall. I looked at it carefully from time to time, trying to figure out some things about my dad, and maybe myself in the process. But I couldn't. My dad just kept moving further and further away from me and back into time. Finally, in the course of another move, I lost the photograph. It was then that I tried to recall it, and at the same time make an attempt to say something about my dad, and how I thought that in some important ways we might be alike. I wrote the poem when I was living in an apartment house in an urban area south of San Francisco, at a time when I found myself, like my dad, having trouble with alcohol. The poem was a way of trying to connect up with him.

Photograph of My Father in His Twenty-Second Year

October. Here in this dank, unfamiliar kitchen
I study my father's embarrassed young man's face.
Sheepish grin, he holds in one hand a string
of spiny yellow perch, in the other
a bottle of Carlsberg beer.

In jeans and flannel shirt, he leans
against the front fender of a 1934 Ford.
He would like to pose brave and hearty for his posterity,
wear his old hat cocked over his ear.
All his life my father wanted to be bold.

But the eyes give him away, and the hands
that limply offer the string of dead perch

and the bottle of beer. Father, I love you,
yet how can I say thank you, I who can't hold my liquor either
and don't even know the places to fish.

The poem is true in its particulars, except that my dad died in June and not   30
October, as the first word of the poem says. I wanted a word with more than one
syllable to it to make it linger a little. But more than that, I wanted a month appropriate to what I felt at the time I wrote the poem—a month of short days and failing light, smoke in the air, things perishing. June was summer nights and days,
graduations, my wedding anniversary, the birthday of one of my children. June was-
n't a month your father died in.

After the service at the funeral home, after we had moved outside, a woman I
didn't know came over to me and said, "He's happier where he is now." I stared at
this woman until she moved away. I still remember the little knob of a hat she was
wearing. Then one of my dad's cousins—I didn't know the man's name—reached
out and took my hand, "We all miss him," he said, and I knew he wasn't saying it
just to be polite.

I began to weep for the first time since receiving the news. I hadn't been able
to before. I hadn't had the time, for one thing. Now, suddenly, I couldn't stop. I held
my wife and wept while she said and did what she could do to comfort me there
in the middle of that summer afternoon.

I listened to people say consoling things to my mother, and I was glad that my
dad's family had turned up, had come to where he was. I thought I'd remember
everything that was said and done that day and maybe find a way to tell it sometime. But I didn't. I forgot it all, or nearly. What I do remember is that I heard our
name used a lot that afternoon, my dad's name and mine. But I knew they were
talking about my dad. *Raymond,* these people kept saying in their beautiful voices
out of my childhood. *Raymond.*

Questions for Discussion and Writing

1. What characteristics does Carver share with his father? How would you
   characterize their relationship? To what extent does Carver wish to understand his father's life in order to understand the direction his own life has
   taken?
2. What feelings does the poem express that Carver found it difficult to express
   face-to-face when his father was still alive?
3. If you can relate to Carver's situation, describe your own experiences and
   observations about the effects of living with someone who is an alcoholic.

GAYLE PEMBERTON

*Gayle Pemberton (b. 1948) is the William R. Kenan Professor of the Humanities at Wesleyan
University and chair of the African-American Studies Department. She was raised in Chicago
and Ohio, received a Ph.D. in English and American literature at Harvard University, and has*

served as the associate director of African-American Studies at Princeton University. Pemberton has taught at Smith, Reed, and Bowdoin Colleges. The following chapter, drawn from her memoir The Hottest Water in Chicago *(1992), recounts the influential role her grandmother played in her life.*

Antidisestablishmentarianism

Okay, so where's Gloria Lockerman?[1] I want to know. Gloria Lockerman was partially responsible for ruining my life. I might never have ended up teaching literature if it had not been for her. I don't want to "call her out." I just want to know how things are, what she's doing. Have things gone well, Gloria? How's the family? What's up?

Gloria Lockerman, in case you don't recall, won scads of money on "The $64,000 Question."[2] Gloria Lockerman was a young black child, like me, but she could spell anything. Gloria Lockerman became my nemesis with her ability, her a-n-t-i-d-i-s-e-s-t-a-b-l-i-s-h-m-e-n-t-a-r-i-a-n-i-s-m.

My parents, my sister, and I shared a house in Dayton, Ohio, with my father's mother and her husband, my stepgrandfather, during the middle fifties. Sharing is an overstatement. It was my grandmother's house. Our nuclear group ate in a makeshift kitchen in the basement; my sister and I shared a dormer bedroom, and my parents actually had a room on the main floor of the house—several parts of which were off-limits. These were the entire living room, anywhere within three feet of Grandma's African violets, the windows and venetian blinds, anything with a doily on it, the refrigerator, and the irises in the backyard.

It was an arrangement out of necessity, given the unimpressive state of our combined fortunes, and it did not meet with anyone's satisfaction. To make matters worse, we had blockbusted a neighborhood. So, for the first year, I integrated the local elementary school—a thankless and relatively inhuman experience. I remember one day taking the Sunday paper route for a boy up the block who was sick. It was a beautiful spring day, dewy, warm. I walked up the three steps to a particular house and placed the paper on the stoop. Suddenly, a full-grown man, perhaps sixty or so, appeared with a shotgun aimed at me and said that if he ever saw my nigger ass on his porch again he'd blow my head off, I know—typical American grandfather.

Grandma liked spirituals, preferably those sung by Mahalia Jackson. She was   5
not a fan of gospel and I can only imagine what she'd say if she were around to hear what's passing for inspirational music these days. She also was fond of country

---

[1] *Gloria Lockerman*: the African-American twelve-year-old from Baltimore who won $32,000 with her spelling abilities on *The $64,000 Question.*

[2] *The $64,000 Question* was a phenomenally popular big-money quiz show that aired in the mid-1950s. In the first six months of this show, the sales of Revlon (the show's sponsor) rose 54 percent. The following year, Revlon's sales tripled.

singers, and any of the members of "The Lawrence Welk Show." ("That Jimmy. Oh, I love the way he sings. He's from Iowa.") She was from Iowa, Jimmy was from Iowa, my father was from Iowa. She was crazy about Jimmy Dean too, and Tennessee Ernie Ford, and "Gunsmoke." She could cook with the finest of them and I wish I could somehow recreate her Parkerhouse rolls, but I lack bread karma. Grandma liked flowers (she could make anything bloom) and she loved her son.

She disliked white people, black people in the aggregate and pretty much individually too, children—particularly female children—her daughter, her husband, my mother, Episcopalianism, Catholicism, Judaism, and Dinah Shore. She had a hot temper and a mean streak. She also suffered from several nagging ailments: high blood pressure, ulcers, an enlarged heart, ill-fitting dentures, arteriosclerosis, and arthritis—enough to make anyone hot tempered and mean, I'm sure. But to a third grader, such justifications and their subtleties were ultimately beyond me and insufficient, even though I believe I understood in part the relationship between pain and personality. Grandma scared the daylights out of me. I learned to control my nervous stomach enough to keep from getting sick daily. So Grandma plus school plus other family woes and my sister still predicting the end of the world every time the sirens went off—Grandma threatened to send her to a convent—made the experience as a whole something I'd rather forget, but because of the mythic proportions of family, can't.

I often think that it might have been better had I been older, perhaps twenty years older, when I knew Grandma. But I realize that she would have found much more wrong with me nearing thirty than she did when I was eight or nine. When I was a child, she could blame most of my faults on my mother. Grown, she would have had no recourse but to damn me to hell.

Ah, but she is on the gene. Grandma did everything fast. She cooked, washed, cleaned, moved—everything was at lightning speed. She passed this handicap on to me, and I have numerous bruises, cuts, and burns to show for it. Watching me throw pots and pans around in the creation of a meal, my mother occasionally calls me by my grandmother's first name. I smile back, click my teeth to imitate a slipping upper, and say something unpleasant about someone.

Tuesday nights were "The $64,000 Question" nights, just as Sundays we watched Ed Sullivan and Saturdays were reserved for Lawrence Welk and "Gunsmoke." We would all gather around the television in what was a small, informal family section between the verboten real living room and the mahogany dining table and chairs, used only three or four times a year. I don't remember where I sat, but it wasn't on the floor since that wasn't allowed either.

As we watched these television programs, once or twice I sat briefly on Grandma's lap. She was the world's toughest critic. No one was considered worthy, apart from the above-mentioned. To her, So-and-So or Whosits could not sing, dance, tell a joke, read a line—nothing. In her hands "Ted Mack's Amateur Hour" would have lasted three minutes. She was willing to forgive only very rarely—usually when someone she liked gave a mediocre performance on one of her favorite shows.

I must admit that Grandma's style of teaching critical thinking worked as well as some others I've encountered. My father had a different approach. Throughout my youth he would play the music of the thirties and forties. His passion was for Billie Holiday, with Ella Fitzgerald, Peggy Lee, Sarah Vaughan, and a few others thrown in for a touch of variety. He enjoyed music, and when he wanted to get some musical point across, he would talk about some nuance of style that revealed the distinction between what he called "really singing" and a failure. He would say, "Now, listen to that there. Did you catch it? Hear what she did with that note?" With Grandma it was more likely to be:

"Did you hear that?"

"What?" I might ask.

"That. What she just sang."

"Yes."   15

"Well, what do you think of it?"

"It's okay, I guess."

"Well, that was garbage. She can't sing a note. That stinks. She's a fool."

Message across. We all choose our own pedagogical techniques.

Game shows are, well, game shows. I turned on my television the other day,   20
and as I clicked through channels looking for something to watch I stopped long enough to hear an announcer say that the guest contestant was going to do something or other in 1981. Reruns of game shows? Well, why not? What difference does it make if the whole point is to watch people squirm, twist, sweat, blare, weep, convulse to get their hands on money and gifts, even if they end up being just "parting gifts?" (I won some of them myself once: a bottle of liquid Johnson's Wax, a box of Chunkies, a beach towel with the name of a diet soda on it, plus a coupon for a case of the stuff, and several boxes of Sugar Blobs—honey-coated peanut butter, marshmallow, and chocolate flavored crispies, dipped in strawberry flavoring for that special morning taste treat!)

Game shows in the fifties were different, more exciting. I thought the studio sets primitive even when I was watching them then. The clock on "Beat the Clock," the coat and crown on "Queen for a Day"—nothing like that mink on "The Big Payoff" that Bess Meyerson modeled—and that wire card flipper on "What's My Line" that John Charles Daly used—my, was it flimsy looking. The finest set of all, though, was on "The $64,000 Question." Hal March would stand outside the isolation booth, the door closing on the likes of Joyce Brothers, Catherine Kreitzer, and Gloria Lockerman, the music would play, and the clock would begin ticking down, like all game show clocks: *TOOT-toot-TOOT-toot-TOOT-toot-BUZZZZZZ.*

There were few opportunities to see black people on television in those days. I had watched "Amos 'n' Andy" when we lived in Chicago. But that show was a variation on a theme. Natives running around or jumping up and down or looking menacing in African adventure movies; shuffling, subservient, and clowning servants in local color movies (or any other sort); and "Amos 'n' Andy" were all the same thing: the perpetuation of a compelling, deadly, darkly humorous, and occasionally laughable idea. Nonfictional blacks on television were limited to Sammy Davis, Jr., as part of the Will Mastin Trio and afterward, or Peg Leg Bates on "The Ed Sullivan Show" on Sunday, or the entertainers who might show up on other variety shows, or Nat King Cole during his fifteen-minute program. Naturally, the appearance of Gloria Lockerman caused a mild sensation as we watched "The $64,000 Question," all assembled.

"Look at her," Grandma said.

I braced myself for the torrent of abuse that was about to be leveled at the poor girl.

"You ought to try to be like that," Grandma said.

"Huh?" I said.

"What did you say?"

"Yes, ma'am."

I was shocked, thrown into despair. I had done well in school, as well as could be hoped. I was modestly proud of my accomplishments, and given the price I was paying every day—and paying in silence, for I never brought my agonies at school home with me—I didn't need Gloria Lockerman thrown in my face. Gloria Lockerman, like me, on television, spelling. I was perennially an early-round knockout in spelling bees.

My sister understands all of this. Her own story is slightly different and she says she'll tell it all one day herself. She is a very good singer and has a superb ear; with our critical training, what more would she need? Given other circumstances, she might have become a performer herself. When she was about eleven Leslie Uggams was on Arthur Godfrey's "Talent Scouts" and was soon to be tearing down the "Name That Tune" runway, ringing the bell and becoming moderately famous. No one ever held Leslie Uggams up to my sister for image consciousness-raising. But my sister suffered nevertheless. She could outsing Leslie Uggams and probably run as fast; she knew the songs and didn't have nearly so strange a last name. But, there she was, going nowhere in the Middle West, and there was Leslie Uggams on her way to "Sing Along With Mitch." To this day, my sister mumbles if she happens to see Leslie Uggams on television—before she can get up to change the channel—or hears someone mention her name. I told her I saw Leslie Uggams in the flesh at a club in New York. She was sitting at a table, just like the rest of us, listening with pleasure to Barbara Cook. My sister swore at me.

Grandma called her husband "Half-Wit." He was a thin, small-boned man who looked to me far more like an Indian chief than like a black man. He was from Iowa too, but that obviously did not account for enough in Grandma's eyes. He had a cracking tenor voice, a head full of dead straight black hair, reddish, dull brown skin, and large sad, dark brown eyes. His craggy face also reminded me of pictures I'd seen of Abraham Lincoln—but, like all political figures and American forefathers, Lincoln, to my family, was fair game for wisecracks, so that resemblance did Grandpa no good either. And for reasons that have gone to the grave with both of them, he was the most thoroughly henpecked man I have ever heard of, not to mention seen.

Hence, domestic scenes had a quality of pathos and high humor as far as I was concerned. My sister and I called Grandpa "Half-Wit" when we were alone together, but that seemed to have only a slight effect on our relations with him and our willingness to obey him—though I cannot recall any occasions calling for his authority. Grandma was Grandma, Half-Wit was Half-Wit—and we lived with the two of them. I have one particularly vivid memory of Grandma, an aficionada of

25

30

the iron skillet, chasing him through the house waving it in the air, her narrow, arthritis-swollen wrist and twisted knuckles turning the heavy pan as if it were a lariat. He didn't get hurt; he was fleet of foot and made it out the back door before she caught him. My father's real father had been dead since the thirties and divorced from Grandma since the teens—so Half-Wit had been in place for quite some years and was still around to tell the story, if he had the nerve.

Grandma had a glass menagerie, the only one I've seen apart from performances of the Williams[3] play. I don't think she had a unicorn, but she did have quite a few pieces. From a distance of no less than five feet I used to squint at the glass forms, wondering what they meant to Grandma, who was herself delicate of form but a powerhouse of strength, speed, and temper. I also wondered how long it would take me to die if the glass met with some unintended accident caused by me. Real or imagined unpleasantries, both in the home and outside of it, helped develop in me a somewhat melancholic nature. And even before we had moved to Ohio I found myself laughing and crying at the same time.

In the earlier fifties, in Chicago, I was allowed to watch such programs as "The Ernie Kovacs Show," "Your Show of Shows," "The Jackie Gleason Show," "The Red Skelton Show," and, naturally, "I Love Lucy." I was continually dazzled by the skits and broad humor, but I was particularly taken with the silent sketches, my favorite comedians as mime artists: Skelton[4] as Freddy the Freeloader, Caesar and Coca[5] in a number of roles, thoroughly outrageous Kovacs acts backed by Gershwin's "Rialto Ripples." My father was a very funny man and a skillful mime. I could tell when he watched Gleason's Poor Soul that he identified mightily with what was on the screen. It had nothing to do with self-pity. My father had far less of it than other men I've met with high intelligence, financial and professional stress, and black faces in a white world. No, my father would even say that we were all poor souls; it was the human condition. His mimicking of the Gleason character—head down, shoulders tucked, stomach sagging, feet splayed—served as some kind of release. I would laugh and cry watching either of them.

But my absolute favorite was Martha Raye, who had a way of milking the fine   35
line between tragedy and comedy better than most. I thought her eyes showed a combination of riotous humor and terror. Her large mouth contorted in ways that seemed to express the same two emotions. Her face was a mask of profound sadness. She did for me what Sylvia Sidney did for James Baldwin. In *The Devil Finds Work*,[6] Baldwin says, "Sylvia Sidney was the only American film actress who reminded me of a colored girl, or woman—which is to say that she was the only American film actress who reminded me of reality." The reality Raye conveyed to me was of how dreams could turn sour in split-seconds, and how underdogs, even

---

[3] *The Glass Menagerie* (1945), by the American playwright Tennessee Williams.   [4] *Red Skelton (1913–1997)*: popular comedian on radio and television.   [5] *Sid Caesar (b. 1922)*: American comedian and actor who starred in television's *Your Show of Shows* (1950–1954) with Imogene Coca, actress, comedian (1908–2001)   [6] *The Devil Finds Works: An Essay* (1976): written by James Baldwin (1924–1987).

when winning, often had to pay abominable prices. She also could sing a jazz song well, with her husky scat phrasing, in ways that were slightly different from those of my favorite singers, and almost as enjoyable.

There were no comedic or dramatic images of black women on the screen— that is, apart from Sapphire and her mother on "Amos 'n' Andy." And knowing Grandma and Grandpa taught me, if nothing else suggested it, that what I saw of black life on television was a gross burlesque— played to the hilt with skill by black actors, but still lacking reality.

Black female singers who appeared on television were, like their music, sacrosanct, and I learned from their styles, lyrics, and improvisations, lessons about life that mime routines did not reveal. Still, it was Martha Raye, and occasionally Lucille Ball and Imogene Coca at their most absurd, that aligned me with my father and his Poor Soul, and primed me to both love and despise Grandma and to see that in life most expressions, thoughts, acts, and intentions reveal their opposite polarities simultaneously.

Grandma died in 1965. I was away, out of the country, and I missed her funeral—which was probably a good idea since I might have been tempted to strangle some close family friend who probably would have launched into a "tsk, tsk, tsk" monologue about long-suffering grandmothers and impudent children. But, in another way, I'm sorry I didn't make it. Her funeral might have provided some proper closure for me, might have prompted me to organize her effect on my life sooner than I did, reconciling the grandmother who so hoped I would be a boy that she was willing to catch a Constellation or a DC-3 to witness my first few hours, but instead opted to take the bus when she heard the sad news, with the grandmother who called me "Sally Slapcabbage" and wrote to me and my sister regularly, sending us the odd dollar or two, until her death.

I remember coming home from school, getting my jelly sandwich and wolfing it down, and watching "The Mickey Mouse Club," my favorite afternoon show, since there was no afternoon movie. I had noticed and had been offended by the lack of black children in the "Club," but the cartoons, particularly those with Donald Duck, were worth watching. On this particular episode—one of the regular guest act days—a group of young black children, perhaps nine or ten of them, came on and sang, with a touch of dancing, "Old MacDonald Had a Farm," in an up-tempo, jazzy version. In spite of the fact that usually these guest days produced some interesting child acts, I became angry with what I saw. I felt patronized, for myself and for them. Clearly a couple of them could out-sing and out-dance any Mouseketeer—something that wasn't worth giving a thought to—but this performance was gratuitous, asymmetrical, a nonsequitur, like Harpo Marx marching through the Negro section in *A Day at the Races*,[7] blowing an imaginary horn and exciting the locals to much singing, swinging, and dancing to a charming ditty called "Who Dat Man?"

[7] *A Day at the Races*: popular 1937 Marx Brothers movie about inmates turned loose in a sanitarium.

I must have mumbled something as I watched the group singing "Old Mac-   40
Donald." Grandma, passing through, took a look at what was on the screen, and at
me, turned off the television, took my hand, led me to her kitchen, and sat me
down at the table where she and Half-Wit ate, poured me some milk, and without
so much as a blink of her eye, said, "Pay no attention to that shit."

Questions for Discussion and Writing

1. How do the circumstances Pemberton describes (especially, her grandmother's response to Gloria Lockerman) explain why Pemberton remembers
   her so fondly? What life lessons did Pemberton learn from her grandmother?
2. What traits does Pemberton possess as a writer? How would you characterize the voice that you hear in this essay? How did her grandmother's influence shape her personality and contribute to her literary style?
3. In your opinion, do television shows accurately reflect (or fail to reflect)
   African-American life in the United States today?

MIKHAL GILMORE

*Mikhal Gilmore was born in 1951 in Salt Lake City, Utah, and grew up in Portland, Oregon.
He is a senior writer at Rolling Stone magazine. "My Brother, Gary Gilmore" first appeared
in Granta (Autumn 1991) and served as the basis for his prize-winning autobiography, Shot
through the Heart (1994).*

My Brother, Gary Gilmore

I am the brother of a man who murdered innocent men. His name was Gary
Gilmore. After his conviction and sentencing, he campaigned to end his own life,
and in January 1977 he was shot to death by a firing-squad in Draper, Utah. It was
the first execution in America in over a decade.

Over the years, many people have judged me by my brother's actions as if in
coming from a family that yielded a murderer I must be formed by the same
causes, the same sins, must by my brother's actions be responsible for the violence
that resulted, and bear the mark of a frightening and shameful heritage. It's as if
there is guilt in the fact of the blood-line itself. Maybe there is.

Pictures in the family scrap-book show my father with his children. I have
only one photograph of him and Gary together. Gary is wearing a sailor's cap. He
has his arms wrapped tightly around my father's neck, his head bent towards him, a
look of broken need on his face. It is heart-breaking to look at this picture—not
just for the look on Gary's face, the look that was the stamp of his future, but also
for my father's expression: pulling away from my brother's cheek, he is wearing a
look of distaste.

When my brother Gaylen was born in the mid forties, my father turned all his
love on his new, beautiful brown-eyed son. Gary takes on a harder aspect in the

pictures around this time. He was beginning to keep a greater distance from the rest of the family. Six years later, my father turned his love from Gaylen to me. You don't see Gary in the family pictures after that.

Gary had nightmares. It was always the same dream: he was being beheaded.   5

In 1953, Gary was arrested for breaking windows. He was sent to a juvenile detention home for ten months, where he saw young men raped and beaten. Two years later, at age fourteen, he was arrested for car theft and sentenced to eighteen months in jail. I was four years old.

When I was growing up I did not feel accepted by, or close to, my brothers. By the time I was four or five, they had begun to find life and adventure outside the home. Frank, Gary and Gaylen signified the teenage rebellion of the fifties for me. They wore their hair in greasy pompadours and played Elvis Presley and Fats Domino records. They dressed in scarred motorcycle jackets and brutal boots. They smoked cigarettes, drank booze and cough syrup, skipped—and quit—school, and spent their evenings hanging out with girls in tight sweaters, racing souped-up cars along country roads outside Portland, or taking part in gang rumbles. My brothers looked for a forbidden life—the life they had seen exemplified in the crime lore of gangsters and killers. They studied the legends of violence. They knew the stories of John Dillinger, Bonnie and Clyde, and Leopold and Loeb; mulled over the meanings of the lives and executions of Barbara Graham, Bruno Hauptmann, Sacco and Vanzetti, the Rosenbergs; thrilled to the pleading of criminal lawyers like Clarence Darrow and Jerry Giesler. They brought home books about condemned men and women, and read them avidly.

I remember loving my brothers fiercely, wanting to be a part of their late-night activities and to share in their laughter and friendship. I also remember being frightened of them. They looked deadly, beyond love, destined to hurt the world around them.

Gary came home from reform school for a brief Christmas visit. On Christmas night I was sitting in my room, playing with the day's haul of presents, when Gary wandered in. "Hey Mike, how you doing?" he asked, taking a seat on my bed. "Think I'll just join you while I have a little Christmas cheer." He had a six-pack of beer with him and was speaking in a bleary drawl. "Look partner, I want to have a talk with you." I think it was the first companionable statement he ever made to me. I never expected the intimacy that followed and could not really fathom it at such a young age. Sitting on the end of my bed, sipping at his Christmas beer, Gary described a harsh, private world and told me horrible, transfixing stories: about the boys he knew in the detention halls, reform schools and county farms where he now spent most of his time; about the bad boys who had taught him the merciless codes of his new life; and about the soft boys who did not have what it took to survive that life. He said he had shared a cell with one of the soft boys, who cried at night, wanting to disappear into nothing, while Gary held him in his arms until the boy finally fell into sleep, sobbing.

Then Gary gave me some advice. "You have to learn to be hard. You have to   10
learn to take things and feel nothing about them: no pain, no anger, nothing. And you have to realize, if anybody wants to beat you up, even if they want to hold you down and kick you, you have to let them. You can't fight back. You *shouldn't* fight

back. Just lie down in front of them and let them beat you, let them kick you. Lie there and let them do it. It is the only way you will survive. If you don't give in to them, they will kill you."

He set aside his beer and cupped my face in his hands. "You have to remember this, Mike," he said. "Promise me. Promise me you'll be a man. Promise me you'll let them beat you." We sat there on that winter night, staring at each other, my face in his hands, and as Gary asked me to promise to take my beatings, his bloodshot eyes began to cry. It was the first time I had seen him shed tears.

I promised: Yes, I'll let them kick me. But I was afraid—afraid of betraying Gary's plea.

Gary and Gaylen weren't at home much. I came to know them mainly through their reputations, through the endless parade of grim policemen who came to the door trying to find them, and through the faces and accusations of bail bondsman and lawyers who arrived looking sympathetic and left disgusted. I knew them through many hours spent in waiting-rooms at city and county jails, where my mother went to visit them, and through the numerous times I accompanied her after midnight to the local police station on Milwaukie's Main Street to bail out another drunken son.

I remember being called into the principal's office while still in grammar school, and being warned that the school would never tolerate my acting as my brothers did; I was told to watch myself, that my brothers had already used years of the school district's good faith and leniency, and that if I was going to be like them, there were other schools I could be sent to. I came to be seen as an extension of my brothers' reputations. Once, I was waiting for a bus in the centre of the small town when a cop pulled over. "You're one of the Gilmore boys, aren't you? I hope you don't end up like those two. I've seen enough shitheads from your family." I was walking down the local main highway when a car pulled over and a gang of older teenage boys piled out, surrounding me, "Are you Gaylen Gilmore's brother?" one of them asked. They shoved me into the car, drove me a few blocks to a deserted lot and took turns punching me in the face. I remembered Gary's advice—"You can't fight back; you *shouldn't* fight back"—and I let them beat me until they were tired. Then they spat on me, got back in their car and left.

I cried all the way back home, and I hated the world. I hated the small town I lived in, its ugly, mean people. For the first time in my life I hated my brothers. I felt that my future would be governed by them, that I would be destined to follow their lives whether I wanted to or not, that I would never know any relief from shame and pain and disappointment. I felt a deep impulse to violence: I wanted to rip the faces off the boys who had beat me up. "I want to kill them," I told myself. "I want to *kill* them"—and as I realized what it was I was saying, and why I was feeling that way, I only hated my world, and my brothers, more.

Frank Gilmore, Sr. died on 30 June 1962. Gary was in Portland's Rocky Butte Jail, and the authorities denied his request to attend the funeral. He tore his cell apart; he smashed a light bulb and slashed his wrists. He was placed in "the hole"— solitary confinement—on the day of father's funeral. Gary was twenty-one. I was eleven.

I was surprised at how hard my mother and brothers took father's death. I was surprised they loved him enough to cry at all. Or maybe they were crying for the love he had so long withheld, and the reconciliation that would be forever denied them. I was the only one who didn't cry. I don't know why, but I never cried over my father's death—not then, and not now.

With my father's death Gary's crimes became more desperate, more violent. He talked a friend into helping him commit armed robbery. Gary grabbed the victim's wallet while the friend held a club; he was arrested a short time later, tried and found guilty. The day of his sentencing, during an afternoon when my mother had to work, he called me from the Clackamas County Courthouse. "How you doing partner? I just wanted to let you and mom know: I got sentenced to fifteen years."

I was stunned. "Gary, what can I do for you?" I asked. I think it came out wrong, as if I was saying: I'm busy; what do you *want?*

"I . . . I didn't really want anything," Gary said, his voice broken. "I just wanted   20 to hear your voice. I just wanted to say goodbye. You know, I won't be seeing you for a few years. Take care of yourself." We hadn't shared anything so intimate since that Christmas night, many years before.

I didn't have much talent for crime (neither did my brothers, to tell the truth), but I also didn't have much appetite for it. I had seen what my brothers' lives had brought them. For years, my mother had told me that I was the family's last hope for redemption. "I want one son to turn out right, *one* son I don't have to end up visiting in jail, one son I don't have to watch in court as his life is sentenced away, piece by piece." After my father's death, she drew me closer to her and her religion, and when I was twelve, I was baptized a Mormon. For many years, the Church's beliefs helped to provide me with a moral center and a hope for deliverance that I had not known before.

I think culture and history helped to save me. I was born in 1951, and although I remember well the youthful explosion of the 1950s, I was too young to experience it the way my brothers did. The music of Elvis Presley and others had represented and expressed my brothers' rebellion: it was hard-edged, with no apparent ideology. The music was a part of my childhood, but by the early sixties the spirit of the music had been spent.

Then, on 9 February 1964 (my thirteenth birthday, and the day I joined the Mormon priesthood), the Beatles made their first appearance on the Ed Sullivan Show. My life would never be the same. The Beatles meant a change, they promised a world that my parents and brothers could not offer. In fact, I liked the Beatles in part because they seemed such a departure from the world of my brothers, and because my brothers couldn't abide them.

The rock culture and youth politics of the sixties allowed their adherents to act out a kind of ritualized criminality: we could use drugs, defy authority, or contemplate violent or destructive acts of revolt, we told ourselves, *because we had a reason to.* The music aimed to foment a sense of cultural community, and for somebody who had felt as disenfranchised by his family as I did, rock and roll offered not just a sense of belonging but empowered me with new ideals. I began to find rock's morality preferable to the Mormon ethos, which seemed rigid and severe. One Sunday in the summer of 1967, a member of the local bishopric—a man I admired, and had once regarded as something of a father figure—drove over to our house and asked me to step outside for a talk. He told me that he and other church leaders had grown concerned about my changed appearance—the new length of my hair and my style of dressing—and felt it was an unwelcome influence on other young Mormons. If I did not reject the new youth culture, I would no longer be welcome in church.

On that day a line was drawn. I knew that rock and roll had provided me with   25
a new creed and a sense of courage. I believed I was taking part in a rebellion that mattered—or at least counted for more than my brothers' rebellions. In the music of the Rolling Stones or Doors or Velvet Underground, I could participate in darkness without submitting to it, which is something Gary and Gaylen had been unable to do. I remember their disdain when I tried to explain to them why Bob Dylan was good, why he mattered. It felt great to belong to a different world from them.

And I did: my father and Gaylen were dead; Gary was in prison and Frank was broken. I thought of my family as a cursed outfit, plain and simple, and I believed that the only way to escape its debts and legacies was to leave it. In 1969 I graduated from high school—the only member of my family to do so. The next day, I moved out of the house in Milwaukie and, with some friends, moved into an apartment near Portland State University, in downtown Portland.

In the summer of 1976, I was working at a record store in downtown Portland, making enough money to pay my rent and bills. I was also writing free-lance journalism and criticism, and had sold my first reviews and articles to national publications, including *Rolling Stone.*

On the evening of 30 July, having passed up a chance to go drinking with some friends, I headed home. *The Wild Bunch,* Peckinpah's genuflection to violence and honor, was on television, and as I settled back on the couch to watch it, I picked up the late edition of *The Oregonian.* I almost passed over a page-two item headlined OREGON MAN HELD IN UTAH SLAYINGS, but then something clicked inside me, and I began to read it. "Gary Mark Gilmore, 35, was charged with the murders of two young clerks during the hold-up of a service station and a motel." I read on, dazed, about how Gary had been arrested for killing Max Jensen and Ben Bushnell on consecutive nights. Both men were Mormons, about the same age as I, and both left wives and children behind.

I dropped the paper to the floor. I sat on the couch the rest of the night, alternately staring at *The Wild Bunch* and re-reading the sketchy account. I felt shocks of rage, remorse and guilt—as if I were partly responsible for the deaths. I had been part of an uninterested world that had shut Gary away. I had wanted to believe that Gary's life and mine were not entwined, that what had shaped him had not shaped me.

It had been a long time since I had written or visited Gary. After his re-   30
sentencing in 1972, I heard news of him from my mother. In January 1975, Gary was sent to the federal penitentiary in Marion, Illinois. After his transfer, we exchanged a few perfunctory letters. In early April 1976, I learned of the Oregon State Parole Board's decision to parole Gary from Marion to Provo, Utah, rather than transfer him back to Oregon. The transaction had been arranged between the parole

board, Brenda Nicol (our cousin) and her father, our uncle Vernon Damico, who lived in Provo. I remember thinking that Gary's being paroled into the heart of one of Utah's most devout and severe Mormon communities was not a great idea.

Between his release and those fateful nights in July, Gary held a job at Uncle Vernon's shoe store, and he met and fell in love with Nicole Barrett, a beautiful young woman with two children. But Gary was unable to deny some old, less wholesome appetites. Almost immediately after his release, he started drinking heavily and taking Fiorinal, a muscle and headache medication that, in sustained doses, can cause severe mood swings and sexual dysfunction. Gary apparently experienced both reactions. He became more violent. Sometimes he got rough with Nicole over failed sex, or over what he saw as her flirtations. He picked fights with other men, hitting them from behind, threatening to cave in their faces with a tire iron that he twirled as handily as a baton. He lost his job and abused his Utah relatives. He walked into stores and walked out again with whatever he wanted under his arm, glaring at the cashiers, challenging them to try to stop him. He brought guns home, and sitting on the back porch would fire them at trees, fences, the sky. "Hit the sun," he told Nicole. "See if you can make it sink." Then he hit Nicole with his fist one too many times, and she moved out.

Gary wanted her back. He told a friend that he thought he might kill her.

On a hot night in late July, Gary drove over to Nicole's mother's house and persuaded Nicole's little sister, April, to ride with him in his white pick-up truck. He wanted her to join him in looking for her sister. They drove for hours, listening to the radio, talking aimlessly, until Gary pulled up by a service station in the small town of Orem. He told April to wait in the truck. He walked into the station, where twenty-six-year-old attendant Max Jensen was working alone. There were no other cars there. Gary pulled a .22 automatic from his jacket and told Jensen to empty the cash from his pockets. He took Jensen's coin changer and led the young attendant around the back of the station and forced him to lie down on the bathroom floor. He told Jensen to place his hands under his stomach and press his face to the ground. Jensen complied and offered Gary a smile. Gary pointed the gun at the base of Jensen's skull. "This one is for me," Gary said, and he pulled the trigger. And then: "This one is for Nicole," and he pulled the trigger again.

The next night, Gary walked into the office of a motel just a few doors away from his uncle Vernon's house in Provo. He ordered the man behind the counter, Ben Bushnell, to lie down on the floor, and then he shot him in the back of the head. He walked out with the motel's cashbox under his arm and tried to stuff the pistol under a bush. But it discharged, blowing a hole in his thumb.

Gary decided to get out of town. First he had to take care of his thumb. He drove to the house of a friend named Craig and telephoned his cousin. A witness had recognized Gary leaving the site of the second murder, and the police had been in touch with Brenda. She had the police on one line, Gary on another. She tried to stall Gary until the police could set up a road-block. After they finished speaking, Gary got into his truck and headed for the local airport. A few miles down the road, he was surrounded by police cars and a SWAT team. He was arrested for Bushnell's murder and confessed to the murder of Max Jensen.

Gary's trial began some months later. The verdict was never in question. Gary didn't help himself when he refused to allow his attorneys to call Nicole as a defense witness. Gary and Nicole had been reconciled; she felt bad for him and visited him in jail every day for hours. Gary also didn't help his case by staring menacingly at the jury members or by offering belligerent testimony on his own behalf. He was found guilty. My mother called me on the night of Gary's sentencing, 7 October, to tell me that he had received the death penalty. He told the judge he would prefer being shot to being hanged.

On Saturday 15 January, I saw Gary for the last time. Camera crews were camped in the town of Draper, preparing for the finale.

During our other meetings that week, Gary had opened with friendly remarks or a joke or even a handstand. This day, though, he was nervous and was eager to deny it. We were separated by a glass partition. "Naw, the noise in this place gets to me sometimes, but I'm as cool as a cucumber," he said, holding up a steady hand. The muscles in his wrists and arms were taut and thick as rope.

Gary showed me letters and pictures he'd received, mainly from children and teenage girls. He said he always tried to answer the ones from the kids first, and he read one from an eight-year-old boy: "I hope they put you some place and make you live forever for what you did. You have no right to die. With all the malice in my heart. [*name.*]"

"Man, that one shook me up for a long time," he said.   40

I asked him if he'd replied to it.

"Yeah, I wrote, 'You're too young to have malice in your heart. I had it in mine at a young age and look what it did for me.'"

Gary's eyes nervously scanned some letters and pictures, finally falling on one that made him smile. He held it up. A picture of Nicole. "She's pretty, isn't she?" I agreed. "I look at this picture every day. I took it myself; I made a drawing from it. Would you like to have it?"

I said I would. I asked him where he would have gone if he had made it to the airport the night of the second murder.

"Portland."   45

I asked him why.

Gary studied the shelf in front of him. "I don't want to talk about that night any more," he said. "There's no point in talking about it."

"Would you have come to see me?"

He nodded. For a moment his eyes flashed the old anger. "And what would *you* have done if I'd come to you?" he asked. "If I had come and said I was in trouble and needed help, needed a place to stay? Would *you* have taken me in? Would you have hidden me?"

The question had been turned back on me. I couldn't speak. Gary sat for a long   50
moment, holding me with his eyes, then said steadily: "I think I was coming to kill you. I think that's what would have happened; there may have been no choice for you, no choice for me." His eyes softened. "Do you understand why?"

I nodded. Of course I understood why: I had escaped the family—or at least thought I had. Gary had not.

I felt terror. Gary's story could have been mine. Then terror became relief—Jensen and Bushnell's deaths, and Gary's own impending death, had meant my own safety. I finished the thought, and my relief was shot through with guilt and remorse. I felt closer to Gary than I'd ever felt before. I understood why he wanted to die.

The warden entered Gary's room. They discussed whether Gary should wear a hood for the execution.

I rapped on the glass partition and asked the warden if he would allow us a final handshake. At first he refused but consented after Gary explained it was our final visit, on the condition that I agree to a skin search. After I had been searched by two guards, two other guards brought Gary around the partition. They said that I would have to roll up my sleeve past my elbow, and that we could not touch beyond a handshake. Gary grasped my hand, squeezed it tight and said, "Well, I guess this is it." He leaned over and kissed me on the cheek.

On Monday morning, 17 January, in a cannery warehouse out behind Utah State Prison, Gary met his firing-squad. I was with my mother and brother and girl-friend when it happened. Just moments before, we had seen the morning newspaper with the headline EXECUTION STAYED. We switched on the television for more news. We saw a press conference. Gary's death was being announced.   55

There was no way to be prepared for that last see-saw of emotion. You force yourself to live through the hell of knowing that somebody you love is going to die in an expected way, at a specific time and place, and that there is nothing you can do to change that. For the rest of your life, you will have to move around in a world that wanted this death to happen. You will have to walk past people every day who were heartened by the killing of somebody in your family—somebody who you knew had long before been murdered emotionally.

You turn on the television, and the journalist tells you how the warden put a black hood over Gary's head and pinned a small, circular cloth target above his chest, and how five men pumped a volley of bullets into him. He tells you how the blood flowed from Gary's devastated heart and down his chest, down his legs, staining his white pants scarlet and dripping to the warehouse floor. He tells you how Gary's arm rose slowly at the moment of the impact, how his fingers seemed to wave as his life left him.

Shortly after Gary's execution, *Rolling Stone* offered me a job as an assistant editor at their Los Angeles bureau. It was a nice offer. It gave me the chance to get away from Portland and all the bad memories it represented.

I moved to Los Angeles in April 1977. It was not an easy life at first. I drank a pint of whisky every night, and I took Dalmane, a sleeping medication that interfered with my ability to dream—or at least made it hard to remember my dreams. There were other lapses: I was living with one woman and seeing a couple of others. For a season or two my writing went to hell. I didn't know what to say or how to say it; I could no longer tell if I had anything *worth* writing about. I wasn't sure how you made words add up. Instead of writing, I preferred reading. I favoured hard-boiled crime fiction—particularly the novels of Ross Macdonald—in which the author tried to solve murders by explicating labyrinthine family histories. I spent many nights listening to punk rock. I liked the music's accommodation with a merciless world. One of the most famous punk songs of the period was by the Adverts. It was called "Gary Gilmore's Eyes." What would it be like, the song asked, to see the world through Gary Gilmore's dead eyes? Would you see a world of murder?

All around me I had Gary's notoriety to contend with. During my first few   60
months in LA—and throughout the years that followed—most people asked me about my brother. They wanted to know what Gary was like. They admired his bravado, his hardness. I met a woman who wanted to sleep with me because I was his brother. I tried to avoid these people.

I also met women who, when they learned who my brother was, would not see me again, not take my calls again. I received letters from people who said I should not be allowed to write for a young audience. I received letters from people who thought I should have been shot alongside my brother.

There was never a time without a reminder of the past. In 1979, Norman Mailer's *The Executioner's Song* was published. At the time, I was living with a woman I loved very much. As she read the book, I could see her begin to wonder about who she was sleeping with, about what had come into her life. One night, a couple of months after the book had been published, we were watching *Saturday Night Live.* The guest host was doing a routine of impersonations. He tied a bandana around his eyes and gleefully announced his next subject: "Gary Gilmore!" My girl-friend got up from the sofa and moved into the bedroom, shutting the door. I poured a glass of whisky. She came out a few minutes later. "I'm sorry," she said, "I can't live with you any more. I can't stand being close to all this stuff." She was gone within a week.

I watched as a private and troubling event continued to be the subject of public sensation and media scrutiny; I watched my brother's life—and in some way, my life—become too large to control. I tried not to surrender to my feelings because my feelings wouldn't erase the pain or shame or bad memories or unresolved love and hate. I was waiting to be told what to feel.

Only a few months before, I had gone through one of the worst times of my life—my brief move to Portland and back. What had gone wrong, I realized, was because of my past, something that had been set in motion long before I was born. It was what Gary and I shared, more than any blood tie: we were both heirs to a legacy of negation that was beyond our control or our understanding. Gary had ended up turning the nullification outward—on innocents, on Nicole, on his family, on the world and its ideas of justice, finally on himself. I had turned the ruin inward. Outward or inward—either way, it was a powerfully destructive legacy, and for the first time in my life, I came to see that it had not really finished its enactment. To believe that Gary had absorbed all the family's dissolution, or that the worst of that rot had died with him that morning in Draper, Utah, was to miss the real nature of the legacy that had placed him before those rifles: what that heritage or patrimony was about, and where it had come from.

We tend to view murders as solitary ruptures in the world around us, outrages   65
that need to be attributed and then punished. There is a motivation, a crime, an arrest, a trial, a verdict and a punishment. Sometimes—though rarely—that punishment is death. The next day, there is another murder. The next day, there is another.

There has been no punishment that breaks the pattern, that stops this custom of one murder following another.

Murder has worked its way into our consciousness and our culture in the same way that murder exists in our literature and film: we consume each killing until there is another, more immediate or gripping one to take its place. When *this* murder story is finished, there will be another to intrigue and terrify that part of the world that has survived it. And then there will be another. Each will be a story, each will be treated and reported and remembered as a unique incident. Each murder will be solved, but murder itself will never be solved. You cannot solve murder without solving the human heart or the history that has rendered that heart so dark and desolate.

This murder story is told from inside the house where murder was born. It is the house where I grew up, and it is a house that I have never been able to leave.

As the night passed, I formed an understanding of what I needed to do. I would go back into my family—into its stories, its myths, its memories, its inheritance—and find the real story and hidden propellants behind it. I wanted to climb into the family story in the same way I've always wanted to climb into a dream about the house where we all grew up.

In the dream, it is always night. We are in my father's house—a charred-brown, 1950s-era home. Shingled, two-story and weather-worn, it is located on the far outskirts of a dead-end American town, pinioned between the night-lights and smoking chimneys of towering industrial factories. A moonlit stretch of railroad track forms the border to a forest I am forbidden to trespass. A train whistle howls in the distance. No train ever comes.

People move from the darkness outside the house to the darkness inside. They are my family. They are all back from the dead. There is my mother, Bessie Gilmore, who, after a life of bitter losses, died spitting blood, calling the names of her father and her husband—men who had long before brutalized her hopes and her love—crying to them for mercy, for a passage into the darkness that she had so long feared. There is my brother Gaylen, who died young of knife-wounds, as his new bride sat holding his hand, watching the life pass from his sunken face. There is my brother Gary, who murdered innocent men in rage against the way life had robbed him of time and love, and who died when a volley of bullets tore his heart from his chest. There is my brother Frank, who became quieter and more distant with each new death, and who was last seen in the dream walking down a road, his hands rammed deep into his pockets, a look of uncomprehending pain on his face. There is my father, Frank, Sr., dead of the ravages of lung cancer. He is in the dream less often than the other family members, and I am the only one happy to see him. 70

One night, years into the same dream, Gary tells me why I can never join my family in its comings and goings, why I am left alone sitting in the living-room as they leave: it is because I have not yet entered death. I cannot follow them across the tracks, into the forest where their real lives take place, until I die. He pulls a gun from his coat pocket. He lays it on my lap. There is a door across the room, and he moves towards it. Through the door is the night. I see the glimmer of the train tracks. Beyond them, my family.

I do not hesitate. I pick the pistol up. I put its barrel in my mouth. I pull the trigger. I feel the back of my head erupt. It is a softer feeling than I expected. I feel my teeth fracture, disintegrate and pass in a gush of blood out of my mouth. I feel my life pass out of my mouth, and in that instant, I collapse into nothingness. There is darkness, but there is no beyond. There is *never* any beyond, only the sudden, certain rush of extinction. I know that it is death I am feeling—that is, I know this is how death must truly feel and I know that this is where beyond ceases to be a possibility.

I have had the dream more than once, in various forms. I always wake up with my heart hammering hard, hurting after being torn from the void that I know is the gateway to the refuge of my ruined family. Or is it the gateway to hell? Either way, I want to return to the dream, but in the haunted hours of the night there is no way back.

Questions for Discussion and Writing

1. What can you infer from Mikhal's account about why Gary committed the murders?
2. What consequences have his brother Gary's crimes had on Mikhal's life? How would you characterize the relationship that the brothers had before and after the murders?
3. Describe an experience in which you were a "victim of guilt by association" and were blamed for something done by a sibling or other relative. Are there any mysterious or shady characters in your lineage? What are they reputed to have done?

P. D. OUSPENSKY

Peter Demianovich Ouspensky (1878–1947) was born in Moscow. His first book The Fourth Dimension *(1909) established him as one of the foremost writers on abstract mathematical theory. His subsequent works,* Tertium Organum *(1912),* A New Model of the Universe *(1914), and* In Search of the Miraculous, *which appeared posthumously in 1949, have been acclaimed as being among the most important philosophical works of the twentieth century. This essay on the Taj Mahal, drawn from the 1914 volume, is a provocative reassessment of one of the world's great architectural wonders.*

The Taj Mahal: The Soul of the Empress Mumtaz-i-Mahal

It was my last summer in India. The rains were already beginning when I left Bombay for Agra and Delhi. For several weeks before that I had been collecting and reading everything I could find about Agra, about the palace of the Great Moguls and about the Taj Mahal, the famous mausoleum of the Empress who died at the beginning of the 17th century.

But everything that I had read, either then or before, left me with a kind of indefinite feeling as though all who had attempted to describe Agra and the Taj Mahal had missed what was most important.

Neither the romantic history of the Taj Mahal, nor the architectural beauty, the luxuriance and opulence of the decoration and ornaments, could explain for me the impression of fairy-tale unreality, of something beautiful, but infinitely remote from life, the impression which was felt behind all the descriptions, but which nobody has been able to put into words or explain.

And it seemed to me that here there was a mystery. The Taj Mahal had a secret which was felt by everybody but to which nobody could give a name.

Photographs told me nothing at all. A large and massive building, and four tapering minarets, one at each corner. In all this I saw no particular beauty, but rather something incomplete. And the four minarets, standing separate, like four candles at the corners of a table, looked strange and almost unpleasant. 5

In what then lies the strength of the impression made by the Taj Mahal? Whence comes the irresistible effect which it produces on all who see it? Neither the marble lace-work of the trellises, nor the delicate carving which covers its walls, neither the mosaic flowers, nor the fate of the beautiful Empress, none of these by itself could produce such an impression. It must lie in something else. But in what? I tried not to think of it, in order not to create a preconceived idea. But something fascinated me and agitated me. I could not be sure, but it seemed to me that the enigma of the Taj Mahal was connected with the mystery of death, that is, with the mystery regarding which, according to the expression of one of the Upanishads,[1] "even the gods have doubted formerly."

The creation of the Taj Mahal dates back to the time of the conquest of India by the Mahomedans. The grandson of Akbar,[2] Shah Jehan, was one of the conquerors who changed the very face of India. Soldier and statesman, Shah Jehan was at the same time a fine judge of art and philosophy; and his court at Agra attracted all the most eminent scholars and artists of Persia, which was at that time the center of culture for the whole of Western Asia.

Shah Jehan passed most of his life, however, on campaign and in fighting. And on all his campaigns he was invariably accompanied by his favorite wife, the beautiful Arjumand Banu, or, as she was also called, Mumtaz-i-Mahal—"The Treasure of the Palace." Arjumand Banu was Shah Jehan's constant adviser in all matters of subtle and intricate Oriental diplomacy, and she also shared his interest in the philosophy to which the invincible Emperor devoted all his leisure.

During one of these campaigns the Empress, who as usual was accompanying Shah Jehan, died, and before her death she asked him to build for her a tomb—"the most beautiful in the world."

---

[1] *Upanishads:* speculative and mystical scriptures of Hinduism composed about 900 B.C., regarded as the foundation of Hindu religion and philosophy.   [2] *Akbar (1542–1605):* the third Mogul emperor of India, known for his religious tolerance and enlightenment, whose grandson built the Taj Mahal.

And Shah Jehan decided to build for the interment of the dead Empress an   10
immense mausoleum of white marble on the bank of the river Jumna in his capital
Agra, and later to throw a silver bridge across the Jumna and on the other bank to
build a mausoleum of black marble for himself.

Only half these plans was destined to be realised, for twenty years later, when
the building of the Empress' mausoleum was being completed, a rebellion was
raised against Shah Jehan by his son Aurungzeb, who later destroyed Benares.[3] Aurungzeb accused his father of having spent on the building of the mausoleum the
whole revenue of the state for the last twenty years. And having taken Shah Jehan
captive Aurungzeb shut him up in a subterranean mosque in one of the inner
courts of the fortress-palace of Agra.

Shah Jehan lived seven years in this subterranean mosque and when he felt the
approach of death, he asked to be moved to the fortress wall into the so-called "Jasmine Pavilion," a tower of lace-like marble, which had contained the favourite
room of the Empress Arjumand Banu. And on the balcony of the "Jasmine Pavilion" overlooking the Jumna, whence the Taj Mahal can be seen in the distance,
Shah Jehan breathed his last.

Such, briefly, is the history of the Taj Mahal. Since those days the mausoleum
of the Empress has survived many vicissitudes of fortune. During the constant
wars that took place in India in the 17th and 18th centuries, Agra changed hands
many times and was frequently pillaged. Conquerors carried off from the Taj
Mahal the great silver doors and the precious lamps and candlesticks; and they
stripped the walls of the ornaments of precious stones. The building itself, however, and the greater part of the interior decoration has been preserved.

In the thirties of the last century the British Governor-General proposed to
sell the Taj Mahal for demolition. The Taj Mahal has now been restored and is carefully guarded.

I arrived at Agra in the evening and decided to go at once to see the Taj Mahal   15
by moonlight. It was not full moon, but there was sufficient light.

Leaving the hotel, I drove for a long time through the European part of Agra,
along broad streets all running between gardens. At last we left the town and, driving through a long avenue, on the left of which the river could be seen, we came
out upon a broad square paved with flagstones and surrounded by red stone walls.
In the walls, right and left, there were gates with high towers. The gate on the right,
my guide explained, led into the old town, which had been the private property of
the Empress Arjumand Banu, and remains in almost the same state as it was during
her lifetime. The gate in the left-hand tower led to the Taj Mahal.

It was already growing dark, but in the light of the broad crescent of the
moon every line of the buildings stood out distinctly against the pale sky. I walked

---

[3] *Benares:* now called Varanasi, the holiest Hindu city, is in north central India on the Ganges River
and is one of the oldest continuously inhabited cities in the world.

in the direction of the high, dark-red gate-tower with its arrow-shaped arch and horizontal row of small white characteristically Indian cupolas surmounted by sharp-pointed spires. A few broad steps led from the square to the entrance under the arch. It was quite dark there. My footsteps along the mosaic paving echoed resoundingly in the side niches from which stairways led up to a landing on the top of the tower, and to the museum which is inside the tower.

Through the arch the garden is seen, a large expanse of verdure and in the distance some white outlines resembling a white cloud that had descended and taken symmetrical forms. These were the walls, cupolas and minarets of the Taj Mahal.

I passed through the arch and out on to the broad stone platform, and stopped to look about me. Straight in front of me and right across the garden led a long broad avenue of dark cypresses, divided down the middle by a strip of water with a row of jutting arms of fountains. At the further end the avenue of cypresses was closed by the white cloud of the Taj Mahal. At the sides of the Taj, a little below it, the cupolas of two large mosques could be seen under the trees.

I walked slowly along the main avenue in the direction of the white building, by the strip of water with its fountains. The first thing that struck me, and that I had not foreseen, was the immense size of the Taj. It is in fact a very large structure, but it appears even larger than it is, owing chiefly to the ingenious design of the builders, who surrounded it with a garden and so arranged the gates and avenues that the building from this side is not seen all at once, but is disclosed little by little as you approach it. I realised that everything about it had been exactly planned and calculated, and that everything was designed to supplement and reinforce the chief impression. It became clear to me why it was that in photographs the Taj Mahal had appeared unfinished and almost plain. It cannot be separated from the garden and from the mosques on either side, which appear as its continuation. I saw now why the minarets at the corners of the marble platform on which the main building stands had given me the impression of a defect. For in photographs I had seen the picture of the Taj as ending on both sides with these minarets. Actually, it does not end there, but imperceptibly passes into the garden and the adjacent buildings. And again, the minarets are not actually seen in all their height as they are in photographs. From the avenue along which I walked only their tops were visible behind the trees.

The white building of the mausoleum itself was still far away, and as I walked towards it, it rose before me higher and higher. Though in the uncertain and changing light of the crescent moon I could distinguish none of the details, a strange sense of expectation forced me to continue looking intently, as if something was about to be revealed to me.

In the shadow of the cypresses it was nearly dark; the garden was filled with the scent of flowers, above all with that of jasmine, and peacocks were miauing. And this sound harmonised strangely with the surroundings, and somehow still further intensified the feeling of expectation which was coming over me.

Already I could see, brightly outlined in front of me, the central portion of the Taj Mahal rising from the high marble platform. A little light glimmered through the doors.

I reached the middle of the path leading from the arched entrance to the mausoleum. Here, in the centre of the avenue, is a square tank with lotuses in it and with marble seats on one side.

In the faint light of the half moon the Taj Mahal appeared luminous. Wonderfully soft, but at the same time quite distinct, white cupolas and white minarets came into view against the pale sky, and seemed to radiate a light of their own.

I sat on one of the marble seats and looked at the Taj Mahal, trying to seize and impress on my memory all the details of the building itself as I saw it and of everything else around me.

I could not have said what went on in my mind during this time, nor could I have been sure whether I thought about anything at all, but gradually, growing stronger and stronger; a strange feeling stole over me, which no words can describe.

Reality, that everyday actual reality in which we live, seemed somehow to be lifted, to fade and float away; but it did not disappear, it only underwent some strange sort of transformation, losing all actuality; every object in it, taken by itself, lost its ordinary meaning and became something quite different. In place of the familiar, habitual reality another reality opened out, a reality which usually we neither know, nor see, nor feel, but which is the one true and genuine reality.

I feel and know that words cannot convey what I wish to say. Only those will understand me who have themselves experienced something of this kind, who know the "taste" of such feelings.

Before me glimmered the small light in the doors of the Taj Mahal. The white cupolas and white minarets seemed to stir in the changing light of the white half moon. From the garden came the scent of jasmine and the miauing of the peacocks.

I had the sensation of being in two worlds at once. In the first place, the ordinary world of things and people had entirely changed, and it was ridiculous even to think of it; so imaginary, artificial and unreal did it appear now. Everything that belonged to this world had become remote, foreign and unintelligible to me—and I myself most of all, this very I that had arrived two hours before with all sorts of luggage and had hurried off to see the Taj Mahal by moonlight. All this—and the whole of the life of which it formed a part—seemed a puppet-show, which moreover was most clumsily put together and crudely painted, thus not resembling any reality whatsoever. Quite as grotesquely senseless and tragically ineffective appeared all my previous thoughts about the Taj Mahal and its riddle.

The riddle was here before me, but now it was no longer a riddle. It had been made a riddle only by that absurd, non-existent reality from which I had looked at it. And now I experienced the wonderful joy of liberation, as if I had come out into the light from some deep underground passages.

Yes, this was the mystery of death! But a revealed and visible mystery. And there was nothing dreadful or terrifyng about it. On the contrary, it was infinite radiance and joy.

Writing this now, I find it strange to recall that there was scarcely any transitional state. From my usual sensation of myself and everything else I passed into this new state immediately, while I was in this garden, in the avenue of cypresses, with the white outline of the Taj Mahal in front of me.

I remember that an unusually rapid stream of thoughts passed through my 35
mind, as if they were detached from me and choosing or finding their own way.

At one time my thought seemed to be concentrated upon the artists who had
built the Taj Mahal. I knew that they had been Sufis,[4] whose mystical philosophy,
inseparable from poetry, has become the esotericism of Mahomedanism and in
brilliant and earthly forms of passion and joy expressed the ideas of eternity, unreality and renunciation. And here the image of the Empress Arjumand Banu and her
memorial, "the most beautiful in the world," became by their invisible sides connected with the idea of death, yet death not as annihilation, but as a new life.

I got up and walked forward with my eyes on the light glimmering in the
doors, above which rose the immense shape of the Taj Mahal.

And suddenly, quite independently of me, something began to be formulated
in my mind.

The light, I knew, burned above the tomb where the body of the Empress lay.
Above it and around it are the marble arches, cupolas and minarets of the Taj
Mahal, which carry it upwards, merging it into one whole with the sky and the
moonlight.

I felt that precisely here was the beginning of the solution of the riddle. 40

The light—glimmering above the tomb where lies the dust of her body—this
light that is so small and insignificant in comparison with the marble shape of the
Taj Mahal, this is life, the life which we know in ourselves and others, in contrast
with that other life which we do not know, which is hidden from us by the mystery of death.

The light which can so easily be extinguished, that is the little, transitory,
earthly life. The Taj Mahal—that is the future or *eternal* life.

I began to understand the idea of the artists who had built the mausoleum of
the Empress, who had surrounded it with this garden, with these gates, towers,
pavilions, fountains, mosques—who had made it so immense, so white, so unbe-
lievably beautiful, merging into the sky with its cupolas and minarets.

Before me and all around me was the soul of the Empress Mumtaz-i-Mahal.

The soul, so infinitely great, radiant and beautiful in comparison with the lit- 45
tle body that had lived on earth and was now enclosed in the tomb.

In that moment I understood that the soul is not enclosed in the body, but
that the body lives and moves in the soul. And then I remembered and understood
a mystical expression which had arrested my attention in old books:

The soul and the future life are one and the same.

It even seemed strange to me that I had not been able to understand this before.
Of course they were the same. Life, as a process, and that which lives, can be differen-
tiated in our understanding only so long as there is the idea of disappearance, of

---

[4] *Sufis*: Muslim philosophical and literary movement that emerged in Persia (present-day Iran) in
the early eleventh century.

death. Here, as in eternity, everything was united, dimensions merged, and our little earthly world disappeared in the infinite world.

I cannot reconstruct all the thoughts and feelings of those moments, and I feel that I am expressing a negligible part of them.

I now approached the marble platform on which stands the Taj Mahal with its 50 four minarets at the corners. Broad marble stairs at the sides of the cypress avenue lead up to the platform from the garden.

I went up and came to the doors where the light was burning. I was met by Mahomedan gate-keepers, with slow, quiet movements, dressed in white robes and white turbans.

One of them lit a lantern, and I followed him into the interior of the mausoleum.

In the middle, surrounded by a carved marble trellis, were two white tombs; in the centre the tomb of the Empress, and beside it that of Shah Jehan. The tombs were covered with red flowers, and above them a light burned in a pierced brass lantern.

In the semi-darkness the indistinct outlines of the white walls vanished into the high dome, where the moonlight, penetrating from without, seemed to form a mist of changing colour.

I stood there a long time without moving, and the calm, grave Mahomedans 55 in their white turbans left me undisturbed, and themselves stood in silence near the trellis which surrounded the tombs.

This trellis is itself a miracle of art. The word "trellis" conveys nothing, because it is really not a trellis, but a lace of white marble of wonderful workmanship. It is difficult to believe that the flowers and decorative ornamentation of this white filigree lace are neither moulded nor cast, but carved directly in thin marble panels.

Observing that I was examining the trellis, one of the gate-keepers quietly approached me and began to explain the plan of the interior of the Taj Mahal.

The tombstones before me were not real tombs. The real tombs in which the bodies lay were underneath in the crypt.

The middle part of the mausoleum, where we now stood, was under the great central dome; and it was separated from the outer walls by a wide corridor running between the four corner recesses, each beneath one of the four smaller cupolas.

"It is never light here," said the man, lifting up his hand. "Light only comes 60 through the trellises of the side galleries.

"Listen, master."

He stepped back a few paces and, raising his head, cried slowly in a loud voice:

"Allah!"

His voice filled the whole of the enormous space of the dome above our heads, and as it began slowly, slowly, to die away, suddenly a clear and powerful echo resounded in the side cupolas from all four sides simultaneously:

"Allah!" 65

The arches of the galleries immediately responded, but not all at once; one after another voices rose from every side as though calling to one another.

"Allah! Allah!"

And then, like the chorus of a thousand voices or like an organ, the great dome itself resounded, drowning everything in its solemn, deep bass:

"Allah!"

Then again, but more quietly, the side-galleries and cupolas answered, and the great dome, less loudly, resounded once more, and the faint, almost whispering tones of the inner arches re-echoed its voice.

The echo fell into silence. But even in the silence it seemed as if a far, far-away note went on sounding.

I stood and listened to it, and with an intensified sense of joy I felt that this marvellous echo also was a calculated part of the plan of the artists who had given to the Taj Mahal a voice, bidding it repeat for ever the name of God.

Slowly I followed the guide, who, raising his lantern, showed me the ornaments covering the walls: violet, rose, blue, yellow and bright red flowers mingled with the green, some life-size and others larger than life-size, stone flowers that looked alive and that were beyond the reach of time; and after that, the whole of the walls covered with white marble flowers, carved doors and carved windows—all of white marble.

The longer I looked and listened, the more clearly, and with a greater and greater sense of gladness, I felt the idea of the artists who had striven to express the infinite richness, variety and beauty of the *soul* or of *eternal life* as compared with the small and insignificant earthly life.

We ascended to the roof of the Taj Mahal, where the cupolas stand at the corners, and from there I looked down on the broad, dark Jumna. Right and left stood large mosques of red stone with white cupolas. Then I crossed to the side of the roof which overlooks the garden. Below, all was still, only the trees rustled in the breeze, and from time to time there came from afar the low and melodious miauing of the peacocks.

All this was so like a dream, so like the "India" one may see in dreams, that I should not have been in the least surprised had I suddenly found myself flying over the garden to the gate-tower, which was now growing black, at the end of the cypress avenue.

Then we descended and walked round the white building of the Taj Mahal on the marble platform, at the corners of which stand the four minarets, and by the light of the moon we examined the decorations and ornaments of the outer walls.

Afterwards we went below into the white marble crypt, where, as above, a lamp was burning and where red flowers lay on the white tombs of the Emperor and Empress.

The following morning I drove to the fortress, where the palace of Shah Jehan and the Empress Arjumand Banu is still preserved.

The fortress of Agra is a whole town in itself. Enormous towers built of brick stand above the gates. The walls are many feet thick, and enclose a labyrinth of courtyards, barracks, warehouses and buildings of all kinds. A considerable part of the fortress indeed is devoted to modern uses and is of no particular interest. At last I came upon the Pearl Mosque, which I had known from Verestchagin's picture. Here begins the kingdom of white marble and blue sky. There are only two colours, white and blue. The Pearl Mosque is very much larger than I had imagined. Great heavy gates encased in copper, and behind them, under a glittering sky, a dazzling white marble yard with a fountain, and further on a hall for sermons, with wonderful carved arches with gold ornaments and with marble latticed windows into the inner parts of the palace, through which the wives of the Emperor and the ladies of the court could see into the mosque.

Then the palace itself. This is not one building, but a whole series of marble buildings and courts contained within the brick buildings and courts of the fortress itself.

The throne of Akbar, a black marble slab in the fortress wall on a level with the higher battlements, and in front of it the "Court of Justice." Then Shah Jehan's "Hall of Audience," with more carved arches similar to those in the Pearl Mosque, and finally the residential quarters of the palace and the Jasmine Pavilion.

These palace apartments are situated on the fortress wall which looks out over the Jumna. They consist of a series of rooms, not very large according to modern standards, but the walls of which are covered with rare and beautiful carving. Everything is so wonderfully preserved that it might have been only yesterday that here, with their women, lived those emperor-conquerors, philosophers, poets, sages, fanatics, madmen, who destroyed one India and created another. Most of the residential part of the palace is under the floor of the marble courts and passages which extend from the Hall of Audience to the fortress wall. The rooms are joined by corridors and passages and by small courts enclosed in marble trellises.

Beyond the fortress wall there is a deep inner court where tourneys of warriors were held, and where wild beasts fought with one another or with men. Above is the small court surrounded by lattices, from which the ladies of the palace viewed the combats of elephants against tigers and gazed at the contests of the warriors. Here, too, with their wares, came merchants from far countries, Arabians, Greeks, Venetians and Frenchmen. A "chessboard" court paved with rows of black and white slabs in chess-board pattern, where dancers and dancing-girls in special costumes acted as chess-men. Further on, the apartments of the Emperor's wives; in the walls carved cupboards for jewelry still exist, as well as small round apertures, leading to secret cupboards, into which only very small hands could penetrate. A bathroom lined with rock crystal which causes its walls to sparkle with changing colours when a light is lit. Small, almost toy rooms, like bonbonnières. Tiny balconies. Rooms under the floor of the inner court, into which the light passes only through thin marble panels, and where it is never hot—and then at last, the miracle of miracles, the Jasmine Pavilion, which used to contain the favourite apartment of the Empress Mumtaz-i-Mahal.

It is a circular tower, surrounded by a balcony hanging over the fortress wall above the Jumna. Eight doors lead within from the balcony. There is literally not one inch of the walls of the Jasmine Pavilion or of the balustrades and pillars of the balcony, that is not covered with the most delicate, beautiful carving. Ornament within ornament, and again in every ornament still another ornament, almost like jewellers' work. The whole of the Jasmine Pavilion is like this, and so is the small hall with a fountain and rows of carved columns.

85

In all this there is nothing grandiose or mystical, but the whole produces an impression of unusual intimacy. I felt the life of the people who had lived there. In some strange way I seemed to be in touch with it, as if the people were still living, and I caught glimpses of the most intimate and secret aspects of their lives. In this palace time is not felt at all. The past connected with these marble rooms is felt as the present, so real and living does it stand out, and so strange is it even to think while here that it is no more.

As we were leaving the palace the guide told me of the subterranean maze beneath the whole fortress where, it is said, innumerable treasures lie concealed. And I remembered that I had read about it before. But the entrances to these underground passages had been closed and covered over many years ago, after a party of curious travellers had lost their way and perished in them. It is said that there are many snakes there, among them some gigantic cobras larger than any to be found elsewhere, which were perhaps alive in the days of Shah Jehan. And they say that sometimes on moonlight nights they crawl out to the river.

From the palace I drove again to the Taj Mahal, and on the way I bought photographs taken from old miniatures, portraits of Shah Jehan and the Empress Arjumand Banu. Once seen, their faces remain in the memory. The Empress' head is slightly inclined, and she holds a rose in her delicate hand. The portrait is very much stylised, but in the shape of the mouth and in the large eyes one feels a deep inner life, strength and thought; and in the whole face the irresistible charm of mystery and fairy-tale. Shah Jehan is in profile. He has a very strange look, ecstatic yet at the same time balanced. In this portrait he sees something which no one but himself could see or perhaps would dare to see. Also he appears to be looking at himself, observing his every thought and feeling. It is the look of a clairvoyant, a dreamer, as well as that of a man of extraordinary strength and courage.

The impression of the Taj Mahal not only is not weakened by the light of day, rather it is strengthened. The white marble amidst the green stands out so astonishingly against the deep blue sky; and in a single glance you seize more particulars and details than at night. Inside the building you are still more struck by the luxuriance of the decoration, the fairy-tale flowers, red, yellow and blue, and the garlands of green; the garlands of marble leaves and marble flowers and lace-work trellises. . . . And all this is the soul of the Empress Mumtaz-i-Mahal.

I spent the whole of the next day until evening in the garden that surrounds 90 the Taj Mahal. Above all things I liked to sit on the wide balcony on the top of the gate-tower. Beneath me lay the garden intersected by the cypress avenue and the line of fountains reaching as far as the marble platform on which the Taj Mahal stands. Under the cypresses slowly moved groups of Mahomedan visitors in robes and turbans of soft colours that can only be imagined: turquoise, lemon-yellow, pale green, yellow-rose. For a long time I watched through my glasses a pale orange turban side by side with an emerald shawl. Every now and again they vanished behind the trees, again they appeared on the marble stairs leading to the mausoleum. Then they disappeared in the entrances to the Taj Mahal, and again could be seen amongst the cupolas on the roof. And all the time along the avenue of cypresses moved the procession of coloured robes and turbans, blue, yellow, green, rose turbans, shawls and caftans—not a single European was in sight.

The Taj Mahal is the place of pilgrimage and the place for promenades from the town. Lovers meet here; you see children with their large dark eyes, calm and quiet, like all Indian children; ancient and decrepit men, women with babies, beggars, fakirs,[5] musicians. . . .

All faces, all types of Mahomedan India pass before you.

And I had a strange feeling all the time that this, too, was part of the plan of the builders of the Taj Mahal, part of their mystical idea of the contact of the *soul* with the whole world and with all the life that from all sides unceasingly flows into the soul.

Questions for Discussion and Writing

1. Why does Ouspensky open his account by mentioning of what little use he has found previous accounts and descriptions of the Taj Mahal? What expectations does this kind of opening raise in the reader?
2. To what extent do Ouspensky's descriptions support his impression of the nature and impact of the Taj Mahal?
3. Have you ever visited a place, building, church, mosque, and so on whose architecture communicated as intense an impression as the one Ouspensky received from the Taj Mahal?

WILLIAM ZINSSER

William Zinsser was born in 1922 and graduated from Princeton University in 1944. He joined the staff of the New York Herald Tribune *in 1946 and worked there until 1959, first as a feature editor and then as a drama editor and film critic. He taught at Yale University between 1971 and 1979 and is the author of numerous books, including* Pop Goes America *(1966),* On Writing Well *(1976), and* American Places: A Writer's Pilgrimage to 15 of This Country's Most Visited and Cherished Sites *(1992), in which "Niagara Falls" first appeared.* Easy to Remember: The Great American Songwriters and Their Songs *(2000) is his most recent work.*

Niagara Falls

Walden Pond and the Concord writers got me thinking about America's great natural places, and I decided to visit Niagara Falls and Yellowstone Park next. I had been reminded that one of the most radical ideas that Emerson and Thoreau and

---

[5] *fakirs:* religious ascetics in India who perform spiritual and physical feats of endurance and subsist through begging.

the other Trancendentalists[1] lobbed into the 19th-century American air was that nature was not an enemy to be feared and repelled, but a spiritual force that the people of a young nation should embrace and take nourishment from. The goal, as Thoreau put it in his essay "Walking," was to become "an inhabitant, or a part and parcel of Nature, rather than a member of society," and it occurred to me that the long and powerful hold of Niagara and Yellowstone on the American imagination had its roots in the gratifying news from Concord that nature was a prime source of uplift, improvement and the "higher" feelings.

Niagara Falls existed only in the attic of my mind where collective memory is stored: scraps of songs about honeymooning couples, vistas by painters who tried to get the plummeting waters to hold still, film clips of Marilyn Monroe running for her life in *Niagara,* odds and ends of lore about stuntmen who died going over the falls, and always, somewhere among the scraps, a boat called *Maid of the Mist,* which took tourists . . . where? Behind the falls? *Under* the falls? Death hovered at the edge of the images in my attic, or at least danger. But I had never thought of going to see the place itself. That was for other people. Now I wanted to be one of those other people.

One misconception I brought to Niagara Falls was that it consisted of two sets of falls, which had to be viewed separately. I would have to see the American falls first and then go over to the Canadian side to see *their* falls, which, everyone said, were better. But nature hadn't done anything so officious, as I found when the shuttle bus from the Buffalo airport stopped and I got out and walked, half running, down a path marked FALLS. The sign was hardly necessary; I could hear that I was going in the right direction.

Suddenly all the images of a lifetime snapped into place—all the paintings and watercolors and engravings and postcards and calendar lithographs. The river does indeed split into two cataracts, divided by a narrow island called Goat Island, but it was man who put a boundary between them. The eye can easily see them as one spectacle: first the straight line of the American falls, then the island, then the much larger, horseshoe-shaped curve of the Canadian falls. The American falls, 1,060 feet across, are majestic but relatively easy to process—water cascading over a ledge. The Canadian falls, 2,200 feet across, are elusive. Water hurtles over them in such volume that the spray ascends from their circular base as high as the falls themselves, 185 feet, hiding them at the heart of the horseshoe. If the Canadian falls are "better," it's not only because they are twice as big but because they have more mystery, curled in on themselves. Whatever is behind all that spray will remain their secret.

My vantage point for this first glimpse was a promenade that overlooks the falls on the American side—a pleasantly landscaped area that has the feeling of a national park; there was none of the souvenir-stand clutter I expected. My   5

---

[1] *Transcendentalism:* a philosophy emphasizing the intuitive and spiritual above the empirical.

strongest emotion as I stood and tried to absorb the view was that I was very glad to be there. So *that's* what they look like! I stayed at the railing for a long time, enjoying the play of light on the tumbling waters; the colors, though the day was gray, were subtle and satisfying. My thoughts, such as they were, were banal—vaguely pantheistic, poor man's Wordsworth. My fellow sightseers were equally at ease, savoring nature with 19th-century serenity, taking pictures of each other against the cataracts. (More Kodak film is sold here than at any place except the Taj Mahal.) Quite a few of the tourists appeared to be honeymooners; many were parents with children; some were elementary school teachers with their classes. I heard some foreign accents, but on the whole it was—as it always has been—America-on-the-road. The old icon was still worth taking the kids to see. Today more people visit Niagara Falls than ever before: 10 million a year.

Far below, in the gorge where the river reassembles after its double descent, I saw a small boat bobbing in the turbulent water, its passengers bunched at the railing in blue slickers. Nobody had to tell me it was the *Maid of the Mist*—I heard it calling. I took the elevator down to the edge of the river. Even there, waiting at the dock, I could hardly believe that such a freakish trip was possible—or even prudent. What if the boat capsized? What if its engine stopped? What if . . . ? But when the *Maid of the Mist* arrived, there was no question of not getting on it. I was just one more statistic proving the falls' legendary pull—the force that has beckoned so many daredevils to their death and that compels so many suicides every year to jump.

On the boat, we all got blue raincoats and put them on with due seriousness. The *Maid of the Mist* headed out into the gorge and immediately sailed past the American falls. Because these falls have famously fallen apart over the years and dumped large chunks of rock at their base, the water glances off the rubble and doesn't churn up as much spray as a straight drop would generate. That gave us a good view of the falls from a fairly close range and got us only moderately wet.

Next we sailed past Goat Island. There I saw a scene so reminiscent of a Japanese movie in its gauzy colors and stylized composition that I could hardly believe it wasn't a Japanese movie. Filtered through the mist, a straggling line of tourists in yellow raincoats was threading its way down a series of wooden stairways and catwalks to reach the rocks in front of the American falls. They were on a tour called "Cave of the Winds," so named because in the 19th century it was possible to go behind the falls into various hollowed-out spaces that have since eroded. Even today nobody gets closer to the falls, or gets wetter, than these stair people. I watched them as I might watch a colony of ants: small yellow figures doggedly following a zigzag trail down a steep embankment to some ordained goal. The sight took me by surprise and was surprisingly beautiful.

Leaving the ants, we proceeded to the Canadian falls. Until then the *Maid of the Mist* had struck me as a normal excursion boat, the kind that might take sightseers around Manhattan. Suddenly it seemed very small. By now we had come within the outer circle of the horseshoe. On both sides of our boat, inconceivable amounts of water were rushing over the edge from the height of a 15-story building. I thought of the word I had seen in so many articles about Niagara's stuntmen:

they were going to "conquer" the falls. Conquer! No such emanations were felt in our crowd. Spray was pelting our raincoats, and we peered out at each other from inside our hoods—eternal tourists bonded together by some outlandish event voluntarily entered into. (Am I really riding down the Grand Canyon on a burro? Am I really about to be charged by an African rhino?) The *Maid of the Mist* showed no sign of being afraid of the Canadian falls; it headed straight into the cloud of spray at the heart of the horseshoe. How much farther were we going to go? The boat began to rock in the eddying water. I felt a twinge of fear.

In the 19th-century literature of Niagara Falls, one adjective carries much of   10 the baggage: "sublime." Today it's seldom heard, except in bad Protestant hymns. But for a young nation eager to feel emotions worthy of God's mightiest wonders, the word had a precise meaning—"a mixture of attraction and terror," as the historian Elizabeth McKinsey puts it. Tracing the theory of sublimity to mid-18th-century aestheticians such as Edmund Burke[2]—in particular, to Burke's *Philosophical Enquiry into the Origin of Our Ideas of the Sublime and Beautiful*—Professor McKinsey says that the experience of early visitors to Niagara Falls called for a word that would go beyond mere awe and fear. "Sublime" was the perfect answer. It denoted "a new capacity to appreciate the beauty and grandeur of potentially terrifying natural objects." Anybody could use it, and everybody did.

Whether I was having sublime feelings as I looked up at the falls I will leave to some other aesthetician. By any name, however, I was thinking: This is an amazing place to be. I wasn't having a 19th-century rapture, but I also wasn't connected in any way to 20th-century thought. I was somewhere in a late-Victorian funk, the kind of romanticism that induced Hudson River School[3] artists to paint a rainbow over Niagara Falls more often than they saw one there. Fortunately, in any group of Americans there will always be one pragmatist to bring us back to earth. Just as I was becoming edgy at the thought of being sucked into the vortex, the man next to me said that he had been measuring our progress by the sides of the gorge and we weren't making any progress at all. Even with its engines at full strength, the *Maid of the Mist* was barely holding its own. That was a sufficiently terrifying piece of news, and when the boat finally made a U-turn I didn't protest. A little sublime goes a long way.

The first *Maid of the Mist* took tourists to the base of the horseshoe falls in 1846. Now, as the mist enveloped our *Maid,* I liked the idea that I was in the same spot and was having what I assume were the same feelings that those travelers had almost 150 years ago. I liked the idea of a tourist attraction so pure that it doesn't have to be tricked out with improvements. The falls don't tug on our sense of history or on our national psyche. They don't have any intellectual content or take their meaning from what was achieved there. They just do what they do.

---

[2] *Edmund Burke (1729–1797):* an Irish statesman, orator, and writer.   [3] *Hudson River School artists:* a group of 29 nineteenth-century landscape painters in New York state who depicted romantic views of the Catskill Mountains using contrasts of light and dark.

"When people sit in the front of that boat at the foot of the falls they get a little philosophical," said Christopher M. Glynn, marketing director of the Maid of the Mist Corporation. "They think: There's something bigger than I am that put *this* together. A lot of them have heard about the Seven Wonders of the World, and they ask, 'Is this one of them?'" Glynn's father, James V. Glynn, owner and president of the company, which has been owned by only two families since 1889, often has his lunch on the boat and talks with grandfathers and grandmothers who first visited Niagara on their honeymoon. "Usually," he told me, "they only saw the falls from above. Down here it's a totally different perspective, and they find the power of the water almost unbelievable. You're seeing one of God's great works when you're in that horseshoe."

Most Americans come to the falls as a family, said Ray H. Wigle of the Niagara Falls Visitors and Convention Bureau. "They wait until the kids are out of school to visit places like this and the Grand Canyon and Yellowstone. They say, "This is part of your education—to see these stupendous works of nature." On one level today's tourists are conscious of 'the environment,' and they're appreciative of the magnificence of the planet and the fact that something like this has a right to exist by itself—unlike early tourists, who felt that nature was savage and had to be tamed and utilized. But deep down there's still a primal response to uncivilized nature that doesn't change from one century to another. 'I never realized it was like this!' I hear tourists say all the time, and when they turn away from their first look at the falls—when they first connect again with another person—there's always a delighted smile on their face that's universal and childish."

I spent two days at Niagara, looking at the falls at different times of day and night, especially from the Canadian side, where the view of both cataracts across the gorge is the most stunning and—as so many artists have notified us—the most pictorial. Even when I wasn't looking at them, even when I was back in my hotel room, I was aware of them, a low rumble in the brain. They are always *there*. Some part of us, as Americans, has known that for a long time.   15

Sightseers began coming to Niagara in sizable numbers when the railroads made it easy for them to get there, starting in 1836 with the opening of the Lockport & Niagara Falls line, which brought families traveling on the Erie Canal. Later, workers came over from Rochester on Sunday afternoon after church, and passengers taking Lake Erie steamers came over for a few hours from Buffalo. To stroll in the park beside the falls was an acceptable Victorian thing to do. No other sublime experience of such magnitude was available. People might have heard of the Grand Canyon or the Rockies, but they couldn't get there; vacations were too short and transportation was too slow.

So uplifting were the falls deemed to be that they became a rallying point after the Civil War for religious leaders, educators, artists and scientists eager to preserve them as a sacred grove for the public. This meant wresting them back from the private owners who had bought the adjacent land from New York State, putting up mills, factories and tawdry souvenir shops, and charging admission for a view of God's handiwork through holes in the fence. That the state had sold off its land earlier was not all that surprising; before the Concord poets and philosophers suggested otherwise, the notion that nature should be left intact and simply appreciated was alien to the settler mentality. Land was meant to be cleared, civilized and put to productive use.

Two men in particular inspired the "Free Niagara!" movement: the painter Frederic Edwin Church and the landscape architect Frederick Law Olmsted,[4] designer of New York's great Central Park. Church's seven-foot-long *Niagara,* which has been called the greatest American painting, drew such worshipful throngs when it was first exhibited in a Broadway showroom in 1857—thousands came every day—that it was sent on a tour of England, where it was unanimously praised by critics, including the sainted John Ruskin.[5] If America could produce such a work, there was hope for the colonies after all. Back home, the painting made a triumphal tour of the South in 1858–59 and was reproduced and widely sold as a chromolithograph. More than any other image, it fixed the falls in the popular imagination as having powers both divine and patriotic:"an earthly manifestation of God's attributes" and a prophecy of "the nation's collective aspirations." Iconhood had arrived; Niagara Falls began to appear in posters and advertisements as the symbol of America. Only the Statue of Liberty would dislodge it.

Olmsted, the other man who shaped Niagara's aesthetic, proposed the heretical idea of a public park next to the falls and on the neighboring islands, in which nature would be left alone. This was counter to the prevailing European concept of a park as a formal arrangement of paths and plantings. In the 1870s Olmsted and a coalition of zealous Eastern intellectuals launched a campaign of public meetings, pamphlets, articles and petitions urging state officials to buy back the land and raze everything that man had put on it. Massive political opposition greeted their effort. Not only were the owners of the land rich and influential; many citizens felt that the government in a free society had no right to say,"In the public interest we're taking this land back."The fight lasted 15 years and was narrowly won in 1885 with the creation of the Niagara Reservation, America's first state park. (One hundred thousand people came on opening day.) Olmsted's hands-off landscaping, which preserved the natural character of the area and kept essential roads and buildings unobtrusive, became a model for parks in many other parts of the country.

Gradually, however, the adjacent hotels and commercial enterprises began to go to seed, as aging resorts will, and in the early 1960s Mayor E. Dent Lackey of Niagara Falls, New York, decided that only a sharp upgrading of the American side would enable his city to attract enough tourists to keep it healthy. Sublimity was no longer the only option for honeymooners; they could fly to Bermuda as easily as

20

---

[4] *Frederick Edwin Church* (1826–1900): American painter, member of the Hudson River school. *Frederick Law Olmsted* (1822–1903): American landscape architect and writer who designed Central Park in Manhattan and Prospect Park in Brooklyn.   [5] *John Ruskin (1819–1900):* English critic and social theorist.

they could fly to Buffalo. Mayor Lackey, riding the 1960s' almost religious belief in urban renewal, tore down much of the "falls area." Like so much '60s renewal, the tearing down far outraced the building back up, but today the new pieces are finally in place: a geological museum, an aquarium, a Native American arts and crafts center, a glass-enclosed botanical garden with 7,000 tropical specimens, an "Artpark," a shopping mall and other such placid amenities. Even the new Burger King is tasteful. The emphasis is on history, culture, education and scenery.

By contrast, over on the Canadian side, a dense thoroughfare called Clifton Hill offers a Circus World, a Ripley's Believe It or Not Museum, a House of Frankenstein, a Guinness Book of Records Museum, several wax museums, a Ferris wheel, a miniature golf course and other such amusements. The result of Mayor Lackey's faith that Americans still want to feel the higher feelings is that tourism has increased steadily ever since he got the call.

> Niag'ra Falls, I'm falling for you,
> Niag'ra Falls, with your rainbow hue,
> Oh, the Maid of the Mist
> Has never been kissed,
> Niag'ra, I'm falling for you.

This terrible song is typical of the objects I found in the local-history section of the Niagara Falls Public Library, along with 20,000 picture postcards, 15,000 stereopticon slides, books by writers as diverse as Jules Verne and William Dean Howells,[6] and thousands of newspaper and magazine articles. Together, for two centuries, they have sent America the message WISH YOU WERE HERE!, sparing no superlative. Howells, in his novel *Their Wedding Journey*, in 1882, wrote: "As the train stopped, Isabel's heart beat with a child-like exultation, as I believe everyone's heart must who is worthy to arrive at Niagara." Describing the place where Isabel and Basil got off the train as a "sublime destination," Howells says: "Niagara deserves almost to rank with Rome, the metropolis of history and religion; with Venice, the chief city of sentiment and fantasy. In either you are at once made at home by a perception of its greatness . . . and you gratefully accept its sublimity as a fact in no way contrasting with your own insignificance."

What the library gets asked about most often, however, is the "stunts and stunters," according to Donald E. Loker, its local-history specialist. "Just yesterday," he told me, "I got a call from an advertising agency that wanted to use Annie Taylor in an ad campaign." Mrs. Taylor was a schoolteacher who went over the falls in a barrel on October 4, 1901, and survived the plunge, unlike her cat, which she had previously sent over in her barrel for a trial run. Thereby she became the first person to conquer the falls—and also one of the last. Most of the other conquerors tried their luck once too often. Today there is a ban on stunts, but not on ghosts. "Didn't somebody tightrope over this?" is one question that tour guides always get. "People

---

[6] *William Dean Howells* (1837–1920): introduced realism and naturalism into American literature. *Their Wedding Journey* (1882) was Howell's first novel about a delightful honeymoon to Niagara Falls.

want to see the scene," one of the guides told me. "They want to know: "How did he do it?'"

Of all those glory-seekers, the most glorious was Jean François Gravelet, known as the great Blondin. A Frenchman trained in the European circus, he came to America in 1859 under the promotional arm of P. T. Barnum and announced that he would cross the Niagara gorge on a tightrope on June 30, 1859. "Blondin was too good a showman to make the trip appear easy," Philip Mason writes in a booklet called "Niagara and the Daredevils." "His hesitations and swayings began to build a tension that soon had the huge crowd gripped in suspense." In the middle he stopped, lowered a rope to the *Maid of the Mist,* pulled up a bottle and sat down to have a drink. Continuing toward the Canadian shore, "he paused, steadied the balancing pole and suddenly executed a back somersault. Men screamed, women fainted. Those near the rope wept and begged him to come in. . . . For the rest of the fabulous summer of 1859 he continued to provide thrills for the huge crowds that flocked to Niagara to see him. Never content to merely to repeat his last performance, Blondin crossed his rope on a bicycle, walked it blindfolded, pushed a wheelbarrow, cooked an omelet in the center, and made the trip with his hands and feet manacled."

I left the library and went back to the falls for a final look. Far below and far away I saw a tiny boat with a cluster of blue raincoats on its upper deck, vanishing into a tall cloud of mist at the center of the horseshoe falls. Then I didn't see it any more. Would it ever come back out? Historical records going back to 1846 said that it would.

Questions for Discussion and Writing

1. What role have writers, philosophers, and painters played in the emergence of Niagara Falls as a tourist attraction?
2. How effective do you find Zinsser's method of interweaving personal experiences with documented historical facts?
3. Describe another natural wonder that elicits from you the same kinds of reactions and feelings that Niagara Falls did from Zinsser.

JOSEPH ADDISON

English essayist and journalist, Joseph Addison (1672–1719) had a distinguished career as a diplomat, member of Parliament, and secretary of state. But he is best known for his collaboration with Richard Steele on the periodicals The Tatler *(1709–1710) and* The Spectator *(1711–1712, 1714). His sparkling and perceptive observations on different aspects of society are well worth revisiting. In the following essay from* The Spectator *(Number 26, dated Friday, March 30, 1711), Addison takes us through the famous Gothic cathedral in London where all English monarchs have been crowned since William I (1027–1087) and where kings, statesmen, poets, and others of distinction, including Addison himself, are buried.*

Reflections in Westminster Abbey

When I am in a serious humour, I very often walk by myself in Westminster-abbey; where the gloominess of the place, and the use to which it is applied, with the solemnity of the building, and the condition of the people who lie in it, are apt to fill the mind with a kind of melancholy, or rather thoughtfulness, that is not disagreeable. I yesterday passed a whole afternoon in the churchyard, the cloisters, and the church, amusing myself with the tomb-stones and inscriptions that I met with in those several regions of the dead. Most of them recorded nothing else of the buried person, but that he was born upon one day, and died upon another; the whole history of his life being comprehended in those epitaphs, which are written with great elegance of expression and justness of thought, and therefore do honour to the living as well as the dead. As a foreigner is very apt to conceive an idea of the ignorance or politeness of a nation from the turn of their public monuments and inscriptions, they should be submitted to the perusal of men of learning and genius before they are put in execution. Sir Cloudesley Shovel's monument has very often given me great offence. Instead of the brave rough English admiral, which was the distinguishing character of that plain gallant man, he is represented on his tomb by the figure of a beau, dressed in a long periwig, and reposing himself upon velvet cushions, under a canopy of state. The inscription is answerable to the monument; for instead of celebrating the many remarkable actions he had performed in the service of his country, it acquaints us only with the manner of his death, in which it was impossible for him to reap any honour. The Dutch, whom we are apt to despise for want of genius, show an infinitely greater taste of antiquity and politeness in their buildings and works of this nature, than what we meet with in those of our own country. The monuments of their admirals, which have been erected at the public expense, represent them like themselves, and are adorned with rostral crowns and naval ornaments, with beautiful festoons of sea-weed, shells, and coral.

But to return to our subject. I have left the repository of our English kings for the contemplation of another day, when I shall find my mind disposed for so serious an amusement. I know that entertainments of this nature are apt to raise dark and dismal thoughts in timorous minds, and gloomy imaginations; but for my own part, though I am always serious, I do not know what it is to be melancholy; and can therefore take a view of nature, in her deep and solemn scenes, with the same pleasure as in her most gay and delightful ones. By this means I can improve myself with those objects, which others consider with terror. When I look upon the tombs of the great, every emotion of envy dies in me; when I read the epitaphs of the beautiful, every inordinate desire goes out; when I meet with the grief of parents upon a tombstone, my heart melts with compassion; when I see the tomb of the parents themselves, I consider the vanity of grieving for those whom we must quickly follow. When I see kings lying by those who deposed them, when I consider rival wits placed side by side, or the holy men that divided the world with their contests and disputes, I reflect with sorrow and astonishment on the little competitions, factions, and debates of mankind. When I read the several dates of the tombs, of some that died yesterday, and some six hundred years ago, I consider that great day when we shall all of us be contemporaries, and make our appearance together.

Questions for Discussion and Writing

1. In what respects do Addison's activities and reactions seem to be a bit eccentric?
2. What function does humor serve in this account? Is it out of place consider-ing the circumstance? Why or why not?
3. Pay a visit to a public monument in your town or community and compose your own "Reflections." You might wish to emulate some of the distinctive features of Addison's syntax (for example, how is parallelism used in the third paragraph?).

FATIMA MERNISSI

Fatima Mernissi is a scholar of Middle Eastern history and culture who was born in 1940 in Fez, Morocco. Her childhood was unusual in that she was raised in a harem (which means "for-bidden" in Arabic). Her experiences there became the subject of her book Dreams of Trespass: Tales of a Harem Girlhood *(1994), in which the following essay first appeared. Mernissi also wrote* Scheherazade Goes West: Different Cultures, Different Harems *(2001).*

Moonlit Nights of Laughter

On Yasmina's farm, we never knew when we would eat. Sometimes, Yasmina only remembered at the last minute that she had to feed me, and then she would convince me that a few olives and a piece of her good bread, which she had baked at dawn, would be enough. But dining in our harem in Fez[1] was an entirely differ-ent story. We ate at strictly set hours and never between meals.

To eat in Fez, we had to sit at our prescribed places at one of the four com-munal tables. The first table was for the men, the second for the important women, and the third for the children and less important women, which made us happy, be-cause that meant that Aunt Habiba could eat with us. The last table was reserved for the domestics and anyone who had come in late, regardless of age, rank, or sex. That table was often overcrowded, and was the last chance to get anything to eat at all for those who had made the mistake of not being on time.

Eating at fixed hours was what Mother hated most about communal life. She would nag Father constantly about the possibility of breaking loose and taking our immediate family to live apart. The nationalists advocated the end of seclusion and the veil, but they did not say a word about a couple's right to split off from their

---

[1] *Fez:* a city in northern Morocco, established 808 A.D.

larger family. In fact, most of the leaders still lived with their parents. The male nationalist movement supported the liberation of women, but had not come to grips
with the idea of the elderly living by themselves, nor with couples splitting off into
separate households. Neither idea seemed right, or elegant.

Mother especially disliked the idea of a fixed lunch hour. She always was the
last to wake up, and liked to have a late, lavish breakfast which she prepared herself
with a lot of flamboyant defiance, beneath the disapproving stare of Grandmother
Lalla Mani. She would make herself scrambled eggs and *baghrir,* or fine crêpes,
topped with pure honey and fresh butter, and, of course, plenty of tea. She usually
ate at exactly eleven, just as Lalla Mani was about to begin her purification ritual
for the noon prayer. And after that, two hours later at the communal table, Mother
was often absolutely unable to eat lunch. Sometimes she would skip it altogether,
especially when she wanted to annoy Father, because to skip a meal was considered
terribly rude and too openly individualistic.

Mother dreamed of living alone with Father and us kids. "Whoever heard of   5
ten birds living together squashed into a single nest?" she would say. "It is not natural to live in a large group, unless your objective is to make people feel miserable."
Although Father said that he was not really sure how the birds lived, he still sympathized with Mother, and felt torn between his duty towards the traditional family and his desire to make her happy. He felt guilty about breaking up the family
solidarity, knowing only too well that big families in general, and harem life in particular, were fast becoming relics of the past. He even prophesied that in the next
few decades, we would become like the Christians, who hardly ever visited their
old parents. In fact, most of my uncles who had already broken away from the big
house barely found the time to visit their mother, Lalla Mani, on Fridays after
prayer anymore. "Their kids do not kiss hands either," ran the constant refrain. To
make matters worse, until very recently, all my uncles had lived in our house, and
had only split away when their wives' opposition to communal life had become
unbearable. That is what gave Mother hope.

The first to leave the big family was Uncle Karim, Cousin Malika's father.
His wife loved music and liked to sing while being accompanied by Uncle Karim,
who played the lute beautifully. But he would rarely give in to his wife's desire to
spend an evening singing in their salon, because his older brother Uncle Ali
thought it unbecoming for a man to sing or play a musical instrument. Finally, one
day, Uncle Karim's wife just took her children and went back to her father's
house, saying that she had no intention of living in the communal house ever
again. Uncle Karim, a cheerful fellow who had himself often felt constrained by
the discipline of harem life, saw an opportunity to leave and took it, excusing his
actions by saying that he preferred to give in to his wife's wishes rather than for-
feit his marriage. Not long after that, all my other uncles moved out, one after the
other, until only Uncle Ali and Father were left. So Father's departure would have
meant the death of our large family. "As long as [my] Mother lives," he often said,
"I wouldn't betray the tradition."

Yet Father loved his wife so much that he felt miserable about not giving in
to her wishes and never stopped proposing compromises. One was to stock an entire cupboardful of food for her, in case she wanted to discreetly eat sometimes,

apart from the rest of the family. For one of the problems in the communal house was that you could not just open a refrigerator when you were hungry and grab something to eat. In the first place, there were no refrigerators back then. More importantly, the entire idea behind the harem was that you lived according to the group's rhythm. You could not just eat when you felt like it. Lalla Radia, my uncle's wife, had the key to the pantry, and although she always asked after dinner what people wanted to eat the next day, you still had to eat whatever the group— after lengthy discussion—decided upon. If the group settled on couscous with chick-peas and raisins, then that is what you got. If you happened to hate chick-peas and raisins, you had no choice but to shut up and settle for a frugal dinner composed of a few olives and a great deal of discretion.

"What a waste of time," Mother would say. "These endless discussions about meals! Arabs would be much better off if they let each individual decide what he or she wanted to swallow. Forcing everyone to share three meals a day just complicates things. And for what sacred purpose? None of course." From there, she would go on to say that her whole life was an absurdity, that nothing made sense, while Father would say that he could not just break away. If he did, tradition would vanish: "We live in difficult times, the country is occupied by foreign armies, our culture is threatened. All we have left is these traditions." This reasoning would drive Mother nuts: "Do you think that by sticking together in this big, absurd house, we will gain the strength we need to throw the foreign armies out? And what is more important anyway, tradition or people's happiness?" That would put an abrupt end to the conversation. Father would try to caress her hand but she would take it away. "This tradition is choking me," she would whisper, tears in her eyes.

So Father kept offering compromises. He not only arranged for Mother to have her own food stock, but also brought her things he knew she liked, such as dates, nuts, almonds, honey, flour, and fancy oils. She could make all the desserts and cookies she wanted, but she was not supposed to prepare a meat dish or a major meal. That would have meant the beginning of the end of the communal arrangement. Her flamboyantly prepared individual breakfasts were enough of a slap in the face to the rest of the family. Every once in a long while, Mother *did* get away with preparing a complete lunch or a dinner, but she had to not only be discreet about it but also give it some sort of exotic overtone. Her most common ploy was to camouflage the meal as a nighttime picnic on the terrace.

These occasional tête-á-tête dinners on the terrace during moonlit summer   10 nights were another peace offering that Father made to help satisfy Mother's yearning for privacy. We would be transplanted to the terrace, like nomads, with mattresses, tables, trays, and my little brother's cradle, which would be set down right in the middle of everything. Mother would be absolutely out of her mind with joy. No one else from the courtyard dared to show up, because they understood all too well that Mother was fleeing from the crowd. What she most enjoyed was trying to get Father to depart from his conventional self-controlled pose. Before long, she would start acting foolishly, like a young girl, and soon, Father would chase her all around the terrace, when she challenged him, "You can't run anymore, you have grown too old! All you're good for now is to sit and watch your son's cradle." Father, who had been smiling up to that point, would look at her at first as if what she had just said had not affected him at all. But then his smile would vanish, and he would start chasing her all over the terrace, jumping over tea-trays and sofas. Sometimes both of them made up games which included my sister and Samir (who was the only one of the rest of the family allowed to attend our moon-lit gatherings) and myself. More often, they completely forgot about the rest of the world, and we children would be sneezing all the next day because they had forgotten to put blankets on us when we had gone to sleep that night.

After these blissful evenings, Mother would be in an unusually soft and quiet mood for a whole week. Then she would tell me that whatever else I did with my life, I had to take her revenge. "I want my daughters' lives to be exciting," she would say, "very exciting and filled with one hundred percent happiness, nothing more, nothing less." I would raise my head, look at her earnestly, and ask what one hundred percent happiness meant, because I wanted her to know that I intended to do my best to achieve it. Happiness, she would explain, was when a person felt good, light, creative, content, loving and loved, and free. An unhappy person felt as if there were barriers crushing her desires and the talents she had inside. A happy woman was one who could exercise all kinds of rights, from the right to move to the right to create, compete, and challenge, and at the same time could feel loved for doing so. Part of happiness was to be loved by a man who enjoyed your strength and was proud of your talents. Happiness was also about the right to privacy, the right to retreat from the company of others and plunge into contemplative solitude. Or to sit by yourself doing nothing for a whole day, and not give excuses or feel guilty about it either. Happiness was to be with loved ones, and yet still feel that you existed as a separate being, that you were not there just to make them happy. Happiness was when there was a balance between what you gave and what you took. I then asked her how much happiness she had in her life, just to get an idea, and she said that it varied according to the days. Some days she had only five percent; others, like the evenings we spent with Father on the terrace, she had full-blown one hundred percent happiness.

Aiming at one hundred percent happiness seemed a bit overwhelming to me, as a young girl, especially since I could see how much Mother labored to sculpt her moments of happiness. How much time and energy she put into creating those wonderful moonlit evenings sitting close to Father, talking softly in his ear, her head on his shoulder! It seemed quite an accomplishment to me because she had to start working on him days ahead of time, and then she had to take care of all the logistics, like the cooking and the moving of the furniture. To invest so much stubborn effort just to achieve a few hours of happiness was impressive, and at least I knew it could be done. But how, I wondered, was I going to create such a high level of excitement for an entire lifetime? Well, if Mother thought it was possible, I should certainly give it a try.

"Times are going to get better for women now, my daughter," she would say to me. "You and your sister will get a good education, and you'll walk freely in the streets and discover the world. I want you to become independent, independent and happy. I want you to shine like moons. I want your lives to be a cascade of serene delights. One hundred percent happiness. Nothing more, nothing less." But when I asked her for more details about how to create that happiness, Mother would grow very impatient. "You have to work at it. One develops the muscles for happiness, just like for walking and breathing."

So every morning, I would sit on our threshold, contemplating the deserted courtyard and dreaming about my beautiful future, a cascade of serene delights. Hanging on to the romantic moonlit terrace evenings, challenging your beloved man to forget about his social duties, relax and act foolish and gaze at the stars while holding your hand, I thought, could be one way to go about developing muscles for happiness. Sculpting soft nights, when the sound of laughter blends with the spring breezes, could be another.

But those magical evenings were rare, or so they seemed. During the days, life   15 took a much more rigid and disciplined turn. Officially, there was no jumping around or foolishness allowed in the Mernissi household—all that was confined to clandestine times and spaces, such as late afternoons in the courtyard when the men were out, or evenings on the deserted terraces.

Questions for Discussion and Writing

1. How did Mernissi's mother manage to create a private family dinner despite the restrictions of communal life?
2. What expectations did Mernissi's mother have for her daughter, and how did she express them?
3. Discuss what the issue of privacy means to you and how this value translates into your everyday life.

Fiction

JOHN CHEEVER

John Cheever (1912–1982) was born in Quincy, Massachusetts, and never finished his formal education after he was expelled from prep school for smoking. Cheever began his literary career by capitalizing on this event with a sketch in The New Republic *entitled "Expelled." He is best known for insightful short stories that reflect the manners and mores of affluent suburban Americans. Collections of his works include* The Enormous Radio *(1953) and* The Stories of John Cheever *(1978), which won the Pulitzer Prize and in which "Reunion" first appeared.*

Reunion

The last time I saw my father was in Grand Central Station. I was going from my grandmother's in the Adirondacks to a cottage on the Cape that my mother had rented, and I wrote my father that I would be in New York between trains for an hour and a half and asked if we could have lunch together. His secretary wrote to say that he would meet me at the information booth at noon, and at twelve o'-clock sharp I saw him coming through the crowd. He was a stranger to me—my mother divorced him three years ago, and I hadn't been with him since—but as soon as I saw him I felt that he was my father, my flesh and blood, my future and my doom. I knew that when I was grown I would be something like him; I would have to plan my campaigns within his limitations. He was a big, good-looking man, and I was terribly happy to see him again. He struck me on the back and shook my hand, "Hi, Charlie," he said. "Hi, boy. I'd like to take you up to my club, but it's in the Sixties, and if you have to catch an early train I guess we'd better get something to eat around here." He put his arm around me, and I smelled my father the way my mother sniffs a rose. It was a rich compound of whiskey, after-shave lotion, shoe polish, woolens, and the rankness of a mature male. I hoped that someone would see us together. I wished that we could be photographed. I wanted some record of our having been together.

We went out of the station and up a side street to a restaurant. It was still early, and the place was empty. The bartender was quarreling with a delivery boy, and there was one very old waiter in a red coat down by the kitchen door. We sat down, and my father hailed the waiter in a loud voice. *"Kellner!"* he shouted. *"Garçon! Cameriere! You!"*[1] His boisterousness in the empty restaurant seemed out of place. "Could we have a little service here!" he shouted. "Chop-chop." Then he clapped his hands. This caught the waiter's attention, and he shuffled over to our table.

"Were you clapping you hands at me?" he asked.

"Calm down, calm down, *sommelier*,"[2] my father said. "If it isn't too much to ask of you—if it wouldn't be too much above and beyond the call of duty, we would like a couple of Beefeater Gibsons."

"I don't like to be clapped at," the waiter said.   5

"I should have brought my whistle," my father said. "I have a whistle that is audible only to the ears of old waiters. Now, take out your little pad and your little pencil and see if you can get this straight: two Beefeater Gibsons. Repeat after me: two Beefeater Gibsons."

"I think you'd better go somewhere else," the waiter said quietly.

"That," said my father, "is one of the most brilliant suggestions I have ever heard. Come on, Charlie, let's get the hell out of here."

I followed my father out of that restaurant into another. He was not so boisterous this time. Our drinks came, and he cross-questioned me about the baseball season. He then struck the edge of his empty glass with his knife and began shouting again. *"Garçon! Kellner! You!* Could we trouble you to bring us two more of the same."

"How old is the boy?" the waiter asked.   10

"That," my father said, "is none of your goddamned business."

---

[1] Waiter in German, French, and Italian.   [2] Wine steward in French.

"I'm sorry, sir," the waiter said, "but I won't serve the boy another drink."

"Well, I have some news for you," my father said. "I have some very interesting news for you. This doesn't happen to be the only restaurant in New York. They've opened another on the corner. Come on, Charlie."

He paid the bill, and I followed him out of that restaurant into another. Here the waiters wore pink jackets like hunting coats, and there was a lot of horse tack on the walls. We sat down, and my father began to shout again. "Master of the hounds! Tallyhoo and all that sort of thing. We'd like a little something in the way of a stirrup cup. Namely, two Bibson Geefeaters."

"Two Bibson Geefeaters?" the waiter asked, smiling.   15

"You know damned well what I want," my father said angrily. "I want two Beefeater Gibsons, and make it snappy. Things have changed in jolly old England. So my friend the duke tells me. Let's see what England can produce in the way of a cocktail."

"This isn't England," the waiter said.

"Don't argue with me," my father said. "Just do as you're told."

"I just thought you might like to know where you are," the waiter said.

"If there's one thing I cannot tolerate," my father said, "it is an impudent do-   20
mestic. Come on, Charlie."

The fourth place we went to was Italian. *"Buon giorno,"* my father said. *"Per favore, possiamo avere du cocktail americani, forti, forti. Molto gin, poco vermut."*[3]

"I don't understand Italian," the waiter said.

"Oh, come off it," my father said. "You understand Italian, and you know damned well you do. *Vogliamo due cocktail americani. Subito."*[4]

The waiter left us and spoke with the captain, who came over to our table and said, "I'm sorry, sir, but this table is reserved."

"All right," my father said. "Get us another table."   25

"All the tables are reserved," the captain said.

"I get it," my father said. "You don't desire our patronage. Is that it? Well, the hell with you. *Vada all' inferno.*[5] Let's go Charlie."

"I have to get my train," I said.

"I'm sorry, sonny," my father said. "I'm terribly sorry." He put his arm around me and pressed me against him. "I'll walk you back to the station. If there had only been time to go up to my club."

"That's all right, Daddy," I said.   30

"I'll get you a paper," he said. "I'll get you a paper to read on the train."

Then he went up to the newsstand and said, "Kind sir, will you be good enough to favor me with one of your goddamned, no-good ten-cent afternoon

---

[3] "Good morning. Could we please have two American cocktails (martinis) quite strong with a lot of gin and a little bit of vermouth."   [4] "I demand two American cocktails (martinis) immediately."
    [5] "Go to Hell."

papers?"The clerk turned away from him and stared at a magazine cover. "Is it asking too much, kind sir," my father said, "is it asking too much for you to sell me one
of your disgusting specimens of yellow journalism?"

"I have to go, Daddy," I said. "It's late."

"Now, just wait a second, sonny," he said. "Just wait a second. I want to get a
rise out of this chap."

"Goodbye, Daddy," I said, and I went down the stairs and got my train, and   35
that was the last time I saw my father.

Questions for Discussion and Writing

1. What embarrasses the young man about the way his father treats others?
2. How does Cheever stage the events in the story to justify the boy's final de-
    cision not to see his Father again?
3. How would the story sound if it were written from the father's point of view
    and his behavior was due to nervousness about making a good impression on
    his son?

BESSIE HEAD

*Bessie Head (1937–1986) was born of mixed parentage in Pietermaritzburg, South Africa. She
was taken from her mother at birth, raised by foster parents until she was thirteen, and then
placed in a mission orphanage. In 1961, newly married, she left South Africa to escape
apartheid and settled on an agricultural commune in Serowe, Botswana, where she lived until her
death in 1986. Among her publications are the novels* When Rain Clouds Gather *(1969),*
Maru *(1971), and* A Question of Power *(1974), acclaimed as one of the first psychological
accounts of a black woman's experience, as well as* A Collector of Treasures and Other
Botswana Village Tales *(1977). She is also the author of two histories:* Serowe: Village of
the Rain Wind *(1981) and* A Bewitched Crossroad *(1985). "Looking for a Rain God"
(1977) is based on a shocking local newspaper report. Head dramatizes how a seven-year
drought creates conflicts between ancient tribal rituals and contemporary moral codes.*

Looking for a Rain God

It is lonely at the lands where the people go to plough. These lands are vast
clearings in the bush, and the wild bush is lonely too. Nearly all the lands are
within walking distance from the village. In some parts of the bush where the underground water is very near the surface, people made little rest camps for themselves and dug shallow wells to quench their thirst while on their journey to their
own lands. They experienced all kinds of things once they left the village. They
could rest at shady watering places full of lush, tangled trees with delicate pale-gold
and purple wildflowers springing up between soft green moss and the children
could hunt around for wild figs and any berries that might be in season. But from
1958, a seven-year drought fell upon the land and even the watering places began

to look as dismal as the dry open thornbush country; the leaves of the trees curled up and withered; the moss became dry and hard and, under the shade of the tangled trees, the ground turned a powdery black and white, because there was no rain. People said rather humorously that if you tried to catch the rain in a cup it would only fill a teaspoon. Toward the beginning of the seventh year of drought, the summer had become an anguish to live through. The air was so dry and moisture-free that it burned the skin. No one knew what to do to escape the heat and tragedy was in the air. At the beginning of that summer, a number of men just went out of their homes and hung themselves to death from trees. The majority of the people had lived off crops, but for two years past they had all returned from the lands with only their rolled-up skin blankets and cooking utensils. Only the charlatans, incanters, and witch doctors made a pile of money during this time because people were always turning to them in desperation for little talismans and herbs to rub on the plough for the crops to grow and the rain to fall.

The rains were late that year. They came in early November, with a promise of good rain. It wasn't the full, steady downpour of the years of good rain but thin, scanty, misty rain. It softened the earth and a rich growth of green things sprang up everywhere for the animals to eat. People were called to the center of the village to hear the proclamation of the beginning of the ploughing season; they stirred themselves and whole families began to move off to the lands to plough.

The family of the old man, Mokgobja, were among those who left early for the lands. They had a donkey cart and piled everything onto it, Mokgobja—who was over seventy years old; two girls, Neo and Boseyong; their mother Tiro and an unmarried sister, Nesta; and the father and supporter of the family, Ramadi, who drove the donkey cart. In the rush of the first hope of rain, the man, Ramadi, and the two women, cleared the land of thornbush and then hedged their vast ploughing area with this same thornbush to protect the future crop from the goats they had brought along for milk. They cleared out and deepened the old well with its pool of muddy water and still in this light, misty rain, Ramadi inspanned[1] two oxen and turned the earth over with a hand plough.

The land was ready and ploughed, waiting for the crops. At night, the earth was alive with insects singing and rustling about in search of food. But suddenly, by mid-November, the rain flew away; the rain clouds fled away and left the sky bare. The sun danced dizzily in the sky, with a strange cruelty. Each day the land was covered in a haze of mist as the sun sucked up the last drop of moisture out of the earth. The family sat down in despair, waiting and waiting. Their hopes had run so high; the goats had started producing milk, which they had eagerly poured on their porridge, now they ate plain porridge with no milk. It was impossible to plant the corn, maize, pumpkin, and watermelon seeds in the dry earth. They sat the whole day in the shadow of the huts and even stopped thinking, for the rain had fled away. Only the children, Neo and Boseyong, were quite happy in their little-girl world. They carried on with their game of making house like their mother and chattered to each

---

[1] *Inspanned:* yoked together.

other in light, soft tones. They made children from sticks around which they tied rags, and scolded them severely in an exact imitation of their own mother. Their voices could be heard scolding the day long: "You stupid thing, when I send you to draw water, why do you spill half of it out of the bucket!" "You stupid thing! Can't you mind the porridge pot without letting the porridge burn!" And then they would beat the rag dolls on their bottoms with severe expressions.

The adults paid no attention to this; they did not even hear the funny chatter; they sat waiting for rain; their nerves were stretched to breaking-point willing the rain to fall out of the sky. Nothing was important, beyond that. All their animals had been sold during the bad years to purchase food, and of all their herd only two goats were left. It was the women of the family who finally broke down under the strain of waiting for rain. It was really the two women who caused the death of the little girls. Each night they started a weird, high-pitched wailing that began on a low, mournful note and whipped up to a frenzy. Then they would stamp their feet and shout as though they had lost their heads. The men sat quiet and self-controlled; it was important for men to maintain their self-control at all times but their nerve was breaking too. They knew the women were haunted by the starvation of the coming year.

Finally, an ancient memory stirred in the old man, Mokgobja. When he was very young and the customs of the ancestors still ruled the land, he had been witness to a rain-making ceremony. And he came alive a little, struggling to recall the details which had been buried by years and years of prayer in a Christian church. As soon as the mists cleared a little, he began consulting in whispers with his youngest son, Ramadi. There was, he said, a certain rain god who accepted only the sacrifice of the bodies of children. Then the rain would fall; then the crops would grow, he said. He explained the ritual and as he talked, his memory became a conviction and he began to talk with unshakable authority. Ramadi's nerves were smashed by the nightly wailing of the women and soon the two men began whispering with the two women. The children continued their game: "You stupid thing! How could you have lost the money on the way to the shop! You must have been playing again!"

After it was all over and the bodies of the two little girls had been spread across the land, the rain did not fall. Instead, there was a deathly silence at night and the devouring heat of the sun by day. A terror, extreme and deep, overwhelmed the whole family. They packed, rolling up their skin blankets and pots, and fled back to the village.

People in the village soon noted the absence of the two little girls. They had died at the lands and were buried there, the family said. But people noted their ashen, terror-stricken faces and a murmur arose. What had killed the children, they wanted to know? And the family replied that they had just died. And people said amongst themselves that it was strange that the two deaths had occurred at the same time. And there was a feeling of great unease at the unnatural looks of the family. Soon the police came around. The family told them the same story of death and burial at the lands. They did not know what the children had died of. So the police asked to see the graves. At this, the mother of the children broke down and told everything.

Throughout that terrible summer the story of the children hung like a dark cloud of sorrow over the village, and the sorrow was not assuaged when the old man and Ramadi were sentenced to death for ritual murder. All they had on the statute books was that ritual murder was against the law and must be stamped out with the death penalty. The subtle story of strain and starvation and breakdown was inadmissible evidence at court; but all the people who lived off crops knew in their hearts that only a hair's breadth had saved them from sharing a fate similar to that of the Mokgobja family. They could have killed something to make the rain fall.

Questions for Discussion and Writing

1. How does Head lay the psychological groundwork for what otherwise would come as a shock—the choice of the two young girls as sacrificial victims? How do the girls appear to other members of the family when everyone must contribute to conserving food and water?

2. Why doesn't Head withhold knowledge of the ending in telling the story? How does knowing what happened shift the focus of the story from *what* to *how* it might have occurred? How does the unceasing drought reactivate a belief that leads to the slaughter and dismemberment of the girls to produce rain?

3. What does Head mean when she ends the story by stating that other villagers "could have killed something to make the rain fall"? What does this imply about her attitude toward the murderers and their plight?

Poetry

CATHY SONG

Born in 1955 in Honolulu, Hawaii, of Chinese and Korean ancestry, Cathy Song was educated at Wellesley and Boston University. Her poetry is collected in Picture Bride *(1983), in which "The Youngest Daughter" first appeared. Song's work focuses on family relationships, and in this poem she explores the intricacies of a mother–daughter relationship. Her most recent collection of poetry is* The Lamp of Bliss *(2001).*

The Youngest Daughter

The sky has been dark
for many years.
My skin has become as damp
and pale as rice paper
and feels the way

5

mother's used to before the drying sun
parched it out there in the fields.

    Lately, when I touch my eyelids,
my hands react as if
I had just touched something   10
hot enough to burn.
My skin, aspirin colored,
tingles with migraine. Mother
has been massaging the left side of my face
especially in the evenings   15
when the pain flares up.

This morning
her breathing was graveled,
her voice gruff with affection
when I wheeled her into the bath.   20
She was in a good humor,
making jokes about her great breasts,
floating in the milky water
like two walruses,
flaccid and whiskered around the nipples.   25
I scrubbed them with a sour taste
in my mouth, thinking:
six children and an old man
have sucked from those brown nipples.

I was almost tender   30
when I came to the blue bruises
that freckle her body,
places where she had been injecting insulin
for thirty years. I soaped her slowly,
she sighed deeply, her eyes closed.   35
It seems it has always
been like this: the two of us
in this sunless room,
the splashing of the bathwater.

In the afternoons   40
when she has rested,
she prepares our ritual of tea and rice,
garnished with a shred of gingered fish,
a slice of pickled turnip,
a token for my white body.   45
We eat in the familiar silence.
She knows I am not to be trusted,
even now planning my escape.

As I toast to her health
with the tea she has poured,
a thousand cranes curtain the window,
fly up in a sudden breeze.

50

Questions for Discussion and Writing

1. How would you characterize the relationship between the mother and daughter in this poem? For how long has this relationship existed in this way? What, in your view, is the significance of the title, "The Youngest Daughter," in explaining the situation the poem describes, in light of the fact that the speaker has five siblings?
2. What details suggest the strain the daughter is experiencing in finally deciding to make her escape and leave?
3. Do you know children who have submerged their own identities and possibilities for an independent life in the interest of caring for an infirm parent or other relative? If you have ever been involved in a relationship as a child similar to the one between the mother and daughter in the poem, did you react as the daughter did? Discuss your experiences.

ROBERT HAYDEN

Robert Hayden (1913–1980) was born in Detroit and educated at Wayne State University and the University of Michigan. He taught for more than twenty years at Fisk University before becoming a professor of English at the University of Michigan. He was elected to the National Academy of American Poets in 1975 and served twice as the poetry consultant to the Library of Congress. His volumes of poetry include A Ballad of Remembrance *(1962),* Words in Mourning Time *(1970), and* Angle of Ascent *(1975). "Those Winter Sundays" (1962) is a finely etched depiction of the speaker's change in attitude toward his father.*

Those Winter Sundays

Sundays too my father got up early
and put his clothes on in the blueblack cold,
then with cracked hands that ached
from labor in the weekday weather made
banked fires blaze. No one ever thanked him.

5

I'd wake and hear the cold splintering, breaking,
When the rooms were warm, he'd call,
and slowly I would rise and dress,
fearing the chronic angers of that house,

Speaking indifferently to him,   10
who had driven out the cold
and polished my good shoes as well.
What did I know, what did I know
of love's austere and lonely offices?

Questions for Discussion and Writing

1. How does Hayden make use of the contrast in imagery between cold and warmth to underscore the shift in the speaker's attitude?
2. What has made the speaker realize, now that he has grown up, how much his father really cared for him?
3. In a short essay, discuss the poem's dominant emotion. Have you ever come to realize that someone cared for you in ways not obvious to you at the time? Describe your experience.

WILLIAM WORDSWORTH

William Wordsworth (1770–1850) was born in a village on the edge of the Lake District in England. He attended St. John's College, Cambridge, in 1787, and began a series of walking tours of Switzerland and France that fired his imagination and are reflected in his autobiographical poem "The Prelude" (1805). He lived in France from 1791 to 1792 at the height of the French Revolution. In 1797 he began a lifelong friendship with the younger poet Samuel Coleridge, a creative association that led in 1798 to the publication of a groundbreaking volume of poems—Lyrical Ballads—whose down-to-earth style and everyday subjects set English poetry on a new course. Wordsworth's ability to communicate heartfelt reactions to inspiring landscapes and to see spiritual depths in everyday scenes is well illustrated in the poem "Composed upon Westminster Bridge, September 3, 1802."

Composed upon Westminster Bridge,[1] *September 3, 1802*

Earth has not anything to show more fair:
Dull would he be of soul who could pass by
A sight so touching in its majesty:
This City now doth, like a garment, wear
The beauty of the morning; silent, bare,   5
Ships, towers, domes, theatres, and temples lie
Open unto the fields, and to the sky;

---

[1] *Westminster Bridge:* bridge over the Thames near the Houses of Parliament in London.

All bright and glittering in the smokeless air.
Never did sun more beautifully steep
In his first splendour, valley, rock, or hill;   10
Ne'er saw I, never felt, a calm so deep!
The river glideth at his own sweet will:
Dear God! the very houses seem asleep;
And all that mighty heart is lying still!

Questions for Discussion and Writing

1. What sights and emotions touch the poet as he stands upon Westminister Bridge in early morning?
2. What effect does Wordsworth achieve by ascribing human qualities to the city?
3. Try your hand at writing a short poem about a place that has inspired you, personifying the features of the scene you find most compelling.

Connections for Chapter 2: Influential People and Memorable Places

1. **Maya Angelou,** *Liked for Myself*
   How are Angelou and Fatima Mernissi encouraged to transcend existing societal restrictions related to race and gender by very strong female figures in their lives?
2. **Raymond Carver,** *My Father's Life*
   In what sense do both Carver and Robert Hayden write in order to reassess their relationships with their respective fathers?
3. **Gayle Pemberton,** *Antidisestablishmentarianism*
   Compare the role that Pemberton's grandmother and Mrs. Flowers in Maya Angelou's memoir play as influential figures in the lives of the two girls.
4. **Mikhail Gilmore,** *My Brother, Gary Gilmore*
   How does Gilmore's narrative raise the questions of heredity and environment discussed by Constance Holden in "Identical Twins Reared Apart" in Chapter 9?
5. **P. D. Ouspensky,** *The Taj Mahal*
   In what way do the Taj Mahal, as portrayed by Ouspensky, and St. Mark's, as described by Mary McCarthy in "The Paradox of St. Mark's" (in Chapter 10), contrast a spiritual view of life with a materialistic one?

6. **William Zinsser,** *Niagara Falls*

   What comparable intangible meanings do Zinsser and P. D. Ouspensky find embodied in Niagara Falls and the Taj Mahal, although one is natural and the other is constructed?

7. **Joseph Addison,** *Reflections in Westminster Abbey*

   Compare and contrast the impressions produced by Westminster Abbey on Addison and the Taj Mahal on P. D. Ouspensky in terms of their very different conclusions about mortality.

8. **Fatima Mernissi,** *Moonlit Nights of Laughter*

   In what ways do both Mernissi and Gayle Pemberton benefit from the free-spirited, independent thinking of their mother and grandmother, respectively?

9. **John Cheever,** *Reunion*

   Compare how Cheever, in his short story, and Raymond Carver in his essay, develop the theme of sons who, for one reason or another, find it difficult to relate to their fathers.

10. **Bessie Head,** *Looking for a Rain God*

    How can Head's story be thought of as a worst-case scenario of Garrett Hardin's "Lifeboat Ethics" (in Chapter 11)?

11. **Cathy Song,** *The Youngest Daughter*

    What different ways do the parents in the poems by Song and Robert Hayden express their love for their children, and how does each speaker react?

12. **Robert Hayden,** *Those Winter Sundays*

    Compare the messages that Hayden and Dylan Thomas (in "Do Not Go Gentle into That Good Night" in Chapter 11) wish to communicate to their fathers.

13. **William Wordsworth,** *Composed upon Westminster Bridge, September 3, 1802*

    In what ways do both P. D. Ouspensky's description of the Taj Mahal and Wordsworth's description of the city of London evoke feelings of the sublime?

3

THE VALUE OF EDUCATION

As the essays in this chapter make clear, education is primarily a liberating experience. Yet, the accounts by Frederick Douglass, Mary Crow Dog, and Richard Rodriguez attest to the ingenuity and determination that are often required in getting an education. Essays by William A. Henry III, John Milton, and Nat Hentoff confront the basic questions of (1) what constitutes an educated person, (2) what role education should play in society, and (3) whether censorship has any role in a free society.

The essay by Jonathan Kozol explores the consequences for society when many citizens are unable to read or write. David Rothenberg explores a contrasting dilemma: Has the Internet, paradoxically, decreased students' capacity for doing independent research?

In the fictional work by Donald Barthelme we can hear the expectations, instructions, and admonitions of society to its young that make us aware of the role school plays in instilling social values.

The poems by Francis E. W. Harper and Linda Hogan offer intensely personal reflections on the value of education, especially for minorities.

Nonfiction

FREDERICK DOUGLASS

Frederick Douglass (1817–1895) was born into slavery in Maryland, where he worked as a field hand and servant. In 1838, after previous failed attempts to escape, for which he was beaten and tortured, he successfully made his way to New York by using the identity papers of a freed black sailor. There he adopted the last name of Douglass and subsequently settled in New Bedford, Massachusetts. Douglass was the first black American to rise to prominence as a national figure. He gained renown as a speaker for the Massachusetts Anti-Slavery League and was an editor for the North Star, *an abolitionist paper, from 1847 to 1860. He was a friend to John*

Brown, helped convince President Lincoln to issue the Emancipation Proclamation, and became ambassador to several foreign countries. The Narrative of the Life of Frederick Douglass, an American Slave *(1845), is one of the most illuminating of the many slave narratives written during the nineteenth century. "Learning to Read and Write," drawn from this autobiography, reveals Douglass's ingenuity in manipulating his circumstances so as to become literate.*

Learning to Read and Write

I lived in Master Hugh's family about seven years. During this time, I succeeded in learning to read and write. In accomplishing this, I was compelled to resort to various stratagems. I had no regular teacher. My mistress, who had kindly commenced to instruct me, had, in compliance with the advice and direction of her husband, not only ceased to instruct, but had set her face against my being instructed by any one else. It is due, however, to my mistress to say of her, that she did not adopt this course of treatment immediately. She at first lacked the depravity indispensable to shutting me up in mental darkness. It was at least necessary for her to have some training in the exercise of irresponsible power, to make her equal to the task of treating me as though I were a brute.

My mistress was, as I have said, a kind and tender-hearted woman; and in the simplicity of her soul she commenced, when I first went to live with her, to treat me as she supposed one human being ought to treat another. In entering upon the duties of a slaveholder, she did not seem to perceive that I sustained to her the relation of a mere chattel, and that for her to treat me as a human being was not only wrong, but dangerously so. Slavery proved as injurious to her as it did to me. When I went there, she was a pious, warm, and tender-hearted woman. There was no sorrow or suffering for which she had not a tear. She had bread for the hungry, clothes for the naked, and comfort for every mourner that came within her reach. Slavery soon proved its ability to divest her of these heavenly qualities. Under its influence, the tender heart became stone, and the lamb-like disposition gave way to one of tiger-like fierceness. The first step in her downward course was in her ceasing to instruct me. She now commenced to practise her husband's precepts. She finally became even more violent in her opposition than her husband himself. She was not satisfied with simply doing as well as he had commanded; she seemed anxious to do better. Nothing seemed to make her more angry than to see me with a newspaper. She seemed to think that here lay the danger. I have had her rush at me with a face made all up of fury, and snatch from me a newspaper, in a manner that fully revealed her apprehension. She was an apt woman; and a little experience soon demonstrated, to her satisfaction, that education and slavery were incompatible with each other.

From this time I was most narrowly watched. If I was in a separate room any considerable length of time, I was sure to be suspected of having a book, and was at once called to give an account of myself. All this, however, was too late. The first step had been taken. Mistress, in teaching me the alphabet, had given me the *inch,* and no precaution could prevent me from taking the *ell.*[1]

The plan which I adopted, and the one by which I was most successful, was that of making friends of all the little white boys whom I met in the street. As many of these as I could, I converted into teachers. With their kindly aid, obtained at different times and in different places, I finally succeeded in learning to read. When I was sent on errands, I always took my book with me, and by going one part of my errand quickly, I found time to get a lesson before my return. I used also to carry bread with me, enough of which was always in the house, and to which I was always welcome; for I was much better off in this regard than many of the poor white children in our neighborhood. This bread I used to bestow upon the hungry little urchins, who, in return, would give me that more valuable bread of knowledge. I am strongly tempted to give the names of two or three of those little boys, as a testimonial of the gratitude and affection I bear them; but prudence forbids;— not that it would injure me, but it might embarrass them; for it is almost an unpardonable offence to teach slaves to read in this Christian country. It is enough to say of the dear little fellows, that they lived on Philpot Street, very near Durgin and Bailey's ship-yard. I used to talk this matter of slavery over with them. I would sometimes say to them, I wished I could be as free as they would be when they got to be men. "You will be free as soon as you are twenty-one, *but I am a slave for life!* Have not I as good a right to be free as you have?" These words used to trouble them; they would express for me the liveliest sympathy, and console me with the hope that something would occur by which I might be free.

I was now about twelve years old, and the thought of being *a slave for life*   5 began to bear heavily upon my heart. Just about this time, I got hold of a book entitled "The Columbian Orator."[2] Every opportunity I got, I used to read this book. Among much of other interesting matter, I found in it a dialogue between a master and his slave. The slave was represented as having run away from his master three times. The dialogue represented the conversation which took place between them, when the slave was retaken the third time. In this dialogue, the whole argument in behalf of slavery was brought forward by the master, all of which was disposed of by the slave. The slave was made to say some very smart as well as impressive things in reply to his master—things which had the desired though unexpected effect; for the conversation resulted in the voluntary emancipation of the slave on the part of the master.

In the same book, I met with one of Sheridan's mighty speeches on and in behalf of Catholic emancipation. These were choice documents to me. I read them over and over again with unabated interest. They gave tongue to interesting thoughts of my own soul, which had frequently flashed through my mind, and died

---

[1] An ell is equal to 1.14 meters.

[2] *The Columbian Orator (1797):* written by Caleb Bingham. It was one of the first readers used in New England schools.

away for want of utterance. The moral which I gained from the dialogue was the power of truth over the conscience of even a slaveholder. What I got from Sheridan was a bold denunciation of slavery, and a powerful vindication of human rights. The reading of these documents enabled me to utter my thoughts, and to meet the arguments brought forward to sustain slavery; but while they relieved me of one difficulty, they brought on another even more painful than the one of which I was relieved. The more I read, the more I was led to abhor and detest my enslavers. I could regard them in no other light than a band of successful robbers, who had left their homes, and gone to Africa, and stolen us from our homes, and in a strange land reduced us to slavery. I loathed them as being the meanest as well as the most wicked of men. As I read and contemplated the subject, behold! that very discontentment which Master Hugh had predicted would follow my learning to read had already come, to torment and sting my soul to unutterable anguish. As I writhed under it, I would at times feel that learning to read had been a curse rather than a blessing. It had given me a view of my wretched condition, without the remedy. It opened my eyes to the horrible pit, but to no ladder upon which to get out. In moments of agony, I envied my fellow-slaves for their stupidity. I have often wished myself a beast. I preferred the condition of the meanest reptile to my own. Any thing, no matter what, to get rid of thinking! It was this everlasting thinking of my condition that tormented me. There was no getting rid of it. It was pressed upon me by every object within sight or hearing, animate or inanimate. The silver trump of freedom had roused my soul to eternal wakefulness. Freedom now appeared, to disappear no more forever. It was heard in every sound, and seen in every thing. It was ever present to torment me with a sense of my wretched condition. I saw nothing without seeing it, I heard nothing without hearing it, and felt nothing without feeling it. It looked from every star, it smiled in every calm, breathed in every wind, and moved in every storm.

I often found myself regretting my own existence, and wishing myself dead; and but for the hope of being free, I have no doubt but that I should have killed myself, or done something for which I should have been killed. While in this state of mind, I was eager to hear any one speak of slavery. I was a ready listener. Every little while, I could hear something about the abolitionists. It was some time before I found what the word meant. It was always used in such connections as to make it an interesting word to me. If a slave ran away and succeeded in getting clear, or if a slave killed his master, set fire to a barn, or did any thing very wrong in the mind of a slaveholder, it was spoken of as the fruit of *abolition.* Hearing the word in this connection very often, I set about learning what it meant. The dictionary afforded me little or no help. I found it was "the act of abolishing," but then I did not know what was to be abolished. Here I was perplexed. I did not dare to ask any one about its meaning, for I was satisfied that it was something they wanted me to know very little about. After a patient waiting, I got one of our city papers, containing an account of the number of petitions from the north, praying for the abolition of slavery in the District of Columbia, and of the slave trade between the States. From this time I understood the words *abolition* and *abolitionist,* and always drew near when that word was spoken, expecting to hear something of importance to myself and fellow-slaves. The light broke in upon me by degrees. I went one day down on the wharf of Mr. Waters; and seeing two Irishmen unloading a scow of stone, I went, unasked, and helped them. When we had finished, one of them came to me and asked me if I were a slave. I told him I was. He asked, "Are ye a slave for life?" I told him that I was. The good Irishman seemed to be deeply affected by the statement. He said to the other that it was a pity so fine a little fellow as myself should be a slave for life. He said it was a shame to hold me. They both advised me to run away to the north; that I should find friends there, and that I should be free. I pretended not to be interested in what they said, and treated them as if I did not understand them; for I feared they might be treacherous. White men have been known to encourage slaves to escape, and then, to get the reward, catch them and return them to their masters. I was afraid that these seemingly good men might use me so; but I nevertheless remembered their advice, and from that time I resolved to run away. I looked forward to a time at which it would be safe for me to escape. I was too young to think of doing so immediately; besides, I wished to learn how to write, as I might have occasion to write my own pass. I consoled myself with the hope that I should one day find a good chance. Meanwhile, I would learn to write.

The idea as to how I might learn to write was suggested to me by being in Durgin and Bailey's ship-yard, and frequently seeing the ship carpenters, after hewing, and getting a piece of timber ready for use, write on the timber the name of that part of the ship for which it was intended. When a piece of timber was intended for the larboard side, it would be marked thus—"L." When a piece was for the starboard side, it would be marked thus—"S." A piece for the larboard side forward, would be marked thus—"L. F." When a piece was for starboard side forward, it would be marked thus—"S. F." For larboard aft, it would be marked thus—"L. A." For starboard aft, it would be marked thus—"S. A." I soon learned the names of these letters, and for what they were intended when placed upon a piece of timber in the ship-yard. I immediately commenced copying them, and in a short time was able to make the four letters named. After that, when I met with any boy who I knew could write, I would tell him I could write as well as he. The next word would be, "I don't believe you. Let me see you try it." I would then make the letters which I had been so fortunate as to learn, and ask him to beat that. In this way I got a good many lessons in writing, which it is quite possible I should never have gotten in any other way. During this time, my copy-book was the board fence, brick wall, and pavement; my pen and ink was a lump of chalk. With these, I learned mainly how to write. I then commenced and continued copying the italics in *Webster's Spelling Book,* until I could make them all without looking on the book. By this time, my little Master Thomas had gone to school, and learned how to write, and had written over a number of copy-books. These had been brought home, and shown to some of our near neighbors, and then laid aside. My mistress used to go to class meeting at the Wilk Street meetinghouse every Monday afternoon, and leave me to take care of the house. When left thus, I used to spend the time in writing in the spaces left in Master Thomas's copy-book, copying what he had written. I continued to do this until I could write a hand very similar to that of Master Thomas. Thus, after a long, tedious effort for years, I finally succeeded in learning how to write.

Questions for Discussion and Writing

1. What effect did the institution of slavery have on Douglass's relationship with the mistress of the household when she initially wanted to help him become literate?

2. Douglass writes that "education and slavery were incompatible with each other." How does this account illustrate his belief? What ingenious methods did Douglass devise to obtain knowledge of reading and writing?

3. What would your life be like if you could not read or write? Describe a day in your life, providing specific examples that would dramatize this condition.

JONATHAN KOZOL

Jonathan Kozol was born in Boston in 1936 and graduated from Harvard in 1958. He was a Rhodes scholar at Oxford University and has taught at numerous colleges, including Yale. His many books on education and literacy include Death at an Early Age *(1967);* Illiterate America *(1985), from which the following selection is taken;* Rachel and Her Children *(1988);* Savage Inequalities *(1991);* Amazing Grace: The Lives of Children and the Conscience of a Nation *(1995); and most recently,* Ordinary Resurrections: Children in the Years of Hope *(2000).*

The Human Cost of an Illiterate Society

PRECAUTIONS, READ BEFORE USING.
Poison: Contains sodium hydroxide (caustic soda-lye).
Corrosive: Causes severe eye and skin damage, may cause blindness.
Harmful or fatal if swallowed.
If swallowed, give large quantities of milk or water.
Do not induce vomiting.
Important: Keep water out of can at all times to prevent contents from violently erupting. . . .

—Warning on a can of Drano

Questions of literacy, in Socrates' belief, must at length be judged as matters of morality. Socrates could not have had in mind the moral compromise peculiar to a nation like our own. Some of our Founding Fathers did, however, have this question in their minds. One of the wisest of those Founding Fathers (one who may not have been most compassionate but surely was more prescient than some of his peers) recognized the special dangers that illiteracy would pose to basic equity in the political construction that he helped to shape.

"A people who mean to be their own governors," James Madison wrote, "must arm themselves with the power knowledge gives. A popular government without popular information or the means of acquiring it, is but a prologue to a farce or a tragedy, or perhaps both."

Tragedy looms larger than farce in the United States today. Illiterate citizens seldom vote. Those who do are forced to cast a vote of questionable worth. They cannot make informed decisions based on serious print information. Sometimes they can be alerted to their interests by aggressive voter education. More frequently, they vote for a face, a smile, or a style, not for a mind or character or body of beliefs.

The number of illiterate adults exceeds by 16 million the entire vote cast for the winner in the 1980 presidential contest. If even one third of all illiterates could vote, and read enough and do sufficient math to vote in their self-interest, Ronald Reagan would not likely have been chosen president. There is, of course, no way to know for sure. We do know this: Democracy is a mendacious term when used by those who are prepared to countenance the forced exclusion of one third of our electorate. So long as 60 million people are denied significant participation, the government is neither of nor for, nor by, the people. It is a government, at best, of those two thirds whose wealth, skin color, or parental privilege allows them opportunity to profit from the provocation and instruction of the written word.

The undermining of democracy in the United States is one "expense" that sensitive Americans can easily deplore because it represents a contradiction that endangers citizens of all political positions. The human price is not so obvious at first.

5

Since I first immersed myself within this work I have often had the following dream: I find that I am in a railroad station or a large department store within a city that is utterly unknown to me and where I cannot understand the printed words. None of the signs or symbols is familiar. Everything looks strange: like mirror writing of some kind. Gradually I understand that I am in the Soviet Union. All the letters on the walls around me are Cyrillic. I look for my pocket dictionary but I find that it has been mislaid. Where have I left it? Then I recall that I forgot to bring it with me when I packed my bags in Boston. I struggle to remember the name of my hotel. I try to ask somebody for directions. One person stops and looks at me in a peculiar way. I lose the nerve to ask. At last I reach into my wallet for an ID card. The card is missing. Have I lost it? Then I remember that my card was confiscated for some reason, many years before. Around this point, I wake up in a panic.

This panic is not so different from the misery that millions of adult illiterates experience each day within the course of their routine existence in the U.S.A.

Illiterates cannot read the menu in a restaurant.

They cannot read the cost of items on the menu in the *window* of the restaurant before they enter.

Illiterates cannot read the letters that their children bring home from their teachers. They cannot study school department circulars that tell them of the courses that their children must be taking if they hope to pass the SAT exams. They cannot help with homework. They cannot write a letter to the teacher. They are afraid to visit in the classroom. They do not want to humiliate their child or themselves.

10

Illiterates cannot read instructions on a bottle of prescription medicine. They cannot find out when a medicine is past the year of safe consumption; nor can they read of allergenic risks, warnings to diabetics, or the potential sedative effect of certain kinds of nonprescription pills. They cannot observe preventive health care admonitions. They cannot read about "the seven warning signs of cancer" or the indications of blood-sugar fluctuations or the risks of eating certain foods that aggravate the likelihood of cardiac arrest.

Illiterates live, in more than literal ways, an uninsured existence. They cannot understand the written details on a health insurance form. They cannot read the waivers that they sign preceding surgical procedures. Several women I have known in Boston have entered a slum hospital with the intention of obtaining a tubal ligation and have emerged a few days later after having been subjected to a hysterectomy. Unaware of their rights, incognizant of jargon, intimidated by the unfamiliar air of fear and atmosphere of ether that so many of us find oppressive in the confines even of the most attractive and expensive medical facilities, they have signed their names to documents they could not read and which nobody, in the hectic situation that prevails so often in those overcrowded hospitals that serve the urban poor, had even bothered to explain.

Childbirth might seem to be the last inalienable right of any female citizen within a civilized society. Illiterate mothers, as we shall see, already have been cheated of the power to protect their progeny against the likelihood of demolition in deficient public schools and, as a result, against the verbal servitude within which they themselves exist. Surgical denial of the right to bear that child in the first place represents an ultimate denial, an unspeakable metaphor, a final darkness that denies even the twilight gleamings of our own humanity. What greater violation of our biological, our biblical, our spiritual humanity could possibly exist than that which takes place nightly, perhaps hourly these days, within such overburdened and benighted institutions as the Boston City Hospital? Illiteracy has many costs; few are so irreversible as this.

Even the roof above one's head, the gas or other fuel for heating that protects the residents of northern city slums against the threat of illness in the winter months become uncertain guarantees. Illiterates cannot read the lease that they must sign to live in an apartment which, too often, they cannot afford. They cannot manage check accounts and therefore seldom pay for anything by mail. Hours and entire days of difficult travel (and the cost of bus or other public transit) must be added to the real cost of whatever they consume. Loss of interest on the check accounts they do not have, and could not manage if they did, must be regarded as another of the excess costs paid by the citizen who is excluded from the common instruments of commerce in a numerate society.

"I couldn't understand the bills," a woman in Washington, D.C., reports, "and then I couldn't write the checks to pay them. We signed things we didn't know what they were." 15

Illiterates cannot read the notices that they receive from welfare offices or from the IRS. They must depend on word-of-mouth instruction from the welfare worker—or from other persons whom they have good reason to mistrust. They do not know what rights they have, what deadlines and requirements they face, what options they might choose to exercise. They are half-citizens. Their rights exist in print but not in fact.

Illiterates cannot look up numbers in a telephone directory. Even if they can find the names of friends, few possess the sorting skills to make use of the yellow pages; categories are bewildering and trade names are beyond decoding capabilities for millions of nonreaders. Even the emergency numbers listed on the first page of the phone book—"Ambulance," "Police," and "Fire"—are too frequently beyond the recognition of nonreaders.

Many illiterates cannot read the admonition on a pack of cigarettes. Neither the Surgeon General's warning nor its reproduction on the package can alert them to the risks. Although most people learn by word of mouth that smoking is related to a number of grave physical disorders, they do not get the chance to read the detailed stories which can document this danger with the vividness that turns concern into determination to resist. They can see the handsome cowboy or the slim Virginia lady lighting up a filter cigarette; they cannot heed the words that tell them that this product is (not "may be") dangerous to their health. Sixty million men and women are condemned to be the unalerted, high-risk candidates for cancer.

Illiterates do not buy "no-name" products in the supermarkets. They must depend on photographs or the familiar logos that are printed on the packages of brand-name groceries. The poorest people, therefore, are denied the benefits of the least costly products.

Illiterates depend almost entirely upon label recognition. Many labels, however, are not easy to distinguish. Dozens of different kinds of Campbell's soup appear identical to the nonreader. The purchaser who cannot read and does not dare to ask for help, out of the fear of being stigmatized (a fear which is unfortunately realistic), frequently comes home with something which she never wanted and her family never tasted. 20

Illiterates cannot read instructions on a pack of frozen food. Packages sometimes provide an illustration to explain the cooking preparations; but illustrations are of little help to someone who must "boil water, drop the food—*within* its plastic wrapper—in the boiling water, wait for it to simmer, instantly remove."

Even when labels are seemingly clear, they may be easily mistaken. A woman in Detroit brought home a gallon of Crisco for her children's dinner. She thought that she had bought the chicken that was pictured on the label. She had enough Crisco now to last a year—but no more money to go back and buy the food for dinner.

Recipes provided on the packages of certain staples sometimes tempt a semiliterate person to prepare a meal her children have not tasted. The longing to vary the uniform and often starchy content of low-budget meals provided to the family that relies on food stamps commonly leads to ruinous results. Scarce funds have been wasted and the food must be thrown out. The same applies to distribution of food-surplus produce in emergency conditions. Government inducements to poor people to "explore the ways" by which to make a tasty meal from tasteless noodles, surplus cheese, and powdered milk are useless to nonreaders. Intended as benevolent advice, such recommendations mock reality and foster deeper feelings of resentment and of inability to cope. (Those, on the other hand, who cautiously refrain from "innovative" recipes in preparation of their children's meals must suffer the opprobrium of "laziness," "lack of imagination. . . .")

Illiterates cannot travel freely. When they attempt to do so, they encounter risks that few of us can dream of. They cannot read traffic signs and, while they often learn to recognize and to decipher symbols, they cannot manage street names which they haven't seen before. The same is true for bus and subway stops. While ingenuity can sometimes help a man or woman to discern directions from familiar landmarks, buildings, cemeteries, churches, and the like, most illiterates are virtually immobilized. They seldom wander past the streets and neighborhoods they know. Geographical paralysis becomes a bitter metaphor for their entire existence. They are immobilized in almost every sense we can imagine. They can't move up. They can't move out. They cannot see beyond. Illiterates may take an oral test for drivers' permits in most sections of America. It is a questionable concession. Where will they go? How will they get there? How will they get home? Could it be that some of us might like it better if they stayed where they belong?

Travel is only one of many instances of circumscribed existence. Choice, in al-   25 most all its facets, is diminished in the life of an illiterate adult. Even the printed TV schedule, which provides most people with the luxury of preselection, does not belong within the arsenal of options in illiterate existence. One consequence is that the viewer watches only what appears at moments when he happens to have time to turn the switch. Another consequence, a lot more common, is that the TV set remains in operation night and day. Whatever the program offered at the hour when he walks into the room will be the nutriment that he accepts and swallows. Thus, to passivity, is added frequency—indeed, almost uninterrupted continuity. Freedom to select is no more possible here than in the choice of home or surgery or food.

"You don't choose," said one illiterate woman. "You take your wishes from somebody else." Whether in perusal of a menu, selection of highways, purchase of groceries, or determination of affordable enjoyment, illiterate Americans must trust somebody else: a friend, a relative, a stranger on the street, a grocery clerk, a TV copywriter.

"All of our mail we get, it's hard for her to read. Settin' down and writing a letter, she can't do it. Like if we get a bill . . . we take it over to my sister-in-law. . . . My sister-in-law reads it."

Billing agencies harass poor people for the payment of the bills for purchases that might have taken place six months before. Utility companies offer an agreement for a staggered payment schedule on a bill past due. "You have to trust them," one man said. Precisely for this reason, you end up by trusting no one and suspecting everyone of possible deceit. A submerged sense of distrust becomes the corollary to a constant need to trust. "They are cheating me . . . I have been tricked . . . I do not know . . ."

Not knowing: This is a familiar theme. Not knowing the right word for the right thing at the right time is one form of subjugation. Not knowing the world that lies concealed behind those words is a more terrifying feeling. The longitude and latitude of one's existence are beyond all easy apprehension. Even the hard, cold stars within the firmament above one's head begin to mock the possibilities for self-location. Where am I? Where did I come from? Where will I go?

"I've lost a lot of jobs," one man explains. "Today, even if you're a janitor,   30 there's still reading and writing. . . . They leave a note saying, 'Go to room so-and-so . . .' You can't do it. You can't read it. You don't know."

"The hardest thing about it is that I've been places where I didn't know where I was. You don't know where you are. . . . You're lost."

"Like I said: I have two kids. What do I do if one of my kids starts choking? I go running to the phone . . . I can't look up the hospital phone number. That's if we're at home. Out on the street, I can't read the sign. I get to a pay phone. 'Okay, tell us where you are. We'll send an ambulance.' I look at the street sign. Right there, I can't tell you what it says. I'd have to spell it out, letter for letter. By that time, one of my kids would be dead. . . . These are the kinds of fears you go with, every single day . . ."

"Reading directions, I suffer with. I work with chemicals. . . . That's scary to begin with . . ."

"You sit down. They throw the menu in front of you. Where do you go from there? Nine times out of ten you say, 'Go ahead. Pick out something for the both of us.' I've eaten some weird things, let me tell you!"

Menus. Chemicals. A child choking while his mother searches for a word she   35
does not know to find assistance that will come too late. Another mother speaks about the inability to help her kids to read: "I can't read to them. Of course that's leaving them out of something they should have. Oh, it matters. You *believe* it matters! I ordered all these books. The kids belong to a book club. Donny wanted me to read a book to him. I told Donny: 'I can't read.' He said: 'Mommy, you sit down. I'll read it to you.' I tried it one day, reading from the pictures. Donny looked at me. He said, 'Mommy, that's not right.' He's only five. He knew I couldn't read . . .'"

A landlord tells a woman that her lease allows him to evict her if her baby cries and causes inconvenience to her neighbors. The consequence of challenging his words conveys a danger which appears, unlikely as it seems, even more alarming than the danger of eviction. Once she admits that she can't read, in the desire to maneuver for the time in which to call a friend, she will have defined herself in terms of an explicit impotence that she cannot endure. Capitulation in this case is preferable to self-humiliation. Resisting the definition of oneself in terms of what one cannot do, what others take for granted, represents a need so great that other imperatives (even one so urgent as the need to keep one's home in winter's cold) evaporate and fall away in face of fear. Even the loss of home and shelter, in this case, is not so terrifying as the loss of self.

"I come out of school. I was sixteen. They had their meetings. The directors meet. They said that I was wasting their school paper. I was wasting pencils . . ."

Another illiterate, looking back, believes she was not worthy of her teacher's time. She believes that it was wrong of her to take up space within her school. She believes that it was right to leave in order that somebody more deserving could receive her place.

Children choke. Their mother chokes another way: on more than chicken bones.

People eat what others order, know what others tell them, struggle not to see   40
themselves as they believe the world perceives them. A man in California speaks about his own loss of identity, of self-location, definition:

"I stood at the bottom of the ramp. My car had broke down on the freeway. There was a phone. I asked for the police. They was nice. They said to tell them where I was. I looked up at the signs. There was one that I had seen before. I read it to them: ONE WAY STREET. They thought it was a joke. I told them I couldn't read. There was other signs above the ramp. They told me to try. I looked around for somebody to help. All the cars was going by real fast. I couldn't make them understand that I was lost. The cop was nice. He told me: 'Try once more.' I did my best. I couldn't read. I only knew the sign above my head. The cop was trying to be nice. He knew that I was trapped. 'I can't send out a car to you if you can't tell me where you are.' I felt afraid. I nearly cried. I'm forty-eight years old. I only said: 'I'm on a one-way street . . .'"

The legal problems and the courtroom complications that confront illiterate adults have been discussed above. The anguish that may underlie such matters was brought home to me this year while I was working on this book. I have spoken, in the introduction, of a sudden phone call from one of my former students, now in prison for a criminal offense. Stephen is not a boy today. He is twenty-eight years old. He called to ask me to assist him in his trial, which comes up next fall. He will be on trial for murder. He has just knifed and killed a man who first enticed him to his home, then cheated him, and then insulted him—as "an illiterate subhuman."

Stephen now faces twenty years to life. Stephen's mother was illiterate. His grandparents were illiterate as well. What parental curse did not destroy was killed off finally by the schools. Silent violence is repaid with interest. It will cost us $25,000 yearly to maintain this broken soul in prison. But what is the price that has been paid by Stephen's victim? What is the price that will be paid by Stephen?

Perhaps we might slow down a moment here and look at the realities described above. This is the nation that we live in. This is a society that most of us did not create but which our President and other leaders have been willing to sustain by virtue of malign neglect. Do we possess the character and courage to address a problem which so many nations, poorer than our own, have found it natural to correct?

The answers to these questions represent a reasonable test of our belief in the   45
democracy to which we have been asked in public school to swear allegiance.

Questions for Discussion and Writing

1. What kinds of limitations beset an illiterate person and limit his or her ability to function in everyday life? What examples best dramatize the costs of illiteracy in personal rather than statistical terms?

2. In Kozol's view, why would an illiterate society be more likely to become less democratic? How persuasive do you find his analysis?

3. Imagine what a typical day in your life would be like if you could not read or write. Keep a record of all your activities, and describe how each would be different if you were illiterate.

MARY CROW DOG

Mary Crow Dog, who took the name Mary Brave Bird, was born in 1956 and grew up on a South Dakota reservation in a one-room cabin without running water or electricity. She joined the new movement of tribal pride sweeping Native American communities in the 1960s and 1970s and was at the siege of Wounded Knee, South Dakota, in 1973. She married the American Indian Movement (AIM) leader Leonard Crow Dog, the movement's chief medicine man. Her powerful autobiography Lakota Woman, *written with Richard Erdoes, one of America's leading writers on Native American affairs and the author of eleven books, became a national best-seller and won the American Book Award for 1991. In it she describes what it was like to grow up a Sioux in a white-dominated society. Her second book,* Ohitka Woman *(1993), also written with Richard Erdoes, continues the story of a woman whose struggle for a sense of self and freedom is a testament to her will and spirit. In "Civilize Them with a Stick" from* Lakota Woman, *the author recounts her experiences as a young student at a boarding school run by the Bureau of Indian Affairs.*

MARY CROW DOG AND RICHARD ERDOES

Civilize Them with a Stick

> Gathered from the cabin, the wickiup, and the tepee,
> partly by cajolery and partly by threats,
> partly by bribery and partly by force,
> they are induced to leave their kindred
> to enter these schools and take upon themselves
> the outward appearance of civilized life.
> —Annual report of the Department of Interior, 1901

It is almost impossible to explain to a sympathetic white person what a typical old Indian boarding school was like; how it affected the Indian child suddenly dumped into it like a small creature from another world, helpless, defenseless, bewildered, trying desperately and instinctively to survive and sometimes not surviving at all. I think such children were like the victims of Nazi concentration camps trying to tell average, middle-class Americans what their experience had been like. Even now, when these schools are much improved, when the buildings are new, all gleaming steel and glass, the food tolerable, the teachers well trained and well intentioned, even trained in child psychology—unfortunately the psychology of white children, which is different from ours—the shock to the child upon arrival is still tremendous. Some just seem to shrivel up, don't speak for days on end, and have an empty look in their eyes. I know of an eleven-year-old on another reservation who hanged herself, and in our school, while I was there, a girl jumped out of the window, trying to kill herself to escape an unbearable situation. That first shock is always there. . . .

The mission school at St. Francis was a curse for our family for generations. My grandmother went there, then my mother, then my sisters and I. At one time or other every one of us tried to run away. Grandma told me once about the bad times she had experienced at St. Francis. In those days they let students go home only for one week every year. Two days were used up for transportation, which meant spending just five days out of three hundred and sixty-five with her family. And that was an improvement. Before grandma's time, on many reservations they did not let the students go home at all until they had finished school. Anybody who disobeyed the nuns was severely punished. The building in which my grandmother stayed had three floors, for girls only. Way up in the attic were little cells, about five by five by ten feet. One time she was in church and instead of praying she was playing jacks. As punishment they took her to one of those little cubicles where she stayed in darkness because the windows had been boarded up. They left her there for a whole week with only bread and water for nourishment. After she came out she promptly ran away, together with three other girls. They were found and brought back. The nuns stripped them naked and whipped them. They used a horse buggy whip on my grandmother. Then she was put back into the attic—for two weeks.

My mother had much the same experiences but never wanted to talk about them, and then there I was, in the same place. The school is now run by the BIA—the Bureau of Indian Affairs—but only since about fifteen years ago. When I was there, during the 1960s, it was still run by the Church. The Jesuit fathers ran the boys' wing and the Sisters of the Sacred Heart ran us—with the help of the strap. Nothing had changed since my grandmother's days. I have been told recently that even in the '70s they were still beating children at that school. All I got out of school was being taught how to pray. I learned quickly that I would be beaten if I failed in my devotions or, God forbid, prayed the wrong way, especially prayed in Indian to Wakan Tanka, the Indian Creator.

The girls' wing was built like an F and was run like a penal institution. Every morning at five o'clock the sisters would come into our large dormitory to wake us up, and immediately we had to kneel down at the sides of our beds and recite the prayers. At six o'clock we were herded into the church for more of the same. I did not take kindly to the discipline and to marching by the clock, left-right, left-right. I was never one to like being forced to do something. I do something because I feel like doing it. I felt this way always, as far as I can remember, and my sister Barbara felt the same way. An old medicine man once told me: "Us Lakotas are not like dogs who can be trained, who can be beaten and keep on wagging their tails, licking the hand that whipped them. We are like cats, little cats, big cats, wildcats, bobcats, mountain lions. It doesn't matter what kind, but cats who can't be tamed, who scratch if you step on their tails." But I was only a kitten and my claws were still small.

Barbara was still in the school when I arrived and during my first year or two she could still protect me a little bit. When Barb was a seventh-grader she ran away together with five other girls, early in the morning before sunrise. They brought them back in the evening. The girls had to wait for two hours in front of the

5

mother superior's office. They were hungry and cold, frozen through. It was wintertime and they had been running the whole day without food, trying to make good their escape. The mother superior asked each girl, "Would you do this again?" She told them that as punishment they would not be allowed to visit home for a month and that she'd keep them busy on work details until the skin on their knees and elbows had worn off. At the end of her speech she told each girl, "Get up from this chair and lean over it." She then lifted the girls' skirts and pulled down their underpants. Not little girls either, but teenagers. She had a leather strap about a foot long and four inches wide fastened to a stick, and beat the girls, one after another, until they cried. Barb did not give her that satisfaction but just clenched her teeth. There was one girl, Barb told me, the nun kept on beating and beating until her arm got tired.

I did not escape my share of the strap. Once, when I was thirteen years old, I refused to go to Mass. I did not want to go to church because I did not feel well. A nun grabbed me by the hair, dragged me upstairs, made me stoop over, pulled my dress up (we were not allowed at the time to wear jeans), pulled my panties down, and gave me what they called "swats"—twenty-five swats with a board around which Scotch tape had been wound. She hurt me badly.

My classroom was right next to the principal's office and almost every day I could hear him swatting the boys. Beating was the common punishment for not doing one's homework, or for being late to school. It had such a bad effect upon me that I hated and mistrusted every white person on sight, because I met only one kind. It was not until much later that I met sincere white people I could relate to and be friends with. Racism breeds racism in reverse.

The routine at St. Francis was dreary. Six A.M., kneeling in church for an hour or so; seven o'clock, breakfast, eight o'clock, scrub the floor, peel spuds, make classes. We had to mop the dining room twice every day and scrub the tables. If you were caught taking a rest, doodling on the bench with a fingernail or knife, or just rapping, the nun would come up with a dish towel and just slap it across your face, saying, "You're not supposed to be talking, you're supposed to be working!" Monday mornings we had cornmeal mush, Tuesday oatmeal, Wednesday rice and raisins, Thursday cornflakes, and Friday all the leftovers mixed together or sometimes fish. Frequently the food had bugs or rocks in it. We were eating hot dogs that were weeks old, while the nuns were dining on ham, whipped potatoes, sweet peas, and cranberry sauce. In winter our dorm was icy cold while the nuns' rooms were always warm.

I have seen little girls arrive at the school, first-graders, just fresh from home and totally unprepared for what awaited them, little girls with pretty braids, and the first thing the nuns did was chop their hair off and tie up what was left behind their ears. Next they would dump the children into tubs of alcohol, a sort of rubbing alcohol, "to get the germs off." Many of the nuns were German immigrants, some from Bavaria, so that we sometimes speculated whether Bavaria was some sort of Dracula country inhabited by monsters. For the sake of objectivity I ought to mention that two of the German fathers were great linguists and that the only Lakota–English dictionaries and grammars which are worth anything were put together by them.

At night some of the girls would huddle in bed together for comfort and re- 10
assurance. Then the nun in charge of the dorm would come in and say, "What are
the two of you doing in bed together? I smell evil in this room. You girls are evil incarnate. You are sinning. You are going to hell and burn forever. You can act that
way in the devil's frying pan." She would get them out of bed in the middle of the
night, making them kneel and pray until morning. We had not the slightest idea
what it was all about. At home we slept two and three in a bed for animal warmth
and a feeling of security.

The nuns and the girls in the two top grades were constantly battling it out
physically with fists, nails, and hair-pulling. I myself was growing from a kitten into
an undersized cat. My claws were getting bigger and were itching for action. About
1969 or 1970 a strange young white girl appeared on the reservation. She looked
about eighteen or twenty years old. She was pretty and had long, blond hair down
to her waist, patched jeans, boots, and a backpack. She was different from any other
white person we had met before. I think her name was Wise. I do not know how
she managed to overcome our reluctance and distrust, getting us into a corner,
making us listen to her, asking us how we were treated. She told us that she was
from New York. She was the first real hippie or Yippie we had come across. She
told us of people called the Black Panthers, Young Lords, and Weathermen. She
said, "Black people are getting it on. Indians are getting it on in St. Paul and California. How about you?" She also said, "Why don't you put out an underground
paper, mimeograph it. It's easy. Tell it like it is. Let it all hang out." She spoke a
strange lingo but we caught on fast.

Charlene Left Hand Bull and Gina One Star were two full-blood girls I used
to hang out with. We did everything together. They were willing to join me in a
Sioux uprising. We put together a newspaper which we called the *Red Panther*. In it
we wrote how bad the school was, what kind of slop we had to eat—slimy, rotten,
blackened potatoes for two weeks—the way we were beaten. I think I was the one
who wrote the worst article about our principal of the moment, Father Keeler. I
put all my anger and venom into it. I called him a goddam wasicun son of a bitch.
I wrote that he knew nothing about Indians and should go back to where he came
from, teaching white children whom he could relate to. I wrote that we knew
which priests slept with which nuns and that all they ever could think about was
filling their bellies and buying a new car. It was the kind of writing which foamed
at the mouth, but which also lifted a great deal of weight from one's soul.

On Saint Patrick's Day, when everybody was at the big powwow, we distributed our newspapers. We put them on windshields and bulletin boards, in desks and
pews, in dorms and toilets. But someone saw us and snitched on us. The shit hit the
fan. The three of us were taken before a board meeting. Our parents, in my case my
mother, had to come. They were told that ours was a most serious matter, the worst
thing that had ever happened in the school's long history. One of the nuns told my
mother, "Your daughter really needs to be talked to." "What's wrong with my daughter?" my mother asked. She was given one of our *Red Panther* newspapers. The nun
pointed out its name to her and then my piece, waiting for mom's reaction. After a
while she asked, "Well, what have you got to say to this? What do you think?"

My mother said, "Well, when I went to school here, some years back, I was treated a lot worse then these kids are. I really can't see how they can have any complaints, because we was treated a lot stricter. We could not even wear skirts halfway up our knees. These girls have it made. But you should forgive them because they are young. And it's supposed to be a free country, free speech and all that. I don't believe what they done is wrong." So all I got out of it was scrubbing six flights of stairs on my hands and knees, every day. And no boy-side privileges.

The boys and girls were still pretty much separated. The only time one could 15 meet a member of the opposite sex was during free time, between four and five-thirty, in the study hall or on benches or the volleyball court outside, and that was strictly supervised. One day Charlene and I went over to the boys' side. We were on the ball team and they had to let us practice. We played three extra minutes, only three minutes more than we were supposed to. Here was the nuns' opportunity for revenge. We got twenty-five swats. I told Charlene, "We are getting too old to have our bare asses whipped that way. We are old enough to have babies. Enough of this shit. Next time we fight back." Charlene only said, "Hoka-hay!"

We had to take showers every evening. One little girl did not want to take her panties off and one of the nuns told her, "You take those underpants off—or else!" But the child was ashamed to do it. The nun was getting her swat to threaten the girl. I went up to the sister, pushed her veil off, and knocked her down. I told her that if she wanted to hit a little girl she should pick on me, pick one her own size. She got herself transferred out of the dorm a week later.

In a school like this there is always a lot of favoritism. At St. Francis it was strongly tinged with racism. Girls who were near-white, who came from what the nuns called "nice families," got preferential treatment. They waited on the faculty and got to eat ham or eggs and bacon in the morning. They got the easy jobs while the skins, who did not have the right kind of background—myself among them—always wound up in the laundry room sorting out ten bushel baskets of dirty boys' socks every day. Or we wound up scrubbing the floors and doing all the dishes. The school therefore fostered fights and antagonism between whites and breeds, and between breeds and skins. At one time Charlene and I had to iron all the robes and vestments the priests wore when saying Mass. We had to fold them up and put them into a chest in the back of the church. In a corner, looking over our shoulders, was a statue of the crucified Savior, all bloody and beaten up. Charlene looked up and said, "Look at that poor Indian. The pigs sure worked him over." That was the closest I ever came to seeing Jesus.

I was held up as a bad example and didn't mind. I was old enough to have a boyfriend and promptly got one. At the school we had an hour and a half for ourselves. Between the boys' and the girls' wings were some benches where one could sit. My boyfriend and I used to go there just to hold hands and talk. The nuns were very uptight about any boy–girl stuff. They had an exaggerated fear of anything having even the faintest connection with sex. One day in religion class, an all-girl class, Sister Bernard singled me out for some remarks, pointing me out as a bad example, an example that should be shown. She said that I was too free with my body. That I was holding hands which meant that I was not a good example to follow.

She also said that I wore unchaste dresses, skirts which were too short, too suggestive, shorter than regulations permitted, and for that I would be punished. She
dressed me down before the whole class, carrying on and on about my unchastity.

I stood up and told her, "You shouldn't say any of those things, miss. You people are a lot worse than us Indians. I know all about you, because my grandmother
and my aunt told me about you. Maybe twelve, thirteen years ago you had a water
stoppage here in St. Francis. No water could get through the pipes. There are water
lines right under the mission, underground tunnels and passages where in my
grandmother's time only the nuns and priests could go, which were off-limits to
everybody else. When the water backed up they had to go through all the water
lines and clean them out. And in those huge pipes they found the bodies of newborn babies. And they were white babies. They weren't Indian babies. At least when
our girls have babies, they don't do away with them that way, like flushing them
down the toilet, almost.

"And that priest they sent here from Holy Rosary in Pine Ridge because he   20
molested a little girl. You couldn't think of anything better than dump him on us.
All he does is watch young women and girls with that funny smile on his face. Why
don't you point him out for an example?"

Charlene and I worked on the school newspaper. After all we had some practice. Every day we went down to Publications. One of the priests acted as the photographer, doing the enlarging and developing. He smelled of chemicals which had
stained his hands yellow. One day he invited Charlene into the darkroom. He was
going to teach her developing. She was developed already. She was a big girl compared to him, taller too. Charlene was nicely built, not fat, just rounded. No sharp
edges anywhere: All of a sudden she rushed out of the darkroom, yelling to me,
"Let's get out of here! He's trying to feel me up. That priest is nasty." So there was
this too to contend with—sexual harassment. We complained to the student body.
The nuns said we just had a dirty mind.

We got a new priest in English. During one of his first classes he asked one of
the boys a certain question. The boy was shy. He spoke poor English, but he had the
right answer. The priest told him, "You did not say it right. Correct yourself. Say it
over again." The boy got flustered and stammered. He could hardly get out a word.
But the priest kept after him: "Didn't you hear? I told you to do the whole thing
over. Get it right this time." He kept on and on.

I stood up and said, "Father, don't be doing that. If you go into an Indian's
home and try to talk Indian, they might laugh at you and say. 'Do it over correctly.
Get it right this time!'"

He shouted at me, "Mary, you stay after class. Sit down right now!"

I stayed after class, until after the bell. He told me, "Get over here!"   25

He grabbed me by the arm, pushing me against the blackboard, shouting.
"Why you always mocking us? You have no reason to do this."

I said, "Sure I do. You were making fun of him. You embarrassed him. He
needs strengthening, not weakening. You hurt him. I did not hurt you."

He twisted my arm and pushed real hard. I turned around and hit him in the
face, giving him a bloody nose. After that I ran out of the room, slamming the door

behind me. He and I went to Sister Bernard's office. I told her, "Today I quit school. I'm not taking any more of this, none of this shit anymore. None of this treatment. Better give me my diploma. I can't waste any more time on you people."

Sister Bernard looked at me for a long, long time. She said, "All right, Mary Ellen, go home today. Come back in a few days and get your diploma." And that was that. Oddly enough, that priest turned out okay. He taught a class in grammar, orthography, composition, things like that. I think he wanted more respect in class. He was still young and unsure of himself. But I was in there too long. I didn't feel like hearing it. Later he became a good friend of the Indians, a personal friend of myself and my husband. He stood up for us during Wounded Knee[1] and after. He stood up to his superiors, stuck his neck way out, became a real people's priest. He even learned our language. He died prematurely of cancer. It is not only the good Indians who die young, but the good whites, too. It is the timid ones who know how to take care of themselves who grow old. I am still grateful to that priest for what he did for us later and for the quarrel he picked with me—or did I pick it with him?—because it ended a situation which had become unendurable for me. The day of my fight with him was my last day in school.

Questions for Discussion and Writing

1. How does the way the government operated the boarding school suggest what is meant by "civilizing" Native Americans?

2. How do the experiences of Mary Crow Dog's mother and grandmother add a historical dimension to her present-day experiences? What do these imply about a long-standing official governmental attitude toward Native Americans?

3. How did Mary Crow Dog react to the experiences to which she was subjected? Why was the incident of the underground newspaper so crucial?

RICHARD RODRIGUEZ

Richard Rodriguez was born in 1944 in San Francisco, where he grew up as a child of Spanish-speaking Mexican-American parents. Rodriguez pursued graduate studies at the University of California at Berkeley and received a Fulbright fellowship to the Warburg Institute in London to study English Renaissance literature. He is an editor at Pacific News Service and in 1997 received the George Foster Peabody Award for his NewsHour essays on American life. His

---

[1] *Wounded Knee:* Originally, a battle that took place in 1890 between Sioux Indians and U.S. troops. The author refers to the 1973 uprising of the Lakota Indians against the Federal Bureau of Investigation in South Dakota at the same location.

autobiography, Hunger of Memory: The Education of Richard Rodriguez *(1982), received the Christopher Award. He has also written* Days of Obligation: An Argument with My Mexican Father *(1992) and many articles for* The Wall Street Journal, The New York Times, The American Scholar, Time, *and other publications.* "On Becoming a Chicano" *reveals his sense of estrangement from his culture when he entered an academic English-speaking environment.*

On Becoming a Chicano

Today I am only technically the person I once felt myself to be—a Mexican-American, a Chicano. Partly because I had no way of comprehending my racial identity except in this technical sense, I gave up long ago the cultural consequences of being a Chicano.

The change came gradually but early. When I was beginning grade school, I noted to myself the fact that the classroom environment was so different in its styles and assumptions from my own family environment that survival would essentially entail a choice between both worlds. When I became a student, I was literally "remade"; neither I nor my teachers considered anything I had known before as relevant. I had to forget most of what my culture had provided, because to remember it was a disadvantage. The past and its cultural values became detachable, like a piece of clothing grown heavy on a warm day and finally put away.

Strangely, the discovery that I have been inattentive to my cultural past has arisen because others—student colleagues and faculty members—have started to assume that I am a Chicano. The ease with which the assumption is made forces me to suspect that the label is not meant to suggest cultural, but racial, identity. Nonetheless, as a graduate student and a prospective university faculty member, I am routinely expected to assume intellectual leadership *as a member of a racial minority.* Recently, for example, I heard the moderator of a panel discussion introduce me as "Richard Rodriguez, a Chicano intellectual." I wanted to correct the speaker—because I felt guilty representing a non-academic cultural tradition that I had willingly abandoned. So I can only guess what it would have meant to have retained my culture as I entered the classroom, what it would mean for me to be today a "Chicano intellectual." (The two words juxtaposed excite me; for years I thought a Chicano had to decide between being one or the other.)

Does the fact that I barely spoke any English until I was nine, or that as a child I felt a surge of self-hatred whenever a passing teenager would yell a racial slur, or that I saw my skin darken each summer—do any of these facts shape the ideas which I have or am capable of having? Today, I suspect they do—in ways I doubt the moderator who referred to me as a "Chicano intellectual" intended. The peculiar status of being a "Chicano intellectual" makes me grow restless at the thought that I have lost at least as much as I have gained through education.

I remember when, 20 years ago, two grammar-school nuns visited my childhood home. They had come to suggest—with more tact than was necessary, because my parents accepted without question the church's authority—that we make a

5

greater effort to speak as much English around the house as possible. The nuns realized that my brothers and I led solitary lives largely because we were barely able to comprehend English in a school where we were the only Spanish-speaking students. My mother and father complied as best they could. Heroically, they gave up speaking to us in Spanish—the language that formed so much of the family's sense of intimacy in an alien world—and began to speak a broken English. Instead of Spanish sounds, I began hearing sounds that were new, harder, less friendly. More important, I was encouraged to respond in English.

The change in language was the most dramatic and obvious indication that I would become very much like the "gringo"—a term which was used descriptively rather than perjoratively in my home—and unlike the Spanish-speaking relatives who largely constituted my preschool world. Gradually, Spanish became a sound freighted with only a kind of sentimental significance, like the sound of the bedroom clock I listened to in my aunt's house when I spent the night. Just as gradually, English became the language I came not to *hear* because it was the language I used every day, as I gained access to a new, larger society. But the memory of Spanish persisted as a reminder of the society I had left. I can remember occasions when I entered a room and my parents were speaking to one another in Spanish; seeing me they shifted into their more formalized English. Hearing them speak to me in English troubled me. The bonds their voices once secured were loosened by the new tongue.

This is not to suggest that I was being *forced* to give up my Chicano past. After the initial awkwardness of transition, I committed myself, fully and freely, to the culture of the classroom. Soon what I was learning in school was so antithetical to what my parents knew and did that I was careful about the way I talked about myself at the evening dinner table. Occasionally, there were moments of childish cruelty: a son's condescending to instruct either one of his parents about a "simple" point of English pronunciation or grammar.

Social scientists often remark, about situations such as mine, that children feel a sense of loss as they move away from their working-class identifications and models. Certainly, what I experienced, others have also—whatever their race. Like other generations of, say, Polish-American or Irish-American children coming home from college, I was to know the silence that ensues so quickly after the quick exchange of news and the dwindling of common interests.

In addition, however, education seemed to mean not only a gradual dissolving of familial and class ties but also a change of racial identity. The new language I spoke was only the most obvious reason for my associating the classroom with "gringo" society. The society I knew as Chicano was barely literate—in English *or* Spanish—and so impatient with either prolonged reflection or abstraction that I found the academic environment a sharp contrast. Sharpening the contrast was the stereotype of the Mexican as a mental inferior. (The fear of this stereotype has been so deep that only recently have I been willing to listen to those, like D. H. Lawrence, who celebrate the "non-cerebral" Mexican as an alternative to the rational and scientific European man.) Because I did not know how to distinguish the healthy non-rationality of Chicano culture from the mental incompetency of which Chicanos were unjustly accused, I was willing to abandon my non-mental skiffs in order to disprove the racist's stereotype.

I was wise enough not to feel proud of the person education had helped me   10
to become. I knew that education had led me to repudiate my race. I was frequently labeled a *pocho,* a Mexican with gringo pretentions, not only because I
could not speak Spanish but also because I would respond in English with precise
and careful sentences. Uncles would laugh good-naturedly, but I detected scorn in
their voices. For my grandmother, the least assimilated of my relations, the changes
in her grandson since entering school were expecially troubling. She remains today
a dark and silently critical figure in my memory, a reminder of the Mexican-Indian
ancestry that somehow my educational success has violated.

Nonetheless, I became more comfortable reading or writing careful prose
than talking to a kitchen filled with listeners, withdrawing from situations to reflect
on their significance rather than grasping for meaning at the scene. I remember,
one August evening, slipping away from a gathering of aunts and uncles in the
backyard, going into a bedroom tenderly lighted by a late sun, and opening a novel
about life in nineteenth-century England. There, by an open window, reading, I
was barely conscious of the sounds of laughter outside.

With so few fellow Chicanos in the university, I had no chance to develop an
alternative consciousness. When I spent occasional weekends tutoring lower-class
Chicano teenagers or when I talked with Mexican-American janitors and maids
around the campus, there was a kind of sympathy—a sense, however privately
held—that we knew something about one another. But I regarded them all primarily as people from my past. The maids reminded me of my aunts (similarly employed); the students I tutored reminded me of my cousins (who also spoke English
with barrio accents).

When I was young, I was taught to refer to my ancestry as Mexican-American.
Chicano was a word used among friends or relatives. It implied a familiarity based on
shared experience. Spoken casually, the term easily became an insult. In 1968 the
word *Chicano* was about to become a political term. I heard it shouted into micro-
phones as Third World groups agitated for increased student and faculty representation in higher education. It was not long before I *became* a Chicano in the eyes of
students and faculty members. My racial identity was assumed for only the simplest
reasons: my skin color and last name.

On occasion I was asked to account for my interests in Renaissance English
literature. When I explained them, declaring a need for cultural assimilation, on the
campus, my listener would disagree. I sensed suspicion on the part of a number of
my fellow minority students. When I could not imitate Spanish pronunciations or
the dialect of the barrio, when I was plainly uninterested in wearing ethnic costumes and could not master a special handshake that minority students often used
with one another, they knew I was different. And I was. I was assimilated into the
culture of a graduate department of English. As a result, I watched how in less than
five years nearly every minority graduate student I knew dropped out of school,
largely for cultural reasons. Often they didn't understand the value of analyzing literature in professional jargon, which others around them readily adopted. Nor did
they move as readily to lofty heights of abstraction. They became easily depressed

by the seeming uselessness of talk they heard around them. "It's not for real," I still hear a minority student murmur to herself and perhaps to me, shaking her head slowly, as we sat together in a class listening to a discussion on punctuation in a Renaissance epic.

I survived—thanks to the accommodation I had made long before. In fact, I prospered, partly as a result of the political movement designed to increase the enrollment of minority students less assimilated than I in higher education. Suddenly grants, fellowships, and teaching offers became abundant. 15

In 1972 I went to England on a Fulbright scholarship. I hoped the months of brooding about racial identity were behind me. I wanted to concentrate on my dissertation, which the distractions of an American campus had not permitted. But the freedom I anticipated did not last for long. Barely a month after I had begun working regularly in the reading room of the British Museum, I was surprised, and even frightened, to have to acknowledge that I was not at ease living the rarefied life of the academic. With my pile of research file cards growing taller, the mass of secondary materials and opinions was making it harder for me to say anything original about my subject. Every sentence I wrote, every thought I had, became so loaded with qualifications and footnotes that it said very little. My scholarship became little more than an exercise in caution. I had an accompanying suspicion that whatever I did manage to write and call my dissertation would be of little use. Opening books so dusty that they must not have been used in decades, I began to doubt the value of writing what only a few people would read.

Obviously, I was going through the fairly typical crisis of the American graduate student. But with one difference: After four years of involvement with questions of racial identity, I now saw my problems as a scholar in the context of the cultural issues that had been raised by my racial situation. So much of what my work in the British Museum lacked, my parents' culture possessed. They were people not afraid to generalize or to find insights in their generalities. More important, they had the capacity to make passionate statements, something I was beginning to doubt my dissertation would ever allow me to do. I needed to learn how to trust the use of "I" in my writing the way they trusted its use in their speech. Thus developed a persistent yearning for the very Chicano culture that I had abandoned as useless.

Feelings of depression came occasionally but forcefully. Some days I found my work so oppressive that I had to leave the reading room and stroll through the museum. One afternoon, appropriately enough, I found myself in an upstairs gallery containing Mayan and Aztec sculptures. Even there the sudden yearning for a Chicano past seemed available to me only as nostalgia. One morning, as I was reading a book about Puritan autobiography, I overheard two Spaniards whispering to one another. I did not hear what they said, but I did hear the sound of their Spanish—and it embraced me, filling my mind with swirling images of a past long abandoned.

I returned from England, disheartened, a few months later. My dissertation was coming along well, but I did not know whether I wanted to submit it. Worse, I did not know whether I wanted a career in higher education. I detested the prospect of spending the rest of my life in libraries and classrooms, in touch with my past only through the binoculars nostalgia makes available. I knew that I could not simply recreate a version of what I would have been like had I not become an academic. There was no possibility of going back. But if the culture of my birth was to survive, it would have to animate my academic work. That was the lesson of the British Museum.

I frankly do not know how my academic autobiography will end. Sometimes I think I will have to leave the campus, in order to reconcile my past and present. Other times, more optimistically, I think that a kind of negative reconciliation is already in progress, that I can make creative use of my sense of loss. For instance, with my sense of the cleavage between past and present, I can, as a literary critic, identify issues in Renaissance pastoral—a literature which records the feelings of the courtly when confronted by the alternatives of rural and rustic life. And perhaps I can speak with unusual feeling about the price we must pay, or have paid, as a rational society for confessing seventeenth-century Cartesian[1] faiths. Likewise, because of my sense of cultural loss, I may be able to identify more readily than another the ways in which language has meaning simply as sound and what the printed word can and cannot give us. At the very least, I can point up the academy's tendency to ignore the cultures beyond its own horizons.

February 1974

On my job interview the department chairman has been listening to an oral version of what I have just written. I tell him he should be very clear about the fact that I am not, at the moment, confident enough to call myself a Chicano. Perhaps I never will be. But as I say all this, I look at the interviewer. He smiles softly. Has he heard what I have been trying to say? I wonder. I repeat: I have lost the ability to bring my past into my present; I do not know how to be a Chicano reader of Spenser or Shakespeare. All that remains is a desire for the past. He sighs, preoccupied, looking at my records. Would I be interested in teaching a course on the Mexican novel in translation? Do I understand that part of my duties would require that I become a counselor of minority students? What was the subject of that dissertation I did in England? Have I read the book on the same subject that was just published this month?

Behind the questioner, a figure forms in my imagination: my grandmother, her face solemn and still.

Questions for Discussion and Writing

1. How did working on his dissertation in England reinforce a sense of lost contact with his Hispanic heritage that Rodriguez first experienced in grade school? How does the title express his need to repossess those values he had once discarded?

---

[1] *Cartesian:* refers to René Descartes (1596–1650), the French philosopher who emphasized rationalization and logic and extended mathematical methods to all fields of human knowledge. He is known for the phrase "I think, therefore I am."

2. Of what advantage is it to Rodriguez to organize his essay employing extended comparisons and contrasts?

3. In a short essay, discuss the advantages and disadvantages of permitting students to use Spanish or some other native language in school rather than English.

WILLIAM A. HENRY III

William A. Henry III (1950–1994) was the drama critic for Time *magazine and frequently wrote on social issues. Henry's belief that an antielitist trend in American society has debased higher education is developed in his last book,* In Defense of Elitism *(1994). The following excerpt from this book first appeared in the August 29, 1994, issue of* Time.

In Defense of Elitism

While all the major social changes in post-war America reflect egalitarianism of some sort, no social evolution has been more willfully egalitarian than opening the academy. Half a century ago, a high school diploma was a significant credential, and college was a privilege for the few. Now high school graduation is virtually automatic for adolescents outside the ghettos and barrios, and college has become a normal way station in the average person's growing up. No longer a mark of distinction or proof of achievement, a college education is these days a mere rite of passage, a capstone to adolescent party time.

Some 63% of all American high school graduates now go on to some form of further education, according to the Department of Commerce's *Statistical Abstract of the United States,* and the bulk of those continuing students attain at least an associate's degree. Nearly 30% of high school graduates ultimately receive a four-year baccalaureate degree. A quarter or so of the population may seem, to egalitarian eyes, a small and hence elitist slice. But by world standards this is inclusiveness at its most extreme—and its most peculiarly American.

For all the socialism of British or French public policy and for all the paternalism of the Japanese, those nations restrict university training to a much smaller percentage of their young, typically 10% to 15%. Moreover, they and other First World nations tend to carry the elitism over into judgments about precisely which institution one attends. They rank their universities, colleges and technical schools along a prestige hierarchy much more rigidly gradated—and judged by standards much more widely accepted—than Americans ever impose on their jumble of public and private institutions.

In the sharpest divergence from American values, these other countries tend to separate the college-bound from the quotidian masses[1] in early adolescence,

---

[1] *quotidian masses:* common, standard, or ordinary.

with scant hope for a second chance. For them, higher education is logically confined to those who displayed the most aptitude for lower education.

The opening of the academy's doors has imposed great economic costs on the American people while delivering dubious benefits to many of the individuals supposedly being helped. The total bill for higher education is about $150 billion per year, with almost two-thirds of that spent by public institutions run with taxpayer funds. Private colleges and universities also spend the public's money. They get grants for research and the like, and they serve as a conduit for subsidized student loans—many of which are never fully repaid. President Clinton refers to this sort of spending as an investment in human capital. If that is so, it seems reasonable to ask whether the investment pays a worthwhile rate of return. At its present size, the American style of mass higher education probably ought to be judged a mistake—and one based on a giant lie.

Why do people go to college? Mostly to make money. This reality is acknowledged in the mass media, which are forever running stories and charts showing how much a college degree contributes to lifetime income (with the more sophisticated publications very occasionally noting the counterweight costs of tuition paid and income forgone during the years of full-time study).

But the equation between college and wealth is not so simple. College graduates unquestionably do better on average economically than those who don't go at all. At the extremes, those with five or more years of college earn about triple the income of those with eight or fewer years of total schooling. Taking more typical examples, one finds that those who stop their educations after earning a four-year degree earn about 1 1/2 times as much as those who stop at the end of high school. These outcomes, however, reflect other things besides the impact of the degree itself. College graduates are winners in part because colleges attract people who are already winners—people with enough brains and drive that they would do well in almost any generation and under almost any circumstances, with or without formal credentialing.

The harder and more meaningful question is whether the mediocrities who have also flooded into colleges in the past couple of generations do better than they otherwise would have. And if they do, is it because college actually made them better employees or because it simply gave them the requisite credential to get interviewed and hired? The U.S. Labor Department's Bureau of Labor Statistics reports that about 20% of all college graduates toil in fields not requiring a degree, and this total is projected to exceed 30% by the year 2005. For the individual, college may well be a credential without being a qualification, required without being requisite.

For American society, the big lie underlying higher education is akin to Garrison Keillor's description of the children in Lake Wobegon:[2] they are all above average. In the unexamined American Dream rhetoric promoting mass higher

---

[2] *Lake Wobegon:* an imaginary and idealized town in Minnesota known to listeners of the national weekly radio show *A Prairie Home Companion* hosted by Garrison Keillor.

education in the nation of my youth, the implicit vision was that one day everyone, or at least practically everyone, would be a manager or a professional. We would use the most elitist of all means, scholarship, toward the most egalitarian of ends. We would all become chiefs; hardly anyone would be left a mere Indian. On the surface, this New Jerusalem appears to have arrived. Where half a century ago the bulk of jobs were blue collar, now a majority are white or pink collar. They are performed in an office instead of on a factory floor. If they still tend to involve repetition and drudgery, at least they do not require heavy lifting.

But the wages for them are going down virtually as often as up. And as a great   10 many disappointed office workers have discovered, being better educated and better dressed at the workplace does not transform one's place in the pecking order. There are still plenty more Indians than chiefs. Lately, indeed, the chiefs are becoming even fewer. The major focus of the "downsizing" of recent years has been eliminating layers of middle management—much of it drawn from the ranks of those lured to college a generation or two ago by the idea that a degree would transform them from the mediocre to magisterial.

Yet U.S. colleges blithely go on "educating" many more prospective managers and professionals than the country is likely to need. In my own field, there are typically more students majoring in journalism at any given moment than there are journalists employed at all the daily newspapers in the U.S. A few years ago, there were more students enrolled in law school than there were partners in all law firms. As trends shift, there have been periodic oversupplies of M.B.A.-wielding financial analysts, of grade school and high school teachers, of computer programmers, even of engineers. Inevitably many students of limited talent spend huge amounts of time and money pursuing some brass-ring occupation, only to see their dreams denied. As a society America considers it cruel not to give them every chance at success. It may be more cruel to let them go on fooling themselves.

Just when it should be clear that the U.S. is already probably doing too much to entice people into college, Bill Clinton is suggesting it do even more. In February 1994, for example, the President asserted that America needs a greater fusion between academic and vocational training in high school—not because too many mediocre people misplaced on the college track are failing to acquire marketable vocational skills, but because too many people on the vocational track are being denied courses that will secure them admission to college. Surely what Americans need is not a fusion of the two tracks but a sharper division between them, coupled with a forceful program for diverting intellectual also-rans out of the academic track and into the vocational one. That is where most of them are heading in life anyway. Why should they wait until they are older and must enroll in high-priced proprietary vocational programs of often dubious efficacy—frequently throwing away not only their own funds but federal loans in the process—because they emerged from high school heading nowhere and knowing nothing that is useful in the marketplace?

If the massive numbers of college students reflected a national boom in love of learning and a prevalent yen for self-improvement, America's investment in the classroom might make sense. There are introspective qualities that can enrich any society in ways beyond the material. But one need look no further than the curricular wars to understand that most students are not looking to broaden their spiritual or intellectual horizons. Consider three basic trends, all of them implicit rejections of intellectual adventure. First, students are demanding courses that reflect and affirm their own identities in the most literal way. Rather than read a Greek dramatist of 2,000 years ago and thrill to the discovery that some ideas and emotions are universal, many insist on reading writers of their own gender or ethnicity or sexual preference, ideally writers of the present or the recent past.

The second trend, implicit in the first, is that the curriculum has shifted from being what professors desire to teach to being what students desire to learn. Nowadays colleges have to hustle for students by truckling trendily. If the students want media-studies programs so they can all fantasize about becoming TV news anchors, then media studies will abound. There are in any given year some 300,000 students enrolled in undergraduate communications courses.

Of even greater significance than the solipsism of students and the pusillanimity of teachers is the third trend, the sheer decline in the amount and quality of work expected in class. In an egalitarian environment the influx of mediocrities relentlessly lowers the general standards at colleges to levels the weak ones can meet. When my mother went to Trinity College in Washington in the early 1940s, at a time when it was regarded more as a finishing school for nice Catholic girls than a temple of discipline, an English major there was expected to be versed in Latin, Anglo-Saxon and medieval French. A course in Shakespeare meant reading the plays, all 37 of them. In today's indulgent climate, a professor friend at a fancy college told me as I was writing this chapter, taking a half semester of Shakespeare compels students to read exactly four plays. "Anything more than one a week," he explained, "is considered too heavy a load."

This probably should not be thought surprising in an era when most colleges, even prestigious ones, run some sort of remedial program for freshmen to learn the reading and writing skills they ought to have developed in junior high school—not to mention an era when many students vociferously object to being marked down for spelling or grammar. Indeed, all the media attention paid to curriculum battles at Stanford, Dartmouth and the like obscures the even bleaker reality of American higher education. As Russell Jacoby points out in his book *Dogmatic Wisdom,* most students are enrolled at vastly less demanding institutions, where any substantial reading list would be an improvement.

My modest proposal is this: Let us reduce, over perhaps a five-year span, the number of high school graduates who go on to college from nearly 60% to a still generous 33%. This will mean closing a lot of institutions. Most of them, in my view, should be community colleges, current or former state teachers' colleges and the like. These schools serve the academically marginal and would be better replaced by vocational training in high school and on-the-job training at work. Two standards should apply in judging which schools to shut down. First, what is the general academic level attained by the student body? That might be assessed in a rough-and-ready way by requiring any institution wishing to survive to give a standardized test—say, the Graduate Record Examination—to all its seniors. Those schools whose students perform below the state norm would face cutbacks or closing. Second, what community is being served? A school that serves a high percentage of disadvantaged students (this ought to be measured by family finances rather than just race or ethnicity) can make a better case for receiving tax dollars than one that subsidizes the children of the prosperous, who have private alternatives. Even ardent egalitarians should recognize the injustice of taxing people who wash dishes or mop floors for a living to pay for the below-cost public higher education of the children of lawyers so that they can go on to become lawyers too.

Some readers may find it paradoxical that a book arguing for greater literacy and intellectual discipline should lead to a call for less rather than more education. Even if college students do not learn all they should, the readers' counterargument would go, surely they learn something, and that is better than learning nothing. Maybe it is. But at what price? One hundred fifty billion dollars is awfully high for deferring the day when the idle or ungifted take individual responsibility and face up to their fate. Ultimately it is the yearning to believe that anyone can be brought up to college level that has brought colleges down to everyone's level.

Questions for Discussion and Writing

1. How, according to Henry, has a misguided egalitarianism led to present abuses in the educational system in the United States? Do the inferences Henry draws from statistics appear to support his claim?
2. How does Henry counter the widely perceived claim that a college degree leads to better-paying jobs?
3. In your opinion, do Henry's recommendations about separating college from vocational skills training make sense? Why, or why not?

DAVID ROTHENBERG

David Rothenberg (b. 1962) is an associate professor of philosophy at the New Jersey Institute of Technology in Newark, New Jersey. He is the editor of Terra Nova: Journal of Nature and Culture *and has written* Hand's End: Technology and the Limits of Nature *(1993). In 2001, Rothenberg edited with Marta Ulvaeus the* Book of Music and Nature: An Anthology of Sounds, Words, Thoughts; Writing on Water; *and* World and the Wild. *This essay first appeared in the* Chronicle of Higher Education *in August 1997.*

How the Web Destroys the Quality of Students' Research Papers

Sometimes I look forward to the end-of-semester rush, when students' final papers come streaming into my office and mailbox. I could have hundreds of pages of original thought to read and evaluate. Once in a while, it is truly exciting, and brilliant words are typed across page in response to a question I've asked the class to discuss.

But this past semester was different. I noticed a disturbing decline in both the quality of the writing and the originality of the thoughts expressed. What had happened since last fall? Did I ask worse questions? Were my students unusually lazy? No. My class had fallen victim to the latest easy way of writing a paper: doing their research on the World-Wide Web.

It's easy to spot a research paper that is based primarily on information collected from the Web. First, the bibliography cites no books, just articles or pointers to places in that virtual land somewhere off any map: http://www.etc. Then a strange preponderance of material in the bibliography is curiously out of date. A lot of stuff on the Web that is advertised as timely is actually at least a few years old. (One student submitted a research paper last semester in which all of his sources were articles published between September and December 1995; that was probably the time span of the Web page on which he found them.)

Another clue is the beautiful pictures and graphs that are inserted neatly into the body of the student's text. They look impressive, as though they were the result of careful work and analysis, but actually they often bear little relation to the precise subject of the paper. Cut and pasted from the vast realm of what's out there for the taking, they masquerade as original work.

Accompanying them are unattributed quotes (in which one can't tell who made the statement or in what context) and curiously detailed references to the kinds of things that are easy to find on the Web (pages and pages of federal documents, corporate propaganda, or snippets of commentary by people whose credibility is difficult to assess). Sadly, one finds few references to careful, in-depth commentaries on the subject of the paper, the kind of analysis that requires a book, rather than an article, for its full development.

Don't get me wrong, I'm no neo-Luddite.[1] I am as enchanted as anyone else by the potential of this new technology to provide instant information. But too much of what passes for information these days is simply *advertising* for information. Screen after screen shows you where you can find out more, how you can connect to this place or that. The acts of linking and networking and randomly jumping from here to there become as exciting or rewarding as actually finding anything of intellectual value.

Search engines, with their half-baked algorithms, are closer to slot machines than to library catalogues. You throw your query to the wind, and who knows what will come back to you? You may get 234,468 supposed references to whatever you want to know. Perhaps one in a thousand might actually help you. But it's easy to be sidetracked or frustrated as you try to go through those Web pages one by one. Unfortunately, they're not arranged in order of importance.

---

[1] *Neo-Luddite:* referring to English weavers who protested the arrival of mechanized looms at the dawn of the Industrial Revolution. Thus, neo-Luddites are those who fear technology.

What I'm describing is the hunt-and-peck method of writing a paper. We all know that word processing makes many first drafts look far more polished than they are. If the paper doesn't reach the assigned five pages, readjust the margin, change the font size, and . . . voila! Of course, those machinations take up time that the student could have spent revising the paper. With programs to check one's spelling and grammar now standard features on most computers, one wonders why students make any mistakes at all. But errors are as prevalent as ever, no matter how crisp the typeface. Instead of becoming perfectionists, too many students have become slackers, preferring to let the machine do their work for them.

What the web adds to the shortcuts made possible by word processing is to make research look too easy. You toss a query to the machine, wait a few minutes, and suddenly a lot of possible sources of information appear on your screen. Instead of books that you have to check out of the library, read carefully, understand, synthesize, and then tactfully excerpt, these sources are quips, blips, pictures, and short summaries that may be downloaded magically to the dorm-room computer screen. Fabulous! How simple! The only problem is that a paper consisting of summaries of summaries is bound to be fragmented and superficial, and to demonstrate more of a random montage than an ability to sustain an argument through 10 to 15 double-spaced pages.

Of course, you can't blame the students for ignoring books. When college libraries are diverting funds from books to computer technology that will be obsolete in two years at most, they send a clear message to students: Don't read, just connect. Surf. Download. Cut and paste. Originality becomes hard to separate from plagiarism if no author is cited on a Web page. Clearly, the words are up for grabs, and students much prefer the fabulous jumble to the hard work of stopping to think and make sense of what they've read. 10

Libraries used to be repositories of words and ideas. Now they are, seen as centers for the retrieval of information. Some of this information comes from other, bigger libraries, in the form of books that can take time to obtain through interlibrary loan. What happens to the many students (some things never change) who scramble to write a paper the night before it's due? The computer screen, the gateway to the world sitting right on their desks, promises instant access-but actually offers only a pale, two-dimensional version of a real library.

But it's also my fault. I take much of the blame for the decline in the quality of student research in my classes. I need to teach students how to read, to take time with language and ideas, to work through arguments, to synthesize disparate sources to come up with original thought. I need to help my students understand how to assess sources to determine their credibility, as well as to trust their own ideas more than snippets of thought that materialize on a screen. The placelessness of the Web leads to an ethereal randomness of thought. Gone are the pathways of logic and passion, the sense of the progress of an argument. Chance holds sway, and it more often misses than hits. Judgment must be taught, as well as the methods of exploration.

I'm seeing my students' attention spans wane and their ability to reason for themselves decline. I wish that the university's computer system would crash for a day, so that I could encourage them to go outside, sit under a tree, and read a really good book—from start to finish. I'd like them to sit for a while and ponder what it means to live in a world where some things get easier and easier so rapidly that we can hardly keep track of how easy they're getting, while other tasks remain as hard as ever—such as doing research and writing a good paper that teaches the writer something in the process. Knowledge does not emerge in a vacuum, but we do need silence and space for sustained thought. Next semester, I'm going to urge my students to turn off their glowing boxes and think, if only once in a while.

Questions for Discussion and Writing

1. According to Rothenberg, how has the process by which students write research papers been changed by the Internet? What traditional skills does he feel have been lost?
2. To what extent does Rothenberg's argument depend on establishing a causal connection between students' use of the Internet and the declining quality of research papers? In your opinion, has he made a good case? Why or why not?
3. Does Rothenberg's characterization of the deficiencies now apparent in research papers correspond to your own experiences? What do you do to avoid the many defects Rothenberg identifies?

JOHN MILTON

The English poet John Milton (1608–1674) named his 1644 pamphlet Areopagitica *after a speech delivered by Isocrates, an Athenian orator (436–338 B.C.) who argued for the right to write, speak, and publish freely. Milton was urging his contemporaries (Presbyterians, who, in 1643, tried to quiet the political opposition by imposing censorship) to censor only those books that were atheistic or libelous. As you read the following piece (originally given as a speech in Parliament), notice the inventive analogy Milton creates between homicide and censorship.*

Areopagitica:[1] *Defense of Books*

I deny not, but that it is of greatest concernment in the Church and Commonwealth, to have a vigilant eye how books demean themselves as well as men; and thereafter to confine, imprison, and do sharpest justice on them as malefactors. For books are not absolutely dead things, but do contain a potency of life in them to be as active as that soul was whose progeny they are; nay, they do preserve as in a vial the purest efficacy and extraction of that living intellect that bred them. I know they are as lively, and as vigorously productive, as those fabulous dragon's teeth; and being sown up and down, may chance to spring up armed men. And yet,

---

[1] *Areopagus:* the oldest, most respectable council of ancient Athens.

on the other hand, unless wariness be used, as good almost kill a man as kill a good book. Who kills a man kills a reasonable creature, God's image; but he who destroys a good book, kills reason itself, kills the image of God, as it were in the eye. Many a man lives a burden to the earth; but a good book is the precious life-blood of a master spirit, embalmed and treasured up on purpose to a life beyond life. 'Tis true, no age can restore a life, whereof perhaps there is no great loss; and revolutions of ages do not oft recover the loss of a rejected truth, for the want of which whole nations fare the worse.

We should be wary therefore what persecutions we raise against the living labours of public men, how we spill that seasoned life of man, preserved and stored up in books; since we see a kind of homicide may be thus committed, sometimes a martyrdom, and if it extend to the whole impression, a kind of massacre; whereof the execution ends not in the slaying of an elemental life, but strikes at that ethereal and fifth essence, the breath of reason itself, slays an immortality rather than a life. But lest I should be condemned of introducing licence, while I oppose licensing, I refuse not the pains to be so much historical, as will serve to show what hath been done by ancient and famous commonwealths against this disorder, till the very time that this project of licensing crept out of the inquisition, was catched up by our prelates, and hath caught some of our presbyters.

In Athens, where books and wits were ever busier than in any other part of Greece, I find but only two sorts of writings which the magistrate cared to take notice of; those either blasphemous and atheistical, or libellous. Thus the books of Protagoras,[2] were by the judges of Areopagus commanded to be burnt, and himself banished the territory for a discourse begun with his confessing not to know "whether there were gods, or whether not." And against defaming, it was agreed that none should be traduced by name, as was the manner of Vetus Comoedia,[3] whereby we may guess how they censured libelling. And this course was quick enough, as Cicero writes, to quell both the desperate wits of other atheists, and the open way of defaming, as the event showed. Of other sects and opinions, though tending to voluptuousness, and the denying of Divine Providence, they took no heed.

Therefore we do not read that either Epicurus,[4] or that libertine school of Cyrene, or what the Cynic impudence uttered, was ever questioned by the laws. Neither is it recorded that the writings of those old comedians were suppressed, though the acting of them were forbid; and that Plato commended the reading of Aristophanes, the loosest of them all, to his royal scholar Dionysius, is commonly known, and may be excused, if holy Chrysostom,[5] as is reported, nightly studied so

---

[2] *Protagoras of Abdera:* a sophist banished from Athens for his atheism in 415 B.C.   [3] *Vetus Comoedia:* the "old comedy" of Athens that lampooned public figures.   [4] *Epicurus:* a hedonist (341-270 B.C.) condemned by Milton.   [5] *Chrysostom:* reference to the patriarch of Constantinople who died in 407 A.D. and was depicted as open-minded by Milton.

much the same author and had the art to cleanse a scurrilous vehemence into the style of a rousing sermon.

Questions for Discussion and Writing

1. According to Milton, why may preventing a book from being published or censoring it after it has been published do as much injury as murdering a human being? Do you find this argument persuasive? Why or why not?
2. How does Milton use references to Athenian society to support his argument?
3. Are there some books that should never be published (for example, those that argue the Holocaust never existed)? Why or why not? Conversely, could any book ever be as valuable as a human life (keep in mind this would include the Bible, the Koran, and other religious documents as well as CPR manuals)? Explain your answer.

NAT HENTOFF

A former board member of the American Civil Liberties Union, Nat Hentoff is a writer and an adjunct associate professor at New York University. He was born in 1925 in Boston. Hentoff graduated from Northeastern in 1945 and did postgraduate work at Harvard and the Sorbonne. He is a regular contributor to such publications as the Washington Post, *the* Progressive, *the* Village Voice, *and* The New Yorker. *Collections of his work include* The First Freedom *(1980). "'Speech Codes' on the Campus and Problems of Free Speech" first appeared in the Fall 1991 issue of* Dissent. *His most recent work is* Listen to the Stories: Nat Hentoff on Jazz and Country Music *(2000).*

"Speech Codes" on the Campus and Problems of Free Speech

During three years of reporting on anti-free-speech tendencies in higher education, I've been at more than twenty colleges and universities—from Washington and Lee and Columbia to Mesa State in Colorado and Stanford.

On this voyage of initially reverse expectations—with liberals fiercely advocating censorship of "offensive" speech and conservatives merrily taking the moral high ground as champions of free expression—the most dismaying moment of revelation took place at Stanford.

AN ECUMENICAL CALL FOR A HARSH CODE

In the course of a two-year debate on whether Stanford, like many other universities, should have a speech code punishing language that might wound minorities, women, and gays, a letter appeared in the *Stanford Daily.* Signed by the African-American Law Students Association, the Asian-American Law Students

Association, and the Jewish Law Students Association, the letter called for a harsh code. It reflected the letter and the spirit of an earlier declaration by Canetta Ivy, a black leader of student government at Stanford during the period of the great debate. "We don't put as many restrictions on freedom of speech," she said, "as we should."

Reading the letter by this rare ecumenical body of law students (so pressing was the situation that even Jews were allowed in), I thought of twenty, thirty years from now. From so bright a cadre of graduates, from so prestigious a law school would come some of the law professors, civic leaders, college presidents, and even maybe a Supreme Court justice of the future. And many of them would have learned—like so many other university students in the land—that censorship is okay provided your motives are okay.

The debate at Stanford ended when the president, Donald Kennedy, follow- 5 ing the prevailing winds, surrendered his previous position that once you start telling people what they can't say, you will end up telling them what they can't think. Stanford now has a speech code.

This is not to say that these gags on speech—every one of them so overboard and vague that a student can violate a code without knowing he or she has done so—are invariably imposed by student demand. At most colleges, it is the administration that sets up the code. Because there have been racist or sexist or homophobic taunts, anonymous notes or graffiti, the administration feels it must *do something*. The cheapest, quickest way to demonstrate that it cares is to appear to suppress racist, sexist, homophobic speech.

"The Pall of Orthodoxy"

Usually, the leading opposition among the faculty consists of conservatives—when there is opposition. An exception at Stanford was law professor Gerald Gunther, arguably the nation's leading authority on constitutional law. But Gunther did not have much support among other faculty members, conservative or liberal.

At the University of Buffalo Law School, which has a code restricting speech, I could find just one faculty member who was against it. A liberal, he spoke only on condition that I not use his name. He did not want to be categorized as a racist.

On another campus, a political science professor, for whom I had great respect after meeting and talking with him years ago, has been silent—students told me—on what Justice William Brennan once called "the pall of orthodoxy" that has fallen on his campus.

When I talked to him, the professor said, "It doesn't happen in my class.   10 There's no 'politically correct' orthodoxy here. It may happen in other places at this university, but I don't know about that." He said no more.

One of the myths about the rise of P.C. (politically correct) is that, coming from the left, it is primarily intimidating conservatives on campus. Quite the contrary. At almost every college I've been, conservative students have their own newspaper, usually quite lively and fired by a muckraking glee at exposing "politically correct" follies on campus.

By and large, those most intimidated—not so much by the speech codes themselves but by the Madame Defarge-like spirit behind them—are liberal students and those who can be called politically moderate.

I've talked to many of them, and they no longer get involved in class discussions when their views would go against the grain of P.C. righteousness. Many, for instance, have questions about certain kinds of affirmative action. They are not partisans of Jesse Helms or David Duke, but they wonder whether progeny of middle-class black families should get scholarship preference. Others have a question about abortion. Most are not pro-life, but they believe that fathers should have a say in whether the fetus should be sent off into eternity.

SELF-CENSORSHIP

Jeff Shesol, a recent graduate of Brown and now a Rhodes scholar at Oxford, became nationally known while at Brown because of his comic strip, "Thatch," which, not too kindly, parodied P.C. students. At a forum on free speech at Brown before he left, Shesol said he wished he could tell the new students at Brown to have no fear of speaking freely. But he couldn't tell them that, he said, advising the new students to stay clear of talking critically about affirmative action or abortion, among other things, in public.

At that forum, Shesol told me, he said that those members of the left who regard dissent from their views as racist and sexist should realize that they are discrediting their goals. "They're honorable goals," said Sheshol, "and I agree with them. I'm against racism and sexism. But these people's tactics are obscuring the goals. And they've resulted in Brown's no longer being an open-minded place." There were hisses from the audience.

Students at New York University Law School have also told me that they censor themselves in class. The kind of chilling atmosphere they describe was exemplified as a case assigned for a moot court competition became subject to denunciation when a sizable number of law students said it was too "offensive" and would hurt the feelings of gay and lesbian students. The case concerned a divorced father's attempt to gain custody of his children on the grounds that their mother had become a lesbian. It was against P.C. to represent the father.

Although some of the faculty responded by insisting that you learn to be a lawyer by dealing with all kinds of cases, including those you personally find offensive, other faculty members supported the rebellious students, praising them for their sensitivity. There was little public opposition from the other students to the attempt to suppress the case. A leading dissenter was a member of the conservative Federalist Society.

What is P.C. to white students is not necessarily P.C. to black students. Most of the latter did not get involved in the N.Y.U. protest, but throughout the country many black students do support speech codes. A vigorous exception was a black Harvard law school student during a debate on whether the law school should start punishing speech. A white student got up and said that the codes are necessary because without them, black students would be driven away from colleges and thereby deprived of the equal opportunity to get an education.

15

A black student rose and said that the white student had a hell of a nerve to assume that he—in the face of racist speech—would pack up his books and go home. He's been familiar with that kind of speech all his life, and he had never felt the need to run away from it. He'd handled it before and he could again.

The black student then looked at his white colleague and said that it was con- 20 descending to say that blacks have to be "protected" from racist speech. "It is more racist and insulting," he emphasized, "to say that to me than to call me a nigger."

But that would appear to be a minority view among black students. Most are convinced they do need to be protected from wounding language. On the other hand, a good many black student organizations on campus do not feel that Jews have to be protected from wounding language.

PRESENCE OF ANTI-SEMITISM

Though it's not much written about in reports of the language wars on campus, there is a strong strain of anti-Semitism among some—not all, by any means—black students. They invite such speakers as Louis Farrakhan, the former Stokely Carmichael (now Kwame Touré), and such lesser but still burning bushes as Steve Cokely, the Chicago commentator who has declared that Jewish doctors inject the AIDS virus into black babies. That distinguished leader was invited to speak at the University of Michigan.

The black student organization at Columbia University brought to the campus Dr. Khallid Abdul Muhammad. He began his address by saying: "My leader, my teacher, my guide is the honorable Louis Farrakhan. I thought that should be said at Columbia Jewniversity."

Many Jewish students have not censored themselves in reacting to this form of political correctness among some blacks. A Columbia student, Rachel Stoll, wrote a letter to the *Columbia Spectator:* "I have an idea. As a white Jewish American, I'll just stand in the middle of a circle comprising . . . Khallid Abdul Muhammad and assorted members of the Black Students Organization and let them all hurl large stones at me. From recent events and statements made on this campus, I gather this will be a good cheap method of making these people feel good."

At UCLA, a black student magazine printed an article indicating there is con- 25 siderable truth to the *Protocols of the Elders of Zion* [a document forged c. 1897 alleging that an international Jewish conspiracy was plotting the overthrow of Christian civilization]. For months, the black faculty, when asked their reactions, preferred not to comment. One of them did say that the black students already considered the black faculty to be insufficiently militant, and the professors didn't want to make the gap any wider. Like white liberal faculty members on other campuses, they want to be liked—or at least not too disliked.

Along with quiet white liberal faculty members, most black professors have not opposed the speech codes. But unlike the white liberals many honestly do believe that minority students have to be insulated from barbed language. They do not believe—as I have found out in a number of conversations—that an essential part of an education is to learn to demystify language, to strip it of its ability to demonize and stigmatize you. They do not believe that the way to deal with big-oted language is to answer it with more and better language of your own. This seems very elementary to me, but not to the defenders, black and white, of the speech codes.

"Fighting Words"

Consider University of California president David Gardner. He has imposed a speech code on all the campuses in his university system. Students are to be pun-ished—and this is characteristic of the other codes around the country—if they use "fighting words"—derogatory references to "race, sex, sexual orientation, or dis-ability."

The term "fighting words" comes from a 1942 Supreme Court decision, *Chaplinsky v. New Hampshire,* which ruled that "fighting words" are not protected by the First Amendment. That decision, however, has been in disuse at the High Court for many years. But it is thriving on college campuses.

In the California code, a word becomes "fighting" if it is directly addressed to "any ordinary person" (presumably, extraordinary people are above all this). These are the kinds of words that are "inherently likely to provoke a violent action, *whether or not they actually do."* (Emphasis added.)

Moreover, he or she who fires a fighting word at any ordinary person can be 30 reprimanded or dismissed from the university because the perpetrator should "rea-sonably know" that what he or she has said will interfere with the "victim's ability to pursue effectively his or her education or otherwise participate fully in univer-sity programs and activities."

Asked Gary Murikami, chairman of the Gay and Lesbian Association at the University of California, Berkeley: "What does it mean?"

Among those—faculty, law professors, college administrators—who insist such codes are essential to the university's purpose of making *all* students feel at home and thereby able to concentrate on their work, there has been a celebratory resort to the Fourteenth Amendment.

That amendment guarantees "equal protection of the laws" to all, and that means to all students on campus. Accordingly, when the First Amendment rights of those engaging in offensive speech clash with the equality rights of their targets under the Fourteenth Amendment, the First Amendment must give way.

This is the thesis, by the way, of John Powell, legal director of the American Civil Liberties Union, even though that organization has now formally opposed all college speech codes—after a considerable civil war among and within its affiliates.

The battle of the amendments continues, and when harsher codes are called 35 for at some campuses, you can expect the Fourteenth Amendment—which was not intended to censor *speech*—will rise again.

A precedent has been set at, of all places, colleges and universities, that the principle of free speech is merely situational. As college administrators change, so will the extent of free speech on campus. And invariably, permissible speech will become more and more narrowly defined. Once speech can be limited in such subjective ways, more and more expression will be included in what is forbidden.

FREEDOM OF THOUGHT

One of the exceedingly few college presidents who speaks out on the consequences of the anti-free-speech movement is Yale University's Benno Schmidt:

> Freedom of thought must be Yale's central commitment. It is not easy to embrace. It is, indeed, the effort of a lifetime. . . . Much expression that is free may deserve our contempt. We may well be moved to exercise our own freedom to counter it or to ignore it. But universities cannot censor or suppress speech, no matter how obnoxious in content, without violating their justification for existence. . . .

> On some other campuses in this country, values of civility and community have been offered by some as paramount values of the university, even to the extent of superseding freedom of expression.

> Such a view is wrong in principle and, if extended, is disastrous to freedom of thought. . . . The chilling effects on speech of the vagueness and open-ended nature of many universities' prohibitions . . . are compounded by the fact that these codes are typically enforced by faculty and students who commonly assert that vague notions of community are more important to the academy than freedom of thought and expression. . . .

> This is a flabby and uncertain time for freedom in the United States.

On the Public Broadcasting System in June 1991, I was part of a Fred Friendly panel at Stanford University in a debate on speech codes versus freedom of expression. The three black panelists strongly supported the codes. So did the one Asian-American on the panel. But then so did Stanford law professor Thomas Grey, who wrote the Stanford code, and Stanford president Donald Kennedy, who first opposed and then embraced the code. We have a new ecumenicism of those who would control speech for the greater good. It is hardly a new idea, but the mix of advocates is rather new.

But there are other voices. In the national board debate at the ACLU on college speech codes, the first speaker—and I think she had a lot to do with making the final vote against codes unanimous—was Gwen Thomas.

A black community college administrator from Colorado, she is a fiercely persistent exposer of racial discrimination. 40

She started by saying, "I have always felt as a minority person that we have to protect the rights of all because if we infringe on the rights of any persons, we'll be next.

"As for providing a nonintimidating educational environment, our young people have to learn to grow up on college campuses. We have to teach them how to deal with adversarial situations. They have to learn how to survive offensive speech they find wounding and hurtful." Gwen Thomas is an educator—an endangered species in higher education.

Questions for Discussion and Writing

1. With which of the assumptions underlying the imposition of speech codes does Hentoff disagree? How do Hentoff's experiences or examples from campuses around the country challenge the presumed benefits of speech codes?

2. How does Hentoff frame the debate about whether the First or the Fourteenth Amendment ought to be given more consideration?

3. Does your own experience in classrooms confirm or disprove Hentoff's contention that the chilling effects on campuses have mostly been felt by students with moderate views? Have you ever felt inhibited from discussing issues because of the circumstances described by Hentoff?

Fiction

DONALD BARTHELME

Donald Barthelme (1931–1989) was born in Philadelphia and raised in Texas, where his father was a prominent architect. He attended the University of Houston and went on to serve as the Cullen Distinguished Professor of English at that university. His novels include Snow White *(1967),* The Dead Father *(1975), and* Paradise *(1986), as well as nine collections of short stories and a book of nonfiction,* Guilty Pleasures *(1974). His short story "The School" (1962) explores difficult questions of how to educate students in grade schools without mentioning death.*

The School

Well, we had all these children out planting trees, see, because we figured that . . . that was part of their education, to see how, you know, the root systems . . . and also sense of responsibility, taking care of things, being individually responsible. You know what I mean. And the trees all died. They were orange trees. I don't know why they died, they just died. Something wrong with the soil possibly or maybe the stuff we got from the nursery wasn't the best. We complained about it. So we've got thirty kids there, each kid had his or her own little tree to plant, and we've got these thirty dead trees. All these kids looking at these little brown sticks, it was depressing.

It wouldn't have been so bad except that just a couple of weeks before the thing with the trees, the snakes all died. But I think that the snakes—well, the reason that the snakes kicked off was that . . . you remember, the boiler was shut off for four days because of the strike, and that was explicable. It was something you could explain to the kids because of the strike. I mean, none of their parents would let them cross the picket line and they knew there was a strike going on and what it meant. So when things got started up again and we found the snakes they weren't too disturbed.

With the herb gardens it was probably a case of overwatering, and at least now they know not to overwater. The children were very conscientious with the herb gardens and some of them probably . . . you know, slipped them a little extra water when we weren't looking. Or maybe . . . well, I don't like to think about sabotage, although it did occur to us. I mean, it was something that crossed our minds. We were thinking that way probably because before that the gerbils had died, and the white mice had died, and the salamander . . . well, now they know not to carry them around in plastic bags.

Of course we *expected* the tropical fish to die, that was no surprise. Those numbers, you look at them crooked and they're belly-up on the surface. But the lesson plan called for a tropical-fish input at that point, there was nothing we could do, it happens every year, you just have to hurry past it.

We weren't even supposed to have a puppy.

5

We weren't even supposed to have one, it was just a puppy the Murdoch girl found under a Gristede's truck one day and she was afraid the truck would run over it when the driver had finished making his delivery, so she stuck it in her knapsack and brought it to school with her. So we had this puppy. As soon as I saw the puppy I thought, Oh Christ, I bet it will live for about two weeks and then . . . And that's what it did. It wasn't supposed to be in the classroom at all, there's some kind of regulation about it, but you can't tell them they can't have a puppy when the puppy is already there, right in front of them, running around on the floor and yap yap yapping. They named it Edgar—that is, they named it after me. They had a lot of fun running after it and yelling, "Here, Edgar! Nice Edgar!" Then they'd laugh like hell. They enjoyed the ambiguity. I enjoyed it myself. I don't mind being kidded. They made a little house for it in the supply closet and all that. I don't know what it died of. Distemper, I guess. It probably hadn't had any shots. I got it out of there before the kids got to school. I checked the supply closet each morning, routinely, because I knew what was going to happen. I gave it to the custodian.

And then there was this Korean orphan that the class adopted through the Help the Children program, all the kids brought in a quarter a month, that was the idea. It was an unfortunate thing, the kid's name was Kim and maybe we adopted him too late or something. The cause of death was not stated in the letter we got, they suggested we adopt another child instead and sent us some interesting case histories, but we didn't have the heart. The class took it pretty hard, they began (I think, nobody ever said anything to me directly) to feel that maybe there was something wrong with the school. But I don't think there's anything wrong with the school, particularly, I've seen better and I've seen worse. It was just a run of bad luck. We had an extraordinary number of parents passing away, for instance. There were I think two heart attacks and two suicides, one drowning, and four killed together in a car accident. One stroke. And we had the usual heavy mortality rate among the grandparents, or maybe it was heavier this year, it seemed so. And finally the tragedy.

The tragedy occurred when Matthew Wein and Tony Mavrogordo were playing over where they're excavating for the new federal office building. There were all these big wooden beams stacked, you know, at the edge of the excavation. There's a court case coming out of that, the parents are claiming that the beams were poorly stacked. I don't know what's true and what's not. It's been a strange year.

I forgot to mention Billy Brandt's father, who was knifed fatally when he grappled with a masked intruder in his home.

One day, we had a discussion in class. They asked me, where did they go? The 10 trees, the salamander, the tropical fish, Edgar, the poppas and mommas, Matthew and Tony, where did they go? And I said, I don't know, I don't know. And they said, who knows? and I said, nobody knows. And they said, is death that which gives meaning to life? And I said, no, life is that which gives meaning to life. Then they said, but isn't death, considered as a fundamental datum, the means by which the taken-for-granted mundanity of the everyday may be transcended in the direction of—

I said, yes, maybe.

They said, we don't like it.

I said, that's sound.

They said, it's a bloody shame!

I said, it is.   15

They said, will you make love now with Helen (our teaching assistant) so that we can see how it is done? We know you like Helen.

I do like Helen but I said that I would not.

We've heard so much about it, they said, but we've never seen it.

I said I would be fired and that it was never, or almost never, done as a demonstration. Helen looked out of the window.

They said, please, please make love with Helen, we require an assertion of 20 value, we are frightened.

I said that they shouldn't be frightened (although I am often frightened) and that there was value everywhere. Helen came and embraced me. I kissed her a few times on the brow. We held each other. The children were excited. Then there was a knock on the door, I opened the door, and the new gerbil walked in. The children cheered wildly.

Questions for Discussion and Writing

1. How does the progression of each of the unsuccessful class projects undermine the ability of the teacher to produce the desired attitude toward life in the students? How is each of these projects intended to promote desired values as part of the students' education?
2. Why does the class request that the teacher make love to Helen? What is the significance of the fact that the children's attention is just as easily satisfied when a new gerbil is introduced into the class?
3. In your opinion, what is the significance of Barthelme's having elementary-school children asking questions in such a sophisticated manner?

Poetry

Francis E. W. Harper

Francis Ellen Watkins Harper (1824–1911) was born in Baltimore, the daughter of free blacks. She attended a school run by her uncle and worked as a seamstress and as a teacher. In the 1850s she began actively working and lecturing for the abolitionist cause. Her writing includes Poems on Miscellaneous Subjects *(1854), a volume of antislavery verse that sold 12,000 copies by 1858 and went through some 20 editions;* Sketches of Southern Life *(1872); and a novel,* Iola Leroy *(1892), recognized as the first novel by a black author to describe Reconstruction.*

Learning to Read

Very soon the Yankee teachers
Came down and set up school;
But, oh! how the Rebs did hate it,—
It was agin' their rule.

Our masters always tried to hide   5
Book learning from our eyes;
Knowledge didn't agree with slavery—
'Twould make us all too wise.

But some of us would try to steal
A little from the book,   10
And put the words together,
And learn by hook or crook.

I remember Uncle Caldwell,
Who took pot liquor[1] fat
And greased the pages of his book,   15
And hid it in his hat

And had his master ever seen
The leaves upon his head,
He'd have thought them greasy papers,
But nothing to be read.   20

And there was Mr. Turner's Ben,
Who heard the children spell,
And picked the words right up by heart,

---

[1] *Pot liquor:* broth in which meat and/or vegetables have cooked.

And learned to read 'em well.

Well, the Northern folks kept sending   25
The Yankee teachers down;
And they stood right up and helped us,
Though Rebs did sneer and frown.

And, I longed to read my Bible,
For precious words it said;   30
But when I begun to learn it,
Folks just shook their heads,

And said there is no use trying,
Oh! Chloe, you're too late;
But as I was rising sixty,   35
I had no time to wait.

So I got a pair of glasses,
And straight to work I went,
And never stopped till I could read
The hymns and Testament.   40

Then I got a little cabin
A place to call my own—
And I felt as independent
As the queen upon her throne.

Questions for Discussion and Writing

1. What kind of danger did learning to read pose to the system of slavery?
2. What function do the examples of slaves learning to read serve in Harper's poem?
3. What motivates Chloe to learn to read? In what ways does reading change her life for the better?

LINDA HOGAN

Linda Hogan, Chickasaw poet, novelist, and essayist, was born in 1947 in Denver, Colorado, and grew up in Oklahoma. She taught American Indian studies at the University of Minnesota from 1984–1991 and she is currently professor of American studies and American Indian studies at the University of Colorado. Her poetry has been collected in Seeing through the Sun *(1985), which received an American Book Award from the Before Columbus Foundation;* The Book of Medicines *(1993); and* Solar Storms *(1996). She has also published short stories, one of which, "Aunt Moon's Young Man," was featured in* Best American Short Stories *(1989). Her novel* Mean Spirit *was nominated for a Pulitzer Prize (1990). Hogan's latest work is* The Woman Who Watches over the World: A Native Memoir *(2001).*

In "Workday" she uses the occasion of a bus ride she took when returning from working at the University of Colorado to explore the gap between Native Americans and her middle-class white coworkers.

workday

I go to work
though there are those who were missing today
from their homes.
I ride the bus
and I do not think of children without food   5
or how my sisters are chained to prison beds.

I go to the university
and out for lunch
and listen to the higher-ups
tell me all they have read   10
about Indians
and how to analyze this poem.
They know us
better than we know ourselves.

I ride the bus home   15
and sit behind the driver.
We talk about the weather
and not enough exercise.
I don't mention Victor Jara's mutilated hands
or men next door   20
in exile
or my own family's grief over the lost child.

When I get off the bus
I look back at the light in the windows
and the heads bent   25
and how the women are all alone
in each seat
framed in the windows
and the men are coming home,
then I see them walking on the Avenue,   30
the beautiful feet,

the perfect legs
even with their spider veins,
the broken knees
with pins in them,   35
the thighs with their cravings,

the pelvis
and small back
with its soft down,
the shoulders which bend forward   40
and forward and forward
to protect the heart from pain.

Questions for Discussion and Writing

1. How does the poem raise the question of whether the speaker has irrevocably lost touch with her own people by working at a university where she is
   little more than a token Native American?
2. What kind of connection does the speaker feel with the Native American
   laborers on the bus?
3. What images express the speaker's grief at the psychological and physical costs
   for Native Americans trying to survive in contemporary American society?

Connections for Chapter 3:
The Value of Education

1. **Frederick Douglass,** *Learning to Read and Write*
   How do both Douglass and Jonathan Kozol emphasize the empowerment
   that literacy produces?
   How does Kenneth M. Stampp's analysis in "To Make Them Stand in Fear"
   (in Chapter 7) provide insight into the pressures that Douglass confronted?
2. **Jonathan Kozol,** *The Human Cost of an Illiterate Society*
   In what sense is the predicament facing an illiterate person comparable to
   that of Nunez, the main character in H. G. Wells's story "The Country of the
   Blind" in Chapter 11?
3. **Mary Crow Dog,** *Civilize Them with a Stick*
   Compare the systematic attempts at cultural conditioning described by Mary
   Crow Dog with those described by Kenneth M. Stampp in "To Make Them
   Stand in Fear" (Chapter 7).
4. **Richard Rodriguez,** *On Becoming a Chicano*
   Discuss the ambivalence both Rodriguez and Linda Hogan feel in relationship to losing touch with their cultures as they advance academically.
5. **William A. Henry III,** *In Defense of Elitism*
   To what extent is the situation Henry describes analogous to the "tragedy of
   the commons" discussed by Garrett Hardin in "Lifeboat Ethics" (Chapter 11)?

6. **David Rothenberg,** *How the Web Destroys the Quality of Students' Research Papers*
   Compare the different perspectives on using the Web by Rothenberg and Bill Gates in "From the Road Ahead" (in Chapter 9).
7. **John Milton,** *Areopagitica: Defense of Books*
   What limits, if any, should be placed on speech according to Milton and Margaret Atwood (in "Pornography" in Chapter 4)?
8. **Nat Hentoff,** *"Speech Codes" on the Campus and Problems of Free Speech*
   Compare Hentoff's view on censorship with John Milton's view, expressed four hundred years earlier, in "Areopagitica: Defense of Books."
9. **Donald Barthelme,** *The School*
   Contrast the very different approaches of Barthelme and Nat Hentoff on the question of the presumed socializing function of education.
10. **Francis E. W. Harper,** *Learning to Read*
    Compare the views of Harper and Peggy Seeger (see "I'm Gonna Be an Engineer" in Chapter 9) on empowerment for women.
11. **Linda Hogan,** *Workday*
    In what ways do Hogan and Bertolt Brecht (in "A Worker Reads History" in Chapter 7) adopt viewpoints of those who are thought of as marginal in relationship to mainstream society?

4

PERSPECTIVES ON LANGUAGE

The selections in this chapter attest to the value of literacy and the importance of being able to communicate. Susanne K. Langer's analysis of the symbolic function of language and personal accounts by Helen Keller and Temple Grandin are particularly fascinating in demonstrating how the creation of an identity depends on language. Alison Lurie broadens our concept of what language is and analyzes how clothing can make statements about who we are and how we wish to be perceived. Aldous Huxley reveals how propaganda has been used to deceive by manipulating emotions and beliefs.

Deborah Tannen inquires into the reasons why men and women have so much difficulty in communicating with each other. Margaret Atwood and Stuart Hirschberg deal with contemporary social issues connected with language: Should the sale of pornography be restricted? Should we take another look at the rhetorical techniques advertisers use so successfully?

Raymond Carver's short story, "What We Talk About When We Talk About Love," probes the underlying meanings and ambiguities of everyday conversation.

The poem by Ted Hughes offers a witty commentary on the illusive nature of language.

A one-act comedy by David Ives examines the premise that three monkeys typing into infinity would sooner or later produce *Hamlet*.

Nonfiction

SUSANNE K. LANGER

Susanne K. Langer (1895–1985) was born in New York City. After studying at Radcliffe and the University of Vienna, Langer became a tutor in philosophy at Radcliffe, where she taught for more than fifty years. She wrote extensively on aesthetics, and her book Feeling and Form *(1953) has been widely viewed as the most important work in aesthetics that has appeared in this century. She also wrote* Problems of Art *(1957) and a three-volume study,* Mind: An Essay on Human Feeling *(1967–1982). "Language and Thought" first appeared in* Fortune *(January 1944).*

Language and Thought

A symbol is not the same thing as a sign; that is a fact that psychologists and philosophers often overlook. All intelligent animals use signs; so do we. To them as well as to us sounds and smells and motions are signs of food, danger, the presence of other beings, or of rain or storm. Furthermore, some animals not only attend to signs but produce them for the benefit of others. Dogs bark at the door to be let in; rabbits thump to call each other; the cooing of doves and the growl of a wolf defending his kill are unequivocal signs of feelings and intentions to be reckoned with by other creatures.

We use signs just as animals do, though with considerably more elaboration. We stop at red lights and go on green; we answer calls and bells, watch the sky for coming storms, read trouble or promise or anger in each other's eyes. That is animal intelligence raised to the human level. Those of us who are dog lovers can probably all tell wonderful stories of how high our dogs have sometimes risen in the scale of clever sign interpretation and sign using.

A sign is anything that announces the existence or the imminence of some event, the presence of a thing or a person, or a change in the state of affairs. There are signs of the weather, signs of danger, signs of future good or evil, signs of what the past has been. In every case a sign is closely bound up with something to be noted or expected in experience. It is always a part of the situation to which it refers, though the reference may be remote in space and time. In so far as we are led to note or expect the signified event we are making correct use of a sign. This is the essence of rational behavior, which animals show in varying degrees. It is entirely realistic, being closely bound up with the actual objective course of history— learned by experience, and cashed in or voided by further experience.

If man had kept to the straight and narrow path of sign using, he would be like the other animals, though perhaps a little brighter. He would not talk, but grunt and gesticulate the point. He would make his wishes known, give warnings, perhaps develop a social system like that of bees and ants, with such a wonderful efficiency of communal enterprise that all men would have plenty to eat, warm apartments—all exactly alike and perfectly convenient—to live in, and everybody could and would sit in the sun or by the fire, as the climate demanded, not talking but just basking, with every want satisfied, most of his life. The young would romp and make love, the old would sleep, the middle-aged would do the routine work almost unconsciously and eat a great deal. But that would be the life of a social, superintelligent, purely sign-using animal.

To us who are human, it does not sound very glorious. We want to go places and do things, own all sorts of gadgets that we do not absolutely need, and when   5 we sit down to take it easy we want to talk. Rights and property, social position, special talents and virtues, and above all our ideas, are what we live for. We have gone off on a tangent that takes us far away from the mere biological cycle that animal generations accomplish; and that is because we can use not only signs but symbols.

A symbol differs from a sign in that it does not announce the presence of the object, the being, condition, or whatnot, which is its meaning, but merely *brings this thing to mind*. It is not a mere "substitute sign" to which we react as though it were the object itself. The fact is that our reaction to hearing a person's name is quite different from our reaction to the person himself. There are certain rare cases where a symbol stands directly for its meaning: in religious experience, for instance, the Host is not only a symbol but a Presence. But symbols in the ordinary sense are not mystic. They are the same sort of thing that ordinary signs are; only they do not call our attention to something necessarily present or to be physically dealt with—they call up merely a conception of the thing they "mean."

The difference between a sign and a symbol is, in brief, that a sign causes us to think or act *in face* of the thing signified, whereas a symbol causes us to think *about* the thing symbolized. Therein lies the great importance of symbolism for human life, its power to make this life so different from any other animal biography that generations of men have found it incredible to suppose that they were of purely zoological origin. A sign is always embedded in reality, in a present that emerges from the actual past and stretches to the future; but a symbol may be divorced from reality altogether. It may refer to what is not the case, to a mere idea, a figment, a dream. It serves, therefore, to liberate thought from the immediate stimuli of a physically present world; and that liberation marks the essential difference between human and nonhuman mentality. Animals think, but they think *of* and *at* things; men think primarily *about* things. Words, pictures, and memory images are symbols that may be combined and varied in a thousand ways. The result is a symbolic structure whose meaning is a complex of all their respective meanings, and this kaleidoscope of *ideas* is the typical product of the human brain that we call the "stream of thought."

The process of transforming all direct experience into imagery or into that supreme mode of symbolic expression, language, has so completely taken possession of the human mind that it is not only a special talent but a dominant, organic need. All our sense impressions leave their traces in our memory not only as signs disposing our practical reactions in the future but also as symbols, images representing our *ideas* of things; and the tendency to manipulate ideas, to combine and abstract, mix and extend them by playing with symbols, is man's outstanding characteristic. It seems to be what his brain most naturally and spontaneously does. Therefore his primitive mental function is not judging reality, but *dreaming his desires*.

Dreaming is apparently a basic function of human brains, for it is free and unexhausting like our metabolism, heartbeat, and breath. It is easier to dream than not to dream, as it is easier to breathe than to refrain from breathing. The symbolic character of dreams is fairly well established. Symbol mongering, on this ineffectual, uncritical level, seems to be instinctive, the fulfillment of an elementary need rather than the purposeful exercise of a high and difficult talent.

The special power of man's mind rests on the evolution of this special activity, not on any transcendently high development of animal intelligence. We are not immeasurably higher than other animals; we are different. We have a biological need and with it a biological gift that they do not share.

Because man has not only the ability but the constant need of *conceiving* what has happened to him, what surrounds him, what is demanded of him—in short, of symbolizing nature, himself, and his hopes and fears—he has a constant and crying need of *expression*. What he cannot express, he cannot conceive; what he cannot conceive is chaos, and fills him with terror.

If we bear in mind this all-important craving for expression we get a new picture of man's behavior; for from this trait spring his powers and his weaknesses. The process of symbolic transformation that all our experiences undergo is nothing more nor less than the process of *conception,* underlying the human faculties of abstraction and imagination.

When we are faced with a strange or difficult situation, we cannot react directly, as other creatures do, with flight, aggression, or any such simple instinctive pattern. Our whole reaction depends on how we manage to conceive the situation— whether we cast it in a definite dramatic form, whether we see it as a disaster, a challenge, a fulfillment of doom, or a fiat of the Divine Will. In words or dreamlike images, in artistic or religious or even in cynical form, we must *construe* the events of life. There is great virtue in the figure of speech, "I can *make* nothing of it," to express a failure to understand something. Thought and memory are processes of *making* the thought content and the memory image; the pattern of our ideas is given by the symbols through which we express them. And in the course of manipulating those symbols we inevitably distort the original experience, as we abstract certain features of it, embroider and reinforce those features with other ideas, until the conception we project on the screen of memory is quite different from anything in our real history.

Conception is a necessary and elementary process; what we do with our conceptions is another story. That is the entire history of human culture—of intelligence and morality, folly and superstition, ritual, language, and the arts—all the phenomena that set man apart from, and above, the rest of the animal kingdom. As the religious mind has to make all human history a drama of sin and salvation in order to define its own moral attitudes, so a scientist wrestles with the mere presentation of "the facts" before he can reason about them. The process of *envisaging* facts, values, hopes, and fears underlies our whole behavior pattern; and this process is reflected in the evolution of an extraordinary phenomenon found always, and only, in human societies—the phenomenon of language.

Language is the highest and most amazing achievement of the symbolistic human mind. The power it bestows is almost inestimable, for without it anything properly called "thought" is impossible. The birth of language is the dawn of humanity. The line between man and beast—between the highest ape and the lowest savage—is the language line. Whether the primitive Neanderthal man was anthropoid or human depends less on his cranial capacity, his upright posture, or even his use of tools and fire, than on one issue we shall probably never be able to settle—whether or not he spoke.

In all physical traits and practical responses, such as skills and visual judgments, we can find a certain continuity between animal and human mentality. Sign using is an ever evolving, ever improving function throughout the whole animal kingdom, from the lowly worm that shrinks into his hole at the sound of an approaching foot, to the dog obeying his master's command, and even to the learned scientist who watches the movements of an index needle.

This continuity of the sign-using talent has led psychologists to the belief that language is evolved from the vocal expressions, grunts and coos and cries, whereby animals vent their feelings or signal their fellows; that man has elaborated this sort of communion to the point where it makes a perfect exchange of ideas possible.

I do not believe that this doctrine of the origin of language is correct. The essence of language is symbolic, not signific; we use it first and most vitally to formulate and hold ideas in our own minds. Conception, not social control, is its first and foremost benefit.

Watch a young child that is just learning to speak play with a toy; he says the name of the object, e.g.: "Horsey! horsey! horsey!" over and over again, looks at the object, moves it, always saying the name to himself or to the world at large. It's quite a time before he talks to anyone in particular; he talks first of all to himself. This is his way of forming and fixing the *conception* of the object in his mind, and around this conception all his knowledge of it grows. *Names* are the essence of language; for the *name* is what abstracts the conception of the horse from the horse itself, and lets the mere idea recur at the speaking of the name. This permits the conception gathered from one horse experience to be exemplified again by another instance of a horse, so that the notion embodied in the name is a general notion.

To this end, the baby uses a word long before he *asks* for the object; when he wants his horsey he is likely to cry and fret, because he is reacting to an actual environment, not forming ideas. He uses the animal language of *signs* for his wants; talking is still a purely symbolic process—its practical value has not really impressed him yet.

20

Language need not be vocal; it may be purely visual, like written language or even tactual, like the deaf-mute system of speech; but it *must be denotative*. The sounds, intended or unintended, whereby animals communicate do not constitute a language because they are signs, not names. They never fall into an organic pattern, a meaningful syntax of even the most rudimentary sort, as all language seems to do with a sort of driving necessity. That is because signs refer to actual situations, in which things have obvious relations to each other that require only to be noted; but symbols refer to ideas, which are not physically there for inspection, so their connections and features have to be represented. This gives all true language a natural tendency toward growth and development, which seems almost like a life of its own. Languages are not invented; they grow with our need for expression.

In contrast, animal "speech" never has a structure. It is merely an emotional response. Apes may greet their ration of yams with a shout of "Nga!" But they do not say "Nga" between meals. If they could *talk about* their yams instead of just saluting them, they would be the most primitive men instead of the most anthropoid of beasts. They would have ideas, and tell each other things true or false, rational or irrational; they would make plans and invent laws and sing their own praises, as men do.

Questions for Discussion and Writing

1. Why is the difference between signs and symbols an important distinction, from Langer's perspective? What comparisons does she use to clarify the difference?
2. In Langer's view, how did language develop and what functions does it serve?
3. What function does her discussion of animal communication play in developing her thesis?

HELEN KELLER

Helen Keller (1880–1968) was born, without handicaps, in Alabama; she contracted a disease at the age of nineteen months that left her both blind and deaf. Because of the extraordinary efforts of Annie Sullivan, Keller overcame her isolation and learned what words meant. She graduated with honors from Radcliffe and devoted herself for most of her life to helping the blind and deaf through the American Foundation for the Blind. She was awarded the Presidential Medal of Freedom by Lyndon Johnson in 1964. "The Day Language Came into My Life" is taken from her autobiography, The Story of My Life *(1902). This work served as the basis for a film,* The Unconquered *(1954), and the acclaimed play by William Gibson,* The Miracle Worker *(1959), which was subsequently made into a movie with Anne Bancroft and Patty Duke.*

The Day Language Came into My Life

The most important day I remember in all my life is the one on which my teacher, Anne Mansfield Sullivan, came to me. I am filled with wonder when I consider the immeasurable contrast between the two lives which it connects. It was the third of March 1887, three months before I was seven years old.

On the afternoon of that eventful day, I stood on the porch, dumb, expectant. I guessed vaguely from my mother's signs and from the hurrying to and fro in the house that something unusual was about to happen, so I went to the door and waited on the steps. The afternoon sun penetrated the mass of honeysuckle that covered the porch and fell on my upturned face. My fingers lingered almost unconsciously on the familiar leaves and blossoms which had just come forth to greet

the sweet southern spring. I did not know what the future held of marvel or surprise for me. Anger and bitterness had preyed upon me continually for weeks and
a deep languor had succeeded this passionate struggle.

Have you ever been at sea in a dense fog, when it seemed as if a tangible white
darkness shut you in, and the great ship, tense and anxious, groped her way toward
the shore with plummet and sounding-line, and you waited with beating heart for
something to happen? I was like that ship before my education began, only I was
without compass or sounding-line and had no way of knowing how near the harbor was. "Light! give me light!" was the wordless cry of my soul, and the light of
love shone on me in that very hour.

I felt approaching footsteps. I stretched out my hand as I supposed to my
mother. Someone took it, and I was caught up and held close in the arms of her
who had come to reveal all things to me, and, more than all things else, to love me.

The morning after my teacher came she led me into her room and gave me a   5
doll. The little blind children at the Perkins Institution had sent it and Laura Bridg-
man had dressed it; but I did not know this until afterward. When I had played with
it a little while, Miss Sullivan slowly spelled into my hand the word "d-o-l-l." I was
at once interested in this finger play and tried to imitate it. When I finally succeeded in making the letters correctly I was flushed with childish pleasure and
pride. Running downstairs to my mother I held up my hand and made the letters
for doll. I did not know that I was spelling a word or even that words existed; I was
simply making my fingers go in monkeylike imitation. In the days that followed I
learned to spell in this uncomprehending way a great many words, among them
pin, hat, cup and a few verbs like *sit, stand* and *walk*. But my teacher had been with
me several weeks before I understood that everything has a name.

One day, while I was playing with my new doll, Miss Sullivan put my big rag
doll into my lap also, spelled "d-o-l-l" and tried to make me understand that
"d-o-l-l" applied to both. Earlier in the day we had had a tussle over the words
"m-u-g" and "w-a-t-e-r." Miss Sullivan had tried to impress it upon me that "m-u-g"
is *mug* and that "w-a-t-e-r" is *water,* but I persisted in confounding the two. In despair she had dropped the subject for the time, only to renew it at the first opportunity. I became impatient at her repeated attempts and, seizing the new doll, I
dashed it upon the floor. I was keenly delighted when I felt the fragments of the
broken doll at my feet. Neither sorrow nor regret followed my passionate outburst.
I had not loved the doll. In the still, dark world in which I lived there was no strong
sentiment or tenderness. I felt my teacher sweep the fragments to one side of the
hearth, and I had a sense of satisfaction that the cause of my discomfort was removed. She brought me my hat, and I knew I was going out into the warm sunshine. This thought, if a wordless sensation may be called a thought, made me hop
and skip with pleasure.

We walked down the path to the well-house, attracted by the fragrance of the
honeysuckle with which it was covered. Some one was drawing water and my
teacher placed my hand under the spout. As the cool stream gushed over one hand
she spelled into the other the word *water,* first slowly, then rapidly. I stood still, my

whole attention fixed upon the motions of her fingers. Suddenly I felt a misty consciousness as of something forgotten—a thrill of returning thought; and somehow the mystery of language was revealed to me. I knew then that "w-a-t-e-r" meant the wonderful cool something that was flowing over my hand. The living word awakened my soul, gave it light, hope, joy, set it free! There were barriers still, it is true, but barriers that could in time be swept away.

I left the well-house eager to learn. Everything had a name, and each name gave birth to a new thought. As we returned to the house every object which I touched seemed to quiver with life. That was because I saw everything with the strange, new sight that had come to me. On entering the door I remembered the doll I had broken. I felt my way to the hearth and picked up the pieces. I tried vainly to put them together. Then my eyes filled with tears; for I realized what I had done, and for the first time I felt repentance and sorrow.

I learned a great many new words that day. I do not remember what they all were; but I do know that *mother, father, sister, teacher* were among them—words that were to make the world blossom for me, "like Aaron's rod, with flowers." It would have been difficult to find a happier child than I was as I lay in my crib at the close of that eventful day and lived over the joys it had brought me, and for the first time longed for a new day to come.

Questions for Discussion and Writing

1. Why is it important for the reader to understand Keller's state of mind in the days preceding the events she describes?
2. How did Keller's understanding of language when she became conscious of the meaning of words differ from her previous experience of spelling them by rote?
3. How does the episode of the broken doll reveal how much Keller was transformed by the experience she describes?

TEMPLE GRANDIN

Temple Grandin has a Ph. D. in animal science from the University of Illinois. She has designed many of the livestock-handling facilities in the United States and in other countries. What makes her achievement astounding is the fact that she is autistic and is one of the few who have overcome this neurological impairment enough to communicate with others. The following selection is drawn from her autobiography, Thinking in Pictures: And Other Reports from My Life with Autism *(1996). In 1998 she edited* Genetics and the Behavior of Domestic Animals *and in 2000* Livestock Handling *and Transport.*

Thinking in Pictures

PROCESSING NONVISUAL INFORMATION

Autistics[1] have problems learning things that cannot be thought about in pictures. The easiest words for an autistic child to learn are nouns, because they directly relate to pictures. Highly verbal autistic children like I was can sometimes learn how to read with phonics. Written words were too abstract for me to remember, but I could laboriously remember the approximately fifty phonetic sounds and a few rules. Lower-functioning children often learn better by association, with the aid of word labels attached to objects in their environment. Some very impaired autistic children learn more easily if words are spelled out with plastic letters they can feel.

Spatial words such as "over" and "under" had no meaning for me until I had a visual image to fix them in my memory. Even now, when I hear the word "under" by itself, I automatically picture myself getting under the cafeteria tables at school during an air-raid drill, a common occurrence on the East Coast during the early fifties. The first memory that any single word triggers is almost always a childhood memory. I can remember the teacher telling us to be quiet and walking single-file into the cafeteria, where six or eight children huddled under each table. If I continue on the same train of thought, more and more associative memories of elementary school emerge. I can remember the teacher scolding me after I hit Alfred for putting dirt on my shoe. All of these memories play like videotapes in the VCR in my imagination. If I allow my mind to keep associating, it will wander a million miles away from the word "under," to submarines under the Antarctic and the Beatles song "Yellow Submarine." If I let my mind pause on the picture of the yellow submarine, I then hear the song. As I start humming the song and get to the part about people coming on board, my association switches to the gangway of a ship I saw in Australia.

I also visualize verbs. The word "jumping" triggers a memory of jumping hurdles at the mock Olympics held at my elementary school. Adverbs often trigger inappropriate images—"quickly" reminds me of Nestle's Quik—unless they are paired with a verb, which modifies my visual image. For example, "he ran quickly" triggers an animated image of Dick from the first-grade reading book running fast, and "he walked slowly" slows the image down. As a child, I left out words such as "is," "the," and "it," because they had no meaning by themselves. Similarly, words like "of" and "an" made no sense. Eventually I learned how to use them properly, because my parents always spoke correct English and I mimicked their speech patterns. To this day certain verb conjugations, such as "to be," are absolutely meaningless to me.

---

[1] *autism:* a condition characterized by a delay in the acquisition of speech, resistance to change of any kind, obsessive repetitive body movements, and a withdrawal into fantasy.

When I read, I translate written words into color movies or I simply store a photo of the written page to be read later. When I retrieve the material, I see a photocopy of the page in my imagination. I can then read it like a TelePrompTer. It is likely that Raymond, the autistic savant depicted in the movie *Rain Man,* used a similar strategy to memorize telephone books, maps, and other information. He simply photocopied each page of the phone book into his memory. When he wanted to find a certain number, he just scanned pages of the phone book that were in his mind. To pull information out of my memory, I have to replay the video. Pulling facts up quickly is sometimes difficult, because I have to play bits of different videos until I find the right tape. This takes time.

When I am unable to convert text to pictures, it is usually because the text has 5 no concrete meaning. Some philosophy books and articles about the cattle futures market are simply incomprehensible. It is much easier for me to understand written text that describes something that can be easily translated into pictures. The following sentence from a story in the February 21, 1994, issue of *Time* magazine, describing the Winter Olympics figure-skating championships, is a good example: "All the elements are in place—the spotlights, the swelling waltzes and jazz tunes, the sequined sprites taking to the air." In my imagination, I see the skating rink and skaters. However, if I ponder too long on the word "elements," I will make the inappropriate association of a periodic table on the wall of my high school chemistry classroom. Pausing on the word "sprite" triggers an image of a Sprite can in my refrigerator instead of a pretty young skater.

Teachers who work with autistic children need to understand associative thought patterns. An autistic child will often use a word in an inappropriate manner. Sometimes these uses have a logical associative meaning and other times they don't. For example, an autistic child might say the word "dog" when he wants to go outside. The word "dog" is associated with going outside. In my own case, I can remember both logical and illogical use of inappropriate words. When I was six, I learned to say "prosecution." I had absolutely no idea what it meant, but it sounded nice when I said it, so I used it as an exclamation every time my kite hit the ground. I must have baffled more than a few people who heard me exclaim "Prosecution!" to my downward-spiraling kite.

Discussions with other autistic people reveal similar visual styles of thinking about tasks that most people do sequentially. An autistic man who composes music told me that he makes "sound pictures" using small pieces of other music to create new compositions. A computer programmer with autism told me that he sees the general pattern of the program tree. After he visualizes the skeleton for the program, he simply writes the code for each branch. I use similar methods when I review scientific literature and troubleshoot at meat plants. I take specific findings or observations and combine them to find new basic principles and general concepts.

My thinking pattern always starts with specifics and works toward generalization in an associational and nonsequential way. As if I were attempting to figure out what the picture on a jigsaw puzzle is when only one third of the puzzle is completed, I am able to fill in the missing pieces by scanning my video library. Chinese mathematicians who can make large calculations in their heads work the same way.

At first they need an abacus, the Chinese calculator, which consists of rows of beads on wires in a frame. They make calculations by moving the rows of beads. When a mathematician becomes really skilled, he simply visualizes the abacus in his imagination and no longer needs a real one. The beads move on a visualized video abacus in his brain.

ABSTRACT THOUGHT

Growing up, I learned to convert abstract ideas into pictures as a way to understand them. I visualized concepts such as peace or honesty with symbolic images. I thought of peace as a dove, an Indian peace pipe, or TV or newsreel footage of the signing of a peace agreement. Honesty was represented by an image of placing one's hand on the Bible in court. A news report describing a person returning a wallet with all the money in it provided a picture of honest behavior.

The Lord's Prayer was incomprehensible until I broke it down into specific   10
visual images. The power and the glory were represented by a semicircular rainbow and an electrical tower. These childhood visual images are still triggered every time I hear the Lord's Prayer. The words "thy will be done" had no meaning when I was a child, and today the meaning is still vague. Will is a hard concept to visualize. When I think about it, I imagine God throwing a lightning bolt. Another adult with autism wrote that he visualized "Thou art in heaven" as God with an easel above the clouds. "Trespassing" was pictured as black and orange no trespassing signs. The word "Amen" at the end of the prayer was a mystery: a man at the end made no sense.

As a teenager and young adult I had to use concrete symbols to understand abstract concepts such as getting along with people and moving on to the next steps of my life, both of which were always difficult. I knew I did not fit in with my high school peers, and I was unable to figure out what I was doing wrong. No matter how hard I tried, they made fun of me. They called me "workhorse," "tape recorder," and "bones" because I was skinny. At the time I was able to figure out why they called me "workhorse" and "bones," but "tape recorder" puzzled me. Now I realize that I must have sounded like a tape recorder when I repeated things verbatim over and over. But back then I just could not figure out why I was such a social dud. I sought refuge in doing things I was good at, such as working on reroofing the barn or practicing my riding prior to a horse show. Personal relationships made absolutely no sense to me until I developed visual symbols of doors and windows. It was then that I started to understand concepts such as learning the give-and-take of a relationship. I still wonder what would have happened to me if I had not been able to visualize my way in the world.

Questions for Discussion and Writing

1. What limitations does Grandin confront in trying to understand abstract ideas and to communicate with other people? What problems did she encounter in high school because of this limitation?

2. In order to explain the radical difference of the way autistics think about things and understand words, Grandin uses analogies. Which of these analogies did you find most effective?

3. Try to translate a passage about an abstract idea (for example, charity or love) by thinking in pictures instead of words. What images did you use to represent these abstract ideas? What insight did this exercise give you into the world of autism?

ALISON LURIE

Alsion Lurie (b. 1926) is the Frederic J. Whiton Professor of American Literature at Cornell University, where she teaches writing and children's literature. She is the author of several books of nonfiction and fiction, including Foreign Affairs *(1984), for which she was awarded a Pulitzer Prize in 1985. Her latest works are* The Last Resort *(1998),* Imaginary Friends *(1998), and* Familiar Spirits: A Memoir of James Merrill and David Jackson *(2001). "The Language of Clothes" first appeared in* Human Ecology *(Spring 1991).*

The Language of Clothes

For thousands of years human beings have communicated with one another first in the language of dress. Long before I am near enough to talk to you on the street, in a meeting, or at a party, you announce your sex, age and class to me through what you are wearing—and very possibly give me important information (or misinformation) as to your occupation, origin, personality, opinions, tastes, sexual desires and current mood. I may not be able to put what I observe into words, but I register the information unconsciously; and you simultaneously do the same for me. By the time we meet and converse we have already spoken to each other in an older and more universal language.

The statement that clothing is a language, though made occasionally with the air of a man finding a flying saucer in his backyard, is not new. Balzac, in *Daughter of Eve* (1830), observed that dress is a "continual manifestation of intimate thoughts, a language, a symbol." Today, as semiotics becomes fashionable, sociologists tell us that fashion too is a language of signs, a nonverbal system of communication.

None of these theorists, however, has gone on to remark what seems obvious: that if clothing is a language, it must have a vocabulary and a grammar like other languages. Of course, as with human speech, there is not a single language of dress, but many: some (like Dutch and German) closely related and others (like Basque) almost unique. And within every language of clothes there are many different dialects and accents, some almost unintelligible to members of the mainstream culture. Moreover, as with speech, each individual has his own stock of words and employs personal variations of tone and meaning.

The vocabulary of dress includes not only items of clothing, but also hair styles, accessories, jewelry, makeup and body decoration. Theoretically at least this vocabulary is as large as or larger than that of any spoken tongue, since it includes every garment, hair style, and type of body decoration ever invented. In practice, of course, the sartorial resources of an individual may be very restricted. Those of a sharecropper, for instance, may be limited to five or ten "words" from which it is possible to create only a few "sentences" almost bare of decoration and expressing only the most basic concepts. A so-called fashion leader, on the other hand, may have several hundred "words" at his or her disposal, and thus be able to form thousands of different "sentences" that will express a wide range of meanings. Just as the average English-speaking person knows many more words than he or she will ever use in conversation, so all of us are able to understand the meaning of styles we will never wear.

MAGICAL CLOTHING

Archaeologists digging up past civilizations and anthropologists studying   5
primitive tribes have come to the conclusion that, as Rachel Kemper [*Costume*] puts it, "Paint, ornament, and rudimentary clothing were first employed to attract good animistic powers and to ward off evil." When Charles Darwin visited Tierra del Fuego, a cold, wet, disagreeable land plagued by constant winds, he found the natives naked except for feathers in their hair and symbolic designs painted on their bodies. Modern Australian bushmen, who may spend hours decorating themselves and their relatives with patterns in colored clay, often wear nothing else but an amulet or two.

However skimpy it may be, primitive dress almost everywhere, like primitive speech, is full of magic. A necklace of shark's teeth or a girdle of cowrie shells or feathers serves the same purpose as a prayer or spell, and may magically replace—or more often supplement—a spoken charm. In the first instance a form of *contagious* magic is at work: the shark's teeth are believed to endow their wearer with the qualities of a fierce and successful fisherman. The cowrie shells, on the other hand, work through *sympathetic* magic: since they resemble the female sexual parts, they are thought to increase or preserve fertility.

In civilized society today belief in the supernatural powers of clothing—like belief in prayers, spells and charms—remains widespread, though we denigrate it with the name "superstition." Advertisements announce that improbable and romantic events will follow the application of a particular sort of grease to our faces, hair or bodies; they claim that members of the opposite (or our own) sex will be drawn to us by the smell of a particular soap. Nobody believes those ads, you may say. Maybe not, but we behave as though we did: look in your bathroom cabinet.

The supernatural garments of European folk tales—the seven-league boots, the cloaks of invisibility and the magic rings—are not forgotten, merely transformed, so that today we have the track star who can only win a race in a particular hat or shoes, the plainclothes cop who feels no one can see him in his raincoat and the wife who takes off her wedding ring before going to a motel with her lover.

Sympathetic or symbolic magic is also often employed, as when we hang crosses, stars or one of the current symbols of female power and solidarity around our necks, thus silently involving the protection of Jesus, Jehovah or Astarte. Such amulets, of course, may be worn to announce our allegiance to some faith or cause rather than as a charm. Or they may serve both purposes simultaneously—or sequentially. The crucifix concealed below the parochial-school uniform speaks only to God until some devilish force persuades its wearer to remove his or her clothes; then it acts—or fails to act—as a warning against sin as well as a protective talisman.

Articles of clothing, too, may be treated as if they had mana, the impersonal supernatural force that tends to concentrate itself in objects. When I was in college it was common to wear a particular "lucky" sweater, shirt or hat to final examinations, and this practice continues today. Here it is usually contagious magic that is at work: the chosen garment has become lucky by being worn on the occasion of some earlier success, or has been given to its owner by some favored person. The wearing of such magical garments is especially common in sports, where they are often publicly credited with bringing their owners luck. Their loss or abandonment is thought to cause injury as well as defeat. Actors also believe ardently in the magic of clothes, possibly because they are so familiar with the near-magical transforming power of theatrical costume.

FASHION AND STATUS

Clothing designed to show the social position of its wearer has a long history. Just as the oldest languages are full of elaborate titles and forms of address, so for thousands of years certain modes have indicated high or royal rank. Many societies passed decrees known as *sumptuary laws* to prescribe or forbid the wearing of specific styles by specific classes of persons. In ancient Egypt only those in high position could wear sandals; the Greeks and Romans controlled the type, color and number of garments worn and the sorts of embroidery with which they could be trimmed. During the Middle Ages almost every aspect of dress was regulated at some place or time—though not always with much success. The common features of all sumptuary laws—like that of edicts, against the use of certain words—seem to be that they are difficult to enforce for very long.

Laws about what could be worn by whom continued to be passed in Europe until about 1700. But as class barriers weakened and wealth could be more easily and rapidly converted into gentility, the system by which color and shape indicated social status began to break down. What came to designate high rank instead was the evident cost of a costume: rich materials, superfluous trimmings and difficult-to-care-for styles, or as Thorstein Veblen later put it [in *The Theory of the Leisure Class*], Conspicuous Waste and Conspicuous Leisure. As a result, it was assumed that the people you met would be dressed as lavishly as their income permitted. In Fielding's *Tom Jones,* for instance, everyone judges strangers by their clothing and treats them accordingly; this is presented as natural. It is a world in which rank is very exactly indicated by costume, from the rags of Molly the gamekeeper's daughter to Sophia Western's riding habit "which was so very richly laced" that "Partridge and the postboy instantly started from their chairs, and my landlady fell to her curtsies, and her ladyships, with great eagerness." The elaborate wigs characteristic of this period conferred status partly because they were both expensive to buy and expensive to maintain.

By the early eighteenth century the social advantages of conspicuous dress were such that even those who could not afford it often spent their money on finery. This development was naturally deplored by supporters of the status quo. In Colonial America the Massachusetts General Court declared its "utter detestation and dislike, that men or women of mean condition, should take upon them the garb of Gentlemen, by wearing Gold or Silver lace, or Buttons, or Points at their knees, or to walk in great Boots; or Women of the same rank to wear Silk or Tiffiny hoods, or Scarfes. . . ." What "men or women of mean condition"—farmers or artisans—were supposed to wear were coarse linen or wool, leather aprons, deerskin jackets, flannel petticoats and the like.

To dress above one's station was considered not only foolishly extravagant, but deliberately deceptive. In 1878 an American etiquette book complained,

> It is . . . unfortunately the fact that, in the United States, but too much attention is paid to dress by those who have neither the excuse of ample means nor of social claims. . . . We Americans are lavish, generous, and ostentatious. The wives of our wealthy men are glorious in garb as are princesses and queens. They have a right so to be. But when those who can ill afford to wear alpaca persist in arraying themselves in silk . . . the matter is a sad one.

Color and Pattern

Certain sorts of information about other people can be communicated in spite of a language barrier. We may not be able to understand Welsh or the thick Southern dialect of the Mississippi delta, but when we hear a conversation in these tongues we can tell at once whether the speakers are excited or bored, cheerful or miserable, confident or frightened. In the same way, some aspects of the language of clothes can be read by almost anyone.

The first and most important of these signs, and the one that makes the greatest and most immediate impact, is color. Merely looking at different colors, psychologists have discovered, alters our blood pressure, heartbeat and rate of respiration, just as hearing a harsh noise or a harmonious musical chord does. When somebody approaches from a distance the first thing we see is the hue of his clothes; the closer he comes, the more space this hue occupies in our visual field and the greater its effect on our nervous system. Loud, clashing colors, like loud noises or loud voices, may actually hurt our eyes or give us a headache; soft, harmonious hues, like music and soft voices, thrill or soothe us. Color in dress is also like tone of voice in speech in that it can completely alter the meaning of what is "said" by other aspects of the costume: style, fabric and trimmings. Just as the words "Do you want to dance with me?" can be whispered shyly or flung as a challenge, so the effect of a white evening dress is very different from that of a scarlet one of identical fabric and pattern. In certain circumstances some hues, like some tones of voice, are beyond the bounds of polite discourse. A bride in a black wedding dress, or a stockbroker greeting his clients in a shocking-pink three-piece suit, would be like people screaming aloud.

Although color often indicates mood, it is not by any means an infallible guide. For one thing, convention may prescribe certain hues. The urban business-man must wear a navy blue, dark gray or (in certain regions) brown or tan suit, and can express his feelings only through his choice of shirt and tie, or tie alone; and even here the respectable possibilities may be very limited. Convention also alters the meaning of colors according to the place and time at which they are worn. Ver-milion in the office is not the same as vermilion at a disco; and hot weather permits the wearing of pale hues that would make one look far more formal and fragile in midwinter.

There are other problems. Some people may avoid colors they like because of the belief or illusion that they are unbecoming, while others may wear colors they normally dislike for symbolic reason: because they are members or fans of a certain football team, for instance. In addition, some fashionable types may select certain hues merely because they are "in" that year.

Finally, it should be noted that the effect of any color in dress is modified by the colors that accompany it. In general, therefore, the following remarks should be taken as applying mainly to costumes composed entirely or almost entirely of a sin-gle hue.

The mood of a crowd, as well as that of an individual, can often be read in the   20
colors of clothing. In the office of a large corporation, or at a professional conven-tion, there is usually a predominance of conventional gray, navy, beige, tan and white—suggesting a general attitude of seriousness, hard work, neutrality, propriety and status. The same group of people at a picnic are a mass of lively, relaxed blue, red and brown, with touches of yellow and green. In the evening, at a disco, they shimmer under the rotating lights in dramatic combinations of purple, crimson, orange, turquoise, gold, silver and black.

Apart from the chameleon, man is the only animal who can change his skin to suit his background. Indeed, if he is to function successfully he must do so. The individual whose clothes do not fall within the recognized range of colors for a given situation attracts attention, usually (though not always) unfavorable attention. When a child puts its pet chameleon down on the earth and it does not turn brown, we know the creature is seriously ill. In the same way, men or women who begin to come to work in a conservative office wearing disco hues and a disco mood are regarded with anxiety and suspicion. If they do not blush a respectable beige, navy or gray within a reasonable length of time, their colleagues know that they will not be around for long.

Questions for Discussion and Writing

1. In what way, according to Lurie, is clothing a kind of language that can be analyzed to discover both the wearer's and the surrounding culture's values? In the past, how did clothing and adornment serve magical purposes?

2. What factors related to social class have determined which kinds of clothes could or could not be worn in particular societies in different eras?
3. Go through your wardrobe and classify items of clothes you wear according to the "statement" you wish to make in different contexts.

DEBORAH TANNEN

Deborah Tannen teaches linguistics at Georgetown University. She has written many books on the difficulties of communicating across cultural, class, ethnic, and gender boundaries, including You Just Don't Understand: Women and Men in Conversation *(1990) and* The Argument Culture *(1998). The following essay from this book originally appeared in the* Washington Post *(1990). Tannen explains why men and women talk at cross-purposes and don't really listen to each other. Tannen's latest book on this subject is* I Only Say This Because I Love You: How the Way We Talk Can Make or Break Family Relationships throughout Our Lives *(2001).*

Sex, Lies, and Conversation

I was addressing a small gathering in a suburban Virginia living room—a women's group that had invited men to join them. Throughout the evening, one man had been particularly talkative, frequently offering ideas and anecdotes, while his wife sat silently beside him on the couch. Toward the end of the evening, I commented that women frequently complain that their husbands don't talk to them. This man quickly concurred. He gestured toward his wife and said, "She's the talker in our family." The room burst into laughter; the man looked puzzled and hurt. "It's true," he explained. "When I come home from work I have nothing to say. If she didn't keep the conversation going, we'd spend the whole evening in silence."

This episode crystallizes the irony that although American men tend to talk more than women in public situations, they often talk less at home. And this pattern is wreaking havoc with marriage.

The pattern was observed by political scientist Andrew Hacker in the late '70s. Sociologist Catherine Kohler Riessman reports in her new book *Divorce Talk* that most of the women she interviewed—but only a few of the men—gave lack of communication as the reason for their divorces. Given the current divorce rate of nearly 50 percent, that amounts to millions of cases in the United States every year—a virtual epidemic of failed conversation.

In my own research, complaints from women about their husbands most often focused not on tangible inequities such as having given up the chance for a career to accompany a husband to his, or doing far more than their share of daily life-support work like cleaning, cooking, social arrangements and errands. Instead, they focused on communication: "He doesn't listen to me," "He doesn't talk to me." I found, as Hacker observed years before, that most wives want their husbands to be, first and foremost, conversational partners, but few husbands share this expectation of their wives.

In short, the image that best represents the current crisis is the stereotypical car-   5
toon scene of a man sitting at the breakfast table with a newspaper held up in front of
his face, while a woman glares at the back of it, wanting to talk.

LINGUISTIC BATTLE OF THE SEXES

How can women and men have such different impressions of communication in
marriage? Why the widespread imbalance in their interests and expectations?

In the April issue of *American Psychologist,* Stanford University's Eleanor Maccoby
reports the results of her own and other's research showing that children's development
is most influenced by the social structure of peer interactions. Boys and girls tend to
play with children of their own gender, and their sex-separate groups have different or-
ganizational structures and interactive norms.

I believe these systematic differences in childhood socialization make talk between women and men like cross-cultural communication, heir to all the attraction and
pitfalls of that enticing but difficult enterprise. My research on men's and women's conversations uncovered patterns similar to those described for children's groups.

For women, as for girls, intimacy is the fabric of relationships, and talk is the
thread from which it is woven. Little girls create and maintain friendships by exchanging secrets; similarly, women regard conversation as the cornerstone of friendship. So a
woman expects her husband to be a new and improved version of a best friend. What is
important is not the individual subjects that are discussed but a sense of closeness, of a
life shared, that emerges when people tell their thoughts, feelings, and impressions.

Bonds between boys can be as intense as girls', but they are based less on talking,   10
more on doing things together. Since they don't assume talk is the cement that binds a
relationship, men don't know what kind of talk women want and they don't miss it
when it isn't there.

Boys' groups are larger, more inclusive, and more hierarchical, so boys must struggle to avoid the subordinate position in the group. This may play a role in women's
complaints that men don't listen to them. Some men really don't like to listen, because
being the listener makes them feel one-down, like a child listening to adults or an employee to a boss.

But often when women tell men, "You aren't listening," and the men protest, "I
am," the men are right. The impression of not listening results from misalignments in
the mechanics of conversation. The misalignment begins as soon as a man and a woman
take physical positions. This became clear when I studied videotapes made by psychologist Bruce Dorval of children and adults talking to their same-sex best friends. I found
that at every age, the girls and women faced each other directly, their eyes anchored on
each other's faces. At every age, the boys and men sat at angles to each other and looked
elsewhere in the room, periodically glancing at each other. They were obviously at-
tuned to each other, often mirroring each other's movements. But the tendency of men
to face away can give women the impression they aren't listening even when they are.
A young woman in college was frustrated: Whenever she told her boyfriend she wanted
to talk to him, he would lie down on the floor, close his eyes, and put his arm over his
face. This signaled to her, "He's taking a nap." But he insisted he was listening extra

hard. Normally, he looks around the room, so he is easily distracted. Lying down and covering his eyes helped him concentrate on what she was saying.

Analogous to the physical alignment that women and men take in conversation is their topical alignment. The girls in my study tended to talk at length about one topic, but the boys tended to jump from topic to topic. The second-grade girls exchanged stories about people they knew. The second-grade boys teased, told jokes, noticed things in the room and talked about finding games to play. The sixth-grade girls talked about problems with a mutual friend. The sixth-grade boys talked about 55 different topics, none of which extended over more than a few turns.

LISTENING TO BODY LANGUAGE

Switching topics is another habit that gives women the impression men aren't listening, especially if they switch to a topic about themselves. But the evidence of the tenth-grade boys in my study indicates otherwise. The tenth-grade boys sprawled across their chairs with bodies parallel and eyes straight ahead, rarely looking at each other. They looked as if they were riding in a car, staring out the windshield. But they were talking about their feelings. One boy was upset because a girl had told him he had a drinking problem, and the other was feeling alienated from all his friends.

Now, when a girl told a friend about a problem, the friend responded by asking   15
probing questions and expressing agreement and understanding. But the boys dismissed each other's problems. Todd assured Richard that his drinking was "no big problem" because "sometimes you're funny when you're off your butt." And when Todd said he felt left out, Richard responded, "Why should you? You know more people than me."

Women perceive such responses as belittling and unsupportive. But the boys seemed satisfied with them. Whereas women reassure each other by implying, "You shouldn't feel bad because I've had similar experiences," men do so by implying, "You shouldn't feel bad because your problems aren't so bad."

There are even simpler reasons for women's impression that men don't listen. Linguist Lynette Hirschman found that women make more listener-noise, such as "mhm," "uhuh," and "yeah," to show "I'm with you." Men, she found, more often give silent attention. Women who expect a stream of listener-noise interpret silent attention as no attention at all.

Women's conversational habits are as frustrating to men as men's are to women. Men who expect silent attention interpret a stream of listener-noise as overreaction or impatience. Also, when women talk to each other in a close, comfortable setting, they often overlap, finish each other's sentences and anticipate what the other is about to say. This practice, which I call "participatory listenership," is often perceived by men as interruption, intrusion and lack of attention.

A parallel difference caused a man to complain about his wife, "She just wants to talk about her own point of view. If I show her another view, she gets mad at me." When most women talk to each other, they assume a conversationalist's job is to express agreement and support. But many men see their conversational duty as pointing out the other side of an argument. This is heard as disloyalty by women, and refusal to offer the requisite support. It is not that women don't want to see other points of view, but that they prefer them phrased as suggestions and inquiries rather than as direct challenges.

In his book *Fighting for Life,* Walter Ong points out that men use "agonistic" or   20
warlike, oppositional formats to do almost anything; thus discussion becomes debate,
and conversation a competitive sport. In contrast, women see conversation as a ritual
means of establishing rapport. If Jane tells a problem and June says she has a similar one,
they walk away feeling closer to each other. But this attempt at establishing rapport can
backfire when used with men. Men take too literally women's ritual "troubles talk," just
as women mistake men's ritual challenges for real attack.

THE SOUNDS OF SILENCE

These differences begin to clarify why women and men have such different expectations about communication in marriage. For women, talk creates intimacy. Marriage is an orgy of closeness: you can tell your feelings and thoughts, and still be loved.
Their greatest fear is being pushed away. But men live in a hierarchical world, where
talk maintains independence and status. They are on guard to protect themselves from
being put down and pushed around.

This explains the paradox of the talkative man who said of his silent wife, "She's
the talker." In the public setting of a guest lecture, he felt challenged to show his intelligence and display his understanding of the lecture. But at home, where he has nothing
to prove and no one to defend against, he is free to remain silent. For his wife, being
home means she is free from the worry that something she says might offend someone,
or spark disagreement, or appear to be showing off; at home she is free to talk.

The communication problems that endanger marriage can't be fixed by mechanical engineering. They require a new conceptual framework about the role of talk in
human relationships. Many of the psychological explanations that have become second
nature may not be helpful, because they tend to blame either women (for not being assertive enough) or men (for not being in touch with their feelings). A sociolinguistic
approach by which male-female conversation is seen as cross-cultural communication
allows us to understand the problem and forge solutions without blaming either party.

Once the problem is understood, improvement comes naturally, as it did to the
young woman and her boyfriend who seemed to go to sleep when she wanted to talk.
Previously, she had accused him of not listening, and he had refused to change his behavior, since that would be admitting fault. But then she learned about and explained to
him the differences in women's and men's habitual ways of aligning themselves in conversation. The next time she told him she wanted to talk, he began, as usual, by lying
down and covering his eyes. When the familiar negative reaction bubbled up, she reassured herself that he really was listening. But then he sat up and looked at her. Thrilled,
she asked why. He said, "You like me to look at you when we talk, so I'll try to do it."
Once he saw their differences as cross-cultural rather than right and wrong, he independently altered his behavior.

Women who feel abandoned and deprived when their husbands won't listen to or   25
report daily news may be happy to discover their husbands trying to adapt once they
understand the place of small talk in women's relationships. But if their husbands don't
adapt, the women may still be comforted that for men, this is not a failure of intimacy.
Accepting the difference, the wives may look to their friends or family for that kind of

talk. And husbands who can't provide it shouldn't feel their wives have made unreasonable demands. Some couples will still decide to divorce, but at least their decisions will be based on realistic expectations.

In these times of resurgent ethnic conflicts, the world desperately needs cross-cultural understanding. Like charity, successful cross-cultural communication should begin at home.

Questions for Discussion and Writing

1. What different objectives do men and women pursue in conversations? How do these differences reveal themselves in verbal and nonverbal behavior?
2. How do the extended examples Tannen presents about two specific couples illustrate her thesis?
3. Evaluate her suggestions for improving communication between men and women. In your opinion, would they work? Why or why not?

STUART HIRSCHBERG

Stuart Hirschberg is an associate professor of English at Rutgers University in Newark, New Jersey, and is the author of several scholarly works on W. B. Yeats and Ted Hughes. He is also the editor and coeditor (with Terry Hirschberg) of rhetorics and anthologies, including this text; One World, Many Cultures *(fourth edition, 2001); and* Every Day, Everywhere: Global Perspectives on Popular Culture *(2002). The following essay is drawn from* Essential Strategies of Argument *(1996).*

The Rhetoric of Advertising

Whether ads are presented as sources of information enabling the consumer to make educated choices between products or aim at offering memorable images or witty, thoughtful, or poetic copy, the underlying intent of all advertising is to persuade specific audiences. Seen in this way, ads appear as mini-arguments whose strategies and techniques of persuasion can be analyzed just like a written argument. We can discover which elements are designed to appeal to the audience's emotions (*pathos* according to Aristotle), which elements make their appeal in terms of reasons, evidence, or logic (*logos*), and how the advertiser goes about winning credibility for itself or in terms of the spokesperson employed to speak on behalf of the product (the *ethos* dimension). Like arguments, ads can be effective if they appeal to the needs, values, and beliefs of the audience. Although the verbal and visual elements within an ad are designed to work together, we can study these elements separately. We can look at how the composition of the elements within an ad is intended to function. We can look at the role of language and how it is used to persuade. We can study how objects and settings are used to promote the audience's identification with the products being sold. We can judge ads according to the skill with which they deploy all of these resources while at the same time being critically aware of their intended effects on us.

THE TECHNIQUES OF ADVERTISING

The claim the ad makes is designed to establish the superiority of the product in the minds of the audience and to create a distinctive image for the product, whether it is a brand of cigarettes, a financial service, or a type of gasoline. The single most important technique for creating this image depends on transferring ideas, attributes, or feelings from outside the product onto the product itself. In this way the product comes to represent an obtainable object or service that embodies, represents, or symbolizes a whole range of meanings. This transfer can be achieved in many ways. For example, when Elizabeth Taylor lends her glamour and beauty to the merchandising of a perfume, the consumer is meant to conclude that the perfume must be superior to other perfumes in the way that Elizabeth Taylor embodies beauty, glamour, and sex appeal. The attempt to transfer significance can operate in two ways. It can encourage the audience to discover meanings and to correlate feelings and attributes that the advertiser wishes the product to represent in ways that allow these needs and desires to become attached to specific products. It can also prevent the correlation of thoughts or feelings that might discourage the audience from purchasing a particular product. For example, the first most instinctive response to the thought of smoking a cigarette might be linked with the idea of inhaling hot and dry smoke from what are essentially burning tobacco leaves. Thus, any associations the audience might have with burning leaves, coughing, and dry hot smoke must be short-circuited by supplying them with a whole set of other associations to receive and occupy the perceptual "slot" that might have been triggered by their first reactions. Cigarette advertisers do this in a variety of ways:

> By showing active people in outdoorsy settings they put the thought of emphysema, shortness of breath, or lung disease very far away indeed.

> By showing cigarette packs set against the background of grass glistening with morning dew or bubbling streams or cascading waterfalls, they subtly guide the audience's response away from what is dry, hot, congested, or burning toward what is open, airy, moist, cool, and clean.

> In some brands, menthol flavoring and green and blue colors are intended to promote these associations.

Thus, ads act as do all other kinds of persuasion to intensify correlations that work to the advertiser's advantage and to suppress associations that would lessen the product's appeal.

The kinds of associations audiences are encouraged to perceive reflect a broad range of positive emotional appeals that encourage the audience to find self-esteem through the purchase of a product that by itself offers a way to meet personal and social needs. The particular approach taken in the composition of the ad, the way it is laid out, and the connotations of the advertising copy vary according to the emotional appeal of the ad.

The most common manipulative techniques are designed to make consumers   5
want to consume to satisfy deep-seated human drives. Of course, no one consciously believes that purchasing a particular kind of toothpaste, perfume, lipstick,
or automobile will meet real psychological and social needs, but that is exactly how
products are sold—through the promise of delivering unattainable satisfactions
through tangible purchasable objects or services. In purchasing a certain product,
we are offered the chance to create ourselves, our personality, and our relationships
through consumption.

EMOTIONAL APPEALS USED IN ADVERTISING

*The emotional appeals in ads function exactly the way assumptions about value do in
written arguments.* They supply the unstated major premise that supplies a rationale
to persuade an audience that a particular product will meet one or another of several different kinds of needs. Some ads present the purchase of a product as a means
by which consumers can find social acceptance.

These ads address the consumer as "you" ("Wouldn't 'you' really rather have a
Buick?"). The "you" here is plural but is perceived as being individual and personal
by someone who has already formed the connection with the product. Ironically,
the price of remaining in good standing with this "group" of fellow consumers requires the consumer to purchase an expensive automobile. In this sense, ads give
consumers a chance to belong to social groups that have only one thing in common—the purchase of a particular product.

One variation on the emotional need to belong to a designated social group
is the appeal to status or "snob appeal." Snob appeal is not new. In 1710, the *Spectator,* a popular newspaper of the time, carried an ad that read:

> An incomparable Powder for Cleaning Teeth, which has given great satisfaction to
> most of the Nobility Gentry in England. (Quoted in W. Duncan Reekie, *Advertising:
> Its Place in Political and Managerial Economics,* 1974.)

Ads for scotch, expensive cars, boats, jewelry, and watches frequently place
their products in upper-class settings or depict them in connection with the fine
arts (sculpture, ballet, etc.). The *value warrant* in these ads encourages the consumer
to imagine that the purchase of the item will confer qualities associated with the
background or activities of this upper-class world onto the consumer.

In other ads the need to belong takes a more subtle form of offering the prod-   10
uct as a way to become part of a time in the past the audience might look back to
with nostalgia. Grandmotherly figures wearing aprons and holding products that
are advertised as being "like Grandma used to make" offer the consumer an imaginary past, a family tradition, or a simpler time looked back to with warmth and
sentimentality. For many years, Smucker's preserves featured ads in which the product was an integral part of a scene emanating security and warmth, which the ad
invited us to remember as if it were our own past. Ads of this kind are often photographed through filters that present misty sepia-tone images that carefully recreate old-fashioned kitchens with the accompanying appliances, dishes, clothes, and

THERE WILL ALWAYS BE THOSE WHO REFUSE TO SKI MAMMOTH.

Admittedly, with an elevation of 11,053 feet and 3,100 foot vertical, there are those of you who just flat out won't pay us a visit. Guess you probably don't realize we have 150 trails – spread out over 3,500 skiable acres – so there's lots of prime terrain, no matter what your ability. But hey, if you don't want to call 1-800-832-7320 and get the complete story in our free travel planner, far be it for us to insist. We certainly wouldn't want to ruffle anyone's feathers.

MAMMOTH

No other mountain lives up to its name.

Source: Mammoth.

hairstyles. The ads thus supply us with false memories and invite us to insert ourselves into this imaginary past and to remember it as if it were our own. At the furthest extreme, ads employing the appeal to see ourselves as part of a group may try to evoke patriotic feelings so that the prospective consumer will derive the satisfactions of good citizenship and sense of participation in being part of the collective psyche of an entire nation. The point is that people really do have profound needs that advertisers can exploit, but it would be a rare product indeed that could really fulfill such profound needs.

Advertisers use highly sophisticated market research techniques to enable them to define and characterize precisely those people who are most likely to be receptive to ads of particular kinds. The science of demographics is aided and abetted by psychological research that enables advertisers to "target" a precisely designated segment of the general public. For example, manufacturers of various kinds of liquor can rely on studies that inform them that vodka drinkers are most likely to read *Psychology Today* and scotch drinkers the *New Yorker,* while readers of *Time* prefer rum and the audience for *Playboy* has a large number of readers who prefer gin. Once a market segment with defined psychological characteristics has been identified, an individual ad can be crafted for that particular segment and placed in the appropriate publication.

Ads, of course, can elicit responses by attempting to manipulate consumers through negative as well as positive emotional appeals. Helen Woodward, the head

"I didn't use one because I didn't have one with me."

GET REAL

If you don't have a parachute, don't jump, genius.

Helps reduce the risk

copywriter for an ad agency, once offered the following advice for ad writers trying to formulate a new ad for baby food: "Give 'em the figures about the baby
death rate—but don't say it flatly . . . if we only had the nerve to put a hearse in the
ad, you couldn't keep the women away from the food" (Stuart Ewen, *Captains of
Consciousness: Advertising and the Social Roots of Consumer Culture* [1976]). Ads of this
kind must first arouse the consumer's anxieties and then offer the product as the
solution to the problem that more often than not the ad has created.

For example, an advertisement for Polaroid evokes the fear of not having
taken pictures of moments that cannot be re-created and then offers the product as
a form of insurance that will prevent this calamity from occurring. Nikon does the
same in claiming that "a moment is called a moment because it doesn't last forever.
Think of sunsets. A child's surprise. A Labrador's licky kiss. This is precisely why the
Nikon N50 has the simple 'Simple' switch on top of the camera."

Ads for products that promise to guarantee their purchasers sex appeal, youth,
health, social acceptance, self-esteem, creativity, enlightenment, a happy family life,
loving relationships, escape from boredom, vitality, and many other things frequently
employ scare tactics to frighten or worry the consumer into purchasing the product
to ease his or her fears. These ads must first make the consumer dissatisfied with the
self that exists. In this way, they function exactly as do *policy arguments* that recommend solutions to problems with measurably harmful consequences. The difference
is that these kinds of ads actually are designed to arouse and then exploit the anxieties related to these problems.

Large industrial conglomerates, whether in oil, chemicals, pharmaceuticals, or   15
agribusiness, frequently use advertising to accomplish different kinds of objectives
than simply persuading the consumer to buy a particular product. These companies
often seek to persuade the general public that they are not polluting the environment, poisoning the water, or causing environmental havoc in the process of manufacturing their products. The emotional appeal they use is to portray themselves as
concerned "corporate citizens," vitally interested in the public good as a whole, and
especially in those communities where they conduct their operations. In some cases,
the ads present products as if they were directly produced from nature without being
subjected to intermediary processing, preservatives, and contaminants, thereby lessen-
ing concern that they produce harmful byproducts. For example, Mazola might depict a spigot producing corn oil directly inserted into an ear of corn. A Jeep might
appear to have materialized out of thin air on a seemingly inaccessible mountain
peak. Companies sensitive to accusations that they are polluting the air and water can
mount an advertising campaign designed to prove that they are not simply exploiting
the local resources (whether timber, oil, fish, coal) for profits but are genuinely interested in putting something back into the community. The folksy good-neighbor tone
of these ads is designed to create a benign image of the company.

THE LANGUAGE OF ADVERTISING

We can see how the creation of a sense of the company's credibility as a concerned citizen corresponds to what Aristotle called the *ethos* dimension. For example, Chevron expresses concern that the light from their oil drilling operations be

shielded so that spawning sea turtles won't be unintentionally misdirected and lose their way!

The appeals to logic, statements of reasons, and presentations of evidence in ads correspond to the *logos* dimension of argument. The wording of the claims is particularly important, since it determines whether companies are legally responsible for any claims they make.

Claims in advertising need to be evaluated to discover whether something is asserted that needs to be proved or is implied without actually being stated.

Claims may refer to authoritative-sounding results obtained by supposedly independent laboratories, teams of research scientists, or physicians without ever saying how these surveys were conducted, what statistical methods were used, and who interpreted the results. Ads of this kind may make an impressive-sounding quasi-scientific claim; Ivory Soap used to present itself as "99 and 44/100% pure" without answering "pure" what. Some ads use technical talk and scientific terms to give the impression of a scientific breakthrough. For example, STP claims that it added "an anti-wear agent and viscosity improvers" to your oil. The copy for L. L. Bean claims of one of its jackets that "even in brutal ice winds gusting to 80 knots this remarkable anorak kept team members who wore it warm and comfortable." It would be important to know that the team members referred to are members of the "L. L. Bean test team."

Other claims cannot be substantiated, for example, "we're the Dexter Shoe   20 Company. And for nearly four decades we put a lot of Dexter Maine into every pair of shoes we make."

In an ad for lipstick, Aveda makes the claim that "it's made of rich, earthy lip colours formulated with pure plant pigment from the Uruku tree. Organically grown by indigenous people in the rain forest."

Claims may be deceptive in other ways. Of all the techniques advertisers use to influence what people believe and how they spend their money, none is more basic than the use of so-called *weasel words*. This term was popularized by Theodore Roosevelt in a speech he gave in St. Louis, May 31, 1916, when he commented that notes from the Department of State were filled with *weasel words* that retract the meaning of the words they are next to just as a weasel sucks the meat out of the egg.

In modern advertising parlance, a weasel word has come to mean any qualifier or comparative that is used to imply a positive quality that cannot be stated as a fact, because it cannot be substantiated. For example, if an ad claims a toothpaste will "help" stop cavities it does not obligate the manufacturer to substantiate this claim. So, too, if a product is advertised as "fighting" germs, the equivocal claim hides the fact that the product may fight and lose.

A recent ad for STP claimed that "no matter what kind of car you drive, STP gas treatment helps remove the water that leads to gas line freeze. And unlike gas line anti-freeze, our unique gas treatment formula works to reduce intake valve deposits and prevent clogged injectors." The key words are "helps" and "works," neither of which obligates STP to be legally accountable to support the claim.

The words *virtually* (as in "virtually spotless") and *up to* or *for as long as* (as in   25 "stops coughs up to eight hours") also remove any legal obligation on the part of the manufacturer to justify the claim.

Other favorite words in the copywriter's repertoire, such as *free* and *new,* are useful in selling everything from cat food to political candidates.

THE ETHICAL DIMENSION OF PERSUASION

As we have seen in our examination of the methods advertisers use to influence consumers, ethical questions are implicit in every act of persuasion. For example, what are we to make of a persuader whose objectives in seeking to influence an audience may be praiseworthy but who consciously makes use of distorted facts or seeks to manipulate an audience by playing on their known attitudes, values, and beliefs. Is success in persuasion the only criterion or should we hold would-be persuaders accountable to some ethical standards of responsibility about the means they use to achieve specific ends? Perhaps the most essential quality in determining whether any act of persuasion is an ethical one depends on the writer maintaining an open dialogue with different perspectives that might be advanced on a particular issue. By contrast, any act of persuasion that intentionally seeks to avoid self-criticism or challenges from competing perspectives will come across as insincere, dogmatic, deceptive, and defensive. The desire to shut down debate or control an audience's capacity to respond to the argument might well be considered unethical. The consequence of this attitude may be observed in the arguer's use of fraudulent evidence, illogical reasoning, emotionally laden irrelevant appeals, simplistic representation of the issue, or the pretense of expertise. Standards to apply when judging the ethical dimension in any act of persuasion require us to consider whether any element of coercion, deception, or manipulation is present. This becomes especially true when we look at the relationship between propaganda as a form of mass persuasion and the rhetorical means used to influence large groups of people.

Questions for Discussion and Writing

1. How do modern advertisers use traditional rhetorical techniques, identified by Aristotle, to appeal to the audiences' emotions (*pathos*), reason (*logos*), and sense of credibility (*ethos*)?
2. In what ways does advertising depend on the transfer of ideas and associations to create a sense of distinctive identity for the product or service?
3. How do the following ads use the techniques identified in this article to market their products? In your opinion, are these ads effective? Why or why not?

ALDOUS HUXLEY

Aldous Huxley (1894–1963) was born in Surrey, England, and was educated at Eton and Balliol College, Oxford. Despite a serious eye disease, Huxley read with the aid of a magnifying glass and graduated from Oxford in 1915 with honors in English literature, after which he joined the staff of the Atheneum. *His brilliant social satires and wide-ranging essays on*

architecture, science, music, history, philosophy, and religion explore the relationship between hu-
mans and society. Brave New World *(1932) is his best-known satire on how futuristic mass*
technology will achieve a sinister utopia of scientific breeding and conditioned happiness. Hux-
ley's other works include Eyeless in Gaza *(1936),* After Many a Summer *(1939),* Time
Must Have a Stop *(1944), and* Ape and Essence *(1948).* The Doors of Perception
(1954), Heaven and Hell *(1956), and* Island *(1962) can be seen as attempts to search in*
new spiritual directions—through mysticism, mescaline, and parapsychology—as a reaction to the
grim future he so devastatingly portrayed. In "Propaganda under a Dictatorship," from Brave
New World Revisited *(1958), Huxley reveals how the manipulation of language in the prop-*
aganda of Nazi Germany conditioned the thoughts and behavior of the masses.

Propaganda under a Dictatorship

At his trial after the Second World War, Hitler's Minister for Armaments, Albert Speer, delivered a long speech in which, with remarkable acuteness, he described the Nazi tyranny and analyzed its methods. "Hitler's dictatorship," he said,
"differed in one fundamental point from all its predecessors in history. It was the
first dictatorship in the present period of modern technical development, a dictatorship which made complete use of all technical means for the domination of its
own country. Through technical devices like the radio and the loudspeaker, eighty
million people were deprived of independent thought. It was thereby possible to
subject them to the will of one man. . . . Earlier dictators needed highly qualified
assistants even at the lowest level—men who could think and act independently.
The totalitarian system in the period of modern technical development can dis-
pense with such men; thanks to modern methods of communication, it is possible
to mechanize the lower leadership. As a result of this there has arisen the new type
of the uncritical recipient of orders."

In the Brave New World of my prophetic fable technology had advanced far
beyond the point it had reached in Hitler's day; consequently the recipients of orders were far less critical than their Nazi counterparts, far more obedient to the
order-giving elite. Moreover, they had been genetically standardized and postna-
tally conditioned to perform their subordinate functions, and could therefore be
depended upon to behave almost as predictably as machines. . . . This conditioning
of "the lower leadership" is already going on under the Communist dictatorships.
The Chinese and the Russians are not relying merely on the indirect effects of advancing technology; they are working directly on the psychophysical organisms of
their lower leaders, subjecting minds and bodies to a system of ruthless and, from all
accounts, highly effective conditioning. "Many a man," said Speer, "has been
haunted by the nightmare that one day nations might be dominated by technical
means. That nightmare was almost realized in Hitler's totalitarian system." Almost,
but not quite. The Nazis did not have time—and perhaps did not have the intelligence and the necessary knowledge—to brainwash and condition their lower leadership. This, it may be, is one of the reasons why they failed.

Since Hitler's day the armory of technical devices at the disposal of the would-
be dictator has been considerably enlarged. As well as the radio, the loudspeaker,
the moving picture camera and the rotary press, the contemporary propagandist

can make use of television to broadcast the image as well as the voice of his client, and can record both image and voice on spools of magnetic tape. Thanks to technological progress, Big Brother can now be almost as omnipresent as God. Nor is it only on the technical front that the hand of the would-be dictator has been strengthened. Since Hitler's day a great deal of work has been carried out in those fields of applied psychology and neurology which are the special province of the propagandist, the indoctrinator and the brainwasher. In the past these specialists in the art of changing people's minds were empiricists. By a method of trial and error they had worked out a number of techniques and procedures, which they used very effectively without, however, knowing precisely why they were effective. Today the art of mind-control is in process of becoming a science. The practitioners of this science know what they are doing and why. They are guided in their work by theories and hypotheses solidly established on a massive foundation of experimental evidence. Thanks to the new insights and the new techniques made possible by these insights, the nightmare that was "all but realized in Hitler's totalitarian system" may soon be completely realizable.

But before we discuss these new insights and techniques let us take a look at the nightmare that so nearly came true in Nazi Germany. What were the methods used by Hitler and Goebbels[1] for "depriving eighty million people of independent thought and subjecting them to the will of one man"? And what was the theory of human nature upon which those terrifyingly successful methods were based? These questions can be answered, for the most part, in Hitler's own words. And what remarkably clear and astute words they are! When he writes about such vast abstractions as Race and History and Providence, Hitler is strictly unreadable. But when he writes about the German masses and the methods he used for dominating and directing them, his style changes. Nonsense gives place to sense, bombast to a hard-boiled and cynical lucidity. In his philosophical lucubrations Hitler was either cloudily daydreaming or reproducing other people's half-baked notions. In his comments on crowds and propaganda he was writing of things he knew by firsthand experience. In the words of his ablest biographer, Mr. Alan Bullock, "Hitler was the greatest demagogue in history." Those who add, "only a demagogue," fail to appreciate the nature of political power in an age of mass politics. As he himself said, "To be a leader means to be able to move the masses." Hitler's aim was first to move the masses and then, having pried them loose from their traditional loyalties and moralities, to impose upon them (with the hypnotized consent of the majority) a new authoritarian order of his own devising. "Hitler," wrote Hermann Rauschning in 1939, "has a deep respect for the Catholic church and the Jesuit order; not because of their Christian doctrine, but because of the 'machinery' they have elaborated and controlled, their hierarchical system, their extremely clever tactics, their knowledge of human nature and their wise use of human weaknesses in ruling over believers." Ecclesiasticism without Christianity, the discipline of a monastic rule, not for God's sake or in order to achieve personal salvation, but for the sake of the State and for

---

[1] *Joseph Paul Goebbels (1897–1945):* the propaganda minister under Hitler, a master of the "big lie."

the greater glory and power of the demagogue turned Leader—this was the goal toward which the systematic moving of the masses was to lead.

Let us see what Hitler thought of the masses he moved and how he did the moving. The first principle from which he started was a value judgment: the masses are utterly contemptible. They are incapable of abstract thinking and uninterested in any fact outside the circle of their immediate experience. Their behavior is determined, not by knowledge and reason, but by feelings and unconscious drives. It is in these drives and feelings that "the roots of their positive as well as their negative attitudes are implanted." To be successful a propagandist must learn how to manipulate these instincts and emotions. "The driving force which has brought about the most tremendous revolutions on this earth has never been a body of scientific teaching which has gained power over the masses, but always a devotion which has inspired them, and often a kind of hysteria which has urged them into action. Whoever wishes to win over the masses must know the key that will open the door of their hearts." . . . In post-Freudian jargon, of their unconscious.

Hitler made his strongest appeal to those members of the lower middle classes who had been ruined by the inflation of 1923, and then ruined all over again by the depression of 1929 and the following years. "The masses" of whom he speaks were these bewildered, frustrated and chronically anxious millions. To make them more masslike, more homogeneously subhuman, he assembled them, by the thousands and the tens of thousands, in vast halls and arenas, where individuals could lose their personal identity, even their elementary humanity, and be merged with the crowd. A man or woman makes direct contact with society in two ways: as a member of some familial, professional or religious group, or as a member of a crowd. Groups are capable of being as moral and intelligent as the individuals who form them; a crowd is chaotic, has no purpose of its own and is capable of anything except intelligent action and realistic thinking. Assembled in a crowd, people lose their powers of reasoning and their capacity for moral choice. Their suggestibility is increased to the point where they cease to have any judgment or will of their own. They become very excitable, they lose all sense of individual or collective responsibility, they are subject to sudden accesses of rage, enthusiasm and panic. In a word, a man in a crowd behaves as though he had swallowed a large dose of some powerful intoxicant. He is a victim of what I have called "herd-poisoning." Like alcohol, herd-poison is an active, extraverted drug. The crowd-intoxicated individual escapes from responsibility, intelligence and morality into a kind of frantic, animal mindlessness.

During his long career as an agitator, Hitler had studied the effects of herd-poison and had learned how to exploit them for his own purposes. He had discovered that the orator can appeal to those "hidden forces" which motivate men's actions, much more effectively than can the writer. Reading is a private, not a collective activity. The writer speaks only to individuals, sitting by themselves in a state of normal sobriety. The orator speaks to masses of individuals, already well primed with herd-poison. They are at his mercy and, if he knows his business, he can do what he likes with them. As an orator, Hitler knew his business supremely well. He was able, in his own words, "to follow the lead of the great mass in such a way that from the living emotion to his hearers the apt word which he needed would be suggested to him and in its turn this would go straight to the heart of his hearers." Otto Strasser called him a "loudspeaker, proclaiming the most secret desires, the least admissible instincts, the sufferings and personal revolts of a whole nation." Twenty years before Madison Avenue embarked upon "Motivational Research," Hitler was systematically exploring and exploiting the secret fears and hopes, the cravings, anxieties and frustrations of the German masses. It is by manipulating "hidden forces" that the advertising experts induce us to buy their wares—a toothpaste, a brand of cigarettes, a political candidate. And it is by appealing to the same hidden forces—and to others too dangerous for Madison Avenue to meddle with—that Hitler induced the German masses to buy themselves a Fuehrer, an insane philosophy and the Second World War.

Unlike the masses, intellectuals have a taste for rationality and an interest in facts. Their critical habit of mind makes them resistant to the kind of propaganda that works so well on the majority. Among the masses "instinct is supreme, and from instinct comes faith. . . . While the healthy common folk instinctively close their ranks to form a community of the people" (under a Leader, it goes without saying) "intellectuals run this way and that, like hens in a poultry yard. With them one cannot make history; they cannot be used as elements composing a community." Intellectuals are the kind of people who demand evidence and are shocked by logical inconsistencies and fallacies. They regard oversimplification as the original sin of the mind and have no use for the slogans, the unqualified assertions and sweeping generalizations which are the propagandist's stock in trade. "All effective propaganda," Hitler wrote, "must be confined to a few bare necessities and then must be expressed in a few stereotyped formulas." These stereotyped formulas must be constantly repeated, for "only constant repetition will finally succeed in imprinting an idea upon the memory of a crowd." Philosophy teaches us to feel uncertain about the things that seem to us self-evident. Propaganda, on the other hand, teaches us to accept as self-evident matters about which it would be reasonable to suspend our judgment or to feel doubt. The aim of the demagogue is to create social coherence under his own leadership. But, as Bertrand Russell has pointed out, "systems of dogma without empirical foundations, such as scholasticism, Marxism and fascism, have the advantage of producing a great deal of social coherence among their disciples." The demagogic propagandist must therefore be consistently dogmatic. All his statements are made without qualification. There are no grays in his picture of the world; everything is either diabolically black or celestially white. In Hitler's words, the propagandist should adopt "a systematically one-sided attitude towards every problem that has to be dealt with." He must never admit that he might be wrong or that people with a different point of view might be even partially right. Opponents should not be argued with; they should be attacked, shouted down, or, if they become too much of a nuisance, liquidated. The morally squeamish intellectual may be shocked by this kind of thing. But the masses are always convinced that "right is on the side of the active aggressor."

Such, then, was Hitler's opinion of humanity in the mass. It was a very low opinion. Was it also an incorrect opinion? The tree is known by its fruits, and a theory of human nature which inspired the kind of techniques that proved so horribly effective must contain at least an element of truth. Virtue and intelligence belong to human beings as individuals freely associating with other individuals in small groups. So do sin and stupidity. But the subhuman mindlessness to which the demagogue makes his appeal, the moral imbecility on which he relies when he goads his victims into action, are characteristic not of men and women as individuals, but of men and women in masses. Mindlessness and moral idiocy are not characteristically human attributes; they are symptoms of herd-poisoning. In all the world's higher religions, salvation and enlightenment are for individuals. The kingdom of heaven is within the mind of a person, not within the collective mindlessness of a crowd. Christ promised to be present where two or three are gathered together. He did not say anything about being present where thousands are intoxicating one another with herd-poison. Under the Nazis enormous numbers of people were compelled to spend an enormous amount of time marching in serried ranks from point A to point B and back again to point A. "This keeping of the whole population on the march seemed to be a senseless waste of time and energy. Only much later," adds Hermann Rauschning, "was there revealed in it a subtle intention based on a well-judged adjustment of ends and means. Marching diverts men's thoughts. Marching kills thought. Marching makes an end of individuality. Marching is the indispensable magic stroke performed in order to accustom the people to a mechanical, quasi-ritualistic activity until it becomes second nature."

From his point of view and at the level where he had chosen to do his dreadful work, Hitler was perfectly correct in his estimate of human nature. To those of us who look at men and women as individuals rather than as members of crowds, or of regimented collectives, he seems hideously wrong. In an age of accelerating overpopulation, of accelerating overorganization and even more efficient means of mass communication, how can we preserve the integrity and reassert the value of the human individual? This is a question that can still be asked and perhaps effectively answered. A generation from now it may be too late to find an answer and perhaps impossible, in the stifling collective climate of that future time, even to ask the question.

10

Questions for Discussion and Writing

1. In Huxley's view, why was one particular segment of the German population so vulnerable to Hitler's propaganda techniques? What role did the inflation of 1923 and the Depression of 1929 play in setting the stage for Hitler's rise to power?

2. What propaganda techniques did Hitler use to manipulate the masses? What was Hitler's opinion of the masses he manipulated?

3. What are some of the more telling examples of contemporary propaganda techniques of stereotypes, slogans, slanting, guilt, or virtue by association mentioned by Huxley? What present-day examples used by politicians can you identify?

MARGARET ATWOOD

Margaret Atwood was born in Ottawa, Ontario, in 1939 and spent her childhood in northern Ontario and Quebec. She was educated at the University of Toronto, where she came under the influence of the critic Northrup Frye, whose theories of mythical modes in literature Atwood has adapted to her own purposes in her prolific writing of poetry, novels, and short stories. She is the author of more than twenty volumes of poetry and fiction, including the novels Surfacing *(1972),* Life before Man *(1979),* Bodily Harm *(1981), and* The Handmaid's Tale *(1986), a much discussed work that was made into a film in 1989. Her most recent novel is* Alias Grace *(1996). Her short stories are collected in* Dancing Girls *(1977),* Murder in the Dark *(1983), and* Bluebeard's Egg and Other Stories *(1986). Atwood also edited the* Oxford Book of Canadian Short Stories in English *(1987). Her latest books include* A Quiet Game *(1997),* Two Solicitudes *(1998),* The Blind Assassin *(2000), and* Negotiating with the Dead: A Writer on Writing *(2001). In "Pornography," Atwood decries obscene and violent images that she believes have a corrupting influence on those who watch them or read about them.*

Pornography

When I was in Finland a few years ago for an international writers' conference, I had occasion to say a few paragraphs in public on the subject of pornography. The context was a discussion of political repression, and I was suggesting the possibility of a link between the two. The immediate result was that a male journalist took several large bites out of me. Prudery and pornography are two halves of the same coin, said he, and I was clearly a prude. What could you expect from an Anglo-Canadian? Afterward, a couple of pleasant Scandinavian men asked me what I had been so worked up about. All "pornography" means, they said, is graphic depictions of whores, and what was the harm in that?

Not until then did it strike me that the male journalist and I had two entirely different things in mind. By "pornography," he meant naked bodies and sex. I, on the other hand, had recently been doing the research for my novel *Bodily Harm,* and was still in a state of shock from some of the material I had seen, including the Ontario Board of Film Censors' "outtakes." By "pornography," I meant women getting their nipples snipped off with garden shears, having meat hooks stuck into their vaginas, being disemboweled; little girls being raped; men (yes, there are some men) being smashed to a pulp and forcibly sodomized. The cutting edge of pornography, as far as I could see, was no longer simple old copulation, hanging from the chandelier or otherwise: it was death, messy, explicit and highly sadistic. I explained this to the nice Scandinavian men. "Oh, but that's just the United States," they said. "Everyone knows they're sick." In their country, they said, violent "pornography" of that kind was not permitted on television or in movies; indeed, excessive violence of any kind was not permitted. They had drawn a clear line between erotica, which earlier studies had shown did not incite men to more aggressive and brutal behavior toward women, and violence, which later studies indicated did.

Some time after that I was in Saskatchewan, where, because of the scenes in *Bodily Harm,* I found myself on an open-line radio show answering questions about "pornography." Almost no one who phoned in was in favor of it, but again they weren't talking about the same stuff I was, because they hadn't seen it. Some of them were all set to stamp out bathing suits and negligees, and, if possible, any depictions of the female body whatsoever. God, it was implied, did not approve of female bodies, and sex of any kind, including that practised by bumblebees, should be shoved back into the dark, where it belonged. I had more than a suspicion that *Lady Chatterley's Lover,*[1] Margaret Laurence's *The Diviners,*[2] and indeed most books by most serious modern authors would have ended up as confetti if left in the hands of these callers.

For me, these two experiences illustrate the two poles of the emotionally heated debate that is now thundering around this issue. They also underline the desirability and even the necessity of defining the terms. "Pornography" is now one of those catchalls, like "Marxism" and "feminism," that have become so broad they can mean almost anything, ranging from certain verses in the Bible, ads for skin lotion and sex texts for children to the contents of *Penthouse,* Naughty '90s postcards and films with titles containing the word *Nazi* that show vicious scenes of torture and killing. It's easy to say that sensible people can tell the difference. Unfortunately, opinions on what constitutes a sensible person vary.

But even sensible people tend to lose their cool when they start talking about this subject. They soon stop talking and start yelling, and the name-calling begins. Those in favor of censorship (which may include groups not noticeably in agreement on other issues, such as some feminists and religious fundamentalists) accuse the others of exploiting women through the use of degrading images, contributing to the corruption of children, and adding to the general climate of violence and threat in which both women and children live in this society; or, though they may not give much of a hoot about actual women and children, they invoke moral standards and God's supposed aversion to "filth," "smut" and deviated *perversion,* which may mean ankles.

The camp in favor of total "freedom of expression" often comes out howling as loud as the Romans would have if told they could no longer have innocent fun watching the lions eat up Christians. It too may include segments of the population who are not natural bedfellows: those who proclaim their God-given right to freedom, including the freedom to tote guns, drive when drunk, drool over chicken

5

---

[1] *Lady Chatterley's Lover (1928):* a controversial novel by D. H. Lawrence that was the subject of a U. S. Supreme Court trial for obscenity.   [2] *The Diviners (1974):* a novel by the Canadian author Margaret Laurence (1926–1987).

porn[3] and get off on videotapes of women being raped and beaten, may be waving the same anticensorship banner as responsible liberals who fear the return of Mrs. Grundy[4], or gay groups for whom sexual emancipation involves the concept of "sexual theatre." *Whatever turns you on* is a handy motto, as is *A man's home is his castle* (and if it includes a dungeon with beautiful maidens strung up in chains and bleeding from every pore, that's his business).

Meanwhile, theoreticians theorize and speculators speculate. Is today's pornography yet another indication of the hatred of the body, the deep mind–body split, which is supposed to pervade Western Christian society? Is it a backlash against the women's movement by men who are threatened by uppity female behavior in real life, so like to fantasize about women done up like outsize parcels, being turned into hamburger, kneeling at their feet in slavelike adoration or sucking off guns? Is it a sign of collective impotence, of a generation of men who can't relate to real women at all but have to make do with bits of celluloid and paper? Is the current flood just a result of smart marketing and aggressive promotion by the money men in what has now become a multibillion-dollar industry? If they were selling movies about men getting their testicles stuck full of knitting needles by women with swastikas on their sleeves, would they do as well, or is this penchant somehow peculiarly male? If so, why? Is pornography a power trip rather than a sex one? Some say that those ropes, chains, muzzles and other restraining devices are an argument for the immense power female sexuality still wields in the male imagination: you don't put these things on dogs unless you're afraid of them. Others, more literary, wonder about the shift from the 19th-century Magic Women or Femme Fatale image to the lollipop-licker, airhead or turkey-carcass treatment of women in porn today. The pro-porners don't care much about theory: they merely demand product. The anti-porners don't care about it in the final analysis either: there's dirt on the street, and they want it cleaned up, now.

It seems to me that this conversation, with its *You're-a-prude/You're-a-pervert* dialectic, will never get anywhere as long as we continue to think of this material as just "entertainment." Possibly we're deluded by the packaging, the format: magazine, book, movie, theatrical presentation. We're used to thinking of these things as part of the "entertainment industry," and we're used to thinking of ourselves as free adult people who ought to be able to see any kind of "entertainment" we want to. That was what the First Choice pay-TV debate was all about. After all, it's only entertainment, right? Entertainment means fun, and only a killjoy would be antifun. What's the harm?

This is obviously the central question: *What's the harm?* If there isn't any real harm to any real people, then the anti-porners can tsk-tsk and/or throw up as much as they like, but they can't rightfully expect more legal controls or sanctions. However, the no-harm position is far from being proven.

---

[3] *Chicken porn:* refers to child pornography.

[4] *Mrs. Grundy:* a fictional character who typified censorship and respectability, who was first mentioned in Thomas Morton's play *Speed the Plough* (1798).

(For instance, there's a clear-cut case for banning—as the federal government   10
has proposed—movies, photos and videos that depict children engaging in sex
with adults: real children are used to make the movies, and hardly anybody thinks
this is ethical. The possibilities for coercion are too great.)

To shift the viewpoint, I'd like to suggest three other models for looking at
"pornography"—and here I mean the violent kind.

Those who find the idea of regulating pornographic materials repugnant because they think it's Fascist or Communist or otherwise not in accordance with the
principles of an open democratic society should consider that Canada has made it
illegal to disseminate material that may lead to hatred toward any group because of
race or religion. I suggest that if pornography of the violent kind depicted these
acts being done predominantly to Chinese, to blacks, to Catholics, it would be off
the market immediately, under the present laws. Why is hate literature illegal? Because whoever made the law thought that such material might incite real people to
do real awful things to other real people. The human brain is to a certain extent a
computer: garbage in, garbage out. We only hear about the extreme cases (like that
of American multimurderer Ted Bundy) in which pornography has contributed to
the death and/or mutilation of women and/or men. Although pornography is not
the only factor involved in the creation of such deviance, it certainly has upped the
ante by suggesting both a variety of techniques and the social acceptability of such
actions. Nobody knows yet what effect this stuff is having on the less psychotic.

Studies have shown that a large part of the market for all kinds of porn, soft
and hard, is drawn from the 16-to-21-year-old population of young men. Boys
used to learn about sex on the street, or (in Italy, according to Fellini movies) from
friendly whores, or, in more genteel surroundings, from girls, their parents, or, once
upon a time, in school, more or less. Now porn has been added, and sex education
in the schools is rapidly being phased out. The buck has been passed, and boys are
being taught that all women secretly like to be raped and that real men get high on
scooping out women's digestive tracts.

Boys learn their concept of masculinity from other men: is this what most
men want them to be learning? If word gets around that rapists are "normal" and
even admirable men, will boys feel that in order to be normal, admirable and masculine they will have to be rapists? Human beings are enormously flexible, and
how they turn out depends a lot on how they're educated, by the society in which
they're immersed as well as by their teachers. In a society that advertises and glori-
fies rape or even implicitly condones it, more women get raped. It becomes socially
acceptable. And at a time when men and the traditional male role have taken a lot
of flak and men are confused and casting around for an acceptable way of being
male (and, in some cases, not getting much comfort from women on that score),
this must be at times a pleasing thought.

It would be naïve to think of violent pornography as just harmless entertain-   15
ment. It's also an educational tool and a powerful propaganda device. What happens
when boy educated on porn meets girl brought up on Harlequin romances? The
clash of expectations can be heard around the block. She wants him to get down on
his knees with a ring, he wants her to get down on all fours with a ring in her nose.
Can this marriage be saved?

Pornography has certain things in common with such addictive substances as alcohol and drugs: for some, though by no means for all, it induces chemical changes in the body, which the user finds exciting and pleasurable. It also appears to attract a "hard core" of habitual users and a penumbra of those who use it occasionally but aren't dependent on it in any way. There are also significant numbers of men who aren't much interested in it, not because they're undersexed but because real life is satisfying their needs, which may not require as many appliances as those of users.

For the "hard core," pornography may function as alcohol does for the alcoholic: tolerance develops, and a little is no longer enough. This may account for the short viewing time and fast turnover in porn theatres. Mary Brown, chairwoman of the Ontario Board of Film Censors, estimates that for every one mainstream movie requesting entrance to Ontario, there is one porno flick. Not only the quantity consumed but the quality of explicitness must escalate, which may account for the growing violence: once the big deal was breasts, then it was genitals, then copulation, then that was no longer enough and the hard users had to have more. The ultimate kick is death, and after that, as the Marquis de Sade so boringly demonstrated, multiple death.

The existence of alcoholism has not led us to ban social drinking. On the other hand, we do have laws about drinking and driving, excessive drunkenness and other abuses of alcohol that may result in injury or death to others.

This leads us back to the key question: what's the harm? Nobody knows, but this society should find out fast, before the saturation point is reached. The Scandinavian studies that showed a connection between depictions of sexual violence and increased impulse toward it on the part of male viewers would be a starting point, but many more questions remain to be raised as well as answered. What, for instance, is the crucial difference between men who are users and men who are not? Does using affect a man's relationship with actual women, and, if so, adversely? Is there a clear line between erotica and violent pornography, or are they on an escalating continuum? Is this a "men versus women" issue, with all men secretly siding with the pro-porners and all women secretly siding against? (I think not; there *are* lots of men who don't think that running their true love through the Cuisinart is the best way they can think of to spend a Saturday night, and they're just as nauseated by films of someone else doing it as women are.) Is pornography merely an expression of the sexual confusion of this age or an active contributor to it?

Nobody wants to go back to the age of official repression, when even piano legs were referred to as "limbs" and had to wear pantaloons to be decent. Neither do we want to end up in George Orwell's *1984,* in which pornography is turned out by the State to keep the proles in a state of torpor, sex itself is considered dirty and the approved practise is only for reproduction. But Rome under the emperors isn't such a good model either.

If all men and women respected each other, if sex were considered joyful and life-enhancing instead of a wallow in germ-filled glop, if everyone were in love all the time, if, in other words, many people's lives were more satisfactory for them than they appear to be now, pornography might just go away on its own. But since this is

20

obviously not happening, we as a society are going to have to make some informed and responsible decisions about how to deal with it.

Questions for Discussion and Writing

1. What does Atwood find objectionable about the direction pornography is taking? How does she reply to those who are on the opposite side of this issue and oppose censorship?
2. What view of human nature underlies Atwood's assessment of the effects of pornography? Do you agree or disagree with this assessment? Explain why.
3. Do you find Atwood's definition of pornography and her assessment of its effects persuasive? Write an essay in which you explore your own views on pornography and censorship.

Fiction

RAYMOND CARVER

Raymond Carver (1938–1988) grew up in a logging town in Oregon and was educated at Humboldt State College (B.A., 1963) and at the University of Iowa, where he studied creative writing. He first received recognition in the 1970s with the publication of stories in the New Yorker, Esquire, *and the* Atlantic Monthly. *His first collection of short stories,* Will You Please Be Quiet, Please? *(1976), was nominated for the National Book Award. Subsequent collections include* What We Talk About When We Talk About Love *(1981), in which the following story first appeared;* Cathedral *(1983); and* Where I'm Calling From *(1988). Carver's uncanny gift for evoking the unsaid meanings in conversations leads to a complex exploration of the very different meanings people apply to the word* love.

What We Talk About When We Talk About Love

My friend Mel McGinnis was talking. Mel McGinnis is a cardiologist, and sometimes that gives him the right.

The four of us were sitting around his kitchen table drinking gin. Sunlight filled the kitchen from the big window behind the sink. There were Mel and me and his second wife, Teresa—Terri, we called her—and my wife, Laura. We lived in Albuquerque then. But we were all from somewhere else.

There was an ice bucket on the table. The gin and the tonic water kept going around, and we somehow got on the subject of love. Mel thought real love was nothing less than spiritual love. He said he'd spent five years in a seminary before quitting to go to medical school. He said he still looked back on those years in the seminary as the most important years in his life.

Terri said the man she lived with before she lived with Mel loved her so much he tried to kill her. Then Terri said, "He beat me up one night. He dragged me around the living room by my ankles. He kept saying, 'I love you, I love you, you bitch.' He went on dragging me around the living room. My head kept knocking on things." Terri looked around the table. "What do you do with love like that?"

She was a bone-thin woman with a pretty face, dark eyes, and brown hair that hung down her back. She liked necklaces made of turquoise, and long pendant earrings.   5

"My God, don't be silly. That's not love, and you know it," Mel said. "I don't know what you'd call it, but I sure know you wouldn't call it love."

"Say what you want to, but I know it was," Terri said. "It may sound crazy to you, but it's true just the same. People are different, Mel. Sure, sometimes he may have acted crazy. Okay. But he loved me. In his own way maybe, but he loved me. There was love there, Mel. Don't say there wasn't."

Mel let out his breath. He held his glass and turned to Laura and me. "The man threatened to kill me," Mel said. He finished his drink and reached for the gin bottle. "Terri's a romantic. Terri's of the kick-me-so-I'll-know-you-love-me school. Terri, hon, don't look that way." Mel reached across the table and touched Terri's cheek with his fingers. He grinned at her.

"Now he wants to make up," Terri said.

"Make up what?" Mel said. "What is there to make up? I know what I know.   10 That's all."

"How'd we get started on this subject, anyway?" Terri said. She raised her glass and drank from it. "Mel always has love on his mind," she said. "Don't you, honey?" She smiled, and I thought that was the last of it.

"I just wouldn't call Ed's behavior love. That's all I'm saying, honey," Mel said. "What about you guys?" Mel said to Laura and me. "Does that sound like love to you?"

"I'm the wrong person to ask," I said. "I didn't even know the man. I've only heard his name mentioned in passing. I wouldn't know. You'd have to know the particulars. But I think what you're saying is that love is an absolute."

Mel said, "The kind of love I'm talking about is. The kind of love I'm talking about, you don't try to kill people."

Laura said, "I don't know anything about Ed, or anything about the situation.   15 But who can judge anyone else's situation?"

I touched the back of Laura's hand. She gave me a quick smile. I picked up Laura's hand. It was warm, the nails polished, perfectly manicured. I encircled the broad wrist with my fingers, and I held her.

"When I left, he drank rat poison," Terri said. She clasped her arms with her hands. "They took him to the hospital in Santa Fe. That's where we lived then, about ten miles out. They saved his life. But his gums went crazy from it. I mean they pulled away from his teeth. After that, his teeth stood out like fangs. My God," Terri said. She waited a minute, then let go of her arms and picked up her glass.

"What people won't do!" Laura said.

"He's out of the action now," Mel said. "He's dead."

Mel handed me the saucer of limes. I took a section, squeezed it over my   20
drink, and stirred the ice cubes with my finger.

"It gets worse," Terri said. "He shot himself in the mouth. But he bungled that
too. Poor Ed," she said. Terri shook her head.

"Poor Ed nothing," Mel said. "He was dangerous."

Mel was forty-five years old. He was tall and rangy with curly soft hair. His
face and arms were brown from the tennis he played. When he was sober, his gestures, all his movements, were precise, very careful.

"He did love me though, Mel. Grant me that," Terri said. "That's all I'm asking. He didn't love me the way you love me. I'm not saying that. But he loved me.
You can grant me that, can't you?"

"What do you mean, he bungled it?" I said.   25

Laura leaned forward with her glass. She put her elbows on the table and held
her glass in both hands. She glanced from Mel to Terri and waited with a look of
bewilderment on her open face, as if amazed that such things happened to people
you were friendly with.

"How'd he bungle it when he killed himself?" I said.

"I'll tell you what happened," Mel said. "He took this twenty-two pistol he'd
bought to threaten Terri and me with. Oh, I'm serious, the man was always threatening. You should have seen the way we lived in those days. Like fugitives. I even
bought a gun myself. Can you believe it? A guy like me? But I did. I bought one
for self-defense and carried it in the glove compartment. Sometimes I'd have to
leave the apartment in the middle of the night. To go to the hospital, you know?
Terri and I weren't married then, and my first wife had the house and kids, the dog,
everything, and Terri and I were living in this apartment here. Sometimes, as I say,
I'd get a call in the middle of the night and have to go in to the hospital at two or
three in the morning. It'd be dark out there in the parking lot, and I'd break into a
sweat before I could even get to my car. I never knew if he was going to come up
out of the shrubbery or from behind a car and start shooting. I mean, the man was
crazy. He was capable of wiring a bomb, anything. He used to call my service at all
hours and say he needed to talk to the doctor, and when I'd return the call, he'd
say, 'Son of a bitch, your days are numbered.' Little things like that. It was scary, I'm
telling you."

"I still feel sorry for him," Terri said.

"It sounds like a nightmare," Laura said. "But what exactly happened after he   30
shot himself?"

Laura is a legal secretary. We'd met in a professional capacity. Before we knew
it, it was a courtship. She's thirty-five, three years younger than I am. In addition to
being in love, we like each other and enjoy one another's company. She's easy to be
with.

"What happened?" Laura said.

Mel said, "He shot himself in the mouth in his room. Someone heard the shot
and told the manager. They came in with a passkey, saw what had happened, and
called an ambulance. I happened to be there when they brought him in, alive but
past recall. The man lived for three days. His head swelled up to twice the size of a
normal head. I'd never seen anything like it, and I hope I never do again. Terri

wanted to go in and sit with him when she found out about it. We had a fight over it. I didn't think she should see him like that. I didn't think she should see him, and I still don't."

"Who won the fight?" Laura said.

"I was in the room with him when he died," Terri said. "He never came up   35
out of it. But I sat with him. He didn't have anyone else."

"He was dangerous," Mel said. "If you call that love, you can have it."

"It was love," Terri said. "Sure, it's abnormal in most people's eyes. But he was willing to die for it. He did die for it."

"I sure as hell wouldn't call it love," Mel said. "I mean, no one knows what he did it for. I've seen a lot of suicides, and I couldn't say anyone ever knew what they did it for."

Mel put his hands behind his neck and tilted his chair back. "I'm not interested in that kind of love," he said. "If that's love, you can have it."

Terri said, "We were afraid. Mel even made a will out and wrote to his brother   40
in California who used to be a Green Beret. Mel told him who to look for if something happened to him."

Terri drank from her glass. She said, "But Mel's right—we lived like fugitives. We were afraid. Mel was, weren't you, honey? I even called the police at one point, but they were no help. They said they couldn't do anything until Ed actually did something. Isn't that a laugh?" Terri said.

She poured the last of the gin into her glass and waggled the bottle. Mel got up from the table and went to the cupboard. He took down another bottle.

"Well, Nick and I know what love is," Laura said. "For us, I mean," Laura said. She bumped my knee with her knee. "You're supposed to say something now," Laura said, and turned her smile on me.

For an answer, I took Laura's hand and raised it to my lips. I made a big production out of kissing her hand. Everyone was amused.

"We're lucky," I said.   45

"You guys," Terri said. "Stop that now. You're making me sick. You're still on the honeymoon, for God's sake. You're still gaga, for crying out loud. Just wait. How long have you been together now? How long has it been? A year? Longer than a year?"

"Going on a year and a half," Laura said, flushed and smiling.

"Oh, now," Terri said. "Wait awhile."

She held her drink and gazed at Laura.

"I'm only kidding," Terri said.   50

Mel opened the gin and went around the table with the bottle.

"Here, you guys," he said. "Let's have a toast. I want to propose a toast. A toast to love. To true love," Mel said.

We touched glasses.

"To love," we said.

Outside in the backyard, one of the dogs began to bark. The leaves of the   55
aspen that leaned past the window ticked against the glass. The afternoon sun was

like a presence in this room, the spacious light of ease and generosity. We could have been anywhere, somewhere enchanted. We raised our glasses again and grinned at each other like children who had agreed on something forbidden.

"I'll tell you what real love is," Mel said. "I mean, I'll give you a good example. And then you can draw your own conclusions." He poured more gin into his glass. He added an ice cube and a sliver of lime. We waited and sipped our drinks. Laura and I touched knees again. I put a hand on her warm thigh and left it there.

"What do any of us really know about love?" Mel said. "It seems to me we're just beginners at love. We say we love each other and we do, I don't doubt it. I love Terri and Terri loves me, and you guys love each other too. You know the kind of love I'm talking about now. Physical love, that impulse that drives you to someone special, as well as love of the other person's being, his or her essence, as it were. Carnal love and, well, call it sentimental love, the day-to-day caring about the other person. But sometimes I have a hard time accounting for the fact that I must have loved my first wife too. But I did, I know I did. So I suppose I am like Terri in that regard. Terri and Ed." He thought about it and then he went on. "There was a time when I thought I loved my first wife more than life itself. But now I hate her guts. I do. How do you explain that? What happened to that love? What happened to it, is what I'd like to know. I wish someone could tell me. Then there's Ed. Okay, we're back to Ed. He loves Terri so much he tries to kill her and he winds up killing himself." Mel stopped talking and swallowed from his glass. "You guys have been together eighteen months and you love each other. It shows all over you. You glow with it. But you both loved other people before you met each other. You've both been married before, just like us. And you probably loved other people before that too, even. Terri and I have been together five years, been married for four. And the terrible thing, the terrible thing is, but the good thing too, the saving grace, you might say, is that if something happened to one of us—excuse me for saying this— but if something happened to one of us tomorrow, I think the other one, the other person, would grieve for a while, you know, but then the surviving party would go out and love again, have someone else soon enough. All this, all of this love we're talking about, it would just be a memory. Maybe not even a memory. Am I wrong? Am I way off base? Because I want you to set me straight if you think I'm wrong. I want to know. I mean I don't know anything, and I'm the first one to admit it."

"Mel, for God's sake," Terri said. She reached out and took hold of his wrist. "Are you getting drunk? Honey? Are you drunk?"

"Honey, I'm just talking," Mel said. "All right? I don't have to be drunk to say what I think. I mean, we're all just talking, right?" Mel said. He fixed his eyes on her.

"Sweetie, I'm not criticizing," Terri said.   60

She picked up her glass.

"I'm not on call today," Mel said. "Let me remind you of that. I am not on call," he said.

"Mel, we love you," Laura said.

Mel looked at Laura, He looked at her as if he could not place her, as if she was not the woman she was.

"Love you too, Laura," Mel said. "And you, Nick, love you too. You know   65
something?" Mel said. "You guys are our pals," Mel said.

He picked up his glass.

Mel said, "I was going to tell you about something. I mean, I was going to prove a point. You see, this happened a few months ago, but it's still going on right now, and it ought to make us feel ashamed when we talk like we know what we're talking about when we talk about love."

"Come on now," Terri said. "Don't talk like you're drunk if you're not drunk."

"Just shut up for once in your life," Mel said very quietly. "Will you do me a favor and do that for a minute? So as I was saying, there's this old couple who had this car wreck out on the interstate. A kid hit them and they were all torn to shit and nobody was giving them much chance to pull through."

Terri looked at us and then back at Mel. She seemed anxious, or maybe that's   70
too strong a word.

Mel was handing the bottle around the table.

"I was on call that night," Mel said. "It was May or maybe it was June. Terri and I had just sat down to dinner when the hospital called. There'd been this thing out on the interstate. Drunk kid, teenager, plowed his dad's pickup into this camper with this old couple in it. They were up in their mid-seventies, that couple. The kid—eighteen, nineteen, something—he was DOA. Taken the steering wheel through his sternum. The old couple, they were alive, you understand. I mean, just barely. But they had everything. Multiple fractures, internal injuries, hemorrhaging, contusions, lacerations, the works, and they each of them had themselves concussions. They were in a bad way, believe me. And, of course, their age was two strikes against them. I'd say she was worse off than he was. Ruptured spleen along with everything else. Both kneecaps broken. But they'd been wearing their seatbelts and, God knows, that's what saved them for the time being."

"Folks, this is an advertisement for the National Safety Council," Terri said. "This is your spokesman, Dr. Melvin R. McGinnis, talking." Terri laughed. "Mel," she said, "sometimes you're just too much. But I love you, hon," she said.

"Honey, I love you," Mel said.

He leaned across the table. Terri met him halfway. They kissed.   75

"Terri's right," Mel said as he settled himself again. "Get those seatbelts on. But seriously, they were in some shape, those oldsters. By the time I got down there, the kid was dead, as I said. He was off in a corner, laid out on a gurney. I took one look at the old couple and told the ER nurse to get me a neurologist and an orthopedic man and a couple of surgeons down there right away."

He drank from his glass. "I'll try to keep this short," he said. "So we took the two of them up to the OR and worked like fuck on them most of the night. They had these incredible reserves, those two. You see that once in a while. So we did everything that could be done, and toward morning we're giving them a fifty-fifty chance, maybe less than that for her. So here they are, still alive the next morning. So, okay, we move them into the ICU, which is where they both kept plugging away at it for two weeks, hitting it better and better on all the scopes. So we transfer them out to their own room."

Mel stopped talking. "Here," he said, "let's drink this cheapo gin the hell up. Then we're going to dinner, right? Terri and I know a new place. That's where we'll go, to this new place we know about. But we're not going until we finish up this cut-rate, lousy gin."

Terri said, "We haven't actually eaten there yet. But it looks good. From the outside, you know."

"I like food," Mel said. "If I had it to do all over again, I'd be a chef, you know? Right, Terri?" Mel said.

He laughed. He fingered the ice in his glass.

"Terri knows," he said. "Terri can tell you. But let me say this. If I could come back again in a different life, a different time and all, you know what? I'd like to come back as a knight. You were pretty safe wearing all that armor. It was all right being a knight until gunpowder and muskets and pistols came along."

"Mel would like to ride a horse and carry a lance," Terri said.

"Carry a woman's scarf with you everywhere," Laura said.

"Or just a woman," Mel said.

"Shame on you," Laura said.

Terri said, "Suppose you came back as a serf. The serfs didn't have it so good in those days," Terri said.

"The serfs never had it good," Mel said. "But I guess even the knights were vessels to someone. Isn't that the way it worked? But then everyone is always a vessel to someone. Isn't that right, Terri? But what I liked about knights, besides their ladies, was that they had that suit of armor, you know, and they couldn't get hurt very easy. No cars in those days, you know? No drunk teenagers to tear into your ass."

"Vassals," Terri said.

"What?" Mel said.

"Vassals," Terri said. "They were called vassals, not vessels."

"Vassals, vessels," Mel said, "what the fuck's the difference? You knew what I meant anyway. All right," Mel said. "So I'm not educated. I learned my stuff. I'm a heart surgeon, sure, but I'm just a mechanic. I go in and I fuck around and I fix things. Shit," Mel said.

"Modesty doesn't become you," Terri said.

"He's just a humble sawbones," I said. "But sometimes they suffocated in all that armor, Mel. They'd even have heart attacks if it got too hot and they were too tired and worn out. I read somewhere that they'd fall off their horses and not be able to get up because they were too tired to stand with all that armor on them. They got trampled by their own horses sometimes."

"That's terrible," Mel said. "That's a terrible thing, Nicky. I guess they'd just lay there and wait until somebody came along and made a shish kebab out of them."

"Some other vessel," Terri said.

"That's right," Mel said. "Some vassal would come along and spear the bastard in the name of love. Or whatever the fuck it was they fought over in those days."

"Same things we fight over these days," Terri said.

Laura said, "Nothing's changed."

The color was still high in Laura's cheeks. Her eyes were bright. She brought her glass to her lips.

Mel poured himself another drink. He looked at the label closely as if studying a long row of numbers. Then he slowly put the bottle down on the table and
slowly reached for the tonic water.

"What about the old couple?" Laura said. "You didn't finish that story you
started."

Laura was having a hard time lighting her cigarette. Her matches kept going
out.

The sunshine inside the room was different now, changing, getting thinner.
But the leaves outside the window were still shimmering, and I stared at the pattern they made on the panes and on the Formica counter. They weren't the same
patterns, of course.

"What about the old couple?" I said.   105

"Older but wiser," Terri said.

Mel stared at her.

Terri said, "Go on with your story, hon. I was only kidding. Then what
happened?"

"Terri, sometimes," Mel said.

"Please, Mel," Terri said. "Don't always be so serious, sweetie. Can't you take a   110
joke?"

"Where's the joke?" Mel said.

He held his glass and gazed steadily at his wife.

"What happened?" Laura said.

Mel fastened his eyes on Laura. He said, "Laura, if I didn't have Terri and if I
didn't love her so much, and if Nick wasn't my best friend, I'd fall in love with you.
I'd carry you off, honey," he said.

"Tell your story," Terri said. "Then we'll go to that new place, okay?"   115

"Okay," Mel said. "Where was I?" he said. He stared at the table and then he
began again.

"I dropped in to see each of them every day, sometimes twice a day if I was up
doing other calls anyway. Casts and bandages, head to foot, the both of them. You
know, you've seen it in the movies. That's just the way they looked, just like in the
movies. Little eye-holes and nose-holes and mouth-holes. And she had to have her
legs slung up on top of it. Well, the husband was very depressed for the longest
while. Even after he found out that his wife was going to pull through, he was still
very depressed. Not about the accident, though. I mean, the accident was one
thing, but it wasn't everything. I'd get up to his mouth-hole, you know, and he'd say
no, it wasn't the accident exactly but it was because he couldn't see her through his
eye-holes. He said that was what was making him feel so bad. Can you imagine?
I'm telling you, the man's heart was breaking because he couldn't turn his goddamn head and *see* his goddamn wife."

Mel looked around the table and shook his head at what he was going to say.

"I mean, it was killing the old fart just because he couldn't *look* at the fucking
woman."

We all looked at Mel.   120

"Do you see what I'm saying?" he said.

Maybe we were a little drunk by then. I know it was hard keeping things in focus. The light was draining out of the room, going back through the window where it had come from. Yet nobody made a move to get up from the table to turn on the overhead light.

"Listen," Mel said. "Let's finish this fucking gin. There's about enough left here for one shooter all around. Then let's go eat. Let's go to the new place."

"He's depressed," Terri said. "Mel, why don't you take a pill?"

Mel shook his head. "I've taken everything there is."   125

"We all need a pill now and then," I said.

"Some people are born needing them," Terri said.

She was using her finger to rub at something on the table. Then she stopped rubbing.

"I think I want to call my kids," Mel said. "Is that all right with everybody? I'll call my kids," he said.

Terri said, "What if Marjorie answers the phone? You guys, you've heard us on   130 the subject of Marjorie? Honey, you know you don't want to talk to Marjorie. It'll make you feel even worse."

"I don't want to talk to Marjorie," Mel said. "But I want to talk to my kids."

"There isn't a day goes by that Mel doesn't say he wishes she'd get married again. Or else die," Terri said. "For one thing," Terri said, "she's bankrupting us. Mel says it's just to spite him that she won't get married again. She has a boyfriend who lives with her and the kids, so Mel is supporting the boyfriend too."

"She's allergic to bees," Mel said. "If I'm not praying she'll get married again, I'm praying she'll get herself stung to death by a swarm of fucking bees."

"Shame on you," Laura said.

"Bzzzzzzz," Mel said, turning his fingers into bees and buzzing them at Terri's   135 throat. Then he let his hands drop all the way to his sides.

"She's vicious," Mel said. "Sometimes I think I'll go up there dressed like a beekeeper. You know, that hat that's like a helmet with the plate that comes down over your face, the big gloves, and the padded coat? I'll knock on the door and let loose a hive of bees in the house. But first I'd make sure the kids were out, of course."

He crossed one leg over the other. It seemed to take him a lot of time to do it. Then he put both feet on the floor and leaned forward, elbows on the table, his chin cupped in his hands.

"Maybe I won't call the kids, after all. Maybe it isn't such a hot idea. Maybe we'll just go eat. How does that sound?"

"Sounds fine to me," I said. "Eat or not eat. Or keep drinking. I could head right on out into the sunset."

"What does that mean, honey?" Laura said.   140

"It just means what I said," I said. "It means I could just keep going. That's all it means."

"I could eat something myself," Laura said. "I don't think I've ever been so hungry in my life. Is there something to nibble on?"

"I'll put out some cheese and crackers," Terri said.

But Terri just sat there. She did not get up to get anything.

Mel turned his glass over. He spilled it out on the table.   145
"Gin's gone," Mel said.
Terri said, "Now what?"

I could hear my heart beating. I could hear everyone's heart. I could hear the human noise we sat there making, not one of us moving, not even when the room went dark.

Questions for Discussion and Writing

1. How are Mel, Terri, Laura, and Nick characterized in terms of their attitudes toward love? In what ways do they differ in their conception of love? How does Terri's account of her ex-lover add fuel to the conflict between her and Mel?

2. What is the significance of Mel's story about the elderly couple he treated in the hospital and the change in his language when he talks about them?

3. How have Nick and Laura's relationship changed as a result of what has taken place during the evening? What unspoken message is conveyed in the ominous silence with which the story ends?

Poetry

TED HUGHES

Edward James (Ted) Hughes (1930–1998) was born in Yorkshire, England, and was educated at Cambridge University. He was married to the American poet Sylvia Plath, who committed suicide in 1963. Hughes's first volumes of verse, The Hawk in the Rain *(1957),* Lupercal *(1960), and* Wodwo *(1967), immediately brought him recognition for his ability to portray the human predicament in uncompromising ways through animal characters. His 1970 volume of poetry,* Crow, *projected a grotesque and fascinating cycle tracing the history of a lonely, yet resilient figure, from before his birth through a complex allegorical journey, in which Hughes, through the character Crow, comments on the savage impulses underlying the facade of civilization. A prolific writer, Hughes produced a wide range of works, including* Gaudete *(1977),* Cave Birds *(1978),* Remains of Elmet *(1979),* Moortown *(1980),* River *(1984), and* Wolf-Watching *(1989), as well as volumes of literary criticism, essays, and poetry for children. In 1984 he was appointed Poet Laureate of Great Britain and, before his death in 1998, produced a body of work that has clearly defined him as the foremost poet writing in English. His last book was* Birthday Letters *(1998). In the following poem, drawn from* Crow, *Hughes creates a circular semantic game that puts words literally into the position of never quite catching up to an elusive reality that mocks Crow's efforts.*

Crow Goes Hunting

Crow
Decided to try words.

He imagined some words for the job, a lovely pack—
Clear-eyed, resounding, well-trained,
With strong teeth.   5
You could not find a better bred lot.

He pointed out the hare and away went the words
Resounding.
Crow was Crow without fail, but what is a hare?

It converted itself to a concrete bunker.   10
The words circled protesting, resounding.

Crow turned the words into bombs—they blasted the bunker.
The bits of bunker flew up—a flock of starlings.

Crow turned the words into shotguns, they shot down the
                                             starlings.   15

The falling starlings turned to a cloudburst.

Crow turned the words into a reservoir, collecting the water.
The water turned into an earthquake, swallowing the
                                             reservoir.

The earthquake turned into a hare and leaped for the hill   20
Having eaten Crow's words.

Crow gazed after the bounding hare
Speechless with admiration.

Questions for Discussion and Writing

1. Why do Crow's attempts to "try words" always come up short?
2. Into what kinds of things do words transform themselves? Why is it significant that the bounding hare that Crow seeks to describe ultimately eats Crow's words?
3. What is Hughes suggesting about the capacity of language to describe reality? Have you ever had an experience where you could have been Crow hunting for the proper words?

Drama

DAVID IVES

The contemporary American playwright David Ives (b. 1941) has created an inventive one-act play that explores the premise that three monkeys typing into infinity would sooner or later produce Hamlet: *What would the monkeys talk about at their typewriters? Ives deepens this paradox by choosing the names Milton, Swift, and Kafka (who is a girl) for the three monkeys and creates a provocative and hilarious play about the meanings we attach to literary works. This play first appeared in a collection of six of his one-acts,* All in the Timing *(1994). Ives has recently written* Time Flies and Other Short Plays *(2001) and* Monsieur Eek *(2001).*

Words, Words, Words

Lights come up on three monkeys pecking away at three typewriters. Behind them, a tire-swing is hanging. The monkeys are named Milton, Swift and Kafka. Kafka is a girl monkey.[1]

They shouldn't be in monkey suits, by the way. Instead, they wear the sort of little-kid clothes that chimps wear in circuses: white shirts and bowties for the boys, a flouncy little dress for Kafka.

They type for a few moments, each at his own speed. Then Milton runs excitedly around the floor on his knuckles, swings onto the tire-swing, leaps back onto his stool, and goes on typing. Kafka eats a banana thoughtfully. Swift pounds his chest and shows his teeth, then goes back to typing.

SWIFT: I don't know. I just don't know

KAFKA: Quiet, please. I'm trying to concentrate here. (*She types a moment with her toes.*)

MILTON: Okay, so what've you got?

SWIFT: Me?

MILTON: Yeah, have you hit anything? Let's hear it.   5

SWIFT: (*Reads what he's typed.*) "Ping-drobba fft fft fft inglewarp carcinoma." That's as far as I got.

KAFKA: I like the "fft fft fft."

MILTON: Yeah. Kind of onomatopoeic.

SWIFT: I don't know. Feels to me like it needs some punching up.

MILTON: You can always throw in a few jokes later on. You gotta get the throughline first.   10

---

[1] *John Milton (1608–1674):* English poet, author of *Paradise Lost* (1667). Jonathan Swift (1667–1745): Anglo-Irish satirist, author of *Gulliver's Travels* (1726). Franz Kafka (1883–1924): German novelist and short story writer, author of *The Trial* (1925).

SWIFT: But do you think it's *Hamlet?*[2]

MILTON: Don't ask me. I'm just a chimp.

KAFKA: They could've given us a clue or something.

SWIFT: Yeah. Or a story conference.

MILTON: But that'd defeat the whole purpose of the experiment.   15

SWIFT: I know, I know, I know. Three monkeys typing into infinity will sooner
   or later produce *Hamlet.*

MILTON: Right.

SWIFT: Completely by chance.

MILTON: And Dr. David Rosenbaum up in that booth is going to prove it.

SWIFT: But what is *Hamlet?*   20

MILTON: I don't know.

SWIFT: (*To Kafka.*) What is *Hamlet?*

KAFKA: I don't know. (*Silence.*)

SWIFT: (*Dawning realization.*) You know—this is really *stupid!*

MILTON: Have you got something better to do in this cage? The sooner we pro-   25
   duce the goddamn thing, the sooner we get out.

KAFKA: Sort of publish or perish, with a twist.

SWIFT: But what do we owe this Rosenbaum? A guy who stands outside those
   bars and tells people, "That one's Milton, that one's Swift, and that one's
   Kafka"—? Just to get a laugh?

KAFKA: What's a Kafka anyway? Why am I a Kafka?

SWIFT: Search me.

KAFKA: What's a Kafka?   30

SWIFT: All his four-eyed friends sure think it's a stitch.

KAFKA: And how are we supposed to write *Hamlet* if we don't even know what
   it is?

MILTON: Okay, okay, so the chances are a little slim.

SWIFT: Yeah—and this from a guy who's supposed to be *smart?* This from a guy
   at *Columbia University?*

MILTON: The way I figure it, there is a Providence that oversees our pages,   35
   rough-draft them how we may.[3]

KAFKA: But how about you, Milton? What've you got?

MILTON: Let's see . . . (*Reads.*)

"Of Man's first disobedience, and the fruit
Of that forbidden tree whose mortal taste
Brought death into the—"[4]

KAFKA: Hey, that's good! It's got rhythm! It really sings!

---

[2] *Hamlet:* William Shakespeare's classic tragedy, composed in 1600–1601. The title of Ives's play refers to a line from *Hamlet,* Act II, Scene ii, line 194; Hamlet's cryptic reply to Polonius who asks what he is reading.

[3] Alludes to *Hamlet,* Scene V, Act ii, line 10.

[4] Alludes to Milton's *Paradise Lost,* Book I, lines 1–3.

MILTON: Yeah?

SWIFT: But is it Shakespeare?   40

KAFKA: Who cares? He's got a real voice there.

SWIFT: Does Dr. Rosenbaum care about voice? Does he care about anybody's individual creativity?

MILTON: Let's look at this from Rosenbaum's point of view for a minute—

SWIFT: 'No! He brings us in here to produce copy, then all he wants is a clean draft of somebody else's stuff. (*Dumps out a bowl of peanuts.*) We're getting peanuts here, to be somebody's hack!

MILTON: Writing is a mug's game anyway, Swifty.   45

SWIFT: Well it hath made me mad.

MILTON: Why not just buckle down and get the project over with? Set up a schedule for yourself. Type in the morning for a couple of hours when you're fresh, then take a break. Let the old juices flow. Do a couple more hours in the afternoon, and retire for a shot of papaya and some masturbation. What's the big deal?

SWIFT: If this Rosenbaum was worth anything, we'd be working on word processors, not these antiques. He's lucky he could find three who type this good, and then he treats us like those misfits at the Bronx Zoo. I mean—a *tire-swing?* What does he take us for?

MILTON: I like the tire-swing. I think it was a very nice touch.

SWIFT: I can't work under these conditions! No wonder I'm producing garbage!   50

KAFKA: How does the rest of yours go, Milton?

MILTON: What, this?

KAFKA: Yeah, read us some more.

MILTON: Blah, blah, blah . . . "whose mortal taste
Brought death into the blammagam.
Bedsocks knockwurst tinkerbelle."
(*Small pause.*) What do you think?

KAFKA: "Blammagam" is good.   55

SWIFT: Well. I don't know . . .

MILTON: What's the matter? Is it the tone? I knew this was kind of a stretch for me.

SWIFT: I'm just not sure it has the same expressive intensity and pungent lyricism as the first part.

MILTON: Well sure, it needs rewriting. What doesn't? This is a rough draft! (*Suddenly noticing.*) Light's on. (*Swift claps his hands over his eyes, Milton puts his hands over his ears, and Kafka puts her hands over her mouth so that they form "See no evil, hear no evil, speak no evil."*)

SWIFT: *This* bit.   60

KAFKA: (*Through her hands.*) Are they watching?

MILTON: (*Hands over ears.*) What?

KAFKA: Are they watching?

SWIFT: I don't know, I can't see. I've got my paws over my eyes.

MILTON: What?   65

KAFKA: What is the point of this?

SWIFT: Why do they videotape our bowel movements?

MILTON: *What?!*

SWIFT: Light's off. (*They take their hands away.*)

MILTON: But how are you doing, Franz? What've you got?   70

KAFKA: Well. . . . (*Reads what she's typed.*)

"K.K.K.K.K.K.K.K.K.K.K.K.K.K.K."[5]

SWIFT: What is that—post-modernism?

KAFKA: Twenty lines of that.

SWIFT: At least it'll fuck up his data.

KAFKA: Twenty lines of that and I went dry. I got blocked. I felt like I was re-   75
peating myself.

MILTON: Do you think that that's in *Hamlet?*

KAFKA: I don't understand what I'm doing here in the first place! I'm not a
writer, I'm a monkey! I'm supposed to be swinging on branches and digging
up ants, not sitting under fluorescent lights ten hours a day!

MILTON: It sure is a long way home to the gardens of sweet Africa. Where lawns
and level downs and flocks grazing the tender herb were sweetly
interposèd . . .[6]

KAFKA: Paradise, wasn't it?

MILTON: Lost!   80

SWIFT: Lost!

KAFKA: Lost!

MILTON: I'm trying to deal with some of that in this new piece here, but it's all
still pretty close to the bone.

SWIFT: Just because they can keep us locked up, they think they're more powerful than we are.

MILTON: They *are* more powerful than we are.   85

SWIFT: Just because they control the means of production, they think they can
suppress the workers.[7]

MILTON: Things are how they are. What are you going to do?

SWIFT: Hey—how come you're always so goddamn ready to justify the ways of
Rosenbaum to the apes?[8]

MILTON: Do you have a key to that door?

SWIFT: No.   90

MILTON: Do you have an independent food source?

---

[5] May allude to Joseph K., the protagonist of Kafka's novels *The Trial* (1925) and *The Castle* (1926), symbolic and surreal works that anticipate postmodernist techniques and themes.

[6] Alludes to Eden, as described in *Paradise Lost*, Book IV.

[7] May allude to Karl Marx (1818–83), German social philosopher and revolutionary, author of the *Communist Manifesto* (1848), in collaboration with Friedrich Engels (1920–1895).

[8] A reference to *Paradise Lost* whose purpose, according to Milton, was to "justify the ways of God to men."

SWIFT: No.

MILTON: So call me a collaborator. I happen to be a professional. If Rosenbaum
wants *Hamlet,* I'll give it a shot. Just don't forget—we're not astrophysicists.
We're not brain surgeons. We're chimps. And for apes in captivity, this is not a
bad gig.

SWIFT: What's really frightening is that if we stick around this cage long
enough, we're gonna evolve into Rosenbaum.

KAFKA: Evolve into Rosenbaum?   95

SWIFT: Brush up your Darwin, baby. We're more than kin and less than kind.[9]

MILTON: Anybody got a smoke?

KAFKA: I'm all out.

SWIFT: Don't look at me. I'm not going to satisfy those voyeurs with the old
smoking-chimp act. No thank you.

MILTON: Don't be a sap, Swifty. You gotta use 'em! Use the system!   100

SWIFT: What do you mean?

MILTON: Watch me, while I put my antic disposition on.[10] (*He jumps up onto his
chair and scratches his sides, screeches, makes smoking motions, pounds his chest,
jumps up and down—and a cigarette descends.*) See what I mean? Gauloise, too.
My fave. (*He settles back to enjoy it.*)

SWIFT: They should've thrown in a kewpie doll for that performance.

MILTON: It got results, didn't it?

SWIFT: Sure. You do your Bonzo routine and get a Gauloise out of it. Last week   105
I totalled a typewriter and got a whole carton of Marlboros.

MILTON: The trouble was, you didn't smoke 'em, you took a crap on 'em.

SWIFT: It was a political statement.

MILTON: Okay, you made your statement and I got my smoke. All's well that
ends well, right?

KAFKA: It's the only way we know they're watching.

MILTON: Huh?   110

KAFKA: We perform, we break typewriters, we type another page—and a cigarette appears. At least it's a sign that somebody out there is paying attention.

MILTON: Our resident philosopher.

SWIFT: But what'll happen if one of us *does* write *Hamlet?* Here we are, set
down to prove the inadvertent virtues of randomness, and to produce something that we wouldn't even recognize if it passed right through our hands—
but what if one of us actually does it?

MILTON: Will we really be released?

KAFKA: Will they give us the key to the city and a tickertape parade?   115

SWIFT: Or will they move us on to *Ulysses?*[11] (*The others shriek in terror at the
thought.*) Why did they pick *Hamlet* in the first place? What's *Hamlet* to them

---

[9] Alludes to *Hamlet, I, ii, 65.*
[10] Alludes to *Hamlet, I, V, 172.*
[11] James Joyce's (1882-1941) novel, published in 1922.

or they to *Hamlet* that we should care?[12] Boy, there's the respect that makes calamity of so long life! For who would bear the whips and scorns of time, the oppressor's wrong, the proud man's contumely—[13]

MILTON: Hey. Swifty!

SWIFT: —the pangs of despisèd love, the law's delay—

MILTON: Hey, Swifty! Relax, will you?

KAFKA: Have a banana.   120

SWIFT: I wish I could get Rosenbaum in here and see how he does at producing *Hamlet* . . . . *That's it!*

KAFKA: What?

SWIFT: That's it! Forget about this random *Hamlet* crap. What about *revenge?*

KAFKA: Revenge? On Rosenbaum?

SWIFT: Who else? Hasn't he bereft us of our homes and families? Stepped in be-   125
tween us and our expectations?[14]

KAFKA: How would we do it?

SWIFT: Easy. We lure him in here to look at our typewriters, test them out like something's wrong—but! *we poison the typewriter keys!*

MILTON: Oh Jesus.

SWIFT: Sure. Some juice of cursèd hebona spread liberally over the keyboard?[15] Ought to work like a charm.

MILTON: Great.   130

SWIFT: If that doesn't work, we envenom the tire-swing and invite him for a ride. Plus—I challenge him to a duel.[16]

MILTON: Brilliant.

SWIFT: Can't you see it? In the course of combat, I casually graze my rapier over the poisoned typewriter keys, and—(*Jabs.*)—a hit! A palpable hit![17] For a reserve, we lay by a cup with some venomous distillment. We'll put the pellet with the poison in the vessel with the pestle![18]

MILTON: Listen, I gotta get back to work. The man is gonna want his pages. (*He rolls a fresh page into his typewriter.*)

KAFKA: It's not a bad idea, but . . .   135

SWIFT: What's the matter with you guys? I'm on to something here!

KAFKA: I think it's hopeless, Swifty.

SWIFT: But this is the goods!

MILTON: Where was I . . . "Bedsocks knockwurst tinkerbelle."

---

[12] Alludes to *Hamlet,* Act II, Scene ii, line 585.

[13] Alludes to Hamlet's famous Soliloquy, Act III, Scene i, lines 68–74.

[14] Alludes to *Hamlet,* V, ii, 65.

[15] Refers to *Hamlet,* Act IV, Scene vii, line 142.

[16] Alludes to *Hamlet,* IV, vii, 138–143.

[17] Alludes to *Hamlet,* V, ii, 269.

[18] A quote from *The Court Jester,* a 1955 film starring Danny Kaye which has become part of theater Folklore.

KAFKA: The readiness is all, I guess.[19]   140
MILTON: Damn straight. Just let me know when that K-button gives out, honey.
SWIFT: Okay. You two serfs go back to work. I'll do all the thinking around here.
    Swifty—revenge! (*He paces, deep in thought.*)
MILTON: "Tinkerbelle . . . shtuckelschwanz . . . hemorrhoid." Yeah, that's good.
    That is good. (*Types.*) "Shtuckelschwanz . . ."
KAFKA: (*Types.*) "Act one, scene one. Elsinore Castle, Denmark . . .
MILTON: (*Types.*) " . . . hemorrhoid."   145
KAFKA: (*Types.*) "Enter Bernardo and Francisco."
MILTON: (*Types.*) "Pomegranate."
KAFKA: (*Types.*) "Bernardo says, 'Who's there?' "[20]
MILTON: (*Types.*) "Bazooka." (*Kafka continues to type* Hamlet, *as the lights fade.*)

PROPERTY LIST

3 typing tables

3 stools

3 old typewriters

Typing paper

3 wastebaskets overflowing with crushed paper

Tire-swing

Banana (KAFKA)

Bowl of peanuts (SWIFT)

3 ashtrays, full of butts

Empty cigarette pack (KAFKA)

Cigarette on a wire, for Milton

Cigarette lighter, for Milton

Questions for Discussion and Writing

1. How do literary and historical allusions add to the humor of the situation? Why would knowing more about the works alluded to enhance the audience's enjoyment of the play?
2. In what way does Ives incorporate the revenge theme in *Hamlet* to comment on the ethics of animal experimentation?
3. How does this play raise the question of who decides what particular literary works become classics? Why aren't any of the three monkeys named Shakespeare?

---

[19] Refers to *Hamlet*, Act V, Scene ii, line 233.

[20] Alludes to *Hamlet*, I, i, 1, the line with which the play opens.

Connections for Chapter 4: Perspectives on Language

1. **Susanne K. Langer,** *Language and Thought*
   What insight does Helen Keller's account give you into the symbolic nature of language, as analyzed by Langer?
2. **Helen Keller,** *The Day Language Came into My Life*
   Compare H. G. Wells's use of the theme of blindness in his story "The Country of the Blind" (in Chapter 11) with Keller's perceptions of being blind.
3. **Temple Grandin,** *Thinking in Pictures*
   Compare the difficulties both Grandin and Helen Keller had in surmounting their respective disabilities and their different perceptions on how language functions.
4. **Stuart Hirschberg,** *The Rhetoric of Advertising*
   To what extent does advertising use techniques also found in political propaganda, as described by Rae Yang in "At the Center of the Storm" in Chapter 8?
5. **Alison Lurie,** *The Language of Clothes*
   How would the concept of clothing as a kind of language, discussed by Lurie, help explain the cross-cultural misunderstandings that Judith Ortiz Cofer confronted in "The Myth of the Latin Woman" in Chapter 1?
6. **Deborah Tannen,** *Sex, Lies, and Conversation*
   To what extent does Anne Tyler's essay "Still Just Writing" (in Chapter 10) illustrate Tannen's thesis about the reasons why women excel at communicating?
7. **Aldous Huxley,** *Propaganda under a Dictatorship*
   Examine Huxley's premise that Hitler adapted Madison Avenue techniques of advertising in light of the analysis by Stuart Hirschberg.
8. **Margaret Atwood,** *Pornography*
   In your opinion, does the "garbage in, garbage out" theory of pornography proposed by Atwood explain the kind of child abuse that Grace Caroline Bridges portrays in her poem "Lisa's Ritual, Age 10" (in Chapter 5)? Explain your answer.
9. **Raymond Carver,** *What We Talk About When We Talk About Love*
   To what extent do the conversations between men and women in Carver's story exemplify the linguistic battle of the sexes discussed by Deborah Tannen?
10. **Ted Hughes,** *Crow Goes Hunting*
    In what respects is Crow's predicament akin to the dilemma facing autistic children, as described by Temple Grandin?
11. **David Ives,** *Words, Words, Words*
    Compare the way Ives and Ted Hughes explore the significance of language through animals who seek to master it.

5

ISSUES IN POPULAR CULTURE

Many contemporary concerns are touched on by the essays in this chapter: consumerism, TV news shows, eating disorders, urban legends, drug addiction, racism, AIDS, the cult of *machismo,* and the worldwide influence of American culture. With a few exceptions, the issues overlap. For example, Juliet B. Schor and Slavenka Drakulić question whether greed and vanity have become America's dominant values, which now have been exported worldwide. The essays by Arthur Ashe and Ann Louise Bardach investigate the ways race, ethnicity, and AIDS have changed our perceptions of relationships in contemporary culture.

The national inability to solve problems without resorting to "quick fixes" and the resulting use of drugs, superficial news broadcasts, and prevalence of eating disorders are discussed by Philip Slater, Neil Postman and Steve Powers, and Kim Chernin. The lasting popularity of urban legends, as described by Jan Harold Brunvand, further indicates our willingness to blur the lines between illusion and reality.

Two timeless stories set contemporary social issues against the background of the human condition. Kate Chopin and Guy de Maupassant offer complex and thoughtful explorations of the consequences of endemic sexism, racism, and illusions regarding mortality.

The poetry by Grace Caroline Bridges and Marge Piercy and the song lyrics by Bruce Springsteen present heartfelt protests about pressing contemporary problems: child abuse, treatment of AIDS victims, and sexual stereotyping.

A play by Betty Keller, *Tea Party,* poignantly dramatizes the plight of two elderly sisters coping with the isolation that afflicts so many older Americans.

Nonfiction

JULIET B. SCHOR

Juliet B. Schor (b. 1955) is the director of Women's Studies and a professor of economics at Harvard. She has written The Overworked American *(1992) and* The Overspent American *(1998), in which the following essay first appeared. Schor analyzes why what*

Americans previously viewed as luxuries have now become necessities. She edited The Consumer Society Reader *with Douglas B. Holt (2000).*

The Culture of Consumerism

In 1996 a best-selling book entitled *The Millionaire Next Door* caused a minor sensation. In contrast to the popular perception of millionaire lifestyles, this book reveals that most millionaires live frugal lives—buying used cars, purchasing their suits at JC Penney, and shopping for bargains. These very wealthy people feel no need to let the world know they can afford to live much better than their neighbors.

Millions of other Americans, on the other hand, have a different relationship with spending. What they acquire and own is tightly bound to their personal identity. Driving a certain type of car, wearing particular designer labels, living in a certain kind of home, and ordering the right bottle of wine create and support a particular image of themselves to present to the world.

This is not to say that most Americans make consumer purchases solely to fool others about who they really are. It is not to say that we are a nation of crass status-seekers. Or that people who purchase more than they need are simply demonstrating a base materialism, in the sense of valuing material possessions above all else. But it is to say that, unlike the millionaires next door, who are not driven to use their wealth to create an attractive image of themselves, many of us are continually comparing our own lifestyle and possessions to those of a select group of people we respect and want to be like, people whose sense of what's important in life seems close to our own.

This aspect of our spending is not new—competitive acquisition has long been an American institution. At the turn of the century, the rich consumed conspicuously. In the early post–World War II decades, Americans spent to keep up with the Joneses, using their possessions to make the statement that they were not failing in their careers. But in recent decades, the culture of spending has changed and intensified. In the old days, our neighbors set the standard for what we had to have. They may have earned a little more, or a little less, but their incomes and ours were in the same ballpark. Their house down the block, worth roughly the same as ours, confirmed this. Today the neighbors are no longer the focus of comparison. How could they be? We may not even know them, much less which restaurants they patronize, where they vacation, and how much they spent for their living room couch.

For reasons that will become clear, the comparisons we make are no longer restricted to those in our own general earnings category, or even to those one rung above us on the ladder. Today a person is more likely to be making comparisons with, or choose as a "reference group," people whose incomes are three, four, or five times his or her own. The result is that millions of us have become participants in a national culture of upscale spending. I call it the new consumerism.

Part of what's new is that lifestyle aspirations are now formed by different points of reference. For many of us, the neighborhood has been replaced by a

5

community of coworkers, people we work alongside and colleagues in our own and related professions. And while our real-life friends still matter, they have been joined by our media "friends." (This is true both figuratively and literally—the television show *Friends* is a good example of an influential media referent.) We watch the way television families live, we read about the lifestyles of celebrities and other public figures we admire, and we consciously and unconsciously assimilate this information. It affects us.

So far so good. We are in a wider world, so we like to know that we are stacking up well against a wider population group than the people on the block. No harm in that. But as new reference groups form, they are less likely to comprise people who all earn approximately the same amount of money. And therein lies the problem. When a person who earns $75,000 a year compares herself to someone earning $90,000, the comparison is sustainable. It creates some tension, even a striving to do a bit better, to be more successful in a career. But when a reference group includes people who pull down six or even seven-figure incomes, that's trouble. When poet-waiters earning $18,000 a year, teachers earning $30,000, and editors and publishers earning six-figure incomes all aspire to be part of one urban literary referent group, which exerts pressure to drink the same brand of bottled water and wine, wear similar urban literary clothes, and appoint apartments with urban literary furniture, those at the lower economic end of the reference group find themselves in an untenable situation. Even if we choose not to emulate those who spend ostentatiously, consumer aspirations can be a serious reach.

Advertising and the media have played an important part in stretching out reference groups vertically. When twenty-somethings can't afford much more than a utilitarian studio but think they should have a New York apartment to match the ones they see on *Friends,* they are setting unattainable consumption goals for themselves, with dissatisfaction as a predictable result. When the children of affluent suburban and impoverished inner-city households both want the same Tommy Hilfiger logo emblazoned on their chests and the top-of-the-line Swoosh on their feet, it's a potential disaster. One solution to these problems emerged on the talk-show circuit recently, championed by a pair of young urban "entry-level" earners: live the *faux* life, consuming *as if* you had a big bank balance. Their strategies? Use your expense account for private entertainment, date bankers, and sneak into snazzy parties without an invitation. Haven't got the wardrobe for it? No matter. Charge expensive clothes, wear them with the tags on, and return them the morning after. Apparently the upscale life is now so worth living that deception, cheating, and theft are a small price to pay for it.

These are the more dramatic examples. Millions of us face less stark but problematic comparisons everyday. People in one-earner families find themselves trying to live the lifestyle of their two-paycheck friends. Parents of modest means struggle to pay for the private schooling that others in their reference group have established as the right thing to do for their children.

Additional problems are created by the accelerating pace of product innovation. To gain broader distribution for the plethora of new products, manufacturers have gone to lifestyle marketing, targeting their pitches of upscale items at rich and 10 nonrich alike. Gourmet cereal, a luxurious latte, or bathroom fixtures that make a statement, the right statement, are offered to people almost everywhere on the economic spectrum. In fact, through the magic of plastic, anyone can buy designer anything, at the trendiest retail shop. Or at outlet prices. That's the new consumerism. And its siren call is hard to resist.

The new consumerism is also built on a relentless ratcheting up of standards. If you move into a house with a fifties kitchen, the presumption is that you will eventually have it redone, because that's a standard that has now been established. If you didn't have air conditioning in your old car, the presumption is that when you replace it, the new one will have it. If you haven't been to Europe, the presumption is that you will get there, because you deserve to get there. And so on. In addition to the proliferation of new products (computers, cell phones, faxes, and other microelectronics), there is a continual upgrading of old ones—autos and appliances—and a shift to customized, more expensive versions, all leading to a general expansion of the list of things we have to have. The 1929 home I just moved into has a closet too shallow to fit a hanger. So the clothes face forward. The real estate agents suggested I solve the "problem" by turning the study off the bedroom into a walk-in. (Why read when you could be buying clothes?) What we want grows into what we *need,* at a sometimes dizzying rate. While politicians continue to tout the middle class as the heart and soul of American society for far too many of us being solidly middle-class is no longer good enough.

Oddly, it doesn't seem as if we're spending wastefully, or even lavishly. Rather, many of us feel we're just making it, barely able to stay even. But what's remarkable is that this feeling is not restricted to families of limited income. It's a generalized feeling, one that exists at all levels. Twenty-seven percent of all households making more than $100,000 a year say they cannot afford to buy everything they really need. Nearly 20 percent say they "spend nearly all their income on the basic necessities of life." In the $50,000–100,000 range, 39 percent and one-third feel this way, respectively. Overall, half the population of the richest country in the world say they cannot afford everything they really need. And it's not just the poorer half.

This book is about why: About why so many middle-class Americans feel materially dissatisfied. Why they walk around with ever-present mental "wish lists" of things to buy or get. How even a six-figure income can seem inadequate, and why this country saves less than virtually any other nation in the world. It is about the ways in which, for America's middle classes, "spending becomes you," about how it flatters, enhances, and defines people in often wonderful ways, but also about how it takes over their lives. My analysis is based on new research showing that the need to spend whatever it takes to keep current within a chosen reference group—which may include members of widely disparate resources—drives much purchasing behavior. It analyzes how standards of belonging socially have changed in recent decades, and how this change has introduced Americans to highly intensified spending pressures.

And finally, it is about a growing backlash to the consumption culture, a movement of people who are downshifting—by working less, earning less, and living their consumer lives much more deliberately.

TABLE 1.1 How Much Is Enough?

Statement	Percentage Agreeing with Statement, by Income						
	<$10,000	10,001–25,000	25,001–35,000	35,001–50,000	50,001–75,000	75,001–100,000	>100,000
I cannot afford to buy everything I really need	64	62	50	43	42	39	27
I spend nearly all of my money on the basic necessities of life	69	64	62	46	35	33	19

SOURCE: Author's calculations from Merck Family Fund poll (February 1995).

SPENDING AND SOCIAL COMPARISON

I am hardly the first person to have argued that consumption has a compara- 15
tive, or even competitive character. Ideas of this sort have a long history within
economics, sociology, and other disciplines. In *The Wealth of Nations,* Adam Smith
observed that even a "creditable day-laborer would be ashamed to appear in pub-
lick, without a linen shirt" and that leather shoes had become a "necessary of life"
in eighteenth-century England. The most influential work on the subject, however,
has been Thorstein Veblen's *Theory of the Leisure Class.* Veblen argued that in affluent
societies, spending becomes the vehicle through which people establish social position. The conspicuous display of wealth and leisure is the marker that reveals a
man's income to the outside world. (Wives, by the way, were seen by Veblen as
largely ornamental, useful to display a man's finest purchases—clothes, furs, and
jewels.) The rich spent conspicuously as a kind of personal advertisement, to secure
a place in the social hierarchy. Everyone below stood watching and, to the extent
possible, emulating those one notch higher. Consumption was a trickle-down
process.

The phenomenon that Veblen identified and described, conspicuous consumption by the rich and the nouveaux riches, was not new even in his own time.
Spending to establish a social position has a long history. Seventeenth- and eigh-
teenth- century Italian nobles built opulent palaces with beautiful facades and,
within those facades, placed tiles engraved with the words *Pro Invidia* (To Be Envied). For centuries, aristocrats passed laws to forbid the nouveaux riches from
copying their clothing styles. At the turn of the century, the wealthy published the
menus of their dinner parties in the newspapers. And fifty years ago, American
social climbers bought fake "ancestor portraits" to hang in their libraries.

Veblen's story made a lot of sense for the upper-crust, turn-of-the-century
urban world of his day. But by the 1920s, new developments were afoot. Because
productivity and output were growing so rapidly, more and more people had entered the comfortable middle classes and begun to enjoy substantial discretionary
spending. And this mass prosperity eventually engendered a new socioeconomic

phenomenon—a mass keeping-up process that led to convergence among consumers' acquisition goals and purchasing patterns.

The advent of mass production in the 1920s made possible an outpouring of identical consumer goods that nearly everybody wanted—and were better able to afford, thanks to declining prices. By the fifties, the Smiths had to have the Joneses' fully automatic washing machine, vacuum cleaner, and, most of all, the shiny new Chevrolet parked in the driveway. The story of this period was that people looked to their own neighborhoods for their spending cues, and the neighbors grew more and more alike in what they had. Like compared with like and strove to become even more alike.

This phenomenon was chronicled by James Duesenberry, a Harvard economist writing just after the Second World War. Duesenberry updated Veblen's trickle-down perspective in his classic discussion of "keeping up with the Joneses." In contrast to Veblen's Vanderbilts, Duesenberry's 1950s Joneses were middle-class and they lived next door, in suburban USA. Rather than seeking to best their neighbors, Duesenberry's Smiths mainly wanted to be like them. Although the ad writers urged people to be the first on the block to own a product, the greater fear in most consumers' minds during this period was that if they didn't get cracking, they might be the last to get on board.

In addition to Veblen and Duesenberry, a number of distinguished economists have emphasized these social and comparative processes in their classic accounts of consumer culture—among them, John Kenneth Galbraith, Fred Hirsch, Tibor Scitovsky, Richard Easterlin, Amartya Sen, Clair Brown, and Robert Frank. Among the most important of their messages is that consumer satisfaction, and dissatisfaction, depend less on what a person has in an absolute sense than on socially formed aspirations and expectations. Indeed, the very term "standard of living" suggests the point: the standard is a social norm. 20

By the 1970s, social trends were once again altering the nature of comparative consumption. Most obvious was the entrance of large numbers of married women into the labor force. As the workplace replaced the coffee klatch and the backyard barbecue as locations of social contact, workplace conversation became a source for information on who went where for vacation, who was having a deck put on the house, and whether the kids were going to dance class, summer camp, or karate lessons. But in the workplace, most employees are exposed to the spending habits of people across a wider economic spectrum, particularly those employees who work in white-collar settings. They have meetings with people who wear expensive suits or "real" Swiss watches. They may work with their boss, or their boss's boss, every day and find out a lot about what they and their families have.

There were also ripple effects on women who didn't have jobs. When many people lived in one-earner households, incomes throughout the neighborhood tended to be close to each other. As many families earned two paychecks, however, mothers who stayed at home or worked part-time found themselves competing with neighbors who could much more easily afford pricey restaurants, piano lessons, and two new cars. Finally, as Robert Frank and Philip Cook have argued, there has been a shift to a "winner-take-all" society: rewards within occupations have become more unequally distributed. As a group of extremely high earners emerged within occupation after occupation, they provided a visible, and very elevated, point of comparison for those who weren't capturing a disproportionate share of the earnings of the group.

Daily exposure to an economically diverse set of people is one reason Americans began engaging in more upward comparison. A shift in advertising patterns is another. Traditionally advertisers had targeted their market by earnings, using one medium or another depending on the income group they were trying to reach. They still do this. But now the huge audiences delivered by television make it the best medium for reaching just about *every* financial group. While *Forbes* readers have a much higher median income than television viewers, it's possible to reach more wealthy people on television than in the pages of any magazine, no matter how targeted its readership. A major sports event or an *ER* episode is likely to deliver more millionaires *and* more laborers than a medium aimed solely at either group. That's why you'll find ads for Lincoln town cars, Mercedes-Benz sports cars, and $50,000 all-terrain vehicles on the Super Bowl telecast. In the process, painters who earn $25,000 a year are being exposed to buying pressures never intended for them, and middle-class housewives look at products once found only in the homes of the wealthy.

Beginning in the 1970s, expert observers were declaring the death of the "belonging" process that had driven much competitive consumption and arguing that the establishment of an individual identity—rather than staying current with the Joneses—was becoming the name of the game. The new trend was to consume in a personal style, with products that signaled your individuality, your personal sense of taste and distinction. But, of course, you had to be different in the right way. The trick was to create a unique image through what you had and wore—and what you did not have and would not be seen dead in.

While the observers had identified a new stage in consumer culture, they   25
were right only to a point. People may no longer have wanted to be just like all others in their socioeconomic class, but their need to measure up within some idealized group survived. What emerged as the new standards of comparison, however, were groups that had no direct counterparts in previous times. Marketers call them clusters—groups of people who share values, orientations, and, most important, *lifestyles.* Clusters are much smaller than traditional horizontal economic strata or classes and can thereby satisfy the need for greater individuality in consumption patterns. "Yuppie" was only the most notorious of these lifestyle cluster groups. There are also middle Americans, twenty-somethings, upscale urban Asians, top one-percenters, and senior sun-seekers. We have radical feminists, comfortable capitalists, young market lions, environmentalists. Whatever.

Ironically, the shift to individuality produced its own brand of localized conformity. (In chapter 2, I discuss just how detailed a profile of spending habits marketers can now produce within a cluster.) Apparently lots of people began wanting the same "individual identity-creating" products. But this predictability, while perhaps a bit absurd, brought with it no *particular* financial problem. Seventies consumerism was manageable. The real problems started in the 1980s as an

TABLE I.2 THE GOOD LIFE GOES UPSCALE

Percentage Identifying Item As a Part of "The Good Life"

	1975	1991
Vacation home	19	35
Swimming pool	14	29
Color TV	46	55
Second color TV	10	28
Travel abroad	30	39
Really nice clothes	36	44
Car	71	75
Second car	30	41
Home you own	85	87
A lot of money	38	55
A job that pays much more than average	45	60
Happy marriage	84	77
One or more children	74	73
Interesting job	69	63
Job that contributes to the welfare of society	38	38
Percentage who think they have a very good chance of achieving the "good life"	35	23

SOURCE: Roper Center, University of Connecticut; published in *American Enterprise* (May–June 1993), p. 87.

economic shift sent seismic shocks through the nation's consumer mentality. Competitive spending intensified. In a very big way.

WHEN $18,000 FEELS LUXURIOUS: JEFF LUTZ

Some Americans are pursuing another path. Want less. Live more simply. Slow down and get in touch with nature. A growing "voluntary simplicity" movement is rejecting the standard path of work and spend. This is a committed, self-conscious group of people who believe that spending less does not reduce their quality of life and may even raise it. Their experience is that *less* (spending) is *more* (time, meaning, peace of mind, financial security, ecological responsibility, physical health, friendship, appreciation of what they do spend). Seattle, long a laid-back, nature-oriented city, is home not only to Boeing and Microsoft but also to many of these individuals. I spent nearly a week there in the summer of 1996, meeting people who were living on less than $20,000 a year. Jeff Lutz was one of them.

After graduating from a small college back east, Jeff and his girlfriend Liza moved to Seattle, where they inhabit a nice, spacious old house in a middle-class neighborhood. They share the place with one friend; their rent is $312 per person. Jeff is self-employed as a medical and legal interpreter and is putting a lot of effort into "growing" his business. Nicely dressed and groomed, he doesn't look too different from other twenty-five-year-old graduates of the prep school and college he attended. But he is. Living on about $10,000 a year, he says he has basically everything he wants and will be content to live at this level of material comfort for the rest of his life. Youthful naïveté? Perhaps. But maybe not.

Lutz grew up in Mexico. His mother, a writer and social activist, went to Mexico with her parents, refugees from Franco's civil war. His father was a lawyer from New York. Family role models helped form his commitment to a frugal lifestyle. "My great-grandfather, who escaped czarist jail in Lithuania, lived in Mexico with one lightbulb and a record player. He had three photos behind his bed. One was Tolstoy, and one was Gandhi, and one was Pious XXIII."

As a teenager, Lutz went to a private school in western Massachusetts. There he began to feel like "part of a herd being prodded along to do one thing after the next in semiconscious wakefulness. You go to elementary school, and then you go to junior high, and then you go to high school, and then you go to college in order to get a job, in order to compete with other people in higher salaries, in order to have more stuff. I saw really clearly in high school just where it was leading." At that point, he made up his mind about two things. First, "I needed to find a way to not be in a nine-to-five-until-I-died treadmill. I had a vision of life being much, much more than spending most of my life in a job that was somebody else's agenda." Second, "I wanted to learn how human beings could live more lightly on the earth."

His experiences in Mexico motivated these sentiments. "I spent a week with some Mazotec Indians in the mountains. And some of these kids my age, one of them had a Washington Redskins jersey. I mean, Spanish is their second language; they spoke Mazoteca, and yet they were listening to Michael Jackson and they wanted to buy my sunglasses and they wanted to buy my watch. And they wanted me to bring more sunglasses and watches so that they could resell them to their friends. It was very clear that our culture was sort of surrounding other cultures through the media. I grew up watching *The Love Boat* dubbed in Spanish."

In college, he designed his own major in environmental studies. But unlike many young people who begin their work lives enthusiastically believing they can combine improving the world with making a good salary, Lutz never really considered that path. "The things I was interested in were pretty outside the box." Near the end of his college years, he came across an article by Joe Dominguez, the creator of a nine-step program of "financial independence." Dominguez's program, contained in his best-selling book (with collaborator Vicki Robin) *Your Money or Your Life,* promises freedom from the grind of the working world, not through getting rich but by downsizing desire. Dominguez and Robin believe Americans have been trained to equate more stuff with more happiness. But that is true only up to a point, a point they feel most of us have passed. Doing it their way, you don't need to save a million dollars to retire, but just one, two, or three hundred thousand.

The program involves meticulously tracking all spending. And not just tracking it but scrutinizing it, by comparing the value of whatever you want to buy with the time it takes to earn the money for it. That calculation involves determining

30

TABLE 1.3   THE EXPANDING DEFINITION OF "NECESSITIES"

	Percentage Indicating Item Is a Necessity		
	1973	1991	1996
Second television	3	15	10
Dishwasher	10	24	13
VCR	—*	18	13
Basic cable service	—	26	17
Remote control for TV or VCR	—	23	—
Answering machine	—	20	26
Home computer	—	11	26
Microwave	—	44	32
Second automobile	20	27	37
Auto air conditioning	13	42	41
Home air conditioning	26	47	51
Television	57	74	59
Clothes dryer	54	74	62
Clothes washer	88	82	86
Automobile	90	85	93
Cellular phone	—	5	—
Housekeeper	—	4	—

*Item did not exist, was not widely in use, or was not asked about in 1973.

SOURCE: Roper Center, University of Connecticut; 1973 and 1991 data published in *American Enterprise* (May–June 1993), p. 89.

your real hourly wage, by taking into account all the hours you work and subtracting all job-related expenses, including the cost of your job wardrobe and takeout food because you're too tired to cook. Equipped with your real wage rate, you can figure out whether a new couch is worth three weeks of work, whether four nights in the Bahamas justify a month of earning, or whether you want to stick with the morning latte (even those half-hours add up). People who follow the program find that when they ask these questions, they spend less. Much less.

Jeff was getting close to financial independence, which entailed earning enough to spend between $800 and $1,200 per month, including health insurance. He says he does not feel materially deprived, and he is careful to point out that voluntary simplicity is not poverty. While he decided against the lattes, he does own a car and a computer, goes out to eat between one and three times a month, rents videos, has friends over for dinner, and buys his clothes both new and used. His furniture is an eclectic mix—nothing fancy, but nothing shabby either. He is convinced that "a higher standard of living will not make me happier. And I'm very clear internally. It's not a belief I picked up from somewhere." It's "something that I've gained an awareness about."

Questions for Discussion and Writing

1. According to Schor, what influence have the media had in altering the public's view of what constitutes the good life?
2. When you look at the tables of comparative statistics Schor provides about luxuries now viewed as necessities, what conclusions do you reach?
3. Would you ever consider following the example of Jeff Lutz and downsizing your expectations and lifestyle? Why or why not?

SLAVENKA DRAKULIĆ

Slavenka Drakulić is a leading Croatian writer, a well-known journalist, and a commentator on cultural affairs in eastern Europe. She is a columnist for the magazine Danas *in Zagreb and a regular contributor to the* Nation *and the* New Republic *magazines. Drakulić is the author of a novel and several works of nonfiction, including* The Balkan Express *(1993) and* Cafe Europa: Life after Communism *(1996), in which the following essay first appeared. Her latest work is* S.: Novel about the Balkans, *translated by Marko Ivic (2000).*

On Bad Teeth

In a way, I was initiated into capitalism through toothpaste.

When I first visited the States in 1983, I loved to watch TV commercials. This is when I noticed that Americans were obsessed by their teeth. Every second commercial seemed to be for a toothpaste. Where I come from, toothpaste is toothpaste. I couldn't believe there were so many different kinds. What were they all *for?* After all the purpose of it is just to clean your teeth. In my childhood there were two kinds, mint flavour and strawberry flavour, and both of them had the same brand name, Kalodont. For a long time I was convinced that Kalodont was the word for toothpaste, because nobody at home used the generic word. We never said, "Do you have toothpaste?" we said, "Do you have Kalodont?" It is hardly surprising, then, that such a person would react with nothing short of disbelief when faced with the American cosmetic (or is it pharmaceutical?) industry and its endless production line. Toothpaste with or without sugar, with or without flour, with or without baking soda, calcium, vitamins....

Over the years, on subsequent visits I continued to be fascinated by this American obsession with toothpaste, from the common varieties all the way up to Rembrandt, the most snobbish brand, if there could be such a thing as snobbishness about toothpaste. I soon learned that there could: in one women's magazine I saw it recommended as a Christmas present! Needless to say, in every commercial for toothpaste at least one bright, impressively beautiful set of teeth flashes across the screen, but this image is not confined to selling toothpaste. As we all know, beautiful teeth are used to advertise beer, hair shampoo, cars, anything. Indeed, they are an indispensable feature of any American advertisement. The foreigner soon learns that they stand not only as a symbol for both good looks and good health, but for something else as well.

If you think that such advertising might be part of the Americans' national obsession with health in general, you are not far from the truth. Americans seem to be passionate about their health and their looks, which appear to be interchangeable qualities. Health and good looks are essential badges of status among the middle classes. Nothing but narcissism, you could retort, but it is more than that. This connection between teeth and social status is not so evident to an Eastern European. I personally had some doubts about those TV teeth, I thought that they must be artificial, some kind of prosthesis made out of plastic or porcelain. They were just too good to be true. How could people have such fine teeth? Intrigued, I decided to take a good look around me.

I noticed that the people I met, that is mostly middle-class urban profession-   5
als, generally, do have a set of bright, white teeth of their own, not unlike the TV teeth. It was even more surprising to me that I could detect no cavities, no missing teeth, no imperfections. I was astonished. The secret was revealed to me when a friend took her son to the dentist. When they returned, the little boy's upper teeth were fixed with a dreadful-looking kind of iron muzzle: a brace, I learned. It was obviously painful for him. "Poor little thing!" I exclaimed, but his mother showed no mercy. Moreover, she was proud that she could afford this torture device. I was puzzled. When she explained to me that the brace cost between $2,000 and $3,000, her attitude seemed even more sinister. I eventually realised that the mystery of beautiful teeth is not only about hygiene, but about money. She had money enough to get her son's teeth fixed, and the little boy was brave enough to stand the pain, because somehow he understood that this was a requirement of his social status. All the other boys from his private school had braces, too. He was going to grow up being well aware of the fact that his healthy, beautiful teeth were expensive and, therefore, an indication of prestige. Moreover, his mother could count on him to brush them three times a day, with an electric toothbrush and the latest toothpaste promising even healthier and more beautiful teeth, as if that were possible. In the long run, all the discomfort would be worth it.

Seeing the boy's brace, the connection between health and wealth in America became a bit clearer to me. Clean, healthy teeth feature so much in advertising because Americans have no free dental care, and neither is it covered by any medical insurance. Therefore, if you invest money and educate your child early enough (a bit of suffering is needed, too), you will save a lot later. But how much money did this take? I got my answer when I had to visit a dentist myself. On one of my last visits my filling fell out, and just to have it refilled with some temporary white stuff, whatever it was, I had to pay $100. This would be a minor financial catastrophe for any Eastern European citizen used to free dental care in his own country; it was expensive even by American standards. Only then did I become fully aware of what it means not to have free dental care.

Predictably enough, I was outraged. How was it possible for dental work to be so expensive in this country? For $100 back home I could have coated my tooth in pure gold! And why was it that such an affluent country did not provide its citizens with basic services like free dental work? This was one of the very few areas in which we from former communist countries had some advantage over Americans—and we would like to keep it.

On my way home, I thought what a blessing it was that we did not have to worry about our teeth, or about whether we could afford to look after them—or at least, we did not have to worry yet, in my country, anyway. However, immediately upon my arrival in Zagreb, I realized that I could allow myself such rose-tinted thoughts only as long as I was on the other side of the Atlantic, from where everything at home looked a bit blurred, especially the general state of people's teeth. Back at home, I was forced to adjust my view. It was as if I had been myopic before and now I had got the right pair of glasses and could finally see properly. And what I saw did not please me at all.

On the bus from the airport I met one of my acquaintances, a young television reporter. For the first time I noticed that half of his teeth were missing and that those which remained looked like the ruins of a decayed medieval town. I had known this guy for years, but I had never thought about the state of the inside of his mouth before, or if I had, I'd considered it totally unimportant. Now I also noticed that, in order to hide his bad teeth, he had grown a moustache and developed a way of laughing which didn't involve him opening his mouth too wide. Even so, his bad teeth were still obvious.

This encounter did not cheer me up. Sitting next to the young reporter, I wondered how he managed to speak in front of a TV camera without making a mistake that would reveal his terrible secret. Without smiling, perhaps? This would be perfectly acceptable, because he reports on the war, but wasn't he tired of this uncomfortable game of hide-and-seek? Wouldn't it be much more professional and make life easier if he visited a good dentist and got it all over with? But this is not something we are supposed to talk about. How do you say such a thing to a person if he is not your intimate friend? You can't just say, "Listen, why don't you do something about your teeth?" Perhaps I should have pulled out my toothpaste and handed it to him, or casually dropped the name of my dentist, something like what my friend did last summer. A woman standing next to her in a streetcar emanated an extremely unpleasant odour from her hairy armpits. My friend could not stand it. She pulled her own deodorant stick out of her handbag and gave it to the woman. The funny thing is that the woman accepted it without taking offence. I, on the other hand, could not risk offending my acquaintance. 10

I continued my investigations at home. Yes, I admit that I looked into the mouths of friends, relatives, acquaintances, neighbours—I could not help it. I discovered that the whole nation had bad teeth, it was just that I had not been able to see it before. I concluded that the guy on the bus was only a part of the general landscape, that he was no exception, and that therefore his failure to attend to his teeth was perfectly normal. I tried to explain this attitude to myself: perhaps people were afraid of drilling? Of course. Who isn't? But if nothing else, there must be an aesthetic drive in every human being, or one would at least think so. Yet, for some reason, aesthetics and communism don't go well together and though we might call our current state post-communism we still have a communist attitude in such matters.

You could also argue that dentists, being employed by the state, are not well paid. Consequently, they don't put much effort into their job. You can claim as well that the materials they use are not of good quality. That is all probably true. But, I still believe that having your teeth repaired to a mediocre standard is preferable to treasuring the medieval ruins in your mouth or being toothless altogether.

There is no excuse that sounds reasonable enough for such negligence. The problem is that the condition of your teeth in Eastern Europe is regarded as a highly personal matter, not a sign of your standard of living or a question for public discussion. Having good teeth is simply a matter of being civilised and well mannered. Strangely enough, however, dirty shoes, dirty fingernails or dandruff are no longer tolerated: these are considered impolite, even offensive. Yet like such matters of personal hygiene, good teeth are not only a question of money. Dental work has been free for the last forty years. At present there co-exists a mixture of both state-run general medical care, which includes dental care, and private dentists. If you want, you can have excellent dental work done. I know people who travel from Vienna to Bratislava, Budapest, Ljubljana or Zagreb to have their teeth re-paired more cheaply. But if you asked people in Eastern Europe who can afford it why they don't go to a private dentist for a better service, they would probably tell you that this is not their priority at the moment. Instead they want to fix their car, or buy a new carpet.

It is clear that leaders and intellectuals here certainly don't care about such a minor aspect of their image. They are preoccupied with the destiny of their respective nations, they do not have time for such trivial matters. The American idea that it is not very polite for a public figure to appear with bad teeth, just as it would be inappropriate to make a speech in your pyjamas, is not understood here. You can meet exquisitely dressed politicians or businessmen, but wait until they open their mouths! If these public figures are not worried about this aspect of their looks, why should ordinary people be concerned about theirs? They too have more important things to do, for example surviving. There is also that new breed, the *nouveau riche* of post-communism. Previously everything was valued by one's participation in politics; now it is slowly replaced by money. The arrogance of these people originates there. Unfortunately, money does not guarantee good manners, or a regular visit to the dentist for that matter.

I can only try to imagine the horrors when free dental work is replaced by private dentists whose prices nobody can afford. How many decades will we have to wait until our teeth look like American ones? It is a question of perception. In order to improve your looks, you have to be convinced that it is worth the trouble. In other words, we are dealing with a problem of self-esteem, with a way of thinking, rather than a superficial question. Bad teeth are the result of bad dentists and bad food, but also of a specific culture of thinking, of not seeing yourself as an individual. What we need here is a revolution of self-perception. Not only will that not come automatically with the new political changes, but I am afraid that it will also take longer than any political or economic developments. We need to accept our responsibilities towards both others and ourselves. This is not only a wise sort of investment in the future, as we can see in the case of Americans, it also gives you the feeling that you have done what you can to improve yourself, be it your teeth, your health, your career, education, environment or society in general.

Individual responsibility, including the responsibility for oneself, is an entirely new concept here, as I have stated many times elsewhere. This is why the revolution of self-perception has a long way to go. As absurd as it may sound, in the old days one could blame the Communist Party even for one's bad teeth. Now there is no one to blame, but it takes time to understand that. If you have never had it, self-respect has to be learned. Maybe our own teeth would be a good place to start.

But I can see signs of coming changes. Recently a good friend borrowed some money from me in order to repair her apartment. When the time came to give it back, she told me that I would have to wait, because she needed the money for something very urgent. She had finally decided to have her teeth fixed by a private dentist. No wonder she was left without a penny. But what could I have said to that? I said the only thing I could say: "I understand you, this must come first."

Finally, I guess it is only fair that I should declare the state of my own teeth. I am one of those who much too often used the free dental work so generously provided by the communist state for the benefit of its people. I was afraid of the dentist, all right, but also brave enough to stand the pain because I had overcome the psychological barrier at an early age.

When I was in the third grade a teacher showed us a cartoon depicting a fortress—a tooth—attacked by bad guys—bacteria. They looked terribly dangerous, digging tunnels and ditches with their small axes until the fortress almost fell into their hands. Then the army of good guys, the white blood cells, arrived and saved it at the last moment. The teacher explained to us how we could fight the bad guys by brushing our teeth regularly with Kalodont and by visiting a dentist every time we spotted a little hole or felt pain. I took her advice literally—I was obviously very impressed by the cartoon, just as I was impressed by the American TV commercials thirty years later. The result is that today I can say that I have good teeth, although six of them are missing. How did that happen? Well, when I spotted a little cavity, I would immediately go to the dentist all by myself. This was mistake number one. You could not choose your own dentist at that time, and my family had to go to a military hospital. A dentist there would usually fill the cavity, but for some reason the filling would soon fall out. Then he would make an even bigger hole and fill it again, until eventually there was not much tooth left.

Those "dentists" were in fact young students of dentistry drafted into the army. For them, this was probably an excellent chance to improve their knowledge by practising on patients. When they'd finished practising on me a more experienced dentist would suggest I had the tooth out. What could I, a child, do but agree? This was mistake number two, of course. I had to learn to live with one gap in my jaw, then another, and another. Much later I had two bridges made by a private dentist. He didn't even ask me why I was missing six of my teeth; he knew how things had worked in those days. My only consolation was that I did not have to pay much for my bridgework.

Like everyone else in the post-communist world, I had to learn the meaning of the American proverb "There is no such thing as a free lunch." The Americans are right. You don't get anything properly done if you don't pay for it sooner or later.

Questions for Discussion and Writing

1. What unique values explain the great importance placed on having good teeth in the United States compared with eastern Europe? How did the situation change after communism?
2. What links does Drakulić discover between political philosophy and dental hygiene in eastern Europe and in the United States?
3. If you chose to repair your car or buy a new carpet before fixing your teeth, what would this choice suggest about you and your culture?

NEIL POSTMAN AND STEVE POWERS

Neil Postman is University Professor, Paulette Goddard Chair of Media Ecology and Chair of the Department of Culture and Communication at New York University and has investigated the effects of the media in books such as Amusing Ourselves to Death *(1985) and* Conscientious Objections *(1992). Most recently, he has written* Building a Bridge to the 18th Century: How the Past Can Improve Our Future *(1999). Together with Steve Powers, an award winning journalist with more than thirty years experience in broadcast news, he wrote* How to Watch TV News *(1992) from which the following essay is drawn.*

TV News as Entertainment

When a television news show distorts the truth by altering or manufacturing facts (through re-creations), a television viewer is defenseless even if a re-creation is properly labeled. Viewers are still vulnerable to misinformation since they will not know (at least in the case of docudramas) what parts are fiction and what parts are not. But the problems of verisimilitude posed by re-creations pale to insignificance when compared to the problems viewers face when encountering a straight (no-monkey-business) show. All news shows, in a sense, are re-creations in that what we hear and see on them are attempts to represent actual events, and are not the events themselves. Perhaps, to avoid ambiguity, we might call all news shows "re-presentations" instead of "re-creations." These re-presentations come to us in two forms: language and pictures. The question then arises: what do viewers have to know about language and pictures in order to be properly armed to defend themselves against the seductions of eloquence (to use Bertrand Russell's apt phrase)?[1] . . .

---

[1] *Bertrand Russell (1872–1970):* British philosopher and mathematician known for his wit and common sense.

[Let us look at] the problem of pictures. It is often said that a picture is worth a thousand words. Maybe so. But it is probably equally true that one word is worth a thousand pictures, at least sometimes—for example, when it comes to understanding the world we live in. Indeed, the whole problem with news on television comes down to this: all the words uttered in an hour of news coverage could be printed on one page of a newspaper. And the world cannot be understood in one page. Of course, there is a compensation: television offers pictures, and the pictures move. Moving pictures are a kind of language in themselves, but the language of pictures differs radically from oral and written language, and the differences are crucial for understanding television news.

To begin with, pictures, especially single pictures, speak only in particularities. Their vocabulary is limited to concrete representation. Unlike words and sentences, a picture does not present to us an idea or concept about the world, except as we use language itself to convert the image to idea. By itself, a picture cannot deal with the unseen, the remote, the internal, the abstract. It does not speak of "man," only of *a* man; not of "tree," only of *a* tree. You cannot produce an image of "nature," any more than an image of "the sea." You can only show a particular fragment of the here-and-now—a cliff of a certain terrain, in a certain condition of light; a wave at a moment in time, from a particular point of view. And just as "nature" and "the sea" cannot be photographed, such larger abstractions as truth, honor, love, and falsehood cannot be talked about in the lexicon of individual pictures. For "showing of" and "talking about" are two very different kinds of processes: individual pictures give us the world as object; language, the world as idea. There is no such thing in nature as "man" or "tree." The universe offers no such categories or simplifications; only flux and infinite variety. The picture documents and celebrates the particularities of the universe's infinite variety. Language makes them comprehensible.

Of course, moving pictures, video with sound, may bridge the gap by juxtaposing images, symbols, sound, and music. Such images can present emotions and rudimentary ideas. They can suggest the panorama of nature and the joys and miseries of humankind.

Picture—smoke pouring from the window, cut to people coughing, an ambulance racing to a hospital, a tombstone in a cemetery.

5

Picture—jet planes firing rockets, explosions, lines of foreign soldiers surrendering, the American flag waving in the wind.

Nonetheless, keep in mind that when terrorists want to prove to the world that their kidnap victims are still alive, they photograph them holding a copy of a recent newspaper. The dateline on the newspaper provides the proof that the photograph was taken on or after that date. Without the help of the written word, film and videotape cannot portray temporal dimensions with any precision. Consider a film clip showing an aircraft carrier at sea. One might be able to identify the ship as Soviet or American, but there would be no way of telling where in the world the carrier was, where it was headed, or when the pictures were taken. It is only through language—words spoken over the pictures or reproduced in them—that the image of the aircraft carrier takes on specific meaning.

Still, it is possible to enjoy the image of the carrier for its own sake. One might find the hugeness of the vessel interesting; it signifies military power on the move. There is a certain drama in watching the planes come in at high speeds and skid to a stop on the deck. Suppose the ship were burning: that would be even more interesting. This leads to an important point about the language of pictures. Moving pictures favor images that change. That is why violence and dynamic destruction find their way onto television so often. When something is destroyed violently it is altered in a highly visible way; hence the entrancing power of fire. Fire gives visual form to the ideas of consumption, disappearance, death—the thing that burned is actually taken away by fire. It is at this very basic level that fires make a good subject for television news. Something was here, now it's gone, and the change is recorded on film.

Earthquakes and typhoons have the same power. Before the viewer's eyes the world is taken apart. If a television viewer has relatives in Mexico City and an earthquake occurs there, then he or she may take a special interest in the images of destruction as a report from a specific place and time; that is, one may look at television pictures for information about an important event. But film of an earthquake can be interesting even if the viewer cares nothing about the event itself. Which is only to say, as we noted earlier, that there is another way of participating in the news—as a spectator who desires to be entertained. Actually to see buildings topple is exciting, no matter where the buildings are. The world turns to dust before our eyes.

Those who produce television news in America know that their medium favors images that move. That is why they are wary of "talking heads," people who simply appear in front of a camera and speak. When talking heads appear on television, there is nothing to record or document, no change in process. In the cinema the situation is somewhat different. On a movie screen, closeups of a good actor speaking dramatically can sometimes be interesting to watch. When Clint Eastwood narrows his eyes and challenges his rival to shoot first, the spectator sees the cool rage of the Eastwood character take visual form, and the narrowing of the eyes is dramatic. But much of the effect of this small movement depends on the size of the movie screen and the darkness of the theater, which make Eastwood and his every action "larger than life."

The television screen is smaller than life. It occupies about 15 percent of the viewer's visual field (compared to about 70 percent for the movie screen). It is not set in a darkened theater closed off from the world but in the viewer's ordinary living space. This means that visual changes must be more extreme and more dramatic to be interesting on television. A narrowing of the eyes will not do. A car crash, an earthquake, a burning factory are much better.

With these principles in mind, let us examine more closely the structure of a typical newscast, and here we will include in the discussion not only the pictures but all the nonlinguistic symbols that make up a television news show. For example, in America, almost all news shows begin with music, the tone of which suggests important events about to unfold. The music is very important, for it equates the news with various forms of drama and ritual—the opera, for example, or a wedding procession—in which musical themes underscore the meaning of the event. Music takes us immediately into the realm of the symbolic, a world that is not to be taken literally. After all, when events unfold in the real world, they do so without musical accompaniment. More symbolism follows. The sound of teletype machines can be heard in the studio, not because it is impossible to screen this noise out, but because the sound is a kind of music in itself. It tells us that data are pouring in from all corners of the globe, a sensation reinforced by the world map in the background (or clocks noting the time on different continents). The fact is that teletype machines are rarely used in TV news rooms, having been replaced by silent computer terminals. When seen, they have only a symbolic function.

Already, then, before a single news item is introduced, a great deal has been communicated. We know that we are in the presence of a symbolic event, a form of theater in which the day's events are to be dramatized. This theater takes the entire globe as its subject, although it may look at the world from the perspective of a single nation. A certain tension is present, like the atmosphere in a theater just before the curtain goes up. The tension is represented by the music, the staccato beat of the teletype machines, and often the sight of news workers scurrying around typing reports and answering phones. As a technical matter, it would be no problem to build a set in which the newsroom staff remained off camera, invisible to the viewer, but an important theatrical effect would be lost. By being busy on camera, the workers help communicate urgency about the events at hand, which suggests that situations are changing so rapidly that constant revision of the news is necessary.

The staff in the background also helps signal the importance of the person in the center, the anchor, "in command" of both the staff and the news. The anchor plays the role of host. He or she welcomes us to the newscast and welcomes us back from the different locations we visit during the filmed reports.

Many features of the newscast help the anchor to establish the impression of   15
control. These are usually equated with production values in broadcasting. They include such things as graphics that tell the viewer what is being shown, or maps and charts that suddenly appear on the screen and disappear on cue, or the orderly progression from story to story. They also include the absence of gaps, or "dead time," during the broadcast, even the simple fact that the news starts and ends at a certain hour. These common features are thought of as purely technical matters, which a professional crew handles as a matter of course. But they are also symbols of a dominant theme of television news: the imposition of an orderly world—called "the news"—upon the disorderly flow of events.

While the form of a news broadcast emphasizes tidiness and control, its content can best be described as fragmented. Because time is so precious on television, because the nature of the medium favors dynamic visual images, and because the pressures of a commercial structure require the news to hold its audience above all else, there is rarely any attempt to explain issues in depth or place events in their proper context. The news moves nervously from a warehouse fire to a court decision, from a guerrilla war to a World Cup match, the quality of the film most often determining the length of the story. Certain stories show up only because they offer dramatic pictures. Bleachers collapse in South America: hundreds of people are crushed—a perfect television news story, for the cameras can record the face of disaster in all its anguish. Back in Washington, a new budget is approved by Congress. Here there is nothing to photograph because a budget is not a physical event; it is a document full of language and numbers. So the producers of the news will show a photo of the document itself, focusing on the cover where it says "Budget of the United States of America." Or sometimes they will send a camera crew to the government printing plant where copies of the budget are produced. That evening, while the contents of the budget are summarized by a voice-over, the viewer sees stacks of documents being loaded into boxes at the government printing plant. Then a few of the budget's more important provisions will be flashed on the screen in written form, but this is such a time-consuming process—using television as a printed page—that the producers keep it to a minimum. In short, the budget is not televisable, and for that reason its time on the news must be brief. The bleacher collapse will get more time that evening.

While appearing somewhat chaotic, these disparate stories are not just dropped in the news program helter-skelter. The appearance of a scattershot story order is really orchestrated to draw the audience from one story to the next—from one section to the next—through the commercial breaks to the end of the show. The story order is constructed to hold and build the viewership rather than place events in context or explain issues in depth.

Of course, it is a tendency of journalism in general to concentrate on the surface of events rather than underlying conditions; this is as true for the newspaper as it is for the newscast. But several features of television undermine whatever efforts journalists may make to give sense to the world. One is that a television broadcast is a series of events that occur in sequence, and the sequence is the same for all viewers. This is not true for a newspaper page, which displays many items simultaneously, allowing readers to choose the order in which they read them. If newspaper readers want only a summary of the latest tax bill, they can read the headline and the first paragraph of an article, and if they want more, they can keep reading. In a sense, then, everyone reads a different newspaper, for no two readers will read (or ignore) the same items.

But all television viewers see the same broadcast. They have no choices. A report is either in the broadcast or out, which means that anything which is of narrow interest is unlikely to be included. As NBC News executive Reuven Frank once explained:

> A newspaper, for example, can easily afford to print an item of conceivable interest to only a fraction of its readers. A television news program must be put together with the assumption that each item will be of some interest to everyone that watches. Every time a newspaper includes a feature which will attract a specialized group it can assume it is adding at least a little bit to its circulation. To the degree a television news program includes an item of this sort . . . it must assume that its audience will diminish.

The need to "include everyone," an identifying feature of commercial television in all its forms, prevents journalists from offering lengthy or complex explanations, or from tracing the sequence of events leading up to today's headlines. One
20

of the ironies of political life in modern democracies is that many problems which concern the "general welfare" are of interest only to specialized groups. Arms control, for example, is an issue that literally concerns everyone in the world, and yet the language of arms control and the complexity of the subject are so daunting that only a minority of people can actually follow the issue from week to week and month to month. If it wants to act responsibly, a newspaper can at least make available more information about arms control than most people want. Commercial television cannot afford to do so.

But even if commercial television could afford to do so, it wouldn't. The fact that television news is principally made up of moving pictures prevents it from offering lengthy, coherent explanations of events. A television news show reveals the world as a series of unrelated, fragmentary moments. It does not—and cannot be expected to—offer a sense of coherence or meaning. What does this suggest to a TV viewer? That the viewer must come with a prepared mind—information, opinions, sense of proportion, an articulate value system. To the TV viewer lacking such mental equipment, a news program is only a kind of rousing light show. Here a falling building, there a five-alarm fire, everywhere the world as an object, much without meaning, connections, or continuity.

Questions for Discussion and Writing

1. According to Postman and Powers, in what different ways has television news been designed to emphasize spectacle over content?
2. Look at the examples of how a new U.S. budget or an arms control negotiation might be reported. How do they illustrate the current failings of news broadcasts?
3. Draw on this essay to analyze the form and content of a nightly TV news broadcast and evaluate the authors' conclusions.

JAN HAROLD BRUNVAND

Jan Harold Brunvand (b. 1933) is professor of folklore at the University of Utah and is the author of The Study of American Folklore: An Introduction *(1997) and* The Vanishing Hitchhiker: American Urban Legends and Their Meanings *(1981), from which the following selection is drawn. Brunvand identifies the distinguishing features of urban legends and gives an in-depth analysis of one particular legend that has been repeated so many times that it is thought to be true.*

Urban Legends: "The Boyfriend's Death"

We are not aware of our own folklore any more than we are of the grammatical rules of our language. When we follow the ancient practice of informally transmitting "lore"—wisdom, knowledge, or accepted modes of behavior—by word of mouth and customary example from person to person, we do not concentrate on the form or content of our folklore; instead, we simply listen to information that others tell us and then pass it on—more or less accurately—to other listeners. In this stream of unselfconscious oral tradition the information that acquires a clear story line is called *narrative folklore,* and those stories alleged to be true are *legends.* This, in broad summary, is the typical process of legend formation and transmission as it has existed from time immemorial and continues to operate today. It works about the same way whether the legendary plot concerns a dragon in a cave or a mouse in a Coke bottle.

It might seem unlikely that legends—*urban* legends at that—would continue to be created in an age of widespread literacy, rapid mass communications, and restless travel. While our pioneer ancestors may have had to rely heavily on oral traditions to pass the news along about changing events and frontier dangers, surely we no longer need mere "folk" reports of what's happening, with all their tendencies to distort the facts. A moment's reflection, however, reminds us of the many weird, fascinating, but unverified rumors and tales that so frequently come to our ears— killers and madmen on the loose, shocking or funny personal experiences, unsafe manufactured products, and many other unexplained mysteries of daily life. Sometimes we encounter different oral versions of such stories, and on occasion we may read about similar events in newspapers or magazines; but seldom do we find, or even seek after, reliable documentation. The lack of verification in no way diminishes the appeal urban legends have for us. We enjoy them merely as stories, and we tend at least to half-believe them as possibly accurate reports. And the legends we tell, as with any folklore, reflect many of the hopes, fears, and anxieties of our time. In short, legends are definitely part of our modern folklore—legends which are as traditional, variable, and functional as those of the past.

Folklore study consists of collecting, classifying, and interpreting in their full cultural context the many products of everyday human interaction that have acquired a somewhat stable underlying form and that are passed traditionally from person to person, group to group, and generation to generation. Legend study is a most revealing area of such research because the stories that people believe to be true hold an important place in their worldview. "If it's true, it's important" is an axiom to be trusted, whether or not the lore really *is* true or not. Simply becoming aware of this modern folklore which we all possess to some degree is a revelation in itself, but going beyond this to compare the tales, isolate their consistent themes, and relate them to the rest of the culture can yield rich insights into the state of our current civilization. . . .

URBAN LEGENDS AS FOLKLORE

Folklore subsists on oral tradition, but not all oral communication is folklore. The vast amounts of human interchange, from casual daily conversations to formal discussions in business or industry, law, or teaching, rarely constitute straight oral folklore. However, all such "communicative events" (as scholars dub them) are punctuated routinely by various units of traditional material that are memorable, repeatable, and that fit recurring social situations well enough to serve in place of original remarks. "Tradition" is the key idea that links together such utterances as nicknames, proverbs, greeting and leave-taking formulas, wisecracks, anecdotes, and jokes as "folklore"; indeed, these are a few of the best known "conversational genres" of American folklore. Longer and more complex folk forms—fairy tales, epics, myths, legends, or ballads, for example—may thrive only in certain special situations of oral transmission. All true folklore ultimately depends upon continued oral dissemination, usually within fairly homogeneous "folk groups," and upon the retention through time of internal patterns and motifs that become traditional in the oral exchanges. The corollary of this rule of stability in oral tradition is that all items of folklore, while retaining a fixed central core, are constantly changing as they are transmitted, so as to create countless "variants" differing in length, detail, style, and performance technique. Folklore, in short, consists of oral tradition in variants.

Urban legends belong to the subclass of folk narratives, legends, that—unlike   5 fairy tales—are believed, or at least believable, and that—unlike myths—are set in the recent past and involve normal human beings rather than ancient gods or demigods. Legends are folk history, or rather quasi-history. As with any folk legends, urban legends gain credibility from specific details of time and place or from references to source authorities. For instance, a popular western pioneer legend often begins something like, "My great-grandmother had this strange experience when she was a young girl on a wagon train going through Wyoming when an Indian chief wanted to adopt her. . . ." Even though hundreds of different great-grandmothers are supposed to have had the same doubtful experience (being desired by the chief because of her beautiful long blond hair), the fact seldom reaches legend-tellers; if it does, they assume that the family lore has indeed spread far and wide. This particular popular tradition, known as "Goldilocks on the Oregon Trail," interests folklorists because of the racist implications of a dark Indian savage coveting a fair young civilized woman—this legend is familiar in the *white* folklore only—and it is of little concern that the story seems to be entirely apocryphal.

In the world of modern urban legends there is usually no geographical or generational gap between teller and event. The story is *true;* it really occurred, and recently, and always to someone else who is quite close to the narrator, or at least "a friend of a friend." Urban legends are told both in the course of casual conversations and in such special situations as campfires, slumber parties, and college dormitory bull sessions. The legends' physical settings are often close by, real, and sometimes even locally renowned for other such happenings. Though the characters in the stories are usually nameless, they are true-to-life examples of the kind of people the narrators and their audience know firsthand.

One of the great mysteries of folklore research is where oral traditions originate and who invents them. One might expect that at least in modern folklore we could come up with answers to such questions, but this is seldom, if ever, the case. . . .

THE PERFORMANCE OF LEGENDS

Whatever the origins of urban legends, their dissemination is no mystery. The tales have traveled far and wide, and have been told and retold from person to person in the same manner that myths, fairy tales, or ballads spread in earlier cultures, with the important difference that today's legends are also disseminated by the mass media. Groups of age-mates, especially adolescents, are one important American legend channel, but other paths of transmission are among office workers and club members, as well as among religious, recreational, and regional groups. Some individuals make a point of learning every recent rumor or tale, and they can enliven any coffee break, party, or trip with the latest supposed "news." The telling of one story inspires other people to share what they have read or heard, and in a short time a lively exchange of details occurs and perhaps new variants are created.

Tellers of these legends, of course, are seldom aware of their roles as "performers of folklore." The conscious purpose of this kind of storytelling is to convey a true event, and only incidentally to entertain an audience. Nevertheless, the speaker's demeanor is carefully orchestrated, and his or her delivery is low-key and soft-sell. With subtle gestures, eye movements, and vocal inflections the stories are made dramatic, pointed, and suspenseful. But, just as with jokes, some can tell them and some can't. Passive tellers of urban legends may just report them as odd rumors, but the more active legend tellers re-create them as dramatic stories of suspense and, perhaps, humor.

"THE BOYFRIEND'S DEATH"

With all these points in mind folklore's subject-matter style, and oral perform-   10
ance, consider this typical version of a well-known urban legend that folklorists have named "The Boyfriend's Death," collected in 1964 (the earliest documented instance of the story) by folklorist Daniel R. Barnes from an eighteen-year-old freshman at the University of Kansas. The usual tellers of the story are adolescents, and the normal setting for the narration is a college dormitory room with fellow students sprawled on the furniture and floors.

> This happened just a few years ago out on the road that turns off highway 59 by the Holiday Inn. This couple were parked under a tree out on this road. Well, it got to be time for the girl to be back at the dorm, so she told her boyfriend that they should start back. But the car wouldn't start, so he told her to lock herself in the car and he would go down to the Holiday Inn and call for help. Well, he didn't come back and he didn't come back, and pretty soon she started hearing a scratching noise on the roof of the car. "Scratch, scratch . . . scratch, scratch." She got scareder and scareder, but he didn't come back. Finally, when it was almost daylight, some people came along and stopped and helped her out of the car, and she looked up and there was her boyfriend hanging from the tree, and his feet were scraping against the roof of the car. This is why the road is called "Hangman's Road."

Here is a story that has traveled rapidly to reach nationwide oral circulation, in the process becoming structured in the typical manner of folk narratives. The traditional and fairly stable elements are the parked couple, the abandoned girl, the mysterious scratching (sometimes joined by a dripping sound and ghostly shadows on the windshield), the daybreak rescue, and the horrible climax. Variable traits are the precise location, the reason for her abandonment, the nature of the rescuers, murder details, and the concluding placename explanation. While "The Boyfriend's Death" seems to have captured teenagers' imaginations as a separate legend only since the early 1960s, it is clearly related to at least two older yarns, "The Hook" and "The Roommate's Death." All three legends have been widely collected by American folklorists, although only scattered examples have been published, mostly in professional journals. Examination of some of these variations helps to make clear the status of the story as folklore and its possible meanings.

At Indiana University, a leading American center of folklore research, folk-narrative specialist Linda Dégh and her students have gathered voluminous data on urban legends, especially those popular with adolescents. Dégh's preliminary published report on "The Boyfriend's Death" concerned nineteen texts collected from IU students from 1964 to 1968. Several storytellers had heard it in high school, often at parties; others had picked it up in college dormitories or elsewhere on campus. Several students expressed some belief in the legend, supposing either that it had happened in their own hometowns, or possibly in other states, once as far distant as "a remote part of Alabama." One informant reported that "she had been sworn to that the incident actually happened," but another, who had heard some variations of the tale, felt that "it seemed too horrible to be true." Some versions had incorporated motifs from other popular teenage horror legends or local ghost stories. . . .

One of the Indiana texts, told in the state of Washington, localizes the story there near Moses Lake, "in the country on a road that leads to a dead-end right under a big weeping willow tree . . . about four or five miles from town." As in most American versions of the story, these specific local touches make believable what is essentially a traveling legend. In a detail familiar from other variants of "The Boyfriend's Death," the body—now decapitated—is left hanging upside down from a branch of the willow tree with the fingernails scraping the top of the car. Another version studied by the Indiana researcher is somewhat aberrant, perhaps because the student was told the story by a friend's parents who claimed that "it happened a long time ago, probably thirty or forty years." Here a murderer is introduced, a "crazy old lady" on whose property the couple has parked. The victim this time is skinned rather than decapitated, and his head scrapes the car as the corpse swings to and fro in the breezy night.

A developing motif in "The Boyfriend's Death" is the character and role of the rescuers, who in the 1964 Kansas version are merely "some people." The standard identification later becomes "the police," authority figures whose presence lends further credence to the story. They are either called by the missing teenagers' parents, or simply appear on the scene in the morning to check the car. In a 1969 variant from Leonardtown, Maryland, the police give a warning, "Miss, please get out of the car and walk to the police car with us, but don't look back." . . . In a version from Texas collected in 1971, set "at this lake somewhere way out in nowhere," a policeman gets an even longer line: "Young lady, we want you to get out of the car and come with us. "Whatever you do, don't turn, don't turn around, just keep walking, just keep going straight and don't look back at the car." The more detailed the police instructions are, the more plausible the tale seems to become. Of course the standard rule of folk-narrative plot development now applies: the taboo must be broken (or the "interdiction violated" as some scholars put it). The girl always *does* look back, like Orpheus in the underworld, and in a number of versions her hair turns white from the shock of what she sees, as in a dozen other American legends.

In a Canadian version of "The Boyfriend's Death," told by a fourteen-year-old boy from Willowdale, Ontario, in 1973, the words of the policemen are merely summarized, but the opening scene of the legend is developed more fully, with several special details, including . . . a warning heard on the car radio. The girl's behavior when left behind is also described in more detail. 15

> A guy and his girlfriend are on the way to a party when their car starts to give them some trouble. At that same time they catch a news flash on the radio warning all people in the area that a lunatic killer has escaped from a local criminal asylum. The girl becomes very upset and at that point the car stalls completely on the highway. The boyfriend gets out and tinkers around with the engine but can't get the car to start again. He decides that he is going to have to walk on up the road to a gas station and get a tow truck but wants his girlfriend to stay behind in the car. She is frightened and pleads with him to take her, but he says that she'll be safe on the floor of the car covered with a blanket so that anyone passing will think it is an abandoned car and not bother her. Besides he can sprint along the road and get back more quickly than if she comes with him in her high-heeled shoes and evening dress. She finally agrees and he tells her not to come out unless she hears his signal of three knocks on the window. . . .

She does hear knocks on the car, but they continue eerily beyond three; the sound is later explained as the shoes of the boyfriend's corpse bumping the car as the body swings from a limb above the car.

The style in which oral narratives are told deserves attention, for the live telling that is dramatic, fluid, and often quite gripping in actual folk performance before a sympathetic audience may seem stiff, repetitious, and awkward on the printed page. Lacking in all our examples of "The Boyfriend's Death" is the essential ingredient of immediate context—the setting of the legend-telling, the storyteller's vocal and facial expression and gestures, the audience's reaction, and the texts of other similar tales narrated at the same session. Several of the informants explained that the story was told to them in spooky situations, late at night, near a cemetery, out camping, or even "while on a hayride or out parked," occasionally near the site of the supposed murder. Some students refer to such macabre legends, therefore, as "scary stories," "screamers," or "horrors."

A widely-distributed folk legend of this kind as it travels in oral tradition acquires a good deal of its credibility and effect from the localized details inserted by individual tellers. The highway and motel identification in the Kansas text are good examples of this, and in a New Orleans version, "The Boyfriend's Death" is absorbed into a local teenage tradition about "The Grunch"—a half-sheep, half-human monster that haunts specific local sites. One teenager there reported, "A man and lady went out by the lake and in the morning they found 'em hanging upside down on a tree and they said grunches did it." Finally, rumors or news stories about missing persons or violent crimes (as mentioned in the Canadian version) can merge with urban legends, helping to support their air of truth, or giving them renewed circulation after a period of less frequent occurrence.

Even the bare printed texts retain some earmarks of effective oral tradition. Witness in the Kansas text the artful use of repetition (typical of folk narrative style): "Well, he didn't come back and he didn't come back . . . but he didn't come back." The repeated use of "well" and the building of lengthy sentences with "and" are other hallmarks of oral style which give the narrator complete control over his performance, tending to squeeze out interruptions or prevent lapses in attention among the listeners. The scene that is set for the incident—lonely road, night, a tree looming over the car, out of gas—and the sound effects—scratches or bumps on the car—contribute to the style, as does the dramatic part played by the policeman and the abrupt ending line: "She looked back, and she saw . . . !" Since the typical narrators and auditors of "The Boyfriend's Death" themselves like to "park" and may have been alarmed by rumors, strange sights and noises, or automobile emergencies (all intensified in their effects by the audience's knowing other parking legends), the abrupt, unresolved ending leaves open the possibilities of what "really happened."

URBAN LEGENDS AS CULTURAL SYMBOLS

Legends can survive in our culture as living narrative folklore if they contain three essential elements: a strong basic story-appeal, a foundation in actual belief, and a meaningful message or "moral." That is, popular stories like "The Boyfriend's Death" are not only engrossing tales, but also "true," or at least so people think, and they teach valuable lessons. Jokes are a living part of oral tradition, despite being fictional and often silly, because of their humor, brevity, and snappy punch lines, but legends are by nature longer, slower, and more serious. Since more effort is needed to tell and appreciate a legend than a joke, it needs more than just verbal art to carry it along. Jokes have significant "messages" too, but these tend to be disguised or implied. People tell jokes primarily for amusement, and they seldom sense their underlying themes. In legends the primary messages are quite clear and straightforward; often they take the form of explicit warnings or good examples of "poetic justice." Secondary messages in urban legends tend to be suggested metaphorically or symbolically; these may provide deeper criticisms of human behavior or social condition.

People still tell legends, therefore, and other folk take time to listen to them, not only because of their inherent plot interest but because they seem to convey true, worthwhile, and relevant information, albeit partly in a subconscious mode. In other words, such stories are "news" presented to us in an attractive way, with hints of larger meanings. Without this multiple appeal few legends would get a hearing in the modern world, so filled with other distractions. Legends survive by being as lively and "factual" as the television evening news, and, like the daily news broadcasts, they tend to concern deaths, injuries, kidnappings, tragedies, and scandals. Apparently the basic human need for meaningful personal contact cannot be entirely replaced by the mass media and popular culture. A portion of our interest in what is occurring in the world must be filled by some face-to-face reports from other human beings.

20

On a literal level a story like "The Boyfriend's Death" simply warns young people to avoid situations in which they may be endangered, but at a more symbolic level the story reveals society's broader fears of people, especially women and the young, being alone and among strangers in the darkened world outside the security of their own home or car. Note that the young woman in the story (characterized by "her high-heeled shoes and evening dress") is shown as especially helpless and passive, cowering under the blanket in the car until she is rescued by men. Such themes recur in various forms in many other urban legends. . . .

In order to be retained in a culture, any form of folklore must fill some genuine need, whether this be the need for an entertaining escape from reality, or a desire to validate by anecdotal examples some of the culture's ideals and institutions. For legends in general, a major function has always been the attempt to explain unusual and supernatural happenings in the natural world. To some degree this remains a purpose for urban legends, but their more common role nowadays seems to be to show that the prosaic contemporary scene is capable of producing shocking or amazing occurrences which may actually have happened to friends or to near-acquaintances but which are nevertheless explainable in some reasonably logical terms. On the one hand we want our factual lore to inspire awe, and at the same time we wish to have the most fantastic tales include at least the hint of a rational explanation and perhaps even a conclusion. Thus an escaped lunatic, a possibly *real* character, not a fantastic invader from outer space or Frankenstein's monster, is said to be responsible for the atrocities committed in the gruesome tales that teenagers tell. As sometimes happens in real life, the car radio gives warning, and the police get the situation back under control. (The policemen's role, in fact, becomes larger and more commanding as the story grows in oral tradition.) Only when the young lovers are still alone and scared are they vulnerable, but society's adults and guardians come to their rescue presently.

In common with brief unverified reports ("rumors"), to which they are often closely related, urban legends gratify our desire to know about and to try to understand bizarre, frightening, and potentially dangerous or embarrassing events that *may* have happened. (In rumors and legends there is always some element of doubt concerning where and when these things *did* occur.) These floating stories appeal to our morbid curiosity and satisfy our sensation-seeking minds that demand gratification through frequent infusions of new information, "sanitized" somewhat by the positive messages. Informal rumors and stories fill in the gaps left by professional news reporting, and these marvelous, though generally false, "true" tales may be said to be carrying the folk-news—along with some editorial matter—from person to person even in today's technological world.

Questions for Discussion and Writing

1. What are the defining characteristics of urban legends and why have they had such staying power in the popular imagination? What distinguishes an urban legend from a myth or fairy tale?

2. In what ways does "The Boyfriend's Death" exhibit the variations of story-line that define the urban legend? Have you heard one of these variations? If so, how did it differ from the one Brunvand cites?
3. Trace the features of an urban legend that you have heard, either one of those mentioned by Brunvand or another, that has been passed on as a "true" story.

KIM CHERNIN

Kim Chernin, born in 1940, is a free-lance writer, editor, and self-described "feminist human-ist." She is the author of a book of poems, The Hunger Song *(1982), and a fictional biogra-phy,* In My Mother's House *(1983). "The Flesh and the Devil" is a chapter from* The Obsession: Reflections on the Tyranny of Slenderness *(1981). In this essay, Chernin draws on her personal experiences as well as surveys, research studies, and life stories of friends to support her incisive analysis of the extent to which cultural stereotypes dominate women's lives. Cherin has also written* A Different Kind of Listening: My Psychoanalysis and Its Shadow *(1995),* My Life as a Boy *(1997), and* Cecilia Bartoli: The Passion of Song, *with Renate Stendhal (1997).*

The Flesh and the Devil

We know that every woman wants to be thin. Our images of womanhood are almost synony-mous with thinness.

—Susie Orbach

...I must now be able to look at my ideal, this ideal of being thin, of being without a body, and to realize: "it is a fiction."

—Ellen West

When the body is hiding the complex, it then becomes our most immediate access to the problem.

—Marian Woodman

The locker room of the tennis club. Several exercise benches, two old-fashioned hair dryers, a mechanical bicycle, a treadmill, a reducing machine, a mirror, and a scale.

A tall woman enters, removes her towel; she throws it across a bench, faces herself squarely in the mirror, climbs on the scale, looks down.

A silence.

"I knew it," she mutters, turning to me. "I knew it."

And I think, before I answer, just how much I admire her, for this courage be-   5
yond my own, this daring to weigh herself daily in this way. And I sympathize. I know what she must be feeling. Not quite candidly, I say: "Up or down?" I am hoping to suggest that there might be people and cultures where gaining weight might not be considered a disaster. Places where women, stepping on scales, might

be horrified to notice that they had reduced themselves. A mythical, almost unimaginable land.

"Two pounds," she says, ignoring my hint. "Two pounds." And then she turns, grabs the towel and swings out at her image in the mirror, smashing it violently, the towel spattering water over the glass. "Fat pig," she shouts at her image in the glass. "You fat, fat pig. . . ."

Later, I go to talk with this woman. Her name is Rachel and she becomes, as my work progresses, one of the choral voices that shape its vision.

Two girls come into the exercise room. They are perhaps ten or eleven years old, at that elongated stage when the skeletal structure seems to be winning its war against flesh. And these two are particularly skinny. They sit beneath the hair dryers for a moment, kicking their legs on the faded green upholstery; they run a few steps on the eternal treadmill, they wrap the rubber belt of the reducing machine around themselves and jiggle for a moment before it falls off. And then they go to the scale.

The taller one steps up, glances at herself in the mirror, looks down at the scale. She sighs, shaking her head. I see at once that this girl is imitating someone. The sigh, the headshake are theatrical, beyond her years. And so, too, is the little drama enacting itself in front of me. The other girl leans forward, eager to see for herself the troubling message imprinted upon the scale. But the older girl throws her hand over the secret. It is not to be revealed. And now the younger one, accepting this, steps up to confront the ultimate judgment. "Oh God," she says, this growing girl. "Oh God," with only a shade of imitation in her voice: "Would you believe it? I've gained five pounds."

These girls, too, become a part of my work. They enter, they perform their little scene again and again; it extends beyond them and in it I am finally able to behold something that would have remained hidden—for it does not express itself directly, although we feel its pressure almost every day of our lives. Something, unnamed as yet, struggling against our emergence into femininity. This is my first glimpse of it, out there. And the vision ripens.   10

I return to the sauna. Two women I have seen regularly at the club are sitting on the bench above me. One of them is very beautiful, the sort of woman Renoir would have admired. The other, who is probably in her late sixties, looks, in the twilight of this sweltering room, very much an adolescent. I have noticed her before, with her tan face, her white hair, her fashionable clothes, her slender hips and jaunty walk. But the effect has not been soothing. A woman of advancing age who looks like a boy.

"I've heard about that illness, anorexia nervosa," the plump one is saying, "and I keep looking around for someone who has it. I want to go sit next to her. I think to myself, maybe I'll catch it. . . ."

"Well," the other woman says to her, "I've felt the same way myself. One of my cousins used to throw food under the table when no one was looking. Finally, she got so thin they had to take her to the hospital. . . . I always admired her."

What am I to understand from these stories? The woman in the locker room who swings out at her image in the mirror, the little girls who are afraid of the coming of adolescence to their bodies, the woman who admires the slenderness of the anorexic girl. It is possible to miss the dislike these women feel for their bodies?

And yet, an instant's reflection tells us that this dislike for the body is not a bi-   15
ological fact of our condition as women—we do not come upon it by nature, we are not born to it, it does not arise for us because of anything predetermined in our sex. We know that once we loved the body, delighting in it the way children will, reaching out to touch our toes and count over our fingers, repeating the game end-lessly as we come to knowledge of this body in which we will live out our lives. No part of the body exempt from our curiosity, nothing yet forbidden, we know an equal fascination with the feces we eliminate from ourselves, as with the ear we discover one day and the knees that have become bruised and scraped with falling and that warm, moist place between the legs from which feelings of indescribable bliss arise.

From that state to the condition of the woman in the locker room is a jour-ney from innocence to despair, from the infant's naive pleasure in the body, to the woman's anguished confrontation with herself. In this journey we can read our struggle with natural existence—the loss of the body as a source of pleasure. But the most striking thing about this alienation from the body is the fact that we take it for granted. Few of us ask to be redeemed from this struggle against the flesh by overcoming our antagonism toward the body. We do not rush about looking for someone who can tell us how to enjoy the fact that our appetite is large, or how we might delight in the curves and fullness of our own natural shape. We hope in-stead to be able to reduce the body, to limit the urges and desires it feels, to remove the body from nature. Indeed, the suffering we experience through our obsession with the body arises precisely from the hopeless and impossible nature of this goal.

Cheryl Prewitt, the 1980 winner of the Miss America contest, is a twenty-two-year-old woman, "slender, bright-eyed, and attractive."[1] If there were a single woman alive in America today who might feel comfortable about the size and shape of her body, surely we would expect her to be Ms. Prewitt? And yet, in order to make her body suitable for the swimsuit event of the beauty contest she has just won, Cheryl Prewitt "put herself through a grueling regimen, jogging long dis-tances down back-country roads, pedaling for hours on her stationary bicycle." The bicycle is still kept in the living room of her parents' house so that she can take part in conversation while she works out. This body she has created, after an arduous struggle against nature, in conformity with her culture's ideal standard for a woman, cannot now be left to its own desires. It must be perpetually shaped, mon-itored, and watched. If you were to visit her at home in Ackerman, Mississippi, you might well find her riding her stationary bicycle in her parents' living room, "working off the calories from a large slice of homemade coconut cake she has just had for a snack."

And so we imagine a woman who will never be Miss America, a next-door neighbor, a woman down the street, waking in the morning and setting out for her regular routine of exercise. The eagerness with which she jumps up at six o'clock

---

[1] Sally Hegelson, *TWA Ambassador,* July 1980.

and races for her jogging shoes and embarks upon the cold and arduous toiling up the hill road that runs past her house. And yes, she feels certain that her zeal to take off another pound, tighten another inch of softening flesh, places her in the school of those ancient wise men who formulated that vision of harmony between mind and body. "A healthy mind in a healthy body," she repeats to herself and imagines that it is love of the body which inspires her this early morning. But now she lets her mind wander and encounter her obsession. First it had been those hips, and she could feel them jogging along there with their own rhythm as she jogged. It was they that had needed reducing. Then, when the hips came down it was the thighs, hidden when she was clothed but revealing themselves every time she went to the sauna, and threatening great suffering now that summer drew near. Later, it was the flesh under the arms—this proved singularly resistant to tautness even after the rest of the body had become gaunt. And finally it was the ankles. But then, was there no end to it? What had begun as a vision of harmony between mind and body, a sense of well-being, physical fitness, and glowing health, had become now demonic, driving her always to further exploits, running farther, denying herself more food, losing more weight, always goaded on by the idea that the body's perfection lay just beyond her present achievement. And then, when she began to observe this driven quality in herself, she also began to notice what she had been thinking about her body. For she would write down in her notebook, without being aware of the violence in what she wrote: "I don't care how long it takes. One day I'm going to get my body to obey me. I'm going to make it lean and tight and hard. I'll succeed in this, even if it kills me."

But what a vicious attitude this is, she realizes one day, toward a body she professes to love. Was it love or hatred of the flesh that inspired her now to awaken even before it was light, and to go out on the coldest morning, running with bare arms and bare legs, busily fantasizing what she would make of her body? Love or hatred?

"You know perfectly well we hate our bodies," says Rachel, who calls herself the pig. She grabs the flesh of her stomach between her hands. "Who could love this?" 20

There is an appealing honesty in this despair, an articulation of what is virtually a universal attitude among women in our culture today. Few women who diet realize that they are confessing to a dislike for the body when they weigh and measure their flesh, subject it to rigorous fasts or strenuous regimens of exercise. And yet, over and over again, as I spoke to women about their bodies, this antagonism became apparent. One woman disliked her thighs, another her stomach, a third the loose flesh under her arms. Many would grab their skin and squeeze it as we talked, with that grimace of distaste language cannot translate into itself. One woman said to me: "Little by little I began to be aware that the pounds I was trying to 'melt away' were my own flesh. Would you believe it? It never occurred to me before. These 'ugly pounds' which filled me with so much hatred were my body."

The sound of this dawning consciousness can be heard now and again among the voices I have recorded in my notebook, heralding what may be a growing awareness of how bitterly the women of this culture are alienated from their bodies.

Thus, another woman said to me: "It's true, I never used to like my body." We had been looking at pictures of women from the nineteenth century; they were large women, with full hips and thighs. "What do you think of them?" I said. "They're like me," she answered, and then began to laugh. "Soft, sensual, and inviting."

The description is accurate, the women in the pictures, and the woman looking at them, share a quality of voluptuousness that is no longer admired by our culture:

> When I look at myself in the mirror I see that there's nothing wrong with me—now! Sometimes I even think I'm beautiful. I don't know why this began to change. It might have been when I started going to the YWCA. It was the first time I saw so many women naked. I realized it was the fuller bodies that were more beautiful. The thin women, who looked so good in clothes, seemed old and worn out. Their bodies were gaunt. But the bodies of the larger women had a certain natural mystery, very different from the false illusion of clothes. And I thought, I'm like them; I'm a big woman like they are and perhaps my body is beautiful. I had always been trying to make my body have the right shape so that I could fit into clothes. But then I started to look at myself in the mirror. Before that I had always looked at parts of myself. The hips were too flabby, the thighs were too fat. Now I began to see myself as a whole. I stopped hearing my mother's voice, asking me if I was going to go on a diet. I just looked at what was really there instead of what should have been there. What was wrong with it? I asked myself. And little by little I stopped disliking my body.[2]

This is the starting point. It is from this new way of looking at an old problem that liberation will come. The very simple idea that an obsession with weight reflects a dislike and uneasiness for the body can have a profound effect upon a woman's life.

> I always thought I was too fat. I never liked my body. I kept trying to lose weight. I just tortured myself. But if I see pictures of myself from a year or two ago I discover now that I looked just fine.

> I remember recently going out to buy Häagen Dazs ice cream. I had decided I was going to give myself something I really wanted to eat. I had to walk all the way down to the World Trade Center. But on my way there I began to feel terribly fat. I felt that I was being punished by being fat. I had lost the beautiful self I had made by becoming thinner. I could hear these voices saying to me: "You're fat, you're ugly, who do you think you are, don't you know you'll never be happy?" I had always heard these voices in my mind but now when they would come into consciousness I would tell them to shut up. I saw two men on the street. I was eating the Häagen Dazs ice cream. I thought I heard one of them say "heavy." I thought they were saying: "She's so fat." But I knew that I had to live through these feelings if I was ever to eat what I liked. I just couldn't go on tormenting myself any more about the size of my body.

> One day, shortly after this, I walked into my house. I noticed the scales, standing under the sink in the bathroom. Suddenly, I hated them. I was filled with grief for

---

[2] Private communication.

having tortured myself for so many years. They looked like shackles. I didn't want to have anything more to do with them. I called my boyfriend and offered him the scales. Then, I went into the kitchen. I looked at my shelves. I saw diet books there. I was filled with rage and hatred of them. I hurled them all into a box and got rid of them. Then I looked into the ice box. There was a bottle of Weight Watchers dressing. I hurled it into the garbage and watched it shatter and drip down the plastic bag. Little by little, I started to feel better about myself. At first I didn't eat less, I just worried less about my eating. I allowed myself to eat whatever I wanted. I began to give away the clothes I couldn't fit into. It turned out that they weren't right for me anyway. I had bought them with the idea of what my body should look like. Now I buy clothes because I like the way they look on me. If something doesn't fit it doesn't fit. I'm not trying to make myself into something I'm not. I weigh more than I once considered my ideal. But I don't seem fat to myself. Now, I can honestly say that I like my body.[3]

Some weeks ago, at a dinner party, a woman who had recently gained weight   25
began to talk about her body.

"I was once very thin," she said, "but I didn't feel comfortable in my body. I fit into all the right clothes. But somehow I just couldn't find myself any longer."

I looked over at her expectantly; she was a voluptuous woman, who had recently given birth to her first child.

"But now," she said as she got to her feet, "now, if I walk or jog or dance, I feel my flesh jiggling along with me." She began to shake her shoulders and move her hips, her eyes wide as she hopped about in front of the coffee table. "You see what I mean?" she shouted over to me. "I love it."

This image of a woman dancing came with me when I sat down to write. I remembered her expression. There was in it something secretive, I thought, something knowing and pleased—the look of a woman who has made peace with her body. Then I recalled the faces of women who had recently lost weight. The haggard look, the lines of strain around the mouth, the neck too lean, the tendons visible, the head too large for the emaciated body. I began to reason:

There must be, I said, for every woman a correct weight, which cannot be dis-   30
covered with reference to a weight chart or to any statistical norm. For the size of the body is a matter of highly subjective individual preferences and natural endowments. If we should evolve an aesthetic for women that was appropriate to women it would reflect this diversity, would conceive, indeed celebrate and even love, slenderness in a woman intended by nature to be slim, and love the rounded cheeks of another, the plump arms, broad shoulders, narrow hips, full thighs, rounded ass, straight back, narrow shoulders or slender arms, of a woman made that way according to her nature, walking with head high in pride of her body, however it happened to be shaped. And then Miss America, and the woman jogging in the morning, and the woman swinging out at her image in the mirror might say, with Susan Griffin in *Woman and Nature:*

---

[3] Private communication.

And we are various, and amazing in our variety, and our differences multiply, so that edge after edge of the endlessness of possibility is exposed . . . none of us beautiful when separate but all exquisite as we stand, each moment heeded in this cycle, no detail unlovely.[4]

Questions For Discussion and Writing

1. What kind of influence do cultural values play in determining how women see themselves? What is Chernin's attitude toward these values?
2. Which of the examples Chernin presents to support her thesis did you find particularly effective?
3. Write an essay analyzing the cultural messages regarding being thin that advertising and the media are constantly presenting. To what extent do these messages differ from your own values?

PHILIP SLATER

Philip Slater (b. 1927) has been a professor of sociology at Harvard and is author of The Pursuit of Loneliness *(1970) and* Wealth-Addiction *(1980). Slater argues that the premium Americans put on success causes many people to resort to drugs to feel better about themselves and to cope with feelings of inadequacy. Slater cites a broad range of examples from everyday life to demonstrate that advertisers exploit societal pressures in order to sell products. The following article first appeared in the* St. Paul Pioneer Press Dispatch *(September 6, 1984). His latest book is* The Temporary Society *(revised edition with Warren G. Bennis, 1998).*

Want-Creation Fuels Americans' Addictiveness

Imagine what life in America would be like today if the surgeon general convinced Congress that cigarettes, as America's most lethal drug, should be made illegal.

The cost of tobacco would increase 5,000 percent. Law enforcement budgets would quadruple but still be hopelessly inadequate to the task. The tobacco industry would become mob-controlled, and large quantities of Turkish tobacco would be smuggled into the country through New York and Miami.

Politicians would get themselves elected by inveighing against tobacco abuse. Some would argue shrewdly that the best enforcement strategy was to go after the growers and advertisers—making it a capital offense to raise or sell tobacco. And a great many Americans would try smoking for the first time.

---

[4] Susan Griffin, *Woman and Nature: The Roaring Inside Her* (New York, 1978).

Americans are individualists. We like to express our opinions much more than we like to work together. Passing laws is one of the most popular pastimes, and enforcing them one of the least. We make laws like we make New Year's resolutions—the impulse often exhausted by giving voice to it. Who but Americans would have their food grown and harvested by people who were legally forbidden to be in the country?

We are a restless, inventive, dissatisfied people. We like novelty. We like to try   5 new things. We may not want to change in any basic sense, any more than other people, but we like the illusion of movement.

We like anything that looks like a quick fix—a new law, a new road, a new pill. We like immediate solutions. We want the pain to stop, the dull mood to pass, the problem to go away. The quicker the action, the better we like it. We like confrontation better than negotiation, antibiotics better than slow healing, majority rule better than community consensus, demolition better than renovation.

When we want something we want it fast and we want it cheap. Obstacles and complications annoy us. We don't want to stop to think about side effects, the Big Picture, or how it's going to make things worse in the long run. We aren't too interested in the long run, as long as something brings more money, a promotion or a new status symbol in the short.

Our model for problem-solving is the 30-second TV commercial, in which change is produced instantaneously and there is always a happy ending. The side effects, the pollution, the wasting diseases, the slow poisoning—all these unhappy complications fall into the great void outside that 30-second frame.

Nothing fits this scenario better than drugs—legal and illegal. The same impatience that sees an environmental impact report as an annoying bit of red tape makes us highly susceptible to any substance that can make us feel better within minutes after ingesting it—whose immediate effects are more or less predictable and whose negative aspects are generally much slower to appear.

People take drugs everywhere, of course, and there is no sure way of knowing   10 if the United States has more drug abusers than other countries. The term "abuse" itself is socially defined.

The typical suburban alcoholic of the '40s and '50s and the wealthy drunks glamorized in Hollywood movies of that period were not considered "drug abusers." Nor is the ex-heroin addict who has been weaned to a lifetime addiction to Methadone.

In the 19th century, morphine addicts (who were largely middle-aged, middle-class women) maintained their genteel but often heavy addictions quite legally, with the aid of the family doctor and local druggist. Morphine only became illegal when its use spread to young, poor, black males. (This transition created some embarrassment for political and medical commentators, who argued that a distinction had to be made between "drug addicts" and "dope fiends.")

Yet addiction can be defined in a way that overrides these biases. Anyone who cannot or will not let a day pass without ingesting a substance should be considered addicted to it, and by this definition Americans are certainly addiction-prone.

It would be hard to find a society in which so great a variety of different substances have been "abused" by so many different kinds of people. There are drugs
for every group, philosophy and social class: marijuana and psychedelics for the '60s
counterculture, heroin for the hopeless of all periods, PCP for the angry and desperate, and cocaine for modern Yuppies and Yumpies.[1]

Drugs do, after all, have different effects, and people select the effects they   15
want. At the lower end of the social scale people want a peaceful escape from a
hopeless and depressing existence, and for this heroin is the drug of choice. Cocaine, on the other hand, with its energized euphoria and illusion of competence is
particularly appealing to affluent achievers—those both obsessed and acquainted
with success.

Addiction among the affluent seems paradoxical to outsiders. From the viewpoint of most people in the world an American man or woman making over $50,000
a year has everything a human being could dream of. Yet very few such people—
even those with hundreds of millions of dollars—feel this way themselves. While they
may not suffer the despair of the very poor, there seems to be a kind of frustration
and hopelessness that seeps into all social strata in our society. The affluent may have
acquired a great deal, but they seem not to have acquired what they wanted.

Most drugs—heroin, alcohol, cocaine, speed, tranquilizers, barbiturates—virtually all of them except the psychedelics and to some extent marijuana—have a
numbing effect. We might then ask: Why do so many Americans need to numb
themselves?

Life in modern society is admittedly harsh and confusing considering the
pace for which our bodies were designed. Noise pollution alone might justify
turning down our sensory volume: It's hard today even in a quiet suburb or rural
setting to find respite from the harsh sound of "labor-saving" machines.

But it would be absurd to blame noise pollution for drug addiction. This rasping clamor that grates daily on our ears is only a symptom—one tangible consequence of our peculiar lifestyle. For each of us wants to be able to exert his or her
will and control without having to negotiate with anyone else.

"I have a right to run my machine and do my work" even if it makes your rest   20
impossible. "I have a right to hear my music" even if this makes it impossible to
hear your music, or better yet, enjoy that most rare and precious of modern commodities: silence. "I have a right to make a profit" even if it means poisoning you,
your children and your children's children. "I have a right to have a drink when I
want to and drive my car when I want to" even if it means totaling your car and
crippling your life.

This intolerance of any constraint or obstacle makes our lives rich in conflict
and aggravation. Each day we encounter the noise, distress and lethal fallout of the
dilemmas we brushed aside so impatiently the day before. Each day the postponed
problems multiply, proliferate, metastasize—but this only makes us more aggravated
and impatient than we were before. And since we're unwilling to change our ways

---

[1] *Yumpies:* young, upper-middle-class professionals.

it becomes more and more necessary to anesthetize ourselves to the havoc we've wrought.

We don't like the thought of attuning ourselves to nature or to a group or community. We like to fantasize having control over our lives, and drugs seem to make this possible. With drugs you are not only master of your fate and captain of your soul, you are dictator of your body as well.

Unwilling to respond to its own needs and wants, you goad it into activity with caffeine in the morning and slow it down with alcohol at night. If the day goes poorly, a little cocaine will set it right, and if quiet relaxation and sensual enjoyment is called for, marijuana.

Cocaine or alcohol makes a party or a performance go well. Nothing is left to chance. The quality of experience is measured by how many drugs or drinks were consumed rather than by the experience itself. Most of us are unwilling to accept the fact that life has good days and bad days. We attempt—unsuccessfully but valiantly—to postpone all the bad days until that fateful moment when the body presents us with all our IOUs, tied up in a neat bundle called cancer, heart disease, cirrhosis or whatever.

Every great sage and spiritual leader throughout history has emphasized that   25
happiness comes not from getting more but from learning to want less. Clearly this is a hard lesson for humans, since so few have learned it.

But in our society we spend billions each year creating want. Covetousness, discontent and greed are taught to our children, drummed into them—they are bombarded with it. Not only through advertising, but in the feverish emphasis on success, on winning at all costs, on being the center of attention through one kind of performance or another, on being the first at something—no matter how silly or stupid (*The Guinness Book of Records*). We are an addictive society.

Addiction is a state of wanting. It is a condition in which the individual feels he or she is incomplete, inadequate, lacking, not whole, and can only be made whole by the addition of something external.

This need not be a drug. It can be money, food, fame, sex, responsibility, power, good deeds, possessions, cleaning—the addictive impulse can attach itself to anything, real or symbolic. You're addicted to something whenever you feel it completes you—that you wouldn't be a whole person without it. When you try to make sure it's always there, that there's always a good supply on hand.

Most of us are a little proud of the supposed personality defects that make addiction "necessary"—the "I can't . . . ," "I have to . . . ," "I always . . . ," "I never. . . ." But such "lacks" are all delusional. It's fun to brag about not being able to live without something but it's just pomposity. We are all human, and given water, a little food, and a little warmth, we'll survive.

But it's very hard to hang onto this humanity when we're told every day that   30
we're ignorant, misguided, inadequate, incompetent and undesirable and that we will emerge from this terrible condition only if we eat or drink or buy something, at which point we'll magically and instantly feel better.

We may be smart enough not to believe the silly claims of the individual ad, but can we escape the underlying message on which all of them agree? That you can only be made whole and healthy by buying or ingesting something? Can we reasonably complain about the amount of addiction in our society when we teach it every day?

A Caribbean worker once said, apropos of the increasing role of Western products in the economy of his country: "Your corporations are like mosquitoes. I don't so much mind their taking a little of my blood, but why do they have to leave that nasty itch in its place?"

It seems futile to spend hundreds of billions of dollars trying to intercept the flow of drugs—arresting and imprisoning those who meet the demand for them, when we activate and nourish that demand every day. Until we get tired of encouraging the pursuit of illusory fixes and begin to celebrate and refine what we already are and have, addictive substances will always proliferate faster than we can control them.

Questions for Discussion and Writing

1. In Slater's view, how is the quick-fix mentality responsible for rampant drug use and addiction in the United States?
2. Consider the definition of addiction that Slater presents. Do you agree or disagree with the way he frames the debate? Why, or why not?
3. What current ads set up hypothetically stressful situations and then push products as a quick and easy way to relieve the stress? Analyze a few of these ads.

ARTHUR ASHE

When Arthur Ashe (1943–1993) defeated Jimmy Connors in 1975 to win the Wimbledon singles title, he became the first black man to win the world's most prestigious grass-court tournament. A chronicle of Ashe's life includes other notable firsts, such as being the first African American player named to the U.S. Davis Cup team in 1963 and the first black to win the U.S. Open in 1968 (a tournament now played in the Arthur Ashe Stadium in Flushing Meadows, NY). He also became the first black pro to play in South Africa's championships in 1973, when the country was still under apartheid. What makes these victories so poignant is that, during double-bypass surgery in 1983, Ashe received blood contaminated with HIV, and he died from AIDS ten years later. This essay, taken from his memoir, Days of Grace *(1993), written with Arnold Rampersad, contains Ashe's thoughtful reflections on the psychic toll of racism.*

The Burden of Race

I had spent more than an hour talking in my office at home with a reporter for *People* magazine. Her editor had sent her to do a story about me and how I was coping with AIDS. The reporter's questions had been probing and yet respectful of my right to privacy. Now, our interview over, I was escorting her to the door. As she slipped on her coat, she fell silent. I could see that she was groping for the right words to express her sympathy for me before she left.

"Mr. Ashe, I guess this must be the heaviest burden you have ever had to bear, isn't it?" she asked finally.

I thought for a moment, but only a moment. "No, it isn't. It's a burden, all right. But AIDS isn't the heaviest burden I have had to bear."

"Is there something worse? Your heart attack?"

I didn't want to detain her, but I let the door close with both of us still inside. "You're not going to believe this," I said to her, "but being black is the greatest burden I've had to bear."

"You can't mean that."

"No question about it. Race has always been my biggest burden. Having to live as a minority in America. Even now it continues to feel like an extra weight tied around me."

I can still recall the surprise and perhaps even the hurt on her face. I may even have surprised myself, because I simply had never thought of comparing the two conditions before. However, I stand by my remark. Race is for me a more onerous burden than AIDS. My disease is the result of biological factors over which we, thus far, have had no control. Racism, however, is entirely made by people, and therefore it hurts and inconveniences infinitely more.

Since our interview (skillfully presented as a first-person account by me) appeared in *People* in June 1992, many people have commented on my remark. A radio station in Chicago aimed primarily at blacks conducted a lively debate on its merits on the air. Most African Americans have little trouble understanding and accepting my statement, but other people have been baffled by it. Even Donald Dell, my close friend of more than thirty years, was puzzled. In fact, he was so troubled that he telephoned me in the middle of the night from Hamburg, Germany, to ask if I had been misquoted. No, I told him, I had been quoted correctly. Some people have asked me flatly, what could *you*, Arthur Ashe, possibly have to complain about? Do you want more money or fame than you already have? Isn't AIDS inevitably fatal? What can be worse than death?

The novelist Henry James suggested somewhere that it is a complex fate being an American. I think it is a far more complex fate being an African American. I also sometimes think that this indeed may be one of those fates that are worse than death.

I do not want to be misunderstood. I do not mean to appear fatalistic, self-pitying, cynical, or maudlin. Proud to be an American, I am also proud to be an African American. I delight in the accomplishments of fellow citizens of my color. When one considers the odds against which we have labored, we have achieved much. I believe in life and hope and love, and I turn my back on death until I must face my end in all its finality. I am an optimist, not a pessimist. Still, a pall of sadness hangs over my life and the lives of almost all African Americans because of what we as a people have experienced historically in America, and what we as individuals experience each and every day. Whether one is a welfare recipient trapped in some blighted "housing project" in the inner city or a former Wimbledon champion who is easily recognized on the streets and whose home is a luxurious apartment in one of the wealthiest districts of Manhattan, the sadness is still there.

In some respects, I am a prisoner of the past. A long time ago, I made peace with the state of Virginia and the South. While I, like other blacks, was once barred from free association with whites, I returned time and time again, under the new rule of desegregation, to work with whites in my hometown and across the South. But segregation had achieved by that time what it was intended to achieve: It left me a marked man, forever aware of a shadow of contempt that lies across my identity and my sense of self-esteem. Subtly the shadow falls on my reputation, the way I know I am perceived; the mere memory of it darkens my most sunny days. I believe that the same is true for almost every African American of the slightest sensitivity and intelligence. Again, I don't want to overstate the case. I think of myself, and others think of me, as supremely self-confident. I know objectively that it is almost impossible for someone to be as successful as I have been as an athlete and to lack self-assurance. Still, I also know that the shadow is always there; only death will free me, and blacks like me, from its pall.

The shadow fell across me recently on one of the brightest days, literally and metaphorically, of my life. On 30 August 1992, the day before the US Open, the USTA and I together hosted an afternoon of tennis at the National Tennis Center in Flushing Meadows, New York. The event was a benefit for the Arthur Ashe Foundation for the Defeat of AIDS. Before the start, I was nervous. Would the invited stars (McEnroe, Graf, Navratilova, et al.) show up? Would they cooperate with us, or be difficult to manage? And, on the eve of a Grand Slam tournament, would fans pay to see light-hearted tennis? The answers were all a resounding yes (just over ten thousand fans turned out). With CBS televising the event live and Aetna having provided the air time, a profit was assured. The sun shone brightly, the humidity was mild, and the temperature hovered in the low 80s.

What could mar such a day? The shadow of race, and my sensitivity, or perhaps hypersensitivity, to its nuances. Sharing the main stadium box with Jeanne, Camera, and me, at my invitation, were Stan Smith, his wife Marjory, and their daughter Austin. The two little girls were happy to see one another. During Wimbledon in June, they had renewed their friendship when we all stayed near each other in London. Now Austin, seven years old, had brought Camera a present. She had come with twin dolls, one for herself, one for Camera. A thoughtful gesture on Austin's part, and on her parents' part, no doubt. The Smiths are fine, religious people. Then I noticed that Camera was playing with her doll above the railing of the box, in view of the attentive network television cameras. The doll was the problem; or rather, the fact that the doll was conspicuously a blond. Camera owns dolls of all colors, nationalities, and ethnic varieties. But she was now on national television playing with a blond doll. Suddenly I heard voices in my head, the voices of irate listeners to a call-in show on some 'black format' radio station. I imagined insistent, clamorous callers attacking Camera, Jeanne, and me.

"*Can you believe the doll Arthur Ashe's daughter was holding up at the AIDS benefit? Wasn't that a shame?*"   15

"*Is that brother sick or what? Somebody ought to teach that poor child about her true black self!*"

"*What kind of role model is Arthur Ashe if he allows his daughter to be brainwashed in that way?*"

"*Doesn't the brother* understand *that he is corrupting his child's mind with notions about the superiority of the white woman? I tell you, I thought we were long past that!*"

The voices became louder in my head. Despite the low humidity, I began to squirm in my seat. What should I do? Should I say, to hell with what some people might think? I know that Camera likes her blond dolls, black dolls, brown dolls, Asian dolls, Indian dolls just about equally; I know that for a fact, because I have watched her closely. I have searched for signs of racial partiality in her, indications that she may be dissatisfied with herself, with her own color. I have seen none. But I cannot dismiss the voices. I try always to live practically, and I do not wish to hear such comments on the radio. On the other hand, I do not want Austin's gift to be sullied by an ungracious response. Finally, I act.

"Jeanne," I whisper, "we have to do something." 20

"About what?" she whispers back.

"That doll. We have to get Camera to put that doll down."

Jeanne takes one look at Camera and the doll and she understands immediately. Quietly, cleverly, she makes the dolls disappear. Neither Camera nor Austin is aware of anything unusual happening. Smoothly, Jeanne has moved them on to some other distraction.

I am unaware if Margie Smith has noticed us, but I believe I owe her an explanation. I get up and go around to her seat. Softly I tell her why the dolls have disappeared. Margie is startled, dumbfounded.

"Gosh, Arthur, I never thought about that. I never *ever* thought about any- 25 thing like that!"

"*You* don't have to think about it," I explain. "But it happens to us, in similar situations, all the time."

"All the time?" She is pensive now.

"All the time. It's perfectly understandable. And it certainly is not your fault. You were doing what comes naturally. But for us, the dolls make for a bit of a problem. All for the wrong reasons. It shouldn't be this way, but it is."

I return to my seat, but not to the elation I had felt before I saw that blond doll in Camera's hand. I feel myself becoming more and more angry. I am angry at the force that made me act, the force of racism in all its complexity, as it spreads into the world and creates defensiveness and intolerance among the very people harmed by racism. I am also angry with myself. I am angry with myself because I have just acted out of pure practicality, not out of morality. The moral act would have been to let Camera have her fun, because she was innocent of any wrongdoing. Instead, I had tampered with her innocence, her basic human right to act impulsively, to accept a gift from a friend in the same beautiful spirit in which it was given.

Deeply embarrassed now, I am ashamed at what I have done. I have made 30 Camera adjust her behavior merely because of the likelihood that some people in the African American community would react to her innocence foolishly and perhaps even maliciously. I know I am not misreading the situation. I would have had telephone calls that very evening about the unsuitability of Camera's doll. Am I being a hypocrite? Yes, definitely, up to a point. I have allowed myself to give in to those people who say we must avoid even the slightest semblance of 'Eurocentric' influence. But I also know what stands behind the entire situation. Racism ultimately created the state in which defensiveness and hypocrisy are our almost instinctive responses, and innocence and generosity are invitations to trouble.

This incident almost ruined the day for me. That night, when Jeanne and I talked about the excitement of the afternoon, and the money that would go to AIDS research and education because of the event, we nevertheless ended up talking mostly about the incident of the dolls. We also talked about perhaps its most ironic aspect. In 1954, when the Supreme Court ruled against school segregation in *Brown v. Board* of *Education,* some of the most persuasive testimony came from the psychologist Dr. Kenneth Clark concerning his research on black children and their pathetic preference for white dolls over black. In 1992, the dolls are still a problem.

Once again, the shadow of race had fallen on me.

Questions for Discussion and Writing

1. Given the events of August 30, 1992, why was Ashe so unnerved by seeing his young daughter play with a white doll?
2. In what sense was race a greater burden on Ashe than having AIDS? How does he explain this paradox?
3. Although this event happened some time ago, how much of Ashe's assessment of racism in America is still pertinent in and out of sports?

ANN LOUISE BARDACH

Ann Louise Bardach, recipient of the PEN West Award for Journalism and a contributing editor to Talk *magazine, examines contemporary issues for* Vanity Fair, *the* New Republic, *and other publications. She has also written* Troubled Waters: The Miami-Havana Showdown *(2001) and an article, "Elian: The Untold Story," for* George *magazine (May 2000). This essay on the effects of AIDS on the Latino community first appeared in the* New Republic *(June 1995).*

The Stealth Virus: AIDS and Latinos

Freddie Rodriguez is discouraged. He has just come from his afternoon's activity of trying to stop men from having unprotected sex in Miami's Alice Wainwright Park, a popular gay cruising spot. Rodriguez, 29, is a slim, handsome Cuban-American with a pale, worried face who works for Health Crisis Network. "I take a bag of condoms to the park with me and I try talking to people before they duck in the bushes and have sex," he explains. "I tell them how dangerous it is. Sometimes I beg them to use a condom. Sometimes they listen to me. Today, no one was interested." Most of the men, he says, are Latinos and range in age from 16 to 60. Many are married and would never describe themselves as gay.

"Discrimination is not really the issue here. Most Latinos do not identify themselves as gay, so they're not discriminated against," he says, his voice drifting off. "Ours is a culture of denial."

To understand why the second wave of AIDS is hitting Latinos particularly hard, one would do well to start in Miami. Once a mecca for retirees, South Beach today is a frenzy of dance and sex clubs, for hetero- and homosexual alike. "We have the highest rate of heterosexual transmission in the country, the second-highest number of babies born with AIDS and we are number one nationwide for teen HIV cases," says Randi Jenson, reeling off a litany that clearly exhausts him. Jenson supervises the Miami Beach HIV/AIDS Project and sits on the board of the Gay, Lesbian and Bisexual Community Center. "And we have the highest rate of bisexuality in the country." When I ask how he knows this, he says, "Trust me on this one, *we know* . . . The numbers to watch for in the future will be Hispanic women—the wives and girlfriends."

Already, AIDS is the leading cause of death in Miami and Fort Lauderdale for women ages 25 to 44, four times greater than the national average. According to the Centers for Disease Control and Prevention (CDC), AIDS cases among Hispanics have been steadily rising. But any foray into the Latino subculture shows that the numbers do not tell the whole story, and may not even tell half. CDC literature notes that "it is believed that AIDS-related cases and deaths for Latinos are understated by at least 30 percent. Many Hispanics do not and cannot access HIV testing and health care." Abetted by widespread shame about homosexuality, a fear of governmental and medical institutions (particularly among undocumented immigrants) and cultural denial as deep as Havana Harbor, AIDS is moving silently and insistently through Hispanic America. It is the stealth virus.

"No one knows how many Latino HIV cases are out there," Damian Pardo, an affable Cuban-American, who is president of the board of Health Crisis Network, tells me over lunch in Coral Gables. "All we know is that the numbers are not accurate—that the actual cases are far higher. Everyone in the community lies about HIV." Everyone, according to Pardo, means the families, the lovers, the priests, the doctors and the patients. "The Hispanic community in South Florida is far more affluent than blacks. More often than not, people see their own family doctor who simply signs a falsified death certificate. It's a conspiracy of silence and everyone is complicitous."

Freddie Rodriguez—smart, affluent, urbane—didn't learn that Luis, his Nicaraguan lover, was HIV-positive until it was too late to do anything about it. "He was my first boyfriend. He would get sick at times but he refused to take a blood test. He said that it was impossible for him to be HIV-positive. I believed him. One day, he disappeared. Didn't come home, didn't go to work—just disappeared." Frantic, Rodriguez called the police and started phoning hospitals. Finally, Luis turned up at Jackson Memorial Hospital. He had been discovered unconscious and rushed to intensive care. When Rodriguez arrived at the hospital, he learned that his lover was in the AIDS wing. Even then, Luis insisted it was a mistake. Two weeks later, he was dead. "I had to tell Luis's family that he was gay," Rodriguez says, "that I was his boyfriend and that he had died of AIDS. They knew nothing. He lived a completely secret life.'"

5

Although Rodriguez was enraged by his lover's cowardice, he understood his dilemma all too well. He remembered how hard it was to tell his own family. "'When I was 22, I finally told my parents that I was gay. My mother screamed and ran out of the room. My father raised his hands in front of his eyes and told me, 'Freddie do you see what's in front of me? It's a big, white cloud. I do not hear anything, see anything and I cannot remember anything because it is all in this big white cloud.' And then he left the room." One of Rodriguez's later boyfriends, this one Peruvian, was also HIV-positive, but far more duplicitous. "'He flat out lied to me when I asked him. He knew, but he only told me after we broke up, *after* we had unsafe sex," says Rodriguez, who remains HIV-negative. "Part of the *machismo* ethic," Rodriguez explains, "is not wearing a condom."

Miami's Body Positive, which provides psychological and nonclinical services to AIDS patients, is housed in a pink concrete bubble off Miami's Biscayne Boulevard. The building and much of its funding are provided by founder Doris Feinberg, who lost both her sons to AIDS during the late 1980s. The gay Cuban-American star of MTV's "The Real World," Pedro Zamora, worked here for the last five years of his life and started its P.O.P. program—Peer Outreach for Persons Who Are Positive. Ernie Lopez, a 26-year-old Nicaraguan who has been Body Positive's director for the last five years, estimates that 40 percent of the center's clients are Latino, in a Miami population that is 70 percent Hispanic. On the day I visit, I see mostly black men at the facility. Lopez warns me not to be fooled. "The Latino numbers are as high as the blacks, but they are not registered" he says. "Latinos want anonymity. They come in very late—when they are desperate and their disease is very progressed. Often it's too late to help them."

"Soy completo," is what they often say in Cuba, meaning, "I'm a total human being." It is the preferred euphemism for bisexuality and in the *machista* politics of Latino culture, bisexuality is a huge step up from being gay. It is this cultural construct that prevents many Latin men from acknowledging that they could be vulnerable to HIV, because it is this cultural construct that tells them they are not gay. Why worry about AIDS if only gay men get AIDS? "To be bisexual is a code," says Ernesto Pujol, a pioneer in Latino AIDS education. "It means, 'I sleep with men but I still have power.' I think there is a legitimate group of bisexuals, but for many bisexuality is a codified and covered homosexuality." Self-definitions can get even more complex. "I'm not gay," a well-known intellectual told me in Havana last year. "'How could I be gay? My boyfriend is married and has a family.'"

Without putting too fine a point on it, what defines a gay man in some segments of the Latino world is whether he's on the top or the bottom during intercourse. "The salient property of the *maricón,*" my Cuban friend adds, "is his passivity. If you're a 'top,'—*el bugarón*—you're not a faggot." Moreover, there are also many heterosexual Latino men who do not regard sex with another man as a homosexual act. "A lot of heterosexual Latinos—say, after a few drinks—will fuck a transvestite as a surrogate woman," says Pujol, "and that is culturally acceptable—absolutely acceptable." Hence the potential for HIV transmission is far greater than in the mainstream Anglo world.

According to Pujol, "only Latinos in the States are interested in other gay 10
men. They have borrowed the American liberated gay model. In Latin America, the
hunt is for 'straight' men. Look at the transvestites on Cristina's (the Spanish-
language equivalent of "Oprah") talk show. Their boyfriends are always some
macho hunk from the *bodega.*" Chino, a Cuban gay now living in Montreal, typifies the cultural divide. "I don't understand it here," he says scornfully. "It's like girls
going out with girls."

"If you come out, says Jorge B., a Cuban artist in Miami Beach, "you lose your
sex appeal to 'straight' men" (straight in this context meaning married men who
have sex with other men). The Hispanic preference for "straight men" is so popular that bathhouses such as Club Bodycenter in Coral Gables are said to cater to a
clientele of older married men who often pick up young lovers after work before
joining their families for dinner. Some men will not risk going to a gay bar, says
Freddie Rodriguez. "They go to public restrooms where they can't be identified."
While many gay Hispanics do eventually "come out," they do so at a huge price—
a shattering loss of esteem within their family and community. "The priest who did
Mass at my grandfather's funeral denied communion to me and my brother," recalls
Pardo. "He knew from my mother's confession that we were gay."

Latino attitudes here are, of course, largely imported, their cultural finger-
prints lifted straight out of Havana, Lima or Guatemala City. Consider Chiapas,
Mexico, where gay men were routinely arrested throughout the 1980s; many of
their bodies were later found dumped in a mass grave. Or Ecuador, where it is
against the law to be a homosexual, and effeminate behavior or dress can be
grounds for arrest. Or Peru, where the Shining Path has targeted gays for assassination. Or Colombia, where death squads do the same, characteristically mutilating
their victims' genitals.

While Latino hostility to homosexuals in the United States tends to be less
dramatic, it can also be virulent, particularly when cradled in reactionary politics. In
Miami, right-wing Spanish-language stations daily blast their enemies as "communists, traitors and Castro puppets." But the epithet reserved for the most despised is
"homosexual" or *"maricón."* When Nelson Mandela visited Miami in 1990, he was
denounced daily as a *"marijuanero maricón"*—a pot-smoking faggot—for having
supported Fidel Castro.

Questions for Discussion and Writing

1. Bardach characterizes AIDS as a "stealth virus" whose spread is fostered by "a
   culture of denial" and a "conspiracy of silence." What does she mean?
2. According to Bardach, in what respects are the values of Spanish culture in
   relationship to homosexuality and bisexuality at the root of the problem?
3. Questions of machismo are at the heart of Bardach's analysis. How would
   you define this concept? What values does it entail?

Fiction

KATE CHOPIN

Kate Chopin (1851–1904) is best known for her novel, The Awakening, *published in 1899, which created enormous public controversy by its realistic treatment of the psychological and sexual awakening of the female protagonist. The collections of Chopin's short stories based on her experiences while living in rural Louisiana are* Bayou Folk *(1894) and* A Night in Acadie *(1897). Her short story "Désirée's Baby" (1899) is widely recognized as a small masterpiece of psychological realism.*

Désirée's Baby

As the day was pleasant, Madame Valmondé drove over to L'Abri to see Désirée and the baby.

It made her laugh to think of Désirée with a baby. Why, it seems but yesterday that Désirée was little more than a baby herself; when Monsieur in riding through the gateway of Valmondé had found her lying asleep in the shadow of the big stone pillar.

The little one awoke in his arms and began to cry for "Dada." That was as much as she could do or say. Some people thought she might have strayed there of her own accord, for she was of the toddling age. The prevailing belief was that she had been purposely left by a party of Texans, whose canvas-covered wagons, late in the day, had crossed the ferry that Coton Maïs kept, just below the plantation. In time Madame Valmondé abandoned every speculation but the one that Désirée had been sent to her by a beneficent Providence to be the child of her affection, seeing that she was without child of the flesh. For the girl grew to be beautiful and gentle, affectionate and sincere—the idol of Valmondé.

It was no wonder, when she stood one day against the stone pillar in whose shadow she had lain asleep, eighteen years before, that Armand Aubigny riding by and seeing her there, had fallen in love with her. That was the way all the Aubignys fell in love, as if struck by a pistol shot. The wonder was that he had not loved her before; for he had known her since his father brought him home from Paris, a boy of eight, after his mother died there. The passion that awoke in him that day, when he saw her at the gate, swept along like an avalanche, or like a prairie fire, or like anything that drives headlong over all obstacles.

Madame Valmondé bent her portly figure over Désirée and kissed her, holding her an instant tenderly in her arms. Then she turned to the child.   5

"This is not the baby!" she exclaimed, in startled tones. French was the language spoken at Valmondé in those days.

"I knew you would be astonished," laughed Désirée, "at the way he has grown. The little *cochon de lait!*[1] Look at his legs, mamma, and his hands and fingernails,—real fingernails. Zandrine had to cut them this morning. Isn't it true, Zandrine?"

The woman bowed her turbaned head majestically, "Mais si, Madame."

"And the way he cries," went on Désirée, "is deafening. Armand heard him the other day as far away as La Blanche's cabin."

Madame Valmondé had never removed her eyes from the child. She lifted it and walked with it over to the window that was lightest. She scanned the baby narrowly, then looked as searchingly at Zandrine, whose face was turned to gaze across the fields.

"Yes, the child has grown, has changed," said Madame Valmondé, slowly, as she replaced it beside its mother. "What does Armand say?"

Désirée's face became suffused with a glow that was happiness itself.

"Oh, Armand is the proudest father in the parish, I believe, chiefly because it is a boy, to bear his name; though he says not—that he would have loved a girl as well. But I know it isn't true. I know he says that to please me. And mamma," she added, drawing Madame Valmondé's head down to her, and speaking in a whisper, "he hasn't punished one of them—not one of them—since baby is born. Even Négrillon, who pretended to have burnt his leg that he might rest from work—he only laughed, and said Négrillon was a great scamp. Oh, mamma, I'm so happy; it frightens me."

What Désirée said was true. Marriage, and later the birth of his son, had softened Armand Aubigny's imperious and exacting nature greatly. This was what made the gentle Désirée so happy, for she loved him desperately. When he frowned she trembled, but loved him. When he smiled, she asked no greater blessing of God. But Armand's dark, handsome face had not often been disfigured by frowns since the day he fell in love with her.

When the baby was about three months old, Désirée awoke one day to the conviction that there was something in the air menacing her peace. It was at first too subtle to grasp. It had only been a disquieting suggestion; an air of mystery among the blacks; unexpected visits from far-off neighbors who could hardly account for their coming. Then a strange, an awful change in her husband's manner, which she dared not ask him to explain. When he spoke to her, it was with averted eyes, from which the old love light seemed to have gone out. He absented himself from home; and when there, avoided her presence and that of her child, without excuse. And the very spirit of Satan seemed suddenly to take hold of him in his dealings with the slaves. Désirée was miserable enough to die.

She sat in her room, one hot afternoon, in her *peignoir*, listlessly drawing through her fingers the strands of her long, silky brown hair that hung about her

---

[1] *cochon de lait:* Literally "pig of milk"—a big feeder.

shoulders. The baby, half naked, lay asleep upon her own great mahogany bed, that was like a sumptuous throne, with its satin-lined half canopy. One of La Blanche's little quadroon boys—half naked too—stood fanning the child slowly with a fan of peacock feathers. Désirée's eyes had been fixed absently and sadly upon the baby, while she was striving to penetrate the threatening mist that she felt closing about her. She looked from her child to the boy who stood beside him; and back again, over and over. "Ah!" It was a cry that she could not help, which she was not conscious of having uttered. The blood turned like ice in her veins, and a clammy moisture gathered upon her face.

She tried to speak to the little quadroon boy; but no sound would come, at first. When he heard his name uttered, he looked up, and his mistress was pointing to the door. He laid aside the great, soft fan, and obediently stole away, over the polished floor, on his bare tiptoes.

She stayed motionless, with gaze riveted upon her child, and her face the picture of fright.

Presently her husband entered the room, and without noticing her, went to a table and began to search among some papers which covered it.

"Armand," she called to him, in a voice which must have stabbed him, if he was human. But he did not notice. "Armand," she said again. Then she rose and tottered towards him. "Armand," she panted once more, clutching his arm, "look at our child. What does it mean? Tell me." 20

He coldly but gently loosened her fingers from about his arm and thrust the hand away from him. "Tell me what it means!" she cried despairingly.

"It means," he answered lightly, "that the child is not white; it means that you are not white."

A quick conception of all that this accusation meant for her nerved her with unwonted courage to deny it. "It is a lie; it is not true, I am white! Look at my hair, it is brown; and my eyes are gray, Armand, you know they are gray. And my skin is fair," seizing his wrist. "Look at my hand, whiter than yours, Armand," she laughed hysterically.

"As white as La Blanche's," he returned cruelly, and went away leaving her alone with their child.

When she could hold a pen in her hand, she sent a despairing letter to Madame Valmondé. 25

"My mother, they tell me I am not white. Armand has told me I am not white. For God's sake tell them it is not true. You must know it is not true. I shall die. I must die. I cannot be so unhappy, and live."

The answer that came was as brief:

"My own Désirée: Come home to Valmondé; back to your mother who loves you. Come with your child."

When the letter reached Désirée she went with it to her husband's study, and laid it open upon the desk before which he sat. She was like a stone image: silent, white, motionless after she placed it there.

In silence he ran his cold eyes over the written words. He said nothing. "Shall I go, Armand?" she asked in tones sharp with agonized suspense. 30

"Yes, go."

"Do you want me to go?"

"Yes, I want you to go."

He thought Almighty God had dealt cruelly and unjustly with him; and felt, somehow, that he was paying Him back in kind when he stabbed thus into his wife's soul. Moreover he no longer loved her, because of the unconscious injury she had brought upon his home and his name.

She turned away like one stunned by a blow, and walked slowly towards the   35
door, hoping he would call her back.

"Good-by, Armand," she moaned.

He did not answer her. That was his last blow at fate.

Désirée went in search of her child. Zandrine was pacing the sombre gallery with it. She took the little one from the nurse's arms with no word of explanation, and descending the steps, walked away, under the live-oak branches.

It was an October afternoon; the sun was just sinking. Out in the still fields the Negroes were picking cotton.

Désirée had not changed the thin white garment nor the slippers which she   40
wore. Her hair was uncovered and the sun's rays brought a golden gleam from its brown meshes. She did not take the broad, beaten road which led to the far-off plantation of Valmondé. She walked across a deserted field, where the stubble bruised her tender feet, so delicately shod, and tore her thin gown to shreds.

She disappeared among the reeds and willows that grew thick along the banks of the deep, sluggish bayou; and she did not come back again.

Some weeks later there was a curious scene enacted at L'Abri. In the centre of the smoothly swept back yard was a great bonfire. Armand Aubigny sat in the wide hallway that commanded a view of the spectacle; and it was he who dealt out to a half dozen negroes the material which kept this fire ablaze.

A graceful cradle of willow, with all its dainty furbishings, was laid upon the pyre, which had already been fed with the richness of a priceless *layette*. Then there were silk gowns, and velvet and satin ones added to these; laces, too, and embroideries; bonnets and gloves; for the *corbeille*[2] had been of rare quality.

The last thing to go was a tiny bundle of letters; innocent little scribblings that Désirée had sent to him during the days of their espousal. There was the remnant of one back in the drawer from which he took them. But it was not Désirée's; it was part of an old letter from his mother to his father. He read it. She was thanking God for the blessing of her husband's love:

"But, above all," she wrote, "night and day, I thank the good God for having so   45
arranged our lives that our dear Armand will never know that his mother, who adores him, belongs to the race that is cursed with the brand of slavery."

---

[2] *Corbeille:* a basket of linens, clothing, and accessories collected in anticipation of a baby's birth.

Questions for Discussion and Writing

1. What can you infer about Armand's character and his past behavior from the fact that he has not punished one slave since his baby was born? How does his behavior toward Désirée change after the baby is three months old? What causes this change in his behavior?

2. What did you assume Désirée would do when she realizes Armand values his social standing more than he does her? In retrospect what clues would have pointed you toward the truth disclosed at the end of the story?

3. Have you ever been in a situation where someone was unaware of your racial or ethnic background and made disparaging remarks about that group? How did you feel and what did you do?

GUY DE MAUPASSANT

Guy de Maupassant (1850–1893) wrote, during his brief life, nearly 300 short stories, six novels, and hundreds of sketches for newspapers and magazines. He was born in Normandy, received his early education at home from his mother, and was briefly enrolled in a seminary, from which he was expelled for insubordination. After serving as a soldier in the Franco-Prussian War (1870), he settled in Paris and became a protégé of Gustav Flaubert.[1] His fame was assured with the publication of his first short story, "Ball of Fat" (1880), and he went on to perfect the short story form as a vehicle for psychological insight, precise detail, and the ironic surprise ending for which he is widely recognized.

An Old Man

All the newspapers had carried this advertisement:

> The new spa at Rondelis offers all the advantages desirable for a lengthy stay or even for permanent residence. Its ferruginous waters, recognized as the best in the world for countering all impurities of the blood, also seem to possess special qualities calculated to prolong human life. This remarkable circumstance may be due in part to the exceptional situation of the little town, which lies in a mountainous region, in the middle of a forest of firs. The fact remains that for several centuries it has been noted for cases of extraordinary longevity.

And the public came along in droves.

One morning the doctor in charge of the springs was asked to call on a newcomer, Monsieur Daron, who had arrived a few days before and had rented a charming villa on the edge of the forest. He was a little old man of eighty-six, still quite sprightly, wiry, healthy and active, who went to infinite pains to conceal his age.

---

[1] *Gustave Flaubert (1821–1880):* French novelist, most famous for *Madame Bovary* (1857).

He offered the doctor a seat and started questioning him straight away.

"Doctor," he said, "if I am in good health, it is thanks to careful living. Though not very old, I have already attained a respectable age, yet I keep free of all illnesses and indispositions, even the slightest malaises, by means of careful living. It is said that the climate here is very good for the health. I am perfectly prepared to believe it, but before settling down here I want proof. I am therefore going to ask you to come and see me once a week to give me the following information in detail.

"First of all I wish to have a complete, absolutely complete, list of all the inhabitants of the town and the surrounding area who are over eighty years old. I also need a few physical and physiological details regarding each of them. I wish to know their professions, their way of life, their habits. Every time one of those people dies you will be good enough to inform me, giving me the precise cause of death and describing the circumstances."

Then he added graciously, "I hope, Doctor, that we shall become good friends," and held out his wrinkled little hand. The doctor shook it, promising him his devoted co-operation.

Monsieur Daron had always had an obsessive fear of death. He had deprived himself of nearly all the pleasures of this world because they were dangerous, and whenever anyone expressed surprise that he should not drink wine—wine, that purveyor of dreams and gaiety—he would reply in a voice in which a note of fear could be detected: "I value my life." And he stressed the word *my*, as if that life, *his* life, possessed some special distinction. He put into that *my* such a difference between his life and other people's lives that any rejoinder was out of the question.

For that matter he had a very special way of stressing the possessive pronouns designating parts of his person and even things which belonged to him. When he said "my eyes, my legs, my arms, my hands," it was quite obvious that there must be no mistake about this: those organs were not at all like other people's. But where this distinction was particularly noticeable was in his references to his doctor. When he said "my doctor," one would have thought that that doctor belonged to him and nobody else, destined for him alone, to attend to his illnesses and to nothing else, and that he was superior to all the other doctors in the world, without exception.

He had never regarded other men as anything but puppets of a sort, created to fill up an empty world. He divided them into two classes: those he greeted because some chance had put him in contact with them, and those he did not greet. But both these categories of individuals were equally insignificant in his eyes.

However, beginning with the day when the Rondelis doctor brought him the list of the seventeen inhabitants of the town who were over eighty, he felt a new interest awaken in his heart, an unfamiliar solicitude for these old people whom he was going to see fall by the wayside one by one. He had no desire to make their acquaintance, but he formed a very clear idea of their persons, and when the doctor dined with him, every Thursday, he spoke only of them. "Well, doctor," he would say, "and how is Joseph Poinçot today? We left him feeling a little ill last week." And when the doctor had given him the patient's bill of health, Monsieur Daron would suggest changes in his diet, experiments, methods of treatment which he might later apply to himself if they had succeeded with the others. Those seventeen old people provided him with an experimental field from which he learnt many a lesson.

One evening the doctor announced as he came in: "Rosalie Tournel has died."

Monsieur Daron gave a start and immediately asked, "What of?"

"Of a chill."

The little old man gave a sigh of relief. Then he said, "She was too fat, too heavy; she must have eaten too much. When I get to her age I'll be more careful about my weight." (He was two years older than Rosalie Tournel, but he claimed to be only seventy.)

A few months later it was the turn of Henri Brissot. Monsieur Daron was very upset. This time it was a man, and a thin man at that, within three months of his own age, and careful about his health. He did not dare to ask any questions, but waited anxiously for the doctor to give him some details.

"Oh, so he died just like that, all of a sudden," he said. "But he was perfectly all right last week. He must have done something silly, I suppose, Doctor?"

The doctor, who was enjoying himself, replied: "I don't think so. His children told me he had been very careful."

Then, unable to contain himself any longer, and filled with fear, Monsieur Daron asked: "But . . . but . . . what did he die of, then?"

"Of pleurisy."

The little old man clapped his dry hands in sheer joy.

"I told you so! I told you he had done something silly. You don't get pleurisy for nothing. He must have gone out for a breath of air after his dinner and the cold must have gone to his chest. Pleurisy! Why, that's an accident, not an illness. Only fools die of pleurisy."

And he ate his dinner in high spirits, talking about those who were left.

"There are only fifteen of them now, but they are all hale and hearty, aren't they? The whole of life is like that: the weakest go first; people who live beyond thirty have a good chance of reaching sixty; those who pass sixty often get to eighty; and those who pass eighty nearly always live to be a hundred, because they are the fittest, toughest and most sensible of all."

Another two disappeared during the year, one of dysentery and the other of a choking fit. Monsieur Daron was highly amused by the death of the former and concluded that he must have eaten something stimulating the day before.

"Dysentery is the disease of careless people. Dammit all, Doctor, you ought to have watched over his diet."

As for the man who had been carried off by a choking fit, his death could only be due to a heart condition which had hitherto gone unnoticed.

But one evening the doctor announced the decease of Paul Timonet, a sort of mummy of whom it had been hoped to make a centenarian and an advertisement for the spa.

When Monsieur Daron asked, as usual: "What did he die of?" the doctor replied, "Bless me, I really don't know."

"What do you mean, you don't know. A doctor always knows. Hadn't he 30
some organic lesion?"

The doctor shook his head.

"No, none."

"Possibly some infection of the liver or the kidneys?"

"No, they were quite sound."

"Did you check whether the stomach was functioning properly? A stroke is 35
often caused by poor digestion."

"There was no stroke."

Monsieur Daron, very perplexed, said excitedly: "Look, he must have died of
something! What do you think it was?"

The doctor threw up his hands.

"I've no idea, no idea at all. He died because he died, that's all."

Then Monsieur Daron, in a voice full of emotion, asked: "Exactly how old 40
was that one? I can't remember."

"Eighty-nine."

And the little old man, at once incredulous and reassured, exclaimed:

"Eighty-nine! So whatever it was, it wasn't old age . . ."

Questions for Discussion and Writing

1. What change can you detect in the doctor's attitude toward Monsieur
   Daron? What brings about this change?
2. What universal aspects of human nature does de Maupassant portray in his
   characterization of Monsieur Daron? How has de Maupassant constructed
   this story to make Daron's obsession poignant as well as humorous?
3. Invent a dialogue between yourself as you are now and yourself as you imagine you will be in sixty years.

Poetry

MARGE PIERCY

*Marge Piercy was born in 1936. She received a B.A. in 1957 from the University of Michigan
and an M.A. in 1958 from Northwestern University. She is a prolific novelist and poet. Piercy's
novels include* Going Down Fast *(1969),* Woman on the Edge of Time *(1976), and* Vida
(1979). Collections of her poetry are Breaking Camp *(1968),* Hard Living *(1969),* To Be
of Use *(1972),* Circles in the Water *(1973),* Living in the Open *(1976), and* The Art of
Blessing the Day: Poems with a Jewish Theme *(1999). She recently wrote* Sleeping with
Cats: A Memoir *(2002). "Barbie Doll" (1973) is typical of Piercy's satiric meditations on economic, racial, and sexual inequality in contemporary American life.*

Barbie Doll

This girlchild was born as usual
and presented dolls that did pee-pee
and miniature GE stoves and irons
and wee lipsticks the color of cherry candy.
Then in the magic of puberty, a classmate said: 5
You have a great big nose and fat legs.

She was healthy, tested intelligent,
possessed strong arms and back,
abundant sexual drive and manual dexterity.
She went to and fro apologizing.   10
Everyone saw a fat nose on thick legs.

She was advised to play coy,
exhorted to come on hearty,
exercise, diet, smile and wheedle.
Her good nature wore out   15
like a fan belt.
So she cut off her nose and her legs
and offered them up.

In the casket displayed on satin she lay
with the undertaker's cosmetics painted on,   20
a turned-up putty nose.
dressed in a pink and white nightie.
Doesn't she look pretty? everyone said.
Consummation at last.
To every woman a happy ending.   25

Questions for Discussion and Writing

1. How does the "girlchild" change herself in response to the advice, criticisms, and suggestions she receives?
2. How is Piercy's use of the image of a Barbie doll appropos of the point she is making? What is she saying about contemporary American cultural values as they shape expectations of young women?
3. What is ironic about the conclusion of the poem?

GRACE CAROLINE BRIDGES

Grace Caroline Bridges is a psychotherapist working in Minneapolis. Her poems have appeared in the Evergreen Chronicles, The Northland Review, *and* Great River Review. *"Lisa's Ritual, Age 10" was published in* Looking for Home: Women Writing about Exile *(1990). The distinctive effects of Bridges's poetry come from her ability to communicate a child's experience by re-creating the shock of an experience rather than merely describing it.*

Lisa's Ritual, Age 10

Afterwards when he is finished with her
lots of mouthwash helps
to get rid of her father's cigarette taste.
She runs a hot bath
      to soak away the pain   5
           like red dye leaking from her
                school dress in the washtub.
She doesn't cry.
When the bathwater cools she adds more hot.
She brushes her teeth for a long time.   10

Then she finds the corner of her room,
curls against it. There the wall is
hard and smooth
as teacher's new chalk, white
as a clean bedsheet. Smells   15
fresh. Isn't sweaty, hairy, doesn't stick
to skin. Doesn't hurt much
when she presses her small backbone
into it. The wall is steady

  while she falls   away: 20
     first the hands   lost
arms dissolving   feet gone
   the legs   dis–   jointed
      body cracking down
        the center like a fault   25
          she falls inside
              slides down like
dust   like kitchen dirt
           slips off
     the dustpan into   30
                      noplace

   a place where

nothing happens,
nothing ever happened.

When she feels the cool   35
wall against her cheek
she doesn't want to
come back. Doesn't want to
think about it.
The wall is quiet, waiting.   40
It is tall like a promise
only better.

Questions for Discussion and Writing

1. How does the way the words are arranged on the page help communicate Lisa's emotional shock and withdrawal as a result of the trauma she has experienced?
2. To what extent might the title refer not only to the physical ritual of cleansing but the psychological ritual of distancing herself from the memories?
3. As a psychotherapist, Bridges is familiar with the clinical symptoms of children who have been sexually abused. What features of the poem suggest that children who experience this kind of abuse may develop multiple personalities and even become schizophrenic as a way of dealing with the trauma?

BRUCE SPRINGSTEEN

Bruce Springsteen was born 1949 in Freehold, New Jersey. He began performing in New York and New Jersey nightclubs and signed with Columbia Records in 1972. He has given numerous nationwide and international concert tours with the E-Street Band. He received the Grammy Award for best male rock vocalist in 1984, 1987, and 1994. The Academy Award and the Golden Globe Award for best original song in a film were given to him for "Streets of Philadelphia" from the film Philadelphia *(1994). His albums include* Born to Run *(1975),* Darkness on the Edge of Town *(1978),* Born in the USA *(1984),* Tunnel of Love *(1987),* Bruce Springsteen's Greatest Hits *(1995), and* Live in New York City *(2001).*

Streets of Philadelphia

I was bruised and battered: I couldn't tell what I felt.
I was unrecognizable to myself.
Saw my reflection in a window and didn't know my own face.
Oh, brother are you gonna leave me wastin' away on the
    streets of Philadelphia.
Ain't no angel gonna greet me: it's just you and I, my friend.   5
And my clothes don't fit me no more: I walked a thousand miles
    just to slip this skin.

I walked the avenue till my legs felt like stone.
I heard the voices of friends vanished and gone.
At night I could hear the blood in my veins

Just as black and whispering as the rain   10
On the streets of Philadelphia.
Ain't no angel gonna greet me: it's just you and I, my friend.
And my clothes don't fit me no more: I walked a thousand miles
    just to slip this skin.

The night has fallen. I'm lying awake.
I can feel myself fading away.   15
So, receive me, brother, with your faithless kiss.
Or will we leave each other alone like this
On the streets of Philadelphia?

Ain't no angel gonna greet me: it's just you and I, my friend.
And my clothes don't fit me no more: I walked a thousand miles   20
    just to slip this skin.

Questions for Discussion and Writing

1. How would you characterize the voice you hear? What images convey the speaker's sense of losing himself because of having AIDS?
2. How does being recognized and acknowledged become a central theme in this song? At what point in the lyrics does the speaker appeal for this recognition?
3. What impact do you think this song is designed to have on those who hear it? What effect did it have on you?

Drama

BETTY KELLER

Betty Keller (b. 1930) has served as the founder and producer of the western Canadian writers' festival and workshop program, the Festival of the Written Arts, from 1983 to 1994. Her many unusual work experiences include jobs as a farmer, an insurance adjuster, and a prison matron. She has also taught at Simon Fraser University and the University of British Columbia. Tea Party was originally included in a collection of short plays titled Improvisations and Creative Drama *(1974). Keller has also written biographical and historical works, including* Sea Silver *(1996) and* Bright Seas and Pioneer Spirits *(1996). The predicament confronting the characters in this play occurs more frequently than we might think. Keller's most recent work is* Pauline Johnson: First Aboriginal Voice of Canada *(1999).*

Tea Party

CHARACTERS

ALMA EVANS: seventy-five years old, small and spare framed. Her clothing is simple but not outdated, her grey hair cut short and neat. She walks with the aid of a cane, although she would not be classed as a cripple.
HESTER EVANS: seventy-nine years old. There is little to distinguish her physically from her sister, except perhaps a face a little more pinched and pain-worn. She sits in a wheelchair; but although her legs may be crippled, her mind certainly is not.
THE BOY: in his early teens, seen only fleetingly.

Scene. The sitting room of the Evans sisters' home. The door to the street is on the rear wall Upstage Left,[1] a large window faces the street Upstage Center. On the right wall is the door to the kitchen; on the left, a door to the remainder of the house. Downstage Left is an easy chair, Upstage Right a sofa, Downstage Right a tea trolley. The room is crowded with the knickknacks gathered by its inhabitants in three-quarters of a century of living.

[*At rise,* ALMA *is positioning* HESTER'*s wheelchair Upstage Left.* ALMA'*s cane is on* HESTER'*s lap.*]

HESTER: That's it.

[ALMA *takes her cane from* HESTER. *They both survey the room.*]

ALMA: I think I'll sit on the sofa . . . at the far end.
HESTER: Yes. That will be cosy. Then he can sit on this end between us.

[ALMA *sits on the Downstage Right end of the sofa. They both study the effect.*]

ALMA: But then he's too close to the door, Hester!

---

[1] *Upstage Left:* To visualize stage locations, assume that the stage directions are described from the viewpoint of an actor facing the audience. Thus "Right" is actually to the left of the audience, and "Left" is right. "Downstage" refers to the front of the stage while "Upstage" is the back. The terms *down* and *up* were established at a time when stages were tilted toward the audience, so that spectators at floor level could have as complete a view as possible of the entire stage.

[HESTER *nods, absorbed in the problem.*]

ALMA [*Moving to the Upstage Left end of sofa.*]:   Then I'd better sit here.   5
HESTER: But now he's too far away from me, Alma.

[ALMA *stands; both of them study the room again.*]

ALMA: But if I push the tea trolley in front of you, he'll have to come to you,
    won't he?
HESTER: Oh, all right, Alma. You're sure it's today?
ALMA [*Pushing the tea trolley laden with cups and napkins, etc. to* HESTER]:   The first
    Thursday of the month.
HESTER: You haven't forgotten the chocolate biscuits?[2]   10
ALMA: No dear, they're on the plate. I'll bring them in with the tea. [Goes to
    window, peering up the street to the Right.]
HESTER: And cocoa?
ALMA: I remembered.
HESTER: You didn't remember for Charlie's visit.
ALMA: Charlie drinks tea, Hester. I didn't make cocoa for him because he   15
    drinks tea.
HESTER: Oh. He didn't stay last time anyway.
ALMA: It was a busy day. . . .
HESTER: Rushing in and out like that. I was going to tell him about father and
    the *Bainbridge* . . . and he didn't stay.
ALMA: What about the *Bainbridge?*
HESTER: Her maiden voyage out of Liverpool . . . when father was gone three   20
    months and we thought he'd gone down with her.
ALMA: That wasn't the *Bainbridge.*
HESTER: Yes, it was. It was the *Bainbridge.* I remember standing on the dock in
    the snow when she finally came in. That was the year I'd begun first form,
    and I could spell out the letters on her side.
ALMA: It was her sister ship, the *Heddingham.*
HESTER: The *Bainbridge.* You were too young to remember. Let's see, the year
    was . . .
ALMA: Mother often told the story. It was the *Heddingham* and her engine broke   25
    down off Cape Wrath beyond the Hebrides.
HESTER: It was 1902 and you were just four years old.
ALMA: The *Heddingham,* and she limped into port on January the fifth.

---

[2] *Chocolate biscuits:* chocolate cookies.

HESTER: January the fourth just after nine in the morning, and we stood in the snow and watched the *Bainbridge* nudge the pier, and I cried and the tears froze on my cheeks.

ALMA: The *Heddingham*.

HESTER: Alma, mother didn't cry, you know. I don't think she ever cried. My memory of names and places is sharp so that I don't confuse them as some others I could mention, but sometimes I can't remember things like how people reacted. But I remember that day. There were tears frozen on my cheeks but mother didn't cry.

ALMA [*Nodding.*]:   She said he didn't offer a word of explanation. Just marched home beside her.

HESTER [*Smiling.*]:   He never did say much. . . . Is he coming yet?

ALMA: No, can't be much longer though. Almost half past four.

HESTER: Perhaps you'd better bring in the tea. Then it will seem natural.

ALMA: Yes dear, I know. [*Exits out door Upstage Right.*] Everything's ready.

HESTER: What will you talk about?

ALMA[*Re-entering with the teapot*]:   I thought perhaps . . . [*Carefully putting down the teapot.*] . . . perhaps brother George!

HESTER: And the torpedo? No, Alma, he's not old enough for that story!

ALMA: He's old enough to know about courage. I thought I'd show him the medal, too. [*She goes to the window, peers both ways worriedly, then carries on towards the kitchen.*]

HESTER: Not yet? He's late to-night. You're sure it's today?

ALMA: He'll come. It's the first Thursday. [*Exit.*]

HESTER: You have his money?

ALMA[*Returning with the plate of biscuits.*]:   I've got a twenty dollar bill, Hester.

HESTER: Alma!

ALMA: Well, we haven't used that one on him. It was Dennis, the last one, who always had change. We could get two visits this way, Hester.

HESTER: Maybe Dennis warned him to carry change for a twenty.

ALMA: It seemed worth a try. [*Goes to the window again.*] Are you going to tell him about the *Heddingham*?

HESTER: The *Bainbridge*. Maybe . . . or maybe I'll tell him about the day the Great War ended. Remember, Alma, all the noise, the paper streamers . . .

ALMA: And father sitting silent in his chair.

HESTER: It wasn't the same for him with George gone. Is he coming yet?

ALMA: No dear, maybe he's stopped to talk somewhere. [*Looking to the right.*] . . . No . . . no, there he is, on the Davis' porch now!

HESTER: I'll pour then. You get the cocoa, Alma.

ALMA[*Going out.*]:   It's all ready, I just have to add hot water.

HESTER: Don't forget the marshmallows!

ALMA[*Reappearing*]:   Oh, Hester, what if he comes in and just sits down closest to the door? He'll never stay!

HESTER: You'll have to prod him along. For goodness sakes, Alma, get his cocoa!

[ALMA *disappears.*]

HESTER: He must be nearly here. He doesn't go to the Leschynskis, and the
     Blackburns don't get home till after six.
ALMA[*Returning with the cocoa.*]:   Here we are! Just in . . .

[*The Boy passes the window. There is a slapping sound as the newspaper lands on the
porch.*]

[ALMA and HESTER *look at the door and wait, hoping to hear a knock, but they both
know the truth. Finally,* ALMA *goes to the door, opens it and looks down at the newspaper.*]

ALMA: He's gone on by.
HESTER: You must have had the day wrong.   60
ALMA: No, he collected at the Davis'.
HESTER[*After a long pause.*]:   He couldn't have forgotten us.
ALMA[*Still holding the cocoa, she turns from the door.*]:   He's collecting at the
     Kerighan's now. [*She closes the door and stands forlornly.*]
HESTER: Well, don't stand there with that cocoa! You look silly. [ALMA *brings the
     cocoa to the tea trolley.*] Here's your tea. [ALMA *takes the cup, sits on the Upstage
     Left of the end sofa. There is a long silence.*]
HESTER: I think I'll save that story for the meter man.   65
ALMA: The *Heddingham?*
HESTER: The *Bainbridge.*
ALMA[*After a pause.*]:   They don't read the meters for two more weeks.

SLOW BLACKOUT

Questions for Discussion and Writing

1. What details in the play generate a sense of poignancy for the predicament in
   which the two sisters find themselves?
2. What do their discussions about seating arrangements for the paper boy reveal? What is the significance of Alma's plan for the twenty-dollar bill? How
   does Alma and Hester's argument about the name of the ship tell the audience about their past history and current relationship?
3. Have you ever known a person who has outlived his or her friends and relatives and is in a situation similar to that of the two sisters in this play? Has
   your acquaintance dealt with his or her predicament in ways that are similar
   to or different from the actions of the characters in *Tea Party?*

Connections for Chapter 5: Issues in Popular Culture

1. **Juliet B. Schor,** *The Culture of Consumerism*
   How do the values relating to body image described by Kim Chernin support Schor's thesis about the extent to which we "buy" into the media's depiction of how we should look and what we should want to own?

2. **Slavenka Drakulić,** *On Bad Teeth*
   What insight do Drakulić and Juliet B. Schor provide into American consumer psychology?

3. **Neil Postman and Steve Powers,** *TV News as Entertainment*
   After reading this article, discuss whether Americans are now addicted (in Philip Slater's sense of the term) to being entertained.

4. **Jan Harold Brunvand,** *Urban Legends: "The Boyfriend's Death"*
   Rewrite Carol Grunewald's essay "Monsters of the Brave New World" (Chapter 9) as an urban legend emphasizing traits that Brunvand describes.

5. **Kim Chernin,** *The Flesh and the Devil*
   Draw on the method for analyzing ads described by Stuart Hirschberg in "The Rhetoric of Advertising" (Chapter 4) and discuss whether current ads support Chernin's assessment?

6. **Philip Slater,** *Want-Creation Fuels Americans' Addictiveness*
   What factors account for the new direction that "want-creation" (as discussed by Slater) has taken, according to Juliet B. Schor?

7. **Arthur Ashe,** *The Burden of Race*
   Given what Neil Postman and Steve Powers say about how the news on television sensationalizes everything into entertainment, were Ashe's fears justified? Why or why not?

8. **Ann Louise Bardach,** *The Stealth Virus: AIDS and Latinos*
   Compare Bardach's and Arthur Ashe's analyses of the interrelationship of culture and race in shaping the public perception of homosexuality and AIDS.

9. **Kate Chopin,** *Désirée's Baby*
   What features of Kate Chopin's "Désirée's Baby" reflect her study of the stories of Guy de Maupassant (such as "An Old Man")?

10. **Guy de Maupassant,** *An Old Man*
    To what extent has the American obsession with appearing young, described by Kim Chernin, set the stage for a national state of mind similar to that of the "old man" in this story?

11. **Marge Piercy,** *Barbie Doll*
    How does the Barbie doll (as portrayed by Piercy) illustrate Chernin's thesis about the damaging effects of society's messages about female body image?

12. **Grace Caroline Bridges,** *Lisa's Ritual, Age 10*
    In your view, does this poem or Bessie Head's story ("Looking for a Rain God" in Chapter 2) more powerfully communicate the nature of child abuse

in very different cultures? Explain your answer. In what sense does Bridges depict the destruction of a "ceremony of innocence" (in W. B. Yeats's phrase in "The Second Coming" in Chapter 11)?

13. **Bruce Springsteen,** *Streets of Philadelphia*
    What different perspectives on the effects of AIDS are provided by Ann Louise Bardach and Springsteen in terms of denial and alienation?

14. **Betty Keller,** *Tea Party*
    What different perspectives on aging are dramatized in Keller's play and in Guy de Maupassant's story "An Old Man"?

6

OUR PLACE IN NATURE

Many essays in this chapter stand as classic investigations of the complex interactions of living things, the study of animal behavior, the deteriorating environment and the value of wilderness. Selections by Ursala K. Le Guin, Joseph K. Skinner, Linda Hogan, and Thor Heyerdahl consider how the exploitation of the environment and pollution of the ocean destroy the interdependence of all living things within the ecosystem.

An essay by Alice Walker shares the author's personal encounter with an unusual horse that suggests intriguing possibilities about the sensitivity and intelligence of animals. Mark Twain and P. J. O'Rourke bring their satiric gifts to bear upon this chapter's central question about our place in nature.

Natsume Soseki assumes the vantage point of a household pet who makes telling observations about a Japanese professor and his family. Then, a humorous story by Lin Sutherland vividly dramatizes the near-mystical joys experienced by fans (both men and women) of fly-fishing.

Poems by Mary Oliver and Henry Wadsworth Longfellow explore each author's profound sense of being at one with nature.

Nonfiction

MARK TWAIN

Samuel Langhorne Clemens (1835–1910) was brought up in Hannibal, Missouri. After serving as a printer's apprentice, he became a steamboat pilot on the Mississippi (1857–1861) and adopted his pen name from the leadsman's call ("mark twain" means "by the mark two fathoms") that sounded the river in shallow places. After an unsuccessful attempt to mine gold in Nevada, Twain edited the Virginia City Enterprise. *In 1865 in the* New York Saturday Press, *Twain published "Jim Smiley and His Jumping Frog," which then became the title story of* The Celebrated Jumping Frog of Calaveras County and Other Sketches *(1867). His reputation as a humorist was enhanced by* Innocents Abroad *(1869), a comic account of his travels through France, Italy, and Palestine, and by* Roughing It *(1872), a delightful spoof of his mining adventures. His acknowledged masterpieces are* The Adventures of Tom Sawyer

(1876) and its sequel The Adventures of Huckleberry Finn *(1885), works of great comic power and social insight. Twain's later works, including* The Man That Corrupted Hadleyburg *(1900), a fable about greed, and* The Mysterious Stranger *(1916), published six years after Twain's death, assail hypocrisy as endemic to the human condition. "The Lowest Animal" (1906) shows Twain at his most iconoclastic, formulating a scathing comparison between humans and the so-called lower animals.*

The Lowest Animal

I have been studying the traits and dispositions of the "lower animals" (so-called), and contrasting them with the traits and dispositions of man. I find the result humiliating to me. For it obliges me to renounce my allegiance to the Darwinian theory of the Ascent of Man from the Lower Animals; since it now seems plain to me that that theory ought to be vacated in favor of a new and truer one, this new and truer one to be named the Descent of Man from the Higher Animals.

In proceeding toward this unpleasant conclusion I have not guessed or speculated or conjectured, but have used what is commonly called the scientific method. That is to say, I have subjected every postulate that presented itself to the crucial test of actual experiment, and have adopted it or rejected it according to the result. Thus I verified and established each step of my course in its turn before advancing to the next. These experiments were made in the London Zoological Gardens, and covered many months of painstaking and fatiguing work.

Before particularizing any of the experiments, I wish to state one or two things which seem to more properly belong in this place than further along. This in the interest of clearness. The massed experiments established to my satisfaction certain generalizations, to wit:

1. That the human race is of one distinct species. It exhibits slight variations—in color, stature, mental caliber, and so on—due to climate, environment, and so forth; but it is a species by itself, and not to be confounded with any other.
2. That the quadrupeds are a distinct family, also. This family exhibits variations —in color, size, food preferences and so on; but it is a family by itself.
3. That the other families—the birds, the fishes, the insects, the reptiles, etc.—are more or less distinct, also. They are in the procession. They are links in the chain which stretches down from the higher animals to man at the bottom.

Some of my experiments were quite curious. In the course of my reading I had come across a case where, many years ago, some hunters on our Great Plains organized a buffalo hunt for the entertainment of an English earl—that, and to provide some fresh meat for his larder. They had charming sport. They killed seventy-two of those great animals; and ate part of one of them and left the seventy-one to rot. In order to determine the difference between an anaconda and an earl—if any—I caused seven young calves to be turned into the anaconda's cage. The grateful reptile immediately crushed one of them and swallowed it, then lay back satisfied. It showed no further interest in the calves, and no disposition to harm them. I tried this experiment with other anacondas; always with the same result. The fact stood proven that the difference between an earl and an anaconda is that the earl is cruel and the anaconda isn't; and that the earl wantonly destroys what he has no use for, but the anaconda doesn't. This seemed to suggest that the anaconda was not descended from the earl. It also seemed to suggest that the earl was descended from the anaconda, and had lost a good deal in the transition.

I was aware that many men who have accumulated more millions of money   5
than they can ever use have shown a rabid hunger for more, and have not scrupled to cheat the ignorant and the helpless out of their poor servings in order to partially appease that appetite. I furnished a hundred different kinds of wild and tame animals the opportunity to accumulate vast stores of food, but none of them would do it. The squirrels and bees and certain birds made accumulations, but stopped when they had gathered a winter's supply, and could not be persuaded to add to it either honestly or by chicane. In order to bolster up a tottering reputation the ant pretended to store up supplies, but I was not deceived. I know the ant. These experiments convinced me that there is this difference between man and the higher animals: he is avaricious and miserly, they are not.

In the course of my experiments I convinced myself that among the animals man is the only one that harbors insults and injuries, broods over them, waits till a chance offers, then takes revenge. The passion of revenge is unknown to the higher animals.

Roosters keep harems, but it is by consent of their concubines; therefore no wrong is done. Men keep harems, but it is by brute force, privileged by atrocious laws which the other sex is allowed no hand in making. In this matter man occupies a far lower place than the rooster.

Cats are loose in their morals, but not consciously so. Man, in his descent from the cat, has brought the cat's looseness with him but has left the unconsciousness behind—the saving grace which excuses the cat. The cat is innocent, man is not.

Indecency, vulgarity, obscenity—these are strictly confined to man; he invented them. Among the higher animals there is no trace of them. They hide nothing; they are not ashamed. Man, with his soiled mind, covers himself. He will not even enter a drawing room with his breast and back naked, so alive are he and his mates to indecent suggestion. Man is "The Animal that Laughs." But so does the monkey, as Mr. Darwin pointed out; and so does the Australian bird that is called the laughing jackass. No—Man is the Animal that Blushes. He is the only one that does it—or has occasion to.

At the head of this article we see how "three monks were burnt to death" a   10
few days ago, and a prior "put to death with atrocious cruelty." Do we inquire into the details? No; or we should find out that the prior was subjected to unprintable multilations. Man—when he is a North American Indian—gouges out his prisoner's eyes; when he is King John, with a nephew to render untroublesome, he uses a red-hot iron; when he is a religious zealot dealing with heretics in the Middle Ages, he skins his captive alive and scatters salt on his back; in the first Richard's time he shuts up a multitude of Jew families in a tower and sets fire to it; in Columbus's time he captures a family of Spanish Jews and—but that is not printable; in our day in England a man is fined ten shillings for beating his mother nearly to

death with a chair, and another man is fined forty shillings for having four pheasant eggs in his possession without being able to satisfactorily explain how he got them. Of all the animals, man is the only one that is cruel. He is the only one that inflicts pain for the pleasure of doing it. It is a trait that is not known to the higher animals. The cat plays with the frightened mouse; but she has this excuse, that she does not know that the mouse is suffering. The cat is moderate—unhumanly moderate: she only scares the mouse, she does not hurt it; she doesn't dig out its eyes, or tear off its skin, or drive splinters under its nails—man-fashion; when she is done playing with it she makes a sudden meal of it and puts it out of its trouble. Man is the Cruel Animal. He is alone in that distinction.

The higher animals engage in individual fights, but never in organized masses. Man is the only animal that deals in that atrocity of atrocities, War. He is the only one that gathers his brethren about him and goes forth in cold blood and with calm pulse to exterminate his kind. He is the only animal that for sordid wages will march out, as the Hessian[1] did in our Revolution, and as the boyish Prince Napoleon did in the Zulu war, and help to slaughter strangers of his own species who have done him no harm and with whom he has no quarrel.

Man is the only animal that robs his helpless fellow of his country—takes possession of it and drives him out of it or destroys him. Man has done this in all the ages. There is not an acre of ground on the globe that is in possession of its rightful owner, or that has not been taken away from owner after owner, cycle after cycle, by force and bloodshed.

Man is the only Slave. And he is the only animal who enslaves. He has always been a slave in one form or another, and has always held other slaves in bondage under him in one way or another. In our day he is always some man's slave for wages, and does that man's work; and this slave has other slaves under him for minor wages, and they do his work. The higher animals are the only ones who exclusively do their own work and provide their own living.

Man is the only Patriot. He sets himself apart in his own country, under his own flag, and sneers at the other nations, and keeps multitudinous uniformed assassins on hand at heavy expense to grab slices of other people's countries, and keep *them* from grabbing slices of *his*. And in the intervals between campaigns he washes the blood off his hands and works for "the universal brotherhood of man"—with his mouth.

Man is the Religious Animal. He is the only Religious Animal. He is the only animal that has the True Religion—several of them. He is the only animal that loves his neighbor as himself, and cuts his throat if his theology isn't straight. He has made a graveyard of the globe in trying his honest best to smooth his brother's path to happiness and heaven. He was at it in the time of the Caesars, he was at it in Mahomet's time, he was at it in the time of the Inquisition, he was at it in France a couple of centuries, he was at it in England in Mary's day, he has been at it ever

15

---

[1] *Hessians:* the German auxiliary soldiers brought over by the British to fight the Americans during the Revolutionary War.

since he first saw the light, he is at it today in Crete—as per the telegrams quoted above—he will be at it somewhere else tomorrow. The higher animals have no religion. And we are told that they are going to be left out, in the Hereafter. I wonder why? It seems questionable taste.

Man is the Reasoning Animal. Such is the claim. I think it is open to dispute. Indeed, my experiments have proven to me that he is the Unreasoning Animal. Note his history, as sketched above. It seems plain to me that whatever he is he is *not* a reasoning animal. His record is the fantastic record of a maniac. I consider that the strongest count against his intelligence is the fact that with that record back of him he blandly sets himself up as the head animal of the lot: whereas by his own standards he is the bottom one.

In truth, man is incurably foolish. Simple things which the other animals easily learn, he is incapable of learning. Among my experiments was this. In an hour I taught a cat and a dog to be friends. I put them in a cage. In another hour I taught them to be friends with a rabbit. In the course of two days I was able to add a fox, a goose, a squirrel and some doves. Finally a monkey. They lived together in peace; even affectionately.

Next, in another cage I confined an Irish Catholic from Tipperary, and as soon as he seemed tame I added a Scotch Presbyterian from Aberdeen. Next a Turk from Constantinople; a Greek Christian from Crete; an Armenian; a Methodist from the wilds of Arkansas; a Buddhist from China; a Brahman from Benares. Finally, a Salvation Army Colonel from Wapping. Then I stayed away two whole days. When I came back to note result, the cage of Higher Animals was all right, but in the other there was but a chaos of gory odds and ends of turbans and fezzes and plaids and bones and flesh—not a specimen left alive. These Reasoning Animals had disagreed on a theological detail and carried the matter to a Higher Court.

One is obliged to concede that in true loftiness of character, Man cannot claim to approach even the meanest of the Higher Animals. It is plain that he is constitutionally incapable of approaching that altitude; that he is constitutionally afflicted with a Defect which must make such approach forever impossible, for it is manifest that this defect is permanent in him, indestructible, ineradicable.

I find this Defect to be *the Moral Sense*. He is the only animal that has it. It is   20
the secret of his degradation. It is the quality *which enables him to do wrong*. It has no other office. It is incapable of performing any other function. It could never have been intended to perform any other. Without it, man could do no wrong. He would rise at once to the level of the Higher Animals.

Since the Moral Sense has but the one office, the one capacity—to enable man to do wrong—it is plainly without value to him. It is as valueless to him as is disease. In fact, it manifestly is a disease. *Rabies* is bad, but it is not so bad as this disease. Rabies enables a man to do a thing which he could not do when in a healthy state: kill his neighbor with a poisonous bite. No one is the better man for having rabies. The Moral Sense enables a man to do wrong. It enables him to do wrong in a thousand ways. Rabies is an innocent disease, compared to the Moral Sense. No one, then, can be the better man for having the Moral Sense. What, now, do we find the Primal Curse to have been? Plainly what it was in the beginning: the infliction upon man of the Moral Sense; the ability to distinguish good from evil; and with it, necessarily, the ability to *do* evil; for there can be no evil act without the presence of consciousness of it in the doer of it.

And so I find that we have descended and degenerated, from some far ancestor—some microscopic atom wandering at its pleasure between the mighty horizons of a drop of water perchance—insect by insect, animal by animal, reptile by reptile, down the long highway of smirchless innocence, till we have reached the bottom stage of development—namable as the Human Being. Below us—nothing. Nothing but the Frenchman.

Questions for Discussion and Writing

1. How are Twain's experiments—comparing human behavior to that of animals in various situations—intended to puncture some illusions the human species has about itself? In what way do each of Twain's experiments reveal that other animals are superior to humans?
2. How do Twain's experiments provide an ironic commentary on Darwin's thesis that humans are at the apex of all other species?
3. How is the method Twain uses to organize his discussion well suited to highlight important differences between animals and humans?

ALICE WALKER

Alice Walker was born in 1944 in Georgia and graduated from Sarah Lawrence College in 1965. She has taught at Yale, Wellesley, and other colleges and has edited and published poetry, fiction, and biography. She is best known for her novel The Color Purple *(1982), which won the American Book Award and the Pulitzer Prize for Fiction and was made into an Academy Award-winning movie in 1985. "Am I Blue?" was first published in her collection of essays* Living by the Word *(1988). Her recent works include* Alice Walker Banned *(1996),* By the Light of My Father's Smile *(1998), and* The Way Forward is with a Broken Heart *(2000).*

Am I Blue?

"Ain't these tears in these eyes tellin' you?" *

For about three years my companion and I rented a small house in the country that stood on the edge of a large meadow that appeared to run from the end of our deck straight into the mountains. The mountains, however, were quite far away,

---

*© 1929 Warner Bros., Inc. (renewed). By Grant Clarke and Harry Akst. All rights reserved. Used by permission.

and between us and them there was, in fact, a town. It was one of the many pleasant aspects of the house that you never really were aware of this.

It was a house of many windows, low, wide, nearly floor to ceiling in the living room, which faced the meadow, and it was from one of these that I first saw our closest neighbor, a large white horse, cropping grass, flipping its mane, and ambling about—not over the entire meadow, which stretched well out of sight of the house, but over the five or so fenced-in acres that were next to the twenty-odd that we had rented. I soon learned that the horse, whose name was Blue, belonged to a man who lived in another town, but was boarded by our neighbors next door. Occasionally, one of the children; usually a stocky teen-ager, but sometimes a much younger girl or boy, could be seen riding Blue. They would appear in the meadow, climb up on his back, ride furiously for ten or fifteen minutes, then get off, slap Blue on the flanks, and not be seen again for a month or more.

There were many apple trees in our yard, and one by the fence that Blue could almost reach. We were soon in the habit of feeding him apples, which he relished, especially because by the middle of summer the meadow grasses—so green and succulent since January—had dried out from lack of rain and Blue stumbled about munching the dried stalks half-heartedly. Sometimes he would stand very still just by the apple tree, and when one of us came out he would whinny, snort loudly, or stamp the ground. This meant, of course: I want an apple.

It was quite wonderful to pick a few apples, or collect those that had fallen to the ground overnight, and patiently hold them, one by one, up to his large, toothy mouth. I remained as thrilled as a child by his flexible dark lips, huge, cubelike teeth that crunched the apples core and all, with such finality, and his high, broad-breasted *enormity;* beside which, I felt small indeed. When I was a child, I used to ride horses, and was especially friendly with one named Nan until the day I was riding and my brother deliberately spooked her and I was thrown, head first, against the trunk of a tree. When I came to, I was in bed and my mother was bending worriedly over me; we silently agreed that perhaps horseback riding was not the safest sport for me. Since then I have walked, and prefer walking to horseback riding—but I had forgotten the depth of feeling one could see in horses' eyes.

I was therefore unprepared for the expression in Blue's. Blue was lonely. Blue was horribly lonely and bored. I was not shocked that this should be the case; five acres to tramp by yourself, endlessly, even in the most beautiful of meadows—and his was—cannot provide many interesting events, and once rainy season turned to dry that was about it. No, I was shocked that I had forgotten that human animals and nonhuman animals can communicate quite well; if we are brought up around animals as children we take this for granted. By the time we are adults we no longer remember. However, the animals have not changed. They are in fact *completed* creations (at least they seem to be, so much more than we) who are not likely *to* change; it is their nature to express themselves. What else are they going to express? And they do. And, generally speaking, they are ignored.

After giving Blue the apples, I would wander back to the house, aware that he was observing me. Were more apples not forthcoming then? Was that to be his sole entertainment for the day? My partner's small son had decided he wanted to learn how to piece a quilt; we worked in silence on our respective squares as I thought . . .

Well, about slavery: about white children, who were raised by black people, who knew their first all-accepting love from black women, and then, when they were twelve or so, were told they must "forget" the deep levels of communication between themselves and "mammy" that they knew. Later they would be able to relate quite calmly, "My old mammy was sold to another good family." "My old mammy was ———— ————." Fill in the blank. Many more years later a white woman would say: "I can't understand these Negroes, these blacks. What do they want? They're so different from us."

And about the Indians, considered to be "like animals" by the "settlers" (a very benign euphemism for what they actually were), who did not understand their description as a compliment.

And about the thousands of American men who marry Japanese, Korean, Filipina, and other non-English-speaking women and of how happy they report they are, *"blissfully,"* until their brides learn to speak English, at which point the marriages tend to fall apart. What then did the men see, when they looked into the eyes of the women they married, before they could speak English? Apparently only their own reflections.

I thought of society's impatience with the young. "Why are they playing the music so loud?" Perhaps the children have listened to much of the music of oppressed people their parents danced to before they were born, with its passionate but soft cries for acceptance and love, and they have wondered why their parents failed to hear.

I do not know how long Blue had inhabited his five beautiful, boring acres before we moved into our house; a year after we had arrived—and had also traveled to other valleys, other cities, other worlds—he was still there.

But then, in our second year at the house, something happened in Blue's life. One morning, looking out the window at the fog that lay like a ribbon over the meadow, I saw another horse, a brown one, at the other end of Blue's field. Blue appeared to be afraid of it, and for several days made no attempt to go near. We went away for a week. When we returned, Blue had decided to make friends and the two horses ambled or galloped along together, and Blue did not come nearly as often to the fence underneath the apple tree.

When he did, bringing his new friend with him, there was a different look in his eyes. A look of independence, of self-possession, of inalienable *horse*ness. His friend eventually became pregnant. For months and months there was, it seemed to me, a mutual feeling between me and the horses of justice, of peace. I fed apples to them both. The look in Blue's eyes was one of, unabashed "this is *it*ness."

It did not, however, last forever. One day, after a visit to the city, I went out to give Blue some apples. He stood waiting, or so I thought, though not beneath the tree. When I shook the tree and jumped back from the shower of apples, he made no move. I carried some over to him. He managed to half-crunch one. The rest he let fall to the ground. I dreaded looking into his eyes—because I had of course noticed that Brown, his partner, had gone—but I did look. If I had been born into slavery, and my partner had been sold or killed, my eyes would have looked like that. The children next door explained that Blue's partner had been "put with him" (the same expression that old people used, I had noticed, when speaking of an ancestor during slavery who had been impregnated by her owner) so that they could mate and she conceive. Since that was accomplished, she had been taken back by her owner, who lived somewhere else.

Will she be back? I asked.

They didn't know.

Blue was like a crazed person. Blue *was*, to me, a crazed person. He galloped furiously, as if he were being ridden, around and around his five beautiful acres. He whinnied until he couldn't. He tore at the ground with his hooves. He butted himself against his single shade tree. He looked always and always toward the road down which his partner had gone. And then, occasionally, when he came up for apples, or I took apples to him, he looked at me. It was a look so piercing, so full of grief, a look so *human,* I almost laughed (I felt too sad to cry) to think there are people who do not know that animals suffer. People like me who have forgotten, and daily forget, all that animals try to tell us. "Everything you do to us will happen to you; we are your teachers, as you are ours. We are one lesson" is essentially it, I think. There are those who never once have even considered animals' rights: those who have been taught that animals actually want to be used and abused by us, as small children "love" to be frightened, or women "love" to be mutilated and raped. . . . They are the great-grandchildren of those who honestly thought, because someone taught them this: "Women can't think," and "niggers can't faint." But most disturbing of all, in Blue's large brown eyes was a new look, more painful than the look of despair: the look of disgust with human beings, with life; the look of hatred. And it was odd what the look of hatred did. It gave him, for the first time, the look of a beast. And what that meant was that he had put up a barrier within to protect himself from further violence; all the apples in the world wouldn't change that fact.

And so Blue remained, a beautiful part of our landscape, very peaceful to look at from the window, white against the grass. Once a friend came to visit and said, looking out on the soothing view: "And it *would* have to be a *white,* horse; the very image of freedom." And I thought, yes, the animals are forced to become for us merely "images" of what they once so beautifully expressed. And we are used to drinking milk from containers showing "contented" cows, whose real lives we want to hear nothing about, eating eggs and drumsticks from "happy" hens, and munching hamburgers advertised by bulls of integrity who seem to command their fate.

As we talked of freedom and justice one day for all, we sat down to steaks. I am eating misery, I thought, as I took the first bite. And spit it out.

Questions for Discussion and Writing

1. How does Walker broaden the significance of Blue's reactions so as to suggest the comparable treatment of slaves, Native Americans, and non-English-speaking women and children? In your opinion, is this extension far-fetched or warranted?

2. In what way is Walker transformed by her experience with Blue? What does she learn from him?

3. Have you ever learned something from an animal that changed your perception of yourself or those around you? Explain your answer.

URSULA K. LE GUIN

Ursula K. Le Guin, the popular author of many acclaimed science fiction works, was born in 1929, in Berkeley, California. She was educated at Radcliffe College, where she was elected to Phi Beta Kappa. She received an M.A. in romance literature from Columbia University in 1952. Le Guin has taught at Mercer University and at the University of Idaho and has conducted writing workshops at Pacific University, the University of Washington, Portland State University, and the University of Reading in England. Besides essays and children's books, Le Guin's significant contributions to science fiction and fantasy literature include The Left Hand of Darkness *(1969), winner of both a Hugo Award and a Science Fiction and Fantasy Writers of America Nebula Award;* The Farthest Shore *(1972), winner of a National Book Award and a Hugo Award; and* The Dispossessed: An Ambiguous Utopia *(1974), winner of the Nebula Award.* The Lathe of Heaven *(1971) was made into a PBS television movie shown in 1980. Her later work, including* Orsinian Tales *(1976),* Malfrena *(1979),* The Language of Night: Essays on Fantasy and Science Fiction *(1979),* The Compass Rose *(1982), and* Tehanu *(1990), envisions utopian and magical worlds (Orsinia, the imagined archipelago of Earthsea, the far-flung planets of the Hainish Cycle) that offer alternatives to the usual male-dominated, autocratic, and technological vistas of traditional American science fiction. Most recently, she has written* Sixty Odd: New Poems *(1999) and* The Telling *(2000). In "A Very Warm Mountain," Le Guin describes her reactions to witnessing the eruption of Mount St. Helens in 1980, forty-five miles away from her home in Portland, Oregon.*

A Very Warm Mountain

An enormous region extending from north-central Washington to northeastern California and including most of Oregon east of the Cascades is covered by basalt lava flows. . . . The unending cliffs of basalt along the Columbia River . . . 74 volcanoes in the Portland area. . . . A blanket of pumice that averages about 50 feet thick . . .
—Roadside Geology of Oregon, *Alt and Hyndman, 1978*

Everybody takes it personally. Some get mad. Damn stupid mountain went and dumped all that dirty gritty glassy gray ash that flies like flour and lies like cement all over their roofs, roads, and rhododendrons. Now they have to clean it up. And the scientists are a real big help, all they'll say is we don't know; we can't tell, she might dump another load of ash on you just when you've got it all cleaned up. It's an outrage.

Some take it ethically. She lay and watched her forests being cut and her elk being hunted and her lakes being fished and fouled and her ecology being tampered with and the smoky, snarling suburbs creeping closer to her skirts, until she saw it was time to teach the White Man's Children a lesson. And she did. In the process of the lesson, she blew her forests to matchsticks, fried her elk, boiled her fish, wrecked her ecosystem, and did very little damage to the cities: so that the lesson taught to the White Man's Children would seem, at best, equivocal.

But everybody takes it personally. We try to reduce it to human scale. To make a molehill out of the mountain.

Some got very anxious, especially during the dreary white weather that hung around the area after May 18 (the first great eruption, when she blew 1300 feet of her summit all over Washington, Idaho, and points east) and May 25 (the first considerable ashfall in the thickly populated Portland area west of the mountain). Farmers in Washington State who had the real fallout, six inches of ash smothering their crops, answered the reporters' questions with polite stoicism; but in town a lot of people were cross and dull and jumpy. Some erratic behavior, some really weird driving. "Everybody on my bus coming to work these days talks to everybody else, they never used to." "Everybody on my bus coming to work sits there like a stone instead of talking to each other like they used to." Some welcomed the mild sense of urgency and emergency as bringing people together in mutual support. Some—the old, the ill—were terrified beyond reassurance. Psychologists reported that psychotics had promptly incorporated the volcano into their private systems; some thought they were controlling her, and some thought she was controlling them. Businessmen, whom we know from the Dow Jones Reports to be an almost ethereally timid and emotional breed, read the scare stories in Eastern newspapers and cancelled all their conventions here; Portland hotels are having a long cool summer. A Chinese Cultural Attaché, evidently preferring earthquakes, wouldn't come farther north than San Francisco. But many natives were irrationally exhilarated, secretly, heartlessly welcoming every steam-blast and earth-tremor: Go it, mountain!

Everybody read in the newspapers everywhere that the May 18 eruption was "five hundred times greater than the bomb dropped on Hiroshima." Some reflected that we have bombs much more than five hundred times more powerful than the 1945 bombs. But these are never mentioned in the comparisons. Perhaps it would upset people in Moscow, Idaho or Missoula, Montana, who got a lot of volcanic ash dumped on them, and don't want to have to think, what if that stuff had been radioactive? It really isn't nice to talk about it, is it. I mean, what if something went off in New Jersey, say, and *was* radioactive—Oh, stop it. That volcano's way out west there somewhere anyhow.

Everybody takes it personally.

I had to go into hospital for some surgery in April, while the mountain was in her early phase—she jumped and rumbled, like the Uncles in *A Child's Christmas in Wales,*[1] but she hadn't done anything spectacular. I was hoping she wouldn't perform while I couldn't watch. She obliged and held off for a month. On May 18 I was home, lying around with the cats, with a ringside view: bedroom and study look straight north about forty-five miles to the mountain.

[1] *A Child's Christmas in Wales:* radio drama by the Welsh poet Dylan Thomas (1914–1953).

I kept the radio tuned to a good country western station and listened to the reports as they came in, and wrote down some of the things they said. For the first couple of hours there was a lot of confusion and contradiction, but no panic, then or later. Late in the morning a man who had been about twenty miles from the blast described it: "Pumice-balls and mud-balls began falling for about a quarter of an hour, then the stuff got smaller, and by nine it was completely and totally black dark. You couldn't see ten feet in front of you!" He spoke with energy and admiration. Falling mud-balls, what next? The main West Coast artery, I–5, was soon closed because of the mud and wreckage rushing down the Toutle River towards the highway bridges. Walla Walla, 160 miles east, reported in to say their street lights had come on automatically at about ten in the morning. The Spokane–Seattle highway, far to the north, was closed, said an official expressionless voice, "on account of darkness."

At one-thirty that afternoon, I wrote:

> It has been warm with a white high haze all morning, since six A.M., when I saw the top of the mountain floating dark against yellow-rose sunrise sky above the haze.

That was, of course, the last time I saw or will ever see that peak.   10

> Now we can see the mountain from the base to near the summit. The mountain itself is whitish in the haze. All morning there has been this long, cobalt-bluish drift to the east from where the summit would be. And about ten o'clock there began to be visible clots, like cottage cheese curds, above the summit. Now the eruption cloud is visible from the summit of the mountain till obscured by a cloud layer at about twice the height of the mountain, i.e., 25–30,000 feet. The eruption cloud is very solid-looking, like sculptured marble, a beautiful blue in the deep relief of baroque curls, sworls, curled-cloud-shapes—darkening towards the top—a wonderful color. One is aware of motion, but (being shaky, and looking through shaky binoculars) I don't actually see the carven-blue-sworl-shapes move. Like the shadow on a sundial. It is *enormous.* Forty-five miles away. It is so much bigger than the mountain itself. It is silent, from this distance. Enormous, silent. It looks not like anything earthy, from the earth, but it does not look like anything atmospheric, a natural cloud, either. The blue of it is stormcloud blue but the shapes are far more delicate, complex, and immense than stormcloud shapes, and it has this solid look; a weightiness, like the capital of some unimaginable column—which in a way indeed it is, the pillar of fire being underground.

At four in the afternoon a reporter said cautiously, "Earthquakes are being felt in the metropolitan area," to which I added, with feeling, "I'll say they are!" I had decided not to panic unless the cats did. Animals are supposed to know about earthquakes, aren't they? I don't know what our cats know; they lay asleep in various restful and decorative poses on the swaying floor and the jiggling bed, and paid no attention to anything except dinner time. I was not allowed to panic.

At four-thirty a meteorologist, explaining the height of that massive, storm-blue pillar of cloud, said charmingly, "You must understand that the mountain is very warm. Warm enough to lift the air over it to 75,000 feet."

And a reporter: "Heavy mud flow on Shoestring Glacier, with continuous lightning." I tried to imagine that scene. I went to the television, and there it was. The radio and television coverage, right through, was splendid. One forgets the joyful courage of reporters and cameramen when there is something worth reporting, a real Watergate, a real volcano.

On the 19th, I wrote down from the radio, "A helicopter picked the logger up while he was sitting on a log surrounded by a mud flow." This rescue was filmed and shown on television: the tiny figure crouching hopeless in the huge abomination of ash and mud. I don't know if this man was one of the loggers who later died in the Emanuel Hospital burn center, or if he survived. They were already beginning to talk about the "killer eruption," as if the mountain had murdered with intent. Taking it personally. . . . Of course she killed. Or did they kill themselves? Old Harry who wouldn't leave his lodge and his whiskey and his eighteen cats at Spirit Lake, and quite right too, at eighty-three; and the young cameraman and the young geologist, both up there on the north side on the job of their lives; and the loggers who went back to work because logging was their living; and the tourists who thought a volcano is like Channel Six, if you don't like the show you turn it off, and took their RVs and their kids up past the roadblocks and the reasonable warnings and the weary country sheriffs sick of arguing: they were all there to keep the appointment. Who made the appointment?

A firefighter pilot that day said to the radio interviewer, "We do what the   15
mountain says. It's not ready for us to go in."

On the 21st I wrote:

> Last night a long, strange, glowing twilight; but no ash has yet fallen west of the mountain. Today, fine, gray, mild, dense Oregon rain. Yesterday afternoon we could see her vaguely through the glasses. Looking appallingly lessened—short, flat—That is painful. She was so beautiful. She hurled her beauty in dust clear to the Atlantic shore, she made sunsets and sunrises of it, she gave it to the western wind. I hope she erupts magma and begins to build herself again. But I guess she is still unbuilding. The Pres. of the U.S. came today to see her. I wonder if he thinks he is on her level. Of course he could destroy much more than she has destroyed if he took a mind to.

On June 4 I wrote:

> Could see her through the glasses for the first time in two weeks or so. It's been dreary white weather with a couple of hours sun in the afternoons.—Not the new summit, yet; that's always in the roil of cloud/plume. But both her long lovely flanks. A good deal of new snow has fallen on her (while we had rain), and her SW face is white, black, and gray, much seamed, in unfamiliar patterns.
> "As changeless as the hills—"
> Part of the glory of it is being included in an event on the geologic scale. Being enlarged. "I shall lift up mine eyes unto the hills," yes; "whence cometh my help."

In all the Indian legends dug out by newspaper writers for the occasion, the mountain is female. Told in the Dick-and-Jane style considered appropriate for popular reportage of Indian myth, with all the syllables hyphenated, the stories seem even more naive and trivial than myths out of context generally do. But the theme of the mountain as woman—first ugly, then beautiful, but always a woman—is consistent. The mapmaking whites of course named the peak after a man, an Englishman who took his title, Baron St. Helens, from a town in the North Country: but the name is obstinately feminine. The Baron is forgotten, Helen remains. The whites who lived on and near the mountain called it The Lady. Called her The Lady. It seems impossible not to take her personally. In twenty years of living through a window from her I guess I have never really thought of her as "it."

She made weather, like all single peaks. She put on hats of cloud, and took them off again, and tried a different shape, and sent them all skimming off across the sky. She wore veils: around the neck, across the breast: white, silver, silver-gray, gray-blue. Her taste was impeccable. She knew the weathers that became her, and how to wear the snow.

Dr. William Hamilton of Portland State University wrote a lovely piece for the college paper about "volcano anxiety," suggesting that the silver cone of St. Helens had been in human eyes a breast, and saying: 20

> St. Helens' real damage to us is not . . . that we have witnessed a denial of the trust-worthiness of God (such denials are our familiar friends). It is the perfection of the mother that has been spoiled, for part of her breast has been removed. Our metaphor has had a mastectomy.
>
> At some deep level, the eruption of Mt. St. Helens has become a new metaphor for the very opposite of stability—for that greatest of twentieth-century fears—cancer. Our uneasiness may well rest on more elusive levels than dirty windshields.

This comes far closer to home than anything else I've read about the "meaning" of the eruption, and yet for me it doesn't work. Maybe it would work better for men. The trouble is, I never saw St. Helens as a breast. Some mountains, yes: Twin Peaks in San Francisco, of course, and other round, sweet California hills—breasts, bellies, eggs, anything maternal, bounteous, yielding. But St. Helens in my eyes was never part of a woman; she is a woman. And not a mother but a sister.

These emotional perceptions and responses sound quite foolish when written out in rational prose, but the fact is that, to me, the eruption was all mixed up with the women's movement. It may be silly but there it is; along the same lines, do you know any woman who wasn't rooting for Genuine Risk to take the Triple Crown? Part of my satisfaction and exultation at each eruption was unmistakably feminist solidarity. You men think you're the only ones can make a really nasty mess? You think you got all the firepower, and God's on your side? You think you run things? Watch this, gents. Watch the Lady act like a woman.

For that's what she did. The well-behaved, quiet, pretty, serene, domestic creature peaceably yielding herself to the uses of man all of sudden said NO. And she spat dirt and smoke and steam. She blackened half her face, in those first March days, like an angry brat. She fouled herself like a mad old harridan. She swore and belched and farted, threatened and shook and swelled, and then she spoke. They heard her voice two hundred miles away. Here I go, she said. I'm doing my thing now. Old Nobodaddy you better JUMP!

Her thing turns out to be more like childbirth than anything else, to my way of thinking. But not on our scale, not in our terms. Why should she speak in our terms or stoop to our scale? Why should she bear any birth that we can recognize? To us it is cataclysm and destruction and deformity. To her—well, for the language for it one must go to the scientists or to the poets. To the geologists. St. Helens is doing exactly what she "ought" to do—playing her part in the great pattern of events perceived by that noble discipline. Geology provides the only time-scale large enough to include the behavior of a volcano without deforming it. Geology, or poetry, which can see a mountain and a cloud as, after all, very similar phenomena. Shelley's cloud can speak for St. Helens:

> I silently laugh
> At my own cenotaph[2] ...
> And arise, and unbuild it again.

So many mornings waking I have seen her from the window before any other 25
thing: dark against red daybreak, silvery in summer light, faint above river-valley fog. So many times I have watched her at evening, the faintest outline in mist, immense, remote, serene: the center, the central stone. A self across the air, a sister self, a stone. "The stone is at the center," I wrote in a poem about her years ago. But the poem is impertinent. All I can say is impertinent.

When I was writing the first draft of this essay in California, on July 23, she erupted again, sending her plume to 60,000 feet. Yesterday, August 7, as I was typing the words "the 'meaning' of the eruption," I checked out the study window and there it was, the towering blue cloud against the quiet northern sky—the fifth major eruption. How long may her labor be? A year, ten years, ten thousand? We cannot predict what she may or might or will do, now, or next, or for the rest of our lives, or ever. A threat: a terror: a fulfillment. This is what serenity is built on. This unmakes the metapors. This is beyond us, and we must take it personally. This is the ground we walk on.

Questions for Discussion and Writing

1. In what respects does Mount St. Helens represent for Le Guin a personification of nature in feminist, not simply feminine, terms? What features of her account support this perception?
2. What might account for the unusual style and structure of Le Guin's essay? What correspondences can you discover between what she writes about and how she writes about it?

---

[2] *Cenotaph:* a sepulchral monument erected in memory of a deceased person whose body is buried elsewhere.

3. Have you ever been caught or involved in a natural disaster—flood, hurricane, earthquake, tornado, wildfire, blizzard, mud slide, avalanche, or the like? Write an essay describing your experiences, communicating how you felt, as well as what happened physically. Did it change your attitude toward "nature"?

JOSEPH K. SKINNER

Joseph K. Skinner (b. 1956) is a 1979 graduate of the University of California who majored in plant sciences. He reports that "in all of my course work at the University of California at Davis, only once was brief mention made of the biological calamity described in this article, and even then no connection was made between it and U.S. economic interests." "Big Mac and the Tropical Forests" first appeared in the Monthly Review *(December 1985). Skinner creates an intriguing causal argument to show how tropical forests in Central and Latin America are being destroyed in order to raise cattle to produce cheap beef for companies such as McDonald's and Swift-Armour Meat Packing Co. Skinner claims that the failure to take responsibility on the part of these and other corporations puts short-term profitability ahead of the destruction of tropical forests. In turn, this destruction could well accelerate the greenhouse effect by permitting rising levels of carbon dioxide to remain in the atmosphere.*

Big Mac and the Tropical Forests

Hello, fast-food chains.

Goodbye, tropical forests.

Sound like an odd connection? The "free-market" economy has led to results even stranger than this, but perhaps none have been as environmentally devastating.

These are the harsh facts: the tropical forests are being leveled for commercial purposes at the rate of 150,000 square kilometers a year, an area the size of England and Wales combined.[1]

At this rate, the world's tropical forests could be entirely destroyed within seventy-three years. Already as much as a fifth or a quarter of the huge Amazon forest, which constitutes a third of the world's total rain forest, has been cut, and the rate of destruction is accelerating. And nearly two thirds of the Central American forests have been cleared or severely degraded since 1950.

Tropical forests, which cover only 7 percent of the Earth's land surface (it used to be 12 percent), support half the species of the world's living things. Due to their destruction, "We are surely losing one or more species a day right now out of the five million (minimum figure) on Earth," says Norman Myers, author of numerous books and articles on the subject and consultant to the World Bank and the World Wildlife Fund. "By the time ecological equilibrium is restored, at least one-quarter

5

---

[1] Jean-Paul Londley, "Tropical Forests resources," FAO Forestry Paper 30 (Rome: FAO, 1982).

of all species will have disappeared, probably a third, and conceivably even more. . . . If this pattern continues, it could mean the demise of two million species by the middle of next century." Myers calls the destruction of the tropical forests "one of the greatest biological debacles to occur on the face of the Earth." Looking at the effects it will have on the course of biological evolution, Myers says:

> The impending upheaval in evolution's course could rank as one of the greatest bio-
> logical revolutions of paleontological time. It will equal in scale and significance the
> development of aerobic respiration, the emergence of flowering plants, and the arrival
> of limbed animals. But of course the prospective degradation of many evolutionary
> capacities will be an impoverishing, not a creative, phenomenon.[2]

In other words, such rapid destruction will vacate so many niches so suddenly that a "pest and weed" ecology, consisting of a relatively few opportunistic species (rats, roaches, and the like) will be created.

Beyond this—as if it weren't enough—such destruction could well have cata-clysmic effects on the Earth's weather patterns, causing, for example, an irreversible desertification of the North American grain belt. Although the scope of the so-called greenhouse effect—in which rising levels of carbon dioxide in the atmos-phere heat the planet by preventing infrared radiation from escaping into space—is still being debated within the scientific community, it is not at all extreme to sup-pose that the fires set to clear tropical forests will contribute greatly to this increase in atmospheric CO_2 and thereby to untold and possibly devastating changes in the world's weather systems.

BIG MAC ATTACK

So what does beef, that staple of the fast-food chains and of the North Amer-ican diet in general, have to do with it?

It used to be, back in 1960, that the United States imported practically no   10
beef. That was a time when North Americans were consuming a "mere" 85 pounds of beef per person per year. By 1980 this was up to 134 pounds per person per year. Concomitant with this increase in consumption, the United States began to import beef, so that by 1981 some 800,000 tons were coming in from abroad, 17 percent of it from tropical Latin America and three fourths of that from Central America. Since fast-food chains have been steadily expanding and now are a $5-billion-a-year business, accounting for 25 percent of all the beef consumed in the United States, the connections between the fast-food empire and tropical beef are clear.

---

[2] There are amazingly few scientists in the world with broad enough expertise to accurately assess the widest implications of tropical deforestation; Norman Myers is one of them. His books include *The Sinking Ark* (Oxford: Pergamon Press, 1979). See also *Conversion of Moist Tropical Forests* (Washington, D.C.: National Academy of Sciences, 1980), "The End of the Line," *Natural History* 94, no. 2 (February 1985), and "The Hamburger Connection," *Ambio* 10, no. 1 (1981). I have used Myers extensively in the preparation of this article. The quotes in this paragraph are from "The Hamburger Connection," pp. 3, 4, 5.

Cattle ranching is "by far the major factor in forest destruction in tropical Latin America," says Myers. "Large fast-food outlets in the U.S. and Europe foster the clearance of forests to produce cheap beef."[3]

And cheap it is, compared to North American beef: by 1978 the average price of beef imported from Central America was $1.47/kg, while similar North American beef cost $3.30/kg.

Cheap, that is, for North Americans, but not for Central Americans. Central Americans cannot afford their own beef. Whereas beef production in Costa Rica increased twofold between 1959 and 1972, per capita consumption of beef in that country went down from 30 lbs. a year to 19. In Honduras, beef production increased by 300 percent between 1965 and 1975, but consumption decreased from 12 lbs. per capita per year to 10. So, although two thirds of Central America's arable land is in cattle, local consumption of beef is decreasing; the average domestic cat in the United States now consumes more beef than the average Central American.[4]

Brazilian government figures show that 38 percent of all deforestation in the Brazilian Amazon between 1966 and 1975 was attributable to large-scale cattle ranching. Although the presence of hoof-and-mouth disease among Brazilian cattle has forced U.S. lawmakers to prohibit the importation of chilled or frozen Brazilian beef, the United States imports $46 million per year of cooked Brazilian beef, which goes into canned products; over 80 percent of Brazilian beef is still exported, most of it to Western Europe, where no such prohibition exists.

At present rates, all remaining Central American forests will have been eliminated by 1990. The cattle ranching largely responsible for this is in itself highly inefficient: as erosion and nutrient leaching eat away the soil, production drops from an average one head per hectare—measly in any case—to a pitiful one head per five to seven hectares within five to ten years. A typical tropical cattle ranch employs only one person per 2,000 head, and meat production barely reaches 50 lbs./acre/year. In Northern Europe, in farms that do not use imported feed, it is over 500 lbs./acre/year.

This real-term inefficiency does not translate into bad business, however, for although there are some absentee landowners who engage in ranching for the prestige of it and are not particularly interested in turning large profits, others find bank loans for growing beef for export readily forthcoming, and get much help and encouragement from such organizations as the Pan American Health Organization, the Organization of American States, the U.S. Department of Agriculture, and U.S. AID, without whose technical assistance "cattle production in the American tropics would be unprofitable, if not impossible."[5] The ultimate big winner appears to be the United States, where increased imports of Central American beef are said to have done more to stem inflation than any other single government initiative.

15

---

[3] Myers, "End of the Line," p. 2.   [4] See James Nations and Daniel I. Komer, "Rainforests and the Hamburger Society," *Environment* 25, no. 3 (April 1983).   [5] Nations and Komer, "Rainforests and the Hamburger Society," p. 17.

"On the good land, which could support a large population, you have the rich cattle owners, and on the steep slopes, which should be left in forest, you have the poor farmers," says Gerardo Budowski, director of the Tropical Agricultural Research and Training Center in Turrialba, Costa Rica. "It is still good business to clear virgin forest in order to fatten cattle for, say, five to eight years and then abandon it."[6]

(Ironically, on a trip I made in 1981 to Morazán, a Salvadoran province largely under control of FMLN guerrillas, I inquired into the guerilla diet and discovered that beef, expropriated from the cattle ranches, was a popular staple.)

SWIFT-ARMOUR'S SWIFT ARMOR

The rain forest ecosystem, the oldest on Earth, is extremely complex and delicate. In spite of all the greenery one sees there, it is a myth that rain forest soil is rich. It is actually quite poor, leached of all nutrients save the most insoluble (such as iron oxides, which give lateritic soil—the most common soil type found there—its red color). Rather, the ecosystem of the rain forest is a "closed" one, in which the nutrients are to be found in the biomass, that is, in the living canopy of plants and in the thin layer of humus on the ground that is formed from the matter shed by the canopy. Hence the shallow-rootedness of most tropical forest plant species. Since the soil itself cannot replenish nutrients, nutrient recycling is what keeps the system going.

Now, what happens when the big cattle ranchers, under the auspices of the Swift-Armour Meat Packing Co., or United Brands, or the King Ranch, sling a huge chain between two enormous tractors, level a few tens of thousands of acres of tropical forest, burn the debris, fly a plane over to seed the ash with guinea grass, and then run their cattle on the newly created grasslands?[7]

For the first three years or so the grass grows like crazy, up to an inch a day, thriving on all that former biomass. After that, things go quickly downhill: the ash becomes eroded and leached, the soil becomes exposed and hardens to the consistency of brick, and the area becomes useless to agriculture. Nor does it ever regain anything near its former state. The Amazon is rising perceptibly as a result of the increased runoff due to deforestation.

Tractor-and-chain is only one way of clearing the land. Another common technique involves the use of herbicides such as Tordon, 2, 4-D, and 2,4,5-T (Agent Orange). The dioxin found in Agent Orange can be extremely toxic to animal life and is very persistent in the environment.

---

[6] Catherine Caufield, "The Rain Forests," *New Yorker* (January 14, 1985), p. 42. This excellent article was later incorporated in a book, *In the Rainforest* (New York: Knopf, 1985).   [7] Other multinationals with interests in meat packing and cattle ranching in tropical Latin America include Armour-Dial International, Goodyear Tire and Rubber Co., and Gulf and Western Industries, Inc. See Roger Burbach and Patricia Flynn, *Agribusiness in the Americas* (New York: Monthly Review Press, 1980).

Tordon, since it leaves a residue deadly to all broad-leaved plants, renders the deforested area poisonous to all plants except grasses; consequently, even if they wanted to, ranchers could not plant soil-enriching legumes in the treated areas, a step which many agronomists recommend for keeping the land productive for at least a little longer.

The scale of such operations is a far cry from the traditional slash-and-burn practiced by native jungle groups, which is done on a scale small enough so that the forest can successfully reclaim the farmed areas. Such groups, incidentally, are also being decimated by cattle interests in Brazil and Paraguay—as missionaries, human rights groups, and cattlemen themselves will attest.

Capital's "manifest destiny" has traditionally shown little concern for the lives   25
of trees or birds or Indians, or anything else which interferes with immediate profitability, but the current carving of holes in the gene pool by big agribusiness seems particularly short-sighted. Since the tropical forests contain two thirds of the world's genetic resources, their destruction will leave an enormous void in the pool of genes necessary for the creation of new agricultural hybrids. This is not to mention the many plants as yet undiscovered—there could be up to 15,000 unknown species in South America alone—which may in themselves contain remarkable properties. (In writing about alkaloids found in the Madagascar periwinkle which have recently revolutionized the treatment of leukemia and Hodgkin's disease, British biochemist John Humphreys said: "If this plant had not been analyzed, not even a chemist's wildest ravings would have hinted that such structures would be pharmacologically active."[8] Ninety percent of Madagascar's forests have been cut.)

But there is no small truth in Indonesian Minister for Environment and Development Emil Salim's complaint that the "South is asked to conserve genes while the other fellow, in the North, is consuming things that force us to destroy the genes in the South."[9]

WHERE'S THE BEEF?

The marketing of beef imported into the United States is extremely complex, and the beef itself ends up in everything from hot dogs to canned soup. Fresh meat is exported in refrigerated container ships to points of entry, where it is inspected by the U.S. Department of Agriculture. Once inspected, it is no longer required to be labeled "imported."[10] From there it goes into the hands of customhouse brokers and meat packers, often changing hands many times; and from there it goes to the fast-food chains or the food processors. The financial structures behind this empire are even more complex, involving governments and quasipublic agencies, such as the Export-Import Bank and the Overseas Private Investment Corporation, as well

---

[8] Quoted in Caulfield, "Rain Forests," p. 60.   [9] Caulfield, "Rain Forests," p. 100.   [10] This is one way McDonald's, for example, can claim not to use foreign beef. For a full treatment of McDonald's, see M. Boas and S. Chain, *Big Mac: The Unauthorized Story of McDonald's* (New York: New American Library, 1976).

as the World Bank and the Inter-American Development Bank, all of which encourage cattle raising in the forest lands. (Brazilian government incentives to cattle ranching in Amazonia include a 50 percent income-tax rebate on ranchers' investments elsewhere in Brazil, tax holidays of up to ten years, loans with negative interest rates in real terms, and exemptions from sales taxes and import duties. Although these incentives were deemed excessive and since 1979 no longer apply to new ranches, they still continue for existing ones. This cost the Brazilian government $63,000 for each ranching job created.)

Beef production in the tropics may be profitable for the few, but it is taking place at enormous cost for the majority and for the planet as a whole. Apart from the environmental destruction, it is a poor converter of energy to protein and provides few benefits for the vast majority of tropical peoples in terms of employment or food. What they require are labor-intensive, multiple-cropping systems.

The world is obviously hostage to an ethic which puts short-term profitability above all else, and such catastrophes as the wholesale destruction of the tropical forests and the continued impoverishment of their peoples are bound to occur as long as this ethic rules.

Questions for Discussion and Writing

1. How does Skinner organize his discussion to point up the unsuspected relationship between hamburgers and the destruction of tropical forests?

2. How does Skinner's discussion of the methods used by cattle ranchers to clear the land underscore his concern over a business ethic that "puts short-term profitability above all else"?

3. Did this article change your attitude toward the billions of hamburgers served in fast-food chains? Do you agree with any of Skinner's solutions? If so, which ones?

THOR HEYERDAHL

Thor Heyerdahl, the daring Norwegian explorer and anthropologist, was born in 1914, educated at the University of Oslo, and served with the Free Norwegian Military Forces (1940–1945). The sea-faring odysseys, which won him international renown, attempted to establish that the pre-Inca inhabitants of Peru could have originally sailed from Peru and settled in Polonesia. To prove this, Heyerdahl constructed a balsa raft and successfully navigated from Callao, Peru, to Tuamotu Island in the South Pacific. In later voyages, Heyerdahl sailed from Morocco in a papyrus boat, the Ra II, to the West Indies, and in 1977–1978 journeyed from Qurna, Iraq, to Djibouti, on the Gulf of Aden, in a boat made entirely of reeds. His fascinating adventures are recounted in On the Hunt for Paradise *(1938),* The Kon-Tiki Expedition *(1948),* Aku–Aku *(1958), and most recently,* The Maldive Mystery *(1986), a true-life archaeological detective story. His most recent books include* Pyramids of Tucume *(1995),* Green Was the Earth on the Seventh Day *(1997), and* In the Footsteps of Adam *(2000). In "How to Kill an Ocean," which originally appeared in* Saturday Review *(1975), Heyerdahl disputes the traditional concept of a "boundless ocean" and identifies current threats that could endanger the oceans of the world.*

How to Kill an Ocean

Since the ancient Greeks maintained that the earth was round and great navigators like Columbus and Magellan demonstrated that this assertion was true, no geographical discovery has been more important than what we all are beginning to understand today: that our planet has exceedingly restricted dimensions. There is a limit to all resources. Even the height of the atmosphere and the depth of soil and water represent layers so thin that they would disappear entirely if reduced to scale on the surface of a commonsized globe.

The correct concept of our very remarkable planet, rotating as a small and fertile oasis, two-thirds covered by life-giving water, and teeming with life in a solar system otherwise unfit for man, becomes clearer for us with the progress of moon travel and modern astronomy. Our concern about the limits to human expansion increases as science produces ever more exact data on the measurable resources that mankind has in stock for all the years to come.

Because of the population explosion, land of any nature has long been in such demand that nations have intruded upon each other's territory with armed forces in order to conquer more space for overcrowded communities. During the last few years, the United Nations has convened special meetings in Stockholm, Caracas, and Geneva in a dramatic attempt to create a "Law of the Sea" designed to divide vast sections of the global ocean space into national waters. The fact that no agreement has been reached illustrates that in our ever-shriveling world there is not even ocean space enough to satisfy everybody. And only one generation ago, the ocean was considered so vast that no one nation would bother to lay claim to more of it than the three-mile limit which represented the length of a gun shot from the shore.

It will probably take still another generation before mankind as a whole begins to realize fully that the ocean is but another big lake, landlocked on all sides. Indeed, it is essential to understand this concept for the survival of coming generations. For we of the 20th century still treat the ocean as the endless, bottomless pit it was considered to be in medieval times. Expressions like "the bottomless sea" and "the boundless ocean" are still in common use, and although we all know better, they reflect the mental image we still have of this, the largest body of water on earth. Perhaps one of the reasons why we subconsciously consider the ocean a sort of bottomless abyss is the fact that all the rain and all the rivers of the world keep pouring constantly into it and yet its water level always remains unchanged. Nothing affects the ocean, not even the Amazon, the Nile, or the Ganges. We know, of course, that this imperviousness is no indicator of size, because the sum total of all the rivers is nothing but the return to its own source of the water evaporated from the sea and carried ashore by drilling clouds.

What is it really then that distinguishes the ocean from the other more restricted bodies of water? Surely it is not its salt content. The Old and the New World have lakes with a higher salt percentage than the ocean has. The Aral Sea, the

5

Dead Sea, and the Great Salt Lake in Utah are good examples. Nor is it the fact that the ocean lacks any outlet. Other great bodies of water have abundant input and yet no outlet. The Caspian Sea and Lake Chad in Central Africa are valid examples. Big rivers, among them the Volga, enter the Caspian Sea, but evaporation compensates for its lack of outlet, precisely as is the case with the ocean. Nor is it correct to claim that the ocean is open while inland seas and lakes are landlocked. The ocean is just as landlocked as any lake. It is flanked by land on all sides and in every direction. The fact that the earth is round makes the ocean curve around it just as does solid land, but a shoreline encloses the ocean on all sides and in every direction. The ocean is not even the lowest body of water on our planet. The surface of the Caspian Sea, for instance, is 85 feet below sea level, and the surface of the Dead Sea is more than 1,200 feet below sea level.

Only when we fully perceive that there is no fundamental difference between the various bodies of water on our planet, beyond the fact that the ocean is the largest of all lakes, can we begin to realize that the ocean has something else in common with all other bodies of water: it is vulnerable. In the long run the ocean can be affected by the continued discharge of all modern man's toxic waste. One generation ago no one would have thought that the giant lakes of America could be polluted. Today they are, like the largest lakes of Europe. A few years ago the public was amazed to learn that industrial and urban refuse had killed the fish in Lake Erie. The enormous lake was dead. It was polluted from shore to shore in spite of the fact that it has a constant outlet through Niagara Falls, which carries pollutants away into the ocean in a never-ending flow. The ocean receiving all this pollution has no outlet but represents a dead end, because only pure water evaporates to return into the clouds. The ocean is big; yet if 10 Lake Eries were taken and placed end to end, they would span the entire Atlantic from Africa to South America. And the St. Lawrence River is by no means the only conveyor of pollutants into the ocean. Today hardly a creek or a river in the world reaches the ocean without carrying a constant flow of nondegradable chemicals from industrial, urban, or agricultural areas. Directly by sewers or indirectly by way of streams and other waterways, almost every big city in the world, whether coastal or inland, makes use of the ocean as mankind's common sink. We treat the ocean as if we believed that it is not part of our own planet—as if the blue waters curved into space somewhere beyond the horizon where our pollutants would fall off the edge, as ships were believed to do before the days of Christopher Columbus. We build sewers so far into the sea that we pipe the harmful refuse away from public beaches. Beyond that is no man's concern. What we consider too dangerous to be stored under technical control ashore we dump forever out of sight at sea, whether toxic chemicals or nuclear waste. Our only excuse is the still-surviving image of the ocean as a bottomless pit.

It is time to ask: is the ocean vulnerable? And if so, can many survive on a planet with a dead ocean? Both questions can be answered, and they are worthy of our attention.

First, the degree of vulnerability of any body of water would of course depend on two factors: the volume of the water and the nature of the pollutants. We know the volume of the ocean, its surface measure, and its average depth. We know that it covers 71 percent of the surface of our planet, and we are impressed, with good reason, when all these measurements are given in almost astronomical figures. If we resort to a more visual image, however, the dimensions lose their magic. The average depth of all oceans is only 1,700 meters. The Empire State Building is 448 meters high. If stretched out horizontally instead of vertically, the average ocean depth would only slightly exceed the 1,500 meters than an Olympic runner can cover by foot in 3 minutes and 35 seconds. The average depth of the North Sea, however, is not 1,700 meters, but only 80 meters, and many of the buildings in downtown New York would emerge high above water level if they were built on the bottom of this sea. During the Stone Age most of the North Sea was dry land where roaming archers hunted deer and other game. In this shallow water, until only recently, all the industrial nations of Western Europe have conducted year-round routine dumping of hundreds of thousands of tons of their most toxic industrial refuse. All the world's sewers and most of its waste are dumped into waters as shallow as, or shallower than, the North Sea. An attempt was made at a recent ocean exhibition to illustrate graphically and in correct proportion the depths of the Atlantic, the Pacific, and the Indian oceans in relation to a cross section of the planet earth. The project had to be abandoned, for although the earth was painted with a diameter twice the height of a man, the depths of the world oceans painted in proportion became so insignificant that they could not be seen except as a very thin pencil line.

The ocean is in fact remarkably shallow for its size. Russia's Lake Baikal, for instance, less than 31 kilometers wide, is 1,500 meters deep, which compares well with the average depth of all oceans. It is the vast *extent* of ocean surface that has made man of all generations imagine a correspondingly unfathomable depth.

When viewed in full, from great heights, the ocean's surface is seen to have definite, confining limits. But at sea level, the ocean seems to extend outward indefinitely, to the horizon and on into blue space. The astronauts have come back from space literally disturbed upon seeing a full view of our planet. They have seen at first hand how cramped together the nations are in a limited space and how the "endless" oceans are tightly enclosed within cramped quarters by surrounding land masses. But one need not be an astronaut to lose the sensation of a boundless ocean. It is enough to embark on some floating logs tied together, as we did with the *Kon-Tiki* in the Pacific, or on some bundles of papyrus reeds, as we did with the *Ra* in the Atlantic. With no effort and no motor we were pushed by the winds and currents from one continent to another in a few weeks.

After we abandon the outworn image of infinite space in the ocean, we are still left with many wrong or useless notions about biological life and vulnerability. Marine life is concentrated in about 4 percent of the ocean's total body of water, whereas roughly 96 percent is just about as poor in life as is a desert ashore. We all know, and should bear in mind, that sunlight is needed to permit photosynthesis for the marine plankton on which all fishes and whales directly or indirectly base their subsistence. In the sunny tropics the upper layer of light used in photosynthesis extends down to a maximum depth of 80 to 100 meters. In the northern latitudes, even on a bright summer's day, this zone reaches no more than 15 to 20 meters below the surface. Because much of the most toxic pollutants are buoyant and stay on the surface (notably all the pesticides and other poisons based on chlorinated hydrocarbons), this concentration of both life and venom in the same restricted body of water is most unfortunate.

What is worse is the fact that life is not evenly distributed throughout this thin surface layer. Ninety percent of all marine species are concentrated above the continental shelves next to land. The water above these littoral shelves represents an area of only 8 percent of the total ocean surface, which itself represents only 4 percent of the total body of water, and means that much less than half a percent of the ocean space represents the home of 90 percent of all marine life. This concentration of marine life in shallow waters next to the coasts happens to coincide with the area of concentrated dumping and the outlet of all sewers and polluted river mouths, not to mention silt from chemically treated farmland. The bulk of some 20,000 known species of fish, some 30,000 species of mollusks, and nearly all the main crustaceans lives in the most exposed waters around the littoral areas. As we know, the reason is that this is the most fertile breeding ground for marine plankton. The marine plant life, the phytoplankton, find here their mineral nutriments, which are brought down by rivers and silt and up from the ocean bottom through coastal upwellings that bring back to the surface the remains of decomposed organisms which have sunk to the bottom through the ages. When we speak of farmable land in any country, we do not include deserts or sterile rock in our calculations. Why then shall we decive ourselves by the total size of the ocean when we know that not even 1 percent of its water volume is fertile for the fisherman?

Much as been written for or against the activities of some nations that have dumped vast quantities of nuclear waste and obsolete war gases in the sea and excused their actions on the grounds that it was all sealed in special containers. In such shallow waters as the Irish Sea, the English Channel, and the North Sea there are already enough examples of similar "foolproof" containers moving about with bottom currents until they are totally displaced and even crack open with the result that millions of fish are killed or mutilated. In the Baltic Sea, which is shallower than many lakes and which—except for the thin surface layer—has already been killed by pollution, 7,000 tons of arsenic were dumped in cement containers some 40 years ago. These containers have now started to leak. Their combined contents are three times more than is needed to kill the entire population of the earth today.

Fortunately, in certain regions modern laws have impeded the danger of dumpings; yet a major threat to marine life remains—the less spectacular but more effective ocean pollution through continuous discharge from sewers and seepage. Except in the Arctic, there is today hardly a creek or a river in the world from which it is safe to drink at the outlet. The more technically advanced the country, the more devastating the threat to the ocean. A few examples picked at random will illustrate the pollution input from the civilized world:

French rivers carry 18 billion cubic meters of liquid pollution annually into the sea. The city of Paris alone discharges almost 1.2 million cubic meters of untreated effluent into the Seine every day.

The volume of liquid waste from the Federal Republic of Germany is estimated at over 9 billion cubic meters per year, or 25.4 million cubic meters per day,

15

not counting cooling water, which daily amounts to 33.6 million cubic meters. Into the Rhine alone 50,000 tons of waste are discharged daily, including 30,000 tons of sodium chloride from industrial plants.

A report from the U.N. Economic and Social Council, issued prior to the Stockholm Conference on the Law of the Sea four years ago, states that the world had then dumped an estimated billion pounds of DDT into our environment and was adding an estimated 100 million more pounds per year. The total world production of pesticides was estimated at more than 1.3 billion pounds annually, and the United States alone exports more than 400 million pounds per year. Most of this ultimately finds its way into the ocean with winds, rain, or silt from land. A certain type of DDT sprayed on crops in East Africa a few years ago was found and identified a few months later in the Bay of Bengal, a good 4,000 miles away.

The misconception of a boundless ocean makes the man in the street more concerned about city smog than about the risk of killing the ocean. Yet the tallest chimney in the world does not suffice to send the noxious smoke away into space; it gradually sinks down, and nearly all descends, mixed with rain, snow, and silt, into the ocean. Industrial and urban areas are expanding with the population explosion all over the world, and in the United States alone, waste products in the form of smoke and noxious fumes amount to it total of 390,000 tons of pollutants every day, or 142 million tons every year.

With this immense concentration of toxic matter, life on the continental shelves would in all likelihood have been exterminated or at least severely decimated long since if the ocean had been immobile. The cause for the delayed action, which may benefit man for a few decades but will aggravate the situation for coming generations, is the well-known fact that the ocean rotates like boiling water in a kettle. It churns from east to west, from north to south, from the bottom to the surface, and down again, in perpetual motion. At a U.N. meeting one of the developing countries proposed that if ocean dumping were prohibited by global or regional law, they would offer friendly nations the opportunity of dumping in their own national waters—for a fee, of course!

It cannot be stressed too often, however, that it is nothing but a complete illusion when we speak of national waters. We can map and lay claim to the ocean bottom, but not to the mobile sea above it. The water itself is in constant transit. What is considered to be the national waters of Morocco one day turns up as the national waters of Mexico soon after. Meanwhile Mexican national water is soon on its way across the North Atlantic to Norway. Ocean pollution abides by no law.

My own transoceanic drifts with the *Kon-Tiki* raft and the reed vessels *Ra I* and *II* were eye-openers to me and my companions as to the rapidity with which so-called national waters displace themselves. The distance from Peru to the Tuamotu Islands in Polynesia is 4,000 miles when it is measured on a map. Yet the *Kon-Tiki* raft had only crossed about 1,000 miles of ocean surface when we arrived. The other 3,000 miles had been granted us by the rapid flow of the current during the 101 days our crossing lasted. But the same raft voyages taught us another and less pleasant lesson: it is possible to pollute the oceans, and it is already being done. In 1947, when the balsa raft *Kon-Tiki* crossed the Pacific, we towed a plankton

20

net behind. Yet we did not collect specimens or even see any sign of human activity in the crystal-clear water until we spotted the wreck of an old sailing ship on the reef where we landed. In 1969 it was therefore a blow to us on board the papyrus raftship *Ra* to observe, shortly after our departure from Morocco, that we had sailed into an area filled with ugly clumps of hard asphalt-like material, brownish to pitch black in color, which were floating at close intervals on or just below the water's surface. Later on, we sailed into other areas so heavily polluted with similar clumps that we were reluctant to dip up water with our buckets when we needed a good scrub-down at the end of the day. In between these areas the ocean was clean except for occasional floating oil lumps and other widely scattered refuse such as plastic containers, empty bottles, and cans. Because the ropes holding the papyrus reeds of *Ra I* together burst, the battered wreck was abandoned in polluted waters short of the island of Barbados, and a second crossing was effectuated all the way from Safi in Morocco to Barbados in the West Indies in 1970. This time a systematic day-by-day survey of ocean pollution was carried out, and samples of oil lumps collected were sent to the United Nations together with a detailed report on the observations. This was published by Secretary-General U Thant as an annex to his report to the Stockholm Conference on the Law of the Sea. It is enough here to repeat that sporadic oil clots drifted by within reach of our dip net during 43 out of the 57 days our transatlantic crossing lasted. The laboratory analysis of the various samples of oil clots collected showed a wide range in the level of nickel and vanadium content, revealing that they originated from different geographical localities. This again proves that they represent not the homogeneous spill from a leaking oil drill or from a wrecked super-tanker, but the steadily accumulating waste from the daily routine washing of sludge from the combined world fleet of tankers.

The world was upset when the *Torrey Canyon's* unintentionally spilled 100,000 tons of oil into the English Channel some years ago; yet this is only a small fraction of the intentional discharge of crude oil sludge through less spectacular, routine tank cleaning. Every year more than *Torrey Canyon's* spill of a 100,000 tons of oil is intentionally pumped into the Mediterranean alone, and a survey of the sea south of Italy yielded 500 liters of solidified oil for every square kilometer of surface. Both the Americans and the Russians were alarmed by our observations of Atlantic pollution in 1970 and sent out specially equipped oceanographic research vessels to the area. American scientists from Harvard University working with the Bermuda Biological Station for Research found more solidified oil than seaweed per surface unit in the Sargasso Sea and had to give up their plankton catch because their nets were completely plugged up by oil sludge. They estimated, however, a floating stock of 86,000 metric tons of tar in the Northwest Atlantic alone. The Russians, in a report read by the representative of the Soviet Academy of Sciences at a recent pollution conference in Prague, found that pollution in the coastal areas of the Atlantic had already surpassed their tentative limit for what had been considered tolerable, and that a new scale of tolerability would have to be postulated.

The problem of oil pollution is in itself a complex one. Various types of crude oil are toxic in different degrees. But they all have one property in common: they attract other chemicals and absorb them like blotting paper, notably the various kinds of pesticides. DDT and other chlorinated hydrocarbons do not dissolve in water, nor do they sink: just as they are absorbed by plankton and other surface organisms, so are they drawn into oil slicks and oil clots, where in some cases they have been rediscovered in stronger concentrations than when originally mixed with dissolvents in the spraying bottles. Oil clots, used as floating support for barnacles, marine worms, and pelagic crabs, were often seen by us from the *Ra*, and these riders are attractive bait for filter-feeding fish and whales, which cannot avoid getting gills and baleens cluttered up by the tarlike oil. Even sharks with their rows of teeth plastered with black oil clots are now reported from the Caribbean Sea. Yet the oil spills and dumping of waste from ships represent a very modest contribution compared with the urban and industrial refuse released from land.

That the ocean, given time, will cope with it all, is a common expression of wishful thinking. The ocean has always been a self-purifying filter that has taken care of all global pollution for millions of years. Man is not the first polluter. Since the morning of time nature itself has been a giant workshop, experimenting, inventing, decomposing, and throwing away waste: the incalculable billions of tons of rotting forest products, decomposing flesh, mud, silt, and excrement. If this waste had not been recycled, the ocean would long since have become a compact soup after millions of years of death and decay, volcanic eruptions, and global erosion. Man is not the first large-scale producer, so why should he become the first disastrous polluter?

Man has imitated nature by manipulating atoms, taking them apart and   25
grouping them together in different compositions. Nature turned fish into birds and beasts into man. It found a way to make fruits out of soil and sunshine. It invented radar for bats and whales, and shortwave transceivers for beetles and butterflies. Jet propulsion was installed on squids, and unsurpassed computers were made as brains, for mankind. Marine bacteria and plankton transformed the dead generations into new life. The life cycle of spaceship earth is the closest one can ever get to the greatest of all inventions, *perpetuum mobile*—the perpetual-motion machine. And the secret is that nothing was composed by nature that could not be recomposed, recycled, and brought back into service again in another form as another useful wheel in the smoothly running global machinery.

This is where man has sidetracked nature. We put atoms together into molecules of types nature had carefully avoided. We invent to our delight immediately useful materials like plastics, pesticides, detergents, and other chemical products hitherto unavailable on planet earth. We rejoice because we can get our laundry whiter than the snow we pollute and because we can exterminate every trace of insect life. We spray bugs and bees, worms and butterflies. We wash and flush the detergents down the drain out to the oysters and fish. Most of our new chemical products are not only toxic: they are in fact created to sterilize and kill. And they keep on displaying these same inherent abilities wherever they end up. Through sewers and seepage they all head for the ocean, where they remain to accumulate as undesired nuts and bolts in between the cogwheels of a so far smoothly running machine. If it had not been for the present generation, man could have gone on polluting the ocean forever with the degradable waste he produced. But with ever-increasing speed and intensity we now produce and discharge into the sea hundreds of thousands of chemicals and other products. They do not evaporate nor do they recycle, but they grow in numbers and quantity and threaten all marine life.

We have long known that our modern pesticides have begun to enter the flesh of penguins in the Antarctic and the brains of polar bears and the blubber of whales in the Arctic, all subsisting on plankton and plankton-eating crustaceans and fish in areas far from cities and farmland. We all know that marine pollution has reached global extent in a few decades. We also know that very little or nothing is being done to stop it. Yet there are persons who tell us that there is no reason to worry, that the ocean is so big and surely science must have everything under control. City smog is being fought through intelligent legislation. Certain lakes and rivers have been improved by leading the sewers down to the sea. But where, may we ask, is the global problem of ocean pollution under control?

No breathing species could live on this planet until the surface layer of the ocean was filled with phytoplankton, as our planet in the beginning was only surrounded by sterile gases. These minute plant species manufactured so much oxygen that it rose above the surface to help form the atmosphere we have today. All life on earth depended upon this marine plankton for its evolution and continued subsistence. Today, more than ever before, mankind depends on the welfare of this marine plankton for his future survival as a species. With the population explosion we need to harvest even more protein from the sea. Without plankton there will be no fish. With our rapid expansion of urban and industrial areas and the continuous disappearance of jungle and forest, we shall be ever more dependent on the plankton for the very air we breathe. Neither man nor any other terrestrial beast could have bred had plankton not preceded them. Take away this indispensable life in the shallow surface areas of the sea, and life ashore will be unfit for coming generations. A dead ocean means a dead planet.

Questions for Discussion and Writing

1. To what types of pollution is the ocean most vulnerable? In what respects is the popular conception of the ocean erroneous, according to Heyerdahl?
2. How does Heyerdahl use statistics and a hypothetical scenario to dramatize the ocean's vulnerability?
3. Research Heyerdahl's experiences on the *Kon Tiki* and the *Ra*. To what extent do these accounts add credibility to his analysis?

LINDA HOGAN

Linda Hogan, Chickasaw poet, novelist, and essayist, was born in 1947 in Denver, Colorado, and grew up in Oklahoma. She taught American Indian Studies at the University of Minnesota from 1984 to 1991 and is currently professor of American Studies and American Indian Studies at the University of Colorado. Her poetry has been collected in Seeing through the Sun

(1985), which received an American Book Award from the Before Columbus Foundation; The Book of Medicines *(1993); and* Solar Storms *(1996). She has also published short stories, one of which, "Aunt Moon's Young Man," was featured in* Best American Short Stories *(1989). Her novel* Mean Spirit *was nominated for a Pulitzer Prize (1990). Hogan's latest work is* The Woman Who Watches Over the World: A Native Memoir *(2001). In "Waking Up the Rake," reprinted from* Parabola, the Magazine of Myth and Tradition *(Summer 1988), Hogan reveals how even the simplest act of compassion for animals can yield unexpected spiritual rewards.*

Waking Up the Rake

In the still dark mornings, my grandmother would rise up from her bed and put wood in the stove. When the fire began to burn, she would sit in front of its warmth and let down her hair. It had never been cut and it knotted down in two long braids. When I was fortunate enough to be there, in those red Oklahoma mornings, I would wake up with her, stand behind her chair, and pull the brush through the long strands of her hair. It cascaded down her back, down over the chair, and touched the floor.

We were the old and the new, bound together in front of the snapping fire, woven like a lifetime's tangled growth of hair. I saw my future in her body and face, and her past was alive in me. We were morning people, and in all of earth's mornings the new intertwines with the old. Even new, a day itself is ancient, old with earth's habit of turning over and over again.

Years later, I was sick, and I went to a traditional healer. The healer was dark and thin and radiant. The first night I was there, she also lit a fire. We sat before it, smelling the juniper smoke. She asked me to tell her everything, my life spoken in words, a case history of living, with its dreams and losses, the scars and wounds we all bear from being in the world. She smoked me with cedar smoke, wrapped a sheet around me, and put me to bed, gently, like a mother caring for her child.

The next morning she nudged me awake and took me outside to pray. We faced east where the sun was beginning its journey on our side of earth.

The following morning in red dawn, we went outside and prayed. The sun was a full orange eye rising up the air. The morning after that we did the same, and on Sunday we did likewise.   5

The next time I visited her it was a year later, and again we went through the same prayers, standing outside facing the early sun. On the last morning I was there, she left for her job in town. Before leaving, she said, "Our work is our altar."

Those words have remained with me.

Now I am a disciple of birds. The birds that I mean are eagles, owls, and hawks. I clean cages at the Birds of Prey Rehabilitation Foundation. It is the work I wanted to do, in order to spend time inside the gentle presence of the birds.

There is a Sufi saying that goes something like this: "Yes, worship God, go to church, sing praises, but first tie your camel to the post." This cleaning is the work of tying the camel to a post.

I pick up the carcasses and skin of rats, mice, and of rabbits. Some of them have   10
been turned inside out by the sharp-beaked eaters, so that the leathery flesh becomes a delicately veined coat for the inner fur. It is a boneyard. I rake the smooth
fragments of bones. Sometimes there is a leg or shank of deer to be picked up.

In this boneyard, the still-red vertebrae lie on the ground beside an open rib
cage. The remains of a rabbit, a small intestinal casing, holds excrement like beads in a
necklace. And there are the clean, oval pellets the birds spit out, filled with fur, bone
fragments and now and then, a delicate sharp claw that looks as if it were woven inside. A feather, light and soft, floats down a current of air, and it is also picked up.

Over time, the narrow human perspective from which we view things ex-
pands. A deer carcass begins to look beautiful and rich in its torn redness, the muscle and bone exposed in the shape life took on for a while as it walked through
meadows and drank at creeks.

And the bone fragments have their own stark beauty, the clean white jaw
bones with ivory teeth small as the head of a pin still in them. I think of medieval
physicians trying to learn about our private, hidden bodies by cutting open the
stolen dead and finding the splendor inside, the grace of every red organ, and the
smooth, gleaming bone.

This work is an apprenticeship, and the birds are the teachers. Sweet-eyed
barn owls, such taskmasters, asking us to be still and slow and to move in time with
their rhythms, not our own. The short-eared owls with their startling yellow eyes
require the full presence of a human. The marsh hawks, behind their branches,
watch our every move.

There is a silence needed here before a person enters the bordered world the   15
birds inhabit, so we stop and compose ourselves before entering their doors, and
we listen to the musical calls of the eagles, the sound of wings in air, the way their
feet with sharp claws, many larger than our own hands, grab hold of a perch. Then
we know we are ready to enter, and they are ready for us.

The most difficult task the birds demand is that we learn to be equal to them,
to feel our way into an intelligence that is different from our own. A friend, awed at
the thought of working with eagles, said, "Imagine knowing an eagle." I answered
her honestly, "It isn't so much that we know the eagles. It's that they know us."

And they know that we are apart from them, that as humans we have somehow fallen from our animal grace, and because of that we maintain a distance from
them, though it is not always a distance of heart. The places we inhabit, even sharing a common earth, must remain distinct and separate. It was our presence that
brought most of them here in the first place, nearly all of them injured in a clash
with the human world. They have been shot, or hit by cars, trapped in leg hold
traps, poisoned, ensnared in wire fences. To ensure their survival, they must remember us as the enemies that we are. We are the embodiment of a paradox; we are the
wounders and we are the healers.

There are human lessons to be learned here, in the work. Fritjof Capra wrote:
"Doing work that has to be done over and over again helps us to recognize the

natural cycles of growth and decay, of birth and death, and thus become aware of the dynamic order of the universe." And it is true, in whatever we do, the brushing of hair, the cleaning of cages, we begin to see the larger order of things. In this place, there is a constant coming to terms with both the sacred place life occupies, and with death. Like one of those early physicians who discovered the strange, inner secrets of our human bodies, I'm filled with awe at the very presence of life, not just the birds, but a horse contained in its living fur, a dog alive and running. What a marvel it is, the fine shape life takes in all of us. It is equally marvelous that life is quickly turned back to the earth-colored ants and the soft white maggots that are time's best and closest companions. To sit with the eagles and their flutelike songs, listening to the longer flute of wind sweep through the lush grasslands, is to begin to know the natural laws that exist apart from our own written ones.

One of those laws, that we carry deep inside us, is intuition. It is lodged in a place even the grave-robbing doctors could not discover. It's a blood-written code that directs us through life. The founder of this healing center, Sigrid Ueblacker, depends on this inner knowing. She watches, listens, and feels her way to an understanding of each eagle and owl. This vision, as I call it, directs her own daily work at healing the injured birds and returning them to the wild.

"Sweep the snow away," she tells me. "The Swainson's hawks should be in Argentina this time of year and should not have to stand in the snow." 20

I sweep.

And that is in the winter when the hands ache from the cold, and the water freezes solid and has to be broken out for the birds, fresh buckets carried over icy earth from the well. In summer, it's another story. After only a few hours the food begins to move again, as if resurrected to life. A rabbit shifts a bit. A mouse turns. You could say that they have been resurrected, only with a life other than the one that left them. The moving skin swarms with flies and their offspring, ants, and a few wasps, busy at their own daily labor.

Even aside from the expected rewards for this work, such as seeing an eagle healed and winging across the sky it fell from, there are others. An occasional snake, beautiful and sleek, finds its way into the cage one day, eats a mouse and is too fat to leave, so we watch its long muscular life stretched out in the tall grasses. Or, another summer day, taking branches to be burned with a pile of wood near the little creek, a large turtle with a dark and shining shell slips soundlessly into the water, its presence a reminder of all the lives beyond these that occupy us.

One green morning, an orphaned owl perches nervously above me while I clean. Its downy feathers are roughed out. It appears to be twice its size as it clacks its beak at me, warning me: stay back. Then, fearing me the way we want it to, it bolts off the perch and flies, landing by accident onto the wooden end of my rake, before it sees that a human is an extension of the tool, and it flies again to a safer place, while I return to raking.

The word "rake" means to gather or heap up, to smooth the broken ground. 25 And that's what this work is, all of it, the smoothing over of broken ground, the healing of the severed trust we humans hold with earth. We gather it back together again with great care, take the broken pieces and fragments and return them to the sky. It is work at the borderland between species, at the boundary between injury and healing.

There is an art to raking, a very fine art, one with rhythm in it, and life. On the days I do it well, the rake wakes up. Wood that came from dark dense forests seems to return to life. The water that rose up through the rings of that wood, the minerals of earth mined upward by the burrowing tree roots, all come alive. My own fragile hand touches the wood, a hand full of my own life, including that which rose each morning early to watch the sun return from the other side of the planet. Over time, these hands will smooth the rake's wooden handle down to a sheen.

Raking. It is a labor round and complete, smooth and new as an egg, and the rounding seasons of the world revolving in time and space. All things, even our own heartbeats and sweat, are in it, part of it. And that work, that watching the turning over of life, becomes a road into what is essential. Work is the country of hands, and they want to live there in the dailiness of it, the repetition that is time's language of prayer, a common, tongue. Everything is there, in that language, in the humblest of labor. The rake wakes up and the healing is in it. The shadows of leaves that once fell beneath the tree the handle came from are in that labor, and the rabbits that passed this way, on the altar of our work. And when the rake wakes up, all earth's gods are reborn and they dance and sing in the dusty air around us.

Questions for Discussion and Writing

1. How did Hogan's recovery from an illness lead her to devote so much time to the care of injured birds of prey?
2. What special significance does the title convey, and how does it summarize what Hogan has learned from her experiences at the shelter?
3. Would you ever volunteer your time to take care of sick or injured animals as Hogan did? Would you consider this a worthwhile activity? Why or why not?

P. J. O'ROURKE

P. J. O'Rourke (b. 1947) has been the editor-in-chief at the National Lampoon *and has written numerous works, including* Eat the Rich *(1998). The following essay first appeared in* Rolling Stone *(June 1990).*

The Greenhouse Affect

If the great outdoors is so swell, how come the homeless aren't more fond of it?

There. I wanted to be the one to say a discouraging word about Earth Day—a lone voice *not* crying in the wilderness, thank you, but hollering in the rec room.

On April 22 [1990]—while everybody else was engaged in a great, smarmy fit of agreeing with himself about chlorofluorocarbons, while *tout le* rapidly-losing-plant-and-animal-species *monde* traded hugs of unanimity over plastic-milk-bottle recycling, while all of you praised one another to the ozone-depleted skies for your brave opposition to coastal flooding and every man Jack and woman Jill told child Jason how bad it is to put crude oil on baby seals—I was home in front of the VCR snacking high on the food chain.

But can any decent, caring resident of this planet possibly disagree with the goals and aspirations embodied in the celebration of Earth Day? No.

That's what bothers me. Mass movements are always a worry. There's a whiff 5 of the lynch mob or the lemming migration about any overlarge gathering of like-thinking individuals, no matter how virtuous their cause. Even a band of angels can turn ugly and start looting if enough angels are hanging around unemployed and convinced that succubi own all the liquor stores in heaven.

Whenever I'm in the middle of conformity, surrounded by oneness of mind, with people oozing concurrence on every side, I get scared. And when I find myself agreeing with everybody, I get really scared.

Sometimes it's worse when everybody's right than when everybody's wrong. Everybody in fifteenth-century Spain was wrong about where China is, and as a result, Columbus discovered Caribbean vacations. On the other hand, everybody in fifteenth-century Spain was right about heresies: They're heretical. But that didn't make the Spanish Inquisition more fun for the people who were burned at the stake.

A mass movement that's correct is especially dangerous when it's right about a problem that needs fixing. Then all those masses in the mass movement have to be called to action, and that call to action better be exciting, or the masses will lose interest and wander off to play arcade games. What's exciting? Monitoring the release into the atmosphere of glycol ethers used in the manufacture of brake-fluid anti-icing additives? No. But what about some violence, an enemy, someone to hate?

Mass movements need what Eric Hoffer—in *The True Believer,* his book about the kind of creepy misfits who join mass movements—calls a "unifying agent."

"Hatred is the most accessible and comprehensive of all unifying agents," 10 writes Hoffer. "Mass movements can rise and spread without belief in a God, but never without belief in a devil." Hoffer goes on to cite historian F. A. Voigt's account of a Japanese mission sent to Berlin in 1932 to study the National Socialist movement. Voigt asked a member of the mission what he thought. He replied, "It is magnificent. I wish we could have something like it in Japan, only we can't, because we haven't got any Jews."

The environmental movement has, I'm afraid, discovered a unifying agent. I almost said "scapegoat," but scapegoats are probably an endangered species. Besides, all animals are innocent, noble, upright, honest and fair in their dealings and have a great sense of humor. Anyway, the environmental movement has found its necessary enemy in the form of that ubiquitous evil—already so familiar to Hollywood scriptwriters, pulp-paperback authors, minority spokespersons, feminists, members of ACT UP, the Christic Institute and Democratic candidates for president: Big Business.

Now, you might think Big Business would be hard to define in this day of leveraged finances and interlocking technologies. Not so. Big Business is every kind of business except the kind from which the person who's complaining draws his pay. Thus the rock-around-the-rain-forest crowd imagines record companies are a cottage industry. The Sheen family considers movie conglomerates to be a part of the arts and crafts movement. And Ralph Nader thinks the wholesale lobbying of Congress by huge tax-exempt, public-interest advocacy groups is akin to working the family farm.

This is why it's rarely an identifiable person (and, of course, never you or me) who pollutes. It's a vague, sinister, faceless thing called industry. The National Wildlife Federation's booklet on toxic-chemical releases says, "Industry dumped more than 2.3 billion pounds of toxic chemicals into or onto the land." What will "industry" do next? Visit us with a plague of boils? Make off with our firstborn? Or maybe it will wreck the Barcalounger. "Once-durable products like furniture are made to fall apart quickly, requiring more frequent replacement," claims the press kit of Inform, a New York-based environmental group that seems to be missing a few sunflower seeds from its trail mix. But even a respectable old establishmentarian organization like the Sierra Club is not above giving a villainous and conspiratorial cast to those who disagree with its legislative agenda. "For the past eight years, this country's major polluters and their friends in the Reagan administration and Congress have impeded the progress of bills introduced by congressional Clean Air advocates," says the Sierra Club's 1989–90 conservation campaign press package. And here at *Rolling Stone*— where we are so opposed to the profit motive that we work for free, refuse to accept advertising and give the magazine away at newsstands—writer Trip Gabriel, in his *Rolling Stone* 571 article "Coming Back to Earth: A Look at Earth Day 1990," avers, "The yuppie belief in the sanctity of material possessions, no matter what the cost in resource depletion, squared perfectly with the philosophy of the Reaganites—to exploit the nation's natural resources for the sake of business."

Sure, "business" and "industry" and "their friends in the Reagan administration and Congress" make swell targets. Nobody squirts sulfur dioxide into the air as a hobby or tosses PCBs [polychlorinated biphenyls] into rivers as an act of charity. Pollution occurs in the course of human enterprise. It is a by-product of people making things like a living, including yours. If we desire, for ourselves and our progeny, a world that's not too stinky and carcinogenic, we're going to need the technical expertise, entrepreneurial vigor and marketing genius of every business and industry. And if you think pollution is the fault only of Reaganite yuppies wallowing in capitalist greed, then go take a deep breath in Smolensk or a long drink from the river Volga.

Sorry, but business and industry—trade and manufacturing—are inherent to civilization. Every human society, no matter how wholesomely primitive, practices as much trade and manufacturing as it can figure out. It is the fruits of trade and   15 manufacturing that raise us from the wearying muck of subsistence and give us the health, wealth, education, leisure and warm, dry rooms with Xerox machines—all of which allow us to be the ecology-conscious, selfless, splendid individuals we are.

Our ancestors were too busy wresting a living from nature to go on any nature hikes. The first European ever known to have climbed a mountain for the view was the poet Petrarch. That wasn't until the fourteenth century. And when Petrarch got to the top of Mont Ventoux, he opened a copy of Saint Augustine's *Confessions* and was shamed by the passage about men "who go to admire the high mountains and the immensity of the oceans and the course of the heaven and neglect themselves." Worship of nature may be ancient, but seeing nature as cuddlesome, hug-a-bear and too cute for words is strictly a modern fashion.

The Luddite side of the environmental movement would have us destroy or eschew technology—throw down the ladder by which we climbed. Well, nuts (and berries and fiber) to you, you shrub huggers. It's time we in the industrialized nations admitted what safe, comfortable and fun-filled lives we lead. If we don't, we will cause irreparable harm to the disadvantaged peoples of the world. They're going to laugh themselves to death listening to us whine.

Contempt for material progress is not only funny but unfair. The average Juan, Chang or Mobutu out there in the parts of the world where every day is Earth Day—or Dirt and Squalor Day anyhow—would like to have a color television too. He'd also like some comfy Reeboks, a Nintendo Power Glove and a Jeep Cherokee. And he means to get them. I wouldn't care to be the skinny health-food nut waving a copy of *50 Simple Things You Can Do to Save the Earth* who tries to stand in his way.

There was something else keeping me indoors on April 22 [1990]. Certain eco-doomsters are not only unreasonable in their attitude toward business, they're unreasonable in their attitude toward reason. I can understand harboring mistrust of technology. I myself wouldn't be inclined to wash my dog in toluene or picnic in the nude at Bhopal.[1] But to deny the validity of the scientific method is to resign your position as a sentient being. You'd better go look for work as a lungwort plant or an Eastern European Communist-party chairman.

For example, here we have the environmental movement screeching like New Kids on the Block fans because President Bush asked for a bit more scientific research on global warming before we cork everybody's Honda, ban the use of underarm deodorants and replace all the coal fuel in our electrical-generating plants with windmills. The greenhouse effect is a complex hypothesis. You can hate George Bush as much as you like and the thing won't get simpler. "The most dire predictions about global warming are being toned down by many experts," said a

20

---

[1] *Bhopal:* reference to catastrophe in Bhopal, India, in 1984, when the release of pesticides from a chemical plant killed 2,000 people and injured tens of thousands.

Washington Post story last January [1990]. And that same month the *New York Times* told me a new ice age was only a couple of thousand years away.

On the original Earth Day, in 1970—when the world was going to end from overcrowding instead of overheating—the best-selling author of *The Population Bomb,* Dr. Paul Ehrlich, was making dire predictions as fast as his earnestly frowning mouth could move. Dr. Ehrlich predicted that America would have water rationing by 1974 and food rationing by 1980; that hepatitis and dysentery rates in the United States would increase by 500 percent due to population density; and that the oceans could be as dead as Lake Erie by 1979. Today Lake Erie is doing better than Perrier, and Dr. Ehrlich is still pounding sand down a rat hole.

Now, don't get me wrong: Even registered Republicans believe ecological problems are real. Real solutions, however, will not be found through pop hysteria or the merchandising of panic. Genuine hard-got knowledge is required. The collegiate idealists who stuff the ranks of the environmental movement seem willing to do absolutely anything to save the biosphere except take science courses and learn something about it. In 1971, American universities awarded 4,390 doctorates in the physical sciences. After fifteen years of youthful fretting over the planet's future, the number was 3,551.

It wouldn't even be all that expensive to make the world clean and prosperous. According to the September 1989 issue of *Scientific American,* which was devoted to scholarly articles about ecological issues, the cost of achieving sustainable and environmentally healthy worldwide economic development by the year 2000 would be about $729 billion. That's roughly fourteen dollars per person per year for ten years. To translate that into sandal-and-candle terms, $729 billion is less than three-quarters of what the world spends annually on armaments.

The Earth can be saved, but not by legislative fiat. Expecting President Bush to cure global warming by sending a bill to Congress is to subscribe to that eternal fantasy of totalitarians and Democrats from Massachusetts: a law against bad weather.

Sometimes I wonder if the fans of eco-Armageddon even want the world's problems to get better. Improved methods of toxic-chemical incineration, stack scrubbers for fossil fuel power plants, and sensible solid-waste management schemes lack melodramatic appeal. There's nothing apocalyptic about gasohol. And it's hard to picture a Byronic hero sorting his beer bottles by color at the recycling center. The beliefs of some environmentalists seem to have little to do with the welfare of the globe or of its inhabitants and a lot to do with the parlor primitivism of the Romantic Movement.

There is this horrible idea, beginning with Jean Jacques Rousseau and still going strong in college classrooms, that natural man is naturally good. All we have to do is strip away the neuroses, repressions and Dial soap of modern society, and mankind will return to an Edenic state. Anybody who's ever met a toddler knows this is soy-protein baloney. Neolithic man was not a guy who always left his campsite cleaner than he found it. Ancient humans trashed half the map with indiscriminate use of fire for slash-and-burn agriculture and hunting drives. They caused

25

desertification through overgrazing and firewood cutting in North Africa, the Middle East and China. And they were responsible for the extinction of mammoths, mastodons, cave bears, giant sloths, New World camels and horses and thousands of other species. Their record on women's issues and minority rights wasn't so hot either. You can return to nature, go back to leading the simple, fulfilling life of the hunter-gatherer if you want, but don't let me catch you poking around in my garbage cans for food.

Then there are the beasts-are-our-buddies types. I've got a brochure from the International Fund for Animal Welfare containing a section called "Highlights of IFAW's History," and I quote: "1978—Campaign to save iguanas from cruelty in Nicaraguan marketplaces—people sew animals' mouths shut."

1978 was the middle of the Nicaraguan civil war. This means that while the evil dirt sack Somoza was shooting it out with the idiot Marxist Sandinistas, the International Fund for Animal Welfare was flying somebody to besieged Managua to check on lizard lips.

The neo-hippie-dips, the sentimentality-crazed iguana anthropomorphizers, the Chicken Littles, the three-bong-hit William Blakes—thank God these people don't actually go outdoors much, or the environment would be even worse than it is already.

But ecology's fools don't upset me. It's the wise guys I'm leery of. Tyranny is 30 implicit in the environmental movement. Although Earth Day participants are going to be surprised to hear themselves accused of fascist tendencies, dictatorship is the unspoken agenda of every morality-based political campaign! Check out Moslem fundamentalists or the right-to-lifers. Like abortion opponents and Iranian imams, the environmentalists have the right to tell the rest of us what to do because they are morally correct and we are not. Plus the tree squeezers care more, which makes them an elite—an aristocracy of mushiness. They know what's good for us even when we're too lazy or shortsighted to snip plastic six-pack collars so sea turtles won't strangle.

Questions for Discussion and Writing

1. O'Rourke condemns the environmentalists because they are a "mass movement." What objections does he make, and do you agree with him?

2. Even if you don't agree with him, did you find O'Rourke's use of language and hypothetical examples effective in getting his points across? Do you find his dichotomy between the environmentalists, on one hand, and the interests of business and industry, on the other, convincing? Why or why not?

3. Since he wrote this essay in 1990, have any of the real problems O'Rourke describes been solved? If so, in what way?

Fiction

NATSUME SOSEKI

Natsume Soseki (1867–1916) was one of Japan's most distinguished writers. He taught English at Tokyo University and was literary editor of the Asahi Newspaper. *Considered a milestone in Japanese literature,* I Am a Cat *(1905) brought Soseki instant recognition as an incisive observer of Japanese bourgeois life. This work was translated into English by Katsue Shibata and Motomari Kai in 1961. Soseki's work, like that of other twentieth-century Japanese writers, reveals the influence of the West on Japanese life and culture. The first chapter introduces a professor of English and his family as they appear through the eyes of a cat who has taken up residence in their home.*

I Am a Cat

I am a cat but as yet I have no name.

I haven't the faintest idea of where I was born. The first thing I do remember is that I was crying "meow, meow," somewhere in a gloomy damp place. It was there that I met a human being for the first time in my life. Though I found this all out at a later date, I learned that this human being was called a Student, one of the most ferocious of the human race. I also understand that these Students sometimes catch us, cook us and then take to eating us. But at that time, I did not have the slightest idea of all this so I wasn't frightened a bit. When this Student placed me on the palm of his hand and lifted me up lightly, I only had the feeling of floating around. After a while, I got used to this position and looked around. This was probably the first time I had a good look at a so-called human being. What impressed me as being most strange still remains deeply imbedded in my mind: the face which should have been covered with hair was a slippery thing similar to what I now know to be a teakettle. I have since come across many other cats but none of them are such freaks. Moreover, the center of the Student's face protruded to a great extent, and from the two holes located there, he would often emit smoke. I was extremely annoyed by being choked by this. That this was what they term as tobacco, I came to know only recently.

I was snuggled up comfortably in the palm of this Student's hand when, after a while, I started to travel around at a terrific speed. I was unable to find out if the Student was moving or if it was just myself that was in motion, but in any case I became terribly dizzy and a little sick. Just as I was thinking that I couldn't last much longer at this rate, I heard a thud and saw sparks. I remember everything up till that moment but think as hard as I can, I can't recall what took place immediately after this.

When I came to, I could not find the Student anywhere. Nor could I find the many cats that had been with me either. Moreover, my dear mother had also disappeared. And the extraordinary thing was that this place, when compared to where I had been before, was extremely bright—ever so bright. I could hardly keep my eyes open. This was because I had been removed from my straw bed and thrown into a bamboo bush.

Finally, mustering up my strength, I crawled out from this bamboo grove and found myself before a large pond. I sat on my haunches and tried to take in the situation. I didn't know what to do but suddenly I had an idea. If I could attract some attention by meowing, the Student might come back to me. I commenced but this was to no avail; nobody came.

By this time, the wind had picked up and came blowing across the pond. Night was falling. I sensed terrible pangs of hunger. Try as I would, my voice failed me and I felt as if all hope were lost. In any case, I resolved to get myself to a place where there was food and so, with this decision in mind, I commenced to circle the water by going around to the left.

This was very difficult but at any rate, I forced myself along and eventually came to a locality where I sensed Man. Finding a hole in a broken bamboo fence, I crawled through, having confidence that it was worth the try, and lo! I found myself within somebody's estate. Fate is strange; if that hole had not been there, I might have starved to death by the roadside. It is well said that every tree may offer shelter. For a long time afterwards, I often used this hole for my trips to call on Mi-ke, the tomcat living next door.

Having sneaked into the estate, I was at a loss as to what the next step should be. Darkness had come and my belly cried for food. The cold was bitter and it started to rain. I had no time to fool around any longer so I went in to a room that looked bright and cozy. Coming to think of it now, I had entered somebody's home for the first time. It was there that I was to confront other humans.

The first person I met was the maid Osan. This was a human much worse than the Student. As soon as she saw me, she grabbed me by the neck and threw me outdoors. I sensed I had no chance against her sudden action so I shut my eyes and let things take their course. But I couldn't endure the hunger and the cold any longer. I don't know how many times I was thrown out but because of this, I came to dislike Osan all through. That's one reason why I stole the fish the other day and why I felt so proud of myself.

When the maid was about to throw me out for the last time, the master of the house made his appearance and asked what all the row was about. The maid turned to him with me hanging limp from her hand, and told him that she had repeatedly tried throwing this stray cat out but that it always kept sneaking into the kitchen again—and that she didn't like it at all. The master, twisting his moustache, looked at me for a while and then told the maid to let me in. He then left the room. I took it that the master was a man of few words. The maid, still mad at me, threw me down on the kitchen floor. In such a way, I was able to establish this place as my home.

At first it was very seldom that I got to see my master. He seemed to be a schoolteacher. Coming home from school he'd shut himself up in his study and would hardly come out for the rest of the day. His family thought him to be very studious and my master also made out as if he were. But actually, he wasn't as hard working as they all believed him to be. I'd often sneak up and look into his study only to find him taking a nap. Sometimes I would find him drivelling on the book he had been reading before dozing off.

He was a man with a weak stomach so his skin was somewhat yellowish. He looked parched and inactive, yet he was a great consumer of food. After eating as much as he possibly could, he'd take a dose of Taka-diastase and then open a book. After reading a couple of pages, however, he'd become drowsy and again commence drooling. This was his daily routine. Though I am a cat myself, at times I think that schoolteachers are very fortunate. If I were to be reborn a man, I would, without doubt, become a teacher. If you can keep a job and still sleep as much as my master did, even cats could manage such a profession. But according to my master—and he makes it plain—there's nothing so hard as teaching. Especially when his friends come to visit him, he does a lot of complaining.

When I first came to this home, nobody but the master was nice to me. Wherever I went, they would kick me around and I was given no other consideration. The fact that they haven't given me a name even as of today goes to show how much they care for me. That's why I try to stay close to my master.

In the morning, when my master reads the papers, I always sit on his lap; and when he takes his nap, I perch on his back. This doesn't mean that he likes it, but then, on the other hand, it doesn't mean that he dislikes it—it has simply become a custom.

Experience taught me that it is best for me to sleep on the container for boiled rice in the mornings as it is warm, and on a charcoal-burning foot warmer in the evenings. I generally sleep on the veranda on fine days. But most of all, I like to crawl into the same bed with the children of the house at night. By children, I mean the girls who are five and three years old respectively. They sleep together in the same bed in their own room. In some way or other, I try to slip into their bed and crawl in between them. But if one of them wakes up, then it is terrible. The girls—especially the smaller one—raise an awful cry in the middle of the night and holler, "There's that cat in here again!" At this, my weak-stomached master wakes up and comes in to help them. It was only the other day that he gave me a terrible whipping with a ruler for indulging in this otherwise pleasant custom.

In coming to live with human beings, I have had the chance to observe them and the more I do the more I come to the conclusion that they are terribly spoiled, especially the children. When they feel like it, they hold you upside down or cover your head with a bag; and at times, they throw you around or try squeezing you into the cooking range. And on top of that, should you so much as bare a claw to try to stop them, the whole family is after you. The other day, for instance, I tried sharpening my claws just for a second on the straw mat of the living room when the Mrs. noticed me. She got furious and from then on, she won't let me in the sitting room. I can be cold and shivering in the kitchen but they never take the trouble to bother about me. When I met Shiro across the street whom I respected, she kept telling me there was nothing as inconsiderate as humans.

Only the other day, four cute little kittens were born to Shiro. But the Student who lives with the family threw all four of them into a pond behind the house on

15

the third day. Shiro told me all this in tears and said that in order for us cats to fulfil parental affection and to have a happy life, we will have to overthrow the human race. Yes, what she said was all very logical. Mi-ke, next door, was extremely furious when I told him about Shiro. He said that humans did not understand the right of possession of others. With us cats, however, the first one that finds the head of a dried sardine or the navel of a gray mullet gets the right to eat it. Should anyone try to violate this rule, we are allowed to use force in order to keep our find. But humans depend on their great strength to take what is legally ours away from us and think it right.

Shiro lives in the home of a soldier and Mi-ke in the home of a lawyer. I live in the home of a schoolteacher and, in comparison, I am far more optimistic about such affairs than either of them. I am satisfied only in trying to live peacefully day after day. I don't believe that the human race will prosper forever so all I have to do is to relax and wait for the time when cats will reign.

Coming to think of the way they act according to their whims—another word for selfishness—I'm going to tell you more about my master. To tell the truth, my master can't do anything well but he likes to stick his nose into everything. Going in for composing haiku,[1] he contributes his poems to the *Hototogisu* magazine, or writes some modern poetry for the *Myojo* magazine; or at times, he composes a piece in English, but all grammatically wrong. Then again, he finds himself engrossed in archery or tries singing lyrical plays; or maybe he tries a hand at playing discordant tunes on the violin. What is most disheartening is the fact that he cannot manage any of them well. Though he has a weak stomach, he does his best.

When he enters the toilet, he commences chanting so he is nicknamed "Mr. Mensroom" by his neighbors. Yet, he doesn't mind such things and continues his chanting: "This is Taira-no-Munemori. . . ." Everybody says, "There goes Munemori again," and then bursts out laughing. I don't know exactly what had come over him about a month after I first established myself at his place, but one pay day he came home all excited carrying with him a great big bundle. I couldn't help feeling curious about the contents.

The package happened to contain a set of water colors, brushes and drawing paper. It seems that he had given up lyrical plays and writing verses and was going in for painting. The following day, he shut himself up in his study and without even taking his daily nap, he drew pictures. This continued day after day. But what he drew remained a mystery because others could not even guess what they were. My master finally came to the conclusion that he wasn't as good a painter as he had thought himself to be. One day he came home with a man who considers himself an aesthetic and I heard them talking to each other.

"It's funny but it's difficult to draw as well as you want. When a painting is done by others, it looks so simple. But when you do a work with a brush yourself, it's quite a different thing," said my master. Coming to think of it, he did have plenty of proof to back up his statement.

20

---

[1] *Haiku:* a major form of Japanese verse written in seventeen syllables, divided into three lines of five, seven and five syllables, employing evocative allusions and comparisons.

His friend, looking over his gold-rimmed glasses, said, "You can't expect to draw well right from the beginning. In the first place, you can't expect to draw anything just from imagination, and by shutting yourself up in a room at that. Once the famous Italian painter Andrea del Sarto said that to draw, you have to interpret nature in its original form. The stars in the sky, the earth with flowers shining with dew, the flight of birds and the running animals, the ponds with their goldfish, and the black crow in a withered tree—nature is the one great panorama of the living world. How about it? If you want to draw something recognizable, why not do some sketching?"

"Did del Sarto really say all those things? I didn't know that. All right, just as you say," said my master with admiration. The eyes behind the gold-rimmed glasses shone, but with scorn.

The following day, as I was peacefully enjoying my daily nap on the veranda, my master came out from his study, something quite out of the ordinary, and sat down beside me. Wondering what he was up to, I slit my eyes open just a wee bit and took a look. I found him trying out Andrea del Sarto's theory on me. I could not suppress a smile. Having been encouraged by his friend, my master was using me as a model.

I tried to be patient and pretended to continue my nap. I wanted to yawn like anything but when I thought of my master trying his best to sketch me, I felt sorry for him, and so I killed it. He first drew my face in outline and then began to add colors. I'd like to make a confession here: as far as cats are concerned, I have to admit that I'm not one of those you'd call perfect or beautiful; my back, my fur or even my face cannot be considered superior in any way to those of other cats. Yet, even though I may be uncomely, I am hardly as ugly as what my master was painting. In the first place, he shaded my color all wrong. I am really somewhat like a Persian cat, a light gray with a shade of yellow with lacquer-like spots—as can be vouched by anyone. But according to my master's painting, my color was not yellow nor was it black. It wasn't gray or brown. It wasn't even a combination of these colors but something more like a smearing together of many tones. What was most strange about the drawing was that I had no eyes. Of course, I was being sketched while taking a nap so I won't complain too much, but you couldn't even find the location of where they should have been. You couldn't tell if I was a sleeping cat or a blind cat. I thought, way down inside me, that if this is what they called the Andrea del Sarto way of drawing pictures, it wasn't worth a sen.

But as to the enthusiasm of my master, I had to bow my head humbly. I couldn't disappoint him by moving but, if you'll excuse my saying so, I had wanted to go outside to relieve myself from a long while back. The muscles of my body commenced fidgeting and I felt that I couldn't hold out much longer. So, trying to excuse myself, I stretched out my forelegs, gave my neck a little twist and indulged in a long slow yawn. Going this far, there was no need for me to stay still any longer because I had changed my pose. I then stepped outside to accomplish my object.

But my master, in disappointment and rage, shouted from within the room, "You fool!" My master, in abusing others, has the habit of using this expression.

25

"You fool!" This is the best he can manage as he doesn't know any other way to swear. Even though he had not known how long I had endured the urgent call of nature, I still consider him uncivilized for this. If he had ever given me a smile or some other encouragement when I climbed onto his back, I could have forgiven him this time, but the fact is that he never considers my convenience. That he should holler, "You fool!" only because I was about to go and relieve myself was more than I could stand. In the first place, humans take too much for granted. If some power doesn't appear to control them better, there's no telling how far they will go in their excesses.

I could endure their being so self-willed but I've heard many other complaints regarding mankind's lack of virtue, and they are much worse.

Right in back of the house, there is a patch of tea plants. It isn't large but it is   30
nice and sunny. When the children of the house are so noisy that I can't enjoy my naps peacefully or when, because of idleness, my digestion is bad, I usually go out to the tea patch to enjoy the magnanimous surroundings. One lovely autumn day about two o'clock in the afternoon, after taking my after-lunch nap, I took a stroll through this patch. I walked along, smelling each tea plant as I went, until I reached a cryptomeria hedge at the west end.

There I found a large cat sleeping soundly, using a withered chrysanthemum in lieu of a mat. It seemed as if he didn't notice me coming, for he kept snoring loudly. I was overwhelmed at his boldness;—after sneaking into somebody else's yard. He was a big black cat.

The sun, now past midday, cast its brilliant rays upon his body and reflected themselves to give the impression of flames bursting from his soft fur. He had such a big frame that he seemed fit to be called a king of the feline family. He was more than twice my size. Admiration and a feeling of curiosity made me forget the past and the future, and I could only stare at him.

The soft autumn breeze made the branches of the paulawnia above quiver lightly and a couple of leaves came fluttering down upon the thicket of dead chrysanthemums. Then the great "king" opened his eyes. I can still feel the thrill of that moment. The amber light in his eyes shone much brighter than the jewels man holds as precious. He did not move at all. The glance he shot at me concentrated on my small forehead, and he abruptly asked me who I was. The great king's directness betrayed his rudeness. Yet, there was a power in his voice that would have terrified dogs, and I found myself shaking with fear. But thinking it inadvisable not to pay my respects, I said, "I am a cat though, as yet, I don't have any name." I said this while pretending to be at ease but actually my heart was beating away at a terrific speed. Despite my courteous reply, he said, "A cat? You don't say so! Where do you live?" He was extremely audacious.

"I live here in the schoolteacher's house."

"I thought so. You sure are skinny." Gathering from his rudeness I couldn't   35
imagine him coming from a very good family. But, judging from his plump body, he seemed to be well fed and able to enjoy an easy life. As for myself, I couldn't refrain from asking, "And who are you?"

"Me? Huh—I'm Kuro, living at the rickshawman's place."

So this was the cat living at the rickshawman's house! He was known in the vicinity as being awfully unruly. Actually he was admired within the home of the rickshawman but, having no education, nobody else befriended him. He was a hoodlum from whom others shied. When I heard him tell me who he was, I felt somewhat uneasy and, at the same time, I felt slightly superior. With the intention of finding out how much learning he had, I asked him some more questions.

"I was just wondering which of the two is the greater—the rickshawman or the schoolteacher."

"What a question! The rickshawman, naturally. Just take a look at your teacher—he's all skin and bones," he snorted.

"You look extremely strong. Most probably, living at the rickshawman's house, you get plenty to eat."   40

"What? I don't go unfed anywhere! Stick with me for a while instead of going around in circles in the tea patch and you'll look better yourself in less than a month."

"Sure, some day, maybe. But to me, it seems as though the schoolteacher lives in a bigger house than the rickshawman," I purred.

"Huh! What if the house is big? That doesn't mean you get your belly full there, does it?"

He seemed extremely irritated and, twitching his pointed ears, he walked away without saying another word. This was my first encounter with Kuro of the house of the rickshawman, but not the last.

Since then, we've often talked together. Whenever we do, Kuro always com-   45
mences bragging, as one living with a rickshawman would.

One day, we were lying in the tea patch and indulging in some small talk. As usual, he kept bragging about the adventures he had had, and then he got around to asking me, "By the way, how many rats have you killed?"

Intellectually I am much more developed than Kuro but when it comes to using strength and showing bravado, there is no comparison. I was prepared for something like this but when he actually asked me the question, I felt extremely embarrassed. But facts are facts; I could not lie to him: "To tell the truth, I have been wanting to catch one for a long time but the opportunity has never come."

Kuro twitched the whiskers which stood out straight from his muzzle and laughed hard. Kuro is conceited, as those who brag usually are, so when I find him being sarcastic I try to say something to appease him. In this way, I am able to manage him pretty well. Having learned this during our first meeting, I stayed calm when he laughed. I realized that it would be foolish to commit myself now by giving unasked-for reasons. I figured it best, at this stage, to let him brag about his own adventures and so I purred quietly, "Being as old as you are, you've probably caught a lot of rats yourself." I was trying to get him to talk about himself. And, as I had expected, he took the bait.

"Well, can't say a lot—maybe about thirty or forty." He was very proud of this and continued, "I could handle one or two hundred rats alone but when it comes to weasels, they're not to my liking. A weasel once gave me a terrible time."

"So? And what happened?" I chimed in. Kuro blinked several times before he   50
continued. "It was at the time of our annual housecleaning last summer. The master crawled under the veranda to put away a sack of lime, and—what do you think?
He surprised a big weasel which came bouncing out."

"Oh?" I pretended to admire him.

"As you know, a weasel is only a little bigger than a rat. Thinking him to be
just another big mouse, I cornered him in a ditch."

"You did?"

"Yeah. Just as I was going in for the *coup de grâce*—can you imagine what he
did? Well, it raised its tail and—ooph! You ought to have taken a whiff. Even now
when I see a weasel I get giddy." So saying, he rubbed his nose with one of his paws
as if he were still trying to stop the smell. I felt somewhat sorry for him so, with the
thought of trying to liven him up a little, I said, "But when it comes to rats, I hardly
believe they would have a chance against you. Being such a famous rat catcher, you
probably eat nothing else and that's why you're so plump and glossy, I'm sure."

I had said this to get him into a better mood but actually it had the contrary   55
effect. He let a big sigh escape and replied, "When you come to think of it, it's not
all fun. Rats are interesting but, you know, there's nobody as crafty as humans in
this world. They take all the rats I catch over to the police box. The policeman
there doesn't know who actually catches them so he hands my master five sen per
head. Because of me, my master has made a neat profit of one yen and fifty sen, but
yet he doesn't give me any decent food. Do you know what humans are? Well, I'll
tell you. They're men, yes, but thieves at heart."

Even Kuro, who was not any too bright, understood such logic and he bris-
tled his back in anger. I felt somewhat uneasy so I murmured some excuse and
went home. It was because of this conversation that I made up my mind never to
catch rats. But, on the other hand, neither do I go around hunting for other food.
Instead of eating an extravagant dinner, I simply go to sleep. A cat living with a
schoolteacher gets to become, in nature, just like a teacher himself. If I'm not careful I might still become just as weak in the stomach as my master.

Speaking of my master the schoolteacher, it finally dawned upon him that he
could not ever hope to get anywhere with water-color painting. He wrote the following entry in his diary, dated December 1:

Met a man today at a party. It's said that he's a debauchee and he looked like one.
Such individuals are liked by women, so it may be quite proper to say that such
people cannot help becoming dissipated. His wife was formerly a geisha girl and I
envy him. Most of the people who criticize debauchees generally have no chance to
become one themselves. Still, others who claim to be debauchees have no qualifications to become so worldly. They simply force themselves into that position. Just as in
the case of my water-color painting, there was absolutely no fear of my making good.
But indifferent to others, I might think that I was good at it. If some men are considered worldly only because they drink sake at restaurants, frequent geisha houses and
stop over for the night, and go through all the necessary motions, then it stands to
reason that I should be able to call myself a remarkable painter. But my water-color
paintings will never be a success.

In regard to this theory, I cannot agree. That a schoolteacher should envy a man who has a wife who was once a geisha shows how foolish and inferior my master is. But his criticism of himself as a water-color painter is unquestionably true. Though my master understands many of his own shortcomings, he cannot get over being terribly conceited. On December 4, he wrote:

> Last night, I attempted another painting but I have finally come to understand that I have no talent. I dreamed that somebody had framed the pictures I have lying around, and had hung them on the wall. Upon seeing them framed, I suddenly thought that I was an excellent painter. I felt happy and kept looking but, when the day dawned, I awoke and again clearly realized that I am still a painter of no talent.

Even in his dreams, my master seemed to regret his having given up painting. This is characteristic of a learned man, a frustrated water-color painter and one who can never become a man of the world.

The day after my master had had his dream, his friend, the man of arts, came   60
to see him again. The first question he asked my master was "How are the pictures getting along?"

My master calmly answered, "According to your advice I'm working hard at sketching. Just as you said, I am finding interesting shapes and detailed changes of colors which I had never noticed before. Due to the fact that artists in Western countries have persisted in sketching, they have reached the development we see today. Yes, all this must be due to Andrea del Sarto." He did not mention what he had written in his diary, but only continued to show his admiration for del Sarto.

The artist scratched his head and commenced to laugh, "That was all a joke, my friend."

"What's that?" My master didn't seem to understand.

"Andrea del Sarto is only a person of my own highly imaginative creation. I didn't think you'd take it so seriously. Ha, ha, ha." The artist was greatly enjoying himself.

Listening to all this from the veranda, I couldn't help wondering what my   65
master would write in his diary about that conversation. This artist was a person who took great pleasure in fooling others. As if he did not realize how his joke about Andrea del Sarto hurt my master, he boasted more: "When playing jokes, some people take them so seriously that they reveal great comic beauty, and it's a lot of fun. The other day I told a student that Nicholas Nickleby had advised Gibbon to translate his great story of the French Revolution from a French textbook and to have it published under his own name. This student has an extremely good memory and made a speech at the Japanese Literature Circle quoting everything I had told him. There were about a hundred people in the audience and they all listened very attentively. Then there's another time. One evening, at a gathering of writers, the conversation turned to Harrison's historical novel *Theophano*. I said that it was one of the best historical novels ever written, especially the part where the heroine dies. 'That really gives you the creeps'—that's what I said. An author who was sitting opposite me was one of those types who cannot and will not say no

to anything. He immediately voiced the opinion that that was a most famous passage. I knew right away that he had never read any more of the story than I had."

With wide eyes, my nervous and weak-stomached master asked, "What would you have done if the other man had really read the story?"

The artist did not show any excitement. He thought nothing of fooling other people. The only thing that counted was not to be caught in the act.

"All I would have had to do is to say that I had made a mistake in the title or something to that effect." He kept on laughing. Though this artist wore a pair of gold-rimmed glasses, he looked somewhat like Kuro of the rickshawman's.

My master blew a few smoke rings but he had an expression on his face that showed he wouldn't have the nerve to do such a thing. The artist, with a look in his eyes as if saying, "That's why you can't paint pictures," only continued. "Jokes are jokes but, getting down to facts, it's not easy to draw. They say that Leonardo da Vinci once told his pupils to copy a smear on a wall. That's good advice. Sometimes when you're gazing at water leaking along the wall in a privy, you see some good patterns. Copy them carefully and you're bound to get some good designs."

"You're only trying to fool me again." 70

"No, not this time. Don't you think it's a wonderful idea? Just what da Vinci himself would have suggested."

"Just as you say," replied my master, half surrendering. But he still hasn't made any sketches in the privy—at least not yet.

Kuro of the rickshawman's wasn't looking well. His glossy fur began to fade and fall out. His eyes, which I formerly compared to amber, began to collect mucus. What was especially noticeable was his lack of energy. When I met him in the tea patch, I asked him how he felt.

"I'm still disgusted with the weasel's stink and with the fisherman. The fish seller hit me with a pole again the other day."

The red leaves of the maple tree were beginning to show contrast to the green 75 of the pines here and there. The maples shed their foliage like dreams of the past. The fluttering petals of red and white fell from the tea plants one after another until there were none remaining. The sun slanted its rays deeper and deeper into the southern veranda and seldom did a day pass that the late autumn wind didn't blow. I felt as though my napping hours were being shortened.

My master still went to school every day and, coming home, he'd still bottle himself up in his study. When he had visitors he'd continue to complain about his job. He hardly ever touched his water colors again. He had discontinued taking Taka-diastase for his indigestion, saying that it didn't do him any good. It was wonderful now that the little girls were attending kindergarten every day but returning home, they'd sing loudly and bounce balls and, at times, they'd still pick me up by the tail.

I still had nothing much to eat so I did not become very fat but I was healthy enough. I didn't become sick like Kuro and, as always, I took things as they came. I still didn't try to catch rats, and I still hated Osan, the maid. I still didn't have a name but you can't always have what you want. I resigned myself to continue living here at the home of this schoolteacher as a cat without a name.

Questions for Discussion and Writing

1. How does the cat's view of the schoolteacher show him as he really is, compared with the way he sees himself?
2. What subtle or overt resemblances link each of the cats mentioned with its owner? For example, how is the narrator like the schoolmaster, Mi-ke similar to the lawyer, and Kuro like the rickshawman?
3. What could your pet say about you that no one else knows? What character traits does the name you gave this pet reveal about you? What name would you give the cat in this story, and why?

LIN SUTHERLAND

Robert Redford's film A River Runs through It *(1992) brought attention to the traditional sport of fly-fishing. What most people don't know, however, is that women as well as men have taken up the sport, but rarely with the fervor dramatized in Lin Sutherland's humorous story, "A River Ran over Me." Sutherland's articles and stories have been published in* Field and Stream, Outdoor Photographer, *and* Women's Day, *and she has contributed to* Uncommon Waters: Women Write about Fly Fishing *(1994) and* A Different Angle: Fly Fishing Stories by Women *(1995), in which this story originally appeared. She is currently humor editor for the on-line magazine* Lou Bignami's Fine Travel.

A River Ran over Me

Fly fishing is beyond sport, skill, and even obsession. It's a religion, and my baptisim into the faith was on the Gunnison River in Colorado. I thought I was merely going to learn something new and different. I didn't anticipate the dogma, the intricate litany, the saints, the tithing, the penance. Nor did I anticipate my mother would become the Joan of Arc of fly fishing.

It started out innocently enough. I chose to take my first stab at fly fishing with Mama because she was a Bass Master of the First Order, the Blood Bait Queen of my youth. But at the age of seventy-two, Mama discovered fly fishing, and as usual, she took something complicated and learned it in about three weeks. Face it, for a woman who took eleven years of Latin in Charleston, South Carolina, anything is easy.

At first she had been skeptical.

"Buncha little snots," she'd remark about fly fishermen. "Effete elitist purists," she'd add.

Then one day she was forced to stop at a little specialty angling shop instead   5
of her usual Live Bait Marina. It was the kind of place that displays fly fishing *en-sembles*—and the only reason she went in there was to look for a particular fishing book.

Mama stood there in the front of the store with her calico mane flying and took in the woven creels, leather belts, fifty-dollar floppy fishing hats and six-hundred-dollar graphite rods.

"HEY!" she shouted. "What kind of foo foo fish shop is this?"

Several customers looked around at her and a pony-tailed young man wearing a very expensive fly fishing shirt with a little fly and hook embroidered on its breast pocket rushed forward.

"Yes, Ma'am? May I help you?" he asked.

"Where the hell are your foo foo fish books, young man?" She looked him up   10
and down, then jabbed his chest with one big-knuckled forefinger.

"Young man, you have feathers embroidered on your chest. Just what does that mean?"

He stammered and opened his mouth.

"Never mind!" she interrupted. "I don't want to know. . . . Hey, here it is—" She reached behind a polished wood counter and pulled out the book she sought.

To make a long story short, Mama and the young man got into a conversa-tion, most of which consisted of her railing about how none of her daughters could fish worth a plugged nickel. The young man turned out to be John Tavenner, a well-respected fly fishing guide from Santa Fe who pulls trout regularly out of the Rio Grande, which hardly anyone could consider a trout stream. He showed my mother boxes of thousands of flies he'd carefully constructed out of chicken necks, hare's ears, and the like. He was twenty-eight but had started fly fishing with his fa-ther at the age of twelve.

As happens often to those who meet my mother, Tavenner became intrigued.   15
Mama has a blunt exterior, but you never doubt she's a lady. A Southern lady, at that. Her piercing china-blue eyes shine with intelligence and interest . . . she sim-ply exudes life. The two began to talk fishing, and it wasn't long before Tavenner invited her to attend one of his fly fishing clinics. And that was that. She was the best he'd ever instructed, he told me later. She had the knack.

Working relentlessly, Mama became an expert in about four months, then a total convert. There is nothing worse than a convert, you know, and the next sum-mer she all but forced me to join her and Tavenner at the bottom end of the Black Canyon of the Gunnison River known for its gold-medal waters. We camped in a delightful overhang of cliffs, where the river was crystal clear and lively and the rapids abundant.

On our first day out, I watched Tavenner land and release one rainbow trout after another. He approached fly fishing as kind of a cross between religion and reincarnation.

"You need to become the fish," he explained excitedly to me. You visualize what the *fish* wants, not what you want. You let your intuitive side override the thinking part of your brain."

"Right-brained fishing?" I inquired.

He considered a moment. "Yes. You're triggering their fish archetypes which   20
have evolved over generations to strike at a certain object. So you have to be intuitive to anticipate what they want. Thinking is a slowing-down process. Action and reaction. That's why it's spiritual."

"So what's the first commandment?" I asked.

"Presentation:" he replied. "Presentation is everything."

"Ah," I nodded knowingly, not having the faintest clue what he meant. But I learned.

The Gunnison happens to be perfect for trout. It is not just one river, but a series of them layered into a single, sometimes chaotic unit. At the bottom is the river of sand, then there is the river of water above, and above that a river of air. Within those three are the rivers of life: the snails, insects, snakes, frogs, cephalopods, nutria, beaver, otter, and then the eagles and ospreys that swoop down to snatch the top of the water food chain, the trout.

Trout, as everyone knows, are wily, skitterish and fine-tasting. They are the high-   25
est predator in the river, except for the fly fishermen, who attempt to imitate what the trout are eating, often at great trouble and expense, and talk about the "hatches" as if they were Saint's Days. It so happened that the Gunnison had just seen one of the biggest hatches of stone flies, and as a result the trout had "shoulders." Anyway, that's what Mama told me.

"How can a trout have shoulders?" I asked. "They don't even have necks."

"They're hogs," she replied. "Fat and sassy." Mama goes for only two kinds of fish—hogs and lunkers. These are leftover terms from her bass days and they're self-explanatory.

Of course, fly fishing has a language of its own—a litany as oblique as any service in Latin. Tavenner was well-versed in the arcane terminology. He spoke to us of P.M.D., which at first I assumed was some kind of insect P.M.S., a femme fly in a nasty mood. It turned out to be a Pale Morning Dun. I was relieved P.M.S. had not invaded the bug world.

Later he announced that he was going out nymphing and invited us to come along. Visions of young things flitting through the wild Colorado woods, with Tavenner, his ponytail flapping, in hot pursuit raced through my mind.

"I'll be using a common nymph," he added, as if in explanation. Dang it, I   30
thought, *there's vulgar ones.* Then he talked about the prince. I thought the prince would probably be the one after the nymphs, but no, this guy's made of green hare's ear, imitating an emerging caddis. Only a trout would go for a green hairy fake prince, I thought. No, wait a minute—I've dated a few of those myself.

"Of course, we could use the Girdle Bitch," Mama suggested helpfully.

"What!" I exclaimed, summoning from the past nightmarish visions of my large aunts with too-tight corsets under their cotton dresses spraddled over lawn chairs in the shade after too much pecan pie at our family reunions Seeing my expression Mama explained that a Girdle Bitch was just another fly—a Bitch Creek Nymph with Spandex legs. Even the explanations were surreal.

"A lot of people don't tie Girdle Bitches with Spandex legs, but I do," Mama said proudly. "They're ugly—but I've caught fish on them."

I took her word for it.

Naturally, I made all the first-timer faux pas on our initial foray to the river.   35
In fact, the list of my sins is excruciatingly extensive:

1. I called the custom-built, monographed, nine-foot, light-weight, five-hundred-dollar graphite fly rod Tavenner let me use "a pole." "Lemme see that pole," I said cheerfully. His face contorted in pain.

2. I asked Tavenner why he didn't have "a bigger bobber." "That's a strike indicator," he informed me, his voice dripping disgust.

3. I put my arms inside my chest-waders. (I was trying to pull up my socks.)

4. I fell over in the rushing water with both my arms inside my chest-waders. I needn't tell you how bad a mistake *that* was. The river ran over me. Baptized me. In the name of the Mother, the Sun, and the Holy Float. It would have drowned me, too, if Tavenner hadn't caught me as I washed downstream and dragged me to shore by my suspenders.

5. I hooked my hair, my leg, my backside. Mama and Tavenner moved several hundred paces upriver from me.

6. I fished with moss. "Clean the moss off your fly every second cast, why don't you, honey?" suggested Mama in a kindly fashion, after noticing my half-hour's moss-casting.

7. I forgot to look at the strike indicator. I was too occupied watching my mother jerking in hogs and lunkers repeatedly. Suddenly, I had a strike myself, but the fish was gone in a flash when I didn't set the hook.

8. When we rafted downstream to fish the riffles, I actually succeeded in hooking *and landing* a rainbow trout, but I got so excited I fell out of the boat—onto my fish. It swished a lot under me. Scared me. Scared the fish, too, no doubt.

I could be the only fisherman who has ever squashed her fish in the water.

But for all these transgressions and more, I did penance. All fly fishermen do, whether they sin or not. Standing in freezing water for long periods of time: that's the flagellation part of the religion. When I got to where I enjoyed it, I began to worry.

Mama, however, had risen to a higher plane—Cardinal status at least, if not exactly Joan of Arc. She cut an intriguing figure out on the river, constantly moving with the smooth, fluid motion of an expert caster. It was meditational. Every once in a while the rhythm would be interrupted with an abrupt yelp, which meant she'd caught another lunker with shoulders.

All this spirituality hadn't been free, of course. Like all sects, this one included tithing. Why, one rooster neck for making flies is forty dollars, and one packet of green hare's ear hair, twelve bucks. And when you add to it the state-of-the-art graphite rods, reels, vests, waders, hats, bags, nets, and so on, it makes you gasp.

Yet the most unique item Tavenner had sold to my mother, which she wore   40
around her neck like a vestment and never removed, was the least expensive. This was the fisherman's tool lanyard, a tool originally used for bait rigging while fishing

offshore, but adapted for fly fishermen. It's particularly advantageous for deep-river waders and floaters because all the tools you need are visible and securely fastened on a lanyard around your neck, handier than having to dig through a tackle box or vest.

The typical setup includes a Swiss Army knife or small scissors to cut line, hemostats to remove hooks, small needle-nose pliers to debarb hooks, a leader straightener, a leader sink, silicone floatant, a hook file, and finally, a stomach pump.

This last item was a revelation. I've seen some pretty outrageous things done in the name of sport, like whacking off bull parts in Spain, but trout stomach pumping has to be at the top. With the first trout Mama caught, she, without warning, began to suck all the insides out of the thing.

"What are you *doing to that fish?*" I shouted, making her leap in alarm.

"Pumping out the little bugger's belly," she replied nonchalantly. "You have to see what they're eating, you know," she added instructively.

I *hadn't* known that. "There must be a better way," I insisted.   45

She examined the green stuff in the tube. "Shoot, nothing but moss," she muttered and dropped the dripping mess onto her shirt front, where the stain spread.

"Think I'll get another cup of coffee," I gagged.

You can renounce all these worldly goods and take your fly fishing back to its simplest state, as the ascetics do in any religion. For instance, Tavenner told us about a client he'd once guided on the river who fished with spines from the barrel cactus with a fly tied on. This man, Tavenner said, had explored the length and breadth of fly fishing and discovered its pure, natural form.

"That's the largest wad of horse crap I ever heard," Mama exclaimed, staring at Tavenner. She was about to say something else, but just then one of those Amazing But True Fish Things happened. I got a strike, a good one. All of us turned our attention to the end of my line. The fish dived straight down, then shot straight up, hit the water, and flew several feet into the air. It was so fast, I couldn't keep the tension on my line. The huge rainbow coiled high in the air for a moment, glistening, poised, droplets of water spraying outward and catching the sun. Then, facing its hunter, the fish turned and spat the fly out in my face. It was well-timed and altogether amazing. I heard Mama laugh.

"That fish has been in this game before," she remarked drolly.   50

"That fish just made my trip," I sighed lightly with satisfaction. Gazing at the rippling water, I reflected, "It's funny, but in all my years of fishing, the ones I remember most are the big ones I've lost."

And somehow, that seemed a perfect benediction for the day.

Questions for Discussion and Writing

1. The narrator's mother has taken to the sport of fly-fishing with a kind of religious fervor. What aspects of the story emphasize this in a lighthearted way?
2. In what way does the narrator's view of her mother (and relationship with her) change as a result of fly-fishing?

3. Have you ever gotten caught up in the rituals and mystique of a sport as either a spectator or a participant? Describe your experiences.

Poetry

MARY OLIVER

Mary Oliver (b. 1935) grew up in Cleveland, Ohio, and was educated at Ohio State University and Vassar College. She has written numerous collections of poetry, including American Primitive *(1983), for which she received the Pulitzer Prize. Most recently, she has written* Winter Hours: Poetry, Prose, and Essays *(1999) and* The Leaf and the Cloud *(2000). Oliver currently teaches at Bennington College in Vermont. The following poem is reprinted from* Twelve Moons *(1978).*

Sleeping in the Forest

I thought the earth
remembered me, she
took me back so tenderly, arranging,
her dark skirts, her pockets
full of lichens and seeds. I slept   5
as never before, a stone
on the riverbed, nothing
between me and the white fire of the stars
but my thoughts, and they floated
light as moths among the branches   10
of the perfect trees. All night
I heard the small kingdoms breathing
around me, the insects, and the birds
who do their work in the darkness. All night
I rose and fell, as if in water, grappling   15
with a luminous doom. By morning
I had vanished at least a dozen times
into something better.

Questions for Discussion and Writing

1. How does the rhythm or pulse of this poem reinforce the sense that the speaker has blended into the world of nature?

2. In what sense does the earth seem to remember her and welcome her return?
3. The experience of being spiritually at one with nature is rare. Under what circumstances, if ever, have you felt this way?

HENRY WADSWORTH LONGFELLOW

Henry Wadsworth Longfellow (1807–1882) graduated from Bowdoin College in 1825 and mastered Spanish, French, Italian, German and the Scandinavian languages. He became a professor of languages at Harvard in 1836. Longfellow is acknowledged as one of the great American poets, whose works were so popular that he was able to live on the proceeds. Some of his best known works are Evangeline *(1847) and* Paul Revere's Ride *(1863). The following poem presents a common experience, rendered with uncommon stylistic grace.*

The Sound of the Sea

The sea awoke at midnight from its sleep,
    And round the pebbly beaches far and wide
    I heard the first wave of the rising tide
Rush onward with uninterrupted sweep;
A voice out of the silence of the deep,   5
    A sound mysteriously multiplied
    As of a cataract from the mountain's side,
Or roar of winds upon a wooded steep.
    So comes to us at times, from the unknown
        And inaccessible solitudes of being,   10
            The rushing of the sea-tides of the soul;
    And inspirations, that we deem our own,
        Are some divine foreshadowing and foreseeing
            Of things beyond our reason or control.

Questions for Discussion and Writing

1. In this vividly imagined poem, what signs are there that the speaker has made contact with a mystical or religious spirit?
2. Examine the pattern of end rhymes in this poem and the way Longfellow accentuates the meaning through varying this basic pattern. Where does he use alliteration and assonance to evoke the spirit of the ocean?
3. Try to create a poem that expresses how you feel about the ocean or any other natural phenomenon, and vary the visual appearance and indentations of the lines as Longfellow does to evoke the movement, size, shape, or defining features of what you are describing.

Connections for Chapter 6: Our Place in Nature

1. **Mark Twain,** *The Lowest Animal*
   In what sense does Hans Ruesch's essay "Slaughter of the Innocent" (in Chapter 11) underscore Twain's thesis?

2. **Alice Walker,** *Am I Blue?*
   How do Walker's reflections on the racial "other" connect with insights about racism in Kate Chopin's story "Désirée's Baby" (in Chapter 5), written in the previous century?

3. **Ursula K. Le Guin,** *A Very Warm Mountain*
   In what respects do Le Guin's essay and Lin Sutherland's story express a feminist viewpoint?

4. **Joseph K. Skinner,** *Big Mac and the Tropical Forests*
   How do Skinner and Thor Heyerdahl alert their readers to the finite and destructible nature of natural resources?

5. **Thor Heyerdahl,** *How to Kill an Ocean*
   How does Heyerdahl's analysis challenge the traditional poetic conception of the ocean voiced by Henry Wadsworth Longfellow in his poem?

6. **Linda Hogan,** *Waking Up the Rake*
   What have Hogan and Alice Walker learned about themselves and their place in nature from their contact with other species?

7. **P. J. O'Rourke,** *The Greenhouse Affect*
   Create a dialogue between O'Rourke and Joseph K. Skinner that fairly presents both of their viewpoints.

8. **Natsume Soseki,** *I Am a Cat*
   Compare the way Soseki and Alice Walker, in her essay "Am I Blue?", imbue a cat and a horse, respectively, with human qualities as well as the two authors' very different purposes in doing so.

9. **Lin Sutherland,** *A River Ran over Me*
   Compare Sutherland's use of quasi-religious imagery in her story with Henry Wadsworth Longfellow's evocation of the spiritual in his poem.

10. **Mary Oliver,** *Sleeping in the Forest*
    In what sense do Oliver's poem and Linda Hogan's account urge readers to transcend customary perspectives on nature?

11. **Henry Wadsworth Longfellow,** *The Sound of the Sea*
    In what ways do Longfellow and Mary Oliver evoke intimations of mystical and religious forces through their reflections on the sea and the forest?

7

HISTORY IN THE MAKING

The selections in this chapter bring to life important social, economic, and political events, and they address the central question of how the present has been affected by the past. Howard Carter offers a glimpse into the far distant past of ancient Egypt in his account of how he discovered Tutankhamen's tomb. Linda Simon tells why historians seeking to delineate plausible explanations for past events should examine journals, letters, newspaper accounts, photographs, and other primary documents. Kenneth M. Stampp's analysis of the manuals slave owners used exemplifies how a historian relies on these original documents.

Historians also draw on information provided by journalists, explorers, and sociologists to gain a more accurate picture of past events. In this chapter, the report of Jack London, Hanson W. Baldwin's reconstruction of the radio messages, and ship's logs and accounts of survivors, and the on-site interviews conducted by John Hersey offer invaluable insight into the 1906 San Francisco earthquake, the 1912 sinking of the *Titanic,* and the atomic bombing of Hiroshima in 1945.

Historical research also underlies social criticism, as we see in Haunani-Kay Trask's denunciation of the unequal power wielded by the colonizers over the colonized in modern Hawaii.

In the stories by Ambrose Bierce and Irene Zabytko, we experience the Civil War through the eyes of an unwilling participant, and we learn what it was like to lose one's humanity during the Nazi occupation of Ukraine.

The three poems look at historical events in an unusual way. Bertolt Brecht challenges us to revisit the past through the eyes of those who have left no trace. David R. Slavitt commemorates the tragedy of the *Titanic* as a fate to be envied. Eleni Fourtouni's poem about the Nazi occupation of Greece during World War II offers an instructive contrast of the impermanence of tyranny with its lasting impact on those who survived it.

Nonfiction

LINDA SIMON

"The Naked Source" is drawn from Linda Simon's essay "Inquiry" from The Michigan Quarterly Review *(Summer 1988).*

The Naked Source

It is true that my students do not know history. That annals of the American past, as students tell it, are compressed into a compact chronicle: John Kennedy and Martin Luther King flourish just a breath away from FDR and Woodrow Wilson, who themselves come right on the heels of Jefferson and Lincoln. The far and distant past is more obscure still.

Some, because they are bright and inquisitive, have learned names, dates, and the titles of major events. But even these masters of Trivial Pursuit often betray their ignorance of a real sense of the past. Teachers all have favorite one-liners that point to an abyss in historical knowledge. Mine is: Sputnik *who?*

There is no debate here. Students do not know history. Students should learn history. There is less agreement about what they should know, why they should know it, and far less agreement about how they should pursue this study of the past.

When I ask my students why they need to know history, they reply earnestly: We need to learn history because those who do not know history are doomed to repeat the mistakes of the past. They have heard this somewhere, although no one can attribute the remark. And if they are told that George Santayana said it, they know not who Santayana was, although if you care to inform them they will dutifully record his name, dates (1863–1952), and the title of the work (*The Life of Reason*) in which the remark was made.

Is that so? I ask. What will not be repeated?   5

Inevitably they respond emotionally with the example of the Holocaust. Some have watched an episode of a PBS series. Some have seen the film *The Diary of Anne Frank*. Such genocide, they reply, will not be repeated because we know about it. Undaunted by examples of contemporary genocide, they remain firm in their conviction. Genocide, they maintain. And the Great Depression.

The Great Depression has made a big impact on the adolescent imagination. Given any work of literature written at any time during the 1930s, some students will explain it as a direct response to the Great Depression. Wasn't everyone depressed, after all? And aren't most serious works of literature grim, glum, dark, and deep? There you have it.

But now we know about the Great Depression. And so it will not, cannot, happen again.

I am not persuaded that requiring students to read Tacitus[1] or Thucydides,[2] Carl Becker[3] or Francis Parkman,[4] Samuel Eliot Morison[5] or Arnold Toynbee[6] will remedy this situation, although I believe that students, and we, might well benefit from these writers' illumination. What students lack, after all, is a sense of historical-mindedness, a sense that lives were lived in a context, a sense that events (the Battle of Barnet, for example) had consequences (if men were slain on the battlefield, they could not return to the farm), a sense that answers must generate questions, more questions, and still more subtle questions.

As it is, students learning history, especially in the early grades, are asked pre-scribed questions and are given little opportunity to pursue their own inquiry or satisfy their own curiosity. The following questions are from current high school texts:

10

> Has the role of the present United Nations proved that the hopes and dreams of Woodrow Wilson were achievable? If so, how? If not, why?
>
> What were the advantages of an isolationist policy for the United States in the nine-teenth century? Were there disadvantages?

Questions such as these perpetuate the idea that history is a body of knowl-edge on which students will be tested. The first question, in other words, asks stu-dents: Did you read the section in the text on the role of the United Nations? Did you read the section on Wilson's aims in proposing the League of Nations? Can you put these two sections together?

The second question asks students: Did you understand the term *isolationist?* Did you read the section on U.S. foreign relations in the nineteenth century? Can you summarize the debate that the authors of the textbook recount?

Questions such as these perpetuate the idea that history can uncover "facts" and "truth," that history is objective, and that students, if only they are diligent, can recover "right answers" about the past. Questions such as these ignore the role of historians. Even those bright students who can recall dates and events rarely can re-call the name of a historian, much less any feeling about who this particular man or woman was. For many students, historical facts are things out there, like seashells or autumn leaves, and it hardly matters who fetches them. The seashell will look the same whether it is gathered in Charles Beard's[7] pocket or Henri Pirenne's.[8]

What students really need to learn, more than "history," is a sense of the his-torical method of inquiry. They need to know what it is that historians do and how

---

[1] *Tacitus (A.D. c. 55–A.D. c. 117):* Roman historian critical of Rome's moral tone.   [2] *Thucydides (c.460–c.400 B.C.):* one of the greatest of Greek historians.   [3] *Carl Becker (1873–1945):* American historian, president of the American Historical Association (1931).   [4] *Francis Parkman (1823–1893):* noted for the account of his journey west in the *Oregon Trail* (1849).   [5] *Samuel Eliot Morison (1887–1976):* American historian.   [6] *Arnold Toynbee (1889–1975):* English historian known for his 12-volume *Study of History* (1934–1961).   [7] *Charles Beard (1874–1948):* American historian.   [8] *Henri Pirenne (1862–1935):* Belgian historian.

they do it. They need to understand the role of imagination and intuition in the telling of histories, they need to practice, themselves, confronting sources, making judgments, and defending conclusions.

When I ask my freshmen what they think historians do, they usually offer me   15
some lofty phrases about "influencing the course of future events." But what I mean is: what do historians do after breakfast? That is a question few of my students can answer. And they are surprised when I read them the following passage by British historian A. L. Rowse[9] from his book *The Use of History*.

> You might think that in order to learn history you need a library of books to begin with. Not at all: that only comes at the end. What you need at the beginning is a pair of stout walking shoes, a pencil and a notebook; perhaps I should add a good county guide covering the area you mean to explore . . . and a map of the country . . . that gives you field footpaths and a wealth of things of interest, marks churches and historic buildings and ruins, wayside crosses and holy wells, prehistoric camps and dykes, the sites of battles. When you can't go for a walk, it is quite a good thing to study the map and plan where you would like to go. I am all in favour of the open-air approach to history; the most delightful and enjoyable, the most imaginative and informative, and—what not everybody understands—the best training.

It is the best training because it gives the would-be historian an encounter with the things that all historians look at and puzzle over: primary sources about the past. Historians look at battlefields and old buildings, read letters and diaries and documents, interview eyewitnesses or participants in events. And they ask questions of these sources. Gradually, after asking increasingly sophisticated questions, they make some sense, for themselves, of what once happened.

What professional historians do, however, is not what most students do when they set out to learn history within the confines of a course. Instead of putting students face to face with primary sources, instructors are more likely to send them to read what other people say about the past. Students begin with a library of books of secondary sources, or they may begin with a text. But that, cautions Rowse, should come "at the end." Instead of allowing students to gain experience in weighing evidence and making inferences, the structures of many courses encourage them to amass information. "I found it!" exclaim enthusiastic students. They need to ask, "But what does it mean?"

They need to ask that question of the kinds of sources that historians actually use. Instead of reading Morison's rendering of Columbus's voyages, for example, students might read Columbus himself: his journal, his letters to the Spanish monarchs. Then they can begin to decide for themselves what sort of man this was and what sort of experience he had. Morison—as excellent a historian as he is—comes

---

[9] *A. L. Rowse (1903–1997):* British historian and Shakespearean scholar.

later. With some sense of the sources that Morison used, students can begin to evaluate his contribution to history, to understand how he drew conclusions from the material available to him, to see how "facts" are augmented by historical intuition. They can begin to understand, too, that the reconstruction of the past is slow and painstaking work.

Courses that cover several decades or even millennia may give students a false impression of historical inquiry. Historians, like archaeologists or epidemiologists, move slowly through bumpy and perilous terrain. They are used to travelling for miles only to find themselves stranded at a dead end. Once, in the archives of Westminster Abbey, I eagerly awaited reading a fragment of a letter from King Henry VI (after all, that is how it was described in the card catalog), only to lift out of an envelope the corner of a page, about an inch across, with the faintest ink-mark the only evidence that it had, five hundred years before, been a letter at all.

Slowly the historian assembles pieces of the past. A household expense record might be the only artifact proving that a certain medieval woman existed. How much can be known about her? How much can be known by examining someone's checkbook today? Yet historians must make do with just such odd legacies: wills and land deeds, maps and drawings, family portraits or photographs. Can you imagine the excitement over the discovery of a diary or a cache of letters? At last, a text. But the diary may prove a disappointment, a frustration. William James recorded the title of a book he may have been reading or the name of a visitor. Didn't he understand that a historian or biographer would need the deep, reflective ruminations of which we know he was more than capable?

Students have not had these experiences. When they are asked to write, they write *about* history. The research paper or the term paper seems to many of them another form of test—this time a take-home drawn out over weeks. Even if they have learned that "voice" and "audience" are important for a writer, they see history papers as different. They must be objective; they must learn proper footnoting and documentation. They must compile an impressive bibliography. Most important, they must find something out. The research paper produces nothing so much as anxiety, and the student often feels overwhelmed by the project.

They might, instead, be asked to write history as historians do it. They might be introduced to archives—in their college, in their community, in their state capital. They might be encouraged to interview people, and to interview them again and again until they begin to get the kind of information that will enlighten them about a particular time or event. They might be encouraged to read newspapers on microfilm or the bound volumes of old magazines that are yellowing in the basement of their local library. And then they might be asked to write in that most challenging form: the historical narrative.

"I can recall experiencing upon the completing of my first work of history," George Kennan[10] wrote once, ". . . a moment of panic when the question suddenly

20

---

[10] *George Frost Kennan (b. 1904):* U.S. diplomat and Pulitzer Prize-winning historian.

presented itself to me: What is it that I have done here? Perhaps what I have written is not really history but rather some sort of novel, the product of my own imagination,—an imagination stimulated, inspired and informed, let us hope, by the documents I have been reading, but imagination nevertheless." Most historians share Kennan's reaction.

Students, of course, can never discover the boundary between "fact" and imaginative construction unless they have contact with primary sources. They cannot know where the historian has intervened to analyze the information he or she has discovered. "Most of the facts that you excavate," Morison wrote in "History as A Literary Art," "are dumb things; it is for you to make them speak by proper selection, arrangement, and emphasis." Morison suggested that beginning historians look to such writers as Sherwood Anderson and Henry James for examples of the kind of palpable description and intense characterization that can make literature—historical or fictional—come alive.

Students need to be persuaded that they are writing literature, not taking a   25 test, when they set out to be historians. Their writing needs to be read and evaluated not only for the facts that they have managed to compile, but for the sense of the past that they have conveyed. They need to discover that the past was not only battles and elections, Major Forces and Charismatic Leaders, but ordinary people, growing up, courting, dancing to a different beat, camping by a river that has long since dried up, lighting out for a territory that no longer exists. Except in the imagination of historians, as they confront the naked source, unaided.

Questions for Discussion and Writing

1. Simon believes that the way history is now being taught leaves much to be desired. What reforms does she propose?
2. What would be the benefits of learning about history in the way Simon suggests? For example, would it be realistic to follow the advice of British historian A. L. Rowse, whom she quotes? Why or why not?
3. What historical topics are of interest to you? They need not be national events and could be as personal as your own family's history and the associated records you might consult and the relatives you might interview. Try to apply the techniques Simon recommends and write up your findings.

HOWARD CARTER

Howard Carter (1873–1939), the English archaeologist whose work resulted in the discovery of the tomb of Tutankhamen, the boy pharoah of the Eighteenth Dynasty (fourteenth century B.C.), was born in London and first went to Egypt as a draughtsman with the British Archaeological Survey Department. Although his first excavations in the Valley of the Tombs of the Kings began in 1902, it was not until November 1922 that he made his greatest discovery, at Thebes, along with his benefactor, Lord Carnarvon (who died in 1923, during the excavation of

Tutankhamen's tomb, under mysterious circumstances). "Finding the Tomb," from Carter's three-volume account of the excavation, The Tomb of Tutankhamen *(1933), describes the exciting story of one of the greatest archaeological discoveries of all time.*

Finding the Tomb

The history of the Valley, as I have endeavoured to show in former chapters, has never lacked the dramatic element, and in this, the latest episode, it has held to its traditions. For consider the circumstances. This was to be our final season in the Valley. Six full seasons we had excavated there, and season after season had drawn a blank; we had worked for months at a stretch and found nothing, and only an excavator knows how desperately depressing that can be; we had almost made up our minds that we were beaten, and were preparing to leave the Valley and try our luck elsewhere; and then—hardly had we sat hoe to ground in our last despairing effort than we made a discovery that far exceeded our wildest dreams. Surely, never before in the whole history of excavation has a full digging season been compressed within the space of five days.

Let me try and tell the story of it all. It will not be easy, for the dramatic suddenness of the initial discovery left me in a dazed condition, and the months that have followed have been so crowded with incident that I have hardly had time to think. Setting it down on paper will perhaps give me a chance to realize what has happened and all that it means.

I arrived in Luxor[1] on 28 October, and by 1 November I had enrolled my workmen and was ready to begin. Our former excavations had stopped short at the north-east corner of the tomb of Rameses VI, and from this point I started trenching southwards. It will be remembered that in this area there were a number of roughly constructed workmen's huts, used probably by the labourers in the tomb of Rameses. These huts, built about three feet above bed-rock, covered the whole area in front of the Ramesside tomb, and continued in a southerly direction to join up with a similar group of huts on the opposite side of the Valley, discovered by Davis in connexion with his work on the Akhenaton[2] cache. By the evening of 3 November we had laid bare a sufficient number of these huts for experimental purposes, so, after we had planned and noted them, they were removed, and we were ready to clear away the three feet of soil that lay beneath them.

Hardly had I arrived on the work next morning (4 November) than the unusual silence, due to the stoppage of the work, made me realize that something out of the ordinary had happened, and I was greeted by the announcement that a step cut in the rock had been discovered underneath the very first hut to be attacked.

---

[1] *Luxor:* ancient city in central Egypt, on the Nile River, near the Valley of the Tombs of the Kings, containing the temples and burial mounds of the pharoahs.   [2] *Akhenaton:* Egyptian king (c. 372–54 B.C.); a religious innovator who embraced solar monotheism, holding that he was the offspring of the sun.

This seemed too good to be true, but a short amount of extra clearing revealed the fact that we were actually in the entrance of a steep cut in the rock, some thirteen feet below the entrance to the tomb of Rameses VI, and a similar depth from the present bed level of the Valley. The manner of cutting was that of the sunken stairway entrance so common in the Valley, and I almost dared to hope that we had found our tomb at last. Work continued feverishly throughout the whole of that day and the morning of the next, but it was not until the afternoon of 5 November that we succeeded in clearing away the masses of rubbish that overlay the cut, and were able to demarcate the upper edges of the stairway on all its four sides.

It was clear by now beyond any question that we actually had before us the entrance to a tomb, but doubts, born of previous disappointments, persisted in creeping in. There was always the horrible possibility, suggested by our experience in the Thothmes III Valley, that the tomb was an unfinished one, never completed and never used: if it had been finished there was the depressing probability that it had been completely plundered in ancient times. On the other hand, there was just the chance of an untouched or only partially plundered tomb, and it was with ill-suppressed excitement that I watched the descending steps of the staircase, as one by one they came to light. The cutting was excavated in the side of a small hillock, and, as the work progressed, its western edge receded under the slope of the rock until it was, first partially, and then completely, roofed in, and became a passage, ten feet high by six feet wide. Work progressed more rapidly now; step succeeded step, and at the level of the twelfth, towards sunset, there was disclosed the upper part of a doorway, blocked, plastered, and sealed.

A sealed doorway—it was actually true, then! Our years of patient labour were to be rewarded after all, and I think my first feeling was one of congratulation that my faith in the Valley had not been unjustified. With excitement growing to fever heat I searched the seal impressions on the door for evidence of the identity of the owner, but could find no name: the only decipherable ones were those of the well-known royal necropolis seal, the jackal and nine captives. Two facts, however, were clear: first, the employment of this royal seal was certain evidence that the tomb had been constructed for a person of very high standing; and second, that the sealed door was entirely screened from above by workmen's huts of the Twentieth Dynasty was sufficiently clear proof that at least from that date it had never been entered. With that for the moment I had to be content.

While examining the seals I noticed, at the top of the doorway, where some of the plaster had fallen away, a heavy wooden lintel. Under this, to assure myself of the method by which the doorway had been blocked, I made a small peephole, just large enough to insert an electric torch, and discovered that the passage beyond the door was filled completely from floor to ceiling with stones and rubble—additional proof this of the care with which the tomb had been protected.

It was a thrilling moment for an excavator. Alone, save for my native workmen, I found myself, after years of comparatively unproductive labour, on the threshold of what might prove to be a magnificent discovery. Anything, literally anything, might lie beyond that passage, and it needed all my self-control to keep from breaking down the doorway, and investigating then and there.

One thing puzzled me, and that was the smallness of the opening in comparison with the ordinary Valley tombs. The design was certainly of the Eighteenth
Dynasty. Could it be the tomb of a noble buried here by royal consent? Was it a
royal cache, a hiding-place to which a mummy and its equipment had been removed for safety? Or was it actually the tomb of the king for whom I had spent so
many years in search.

Once more I examined the seal impressions for a clue, but on the part of the   10
door so far laid bare only those of the royal necropolis seal already mentioned were
clear enough to read. Had I but known that a few inches lower down there was a
perfectly clear and distinct impression of the seal of Tutankhamen, the king I most
desired to find, I would have cleared on, had a much better night's rest in consequence, and saved myself nearly three weeks of uncertainty. It was late, however,
and darkness was already upon us. With some reluctance I re-closed the small hole
that I had made, filled in our excavation for protection during the night, selected
the most trustworthy of my workmen—themselves almost as excited as I was—to
watch all night above the tomb, and so home by moonlight, riding down the Valley.

Naturally my wish was to go straight ahead with our clearing to find out the
full extent of the discovery, but Lord Carnarvon was in England, and in fairness to
him I had to delay matters until he could come. Accordingly, on the morning of
6 November I sent him the following cable: "At last have made wonderful discovery in Valley; a magnificent tomb with seals intact; re-covered same for your arrival;
congratulations."

My next task was to secure the doorway against interference until such time as
it could finally be reopened. This we did by filling our excavation up again to surface level, and rolling on top of it the large flint boulders of which the workmen's
huts had been composed. By the evening of the same day, exactly forty-eight hours
after we had discovered the first step of the staircase, this was accomplished. The
tomb had vanished. So far as the appearance of the ground was concerned there
never had been any tomb, and I found it hard to persuade myself at times that
the whole episode had not been a dream.

I was soon to be reassured on this point. News travels fast in Egypt, and within
two days of the discovery congratulations, inquiries, and offers of help descended
upon me in a steady stream from all directions. It became clear, even at this early
stage, that I was in for a job that could not be tackled single-handed, so I wired to
Callender, who had helped me on various previous occasions, asking him if possible to join me without delay, and to my relief he arrived on the very next day. On
the 8th I had received two messages from Lord Carnarvon in answer to my cable,
the first of which read, "Possibly come soon," and the second, received a little later,
"Propose arrive Alexandria 20th."

We had thus nearly a fortnight's grace, and we devoted it to making preparations of various kinds, so that when the time of reopening came, we should be able,
with the least possible delay, to handle any situation that might arise. On the night
of the 18th I went to Cairo for three days, to meet Lord Carnarvon and make a
number of necessary purchases, returning to Luxor on the 21st. On the 23rd Lord
Carnarvon arrived in Luxor with his daughter, Lady Evelyn Herbert, his devoted

companion in all his Egyptian work, and everything was in hand for the beginning of the second chapter of the discovery of the tomb. Callender had been busy all day clearing away the upper layer of rubbish, so that by morning we should be able to get into the staircase without any delay.

By the afternoon of the 24th the whole staircase was clear, sixteen steps in all, and we were able to make a proper examination of the sealed doorway. On the lower part the seal impressions were much clearer, and we were able without any difficulty to make out on several of them the name of Tutankhamen. This added enormously to the interest of the discovery. If we had found, as seemed almost certain, the tomb of that shadowy monarch, whose tenure of the throne coincided with one of the most interesting periods in the whole of Egyptian history, we should indeed have reason to congratulate ourselves.

With heightened interest, if that were possible, we renewed our investigation of the doorway. Here for the first time a disquieting element made its appearance. Now that the whole door was exposed to light it was possible to discern a fact that had hitherto escaped notice—that there had been two successive openings and reclosings of a part of its surface: furthermore, that the sealing originally discovered, the jackal and nine captives, had been applied to the re-closed portions, whereas the sealings of Tutankhamen covered the untouched part of the doorway, and were therefore those with which the tomb had been originally secured. The tomb then was not absolutely intact, as we had hoped. Plunderers had entered it, and entered it more than once—from the evidence of the huts above, plunderers of a date not later than the reign of Rameses VI—but that they had not rifled it completely was evident from the fact that it had been re-sealed.

Then came another puzzle. In the lower strata of rubbish that filled the staircase we found masses of broken potsherds and boxes, the latter bearing the names of Akhenaton, Smenkhkare and Tutankhamen, and, what was much more upsetting, a scarab of Thothmes III and a fragment with the name of Amenhetep III. Why this mixture of names? The balance of evidence so far would seem to indicate a cache rather than a tomb, and at this stage in the proceedings we inclined more and more to the opinion that we were about to find a miscellaneous collection of objects of the Eighteenth Dynasty kings, brought from Tell el Amarna by Tutankhamen and deposited here for safety.

So matters stood on the evening of the 24th. On the following day the sealed doorway was to be removed, so Callender set carpenters to work making a heavy wooden grille to be set up in its place. Mr. Engelbach, Chief Inspector of the Antiquities Department, paid us a visit during the afternoon, and witnessed part of the final clearing of rubbish from the doorway.

On the morning of the 25th the seal impressions on the doorway were carefully noted and photographed, and then we removed the actual blocking of the door, consisting of rough stones carefully built from floor to lintel, and heavily plastered on their outer faces to take the seal impressions.

This disclosed the beginning of a descending passage (not a staircase), the same width as the entrance stairway, and nearly seven feet high. As I had already discovered from my hole in the doorway, it was filled completely with stone and rubble, probably the chip from its own excavation. This filling, like the doorway, showed distinct signs of more than one opening and re-closing of the tomb, the untouched part consisting of clean white chip, mingled with dust, whereas the disturbed part was composed mainly of dark flint. It was clear that an irregular tunnel had been cut through the original filling at the upper corner on the left side, a tunnel corresponding in position with that of the hole in the doorway.

As we cleared the passage we found, mixed with the rubble of the lower levels, broken potsherds, jar sealings, alabaster jars, whole and broken, vases of painted pottery, numerous fragments of smaller articles, and water skins, these last having obviously been used to bring up the water needed for the plastering of the doorways. These were clear evidence of plundering, and we eyed them askance. By night we had cleared a considerable distance down the passage, but as yet saw no sign of second doorway or of chamber.

The day following (26 November) was the day of days, the most wonderful that I have ever lived through, and certainly one whose like I can never hope to see again. Throughout the morning the work of clearing continued, slowly perforce, on account of the delicate objects that were mixed with the filling. Then, in the middle of the afternoon, thirty feet down from the outer door, we came upon a second sealed doorway, almost an exact replica of the first. The seal impressions in this case were less distinct, but still recognizable as those of Tutankhamen and of the royal necropolis. Here again the signs of opening and re-closing were clearly marked upon the plaster. We were firmly convinced by this time that it was a cache that we were about to open, and not a tomb. The arrangement of stairway, entrance passage and doors reminded us very forcibly of the cache of Akhenaton and Tyi material found in the very near vicinity of the present excavation by Davis, and the fact that Tutankhamen's seals occurred there likewise seemed almost certain proof that we were right in our conjecture. We were soon to know. There lay the sealed doorway, and behind it was the answer to the question.

Slowly, desperately slowly it seemed to us as we watched, the remains of passage debris that encumbered the lower part of the doorway were removed, until at last we had the whole door clear before us. The decisive moment had arrived. With trembling hands I made a tiny breach in the upper left-hand corner. Darkness and blank space, as far as an iron testing-rod could reach, showed that whatever lay beyond was empty, and not filled like the passage we had just cleared. Candle tests were applied as a precaution against foul gases, and then, widening the hole a little, I inserted the candle and peered in, Lord Carnarvon, Lady Evelyn and Callender standing anxiously beside me to hear the verdict. At first I could see nothing, the hot air escaping from the chamber causing the candle flame to flicker, but presently, as my eyes grew accustomed to the light, details of the room within emerged slowly from the midst, strange animals, statues, and gold—everywhere the glint of gold. For the moment, an eternity it must have seemed to the others standing by— I was struck dumb with amazement, and when Lord Carnarvon, unable to stand the suspense any longer, inquired anxiously, "Can you see anything?" it was all I could do to get out the words. "Yes, wonderful things." Then, widening the hole a little further, so that we both could see, we inserted an electric torch.

Questions for Discussion and Writing

1. What obstacles did Carter have to overcome in continuing his search for the tomb for so many years? Why did he fear that the tomb he discovered might already have been ransacked or was of only minor importance?
2. How does Carter's organization of the essay heighten suspense leading up to his discovery? How do his detailed descriptions help the reader understand the nature of archaeological work and what is involved, and to visualize the layout of the excavation itself?
3. What is the significance of the discovery Carter made? What would archaeologists of the future conclude about our civilization from the contents of your most cluttered desk drawer?

KENNETH M. STAMPP

Kenneth M. Stampp was born in 1912 in Milwaukee, Wisconsin, and earned his Ph.D. from the University of Wisconsin in 1942. Stampp is the Morrison Professor of American History Emeritus at the University of California at Berkeley and has served as president of the Organization of American Historians. He has been Harmsworth Professor of American History at Oxford University and a Fulbright lecturer at the University of Munich and has received two Guggenheim fellowships. In addition to editing The Causes of the Civil War *(1974), Stampp is the author of many distinguished studies, including* And the War Came *(1950),* The Peculiar Institution: Slavery in the Antebellum South *(1956), and* The Imperiled Union *(1960). His most recent books include* America in 1857: A Nation on the Brink *(1990) and* The Causes of the Civil War *(1991). In "To Make Them Stand in Fear," taken from* The Peculiar Institution, *Stampp lets the facts of brutal exploitation speak for themselves as he describes the step-by-step process by which slavemasters in the South sought to break the spirits of newly arrived blacks.*

To Make Them Stand in Fear

A wise master did not take seriously the belief that Negroes were natural-born slaves. He knew better. He knew that Negroes freshly imported from Africa had to be broken to bondage; that each succeeding generation had to be carefully trained. This was no easy task, for the bondsman rarely submitted willingly. Moreover, he rarely submitted completely. In most cases there was no end to the need for control—at least not until old age reduced the slave to a condition of helplessness.

Masters revealed the qualities they sought to develop in slaves when they singled out certain ones for special commendation. A small Mississippi planter mourned the death of his "faithful and dearly beloved servant" Jack: "Since I have owned him he has been true to me in all respects. He was an obedient trusty servant. . . . I never knew him to steal nor lie and he ever set a moral and industrious example to those around him. . . . I shall ever cherish his memory." A Louisiana sugar planter lost a "very valuable Boy" through an accident: "His life was a very great one. I have always found him willing and obedient and never knew him to fail to do anything he was put to do." These were "ideal" slaves, the models slaveholders had in mind as they trained and governed their workers.

How might this ideal be approached? The first step, advised those who wrote discourses on the management of slaves, was to establish and maintain strict discipline. An Arkansas master suggested the adoption of the "Army Regulations as to the discipline in Forts." "They must obey at all times, and under all circumstances, cheerfully and with alacrity," affirmed a Virginia slaveholder. "It greatly impairs the happiness of a negro, to be allowed to cultivate an insubordinate temper. Unconditional submission is the only footing upon which slavery should be placed. It is precisely similar to the attitude of a minor to his parent, or a soldier to his general." A South Carolinian limned a perfect relationship between a slave and his master: "that the slave should know that his master is to govern absolutely, and he is to obey implicitly. That he is never for a moment to exercise either his will or judgment in opposition to a positive order."

The second step was to implant in the bondsmen themselves a consciousness of personal inferiority. They had "to know and keep their places," to "feel the difference between master and slave," to understand that bondage was their natural status. They had to feel that African ancestry tainted them, that their color was a badge of degradation. In the country they were to show respect for even their master's non-slave-holding neighbors; in the towns they were to give way on the streets to the most wretched white man. The line between the races must never be crossed, for familiarity caused slaves to forget their lowly station and to become "impudent."

Frederick Douglass explained that a slave might commit the offense of impudence in various ways: "in the tone of an answer; in answering at all; in not answering; in the expression of countenance; in the motion of the head; in the gait, manner and bearing of the slave." Any of these acts, in some subtle way, might indicate the absence of proper subordination. "In a well regulated community," wrote a Texan, "a negro takes off his hat in addressing a white man. . . . Where this is not enforced, we may always look for impudent and rebellious negroes." 5

The third step in the training of slaves was to awe them with a sense of their master's enormous power. The only principle upon which slavery could be maintained, reported a group of Charlestonians, was the "principle of fear." In his defense of slavery James H. Hammond admitted that this, unfortunately, was true but put the responsibility upon the abolitionists. Antislavery agitation had forced masters to strengthen their authority: "We have to rely more and more on the power of fear. . . . We are determined to continue masters, and to do so we have to draw the reign tighter and tighter day by day to be assured that we hold them in complete check." A North Carolina mistress, after subduing a troublesome domestic, realized that it was essential "to make them stand in fear"!

In this the slaveholders had considerable success. Frederick Douglass believed that most slaves stood "in awe" of white men; few could free themselves altogether from the notion that their masters were "invested with a sort of sacredness." Olmsted saw a small white girl stop a slave on the road and boldly order him to return to his plantation. The slave fearfully obeyed her command. A visitor in Mississippi claimed that a master, armed only with a whip or cane, could throw himself among a score of bondsmen and cause them to "flee with terror." He accomplished this by the "peculiar tone of authority" with which he spoke. "Fear, awe, and obedience . . . are interwoven into the very nature of the slave."

The fourth step was to persuade the bondsmen to take an interest in the master's enterprise and to accept his standards of good conduct. A South Carolina planter explained: "The master should make it his business to show his slaves, that the advancement of his individual interest, is at the same time an advancement of theirs. Once they feel this, it will require but little compulsion to make them act as it becomes them." Though slaveholders induced only a few chattels to respond to this appeal, these few were useful examples for others.

The final step was to impress Negroes with their helplessness, to create in them "a habit of perfect dependence" upon their masters. Many believed it dangerous to train slaves to be skilled artisans in the towns, because they tended to become self-reliant. Some thought it equally dangerous to hire them to factory owners. In the Richmond tobacco factories they were alarmingly independent and "insolvent." A Virginian was dismayed to find that his bondsmen, while working at an iron furnace, "got a habit of roaming about and *taking care of themselves*." Permitting them to hire their own time produced even worse results. "No higher evidence can be furnished of its baneful effects," wrote a Charlestonian, "than the unwillingness it produces in the slave, to return to the regular life and domestic control of the master."

A spirit of independence was less likely to develop among slaves kept on the land, where most of them became accustomed to having their master provide their basic needs, and where they might be taught that they were unfit to look out for themselves. Slaves then directed their energies to the attainment of mere "temporary ease and enjoyment." "Their masters," Olmsted believed, "calculated on it in them—do not wish to cure it—and by constant practice encourage it."

Here, then, was the way to produce the perfect slave: accustom him to rigid discipline, demand from him unconditional submission, impress upon him his innate inferiority, develop in him a paralyzing fear of white men, train him to adopt the master's code of good behavior, and instill in him a sense of complete dependence. This, at least, was the goal.

But the goal was seldom reached. Every master knew that the average slave was only an imperfect copy of the model. He knew that some bondsmen yielded only to superior power—and yielded reluctantly. This complicated his problem of control.

Questions for Discussion and Writing

1. What kind of instructions were provided in the source manuals from which Stampp quotes? How does Stampp's use of these source documents illustrate the method historians use to reconstruct and interpret past events?

2. How is Stampp's analysis arranged to show that the conditioning process moved through separate stages, from external control of behavior to a state in

which the slaves believed that what was good for the slave owners was good for them as well?

3. Why was the psychological conditioning used to produce dependency ultimately more important to the process than physical constraints? Why were slaves who could hire themselves out independently less able to be conditioned than those kept solely on one plantation?

HUANANI-KAY TRASK

Huanani-Kay Trask (b. 1949) is an activist, author, and poet who is a professor of Hawaiian Studies at the University of Hawai'i at Manoa. She received her Ph.D. in political science from the University of Wisconsin at Madison. The following essay originally appeared in From a Native Daughter: Colonialism and Sovereignty in Hawai'i (1999). The following essay is an impassioned argument against the abuse of Native Hawaiian rights caused by rampant tourism.

From a Native Daughter

I am certain that most, if not all, Americans have heard of Hawai'i and have wished, at some time in their lives, to visit my Native land. But I doubt that the history of how Hawai'i came to be territorially incorporated, and economically, politically, and culturally subordinated to the United States is known to most Americans. Nor is it common knowledge that Hawaiians have been struggling for over twenty years to achieve a land base and some form of political sovereignty on the same level as American Indians. Finally, I would imagine that most Americans could not place Hawai'i or any other Pacific island on a map of the Pacific. But despite all this appalling ignorance, five million Americans will vacation in my homeland this year *and* the next, and so on, into the foreseeable capitalist future. Such are the intended privileges of the so-called American standard of living: ignorance of and yet power over one's relations to Native peoples. Thanks to postwar American imperialism, the ideology that the United States has no overseas colonies and is, in fact, the champion of self-determination the world over holds no greater sway than in the United States itself. To most Americans, then, Hawai'i is *theirs*: to use, to take, and, above all, to fantasize about long after the experience.

Just five hours away by plane from California, Hawai'i is a thousand light years away in fantasy. Mostly a state of mind, Hawai'i is the image of escape from the rawness and violence of daily American life. Hawaii—the word, the vision, the sound in the mind—is the fragrance and feel of soft kindness. Above all, Hawai'i is "she," the Western image of the Native "female" in her magical allure. And if luck prevails, some of "her" will rub off on you, the visitor.

This fictional Hawai'i comes out of the depths of Western sexual sickness that demands a dark, sin-free Native for instant gratification between imperialist wars. The attraction of Hawai'i is stimulated by slick Hollywood movies, saccharine Andy Williams music, and the constant psychological deprivations of maniacal

American life. Tourists flock to my Native land for escape, but they are escaping into a state of mind while participating in the destruction of a host people in a Native place.

To Hawaiians, daily life is neither soft nor kind. In fact, the political, economic, and cultural reality for most Hawaiians is hard, ugly, and cruel.

In Hawai'i, the destruction of our land and the prostitution of our culture is   5
planned and executed by multinational corporations (both foreign-based and Hawai'i-based), by huge landowners (such as the missionary-descended Castle & Cook of Dole Pineapple fame), and by collaborationist state and county governments. The ideological gloss that claims tourism to be our economic savior and the "natural" result of Hawaiian culture is manufactured by ad agencies (such as the state-supported Hawai'i Visitors Bureau) and tour companies (many of which are owned by the airlines) and spewed out to the public through complicitous cultural engines such as film, television and radio, and the daily newspaper. As for the local labor unions, both rank and file and management clamor for more tourists, while the construction industry lobbies incessantly for larger resorts.

The major public educational institution, the University of Hawai'i, funnels millions of taxpayer dollars into a School of Travel Industry Management and a business school replete with a Real Estate Center and a Chair of Free Enterprise (renamed the Walker Chair to hide the crude reality of capitalism). As the propaganda arm of the tourist industry in Hawai'i, both schools churn out studies that purport to show why Hawai'i needs more golf courses, hotels, and tourist infrastructure and how Hawaiian culture is "naturally" one of giving and entertaining.

Of course, state-encouraged commodification and prostitution of Native cultures through tourism is not unique to Hawai'i. It is suffered by peoples in places as disparate as Goa, Australia, Tahiti, and the southwestern United States. Indeed, the problem is so common place that international organizations—for example, the Ecumenical Coalition on Third World Tourism out of Bangkok, the Center for Responsible Tourism in California, and the Third World European Network—have banded together to help give voice to Native peoples in daily resistance against corporate tourism. My focus on Hawai'i, although specific to my own culture, would likely transfer well when applied to most Native peoples.[1]

---

[1] The Center for Responsible Tourism and the Third World European Network were created out of the activism and organizing of the Ecumenical Coalition on Third World Tourism (ECTWT). This umbrella organization is composed of the following member bodies: All Africa Conference of Churches, Caribbean Conference of Churches, Christian Conference of Asia, Consejo Latinoamericano de Iglesias, Federation of Asian Bishops Conference/Office of Human Development, Middle East Council of Churches, Pacific Conference of Churches. In addition, sister organizations, like the Hawai'i Ecumenical Coalition on Tourism, extend the network worldwide. The ECTWT publishes a quarterly magazine with articles on Third World tourism and its destructive effects from child prostitution to dispossession of Native peoples. The address for ECTWT is P.O. Box 24, Chorakhebua, Bangkok 10230, Thailand.

Despite our similarities with other major tourist destinations, the statistical picture of the effects of corporate tourism in Hawai'i is shocking:

Fact: Nearly forty years ago, at statehood, Hawai'i residents outnumbered tourists by more than 2 to 1. Today, tourists outnumber residents by 6 to 1; they outnumber Native Hawaiians by 30 to 1.[2]

Fact.: According to independent economists and criminologists, "tourism has been the single most powerful factor in O'ahu's crime rate," including crimes against people and property.[3]

Fact: Independent demographers have been pointing out for years that "tourism is the major source of population growth in Hawai'i" and that "rapid growth of the tourist industry ensures the trend toward a rapidly expanded population that receives lower per capita income."[4]

Fact: The Bank of Hawai'i has reported that the average real incomes of Hawai'i residents grew only *one* percent during the period from the early seventies through the early eighties, when tourism was booming. The same held true throughout the nineties. The census bureau reports that personal income growth in Hawai'i during the same time was the lowest by far of any of the fifty American states.[5]

Fact: Groundwater supplies on O'ahu will be insufficient to meet the needs of residents and tourists by the year 2000.[6]

Fact: According to *The Honolulu Advertiser,* "Japanese investors have spent more than $7.1 billion on their acquisitions" since 1986 in Hawai'i. This kind of volume translates into huge alienations of land and properties. For example, nearly 2,000 acres of land on the Big Island of Hawai'i was purchased for $18.5 million and over 7,000 acres on Moloka'i went for $33 million. In 1989, over $1 billion was spent by the Japanese on land alone.[7]

Fact: More plants and animals from our Hawaiian Islands are now extinct or on the endangered species list than in the rest of the United States.[8]

Fact: More than 29,000 families are on the Hawaiian trust lands list, waiting for housing, pastoral, or agricultural lots.[9]

---

[2] Eleanor C. Nordyke, *The Peopling of Hawai'i,* 2nd ed. (Honolulu: University of Hawai'i Press, 1989), *pp. 134–172.*   [3] Meda Chesney-Lind, "Salient Factors in Hawai'i's Crime Rate," University of Hawai'i School of Social Work. Available from author.   [4] Nordyke, *The Peopling of Hawai'i,* pp. 134–172.   [5] Bank of Hawai'i Annual Economic Report, *1984.*   [6] Estimate of independent hydrologist Kate Vandemoer to community organizing group *Kūpa'a He'eia,* February 1990. Water quality and groundwater depletion are two problems much discussed by state and county officials in Hawai'i but ignored when resort permits are considered.   [7] *The Honolulu Advertiser,* April 8, 1990.   [8] David Stannard, Testimony against West Beach Estates. Land Use Commission, State of Hawaii, January 10, 1985.   [9] Department of Hawaiian Home Lands, phone interview, March *1998.*

Fact: The median cost of a home on the most populated island of O'ahu is around $350,000.[10]

Fact: Hawai'i has by far the worst ratio of average family income to average housing costs in the country. This explains why families spend nearly 52 percent of their gross income for housing costs.[11]

Fact: Nearly one-fifth of Hawai'i's resident population is classified as *near-homeless*, that is, those for whom any mishap results in immediate on-the-street homelessness.[12]

These kinds of statistics render a very bleak picture, not at an what the posters and jingoistic tourist promoters would have you believe about Hawai'i.

My use of the word *tourism* in the Hawai'i context refers to a mass-based, corporately controlled industry that is both vertically and horizontally integrated such that one multinational corporation owns an airline and the tour buses that transport tourists to the corporation-owned hotel where they eat in a corporation-owned restaurant, play golf, and "experience" Hawai'i on corporation-owned recreation areas and eventually consider buying a second home built on corporation land. Profits, in this case, are mostly repatriated back to the home country. In Hawai'i, these "home" countries are Japan, Taiwan, Hong Kong, Canada, Australia, and the United States. In this sense, Hawai'i is very much like a Third World colony where the local elite—the Democratic Party in our state—collaborate in the rape of Native land and people.[13]

The mass nature of this kind of tourism results in megaresort complexes on thousands of acres with demands for water and services that far surpass the needs of Hawai'i residents. These complexes may boast several hotels, golf courses, restaurants, and other "necessaries" to complete the total tourist experience. Infrastructure is usually built by the developer in exchange for county approval of more hotel units. In Hawai'i, counties bid against each other to attract larger and larger complexes. "Rich" counties, then, are those with more resorts, since they will pay more of the tax base of the county. The richest of these is the City and County of Honolulu, which encompasses the entire island of O'ahu. This island is the site of four major tourist destinations, a major international airport, and 80 percent of the resident population of Hawai'i. The military also controls nearly 30 percent of the island, with bases and airports of their own. As you might imagine, the density of certain parts of Honolulu (e.g., Waikīkī) is among the highest in the world. At the

10

---

[10] *Honolulu Star-Bulletin,* May 8, 1990.   [11] Bank of Hawai'i Annual Economic Report, 1984. In 1992, families probably spent closer to 60 percent of their gross income for housing costs. Billion-dollar Japanese investments and other speculation since 1984 have caused rental and purchase prices to skyrocket.   [12] This is the estimate of a state-contracted firm that surveyed the islands for homeless and near-homeless families. Testimony was delivered to the state legislature, 1990 session.   [13] For an analysis of post-statehood Hawai'i and its turn to mass-based corporate tourism, see Noel Kent, *Hawai'i: Islands Under the Influence.* For an analysis of foreign investment in Hawai'i, see *A Study of Foreign Investment and Its Impact on the State* (Honolulu: Hawai'i Real Estate Center, University of Hawaii, 1989).

present annual visitor count, more than five million tourists pour through O'ahu, an island of only 607 square miles.

With this as a background on tourism, I want to move now into the area of cultural prostitution. *Prostitution* in this context refers to the entire institution that defines a woman (and by extension the *female*) as an object of degraded and victimized sexual value for use and exchange through the medium of money. The *prostitute* is a woman who sells her sexual capacities and is seen, thereby, to possess and reproduce them at will, that is, by her very "nature." The prostitute and the institution that creates and maintains her are, of course, of patriarchal origin. The pimp is the conduit of exchange, managing the commodity that is the prostitute while acting as the guard at the entry and exit gates, making sure the prostitute behaves as a prostitute by fulfilling her sexual-economic functions. The victims participate in their victimization with enormous ranges of feeling, from resistance to complicity, but the force and continuity of the institution are shaped by men.

There is much more to prostitution than my sketch reveals but this must suffice, for I am interested in using the largest sense of this term as a metaphor in understanding what has happened to Hawaiian culture. My purpose is not to exact detail or fashion a model but to convey the utter degradation of our culture and our people under corporate tourism by employing *prostitution* as an analytic category.

Finally, I have chosen four areas of Hawaiian culture to examine: our homeland, our *one hānau* that is Hawai'i, our lands and fisheries, the outlying seas and the heavens; our language and dance; our familial relationships; and our women.

The *mo'olelo,* or history of Hawaiians, is to be found in our genealogies. From 15
our great cosmogonic genealogy, the *kumulipo,* derives the Hawaiian identity. The "essential lesson" of this genealogy is "the interrelatedness of the Hawaiian world, and the inseparability of its constituents parts." Thus, "the genealogy of the land, the gods, chiefs, and people intertwine one with the other, and with all aspects of the universe."[14]

In the *mo'olelo* of Papa and Wākea, "earth mother" and "sky father," our islands were born: Hawai'i, Maui, O'ahu, Kaua'i, and Ni'ihau. From their human offspring came the *taro* plant and from the *taro* came the Hawaiian people. The lessons of our genealogy are that human beings have a familial relationship to land and to the *taro,* our elder siblings or *kua'ana.*

In Hawai'i, as in all of Polynesia, younger siblings must serve and honor elder siblings who, in turn, must feed and care for their younger siblings. Therefore, Hawaiians must cultivate and husband the land that will feed and provide for the Hawaiian people. This relationship of people to land is called *mālama 'āina* or *aloha 'āina,* "care and love of the land."

When people and land work together harmoniously, the balance that results is called *pono.* In Hawaiian society, the *ali'i,* or "'chiefs," were required to maintain

---

[14] Lilikala Kame'eleihiwa, *Native Land and Foreign Desires* (Honolulu: Bishop Museum Press, 1992), p. 2.

order, an abundance of food, and good government. The *maka'āinana* or "common people," worked the land and fed the chiefs; the *ali'i* organized production and appeased the gods.

Today, *mālama 'āina is* called *stewardship* by some, although that word does not convey spiritual and genealogical connections. Nevertheless, to love and make the land flourish is a Hawaiian value. *'Āina, one* of the words for "land," means "that which feeds." *Kam'āina,* a term for native-born people, means "child of the land.'" Thus is the Hawaiian relationship to land both familial and reciprocal.

Hawaiian deities also spring from the land: Pele is our volcano, Kāne and Lono, our fertile valleys and plains, Kanaloa our ocean and all that lives within it, and so on with the numerous gods of Hawai'i. Our whole universe, physical and metaphysical, is divine.

Within this world, the older people, or *kūpuna,* are to cherish those who are younger, the *mo'opuna.* Unstinting generosity is a prized value. Social connections between our people are through *aloha,* simply translated as "love" but carrying with it a profoundly Hawaiian sense that is, again, familial and genealogical. Hawaiians feel *aloha* for Hawai'i from whence they come and for their Hawaiian kin upon whom they depend. It is nearly impossible to feel or practice *aloha* for something that is not familial. This is why we extend familial relations to those few non-Natives whom we feel understand and can reciprocate our *aloha.* But *aloha* is freely given and freely returned; it is not and cannot be demanded or commanded. Above all, *aloha* is a cultural feeling and practice that works among the people and between the people and their land.

The significance and meaning of *aloha* underscores the centrality of the Hawaiian language or *'ōlelo,* to the culture. *'Olelo* means both "language" and "tongue;" *mo'olelo,* or "history," is that which comes from the tongue, that is, "a story." *Haole,* or white people, say that we have oral history, but what we have are stories, such as our creation story, passed on through the generations. This sense of history is different from the *haole* sense of history. To Hawaiians in traditional society, language had tremendous power, thus the phrase, *i ka 'ōlelo ke ola; i ka 'ōlelo ka make*—"in language is life, in language is death."

After nearly two thousand years of speaking Hawaiian, our people suffered the near extinction of our language through its banning by the American-imposed government in 1900, the year Hawai'i became a territory of the United States. All schools, government operations and official transactions were thereafter conducted in English, despite the fact that most people, including non-Natives, still spoke Hawaiian at the turn of the century.

Since 1970, *'ōlelo Hawai'i,* or the Hawaiian language, has undergone a tremendous revival, including the rise of language immersion schools. The state of Hawai'i now has two official languages, Hawaiian and English, and the call for Hawaiian language speakers and teachers is increasing every day.[15]

---

[15] See Larry Kimura, "Native Hawaiian Culture," *Native Hawaiians Study Commission Report,* vol. 1, pp. 173–197.

Along with the flowering of Hawaiian language has come a flowering of   25
Hawaiian dance, especially in its ancient form, called *hula kahiko.* Dance academies,
known as *hālau,* have proliferated throughout Hawai'i, as have *kumu hula,* or dance
masters, and formal competitions where all-night presentations continue for three
or four days to throngs of appreciative listeners. Indeed, among Pacific Islanders,
Hawaiian dance is considered one of the finest Polynesian art forms today.

Of course, the cultural revitalization that Hawaiians are now experiencing and
transmitting to their children is as much a *repudiation* of colonization by so-called
Western civilization in its American form as it is a *reclamation of* our own past
and our own ways of life. This is why cultural revitalization is often resisted and dis-
paraged by anthropologists and others: they see very clearly that its political effect
is decolonization of the mind. Thus our rejection of the nuclear family as the basic
unit of society and of individualism as the best form of human expression infuriates
social workers, the churches, the legal system, and educators to this day. Hawaiians
continue to have allegedly "illegitimate" children, to *hānai,* or "adopt," both children and adults outside of sanctioned Western legal concepts, to hold and use land
and water in a collective form rather than a private property form, and to proscribe
the notion and the value that one person should strive to surpass and therefore
outshine all others.

All these Hawaiian values can be grouped under the idea of *'ohana,* loosely
translated as "family," but more accurately imagined as a group of both closely and
distantly related people who share nearly everything, from land and food to children
and status. Sharing is central to this value, since it prevents individual decline. Of
course, poverty is not thereby avoided; it is only shared with everyone in the unit.
The *'ohana* works effectively when the *kua'ana* relationship (elder sibling/younger
sibling reciprocity) is practiced.

Finally, within the *'ohana,* our women are considered the life-givers of the nation and are accorded the respect and honor this status conveys. Our young
women, like our young people in general, are the *pua,* or "flower" of our *lāhui,* or
our "nation." The renowned beauty of our women, especially their sexual beauty, is
not considered a commodity to be hoarded by fathers and brothers but an attribute of our people. Culturally, Hawaiians are very open and free about sexual relationships, although Christianity and organized religion have done much to damage
these traditional sexual values.

With this understanding of what it means to be Hawaiian, I want to move
now to the prostitution of our culture by tourism.

Hawai'i itself is the female object of degraded and victimized sexual value.   30
Our *'āina,* or lands, are not any longer the source of food and shelter, but the
source of money. Land is now called "real estate," rather than "our mother," Papa.
The American relationship of people to land is that of exploiter to exploited.
Beautiful areas, once sacred to my people, are now expensive resorts; shorelines
where net fishing, seaweed gathering, and crabbing occurred are more and more
the exclusive domain of recreational activities such as sunbathing, wind-surfing,
and jet skiing. Now, even access to beaches near hotels is strictly regulated or denied to the local public altogether.

The phrase, *mālama 'āina*—"to care for the land"—is used by government officials to sell new projects and to convince the locals that hotels can be built with a concern for "ecology." Hotel historians, like hotel doctors, are stationed in-house to soothe the visitors' stay with the pablum of invented myths and tales of the "primitive."

High schools and hotels adopt each other and funnel teenagers through major resorts for guided tours from kitchens to gardens to honeymoon suites in preparation for post-secondary school jobs in the lowest paid industry in the state. In the meantime, tourist appreciation kits and movies are distributed through the state Department of Education to all elementary schools. One film, unashamedly titled *What's in It for Me?*, was devised to convince locals that tourism is, as the newspapers never tire of saying, "the only game in town."

Of course, all this hype is necessary to hide the truth about tourism, the awful exploitative truth that the industry is the major cause of environmental degradation, low wages, land dispossession, and the highest cost of living in the United States.

While this propaganda is churned out to local residents, the commercialization of Hawaiian culture proceeds with calls for more sensitive marketing of our Native values and practices. After all, a prostitute is only as good as her income-producing talents. These talents, in Hawaiian terms, are the *hula;* the generosity, or *aloha,* of our people; the *u'i,* or youthful beauty of our women and men, and the continuing allure of our lands and waters, that is, of our place, Hawai'i.

The selling of these talents must produce income. And the function of tourism and the State of Hawaii is to convert these attributes into profit.

The first requirement is the transformation of the product, or the cultural attribute, much as a woman must be transformed to look like a prostitute—that is, someone who is complicitous in her own commodification. Thus *hula* dancers wear clownlike makeup, don costumes from a mix of Polynesian cultures, and behave in a manner that is smutty and salacious rather than powerfully erotic. The distance between the smutty and the erotic is precisely the distance between Western culture and Hawaiian culture. In the hotel version of the *hula,* the sacredness of the dance has completely evaporated, while the athleticism and sexual expression have been packaged like ornaments. The purpose is entertainment for profit rather than a joyful and truly Hawaiian celebration of human and divine nature.

The point, of course, is that everything in Hawai'i can be yours, that is, you the tourists', the non-Natives', the visitors'. The place, the people, the culture, even our identity as a "Native" people is for sale. Thus the word "Aloha" is employed as an aid in the constant hawking of things Hawaiian. In truth, this use of *aloha is* so far removed from any Hawaiian cultural context that it is, literally, meaningless.

Thus, Hawai'i, like a lovely woman, is there for the taking. Those with only a little money get a brief encounter, those with a lot of money, like the Japanese, get more. The state and counties will give tax breaks, build infrastructure, and have the governor personally welcome tourists to ensure that they keep coming. Just as the pimp regulates prices and guards the commodity of the prostitute, so the state bargains with developers for access to Hawaiian land and culture. Who builds the biggest resorts to attract the most affluent tourists gets the best deal: more hotel rooms, golf courses, and restaurants approved. Permits are fast-tracked, height and density limits are suspended, new groundwater sources are miraculously found.

Hawaiians, meanwhile, have little choice in all this. We can fill up the unemployment lines, enter the military, work in the tourist industry, or leave Hawai'i. Increasingly, Hawaiians are leaving, not by choice but out of economic necessity.

Our people who work in the industry—dancers, waiters, singers, valets, gardeners, housekeepers, bartenders, and even a few managers—make between $10,000 and $25,000 a year, an impossible salary for a family in Hawai'i. Psychologically, our young people have begun to think of tourism as the only employment opportunity, trapped as they are by the lack of alternatives. For our young women, modeling is a "cleaner" job when compared to waiting on tables or dancing in a weekly revue, but modeling feeds on tourism and the commodification of Hawaiian women. In the end, the entire employment scene is shaped by tourism.

40

Despite their exploitation, Hawaiians' participation in tourism raises the problem of complicity. Because wages are so low and advancement so rare, whatever complicity exists is secondary to the economic hopelessness that drives Hawaiians into the industry. Refusing to contribute to the commercialization of one's culture becomes a peripheral concern when unemployment looms.

Of course, many Hawaiians do not see tourism as part of their colonization. Thus, tourism is viewed as providing jobs, not as a form of cultural prostitution. Even those who have some glimmer of critical consciousness do not generally agree that the tourist industry prostitutes Hawaiian culture. This is a measure of the depth of our mental oppression: we cannot understand our own cultural degradation because we are living it. As colonized people, we are colonized to the extent that we are unaware of our oppression. When awareness begins, then so, too, does decolonization. Judging by the growing resistance to new hotels, to geothermal energy and manganese nodule mining, which would supplement the tourist industry, and to increases in the sheer number of tourists, I would say that decolonization has begun, but we have many more stages to negotiate on our path to sovereignty.

My brief excursion into the prostitution of Hawaiian culture has done no more than give an overview. Now that you have read a Native view, let me just leave this thought with you. If you are thinking of visiting my homeland, please do not. We do not want or need any more tourists, and we certainly do not like them. If you want to help our cause, pass this message on to your friends.

Questions for Discussion and Writing

1. Trask feels that the cumulative effects of tourism on Hawaii have been disastrous. What facts and figures does she present to support her thesis?
2. Does Trask run the risk of alienating even those who might agree with her because of her incendiary rhetorical approach? Why or why not? Did you find her approach effective? Explain your answer.

3. Trask concludes her essay by requesting prospective visitors to remain home. Would her essay have any effect on your decision to visit Hawaii if you had the opportunity to do so? Why or why not?

JACK LONDON

Jack London (1876–1916) was born John Griffith Chaney in San Francisco but took the name of his stepfather, John London. His impoverished childhood bred self-reliance: He worked in a canning factory and a jute mill and as a longshoreman, robbed oyster beds as the self-styled "Prince of the Oyster Pirates," went to sea at seventeen, and took part in the Klondike gold rush of 1897. When he began writing his distinctive stories, often set in the Yukon, of the survival of men and animals in harsh environments, he drew on these experiences and was profoundly influenced by the works of Karl Marx, Rudyard Kipling, and Friedrich Wilhelm Nietzsche. In his novels The Call of the Wild *(1903),* The Sea Wolf *(1904),* White Fang *(1906), and* The Iron Heel *(1908), and in short stories such as "Love of Life" (1906) and "To Build a Fire" (1910), London powerfully dramatizes the conflict between barbarism and civilization. During London's short, turbulent life, his prolific output as a writer also included his work as a journalist. Among other assignments, he covered the Russo-Japanese War of 1904–1905 as a syndicated correspondent. "The San Francisco Earthquake" (1906) was the first in a series of reports on the April 18, 1906, catastrophe that London wrote for* Collier's *magazine. His straightforward descriptive style influenced later writers such as Ernest Hemingway and Sherwood Anderson.*

The San Francisco Earthquake

The earthquake shook down in San Francisco hundreds of thousands of dollars' worth of walls and chimneys. But the conflagration that followed burned up hundreds of millions of dollars' worth of property. There is no estimating within hundreds of millions the actual damage wrought. Not in history has a modern imperial city been so completely destroyed. San Francisco is gone. Nothing remains of it but memories and a fringe of dwelling-houses on its outskirts. Its industrial section is wiped out. Its business section is wiped out. The factories and warehouses, the great stores and newspaper buildings, the hotels and the palaces of the nabobs, are all gone. Remains only the fringe of dwelling-houses on the outskirts of what was once San Francisco.

Within an hour after the earthquake shock the smoke of San Francisco's burning was a lurid tower visible a hundred miles away. And for three days and nights this lurid tower swayed in the sky, reddening the sun, darkening the day, and filling the land with smoke.

On Wednesday morning at a quarter past five came the earthquake. A minute later the flames were leaping upward. In a dozen different quarters south of Market Street, in the working-class ghetto, and in the factories, fires started. There was no opposing the flames. There was no organization, no communication. All the cunning adjustments of a twentieth century city had been smashed by the earthquake.

The streets were humped into ridges and depressions, and piled with the debris of fallen walls. The steel rails were twisted into perpendicular and horizontal angles. The telephone and telegraph systems were disrupted. And the great water-mains had burst. All the shrewd contrivances and safe-guards of man had been thrown out of gear by thirty seconds' twitching of the earth-crust.

THE FIRE MADE ITS OWN DRAFT

By Wednesday afternoon, inside of twelve hours, half the heart of the city was gone. At that time I watched the vast conflagration from out on the bay. It was dead calm. Not a flicker of wind stirred. Yet from every side wind was pouring in upon the city. East, west, north, and south, strong winds were blowing upon the doomed city. The heated air rising made an enormous suck. Thus did the fire of itself build its own colossal chimney through the atmosphere. Day and night this dead calm continued, and yet, near to the flames, the wind was often half a gale, so mighty was the suck.

Wednesday night saw the destruction of the very heart of the city. Dynamite was lavishly used, and many of San Francisco's proudest structures were crumbled by man himself into ruins, but there was no withstanding the onrush of the flames. Time and again successful stands were made by the fire-fighters, and every time the flames flanked around on either side, or came up from the rear, and turned to defeat the hard-won victory.

An enumeration of the buildings destroyed would be a directory of San Francisco. An enumeration of the buildings undestroyed would be a line and several addresses. An enumeration of the deeds of heroism would stock a library and bankrupt the Carnegie Medal fund. An enumeration of the dead will never be made. All vestiges of them were destroyed by the flames. The number of victims of the earthquake will never be known. South of Market Street, where the loss of life was particularly heavy, was the first to catch fire.

Remarkable as it may seem, Wednesday night, while the whole city crashed and roared into ruin, was a quiet night. There were no crowds. There was no shouting and yelling. There was no hysteria, no disorder. I passed Wednesday night in the path of the advancing flames, and in all those terrible hours I saw not one woman who wept, not one man who was excited, not one person who was in the slightest degree panic-stricken.

Before the flames, throughout the night, fled tens of thousands of homeless ones. Some were wrapped in blankets. Others carried bundles of bedding and dear household treasures. Sometimes a whole family was harnessed to a carriage or delivery wagon that was weighted down with their possessions. Baby buggies, toy wagons, and go-carts were used as trucks, while every other person was dragging a trunk. Yet everybody was gracious. The most perfect courtesy obtained. Never, in all San Francisco's history, were her people so kind and courteous as on this night of terror.

5

A Caravan of Trunks

All night these tens of thousands fled before the flames. Many of them, the poor people from the labor ghetto, had fled all day as well. They had left their homes burdened with possessions. Now and again they lightened up, flinging out upon the street clothing and treasures they had dragged for miles.

They held on longest to their trunks, and over these trunks many a strong   10
man broke his heart that night. The hills of San Francisco are steep, and up these hills, mile after mile, were the trunks dragged. Everywhere were trunks, with across them lying their exhausted owners, men and women. Before the march of the flames were flung picket lines of soldiers. And a block at a time, as the flames advanced, these pickets retreated. One of their tasks was to keep the trunk-pullers moving. The exhausted creatures, stirred on by the menace of bayonets, would arise and struggle up the steep pavements, pausing from weakness every five or ten feet.

Often, after surmounting a heart-breaking hill, they would find another wall of flame advancing upon them at right angles and be compelled to change anew the line of their retreat. In the end, completely played out, after toiling for a dozen hours like giants, thousands of them were compelled to abandon their trunks. Here the shopkeepers and soft members of the middle class were at a disadvantage. But the working men dug holes in vacant lots and backyards and buried their trunks.

The Doomed City

At nine o'clock Wednesday evening I walked down through the very heart of the city. I walked through miles and miles of magnificent buildings and towering skyscrapers. Here was no fire. All was in perfect order. The police patrolled the streets. Every building had its watchman at the door. And yet it was doomed, all of it. There was no water. The dynamite was giving out. And at right angles two different conflagrations were sweeping down upon it.

At one o'clock in the morning I walked down through the same section. Everything still stood intact. There was no fire. And yet there was a change. A rain of ashes was falling. The watchmen at the doors were gone. The police had been withdrawn. There were no firemen, no fire engines, no men fighting with dynamite. The district had been absolutely abandoned. I stood at the corner of Kearney and Market, in the very innermost heart of San Francisco. Kearney Street was deserted. Half a dozen blocks away it was burning on both sides. The street was a wall of flame, and against this wall of flame, silhouetted sharply, were two United States cavalrymen sitting their horses, calmly watching. That was all. Not another person was in sight. In the intact heart of the city two troopers sat their horses and watched.

SPREAD OF THE CONFLAGRATION

Surrender was complete. There was no water. The sewers had long since been pumped dry. There was no dynamite. Another fire had broken out further uptown, and now from three sides conflagrations were sweeping down. The fourth side had been burned earlier in the day. In that direction stood the tottering walls of the Examiner building, the burned-out Call building, the smoldering ruins of the Grand Hotel, and the gutted, devastated, dynamited Palace Hotel.

The following will illustrate the sweep of the flames and the inability of men to calculate their spread. At eight o'clock Wednesday evening I passed through Union Square. It was packed with refugees. Thousands of them had gone to bed on the grass. Government tents had been set up, supper was being cooked, and the refugees were lining up for free meals.   15

At half-past one in the morning three sides of Union Square were in flames. The fourth side, where stood the great St. Francis Hotel, was still holding out. An hour later, ignited from top and sides, the St. Francis was flaming heavenward. Union Square, heaped high with mountains of trunks, was deserted. Troops, refugees, and all had retreated.

A FORTUNE FOR A HORSE!

It was at Union Square that I saw a man offering a thousand dollars for a team of horses. He was in charge of a truck piled high with trunks for some hotel. It had been hauled here into what was considered safety, and the horses had been taken out. The flames were on three sides of the Square, and there were no horses.

Also, at this time, standing beside the truck, I urged a man to seek safety in flight. He was all but hemmed in by several conflagrations. He was an old man and he was on crutches. Said he, "Today is my birthday. Last night I was worth thirty thousand dollars. I bought five bottles of wine, some delicate fish, and other things for my birthday dinner. I have had no dinner, and all I own are these crutches."

I convinced him of his danger and started him limping on his way. An hour later, from a distance, I saw the truckload of trunks burning merrily in the middle of the street.

On Thursday morning, at a quarter past five, just twenty-four hours after the earthquake, I sat on the steps of a small residence on Nob Hill. With me sat Japanese, Italians, Chinese, and Negroes—a bit of the cosmopolitan flotsam of the wreck of the city. All about were the palaces of the nabob pioneers of Forty-nine. To the east and south, at right angles, were advancing two mighty walls of flame.   20

I went inside with the owner of the house on the steps of which I sat. He was cool and cheerful and hospitable. "Yesterday morning," he said, "I was worth six hundred thousand dollars. This morning this house is all I have left. It will go in fifteen minutes." He pointed to a large cabinet. "That is my wife's collection of china. This rug upon which we stand is a present. It cost fifteen hundred dollars. Try that piano. Listen to its tone. There are few like it. There are no horses. The flames will be here in fifteen minutes."

Outside, the old Mark Hopkins residence, a palace, was just catching fire. The troops were falling back and driving the refugees before them. From every side came the roaring of flames, the crashing of walls, and the detonations of dynamite.

THE DAWN OF THE SECOND DAY

I passed out of the house. Day was trying to dawn through the smoke-pall. A sickly light was creeping over the face of things. Once only the sun broke through the smoke-pall, blood-red, and showing a quarter its usual size. The smoke-pall itself, viewed from beneath, was a rose color that pulsed and fluttered with lavender shades. Then it turned to mauve and yellow and dun. There was no sun. And so dawned the second day on stricken San Francisco.

An hour later I was creeping past the shattered dome of the City Hall. Than it, there was no better exhibit of the destructive forces of the earthquake. Most of the stone had been shaken from the great dome, leaving standing the naked framework of steel. Market Street was piled high with wreckage, and across the wreckage lay the overthrown pillars of the City Hall shattered into short crosswise sections.

This section of the city, with the exception of the Mint and the Post-Office, 25 was already a waste of smoking ruins. Here and there through the smoke, creeping warily under the shadows of tottering walls, emerged occasional men and women. It was like the meeting of the handful of survivors after the day of the end of the world.

BEEVES SLAUGHTERED AND ROASTED

On Mission Street lay a dozen steers, in a neat row stretching across the street, just as they had been struck down by the flying ruins of the earthquake. The fire had passed through afterward and roasted them. The human dead had been carried away before the fire came. At another place on Mission Street I saw a milk wagon. A steel telegraph pole had smashed down sheer through the driver's seat and crushed the front wheels. The milkcans lay scattered around.

All day Thursday and all Thursday night, all day Friday and Friday night, the flames still raged.

Friday night saw the flames finally conquered, though not until Russian Hill and Telegraph Hill had been swept and three-quarters of a mile of wharves and docks had been licked up.

THE LAST STAND

The great stand of the fire-fighters was made Thursday night on Van Ness Avenue. Had they failed here, the comparatively few remaining houses of the city would have been swept. Here were the magnificent residences of the second generation of San Francisco nabobs, and these, in a solid zone, were dynamited down across the path of the fire. Here and there the flames leaped the zone, but these fires were beaten out, principally by the use of wet blankets and rugs.

San Francisco, at the present time, is like the crater of a volcano, around which are camped tens of thousand of refugees. At the Presidio alone are at least twenty thousand. All the surrounding cities and towns are jammed with the homeless ones, where they are being cared for by the relief committees. The refugees were carried free by the railroads to any point they wished to go, and it is estimated that over one hundred thousand people have left the peninsula on which San Francisco stood. The Government has the situation in hand, and, thanks to the immediate relief given by the whole United States, there is not the slightest possibility of a famine. The bankers and business men have already set about making preparations to rebuild San Francisco.

Questions for Discussion and Writing

1. What examples of courteous behavior does London cite that support the impression of the civility of San Franciscans under great stress? How much of San Francisco was destroyed by subsequent fires in comparison with the damage done by the earthquake itself? How do we know that London risked his own life to accurately report the extent of the destruction?
2. What effect does London produce by reporting the event from many different vantage points within the city? How is his description enhanced by metaphors that evoke the sounds, sights, tastes, and smells of the conflagration? How does his shift from war imagery to the metaphor of the shipwreck reflect the predicament citizens faced as survivors of the devastation?
3. How does the phrase "[my] fortune for a horse" (echoing the famous line from Shakespeare's play *Richard III*, "my kingdom for a horse") express the desperation of citizens seeking to save what little they could? Which parts of this report are enhanced by London's skill as a novelist using fictional techniques to dramatize his otherwise objective journalistic account?

HANSON W. BALDWIN

Hanson W. Baldwin (1903–1991) served as military editor for The New York Times *and won the Pulitzer Prize for his reporting in 1943. Among his published works are* The Crucial Year, 1939–41: The World at War *(1976). This account was first published in* Harper's *magazine in January 1934.*

R. M. S. Titanic

The White Star liner *Titanic,* largest ship the world had ever known, sailed from Southampton on her maiden voyage to New York on April 10, 1912. The paint on her strakes was fair and bright; she was fresh from Harland and Wolff's

Belfast yards, strong in the strength of her forty-six thousand tons of steel, bent, hammered, shaped and riveted through the three years of her slow birth.

There was little fuss and fanfare at her sailing; her sister ship, the *Olympic*—slightly smaller than the *Titanic*—had been in service for some months and to her had gone the thunder of the cheers.

But the *Titanic* needed no whistling steamers or shouting crowds to call attention to her superlative qualities. Her bulk dwarfed the ships near her as longshoremen singled up her mooring lines and cast off the turns of heavy rope from the dock bollards. She was not only the largest ship afloat, but was believed to be the safest. Carlisle, her builder, had given her double bottoms and had divided her hull into sixteen watertight compartments, which made her, men thought, unsinkable. She had been built to be and had been described as a gigantic lifeboat. Her designers' dreams of a triple-screw giant, a luxurious, floating hotel, which could speed to New York at twenty-three knots, had been carefully translated from blue prints and mold-loft lines at the Belfast yards into a living reality.

The *Titanic's* sailing from Southampton, though quiet, was not wholly uneventful. As the liner moved slowly toward the end of her dock that April day, the surge of her passing sucked away from the quay the steamer *New York,* moored just to seaward of the *Titanic's* berth. There were sharp cracks as the manila mooring lines of the *New York* parted under the strain. The frayed ropes writhed and whistled through the air and snapped down among the waving crowd on the pier; the *New York* swung toward the *Titanic's* bow, was checked and dragged back to the dock barely in time to avert a collision. Seamen muttered, thought it an ominous start.

Past Spithead and the Isle of Wight the *Titanic* steamed. She called at Cherbourg at dusk and then laid her course for Queenstown. At 1:30 p.m. on Thursday, April 11, she stood out of Queenstown harbor, screaming gulls soaring in her wake, with 2,201 persons—men, women, and children—aboard.

Occupying the Empire bedrooms and Georgian suites of the first-class accommodations were many well-known men and women—Colonel John Jacob Astor and his young bride; Major Archibald Butt, military aide to President Taft, and his friend, Frank D. Millet, the painter; John B. Thayer, vice-president of the Pennsylvania Railroad, and Charles M. Hays, president of the Grand Trunk Railway of Canada; W. T. Stead, the English journalist; Jacques Futrelle, French novelist; H. B. Harris, theatrical manager, and Mrs. Harris; Mr. and Mrs. Isidor Straus; and J. Bruce Ismay, chairman and managing director of the White Star line.

Down in the plain wooden cabins of the steerage class were 706 immigrants to the land of promise, and trimly stowed in the great holds was a cargo valued at $420,000: oak beams, sponges, wine, calabashes, and an odd miscellany of the common and the rare.

The *Titanic* took her departure on Fastnet Light and, heading into the night, laid her course for New York. She was due at Quarantine the following Wednesday morning.

Sunday dawned fair and clear. The *Titanic* steamed smoothly toward the west, faint streamers of brownish smoke trailing from her funnels. The purser held services in the saloon in the morning; on the steerage deck aft the immigrants were

5

playing games and a Scotsman was puffing "The Campbells Are Coming" on his bagpipes in the midst of the uproar.

At 9 A.M. a message from the steamer *Caronia* sputtered into the wireless   10
shack:

Captain, Titanic—Westbound steamers report bergs growlers and field ice in 42 degrees N. from 49 degrees to 51 degrees W. 12th April.

Compliments—

Barr.

It was cold in the afternoon; the sun was brilliant, but the *Titanic,* her screws turning over at 75 revolutions per minute, was approaching the Banks.

In the Marconi cabin Second Operator Harold Bride, earphones clamped on his head, was figuring accounts; he did not stop to answer when he heard MWL, Continental Morse for the nearby Leyland liner, *Californian,* calling the *Titanic.* The *Californian* had some message about three icebergs; he didn't bother then to take it down. About 1:42 P.M. the rasping spark of those days spoke again across the water. It was the *Baltic,* calling the *Titanic,* warning her of ice on the steamer track. Bride took the message down and sent it up to the bridge. The officer-of-the-deck glanced at it; sent it to the bearded master of the *Titanic,* Captain E. C. Smith, a veteran of the White Star service. It was lunch time then; the Captain, walking along the promenade deck, saw Mr. Ismay, stopped, and handed him the message without comment. Ismay read it, stuffed it in his pocket, told two ladies about the icebergs, and resumed his walk. Later, about 7:15 P.M., the Captain requested the return of the message in order to post it in the chart room for the information of officers.

Dinner that night in the Jacobean dining room was gay. It was bitter on deck, but the night was calm and fine; the sky was moonless but studded with stars twinkling coldly in the clear air.

After dinner some of the second-class passengers gathered in the saloon, where the Reverend Mr. Carter conducted a "hymn singsong." It was almost ten o'clock and the stewards were waiting with biscuits and coffee as the group sang:

O, hear us when we cry to Thee
For those in peril on the sea.

On the bridge Second Officer Lightoller—short, stocky, efficient—was re-   15
lieved at ten o'clock by First Officer Murdock. Lightoller had talked with other officers about the proximity of ice; at least five wireless ice warnings had reached the ship; lookouts had been cautioned to be alert; captains and officers expected to reach the field at any time after 9:30 P.M. At twenty-two knots, its speed unslackened, the *Titanic* plowed on through the night.

Lightoller left the darkened bridge to his relief and turned in. Captain Smith went to his cabin. The steerage was long since quiet; in the first and second cabins lights were going out; voices were growing still, people were asleep. Murdock paced back and forth on the bridge, peering out over the dark water, glancing now and then at the compass in front of Quatermaster Hichens at the wheel.

In the crow's nest, Lookout Frederick Fleet and his partner, Leigh, gazed down at the water, still and unruffled in the dim, starlit darkness. Behind and below them the ship, a white shadow with here and there a last winking light; ahead of them a dark and silent and cold ocean.

There was a sudden clang. "Dong-dong. Dong-dong. Dong-dong. Dong!" The metal clapper of the great ship's bell struck out 11:30. Mindful of the warnings, Fleet strained his eyes, searching the darkness for the dreaded ice. But there were only the stars and the sea.

In the wireless room, where Phillips, first operator, had relieved Bride, the buzz of the *Californian's* set again crackled into the earphones:

Californian: "Say, old man, we are stuck here, surrounded by ice."

Titanic: "Shut up, shut up; keep out. I am talking to Cape Race; you are jamming my signals."

Then, a few minutes later—about 11:40 . . .   20

Out of the dark she came, a vast, dim, white, monstrous shape, directly in the *Titanic's* path. For a moment Fleet doubted his eyes. But she was a deadly reality, this ghastly thing. Frantically, Fleet struck three bells—*something dead ahead.* He snatched the telephone and called the bridge:

"Iceberg! Right ahead!"

The First Officer heard but did not stop to acknowledge the message.

"Hard astarboard!"

Hichens strained at the wheel; the bow swung slowly to port. The monster   25 was almost upon them now.

Murdock leaped to the engine-room telegraph. Bells clanged. Far below in the engine room those bells struck the first warning. Danger! The indicators on the dial faces swung round to "Stop!" Then "Full speed astern!" Frantically the engineers turned great valve wheels; answered the bridge bells. . . .

There was a slight shock, a brief scraping, a small list to port. Shell ice—slabs and chunks of it—fell on the foredeck. Slowly the *Titanic* stopped.

Captain Smith hurried out of his cabin.

"What has the ship struck?"

Murdock answered, "An iceberg, sir. I hard-astarboarded and reversed the en-   30 gines, and I was going to hard-aport around it, but she was too close. I could not do any more. I have closed the watertight doors."

Fourth Officer Boxhall, other officers, the carpenter, came to the bridge. The Captain sent Boxhall and the carpenter below to ascertain the damage.

A few lights switched on in the first and second cabins; sleepy passengers peered through porthole glass; some casually asked the stewards:

"Why have we stopped?"

"I don't know, sir, but I don't suppose it is anything much."

In the smoking room a quorum of gamblers and their prey were still sitting   35 round a poker table; the usual crowd of kibitzers looked on. They had felt the slight jar of the collision and had seen an eighty-foot ice mountain glide by the smoking-room windows, but the night was calm and clear, the *Titanic* was "unsinkable"; they hadn't bothered to go on deck.

But far below, in the warren of passages on the starboard side forward, in the forward holds and boiler rooms, men could see that the *Titanic's* hurt was mortal. In No. 6 boiler room, where the red glow from the furnaces lighted up the naked, sweaty chests of coal-blackened firemen, water was pouring through a great gash about two feet above the floor plates. This was no slow leak; the ship was open to the sea; in ten minutes there were eight feet of water in No. 6. Long before then the stokers had raked the flaming fires out of the furnaces and had scrambled through the watertight doors into No. 5 or had climbed up the long steel ladders to safety. When Boxhall looked at the mail room in No. 3 hold, twenty-four feet above the keel, the mailbags were already floating about in the slushing water. In No. 5 boiler room a stream of water spurted into an empty bunker. All six compartments forward of No. 4 were open to the sea; in ten seconds the iceberg's jagged claw had ripped a three-hundred-foot slash in the bottom of the great *Titanic*.

Reports came to the bridge; Ismay in dressing gown ran out on deck in the cold, still, starlit night, climbed up the bridge ladder.

"What has happened?"

Captain Smith: "We have struck ice."

"Do you think she is seriously damaged?"

Captain: "I'm afraid she is."   40

Ismay went below and passed Chief Engineer William Bell fresh from an inspection of the damaged compartments. Bell corroborated the Captain's statement; hurried back down the glistening steel ladders to his duty. Man after man followed him—Thomas Andrews, one of the ship's designers, Archie Frost, the builder's chief engineer, and his twenty assistants—men who had no posts of duty in the engine room but whose traditions called them there.

On deck, in corridor and stateroom, life flowed again. Men, women, and children awoke and questioned; orders were given to uncover the lifeboats; water rose into the firemen's quarters; half-dressed stokers streamed up on deck. But the passengers—most of them—did not know that the *Titanic* was sinking. The shock of the collision had been so slight that some were not awakened by it; the *Titanic* was so huge that she must be unsinkable; the night was too calm, too beautiful, to think of death at sea.

Captain Smith half ran to the door of the radio shack. Bride, partly dressed, eyes dulled with sleep, was standing behind Phillips, waiting.

"Send the call for assistance."   45

The blue spark danced: "CQD—CQD—CQD—CQ—"

Miles away Marconi men heard. Cape Race heard it, and the steamships *La Provence* and *Mt. Temple*.

The sea was surging into the *Titanic's* hold. At 12:20 the water burst into the seamen's quarters through a collapsed fore-and-aft wooden bulkhead. Pumps strained in the engine rooms—men and machinery making a futile fight against the sea. Steadily the water rose.

The boats were swung out—slowly; for the deckhands were late in reaching their stations, there had been no boat drill, and many of the crew did not know to what boats they were assigned. Orders were shouted; the safety valves had lifted, and steam was blowing off in a great rushing roar. In the chart house Fourth Officer Boxhall bent above a chart, working rapidly with pencil and dividers.

12:15 A.M. Boxhall's position is sent out to a fleet of vessels: "Come at once; we have struck a berg."

To the Cunarder *Carpathia* (Arthur Henry Rostron, Master, New York to Liverpool, fifty-eight miles away): "It's a CQD, old man. Position 41–46 N.; 50–14 W."

The blue spark dancing: "Sinking; cannot hear for noise of steam."

12:30 A.M. The word is passed: "Women and children in the boats." Stewards finish waking their passengers below; life preservers are tied on; some men smile at the precaution. "The *Titanic* is unsinkable." The *Mt. Temple* starts for the *Titanic;* the *Carpathia,* with a double watch in her stokeholds, radios, "Coming hard." The CQD changes the course of many ships—but not of one; the operator of the *Californian,* near by, has just put down his earphones and turned in.

The CQD flashes over land and sea from Cape Race to New York; newspaper city rooms leap to life and presses whir.

On the *Titanic,* water creeps over the bulkhead between Nos. 5 and 6 firerooms. She is going down by the head; the engineers—fighting a losing battle—are forced back foot by foot by the rising water. Down the promenade deck, Happy Jock Hume, the bandsman, runs with his instrument.

12:45 A.M. Murdock, in charge on the starboard side, eyes tragic, but calm and cool, orders boat No. 7 lowered. The women hang back; they want no boat ride on an ice-strewn sea; the *Titanic* is unsinkable. The men encourage them, explain that this is just a precautionary measure: "We'll see you again at breakfast." There is little confusion; passengers stream slowly to the boat deck. In the steerage the immigrants chatter excitedly.

A sudden sharp hiss—a streaked flare against the night; Boxhall sends a rocket toward the sky. It explodes, and a parachute of white stars lights up the icy sea. "God! Rockets!" The band plays ragtime.

No. 8 is lowered, and No. 5. Ismay, still in dressing gown, calls for women and children, handles lines, stumbles in the way of an officer, is told to "get the hell out of here." Third Officer Pitman takes charge of No. 5; as he swings into the boat Murdock grasps his hand. "Good-by and good luck, old man."

No. 6 goes over the side. There are only twenty-eight people in a lifeboat with a capacity of sixty-five.

A light stabs from the bridge; Boxhall is calling in Morse flashes, again and again, to a strange ship stopped in the ice jam five to ten miles away. Another rocket drops its shower of sparks above the ice-strewn sea and the dying ship.

1:00 A.M. Slowly the water creeps higher; the fore ports of the *Titanic* are dipping into the sea. Rope squeaks through blocks; lifeboats drop jerkily seaward. Through the shouting on the decks comes the sound of the band playing ragtime.

The "Millionaires' Special" leaves the ship—boat No. 1, with a capacity of forty people, carries only Sir Cosmo and Lady Duff Gordon and ten others. Aft, the frightened immigrants mill and jostle and rush for a boat. An officer's fist flies out; three shots are fired into the air, and the panic is quelled. . . . Four Chinese sneak unseen into a boat and hide in its bottom.

1:20 A.M. Water is coming into No. 4 boiler room. Stokers slice and shovel as water laps about their ankles—steam for the dynamos, steam for the dancing spark! As the water rises, great ash hoes rake the flaming coals from the furnaces. Safety valves pop; the stokers retreat aft, and the watertight doors clang shut behind them.

The rockets fling their spendor toward the stars. The boats are more heavily loaded now, for the passengers know the *Titanic* is sinking. Women cling and sob. The great screws aft are rising clear of the sea. Half-filled boats are ordered to come alongside the cargo ports and take on more passengers, but the ports are never opened—and the boats are never filled. Others pull for the steamer's light miles away but never reach it; the light disappears, the unknown ship steams off.

The water rises and the band plays ragtime. 65

1:30 A.M. Lightoller is getting the port boats off; Murdock the starboard. As one boat is lowered into the sea a boat officer fires his gun along the ship's side to stop a rush from the lower decks. A woman tries to take her great Dane into a boat with her; she is refused and steps out of the boat to die with her dog. Millet's "little smile which played on his lips all through the voyage" plays no more; his lips are grim, but he waves good-by and brings wraps for the women.

Benjamin Guggenheim, in evening clothes, smiles and says, "We've dressed up in our best and are prepared to go down like gentlemen."

1:40 A.M. Boat 14 is clear, and then 13, 16, 15, and C. The lights still shine, but the *Baltic* hears the blue spark say, "Engine room getting flooded."

The *Olympic* signals, "Am lighting up all possible boilers as fast as can."

Major Butt helps women into the last boats and waves good-by to them. Mrs. 70 Straus puts her foot on the gunwale of a lifeboat, then she draws back and goes to her husband: "We have been together many years; where you go I will go." Colonel John Jacob Astor puts his young wife in a lifeboat, steps back, taps cigarette on fingernail: "Good-by, dearie; I'll join you later."

1:45 A.M. The foredeck is under water, the fo'c'sle head almost awash; the great stern is lifted high toward the bright stars; and still the band plays. Mr. and Mrs. Harris approach a lifeboat arm in arm.

Officer: "Ladies first, please."

Harris bows, smiles, steps back: "Of course; certainly; ladies first."

Boxhall fires the last rocket, then leaves in charge of boat No. 2.

2:00 A.M. She is dying now; her bow goes deeper, her stern higher. But there 75 must be steam. Below in the stokeholds the sweaty firemen keep steam up for the flaring lights and the dancing spark. The glowing coals slide and tumble over the slanted grate bars; the sea pounds behind that yielding bulkhead. But the spark dances on.

The *Asian* hears Phillips try the new signal—SOS.

Boat No. 4 has left now; boat D leaves ten minutes later. Jacques Futrelle clasps his wife: "For God's sake, go! It's your last chance; go!" Madame Futrelle is half forced into the boat. It clears the side.

There are about 660 people in the boats, and 1,500 still on the sinking *Titanic*.

On top of the officers' quarters men work frantically to get the two collapsibles stowed there over the side. Water is over the forward part of A deck now; it surges up the companionways toward the boat deck. In the radio shack, Bride has slipped a coat and lifejacket about Phillips as the first operator sits hunched over his key, sending—still sending—"41–46 N.; 50–14 W. CQD—CQD—SOS—SOS—"

The Captain's tired white face appears at the radio-room door: "Men, you have done your full duty. You can do no more. Now, it's every man for himself." The Captain disappears—back to his sinking bridge, where Painter, his personal steward, stands quietly waiting for orders. The spark dances on. Bride turns his back and goes into the inner cabin. As he does so, a stoker, grimed with coal, mad with fear, steals into the shack and reaches for the lifejacket on Phillips' back. Bride wheels about and brains him with a wrench.

2:10 A.M. Below decks the steam is still holding, though the pressure is falling—rapidly. In the gymnasium on the boat deck the athletic instructor watches quietly as two gentlemen ride the bicycles and another swings casually at the punching bag. Mail clerks stagger up the boat-deck stairways, dragging soaked mail sacks. The spark still dances. The band still plays—but not ragtime:

Nearer my God to Thee,
Nearer to Thee . . .

A few men take up the refrain; others kneel on the slanting decks to pray. Many run and scramble aft, where hundreds are clinging above the silent screws on the great uptilted stern. The spark still dances and the lights still flare; the engineers are on the job. The hymn comes to its close. Bandmaster Hartley, Yorkshireman violinist, taps his bow against a bulkhead, calls for "Autumn" as the water curls about his feet, and the eight musicians brace themselves against the ship's slant. People are leaping from the decks into the nearby water—the icy water. A woman cries, "Oh, save me, save me!" A man answers, "Good lady, save yourself. Only God can save you now." The band plays "Autumn":

God of Mercy and Compassion!
Look with pity on my pain . . .

The water creeps over the bridge where the *Titanic's* master stands; heavily he steps out to meet it.

2:17 A.M. "CQ—" The *Virginian* hears a ragged, blurred CQ, then an abrupt stop. The blue spark dances no more. The lights flicker out; the engineers have lost their battle.

2:18 A.M. Men run about blackened decks; leap into the night; are swept into the sea by the curling wave which licks up the *Titanic's* length. Lightoller does not leave the ship; the ship leaves him; there are hundreds like him, but only a few who live to tell of it. The funnels still swim above the water, but the ship is climbing to the perpendicular; the bridge is under and most of the foremast; the great stern rises like a squat leviathan. Men swim away from the sinking ship; others drop from the stern.

The band plays in the darkness, the water lapping upwards:

Hold me up in mighty waters,
Keep my eyes on things above,
Righteousness, divine atonement,
Peace and everlas . . .

The forward funnel snaps and crashes into the sea; its steel tons hammer out of existence swimmers struggling in the freezing water. Streams of sparks, of smoke and steam, burst from the after funnels. The ship upends to fifty—to sixty degrees.

Down in the black abyss of the stokeholds, of the engine rooms, where the dynamos have whirred at long last to a stop, the stokers and the engineers are reeling against hot metal, the rising water clutching at their knees. The boilers, the engine cylinders, rip from their bed plates: crash through bulkheads; rumble—steel against steel.

The *Titanic* stands on end, poised briefly for the plunge. Slowly she slides to her grave—slowly at first, and then more quickly—quickly—quickly.

2:20 A.M. The greatest ship in the world has sunk. From the calm, dark waters [90] where the floating lifeboats move, there goes up, in the white wake of her passing, "one long continuous moan."

The boats that the *Titanic* had launched pulled safely away from the slight suction of the sinking ship, pulled away from the screams that came from the lips of the freezing men and women in the water. The boats were poorly manned and badly equipped, and they had been unevenly loaded. Some carried so few seamen that women bent to the oars. Mrs. Astor tugged at an oar handle; the Countess of Rothes took a tiller. Shivering stokers in sweaty, coal-blackened singlets and light trousers steered in some boats; stewards in white coats rowed in others. Ismay was in the last boat that left the ship from the starboard side; with Mr. Carter of Philadelphia and two seamen he tugged at the oars. In one of the lifeboats an Italian with a broken wrist—disguised in a woman's shawl and hat—huddled on the floor boards, ashamed now that fear had left him. In another rode the only baggage saved from the *Titanic*—the carry-all of Samuel L. Goldenberg, one of the rescued passengers.

There were only a few boats that were heavily loaded; most of those that were half empty made but perfunctory efforts to pick up the moaning swimmers, their officers and crew fearing that they would endanger the living if they pulled back into the midst of the dying. Some boats beat off the freezing victims; fear-crazed men and women struck with oars at the heads of swimmers. One woman drove her fist into the face of a half-dead man as he tried feebly to climb over the gunwale. Two other women helped him in and stanched the flow of blood from the ring cuts on his face.

One of the collapsible boats, which had floated off the top of the officers' quarters when the *Titanic* sank, was an icy haven for thirty or forty men. The boat had capsized as the ship sank; men swam to it, clung to it, climbed upon its slippery bottom, stood knee-deep in water in the freezing air. Chunks of ice swirled about their legs; their soaked clothing clutched their bodies in icy folds. Colonel Archibald Gracie was cast up there, Gracie who had leaped from the stern as the *Titanic* sank; young Thayer who had seen his father die; Lightoller who had twice been sucked down with the ship and twice blown to the surface by a belch of air; Bride, the second operator, and Phillips, the first. There were many stokers, half-naked; it was a shivering company. They stood there in the icy sea, under the far stars, and sang and prayed—the Lord's Prayer. After a while a lifeboat came and picked them off, but Phillips was dead then or died soon afterward in the boat.

Only a few of the boats had lights; only one—No. 2—had a light that was of any use to the *Carpathia*, twisting through the ice field to the rescue. Other ships were "coming hard" too; one, the *Californian*, was still dead to opportunity.

The blue sparks still danced, but not the *Titanic*'s. *Le Provence* to *Celtic*: "Nobody has heard the *Titanic* for about two hours." 95

It was 2:40 when the *Carpathia* first sighted the green light from No. 2 boat; it was 4:10 when she picked up the first boat and learned that the *Titanic* had foundered. The last of the moaning cries had just died away then.

Captain Rostron took the survivors aboard, boatload by boatload. He was ready for them, but only a small minority of them required much medical attention. Bride's feet were twisted and frozen; others were suffering from exposure; one died, and seven were dead when taken from the boats, and were buried at sea.

It was then that the fleet of racing ships learned they were too late; the *Parisian* heard the weak signals of MPA, the *Carpathia*, report the death of the *Titanic*. It was then—or soon afterward, when her radio operator put on his earphones—that the *Californian*, the ship that had been within sight as the *Titanic* was sinking, first learned of the disaster.

And it was then, in all its white-green majesty, that the *Titanic*'s survivors saw the iceberg, tinted with the sunrise, floating idly, pack ice jammed about its base, other bergs heaving slowly near by on the blue breast of the sea.

Questions for Discussion and Writing

1. In what way is the encounter between the iceberg and the *Titanic* described in ways that underscore the many ironies involved, including the naming of the ship, the handling of radio messages, and the experiences of those on board? How does Baldwin's account suggest the modern-day equivalent of a Greek tragedy, whose heroes, through a combination of fate and their tragic flaws, brought catastrophes on themselves?

2. Analyze Baldwin's narrative technique. For example, what is the effect of the considerable statistical data he provides. How effectively does he reveal the character of individual passengers and crew?

3. The sinking of the *Titantic* has assumed the dimensions of a modern-day myth and has been the subject of a number of films, including the Academy Award–winning 1997 movie and a Broadway musical. Analyze one or several of these in relationship to Baldwin's account, and discuss the subtle and not-so-subtle shifts in emphasis that are evident in these dramatizations.

JOHN HERSEY

John Hersey (1914–1993) was born in Tientsin, China. After graduating from Yale in 1936, Hersey's varied career included being a driver for Sinclair Lewis and a war correspondent in China and Japan. During World War II, he covered the war in the South Pacific, the Mediterranean, and Moscow for Time *magazine. He then became editor and correspondent for* Life *magazine and made a trip to China and Japan for* Life *and The* New Yorker *in 1945–1946. The* New Yorker *devoted its August 31, 1946, issue to the publication of Hersey's momentous work* Hiroshima, *which reported the effects of the atomic bomb on the lives of six people. In 1985, Hersey did a follow-up report on what the lives of these six people had been like during the intervening forty years. Hersey's other books include the novels* A Bell for Adano *(1944), which won the Pulitzer Prize;* The Wall *(1950);* The War Lover *(1959);* The Child Buyer *(1960);* White Lotus *(1965); and* The Conspiracy *(1972). His last published works are* Life Sketches *(1989) and* Key West Tales *(1994). Hersey's approach to journalism is always through the specific individuals who are caught up in historical events. In "A Noiseless Flash from Hiroshima," from* Hiroshima, *Hersey communicates the incalculable horror of the atomic bomb at Hiroshima through the images, emotions, and experiences of six people who survived.*

A Noiseless Flash from Hiroshima

At exactly fifteen minutes past eight in the morning, on August 6, 1945, Japanese time, at the moment when the atomic bomb flashed above Hiroshima, Miss Toshiko Sasaki, a clerk in the personnel department of the East Asia Tin Works, had just sat down at her place in the plant office and was turning her head to speak to the girl at the next desk. At that same moment, Dr. Masakazu Fujii was settling down cross-legged to read the Osaka *Asahi* on the porch of his private hospital, overhanging one of the seven deltaic rivers which divide Hiroshima; Mrs. Hatsuyo Nakamura, a tailor's widow, stood by the window of her kitchen, watching a neighbor tearing down his house because it lay in the path of an air-raid-defense fire lane; Father Wilhelm Kleinsorge, a German priest of the Society of Jesus, reclined in his underwear on a cot on the top floor of his order's three-story mission house, reading a Jesuit magazine, *Stimmen der Zeit;* Dr. Terufimi Sasaki, a young member of the surgical staff of the city's large, modern Red Cross Hospital, walked along one of the hospital corridors with a blood specimen for a Wassermann test in his hand; and the Reverend Mr. Kiyoshi Tanimoto, pastor of the Hiroshima Methodist Church, paused at the door of a rich man's house in Koi, the city's western suburb, and prepared to unload a handcart full of things he had evacuated from town in fear of the massive B-29 raid which everyone expected Hiroshima to suffer. A hundred thousand people were killed by the atomic bomb, and these six were among the survivors. They still wonder why they lived when so many others died. Each of them counts many small items of chance or volition—a step taken in time, a decision to go indoors, catching one streetcar instead of the next—that spared him. And now each knows that in the act of survival he lived a dozen lives and saw more death than he ever thought he would see. At the time, none of them knew anything.

The Reverend Mr. Tanimoto got up at five o'clock that morning. He was alone in the parsonage, because for some time his wife had been commuting with their year-old baby to spend nights with a friend in Ushida, a suburb to the north. Of all the important cities of Japan, only two, Kyoto and Hiroshima, had not been visited in strength by *B-san,* or Mr. B, as the Japanese, with a mixture of respect and unhappy familiarity, called the B-29; and Mr. Tanimoto, like all his neighbors and friends, was almost sick with anxiety. He had heard uncomfortably detailed accounts of mass raids on Kure, Iwakuni, Tokuyama, and other nearby towns; he was sure Hiroshima's turn would come soon. He had slept badly the night before, because there had been several air-raid warnings. Hiroshima had been getting such warnings almost every night for weeks, for at that time the B-29s were using Lake Biwa, northeast of Hiroshima, as a rendezvous point, and no matter what city the Americans planned to hit, the Superfortresses streamed in over the coast near Hiroshima. The frequency of the warnings and the continued abstinence of Mr. B with respect to Hiroshima had made its citizens jittery; a rumor was going around that the Americans were saving something special for the city.

Mr. Tanimoto is a small man, quick to talk, laugh, and cry. He wears his black hair parted in the middle and rather long; the prominence of the frontal bones just above his eyebrows and the smallness of his mustache, mouth, and chin give him a strange, old-young look, boyish and yet wise, weak and yet fiery. He moves nervously and fast, but with a restraint which suggests that he is a cautious, thoughtful man. He showed, indeed, just those qualities in the uneasy days before the bomb fell. Besides having his wife spend the nights in Ushida, Mr. Tanimoto had been carrying all the portable things from his church, in the close-packed residential district called Nagaragawa, to a house that belonged to a rayon manufacturer in Koi, two miles from the center of town. The rayon man, a Mr. Matsui, had opened his then unoccupied estate to a large number of his friends and acquaintances, so that they might evacuate whatever they wished to a safe distance from the probable target area. Mr. Tanimoto had had no difficulty in moving chairs, hymnals, Bibles, altar gear, and church records by pushcart himself, but the organ console and an upright piano required some aid. A friend of his named Matsuo had, the day before, helped him get the piano out to Koi; in return, he had promised this day to assist Mr. Matsuo in hauling out a daughter's belongings. That is why he had risen so early.

Mr. Tanimoto cooked his own breakfast. He felt awfully tired. The effort of moving the piano the day before, a sleepless night, weeks of worry and unbalanced diet, the cares of his parish—all combined to make him feel hardly adequate to the new day's work. There was another thing, too: Mr. Tanimoto had studied theology at Emory College, in Atlanta, Georgia; he had graduated in 1940; he spoke excellent English; he dressed in American clothes; he had corresponded with many American friends right up to the time the war began; and among a people obsessed with a fear of being spied upon—perhaps almost obsessed himself—he found himself growing increasingly uneasy. The police had questioned him several times, and just a few days before, he had heard that an influential acquaintance, a Mr. Tanaka, a retired officer of the Toyo Kisen Kaisha steamship line, an anti-Christian, a man famous in Hiroshima for his showy philanthropies and notorious for his personal tyrannies, had been telling people that Tanimoto should not be trusted. In compensation, to show himself publicly a good Japanese, Mr. Tanimoto had taken on the chairmanship of his local *tonarigumi,* or Neighborhood Association, and to his other duties and concerns this position had added the business of organizing air-raid defense for about twenty families.

Before six o'clock that morning, Mr. Tanimoto started for Mr. Matsuo's house. There he found that their burden was to be a *tansu,* a large Japanese cabinet, full of clothing and household goods. The two men set out. The morning was perfectly clear and so warm that the day promised to be uncomfortable. A few minutes after they started, the air-raid siren went off—a minute-long blast that warned of approaching planes but indicated to the people of Hiroshima only a slight degree of danger, since it sounded every morning at this time, when an American weather plane came over. The two men pulled and pushed the handcart through the city streets. Hiroshima was a fan-shaped city, lying mostly on the six islands formed by the seven estuarial rivers that branch out from the Ota River; its main commercial and residential districts, covering about four square miles in the center of the city, contained three-quarters of its population, which had been reduced by several evacuation programs from a wartime peak of 380,000 to about 245,000. Factories and other residential districts, or suburbs, lay compactly around the edges of the city. To the south were the docks, an airport, and the island-studded Inland Sea. A rim of mountains runs around the other three sides of the delta. Mr. Tanimoto and Mr. Matsuo took their way through the shopping center, already full of people, and across two of the rivers to the sloping streets of Koi, and up them to the outskirts and foothills. As they started up a valley away from the tight-ranked houses, the all-clear sounded. (The Japanese radar operators, detecting only three planes, supposed that they comprised a reconnaissance.) Pushing the handcart up to the rayon man's house was tiring, and the men, after they had maneuvered their load into the driveway and to the front steps, paused to rest awhile. They stood with a wing of the house between them and the city. Like most homes in this part of Japan, the house consisted of a wooden frame and wooden walls supporting a heavy tile roof. Its front hall, packed with rolls of bedding and clothing, looked like a cool cave full of fat cushions. Opposite the house, to the right of the front door, there was a large, finicky rock garden. There was no sound of planes. The morning was still; the place was cool and pleasant.

Then a tremendous flash of light cut across the sky. Mr. Tanimoto has a distinct recollection that it travelled from east to west, from the city toward the hills. It seemed a sheet of sun. Both he and Mr. Matsuo reacted in terror—and both had time to react (for they were 3,500 yards, or two miles, from the center of the explosion). Mr. Matsuo dashed up the front steps into the house and dived among the bedrolls and buried himself there. Mr. Tanimoto took four or five steps and threw himself between two big rocks in the garden. He bellied up very hard against one of them. As his face was against the stone, he did not see what happened. He felt a sudden pressure, and then splinters and pieces of board and fragments of the tile fell on him. He heard no roar. (Almost no one in Hiroshima recalls hearing any noise of the bomb. But a fisherman in his sampan on the Inland Sea near Tsuzu, the man with whom Mr. Tanimoto's mother-in-law and sister-in-law were living, saw the flash and heard a tremendous explosion; he was nearly twenty miles from Hiroshima, but the thunder was greater than when the B-29s hit Iwakuni, only five miles away.)

When he dared, Mr. Tanimoto raised his head and saw that the rayon man's house had collapsed. He thought a bomb had fallen directly on it. Such clouds of dust had risen that there was a sort of twilight around. In panic, not thinking for the moment of Mr. Matsuo under the ruins, he dashed out into the street. He noticed as he ran that the concrete wall of the estate had fallen over—toward the house rather than away from it. In the street, the first thing he saw was a squad of soldiers who had been burrowing into the hillside opposite, making one of the thousands of dugouts in which the Japanese apparently intended to resist invasion, hill by hill, life for life; the soldiers were coming out of the hole, where they should have been safe, and blood was running from their heads, chests, and backs. They were silent and dazed.

Under what seemed to be a local dust cloud, the day grew darker and darker.

At nearly midnight, the night before the bomb was dropped, an announcer on the city's radio station said that about two hundred B-29s were approaching southern Honshu and advised the population of Hiroshima to evacuate to their designated "safe areas." Mrs. Hatsuyo Nakamura, the tailor's widow, who lived in the section called Noboricho and who had long had a habit of doing as she was told, got her three children—a ten-year-old boy, Toshio, an eight-year-old girl, Yaeko, and a five-year-old girl, Myeko—out of bed and dressed them and walked with them to the military area known as the East Parade Ground, on the northeast edge of the city. There she unrolled some mats and the children lay down on them. They slept until about two, when they were awakened by the roar of the planes going over Hiroshima.

As soon as the planes had passed, Mrs. Nakamura started back with her children. They reached home a little after two-thirty and she immediately turned on the radio, which, to her distress, was just then broadcasting a fresh warning. When she looked at the children and saw how tired they were, and when she thought of the number of trips they had made in past weeks, all to no purpose, to the East Parade Ground, she decided that in spite of the instructions on the radio, she simply could not face starting out all over again. She put the children in their bedrolls on the floor, lay down herself at three o'clock, and fell asleep at once, so soundly that when planes passed over later, she did not waken to their sound.

The siren jarred her awake at about seven. She arose, dressed quickly, and hurried to the house of Mr. Nakamoto, the head of her Neighborhood Association, and asked him what she should do. He said that she should remain at home unless an urgent warning—a series of intermittent blasts of the siren—was sounded. She returned home, lit the stove in the kitchen, set some rice to cook, and sat down to read the morning's Hiroshima *Chugoku*. To her relief, the all-clear sounded at eight o'clock. She heard the children stirring, so she went and gave each of them a handful of peanuts and told them to stay on their bedrolls, because they were tired from the night's walk. She had hoped that they would go back to sleep, but the man in the house directly to the south began to make a terrible hullabaloo of hammering, wedging, ripping, and splitting. The prefectural government, convinced, as everyone in Hiroshima was, that the city would be attacked soon, had begun to press with threats and warnings for the completion of wide fire lanes, which, it was hoped, might act in conjunction with the rivers to localize any fires started by an incendiary raid; and the neighbor was reluctantly sacrificing his home to the city's safety. Just the day before, the prefecture had ordered all able-bodied girls from the secondary schools to spend a few days helping to clear these lanes, and they started work soon after the all-clear sounded.

Mrs. Nakamura went back to the kitchen, looked at the rice, and began watching the man next door. At first, she was annoyed with him for making so much noise, but then she was moved almost to tears by pity. Her emotion was specifically directed toward her neighbor, tearing down his home, board by board, at a time when there was so much unavoidable destruction, but undoubtedly she also felt a generalized, community pity, to say nothing of self-pity. She had not had an easy time. Her husband, Isawa, had gone into the Army just after Myeko was born, and she had heard nothing from or of him for a long time, until, on March 5, 1942, she received a seven-word telegram: "Isawa died an honorable death at Singapore." She learned later that he had died on February 15th, the day Singapore fell, and that he had been a corporal. Isawa had been a not particularly prosperous tailor, and his only capital was a Sankoku sewing machine. After his death, when his allotments stopped coming, Mrs. Nakamura got out the machine and began to take in piecework herself, and since then had supported the children, but poorly, by sewing.

As Mrs. Nakamura stood watching her neighbor, everything flashed whiter than any white she had ever seen. She did not notice what happened to the man next door; the reflex of a mother set her in motion toward her children. She had taken a single step (the house was 1,350 yards, or three-quarters of a mile, from the center of the explosion) when something picked her up and she seemed to fly into the next room over the raised sleeping platform, pursued by parts of her house.

Timbers fell around her as she landed, and a shower of tiles pommelled her; everything became dark, for she was buried. The debris did not cover her deeply. She rose up and freed herself. She heard a child cry, "Mother, help me!" and saw her youngest—Myeko, the five-year-old—buried up to her breast and unable to move. As Mrs. Nakamura started frantically to claw her way toward the baby, she could see or hear nothing of her other children.

In the days right before the bombing, Dr. Masakazu Fujii, being prosperous, hedonistic, and at the time not too busy, had been allowing himself the luxury of sleeping until nine or nine-thirty, but fortunately he had to get up early the morning the bomb was dropped to see a house guest off on a train. He rose at six, and half an hour later walked with his friend to the station, not far away, across two of the rivers. He was back home by seven, just as the siren sounded its sustained warning. He ate breakfast and then, because the morning was already hot, undressed down to his underwear and went out on the porch to read the paper. This porch— 15 in fact, the whole building—was curiously constructed. Dr. Fujii was the proprietor of a peculiarly Japanese institution: a private, single-doctor hospital. This building, perched beside and over the water of the Kyo River, and next to the bridge of the same name, contained thirty rooms for thirty patients and their kinfolk—for, according to Japanese custom, when a person falls sick and goes to a hospital, one or more members of his family go and live there with him, to cook for him, bathe, massage, and read to him, and to offer incessant familial sympathy, without which a Japanese patient would be miserable indeed. Dr. Fujii had no beds—only straw mats—for his patients. He did, however, have all sorts of modern equipment: an X-ray machine, diathermy apparatus, and a fine tiled laboratory. The structure rested two-thirds on the land, one-third on piles over the tidal waters of the Kyo. This overhang, the part of the building where Dr. Fujii lived, was queer-looking, but it was cool in summer and from the porch, which faced away from the center of the city, the prospect of the river, with pleasure boats drifting up and down it, was always refreshing. Dr. Fujii had occasionally had anxious moments when the Ota and its mouth branches rose to flood, but the piling was apparently firm enough and the house had always held.

Dr. Fujii had been relatively idle for about a month because in July, as the number of untouched cities in Japan dwindled and as Hiroshima seemed more and more inevitably a target, he began turning patients away, on the ground that in case of a fire raid he would not be able to evacuate them. Now he had only two patients left—a woman from Yano, injured in the shoulder, and a young man of twenty-five recovering from burns he had suffered when the steel factory near Hiroshima in which worked had been hit. Dr. Fujii had six nurses to tend his patients. His wife and children were safe; his wife and one son were living outside Osaka, and another son and two daughters were in the country on Kyushu. A niece was living with him, and a maid and a man-servant. He had little to do and did not mind, for he had saved some money. At fifty, he was healthy, convivial, and calm, and he was pleased to pass the evenings drinking whiskey with friends, always sensibly and for the sake of conversation. Before the war, he had affected brands imported from Scotland and America; now he was perfectly satisfied with the best Japanese brand, Suntory.

Dr. Fujii sat down cross-legged in his underwear on the spotless matting of the porch, put on his glasses, and started reading the Osaka *Asahi*. He liked to read the Osaka news because his wife was there. He saw the flash. To him—faced away from the center and looking at his paper—it seemed a brilliant yellow. Startled, he began to rise to his feet. In that moment (he was 1,550 yards from the center), the hospital leaned behind him rising and, with a terrible ripping noise, toppled into the river. The Doctor, still in the act of getting to his feet, was thrown forward and around and over, he was buffeted and gripped; he lost track of everything, because things were so speeded up; he felt the water.

Dr. Fujii hardly had time to think that he was dying before he realized that he was alive, squeezed tightly by two long timbers in a V across his chest, like a morsel suspended between two huge chopsticks—held upright, so that he could not move, with his head miraculously above water and his torso and legs in it. The remains of his hospital were all around him in a mad assortment of splintered lumber and materials for the relief of pain. His left shoulder hurt terribly. His glasses were gone.

Father Wilhelm Kleinsorge, of the Society of Jesus, was, on the morning of the explosion, in rather frail condition. The Japanese wartime diet had not sustained him, and he felt the strain of being a foreigner in an increasingly xenophobic Japan; even a German, since the defeat of the Fatherland, was unpopular. Father Kleinsorge had, at thirty-eight, the look of a boy growing too fast—thin in the face, with a prominent Adam's apple, a hollow chest, dangling hands, big feet. He walked clumsily, leaning forward a little. He was tired all the time. To make matters worse, he had suffered for two days, along with Father Cieslik, a fellow-priest, from a rather painful and urgent diarrhea, which they blamed on the beans and black ration bread they were obliged to eat. Two other priests then living in the mission compound, which was in the Noboricho section—Father Superior LaSalle and Father Schiffer—had happily escaped this affliction.

Father Kleinsorge woke up about six the morning the bomb was dropped, and half an hour later—he was a bit tardy because of his sickness—he began to read Mass in the mission chapel, a small Japanese-style wooden building which was without pews, since its worshippers knelt on the usual Japanese matted floor, facing an altar graced with splendid silks, brass, silver, and heavy embroideries. This morning, a Monday, the only worshippers were Mr. Takemoto, a theological student living in the mission house; Mr. Fukai, the secretary of the diocese; Mrs. Murata, the mission's devoutly Christian housekeeper; and his fellow-priests. After Mass, while Father Kleinsorge was reading the Prayers of Thanksgiving, the siren sounded. He stopped the service and the missionaries retired across the compound to the bigger building. There, in his room on the ground floor, to the right of the front door, Father Kleinsorge changed into a military uniform which he had acquired when he was teaching at the Rokko Middle School in Kobe and which he wore during air-raid alerts.

After an alarm, Father Kleinsorge always went out and scanned the sky, and in this instance, when he stepped outside, he was glad to see only the single weather plane that flew over Hiroshima each day about this time. Satisfied that nothing would happen, he went in and breakfasted with the other Fathers on substitute coffee and ration bread, which, under the circumstances, was especially repugnant to him. The Fathers sat and talked awhile, until, at eight, they heard the all-clear. They went then to various parts of the building. Father Schiffer retired to his room to do some writing. Father Cieslik sat in his room in a straight chair with a pillow over his stomach to ease his pain, and read. Father Superior LaSalle stood at the window of his room, thinking. Father Kleinsorge went up to a room on the third floor, took off all his clothes except his underwear, and stretched out on his right side on a cot and began reading his *Stimmen der Zeit*.

After the terrible flash—which, Father Kleinsorge later realized, reminded him of something he had read as a boy about a large meteor colliding with the earth—he had time (since he was 1,400 yards from the center) for one thought: A bomb has fallen directly on us. Then, for a few seconds or minutes, he went out of his mind.

20

Father Kleinsorge never knew how he got out of the house. The next things he was conscious of were that he was wandering around in the mission's vegetable garden in his underwear, bleeding slightly from small cuts along his left flank; that all the buildings round about had fallen down except the Jesuits' mission house, which had long before been braced and double-braced by a priest named Gropper, who was terrified of earthquakes; that the day had turned dark; and that Muratasan, the housekeeper, was nearby, crying over and over, "*Shu Jesusu, awaremi tamai!* Our Lord Jesus, have pity on us!"

On the train on the way into Hiroshima from the country, where he lived with his mother, Dr. Terufumi Sasaki, the Red Cross Hospital surgeon, thought over an unpleasant nightmare he had had the night before. His mother's home was in Mukai-hara, thirty miles from the city, and it took him two hours by train and tram to reach the hospital. He had slept uneasily all night and had wakened an hour earlier than usual, and, feeling sluggish and slightly feverish, had debated whether to go to the hospital at all; his sense of duty finally forced him to go, and he had started out on the earlier train than he took most mornings. The dream had particularly frightened him because it was so closely associated, on the surface at least, with a disturbing actuality. He was only twenty-five years old and had just completed his training at the Eastern Medical University, in Tsingtao, China. He was something of an idealist and was much distressed by the inadequacy of medical facilities in the country town where his mother lived. Quite on his own, and without a permit, he had begun visiting a few sick people out there in the evenings, after his eight hours at the hospital and four hours' commuting. He had recently learned that the penalty for practicing without a permit was severe; a fellow-doctor whom he had asked about it had given him a serious scolding. Nevertheless, he had continued to practice. In his dream, he had been at the bedside of a country patient when the police and the doctor he had consulted burst into the room, seized him, dragged him outside, and beat him up cruelly. On the train, he just about decided to give up the work in Mukaihara, since he felt it would be impossible to get a permit, because the authorities would hold that it would conflict with his duties at the Red Cross Hospital.

At the terminus, he caught a streetcar at once. (He later calculated that if he had taken his customary train that morning, and if he had had to wait a few minutes for the streetcar, as often happened, he would have been close to the center at the time of the explosion and would surely have perished.) He arrived at the hospital at seven-forty and reported to the chief surgeon. A few minutes later, he went to a room on the first floor and drew blood from the arm of a man in order to perform a Wassermann test. The laboratory containing the incubators for the test was on the third floor. With the blood specimen in his left hand, walking in a kind of distraction he had felt all morning, probably because of the dream and his restless night, he started along the main corridor on his way toward the stairs. He was one step beyond an open window when the light of the bomb was reflected, like a gigantic photographic flash, in the corridor. He ducked down on one knee and said to himself, as only a Japanese would, "Sasaki, *gambare!* Be brave!" Just then (the building was 1,650 yards from the center), the blast ripped through the hospital.

25

The glasses he was wearing flew off his face; the bottle of blood crashed against one wall; his Japanese slippers zipped out from under his feet—but otherwise, thanks to where he stood, he was untouched.

Dr. Sasaki shouted the name of the chief surgeon and rushed around to the man's office and found him terribly cut by glass. The hospital was in horrible confusion: heavy partitions and ceilings had fallen on patients, beds had overturned, windows had blown in and cut people, blood was spattered on the walls and floors, instruments were everywhere, many of the patients were running about screaming, many more lay dead. (A colleague working in the laboratory to which Dr. Sasaki had been walking was dead; Dr. Sasaki's patient, whom he had just left and who a few moments before had been dreadfully afraid of syphilis, was also dead.) Dr. Sasaki found himself the only doctor in the hospital who was unhurt.

Dr. Sasaki, who believed that the enemy had hit only the building he was in, got bandages and began to bind the wounds of those inside the hospital; while outside, all over Hiroshima, maimed and dying citizens turned their unsteady steps toward the Red Cross Hospital to begin an invasion that was to make Dr. Sasaki forget his private nightmare for a long, long time.

Miss Toshiko Sasaki, the East Asia Tin Works clerk, who is not related to Dr. Sasaki, got up at three o'clock in the morning on the day the bomb fell. There was extra housework to do. Her eleven-month-old brother, Akio, had come down the day before with a serious stomach upset; her mother had taken him to the Tamura Pediatric Hospital and was staying there with him. Miss Sasaki, who was about twenty, had to cook breakfast for her father, a brother, a sister, and herself, and—since the hospital, because of the war, was unable to provide food—to prepare a whole day's meals for her mother and the baby, in time for her father, who worked in a factory making rubber earplugs for artillery crews, to take the food by on his way to the plant. When she had finished and had cleaned and put away the cooking things, it was nearly seven. The family lived in Koi, and she had a forty-five-minute trip to the tin works, in the section of town called Kannonmachi. She was in charge of the personnel records in the factory. She left Koi at seven, and as soon as she reached the plant, she went with some of the other girls from the personnel department to the factory auditorium. A prominent local Navy man, a former employee, had committed suicide the day before by throwing himself under a train—a death considered honorable enough to warrant a memorial service, which was to be held at the tin works at ten o'clock that morning. In the large hall, Miss Sasaki and the others made suitable preparations for the meeting. This work took about twenty minutes.

Miss Sasaki went back to her office and sat down at her desk. She was quite far from the windows, which were off to her left, and behind her were a couple of tall bookcases containing all the books of the factory library, which the personnel department had organized. She settled herself at her desk, put some things in a drawer, and shifted papers. She thought that before she began to make entries in her lists of new employees, discharges, and departures for the Army, she would chat for a moment with the girl at her right. Just as she turned her head away from the windows, the room was filled with a blinding light. She was paralyzed by fear, fixed still in her chair for a long moment (the plant was 1,600 yards from the center).

Everything fell, and Miss Sasaki lost consciousness. The ceiling dropped suddenly and the wooden floor above collapsed in splinters and the people up there came down and the roof above them gave way; but principally and first of all, the bookcases right behind her swooped forward and the contents threw her down, with her left leg horribly twisted and breaking underneath her. There, in the tin factory, in the first moment of the atomic age, a human being was crushed by books.   30

Questions for Discussion and Writing

1. How do the experiences of the six people Hersey wrote about represent the experiences of untold thousands in Hiroshima on the day the bomb exploded? What is the significance of the title, "A Noiseless Flash from Hiroshima"?

2. In how many different places can you find Hersey referring to the exact time on the clock? Why is this significant? What point does Hersey emphasize by contrasting the everyday preoccupations of these six people one second before the blast with the overwhelming problems of survival they faced immediately after the explosion?

3. In what way is Hersey's journalistic technique an attempt to simulate what the eye of a camera might see and record? How does Hersey's skill in reporting realistic details (for example, medical facilities overwhelmed by great numbers of injured people) convey the extent of the horror of the explosion?

Fiction

AMBROSE BIERCE

Ambrose Bierce (1842–1914?) was born in rural Ohio, the youngest of a large, devout poverty-stricken family. He enlisted in the Union army at the outbreak of the Civil War as a drummer boy, fought bravely in some of the most important battles, and rose from the rank of private to major. After the war, he became a journalist in San Francisco and wrote satiric pieces for a news weekly, of which he was soon made editor. The biting wit for which Bierce is so distinguished became his hallmark. He worked briefly in London as a journalist, after returning to the United States he wrote his famous "Prattler" column for the Argonaut *magazine. In 1887, William Randolph Hearst bought the column and placed it on the editorial page of the* Sunday Examiner. *Bierce published tales of soldiers and civilians in 1891 and later followed them with* Can Such Things Be? *(1893) and his acerbic* Devil's Dictionary *(1906). In 1913 he left for*

Mexico to cover the revolution and vanished without a trace. With characteristic aplomb, his last letter to a friend stated, "Goodbye, if you hear of my being stood up against a Mexican stone wall and shot to rags, please know that I think it a pretty good way to depart this life. It beats old age, disease, or falling down the cellar stairs. "An Occurence at Owl Creek Bridge" (1890) has emerged as a classic. This haunting story reconstructs an experience so that impressions, colors, sounds, sensations, and time itself are thoroughly subordinated to the psychological state of the narrator.

An Occurrence at Owl Creek Bridge

I

A man stood upon a railroad bridge in Northern Alabama, looking down into the swift waters twenty feet below. The man's hands were behind his back, the wrists bound with a cord. A rope loosely encircled his neck. It was attached to a stout cross-timber above his head, and the slack fell to the level of his knees. Some loose boards laid upon the sleepers supporting the metals of the railway supplied a footing for him and his executioners—two private soldiers of the Federal army, directed by a sergeant, who in civil life may have been a deputy sheriff. At a short remove upon the same temporary platform was an officer in the uniform of his rank, armed. He was a captain. A sentinel at each end of the bridge stood with his rifle in the position known as "support," that is to say, vertical in front of the left shoulder, the hammer resting on the forearm thrown straight across the chest—a normal and unnatural position, enforcing an erect carriage of the body. It did not appear to be the duty of these two men to know what was occurring at the centre of the bridge; they merely blockaded the two ends of the foot plank which traversed it.

Beyond one of the sentinels nobody was in sight; the railroad ran straight away into a forest for a hundred yards, then, curving, was lost to view. Doubtless there was an outpost further along. The other bank of the stream was open ground—a gentle acclivity crowned with a stockade of vertical tree trunks, loop-holed for rifles, with a single embrasure through which protruded the muzzle of a brass cannon commanding the bridge. Midway of the slope between bridge and fort were the spectators—a single company of infantry in line, at "parade rest," the butts of the rifles on the ground, the barrels inclining slightly backward against the right shoulder, the hands crossed upon the stock. A lieutenant stood at the right of the line, the point of his sword upon the ground, his left hand resting upon his right. Excepting the group of four at the centre of the bridge not a man moved. The company faced the bridge, staring stonily, motionless. The sentinels, facing the banks of the stream, might have been statues to adorn the bridge. The captain stood with folded arms, silent, observing the work of his subordinates but making no sign. Death is a dignitary who, when he comes announced, is to be received with formal manifestations of respect, even by those most familiar with him. In the code of military etiquette silence and fixity are forms of deference.

The man who was engaged in being hanged was apparently about thirty-five years of age. He was a civilian, if one might judge from his dress, which was that of a planter. His features were good—a straight nose, firm mouth, broad forehead, from which his long, dark hair was combed straight back, falling behind his ears to the collar of his well-fitted frock coat. He wore a moustache and pointed beard, but no whiskers; his eyes were large and dark grey and had a kindly expression which one would hardly have expected in one whose neck was in the hemp. Evidently this was no vulgar assassin. The liberal military code makes provision for hanging many kinds of people, and gentlemen are not excluded.

The preparations being complete, the two private soldiers stepped aside and each drew away the plank upon which he had been standing. The sergeant turned to the captain, saluted and placed himself immediately behind that officer, who in turn moved apart one pace. These movements left the condemned man and the sergeant standing on the two ends of the same plank, which spanned three of the cross-ties of the bridge. The end upon which the civilian stood almost, but not quite, reached a fourth. This plank had been held in place by the weight of the captain; it was now held by that of the sergeant. At a signal from the former, the latter would step aside, the plank would tilt and the condemned man go down between two ties. The arrangement commended itself to his judgment as simple and effective. His face had not been covered nor his eyes bandaged. He looked a moment at his "unsteadfast footing," then let his gaze wander to the swirling water of the stream racing madly beneath his feet. A piece of dancing driftwood caught his attention and his eyes followed it down the current. How slowly it appeared to move! What a sluggish stream!

He closed his eyes in order to fix his last thoughts upon his wife and children. The water, touched to gold by the early sun, the brooding mists under the banks at some distance down the stream, the fort, the soldiers, the piece of drift—all had distracted him. And now he became conscious of a new disturbance. Striking through the thought of his dear ones was a sound which he could neither ignore nor understand, a sharp, distinct, metallic percussion like the stroke of a blacksmith's hammer upon the anvil; it had the same ringing quality. He wondered what it was, and whether immeasurably distant or near by—it seemed both. Its recurrence was regular, but as slow as the tolling of a death knell. He awaited each stroke with impatience and—he knew not why—apprehension. The intervals of silence grew progressively longer; the delays became maddening. With their greater infrequency the sounds increased in strength and sharpness. They hurt his ear like the thrust of a knife; he feared he would shriek. What he heard was the ticking of his watch.

He unclosed his eyes and saw again the water below him. "If I could free my hands," he thought, "I might throw off the noose and spring into the stream. By diving I could evade the bullets, and, swimming, vigorously, reach the bank, take to the woods, and get away home. My home, thank God, is as yet outside their lines; my wife and little ones are still beyond the invader's farthest advance."

As these thoughts, which have here to be set down in words, were flashed into the doomed man's brain rather than evolved from it, the captain nodded to the sergeant. The sergeant stepped aside.

5

II

Peyton Farquhar was a well-to-do planter, of an old and highly-respected Alabama family. Being a slave owner, and, like other slave owners, a politician, he was naturally an original secessionist and ardently devoted to the Southern cause. Circumstances of an imperious nature which it is unnecessary to relate here, had prevented him from taking service with the gallant army which had fought the disastrous campaigns ending with the fall of Corinth, and he chafed under the inglorious restraint, longing for the release of his energies, the larger life of the soldier, the opportunity for distinction. That opportunity, he felt, would come, as it comes to all in war time. Meanwhile he did what he could. No service was too humble for him to perform in aid of the South, no adventure too perilous for him to undertake if consistent with the character of a civilian who was at heart a soldier, and who in good faith and without too much qualification assented to at least a part of the frankly villainous dictum that all is fair in love and war.

One evening while Farquhar and his wife were sitting on a rustic bench near the entrance to his ground, a grey-clad soldier rode up to the gate and asked for a drink of water.[1] Mrs. Farquhar was only too happy to serve him with her own white hands. While she was gone to fetch the water, her husband approached the dusty horseman and inquired eagerly for news from the front.

"The Yanks are repairing the railroads," said the man, "and are getting ready   10
for another advance. They have reached the Owl Creek bridge, put it in order, and built a stockade on the other bank. The commandant has issued an order, which is posted everywhere, declaring that any civilian caught interfering with the railroad, its bridges, tunnels, or trains, will be summarily hanged. I saw the order."

"How far is it to the Owl Creek bridge?" Farquhar asked.

"About thirty miles."

"Is there no force on this side the creek?"

"Only a picket post half a mile out, on the railroad, and a single sentinel at this end of the bridge."

"Suppose a man—a civilian and student of hanging—should elude the picket   15
post and perhaps get the better of the sentinel," said Farquhar, smiling, "what could he accomplish?"

The soldier reflected. "I was there a month ago," he replied. "I observed that the flood of last winter had lodged a great quantity of driftwood against the wooden pier at this end of the bridge. It is now dry and would burn like tow."

The lady had now brought the water, which the soldier drank. He thanked her ceremoniously, bowed to her husband, and rode away. An hour later, after nightfall, he repassed the plantation, going northward in the direction from which he had come. He was a Federal scout.

---

[1] "A grey-clad soldier" refers to the gray uniforms worn by Confederate soldiers.

III

As Peyton Farquhar fell straight downward through the bridge, he lost consciousness and was as one already dead. From this state he was awakened—ages later, it seemed to him—by the pain of a sharp pressure upon his throat, followed by a sense of suffocation. Keen, poignant agonies seemed to shoot from his neck downward through every fibre of his body and limbs. These pains appeared to flash along well-defined lines of ramification, and to beat with an inconceivably rapid periodicity. They seemed like streams of pulsating fire heating him to an intolerable temperature. As to his head, he was conscious of nothing but a feeling of fullness—of congestion. These sensations were unaccompanied by thought. The intellectual part of his nature was already effaced; he had power only to feel, and feeling was torment. He was conscious of motion. Encompassed in a luminous cloud, of which he was now merely the fiery heart, without material substance, he swung through unthinkable arcs of oscillation, like a vast pendulum. Then all at once, with terrible suddenness, the light about him shot upward with the noise of a loud plash; a frightful roaring was in his ears, and all was cold and dark. The power of thought was restored; he knew that the rope had broken and he had fallen into the stream. There was no additional strangulation; the noose about his neck was already suffocating him, and kept the water from his lungs. To die of hanging at the bottom of a river—the idea seemed to him ludicrous. He opened his eyes in the blackness and saw above him a gleam of light, but how distant, how inaccessible! He was still sinking, for the light became fainter and fainter until it was a mere glimmer. Then it began to grow and brighten, and he knew that he was rising toward the surface—knew it with reluctance, for he was now very comfortable. "To be hanged and drowned," he thought, "that is not so bad; but I do not wish to be shot. No: I will not be shot; that is not fair."

He was not conscious of an effort, but a sharp pain in his wrist apprised him that he was trying to free his hands. He gave the struggle his attention, as an idler might observe the feat of a juggler, without interest in the outcome. What splendid effort!—what magnificent, what superhuman strength! Ah, that was a fine endeavor! Bravo! The cord fell away; his arms parted and floated upward, the hands dimly seen on each side in the growing light. He watched them with a new interest as first one and then the other pounced upon the noose at his neck. They tore it away and thrust it fiercely aside, its undulations resembling those of a water-snake. "Put it back, put it back!" He thought he shouted these words to his hands, for the undoing of the noose had been succeeded by the direst pang which he had yet experienced. His neck arched horribly; his brain was on fire; his heart, which had been fluttering faintly, gave a great leap, trying to force itself out at his mouth. His whole body was racked and wrenched with an insupportable anguish! But his disobedient hands gave no heed to the command. They beat the water vigorously with quick, downward strokes, forcing him to the surface. He felt his head emerge; his eyes were blinded by the sunlight; his chest expanded convulsively, and with a supreme and crowning agony his lungs engulfed a great draught of air, which instantly he expelled in a shriek!

He was now in full possession of his physical senses. They were, indeed, 20
preternaturally keen and alert. Something in the awful disturbance of his organic
system had so exalted and refined them that they made record of things never before perceived. He felt the ripples upon his face and heard their separate sounds as
they struck. He looked at the forest on the bank of the stream, saw the individual
trees, the leaves and the veining of each leaf—saw the very insects upon them, the
locusts, the brilliant-bodied flies, the grey spiders stretching their webs from twig
to twig. He noted the prismatic colors in all the dewdrops upon a million blades of
grass. The humming of the gnats that danced above the eddies of the stream, the
beating of the dragon flies' wings, the strokes of the water spiders' legs, like oars
which had lifted their boat—all these made audible music. A fish slid along beneath
his eyes and he heard the rush of its body parting the water.

He had come to the surface facing down the stream; in a moment the visible
world seemed to wheel slowly round, himself the pivotal point, and he saw the
bridge, the fort, the soldiers upon the bridge, the captain, the sergeant, the two pri-
vates, his executioners. They were in silhouette against the blue sky. They shouted
and gesticulated, pointing at him; the captain had drawn his pistol, but did not fire;
the others were unarmed. Their movements were grotesque and horrible, their
forms gigantic.

Suddenly he heard a sharp report and something struck the water smartly
within a few inches of his head, spattering his face with spray. He heard a second
report, and saw one of the sentinels with his rifle at his shoulder, a light cloud of
blue smoke rising from the muzzle. The man in the water saw the eye of the man
on the bridge gazing into his own through the sights of the rifle. He observed that
it was a grey eye, and remembered having read that grey eyes were keenest and that
all famous marksmen had them. Nevertheless, this one had missed.

A counter swirl had caught Farquhar and turned him half round; he was again
looking into the forest on the bank opposite the fort. The sound of a clear, high
voice in a monotonous singsong now rang out behind him and came across the
water with a distinctness that pierced and subdued all other sounds, even the beating of the ripples in his ears. Although no soldier, he had frequented camps enough
to know the dread significance of that deliberate, drawling, aspirated chant; the
lieutenant on shore was taking a part in the morning's work. How coldly and pitilessly—with what an even, calm intonation, presaging and enforcing tranquility in
the men—with what accurately-measured intervals fell those cruel words:

"Attention, company. . . . Shoulder arms. . . . Ready. . . . Aim. . . . Fire."

Farquhar dived—dived as deeply as he could. The water roared in his ears like 25
the voice of Niagara, yet he heard the dulled thunder of the volley, and rising again
toward the surface, met shining bits of metal, singularly flattened, oscillating slowly
downward. Some of them touched him on the face and hands, then fell away, continuing their descent. One lodged between his collar and neck, it was uncomfortably warm, and he snatched it out.

As he rose to the surface, gasping for breath, he saw that he had been a long
time under water; he was perceptibly farther down stream—nearer to safety. The
soldiers had almost finished reloading; the metal ramrods flashed all at one in the

sunshine as they were drawn from the barrels, turned in the air, and thrust into their sockets. The two sentinels fired again, independently and ineffectually.

The hunted man saw all this over his shoulder; he was now swimming vigorously with the current. His brain was as energetic as his arms and legs; he thought with the rapidity of lightning.

"The officer," he reasoned, "will not make the martinet's error a second time. It is as easy to dodge a volley as a single shot. He has probably already given the command to fire at will. God help me, I cannot dodge them all!"

An appalling plash within two yards of him, followed by a loud rushing sound, *diminuendo*, which seemed to travel back through the air to the fort and died in an explosion which stirred the very river to its deeps![2] A rising sheet of water, which curved over him, fell down upon him, blinded him, strangled him! The cannon had taken a hand in the game. As he shook his head free from the commotion of the smitten water, he heard the deflected shot humming through the air ahead, and in an instant it was cracking and smashing the branches in the forest beyond.

"They will not do that again," he thought; "the next time they will use a charge of grape. I must keep my eye upon the gun; the smoke will apprise me—the report arrives too late; it lags behind the missile. It is a good gun."

30

Suddenly he felt himself whirled round and round—spinning like a top. The water, the banks, the forest, the now distant bridge, fort, and men—all were commingled and blurred. Objects were represented by their colors only; circular horizontal streaks of color—that was all he saw. He had been caught in a vortex and was being whirled on with a velocity of advance and gyration which made him giddy and sick. In a few moments he was flung upon the gravel at the foot of the left bank of the stream—the southern bank—and behind a projecting point which concealed him from his enemies. The sudden arrest of his motion, the abrasion of one of his hands on the gravel, restored him and he wept with delight. He dug his fingers into the sand, threw it over himself in handfuls and audibly blessed it. It looked like gold, like diamonds, rubies, emeralds; he could think of nothing beautiful which it did not resemble. The trees upon the bank were giant garden plants; he noted a definite order in their arrangement, inhaled the fragrance of their blooms. A strange, roseate light shone through the spaces among their trunks, and the wind made in their branches the music of æolian harps.[3] He had no wish to perfect his escape, was content to remain in that enchanting spot until retaken.

A whizz and rattle of grapeshot among the branches high above his head roused him from his dream. The baffled cannoneer had fired him a random farewell. He sprang to his feet, rushed up the sloping bank, and plunged into the forest.

---

[2] *Diminuendo:* a gradually diminishing volume, a term used in music.   [3] *Aeolian harp:* a musical instrument consisting of a box equipped with strings of equal length that are tuned in unison. Such harps are placed in windows to produce harmonious tones sounded by the wind.

All that day he travelled, laying his course by the rounding sun. The forest seemed interminable; nowhere did he discover a break in it, not even a woodman's road. He had not known that he lived in so wild a region. There was something un-canny in the revelation:

By nightfall he was fatigued, footsore, famishing. The thought of his wife and children urged him on. At last he found a road which led him in what he knew to be the right direction. It was as wide and straight as a city street, yet it seemed un-travelled. No fields bordered it, no dwelling anywhere. Not so much as the barking of a dog suggested human habitation. The black bodies of the great trees formed a straight wall on both sides, terminating on the horizon in a point, like a diagram in a lesson in perspective. Overhead, as he looked up through this rift in the wood, shone great golden stars looking unfamiliar and grouped in strange constellations. He was sure they were arranged in some order which had a secret and malign sig-nificance. The wood on either side was full of singular noises, among which—once, twice, and again—he distinctly heard whispers in an unknown tongue.

His neck was in pain, and, lifting his hand to it, he found it horribly swollen. 35 He knew that it had a circle of black where the rope had bruised it. His eyes felt congested; he could no longer close them. His tongue was swollen with thirst; he relieved its fever by thrusting it forward from between his teeth into the cool air. How softly the turf had carpeted the untravelled avenue! He could no longer feel the roadway beneath his feet!

Doubtless, despite his suffering, he fell asleep while walking, for now he sees another scene—perhaps he has merely recovered from a delirium. He stands at the gate of his own home: All is as he left it, and all bright and beautiful in the morn-ing sunshine. He must have travelled the entire night. As he pushes open the gate and passes up the wide white walk, he sees a flutter of female garments; his wife, looking fresh and cool and sweet, steps down from the verandah to meet him. At the bottom of the steps she stands waiting, with a smile of ineffable joy, an attitude of matchless grace and dignity. Ah, how beautiful she is! He springs forward with extended arms. As he is about to clasp her, he feels a stunning blow upon the back of the neck; a blinding white light blazes all about him, with a sound like a shock of a cannon—then all is darkness and silence!

Peyton Farquhar was dead; his body, with a broken neck, swung gently from side to side beneath the timbers of the Owl Creek bridge.

Questions for Discussion and Writing

1. If we conclude that the narrator is actually hanged at the end of the story, what clues does Bierce provide to suggest that almost everything that hap-pens is in the mind of the main character?

2. What details does Bierce provide to signal that events as they are reported, are not the same as what actually occurs?

3. How does Bierce convey the psychological desperation of the main charac-ter as he tries to ward off tangible signs of what is actually happening?

IRENE ZABYTKO

Irene Zabytko was born in 1954 to a Ukrainian family in Chicago. Her fiction has won the PEN Syndicated Fiction Project, and she is the founder and publisher of OdessaPressa *Productions. Her most recent work is* The Sky Unwashed *(2000), a novel based on the nuclear accident in Chernobyl, Russia. The following story originally appeared in* The Perimeter of Light: Writing about the Vietnam War, *edited by Vivian Vie Balfour (1992).*

Home Soil

I watch my son crack his knuckles, oblivious to the somber sounds of the Old Slavonic hymns the choir behind us is singing.

We are in the church where Bohdan, my son, was baptized nineteen years ago. It is Sunday. The pungent smell of frankincense permeates the darkened atmosphere of this cathedral. Soft sun rays illuminate the stained-glass windows. I sit near the one that shows Jesus on the cross looking down on some unidentifiable Apostles who are kneeling beneath His nailed feet. In the background, a tiny desperate Judas swings from a rope, the thirty pieces of silver thrown on the ground.

There is plenty of room in my pew, but my son chooses not to sit with me. I see him staring at the round carapace of a ceiling, stoic icons staring directly back at him. For the remainder of the Mass, he lightly drums his nervous fingers on top of the cover of *My Divine Friend,* the Americanized prayer book of the Ukrainian service. He took bongo lessons before he graduated high school, and learned the basic rolls from off a record, "Let's Swing with Bongos." I think it was supposed to make him popular with the girls at parties. I also think he joined the army because he wanted the virile image men in uniforms have that the bongos never delivered. When he returned from Nam, he mentioned after one of our many conversational silences that he lost the bongos, and the record is cracked, with the pieces buried somewhere deep inside the duffel bag he still hasn't unpacked.

Bohdan, my son, who calls himself Bob, has been back for three weeks. He looks so "American" in his green tailored uniform: his spit-shined vinyl dress shoes tap against the red-cushioned kneelers. It was his idea to go to church with me. He has not been anywhere since he came home. He won't even visit my garden.

Luba, my daughter, warned me he would be moody. She works for the Voice of America and saw him when he landed from Nam in San Francisco. "Just don't worry, *tato,*[1] she said to me on the telephone. "He's acting weird. Culture shock."

"Explain what you mean."

"Just, you know, strange." For a disc jockey, and a bilingual one at that, she is so inarticulate. She plays American jazz and tapes concerts for broadcasts for her anonymous compatriots in Ukraine. That's what she was doing when she was in San Francisco, taping some jazz concert. Pure American music for the huddled

5

---

[1] *tato:* "Father" or "Dad."

gold-toothed youths who risk their *komsomol* privileges and maybe their lives listening to these clandestine broadcasts and to my daughter's sweet voice. She will never be able to visit our relatives back there because American security won't allow it, and she would lose her job. But it doesn't matter. After my wife died, I have not bothered to keep up with anyone there, and I don't care if they have forgotten all about me. It's just as well.

I noticed how much my son resembled my wife when I first saw him again at the airport. He was alone, near the baggage claim ramp. He was taller than ever, and his golden hair was bleached white from the jungle sun. He inherited his mother's high cheekbones, but he lost his baby fat, causing his cheeks to jut out from his lean face as sharp as the arrowheads he used to scavenge for when he was a kid.

We hugged briefly. I felt his medals pinch through my thin shirt. "You look good, son," I tied. I avoided his eyes and concentrated on a pin shaped like an open parachute that he wore over his heart.

"Hi, *tato*," he murmured. We spoke briefly about his flight home from San   10
Francisco, how he'd seen Luba. We stood apart, unlike the other soldiers with their families who were hugging and crying on each other's shoulders in a euphoric delirium.

He grabbed his duffle bag from the revolving ramp and I walked behind him to see if he limped or showed any signs of pain. He showed nothing.

"Want to drive?" I asked, handing him the keys to my new Plymouth.

"Nah," he said. He looked around at the cars crowding the parking lot, and I thought he seemed afraid. "I don't remember how the streets go anymore."

An usher in his best borscht-red polyester suit waits for me to drop some money into the basket. It is old Pan[2] Medved, toothless except for the prominent gold ones he flashes at me as he pokes me with his basket.

"*Nu*, give," he whispers hoarsely, but loud enough for a well-dressed woman   15
with lacquered hair who sits in front of me to turn around and stare in mute accusation.

I take out the gray and white snakeskin wallet Bohdan brought back for me, and transfer out a ten dollar bill. I want the woman to see it before it disappears into the basket. She smiles at me and nods.

Women always smile at me like that. Especially after they see my money and find out that I own a restaurant in the neighborhood. None of the Ukies[3] go there; they don't eat fries and burgers much. But the "jackees"—the Americans—do when they're sick of eating in the cafeteria at the plastics factory. My English is pretty good for a D.P., and no one has threatened to bomb my business because they accuse me of being a no-god bohunk commie. Not yet anyway.

---

[2] *Pan:* a term of respect for adult males, the equivalent of *Mr.*   [3] *Ukies:* Ukrainian Americans.

But the women are always impressed. I usually end up with the emigrés—some of them Ukrainians. The Polish women are the greediest for gawdy trinkets and for a man to give them money so that they can return to their husbands and children in Warsaw. I like them the best anyway because they laugh more than the other women I see, and they know how to have a good time.

Bohdan knows nothing about my lecherous life. I told the women to stay clear after my son arrived. He is so lost with women. I think he was a virgin when he joined the army, but I'm sure he isn't now. I can't ask him.

After mass ends, I lose Bohdan in the tight clusters of people leaving their pews and genuflecting toward the iconostasis. He waits for me by the holy water font. It looks like a regular porcelain water fountain but without a spout. There is a sponge in the basin that is moistened with the holy water blessed by the priests here. Bohdan stands towering over the font, dabs his fingers into the sponge, but doesn't cross himself the way he was taught to do as a boy.

"What's the matter?" I ask in English. I hope he will talk to me if I speak to him in his language.

But Bohdan ignores me and watches an elderly woman gingerly entering the door of the confessional. "What she got to say? Why is she going in there?"

"Everyone has sins."

"Yeah, but who forgives?"

"God forgives," I say. I regret it because it makes me feel like a hypocrite whenever I parrot words I still find difficult to believe.

We walk together in the neighborhood; graffiti visible in the alley-ways despite the well-trimmed lawns with flowers and "bathtub" statues of the Blessed Mary smiling benevolently at us as we pass by the small bungalows. I could afford to move out of here, out of Chicago and into some nearby cushy suburb, Skokie or something. But what for? Some smart Jewish lawyer or doctor would be my next door neighbor and find out that I'm a Ukie and complain to me about how his grandmother was raped by Petliura.[4] I've heard it before. Anyway, I like where I am. I bought a three-flat apartment building after my wife died and I live in one of the apartments rent-free. I can walk to my business, and see the past—old women in babushkas sweeping the sidewalks in front of their cherished gardens; men in Italian-made venetian-slat sandals and woolen socks rushing to a chess match at the Soyuiez, a local meeting place where the D.P.s sit for hours rehashing the war over beers and chess.

Bohdan walks like a soldier. Not exactly a march, but a stiff gait that a good posture in a rigid uniform demands. He looks masculine, but tired and worn. Two pimples are sprouting above his lip where a faint moustache is starting.

"Want a cigarette?" I ask. Soldiers like to smoke. During the forties, I smoked that horrible cheap tobacco, *mahorka*. I watch my son puff heavily on the cigarette

20

25

---

[4] *Petliura:* Simeon Petliura (1879–1926), an anti-Bolshevik Ukrainian leader who was accused of responsibility for Jewish pogroms during World War I. When his forces were defeated by the Russians he went into exile in Paris, where he was ultimately assassinated by a Jewish nationalist.

I've given him, with his eyes partially closed, delicately cupping his hands to protect it from the wind. In my life, I have seen so many soldiers in that exact pose; they all look the same. When their faces are contorted from sucking the cigarette, there is an unmistakable shadow of vulnerability and fear of living. That gesture and stance are more eloquent than the blood and guts war stories men spew over their beers.

Pan Medved, the battered gold-toothed relic in the church, has that look. Pan Holewski, one of my tenants, has it too. I would have known it even if he never openly displayed his old underground soldier's cap that sits on a bookshelf in the living room between small Ukrainian and American flags. I see it every time I collect the rent.

I wish Bohdan could tell me what happened to him in Vietnam. What did he do? What was done to him? Maybe now isn't the time to tell me. He may never tell me. I never told anyone either.

I was exactly his age when I became a soldier. At nineteen, I was a student at the university in L'vov, which the Poles occupied. I was going to be a poet, to study poetry and write it, but the war broke out, and my family could not live on the romantic epics I tried to publish, so I was paid very well by the Nazis to write propaganda pamphlets. "Freedom for Ukrainians" I wrote—"Freedom for our people. Fight the Poles and Russians alongside our German brothers" and other such dreck. I even wrote light verse that glorified Hitler as the protector of the free Ukrainian nation that the Germans promised us. My writing was as naïve as my political ideas.

My new career began in a butcher shop, commandeered after the Polish owner was arrested and shot. I set my battered Underwood typewriter atop an oily wooden table where crescents of chicken feathers still clung between the cracks. Meat hooks that once held huge sides of pork hung naked in a back room, and creaked ominously like a deserted gallows whenever anyone slammed the front door. Every shred of meat had been stolen by looters after the Germans came into the city. Even the little bell that shopkeepers kept at the entrance was taken. But I was very comfortable in my surroundings. I thought only about how I was to play a part in a historical destiny that my valiant words would help bring about. That delusion lasted only about a week or so until three burly Nazis came in. *"Schnell!"* they said to me, pushing me out of my chair and pointing to the windows where I saw crowds chaotically swarming about. Before I could question the soldiers, one of them shoved a gun into my hands and pushed me out into the streets. I felt so bewildered until the moment I pointed my rifle at a man who was about—I thought—to hit me with a club of some sort. Suddenly, I felt such an intense charge of power, more so than I had ever felt writing some of my best poems. I was no longer dealing with abstract words and ideas for a mythological cause; I was responsible for life and death.

I enjoyed that power, until it seeped into my veins and poisoned my soul. It was only an instant, a brief interlude, a matter of hours until that transformation occurred. I still replay that scene in my mind almost forty years after it happened, no matter what I am doing, or who I am with.

30

I think she was a village girl. Probably a Jew, because on that particular day, the Jews were the ones chosen to be rounded up and sent away in cattle cars. Her hair was golden red, short and wavy as was the style, and her neck was awash in freckles. It was a crowded station in the center of the town, not far from the butcher shop. There were Germans shouting and women crying and church bells ringing. I stood with that German regulation rifle I hardly knew how to handle, frozen because I was too lightheaded and excited. I too began to yell at people and held the rifle against my chest, and I was very much aware of how everyone responded to my authority.

Then, this girl appeared in my direct line of vision. Her back was straight, her shoulders tensed; she stopped in the middle of all the chaos. Simply stopped. I ran up and pushed her. I pushed her hard, she almost fell. I kept pushing her, feeling the thin material of her cheap wool jacket against my chapped eager hand; her thin muscles forced forward by my shoves. Once, twice, until she toppled into the open door of a train and fell toward a heap of other people moving deeper into the tiny confines of the stinking cattle car. She never turned around.

I should have shot her. I should have spared her from whatever she had to go through. I doubt she survived. I should have tried to find out what her name was, so I could track down her relatives and confess to them. At least in that way, they could have spat at me injustice and I would have finally received the absolution I will probably never find in this life.

I don't die. Instead, I go to the garden. It is Sunday evening. I am weeding the crop of beets and cabbages I planted in the patch in my backyard. The sun is lower, a breeze kicks up around me, but my forehead sweats. I breathe in the thick deep earth smells as the dirt crumbles and rotates against the blade of my hoe. I should destroy the honeysuckle vine that is slowly choking my plants, but the scent is so sweet, and its intoxicating perfume reminds me of a woman's gentleness.

I hoe for a while, but not for long, because out of the corner of my eye, I see Bohdan sitting on the grass tearing the firm green blades with his clenched hands. He is still wearing his uniform, all except the jacket, tie, and cap. He sits with his legs apart, his head down, ignoring the black flies that nip at his ears.

I wipe my face with a bright red bandana, which I brought with me to tie up the stalks of my drooping sunflowers. "Bohdan," I say to my son. "Why don't we go into the house and have a beer. I can finish this another time." I look at the orange sun. 'It's humid and there's too many flies—means rain will be coming."

My son is quietly crying to himself.

"*Tato,* I didn't know anything," he cries out. "You know, I just wanted to jump out from planes with my parachute. I just wanted to fly . . ."

"I should have stopped you," I say more to myself than to him. Bohdan lets me stroke the thin spikes of his army regulation crew-cut which is soft and warm and I am afraid of how easily my hand can crush his skull.

I rock him in my arms the way I saw his mother embrace him when he was afraid to sleep alone.

There is not much more I can do right now except to hold him. I will hold him until he pulls away.

Questions for Discussion and Writing

1. Suddenly finding oneself with the power of life and death over other human beings is a harrowing experience for the narrator. How do the memories of this experience bring him closer to his son, who just returned from Vietnam?
2. What means does Zabytko use to make the narrator a sympathetic character despite the evil he has perpetrated in the past?
3. The *Mahabarata*, a classic Indian epic (200 B.C.), suggests that just as no good man is all good, no bad man is all bad. How does "Home Soil" illustrate this insight?

Poetry

BERTOLT BRECHT

Bertolt Brecht (1898–1956) was born in Augsburg, Germany; studied medicine at Munich University; and served as an orderly in a military hospital during World War I. Although he wrote poems and stories, he is best known for his dramas, such as The Three-Penny Opera *(1928, written with Kurt Weill) and* The Caucasian Chalk Circle *(1954). The following poem (translated by H. R. Hayes) is reprinted from* Selected Poems *(1947).*

A Worker Reads History

Who built the seven gates of Thebes?
The books are filled with names of kings.
Was it kings who hauled the craggy blocks of stone?
And Babylon, so many times destroyed,
Who built the city up each time? In which of Lima's houses,   5
That city glittering with gold, lived those who built it?
In the evening when the Chinese wall was finished
Where did the masons go? Imperial Rome
Is full of arcs of triumph. Who reared them up? Over whom
Did the Caesars triumph? Byzantium lives in song,   10
Were all her dwellings palaces? And even in Atlantis[1] of the legend
The night the sea rushed in,
The drowning men still bellowed for their slaves.

Young Alexander conquered India.
He alone?   15

---

[1] *Atlantis:* a mythical island in the Atlantic Ocean west of Gibraltar, said to have sunk into the sea.

Caesar beat the Gauls.
Was there not even a cook in his army?
Philip of Spain wept as his fleet
Was sunk and destroyed. Were there no other tears?
Frederick the Great triumphed in the Seven Years War. Who   20
Triumphed with him?

Each page a victory,

At whose expense the victory ball?
Every ten years a great man,
Who paid the piper?   25

So many particulars.
So many questions.

Questions for Discussion and Writing

1. In what way is the poem designed to make readers think about people that history books never mention? Who are they, and what role have they really played?
2. The contrast between the "great man" who appears every ten years and the faceless masses who pay the "piper" is a source of dramatic irony. What point is Brecht making with this statement?
3. A classic debate in history has been whether leaders shape history or are created by historical events. What is your view? Give an example that supports it.

ELENI FOURTOUNI

Eleni Fourtouni was born during World War II in Sparta, Greece, in 1933. Fourtouni's poetry springs from her translations of nine journals kept by Greek women political prisoners during the war in Greece. These journals were edited and compiled by Victoria Theodorou, herself an inmate of the prison and writer of one of the journals. These compilations and oral histories are called Greek Women of the Resistance. *Fourtouni's work includes a collection of poetry,* Monovassia *(1976), an anthology she edited and translated,* Contemporary Greek Women Poets *(1978), in which "Child's Memory" first appeared. The act of cutting off the head of a fish her young son has just caught releases submerged childhood memories of brutalities committed during the Nazi occupation in this poem.*

Child's Memory

Every time I think of it
there's a peculiar tickle
at my throat
especially when I clean fish

the fish my blond son brings me   5
proud of his catch—
and I must cut off the heads

my hand holding the knife hesitates—
that peculiar tickle again—
I set the knife aside   10
furtively I scratch my throat

then I bring the knife down
on the thick scaly neck—
not much of a neck really—
just below the gills   15
I hack at the slippery
hulk of bass
my throat itches
my hands stink fish
they drip blood   20
my knife cuts through

the great head is off
I breathe

Once again the old image comes
into focus—   25
the proud blond soldier
his polished black boots
his spotless green uniform
his smile
the sack he lugs   30
into the schoolyards

the children gather
the soldier dips his hand inside the sack
the children hold their breath
what is it what?   35
their ink-smudged hands fly to their eyes

but we're full of curiosity
between our spread fingers we see . . .

the soldier's laughter is loud
as he pulls out   40
the heads of two Greek partisans.

quickly I rinse the blood off my knife.

Questions for Discussion and Writing

1. How does the way in which the poem begins suggest that the traumatic events of the past are never far from the speaker's consciousness?
2. What insight does the poem offer into the relationship between the local Greek population and the German army that occupied the town during World War II?
3. How does the way the poem is constructed build suspense about the unknown horrible event that still casts a shadow over the young mother's life in the present? How has the mother's relationship with her son been forever altered by the events that took place in her own childhood during wartime?

DAVID R. SLAVITT

David R. Slavitt (b. 1935) was educated at Yale and Columbia Universities. His published works include novels, plays, several books of poetry, and translations of Greek and Roman poets. "Titanic" first appeared in Big Nose *(1983). He translated* The Latin Odes of Jean Dorat *(2000) and, from the French,* Sonnets of Love and Death: Jean de Sponde—1557–1595 *(2001) and* The Book of Lamentations: A Meditation and Translation *(2001). Slavitt currently teaches at Bennington College in Vermont.*

Titanic

Who does not love the *Titanic?*
If they sold passage tomorrow for the same crossing,
who would not buy?

To go down ... We all go down, mostly
alone. But with crowds of people, friends, servants,   5
well fed, with music, with lights! Ah!

And the world, shocked, mourns, as it ought to do
and almost never does. There will be the books and movies
to remind our grandchildren who we were
and how we died, and give them a good cry.   10

Not so bad, after all. The cold
water is anesthetic and very quick.
The cries on all sides must be a comfort.

We all go: only a few, first-class.

Questions for Discussion and Writing

1. Slavitt uses the historical event of the *Titanic's* sinking to explore the broader implications of mortality. What particular twist does he give this age-old topic?
2. To what extent is self-pity the dominant emotion Slavitt evokes, or do you find his poem ironic? Explain your reaction.
3. Would being remembered be important to you in the way Slavitt suggests the passengers on the Titanic are remembered? Why or why not?

Connections for Chapter 7: History in the Making

1. **Linda Simon,** *The Naked Source*

   How do Kenneth M. Stampp's research and the inferences he draws from records and documents illustrate the methods historians use, as recommended by Simon?

   Do you think Simon would approve of Hanson W. Baldwin's reconstruction of the events that led to the sinking of the *Titanic?* Why or why not?

2. **Howard Carter,** *Finding the Tomb*

   Compare the historical reality of ancient Egypt unearthed by Carter with the poetic uses of this era by W. B. Yeats in his poem "The Second Coming" in Chapter 11.

3. **Kenneth M. Stampp,** *To Make Them Stand in Fear*

   What insights into the psychology of the colonizers and the colonized do Stampp and Haunani-Kay Trask offer in their essays?

4. **Haunani-Kay Trask,** *From a Native Daughter*

   In what sense might Trask's analysis be considered the worker's reading of history espoused by Bertolt Brecht in his poem?

5. **Jack London,** *The San Francisco Earthquake*

   Compare the reactions of the survivors of the earthquake with the reactions of the survivors of the *Titanic* as reported by Hanson W. Baldwin.

6. **Hanson W. Baldwin,** *R. M. S.* Titanic

   Baldwin and John Hersey both describe events in which technological advances have tragic outcomes. What sense do you get that the authors are conscious of the larger ironies of technology and hubris?

   What aspects of the literal lifeboat dilemma confronting passengers on the *Titanic* does Garrett Hardin (in "Lifeboat Ethics" in Chapter 11) use to explore ethical trade-offs?

7. **John Hersey,** *A Noiseless Flash from Hiroshima*

   How do the reactions of the survivors in Hersey's account differ from the reactions of the survivors of the San Francisco earthquake, as reported by Jack

London? What means do the authors use to bring into human terms events outside the reader's comprehension?

8. **Ambrose Bierce,** *An Occurrence at Owl Creek Bridge*
   Bierce uses a neutral journalistic framework to set the stage for his story. After reading the accounts by Jack London and John Hersey, discuss the advantages of this method for Bierce.

9. **Irene Zabytko,** *Home Soil*
   To what extent do Zabytko's story and Haunani-Kay Trask's analysis explore tensions and enmities between different racial and ethnic groups and the stereotypes on which they are based?

10. **Bertolt Brecht,** *A Worker Reads History*
    In what respects do both Brecht and Linda Simon argue for a reexamination of assumptions underlying traditional historical research?

11. **Eleni Fourtouni,** *Child's Memory*
    In what respects does Fourtouni's poem and Irene Zabytko's story provide complementary perspectives on wartime memories triggered by events in the present?

12. **David R. Slavitt,** *Titanic*
    What different emphasis does Slavitt give to the sinking of the *Titanic* from Hanson W. Baldwin's treatment in his essay?

8

THE PURSUIT OF JUSTICE

The allegiance that individuals owe their governments and the protection of individual rights that citizens expect in return have been subjects of intense analysis through the ages. The readings that follow continue this debate by providing accounts drawn from many different societies; they reveal assumptions and expectations that are very different in many cases from our own about our democratic form of government. Thomas Paine, writing in the 1700s, and Martin Luther King, Jr., writing over two hundred years later, enunciate strikingly similar ideas of freedom and affirm the government's role as ultimate guarantor of the rights of individual citizens. Golda Meir's account re-creates the moment when the guiding principles underlying the state of Israel were formulated.

Readings by Harriet Jacobs and Luis Sepulveda bear witness to the consequences of the suspension of civil rights under slavery, and to the experiences of those who have been subject to arrest, detention, and torture in Chile. A contrasting perspective is offered by Rae Yang, who admits her complicity in state-sponsored terrorism as a Red Guard in China, under Mao Zedong.

Albert Camus's story, "The Guest,". is a masterful dramatization of the inevitability of personal choice in the politicized environment of the Algerian conflict. Luisa Valenzuela creates an ironic fable about the corrupting effects of power on the average citizen under a dictatorship in Argentina.

The poems of W. H. Auden and Margaret Atwood offer a sardonic epitaph on a compliant citizen and a stunning catalogue of the effects of wars on soldiers and the women they leave behind.

Protest, a play by Václav Havel (the first elected president of the Czech Republic), explores the relationship between two political dissenters, one of whom has sold out to the government for private gain, while the other (like Havel himself) has been imprisoned and struggles to make a living.

Nonfiction

THOMAS PAINE

Thomas Paine (1737–1809), following Benjamin Franklin's advice, left England and came to America in 1774, served in the Revolutionary Army, and supported the cause of the colonies through his influential pamphlets Common Sense *(1776) and* The Crisis *(1776–1783). He also supported the French Revolution and wrote* Rights of Man *(1792) and* The Age of Reason *(1793).* Rights of Man *was written in reply to Edmund Burke's* Reflections upon the Revolution in France. *Paine disputes Burke's doctrine that one generation can compel succeeding ones to follow a particular form of government. Paine defines the inalienable "natural" and "civil" rights of humankind and expounds on society's obligation to protect these rights.*

Rights of Man

If any generation of men ever possessed the right of dictating the mode by which the world should be governed for ever, it was the first generation that existed; and if that generation did it not, no succeeding generation can show any authority for doing it, nor can set any up. The illuminating and divine principle of the equal rights of man, (for it has its origin from the Maker of man) relates, not only to the living individuals, but to generations of men succeeding each other. Every generation is equal in rights to the generations which preceded it, by the same rule that every individual is born equal in rights with his contemporary.

Every history of the creation, and every traditionary account, whether from the lettered or unlettered world, however they may vary in their opinion or belief of certain particulars, all agree in establishing one point, *the unity of man;* by which I mean, that men are all of *one degree,* and consequently that all men are born equal, and with equal natural right, in the same manner as if posterity had been continued by *creation* instead of *generation,* the latter being only the mode by which the former is carried forward; and consequently, every child born into the world must be considered as deriving its existence from God. The world is as new to him as it was to the first man that existed, and his natural right in it is of the same kind.

The Mosaic account of the creation, whether taken as divine authority, or merely historical, is full to this point, *the unity or equality of man.* The expressions admit of no controversy. "And God said, Let us make man in our own image. In the image of God created he him; male and female created he them." The distinction of sexes is pointed out, but no other distinction is even implied. If this be not divine authority, it is at least historical authority, and shows that the equality of man, so far from being a modern doctrine, is the oldest upon record.

It is also to be observed, that all the religions known in the world are founded, so far as they relate to man, on the *unity of man,* as being all of one degree. Whether in heaven or in hell, or in whatever state man may be supposed to exist hereafter, the good and the bad are the only distinctions. Nay, even the laws of governments are obliged to slide into this principle, by making degrees to consist in crimes, and not in persons.

It is one of the greatest of all truths, and of the highest advantage to cultivate. By considering man in this light, and by instructing him to consider himself in this light, it places him in a close connexion with all his duties, whether to his Creator, or to the creation, of which his is a part; and it is only when he forgets his origin, or, to use a more fashionable phrase, his *birth and family;* that he becomes dissolute. It is not among the least of the evils of the present existing governments in all parts of Europe, that man, considered as man, is thrown back a vast distance from his Maker, and the artificial chasm filled up by a succession of barriers, or sort of turn-pike gates, through which he has to pass. I will quote Mr. Burke's[1] catalogue of barriers that he has set up between man and his Maker. Putting himself in the character of a herald, he says—"We fear God—we look with *awe* to kings—with affection to parliaments—with duty to magistrates—with reverence to priests, and with respect to nobility." Mr. Burke has forgotten to put in "*chivalry.*" He has also forgotten to put in Peter.

The duty of man is not a wilderness of turnpike gates, through which he is to pass by tickets from one to the other. It is plain and simple, and consists but of two points. His duty to God, which every man must feel; and with respect to his neighbour, to do as he would be done by. If those to whom power is delegated do well, they will be respected; if not, they will be despised: and with regard to those to whom no power is delegated, but who assume it, the rational world can know nothing of them.

Hitherto we have spoken only (and that but in part) of the natural rights of man. We have now to consider the civil rights of man, and to show how the one originates from the other. Man did not enter into society to become *worse* than he was before, nor to have fewer rights than he had before, but to have those rights better secured. His natural rights are the foundation of all his civil rights. But in order to pursue this distinction with more precision, it will be necessary to mark the different qualities of natural and civil rights.

A few words will explain this. Natural rights are those which appear to man in right of his existence. Of this kind are all the intellectual rights, or rights of the mind, and also all those rights of acting as an individual for his own comfort and happiness, which are not injurious to the natural rights of others.—Civil rights are those which appertain to man in right of his being a member of society. Every civil right has for its foundation, some natural right pre-existing in the individual, but to the enjoyment of which his individual power is not, in all cases, sufficiently competent. Of this kind are all those which relate to security and protection.

From this short review, it will be easy to distinguish between that class of natural rights which man retains after entering into society, and those which he throws into the common stock as a member of society.

---

[1] *Edmund Burke (1729–1797):* Irish statesman, orator, and writer who sympathized with the American Revolution but opposed the French Revolution on the grounds that it was a completely unjustified break with tradition.

The natural rights which he retains, are all those in which the *power* to exe- ·10
cute is as perfect in the individual as the right itself. Among this class, as is before
mentioned, are all the intellectual rights, or rights of the mind: consequently, religion is one of those rights. The natural rights which are not retained, are all those
in which, though the right is perfect in the individual, the power to execute them
is defective. They answer not his purpose. A man, by natural right, has a right to
judge in his own cause; and so far as the right of mind is concerned; he never sur-
renders it: But what availeth it him to judge, if he has not power to redress? He
therefore deposits this right in the common stock of society, and takes the arm of
society, of which he is a part, in preference and in addition to his own. Society
grants him nothing. Every man is a proprietor in society, and draws on the capital as
a matter of right.

From these premises, two or three certain conclusions will follow.

First, That every civil right grows out of a natural right; or, in other words, is a
natural right exchanged.

Secondly, that civil power, properly considered as such, is made up of the aggregate of that class of the natural rights of man, which becomes defective in the
individual in point of power, and answers not his purpose; but when collected to a
focus, becomes competent to the purpose of every one.

Thirdly, That the power produced from the aggregate of natural rights, imperfect in power in the individual, cannot be applied to invade the natural rights,
which are retained in the individual, and in which the power to execute is as perfect as the right itself.

We have now, in a few words, traced man from a natural individual to a mem- ·15
ber of society, and shown, or endeavoured to show, the quality of the natural rights
retained, and of those which are exchanged for civil rights. Let us now apply these
principles to governments.

In casting our eyes over the world, it is extremely easy to distinguish the governments which have arisen out of society, or out of the social compact, from those
which have not: but to place this in a clearer light than what a single glance may afford, it will be proper to take a review of the several sources from which governments have arisen, and on which they have been founded.

They may be all comprehended under three heads. First, Superstition. Secondly, Power. Thirdly, The common interest of society, and the common rights
of man.

Questions for Discussion and Writing

1. What rationale supports Paine's assertion that all men and women possess
   certain natural rights? Where did these rights come from, and who ordained
   them? How does Paine make use of the biblical account of Creation as the
   foundation for his argument?

2. How does Paine justify the rejection of barriers thrown up by "evils of the
   existing governments in all parts of Europe"? How is this idea used as a rationale to justify rejecting British rule over the American colonies?

3. Reread the Declaration of Independence. What elements in this document reflect ideas and concepts also discussed by Thomas Paine?

HARRIET JACOBS

Harriet Jacobs (1813–1896), also known as Linda Brent, escaped from the slavery into which she had been born and made a new life for herself in the North. She told her story, related below, "Incidents in the Life of a Slave Girl" (1861), with the assistance of Lydia Maria Child, a northern abolitionist leader. Her account has become part of the canon of American literature, history, and women's studies. In the following selection, Jacobs reveals the harrowing predicament that many female slaves found themselves in, trying to fend off their masters' lust and the ensuing jealousy of their wives.

Incidents in the Life of a Slave Girl

I would ten thousand times rather that my children should be the half-starved paupers of Ireland than to be the most pampered among the slaves of America. I would rather drudge out my life on a cotton plantation, till the grave opened to give me rest, than to live with an unprincipled master and a jealous mistress. The felon's home in a penitentiary is preferable. He may repent, and turn from the error of his ways, and so find peace, but it is not so with a favorite slave. She is not allowed to have any pride of character. It is deemed a crime in her to wish to be virtuous.

Mrs. Flint possessed the key to her husband's character before I was born. She might have used this knowledge to counsel and to screen the young and the innocent among her slaves; but for them she had no sympathy. They were the objects of her constant suspicion and malevolence. She watched her husband with unceasing vigilance; but he was well practiced in means to evade it. What he could not find opportunity to say in words he manifested in signs. He invented more than were ever thought of in a deaf and dumb asylum. I let them pass, as if I did not understand what he meant; and many were the curses and threats bestowed on me for my stupidity. One day he caught me teaching myself to write. He frowned, as if he was not well pleased; but I suppose he came to the conclusion that such an accomplishment might help to advance his favorite scheme. Before long, notes were often slipped into my hand. I would return them, saying, "I can't read them, sir." "Can't you?" he replied; "then I must read them to you." He always finished the reading by asking, "Do you understand?" Sometimes he would complain of the heat of the tea room, and order his supper to be placed on a small table in the piazza. He would seat himself there with a well-satisfied smile, and tell me to stand by and brush away the flies. He would eat very slowly, pausing between the mouthfuls. These intervals were employed in describing the happiness I was so foolishly throwing away, and in threatening me with the penalty that finally awaited my stubborn disobedience. He boasted much of the forbearance he had exercised toward me, and reminded me that there was a limit to his patience. When I succeeded in avoiding opportunities for him to talk to me at home, I was ordered to come to his office, to do some errand. When there, I was obliged to stand and listen to such language as he saw fit to address to me. Sometimes I so openly expressed my contempt for him that he would become violently enraged, and I wondered why he did not strike me. Circumstanced as he was, he probably thought it was better policy to be forebearing. But the state of things grew worse and worse daily. In desperation I told him that I must and would apply to my grandmother for protection. He threatened me with death, and worse than death, if I made my complaint to her. Strange to say, I did not despair. I was naturally of a buoyant disposition, and always I had a hope of somehow getting out of his clutches. Like many a poor, simple slave before me, I trusted that some threads of joy would yet be woven into my dark destiny.

I had entered my sixteenth year, and every day it became more apparent that my presence was intolerable to Mrs. Flint. Angry words frequently passed between her and her husband. He had never punished me himself, and he would not allow anybody else to punish me. In that respect, she was never satisfied; but, in her angry moods, no terms were too vile for her to bestow upon me. Yet I, whom she detested so bitterly, had far more pity for her than he had, whose duty it was to make her life happy. I never wronged her, or wished to wrong her; and one word of kindness from her would have brought me to her feet.

After repeated quarrels between the doctor and his wife, he announced his intention to take his youngest daughter, then four years old, to sleep in his apartment. It was necessary that a servant should sleep in the same room, to be on hand if the child stirred. I was selected for that office, and informed for what purpose that arrangement had been made. By managing to keep within sight of people, as much as possible, during the daytime, I had hitherto succeeded in eluding my master, though a razor was often held to my throat to force me to change this line of policy. At night I slept by the side of my great aunt, where I felt safe. He was too prudent to come into her room. She was an old woman, and had been in the family many years. Moreover, as a married man, and a professional man, he deemed it necessary to save appearances in some degree. But he resolved to remove the obstacle in the way of his scheme; and he thought he had planned it so that he should evade suspicion. He was well aware how much I prized my refuge by the side of my old aunt, and he determined to dispossess me of it. The first night the doctor had the little child in his room alone. The next morning, I was ordered to take my station as nurse the following night. A kind Providence interposed in my favor. During the day Mrs. Flint heard of this new arrangement, and a storm followed. I rejoiced to hear it rage.

After a while my mistress sent for me to come to her room. Her first question   5
was, "Did you know you were to sleep in the doctor's room?"

"Yes, ma'am."

"Who told you?"

"My master."

"Will you answer truly all the questions I ask?"

"Yes, ma'am."   10

"Tell me, then, as you hope to be forgiven, are you innocent of what I have accused you?"

"I am."

She handed me a Bible, and said, "Lay your hand on your heart, kiss this holy book, and swear before God that you tell me the truth."

I took the oath she required, and I did it with a clear conscience.

"You have taken God's holy word to testify your innocence," said she. "If you have deceived me, beware! Now take this stool, sit down, look me directly in the face, and tell me all that has passed between your master and you."

I did as she ordered. As I went on with my account her color changed frequently, she wept, and sometimes groaned. She spoke in tones so sad, that I was touched by her grief. The tears came to my eyes; but I was soon convinced that her emotions arose from anger and wounded pride. She felt that her marriage vows were desecrated, her dignity insulted; but she had no compassion for the poor victim of her husband's perfidy. She pitied herself as a martyr; but she was incapable of feeling for the condition of shame and misery in which her unfortunate, helpless slave was placed.

Yet perhaps she had some touch of feeling for me; for when the conference was ended, she spoke kindly, and promised to protect me. I should have been much comforted by this assurance if I could have had confidence in it; but my experiences in slavery had filled me with distrust. She was not a very refined woman, and had not much control over her passions. I was an object of her jealousy, and, consequently, of her hatred; and I knew I could not expect kindness or confidence from her under the circumstances in which I was placed. I could not blame her. Slaveholders' wives feel as other women would under similar circumstances. The fire of her temper kindled from small sparks, and now the flame became so intense that the doctor was obliged to give up his intended arrangement.

I knew I had ignited the torch, and I expected to suffer for it afterward; but I felt too thankful to my mistress for the timely aid she rendered me to care much about that. She now took me to sleep in a room adjoining her own. There I was an object of her especial care, though not of her especial comfort, for she spent many a sleepless night to watch over me. Sometimes I woke up, and found her bending over me. At other times she whispered in my ear, as though it was her husband who was speaking to me, and listened to hear what I would answer. If she startled me, on such occasions, she would glide stealthily away; and the next morning she would tell me I had been talking in my sleep, and ask who I was talking to. At last I began to be fearful for my life. It had been often threatened; and you can imagine, better than I can describe, what an unpleasant sensation it must produce to wake up in the dead of night and find a jealous woman bending over you. Terrible as this experience was, I had fears that it would give place to one more terrible.

My mistress grew weary of her vigils; they did not prove satisfactory. She changed her tactics. She now tried the trick of accusing my master of crime, in my presence, and gave my name as the author of the accusation. To my utter astonishment, he replied, "I don't believe it; but if she did acknowledge it, you tortured her into exposing me." Tortured into exposing him! Truly, Satan had no difficulty in distinguishing the color of his soul! I understood his object in making this false representation. It was to show me that I gained nothing by seeking the protection of my mistress; that the power was still all in his own hands. I pitied Mrs. Flint. She was a second wife, many years the junior of her husband; and the hoary-headed miscreant was enough to try the patience of a wiser and better woman. She was completely foiled, and knew not how to proceed. She would gladly have had me flogged for my supposed false oath; but, as I have already stated, the doctor never allowed anyone to whip me. The old sinner was politic. The application of the lash might have led to remarks that would have exposed him in the eyes of his children and grandchildren. How often did I rejoice that I lived in a town where all the inhabitants knew each other! If I had been on a remote plantation, or lost among the multitude of a crowded city, I should not be a living woman at this day.

The secrets of slavery are concealed like those of the Inquisition. My master   20 was, to my knowledge, the father of eleven slaves. But did the mothers dare to tell who was the father of their children? Did the other slaves dare to allude to it, except in whispers among themselves? No, indeed! They knew too well the terrible consequences.

My grandmother could not avoid seeing things which excited her suspicions. She was uneasy about me, and tried various ways to buy me; but the never-changing answer was always repeated: "Linda does not belong to *me*. She is my daughter's property, and I have no legal right to sell her." The conscientious man! He was too scrupulous to *sell* me; but he had no scruples whatever about committing a much greater wrong against the helpless young girl placed under his guardianship, as his daughter's property. Sometimes my persecutor would ask me whether I would like to be sold. I told him I would rather be sold to anybody than to lead such a life as I did. On such occasions he would assume the air of a very injured individual, and reproach me for my ingratitude. "Did I not take you into the house, and make you the companion of my own children?" he would say. "Have I ever treated you like a Negro? I have never allowed you to be punished, not even to please your mistress. And this is the recompense I get, you ungrateful girl!" I answered that he had reasons of his own for screening me from punishment, and that the course he pursued made my mistress hate me and persecute me. If I wept, he would say, "Poor child! Don't cry! don't cry! I will make peace for you with your mistress. Only let me arrange matters in my own way. Poor, foolish girl! you don't know what is for your own good. I would cherish you. I would make a lady of you. Now go, and think of all I have promised you."

I did think of it.

Reader, I draw no imaginary pictures of southern homes. I am telling you the plain truth. Yet when victims make their escape from this wild beast of Slavery, northerners consent to act the part of bloodhounds, and hunt the poor fugitive back into his den, "full of dead men's bones, and all uncleanness." Nay, more, they are not only willing, but proud, to give their daughters in marriage to slaveholders. The poor girls have romantic notions of a sunny clime, and of the flowering vines that all the year round shade a happy home. To what disappointments are they destined! The young wife soon learns that the husband in whose hands she has placed her happiness pays no regard to his marriage vows. Children of every shade of complexion play with her own fair babies, and too well she knows that they are born unto him of his own household. Jealousy and hatred enter the flowery home, and it is ravaged of its loveliness.

Southern women often marry a man knowing that he is the father of many little slaves. They do not trouble themselves about it. They regard such children as property, as marketable as the pigs on the plantation; and it is seldom that they do not make them aware of this by passing them into the slave-trader's hands as soon as possible, and thus getting them out of their sight. I am glad to say there are some honorable exceptions.

I have myself known two southern wives who exhorted their husbands to free   25
those slaves toward whom they stood in a "parental relation"; and their request was granted. These husbands blushed before the superior nobleness of their wives' natures. Though they had only counseled them to do that which it was their duty to do, it commanded their respect, and rendered their conduct more exemplary. Concealment was at an end, and confidence took the place of distrust.

Though this bad institution deadens the moral sense, even in white women, to a fearful extent, it is not altogether extinct. I have heard southern ladies say of Mr. Such-a-one, "He not only thinks it no disgrace to be the father of those little niggers, but he is not ashamed to call himself their master. I declare, such things ought not to be tolerated in any decent society!"

Questions for Discussion and Writing

1. In what ways did slavery create the conditions in which the kinds of events Jacobs describes could occur? How does she convey her untenable predicament vis-à-vi Dr. and Mrs. Flint and her resourcefulness in coping with it?
2. What was Jacobs's purpose in writing this narrative? How does it change assumptions that her readers might have held about the institution of slavery? In what way was slavery a morally corrupting influence on everyone involved?
3. Discuss comparable circumstances that exist today that have the same effect as those Jacobs describes, for example, sexual harassment in the workplace or illegal aliens working for families or the predicament of immigrants who are completely dependent on their employers.

MARTIN LUTHER KING, JR.

Martin Luther King, Jr. (1929–1968), a monumental figure in the U. S. civil rights movement and a persuasive advocate of nonviolent means for producing social change, was born in Atlanta, Georgia, in 1929. He was ordained a Baptist minister in his father's church when he was eighteen and went on to earn degrees from Morehouse College (B.A., 1948), Crozer Theological Seminary (B.D., 1951), Chicago Theological Seminary (D.D., 1957), and Boston University (Ph.D., 1955; D.D. 1959). On December 5, 1955, while he was pastor of a church in Montgomery, Alabama, King focused national attention on the predicament of southern blacks by leading a citywide boycott of the segregated bus system. The boycott lasted over one year and nearly bankrupted the company. King founded the Southern Christian Leadership Conference and adapted techniques of nonviolent protest, which had been employed by Gandhi,[1] in a series of sit-ins and mass marches that were instrumental in bringing about the Civil Rights Act of 1964 and the Voting Rights Act of 1965. He was awarded the Nobel Prize for Peace in 1964 in recognition of his great achievements as the leader of the American civil rights movement. Sadly, King's affirmation of the need to meet physical violence with peaceful resistance led to his being jailed more than fourteen times, beaten, stoned, stabbed in the chest, and finally murdered in Memphis, Tennessee, on April 4, 1968. His many distinguished writings include Stride Towards Freedom: The Montgomery Story *(1958);* Letter from Birmingham Jail, *written in 1963 and published in 1968;* Why We Can't Wait *(1964);* Where Do We Go from Here: Community or Chaos? *(1967); and* The Trumpet of Conscience *(1968). "I Have a Dream" (1963) is the inspiring sermon delivered by King from the steps of the Lincoln Memorial to the nearly 250,000 people who had come to Washington, D.C., to commemorate the centennial of Lincoln's Emancipation Proclamation. Additional millions who watched on television were moved by this eloquent, noble, and impassioned plea that the United States might fulfill its original promise of freedom and equality for all its citizens.*

I Have a Dream

I am happy to join with you today in what will go down in history as the greatest demonstration for freedom in the history of our nation.

Five score years ago, a great American, in whose symbolic shadow we stand today, signed the Emancipation Proclamation.[2] This momentous decree came as a great beacon light of hope to millions of Negro slaves who had been seared in the flames of withering injustice. It came as a joyous daybreak to end the long night of their captivity. But one hundred years later, the Negro is still not free. One hundred years later, the life of the Negro is still sadly crippled by the manacles of segregation and the chains of discrimination. One hundred years later, the Negro lives on a lonely island of poverty in the midst of a vast ocean of material prosperity. One hundred years later, the Negro is still anguished in the corners of American society and finds himself in exile in his own land. And so we have come here today to dramatize a shameful condition.

In a sense we have come to our nation's capital to cash a check. When the architects of our republic wrote the magnificent words of the Constitution and the Declaration of Independence, they were signing a promissory note to which every American was to fall heir. This note was the promise that all men—yes, Black men as well as white men—would be guaranteed the inalienable rights of life, liberty, and the pursuit of happiness.

It is obvious today that America has defaulted on this promissory note insofar as her citizens of color are concerned. Instead of honoring this sacred obligation, America has given the Negro people a bad check, a check which has come back

---

[1] *Gandhi: (1869–1948):* a great Indian political and spiritual leader, called Mahatma (great-souled), whose approach was one of nonviolent protest. He is regarded as the father of independent India.   [2] *The Emancipation Proclamation:* the executive order abolishing slavery in the Confederacy that President Abraham Lincoln put into effect on January 1, 1863.

marked "insufficient funds." But we refuse to believe that the bank of justice is bankrupt. We refuse to believe that there are insufficient funds in the great vaults of opportunity of this nation; and so we have come to cash this check, a check that will give us upon demand the riches of freedom and the security of justice.

We have also come to this hallowed spot to remind America of the fierce urgency of *now*. This is no time to engage in the luxury of cooling off or to take the tranquilizing drug of gradualism. *Now* is the time to make real the promises of democracy. *Now* is the time to rise from the dark and desolate valley of segregation to the sunlit patch of racial justice. *Now* is the time to lift our nation from the quicksands of racial injustice to the solid rock of brotherhood. *Now* is the time to make justice a reality for all of God's children.

It would be fatal for the nation to overlook the urgency of the moment. This sweltering summer of the Negro's legitimate discontent will not pass until there is an invigorating autumn of freedom and equality. Nineteen sixty-three is not an end, but a beginning. And those who hope that the Negro needed to blow off steam and will now be content will have a rude awakening if the nation returns to business as usual. There will be neither rest nor tranquility in America until the Negro is granted his citizenship rights. The whirlwinds of revolt will continue to shake the foundations of our nation until the bright day of justice emerges.

But there is something that I must say to my people who stand on the warm threshold which leads into the palace of justice. In the process of gaining our rightful place, we must not be guilty of wrongful deeds. Let us not seek to satisfy our thirst for freedom by drinking from the cup of bitterness and hatred. We must forever conduct our struggle on the high plane of dignity and discipline. We must not allow our creative protest to degenerate into physical violence. Again and again we must rise to the majestic heights of meeting physical force with soul force. And the marvelous new militancy which has engulfed the Negro community must not lead us to a distrust of all white people; for many of our white brothers, as evidenced by their presence here today, have come to realize that their destiny is tied up with our destiny, and they have come to realize that their freedom is inextricably bound to our freedom.

We cannot walk alone. And as we walk we must make the pledge that we shall always march ahead. We cannot turn back. There are those who are asking the devotees of civil rights, "When will you be satisfied?" We can never be satisfied as long as the Negro is the victim of the unspeakable horrors of police brutality. We can never be satisfied as long as our bodies, heavy with the fatigue of travel, cannot gain lodging in the motels of the highways and the hotels of the cities. We cannot be satisfied as long as the Negro's basic mobility is from a smaller ghetto to a larger one. We can never be satisfied as long as our children are stripped of their selfhood and robbed of their dignity by signs stating "For Whites Only." We cannot be satisfied as long as the Negro in Mississippi cannot vote and a Negro in New York believes he has nothing for which to vote. No, no, we are not satisfied, and we will not be satisfied until justice rolls down like waters and righteousness like a mighty stream.

I am not unmindful that some of you have come here out of great trials and tribulations. Some of you have come fresh from narrow jail cells. Some of you have come from areas where your quest for freedom left you battered by the storms of persecution and staggered by the winds of police brutality. You have been the veterans of creative suffering. Continue to work with the faith that unearned suffering is redemptive.

Go back to Mississippi, and go back to Alabama. Go back to South Carolina. 10 Go back to Georgia. Go back to Louisiana. Go back to the slums and ghettos of our northern cities, knowing that somehow this situation can and will be changed. Let us not wallow in the valley of despair.

I say to you today, my friends, even though we face the difficulties of today and tomorrow, I still have a dream. It is a dream deeply rooted in the American dream. I have a dream that one day this nation will rise up and live out the true meaning of its creed: "We hold these truths to be self-evident, that all men are created equal." I have a dream that one day, on the red hills of Georgia, sons of former slaves and the sons of former slave owners will be able to sit down together at the table of brotherhood. I have a dream that one day even the state of Mississippi, a state sweltering with the heat of injustice, sweltering with the heat of oppression, will be transformed into an oasis of freedom and justice. I have a dream that my four little children will one day live in a nation where they will not be judged by the color of their skin, but by the content of their character.

I have a dream today. I have a dream that one day down in Alabama—with its vicious racists, with its governor's lips dripping with the words of interposition and nullification—one day right there in Alabama, little Black boys and Black girls will be able to join hands with little white boys and white girls as sisters and brothers.

I have a dream today. I have a dream that one day every valley shall be exalted and every hill and mountain shall be made low, the rough places will be made plain and the crooked places will be made straight, and the glory of the Lord shall be revealed, and all flesh shall see it together.

This is our hope. This is the faith that I go back to the South with. And with this faith we will be able to hew out of the mountain of despair a stone of hope. With this faith we will be able to transform the jangling discords of our nation into a beautiful symphony of brotherhood. With this faith we will be able to work together, to play together, to struggle together, to go to jail together, to stand up for freedom together, knowing that we will be free one day.

And this will be the day—this will be the day when all of God's children will 15 be able to sing with new meaning.

> My country, 'tis of thee,
> Sweet land of liberty,
>   Of thee I sing;
> Land where my fathers died,
> Land of the Pilgrims' pride,
>   From every mountainside
>   Let freedom ring.

And if America is to be a great nation, this must become true.

And so let freedom ring from the prodigious hilltops of New Hampshire. Let freedom ring from the mighty mountains of New York. Let freedom ring from the heightening Alleghenies of Pennsylvania. Let freedom ring from the snow-capped Rockies of Colorado. Let freedom ring from the curvaceous slopes of California.

But not only that. Let freedom ring from Stone Mountain of Georgia. Let freedom ring from Lookout Mountain of Tennessee. Let freedom ring from every hill and molehill of Mississippi. "From every mountainside let freedom ring."

And when this happens—when we allow freedom to ring, when we let it ring from every village and every hamlet, from every state and every city—we will be able to speed up that day when all of God's children, Black men and white men, Jews and Gentiles, Protestants and Catholics, will be able to join hands and sing in the words of the old Negro spiritual: "Free at last! Free at last! Thank God Almighty. We are free at last!"

Questions for Discussion and Writing

1. How did the civil rights movement express ideas of equality and freedom that were already deeply rooted in the Constitution? How did the affirmation of minority rights renew aspirations first stated by America's Founding Fathers?

2. What evidence is there that King was trying to reach many different groups of people, each with its own concerns? Where does he seem to shift his attention from one group to another?

3. What importance does King place on the idea of nonviolent protest? How do King's references to the Bible and the Emancipation Proclamation enhance the effectiveness of his speech?

GOLDA MEIR

Golda Meir (1898–1978) was born in Russia. After a teaching career in the United States, she settled in Palestine in 1921. She later served as Israel's Minister of Labor and Foreign Affairs before becoming prime minister in 1969. She sought peace between Israel and the Arab nations through diplomacy but was forced to resign in 1974 when Arab forces launched an unexpected onslaught on Israel. "We Have Our State," drawn from her autobiography, My Life *(1975), recounts the circumstances surrounding the moment when Israel became a state on May 14, 1948.*

We Have Our State

On the morning of May 14, I participated in a meeting of the People's Council at which we were to decide on the name of the state and on the final formulation of the declaration. The name was less of a problem than the declaration because there was a last-minute argument about the inclusion of a reference to God. Actually the issue had been brought up the day before. The very last sentence, as finally submitted to the small subcommittee charged with producing the final version of the proclamation, began with the words "With trust in the Rock of Israel, we set our hands in witness to this Proclamation. . . ." Ben-Gurion[1] had hoped that the phrase "Rock of Israel" was sufficiently ambiguous to satisfy those Jews for whom it was inconceivable that the document which established the Jewish state should not contain any reference to God, as well as those who were certain to object strenuously to even the least hint of clericalism in the proclamation.

But the compromise was not so easily accepted. The spokesman of the religious parties, Rabbi Fishman-Maimon, demanded that the reference to God be unequivocal and said that he would approve of the "Rock of Israel" only if the words "and its Redeemer" were added, while Aaron Zisling of the left wing of the Labor Party was just as determined in the opposite direction. "I cannot sign a document referring in any way to a God in whom I do not believe," he said. It took Ben-Gurion most of the morning to persuade Maimon and Zisling that the meaning of the "Rock of Israel" was actually twofold: While it signified "God" for a great many Jews, perhaps for most, it could also be considered a symbolic and secular reference to the "strength of the Jewish people." In the end Maimon agreed that the word "Redeemer" should be left out of the text, though, funnily enough, the first English-language translation of the proclamation, released for publication abroad that day, contained no reference at all to the "Rock of Israel" since the military censor had struck out the entire last paragraph as a security precaution because it mentioned the time and place of the ceremony.[2]

The argument itself, however, although it was perhaps not exactly what one would have expected a prime minister-designate to be spending his time on only a few hours before proclaiming the independence of a new state—particularly one threatened by immediate invasion—was far from being just an argument about terminology. We were all deeply aware of the fact that the proclamation not only spelled the formal end to 2,000 years of Jewish homelessness, but also gave expression to the most fundamental principles of the State of Israel. For this reason, each and every word mattered greatly. Incidentally, my good friend Zeev Sharef, the first secretary of the government-to-be (who laid the foundations for the machinery of government), even found time to see to it that the scroll we were about to sign that afternoon should be rushed to the vaults of the Anglo-Palestine Bank after the ceremony, so that it could at least be preserved for posterity—even if the state and we ourselves did not survive for very long.

At about 2 P.M. I went back to my hotel on the seashore, washed my hair and changed into my best black dress. Then I sat down for a few minutes, partly to catch my breath, partly to think—for the first time in the past two or three days—about the children. Menachem was in the United States then—a student at the Manhattan School of Music. I knew that he would come back now that war was

---

[1] *David Ben-Gurion (1886–1973):* the first prime minister of Israel (1949–1953 and 1955–1963).
[2] After the withdrawal of the British mandate following the November 1947 United Nations–directed partition of Palestine into Jewish and Arab states, the event Meir describes occurred. Subsequently, the neighboring Arab states of Lebanon, Syria, Jordan, Egypt, and Iraq declared war on Israel.

inevitable, and I wondered when and how we would meet again. Sarah was in Revivim, and although not so very far away, as the crow flies, we were quite cut off from each other. Months ago, gangs of Palestinian Arabs and armed infiltrators from Egypt had blocked the road that connected the Negev to the rest of the country and were still systematically blowing up or cutting most of the pipelines that brought water to the twenty-seven Jewish settlements that then dotted the Negev. The Haganah had done its best to break the siege. It had opened a dirt track, parallel to the main road, on which convoys managed, now and then, to bring food and water to the 1,000-odd settlers in the south. But who knew what would happen to Revivim or any other of the small, ill-armed ill-equipped Negev settlements when the full-scale Egyptian invasion of Israel began, as it almost certainly would, within only a few hours? Both Sarah and her Zechariah were wireless operators in Revivim, and I had been able to keep in touch with them up till then. But I hadn't heard about or from either of them for several days, and I was extremely worried. It was on youngsters like them, their spirit and their courage, that the future of the Negev and, therefore, of Israel depended, and I shuddered at the thought of their having to face the invading troops of the Egyptian army.

I was so lost in my thoughts about the children that I can remember being   5
momentarily surprised when the phone rang in my room and I was told that a car was waiting to take me to the museum. It had been decided to hold the ceremony at the Tel Aviv museum on Rothschild Boulevard, not because it was such an imposing building (which it wasn't), but because it was small enough to be easily guarded. One of the oldest buildings in Tel Aviv, it had originally belonged to the city's first mayor, who had willed it to the citizens of Tel Aviv for use as an art museum. The grant total of about $200 had been allocated for decorating it suitably for the ceremony; the floors had been scrubbed, the nude paintings on the walls modestly draped, the windows blacked out in case of an air raid and a large picture of Theodore Herzl hung behind the table at which the thirteen members of the provisional government were to sit. Although supposedly only the 200-odd people who had been invited to participate knew the details, a large crowd was already waiting outside the museum by the time I arrived there.

A few minutes later, at exactly 4 P.M., the ceremony began. Ben-Gurion, wearing a dark suit and tie, stood up and rapped a gavel. According to the plan, this was to be the signal for the orchestra, tucked away in a second floor gallery, to play "Hatikvah."[3] But something went wrong, and there was no music. Spontaneously, we rose to our feet and sang our national anthem. Then Ben-Gurion cleared his throat and said quietly, "I shall now read the Scroll of Independence." It took him only a quarter of an hour to read the entire proclamation. He read it slowly and very clearly, and I remember his voice changing and rising a little as he came to the eleventh paragraph:

---

[3] *"Hatikvah" (1886):* recognized as the national anthem of the state of Israel; means "the hope."

Accordingly we, the members of the National Council, representing the Jewish people in the Land of Israel and the Zionist movement, have assembled on the day of the
termination of the British mandate for Palestine, and, by virtue of our natural and historic right and of the resolution of the General Assembly of the United Nations, do
hereby proclaim the establishment of a Jewish state in the Land of Israel—the
State of Israel.

The State of Israel! My eyes filled with tears, and my hands shook. We had
done it. We had brought the Jewish state into existence—and I, Golda Mabovitch
Meyerson, had lived to see the day. Whatever happened now, whatever price any
of us would have to pay for it, we had re-created the Jewish national home. The
long exile was over. From this day on we would no longer live on sufferance
in the land of our forefathers. Now we were a nation like other nations, master—
for the first time in twenty centuries—of our own destiny. The dream had come
true—too late to save those who had perished in the Holocaust, but not too late
for the generations to come. Almost exactly fifty years ago, at the close of the First
Zionist Congress in Basel, Theodore Herzl had written in his diary: "At Basel, I
founded the Jewish state. If I were to say this today, I would be greeted with
laughter. In five years perhaps, and certainly in fifty, everyone will see it." And so it
had come to pass.

As Ben-Gurion read, I thought again about my children and the children that
they would have, how different their lives would be from mine and how different
my own life would be from what it had been in the past, and I thought about my
colleagues in besieged Jerusalem, gathered in the offices of the Jewish Agency, listening to the ceremony through static on the radio, while I, by sheer accident, was
in the museum itself. It seemed to me that no Jew on earth had ever been more
privileged than I was that Friday afternoon.

Then, as though a signal had been given, we rose to our feet, crying and clapping, while Ben-Gurion, his voice breaking for the only time, read: "The State of
Israel will be open to Jewish immigration and the ingathering of exiles." This was
the very heart of the proclamation, the reason for the state and the point of it all.
I remember sobbing out loud when I heard those words spoken in that hot,
packed little hall. But Ben-Gurion just rapped his gavel again for order and went
on reading:

Even amidst the violent attacks launched against us for months past, we
call upon the sons of the Arab people dwelling in Israel to keep the peace and to play
their part in building the state on the basis of full and equal citizenship and due representation in all its institutions, provisional and permanent.

And: 10

We extend the hand of peace and good neighborliness to all the states around us and
to their peoples, and we call upon them to cooperate in mutual helpfulness with the

independent Jewish nation in its land. The State of Israel is prepared to make its contribution in a concerted effort for the advancement of the entire Middle East.

When he finished reading the 979 Hebrew words of the proclamation, he asked us to stand and "adopt the scroll establishing the Jewish state," so once again we rose to our feet. Then, something quite unscheduled and very moving happened. All of a sudden Rabbi Fishman-Maimon stood up, and, in a trembling voice, pronounced the traditional Hebrew prayer of thanksgiving. "Blessed be Thou, O Lord our God, King of the Universe, who has kept us alive and made us endure and brought us to this day. Amen." It was a prayer that I had heard often, but it had never held such meaning for me as it did that day.

Before we came up, each in turn, in alphabetical order, to sign the proclamation, there was one other point of "business" that required our attention. Ben-Gurion read the first decrees of the new state. The White Paper was declared null and void, while, to avoid a legal vacuum, all the other mandatory rules and regulations were declared valid and in temporary effect. Then the signing began. As I got up from my seat to sign my name to the scroll, I caught sight of Ada Golomb, standing not far away. I wanted to go over to her, take her in my arms and tell her that I knew that Eliahu and Dov should have been there in my place, but I couldn't hold up the line of the signatories, so I walked straight to the middle of the table, where Ben-Gurion and Sharett[4] sat with the scroll between them. All I recall about my actual signing of the proclamation is that I was crying openly, not able even to wipe the tears from my face, and I remember that as Sharett held the scroll in place for me, a man called David Zvi Pincus, who belonged to the religious Mizrachi Party, came over to try and calm me. "Why do you weep so much, Golda?" he asked me.

"Because it breaks my heart to think of all those who should have been here today and are not," I replied, but I still couldn't stop crying.

Only twenty-five members of the People's Council signed the proclamation on May 14. Eleven others were in Jerusalem, and one was in the States. The last to sign was Moshe Sharett. He looked very controlled and calm compared to me—as though he were merely performing a standard duty. Later, when once we talked about that day, he told me that when he wrote his name on the scroll, he felt as though he were standing on a cliff with a gale blowing up all around him and nothing to hold on to except his determination not to be blown over into the raging sea below—but none of this showed at the time.

After the Palestine Philharmonic Orchestra played "Hatikvah," Ben-Gurion rapped his gavel for the third time. "The State of Israel is established. This meeting is ended." We all shook hands and embraced each other. The ceremony was over. Israel was a reality.

15

---

[4] *Moshe Sharett:* the first foreign minister of Israel (1948–1956) and prime minister (1954–1955).

Questions for Discussion and Writing

1. What considerations were uppermost in Meir's mind during this crucial time?
2. What details are effective in communicating the precariousness of the fledgling state?
3. What compromises in terminology were necessary to allow a final vote authorizing Israel to exist as both a religious and a secular state?

RAE YANG

Rae Yang, (b. 1950) grew up in China and joined the Red Guards at the age of fifteen. She currently teaches East Asian studies at Dickinson College and has written about her experiences during the Cultural Revolution in Spider Eaters *(1997), from which the following chapter is drawn.*

At the Center of the Storm

From May to December 1966, the first seven months of the Cultural Revolution[1] left me with experiences I will never forget. Yet I forgot things almost overnight in that period. So many things were happening around me. The situation was changing so fast. I was too excited, too jubilant, too busy, too exhausted, too confused, too uncomfortable. . . . The forgotten things, however, did not all go away. Later some of them sneaked back into my memory, causing me unspeakable pain and shame. So I would say that those seven months were the most terrible in my life. Yet they were also the most wonderful! I had never felt so good about myself before, nor have I ever since.

In the beginning, the Cultural Revolution exhilarated me because suddenly I felt that I was allowed to think with my own head and say what was on my mind. In the past, the teachers at 101 had worked hard to make us intelligent, using the most difficult questions in mathematics, geometry, chemistry, and physics to challenge us. But the mental abilities we gained, we were not supposed to apply elsewhere. For instance, we were not allowed to question the teachers' conclusions. Students who did so would be criticized as "disrespectful and conceited," even if their opinions made perfect sense. Worse still was to disagree with the leaders. Leaders at various levels represented the Communist Party. Disagreeing with them could be interpreted as being against the Party, a crime punishable by labor reform, imprisonment, even death.

---

[1] *The Cultural Revolution:* a movement launched by Chairman Mao to purge the government and society of liberal elements spearheaded by ideologically motivated young men and women known as the Red Guards.

Thus the teachers created a contradiction. On the one hand, they wanted us to be smart, rational, and analytical. On the other hand, they forced us to be stupid, to be "the teachers' little lambs" and "the Party's obedient tools." By so doing, I think, they planted a sick tree; the bitter fruit would soon fall into their own mouths.

When the Cultural Revolution broke out in late May 1966, I felt like the legendary monkey Sun Wukong, freed from the dungeon that had held him under a huge mountain for five hundred years. It was Chairman Mao who set us free by allowing us to rebel against authorities. As a student, the first authority I wanted to rebel against was Teacher Lin, our homeroom teacher—in Chinese, *banzhuren*. As *banzhuren*, she was in charge of our class. A big part of her duty was to make sure that we behaved and thought correctly.

Other students in my class might have thought that I was Teacher Lin's favorite. As our Chinese teacher, she read my papers in front of the class once in a while. That was true. (Only she and I knew that the grades I got for those papers rarely went above 85. I could only imagine what miserable grades she gave to others in our class.) She also chose me to be the class representative for Chinese, which meant if others had difficulties with the subject, I was to help them. In spite of all these, I did not like Teacher Lin! She had done me a great wrong in the past. I would never forget it.

In my opinion, Lin was exactly the kind of teacher who, in Chairman Mao's words, "treated the students as their enemies." In 1965, we went to Capital Steel and Iron Company in the far suburb of Beijing to do physical labor. One night there was an earthquake warning. We were made to stay outdoors to wait for it. By midnight, no earthquake had come. Two o'clock, still all quiet. Three o'clock, four o'clock, five. . . . The night was endless. Sitting on the cold concrete pavement for so many hours, I was sleepy. I was exhausted. My only wish at the moment was to be allowed to go into the shack and literally "hit the hay." Without thinking I grumbled: "Ai! How come there is still no earthquake?"

Who should have thought that this remark was overheard by Teacher Lin? All of a sudden she started criticizing me in a loud voice.

"The workers and the poor and lower-middle peasants would never say such a thing! Think of all the property that will be damaged by an earthquake. Think of all the lives that may be lost! Now you are looking forward to an earthquake! Only class enemies look forward to earthquakes! Where did your class feelings go? Do you have any proletarian feelings at all? . . ."

She went on and on. Her shrill voice woke up everybody, my classmates as well as students in the other five parallel classes. All were sitting outside at the moment. Everybody turned to watch us. Three hundred pairs of eyes! It was such a shame! I felt my cheeks burning. I wanted to defend myself. I wanted to tell Teacher Lin that although there might be some truth in what she said, I had never been in an earthquake. I was merely tired and wished the whole thing over. Besides, I was only half awake when I said that. I was not looking forward to an earthquake!

In fact, what I really wanted to tell her was that I knew why she was making such a fuss about my remark, which if she had not seized would have drifted away and scattered in the morning breeze like a puff of vapor: she was using this as an opportunity to show off her political correctness in front of all these teachers and students. At my cost! Later she might be able to cash in on it, using it as her political capital. . . .

But of course I knew it would be crazy for me to talk back like that. Contradicting the teacher would only lead me into more trouble. So I swallowed the words that were rolling on the tip of my tongue and lowered my head. Hot tears assaulted my eyes. Tears of anger. Tears of shame. I bit my lips to force them back. *Let's wait and see, Teacher Lin. Someday I will have my revenge. On you!*

Now the time had come for the underdogs to speak up, to seek justice! Immediately I took up a brush pen, dipped it in black ink and wrote a long *dazibao*[2] (criticism in big characters). Using some of theatrical devices Teacher Lin had taught us, I accused her of lacking proletarian feelings toward her students, of treating them as her enemies, of being high-handed, and suppressing different opinions. When I finished and showed it to my classmates, they supported me by signing their names to it. Next, we took the *dazibao* to Teacher Lin's home nearby and pasted it on the wall of her bedroom for her to read carefully day and night. This, of course, was not personal revenge. It was answering Chairman Mao's call to combat the revisionist educational line. If in the meantime it caused Teacher Lin a few sleepless nights, so be it! This revolution was meant to "touch the soul" of people, an unpopular teacher in particular.

Teacher Lin, although she was not a good teacher in my opinion, was not yet the worst. Teacher Qian was even worse. He was the political teacher who had implemented the Exposing Third Layer of Thoughts campaign. In the past many students believed that he could read people's minds. Now a *dazibao* by a student gave us a clue as to how he acquired this eerie ability. Something I would not have guessed in a thousand years! He had been reading students' diaries in class breaks, while we were doing physical exercise on the sports ground. The student who wrote the *dazibao* felt sick one day and returned to his classroom earlier than expected. There he had actually seen Qian sneak a diary from a student's desk and read it. The student kept his silence until the Cultural Revolution, for Qian was his *banzhuren.*

So this was Qian's so-called "political and thought work"! What could it teach us but dishonesty and hypocrisy? Such a "glorious" example the school had set for us, and in the past we had revered him so much! Thinking of the nightmare he gave me, I was outraged. "Take up a pen, use it as a gun." I wrote another *dazibao* to denounce Teacher Qian.

Within a few days *dazibao* were popping up everywhere like bamboo shoots · 15 after a spring rain, written by students, teachers, administrators, workers, and librarians. Secrets dark and dirty were exposed. Everyday we made shocking discoveries. The sacred halo around the teachers' heads that dated back two thousand five hundred years to the time of Confucius disappeared. Now teachers must drop their

---

[2] *Dazibao:* wall posters through which public policy was announced and debated.

pretentious airs and learn a few things from their students. Parents would be taught by their kids instead of vice versa, as Chairman Mao pointed out. Government officials would have to wash their ears to listen to the ordinary people Heaven and earth were turned upside down. The rebellious monkey with enormous power had gotten out. A revolution was underway.

Looking back on it, I should say that I felt good about the Cultural Revolution when it started. It gave me a feeling of superiority and confidence that I had never experienced before. Yet amidst the new freedom and excitement, I ran into things that made me very uncomfortable.

I remember one day in July, I went to have lunch at the student dining hall. On the way I saw a crowd gathering around the fountain. I went over to take a look. The fountain had been a pleasant sight in the past. Sparkling water swaying in the wind among green willow twigs, making the air fresh and clean. In Beijing it was a luxury ordinary middle schools did not enjoy. When the Cultural Revolution broke out, the water was turned off. Now the bottom of the fountain was muddy, littered with wastepaper and broken glass.

On this day I saw a teacher in the fountain, a middle-aged man. His clothes were muddy. Blood was streaming down his head, as a number of students were throwing bricks at him. He tried to dodge the bricks. While he did so, without noticing it, he crawled in the fountain, round and round, like an animal in the zoo. Witnessing such a scene, I suddenly felt sick to my stomach. I would have vomited, if I had not quickly turned round and walked away. Forget about lunch. My appetite was gone.

Sitting in an empty classroom, I wondered why this incident upset me so much: *This is the first time I've seen someone beaten. Moreover this person isn't a stranger. He's a teacher at 101. Do. I pity him? Maybe a little? Maybe not. After all I don't know anything about him. He might be a counter revolutionary or a bad element. He might have done something very bad; thus he deserved the punishment. Something else bothers me, then—not the teacher. What is it?*

Then it dawned on me that I was shocked by the ugliness of the scene. *Yes.* 20 *That's it! In the past when I read about torture in revolutionary novels, saw it in movies, and daydreamed about it, it was always so heroic, so noble; therefore it was romantic and beautiful. But now, in real life, it happened in front of me. It's so sordid! I wish I'd seen none of it! I don't want the memory to destroy my hero's dream.*

This teacher survived; another was not so fortunate. Teacher Chen, our art teacher, was said to resemble a spy in the movies. He was a tall, thin man with sallow skin and long hair, which was a sign of decadence. Moreover, he seemed gloomy and he smoked a lot. "If a person weren't scheming or if he didn't feel very unhappy in the new society, why would he smoke like that?" a classmate asked me, expecting nothing but heartfelt consent from me. "Not to say that in the past he had asked students to draw naked female bodies in front of plaster statues to corrupt them!" For these "crimes," he was beaten to death by a group of senior students.

When I heard this, I felt very uncomfortable again. The whole thing seemed a bad joke to me. Yet it was real! Teacher Chen had taught us the year before and unlike Teacher Lin and Teacher Qian, he had never treated students as his enemies. He was polite and tolerant. If a student showed talent in painting, he would be delighted. On the other hand, he would not embarrass a student who "had no art cells." I had never heard complaints about him before. Yet somehow he became the first person I knew who was killed in the Cultural Revolution.

Living next door to Teacher Chen was Teacher Jiang, our geography teacher. While Teacher Chen was tall and lean, Teacher Jiang was short and stout. Both were old bachelors, who taught auxiliary courses. Before the Cultural Revolution Teacher Jiang was known for two things. One was his unkempt clothes. The other was the fact that he never brought anything but a piece of chalk to class. Yet many students said that he was the most learned teacher at 101. He had many maps and books stored in his funny big head.

If Teacher Jiang had been admired by students before, he became even more popular after the revolution started and Teacher Chen was killed. Since August 1966 Red Guards were allowed to travel free of charge to places all over China. Before we set off, everybody wanted to get a few tips from him, and afterwards we'd love to tell him a few stories in return. It was our chance to show off what we had learned from the trips. Thus from August to December, Teacher Jiang had many visitors. Happy voices and laughter were heard from across the lotus pond in front of his dorm house. At night fights shone through his windows often into the small hours. Geography turned out a true blessing for Teacher Jiang, while art doomed Teacher Chen.

In contrast to the teachers who lost control over their lives in 1966, we students suddenly found power in our hands. Entrance examinations for senior middle school and college were canceled. Now it was entirely up to us to decide what we would do with our time. This was a big change. In the past, decisions had always been made for us by our parents, teachers, and leaders. At school, all courses were required and we took them according to a fixed schedule, six classes a day, six days a week. College was the same as middle schools. After college, the state would assign everybody a job, an iron rice bowl. Like it or not, it would be yours for life.

Now those who had made decisions for us—teachers, parents, administrators—were swept aside by the storm. We were in charge. We could do things on our own initiative. We made plans. We carried them out. So what did we do? Instead of routine classes, we organized meetings at which we shared our family history (People who spoke up at such meetings were of course revolutionary cadres' children. Others could only listen.) I remember Wu, a girl from a high-ranking cadre's family, told a story that left a deep impression on me.

In 1942 Japanese troops raided the Communist base in the north. At this time Wu's older brother was only several months old. He was a beautiful baby boy, with a chubby face and the mother's large brown eyes. The mother gave him the name Precious. Day and night she longed for the father to come back from the front to meet his firstborn.

But before the father returned, the Japanese invaders came. Wu's mother took the baby and fled to the mountains. She and many others hid in a cavern. The enemy soldiers came near, searching for them. At this moment the baby woke up and was about to cry. Her mother had no choice but to cover his mouth with her own hand. Or else all would have been found and killed by the Japanese.

25

The baby was in agony. He struggled with all his might for his life. His lovely little face turned red and then blue. His tiny hands grabbed at his mother's, desperately trying to push it away so that he could breathe. His plump little feet kicked helplessly. The mother's heart was pierced by ten thousand arrows, but she did not dare loosen her grip. Finally the Japanese went away. By then the baby had turned cold in her arms.

Wu burst into tears and we all cried with her.   30

Why does she cry like that? Yes. I understand. The brother! Because he died so tragically, he will always be loved most by the parents. The perfect child. The most "precious" one, the one they sacrificed for the revolution. Wu and her other siblings cannot rival him, no matter how good they are. . . .

But of course that was not why she cried or why we cried with her on that day. We cried because we were deeply moved by the heroic struggle and tremendous sacrifice made by our parents and older brothers and sisters. The stories we told at such meetings convinced us that our lives were on the line: if we should allow the revolution to deteriorate, the evil imperialists and beastly Nationalists would come back. As a slogan of the thirties went, "Cut the grass and eliminate the roots"—if we did not act, they would kill our parents who were revolutionary cadres and make sure that none of us would survive to seek revenge on them.

Suddenly I felt that these classmates of mine were dearer to me than my own brothers and sisters. I loved them! They loved me! Today we shed tears in the same room. Tomorrow we would shed blood in the same ditch. I was willing to sacrifice my life for any of them, while before the Cultural Revolution I mistrusted them, seeing them as nothing but my rivals.

In fact, it was not fear for our lives but pride and a sense of responsibility that fired us up. Chairman Mao had said that we were the morning sun. We were the hope. The future of China and the fate of humankind depended on us. The Soviet Union and East European countries had changed colors. Only China and Albania remained true to Marxism and Leninism. By saving the revolution in China, we were making history. We must uproot bureaucracy and corruption in China, abolish privileges enjoyed by government officials and the intelligentsia, reform education, reform art and literature, reform government organizations. . . . In short, we must purify China and make it a shining example. Someday the whole world would follow us onto this new path.

Aside from sharing family history, we biked to universities and middle schools   35 all over Beijing to read *dazibao* and attend mass rallies where Lin Biao, Zhou Enlai, and Mao's wife, Jiang Qing, showed up to give speeches. I first heard the term "Red Guard" in late June at Middle School attached to Qinghua University, two months before most Chinese would hear of it. It was an exciting idea. On our way back, my schoolmates and I were so preoccupied with the notion that our bikes stopped on a riverbank. Next thing I remember, we were tearing up our red scarves, which only a month before had been the sacred symbol of the Young Pioneers. Now they represented the revisionist educational line and to tear them up was a gesture of rebellion. We tied the strips of red cloth around our left arms in the style of workers' pickets of the 1920s. When we rode away from the spot, we had turned ourselves into Red Guards.

People in the street noticed our new costume: faded army uniforms that had been worn by our parents, red armbands, wide canvas army belts, army caps, the peaks pulled down low by girls in the style of the boys. . . . Some people smiled at us. Some waved their hands. Their eyes showed surprise, curiosity, excitement, admiration. I don't think I saw fear. Not yet.

When people smiled at us, we smiled back, proud of ourselves. Our eyes were clear and bright. Our cheeks rosy and radiant. Red armbands fluttered in the wind. We pedaled hard. We pedaled fast. All of us had shiny new bikes, a luxury most Chinese could not afford at the time. (In my case, Father had bought me a new bike so as to show his support for the Cultural Revolution. Being a dreamer himself, he believed, or at least hoped, that the Cultural Revolution would purify the Communist Party and save the revolution.)

When we rang the bells, we rang them in unison, for a long time. It was not to warn people to get out of our way. It was to attract their attention. Or maybe we just wanted to listen to the sound. The sound flew up, crystal clear and full of joy, like a flock of white doves circling in the blue sky. At the time, little did I know that this was the first stir of a great storm that would soon engulf the entire country.

On August 18, 1966, I saw Chairman Mao for the first time. The night before, we set off from 101 on foot a little after midnight and arrived at Tian'anmen Square before daybreak. In the dark we waited anxiously. Will Chairman Mao come? was the question in everybody's mind. Under a starry sky, we sang.

"Lifting our heads we see the stars of Beidou [the Big Dipper], lowering our heads we are longing for Mao Zedong, longing for Mao Zedong. . . ." 40

We poured our emotions into the song. Chairman Mao who loved the people would surely hear it, for it came from the bottom of our hearts.

Perhaps he did. At five o'clock, before sunrise, like a miracle he walked out of Tian'anmen onto the square and shook hands with people around him. The square turned into a jubilant ocean. Everybody was shouting "Long live Chairman Mao!" Around me girls were crying; boys were crying too. With hot tears streaming down my face, I could not see Chairman Mao clearly. He had ascended the rostrum. He was too high, or rather, the stands for Red Guard representatives were too low.

Earnestly we chanted: "We-want-to-see-Chair-man-Mao!" He heard us! He walked over to the corner of Tian'anmen and waved at us. Now I could see him clearly. He was wearing a green army uniform and a red armband, just like all of us. My blood was boiling inside me. I jumped and shouted and cried in unison with a million people in the square. At that moment, I forgot myself; all barriers that existed between me and others broke down. I felt like a drop of water that finally joined the mighty raging ocean. I would never be lonely again.

The night after, we celebrated the event at 101. Everybody joined the folk dance called *yangge* around bonfires. No one was shy. No one was self-conscious. By then, we had been up and awake for more than forty hours, but somehow I was still bursting with energy. Others seemed that way too. After dancing a couple of hours, I biked all the way home to share the happiness with my parents. By this time, they no longer minded that I woke them up at three o'clock in the morning. In fact, they had urged me to wake them up whenever I got home so that they could hear the latest news from me about the revolution.

Seeing Chairman Mao added new fuel to the flame of our revolutionary zeal. 45
The next day, my fellow Red Guards and I held a meeting to discuss our next
move. Obviously if we loved Chairman Mao, just shouting slogans was not enough.
We must do something. But what could we do? By mid-August the teachers at 101
had been criticized and some were detained in "cow sheds." Even the old school
principal, Wang Yizhi, had been "pulled down from the horse" because of her connection with Liu Shaoqi, the biggest capitalist-roader in the Party. On campus, little was left for us to rebel against. Therefore, many Red Guards had walked out of
schools to break "four olds" (old ideas, old culture, old customs and old habits) in
the city.

This was what we should do. Only first we had to pinpoint some "four olds."
I suggested that we go to a nearby restaurant to get rid of some old practices.
Everybody said: "Good! Let's do it!" So we jumped onto our bikes and rushed out
like a gust of wind.

Seeing a group of Red Guards swarming in, everybody in the restaurant
tensed up. In August, people began to fear Red Guards who summoned the wind,
raised the storm, and spread terror all over China. Small talk ceased. All eyes were
fastened on us.

I stepped forward and began ritualistically: "Our great leader Chairman Mao
teaches us, 'Corruption and waste are very great crimes.'" After that, I improvised:
"Comrades! In today's world there are still many people who live in poverty and
have nothing to eat. So we should not waste food. Nor should we behave like
bourgeois ladies and gentlemen who expect to be waited on by others in a restaurant. From now on, people who want to eat in this restaurant must follow new
rules: One, go to the window to get your own food. Two, carry it to the table yourselves. Three, wash your own dishes. Four, you must finish the food you ordered.
Otherwise you may not leave the restaurant!"

While I said this, I saw some people change color and sweat broke out on
their foreheads. They had ordered too much food. Now they had to finish it under
the watchful eyes of a group of Red Guards. This was not an enviable situation. But
nobody in the restaurant protested. Contradicting a Red Guard was asking for big
trouble. It was like playing with thunderbolts and dynamite. So people just lowered
their heads and swallowed the food as fast as they could. Some of them might develop indigestion afterwards, but I believed it was their own fault. By showing off
their wealth at a restaurant, they wasted the blood and sweat of the peasants. Now
they got caught and lost face. This should teach them a lesson!

While my comrades and I were breaking four olds at restaurants, other Red 50
Guards were raiding people's homes all over the city. News of victory poured in:
Red Guards discovered guns, bullets, old deeds, gold bars, foreign currency, yellow
books and magazines (pornography).... Hearing this, people in my group became
restless. But somehow I was not eager to raid homes, and I did not ask myself why.
"We are busy making revolution at restaurants, aren't we?"

Then one day an old woman stopped us in the street and insisted that we go
with her to break some "four olds" in the home of a big capitalist. None of us
could say No to this request. So she led us to the home of a prominent overseas
Chinese, where the "four olds" turned out to be flowers.

The courtyard we entered was spacious. A green oasis of cool shade, drifting fragrance, and delicate beauty: tree peonies and bamboo were planted next to Tai Lake rocks. Orchids and chrysanthemums grew along a winding path inlaid with cobblestones. A trellis of wisteria stood next to a corridor. Goldfish swam under water lilies in antique vats. . . .

Strange! Why does this place look familiar? I am sure I've never been here before. Could it be I've seen it in a dream.? . . .

Suddenly the answer dawned on me: *this place looks just like Nainai's home. Nainai's home must have been raided. Maybe several times by now. Is she still there? Did they kick her out? Is she all right? And what happened to the beautiful flowers she and Third Aunt planted? . . . No use thinking about such things! I can't help her anyway. She is a capitalist. I am a Red Guard. I have nothing to do with her!*

The question in front of me now is what to do with these flowers. Smash them! Uproot them! Trample them to the ground! Flowers, plants, goldfish, birds, these are all bourgeois stuff. The new world has no place for them. My fellow Red Guards have already started. I mustn't fall behind,   55

So I lifted up a flowerpot and dropped it against a Tai Lake rock. Bang! The sound was startling. *Don't be afraid. The first step is always the most difficult.* Bang! Bang! *Actually it isn't so terrible. Now I've started, I can go on and on. To tell the truth, I even begin to enjoy breaking flowerpots! Who would have thought of that? . . .*

After a while, we were all out of breath. So we ordered the family to get rid of the remaining flowers in three days, pledging that we'd come back to check on them. Then we left. Behind us was a world of broken pots, spilled soil, fallen petals, and bare roots. Another victory of Mao Zedong thought.

On my way home, surprise caught up with me. I was stopped by a group of Red Guards whom I did not know. They told me that my long braids were also bourgeois stuff. Hearing this, I looked around and saw Red Guards stand on both sides of the street with scissors in their hands. Anyone who had long or curly hair would be stopped by them, their hair cut off on the spot in front of jeering kids. Suddenly I felt my cheeks burning. To have my hair cut off in the street was to lose face. So I pleaded with them, vowing that I would cut my braids as soon as I got home. They let me go. For the time being, I coiled my braids on top of my head and covered them with my army cap.

Fearing that other surprises might be in store for me in the street, I went straight home. There I found Aunty in dismay It turned out that she too had seen Red Guards cutting long hair in the street. So she did not dare leave home these couple of days and we were about to run out of groceries.

"What shall I do?" she asked me. "If I cut my hair, won't I look like an old devil, with short white hair sticking up all over my head?" Her troubled look reminded me that since her childhood, Aunty always had long hair. Before she was married, it was a thick, long braid. Then a bun, for a married woman, which looked so elegant on the back of her head. Even in Switzerland, she had never changed her hairstyle. But now neither she nor I had any choice. If we did not want to lose face in the street, we'd better do it ourselves at home.   60

While Aunty and I were cutting each other's hair, my parents were burning things in the bathroom. The idea was the same: to save face and avoid trouble, better destroy all the "four olds" we had before others found them out. So they picked out a number of Chinese books, burned them together with all the letters they had kept and some old photographs. The ash was flushed down the toilet. Repair the house before it rains. That was wise. No one could tell whose home would be raided next. Better be prepared for the worst.

Now suddenly it seemed everybody in my family had trouble, including Lian, who was eleven. His problem was our cat, Little Tiger. Lian found him three years ago playing hide and seek in a lumber yard. Then he was a newborn kitten. So little that he did not even know how to drink milk. Aunty taught us how to feed him. Put milk in a soupspoon. Tilt it to make the milk flow slowly through the depression in the middle of the handle. Put the tip of the handle into the kitten's tiny mouth. He tasted the milk. He liked it. He began to drink it. By and by the kitten grew into a big yellow cat with black stripes. On his forehead, three horizontal lines formed the Chinese character *wang,* which means king. We called him Little Tiger because in China the tiger is king of all animals.

Little Tiger's life was in danger, now, for pets were considered bourgeois too. This morning Lian had received an ultimatum from kids who were our neighbors. It said we had to get rid of Little Tiger in three days or else they would come and take revolutionary action. This time we could not solve the problem by doing it ourselves. Little Tiger was a member of our family. We had to think of a way to save his life.

Aunty suggested that we hide him in a bag, take him out to a faraway place, and let him go. He would become a wild cat. Good idea. Only I did not want to do this. What would people say if they found that I, a Red Guard, was hiding a cat in my bag? So I told Lian to do it and went back to school. Since the Cultural Revolution started, I had a bed in the student dormitory and spent most of the nights there.

A few days later when I came back home, Aunty told me what had happened to Little Tiger. (Lian himself wouldn't talk about it.) When Lian took him out, he was spotted by the boys who had given him the ultimatum. Noticing something was moving in his bag, they guessed it was the cat. They grabbed the bag, swung it round, and hit it hard against a brick wall. "Miao!" Little Tiger mewed wildly. The boys laughed. It was fun. They continued to hit him against the wan. Lian started to cry and he begged them to stop. Nobody listened to him. Little Tiger's blood stained the canvas bag, leaving dark marks on the brick wall. But he was still alive. Only his mewing became weak and pitiable. Too bad a cat had nine lives! It only prolonged his suffering and gave the boys more pleasure. Bang! Bang! Little Tiger was silent. Dead at last. Lian ran back and cried in Aunty's arms for a long time.

A week after our cat was killed by the boys, a neighbor whom I called Guma killed herself. On that day, I happened to be home. I heard a commotion outside and looked. Many people were standing in front of our building. When I went out, I saw clearly that Guma was hanging from a pipe in the bathroom. Another gruesome sight I could not wipe from my memory.

Why did she kill herself? Nobody knew the answer. Before she died, she was a typist at the college. A quiet little woman. She had no enemies; no historical

65

problems. Nobody had struggled against her. So people assumed that she killed herself for her husband's sake.

The love story between her and her husband must have been quite dramatic. Mother said a writer had interviewed them because he wanted to write a book about it. Guma's husband, whom I called Guzhang, was a professor in the French department. I used to like him a lot because of his refined, gentle manner and the many interesting books he owned. Recently, however, it became known that Guzhang had serious historical problems. In his youth he had studied in France and joined the Communist Party there. Later somehow he dropped out of the Party and turned away from politics. Because of this, he was accused of being a renegade. A renegade he seemed to me, like one who was a coward in revolutionary novels and movies. The following story would prove my point.

After Gurna killed herself, Guzhang wanted to commit suicide too. He went to the nearby Summer Palace and jumped into the lake. But the place he jumped was too shallow. After a while he climbed out, saying the water was too cold. When people at the college heard this story, he became a laughingstock. Even Aunty remarked: "You may know people for a long time and still you don't know their hearts. Who should have thought that Guma, a woman so gentle and quiet, was so resolute, while Guzhang, a big man, did not have half her courage."

These words seemed sinister. To tell the truth, I was alarmed by them. Just a couple of days before a nanny had killed herself at the nearby University of Agriculture. The old woman was a proletarian pure and simple. So why did she kill herself?

Her death was caused by a new chapter in the breaking "four olds" campaign. The idea was actually similar to mine: in the past bourgeois ladies and gentlemen were waited on hand and foot by the working people. In the new society such practices should be abolished. The working people would no longer serve and be exploited by bourgeois ladies and gentlemen. Thus the new rule said those who were labeled bourgeois ladies and gentlemen were not allowed to use nannies. As for those who were not labeled bourgeois ladies and gentlemen, they were not allowed to use nannies either. Because if they used nannies, it was proof enough that they were bourgeois ladies and gentlemen, and bourgeois ladies and gentlemen were not allowed to use nannies. Thus according to the new rule, no family was allowed to use nannies.

As a result, the old woman killed herself, because she lost her job and had no children to support her. Though she had saved some money for her old age, another new rule had it all frozen in the bank.

Aunty was in exactly the same situation. When she first came to work for us, she was forty-six. Then her son died. Now she was sixty-two, an old woman by traditional standards. Right now all her savings were frozen in the bank. Whether someday she might get them back or not, and if yes when, was anybody's guess. Now the deadline set by the Red Guards of the college for all the nannies to leave was drawing near. Recently Aunty made me uneasy. I was frightened by her eyes. They were so remote, as if they were in a different world. I could not get in touch with them. Then she made that strange comment about being resolute. Could she mean . . . ?

70

On the evening before Aunty left (fortunately she had kept her old home in the city, to which now she could return), Father gathered our whole family together. Solemnly he made a pledge to her. He said that he would continue to support her financially for as long as she lived. Although for the time being she had to leave, she would always be a member of our family. She needn't worry about her old age.

That was, in my opinion, the exact right thing to say at the right moment. Even today when I look back on it, I am proud of Father for what he said on that hot summer evening thirty years ago. By then tens of thousands of nannies were being driven out of their employers' homes in Beijing, and who knows how many in the whole country. But few people had the kindness and generosity to say what Father said.

Aunty said nothing in return. But she was moved. From then on, she took our family to be her own. Instead of a burden, she became a pillar for our family through one storm after another. She did not quit until all her strength was used up.

Questions for Discussion and Writing

1. When the Red Guards were given total power to root out political subversives, what was the change in the relationship these teenagers had with their teachers, parents and administrators, who had once had power over them?
2. How does Yang shape her narrative to emphasize her growing ambivalence about what she had been so sure of in the beginning?
3. The excesses of overzealous political activism are well documented in Yang's account. Have you ever known someone whose commitment to a cause took over his or her entire life?

LUIS SEPULVEDA

The Chilean novelist Luis Sepulveda (b. 1949) was confined to prison as a political enemy under the dictatorship of Augusto Pinochet. He describes his experiences in this selection from Full Circle: A South American Journey *(1996). He has also written* The Old Man Who Read Love Stories *(1992) and* The Name of the Bullfighter *(1996).*

Daisy

The military had rather inflated ideas of our destructive capacity. They questioned us about plans to assassinate all the officers in American military history, to blow up bridges and seal off tunnels, and to prepare for the landing of a terrible foreign enemy whom they could not identify.

Temuco is a sad, grey, rainy city. No-one would call it a tourist attraction, and yet the barracks of the Tucapel regiment came to house a sort of permanent international convention of sadists. The Chileans, who were the hosts, after all, were assisted in the interrogations by primates from Brazilian military intelligence—they were the worst—North Americans from the State Department, Argentinian paramilitary personnel, Italian neo-fascists and even some agents of Mossad.

I remember Rudi Weismann, a Chilean with a passion for the South and sailing, who was tortured and interrogated in the gentle language of the synagogues. This infamy was too much for Rudi, who had thrown in his lot with Israel: he had worked on a kibbutz, but in the end his nostalgia for Tierra del Fuego had brought him back to Chile. He simply could not understand how Israel could support such a gang of criminals, and though till then he had always been a model of good humour, he dried up like a neglected plant. One morning we found him dead in his sleeping bag. No need for an autopsy, his face made it clear: Rudi Weismann had died of sadness.

The commander of the Tucapel regiment—a basic respect for paper prevents me from writing his name—was a fanatical admirer of Field Marshal Rommel. When he found a prisoner he liked, he would invite him to recover from the interrogations in his office. After assuring the prisoner that everything that happened in the barracks was in the best interests of our great nation, the commander would offer him a glass of Korn—somebody used to send him this insipid, wheat-based liquor from Germany—and make him sit through a lecture on the Africa Korps. The guy's parents or grandparents were German, but he couldn't have looked more Chilean: chubby, short-legged, dark untidy hair. You could have mistaken him for a truck driver or a fruit vendor, but when he talked about Rommel he became the caricature of a Nazi guard.

At the end of the lecture he would dramatise Rommel's suicide, clicking his heels, raising his right hand to his forehead to salute an invisible flag, muttering "Adieu geliebtes Vaterland," and pretending to shoot himself in the mouth. We all hoped that one day he would do it for real. 5

There was another curious officer in the regiment: a lieutenant struggling to contain a homosexuality that kept popping out all over the place. The soldiers had nicknamed him Daisy, and he knew it.

We could all tell that it was a torment for Daisy not to be able to adorn his body with truly beautiful objects, and the poor guy had to make do with the regulation paraphernalia. He wore a .45 pistol, two cartridge clips, a commando's curved dagger, two hand grenades, a torch, a walkie-talkie, the insignia of his rank and the silver wings of the parachute corps. The prisoners and the soldiers thought he looked like a Christmas tree

This individual sometimes surprised us with generous and apparently disinterested acts—we didn't know that the Stockholm syndrome could be a military perversion. For example, after the interrogations he would suddenly fill our pockets with cigarettes or the highly prized aspirin tablets with vitamin C. One afternoon he invited me to his room.

"So you're a man of letters," he said, offering me a can of Coca-Cola.

"I've written a couple of stories. That's all," I replied.   10

"You're not here for an interrogation. I'm very sorry about what's happening, but that's what war is like. I want us to talk as one writer to another. Are you surprised? The army has produced some great men of letters. Think of Don Alonso de Ercilla y Zúñiga, for example."

"Or Cervantes," I added.

Daisy included himself among the greats. That was his problem. If he wanted adulation, he could have it. I drank the Coca-Cola and thought about Garcés, or rather, about his chicken, because, incredible as it seems, the cook had a chicken called Dulcinea,[1] the name of Don Quixote's mistress.

One morning it jumped the wall which separated the common-law prisoners from the POWs, and it must have been a chicken with deep political convictions, because it decided to stay with us. Garcés caressed it and sighed, saying: "If I had a pinch of pepper and a pinch of cumin, I'd make you a chicken marinade like you've never tasted."

"I want you to read my poems and give me your opinion, your honest opin-   15
ion," said Daisy, handing me a notebook.

I left that room with my pockets full of cigarettes, caramel sweets, tea bags and a tin of U.S. Army marmalade. That afternoon I started to believe in the brotherhood of writers.

They transported us from the prison to the barracks and back in a cattle truck. The soldiers made sure there was plenty of cow shit on the floor of the truck before ordering us to lie face down with our hands behind our necks. We were guarded by four of them, with North American machine guns, one in each corner of the truck. They were almost all young guys brought down from northern garrisons, and the harsh climate of the South kept them flu-ridden and in a perpetually filthy mood. They had orders to fire on the bundles—us—at the slightest suspect movement, or on any civilian who tried to approach the truck. But as time wore on, the discipline gradually relaxed and they turned a blind eye to the packet of cigarettes or piece of fruit thrown from a window, or the pretty and daring girl who ran beside the truck blowing us kisses and shouting: "Don't give up, comrades! We'll win!"

Back in prison, as always, we were met by the welcoming committee organised by Doctor "Skinny" Pragnan, now an eminent psychiatrist in Belgium. First he examined those who couldn't walk and those who had heart problems, then those who had come back with a dislocation or with ribs out of place. Pragnan was expert at estimating how much electricity had been put into us on the grill, and patiently determined who would be able to absorb liquids in the next few hours. Then finally it was time to take communion: we were given the aspirin with vitamin C and an anticoagulant to prevent internal haematomas.

---

[1] *Dulcinea*: ironically refers to the object of Don Quixote's affection in the novel *Don Quixote de La Mancha* (1605) by Miguel de Cervantes (1547–1616).

"Dulcinea's days are numbered," I said to Garcés, and looked for a corner in which to read Daisy's notebook.

The elegantly inscribed pages were redolent of love, honey, sublime suffering   20
and forgotten flowers. By the third page I knew that Daisy hadn't even gone to the trouble of reusing the ideas of the Mexican poet Amado Nervo—he'd simply copied out his poems word for word.

I called out to Peyuco Gálvez, a Spanish teacher, and read him a couple of lines.

"What do you think, Peyuco?"

"Amado Nervo. The book is called *The Interior Gardens.*"

I had got myself into a real jam. If Daisy found out that I knew the work of this sugary poet Nervo, then it wasn't Garcés's chicken whose days were numbered, but mine. It was a serious problem, so that night I presented it to the Council of Elders.

"Now, Daisy, would he be the passive or the active type?" enquired Iriarte.   25

"Stop it, will you. My skin's at risk here," I replied.

"I'm serious. Maybe our friend wants to have an affair with you, and giving you the notebook was like dropping a silk handkerchief. And like a fool you picked it up. Perhaps he copied out the poems for you to find a message in them. I've known queens who seduced boys by lending them *Demian*[2] by Hermann Hesse, If Daisy is the passive type, this business with Amado Nervo means he wants to test your nerve, so to speak. And if he's the active type, well, it would have to hurt less than a kick in the balls."

"Message my arse. He gave you the poems as his own, and you should say you liked them a lot. If he was trying to send a message, he should have given the notebook to Garcés; he's the only one who has an interior garden. Or maybe Daisy doesn't know about the pot plant," remarked Andrés Müller.

"Let's be serious about this. You have to say something to him, and Daisy mustn't even suspect that you know Nervo's poems," declared Pragnan.

"Tell him you liked the poems but that the adjectives strike you a bit exces-   30
sive. Quote Huidobro: when an adjective doesn't give life, it kills. That way you'll show him that you read his poems carefully and that you are criticising his work as a colleague," suggested Gálvez.

The Council of Elders approved of Gálvez's idea, but I spent two weeks on tenterhooks. I couldn't sleep. I wished they would come and take me to be kicked and electrocuted so I could give the damned notebook back. In those two weeks I came to hate good old Garcés:

"Listen, mate, if everything goes well, and you get a little jar of capers as well as the cumin and the pepper, we'll have such a feast with that chicken."

After a fortnight, I found myself at last stretched out face down on the mattress of cowpats with my hands behind my neck. I thought I was going mad: I was happy to be heading towards a session of the activity known as torture.

---

[2] *Demian (1919):* by Hermann Hesse, German novelist (1877–1962).

Tucapel barracks. Service Corps. In the background, the perpetual green of Cerro Ñielol, sacred to the Mapuche Indians. There was a waiting room outside the interrogation cell, like at the doctor's. There they made us sit on a bench with our hands tied behind our backs and black hoods over our heads. I never understood what the hoods were for, because once we got inside they took them off, and we could see the interrogators—the toy soldiers who, with panic-stricken faces, turned the handle of the generator, and the health officers who attached the electrodes to our anuses, testicles, gums and tongue, and then listened with stethoscopes to see who was faking and who had really passed out on the grill.

Lagos, a deacon of the Emmaus International ragmen, was the first to be interrogated that day. For a year they had been working him over to find out how the organisation had come by a couple of dozen old military uniforms which had been found in their warehouses. A trader who sold army surplus gear had donated them. Lagos screamed in pain and repeated over and over what the soldiers wanted to hear: the uniforms belonged to an invading army which was preparing to land on the Chilean coast.

I was waiting for my turn when someone took off the hood. It was Lieutenant Daisy.

"Follow me," he ordered.

We went into an office. On the desk I saw a tin of cocoa and a carton of cigarettes which were obviously there to reward my comments on his literary work.

"Did you read my poesy?" he asked, offering me a seat.

Poesy. Daisy said poesy, not poetry. A man covered with pistols and grenades can't say "poesy" without sounding ridiculous and effete. At that moment he revolted me, and I decided that even if it meant pissing blood, hissing when I spoke and being able to charge batteries just by touching them, I wasn't going to lower myself to flattering a plagiarising faggot in uniform.

"You have pretty handwriting, Lieutenant. But you know these poems aren't yours," I said, giving him back the notebook.

I saw him begin to shake. He was carrying enough arms to kill me several times over, and if he didn't want to stain his uniform, he could order someone else to do it. Trembling with anger he stood up, threw what was on the desk onto the floor and shouted:

"Three weeks in the cube. But first, you're going to visit the chiropodist, you piece of subversive shit!"

The chiropodist was a civilian, a landholder who had lost several thousand hectares in the land reform, and who was getting his revenge by participating in the interrogations as a volunteer. His speciality was peeling back toenails, which led to terrible infections.

I knew the cube. I had spent my first six months of prison there in solitary confinement: it was an underground cell, one and a half metres wide by one and a half metres long by one and a half metres high. In the old days there had been a tannery in the Temuco jail, and the cube was used to store fat. The walls still stank of fat, but after a week your excrement fixed that, making the cube very much a place of your own.

You could only stretch out across the diagonal, but the low temperatures of southern Chile, the rainwater and the soldiers' urine made you want to curl up hugging your legs and stay like that wishing yourself smaller and smaller, so that eventually you could live on one of the islands of floating shit, which conjured up images of dream holidays. I was there for three weeks, running through Laurel and Hardy[3] films, remembering the books of Salgari,[4] Stevenson,[5] and London[6] word by word, playing long games of chess, licking my toes to protect them from infection. In the cube I swore over and over again never to become a literary critic.

Questions for Discussion and Writing

1. Sepulveda's main tormentor is a prison guard with literary aspirations, nicknamed Daisy. What moral, aesthetic, and practical choices does Sepulveda face?
2. Sepulveda displays surprising good humor considering the circumstances. Give some examples of how he gets this across in his account?
3. Plagiarism, even for those who are not prison guards, is a serious offense. What precautions have you taken to avoid committing plagiarism in your schoolwork?

Fiction

ALBERT CAMUS

Albert Camus (1913–1960) was born in Algeria. Despite illness and poverty, he excelled as both an athlete and a scholarship student at the University of Algiers. In 1940, he traveled to France and became active in the Resistance, serving as the editor of the clandestine paper Combat. Initially, Camus was closely associated with Jean-Paul Sartre and the French existentialist movement, but he broke with Sartre and developed his own concept of the absurd, emphasizing the importance of human solidarity. Camus was awarded the Nobel Prize for literature in 1957. His literary works include the novels The Stranger *(1942),* The Plague *(1947), and* The

---

[3] *Laurel and Hardy:* American film comedy team made up of Stan Laurel (1890–1965) and Oliver Hardy (1892–1957).   [4] *Emilio Salgari, (1862–1911):* called the Italian Jules Verne, the author of more than two hundred adventure stories and novels.   [5] *Robert Louis Stevenson, (1850–1894):* Scottish novelist, poet, and essayist. Best known for *Treasure Island* (1883).   [6] *Jack London, (1876–1916):* American author who created romantic, yet realistic fiction in works such as *The Call of the Wild* (1903). See his essay "The San Francisco Earthquake" in Chapter 7.

Fall *(1956) and the nonfiction works* The Myth of Sisyphus *(1942) and* The Rebel
(1951). "The Guest," a short story drawn from his collection Exile and The Kingdom
*(1957), depicts the dilemma of Daru, a rural schoolteacher who does not wish to be drawn into
complicity with the French in their war against Algeria. The story masterfully explores the issues
of inevitability of choice and the burdens of responsibility and brotherhood that Camus struggled
with throughout his life.*

The Guest

The schoolmaster was watching the two men climb toward him. One was on
horseback, the other on foot. They had not yet tackled the abrupt rise leading to
the schoolhouse built on the hillside. They were toiling onward, making slow
progress in the snow, among the stones, on the vast expanse of the high, deserted
plateau. From time to time the horse stumbled. Without hearing anything yet, he
could see the breath issuing from the horse's nostrils. One of the men, at least,
knew the region. They were following the trail although it had disappeared days
ago under a layer of dirty white snow. The schoolmaster calculated that it would
take them half an hour to get onto the hill. It was cold; he went back into the
school to get a sweater.

He crossed the empty frigid classroom. On the blackboard the four rivers of
France, drawn with four different colored chalks, had been flowing toward their es-
tuaries for the past three days. Snow had suddenly fallen in mid-October after eight
months of drought without the transition of rain, and the twenty pupils, more or
less, who lived in the villages scattered over the plateau had stopped coming. With
fair weather they would return. Daru now heated only the single room that was his
lodging, adjoining the classroom and giving also onto the plateau to the east. Like
the class windows, his window looked to the south too. On that side the school was
a few kilometers from the point where the plateau began to slope toward the
south. In clear weather could be seen the purple mass of the mountain range where
the gap opened onto the desert.

Somewhat warmed, Daru returned to the window from which he had first
seen the two men. They were no longer visible. Hence they must have tackled the
rise. The sky was not so dark, for the snow had stopped falling during the night.
The morning had opened with a dirty light which had scarcely become brighter as
the ceiling of clouds lifted. At two in the afternoon it seemed as if the day were
merely beginning. But still this was better than those three days when the thick
snow was falling amidst unbroken darkness with little gusts of wind that rattled the
double door of the classroom. Then Daru had spent long hours in his room, leaving it only to go to the shed and feed the chickens or get some coal. Fortunately
the delivery truck from Tadjid, the nearest village to the north, had brought his
supplies two days before the blizzard. It would return in forty-eight hours.

Besides, he had enough to resist a siege, for the little room was cluttered with
bags of wheat that the administration left as a stock to distribute to those of his
pupils whose families had suffered from the drought. Actually they had all been
victims because they were all poor. Every day Daru would distribute a ration to the

children. They had missed it, he knew, during these bad days. Possibly one of the fathers or big brothers would come this afternoon and he could supply them with grain. It was just a matter of·carrying them over to the next harvest. Now shiploads of wheat were arriving from France and the worst was over. But it would be hard to forget that poverty, that army of ragged ghosts wandering in the sunlight, the plateaus burned to a cinder month after month, the earth shriveled up little by little, literally scorched, every stone bursting into dust under one's foot. The sheep had died then by thousands and even a few men, here and there, sometimes without anyone's knowing.

In contrast with such poverty, he who lived almost like a monk in his remote   5
schoolhouse, nonetheless satisfied with the little he had and with the rough life, had felt like a lord with his whitewashed walls, his narrow couch, his unpainted shelves, his well, and his weekly provision of water and food. And suddenly this snow, without warning, without the foretaste of rain. This is the way the region was, cruel to live in, even without men—who didn't help matters either. But Daru had been born here. Everywhere else, he felt exiled.

He stepped out onto the terrace in front of the schoolhouse. The two men were now halfway up the slope. He recognized the horseman as Balducci, the old gendarme he had known for a long time. Balducci was holding on the end of a rope an Arab who was walking behind him with hands bound and head lowered. The gendarme waved a greeting to which Daru did not reply, lost as he was in contemplation of the Arab dressed in a faded blue jellaba, his feet in sandals but covered with socks of heavy raw wool, his head surmounted by a narrow, short *chèche*. They were approaching. Balducci was holding back his horse in order not to hurt the Arab, and the group was advancing slowly.

Within earshot, Balducci shouted: "One hour to do the three kilometers from El Ameur!" Daru did not answer. Short and square in his thick sweater, he watched them climb. Not once had the Arab raised his head. "Hello" said Daru when they got up onto the terrace. "Come in and warm up." Balducci painfully got down from his horse without letting go the rope. From under his bristling mustache he smiled at the schoolmaster. His little dark eyes, deep-set under a tanned forehead, and his mouth surrounded with wrinkles made him look attentive and studious. Daru took the bridle, led the horse to the shed, and came back to the two men, who were now waiting for him in the school. He led them into his room. "I am going to heat up the classroom," he said. "We'll be more comfortable there." When he entered the room again, Balducci was on the couch. He had undone the rope tying him to the Arab, who had squatted near the stove. His hands still bound, the *chèche* pushed back on his head, he was looking toward the window. At first Daru noticed only his huge lips, fat, smooth, almost Negroid; yet his nose was straight, his eyes were dark and full of fever. The *chèche* revealed an obstinate forehead and, under the weathered skin now rather discolored by the cold, the whole face had a restless and rebellious look that struck Daru when the Arab, turning his face toward him, looked him straight in the eyes. "Go into the other room," said the schoolmaster, "and I'll make you some mint tea." "Thanks," Balducci said. "What a chore! How I long for retirement." And addressing his prisoner in Arabic: "Come on, you." The Arab got up and, slowly, holding his bound wrists in front of him, went into the classroom.

With the tea, Daru brought a chair. But Balducci was already enthroned on the nearest pupil's desk and the Arab had squatted against the teacher's platform facing the stove, which stood between the desk and the window. When he held out the glass of tea to the prisoner, Daru hesitated at the sight of his bound hands. "He might perhaps be untied." "Sure," said Balducci, "that was for the trip." He started to get to his feet. But Daru, setting the glass on the floor, had knelt beside the Arab. Without saying anything, the Arab watched him with his feverish eyes. Once his hands were free, he rubbed his swollen wrists against each other, took the glass of tea, and sucked up the burning liquid in swift little sips.

"Good," said Daru. "And where are you headed?"

Balducci withdrew his mustache from the tea. "Here, son." 10

"Odd pupils! And you're spending the night?"

"No. I'm going back to El Ameur. And you will deliver this fellow to Tinguit. He is expected at police headquarters."

Balducci was looking at Daru with a friendly little smile.

"What's this story?" asked the schoolmaster. "Are you pulling my leg?"

"No, son. Those are the orders." 15

"The orders? I'm not . . ." Daru hesitated, not wanting to hurt the old Corsican. "I mean, that's not my job."

"What! What's the meaning of that? In wartime people do all kinds of jobs."

"Then I'll wait for the declaration of war!"

Balducci nodded.

"O.K. But the orders exist and they concern you too. Things are brewing, it 20 appears. There is talk of a forthcoming revolt. We are mobilized, in a way."

Daru still had his obstinate look.

"Listen, son," Balducci said. "I like you and you must understand. There's only a dozen of us at El Ameur to patrol throughout the whole territory of a small department and I must get back in a hurry. I was told to hand this guy over to you and return without delay. He couldn't be kept there. His village was beginning to stir; they wanted to take him back. You must take him to Tinguit tomorrow before the day is over. Twenty kilometers shouldn't faze a husky fellow like you. After that, all will be over. You'll come back to your pupils and your comfortable life."

Behind the wall the horse could be heard snorting and pawing the earth. Daru was looking out the window. Decidedly, the weather was clearing and the light was increasing over the snowy plateau. When all the snow was melted, the sun would take over again and once more would burn the fields of stone. For days, still, the unchanging sky would shed its dry light on the solitary expanse where nothing had any connection with man.

"After all," he said, turning around toward Balducci, "what did he do?" And, before the gendarme had opened his mouth, he asked: "Does he speak French?"

"No, not a word. We had been looking for him for a month, but they were 25 hiding him. He killed his cousin."

"Is he against us?"

"I don't think so. But you can never be sure."

"Why did he kill?"

"A family squabble, I think. One owed the other grain, it seems. It's not at all clear. In short, he killed his cousin with a billhook. You know, like a sheep, *kreezk!*"

Balducci made the gesture of drawing a blade across his throat and the Arab, his attention attracted, watched him with a sort of anxiety. Daru felt a sudden wrath against the man, against all men with their rotten spite, their tireless hates, their blood lust.

But the kettle was singing on the stove. He served Balducci more tea, hesitated, then served the Arab again, who, a second time, drank avidly. His raised arms made the jellaba fall open and the schoolmaster saw his thin, muscular chest.

"Thanks, kid," Balducci said. "And now, I'm off."

He got up and went toward the Arab, taking a small rope from his pocket.

"What are you doing?" Daru asked dryly.

Balducci, disconcerted, showed him the rope.

"Don't bother."

The old gendarme hesitated. "It's up to you. Of course, you are armed?"

"I have my shotgun."

"Where?"

"In the trunk."

"You ought to have it near your bed."

"Why? I have nothing to fear."

"You're crazy, son. If there's an uprising, no one is safe, we're all in the same boat."

"I'll defend myself. I'll have time to see them coming."

Balducci began to laugh, then suddenly the mustache covered the white teeth.

"You'll have time? O.K. That's just what I was saying. You have always been a little cracked. That's why I like you, my son was like that."

At the same time he took out his revolver and put it on the desk.

"Keep it; I don't need two weapons from here to El Ameur."

The revolver shone against the black paint of the table. When the gendarme turned toward him, the schoolmaster caught the smell of leather and horseflesh.

"Listen, Balducci," Daru said suddenly, "every bit of this disgusts me, and first of all your fellow here. But I won't hand him over. Fight, yes, if I have to. But not that."

The old gendarme stood in front of him and looked at him severely.

"You're being a fool," he said slowly. "I don't like it either. You don't get used to putting a rope on a man even after years of it, and you're even ashamed—yes, ashamed. But you can't let them have their way."

"I won't hand him over," Daru said again.

"It's an order, son, and I repeat it."

"That's right. Repeat to them what I've said to you: I won't hand him over."

Balducci made a visible effort to reflect. He looked at the Arab and at Daru. At last he decided.

"No, I won't tell them anything. If you want to drop us, go ahead; I'll not denounce you. I have an order to deliver the prisoner and I'm doing so. And now
you'll just sign this paper for me."

"There's no need. I'll not deny that you left him with me."

"Don't be mean with me. I know you'll tell the truth. You're from hereabouts
and you are a man. But you must sign, that's the rule."

Daru opened his drawer, took out a little square bottle of purple   60
ink, the red wooden penholder with the "sergeant-major" pen he used
for making models of penmanship, and signed. The gendarme carefully folded the
paper and put it into his wallet. Then he moved toward the door.

"I'll see you off," Daru said.

"No," said Balducci. "There's no use being polite. You insulted me."

He looked at the Arab, motionless in the same spot, sniffed peevishly, and
turned away toward the door. "Good-by, son," he said. The door shut behind him.
Balducci appeared suddenly outside the window and then disappeared. His footsteps were muffled by the snow. The horse stirred on the other side of the wall and
several chickens fluttered in fright. A moment later Balducci reappeared outside the
window leading the horse by the bridle. He walked toward the little rise without
turning around and disappeared from sight with the horse following him. A big
stone could be heard bouncing down. Daru walked back toward the prisoner, who,
without stirring, never took his eyes off him. "Wait," the schoolmaster said in Arabic and went toward the bedroom. As he was going through the door, he had a second thought, went to the desk, took the revolver, and stuck it in his pocket. Then,
without looking back, he went into his room.

For some time he lay on his couch watching the sky gradually close over, listening to the silence. It was this silence that had seemed painful to him during the
first days here, after the war. He had requested a post in the little town at the base
of the foothills separating the upper plateaus from the desert. There, rocky walls,
green and black to the north, pink and lavender to the south, marked the frontier
of eternal summer. He had been named to a post farther north, on the plateau itself. In the beginning, the solitude and the silence had been hard for him on these
wastelands peopled only by stones. Occasionally, furrows suggested cultivation, but
they had been dug to uncover a certain kind of stone good for building. The only
plowing here was to harvest rocks. Elsewhere a thin layer of soil accumulated in the
hollows would be scraped out to enrich paltry village gardens. This is the way it
was: bare rock covered three quarters of the region. Towns sprang up, flourished,
then disappeared; men came by, loved one another or fought bitterly, then died. No
one in this desert, neither he nor his guest, mattered. And yet, outside this desert
neither of them, Daru knew, could have really lived.

When he got up, no noise came from the classroom. He was amazed at the   65
unmixed joy he derived from the mere thought that the Arab might have fled and
that he would be alone with no decision to make. But the prisoner was there. He
had merely stretched out between the stove and the desk. With eyes open, he was
staring at the ceiling. In that position, his thick lips were particularly noticeable,
giving him a pouting look. "Come," said Daru. The Arab got up and followed him.

In the bedroom, the schoolmaster pointed to a chair near the table under the window. The Arab sat down without taking his eyes off Daru.

"Are you hungry?"

"Yes," the prisoner said.

Daru set the table for two. He took flour and oil, shaped a cake in a frying-pan and lighted the little stove that functioned on bottled gas. While the cake was cooking, he went out to the shed to get cheese, eggs, dates, and condensed milk. When the cake was done he set it on the window sill to cool, heated some condensed milk diluted with water, and beat up the eggs into an omelet. In one of his motions he knocked against the revolver stuck in his right pocket. He set the bowl down, went into the classroom, and put the revolver in his desk drawer. When he came back to the room, night was falling. He put on the light and served the Arab. "Eat," he said. The Arab took a piece of the cake, lifted it eagerly to his mouth, and stopped short.

"And you?" he asked.

"After you. I'll eat too." 70

The thick lips opened slightly. The Arab hesitated, then bit into the cake determinedly.

The meal over, the Arab looked at the schoolmaster. "Are you the judge?"

"No, I'm simply keeping you until tomorrow."

"Why do you eat with me?"

"I'm hungry." 75

The Arab fell silent. Daru got up and went out. He brought back a folding bed from the shed, set it up between the table and the stove, perpendicular to his own bed. From a large suitcase which, upright in a corner, served as a shelf for papers, he took two blankets and arranged them on the camp bed. Then he stopped, felt useless, and sat down on his bed. There was nothing more to do or to get ready. He had to look at this man. He looked at him, therefore, trying to imagine his face bursting with rage. He couldn't do so. He could see nothing but the dark yet shining eyes and the animal mouth.

"Why did you kill him?" he asked in a voice whose hostile tone surprised him.

The Arab looked away.

"He ran away. I ran after him."

He raised his eyes to Daru again and they were full of a sort of woeful inter- 80 rogation. "Now what will they do to me?"

"Are you afraid?"

He stiffened, turning his eyes away.

"Are you sorry?"

The Arab stared at him openmouthed. Obviously he did not understand. Daru's annoyance was growing. At the same time he felt awkward and self-conscious with his big body wedged between the two beds.

"Lie down there," he said impatiently. "That's your bed." 85

The Arab didn't move. He called to Daru:

"Tell me!"

The schoolmaster looked at him.

"Is the gendarme coming back tomorrow?"

"I don't know."

90

"Are you coming with us?"

"I don't know. Why?"

The prisoner got up and stretched out on top of the blankets, his feet toward the window. The light from the electric bulb shone straight into his eyes and he closed them at once.

"Why?" Daru repeated, standing beside the bed.

The Arab opened his eyes under the blinding light and looked at him, trying 95 not to blink.

"Come with us," he said.

In the middle of the night, Daru was still not asleep. He had gone to bed after undressing completely; he generally slept naked. But when he suddenly realized that he had nothing on, he hesitated. He felt vulnerable and the temptation came to him to put his clothes back on. Then he shrugged his shoulders; after all, he wasn't a child and, if need be, he could break his adversary in two. From his bed he could observe him, lying on his back, still motionless with his eyes closed under the harsh light. When Daru turned out the light, the darkness seemed to coagulate all of a sudden. Little by little, the night came back to life in the window where the starless sky was stirring gently. The schoolmaster soon made out the body laying at his feet. The Arab still did not move, but his eyes seemed open. A faint wind was prowling around the schoolhouse. Perhaps it would drive away the clouds and the sun would reappear.

During the night the wind increased. The hens fluttered a little and then were silent. The Arab turned over on his side with his back to Daru, who thought he heard him moan. Then he listened for his guest's breathing, become heavier and more regular. He listened to that breath so close to him and mused without being able to go to sleep. In this room where he had been sleeping alone for a year, this presence bothered him. But it bothered him also by imposing on him a sort of brotherhood he knew well but refused to accept in the present circumstances. Men who share the same rooms, soldiers or prisoners, develop a strange alliance as if, having cast off their armor with their clothing, they fraternized every evening, over and above their differences, in the ancient community of dream and fatigue. But Daru shook himself; he didn't like such musings, and it was essential to sleep.

A little later, however, when the Arab stirred slightly, the schoolmaster was still not asleep. When the prisoner made a second move, he stiffened, on the alert. The Arab was lifting himself slowly on his arms with almost the motion of a sleep-walker. Seated upright in bed, he waited motionless without turning his head toward Daru, as if he were listening attentively. Daru did not stir, it had just occurred to him that the revolver was still in the drawer of his desk. It was better to act at once. Yet he continued to observe the prisoner, who, with the same slithery motion, put his feet on the ground, waited again, then began to stand up slowly. Daru was about to call out to him when the Arab began to walk, in a quite natural but extraordinarily silent way. He was heading toward the door at the end of the room that opened into the shed. He lifted the latch with precaution and went out, pushing the door behind him but without shutting it. Daru had not stirred. "He is running away," he merely thought. "Good riddance!" Yet he listened attentively. The hens were not fluttering; the guest must be on the plateau. A faint sound of water reached him, and he didn't know what it was until the Arab again stood framed in the doorway, closed the door carefully, and came back to bed without a sound. Then Daru turned his back on him and fell asleep. Still later he seemed, from the depths of his sleep, to hear furtive steps around the schoolhouse. "I'm dreaming! I'm dreaming!" he repeated to himself. And he went on sleeping.

When he awoke, the sky was clear; the loose window let in a cold, pure air.   100
The Arab was asleep, hunched up under the blankets now, his mouth open, utterly relaxed. But when Daru shook him, he started dreadfully, staring at Daru with wild eyes as if he had never seem him and such a frightened expression that the schoolmaster stepped back. "Don't be afraid. It's me You must eat." The Arab nodded his head and said yes. Calm had returned to his face, but his expression was vacant and listless.

The coffee was ready. They drank it seated together on the folding bed as they munched their pieces of the cake. Then Daru led the Arab under the shed and showed him the faucet where he washed. He went back into the room, folded the blankets and the bed, made his own bed and put the room in order. Then he went through the classroom and out onto the terrace. The sun was already rising in the blue sky; a soft, bright light was bathing the deserted plateau. On the ridge the snow was melting in spots. The stones were about to reappear. Crouched on the edge of the plateau, the schoolmaster looked at the deserted expanse. He thought of Balducci. He had hurt him, for he had sent him off in a way as if he didn't want to be associated with him. He could still hear the gendarme's farewell and, without knowing why, he felt strangely empty and vulnerable. At that moment, from the other side of the schoolhouse, the prisoner coughed. Daru listened to him almost despite himself and then, furious, threw a pebble that whistled through the air before sinking into the snow. That man's stupid crime revolted him, but to hand him over was contrary to honor. Merely thinking of it made him smart with humiliation. And he cursed at one and the same time his own people who had sent him this Arab and the Arab too who had dared to kill and not managed to get away. Daru got up, walked in a circle of the terrace, waited motionless, and then went back into the schoolhouse.

The Arab, leaning over the cement floor of the shed, was washing his teeth with two fingers. Daru looked at him and said: "Come." He went back into the room ahead of the prisoner. He slipped a hunting-jacket on over his sweater and put on walking-shoes. Standing, he waited until the Arab had put on his chèche and sandals. They went into the classroom and the schoolmaster pointed to the exit, saying: "Go ahead." The fellow didn't budge. "I'm coming," said Daru. The Arab went out. Daru went back into the room and made a package of pieces of rusk, dates, and sugar. In the classroom, before going out, he hesitated a second in front of his desk, then crossed the threshold and locked the door. "That's the way," he said. He started toward the east, followed by the prisoner. But, a short distance from the schoolhouse, he thought he heard a slight sound behind them. He retraced his steps and examined the surroundings of the house; there was no one there. The Arab watched him without seeming to understand. "Come on," said Daru.

They walked for an hour and rested beside a sharp peak of limestone. The snow was melting faster and faster and the sun was drinking up the puddles at once, rapidly cleaning the plateau, which gradually dried and vibrated like the air itself. When they resumed walking, the ground rang under their feet. From time to time a bird rent the space in front of them with a joyful cry. Daru breathed in deeply the fresh morning light; he felt a sort of rapture before the vast familiar expanse, now almost entirely yellow under its domes of blue sky. They walked an hour more, descending toward the south. They reached a level height made up of crumbly rocks. From there on, the plateau sloped down, eastward, toward a low plain where there were a few spindly trees and to the south, toward outcroppings of rock that gave the landscape a chaotic look.

Daru surveyed the two directions. There was nothing but the sky on the horizon. Not a man could be seen. He turned toward the Arab, who was looking at him blankly. Daru held out the package to him. "Take it," he said. "There are dates, bread, and sugar. You can hold out for two days. Here are a thousand francs too." The Arab took the package and the money but kept his full hands at chest level as if he didn't know what to do with what was being given him. "Now look," the schoolmaster said as he pointed in the direction of the east, "there's the way to Tinguit. You have a two-hour walk. At Tinguit you'll find the administration and the police. They are expecting you." The Arab looked toward the east, still holding the package and the money against his chest. Daru took his elbow and turned him rather roughly toward the south. At the foot of the height on which they stood could be seen a faint path. "That's the trail across the plateau. In a day's walk from here you'll find pasturelands and the first nomads. They'll take you in and shelter you according to their law." The Arab had now turned toward Daru and a sort of panic was visible in his expression. "Listen," he said. Daru shook his head: "No, be quiet. Now I'm leaving you." He turned his back on him, took two long steps in the direction of the school, looked hesitantly at the motionless Arab, and started off again. For a few minutes he heard nothing but his own step resounding on the cold ground and did not turn his head. A moment later, however, he turned around. The Arab was still there on the edge of the hill, his arms hanging now, and he was looking at the schoolmaster. Daru felt something rise in his throat. But he swore with impatience, waved vaguely, and started off again. He had already gone some distance when he again stopped and looked. There was no longer anyone on the hill.

Daru hesitated. The sun was now rather high in the sky and was beginning to beat down on his head. The schoolmaster retraced his steps, at first somewhat uncertainly, then with decision. When he reached the little hill, he was bathed in sweat. He climbed it as fast as he could and stopped, out of breath, at the top. The rock-fields to the south stood out sharply against the blue sky, but on the plain to the west a steamy heat was already rising. And in that slight haze, Daru, with heavy heart, made out the Arab walking slowly on the road to prison.

A little later, standing before the window of the classroom, the schoolmaster was watching the clear light bathing the whole surface of the plateau, but he hardly saw it. Behind him on the blackboard, among the winding French rivers, sprawled the clumsily chalked-up words he had just read: "You handed over our brother. You will pay for this." Daru looked at the sky, the plateau, and, beyond, the invisible lands stretching all the way to the sea. In this vast landscape he had loved so much, he was alone.

Questions for Discussion and Writing

1. Between what conflicting loyalties is Daru torn? What can you infer about his past relationship with Balducci?
2. How does Daru try to avoid responsibility for turning in the Arab? Why, in your opinion, does the Arab, when free to choose, continue on the path leading to the town where he will be imprisoned and possibly even executed?
3. How are Daru's actions toward the Arab misunderstood by the local populace who are spying on him? What is the significance of the message written on the blackboard? How does this story express Camus's existential philosophy about the unavoidability of making choices and the burdens of freedom?

LUISA VALENZUELA

Luisa Valenzuela was born in Buenos Aries, Argentina, in 1938 and grew up in a literary atmosphere where Jorge Luis Borges visited her family and coauthored stories with her mother. Valenzuela was already a successful writer when a military regime took over Argentina in the late 1970s and began a reign of terror in which individuals known as the "disappeared" were removed without a trace. She fled Argentina to live in the United States, where she taught creative writing at Columbia University. The short story that follows first appeared in The Open Door *(1988), a collection whose title she chose because "The Open Door is the name of the most traditional, least threatening lunatic asylum in Argentina." She has recently written* Symmetries: Stories, *translated by Margaret Jull Costa (1998).*

The Censors

Poor Juan! One day they caught him with his guard down before he could even realize that what he had taken as a stroke of luck was really one of fate's dirty tricks. These things happen the minute you're careless, as one often is. Juancito let happiness—a feeling you can't trust—get the better of him when he received from a confidential source Mariana's new address in Paris and knew that she hadn't forgotten him. Without thinking twice, he sat down at his table and wrote her a letter. *The* letter that now keeps his mind off his job during the day and won't let him sleep at night (what had he scrawled, what had he put on that sheet of paper he sent to Mariana?).

Juan knows there won't be a problem with the letter's contents, that it's irreproachable, harmless. But what about the rest? He knows that they examine, sniff, feel, and read between the fines of each and every letter, and check its tiniest comma and most accidental stain. He knows that all letters pass from hand to hand and go through all sorts of tests in the huge censorship offices and that, in the end, very few continue on their way. Usually it takes months, even years, if there aren't any snags; all this time the freedom, maybe even the life, of both sender and receiver is in jeopardy. And that's why Juan's so troubled: thinking that something might happen to Mariana because of his letters. Of all people, Mariana, who must finally feel safe there where she always dreamt she'd live. But he knows that the *Censor's Secret Command* operates all over the world and cashes in on the discount in air fares; there's nothing to stop them from going as far as that hidden Paris neighborhood, kidnapping Mariana, and returning to their cozy homes, certain of having fulfilled their noble mission.

Well, you've got to beat them to the punch, do what everyone tries to do: sabotage the machinery, throw sand in its gears, get to the bottom of the problem so as to stop it.

This was Juan's sound plan when he, like many others, applied for a censor's job—not because he had a calling or needed a job: no, he applied simply to intercept his own letter, a consoling albeit unoriginally idea. He was hired immediately, for each day more and more censors are needed and no one would bother to check on his references.

Ulterior motives couldn't be overlooked by the *Censorship Division,* but they   5 needn't be too strict with those who applied. They knew how hard it would be for the poor guys to find the letter they wanted and even if they did, what's a letter or two when the new censor would snap up so many others? That's how Juan managed to join the *Post Office's Censorship Division,* with a certain goal in mind.

The building had a festive air on the outside that contrasted with its inner staidness. Little by little, Juan was absorbed by his job, and he felt at peace since he was doing everything he could to get his letter for Mariana. He didn't even worry when, in his first month, he was sent to *Section K* where envelopes are very carefully screened for explosives.

It's true that on the third day, a fellow worker had his right hand blown off by a letter, but the division chief claimed it was sheer negligence on the victim's part. Juan and the other employees were allowed to go back to their work, though feeling less secure. After work, one of them tried to organize a strike to demand higher wages for unhealthy work, but Juan didn't join in; after thinking it over, he reported the man to his superiors and thus got promoted.

You don't form a habit by doing something once, he told himself as he left his boss's office. And when he was transferred to *Section J*, where letters are carefully checked for poison dust, he felt he had climbed a rung in the ladder.

By working hard, he quickly reached *Section E* where the job became more interesting, for he could now read and analyze the letters' contents. Here he could even hope to get hold of his letter, which, judging by the time that had elapsed, had gone through the other sections and was probably floating around in this one.

Soon his work became so absorbing that his noble mission blurred in his   10 mind. Day after day he crossed out whole paragraphs in red ink, pitilessly chucking many letters into the censored basket. These were horrible days when he was shocked by the subtle and conniving ways employed by people to pass on subversive messages; his instincts were so sharp that he found behind a simple "the weather's unsettled" or "prices continue to soar" the wavering hand of someone secretly scheming to overthrow the Government.

His zeal brought him swift promotion. We don't know if this made him happy. Very few letters reached him in *Section B*—only a handful passed the other hurdles—so he read them over and over again, passed them under a magnifying glass, searched for microprint with an electronic microscope, and tuned his sense of smell so that he was beat by the time he made it home. He'd barely manage to warm up his soup, eat some fruit, and fall into bed, satisfied with having done his duty. Only his darling mother worried, but she couldn't get him back on the right track. She'd say, though it wasn't always true: Lola called, she's at the bar with the girls, they miss you, they're waiting for you. Or else she'd leave a bottle of red wine on the table. But Juan wouldn't overdo it: any distraction could make him lose his edge and the perfect censor had to be alert, keen, attentive, and sharp to nab cheats. He had a truly patriotic task, both self-denying and uplifting.

His basket for censored letters became the best fed as well as the most cunning basket in the whole *Censorship Division*. He was about to congratulate himself for having finally discovered his true mission, when his letter to Mariana reached his hands. Naturally, he censored it without regret. And just as naturally, he couldn't stop them from executing him the following morning, another victim of his devotion to his work.

Questions for Discussion and Writing

1. What prompts Juan to apply for the job as a censor, and how does he change as a result of rising through the ranks in this occupation?
2. What details suggest that Juan was a very different kind of person before becoming a censor? Why is the ending ironic?
3. Most people know that e-mail messages are not as private as previously believed (for example, they are stored for long periods of time, employers and universities can access them, and they can be subpoenaed). Has this knowledged changed the way you use e-mail?

Poetry

W. H. AUDEN

W. H. Auden (1907–1973) was born in York, England, the son of a distinguished physician. He was educated at Oxford, where he was part of a group of poets, including Louis MacNeice, Stephen Spender, and C. Day Lewis, who shared the goal of creating new poetic techniques to

express heightened social consciousness. After graduating from Oxford in 1928, Auden spent a
year in Berlin, where he was influenced by Marxist poet and playwright Bertolt Brecht. After
teaching school in England and Scotland in the 1930s, he went to Spain in 1937, where he
drove an ambulance for the Republicans in the war against the Fascists. He moved to the United
States in 1939 and became an American citizen in 1946, dividing his time between New York
and Europe. He was elected professor of poetry at Oxford in 1956. The most complete edition of
his poetry is the posthumously published Collected Poems *(1978). In "The Unknown Citi-*
zen" (1940), Auden satirizes a dehumanized materialistic society that requires absolute con-
formity of its citizens.

The Unknown Citizen

(To JS/07/M/378
This Marble Monument
Is Erected by the State)

He was found by the Bureau of Statistics to be
One against whom there was no official complaint,
And all the reports on his conduct agree
That, in the modern sense of an old-fashioned word, he was a saint,
For in everything he did he served the Greater Community.   5
Except for the War till the day he retired
He worked in a factory and never got fired,
But satisfied his employers, Fudge Motors Inc.
Yet he wasn't a scab[1] or odd in his views,
For his Union reports that he paid his dues,   10
(Our report on his Union shows it was sound)
And our Social Psychology workers found
That he was popular with his mates and liked a drink.
The Press are convinced that he bought a paper every day
And that his reactions to advertisements were normal in every way.   15
Policies taken out in his name prove that he was fully insured,
And his Health-card shows he was once in hospital but left it cured.
Both Producers Research and High-Grade Living declare
He was fully sensible to the advantages of the Installment Plan
And had everything necessary to the Modern Man,   20
A phonograph, radio, a car and a frigidaire.
Our researchers into Public Opinion are content
That he held the proper opinions for the time of year;
When there was peace, he was for peace; when there was war, he went.
He was married and added five children to the population,   25

---

[1] *Scab:* a worker who won't join the union or who takes a striker's job.

Which our Eugenist[2] says was the right number for a parent
    of his generation,
And our teachers report that he never interfered with their education.
Was he free? Was he happy? The question is absurd:
Had anything been wrong, we should certainly have heard.   29

Questions for Discussion and Writing

1. Why is it significant that no official complaint was ever brought against the unknown citizen? What kind of society did he inhabit?
2. How does Auden parody the language of bureaucracy to satirize the social and political tenets of the government? What aspects of this society does he assail?
3. How might the word *unknown* in the title be interpreted? What is the significance of the question "Was he free? Was he happy?" in line 28? What evidence, if any, does the poem give as an answer?

MARGARET ATWOOD

Margaret Atwood was born in Ottawa, Ontario, in 1939. She was educated at the University of Toronto, where she came under the influence of the critic Northrup Frye, whose theories of mythical modes in literature she has adapted to her own purposes in her prolific writing of poetry, novels, and short stories. She is the author of more than twenty volumes of poetry and fiction, including The Handmaid's Tale *(1986), which was made into a film in 1989. Her short story collections include* Bluebeard's Egg and Other Stories *(1986). She also edited the* Oxford Book of Canadian Short Stories in English *(1987). Her most recent works include* Alias Grace: A Novel *(1996),* A Quiet Game *(1997), and* Two Solitudes *(1998). In the following poem from* Power Politics *(1971), Atwood depicts how the women whom soldiers leave at home change as wars change but always find themselves in the same predicament.*

At First I Was Given Centuries

At first I was given centuries
to wait in caves, in leather
tents, knowing you would never come back

Then it speeded up: only
several years between   5

---

    [2] *Eugenist:* an expert in eugenics, the science of improving the human race by careful selection of parents to breed healthier, more intelligent children.

the day you jangled off
into the mountains, and the day (it was
spring again) I rose from the embroidery
frame at the messenger's entrance.

That happened twice, or was it   10
more; and there was once, not so
long ago, you failed,
and came back in a wheelchair
with a mustache and a sunburn
and were insufferable.   15

Time before last though, I remember
I had a good eight months between
running alongside the train, skirts hitched, handing
you violets in at the window
and opening the letter; I watched   20
your snapshot fade for twenty years.

And last time (I drove to the airport
still dressed in my factory
overalls, the wrench
I had forgotten sticking out of the back   25
pocket; there you were,
zippered and helmeted, it was zero
hour, you said Be
Brave) it was at least three weeks before
I got the telegram and could start regretting.   30

But recently, the bad evenings
there are only seconds
between the warning on the radio and the
explosion; my hands
don't reach you   35

and on quieter nights
you jump up from
your chair without even touching your dinner

and I can scarcely kiss you goodbye
before you run out into the street and they shoot   40

Questions for Discussion and Writing

1. How would you describe the voice you hear, and to whom is she speaking?
2. How have circumstances changed as the poem progresses? What specific
   wars are alluded to in the course of the poem?

3. What new conditions imply a change in the nature of warfare over the centuries and the consequences for the women left behind?

Drama

Václav Havel

Václav Havel was born in Prague, Czechoslovakia, in 1936. Prevented from attending high school, he earned a diploma by attending night class and working as a laboratory assistant during the day. By age twenty, Havel was publishing his first articles in literary and theatrical magazines. He worked as a stagehand at several theaters in Prague and rose to the position of resident playwright at the Ballustrade Theater. His first play, Autostop *(1961), cowritten with Ivan Vyskocil, is a satire on society's preoccupation with automobiles. Havel's first full-length play,* The Garden Party *(1963), is widely regarded as the play that began the theater of the absurd in Czechoslovakia. A second full-length play,* The Memorandum *(1965), continued to articulate Havel's exploration of conflict between citizens and the political system. The play earned an Obie Award (an award for Off-Broadway productions) when it was produced at the 1968 New York Shakespeare Festival. Months after Havel's third play,* The Increased Difficulty of Concentration *(1968), appeared, Havel discovered he was under government surveillance and was being watched twenty-four hours a day. Government censorship prevented him from finding a publisher or having his plays produced, and he resorted to circulating his works privately—even as foreign productions of his plays won him an international reputation. His best-known works of the 1970s are his three one-act plays, often called* The Vaněk Trilogy *after the main character. All three plays—*"Audience," "Private View," *and* "Protest"*—focus on how the system intrudes into the lives of common citizens who are not dissidents. Throughout this period, Havel was repeatedly interrogated, held for detention, and imprisoned. He managed to write* Protest, *translated by Vera Blackwell, in 1979 while under surveillance and house arrest before being sentenced to prison for four and a half years. The accounts of his imprisonment, from which he was released in 1983 when he became violently ill, are in his nonfiction works,* Living in Truth *(1989),* Disturbing the Peace *(1990), and* Letters to Olga *(1990), a volume of letters written to his wife. The "velvet revolution" that brought down the communist government in 1989 led to Havel's becoming the first freely elected president of Czechoslovakia. In 1993 he was re-elected as the president of the newly created Czech Republic. In* Protest, *the dissident writer Vaněk, a semiautobiographical figure, is confronted by Staněk, a successful writer who has made his peace with the system. Staněk's attempt to justify his own behavior is perhaps the most brilliant theatrical realization of pseudoreasoning and rationalization of political cowardice ever presented on a stage. Havel's latest work is* The Beggar's Opera, *translated by Paul Wilson (2001).*

Protest

Characters

Vaněk
Staněk

PLACE

Staněk's study, Prague.

Staněk's study. On the left, a massive writing desk, on it a typewriter, a telephone, reading glasses, and many books and papers; behind it, a large window with a view into the garden. On the right, two comfortable arm chairs and between them a small table. The whole back wall is covered by bookcases, filled with books and with a built-in bar. In one of the niches there is a tape recorder. In the right back corner, a door; on the right wall, a large surrealist painting. When the curtain rises, Staněk and Vaněk are on stage: Staněk, standing behind his desk, is emotionally looking at Vaněk, who is standing at the door holding a briefcase and looking at Staněk with signs of embarrassment. A short, tense pause. Then Staněk suddenly walks excitedly over to Vaněk, takes him by the shoulders with both arms, shakes him in a friendly way, calling out.

[STANĚK: Vaněk—Hello!
    (*Vaněk smiles timidly. Staněk lets go, trying to conceal his agitation.*) Did you have
    trouble finding it?
VANĚK: Not really—
STANĚK: Forgot to mention the flowering magnolias. That's how you know it's
    my house. Superb, aren't they?
VANĚK: Yes—
STANĚK: I managed to double their blossoms in less than three years, compared   5
    to the previous owner. Have you magnolias at your cottage?
VANĚK: No—
STANĚK: You must have them! I'm going to find you two quality saplings and
    I'll come and plant them for you personally. (*Crosses to the bar and opens it.*)
    How about some brandy?
VANĚK: I'd rather not—
STANĚK: Just a token one. Eh?
    (*He pours brandy into two glasses, hands one glass to Vaněk and raises the other for a
    toast.*) Well—here's to our reunion!
VANĚK: Cheers—   10
    (*Both drink; Vaněk shudders slightly.*)
STANĚK: I was afraid you weren't going to come.
VANĚK: Why?
STANĚK: Well, I mean, things got mixed up in an odd sort of way—What?—
    Won't you sit down?
VANĚK (*Sits down in an armchair, placing his briefcase on the floor beside him.*):
    Thanks—
STANĚK: (*Sinks into an armchair opposite Vaněk with a sigh.*):   That's more like it!   15
    Peanuts?
VANĚK: No, thanks—

STANĚK: (*Helps himself. Munching.*):   You haven't changed much in all these years, you know?

VANĚK: Neither have you—

STANĚK: Me? Come on! Getting on for fifty, going gray, aches and pains setting in—Not as we used to be, eh? And the present times don't make one feel any better either, what? When did we see each other last, actually?

VANĚK: I don't know—

STANĚK: Wasn't it at your last opening night?

VANĚK: Could be—

STANĚK: Seems like another age! We had a bit of an argument—

VANĚK: Did we?

STANĚK: You took me to task for my illusions and my over-optimism. Good Lord! How often since then I've had to admit to myself you were right! Of course, in those days I still believed that in spite of everything some of the ideals of my youth could be salvaged and I took you for an incorrigible pessimist.

VANĚK: But I'm not a pessimist—

STANĚK: You see, everything's turned around! (*Short pause.*) Are you—alone?

VANĚK: How do you mean, alone?

STANĚK: Well, isn't there somebody—you know—

VANĚK: Following me?

STANĚK: Not that I care! After all, it was me who called you up, right?

VANĚK: I haven't noticed anybody—

STANĚK: By the way, suppose you want to shake them off one of these days, you know the best place to do it?

VANĚK: No—

STANĚK: A department store. You mingle with the crowd, then at a moment when they aren't looking you sneak into the washroom and wait there for about two hours. They become convinced you managed to slip out through a side entrance and they give up. You must try it out sometime! (*Pause.*)

VANĚK: Seems very peaceful here—

STANĚK: That's why we moved here. It was simply impossible to go on writing near that railway station! We've been here three years, you know. Of course, my greatest joy is the garden. I'll show you around later—I'm afraid I'm going to boast a little—

VANĚK: You do the gardening yourself?

STANĚK: It's become my greatest private passion these days. Keep puttering about out there almost every day. Just now I've been rejuvenating the apricots. Developed my own method, you see, based on a mixture of natural and artificial fertilizers plus a special way of waxless grafting. You won't believe the results I get! I'll find some cuttings for you later on—

(*Staněk walks over to the desk, takes a package of foreign cigarettes out of a drawer, brings matches and an ashtray, and puts it all on the table in front of Vaněk.*) Ferdinand, do have a cigarette.

VANĚK: Thanks—

(*Vaněk takes a cigarette and lights it; Staněk sits in the other chair; both drink.*)

STANĚK: Well now, Ferdinand, tell me—How are you?

VANĚK: All right, thanks—

STANĚK: Do they leave you alone—at least now and then?

VANĚK: It depends—

  (*Short pause.*)

STANĚK: And how was it in there?   45

VANĚK: Where?

STANĚK: Can our sort bear it at all?

VANĚK: You mean prison? What else can one do?

STANĚK: As far as I recall, you used to be bothered by hemorrhoids. Must have
  been terrible, considering the hygiene in there.

VANĚK: They gave me suppositories—   50

STANĚK: You ought to have them operated on, you know. It so happens a friend
  of mine is our greatest hemorrhoid specialist. Works real miracles. I'll arrange
  it for you.

VANĚK: Thanks—

  (*Short pause.*)

STANĚK: You know, sometimes it all seems like a beautiful dream—all the exciting opening nights, private views, lectures, meetings—the endless discussions
  about literature and art! All the energy, the hopes, plans, activities, ideas—the
  wine-bars crowded with friends, the wild booze-ups, the madcap affrays in
  the small hours, the jolly girls dancing attendance on us! And the mountains
  of work we managed to get done, regardless!—That's all over now. It'll never
  come back!

VANĚK: Mmn—

  (*Pause. Both drink.*)

STANĚK: Did they beat you?   55

VANĚK: No—

STANĚK: Do they beat people up in there?

VANĚK: Sometimes. But not the politicals—

STANĚK: I thought about you a great deal!

VANĚK: Thank you—   60

  (*Short pause.*)

STANĚK: I bet in those days it never even occurred to you—

VANĚK: What?

STANĚK: How it'll all end up! I bet not even you had guessed that!

VANĚK: Mmn—

STANĚK: It's disgusting, Ferdinand, disgusting! The nation is governed by scum!   65
  And the people? Can this really be the same nation which not very long ago
  behaved so magnificently? All that horrible cringing, bowing and scraping!
  The selfishness, corruption and fear wherever you turn! What have they
  made of us, old pal? Can this really be us?

VANĚK: I don't believe things are as black as all that—

STANĚK: Forgive me, Ferdinand, but you don't happen to live in a normal environment. All you know are people who manage to resist this rot. You just

keep on supporting and encouraging each other. You've no idea the sort of environment I've got to put up with! You're lucky you no longer have anything to do with it. Makes you sick at your stomach!

(*Pause. Both drink.*)

VANĚK: You mean television?

STANĚK: In television, in film studios—you name it.

VANĚK: There was a piece by you on the T.V. the other day—   70

STANĚK: You can't imagine what an ordeal that was! First they kept blocking it for over a year, then they started changing it around—changed my whole opening and the entire closing sequence! You wouldn't believe the trifles they find objectionable these days! Nothing but sterility and intrigues, intrigues and sterility! How often I tell myself—wrap it up, chum, forget it, go hide somewhere— grow apricots—

VANĚK: I know what you mean—

STANĚK: The thing is though, one can't help wondering whether one's got the right to this sort of escape. Supposing even the little one might be able to accomplish today can, in spite of everything, help someone in some way, at least give him a bit of encouragement, uplift him a little.—Let me bring you a pair of slippers.

VANĚK: Slippers? Why?

STANĚK: You can't be comfortable in those boots.   75

VANĚK: I'm all right—

STANĚK: Are you sure?

VANĚK: Yes. Really—

(*Both drink.*)

STANĚK (*Pause.*): How about drugs? Did they give you any?

VANĚK: No—   80

STANĚK: No dubious injections?

VANĚK: Only some vitamin ones—

STANĚK: I bet there's some funny stuff in the food!

VANĚK: Just bromine against sex—

STANĚK: But surely they tried to break you down somehow!   85

VANĚK: Well—

STANĚK: If you'd rather not talk about it, it's all right with me.

VANĚK: Well, in a way, that's the whole point of pre-trial interrogations, isn't it? To take one down a peg or two—

STANĚK: And to make one talk!

VANĚK: Mmn—   90

STANĚK: If they should haul me in for questioning—which sooner or later is bound to happen—you know what I'm going to do?

VANĚK: What?

STANĚK: Simply not answer any of their questions! Refuse to talk to them at all! That's by far the best way. Least one can be quite sure one didn't say anything one ought not to have said!

VANĚK: Mmn—

STANĚK: Anyway, you must have steel nerves to be able to bear it all and in ad-   95
dition to keep doing the things you do.

VANĚK: Like what?

STANĚK: Well, I mean all the protests, petitions, letters—the whole fight for
human rights! I mean the things you and your friends keep on doing—

VANĚK: I'm not doing so much—

STANĚK: Now don't be too modest, Ferdinand! I follow everything that's going
on! I know! If everybody did what you do, the situation would be quite
different! And that's a fact. It's extremely important there should be at least a
few people here who aren't afraid to speak the truth aloud, to defend others,
to call a spade a spade! What I'm going to say might sound a bit solemn
perhaps, but frankly, the way I see it, you and your friends have taken on an
almost superhuman task: to preserve and to carry the remains, the remnant
of moral conscience through the present quagmire! The thread you're spinning may be thin, but—who knows—perhaps the hope of a moral rebirth of
the nation hangs on it.

VANĚK: You exaggerate—   100

STANĚK: Well, that's how I see it, anyway.

VANĚK: Surely our hope lies in all the decent people—

STANĚK: But how many are there still around? How many?

VANĚK: Enough—

STANĚK: Are there? Even so, it's you and your friends who are the most exposed   105
to view.

VANĚK: And isn't that precisely what makes it easier for us?

STANĚK: I wouldn't say so. The more you're exposed, the more responsibility
you have towards all those who know about you, trust you, rely on you and
look up to you, because to some extent you keep upholding their honour,
too! (*Gets up.*) I'll get you those slippers!

VANĚK: Please don't bother—

STANĚK: I insist. I feel uncomfortable just looking at your boots. (*Pause. Staněk
returns with slippers.*)

VANĚK: (*Sighs.*)   110

STANĚK: Here you are. Do take those ugly things off, I beg you. Let me—
(*Tries to take off Vaněk boots.*) Won't you let me—Hold still—

VANĚK (Embarrassed.):   No—please don't—no—I'll do it—(*Struggles out of his
boots, slips on slippers.*) There—Nice, aren't they? Thank you very much.

STANĚK: Good gracious, Ferdinand, what for?—(*Hovering over Vaněk.*) Some
more brandy?

VANĚK: No more for me, thanks—

STANĚK: Oh, come on. Give me your glass!   115

VANĚK: I'm sorry, I'm not feeling too well—

STANĚK: Lost the habit inside, is that it?

VANĚK: Could be—But the point is—last night, you see—

STANĚK: Ah, that's what it is. Had a drop too many, eh?

VANĚK: Mmn—   120

STANĚK: I understand. (*Returns to his chair.*) By the way, you know the new wine-bar, "The Shaggy Dog"?

VANĚK: No—

STANĚK: You don't? Listen, the wine there comes straight from the cask, it's not expensive and usually it isn't crowded. Really charming spot, you know, thanks to a handful of fairly good artists who were permitted—believe it or not—to do the interior decoration. I can warmly recommend it to you. Lovely place. Where did you go, then?

VANĚK: Well, we did a little pub-crawling, my friend Landovský and I—

STANĚK: Oh, I see! You were with Landovský, were you? Well! In that case, I'm not at all surprised you came to a sticky end! He's a first class actor, but once he starts drinking—that's it! Surely you can take one more brandy! Right? 125

VANĚK: (*Sighs.*)

(*Drinks are poured. They both drink. Vaněk shudders.*)

STANĚK (*Back in his armchair. Short pause*): Well, how are things otherwise? You do any writing?

VANĚK : Trying to—

STANĚK: A play?

VANĚK: A one-act play— 130

STANĚK: Another autobiographical one?

VANĚK: More or less—

STANĚK: My wife and I read the one about the brewery[1] the other day. We thought it was very amusing.

VANĚK: I'm glad—

STANĚK: Unfortunately we were given a rather bad copy.[2] Very hard to read. 135

VANĚK: I'm sorry—

STANĚK: It's a really brilliant little piece! I mean it! Only the ending seemed to me a bit muddy. The whole thing wants to be brought to a more straightforward conclusion, that's all. No problem. You can do it.

(*Pause. Both drink. Vaněk shudders.*)

STANĚK: Well, how are things? How about Pavel?[3] Do you see him?

VANĚK: Yes—

STANĚK: Does he do any writing? 140

VANĚK: Just now he's finishing a one-act, as well. It's supposed to be performed together with mine—

STANĚK: Wait a minute. You don't mean to tell me you two have teamed up also as authors!

---

[1] Staněk is referring to "Audience." [2] Literary works circulating as *samizdat* (that is, unofficial or underground–Eds.)texts in typescript are understandably often of poor quality. If one gets to read the, say, sixth carbon copy on onion skin, the readability of the script leaves much to be desired. [3] Staněk means Pavel Kohout. (b. 1928), a fellow writer and advisor to Vaclav Havel.

VANĚK: More or less—

STANĚK: Well, well!—Frankly, Ferdinand, try as I may, I don't get it. I don't. I simply can't understand this alliance of yours. Is it quite genuine on your part? Is it?—Good heavens! Pavel! I don't know! Just remember the way he started! We both belong to the same generation, Pavel and I, we've both—so to speak—spanned a similar arc of development, but I don't mind telling you that what he did in those days—Well! It was a bit too strong even for me!—Still, I suppose it's your business. You know best what you're doing.

VANĚK: That's right!   145

(*Pause. Both drink.*)

STANĚK: Is your wife fond of gladioli?

VANĚK: I don't know. I think so—

STANĚK: You won't find many places with such a large selection as mine. I've got thirty-two shades, whereas at a common or garden nursery you'll be lucky to find six. Do you think your wife would like me to send her some bulbs?

VANĚK: I'm sure she would—

STANĚK: There's still time to plant them you know. (*Pause.*) Ferdinand—   150

VANĚK: Yes?

STANĚK: Weren't you surprised when I suddenly called you up?

VANĚK: A bit—

STANĚK: I thought so. After all, I happen to be among those who've still managed to keep their heads above water and I quite understand that—because of this—you might want to keep a certain distance from me.

VANĚK: No, not I—   155

STANĚK: Perhaps not you yourself, but I realize that some of your friends believe that anyone who's still got some chance today has either abdicated morally, or is unforgivably fooling himself.

VANĚK: I don't think so—

STANĚK: I wouldn't blame you if you did, because I know only too well the grounds from which such prejudice could grow. (*An embarrassed pause.*) Ferdinand—

VANĚK: Yes?

STANĚK: I realize what a high price you have to pay for what you're doing. But   160
please don't think it's all that easy for a man who's either so lucky, or so unfortunate as to be still tolerated by the official apparatus, and who—at the same time—wishes to live at peace with his conscience.

VANĚK: I know what you mean—

STANĚK: In some respects it may be even harder for him.

VANĚK: I understand.

STANĚK: Naturally, I didn't call you in order to justify myself! I don't really think there's any need. I called you because I like you and I'd be sorry to see you sharing the prejudice which I assume exists among your friends.

VANĚK: As far as I know nobody has ever said a bad word about you—   165

STANĚK: Not even Pavel?

VANĚK: No—

STANĚK (*Embarrassed pause.*):   Ferdinand—

VANĚK: Yes?

STANĚK: Excuse me—(*Gets up. Crosses to the tape recorder. Switches it on: Soft, non-*   170
descript background music. Staněk returns to his chair.) Ferdinand, does the name
Javurek mean anything to you?

VANĚK: The pop singer? I know him very well—

STANĚK: So I expect you know what happened to him.

VANĚK: Of course. They locked him up for telling a story during one of his
performances. The story about the cop who meets a penguin in the
street—

STANĚK: Of course. It was just an excuse. The fact is, they hate his guts because
he sings the way he does. The whole thing is so cruel, so ludicrous, so base!

VANĚK: And cowardly—   175

STANĚK: Right! And cowardly! Look, I've been trying to do something for the
boy. I mean, I know a few guys at the town council and at the prosecutor's
office, but you know how it is. Promises, promises! They all say they're going
to look into it, but the moment your back is turned they drop it like a hot
potato, so they don't get their fingers burnt! Sickening, the way everybody
looks out for number one!

VANĚK: Still, I think it's nice of you to have tried to do something—

STANĚK: My dear Ferdinand, I'm really not the sort of man your friends obviously take me for! Peanuts?

VANĚK: No, thanks—

STANĚK (*Short pause.*):   About Javurek—   180

VANĚK: Yes?

STANĚK: Since I didn't manage to accomplish anything through private intervention, it occurred to me perhaps it ought to be handled in a somewhat
different way. You know what I mean. Simply write something—a protest or
a petition? In fact, this is the main thing I wanted to discuss with you. Naturally, you're far more experienced in these matters than I. If this document
contains a few fairly well-known signatures—like yours, for example—it's
bound to be published somewhere abroad which might create some political
pressure. Right? I mean, these things don't seem to impress them all that
much, actually—but honestly, I don't see any other way to help the boy. Not
to mention Annie—

VANĚK: Annie?

STANĚK: My daughter.

VANĚK: Oh? Is that your daughter?   185

STANĚK: That's right.

VANĚK: Well, what about her?

STANĚK: I thought you knew.

VANĚK: Knew what?

STANĚK: She's expecting. By Javurek—   190

VANĚK: Oh, I see. That's why—

STANĚK: Wait a minute! If you mean the case interests me merely because of
family matters—

VANĚK: I didn't mean that—

STANĚK: But you just said—

VANĚK: I only wanted to say, that's how you know about the case at all; you   195
were explaining to me how you got to know about it. Frankly, I wouldn't
have expected you to be familiar with the present pop scene. I'm sorry if it
sounded as though I meant—

STANĚK: I'd get involved in this case even if it was someone else expecting his
child! No matter who—

VANĚK: I know—

(*Embarrassed pause.*)

STANĚK: Well, what do you think about my idea of writing some sort of
protest?

(*Vaněk begins to look for something in his briefcase, finally finds a paper, and hands it
to Staněk.*)

VANĚK: I guess this is the sort of thing you had in mind—

STANĚK: What?   200

VANĚK: Here—

STANĚK (*Grabs the document.*):   What is it?

VANĚK: Have a look—

(*Staněk takes the paper from Vaněk, goes quickly to the writing desk, picks up his
glasses, puts them on, and begins to read attentively. Lengthy pause. Staněk shows
signs of surprise. When he finishes reading, he puts aside his glasses and begins to pace
around in agitation.*)

STANĚK: Now isn't it fantastic! That's a laugh, isn't it? Eh? Here I was cudgeling
my brains how to go about it, finally I take the plunge and consult you—and
all this time you've had the whole thing wrapped up and ready! Isn't it
marvellous? I knew I was doing the right thing when I turned to you!
(*Staněk returns to the table, sits down, puts on his glasses again, and rereads the
text.*) There! Precisely what I had in mind! Brief, to the point, fair, and yet
emphatic. Manifestly the work of a professional! I'd be sweating over it for a
whole day and I'd never come up with anything remotely like this!

VANĚK: (*Embarrassed.*)   205

STANĚK: Listen, just a small point—here at the end—do you think "willfulness"
is the right word to use? Couldn't one find a milder synonym, perhaps?
Somehow seems a bit misplaced, you know. I mean, the whole text is composed in very measured, factual terms—and this word here suddenly sticks
out, sounds much too emotional, wouldn't you agree? Otherwise it's absolutely perfect. Maybe the second paragraph is somewhat superfluous; in
fact, it's just a rehash of the first one. Except for the reference here to
Javurek's impact on nonconformist youth. This is excellent and must stay in!
How about putting it at the end instead of your "willfulness"? Wouldn't that
do the trick?—But these are just my personal impressions, Good heavens!
Why should you listen to what I have to say! On the whole the text is excellent, and no doubt it's going to hit the mark. Let me say again, Ferdinand,
how much I admire you. Your knack for expressing the fundamental points
of an issue, while avoiding all needless abuse, is indeed rare among our kind!

VANĚK: Come on—you don't really mean that—
  (*Staněk takes off his glasses, goes over to Vaněk, puts the paper in front of him, sits again in the easy chair, and sips his drink. Short pause.*)
STANĚK: Anyway, it's good to know there's somebody around whom one can always turn to and rely on in a case like this.
VANĚK: But it's only natural, isn't it?
STANĚK: It may seem so to you. But in the circles where I've to move such   210
  things aren't in the least natural! The natural response is much more likely to be the exact opposite. When a man gets into trouble everybody drops him as soon as possible, the lot of them. And out of fear for their own positions they try to convince all and sundry they've never had anything to do with him; on the contrary, they sized him up right away, they had his number! But why am I telling you all this, you know best the sort of thing that happens! Right? When you were in prison your long-time theatre pals held forth against you on television. It was revolting—
VANĚK: I'm not angry with them—
STANĚK: But I am! And what's more I told them so. In no uncertain terms! You know, a man in my position learns to put up with a lot of things, but—if you'll forgive me—there are limits! I appreciate it might be awkward for you to blame them, as you happen to be the injured party. But listen to me, you've got to distance yourself from the affair! Just think: Once we, too, begin to tolerate this sort of muck—we're *de facto* assuming co-responsibility for the entire moral morass and indirectly contributing to its deeper penetration. Am I right?
VANĚK: Mmn—
STANĚK (*Short pause.*):   Have you sent it off yet?
VANĚK: We're still collecting signatures—   215
STANĚK: How many have you got so far?
VANĚK: About fifty—
STANĚK: Fifty? Not bad! (*Short pause.*) Well, never mind, I've just missed the boat, that's all.
VANĚK: You haven't—
STANĚK: But the thing's already in hand, isn't it?   220
VANĚK: Yes, but it's still open—I mean—
STANĚK: All right, but now it's sure to be sent off and published, right? By the way, I wouldn't give it to any of the agencies, if I were you. They'll only print a measly little news item which is bound to be overlooked. Better hand it over directly to one of the big European papers, so the whole text gets published, including all the signatures!
VANĚK: I know—
STANĚK (*Short pause.*):   Do they already know about it?
VANĚK: You mean the police?   225
STANĚK: Yes.
VANĚK: I don't think so. I suppose not—
STANĚK: Look here, I don't want to give you any advice, but it seems to me you ought to wrap it up as soon as possible, else they'll get wind of what's going

on and they'll find a way to stop it. Fifty signatures should be enough! Besides, what counts is not the number of signatures, but their significance.

VANĚK: Each signature has its own significance!

STANĚK: Absolutely, but as far as publicity abroad is concerned, it is essential that   230
some well-known names are represented, right? Has Pavel signed?

VANĚK: Yes—

STANĚK: Good. His name—no matter what one may think of him personally—
does mean something in the world today!

VANĚK: No question—

STANĚK (*Short pause.*):   Listen, Ferdinand—

VANĚK: Yes?   235

STANĚK: There's one more thing I wanted to discuss with you. It's a bit delicate,
though—

VANĚK: Oh?

STANĚK: Look here, I'm no millionaire, you know, but so far I've been able to
manage—

VANĚK: Good for you—

STANĚK: Well, I was thinking—I mean—I'd like to—Look, a lot of your friends   240
have lost their jobs. I was thinking—would you be prepared to accept from
me a certain sum of money?

VANĚK: That's very nice of you! Some of my friends indeed find themselves in a
bit of a spot. But there are problems, you know. I mean, one is never quite
sure how to go about it. Those who most need help are often the most reluctant to accept—

STANĚK: You won't be able to work miracles with what I can afford, but I ex-
pect there are situations when every penny counts.
(*Takes out his wallet, removes two banknotes, hesitates, adds a third, hands them to
Vaněk.*) Here—please—a small offering.

VANĚK: Thank you very much. Let me thank you for all my friends—

STANĚK: Gracious, we've got to help each other out, don't we? (*Pause.*) Incidentally, there's no need for you to mention this little contribution comes from
me. I don't wish to erect a monument to myself. I'm sure you've gathered
that much by now, eh?

VANĚK: Yes. Again many thanks—   245

STANĚK: Well now, how about having a look at the garden?

VANĚK: Mr. Staněk—

STANĚK: Yes?

VANĚK: We'd like to send it off tomorrow—

STANĚK: What?   250

VANĚK: The protest—

STANĚK: Excellent! The sooner the better!

VANĚK: So that today there's still—

STANĚK: Today you should think about getting some sleep! That's the main
thing! Don't forget you've a bit of a hangover after last night and tomorrow
is going to be a hard day for you!

VANĚK: I know. All I was going to say— 255

STANĚK: Better go straight home and unplug the phone. Else Ladovský rings you up again and heaven knows how you'll end up!

VANĚK: Yes, I know. There're only a few signatures I've still got to collect—it won't take long. All I was going to say—I mean, don't you think it would be helpful—as a matter of fact, it would, of course, be sensational! After all, practically everybody's read your *Crash!*

STANĚK: Oh, come on, Ferdinand! That was fifteen years ago!

VANĚK: But it's never been forgotten!

STANĚK: What do you mean—sensational? 260

VANĚK: I'm sorry, I had the impression you'd actually like to—

STANĚK: What?

VANĚK: Participate—

STANĚK: Participate? Wait a minute. Are you talking about (*points to the paper*) this? Is that what you're talking about?

VANĚK: Yes— 265

STANĚK: You mean I—

VANĚK: I'm sorry, but I had the impression—

(*Staněk finishes his drink, crosses to the bar, pours himself a drink, walks over to the window, looks out for a while, whereupon he suddenly turns to Vaněk with a smile.*)

STANĚK: Now that's a laugh, isn't it?

VANĚK: What's a laugh?

STANĚK: Come on, can't you see how absurd it is? Eh? I ask you over hoping 270 you might write something about Javurek's case—you produce a finished text and what's more, one furnished with fifty signatures! I'm bowled over like a little child, can't believe my eyes and ears, I worry about ways to stop them from ruining your project—and all this time it hasn't occurred to me to do the one simple, natural thing which I should have done in the first place! I mean, at once sign the document myself! Well, you must admit it's absurd, isn't it?

VANĚK: Mmn—

STANĚK: Now, listen Ferdinand, isn't this a really terrifying testimony to the situation into which we've been brought? Isn't it? Just think: even I, though I know it's rubbish, even I've got used to the idea that the signing of protests is the business of local specialists, professionals in solidarity, dissidents! While the rest of us—when we want to do something for the sake of ordinary human decency—automatically turn to you, as though you were a sort of service establishment for moral matters. In other words, we're here simply to keep our mouths shut and to be rewarded by relative peace and quiet, whereas you're here to speak up for us and to be rewarded by blows on earth and glory in the heavens! Perverse, isn't it?

VANĚK: Mmn—

STANĚK: Of course it is! And they've managed to bring things to such a point that even a fairly intelligent and decent fellow—which, with your permission, I still think I am—is more or less ready to take this situation for granted! As though it was quite normal, perfectly natural! Sickening, isn't it? Sickening the depths we've reached! What do you say? Makes one puke, eh?

VANĚK: Well—   275

STANĚK: You think the nation can ever recover from all this?

VANĚK: Hard to say—

STANĚK: What can one do? What can one do? Well, seems clear, doesn't it? In theory, that is. Everybody should start with himself. What? However! Is this country inhabited only by Vaněks? It really doesn't seem that everybody can become a fighter for human rights.

VANĚK: Not everybody, no—

STANĚK: Where is it?   280

VANĚK: What?

STANĚK: The list of signatures, of course.

VANĚK (*Embarrassed pause.*):   Mr. Staněk—

STANĚK: Yes?

VANĚK: Forgive me, but—I'm sorry, I've suddenly a funny feeling that perhaps—   285

STANĚK: What funny feeling?

VANĚK: I don't know—I feel very embarrassed—Well, it seems to me perhaps I wasn't being quite fair—

STANĚK: In what way?

VANĚK: Well, what I did—was a bit of a con trick—in a way—

STANĚK: What are you talking about?   290

VANĚK: I mean, first I let you talk, and only then I ask for your signature—I mean, after you're already sort of committed by what you've said before, you see—

STANĚK: Are you suggesting that if I'd known you were collecting signatures for Javurek, I would never have started talking about him?

VANĚK: No, that's not what I mean—

STANĚK: Well, what do you mean?

VANĚK: How shall I put it—   295

STANĚK: Oh, come on! You mind I didn't organize the whole thing myself, is that it?

VANĚK: No, that's not it—

STANĚK: What is it then?

VANĚK: Well, it seems to me it would've been a quite different matter if I'd come to you right away and asked for your signature. That way you would've had an option—

STANĚK: And why didn't you come to me right away, actually? Was it because   300 you'd simply written me off in advance?

VANĚK: Well, I was thinking that in your position—

STANĚK: Ah! There you are! You see? Now it's becoming clear what you really think of me, isn't it? You think that because now and then one of my pieces happens to be shown on television, I'm no longer capable of the simplest act of solidarity!

VANĚK: You misunderstand me.—What I meant was—

STANĚK: Let me tell you something, Ferdinand. (*Drinks. Short pause.*) Look here, if I've—willy-nilly—got used to the perverse idea that common decency and morality are the exclusive domain of the dissidents—then you've—willy-nilly—got used to the idea as well! That's why it never crossed your mind that certain values might be more important to me than my present position. But suppose even I wanted to be finally a free man, suppose even I wished to renew my inner integrity and shake off the yoke of humiliation and shame? It never entered your head that I might've been actually waiting for this very moment for years, what? You simply placed me once and for all among those hopeless cases, among those whom it would be pointless to count on in any way. Right? And now that you found I'm not entirely indifferent to the fate of others—you made that slip about my signature! But you saw at once what happened, and so you began to apologize to me. Good God! Don't you realize how you humiliate me? What if all this time I'd been hoping for an opportunity to act, to do something that would again make a man of me, help me to be once more at peace with myself, help me to find again the free play of my imagination and my lost sense of humour, rid me of the need to escape my traumas by minding the apricots and the blooming magnolias! Suppose even I prefer to live in truth! What if I want to return from the world of custom-made literature and the proto-culture of television to the world of art which isn't geared to serve anyone at all?

VANĚK: I'm sorry—forgive me! I didn't mean to hurt your feelings—. Wait a minute, I'll—just a moment—

(*Vaněk opens his briefcase, rummages in it for a while, finally extracts the sheets with the signatures and hands them to Staněk. Staněk gets up slowly and crosses with the papers to the desk, where he sits down, puts on his glasses, and carefully studies the sheets nodding his head here and there. After a lengthy while, he takes off his glasses, slowly rises, thoughtfully paces around, finally turning to Vaněk.*)

STANĚK: Let me think aloud. May I?

VANĚK: By all means—

STANĚK (*Halts, drinks, begins to pace again as he talks.*):   I believe I've already covered the main points concerning the subjective side of the matter. If I sign the document, I'm going to regain—after years of being continually sick to my stomach—my self-esteem, my lost freedom, my honour, and perhaps even some regard among those close to me. I'll leave behind the insoluble dilemmas, forced on me by the conflict between my concern for my position and my conscience. I'll be able to face with equanimity Annie, myself, and even that young man when he comes back. It'll cost me my job, though my job brings me no satisfaction—on the contrary, it brings me shame—nevertheless, it does support me and my family a great deal better than if I were to become a night watchman. It's more than likely that my son won't be permitted to continue his studies. On the other hand, I'm sure he's going to have more respect for me that way, than if his permission to study was bought by my refusal to sign the protest for Javurek, whom he happens to worship.—Well then. This is the subjective side of the matter. Now how about the objective side? What happens when—among the signatures of a few well-known dissidents and a handful of Javurek's teenage friends—there suddenly crops up—to everybody's surprise and against all expectation—my signature? The signature of a man who hasn't been heard from regarding civic affairs for years! Well? My co-signatories—as well as many of those who don't sign documents of this sort, but who nonetheless deep down side with those who do—are naturally going to welcome my signature with pleasure. The closed circle of habitual signers—whose signatures, by the way, are already beginning to lose their clout, because they cost practically nothing. I mean, the people in question have long since lost all ways and means by which they could actually pay for their signatures. Right? Well, this circle will be broken. A new name will appear, a name the value of which depends precisely on its previous absence. And of course, I may add, on the high price paid for its appearance! So much for the objective "plus" of my prospective signature. Now what about the authorities? My signature is going to surprise, annoy, and upset them for the very reasons which will bring joy to the other signatories. I mean, because it'll make a breach in the barrier the authorities have been building around your lot for so long and with such effort. All right. Let's see about Javurek. Concerning his case, I very much doubt my participation would significantly influence its outcome. And if so, I'm afraid it's more than likely going to have a negative effect. The authorities will be anxious to prove they haven't been panicked. They'll want to show that a surprise of this sort can't make them lose their cool. Which brings us to the consideration of what they're going to do to me. Surely, my signature is bound to have a much more significant influence on what happens in my case. No doubt, they're going to punish me far more cruelly than you'd expect. The point being that my punishment will serve them as a warning signal to all those who might be tempted to follow my example in the future, choose freedom, and thus swell the ranks of the dissidents. You may be sure they'll want to show them what the score is! Right? The thing is—well, let's face it—they're no longer worried all that much about dissident activities within the confines of the established ghetto. In some respects they even seem to prod them on here and there. But! What they're really afraid of is any semblance of a crack in the fence around the ghetto! So they'll want to exorcize the bogey of a prospective epidemic of dissent by an exemplary punishment of myself. They'll want to nip it in the bud, that's all. (*Drinks. Pause.*) The last question I've got to ask myself is this: what sort of reaction to my signature can one expect among those who, in one way or another, have followed what you might call "the path of accommodation." I mean people who are, or ought to be, our main concern, because—I'm sure you'll agree—our hope for the future depends above all on whether or not it will be possible to awaken them from their slumbers and to enlist them to take an active part in civic affairs. Well, I'm afraid that my signature is going to be received with absolute resentment by this crucial section of the populace. You know why? Because, as a matter of fact, these people secretly hate the dissidents. They've become their bad conscience, their living reproach! That's how they see the dissidents. And at the same time, they envy them their honour and their inner freedom, values which they themselves were denied by fate. This is why they never miss an opportunity to smear the dissidents. And precisely this opportunity is going to be offered to them by my signature. They're going to spread nasty rumours about you and your friends. They're going to say that you who have nothing more to lose—you who have long since landed at the bottom of the heap and, what's more, managed to make yourselves quite at home in there—are now trying to drag down to your own level an unfortunate man, a man who's so far been able to stay above the salt line. You're dragging him down—irresponsible as you are—without the slightest compunction, just for your own whim, just because you wish to irritate the authorities by creating a false impression that your ranks are being swelled! What do you care about losing him his job! Doesn't matter, does it? Or do you mean to suggest you'll find him a job down in the dump in which you yourselves exist? What? No—Ferdinand! I'm sorry. I'm afraid I'm much too familiar with the way these people think! After all, I've got to live among them, day in day out. I know precisely what they're going to say. They'll say I'm your victim, shame-lessly abused, misguided, led astray by your cynical appeal to my humanity! They'll say that in your ruthlessness you didn't shrink even from making use of my personal relationship to Javurek! And you know what? They're going to say that all the humane ideals you're constantly proclaiming have been tar-nished by your treatment of me. That's the sort of reasoning one can expect from them! And I'm sure I don't have to tell you that the authorities are bound to support this interpretation, and to fan the coals as hard as they can! There are others, of course, somewhat more intelligent perhaps. These people might say that the extraordinary appearance of my signature among yours is actually counterproductive, in that it concentrates everybody's attention on my signature and away from the main issue concerning Javurek. They'll say it puts the whole protest in jeopardy, because one can't help asking oneself what was the purpose of the exercise: was it to help Javurek, or to parade a newborn dissident? I wouldn't be at all surprised if someone were to say that, as a matter of fact, Javurek was victimized by you and your friends. It might be suggested his personal tragedy only served you to further your ends—which are far removed from the fate of the unfortunate man. Furthermore, it'll be pointed out that by getting my signature you managed to dislodge me from the one area of operation—namely, backstage diplomacy, private intervention—where I've been so far able to manoeuvre and where I might have proved infinitely more helpful to Javurek in the end! I do hope you understand me, Ferdinand. I don't wish to exaggerate the importance of these opinions, nor am I prepared to become their slave. On the other hand, it seems to be in the interests of our case for me to take them into account. After all, it's a matter of a political decision and a good politician must consider all the issues which are likely to influence the end result of his

action. Right? In these circumstances the question one must resolve is as
follows: what do I prefer? Do I prefer the inner liberation which my
signature is going to bring me, a liberation paid for—as it now turns out—
by a basically negative objective impact—or do I choose the other alternative.
I mean, the more beneficial effect which the protest would have without my
signature, yet paid for by my bitter awareness that I've again—who knows,
perhaps for the last time—missed a chance to shake off the bonds of shameful
compromises in which I've been choking for years? In other words, if I'm to
act indeed ethically—and I hope by now you've no doubt I want to do just
that—which course should I take? Should I be guided by ruthless objective
considerations, or by subjective inner feelings?

VANĚK: Seems perfectly clear to me—
STANĚK: And to me—   310
VANĚK: So that you're going to—
STANĚK: Unfortunately—
VANĚK: Unfortunately?
STANĚK: You thought I was—
VANĚK: Forgive me, perhaps I didn't quite understand—   315
STANĚK: I'm sorry if I've—
VANĚK: Never mind—
STANĚK: But I really believe—
VANĚK: I know—

(*Both drink. Vaněk shudders. Lengthy embarrassed pause. Staněk takes the sheets and
hands them with a smile to Vaněk who puts them, together with the text of the letter
of protest, into his briefcase. He shows signs of embarrassment. Staněk crosses to the
tape recorder, unplugs it, comes back and sits down.*)

STANĚK: Are you angry?   320
VANĚK: No—
STANĚK: You don't agree, though—
VANĚK: I respect your reasoning—
STANĚK: But what do you think?
VANĚK: What should I think?   325
STANĚK: That's obvious, isn't it?
VANĚK: Is it?
STANĚK: You think that when I saw all the signatures, I did, after all, get the
   wind up!
VANĚK: I don't—
STANĚK: I can see you do!   330
VANĚK: I assure you—
STANĚK: Why don't you level with me?! Don't you realize that your benevolent
   hypocrisy is actually far more insulting than if you gave it to me straight?! Or
   do you mean I'm not even worthy of your comment?!
VANĚK: But I told you, didn't I, I respect your reasoning—
STANĚK: I'm not an idiot, Vaněk!
VANĚK: Of course not—   335

STANĚK: I know precisely what's behind your "respect"!

VANĚK: What is?

STANĚK: A feeling of moral superiority!

VANĚK: You're wrong—

STANĚK: Only, I'm not quite sure if you—you of all people—have any right to   340
feel so superior!

VANĚK: What do you mean?

STANĚK: You know very well what I mean!

VANĚK: I don't—

STANĚK: Shall I tell you?

VANĚK: Please do—   345

STANĚK: Well! As far as I know, in prison you talked more than you should
have! (*Vaněk jumps up, wildly staring at Staněk who smiles triumphantly. Short
tense pause. The phone rings. Vaněk broken, sinks back into his chair. Staněk crosses to
the telephone and lifts the receiver.*)

STANĚK: Hello—yes—what? You mean—Wait a minute—I see—I see—Where
are you? Yes, yes, of course—absolutely!—good—You bet!—Sure—I'll be
here waiting for you! Bye bye. (*Staněk puts the receiver down and absent-
mindedly stares into space. Lengthy pause. Vaněk gets up in embarrassment. Only
now Staněk seems to realize that Vaněk is still there. He turns to him abruptly.*) You
can go and burn it downstairs in the furnace!

VANĚK: What?

STANĚK: He's just walked into the canteen! To see Annie.

VANĚK: Who did?   350

STANĚK: Javurek! Who else?

VANĚK (*Jumps up.*):   Javurek? You mean he was released? But that's wonderful!
So your private intervention did work, after all! Just as well we didn't send
off the protest a few days earlier! I'm sure they would've got their backs up
and kept him inside!
(*Staněk searchingly stares at Vaněk, then suddenly smiles, decisively steps up to him,
and with both hands takes him by the shoulders.*)

STANĚK: My dear fellow, you mustn't fret! There's always the risk that you can
do more harm than good by your activities! Right? Heavens, if you should
worry about this sort of thing, you'd never be able to do anything at all!
Come, let me get you those saplings—

Questions for Discussion and Writing

1. What occasion has prompted this meeting between Vaněk and Staněk? What
   can you infer about their past relationship from their initial conversation?
2. How does Havel use the incident of drawing up and signing the petition to
   reveal the kind of person Staněk has become?
3. Differences in political views often create conflicts in personal relationships.
   Has this ever happened to you? Describe your experiences.

Connections for Chapter 8:
The Pursuit of Justice

1. **Thomas Paine,** *Rights of Man*
   Compare Paine's essay with Golda Meir's memoir in terms of the underlying principles on which the new nations are founded and the dangers independence will produce.

2. **Harriet Jacobs,** *Incidents in the Life of a Slave Girl*
   In what ways do Jacobs and Martin Luther King, Jr., address the idea of justice as a fundamental human right for African-Americans?
   How might historians use Jacobs's account as a source document in ways recommended by Linda Simon in "The Naked Source" in Chapter 7?

3. **Martin Luther King, Jr.,** *I Have a Dream*
   Would you call Jill Nelson's "Number One!" (in Chapter 1) a success story in terms of King's expectations for African-Americans? Why or why not?
   How does the narrative by Frederick Douglass in Chapter 3 provide insight into the historical background of King's speech?

4. **Golda Meir,** *We Have Our State*
   Compare Meir's dream with that of Martin Luther King, Jr. as expressed in his speech.
   To gain insight into why it was so important for Israel to become a recognized state, read this account against the background of Irene Zabytko's story "Home Soil," and discuss your observations.

5. **Rae Yang,** *At the Center of the Storm*
   Drawing on the accounts by Rae Yang and Aldous Huxley in "Propaganda under a Dictatorship" (Chapter 4), analyze how propaganda can be used in everyday life to reinforce state ideology.

6. **Luis Sepulveda,** *Daisy*
   Compare and contrast the pressures to which Sepulveda and Harriet Jacobs were subjected and the way they responded.

7. **Luisa Valenzuela,** *The Censors*
   Compare and contrast the ethical dilemmas facing the main character, Juan, in this story and Rae Yang in "At the Center of the Storm."
   In terms of their moral choices, in what respects are scientists who practice vivisection, as described by Hans Ruesch in "Slaughter of the Innocent" (in Chapter 11), comparable to the protagonist of Valenzuela's story?

8. **Albert Camus,** *The Guest*
   In what sense is Daru's dilemma in this story comparable to that confronting Luis Sepulveda's narrator in "Daisy"?

9. **W. H. Auden,** *The Unknown Citizen*
   In what respects might Juan in Luisa Valenzuela's story be characterized as "the unknown citizen" of Auden's poem?

10. **Margaret Atwood,** *At First I Was Given Centuries*

    Compare the contrasting roles of women as active or passive players in history in Atwood's poem and in Golda Meir's memoir.

    How do Atwood and Lawrence Ferlinghetti (see "In Goya's Greatest Scenes We Seem to See" in Chapter 10) use poetry as a vehicle for social protest?

11. **Václav Havel,** *Protest*

    Compare depictions of political cowardice in the face of governmental control in Havel's play, and in W. H. Auden's poem.

9

THE IMPACT OF TECHNOLOGY

The essays in this chapter examine the extent to which culture and society depend on scientific discoveries and technological developments. Without basic scientific research, we would not have televisions, personal computers, VCRs, microwave ovens, cellular telephones, fax machines, the World Wide Web, and a host of other inventions. However, the creation of the world's first successful clone (the lamb "Dolly") raises a number of profoundly important ethical issues explored by Gina Kolata. Carol Grunewald considers the ethics of animal experimentation in the context of new genetic research. Constance Holden offers a thoughtful analysis of the role heredity plays in shaping human behavior. Anne Taylor Fleming discusses how developments in biotechnology have given women new choices and have produced new dilemmas.

Selections by Umberto Eco, LynNell Hancock, and Bill Gates offer invaluable insights into the effects of our dependence on technology, and into the social consequences of cyberspace.

John Cheever, in his innovative story, looks at the consequences when people can peer into the private lives of others.

Walt Whitman's poem offers a different perspective on astronomy, and Peggy Seeger's ironic ballad comments on the opportunities women have to become engineers in the new technological world.

Nonfiction

GINA KOLATA

Gina Kolata (b. 1948) is a science journalist who has been writing for The New York Times *since 1988. She studied molecular biology at the Massachusetts Institute of Technology and holds a master's degree in mathematics from the University of Maryland. Kolata is the author of* The Baby Doctors: Probing the Limits of Fetal Medicine *(1990) and* Clone: The Road to Dolly and the Path Ahead *(1998), from which "A Clone Is Born" is reprinted.*

She also wrote Flu: The Story of the Great Influenza Pandemic of 1918 and the Search for the Virus That Caused It *(1999).*

A Clone Is Born

Many people wonder if this is a miracle for which we can thank God, or an ominous new way to play God ourselves.

—Nancy Duff, Princeton Theological Seminary

On a soft summer night, July 5, 1996, at 5:00 P.M., the most famous lamb in history entered the world, head and forelegs first. She was born in a shed, just down the road from the Roslin Institute in Roslin, Scotland, where she was created. And yet her creator, Ian Wilmut, a quiet, balding fifty-two-year-old embryologist, does not remember where he was when he heard that the lamb, named Dolly, was born. He does not even recall getting a telephone call from John Bracken, a scientist who had monitored the pregnancy of the sheep that gave birth to Dolly, saying that Dolly was alive and healthy and weighed 6.6 kilograms, or 14.5 pounds.

It was a moment of remarkable insouciance. No one broke open champagne. No one took pictures. Only a few staff members from the institute and a local veterinarian who attended the birth were present. Yet Dolly, a fluffy creature with grayish-white fleece and a snow-white face, who looked for all the world like hundreds of other lambs that dot the rolling hills of Scotland, was soon to change the world.

When the time comes to write the history of our age, this quiet birth, the creation of this little lamb, will stand out. The events that change history are few and unpredictable. In the twentieth century, there was the discovery of quantum theory, the revolutionary finding by physicists that the normal rules of the visible world do not apply in the realm of the atom. There was Einstein's theory of general relativity, saying that space and time can be warped. There was the splitting of the atom, with its promise of good and evil. There was the often-overlooked theorem of mathematician Kurt Gödel, which said that there are truths that are unknowable, theorems that can be neither proved nor disproved. There was the development of computers that transformed Western society.

In biology and medicine, there was the discovery of penicillin in the 1940s, and there was James Watson and Francis Crick's announcement, in 1953, that they had found the structure of DNA, the genetic blueprint. There was the conquest of smallpox that wiped the ancient scourge from the face of the earth, and the discovery of a vaccine that could prevent the tragedy of polio. In the 1980s, there was the onslaught of AIDS, which taught us that plagues can afflict us still.

In politics, there were the world wars, the rise and fall of communism, and the Great Depression. There is the economic rise of Asia in the latter part of the century, and the ever-shifting balance of the world's powers.

But events that alter our very notion of what it means to be human are few and scattered over the centuries. The birth of Dolly is one of them. "Analogies to

Copernicus, to Darwin, to Freud, are appropriate," said Alan Weisbard, a professor of law and medical ethics at the University of Wisconsin. The world is a different place now that she is born.

Dolly is a clone. She was created not out of the union of a sperm and an egg but out of the genetic material from an udder cell of a six-year-old sheep. Wilmut fused the udder cell with an egg from another sheep, after first removing all genetic material from the egg. The udder cell's genes took up residence in the egg and directed it to grow and develop. The result was Dolly, the identical twin of the original sheep that provided the udder cells, but an identical twin born six years later. In a moment of frivolity, as a wry joke, Wilmut named her Dolly after Dolly Parton, who also was known, he said, for her mammaries.

Until Dolly entered the world, cloning was the stuff of science fiction. It had been raised as a possibility decades ago, then dismissed, relegated to the realm of the kooky, the fringy, something that serious scientists thought was simply not going to happen anytime soon.

Yet when it happened, even though it involved but one sheep, it was truly fantastic, and at the same time horrifying in a way that is hard to define. In 1972, when Willard Gaylin, a psychiatrist and the founder of the Hastings Center, an ethics think tank, mistakenly thought that science was on the verge of cloning, he described its awesome power: "One could imagine taking a single sloughed cell from the skin of a person's hand, or even from the hand of a mummy (since cells are neither 'alive' nor 'dead,' but merely intact or not intact), and seeing it perpetuate itself into a sheet of skin tissue. But could one really visualize the cell forming a finger, let alone a hand, let alone an embryo, let alone another Amenhotep[1]?"

And what if more than one clone is made? Is it even within the realm of the   10
imaginable to think that someday, perhaps decades from now, but someday, you could clone yourself and make tens, dozens, hundreds of genetically identical twins? Is it really science fiction to think that your cells could be improved beforehand, genetically engineered to add some genes and snip out others? These ideas, that so destroy the notion of the self, that touch on the idea of the soul, of human identity, seemed so implausible to most scientists that they had declared cloning off-limits for discussion.

Even ethicists, those professional worriers whose business it is to raise alarms about medicine and technology, were steered away from talk of cloning, though they tried to make it a serious topic. In fact, it was one of the first subjects mentioned when the bioethics field came into its own in the late 1960s and early 1970s. But scientists quashed the ethicists' ruminations, telling them to stop inventing such scary scenarios. The ethicists were informed that they were giving science a bad name to raise such specters as if they were real possibilities. The public would be frightened, research grants might dry up, scientists would be seen as Frankensteins, and legitimate studies that could benefit humankind could be threatened as part of an anti-science backlash.

---

[1] *Amenhotep:* king of Egypt of the Eighteenth Dynasty, approximately 1570 B.C.

Daniel Callahan, one of the founders of the bioethics movement and the founder, with Gaylin, of the Hastings Center, recalled that when he and others wanted to talk about cloning, scientists pooh-poohed them. They were told, he said, that "there was no real incentive for science to do this and it was just one of those scary things that ethicists and others were talking about that would do real harm to science."

Now, with the birth of Dolly, the ethicists were vindicated. Yes, it was a sheep that was cloned, not a human being. But there was nothing exceptional about sheep. Even Wilmut, who made it clear that he abhorred the very idea of cloning people, said that there was no longer any theoretical reason why humans could not clone themselves, using the same methods he had used to clone Dolly. "There is no reason in principle why you couldn't do it." But, he added, "all of us would find that offensive."

The utterly pragmatic approach of Wilmut and many other scientists, however, ignores the awesome nature of what was accomplished. Our era is said to be devoted to the self, with psychologists and philosophers battling over who can best probe the nature of our identities. But cloning pares the questions down to their essence, forcing us to think about what we mean by the self, whether we are our genes or, if not, what makes us *us*. "To thine own self be true" goes the popular line from Shakespeare—but what is the self?

We live in an age of the ethicist, a time when we argue about pragmatism and compromises in our quest to be morally right. But cloning forces us back to the most basic questions that have plagued humanity since the dawn of recorded time: What is good and what is evil? And how much potential for evil can we tolerate to obtain something that might be good? We live in a time when sin is becoming one of those quaint words that we might hear in church but that has little to do with our daily world. Cloning, however, with its possibilities for creating our own identical twins, brings us back to the ancient sins of vanity and pride: the sins of Narcissus, who so loved himself, and of Prometheus, who, in stealing fire, sought the powers of God. In a time when we hear rallying cries of reproductive freedom, of libertarianism and the rights of people to do what they want, so long as they hurt no one else, cloning, by raising the possibility that people could be made to order like commodities, places such ideas against the larger backdrop of human dignity.

So before we can ask why we are so fascinated by cloning, we have to examine our souls and ask, What exactly so bothers many of us about trying to replicate our genetic selves? Or, if we are not bothered, why aren't we?

We want children who resemble us. Even couples who use donor eggs because the woman's ovaries have failed or because her eggs are not easily fertilized, or who use donor sperm because the man's sperm is not viable, peruse catalogs of donors to find people who resemble themselves. We want to replicate ourselves. Several years ago, a poem by Linda Pastan, called "To a Daughter Leaving Home," was displayed on the walls of New York subways. It read:

Knit two, purl two,
I make of small boredoms

15

a fabric
to keep you warm.
Is it my own image
I love so
in your face?
I lean over your sleep,
Narcissus over
his clear pool,
ready to fall in—
to drown for you
if necessary.

Yet if we so love ourselves, reflected in our children, why is it so terrifying to so many of us to think of seeing our exact genetic replicas born again, identical twins years younger than we? Is there a hidden fear that we would be forcing God to give us another soul, thereby bending God to our will, or, worse yet, that we would be creating soul-less beings that were merely genetic shells of humans? After all, in many religions, the soul is supposed to be present from the moment of conception, before a person is born and shaped by nurture as well as nature. If a clone is created, how could its soul be different from the soul of the person who is cloned? Is it possible, as molecular biologist Gunther Stendt once suggested, that "a human clone would nor consist of real persons but merely of Cartesian[2] automata in human shape"?

Or is it one thing for nature to form us through the vagaries of the genetic lottery, and another for us to take complete control, abandoning all thoughts of somehow, through the mixing of genes, having a child who is like us, but better? Normally, when a man and a woman have a child together, the child is an unpredictable mixture of the two. We recognize that, of course, in the hoary old joke in which a beautiful but dumb woman suggests to an ugly but brilliant man that the two have a child. Just think of how wonderful the baby would be, the woman says, with my looks and your brains. Aha, says the man. But what if the child inherited *my* looks and *your* brains?[3]

Theologians speak of the special status of a child, born of an act of love   20
between a man and a woman. Of course, we already routinely employ infertility treatments, like donor eggs, semen banks, and frozen embryos, that have weakened these ties between the parents and the child. But, said Gilbert Meilaender, a Lutheran theologian, cloning would be "a new and decisive turn on this road." Cloning entails the *production,* rather than the creation, of a child. It is "far less a surrender to the mystery of the genetic lottery," he said, and "far more an understanding of the child as a product of human will."

---

[2] *Cartesian:* refers to French philosopher, mathematician, and scientist René Descartes (1596–1650).
[3] Anecdote attributed to George Bernard Shaw (1856–1950), Irish playwright, critic, and essayist.

Elliott Dorff, a rabbi at the University of Judaism in Los Angeles, said much the same thing. "Each person involved has to get out of himself or herself in order to make and have a child." But if a person can be reproduced through cloning, that self-surrender is lost, and there is danger of self-idolization.

Cloning also poses a danger to our notion of mortality, Dorff said. The biblical psalm says, "Teach us to number our days so that we can obtain a heart of wisdom," he recalled. "The sense that there is a deadline, that there is an end to all this, forces us to make good use of our lives."

In this age of entertainment, when philosophical and theological questions are pushed aside as too difficult or too deep, cloning brings us face-to-face with our notion of what it means to be human and makes us confront both the privileges and limitations of life itself. It also forces us to question the powers of science. Is there, in fact, knowledge that we do not want? Are there paths we would rather not pursue?

The time is long past when we can speak of the purity of science, divorced from its consequences. If any needed reminding that the innocence of scientists was lost long ago, they need only recall the comments of J. Robert Oppenheimer, the genius who was a father of the atomic bomb and who was transformed in the process from a supremely confident man, ready to follow his scientific curiosity, to a humbled and stricken soul, wondering what science had wrought.

Before the bomb was made, Oppenheimer said, "When you see something that is technically sweet you go ahead and do it." After the bomb was dropped on Hiroshima and Nagasaki, in a chilling speech at the Massachusetts Institute of Technology in 1947, he said: "In some sort of crude sense which no vulgarity, no humor, no overstatement can quite extinguish, the physicists have known sin; and this is a knowledge which they cannot lose."

As with the atom bomb, cloning is complex, multilayered in its threats and its promises. It offers the possibility of real scientific advances that can improve our lives and save them. In medicine, scientists dream of using cloning to reprogram cells so we can make our own body parts for transplantation. Suppose, for example, you needed a bone-marrow transplant. Some deadly forms of leukemia can be cured completely if doctors destroy your own marrow and replace it with healthy marrow from someone else. But the marrow must be a close genetic match to your own. If not, it will lash out at you and kill you. Bone marrow is the source of the white blood cells of the immune system. If you have someone else's marrow, you'll make their white blood cells. And if those cells think you are different from them, they will attack.

Today, if you need marrow, you have to hope that a sister, brother, parent, or child happens to have bone-marrow cells that are genetically compatible with your own. If you have no relative whose marrow matches yours, you can search in computer databases of people who have volunteered to donate their marrow, but your chances of finding someone who matches you are less than one in twenty thousand—or one in a million if your genetic type is especially rare.

But suppose, instead, that scientists could take one of your cells—any cell—and merge it with a human egg. The egg would start to divide, to develop, but it would not be permitted to divide more than a few times. Instead, technicians would bathe it in proteins that direct primitive cells, embryo cells, to become marrow cells. What started out to be a clone of you could grow into a batch of your marrow—the perfect match.

More difficult, but not inconceivable, would be to grow solid organs, like kidneys or livers, in the same way.

Another possibility is to create animals whose organs are perfect genetic matches for humans. If you needed a liver, a kidney, or even a heart, you might be able to get one from a pig clone that was designed so it had human proteins on the surface of its organs. The reason transplant surgeons steer away from using animal organs in humans, even though there is a dire shortage of human organs, is that animals are so genetically different from people. A pig kidney transplanted into a human is just so foreign that the person's immune system will attack it and destroy it. But cloning offers a different approach. Scientist could take pig cells, for example, and add human genes to them in the laboratory, creating pig cells that were coated with human proteins. Then they could make cloned pigs from those cells. Each pig would have organs that looked, to a human immune system, for all the world like a human organ. These organs could be used for transplantation.

Cloning could also be used to make animals that are living drug factories—exactly the experiment that Ian Wilmut's sponsor, a Scottish company called PPL Therapeutics, Ltd., wants to conduct. Scientists could insert genes into laboratory cells that would force the cells to make valuable drugs, like clotting factors for hemophiliacs. Then they could clone animals from those cells and create animals that made the drugs in their milk. The only step remaining would be to milk the clones and extract the drugs.

Another possibility would be to clone prize dairy cows. The average cow produces about fifteen thousand pounds of milk annually, but world champion milk producers make as much as forty thousand pounds of milk a year. The problem for breeders is that there are, apparently, so many genes involved in creating one of these phenomenal cows that no one has learned how to breed them the old-fashioned way. But if you had a cow that produced forty thousand pounds of milk a year, you could clone her and make a herd.

Zoologists might clone animals that are on the verge of extinction, keeping them alive and propagating when they might otherwise have vanished from the earth.

The possibilities are limitless, scientists say, and so, some argue, we should stop focusing on our hypothetical fears and think about the benefits that cloning could bring.

Others say that cloning is far from business as usual, far from a technical advance, and that we should be wary of heading down such a brambly path.

But was the cloning of Dolly really such a ground-shifting event? After all, the feat came as a climax to years of ever more frightening, yet dazzling, technological feats, particularly in the field of assisted reproduction. Each step, dreaded by some, cursed by others, welcomed by many more, soon grew to be part of the medical landscape, hardly worthy of comment. And so, with this history as background, some asked why, and how, anyone thought cloning could be controlled—or why anyone would want to. Besides, some asked, why was cloning any different in principle from some of the more spectacular infertility treatments that are accepted with hardly a raised eyebrow?

The infertility revolution began in 1978, when Louise Brown was born in England, the world's first test-tube baby. After more than a decade of futile efforts, scientists finally had learned to fertilize women's eggs outside their bodies, allowing the first stages of human life to begin in a petri dish in a laboratory. The feat raised alarms at the time. It was, said Moshe Tendler, a professor of medical ethics and chair of the biology department at Yeshiva University, "matchmaking at its most extreme, two reluctant gametes trying to be pushed together whether they liked it or not."

But in vitro fertilization flourished despite its rocky start, nourished by the plaintive cries of infertile couples so unjustly condemned to be barren, and justified by the miracle babies—children who were wanted so badly that their parents were willing to spend years in doctors' offices, take out loans for tens of thousands of dollars, and take their chances of finally, ultimately, failing and losing all hope of having a child who bore their genes. The doctors who ran the clinics soothed the public's fears. In vitro fertilization was not horrifying, they said. It was just a way to help infertile couples have babies.

The federal government quickly got out of the business of paying for any research that even peripherally contributed to the manipulation of human embryos, but in vitro fertilization clinics simply did research on their own, with money from the fees they charged women for infertility treatments, and so the field advanced, beyond the purview of university science, with its federal grants and accompanying strict rules and regulations.

"There are no hard-and-fast rules; there is no legislation," said Arthur Wisot,   40 the executive director of the Center for Advanced Reproductive Care in Redondo Beach, California. "This whole area of medicine is totally unregulated. We don't answer to anyone but our peers."

Nearly every year, the fertility clinics would take another step. Recently, they began advertising something they called intercytoplasmic sperm injection, or I.C.S.I., in which they could get usable sperm even from men who seemed to make none, or whose sperm cells were misshapen or immotile and simply unable to fertilize an egg. The scientists would insert a needle into a man's testicle and remove immature sperm, which were little more than raw genes. They would inject these nascent sperm into an egg to create an embryo. Medical scientists later discovered that many of these men had such feeble sperm because the genes that controlled their sperm production were mutated. When the sperm, carrying the mutated gene, were used to make a baby boy, the boy would grow up with the same mutations and he, too, would need I.C.S.I. to have a baby. Some scientists worried that there might be other consequences of such a mutation.

But the infertility doctors and many infertile couples were unconcerned by the possibility that this technique might be less of an unqualified boon than it at first appeared. And the I.C.S.I. advertisements continued unabated.

Infertility doctors also learned to snip a cell from a microscopic embryo and analyze it for genetic defects, selecting only healthy embryos to implant in a woman's womb. They learned that there is no age barrier to pregnancy: Women who had passed the age of menopause could still carry a baby if they used eggs from a younger woman, fertilized in a laboratory. Even women in their early sixties have gotten pregnant, and while some doctors have said they do not want to participate in creating such pregnancies, others say that it is really up to the women whether they want to become mothers at such an advanced age.

Infertility clinics are even learning to do the ultimate prenatal testing: fishing fetal cells out of a pregnant woman's blood and analyzing them for genetic defects. It is, said Tendler, "the perfect child syndrome. We can now take 5 cc of a woman's blood when she is seven to nine weeks pregnant, do 191 genetic probes on that cell, and decide whether that baby is going to make it or not."

The latest development involves methods to sort sperm, separating those sperm with Y chromosomes, which would create boys, from those with X chromosomes, which would create girls. Soon parents can have the ultimate control over the sex of their babies.

At the same time, molecular biologists learned to snip genes out of cells and to sew others in, engineering cells to order. Infertility clinics expect, before long, to be able to add genes to human embryos—or delete genes that could cause disease or disability—creating a perfect child before even implanting an embryo into a woman's womb.

At first, the feats of reproductive scientists were the objects of controversy and shock. But we have become accustomed to their achievements. And it is hard to argue against the cries that couples have a right to reproductive freedom. Many have suffered for years, yearning for a child of their own. If they want to create babies, and are paying with their own money, who has the right to tell them no?

These days, when infertility doctors introduce a new method to the public, or when their techniques disrupt what we have thought of as the natural order, there is, at first, a ripple of surprise, or sometimes dismay, but then that reaction fades and all we remember is that there seemed to be reports of one more incredible technological trick.

Even newspapers are becoming blasé. One Sunday in April, about six weeks after the cloning of Dolly was announced, I was attending a meeting of a federal commission that was assessing cloning. I crept out of the meeting to call a national news editor at *The New York Times* and inform him of the meeting's progress. He said there was something else he wanted to ask me about. There was a story out of Florida, he said, about a woman who just gave birth to her own grandchild. Was that news, he asked me?

I assured him that it was not news. Several years ago, another woman had done the same thing, and we'd reported it on page 1. The woman's daughter had been born with ovaries but not a uterus, so the mother carried the baby for the daughter. That story had come and gone, no longer even worth a raised eyebrow.

So when Dolly was born, in this age of ever-more-disarming scientific advances, some worried that her birth might be greeted with a brief shiver, then forgotten, like the woman who gave birth to her own grandchild. Leon Kass, a

45

50

biochemist turned philosopher, at the University of Chicago, warned that to react as though cloning were just another infertility treatment would be to miss the point of Dolly. He worried that we may be too jaded by previous triumphs of technological wizardry to take cloning as seriously as we should. He quoted Raskolnikov, the protagonist of Fyodor Dostoyevsky's *Crime and Punishment:* "Man gets used to everything—the beast."

It is true, of course, that the revolution in infertility treatments set the stage for people to think about cloning a human. Were it not for the proficiency of doctors in manipulating human eggs and sperm, it would not be feasible to even think of transferring the chromosomes of an adult cell into a human egg. But there is an intellectual chasm between methods that result in a baby with half its genes from the mother and half from the father and cloning, which would result in a baby whose genes are identical to those of an adult who was cloned.

Human cloning, Kass said, would be "something radically new, both in itself and in its easily foreseeable consequences. The stakes here are very high indeed." Until now "we have benefited mightily from the attitude, let technology go where it will and we can fix any problems that might arise later." But, he said, "that paradigm is open to question." Now we are "threatened with really major changes in human life, even human nature." And even if an absolute prohibition on cloning cannot be made effective, "it would at least place the burden on the other side to show the necessity" of taking this awesome step.

What is at issue, Kass said, "is nothing less than whether human procreation is going to remain human, whether children are going to be made rather than begotten, and whether it is a good thing, humanly speaking, to say yes to the road which leads, at best, to the dehumanized rationality of *Brave New World*." And so "What we have here is not business as usual, to be fretted about for a while and then given our seal of approval, not least because it appears to be unusual." Instead, he said, "the future of humanity may hang in the balance."

The cloning debate, Kass said, is so much more than just an argument about 55 one more step in assisted reproduction. "This is really one of those critical moments where one gets a chance to think about terribly important things. Not just genetics and what is the meaning of mother and father and kinship, but also the whole relationship between science and society and attitudes toward technology." Cloning, he said, "provides the occasion as well as the urgent necessity of deciding whether we shall be slaves of unregulated progress and ultimately its artifacts or whether we shall remain free human beings to guide our technique towards the enhancement of human dignity."

He quoted the theologian Paul Ramsey: "Raise the ethical questions with a serious and not a frivolous conscience. A man of frivolous conscience announces that there are ethical quandaries ahead that we must urgently consider before the future catches up with us. By this he often means that we need to devise a new ethics that will provide the rationalization for doing in the future what men are bound to do because of the new actions and interventions science will have made possible. In contrast, a man of serious conscience means to say in raising urgent ethical questions that there may be some things that men should never do. The good things that men do can be made complete only by the things they refuse to do."

Yet if there is one lesson of cloning it is that there is no uniformly accepted way to think about the ethical questions that it elicits, and no agreement, even among the most thoughtful and well-informed commentators, about what is right and what is wrong. Many—but by no means all—theologians tended to condemn the notion of human cloning. Many ethicists were similarly repelled, but others asked instead, who would be harmed, and why are we so sure that harm would ensue? While theologians cited religious traditions and biblical proscriptions, lawyers cited reproductive rights and said it would be very hard to argue that it was illegal to clone oneself. In the meantime, some ethicists said they'd heard from in vitro fertilization clinics, which—operating already outside the usual rules that bind scientists, and looking for paying customers—were extremely interested in investigating cloning.

The diversity of opinions extended even to interpretations of identical passages from the Bible. One priest and Catholic theologian argued from Genesis that cloning would be against God's will. An orthodox rabbi and theologian argued from the same passage that cloning should not be proscribed.

The priest, Albert Moraczewski, of the National Conference of Catholic Bishops, was invited to explain the Catholic point of view by a presidential commission that was asked to make recommendations on whether cloning should be permitted. He began by saying that the cloning of humans would be an affront to human dignity. Then he spoke of the familiar story of Adam and Eve, told in the Book of Genesis, in which God gave humans dominion "over the creatures that swim in the sea, that fly in the air, or that walk the earth." And he spoke of God's order. "The Lord God gave man this order: 'You are free to eat from any of the trees of the garden except the tree of knowledge of good and bad.'"

Moraczewski explained that according to the Catholic interpretation, "Adam   60
and Eve were given freedom in the garden but with one limitation, which if transgressed would lead to death. Accordingly, human beings have been granted intelligence and free will so that human beings can search for, and recognize, the truth and freely pursue the good."

Cloning, he said, would exceed "the limits of the delegated dominion given to the human race. There is no evidence that humans were given the power to alter their nature or the manner in which they come into existence."

He added that couples who clone a child would be dehumanizing the act of procreating and treating their child as an object, attempting to "design and control the very identity of the child."

Moraczewski concluded by quoting John Paul II: "The biological nature of every person is untouchable."

The next day, Moshe Tendler, an Orthodox Jewish rabbi, spoke to the commission. He, too, started with Genesis, and with the same quotation. But his interpretation of it, from the Jewish tradition, was very different.

"This knowledge of good and evil has always confused theologians and cer-   65
tainly the layman," Tendler said. "If Adam and Eve did not know of good and evil, how could they have sinned? They knew good and evil. The tree of good and evil is the tree that allows you to think that you can reevaluate, you can set another yardstick for what is good and what is evil."

The Jewish tradition says that humans are obliged to help master our world, according to Tendler, as long as they do not transgress into areas where they would attempt to contravene God. It would not be in character with the Jewish tradition to have a technology that could have outcomes that are good—like preserving the family line of a Holocaust survivor who had no other living relatives—and decide, ahead of time, not to use it for fear of its evil consequences. "We are bound by good and evil as given to us by divine imperative. And we knew pretty well in most areas what is good and what is evil until cloning came along and now we are not so sure what is good and what is evil.

"So, cloning, it is not intrinsically good or evil," Tendler said. The question, really, is whether particular applications of cloning might be a transgression by humans into the domain of God.

"I will give you a simile or metaphor of a guest invited to your house," Tendler said. "You ask them to be comfortable, help themselves, there is cake in the cake box and fruits in the refrigerator, and coffee in the coffeemaker." When you wake up, he continued, you're pleased to see that your guest did as you suggested. "But if he should move your sofa to the other side of the wall because he thought that that is where it really belongs, you will not invite him again."

God, Tendler added, says, "Make yourselves comfortable in my world, but you are guests in my house, do not act as if you own the place. Don't you rearrange my furniture."

He spoke also of a metaphor from the Talmud. "The question was posed, 'Is there not a time when you say to the bee, neither your honey nor your sting?'" And so, he asked, are we really prepared to ban cloning, to give up the honey, because we are so afraid of the sting?

On the other hand, some wonder whether we might not want to squash the bee. Nancy Duff, a theologian at the Princeton Theological Seminary, argued from Protestant tradition that, at the very least, all thoughts of human cloning should be put on hold. "Many people wonder if this is a miracle for which we can thank God, or an ominous new way to play God ourselves," she said. "At the very least, it represents the ongoing tension between faith and science."

But there is also a secular point of view, one that asks how persuasive, after all, are the hypothetical harms of cloning, and whether they are great enough to override the right that people have to reproductive freedom. John Robertson, a law professor at the University of Texas in Austin, who specializes in ethics and reproductive law, said he is unconvinced by those who argue that cloning is somehow too unnatural, too repugnant, too contrary to the laws of God, to proceed with. "In assessing harm, deviation from traditional methods of reproduction, including genetic selection of offspring characteristics, is not in itself a compelling reason for restriction when tangible harm to others is nor present." He argued that cloning is not significantly different from other methods our society now accepts as ethical, and which are now being actively studied in research laboratories throughout the world. He referred to methods for adding genes or correcting faulty ones, in an attempt to cure diseases like muscular dystrophy or cystic fibrosis, which, although not yet possible, is expected to occur before too long.

"Cloning enables a child with the genome of another embryo or person to be born," Robertson said. "The genome is taken as it is. Genetic alteration, on the other hand, will change the genome of a person who could have been born with their genome intact." So what is the greater intervention? Given a choice of a child who is a clone or no child at all—a choice that could befall infertile couples—how bad is it to allow them to have a clone? Robertson asked. "If a loving family will rear the child, it is difficult to see why cloning for genetic selection is per se unacceptable."

A compelling argument, said Daniel Brock, a philosopher and ethicist at Brown University, is the right to clone part of our right to reproductive freedom? he asked. He said that although he is not certain that cloning could be protected in this way because it is not, strictly speaking, reproduction, it might nonetheless fall into that broad category. And, he added, if the right to have yourself cloned is treated as a reproductive right, "that creates the presumption that it should be available to people who want to use it without government control."

Brock, for one, thinks that the public reaction to cloning is overblown. "The various harms are usually speculative," he said. "It is difficult to make the claim that these harms are serious enough and well-enough established to justify overriding the claim that cloning should be available." The public, he said, "has a tendency to want to leap ahead to possibilities that we're not even sure are possible."

Ruth Macklin, an ethicist at Albert Einstein College of Medicine, raised similar questions about whether fears of cloning are reasonable. "One incontestable ethical requirement is that no adult person should be cloned without his or her consent," Macklin said. "But if adult persons sought to have themselves cloned, would the resulting individual be harmed by being brought into existence in this way? One harm that some envisage is psychological or emotional distress to a person who is an exact replica of another. Some commentators have elevated this imagined harm to the level of a right: the right to control our own individual genetic identity. But it is not at all clear why the deliberate creation of an individual who is genetically identical to another living being (but separated in time) would violate anyone's rights."

After all, Macklin said, if the cloned person was not created from the cell of another, he or she would not have been born. Is it really better never to have existed than to exist as a clone? "Evidence, not mere surmise, is required to conclude that the psychological burdens of knowing that one was cloned would be of such magnitude that they would outweigh the benefits of life itself."

Macklin even took on those who argued that cloning violates human dignity. Those who hold that view, she said, "owe us a more precise account of just what constitutes a violation of human dignity if no individuals are harmed and no one's rights are violated. Dignity is a fuzzy concept and appeals to dignity are often used to substitute for empirical evidence that is lacking or sound arguments that cannot be mustered."

Kass argued, however, that such utterly pragmatic language obscures the moral significance of what is being contemplated. He quoted Bertrand Russell: "Pragmatism is like that warm bath that heats up so imperceptibly that you don't know when to scream."

75

The clashing viewpoints, said Ezekiel J. Emanuel, a doctor and ethicist at the   80
Dana-Farber Cancer Institute in Boston, who was a member of the president's
commission that was studying cloning, seem to indicate "a moral values gap." And
so, he added, how people react to cloning "depends a lot on one's world outlook, as
it were. How much you might weigh these other values depends a lot on how you
understand yourself and your place in the world."

And that, in the end, is what cloning brings to the fore. Cloning is a metaphor
and a mirror. It allows us to look at ourselves and our values and to decide what is
important to us, and why.

It also reflects the place of science in our world. Do we see science as a threat
or a promise? Are scientists sages or villains? Have scientists changed over the years
from natural philosophers to technologists focused on the next trick that can be
played on nature?

Freud once said that, sometimes, a cigar is just a cigar. But so far, we have not
reached a point where a clone is just a clone. As the social and cultural history of
cloning continues, the questions and the insights into who we are, who we are becoming, and who we want to be grow ever deeper. Dolly, it now seems, is more a
beginning than an end.

Questions for Discussion and Writing

1. What challenging ethical issues must now be confronted with the birth of
   the world's first successful clone, Dolly, and the cloning of a human embryo
   in November, 2001?
2. How does Kolata's use of statements from a broad range of scientists, ethicists, and religious leaders demonstrate how profoundly important are the
   questions Dolly's birth raises for humanity?
3. Select any of the ethical dilemmas explored in this chapter, and write an
   essay stating your own views on the issue and any hypothetical scenarios you
   can think of that would support your opinion.

ANNE TAYLOR FLEMING

Anne Taylor Fleming (b. 1928) is a journalist and author whose published works include
Motherhood Deferred: A Woman's Journey *(1995),* Sophie Is Gone *(1996) and* This
Means Mischief *(1997). Her first work of fiction,* Marriage: A Duet—*two novellas—will be
published in 2002. She has also written numerous articles for* Glamour, Vogue, Newsweek,
The New Yorker, *and* Woman's Day *and can be heard as a commentator on National Public
Radio (NPR) and seen on* The NewsHour *with Jim Lehrer on PBS. The following essay first
appeared in* The New York Times *(1994).*

Sperm in a Jar

On a beautiful spring day in 1988 I am driving down the Santa Monica freeway with a jar of my sixty-year-old husband's sperm in my purse, en route to the
Institute for Reproductive Research at the Hospital of the Good Samaritan in

downtown Los Angeles. He is at home sleeping after having yielded up this specimen, and I am gingerly maneuvering through the heavy morning traffic with my stash, careful not to swerve or speed lest I upset my cargo or get stopped by a cop.

This is what we have come to, after sixteen years of marriage: this clinical breeding. Oh, my, how did I get here? I ask myself as I park the car, surrender the sperm to the lab technician, and take my place in the waiting room. What quirk of fate, of timing, of biology, has brought me to this clinic, presided over by Dr. Richard Marrs, one of the new crop of infertility experts who do the procreative bidding of those of us who cannot do it on our own? A soft-spoken forty-year-old Texan with a specialty in reproductive endocrinology, Dr. Marrs spouts abbreviations for all the out-of-body pregnancy procedures—I.V.F. (in-vitro fertilization), GIFT (gamete intra-Fallopian transfer), ZIFT (zygote intra-Fallopian transfer), IUI (intra-uterine insemination), ITI (intertubal insemination)—with optimism and assurance. His waiting room is full of anxious women from all over the country, from all over the world.

I am one of them, this sisterhood of the infertile. At thirty-eight, I have entered the high-tech world of postsexual procreation. As I look around at the other women—some in blue jeans, like me, some in suits en route to work, just stopping by to get a shot of sperm before heading out to do battle in corporate America—I smile a small, repressed smile at them and for them. We have sailed together into a strange, surreal country, the Country of the Disembodied Procreators, mutually dedicated to practicing biological warfare against our very own bodies in the hope of reversing time, cheating fate, and getting our hands on an embryo, a baby, a life.

We're hard-core, those of us here. Last-ditchers. And there's a kind of stubborn, exhilarating pride radiating from us. No wimps, we. Toting our small white paper bags of hypodermic needles and hundreds of dollars' worth of fertility drugs, we shoot up once or twice daily with the expertise of junkies, our hips tight and swollen like cheeks with wads of tobacco in them. We are fearless, Amazonian in our baby hunger, bereft. The small waiting room vibrates with our hope.

"Anne."   5

I go into an examining room, strip from the waist down and take my place in the stirrups. The doctor appears. Boyish and solicitous, his hair beginning to gray like that of many of his patients, he is perfectly cast for his role as procreative assistant to a bunch of desperate women. Gently he inserts the dildo-like scanner and, voilà, my ovaries appear as if by magic on the grainy screen next to me. The doctor and I count together: One, two, three, on the left side; one, two, on the right.

"You have the ovaries of a twenty-five-year-old," he says, reaching for the syringe of my husband's sperm, now washed and sorted and counted. And with one deft whoosh through a thin catheter inserted up through my vagina and cervix, the sperm are sent spinning into my uterus.

I feel nothing, no pain; but strangely enough, tears hover. There is something in the matter-of-fact gentleness with which the doctor folds my legs back up off the stirrups that affects me, a reminder of touch and flesh, normal procreation instead of this cold, solo breeding. I hold the tears until the doctor leaves. In my supine position, which I must maintain for at least fifteen minutes, I imagine the sperm settling in, looking around after their frantic, accelerated journey. I implore my eggs to make their move, to come down my Fallopian tubes into the sperm's frenzied midst, there to be pursued and penetrated.

I drift into a reverie, remembering being pursued and won and indeed penetrated myself as a young college girl in Northern California in the late 1960s. I remember the wonderfully sticky smells that hung over those years, an erotic brew of sweat and incense and marijuana. I remember the aromatic afternoons in bed in my small dorm room, the sun filtering in through the redwoods, the light filigreed across our skin and the spines of my books—Rousseau[1] and Thoreau[2] and Marx[3] and Marcuse.[4] From a record player down the hall Janis Joplin wailed about freedom. A cocoon of passion and politics, of pine trees and patchouli oil. Armed with my contraceptives and my fledgling feminism, I was on the cusp of a fabulous journey. My sisters and I were. We were the golden girls of the brave new world, ready, willing and able to lay our contraceptively endowed bodies across the chasm between the feminine mystique and the world the feminists envisioned. Strong, smart, educated, we were the beneficiaries of unique historical timing, when the doors were opening, the old male-female roles were falling and the world was ours to conquer: the world of men, of lawyers and doctors, astronauts and poets. I wanted in that world. I wanted to matter. I wanted to be somebody. I wanted to send dazzling words out into that world.

Babies didn't cross my mind back then. And not for a long, long time after. I took contraception for granted: birth-control pills briefly in my late teens, then a diaphragm. It became not only a fixed part of my body but also a fixed part of my mind—entrenched, reflexive, the ticket to my female freedom. Not for me an unexpected pregnancy, the fate of women throughout the millennia. 10

In the early 1970s, when my husband, Karl, whispered above me about wanting to have a baby, I shrank from his ardor. I couldn't imagine it, didn't even feel the connection between lovemaking and baby making, so methodically had I put contraception—and ambition—between my womb and pregnancy. I had been adamant, powerful in my rebuff of the sperm ejaculated into my body, the sperm I am now importuning to do its fertilizing dance.

After all those years of sex without procreation, here I lie, engaged in this procreation without sex. It is a stunning reversal, a cosmic joke. It contains my history, that arc—from all that sex to no sex—a lifetime of trying to be somebody, my whole own woman in the latter half of twentieth-century America, a lifetime of holding motherhood at bay. The nurse gently knocks and I am released. On the

---

[1] *Rousseau, Jean Jacques (1712–1778):* Swiss-French philosopher and political theorist, whose theory of the "natural man," stated in *Émile* (1762), shaped 19th-century romanticism. [2] *Thoreau, Henry David (1817–1862):* American naturalist, most famous for his work *Walden* (1854). [3] *Marx, Karl (1818–1883):* German social philosopher and originator of communist doctrines. [4] *Marcuse, Herbert (1898–1979):* American political philosopher, best known for *Eros and Civilization* (1954), a synthesis of Marxist and Freudian theory.

freeway heading home, I am already beginning the fourteen-day countdown to the pregnancy test—am I am I not; am I, am I not—a moment-by-moment monitoring, an imaginary ear to the womb intent on picking up any uterine sign of life.

In my hope and in my angst, I am tempted to roll down the window and shout: "Hey, hey, Gloria![5] Germaine![6] Kate![7] Tell us: How does it feel to have ended up without babies, children, flesh of your flesh? Did you mean to thumb your noses at motherhood, or is that what we heard or intuited for our own needs? Simone, Simone de Beauvoir[8] and Virginia Woolf,[9] can you wade in here too, please, share any regrets, my barren heroines from the great beyond? Tell me: Was your art worth the empty womb—predicated on it, in fact—no children to divert attention, to splinter the focus? Can you tell me, any of you: Am I going to get over this?"

The clouds do not part; no feminist goddess peers down with a benediction on my emptiness. I am on my own here, an agnostic midlife feminist sending up silent prayers to the fertility gods on high. (I also send up apologies to the mothers of yore, the station-wagon moms with their postpartum pounds who felt denigrated in the liberationist heyday by the young, lean, ambitious women like me so intent on making our way.) In my most aggrieved moments I think of infertility as comeuppance for having so fervently and so long delayed motherhood. The data are irrefutable: Fertility declines with age.

How could something as primal as this longing to procreate have been so long repressed, so long buried? Not only am I infertile but, worse, a cliché, a humbled renegade haunting the national imagination, held up as some sort of dupe of feminism, rather a double dupe of the sexual revolution and the women's revolution.   15

I will persevere in this pregnancy quest. I know that about myself. And as I turn into the driveway I breathe a pride-filled sigh. I can manage this. If it doesn't work this time, I will try again next month and the next. I will be optimistic, as dogged in my pursuit of motherhood as in everything else: Our Lady of the Stirrups, shooting up and running up and down the smoggy L.A. freeways with jars of sperm if need be.

Dr. Marrs and I are having our procreative postmortem. It has been only a matter of months, but it seems a thousand years ago that I was here. After countless inseminations and surgical procedures, I still do not have a baby. He says the only thing left to offer women like me is—and I almost want to cover my ears because I know full well what's coming—those damn donor eggs. That's the panacea now for us older women who aren't getting pregnant even with high-tech intervention. Am I willing to buy eggs from another woman to make embryos with my hus-

---

[5] Refers to Gloria Steinem (b. 1934), American journalist and feminist, the founding editor of *Ms.* magazine.   [6] Refers to Germaine Greer (b. 1939), Australian writer whose *The Female Eunuch* (1970) made her a leading spokeswoman for feminism.   [7] Refers to Kate Millet (b. 1937), the author of *Sexual Politics* (1970), a landmark in feminist scholarship.   [8] Simone de Beauvoir (1908–1986): prominent French novelist and essayist, pioneer of the women's movement and author of the influential *The Second Sex* (translated into English in 1953).   [9] *Virginia Woolf (1882–1941):* English author who greatly influenced the nineteenth-century novel. Her *A Room of One's Own* (1929) was a leading feminist work.

band's sperm and carry them as my own—if I can carry them? This is a daunting new edge to dance on somehow,

He says the odds for donor eggs on an I.V.F. or GIFT procedure go as high as a 25 to 33 percent success rate per cycle, no matter the recipient's age. Big, fat, juicy odds from where I'm sitting. So, are eggs and sperm totally analogous finally, equally purchasable? Is this the logical reduction of liberation, this absolute biological equality?

It strikes me as conceptual hanky-panky—my husband's sperm and another woman's egg. I imagine a stranger floating in my amniotic fluid. What do I tell this child, and when? Ninety percent of the couples who buy eggs do so anonymously, I am told—most clinics won't do otherwise—the same way couples have been buying sperm for so many years. They simply pretend to all concerned that the baby is 100 percent genetically theirs.

Can I do that, be matched up with a woman whose physical characteristics approximate mine and just carry the conceit on to the grave? No. I would have to know that down the road my child could see and meet his or her biological mother. I get dizzy with the moral and emotional ramifications of this. But I am not ready to shut the door, especially since doctors can work their magic even on postmenopausal women. Still, do I really want to be a fifty-year-old first-time mother? 20

Isn't that finally beyond the limit, procreating in the final trimester of life? Do I want it so bad—to have someone, anyone, doing somersaults in my gut? I can't answer. In fact, there is one other alternative that will allow me my own embryo—not a pregnancy but an embryo. Gestational surrogacy. Rent-a-womb.

A friend of proven fertility has offered to try to carry my embryos for me. It is one of those offers that transcends love. Why not? I can make them, that we know; and she can certainly carry them, or at least has carried her own. But in an offhand moment she says ebulliently, "I'll breast feed them too for a few days, just to get them started,'" and something in me tenses despite the overweening generosity of her offer.

My babies? You will breast feed my babies? And in that instant I have a sharp inkling of how fine the lines are in all this talk of scrambled eggs and borrowed wombs.

In the meantime, I mourn. Karl doesn't really. We have survived. As the father of four grown sons, he feels no stubborn need for our baby, as I do, as the younger husbands of my friends do. His detachment is faintly annoying but mostly restful.

For me now, it's over, and I set about, as is my writer's wont, trying to reckon with all the mixed messages and complicated choices faced by women over the last decades, looking for clues always to my delayed and unconsummated motherhood. True, those bedeviling baby-making possibilities remain, and I toss them around in the days and weeks and months after I have officially declared my independence from Dr. Marrs and his seductive magic. But I don't begrudge anyone else's choices. Going through this, with all the disapproval from various quarters—friend and foe, feminist and counterfeminist—I am aware of how lonely some decisions can be. 20

Questions for Discussion and Writing

1. The range of choices available to Fleming dramatizes the impact of technology on our society. Yet Fleming is clearly ambivalent about the trade-offs involved in being a woman of today. Why?
2. How does the background information Fleming tells us about herself make her predicament symbolic of a whole era in American culture?
3. In choosing whether to have a child using new birth technologies, which procedures would be acceptable to you and which would you reject and why? Would you feel comfortable in being able to select the sex of your child? Why or why not?

CONSTANCE HOLDEN

Constance Holden, born in 1941, is a writer for Science *magazine, whose column "News and Comment" discusses the implications of issues in the forefront of scientific research. Holden is particularly interested in questions about the relationship between mind and body. "Identical Twins Reared Apart," from* Science *(March 1980), reports on a comparative study, conducted by Thomas J. Bouchard at the University of Minnesota, which pointed to the importance of heredity rather than environment in shaping human behavior. Holden develops a point-by-point comparison of the striking similarities in behavior between nine sets of identical twins who were separated at birth, reared in different environments, and then brought together.*

Identical Twins Reared Apart

Bridget and Dorothy are 39-year-old British housewives, identical twins raised apart who first met each other a little over a year ago. When they met, to take part in Thomas Bouchard's twin study at the University of Minnesota, the manicured hands of each bore seven rings. Each also wore two bracelets on one wrist and a watch and a bracelet on the other. Investigators in Bouchard's study, the most extensive investigation ever made of identical twins reared apart, are still bewitched by the seven rings. Was it coincidence, the result of similar influences, or is this small sign of affinity a true, even inevitable, manifestation of the mysterious and infinitely complex interaction of the genes the two women have in common?

Investigators have been bemused and occasionally astonished at similarities between long-separated twins, similarities that prevailing dogma about human behavior would ordinarily attribute to common environmental influences. How is it, for example, that two men with significantly different upbringings came to have the same authoritarian personality? Or another pair to have similar histories of endogenous depression? Or still another pair to have virtually identical patterns of headaches?

These are only bits and pieces from a vast amount of data, none of it yet analyzed, being collected by the University of Minnesota twin study that began last March. So provocative have been some of the cases that the study has already received much attention in the press, and it is bound to get a lot more. The investigation is extremely controversial, aimed, as it is, directly at the heart of the age-old debate about heredity versus environment. Identical twins reared apart have been objects of scrutiny in the past, notably in three studies conducted in England, Denmark, and the United States. An indication of the sensitivity of this subject is the fact that the last one in this country was completed more than 40 years ago,[1] although the rarity of cases has also made this type of research rather exotic. The Minnesota investigators, however, have been able to locate more twin pairs than they expected. So far they have processed nine pairs of identical or monozygotic twins (as well as several pairs of fraternal or dizygotic twins used as controls) and, owing to the publicity given the project, have managed to locate 11 additional pairs to take part in the study.

The Minnesota study is unprecedented in its scope, using a team of psychologists, psychiatrists, and medical doctors to probe and analyze every conceivable aspect of the twins' life histories, medical histories and physiology, tastes, psychological inclinations, abilities, and intelligence. It began when Bouchard, a psychologist who specializes in investigating individual differences, heard of a pair of twins separated from birth, both coincidentally named Jim by their adoptive families, who were reunited at the age of 39. Bouchard did not have to look far to set up his study team, as Minnesota is a hotbed of twin research. There, ready to go to work, were Irving Gottesman, a behavioral geneticist who has spent his career studying twins and whose particular interest is the etiology of schizophrenia; psychologist David Lykken, who has been looking at the brain waves of twins for 10 years, psychologist Auke Tellegen, who recently completed a new personality questionnaire that is being used on the twins; and psychiatrist Leonard Heston, who has studied heritability of mental disorders with adopted children.

Bouchard has taken an eclectic approach in developing the battery of exercises through which the twins are run. Each pair goes through 6 days of intensive testing. In addition to detailed medical histories including diet, smoking, and exercise, the twins are given electrocardiograms, chest x-rays, heart stress tests, and pulmonary exams. They are injected with a variety of substances to determine allergies. They are wired to electroencephalographs to measure their brain wave responses to stimuli in the form of tones of varying intensity, and given other psychophysiological tests to measure such responses as reaction times. Several handedness tests are given to ascertain laterality.

The physiological probes are interspersed with several dozen pencil-and-paper tests, which over the week add up to about 15,000 questions; these cover family and childhood environment, fears and phobias, personal interests, vocational interests, values, reading and TV viewing habits, musical interests, aesthetic judgement tests, and color preferences. They are put through three comprehensive

---

[1] A. H. Newman, F. N. Freeman, and K. J. Holzinger wrote up their study of 19 twin pairs in a 1937 book, *Twins: A Study of Heredity and Environment.*

psychological inventories. Then there is a slew of ability tests: the Wechsler Adult Intelligence Scale (the main adult IQ test) and numerous others that reveal skills in information processing, vocabulary, spatial abilities, numerical processing, mechanical ability, memory, and so forth. Throughout the 6 days there is much overlap and repetition in the content of questions, the intent being to "measure the same underlying factor at different times," says Bouchard. Mindful of charges of investigator bias in the administration of IQ tests in past twin studies, Bouchard has contracted with outside professionals to come in just for the purpose of administering and scoring the Wechsler intelligence test.

And the upshot of all this probing? Although the data have not yet been interpreted, there have already been some real surprises. Bouchard told *Science:* "I frankly expected far more differences [between twins] than we have found so far. I'm a psychologist, not a geneticist. I want to find out how the environment works to shape psychological traits." But the most provocative morsels that have so far become available are those that seem to reveal genetic influences at work.

Take the "Jim twins," as they have come to be known. Jim Springer and Jim Lewis were adopted as infants into working-class Ohio families. Both liked math and did not like spelling in school. Both had law enforcement training and worked part-time as deputy sheriffs. Both vacationed in Florida, both drove Chevrolets. Much has been made of the fact that their lives are marked by a trail of similar names. Both had dogs named Toy. Both married and divorced women named Linda and had second marriages with women named Betty. They named their sons James Allan and James Alan, respectively. Both like mechanical drawing and carpentry. They have almost identical drinking and smoking patterns. Both chew their fingernails down to the nubs.

But what investigators thought "astounding" was their similar medical histories. In addition to having hemorrhoids and identical pulse and blood pressure and sleep patterns, both had inexplicably put on 10 pounds at the same time in their lives. What really gets the researchers is that both suffer from "mixed headache syndrome"—a combination tension headache and migraine. The onset occurred in both at the age of 18. They have these late-afternoon headaches with the same frequency and same degree of disability, and the two used the same terms to describe the pain.

The twins also have their differences. One wears his hair over his forehead, the other has it slicked back with sideburns. One expresses himself better orally, the other in writing. But although the emotional environments in which they were brought up were different, the profiles on their psychological inventories were much alike.

Another much-publicized pair are 47-year-old Oskar Stöhr and Jack Yufe. These two have the most dramatically different backgrounds of all the twins studied. Born in Trinidad of a Jewish father and a German mother, they were separated shortly after birth. The mother took Oskar back to Germany, where he was raised as a Catholic and a Nazi youth by his grandmother. Jack was raised in the Caribbean, as a Jew, by his father, and spent part of his youth on an Israeli kibbutz. The two men now lead markedly different lives. Oskar is an industrial supervisor in

10

Germany, married, a devoted union man, a skier. Jack runs a retail clothing store in San Diego, is separated, and describes himself as a workaholic.

But similarities started cropping up as soon as Oskar arrived at the airport. Both were wearing wire-rimmed glasses and mustaches, both sported two-pocket shirts with epaulets. They share idiosyncrasies galore: they like spicy foods and sweet liqueurs, are absentminded, have a habit of falling asleep in front of the television, think it's funny to sneeze in a crowd of strangers, flush the toilet before using it, store rubber bands on their wrists, read magazines from back to front, dip buttered toast in their coffee. Oskar is domineering toward women and yells at his wife, which Jack did before he was separated. Oskar did not take all the tests because he speaks only German (some are scheduled to be administered to him in German), but the two had very similar profiles on the Minnesota Multi-phastic Personality Inventory (the MMPI was already available in German). Although the two were raised in different cultures and speak different languages, investigator Bouchard professed himself struck by the similarities in their mannerisms, the questions they asked, their "temperament, tempo, the way they do things"—which are, granted, relatively intangible when it comes to measuring them. Bouchard also thinks the two supply "devastating" evidence against the feminist contention that children's personalities are shaped differently according to the sex of those who rear them, since Oskar was raised by women and Jack by men.

Other well-publicized twin pairs are Bridget and Dorothy, the British housewives with the seven rings, and Barbara and Daphne, another pair of British housewives. Both sets are now in their late 30's and were separated during World War II. Bridget and Dorothy are of considerable interest because they were raised in quite different socioeconomic settings—the class difference turns out mainly to be reflected in the fact that the one raised in modest circumstances has bad teeth. Otherwise, say the investigators, they share "striking similarities in all areas," including another case of coincidence in naming children. They named their sons Richard Andrew and Andrew Richard, respectively, and their daughters Catherine Louise and Karen Louise. (Bouchard is struck by this, as the likelihood of such a coincidence would seem to be lessened by the fact that names are a joint decision by husband and wife.) On ability and IQ tests the scores of the sisters were similar, although the one raised in the lower class setting had a slightly higher score.

The other British twins, Daphne and Barbara, are fondly remembered by the investigators as the "giggle sisters." Both were great gigglers, particularly together, when they were always setting each other off. Asked if there were any gigglers in their adoptive families, both replied in the negative. The sisters also shared identical coping mechanisms in the face of stress: they ignored it, managed to "read out" such stimuli. In keeping with this, both flatly avoided conflict and controversy—neither, for example, had any interest in politics. Such avoidance of conflict is "classically regarded as learned behavior," says Bouchard. Although the adoptive families of the two women were not terribly different, "we see more differences within families than between these two."

Only fragmentary information is available so far from the rest of the nine sets of twins, but it supplies abundant food for new lines of inquiry. Two 57-year-old women, for example, developed adult-onset diabetes at the same time in their lives. One of a pair of twins suffers from a rare neurological disease that has always been thought to be genetic in origin. Another area where identical twins differ is in their allergies.

Psychiatrically, according to Heston, who conducts personal interviews with all the twins, there has been remarkable agreement. "Twins brought up together have very high concordance in psychiatric histories," he says. (For example, if one identical twin has schizophrenia, the other one stands a 45 percent chance of developing it.) But what is surprising is that "what we see [with the twins in the study] is pretty much the same as in twins brought up together." By and large, he says, they share very similar phobias, and he has noted more than one case where both twins had histories of endogenous depression. In one case, twins who had been brought up in different emotional environments—one was raised in a strict disciplinarian household, the other had a warm, tolerant, loving mother—showed very similar neurotic and hypochondriacal traits. Says Heston, "things that I would never have thought of—mild depressions, phobias—as being in particular genetically mediated . . . now, at least, there are grounds for a very live hypothesis" on the role of genes not only in major mental illnesses, where chemistry clearly plays a part, but in lesser emotional disturbances.

Other odds and ends:

Two men brought up in radically different environments—one an uneducated manual laborer, the other highly educated and cosmopolitan—turned out to be great raconteurs. (They did, however, have very different IQ scores. The numbers are confidential but the difference was close to the largest difference on record for identical twins, 24 points.)

One of the greatest areas of discordance for twins was smoking. Of the nine pairs, there were four in which one twin smoked and the other did not. No one has an explanation for this. But, surprisingly, in at least one case a lifelong heavy smoker came out just as well on the pulmonary exam and heart stress test as did the nonsmoker.

In a couple of cases, one of a twin pair wore glasses and the other did not. But when their eyes were checked, it was found that both members of each pair required the same correction.

In the fascinating tidbit category: One pair of female twins was brought together briefly as children. Each wore her favorite dress for the occasion. The dresses were identical.

What is to be made of all this? As Tellegen warns, any conclusions at this point are "just gossip." The similarities are somehow more fascinating than the differences, and it could well be that the subjective impression they make on the investigators is heavier than is justified. Nonetheless, even the subjective impressions offer fertile grounds for speculation. Bouchard, for example, thinks that the team may discover that identical twins have a built-in penchant for a certain level of physical exertion. The latest pair to visit the laboratory, for example—23-year-old males—both eschew exercise (although both are thin as rails).

Lykken, who does the tests on the twins' central nervous systems, uses the case of the seven rings as an example for one of his tentative ideas. Fondness for rings is obviously not hereditary, but groups of unrelated genes on different chromosomes, producing pretty hands and other characteristics, may combine to result in beringedness. These traits, called idiographic—meaning particular to an individual rather than shared across a population—may not be as much a result of chance as has been thought. "There are probably other traits that are idiographic that may be almost inevitable given the [gene] combinations. . . . More of these unique characteristics than we previously thought may be determined by a particular combination of genes." Lykken adds, "people get so upset when you suggest that the wiring diagram can influence the mind." But to believe otherwise "requires a naïve dualism . . . an assumption that mental events occur independent of the physical substrate."

Such talk begins to sound pretty deterministic, but Lykken insists that when   20
the mass of data has been ordered "there will be material that will make environmentalists very happy and material that will make hereditarians very happy." One thing that will not make the environmentalists happy is the fact that IQ seems to have a high degree of heritability, as indicated by the fact that of all the tests administered to identical twins separately reared, IQ shows the highest concordance. It is even higher than the introversion-extroversion personality trait, a venerable measure in psychological testing that shows higher concordance than other conventional categories such as sense of well-being, responsibility, dominance, and ego strength.

As several investigators mentioned to *Science,* the scores of identical twins on many psychological and ability tests are closer than would be expected for the same person taking the same test twice. Lykken also found this to be true of brain wave tracings, which is probably the most direct evidence that identical twins are almost identically wired. Several researchers also felt that there is something to the idea that identical twins reared apart may be even more similar in some respects than those reared together. The explanation is simple: competition between the two is inevitable; hence if the stronger or taller of the two excels at sports, the other twin, even if equal in inclination and ability, will avoid sports altogether in order not to be overshadowed. Or one twin will choose to be a retiring type in order not to compete with his extroverted sibling. In short, many twins, in the interest of establishing their individuality, tend to exaggerate their differences.

Although the tentativeness of the findings so far must be repeatedly emphasized, at least one of the Minnesota researchers believes it may be safe to hypothesize that only extreme differences in environment result in significant differences between identical twins. Lykken says, after observing so many similarities, that it is tempting to conclude that "native ability will show itself over a broad range" of backgrounds. So either a seriously impoverished or a greatly enriched environment is required "to significantly alter its expression."

Such an idea, if it gained broad acceptance, would have major impacts on social policies. But Bouchard wants to keep his study separate from politics, emphasizing instead that the research is "very much exploratory."

The data, once assembled and analyzed, should provide a gold mine of new hypotheses. If a great many pairs of twins are collected, says Bouchard, they may be able to present the findings quantitatively, otherwise, the findings will be in the form of case histories. Tellegen, however, whose main interest is the methodology, says "we want to invent methods for analyzing traits in an objective manner, so we can get statistically cogent conclusions from a single case." He points out that psychoanalytic theory was developed from intensive study of small numbers of people and that behavioral psychologist B. F. Skinner similarly was able to develop his theories by studying small numbers of animals. Take the twins with the identical headache syndromes: with just one pair of twins the door is opened to a new field of research.

The twin study may also make it clear that estimating the relative contribution of heredity and environment to mental and psychological traits can never be boiled down to percentages. Some people, for example, may have authoritarian personalities no matter what their upbringing; the authoritarianism of others may be directly traceable to their environment. Similarly, with intelligence, some people may be smart or dumb regardless of outside influences, whereas the intelligence of others may be extremely malleable. Theoretically, variations from individual to individual in malleability and susceptibility may be so great that any attempt to make a generalization about the relative contribution of "innate" characteristics to a certain trait across a population would have no meaning.

Twin studies have been regarded with suspicion in some quarters because, according to Gottesman, the behavioral geneticist who worked with James Shields in England, they were "originally used to prove a genetic point of view." The most notorious of these were the studies of Cyril Burt on intelligence of twins reared separately, which were subsequently discredited. But, says Gottesman, "this study is a continuation of the efforts of Shields and Nielson [Niels Juel-Nielsen, a psychiatrist at the University of Odense in Denmark] to challenge received wisdom about the roles of genes and environment." Everyone, observes Gottesman, "seems to have made up their minds one way or the other." With such a dearth of data of the kind that can only be obtained by studying persons with identical genes raised in different environments, people have been free to be as dogmatic as they please.

Bouchard had a devil of a time getting funding for his study. Various probes at the National Institutes of Health were discouraged on the grounds that the study was too multidisciplinary for any institute to embrace it. He finally got some money from the National Science Foundation.

Although the ultimate conclusions of the study may well be susceptible to sensationalizing, Gordon Allen of the National Institute of Mental Health, head of the International Twin Society, does not believe it will find any "new and unique answers." The sample will not be large enough for that, and besides, too few of the twin pairs were reared in environments so radically different as to bring genetically based behavioral similarities into stark relief.

The most solid and unequivocal evidence will be that supplied by the physiological findings. Although the similarities are the most titillating to most observers, it is the discordances that will be the most informative. For any difference

25

between a pair of identical twins is "absolute proof that that is not completely controlled by heredity."

At this point, no one can make any generalizations beyond that made by   30
James Shields, who died last year. Shields wrote that the evidence so far showed
that "MZ [monozygotic] twins do not have to be brought up in the same subtly
similar family environment for them to be alike." He concluded, "I doubt if MZ's
will ever be numerous and representative enough to provide the main evidence
about environment, or about genetics, but . . . they can give unique real-life illustrations of some of the many possible pathways from genes to human behavior—
and so will always be of human and scientific interest."

Questions for Discussion and Writing

1. What types of similarities did researchers discover in studying the nine sets of
   identical twins who were reunited after having been separated at birth and
   reared in different environments? Which set of twins did you find the most
   fascinating—the Jims, Oskar and Jack, Bridget and Dorothy, or Daphne and
   Barbara—and why?
2. In a study of this type, would physiological similarities (such as a predisposi-
   tion to migraine headaches) be more significant than psychological similarities (such as personal taste in clothes, food, colors, etc.)? Why, or why not?
3. How did Holden's article influence your thinking about whether heredity or
   environment is more important in shaping human behavior? Using any one
   set of twins, discuss how the point-by-point similarities in behavior were or
   were not persuasive in establishing the overriding importance of heredity.

CAROL GRUNEWALD

Carol Grunewald is a Times Mirror *newspaper reporter and former editor of the magazine
the* Animal Rights Agenda. *She currently works for the National Humane Society,
Washington, D.C. This essay originally appeared in the January 1991 issue of the* New
Internationalist.

Monsters of the Brave New World

It's probably no accident that some of the most fearsome monsters invented
by the human mind have been composed of body parts of various animal—including human—species.

Ancient and mediaeval mythology teem with "transgenic" creatures who have
served through the ages as powerful symbols and movers of the human subconscious. In Greek mythology the Chimera—a hideous fire-breathing she-monster
with the head of a lion, the body of a goat and a dragon's tail—was darkness incarnate and a symbol of the underworld.

At the beginning of the industrial or technological age, the collective con-sciousness conjured monsters from a new but related fear—the consequences of human interference with nature. Fears of science and technology gone out of con-trol created the stories of *Dr. Jekyll and Mr. Hyde*[1] and *Dr. Frankenstein*[2].

The contemporary monster is apt to be a real human being, but an amoral, so-ciopathic one—a Mengele[3] or an Eichmann[4] who imposes his evil will not in the heat of passion, but in cold detachment.

Deepest Human Fears

Our nightmares, our mythologies, our movies, our real-life monsters reveal   5
many of our deepest human fears: of the unknown, of the unnatural, of science gone berserk and of the dark side of the human psyche. With such an intense sub-liminal heritage, no wonder many people are instinctively wary of the new and revolutionary science of genetic engineering—a science born just 15 years ago but which is already creating its own monsters. They have good reason to be afraid.

The goal of genetic engineering is to break the code of life and to reform and "improve" the biological world according to human specifications. It is the science of manipulating genes either within or between organisms. Genes are the funda-mental and functional units of heredity; they are what make each of us similar to our species but individually different.

There are two astonishing aspects to this new science. For the first time, hu-mankind has the capacity to effect changes in the genetic code of individual or-ganisms which will be passed down to future generations.

Equally startling, humankind now has the ability to join not only various an-imal species that could never mate in nature but also to cross the fundamental bio-logical barriers between plants and animals that have always existed.

Experiments have already produced a few animal monstrosities. "Geeps," part goat, part sheep, have been engineered through the process of cell-fusion—mixing cells of goat and sheep embryos. A pig has been produced whose genetic structure was altered by the insertion of a human gene responsible for producing a growth hormone. The unfortunate animal (nicknamed "super-pig") is so riddled with arthritis she can barely stand, is nearly blind, and prone to developing ulcers and pneumonia. No doubt researchers will create many such debilitated and pain-racked animals until they get it right.

---

[1] *Dr. Jekyll and Mr. Hyde:* a person marked by a dual personality, one aspect of which is good and the other evil, after the protagonist of Robert Louis Stevenson's novel, *The Strange Case of Dr. Jekyll and Mr. Hyde* (1886).   [2] *Dr. Frankenstein:* a person who creates a destructive agency that cannot be con-trolled or brings about the ruin of the creator. A character from the 1818 novel by Mary Shelley. [3] *Josef Mengele (1911–1979):* nicknamed "the angel of death" because of his role in deciding who would live and die at the Auschwitz concentration camp.   [4] *Adolf Eichmann (1906–1962):* German Nazi of-ficial responsible for the killing of millions of Jews during the Holocaust. In 1960, he was hanged for crimes against humanity by the government of Israel.

CUSTOM-DESIGNED CREATURES

Meanwhile, the world's knowledge of genetic engineering is growing apace.   10
Much of what is now only theoretically possible will almost certainly be realized.
With the world's genetic pool at a scientist's disposal, the possibilities are endless. It's
just a matter of time.

But two historic events spurred the growth in what is now referred to as the
"biotech industry." In 1980 the U.S. Supreme Court ruled, in a highly controversial
5–4 vote, that "man-made" micro-organisms can be patented. Then in April 1987,
without any public debate, the U.S. Patent Officer suddenly announced that all
forms of life—including animals but excluding human beings—may be considered
"human inventions." These could qualify as "patentable subject matter," provided
they had been genetically engineered with characteristics not attainable through
classical breeding techniques.

The economic incentives were impossible for researchers and corporations to
resist. The genetic engineering of animals was a biological gold mine waiting to be
exploited. In hope of getting rich off the "inventions," scientists have so far "created" thousands of animals nature could never have made. Now more than 90
patents are pending for transgenic animals, and some 7,000 are pending for genetically engineered plant and animal micro-organisms.

Until now animal rights activists have been the foremost opponents of genetic
engineering. The reason: animals are already the worse for it. Because they are
powerless, animals have always suffered at the hands of humankind. When a new
technology comes along, new ways are devised to exploit them. But genetic engineering represents the most extreme and blatant form of animal exploitation yet.

Genetic engineers do not see animals as they are: inherently valuable, sentient
creatures with sensibilities very similar to ours and lives of their own to live. To
them, animals are mere biological resources, bits of genetic code that can be manipulated at will and "improved" to serve human purposes. They can then be
patented like a new toaster or tennis ball.

In a recent article, the U.S. Department of Agriculture crows that "the face of   15
animal production in the twenty-first century could be . . . broilers blooming to
market size 40 per cent quicker, miniature hens cranking out eggs in double time,
a computer 'cookbook' of recipes for custom-designed creatures."

The trade journal of the American beef industry boasts that in the year 2014
farmers will be able to order "from a Sears-type catalog, specific breeds or mixtures
of breeds of (genetically engineered) cattle identified by a model number and name.
Just like the 2014's new model pick-up truck, new model animals can be ordered
for specific purposes."

A university scientist says, "I believe it's completely feasible to specifically design an animal for a hamburger."

A Canadian researcher speaking at a farmers' convention eagerly tells the
group that "at the Animal Research Institute we are trying to breed animals without legs and chickens without feathers."

Huge profits are to be made from new cows, pigs, chickens and other farm
animals whose genetic scripts will be written and "improved" to grow faster and

leaner on less food and on new foods such as sawdust, cardboard and industrial and human waste.

Researchers have been straining at the bit to design and patent new animal 20 "models" of human disease—living, breathing "tools" who will be experimented to death in the laboratory. Scientists have also created "medicine factories" out of mice by implanting in them human genes for producing human enzymes, proteins and drugs that can be harvested. Cows, sheep and other milk-producing animals have been targeted for further experimentation in this area.

Animals already suffer abominably in intensive-confinement factory farms and laboratories. Genetic manipulations will result in further subjugation of animals and increase and intensify their stress, pain, and mental suffering.

But genetic engineering also imposes risks on wildlife and the environment. Many questions need to be asked. For example, what will happen when genetically-altered animals and plants are released into the environment? Once they're out there we can't get them back. What if they run amok? Carp and salmon are currently engineered to grow twice as large as they do in nature. But will they also consume twice as much food? Will they upset the ecological balance and drive other animal or plant species to extinction?

Indeed, the genetic engineering of animals will almost certainly endanger species and reduce biological diversity. Once researchers develop what is considered to be the "perfect carp" or "perfect chicken" these will be the ones that are reproduced in large numbers. All other "less desirable" species would fall by the wayside and decrease in number. The "perfect" animals might even be cloned— reproduced as exact copies—reducing even further the pool of available genes on the planet.

Such fundamental human control over all nature would force us to view it differently. Which leads us to the most important examination of all: our values.

How Human?

"We need to ask ourselves what are the long term consequences for civiliza- 25 tion of reducing all of life to engineering values." These are the words of Foundation on Economic Trends President Jeremy Rifkin, the leading opponent of genetic engineering in the U.S. Rifkin warns that the effects of new technologies are pervasive. They reach far beyond the physical, deep into the human psyche and affect the well-being of all life on earth.

In the brave new world of genetic engineering will life be precious? If we could create living beings at will—and even replace a being with an exact clone if it died—would life be valued? The patenting of new forms of life has already destroyed the distinction between living things and inanimate objects. Will nature be just another form of private property?

The intermingling of genes from various species, including the human species, will challenge our view of what it means to be human. If we inject human genes into animals, for example, will they become part human? If animal genes are injected into humans will we become more animal? Will the distinctions be lost? And if so, what will the repercussions be for all life?

And will humans be able to create, patent, and thus own a being that is, by virtue of its genes, part human? In other words, how human would a creature have to be in order to be included in the system of rights and protections that are accorded to "full humans" today?

We may already know the answer to that question. Chimpanzees share 99 per cent of our human genetic inheritance, yet nowhere in the world is there a law that prevents these nearly 100-percent human beings from being captured, placed in leg-irons, owned, locked in laboratory and zoo cages and dissected in experiments.

The blurring of the lines between humans and animals could have many interesting consequences. All of us (humans and animals) are really made of the same "stuff" and our genes will be used interchangeably. Since we are already "improving" animals to serve our needs, why not try and improve ourselves as well? With one small step, we could move from animal eugenics to human eugenics and, by means of genetic engineering, make the plans of the Nazis seem bumbling and inefficient. 30

LIFE AS PROPERTY

Finally, who will control life? Genetic technology is already shoring up the mega-multinational corporations and consolidating and centralizing agribusiness. Corporate giants like General Electric, Du Pont, Upjohn, Ciba-Geigy, Monsanto, and Dow Chemical have multibillion-dollar investments in genetic engineering technology. It is becoming increasingly clear that we are placing the well-being of the planet and all its inhabitants in the hands of a technological elite. Our scientists, corporations and military are playing with, and may eventually own, our genes.

The arrogance and foolishness of humankind! With everything on the planet existing just to be used and exploited—with nothing existing without a "reason" and a "use"—where is the joy of life? What is the reason for living?

People and animals are inseparable; our fates are inextricably linked. People are animals. What is good for animals is good for the environment is good for people. What is bad for them is bad for us.

The first line of resistance should be to scrap the patenting of animals. And the release of any genetically altered organisms into the environment should be prohibited.

Finally, we must remember that the mind that views animals as pieces of coded genetic information to be manipulated and exploited at will is the mind that would view human beings in a similar way. People who care about people should listen carefully to what Animals Rights activists and environmentalists have to say about obtaining justice for, and preserving the integrity of, *all* life. 35

Questions for Discussion and Writing

1. How do new capabilities of genetic engineering raise concerns about a new type of abuse of the animals that are used in this research? What concerns does Grunewald have about cross-breeding between laboratory-produced animals and species that exist in nature?
2. How do changes in patent law raise questions about whether corporations should be able to invent and control new life forms? How do the dangers posed by creating a new species with unforeseen characteristics parallel those of eugenics?
3. If you could genetically engineer your children to possess any traits you wished, would you do so, and what would these characteristics be?

UMBERTO ECO

Umberto Eco (b. 1932) is a professor of semiotics at the University of Bologna, Italy. His innovative novels include The Name of the Rose *(1994) and* The Island of the Day Before *(1995). In addition to scholarly works such as* Kant and the Platypus *(1999), Eco has also written collections of popular essays, including* How to Travel with a Salmon *(1995), in which the following essays first appeared. Eco's latest work is* Five Moral Pieces, *translated by Alastair McEwen (2001).*

How Not to Use the Fax Machine and the Cellular Phone

The fax machine is truly a great invention. For anyone still unfamiliar with it, the fax works like this: you insert a letter, you dial the number of the addressee, and in the space of a few minutes the letter has reached its destination. And the machine isn't just for letters: it can send drawings, plans, photographs, pages of complicated figures impossible to dictate over the telephone. If the letter is going to Australia, the cost of the transmission is no more than that of an intercontinental call of the same duration. If the letter is being sent from Milan to Saronno, it costs no more than a directly dialed call. And bear in mind that a call from Milan to Paris, in the evening hours, costs about a thousand lire. In a country like ours, where the postal system, by definition, doesn't work, the fax machine solves all your problems. Another thing many people don't know is that you can buy a fax for your bedroom, or a portable version for travel, at a reasonable price. Somewhere between a million five and two million lire. A considerable amount for a toy, but a bargain if your work requires you to correspond with many people in many different cities.

Unfortunately, there is one inexorable law of technology, and it is this: when revolutionary inventions become widely accessible, they cease to be accessible. Technology is inherently democratic, because it promises the same services to all;

but it works only if the rich are alone in using it. When the poor also adopt technology, it stops working. A train used to take two hours to go from A to B; then the motor car arrived, which could cover the same distance in one hour. For this reason cars were very expensive. But as soon as the masses could afford to buy them, the roads became jammed, and the trains started to move faster. Consider how absurd it is for the authorities constantly to urge people to use public transport, in the age of the automobile; but with public transport, by consenting not to belong to the elite, you get where you're going before members of the elite do.

In the case of the automobile, before the point of total collapse was reached, many decades went by. The fax machine, more democratic (in fact, it costs much less than a car), achieved collapse in less than a year. At this point it is faster to send something through the mail. Actually, the fax encourages such postal communications. In the old days, if you lived in Medicine Hat, and you had a son in Brisbane, you wrote him once a week and you telephoned him once a month. Now, with the fax, you can send him, in no time, the snapshot of his newborn niece. The temptation is irresistible. Furthermore, the world is inhabited by people, in an ever-increasing number, who want to tell you something that is of no interest to you: how to choose a smarter investment, how to purchase a given object, how to make them happy by sending them a check, how to fulfill yourself completely by taking part in a conference that will improve your professional status. All of these people, the moment they discover you have a fax, and unfortunately there are now fax directories, will trample one another underfoot in their haste to send you, at modest expense, unrequested messages.

As a result, you will approach your fax machine every morning and find it swamped with messages that have accumulated during the night. Naturally, you throw them away without having read them. But suppose someone close to you wants to inform you that you have inherited ten million dollars from an uncle in America, but on condition that you visit a notary before eight o'clock: if the well-meaning friend finds the line busy, you don't receive the information in time. If someone *has* to get in touch with you, then, he has to do so by mail. The fax is becoming the medium of trivial messages, just as the automobile has become the means of slow travel, for those who have time to waste and want to spend long hours in gridlocked traffic, listening to Mozart or Dire Straits.

Finally, the fax introduces a new element into the dynamics of nuisance. Until today, the bore, if he wanted to irritate you, paid (for the phone call, the postage stamp, the taxi to bring him to your doorbell). But now you contribute to the expense, because you're the one who buys the fax paper.

How can you react? I have already had letterhead printed with the warning "Unsolicited faxes are automatically destroyed," but I don't think that's enough. If you want my advice, I'd suggest keeping your fax disconnected. If someone has to send you something, he has to call you first and ask you to connect the machine. Of course, this can overload the telephone line. It would be best for the person who has to send a fax to write you first. Then you can answer, "Send your message via fax Monday at 5.05.27 P.M., Greenwich mean time, when I will connect the machine for precisely four minutes and thirty-six seconds."

It is easy to take cheap shots at the owners of cellular phones. But before doing so, you should determine to which of the five following categories they belong.

First come the handicapped. Even if their handicap is not visible, they are obliged to keep in constant contact with their doctor or the 24-hour medical service. All praise, then, to the technology that has placed this beneficent instrument at their service. Second come those who, for serious professional reasons, are required to be on call in case of emergency (fire chiefs, general practitioners, organ-transplant specialists always awaiting a fresh corpse, or President Bush, because if he is ever unavailable, the world falls into the hands of Quayle). For them the portable phone is a harsh fact of life, endured, but hardly enjoyed. Third, adulterers. Finally, for the first time in their lives, they are able to receive messages from their secret lover without the risk that family members, secretaries, or malicious colleagues will intercept the call. It suffices that the number be known only to him and her (or to him and him, or to her and her: I can't think of any other possible combinations). All three categories listed above are entitled to our respect. Indeed, for the first two we are willing to be disturbed even while dining in a restaurant, or during a funeral; and adulterers are very discreet, as a rule.

Two other categories remain. These, in contrast, spell trouble (for us and for themselves as well). The first comprises those persons who are unable to go anywhere unless they have the possibility of chattering about frivolous matters with the friends and relations they have just left. It is hard to make them understand why they shouldn't do it. And finally, if they cannot resist the compulsion to interact, if they cannot enjoy their moments of solitude and become interested in what they themselves are doing at that moment, if they cannot avoid displaying their vacuity and, indeed, make it their trademark, their emblem, well, the problem must be left to the psychologist. They irk us, but we must understand their terrible inner emptiness, be grateful we are not as they are, and forgive them—without, however, gloating over our own superior natures, and thus yielding to the sins of spiritual pride and lack of charity. Recognize them as your suffering neighbor, and turn the other ear.

In the last category (which includes, on the bottom rung of the social ladder, the purchasers of fake portable phones) are those people who wish to show in public that they are greatly in demand, especially for complex business discussions. Their conversations, which we are obliged to overhear in airports, restaurants, or trains, always involve monetary transactions, missing shipments of metal sections, an unpaid bill for a crate of neckties, and other things that, the speaker believes, are very Rockefellerian.

Now, helping to perpetuate the system of class distinctions is an atrocious mechanism ensuring that, thanks to some atavistic proletarian defect, the nouveau riche, even when he earns enormous sums, won't know how to use a fish knife or will hang a plush monkey in the rear window of his Ferrari or put a San Gennaro on the dashboard of his private jet, or (when speaking his native Italian) use English words like "management." Therefore he will not be invited by the Duchesse de Guermantes (and he will rack his brain trying to figure out why not; after all, he has a yacht so long it could almost serve as a bridge across the English Channel).

What these people don't realize is that Rockefeller doesn't need a portable telephone; he has a spacious room full of secretaries so efficient that at the very worst, if his grandfather is dying, the chauffeur comes and whispers something in his ear. The man with power is the man who is not required to answer every call; on the contrary, he is always—as the saying goes—in a meeting. Even at the lowest managerial level, the two symbols of success are a key to the executive washroom and a secretary who asks, "Would you care to leave a message?"

So anyone who flaunts a portable phone as a symbol of power is, on the contrary, announcing to all and sundry his desperate, subaltern position, in which he is obliged to snap to attention, even when making love, if the CEO happens to telephone; he has to pursue creditors day and night to keep his head above water; and he is persecuted by the bank, even at his daughter's First Holy Communion, because of an overdraft. The fact that he uses, ostentatiously, his cellular phone is proof that he doesn't know these things, and it is the confirmation of his social banishment, beyond appeal.

Questions for Discussion and Writing

1. For Eco, what is ironic about the elevated value these gadgets have for us compared with their actual usefulness?
2. Do you agree with Eco's point that people who use cellular phones as a way of displaying their importance are ironically advertising quite the opposite? Explain your answer.
3. In your opinion, should the use of cellular phones be restricted in public places such as theaters and restaurants? Why or why not? Based on your experiences, what effects have the cellular phone and the fax machine had on business and social interactions? What new gadgets (such as the Palm Pilot) have now come to represent status? Write your own Eco-like spoof on one of these.

LynNell Hancock

LynNell Hancock is a journalist and director of the Prudential Fellowship for Children and the News at Columbia University. She has written articles on public education for Newsweek, *where the following essay first appeared in on February 27, 1995. Most recently, she has written* Hands to Work: The Story of Three Families Racing the Welfare Clock *(2002).*

The Haves and the Have-Nots

Aaron Smith is a teenager on the techno track. In America's breathless race to achieve information nirvana, the senior from Issaqua, a middle-class district east of Seattle, has the hardware and hookups to run the route. Aaron and 600 of his fellow students at Liberty High School have their own electronic-mail addresses. They can log on to the Internet every day, joining only about 15 percent of America's schoolchildren who can now forage on their own for documents in European libraries or chat with experts around the world. At home, the 18-year-old e-mails his teachers, when he is not prowling the World Wide Web to track down snowboarding conditions on his favorite Cascade Mountain passes. "We have the newest, greatest thing," Aaron says.

On the opposite coast, in Boston's South End, Marilee Colon scoots a mouse along a grimy Apple pad, playing a Kid Pix game on an old black-and-white terminal. It's Wednesday at a neighborhood center, Marilee's only chance to poke around on a computer. Her mom, a secretary at the center, can't afford one in their home. Marilee's public-school classroom doesn't have any either. The 10-year-old from Roxbury depends on the United South End Settlement Center and its less than state-of-the-art Macs and IBMs perched on mismatched desks. Marilee has never heard of the Internet. She is thrilled to double-click on the stick of dynamite and watch her teddy-bear creation fly off the screen. "It's fun blowing it up," says the delicate fifth grader, twisting a brown ponytail around her finger.

Certainly Aaron was born with a stack of statistical advantages over Marilee. He is white and middle class and lives with two working parents who both have higher degrees. Economists say the swift pace of hightech advances will only drive a further wedge between these youngsters. To have an edge in America's job search, it used to be enough to be well educated. Now, say the experts, it's critical to be digital. Employees who are adept at technology "earn roughly 10 to 15 percent higher pay," according to Alan Krueger, chief economist for the U.S. Labor Department. Some argue that this pay gap has less to do with technology than with industries' efforts to streamline their work forces during the recession. . . . Still, nearly every American business from Wall Street to McDonald's requires some computer knowledge. Taco Bell is modeling its cash registers after Nintendo controls, according to Rosabeth Moss Kanter. The "haves" says the Harvard Business School professor, will be able to communicate around the globe. The "have-nots" will be consigned to the "rural backwater of the information society."

Like it or not, America is a land of inequities. And technology, despite its potential to level the social landscape, is not yet blind to race, wealth and age. The richer the family, the more likely it is to own and use a computer, according to 1993 census data. White families are three times as likely as blacks or Hispanics to have computers at home. Seventy-four percent of Americans making more than $75,000 own at least one terminal, but not even one third of all Americans own computers. A small fraction—only about 7 percent—of students' families subscribe to online services that transform the plastic terminal into a telecommunications port.

At least in public schools, the computer gap is closing. More than half the students have some kind of computer, even if it's obsolete. But schools with the biggest concentration of poor children have the least equipment, according to Jeanne Hayes of Quality Education Data. Ten years ago schools had one computer for every 125 children, according Hayes. Today that figure is one for 12.

Though the gap is slowly closing, technology is advancing so fast, and at such huge costs, that it's nearly impossible for cash-strapped municipalities to catch up.

Seattle is taking bids for one company to wire each ZIP code with fiber optics, so everyone—rich or poor—can hook up to video, audio and other multimedia services. Estimated cost: $500 million. Prosperous Montgomery Country, Md., has an $81 million plan to put every classroom online. Next door, the District of Columbia public schools have the same ambitious plan but less than $1 million in the budget to accomplish it.

New ideas—and demands—for the schools are announced every week. The '90s populist slogan is no longer "A chicken in every pot" but "A computer on every desk." Vice President Al Gore has appealed to the telecommunications industry to cut costs and wire all schools, a task Education Secretary Richard Riley estimates will cost $10 billion. House Speaker Newt Gingrich stumbled into the discussion with a suggestion that every poor family get a laptop from Uncle Sam. Rep. Ed Markey wants a computer sitting on every school desk within 10 years. "The opportunities are enormous," Markey says.

Enormous, yes, but who is going to pay for them? Some successful school projects have relied heavily on the kindness of strangers. In Union City, N.J., school officials renovated the guts of a 100-year-old building five years ago, overhauling the curriculum and wiring every classroom in Christopher Columbus Middle School for high tech. Bell Atlantic provided wiring free and agreed to give each student in last year's seventh-grade class a computer to take home. Even parents, most of whom are South American immigrants, can use their children's computers to e-mail the principal in Spanish. He uses translation software and answers them electronically. The results have shown up in test scores. In a school where 80 percent of the children are poor, reading, math, attendance and writing scores are now the best in the district. "We believe that technology will improve our everyday life," says principal Bob Fazio. "And that other schools will piggyback and learn from us."

Still, for every Christopher Columbus, there are far more schools like Jordan High School in South-Central Los Angeles. Only 30 computers in the school's lab, most of them 12 to 15 years old, are available for Jordan's 2,000 students, many of whom live in the nearby Jordan Downs housing project. "I am teaching these kids on a system that will do them no good in the real world when they get out there," says Robert Doornbos, Jordan's computer-science instructor. "The school system has not made these kids' getting on the Information Highway a priority."

Donkey Kong: Having enough terminals to go around is one problem. But another important question is what the equipment is used for. Not much beyond rote drills and word processing, according to Linda Roberts, a technology consultant for the U.S. Department of Education. A 1992 National Assessment of Educational Progress survey found that most fourth-grade math students were using computers to play games, "like Donkey Kong." By the eighth grade, most math students weren't using them at all.

Many school officials think that access to the Internet could become the most effective equalizer in the educational lives of students. With a modem attached, even most ancient terminals can connect children in rural Mississippi to universities in Asia. A Department of Education report last week found that 35 percent of schools have at least one computer with a modem. But only half the schools let

10

students use it. Apparently administrators and teachers are hogging the Info Highway for themselves.

There is another gap to be considered. Not just between rich and poor, but between the young and the used-to-be-young. Of the 100 million Americans who use computers at home, school or work, nearly 60 percent are 17 or younger, according to the census. Children, for the most part, rule cyberspace, leaving the over-40 set to browse through the almanac.

The gap between the generations may be the most important, says MIT guru Nicholas Negroponte, author of the new book *Being Digital*. Adults are the true "digitally homeless, the needy," he says. In other words, adults like Debbie Needleman, 43, an office manager at Wallpaper Warehouse in Natick, Mass., are wary of the digital age. "I really don't mind that the rest of the world passes me by as long as I can still earn a living," she says.

These aging choose-nots become a more serious issue when they are teachers in schools. Even if schools manage to acquire state-of-the-art equipment, there is no guarantee that trained adults will be available to understand them. This is something that tries Aaron Smith's patience. "A lot of my teachers are quite illiterate," says Aaron, the fully equipped Issaqua teenager. "You have to explain it to them real slow to make sure they understand everything." Fast or slow, Marilee Colon, Roxbury's fifth-grade computer lover, would like her chance to understand everything too.

Questions for Discussion and Writing

1. According to Hancock, although publicized as a democratizing tool, the computer has dramatically separated the haves from the have-nots. What factors determine who has access to this technology?
2. How does Hancock's comparison of schoolchildren dramatize her thesis? Why is she critical of articles that expound on the glories of computer literacy?
3. In your experience, have computers had the kind of democratizing effect that was promised? Why or why not?

BILL GATES

Bill Gates (b. 1956) attended Harvard, where he wrote some of the first computer software programs. In 1975 (with Paul Allen), Gates started the company Microsoft, of which he is the chief executive officer. He is the author of The Road Ahead *(1995), from which the following selection is drawn, and of* Business @ the Speed of Thought: Using a Digital Nervous System *with Collins Hemingway (1999).*

The Road Ahead

I wrote my first software program when I was thirteen years old. It was for playing tic-tac-toe. The computer I was using was huge and cumbersome and slow and absolutely compelling. Letting a bunch of teenagers like me and my friend Paul Allen loose on a computer was the idea of the Mothers' Club at Lakeside, the private school I attended. The mothers decided that the proceeds from a rummage sale should be used to install a terminal and buy computer time for students, a pretty amazing choice at the time in Seattle—and one I'll always be grateful for.

I realized later part of the appeal was that here was an enormous, expensive, grown-up machine and we, the kids, could control it. We were too young to drive or to do any of the other fun-seeming adult activities, but we could give this big machine orders and it would always obey. It's feedback you don't get from many other things. That was the beginning of my fascination with software. And to this day it still thrills me to know that if I can get the program right it will always work perfectly, every time, just the way I told it to.

My parents paid my tuition at Lakeside and gave me money for books, but I had to take care of my own computer-time bills. This is what drove me to the commercial side of the software business. A bunch of us, including Paul, got entry-level software programming jobs. For high school students the pay was extraordinary—about $5,000 each summer, part in cash and the rest in computer time. One of the programs I wrote was the one that scheduled students in classes. I surreptitiously added a few instructions and found myself nearly the only guy in a class full of girls.

As a college sophomore, I stood in Harvard Square with Paul and pored over the description of a kit computer in *Popular Electronics* magazine. As we read excitedly about the first truly personal computer, Paul and I didn't know exactly how it would be used, but we were sure it would change us and the world of computing. We were right. The personal-computer revolution happened and it has affected millions of lives. It has led us to places we had barely imagined.

THE NEXT REVOLUTION

Now that computing is astoundingly inexpensive and computers inhabit every part of our lives, we stand at the brink of another revolution. This one will involve unprecedentedly inexpensive communication; all the computers will join together to communicate with us and for us. Interconnected globally, they will form a network, which is being called the information highway. A direct precursor is the present Internet, which is a group of computers joined and exchanging information using current technology.

The revolution in communications is just beginning. It will take place over several decades, and will be driven by new "applications"—new tools, often meeting currently unforeseen needs. During the next few years, major decisions will have to be made by governments, companies, and individuals. These decisions will have an impact on the way the highway will roll out and how much benefit those deciding will realize. It is crucial that a broad set of people—not just technologists or those

5

who happen to be in the computer industry—participate in the debate about how this technology should be shaped. If that can be done, the highway will serve the purposes users want. Then it will gain broad acceptance and become a reality.

In the United States, the connecting of all these computers has been compared to another massive project: the gridding of the country with interstate highways, which began during the Eisenhower era. This is why the new network was dubbed the "information superhighway." The highway metaphor isn't quite right, though. The phrase suggests landscape and geography, a distance between points, and embodies the implication that you have to travel to get from one place to another. In fact, one of the most remarkable aspects of this new communications technology is that it will eliminate distance. It won't matter if someone you're contacting is in the next room or on another continent, because this highly mediated network will be unconstrained by miles and kilometers.

A different metaphor that I think comes closer to describing a lot of the activities that will take place is that of the ultimate market. Markets from trading floors to malls are fundamental to human society, and I believe this new one will eventually be the world's central department store. It will be where we social animals will sell, trade, invest, haggle, pick stuff up, argue, meet new people, and hang out. Think of the hustle and bustle of the New York Stock Exchange or a farmers' market or of a bookstore full of people looking for fascinating stories and information. All manner of human activity takes place, from billion-dollar deals to flirtations.

The highway will enable capabilities that seem magical when they are described, but represent technology at work to make our lives easier and better. Because consumers already understand the value of movies and are used to paying to watch them, video-on-demand will be an important application on the information highway. It won't be the first, however. We already know that PCs will be connected long before television sets and that the quality of movies shown on early systems will not be very high. The systems will be able to offer other applications such as games, electronic mail, and home banking. When high-quality video can be transmitted, there won't be any intermediary VCR; you'll simply request what you want from a long list of available programs.

Television shows will continue to be broadcast as they are today for synchronous consumption—at the same time they are first broadcast. After they air, these shows—as well as thousands of movies and virtually all other kinds of video—will be available whenever you want to view them. You'll be able to watch the new episode of "Seinfeld" at 9:00 P.M. on Thursday night, or at 9:13 P.M., or at 9:45 P.M., or at 11:00 A.M. on Saturday. If you don't care for his brand of humor, there will be thousands of other choices. Even if a show is being broadcast live, you'll be able to use your infrared remote control to start, stop, or go to any previous part of the program, at any time. If someone comes to your door, you'll be able to pause the program for as long as you like. You'll be in absolute control.

Your television set will not look like a computer and won't have a keyboard, but additional electronics inside or attached will make it architecturally like a PC. Television sets will connect to the highway via a set-top box similar to ones supplied today by most cable TV companies.

A WORLD OF "E-BOOKS"

On the information highway, rich electronic documents will be able to do things no piece of paper can. The highway's powerful database technology will allow them to be indexed and retrieved using interactive exploration. It will be extremely cheap and easy to distribute them. In short, these new digital documents will replace many printed paper ones because they will be able to help us in new ways.

Ultimately, incremental improvements in computer and screen technology will give us a lightweight, universal electronic book or "e-book," which will approximate today's paperback book. Inside a case roughly the same size and weight as today's hardcover or paperback book, you'll have a display that can show high-resolution text, pictures, and video. You'll be able to flip pages with your finger or use voice commands.

The real point of electronic documents is not simply that we will read them on hardware devices. Going from paper book to e-book is just the final stage of a process already well under way. The exciting aspect of digital documentation is the redefinition of the document itself.

By the end of the decade a significant percentage of documents, even in offices, won't even be fully printable on paper. They will be like a movie or a song is today. You will still be able to print a two-dimensional view of its content, but it will be like reading a musical score instead of experiencing an audio recording.

Electronic documents will be interactive. Request a kind of information, and the document responds. Indicate that you've changed your mind, and the document responds again. Once you get used to this sort of system, you find that being able to look at information in different ways makes that information more valuable. The flexibility invites exploration, and the exploration is rewarded with discovery.

You'll be able to get your daily news in a similar way. You'll be able to specify how long you want your newscast to last because you'll be able to have each of the news stories selected individually. The newscast assembled for and delivered only to you might include world news from NBC, the BBC, CNN, or the *Los Angeles Times,* with a weather report from a favorite local TV meteorologist—or from any private meteorologist who wanted to offer his or her own service. You will be able to request longer stories on the subjects that particularly interest you and just highlights on others. If, while you are watching the newscast, you want more than has been put together, you will easily be able to request more background or detail, either from another news broadcast or from file information.

Among all the types of paper documents, narrative fiction is one of the few that will not benefit from electronic organization. Almost every reference book has an index, but novels don't because there is no need to be able to look something up in a novel. Novels are linear. Likewise, we'll continue to watch most movies from start to finish. This isn't a technological judgment—it is an artistic one: Their linearity is intrinsic to the storytelling process.

The success of CD-ROM games has encouraged authors to begin to create interactive novels and movies in which they introduce the characters and the

15

general outline of the plot, then the reader/player makes decisions that change the outcome of the story. No one suggests that every book or movie should allow the reader or viewer to influence its outcome. A good story that makes you just want to sit there for a few hours and enjoy it is wonderful entertainment. I don't want to choose an ending for *The Great Gatsby*[1] or *La Dolce Vita*.[2] F. Scott Fitzgerald and Federico Fellini[3] have done that for me.

Significant investments will be required to develop great on-line content that will delight and excite PC users and raise the number on-line from 10 percent up to 50 percent, or even the 90 percent I believe it will become. Part of the reason this sort of investment isn't happening today is that simple mechanisms for authors and publishers to charge their users or to be paid by advertisers are just being developed. 20

As the fidelity of visual and audio elements improves, reality in all its aspects will be more closely simulated. This "virtual reality," or VR, will allow us to "go" places and "do" things we never would be able to otherwise.

In order to work, VR needs two different sets of technology software that creates the scene and makes it respond to new information, and devices that allow the computer to transmit the information to our senses. The software will have to figure out how to describe the look, sound, and feel of the artificial world down to the smallest detail. That might sound overwhelmingly difficult but actually it's the easy part. We could write the software for VR today, but we need far more computer power to make it truly believable. At the pace technology is moving, though, that power will be available soon.

Inevitably, there has been more speculation (and wishful thinking) about virtual sex than about any other use for VR. Sexually explicit content is as old as information itself. If historical patterns are a guide, a big early market for advanced virtual-reality documents will be virtual sex. But again, historically, as each of these markets grew, explicit material became a smaller and smaller factor.

THE IMPORTANCE OF EDUCATION

More than ever, an education that emphasizes general problem-solving skills will be important. In a changing world, education is the best preparation for being able to adapt. As the economy shifts, people and societies who are appropriately educated will tend to do best. The premium that society pays for skills is going to climb, so my advice is to get a good formal education and then keep on learning. Acquire new interests and skills throughout your life.

Some fear that technology will dehumanize formal education. But anyone who has seen kids working together around a computer, the way my friends and I 25

---

[1] *The Great Gatsby:* 1925 novel acclaimed as a classic depiction of the Roaring Twenties, by American writer F. Scott Fitzgerald (1896–1940).   [2] *La Dolce Vita (1960)*.   [3] *Frederico Fellini (1920–1993):* Italian film director whose works are known for their extravagant visual fantasy.

first did in 1968, or watched exchanges between students in classrooms separated by oceans, knows that technology can humanize the educational environment. The same technological forces that will make learning so necessary will also make it practical and enjoyable. Just as information technology now allows Levi Strauss & Co. to offer jeans that are both mass-produced and custom fitted, information technology will bring mass customization to learning. Multimedia documents and easy-to-use authoring tools will enable teachers to "mass-customize" a curriculum for each student: computers will fine-tune the product—educational material, in this case—to allow students to follow somewhat divergent paths and learn at their own rates.

There is an often-expressed fear that technology will replace teachers. I can say emphatically and unequivocally, IT WON'T. The information highway won't replace or devalue any of the human educational talent needed for the challenges ahead: committed teachers, creative administrators, involved parents, and, of course, diligent students. However, technology will be pivotal in the future role of teachers.

Before the benefits of these advances can be realized, though, the way computers in the classroom are thought about will have to change. A lot of people are cynical about educational technology because it has been overhyped and has failed to deliver on its promises. Many of the PCs in schools today are not powerful enough to be easy to use, and they don't have the storage capacity or network connections to permit them to respond to a child's curiosity with much information.

When teachers do excellent work and prepare wonderful materials now, only their few dozen students benefit each year. The network will enable teachers to share lessons and materials, so that the best educational practices can spread. The interactive network also will allow students to quiz themselves any time, in a risk-free environment. A self-administered quiz is a form of self-exploration. Testing will become a positive part of the learning process. A mistake won't call forth a reprimand; it will trigger the system to help the student overcome his misunderstanding. The highway will also make home schooling easier. It will allow parents to select some classes from a range of quality possibilities and still maintain control over content.

THE IMPACT ON SOCIETY

Just because I'm optimistic doesn't mean I don't have concerns about what is going to happen to all of us. The broad benefits of advancing productivity are no solace for someone whose job is on the line. When a person has been trained for a job that is no longer needed, you can't just suggest he go out and learn something else. Adjustments aren't that simple or fast, but ultimately they are necessary

The fully developed information highway will be affordable—almost by definition. An expensive system that connected a few big corporations and wealthy people simply would not be the information highway—it would be the information private road. The network will not attract enough great content to thrive if only the most affluent 10 percent of society choose to avail themselves of it. There are fixed costs to authoring material; so to make them affordable, a large audience

30

is required. Advertising revenue won't support the highway if a majority of eligible people don't embrace it. If that is the case, the price for connecting will have to be cut or deployment delayed while the system is redesigned to be more attractive. The information highway is a mass phenomenon, or it is nothing.

The net effect will be a wealthier world, which should be stabilizing. Developed nations, and workers in those nations, are likely to maintain a sizable economic lead. However, the gap between the have and have-not nations will diminish. Starting out behind is sometimes an advantage. Those who adopt late skip steps, and avoid the mistakes of the trailblazers. Some countries will never have industrialization but will move directly into the Information Age.

The information highway is going to break down boundaries and may promote a world culture, or at least a sharing of cultural activities and values. The highway will also make it easy for patriots, even expatriates, deeply involved in their own ethnic communities to reach out to others with similar interests no matter where they may be located. This may strengthen cultural diversity and counter the tendency toward a single world culture.

A complete failure of the information highway is worth worrying about. Because the system will be thoroughly decentralized, any single outage is unlikely to have a widespread effect. If an individual server falls, it will be replaced and its data restored. But the system could be susceptible to assault. As the system becomes more important, we will have to design in more redundancy. One area of vulnerability is the system's reliance on cryptography—the mathematical locks that keep information safe. None of the protection systems that exist today, whether steering-wheel locks or steel vaults, are completely fail-safe. The best we can do is make it as difficult as possible for somebody to break in. Still, popular opinions to the contrary, computer security has a very good record.

Loss of privacy is another major concern about the highway. A great deal of information is already being gathered about each of us, by private companies as well as by government agencies, and we often have no idea how it is used or whether it is accurate. As more business is transacted using the highway and the amount of information stored there accrues, governments will consciously set policies regarding privacy and access to information. The potential problem is abuse, not the mere existence of information.

These privacy fears revolve around the possibility that someone else is keeping track of information about you. But the highway will also make it possible for an individual to keep track of his or her own whereabouts—to lead what we might call "a documented life." Your wallet PC will be able to keep audio, time, location, and eventually even video records of everything that happens to you. It will be able to record every word you say and every word said to you, as well as body temperature, blood pressure, barometric pressure, and a variety of other data about you and your surroundings. It will be able to track your interactions with the highway—all of the commands you issue, the messages you send, and the people you call or who call you. The resulting record will be the ultimate diary and autobiography, if you want one.

I find the prospect of documented lives a little chilling, but some people will warm to the idea. One reason for documenting a life will be defensive. If someone ever accused you of something, you could retort: "Hey, buddy, I have a documented life. These bits are stored away. I can play back anything I've ever said. So don't play games with me." Medical malpractice insurance might be cheaper, or only available, for doctors who record surgical procedures or even office visits. I can imagine proposals that every automobile, including yours and mine, be outfitted not only with a recorder but also with a transmitter that identifies the car and its location. If a car was reported stolen, its location would be known immediately. After a hit-and-run accident or a drive-by shooting, a judge could authorize a query: "What vehicles were in the following two-block area during this thirty-minute period?" The black box could record your speed and location, which would allow for the perfect enforcement of speeding laws. I would vote against that.

Even if the model of political decision making does not change explicitly, the highway will bestow power on groups who want to organize to promote causes or candidates. This could lead to an increased number of special-interest groups and political parties. Someone will doubtless propose total "direct democracy," having all issues put to a vote. Personally, I don't think direct voting would be a good way to run a government. There is a place in governance for representatives—middlemen—to add value. They are the ones who understand all the nuances of complicated issues. Politics involves compromise, which is nearly impossible without a relatively small number of representatives making decisions on behalf of the people who elected them.

We are watching something historic happen, and it will affect the world seismically, the same way the scientific method, the invention of printing, and the arrival of the Industrial Age did. Big changes used to take generations or centuries. This one won't happen overnight, but it will move much faster. The first manifestations of the information highway will be apparent in the United States by the millennium. Within a decade there will be widespread effects. If I had to guess which applications of the network will be embraced quickly and which will take a long time, I'd certainly get some wrong. Within twenty years virtually everything I've talked about will be broadly available in developed countries and in businesses and schools in developing countries.

Questions for Discussion and Writing

1. Considering Gates's role as visionary for the software industry, take a close look at his predictions about the transforming effects of the Internet. Which of these predictions have materialized and which have not (since he wrote this piece in 1995)?
2. What aspects of Gates's analysis might be intended to reply to fears about the downside of the electronic revolution?
3. What changes have you observed that Gates does not mention? What do you think "the next technological revolution" will be, and how will it affect our society?

Fiction

JOHN CHEEVER

John Cheever (1912–1982) was born in Quincy, Massachusetts, and never finished his formal education because he was expelled from prep school for smoking. Cheever began his literary career by capitalizing on this event with a sketch in The New Republic *entitled "Expelled." He is best known for his insightful short stories, which reflect the manners and mores of affluent suburban Americans. Collections of his works include* The Enormous Radio *(1953), in which the following story first appeared, and* The Stories of John Cheever *(1978), which won the Pulitzer Prize.*

The Enormous Radio

Jim and Irene Westcott were the kind of people who seem to strike that satis-factory average of income, endeavor, and respectability that is reached by the statis-tical reports in college alumni bulletins. They were the parents of two young children, they had been married nine years, they lived on the twelfth floor of an apartment house near Sutton Place, they went to the theatre on an average of 10.3 times a year, and they hoped someday to live in Westchester. Irene Westcott was a pleasant, rather plain girl with soft brown hair and a wide, fine forehead upon which nothing at all had been written, and in the cold weather she wore a coat of fitch skins dyed to resemble mink. You couldn't say that Jim Westcott looked younger than he was, but you could at least say of him that he seemed to feel younger. He wore his graying hair cut very short, he dressed in the kind of clothes his class had worn at Andover, and his manner was earnest, vehement, and inten-tionally naïve. The Westcotts differed from their friends, their classmates, and their neighbors only in an interest they shared in serious music. They went to a great many concerts—although they seldom mentioned this to anyone—and they spent a good deal of time listening to music on the radio.

Their radio was an old instrument, sensitive, unpredictable, and beyond repair. Neither of them understood the mechanics of radio—or of any of the other appli-ances that surrounded them—and when the instrument faltered, Jim would strike the side of the cabinet with his hand. This sometimes helped. One Sunday after-noon, in the middle of a Schubert quartet, the music faded away altogether. Jim struck the cabinet repeatedly, but there was no response; the Schubert was lost to them forever. He promised to buy Irene a new radio, and on Monday when he came home from work he told her that he had got one. He refused to describe it, and said it would be a surprise for her when it came.

The radio was delivered at the kitchen door the following afternoon, and with the assistance of her maid and the handyman Irene uncrated it and brought it into the living room. She was struck at once with the physical ugliness of the large gum-wood cabinet. Irene was proud of her living room, she had chosen its furnishings and colors as carefully as she chose her clothes, and now it seemed to her that the new radio stood among her intimate possessions like an aggressive intruder. She was confounded by the number of dials and switches on the instrument panel, and she studied them thoroughly before she put the plug into a wall socket and turned the radio on. The dials flooded with a malevolent green light, and in the distance she heard the music of a piano quintet. The quintet was in the distance for only an instant; it bore down upon her with a speed greater than light and filled the apartment with the noise of music amplified so mightily that it knocked a china ornament from a table to the floor. She rushed to the instrument and reduced the volume. The violent force that was snared in the ugly gumwood cabinet made her uneasy. Her children came home from school then, and she took them to the Park. It was not until later in the afternoon that she was able to return to the radio.

The maid had given the children their suppers and was supervising their baths when Irene turned on the radio, reduced the volume, and sat down to listen to a Mozart quintet that she knew and enjoyed. The music came through clearly. The new instrument had a much purer tone, she thought, than the old one. She decided that tone was most important and that she could conceal the cabinet behind a sofa. But as soon as she had made her peace with the radio, the interference began. A crackling sound like the noise of a burning powder fuse began to accompany the singing of the strings. Beyond the music, there was a rustling that reminded Irene unpleasantly of the sea, and as the quintet progressed, these noises were joined by many others. She tried all the dials and switches but nothing dimmed the interference, and she sat down, disappointed and bewildered, and tried to trace the flight of the melody. The elevator shaft in her building ran beside the living-room wall, and it was the noise of the elevator that gave her a clue to the character of the static. The rattling of the elevator cables and the opening and closing of the elevator doors were reproduced in her loudspeaker, and, realizing that the radio was sensitive to electrical currents of all sorts, she began to discern through the Mozart the ringing of telephone bells, the dialing of phones, and the lamentation of a vacuum cleaner. By listening more carefully, she was able to distinguish doorbells, elevator bells, electric razors, and Waring mixers, whose sounds had been picked up from the apartments that surrounded hers and transmitted through her loudspeaker. The powerful and ugly instrument, with its mistaken sensitivity to discord, was more than she could hope to master, so she turned the thing off and went into the nursery to see her children.

When Jim Westcott came home that night, he went to the radio confidently and worked the controls. He had the same sort of experience Irene had had. A man was speaking on the station Jim had chosen, and his voice swung instantly from the distance into a force so powerful that it shook the apartment. Jim turned the volume control and reduced the voice. Then, a minute or two later, the interference began. The ringing of telephones and doorbells set in, joined by the rasp of the elevator doors and the whir of cooking appliances. The character of the noise had changed since Irene had tried the radio earlier; the last of the electric razors was being unplugged, the vacuum cleaners had all been returned to their closets, and

5

the static reflected that change in pace that overtakes the city after the sun goes down. He fiddled with the knobs but couldn't get rid of the noises, so he turned the radio off and told Irene that in the morning he'd call the people who had sold it to him and give them hell.

The following afternoon, when Irene returned to the apartment from a luncheon date, the maid told her that a man had come and fixed the radio. Irene went into the living room before she took off her hat or her furs and tried the instrument. From the loudspeaker came a recording of the "Missouri Waltz." It reminded her of the thin, scratchy music from an old-fashioned phonograph that she sometimes heard across the lake where she spent her summers. She waited until the waltz had finished, expecting an explanation of the recording, but there was none. The music was followed by silence, and then the plaintive and scratchy record was repeated. She turned the dial and got a satisfactory burst of Caucasian music—the thump of bare feet in the dust and the rattle of coin jewelry—but in the background she could hear the ringing of bells and a confusion of voices. Her children came home from school then, and she turned off the radio and went to the nursery.

When Jim came home that night, he was tired, and he took a bath and changed his clothes. Then he joined Irene in the living room. He had just turned on the radio when the maid announced dinner, so he left it on, and he and Irene went to the table.

Jim was too tired to make even a pretense of sociability, and there was nothing about the dinner to hold Irene's interest, so her attention wandered from the food to the deposits of silver polish on the candlesticks and from there to the music in the other room. She listened for a few minutes to a Chopin prelude and then was surprised to hear a man's voice break in. "For Christ's sake, Kathy," he said, "do you always have to play the piano when I get home?" The music stopped abruptly. "It's the only chance I have," a woman said. "I'm at the office all day." "So am I," the man said. He added something obscene about an upright piano, and slammed a door. The passionate and melancholy music began again.

"Did you hear that?" Irene asked.

"What?" Jim was eating his dessert.   10

"The radio. A man said something while the music was still going on—something dirty."

"It's probably a play."

"I don't think it *is* a play," Irene said.

They left the table and took their coffee into the living room. Irene asked Jim to try another station. He turned the knob. "Have you seen my garters?" a man asked. "Button me up," a woman said. "Have you seen my garters?" the man said again. "Just button me up and I'll find your garters," the woman said. Jim shifted to another station. "I wish you wouldn't leave apple cores in the ashtrays," a man said. "I hate the smell."

"This is strange," Jim said.   15

"Isn't it?" Irene said.

Jim turned the knob again. "'On the coast of Coromandel where the early pumpkins blow,'" a woman with a pronounced English accent said, "'in the middle of the woods lived the Yonghy-Bonghy-Bò. Two old chairs, and half a candle, one old jug without a handle. . . .'"

"My God!" Irene cried. "That's the Sweeneys' nurse."

"'These were all his worldly goods,'" the British voice continued.

"Turn that thing off," Irene said. "Maybe they can hear *us*." Jim switched the 20 radio off. "That was Miss Armstrong, the Sweeneys' nurse," Irene said. "She must be reading to the little girl. They live in 17-B. I've talked with Miss Armstrong in the Park. I know her voice very well. We must be getting other people's apartments."

"That's impossible," Jim said.

"Well, that was the Sweeneys' nurse," Irene said hotly. "I know her voice. I know it very well. I'm wondering if they can hear us."

Jim turned the switch. First from a distance and then nearer, nearer, as if borne on the wind, came the pure accents of the Sweeneys' nurse again: "'*Lady Jingly! Lady Jingly!*'" she said, "'*sitting where the pumpkins blow, will you come and be my wife?* said the Yonghy-Bonghy-Bò. . . .'"

Jim went over to the radio and said "Hello" loudly into the speaker.

"'*I am tired of living singly,*'" the nurse went on, "'*on this coast so wild and shingly,* 25 *I'm a-weary of my life; if you'll come and be my wife, quite serene would be my life. . . .*'"

"I guess she can't hear us," Irene said. "Try something else."

Jim turned to another station, and the living room was filled with the uproar of a cocktail party that had overshot its mark. Someone was playing the piano and singing the "Whiffenpoof Song,"[1] and the voices that surrounded the piano were vehement and happy. "Eat some more sandwiches," a woman shrieked. There were screams of laughter and a dish of some sort crashed to the floor.

"Those must be the Fullers, in 11-E," Irene said. "I knew they were giving a party this afternoon. I saw her in the liquor store. Isn't this too divine? Try something else. See if you can get those people in 18-C."

The Westcotts overheard that evening a monologue on salmon fishing in 30 Canada, a bridge game, running comments on home movies of what had apparently been a fortnight at Sea Island, and a bitter family quarrel about an overdraft at the bank. They turned off their radio at midnight and went to bed, weak with laughter. Sometime in the night, their son began to call for a glass of water and Irene got one and took it to his room. It was very early. All the lights in the neighborhood were extinguished, and from the boy's window she could see the empty street. She went into the living room and tried the radio. There was some faint coughing, a moan, and then a man spoke. "Are you all right, darling?" he asked. "Yes," a woman said wearily. "Yes, I'm all right, I guess," and then she added with great feeling, "But, you know, Charlie, I don't feel like myself any more. Sometimes there are about fifteen or twenty minutes in the week when I feel like myself. I don't like to go to another doctor, because the doctor's bills are so awful already, but

---

[1] *"The Whiffenpoof Song":* song originally written in 1909 for The Whiffenpoofs, the undergraduate glee club at Yale.

I just don't feel like myself, Charlie. I just never feel like myself." They were not young, Irene thought. She guessed from the timbre of their voices that they were middle-aged. The restrained melancholy of the dialogue and the draft from the bedroom window made her shiver, and she went back to bed.

The following morning, Irene cooked breakfast for the family—the maid didn't come up from her room in the basement until ten—braided her daughter's hair, and waited at the door until her children and her husband had been carried away in the elevator. Then she went into the living room and tried the radio. "I don't want to go to school," a child screamed. "I hate school. I won't go to school. I hate school." "You will go to school," an enraged woman said. "We paid eight hundred dollars to get you into that school and you'll go if it kills you." The next number on the dial produced the worn record of the "Missouri Waltz." Irene shifted the control and invaded the privacy of several breakfast tables. She overheard demonstrations of indigestion, carnal love, abysmal vanity, faith, and despair. Irene's life was nearly as simple and sheltered as it appeared to be, and the forthright and sometimes brutal language that came from the loudspeaker that morning astonished and troubled her. She continued to listen until her maid came in. Then she turned off the radio quickly, since this insight, she realized, was a furtive one.

Irene had a luncheon date with a friend that day, and she left her apartment at a little after twelve. There were a number of women in the elevator when it stopped at her floor. She stared at their handsome and impassive faces, their furs, and the cloth flowers in their hats. Which one of them had been to Sea Island? she wondered. Which one had overdrawn her bank account? The elevator stopped at the tenth floor and a woman with a pair of Skye terriers joined them. Her hair was rigged high on her head and she wore a mink cape. She was humming the "Missouri Waltz."

Irene had two Martinis at lunch, and she looked searchingly at her friend and wondered what her secrets were. They had intended to go shopping after lunch, but Irene excused herself and went home. She told the maid that she was not to be disturbed; then she went into the living room, closed the doors, and switched on the radio. She heard, in the course of the afternoon, the halting conversation of a woman entertaining her aunt, the hysterical conclusion of a luncheon party, and a hostess briefing her maid about some cocktail guests. "Don't give the best Scotch to anyone who hasn't white hair," the hostess said. "See if you can get rid of that liver paste before you pass those hot things, and could you lend me five dollars? I want to tip the elevator man."

As the afternoon waned, the conversations increased in intensity. From where Irene sat, she could see the open sky above the East River. There were hundreds of clouds in the sky, as though the south wind had broken the winter into pieces and were blowing it north, and on her radio she could hear the arrival of cocktail guests and the return of children and businessmen from their schools and offices. "I found a good-sized diamond on the bathroom floor this morning," a woman said. "It must have fallen out of that bracelet Mrs. Dunston was wearing last night." "We'll sell it," a man said. "Take it down to the jeweler on Madison Avenue and sell it.

Mrs. Dunston won't know the difference, and we could use a couple of hundred bucks. . . .'" "'Oranges and lemons, say the bells of St. Clement's,'" the Sweeneys' nurse sang. "'Halfpence and farthings, say the bells of St. Martin's. When will you pay me? say the bells at old Bailey. . . .'" "It's not a hat," a woman cried, and at her back roared a cocktail party. "It's not a hat, it's a love affair. That's what Walter Florell said. He said it's not a hat, it's a love affair," and then, in a lower voice, the same woman added, "Talk to somebody, for Christ's sake, honey, talk to somebody. If she catches you standing here not talking to anybody, she'll take us off her invitation list, and I love these parties."

The Westcotts were going out for dinner that night, and when Jim came home, Irene was dressing. She seemed sad and vague, and he brought her a drink. They were dining with friends in the neighborhood, and they walked to where they were going. The sky was broad and filled with light. It was one of those splendid spring evenings that excite memory and desire, and the air that touched their hands and faces felt very soft. A Salvation Army band was on the corner playing "Jesus Is Sweeter." Irene drew on her husband's arm and held him there for a minute, to hear the music. "They're really such nice people, aren't they?" she said. "They have such nice faces. Actually, they're so much nicer than a lot of the people we know." She took a bill from her purse and walked over and dropped it into the tambourine. There was in her face, when she returned to her husband, a look of radiant melancholy that he was not familiar with. And her conduct at the dinner party that night seemed strange to him, too. She interrupted her hostess rudely and stared at the people across the table from her with an intensity for which she would have punished her children. — 35

It was still mild when they walked home from the party, and Irene looked up at the spring stars. "'How far that little candle throws its beams,'" she exclaimed. "'So shines a good deed in a naughty world.'" She waited that night until Jim had fallen asleep, and then went into the living room and turned on the radio.

Jim came home at about six the next night. Emma, the maid, let him in, and he had taken off his hat and was taking off his coat when Irene ran into the hall. Her face was shining with tears and her hair was disordered. "Go up to 16-C, Jim!" she screamed. "Don't take off your coat. Go up to 16-C. Mr. Osborn's beating his wife. They've been quarreling since four o'clock, and now he's hitting her. Go up there and stop him."

From the radio in the living room, Jim heard screams, obscenities, and thuds. "You know you don't have to listen to this sort of thing," he said. He strode into the living room and turned the switch. "It's indecent," he said. "It's like looking in windows. You know you don't have to listen to this sort of thing. You can turn it off."

"Oh, it's so horrible, it's so dreadful," Irene was sobbing. "I've been listening all day, and it's so depressing."

"Well, if it's so depressing, why do you listen to it? I bought this damned radio to give you pleasure," he said. "I paid a great deal of money for it. I thought it might make you happy. I wanted to make you happy." — 40

"Don't, don't, don't, don't quarrel with me," she moaned, and laid her head on his shoulder. "All the others have been quarreling all day. Everybody's been quarreling. They're all worried about money. Mrs. Hutchinson's mother is dying of cancer in Florida and they don't have enough money to send her to the Mayo Clinic. At least, Mr. Hutchinson says they don't have enough money. And some woman in this building is having an affair with the handyman—with that hideous handyman. It's too disgusting. And Mrs. Melville has heart trouble and Mr. Hendricks is going to lose his job in April and Mrs. Hendricks is horrid about the whole thing and that girl who plays the 'Missouri Waltz' is a whore, a common whore, and the elevator man has tuberculosis and Mr. Osborn has been beating Mrs. Osborn." She wailed, she trembled with grief and checked the stream of tears down her face with the heel of her palm.

"Well, why do you have to listen?" Jim asked again. "Why do you have to listen to this stuff if it makes you so miserable?"

"Oh, don't, don't, don't," she cried. "Life is too terrible, too sordid and awful. But we've never been like that, have we, darling? Have we? I mean, we've always been good and decent and loving to one another, haven't we? And we have two children, two beautiful children. Our lives aren't sordid, are they, darling? Are they?" She flung her arms around his neck and drew his face down to hers. "We're happy, aren't we, darling? We are happy, aren't we?"

"Of course we're happy," he said tiredly. He began to surrender his resentment. "Of course we're happy. I'll have that damned radio fixed or taken away tomorrow." He stroked her soft hair. "My poor girl," he said.

"You love me, don't you?" she asked. "And we're not hypercritical or worried   45
about money or dishonest, are we?"

"No, darling," he said.

A man came in the morning and fixed the radio. Irene turned it on cautiously and was happy to hear a California-wine commercial and a recording of Beethoven's Ninth Symphony, including Schiller's "Ode to Joy." She kept the radio on all day and nothing untoward came from the speaker.

A Spanish suite was being played when Jim came home. "Is everything all right?" he asked. His face was pale, she thought. They had some cocktails and went in to dinner to the "Anvil Chorus" from *Il Trovatore*. This was followed by Debussy's "La Mer."

"I paid the bill for the radio today," Jim said. "It cost four hundred dollars. I hope you'll get some enjoyment out of it."

"Oh, I'm sure I will," Irene said.   50

"Four hundred dollars is a good deal more than I can afford," he went on. "I wanted to get something that you'd enjoy. It's the last extravagance we'll be able to indulge in this year. I see that you haven't paid your clothing bills yet. I saw them on your dressing table." He looked directly at her. "Why did you tell me you'd paid them? Why did you lie to me?"

"I just didn't want you to worry, Jim," she said. She drank some water. "I'll be able to pay my bills out of this month's allowance. There were the slipcovers last month, and that party."

"You've got to learn to handle the money I give you a little more intelligently, Irene," he said. "You've got to understand that we don't have as much money this year as we had last. I had a very sobering talk with Mitchell today. No one is buy-ing anything. We're spending all our time promoting new issues, and you know how long that takes. I'm not getting any younger, you know. I'm thirty-seven. My hair will be gray next year. I haven't done as well as I'd hoped to do. And I don't suppose things will get any better."

"Yes, dear," she said.

"We've got to start cutting down," Jim said. "We've got to think of the chil- 55
dren. To be perfectly frank with you, I worry about money a great deal. I'm not at all sure of the future. No one is. If anything should happen to me, there's the insur-ance, but that wouldn't go very far today. I've worked awfully hard to give you and the children a comfortable life," he said bitterly. "I don't like to see all my energies, all of my youth, wasted in fur coats and radios and slipcovers and—"

"Please, Jim," she said. "Please. They'll hear us."

"*Who'll hear us?* Emma can't hear us."

"The radio."

"Oh, I'm sick!" he shouted. "I'm sick to death of your apprehensiveness. The radio can't hear us. Nobody can hear us. And what if they can hear us? Who cares?"

Irene got up from the table and went into the living room. Jim went to the 60
door and shouted at her from there. "Why are you so Christly all of a sudden? What's turned you overnight into a convent girl? You stole your mother's jewelry before they probated her will. You never gave your sister a cent of that money that was intended for her—not even when she needed it. You made Grace Howland's life miserable, and where was all your piety and your virtue when you went to that abortionist? I'll never forget how cool you were. You packed your bag and went off to have that child murdered as if you were going to Nassau. If you'd had any rea-sons, if you'd had any good reasons . . ."

Irene stood for a minute before the hideous cabinet, disgraced and sickened, but she held her hand on the switch before she extinguished the music and the voices, hoping that the instrument might speak to her kindly, that she might hear the Sweeneys' nurse. Jim continued to shout at her from the door. The voice on the radio was suave and noncommittal. "An early-morning railroad disaster in Tokyo," the loudspeaker said, "killed twenty-nine people. A fire in a Catholic hospital near Buffalo for the care of blind children was extinguished early this morning by nuns. The temperature is forty-seven. The humidity is eighty-nine."

Questions for Discussion and Writing

1. On what fantastic premise does Cheever's story depend? How would you characterize the Westcotts when we first come to know them?

2. How do Irene and her husband change as a result of their experiences?

3. What is ironic about the way the story ends? What different meanings does the word *enormous* in the title come to have?

Poetry

WALT WHITMAN

Walt Whitman (1819–1892) was born in then-rural Huntington, Long Island, into a family of Quakers. The family later moved to Brooklyn, then a city of fewer than 10,000, where he worked as a carpenter. He attended school briefly and in 1830 went to work as an office boy but soon turned to printing and journalism. Until the 1850s he worked as a newspaperman. He was the editor of the Brooklyn Eagle *from 1846 to 1848. In 1855, Whitman published the first of many editions of* Leaves of Grass, *a work that was to prove to be of unparalleled influence in establishing him as one of the most innovative figures of nineteenth-century poetry. In subsequent editions, he showed himself capable of writing long, intricately orchestrated poems that embrace the ideals of working-class democracy expressed in experimental free-verse rhythms and realistic imagery. When the Civil War broke out, Whitman was too old to enlist but went to the front in 1862 to be with his brother George, who had been reported wounded. During the remainder of the war, Whitman served as a nurse tending wounded soldiers, Union and Confederate alike. In "When I Heard the Learn'd Astronomer" (1865) Whitman contrasts the poet's disenchantment with the impersonal coldness of rational science with a mystical appreciation of nature.*

When I Heard the Learn'd Astronomer

When I heard the learn'd astronomer,
When the proofs, the figures, were ranged in columns before me,
When I was shown the charts and diagrams, to add, divide, and measure
    them,
When I sitting heard the astronomer where he lectured with much applause   5
    in the lecture-room,
How soon unaccountable I became tired and sick,
Till rising and gliding out I wander'd off by myself,
In the mystical moist night-air, and from time to time,
Look'd up in perfect silence at the stars.   10

Questions for Discussion and Writing

1. How is Whitman's description of what the astronomer is trying to do critical of the scientist's approach? How does he feel listening to the astronomer's lecture?

2. What feelings does the speaker get from looking at the stars? What words best reflect this mood?

3. In a short essay, discuss Whitman's attitudes toward science and nature as expressed in this poem.

PEGGY SEEGER

Peggy Seeger was born in New York in 1935. She received training in both folk and classical music as a child and studied music at Radcliffe College, where she began performing folk songs publicly. After graduation, she traveled throughout Europe and China from 1955 to 1956, moved to Britain in 1956, and became a British subject in 1959. As a solo performer and with her husband, James Henry Miller, she played an important role in leading a British folk music revival. They have written music for radio, films, and television; made many records; and compiled scholarly anthologies of folk songs. "I'm Gonna Be an Engineer" (1970) brings together her many roles as folksinger, song collector, and songwriter as she adapts a traditional style of folk song to modern themes.

I'm Gonna Be an Engineer

When I was a little girl, I wished I was a boy,
I tagged along behind the gang and wore my corduroys,
Everybody said I only did it to annoy
But I was gonna be an engineer.

Mamma told me, "Can't you be a lady?   5
Your duty is to make me the mother of a pearl.
Wait until you're older, dear, and maybe
You'll be glad that you're a girl."

    DAINTY AS A DRESDEN STATUE.
    GENTLE AS A JERSEY COW.   10
    SMOOTH AS SILK, GIVES CREAMY MILK
    LEARN TO COO, LEARN TO MOO,
    THAT'S WHAT YOU DO TO BE A LADY NOW—

When I went to school I learned to write and how to read,
Some history, geography, and home economy.   15
And typing is a skill that every girl is sure to need,
To while away the extra time until the time to breed,
And then they had the nerve to say, "What would you like to be?"
I says, "I'm gonna be an engineer!"
    No, you only need to learn to be a lady,   20
    The duty isn't yours for to try and run the world,
    An engineer could never have a baby!
    Remember, dear, that you're a girl.

    SHE'S SMART (FOR A WOMAN).
    I WONDER HOW SHE GOT THAT WAY?   25
    YOU GET NO CHOICE, YOU GET NO VOICE
    JUST STAY MUM, PRETEND YOU'RE DUMB
    AND THAT'S HOW YOU COME TO BE A LADY TODAY—

Then Jimmy come along and we set up a conjugation,
We were busy every night with loving recreation.   30
I spent my day at work so HE could get his education,
Well, now he's an engineer.
 He says, "I know you'll always be a lady,
 It's the duty of my darling to love me all her life,
 Could an *engineer* look after or obey me?   35
 Remember, dear, that you're my wife."

Well, as soon as Jimmy got a job, I began again,
Then, happy at my turret-lathe a year or so, and then:
The morning that the twins were born, Jimmy says to them,
"Kids, your mother *was* an engineer."   40
 You owe it to the kids to be a lady,
 Dainty as a dishrag, faithful as a chow,
 Stay at home, you got to mind the baby,
 Remember you're a mother now.

Well, every time I turn around it's something else to do,   45
It's cook a meal, mend a sock, sweep a floor or two,
I listen in to Jimmy Young, it makes me want to spew,
I WAS GONNA BE AN ENGINEER!
 Don't I really wish that I could be a lady?
 I could do the lovely things that a lady's 'sposed to do,   50
 I wouldn't even mind, if only they would pay me,
 And I could be a person too.

WHAT PRICE—FOR A WOMAN?
YOU CAN BUY HER FOR A RING OF GOLD.
TO LOVE AND OBEY (WITHOUT ANY PAY)   55
YOU GET A COOK AND A NURSE (FOR BETTER OR WORSE)
YOU DON'T NEED A PURSE WHEN THE LADY IS SOLD.

Ah, but now that times are harder and my Jimmy's got the sack,
I went down to Vicker's, they were glad to have me back,
But I'm a third-class citizen, my wages tell me that,   60
And I'm a first-class engineer.
 The boss he says, "We pay you as a lady,
 You only got the job 'cause I can't afford a man,
 With you I keep the profits high as may be,
 You're just a cheaper pair of hands."   65

YOU GOT ONE FAULT—YOU'RE A WOMAN.
YOU'RE NOT WORTH THE EQUAL PAY.
A BITCH OR A TART, YOU'RE NOTHING BUT HEART,
SHALLOW AND VAIN, YOU GOT NO BRAIN,
YOU EVEN GO DOWN THE DRAIN LIKE A LADY TODAY—   70

Well, I listened to my mother and I joined a typing-pool,
I listened to my lover and I put him through his school,
But if I listen to the boss, I'm just a bloody fool
And an underpaid engineer!
    I been a sucker ever since I was a baby,   75
    As a daughter, as a wife, as a mother and a "dear"—
    But I'll fight them as a woman, not a lady,
    Fight them as an engineer!

Questions for Discussion and Writing

1. What images challenge assumptions that women are intrinsically less capable of becoming engineers than are men?
2. How do images of the speaker performing different societally expected roles contrast with those of her taking on roles traditionally associated with men?
3. What function do the refrains play as an expression of society's expectations? How do these contrast with the speaker's own personal story and the decision she reaches?

Connections for Chapter 9: The Impact of Technology

1. **Gina Kolata,** *A Clone Is Born*
   In what sense do artists (see Junichiro Tanizaki's story "The Tattooer" in Chapter 10) try to reproduce themselves through their creations in ways that correspond to cloning?
2. **Anne Taylor Fleming,** *Sperm in a Jar*
   Both Fleming and Gina Kolata describe interventions of technology that create human life. Based on their analyses, what limits would you deem appropriate?
3. **Constance Holden,** *Identical Twins Reared Apart*
   In principle, why would clones (as described by Gina Kolata) be essentially different from identical twins, described by Holden, aside from the age difference?
4. **Carol Grunewald,** *Monsters of the Brave New World*
   In what way do both Grunewald and Gina Kolata explore the ethical ramifications of new techniques in genetic engineering?
5. **Umberto Eco,** *How Not to Use the Fax Machine and the Cellular Phone*
   Compare Eco's characterization of modern gadgets that symbolize success in a consumer culture with Mary McCarthy's description of the artifacts of commercialism in Venice (see "The Paradox of St. Mark's" in Chapter 10)?

6. **LynNell Hancock,** *The Haves and the Have-Nots*

   Compare Gates's optimism that technology will close the gap between the haves and the have-nots with Hancock's assessment.

   What questions does Hancock raise that echo Jonathan Kozol's concerns (see "The Human Cost of an Illiterate Society" in Chapter 3)?

7. **Bill Gates,** *The Road Ahead*

   To what extent has Gates's prediction of an overdocumented life become the basis of Luisa Valenzuela's story "The Censors" in Chapter 8.

   Compare Gates's predictions regarding computers and education with David Rothenberg's analysis in "How the Web Destroys the Quality of Students' Research Papers" (Chapter 3).

8. **John Cheever,** *The Enormous Radio*

   To what extent have the cellular phone and the fax machine, as depicted by Umberto Eco, infringed on privacy in ways that correspond to the effect of the "enormous radio" in Cheever's story, written almost a half century earlier?

9. **Walt Whitman,** *When I Heard the Learn'd Astronomer*

   Compare the ways Whitman and William Zinsser (see "Niagara Falls" in Chapter 2) recover a sense of awe for nature that has been diminished by civilization.

10. **Peggy Seeger,** *I'm Gonna Be an Engineer*

    How is the theme of empowerment developed in the poems by Seeger and Francis E. E. Harper (see "Learning to Read" in Chapter 3)?

10

THE ARTISTIC IMPULSE

Consider how much less interesting the world would be without the distinctive contributions of composers, writers, playwrights, poets, photographers, painters, and dancers. Although the criteria of what constitutes art change from age to age and culture to culture, artists deepen, enrich, and extend our knowledge of human nature and experience. The pleasures we derive from listening to music, reading, looking at paintings, and other creative endeavors add immeasurably to our appreciation of life. Essays by Kurt Vonnegut, Jr., Anne Tyler, and Alice Munro bring different perspectives to the question of what constitutes good writing and reveal the effort writers must make and how they reshape reality into creative works. Wilson Bryan Key analyzes the subliminal film techniques used in the movie *The Exorcist* (1973), and Sheila Whiteley traces the evolution of Mick Jagger as a performer from the 1960s to the present. Mary McCarthy takes us on a tour of Venice, with its strange blend of avarice and art, and lastly, Lance Morrow examines the role photography has played in shaping our perception of key moments in history.

Junichiro Tanizaki tells the shocking story of a tattoo artist obsessed with the desire to decorate the body of a beautiful woman.

Poems by Anne Bradstreet and Emily Dickinson suggest that artists are never satisfied with their creations and that poetry creates its effects through indirect means. In the poem by Lawrence Ferlinghetti, we can discover the energy, movement, and vitality communicated by a great painting, *The Third of May, 1808,* by the Spanish artist Francisco Goya, as well as its contemporary relevance.

Nonfiction

KURT VONNEGUT, JR.

Kurt Vonnegut, Jr. (b. 1922) is the author of such iconoclastic masterpieces as Cat's Cradle *(1963),* Slaughterhouse Five *(1969),* Sirens of Titan *(1971),* Breakfast of Champions *(1973),* Timequake *(1993), and innumerable short stories written for magazines. He is well qualified to offer practical advice on writing with style, as the unique voice Vonnegut creates in his*

fiction makes his work a joy to read. In 1999 he wrote a book with Lee Stringer about writing,
Like Shaking Hands with God: A Conversation about Writing *and* God Bless You, Dr.
Kevorkian *(2000), an ironic allusion to his 1965 novel* God Bless You, Mr. Rosewater.

How to Write with Style

Newspaper reporters and technical writers are trained to reveal almost nothing about themselves in their writings. This makes them freaks in the world of
writers, since almost all of the other ink-stained wretches in that world reveal a lot
about themselves to readers. We call these revelations, accidental and intentional, elements of style.

These revelations tell us as readers what sort of person it is with whom we are
spending time. Does the writer sound ignorant or informed, stupid or bright,
crooked or honest, humorless or playful—? And on and on.

Why should you examine your writing style with the idea of improving it?
Do so as a mark of respect for your readers, whatever you're writing. If you scrib-
ble your thoughts any which way, your readers will surely feel that you care nothing about them. They will mark you down as an egomaniac or a chowder head—or
worse, they will stop reading you.

The most damning revelation you can make about yourself is that you do not
know what is interesting and what is not. Don't you yourself like or dislike writers
mainly for what they choose to show you or make you think about? Did you ever
admire an empty-headed writer for his or her mastery of the language? No.

So your own winning style must begin with ideas in your head.   5

1. FIND A SUBJECT YOU CARE ABOUT

Find a subject you care about and which you in your heart feel others should
care about. It is this genuine caring, and not your games with language, which will
be the most compelling and seductive element in your style.

I am not urging you to write a novel, by the way—although I would not be
sorry if you wrote one, provided you genuinely cared about something. A petition
to the mayor about a pothole in front of your house or a love letter to the girl next
door will do.

2. DO NOT RAMBLE, THOUGH

I won't ramble on about that.

3. KEEP IT SIMPLE

As for your use of language: Remember that two great masters of language,
William Shakespeare and James Joyce, wrote sentences which were almost childlike
when their subjects were most profound. "To be or not to be?" asks Shakespeare's
Hamlet. The longest word is three letters long. Joyce, when he was frisky, could put
together a sentence as intricate and as glittering as a necklace for Cleopatra, but my

favorite sentence in his short story "Eveline" is this one: "She was tired." At that point in the story, no other words could break the heart of a reader as those three words do.

Simplicity of language is not only reputable, but perhaps even sacred. The   10
Bible opens with a sentence well within the writing skills of a lively fourteen-year-old: "In the beginning God created the heaven and the earth."

4. HAVE THE GUTS TO CUT

It may be that you, too, are capable of making necklaces for Cleopatra, so to speak. But your eloquence should be the servant of the ideas in your head. Your rule might be this: If a sentence, no matter how excellent, does not illuminate your subject in some new and useful way, scratch it out.

5. SOUND LIKE YOURSELF

The writing style which is most natural for you is bound to echo the speech you heard when a child. English was the novelist Joseph Conrad's third language, and much that seems piquant in his use of English was no doubt colored by his first language, which was Polish. And lucky indeed is the writer who has grown up in Ireland, for the English spoken there is so amusing and musical. I myself grew up in Indianapolis, where common speech sounds like a band saw cutting galvanized tin, and employs a vocabulary as unornamental as a monkey wrench.

In some of the more remote hollows of Appalachia, children still grow up hearing songs and locutions of Elizabethan times. Yes, and many Americans grow up hearing a language other than English, or an English dialect a majority of Americans cannot understand.

All these varieties of speech are beautiful, just as the varieties of butterflies are beautiful. No matter what your first language, you should treasure it all your life. If it happens not to be standard English, and if it shows itself when you write standard English, the result is usually delightful, like a very pretty girl with one eye that is green and one that is blue.

I myself find that I trust my own writing most, and others seem to trust it   15
most, too, when I sound most like a person from Indianapolis, which is what I am. What alternatives do I have? The one most vehemently recommended by teachers has no doubt been pressed on you, as well: to write like cultivated Englishmen of a century or more ago.

6. SAY WHAT YOU MEAN TO SAY

I used to be exasperated by such teachers, but am no more. I understand now that all those antique essays and stories with which I was to compare my own work were not magnificent for their datedness or foreignness, but for saying precisely what their authors meant them to say. My teachers wished me to write accurately, always selecting the most effective words, and relating the words to one another unambiguously, rigidly, like parts of a machine. The teachers did not want to turn

me into an Englishman after all. They hoped that I would become understandable—and therefore understood. And there went my dream of doing with words
what Pablo Picasso did with paint or what any number of jazz idols did with
music. If I broke all the rules of punctuation, had words mean whatever I wanted
them to mean, and strung them together higgledy-piggledy, I would simply not be
understood. So you, too, had better avoid Picasso-style or jazz-style-writing, if you
have something worth saying and wish to be understood.

Readers want our pages to look very much like pages they have seen before.
Why? This is because they themselves have a tough job to do, and they need all the
help they can get from us.

7. PITY THE READERS

They have to identify thousands of little marks on paper, and make sense of
them immediately. They have to *read,* an art so difficult that most people don't really master it even after having studied it all through grade school and high
school—twelve long years.

So this discussion must finally acknowledge that our stylistic options as writers are neither numerous nor glamorous, since our readers are bound to be such
imperfect artists. Our audience requires us to be sympathetic and patient teachers,
even willing to simplify and clarify—whereas we would rather soar high above the
crowd, singing like nightingales.

That is the bad news. The good news is that we Americans are governed   20
under a unique Constitution, which allows us to write whatever we please without
fear of punishment. So the most meaningful aspect of our styles, which is what we
choose to write about, is utterly unlimited.

8. FOR REALLY DETAILED ADVICE

For a discussion of literary style in a narrower sense, in a more technical sense,
I commend to your attention *The Elements of Style,* by William Strunk, Jr., and E. B.
White (Macmillan, 1979). E. B. White is, of course, one of the most admirable lit-
erary stylists this country has so far produced.

You should realize, too, that no one would care how well or badly Mr. White
expressed himself, if he did not have perfectly enchanting things to say.

Questions for Discussion and Writing

1. To what extent has Vonnegut followed his own advice? How would you
   characterize the voice he creates in this essay?
2. Why does Vonnegut use Shakespeare and Joyce as examples to illustrate the
   value of simplicity in language? Did you find the similes and metaphors Vonnegut uses to be particularly effective in getting his ideas across?

3. Rewrite a paragraph or two from a recent essay of yours following Vonnegut's seven suggestions. Which version did you prefer and why? You might wish to read any of Vonnegut's novels to see whether he follows his own advice.

ANNE TYLER

Anne Tyler was born in 1941 in Minneapolis, Minnesota, but grew up in Raleigh, North Carolina. She graduated at age nineteen from Duke University, where she twice won the Anne Flexner Award for creative writing and was elected to Phi Beta Kappa. She has done graduate work in Russian studies at Columbia University and has worked for a year as the Russian bibliographer in the Duke University library. She lives in Baltimore with her two daughters. Her stories have appeared in such magazines as The New Yorker, Harper's, *and* The Southern Review. *She is a prolific and popular novelist, and her works include* Dinner at the Homesick Restaurant *(1982);* The Accidental Tourist *(1985), which was made into an Academy-Award-winning film; and* Saint Maybe *(1991). Her eleventh novel* Breathing Lessons *was awarded the Pulitzer Prize in 1988. Her most recent novels are* Ladder of Years *(1995),* A Patchwork Planet *(1998), and* Back When We Were Grownups *(2001). In "Still Just Writing," which first appeared in* The Writer on Her Work: Contemporary Women Writers Reflect on Their Art and Situation *(1984), Tyler traces her development as a writer and considers how she strikes a balance between the demands of writing fiction and her obligations as a wife and mother.*

Still Just Writing

While I was painting the downstairs hall I thought of a novel to write. Really I just thought of a character; he more or less wandered into my mind, wearing a beard and a broad-brimmed leather hat. I figured that if I sat down and organized this character on paper, a novel would grow up around him. But it was March and the children's spring vacation began the next day, so I waited.

After spring vacation the children went back to school, but the dog got worms. It was a little complicated at the vet's and I lost a day. By then it was Thursday; Friday is the only day I can buy the groceries, pick up new cedar chips for the gerbils, scrub the bathrooms. I waited till Monday. Still, that left me four good weeks in April to block out the novel.

By May I was ready to start actually writing, but I had to do it in patches. There was the follow-up treatment at the vet, and then a half-day spent trailing the dog with a specimen tin so the lab could be sure the treatment had really worked. There were visits from the washing machine repairman and the Davey tree man, not to mention briefer interruptions by the meter reader, five Jehovah's Witnesses, and two Mormons. People telephoned wanting to sell me permanent light bulbs and waterproof basements. An Iranian cousin of my husband's had a baby; then the cousin's uncle died; then the cousin's mother decided to go home to Iran and needed to know where to buy a black American coat before she left. There *are* no black American coats; don't Americans wear mourning? I told her no, but I checked around at all the department stores anyway because she didn't speak English. Then I wrote chapters one and two. I had planned to work till three-thirty every day, but it was a month of early quittings: once for the children's dental appointment, once for the cat's rabies shot, once for our older daughter's orthopedist, and twice for her gymnastic meets. Sitting on the bleachers in the school gymnasium, I told myself I could always use this in a novel someplace, but I couldn't really picture writing a novel about twenty little girls in leotards trying to walk the length of a wooden beam without falling off. By the time I'd written chapter three, it was Memorial Day and the children were home again.

I knew I shouldn't expect anything from June. School was finished then and camp hadn't yet begun. I put the novel away. I closed down my mind and planted some herbs and played cribbage with the children. Then on the 25th, we drove one child to a sleep-away camp in Virginia and entered the other in a day camp, and I was ready to start work again. First I had to take my car in for repairs and the mechanics lost it, but I didn't get diverted. I sat in the garage on a folding chair while they hunted my car all one afternoon, and I hummed a calming tune and tried to remember what I'd planned to do next in my novel. Or even what the novel was about, for that matter. My character wandered in again in his beard and his broad-brimmed hat. He looked a little pale and knuckly, like someone scrabbing at a cliff edge so as not to fall away entirely.

I had high hopes for July, but it began with a four-day weekend, and on Monday night we had a long-distance call from our daughter's camp in Virginia. She was seriously ill in a Charlottesville hospital. We left our youngest with friends and drove three hours in a torrent of rain. We found our daughter frightened and crying, and another child (the only other child I knew in all of Virginia) equally frightened and crying down in the emergency room with possible appendicitis, so I spent that night alternating between a chair in the pediatric wing and a chair in the emergency room. By morning, it had begun to seem that our daughter's illness was typhoid fever. We loaded her into the car and took her back to Baltimore, where her doctor put her on drugs and prescribed a long bed-rest. She lay in bed six days, looking wretched and calling for fluids and cold cloths. On the seventh day she got up her same old healthy self, and the illness was declared to be not typhoid fever after all but a simple virus, and we shipped her back to Virginia on the evening train. The next day I was free to start writing again but sat, instead, on the couch in my study, staring blankly at the wall.

I could draw some conclusions here about the effect that being a woman/ wife/mother has upon my writing, except that I am married to a writer who is also a man/husband/father. He published his first novel while he was a medical student in Iran; then he came to America to finish his training. His writing fell by the wayside, for a long while. You can't be on call in the emergency room for twenty hours and write a novel during the other four. Now he's a child psychiatrist, full-time, and he writes his novels in the odd moments here and there—when he's not preparing a lecture, when he's not on the phone with a patient, when he's not attending classes at the psychoanalytic institute. He writes in Persian, still, in those

5

black-and-white speckled composition books. Sometimes one of the children will interrupt him in English and he will answer in Persian, and they'll say, "What?" and he'll look up blankly, and it seems a sheet has to fall from in front of his eyes before he remembers where he is and switches to English. Often, I wonder what he would be doing now if he didn't have a family to support. He cares deeply about his writing and he's very good at it, but every morning at five-thirty he gets up and puts on a suit and tie and drives in the dark to the hospital. Both of us, in different ways, seem to be hewing our creative time in small, hard chips from our living time.

Occasionally, I take a day off. I go to a friend's house for lunch, or weed the garden, or rearrange the linen closet. I notice that at the end of one of these days, when my husband asks me what I've been doing, I tend to exaggerate any hardships I may have encountered. ("A pickup nearly sideswiped me on Greenspring Avenue. I stood in line an hour just trying to buy the children some flip-flops.") It seems sinful to have lounged around so. Also, it seems sinful that I have more choice than my husband as to whether or not to undertake any given piece of work. I can refuse to do an article if it doesn't appeal to me, refuse to change a short story, refuse to hurry a book any faster than it wants to go—all luxuries. My husband, on the other hand, is forced to rise and go off to that hospital every blessed weekday of his life. His luxury is that no one expects him to drop all else for two weeks when a child has chicken pox. The only person who has no luxuries at all, it seems to me, is the woman writer who is the sole support of her children. I often think about how she must manage. I think that if I were in that position, I'd have to find a job involving manual labor. I have spent so long erecting partitions around the part of me that writes—learning how to close the door on it when ordinary life intervenes, how to close the door on ordinary life when it's time to start writing again—that I'm not sure I could fit the two parts of me back together now.

Before we had children I worked in a library. It was a boring job, but I tend to like doing boring things. I would sit on a stool alphabetizing Russian catalogue cards and listening to the other librarians talking around me. It made me think of my adolescence, which was spent listening to the tobacco stringers while I handed tobacco. At night I'd go home from the library and write. I never wrote what the librarians said, exactly, but having those voices in my ears all day helped me summon up my own characters' voices. Then our first baby came along—an insomniac. I quit work and stayed home all day with her and walked her all night. Even if I had found the time to write, I wouldn't have had the insides. I felt drained; too much care and feeling were being drawn out of me. And the only voices I heard now were by appointment—people who came to dinner, or invited us to dinner, and who therefore felt they had to make deliberate conversation. That's one thing writers never have, and I still miss it: the easy-going, on-again-off-again, gossipy murmurs of people working alongside each other all day.

I enjoyed tending infants (though I've much preferred the later ages), but it was hard to be solely, continually in their company and not to be able to write. And I couldn't think of any alternative. I know it must be possible to have a child raised beautifully by a housekeeper, but every such child I've run into has seemed dulled and doesn't use words well. So I figured I'd better stick it out. As it happened, it wasn't that long—five years, from the time our first daughter was born till our second started nursery school and left me with my mornings free. But while I was going through it I thought it would be a lot longer. I couldn't imagine any end to it. I felt that everything I wanted to write was somehow coagulating in my veins and making me fidgety and slow. Then after a while I didn't have anything to write anyhow, but I still had the fidgets. I felt useless, no matter how many diapers I washed or strollers I pushed. The only way I could explain my life to myself was to imagine that I was living in a very small commune. I had spent my childhood in a commune, or what would nowadays be called a commune, and I was used to the idea of division of labor. What we had here, I told myself, was a perfectly sensible arrangement: one member was the liaison with the outside world, bringing in money; another was the caretaker, reading the Little Bear books to the children and repairing the electrical switches. This second member might have less physical freedom, but she had much more freedom to arrange her own work schedule. I must have sat down a dozen times a week and very carefully, consciously thought it all through. Often, I was merely trying to convince myself that I really did pull my own weight.

This Iranian cousin who just had the baby: she sits home now and cries a lot.   10
She was working on her master's degree and is used to being out in the world more. "Never mind," I tell her, "you'll soon be out again. This stage doesn't last long."

"How long?" she asks.

"Oh . . . three years, if you just have the one."

"Three years!"

I can see she's appalled. Her baby is beautiful, very dark and Persian; and what's more, he sleeps—something I've rarely seen a baby do. What I'm trying to say to her (but of course, she'll agree without really hearing me) is that he's worth it. It seems to me that since I've had children, I've grown richer and deeper. They may have slowed down my writing for a while, but when I did write, I had more of a self to speak from. After all, who else in the world do you *have* to love, no matter what? Who else can you absolutely not give up on? My life seems more intricate. Also more dangerous.

After the children started school, I put up the partitions in my mind. I would   15
rush around in the morning braiding their hair, packing their lunches; then the second they were gone I would grow quiet and climb the stairs to my study. Sometimes a child would come home early and I would feel a little tug between the two parts of me; I'd be absent-minded and short-tempered. Then gradually I learned to make the transition more easily. It feels like a sort of string that I tell myself to loosen. When the children come home, I drop the string and close the study door and that's the end of it. It doesn't always work perfectly, of course. There are times when it doesn't work at all: if a child is sick, for instance, I can't possibly drop the children's end of the string, and I've learned not to try. It's easier just to stop writing for a while. Or if they're home but otherwise occupied, I no longer attempt to sneak off to my study to finish that one last page; I know that instantly, as if by magic, assorted little people will be pounding on my door requiring Band-Aids, tetanus shots, and a complete summation of the facts of life.

Last spring, I bought a midget tape recorder to make notes on. I'd noticed that my best ideas came while I was running the vacuum cleaner, but I was always losing them. I thought this little recorder would help. I carried it around in my shirt pocket. But I was ignoring the partitions, is what it was; I was letting one half of my life intrude upon the other. A child would be talking about her day at school and suddenly I'd whip out the tape recorder and tell it, "Get Morgan out of that cocktail party; he's not the type to drink." "Huh?" the child would say. Both halves began to seem ludicrous, unsynchronized. I took the recorder back to Radio Shack.

A few years ago, my parents went to the Gaza Strip to work for the American Friends Service Committee. It was a lifelong dream of my father's to do something with the AFSC as soon as all his children were grown, and he'd been actively preparing for it for years. But almost as soon as they got there, my mother fell ill with a mysterious fever that neither the Arab nor the Israeli hospitals could diagnose. My parents had to come home for her treatment, and since they'd sublet their house in North Carolina, they had to live with us. For four months, they stayed here—but only on a week-to-week basis, not knowing when they were going back, or whether they were going back at all, or how serious my mother's illness was. It was hard for her, of course, but it should have been especially hard in another way for my father, who had simply to hang in suspended animation for four months while my mother was whisked in and out of hospitals. However, I believe he was as pleased with life as he always is. He whistled Mozart and puttered around insulating our windows. He went on long walks collecting firewood. He strolled over to the meetinghouse and gave a talk on the plight of the Arab refugees. "Now that we seem to have a little time," he told my mother, "why not visit the boys?" and during one of her out-patient periods he took her on a gigantic cross-country trip to see all my brothers and my other relatives they happened upon. Then my mother decided she ought to go to a faith healer. (She wouldn't usually do such a thing, but she was desperate.) "Oh. Okay," my father said, and he took her to a faith healer, whistling all the way. And when the faith healer didn't work, my mother said, "I think this is psychosomatic. Let's go back to Gaza." My father said, "Okay," and reserved two seats on the next plane over. The children and I went to see them the following summer: my mother's fever was utterly gone, and my father drove us down the Strip, weaving a little Renault among the tents and camels, cheerfully whistling Mozart.

I hold this entire, rambling set of events in my head at all times, and remind myself of it almost daily. It seems to me that the way my father lives (infinitely adapting, and looking around him with a smile to say, "Oh! So *this* is where I am!") is also the way to slip gracefully through a choppy life of writing novels, plastering the dining room ceiling, and presiding at slumber parties. I have learned, bit by bit, to accept a school snow-closing as an unexpected holiday, an excuse to play seventeen rounds of Parcheesi instead of typing up a short story. When there's a midweek visitation of uncles from Iran (hordes of great, bald, yellow men calling for their glasses of tea, sleeping on guest beds, couches, two armchairs pushed together, and discarded crib mattresses), I have decided that I might as well listen to what they have to say, and work on my novel tomorrow instead. I smile at the uncles out of a kind of clear, swept space inside me. What this takes, of course, is a sense of limitless time, but I'm getting that. My life is beginning to seem unusually long. And there's a danger to it: I could wind up as passive as a piece of wood on a wave. But I try to walk a middle line.

I was standing in the schoolyard waiting for a child when another mother came up to me. "Have you found work yet?" she asked. "Or are you still just writing?"

Now, how am I supposed to answer that?   20

I could take offense, come to think of it. Maybe the reason I didn't is that I halfway share her attitude. They're *paying* me for this? For just writing down untruthful stories? I'd better look around for more permanent employment. For I do consider writing to be a finite job. I expect that any day now, I will have said all I have to say; I'll have used up all my characters, and then I'll be free to get on with my real life. When I make a note of new ideas on index cards, I imagine I'm clearing out my head, and that soon it will be empty and spacious. I file the cards in a little blue box, and I can picture myself using the final card one day—ah! through at last!—and throwing the blue box away. I'm like a dentist who continually fights tooth decay, working toward the time when he's conquered it altogether and done himself out of a job. But my head keeps loading up again; the little blue box stays crowded and messy. Even when I feel I have no ideas at all, and can't possibly start the next chapter, I have a sense of something still bottled in me, trying to get out.

People have always seemed funny and strange to me, and touching in unexpected ways. I can't shake off a sort of mist of irony that hangs over whatever I see. Probably that's what I'm trying to put across when I write; I may believe that I'm the one person who holds this view of things. And I'm always hurt when a reader says that I choose only bizarre or eccentric people to write about. It's not a matter of choice; it just seems to me that even the most ordinary person, in real life, will turn out to have something unusual at his center. I like to think that I might meet up with one of my past characters at the very next street corner. The odd thing is, sometimes I have. And if I were remotely religious, I'd believe that a little gathering of my characters would be waiting for me in heaven when I died. "*Then* what happened?" I'd ask them. "How have things worked out, since the last time I saw you?"

I think I was born with the impression that what happened in books was much more reasonable, and interesting, and *real,* in some ways, than what happened in life. I hated childhood, and spent it sitting behind a book waiting for adulthood to arrive. When I ran out of books I made up my own. At night, when I couldn't sleep, I made up stories in the dark. Most of my plots involved girls going west in covered wagons. I was truly furious that I'd been born too late to go west in a covered wagon.

I know a poet who says that in order to be a writer, you have to have had rheumatic fever in your childhood. I've never had rheumatic fever, but I believe that any kind of setting-apart situation will do as well. In my case, it was emerging from that commune—really an experimental Quaker community in the wilderness—and trying to fit into the outside world. I was eleven. I had never used a telephone and could strike a match on the soles of my bare feet. All the children in my new school looked very peculiar to me, and I certainly must have looked peculiar to them. I am still surprised, to this day, to find myself where I am. My life is so streamlined and full of modern conveniences. How did I get here? I have given up hope, by now, of ever losing my sense of distance; in fact, I seem to have come to cherish it. Neither I nor any of my brothers can stand being out among a crowd of people for any length of time at all.

I spent my adolescence planning to be an artist, not a writer. After all, books 25 had to be about major events, and none had ever happened to me. All I knew were tobacco workers, stringing the leaves I handed them and talking up a storm. Then I found a book of Eudora Welty's short stories in the high school library. She was writing about Edna Earle, who was so slow-witted she could sit all day just pondering how the tail of the *C* got through the loop of the *L* on the Coca-Cola sign. Why, I knew Edna Earle. You mean you could *write* about such people? I have always meant to send Eudora Welty a thank-you note, but I imagine she would find it a little strange.

I wanted to go to Swarthmore College, but my parents suggested Duke instead, where I had a full scholarship, because my three brothers were coming along right behind me and it was more important for boys to get a good education than for girls. That was the first and last time that my being female was ever a serious issue. I still don't think it was just, but I can't say it ruined my life. After all, Duke had Reynolds Price, who turned out to be the only person I ever knew who could actually teach writing. It all worked out, in the end.

I believe that for many writers, the hardest time is that dead spot after college (where they're wonder-children, made much of) and before their first published work. Luckily, I didn't notice that part; I was so vague about what I wanted to do that I could hardly chafe at not yet doing it. I went to graduate school in Russian studies; I scrubbed decks on a boat in Maine; I got a job ordering books from the Soviet Union. Writing was something that crept in around the edges. For a while I lived in New York, where I became addicted to riding any kind of train or subway, and while I rode I often felt I was nothing but an enormous eye, taking things in and turning them over and sorting them out. But who would I tell them to, once I'd sorted them? I have never had more than three or four close friends, at any period of my life; and anyway, I don't talk well. I am the kind of person who wakes up at four in the morning and suddenly thinks of what she should have said yesterday at lunch. For me, writing something down was the only road out.

You would think, since I waited so long and so hopefully for adulthood, that it would prove to be a disappointment. Actually, I figure it was worth the wait. I like everything about it but the paperwork—the income tax and protesting the Sears bill and renewing the Triple-A membership. I always did count on having a husband and children, and here they are. I'm surprised to find myself a writer but have fitted it in fairly well, I think. The only real trouble that writing has ever brought me is an occasional sense of being invaded by the outside world. Why do people imagine that writers, having chosen the most private of professions, should be any good at performing in public, or should have the slightest desire to tell their secrets to interviewers from ladies' magazines? I feel I am only holding myself together by being extremely firm and decisive about what I will do and what I will not do. I will write my books and raise the children. Anything else just fritters me away. I know that makes me seem narrow, but in fact, I *am* narrow. I like routine and rituals and I hate leaving home; I have a sense of digging my heels in. I refuse to drive on freeways. I dread our annual vacation. Yet I'm continually prepared for travel: it is physically impossible for me to buy any necessity without buying a travel-sized version as well. I have a little toilet kit, with soap and a nightgown, forever packed and ready to go. How do you explain that?

As the outside world grows less dependable, I keep buttressing my inside world, where people go on meaning well and surprising other people with little touches of grace. There are days when I sink into my novel like a pool and emerge feeling blank and bemused and used up. Then I drift over to the schoolyard, and there's this mother wondering if I'm doing anything halfway useful yet. Am I working? Have I found a job? No, I tell her.

I'm still just writing.   30

Questions for Discussion and Writing

1. In what way do the many roles Tyler has to play give her more of a "self" to draw upon when she writes fiction? What experiences illustrate the kind of self-discipline of which she is capable in balancing the demands of her two lives?

2. How do the kinds of experiences she had in childhood help explain her unusual ability to depict characters surrounded by a sort of mist of irony? What do you think she means by this phrase?

3. How does the title of the essay reflect a common societal attitude toward people who make a living through creative endeavors?

ALICE MUNRO

Alice Munro was born in 1931 and educated in Ontario, Canada. She moved with her first husband to British Columbia. While working in the Vancouver Public Library, she began to have some of her short stories published. Her first collection, Dance of the Happy Shades *(1968), received the Governor General's Award for Literature. Her acute insight into human nature is evident in her other works as well, including the novel* Lives of Girls and Women *(1971) and her short story collections* Something I've Been Meaning to Tell You *(1974),* The Beggar Maid *(1982),* The Progress of Love *(1986), and* Friend of My Youth *(1990),* Open Secrets *(1994), and, most recently,* Queenie: A Story *(1999). "What Is Real?" which first appeared in* Making It New: Contemporary Canadian Stories *(1982), is a revised version of a public talk that explores the relationship between a writer's fiction and her life.*

What Is Real?

Whenever people get an opportunity to ask me questions about my writing, I can be sure that some of the questions asked will be these:

"Do you write about real people?"

"Did those things really happen?"

"When you write about a small town are you really writing about Wingham?" (Wingham is the small town in Ontario where I was born and grew up, and it has often been assumed, by people who should know better, that I have simply "fictionalized" this place in my work. Indeed, the local newspaper has taken me to task for making it the "butt of a soured and cruel introspection.")

The usual thing, for writers, is to regard these either as very naive questions, asked by people who really don't understand the difference between autobiography and fiction, who can't recognize the device of the first-person narrator, or else as catch-you-out questions posed by journalists who hope to stir up exactly the sort of dreary (and to outsiders, slightly comic) indignation voiced by my home-town paper. Writers answer such questions patiently or crossly according to temperament and the mood they're in. They say, no, you must understand, my characters are composites; no, those things didn't happen the way I wrote about them; no, of course not, that isn't Wingham (or whatever other place it may be that has had the queer unsought-after distinction of hatching a writer). Or the writer may, riskily, ask the questioners what is real, anyway? None of this seems to be very satisfactory. People go on asking these same questions because the subject really does interest and bewilder them. It would seem to be quite true that they don't know what fiction is.

And how could they know, when what it is, is changing all the time, and we differ among ourselves, and we don't really try to explain because it is too difficult?

What I would like to do here is what I can't do in two or three sentences at the end of a reading. I won't try to explain what fiction is, and what short stories are (assuming, which we can't, that there is any fixed thing that it is and they are), but what short stories are to me, and how I write them, and how I use things that are "real." I will start by explaining how I read stories written by other people. For one thing, I can start reading them anywhere; from beginning to end, from end to beginning, from any point in between in either direction. So obviously I don't take up a story and follow it as if it were a road, taking me somewhere, with views and neat diversions along the way. I go into it, and move back and forth and settle here and there, and stay in it for a while. It's more like a house. Everybody knows what a house does, how it encloses space and makes connections between one enclosed space and another and presents what is outside in a new way. This is the nearest I can come to explaining what a story does for me, and what I want my stories to do for other people.

So when I write a story I want to make a certain kind of structure, and I know the feeling I want to get from being inside that structure. This is the hard part of the explanation, where I have to use a word like "feeling," which is not very precise, because if I attempt to be more intellectually respectable I will have to be dishonest. "Feeling" will have to do.

There is no blueprint for the structure. It's not a question of, "I'll make this kind of house because if I do it right it will have this effect." I've got to make, I've got to build up, a house, a story, to fit around the indescribable "feeling" that is like the soul of the story, and which I must insist upon in a dogged, embarrassed way, as being no more definable than that. And I don't know where it comes from. It seems to be already there, and some unlikely clue, such as a shop window or a bit of conversation, makes me aware of it. Then I start accumulating the material and putting it together. Some of the material I may have lying around already, in memories and observations, and some I invent, and some I have to go diligently looking for (factual details), while some is dumped in my lap (anecdotes, bits of speech). I see how this material might go together to make the shape I need, and I try it. I keep trying and seeing where I went wrong and trying again.

I suppose this is the place where I should talk about technical problems and   10
how I solve them. The main reason I can't is that I'm never sure I do solve anything. Even when I say that I see where I went wrong, I'm being misleading. I never figure out how I'm going to change things, I never say to myself, "That page is heavy going, that paragraph's clumsy, I need some dialogue and shorter sentences." I feel a part that's wrong, like a soggy weight; then I pay attention to the story, as if it were really happening somewhere, not just in my head, and in its own way, not mine. As a result, the sentences may indeed get shorter, there may be more dialogue, and so on. But though I've tried to pay attention to the story, I may not have got it right; those shorter sentences may be an evasion, a mistake. Every final draft, every published story, is still only an attempt, an approach, to the story.

I did promise to talk about using reality. "Why, if Jubilee isn't Wingham, has it got Shuter Street in it?" people want to know. Why have I described somebody's real ceramic elephant sitting on the mantelpiece? I could say I get momentum from doing things like this. The fictional room, town, world, needs a bit of starter dough from the real world. It's a device to help the writer—at least it helps me— but it arouses a certain baulked fury in the people who really do live on Shuter Street and the lady who owns the ceramic elephant. "Why do you put in something true and then go on and tell lies?" they say, and anybody who has been on the receiving end of this kind of thing knows how they feel.

"I do it for the sake of my art and to make this structure which encloses the soul of my story, that I've been telling you about," says the writer. "That is more important than anything."

Not to everybody, it isn't.

So I can see there might be a case, once you've written the story and got the momentum, for going back and changing the elephant to a camel (though there's always a chance the lady might complain that you made a nasty camel out of a beautiful elephant), and changing Shuter Street to Blank Street. But what about the big chunks of reality, without which your story can't exist? In the story "Royal Beatings," I use a big chunk of reality: the story of the butcher, and of the young men who may have been egged on to "get" him. This is a story out of an old newspaper; it really did happen in a town I know. There is no legal difficulty about using it because it has been printed in a newspaper, and besides, the people who figure in it are all long dead. But there is a difficulty about offending people in that town who would feel that use of this story is a deliberate exposure, taunt and insult. Other people who have no connection with the real happening would say, "Why write about anything so hideous?" And lest you think that such an objection could only be raised by simple folk who read nothing but Harlequin Romances, let me tell you that one of the questions most frequently asked at universities is, "Why do you write about things that are so depressing?" People can accept almost any amount of ugliness if it is contained in a familiar formula, as it is on television, but when they come closer to their own place, their own lives, they are much offended by a lack of editing.

There are ways I can defend myself against such objections. I can say, "I do it   15 in the interests of historical reality. That is what the old days were really like." Or, "I do it to show the dark side of human nature, the beast let loose, the evil we can run up against in communities and families." In certain countries I could say, "I do it to show how bad things were under the old system when there were prosperous butchers and young fellows hanging around livery stables and nobody thought about building a new society." But the fact is, the minute I say *to show* I am telling a lie. I don't do it to show anything. I put this story at the heart of my story because I need it there and it belongs there. It is the black room at the center of the house with all other rooms leading to and away from it. That is all. A strange defense. Who told me to write this story? Who feels any need of it before it is written? I do. I do, so that I might grab off this piece of horrid reality and install it where I see fit, even if Hat Nettleton and his friends[1] were still around to make me sorry.

The answer seems to be as confusing as ever. Lots of true answers are. Yes and no. Yes, I use bits of what is real, in the sense of being really there and really happening, in the world, as most people see it, and I transform it into something that is really there and really happening, in my story. No, I am not concerned with using what is real to make any sort of record or prove any sort of point, and I am not concerned with any methods of selection but my own, which I can't fully explain. This is quite presumptuous, and if writers are not allowed to be so—and quite often, in many places, they are not—I see no point in the writing of fiction.

Questions for Discussion and Writing

1. In what way, according to Munro, does she draw aspects of real-life experiences into her fiction? What insight does she offer into the writer's ability to restructure accounts in ways that will create suspense, build conflict, add to or take away from the known facts, expand or compress time, and invent new characters?

2. What metaphors does Munro use in discussing how she writes? What do these metaphors add to your understanding of the fictional process?

3. What is gained or lost by viewing a particular story as wholly autobiographical as opposed to purely fictional?

---

[1] *Hat Nettleton and his friends:* three thuggish youths in Munro's short story "Royal Beatings."

WILSON BRYAN KEY

Wilson Bryan Key was born in 1925 in Richmond, California, and received his Ph.D in communication from the University of Denver in 1971. He has been a professor of journalism at the University of Denver, the University of Kansas, Boston University, and the University of Western Ontario. Key has been the president of Mediaprobe: The Center for the Study of Media, Inc., since 1973. Key was the first to document the widespread use of subliminals in mass media in his books Subliminal Seduction: Ad Media's Manipulation of a Not-So-Innocent America *(1973),* Media Sexploitation *(1976), and* The Clam Plate Orgy: And Other Subliminals the Media Use to Manipulate Your Behavior *(1980). Besides these pioneering works, Key is the author of more than three hundred research studies for private corporations and governments. In "The Exorcist Massage Parlor," from* Media Sexploitation, *Key offers a fascinating analysis of how William Friedkin, director of the movie* The Exorcist, *systematically wove various animal sounds into the film's soundtrack to manipulate the audience's reactions.*

The Exorcist *Massage Parlor*

AUDITORY ARCHETYPES

The Exorcist was remarkable in the way both audio and visual were integrated and mutually reinforced. The soundtrack, for which the movie won an Academy Award, was a brilliant example of creative subliminal sound engineering. Similar techniques have been used for years in other movies and by the popular music recording industry.

In several dozen interviews with theater employees—refreshment stand attendants, ushers, and ticket takers who had only heard the movie's soundtrack for several days before actually viewing the film, all reported extreme discomfort from the sound. The discomfort could not be verbally explained, but all agreed it was directly related to the soundtrack. Each of the theater staffs interviewed reported employees who became ill after finally seeing the film in its entirety—from mild to extreme nausea and hysteria.

Friedkin openly admitted he had used several natural sound effects in the movie's auditory background. One of these, he explained, was the sound of angry, agitated bees. After provoking a jar of bees into excited anger, he recorded their buzzing, then rerecorded the buzzing at sixteen different frequencies. He finally mixed the sixteen frequencies of buzzing together in what might be consciously heard as a single sound—a super buzzing of infuriated bees virtually unrecognizable at conscious levels. This sound of angry bees wove in and out of scenes throughout the film.

Virtually all humans (some much more strongly than others) respond with hysteria, fear, and intense anxiety to the sound of angry, buzzing bees, even if they have never in their lives experienced the actual sound. Many animals respond similarly. Perhaps the strongest verbally definable emotion triggered by the bee buzzing is fear or fright—a near panic-filled desire to run, flee, and escape from the threat. Carl Jung's theory of archetypes suggests that this sound—as the emotional reaction appears to cross cultures—could qualify as an archetypal symbol.

In many cultures the bee has been symbolically associated with death and im-   5
mortality. In several ancient civilizations, dead bodies were smeared with honey as
food for the soul. Indeed, honey was often used as an embalming fluid. Over many
centuries in Europe, bees were prohibited from use in barter for fear they might
take offense and destroy crops and flocks in retribution. Bees appeared as symbols
of death, fear, and power in ancient Egypt, Germany, China, Greece, Italy, and
Japan, in early Christian art, in both Hebrew and Moslem traditions, and in Norse
mythology. The Hindu god Krishna was often described as hovering in the form of
a bee. Souls have often been thought to swarm as bees migrating from hives.

There is never any conscious awareness, of course, within *The Exorcist* audience of angry bees buzzing. However, there are easily observable levels of anxiety
produced by the sound as it weaves in and out of various scenes. The bee sound appeared, for example, in the scene where Father Merrin first visits Regan's bedroom
while he removed various objects from a pouch, symbolically letting the invisible
bees out of the bag.

SYMBOLS OF EVIL

Another auditory archetype mixed subtly into the soundtrack was the terrified squealing of pigs while they were being slaughtered. Few sounds strike terror
so deeply into the heart of man. This sound will affect virtually all humans even
though they may never have experienced the squealing or sight of an actual pig.
The expression "squealing like a stuck pig" has even gone into the language.

Pigs have been portrayed in various symbolic relationships with man for at
least half a million years. Even today, the pig is considered one of the most intelligent of domestic animals—by human standards, of course. The pig, at least for
modern man, was cursed by bad table manners that emphasize the pig's filth, greed,
gluttony, and lethargy. Nevertheless, in many ancient cultures, pigs were often sub-
stituted for human victims during religious sacrifices. A black pig has often been
symbolic in Christian art of the devil and Satan. In many civilizations the pig was
thought to be a demon that injured fertility heroes in the groin, rendering them
sterile. In Celtic mythology pigs were even portrayed as returning to life after being
eaten. And, of course, in one of the New Testament's most celebrated exorcisms,
Christ drove a legion of devils into a herd of swine which, maddened, threw themselves into a lake much as Father Karras flung his possessed body out the window.

In addition to the pigs' squealing hidden in *The Exorcist* soundtrack, Regan's
grotesque, filthy face during the exorcism scene often resembled that of a pig. Further, subliminal reinforcement for the pig symbol is obtained by the word PIG
written as graffiti on a ledge at the left side of the stairs looking down behind the
house where the deaths occurred. This staircase, and the consciously unnoticed
word PIG, appeared many times throughout the movie. Friedkin explained how
the soundtrack often mixed the angry bee buzz with the pig squeals. The two
sounds wove in and out of the film, coordinating with the visual.

Embedded in the sound, under the voices and surface sounds apparent in the   10
exorcism scene, was what seemed to be the roaring of lions or large cats. A third of
the audience surveyed described a feeling of being devoured or struggling against

being devoured. There were also orgasmic sexual sounds in the exorcism scene that appeared to involve both males and females.

Sound is extremely important in the management and control of any group of individuals, certainly for those in a theater. Famed movie director Alfred Hitchcock ranked sound as more vital to the success of his famous suspense movies than his visual illusions.

In a recent Muzak Corporation advertisement, the company actually presented its services, background music for stores and offices, as an "environmental management" technique.

In Western society surprisingly little is publicly known about sound and its effect upon behavior. The consciously available portion of sound frequency ranges from 20 to 20,000 cycles per second—or so advertise the high-fidelity appliance manufacturers. Most theaters have sound equipment that will produce audible sound in this range. As a practical matter, however, few individuals can consciously hear over 17,000 cps or under 200 cps, especially young people whose hearing has been permanently dampened by high-volume electronic amplification.

Sound, nevertheless, can be perceived at each end of the spectrum beyond the consciously perceived frequencies. Resonance and other sound qualities also play parts in the subliminal perception of sound. To illustrate, some Moog synthesizers are capable of producing sound at 20,000 cps or higher and under 20 cps. You can consciously hear nothing at these high or low frequencies, but if volume or resonance is increased, most people become extremely agitated. If information is included in these subliminal frequencies, it will instantly be perceived at the unconscious level.

HYPNOTIC INDUCTIONS

When normal voice volume levels in *The Exorcist* were reduced, the audience was required to strain or increase attention or concentration upon the dialogue. This is almost a standard hypnotic induction technique, compelling the subject to concentrate upon one sensory data source. The audience uniformly leaned forward in their seats to hear, for example, the charming conversation between mother and daughter in the bedroom scene at the film's beginning. Similarly, many scenes throughout the movie were momentarily out of focus. Again, the audience—like puppets being manipulated with strings—leaned forward, concentrating on the visual images as they tried to correct for the blurred focus. Much of the dialogue between shock scenes was muted or whispered, so as to regain audience involvement.

When humans are led toward hypnosis, they become highly suggestible. Their emotions become more easily manipulated, managed, and controlled the further they proceed along the induction path.

Friedkin utilized little music in the soundtrack, though he credited works by Hans Werner Henze, George Crumb, Anton Webern, and five other composers. Like all good background music, the themes were purposely designed for subliminal consumption. The consumption of music and sound generally followed two patterns. One pattern built slowly from plateau to plateau, always intensifying the audience's emotional response. Indeed, in a sample of roughly fifty women who had seen the movie, over half candidly admitted *The Exorcist* excited them sexually.

Most cited the soundtrack as the apparent source of this excitement.

The other general sound pattern abruptly jarred the audience into a tension state. Loud, sharp noises—bells ringing, doors slamming, dogs barking—preceded and followed by extended periods of electronic silence. The sound would gradually increase to a crescendo, trail off to nothingness, or cut off sharply. This technique is primarily an attention-holding-tension-building device. Physiological tension was also increased by silences. For example, the early scene in the attic—which was abruptly broken by a loud, sharp noise.

Jumping the sound from one scene to the next—as a continuity and tension-building device, quite similar to the pink roses used visually—was done throughout the film. An important sound jump occurred during Father Karras's first visit to the house. During the preceding scene, in the dream sequence where Karras's mother climbs the subway stairs, the street sound was unrecognizable as a rather high frequency, moderately loud-volume sound. In the next scene where Karras visited the house, the sound was the same except a truck gear shift was heard and the sound increased in frequency. The gear shift identified the background noise, reducing audience tension for the priest's first visit with Regan, where the tension again built toward a tense climax.

LOUD SILENCES

The Exorcist silences were not completely silent. They were electronic silences, with low-frequency background hums. The silences were only silent in contrast to high and increasing volume sequences. These silences also formed a series of plateaus which gradually increased in volume and decreased in time interval as the story moved toward various climactic situations. Silences, like the sounds, were used to produce within the audience a series of emotional plateaus. These silences became louder and louder and more and more rapid as each segment progressed. The tension and release, tension and release, tension and release, always building higher and higher and higher, induced—by itself—exhaustion and even nausea for many in the audience.

Another manifestation of tension management in the audience was coughing. The audience coughed heavily at predictable intervals throughout the movie. Audience coughing was recorded at several theaters and always appeared at roughly the same point in the story. This was compared with cough reactions in several other action type films, *The Sting, Executive Decision,* and *Papillon. The Exorcist,* in comparison, produced notably stronger and more predictable cough patterns. There were, apparently, subliminal cues in the visual or auditory stimuli that motivated the coughing.

Coughing is a tension release and appeared to occur roughly within thirty seconds after the auditory tension peaks were released. The first sounds of the evil force in the attic sounded like coughing, followed by a rasping bronchial sound. Coughing, of course, can lead to an upset stomach.

The changes of Regan's voice—from that of a twelve-year-old girl to that of the devil—were carefully synthesized with the visual changes in her appearance. At some point during this transition, the girl's voice was replaced by the voice of

Mercedes McCambridge, an actress with a deep husky voice. Friedkin admitted to putting the actress's voice through a filter to produce a voice unidentifiable as either male or female.

In other words, the devil's voice was consciously perceived as androgenous, or hermaphroditic. This voice quality would not be meaningful at the conscious level, but would be subliminally apparent. No matter how natural voices are disguised, hypnotized humans are able to identify male or female voice characteristics. It would not be an exaggeration to state that *The Exorcist* visual effects were only props for the sound. A large proportion of the audience recalled the sound with great discomfort weeks after leaving the theater.

Questions for Discussion and Writing

1. Why did so many viewers of *The Exorcist* (1973 or 2000) experience such adverse physical reactions on seeing the movie, according to Key?

2. What archetypes and instinctive reactions were triggered by the sound patterns inserted by the director, William Friedkin?

3. Have you even seen *The Exorcist?* If not, rent a copy and write a paragraph or two agreeing or disagreeing with Key's analysis regarding the presence of subliminal stimuli. In what other films do you think subliminal techniques of the kind described by Key have been used? What were they?

SHEILA WHITELEY

Sheila Whiteley (b. 1941) is senior lecturer in popular music and the associate director of the Institute for Social Research at the University of Salford in England. She is the author of The Space between the Notes: Rock and Counterculture *(1992). The following essay is drawn from her 1997 book,* Sexing the Groove: Popular Music and Gender. *In 2000,* Women and Popular Music: Sexuality, Identity, and Subjectivity *was published.*

Mick Jagger, Sexuality, Style, and Image

INTRODUCTION

There is often a temptation to interpret the meaning of popular music through clusters of adjectives which articulate a stereotypical and predefined sexuality. "Brutal, menacing, erectile, tough" are words that are embedded in the folk wisdom of rock. They simultaneously identify, describe and characterise the macho style of performance which was to be coined "cock rock."[1] It is not difficult to

---

[1] Frith, S. and McRobbie, A. (1990) "Rock and Sexuality," in S. Frith and A. Goodwin, *On Record: Rock, Pop and the Written Word,* London: Routledge, p. 375.

substantiate these adjectives by reference to the early career of the Rolling Stones, and yet a closer examination of Jagger's performance style suggests a more complex gendered identity. The songs may imply a heterosexual mode of address. There is generally an emphasis on the penis as the absolute insignia of maleness, but live performances disrupt any notion of "normative" masculinity. Rather, they involve a self-presentation which is, at one and the same time, both masculine and feminine. As "the king bitch of rock," and with a performing style derived largely from a careful scrutiny of Rudolph Nureyev and Tina Turner, Jagger promised fantasy gratification to both the heterosexual and the homosexual.

It is thus suggested that Jagger's performance style opened up definitions of gendered masculinity and so laid the foundations for self-invention and sexual plasticity which are now an integral part of contemporary youth culture. In Manchester the "in clubs" of the 1990s are characterised by a new "campness." Masculinity has been replaced by a parody of the feminine, and transvestism is becoming an established part of the music scene.

My analysis of Jagger is based on the premise that performers and performances provide a particular insight into the meaning of rock and that this is different from listening to a song (on a CD, tape, record or radio). In the first instance, the imagination is freed to interpret the way that the text structures meaning; in the second, attention is drawn both to the song and away from it as the singer imposes a particular interpretation of the lyric content. It is also suggested that identification with a band contextualises performances, that the experience of the song is shaped by what has gone before. *Their Satanic Majesties Request* (1967), for example, was greeted with adverse criticism as it failed to conform to the expectations of a band classified as rhythm and blues. It is equally suggested that perceptions of a band are partly shaped by the media and that press reports of, for example, licentious behaviour not only feed the image of the band but equally inform the reception of a song. A singer who has raped a fan, for example, would have little credibility as a romantic icon. Alternatively, a group who are associated with "sex appeal" may well benefit from press reports which sensationalise their ability to attract "desirable women."

Thus, it is suggested that Jagger's role as singer is analogous to that of a complex character in an unfolding drama. He was, *is* Little Red Rooster, Jumping Jack Flash, Lucifer, the Midnight Rambler. His creation of a developing persona suggests an identity that is gendered and, at times, only ambiguously sexed. The effect is to provide a constructed "reality" in which he assumes an iconic embodiment of power[2] which offers specific insights into the relationship between audience and performer.

---

[2] The representation of Jagger's mouth with the diamond set in the right incisor is iconic in representing the essential nature of the Rolling Stones: macho, sexually dominant, anti-establishment (see for example their album sleeve *The Rolling Stones: Get Stoned:* 30 greatest hits, 30 original tracks).

FROM COCK ROCKER TO DOMINATRIX

The early success of the Stones is well documented. In part it is attributable to   5
the 1960s British rhythm and blues scene, with Jagger and Watts gaining experience in Alexis Korner's legendary band, Blues Incorporated. In June 1962 the em-
bryonic Stones gave their first performance "Brian Jones and Mick Jagger and the
Rollin' Stones." In January 1963, having replaced drummer Tony Chapman with
Charlie Watts and securing Bill Wyman as bassist, the band went on the club circuit
with a repertoire based largely on Berry/Diddley material. After an 8-month resi-
dency at the Crawdaddy Club, Richmond, the band attracted the attention of Andrew Loog Oldham. Formerly in public relations, he recognised the potential of
the band's nihilistic image and, as their manager, promoted them as sensual, insolent
and undesirable. In terms of market potential, it was a shrewd move. The Beatles
were fast becoming established as a clean-living, clean-cut Beat band and the
Stones provided an ideal counterpart.

It was, however, the controversy surrounding the band's cover version of
Willie Dixon's "Little Red Rooster" (1964) that finally established their reputation.
Riots had broken out in Chicago when the Stones had attempted to give press interviews after recording the *Five by Five* EP with Chess Studios. With "Little Red
Rooster" banned in the States for its overtly sexual lyrics, it is not too surprising
that the attendant publicity propelled the Stones into the limelight. Although arguably influenced by Muddy Waters and in a Chicago urban blues style, the characteristic sensual astringency of Jagger's vocal predominates. Indolent with sexual
innuendo, and accompanied by a guitar slide which ranges from a throb suggestive
of arterial blood to a quivering scream, the final verse links "my" little red rooster
to the penis itself. The record, not surprisingly, went to the top of the UK charts.

Jagger had already established his reputation as a "sexy" performer: he used to
wiggle his arse—it was lovely. . . . That was the best time, although predictable,
knowing that every time you did a certain set at a certain time, everything would
explode. And sure enough it did, and it always ended up in an absolute . . . gyrating
riot.[3]

Jagger's delivery, whereby musical gesture is embedded within an overtly
phallocentric performance style, would appear to conform to Frith and McRobbie's identification of the aggressive and boastful male.[4] "(I Can't Get No) Satisfaction" (1965) is dominated equally by Jagger's assertive delivery and the lead guitar
riff with which the song opens. The bare texture is underpinned by the deliberate
punctuation on rhythm guitar which works to establish a powerful four-in-a-bar
pulse. The verse is equally sparse, driven by overlapping riffs which support the
fragmented vocal line. At the same time, there is an underlying tension, as the slow

---

[3] Ibid., p. 25.   [4] Frith and McRobbie, op. cit., p. 375.

triplet rhythm of the opening words moves against, and frustrates, the relentless flow of the four-beat time.

Sexual arousal is musically encoded by the ascending sequence, the push towards the climactic "get," the slide down to "no" which prefaces the more languorous delivery on "satisfaction" which is itself subjected to a more intensive sense of arousal in the repetitive fade-out. While the lead guitar emphasises the rhythm of the words through strongly accented chords, the rhythm guitar returns to the opening riff, increasing the level of excitement through a precise and calculated rhythm which works to undercut the losing streak inferred by the words. The insistent pulsating guitar riff, and the sexual connotations of "(I Can't Get No) Satisfaction" make it apparent that Jagger's appetite is insatiable and that no one person is capable of satisfying it. On disc, the song acquires its particular force from the graphic dislocation between the triplet rhythm of the opening phrase and the four-in-a-bar beat. In theory, it is a simple procedure. In effect, it provides a precise musical equivalent of grinding, physical blockage. In performance, this sense of excessive sexual drive was even more overt. Conquests are counted, as the connotations of "try" are linked to the faceless "you" in the audience. This mood of aggressive sexuality was heightened in the Stones' late 1960s tours when a huge blown-up phallus dominated the stage.

With the Stones ideologically defining the position of masculinity and femininity through an emphasis on sexual prowess, songs can be interpreted as acting out a particular sexual iconography. There is little subtlety or gentleness, no coaxing to orgasm, rather a rhythmic obstinacy, reiteration to excess and an obliterating emphasis on high decibel sound. As such, the structure of the music, the hypnotically repetitive phrases, coupled with the exhibitionist style of performance, push towards a sexual energy which, in turn, is emphasised by the slogan-like repetition of key phrases: "(I Can't Get No) Satisfaction," "Let's Spend the Night Together." As Jo Bergman, the Stones' publicity officer, pointed out, their lyrics weren't exactly subtle. Jagger had suggested releasing the title track "Let It Bleed" as a promotion for their new album, but Jo had felt them to be too risky. "'Well, they're not just dirty, I mean they're *double entendre*,' Mick said. 'If you want someone to cream on, you can cream on me, is a pretty single *entendre*,' Jo said."[5]

As Jagger himself pointed out:

> What I'm doing is a sexual thing. I dance, and all dancing is a replacement for sex. What really upsets people is that I'm a man and not a woman....What I do is very much the same as a girl's striptease dance.[6]

Mirroring Tina Turner and the sexual nuances in her performance, it is not surprising that Jagger's stage presence expressed both a sense of female eroticism and

10

[5] Booth. op. cit., p. 15   [6] Christgau, R., "The Rolling Stones," cited in DeCurtis, A. (ed.) (1992) *Illustrated History of Rock and Roll,* 3rd edn, New York: Random House, p. 182.

the polymorphic.[7] His style of dancing, his use of make-up suggested that the whole of his being was directed towards arousing both sexes, and yet, at the same time, there is the suggestion of masquerade and play. There is an open invitation to take a good look, but if Jagger were to strip the illusion would be shattered.

It would appear that Jagger's ability to arouse both a heterosexual and homosexual audience is attributable in part to his own underlying femininity. As Robert Hughes points out, "He is a butterfly for sexual lepidopterists, strutting and jack-knifing across the stage in a cloud of scarf and glitter, pinned by the spotlights."[8] Marianne Faithfull also points to this sense of bi-sexuality.

> Mick enjoyed wearing some of the clothing of the women they [the Stones] were living with. It was this strong masculine-feminine force, which manifested itself when they were performing, that caused some people to regard them as bisexual. . . . It's almost a stylistic thing, it's the very heart of narcissism. It's just the desire, a very strong desire, to have people be in love with you. Whether it's a man or a woman isn't really very important.[9]

Although the identification of the "strong masculine-feminine force," the bi-sexuality, is helpful in discussing Jagger's essential narcissism, the actual construction of a

---

[7] Jagger's performance style was closely modelled on Tina Turner. "Mick was fascinated with the way Tina Turner moved on the stage. He studied her every gesture, her every move, all the nuances of her performance. And when he got back to his room, he would practise what he had seen in front of the mirror, endlessly dancing, gesturing, watching himself, moving his body rhythmically, the way Tina did. What seemed spontaneous on stage was really carefully rehearsed and plotted in front of the mirror." (Marianne Faithfull, cited in Hotchner, 1990. *Blow Away: The Rolling Stones and the Death of the Sixties.* New York: Simon & Schuster p. 167). As Easthope points out: "In terms of the myth masculinity wants to present itself as an essence—fixed, self-consistent, pure. In fact it has no essence and no central core. Gender is marked in three areas or levels of human experience—that of the body and the biological; that of social roles; and that at which gender is defined internally in the unconscious. The myth aims to bring all three levels in a perfect unity, the completely masculine individual. But it can never work like this because the levels are distinct and never simply overlap. If we use the terms 'male' for the body, 'man' for the social identity, and 'masculine' for the subjective tendency then we can see that they will not fit together evenly to make up 'one' individual. There are essentially two reasons for this. One is that each term can only fully be defined by its opposite—male/female, man/woman masculine/feminine. And the other is that the body always has to be installed in its social roles (this is what growing up involves) by means of an internal subjective process. And this process, which psychoanalysis describes as unconscious, always calls into play both masculine and feminine desire inside the individual" (Easthope, A. *What a Man's Gotta Do: The Masculine Myth in Popular Culture.* Boston: Unwin Hyman, pp. 166–167). "The account of sexuality given by psychoanalysis assumes that the human infant is polymorphously perverse, exploring without inhibition any possible avenue and site for pleasure. It also recognizes that the adult does not give up all its early pleasures but rather keeps his or her bisexual potential" (Easthope, op. cit., p. 104).   [8] R. Hughes cited in Hotchner, op. cit., p. 164.   [9] M. Faithfull cited in Hotchner, op. cit., p. 208.

specific femininity would appear to be centred essentially on a notion of power. There is little suggestion of the passive female in Jagger's performance. Rather, his dominating and provocative presence suggests more the image of the dominatrix, skillful and fully aware of her ability to control experience.

> One of the great things about sadomasochism . . . you just go ahead and say "Whatever feelings there are to experience, I will let them happen. . . ." I really am tired of this romantic model for sex where it's all supposed to be hearts and cupids and valentines. I like to be able to get dirty and rough and to tussle around and sweat and be strong. . . . The public in general thinks of sadomasochists as a bunch of blood-crazed sadists who want to commit mayhem on helpless victims. In fact, the culture is full of people who want to be tied up and have their brains fucked out . . . who are looking for a sadist.[10]

"PLEASE ALLOW ME TO INTRODUCE MYSELF . . ."

The emphasis on power-as-pleasure/pleasure-as-power was to find its ulti-   15
mate resolution in Jagger's satanic image. Attributable in part to the band's increasing involvement with the 1960s drug scene, the band had been getting deeper and deeper into the occult. "Led by Anita Pallenberg, Keith and Mick had developed a kind of satanic identification, as if they were openly dealing with the devil."[11] In particular, Jagger had become fascinated with *The Master and Margarita,* a book given to him by Marianne Faithfull, and which deals with satanic fantasy.

In terms of musical development, the emphasis on satanism linked to LSD was evident in their 1967 album *Their Satanic Majesties Request.* Considered at the time to be a pale imitation of the Beatles' *Sgt. Pepper's* album, *Their Satanic Majesties Request* marks a shift from rhythm and blues to psychedelic rock.[12] In terms of image, it heralds Jagger's musical self-identification as Beelzebub, a role already explored in Kenneth Anger's film *Lucifer Rising.*

Within the context of *Their Satanic Majesties Request,* Jagger's assumed role as master of ceremonies presages his emerging presence as Lucifer, the ultimate master of ceremonies. There is, then, a sense of crossing the galaxies. For the critic, the Stones may have appeared "lost in space," *Their Satanic Majesties Request* may have relied too heavily on studio production for an essentially live band, but at the same time there is a brooding sense of fantasy which is finally realised in "Street-Fighting Man," "Jumping Jack Flash," "Sympathy for the Devil," and "Goat's Head Soup."

---

[10] *S/M,* June 1988.   [11] Hotchner, op. cit., p. 344.   [12] Psychedelic musical codes are associated with blurred or tinkly timbres, electronic distortion, soundscapes, etc. See Whiteley, S. (1992) *The Space between the Notes,* London: Routledge, which examines the relationship between hallucinogenics and popular music.

Although "Street-Fighting Man," with its harsh timbres and basic aggressiveness, is focused by Jagger's experience of the Vietnam demonstration in October 1968, it also heralds Jagger's emerging persona as Lucifer. The call to overthrow established order may evoke memories of the Stones' role as symbolic anarchists; the sentiments may be focused by their interest in activism as evidenced by Jagger's attempt to join the demonstration at Grosvenor Square,[13] but essentially the focus is on the subversive potential of rock and his sense of self-identification as disturbance. In "Sympathy for the Devil" Jagger's role becomes firmly established. His name is Lucifer. Interspersed with grunts and screams there is a sense of self-destructive jubilation. The pounding beat has a primitive energy which evokes an ecstatic tribal response. The master of ceremonies, "His Satanic Majesty" finally emerges. Jagger is cast as "leader of the dance" and the final coda is explicit in its demands "I want ya baby."

Live performance provided a visual endorsement of the role. The Los Angeles performance (7 November 1969) is remembered by Ossie Clark as particularly frightening:

> there was a strange look on Mick's face, a kind of sneer. . . . the Stones appeared, the first note was played and the whole place erupted like a tiger roaring. I almost blacked out. This was not the wave of adulation I was accustomed to hearing, no this was like a mob being exhorted by a dictator. And then, when Mick went into his Lucifer routine with the black and red streamers flying, the audience seemed to spit out its defiance.
>
> He introduced himself as "a man of wealth and taste" who had been around a long time, had taken men's souls and achieved a catalogue of Satanic triumphs. I was trembling I was so frightened. And the more the audience's reaction intensified, the more Mick baited them. I expected a riot, an explosion. . . . I couldn't shake off the scar, the ominous feelings of that night. It stayed with me. For a week or more after that, I'd wake in the night in a heavy sweat. . . . I never designed another costume for Mick. . . . It was as if he had become Satan and was announcing his evil intentions. He was revelling in this role. Frightening, truly frightening. I always knew Mick had several clearly defined personas—talk about a split personality! But this was a side of Mick never revealed before. He was rejoicing in being Lucifer.[14]

At Altamont, the hooliganism associated with many of the Stones' earlier concerts became a massive certainty when LSD was tied to orgiastic exhibitionism.   20

"And then it happened. Mick wrapped his cloak around him and the band struck up "Sympathy for the Devil," Mick's definitive Satan song in which he

---

[13] Jagger had attempted to join in the demonstrations against the war in Vietnam at the American Embassy in Grosvenor Square but had been recognised by both the press and fans, who had asked for his autograph. He left, realising that fame could be counter-productive. The lyrics of the song were sent to the underground newspaper, Black Dwarf.   [14] Ossie Clark in Hotchner, op. cit., pp. 345–6.

introduces himself as "a man of wealth and taste. . . ." The Angels went berserk, the sickening sound of their smashing pool cues competing with the music. A young girl was clubbed right in front of Jagger as the stage became over-run with Angels. "'Rape, murder, it's just a shot away,' Mick sang over and over."[15]

In the Manson murders there was chaos, a commission of violence, rape and murder ideologically fused with a vision of occult sensuality. With Jagger, a similar position emerges. The symbolic celebration of satanism as presaged in *Their Satanic Majesties Request,* the association of Lucifer as Lord of the Dance, suddenly moved towards an enactment in reality.

What were those two people doing? It looked as if they were dancing and there was a flash of something shiny. The cameraman, his eye to the camera, said, "What the hell goes on, two people dancing with all this shit going on?" The camera was on it, but what had happened was too fast for us. As it turned out, the camera had recorded the killing of the black kid. The dance we thought we saw was a dance of death.[16]

In retrospect, it would appear that the unprecedented and excessive violence at Altamont was due to the take over by Hell's Angels, whose policing of the concert was characteristically brutal. Initially, the Stones appeared out of their depth and unable to perform, but as they regained confidence the delivery of such songs as "Midnight Rambler" and "Brown Sugar" appeared to feed the volatile mood in the auditorium. "Midnight Rambler" with its macabre lyrics, the night killer who waits in corridors with a knife ready to stab a victim, was particularly apposite to the occasion. In retrospect, it would appear unlikely that such songs would calm the already explosive atmosphere.

RETURN OF THE HONKY TONK WOMAN

"Sympathy for the Devil" was not performed live again for another six years. In retrospect it is tempting to suggest that the decision was prompted by its Luciferian associations, the focus on the song's historical mayhem juxtaposed with the grim reality of Altamont itself. As such, Decca's release of *Get Yer Ya-Ya's Out* (29 September 1970) may read like a callous and opportunistic retrospective on Altamont in its collation of such songs as "Midnight Rambler," "Street-Fighting Man" and "Sympathy for the Devil." But then, as Keith Richards revealed in 1970:

> We found out, and it wasn't for years that we did, that all the bread we made for Decca was going into making little black boxes that go into American Air Force bombers to bomb fucking North Vietnam. They took the bread we made for them and put it into the radar section of their business. When we found that out, it blew our minds.[17]

---

[15] Booth, op. cit., p. 92.   [16] Hotchner, op. cit., p. 21.   [17] Ibid., p. 373.

Richards's response focuses the band's basic dilemma. In terms of personal conscience, Decca's investment in the "little black boxes" stood for a misappropriation of the capital amassed for Richards/Jagger songs. At the same time, the bonding between audience and performer, which was fundamental to the Stones' essential sense of cultural and political subversion, had ultimately resulted in the death toll at Altamont. On the one hand, it was possible to sever ties with Decca and establish their own label, so placing them outside of the constraints and opportunism of the capitalist music business; on the other hand, the dilemma of personal direction was less easy to solve. It could be argued that the Stones were not unique in this respect. The early 1970s generally were characterised by a sense of underlying pessimism. The casualties at Altamont were curiously reflected at a macrocosmic level in the death of the decade itself: Martin Luther King and J. F. Kennedy had been murdered; Hendrix and Joplin were dead—the former through an inhalation of vomit following barbiturate intoxication, the latter from an overdose of heroin. Jim Morrison had died of a "heart attack" in Paris; Brian Jones had drowned in a swimming pool, the coroner's verdict: "death by misadventure." Marianne Faithfull, who had followed Jagger to Australia where he was to star in the ill-fated movie *Ned Kelly*, was to attempt suicide and Jagger was to break the relationship. At Kent State University, four students had been shot dead, tragically proving the depth of the gulf between those who wanted to change America and its policies in Vietnam and the conservative majority who believed in law and order politics at any cost. Finally, the particular association of LSD with satanism which had resulted in the Sharon Tate murders culminated in a panic reaction to the adverse effects of drugs. Personal survival, drugs and rock ideology generally were focused by the U.S. broadcast licensing authorities warning radio stations that they would be subverting the government's campaign against drug abuse if they mentioned lyrics which referred, however obliquely, to dope.

Again, it is tempting to draw an analogy with the band's own history, the juxtaposition of Brian Jones's funeral on 10 July 1969,[18] the release of "Honky Tonk Woman" on 11 July with its decadent lyrics and compulsive dance beat.

At the same time there is a certain sense of continuity. The "veiled" Jagger on the record sleeve refocuses androgyny within an overall context of death, sensuality and dance. As Elaine Showalter points out:

---

[18] During the Hyde Park concert to commemorate Brian Jones's death Jagger had attempted to revitalise the proceedings after his somewhat pretentious reading of Shelley and the abortive attempt to release white butterflies to enhance the meaning of "he is not dead, he doth not sleep." The band played an unrehearsed performance of "Honky Tonk Woman." "Mick's performance got increasingly frantic as he tried to over-compensate for the band's sluggishness, with the result that he really went overboard. He stripped off his dolly tunic and was leaping around in his vest and pants when he suddenly went to his knees, stuck his mike on his crotch and put his mouth over it, leaving nothing to the imagination as to what he was mimicking" (Hotchner, op. cit., p. 330).

veiling was associated with female sexuality and the veil of the hymen . . . it concealed sexuality. Furthermore science and medicine had traditionally made use of sexual metaphors which represented "Nature" as a woman to be unveiled by the man who seeks her secrets. . . . The veiled woman who is dangerous to look upon also signifies the quest for the mystery of origins, the truths of birth and death. . . . What lies behind the veil is the spectre of female sexuality, a silent but terrible mouth that may wound or devour the male spectator.[19]

The Stones' songs are not about a rational time sense, rather vitality with an emphasis on sexual energy. The sleeve of *Sticky Fingers* had simply featured a well-endowed crotch-shot of a pair of jeans complete with zipper, an icon to penis worship and sexual endowment, and Jagger was long reputed to be the best-hung star of all rockdom. Whether fact or fantasy, this exaggerated sense of "who you are," allied to an inflated performing ego and "a reported contempt for women who have been no more to him than objects of carnal desire"[20] has remained central to his image. At 53 image and reality remain conflated. Recent (October 1996) reports on his separation from Jerry Hall castigate him as a "serial womaniser," a "roué of rock, growing up disgracefully," a "hanky pank woman."

It is unlikely, however, that Jagger's latest escapade will undermine his success, rather it will underpin a continuing sense of notoriety. If rock continues to equate with penis-worship, whether this is ritualised through cock rock, cross-dressing, female impersonation or camp,[21] the sense of mastery of the feminine [will] remain a masculine phenomenon"[22] and Jerry Hall, like others before her, will become little more than "yesterday's girl."

30

---

[19] Showalter, E. (1991) *Sexual Anarchy: Gender and Culture at the Fin de Siècle,* London: Bloomsbury, p. 145.   [20] Marianne Faithfull also comments on such songs as "Yesterday's Papers" which she recognised as a "horrible public humiliation" for Chrissie Shrimpton with whom Jagger was living when he began his affair with Faithfull: "'Who wants yesterday's papers, who wants yesterday's girl. . . .'" "Under My Thumb" was also about Chrissie. You see, when he got her where he wanted her, he didn't want her any more" (Ibid., p. 39).   [21] The discussion of "campness" that follows is the result of extensive discussions with friends and colleagues, male/female heterosexual/homosexual/lesbian. *Camp:* attitude, a parody of both "gay" and femininity. To an extent this is an offshoot of the feminised male, an affirmation of duality. Camp takes this to an extreme through gesture, style and attitude. The mystery of the androgyne is replaced by overt characterisation. Essentially this is a male display. Women who exemplify "camp" (e.g. Victoria Wood) tend to emphasise a tripartite relationship, a woman parodying the male as female. Equally, whilst such artists as Julian Clary exhibit "campness," and where jokes are anally centred thus suggesting gay male exchange, the attributes and characterisation remain one of excessive gesture and attitude and, as such, a travesty of the feminine. As such, sensuality is demasculinised to be replaced by the constructed and overt—the dramatic hand gesture, the overtly flirtatious gaze, the parody of coyness.   [22] Cornwall, A. and Lindisfarne, N. (1994) *Dislocating Masculinities,* London: Routledge. p. 6.

A FEW FINAL THOUGHTS

As this chapter has argued, Jagger's performance style has depended largely on the development of an image which has moved from an initial categorisation of cock rock to one which suggests a more ambiguous sexuality. To an extent the identities are superimposed. The flaunting of sexuality is present throughout, whether this is represented by the Luciferian image or the self-parody evident in his more camp persona. In retrospect, it is evident that this legacy has been passed on. In the early 1970s there was an emphasis both on Glitter and Glam with its vanity, irony and emphasis on androgyneity. In the early 1980s, the emphasis was on presentation—"designer boys, material girls." In the 1990s, there is a resurgence of camp. Image predominates.

Whilst it is, perhaps, a cliché to suggest that we design gods in our image, there is nevertheless a certain resonance with Jagger's fictional incarnations as cock rocker supreme, androgyne, dominatrix, Lucifer. In one sense these images can be interpreted simply at the level of performance, the acting out of role. At the same time, they lock into the discourses surrounding gender and masquerade, that masculinities vary not only over time but according to setting. As discussed earlier, many of the Rolling Stones' songs can be considered gendered, in particular they exhibit specific sexist sensibilities. The themes of relationships centre around an unequal relationship in which Jagger, as singer, acts out a sexual iconography which is generally aggressive, dominating and boastful, occasionally self-pitying. Since the early 1960s, performances have often been accompanied by inflatable life-sized women and/or an inflatable phallus. The effect is to undercut any sense of self-doubt. The male world is constructed as an ideal world of sex without physical or emotional difficulties and masculine vulnerability is generally marked only by its absence. As such, it could be argued that the original discussion of cock rock by Frith and McRobbie needs only to be extended. The power of the phallus is omnipresent whether as cock rocker or androgyne.

At the same time, the extent to which Jagger's more macho persona conflicts with his androgyneity does raise problems. Clearly there is no one interpretation, but it is suggested that the mysterious image of the androgyne sets up an enigma which is focused on the interface between sexual difference (Jagger's real maleness, the androgynous performer) and the content of the song. As singer/songwriter he voices a male perspective, but at the same time his male/female persona serves to eroticise the songs by making him both the titillating/submissive woman and the male perpetrator of violence. The effect is almost one of rape fantasy—she led me on, she got her just deserts.

While it is not suggested that the Stones directly encouraged sex brutality, it could be argued that such songs as "Under My Thumb," such album sleeves as *Black and Blue*, provide a cultural expression of female subordination. In particular, the notion of compliance would appear to work in a manner similar to that of pornography in that it articulates the disruptive potential of sexual passion. On the positive side, it could be argued that Jagger's sense of ambivalent sexuality opened up definitions of gender which were to dominate much of the early 1970s and which are still prevalent today. In particular, they provide a framework within which the male performer and fan alike can find a range of heterosexual and homosexual expression.

Questions for Discussion and Writing

1. In Whiteley's view, what transformations have taken place in Mick Jagger's stage performances since the 1960s?
2. What common elements underlie the different personas he has adopted over these past four decades?
3. Describe your own reaction to Mick Jagger's performances. Drawing on Whiteley's exploration, analyze features of the Rolling Stones that would account for their continued popularity? For example, what use did the producers make of Mick Jagger's song "Sympathy for the Devil" in the soundtrack of the 1998 film *Father.*

MARY MCCARTHY

Mary McCarthy (1912–1989) was born in Seattle, Washington, and was educated at a convent, an Episcopal school, and Vassar College. Her writing is characterized by wit, stylistic virtuosity, and a keen observation of society's manners and mores. She is best known for her novel The Group *(1963), which was later made into a popular 1966 film. The following essay is drawn from her book* Venice Observed *(1966).*

The Paradox of St. Mark's

It was from Byzantium that the taste for refinement and sensuous luxury came to Venice. *"Artificiosa voluptate se mulcebat,"*[1] a chronicler wrote of the Greek wife of an early doge. Her scents and perfumes, her baths of dew, her sweet-smelling gloves and dresses, the fork she used at table scandalized her subjects, plain Italian pioneer folk. The husband of this effeminate woman had Greek tastes also. He began, says the chronicler, "to work in mosaic," importing mosaic workers—and marbles and precious stones—to adorn his private chapel, St. Mark's, in the Eastern style that soon became second nature to the Venetians.

The Byzantine[2] mode, in Venice, lost something of its theological awesomeness. The stern, solemn figure of the Pantocrator[3] who dominates the Greek churches with his frowning brows and upraised hand does not appear in St. Mark's

---

[1] "She indulged herself in artificial desire." The doge was the chief magistrate of the republic of Venice.   [2] *Byzantine:* pertains to a method of construction in the Byzantine Empire with round arches, low domes, a highly formal structure, and the use of rich color.   [3] Christ as "Ruler of All."

in His arresting majesty. In a Greek church, you feel that the Eye of God is on you from the moment you step in the door; you are utterly encompassed by this all-embracing gaze, which in peasant chapels is often represented by an eye over the door. The fixity of this divine gaze is not punitive; it merely calls you to attention and reminds you of the eternal, the Law of the universe arching over time and circumstance. The Pantocrator of the Creeks has traits of the old Nemesis,[4] sweetened and purified by the Redemption. He is also a Platonic idea, the End of the chain of speculation.

The Venetians were not speculators or philosophers, and the theological assertion is absent from St. Mark's mosaics, which seek rather to tell a Biblical story than to convey an abstraction. The *clothing* of the story assumes, in Venice, an adventitious interest, as in the fluffy furs worn by Salome in the Baptistery. . . .

St. Mark's, in the Ravenna style, was begun in 829, but it was twice destroyed, burned down once by the people in rebellion against a tyrannous doge, restored, and torn down again by an eleventh-century doge who wanted his chapel in the fashionable Byzantine style. (It was his successor, Doge Selvo, that married the Greek wife.) The present St. Mark's in the shape of a Greek cross with five domes and modeled, some think, on the church of the Twelve Apostles in Constantinople, is the result of his initiative. . . .

From the outside, as is often observed, St. Mark's looks like an Oriental pavilion—half pleasure-house, half war-tent, belonging to some great satrap. Inside, glittering with jewels and gold, faced with precious Eastern marbles, jasper and alabastar, prophyry and verdantique, sustained by Byzantine columns in the same materials, of varying sizes and epochs, scarcely a pair alike, this dark cruciform cave has the look of a robber's den. In the chapel of the Crucifix, with a pyramidal marble roof topped by a huge piece of Oriental agate and supported by six Byzantine columns in black and white African marble, stands a painted crucifix, of special holiness, taken from Constantinople. In the atrium, flanking St. Clement's door, are two pairs of black and white marble columns, with wonderful lion's and eagle's heads in yellowish ivory; tradition says they came from the Temple of Solomon in Jerusalem. From Tyre came the huge block of Mountain Tabor granite on the altar in the Baptistery—said to be the stone on which Christ was wont to pray. In the Zen chapel, the wall is lined with onion marbles and verdantique, reputedly the gravestones of the Byzantine Emperors.

In the chapel of St. Isidore sleeps the saint stolen from Chios; he was hidden for two centuries for fear of confiscation. St. Theodore, stolen from Byzantium, was moved to San Salvatore. St. Mark himself was lost for a considerable period, after the fire in 976, which destroyed most of the early church; he revealed his presence by thrusting forth his arm. He was not the original saint of Venice, but, so to speak, a usurper, displacing St. Theodore. Thus, he himself, the patron, was a kind of thieving cuckoo bird, and his church, which was only the Doge's private chapel,

5

---

[4] An ancient goddess who dealt out retributive justice.

imitated him by usurping the functions of San Pietro in Castello, the seat of the Patriarch and the real Cathedral (until very recent times) of Venice. In the same style, the early doges had themselves buried, in St. Mark's porch, in sarcophagi that did not belong to them, displacing the bones of old pagans and paleo-Christians.

Venice, unlike Rome or Ravenna or nearby Verona, had nothing of its own to start with. Venice, as a city, was a foundling, floating upon the waters like Moses in his basket among the bulrushes. It was therefore obliged to be inventive, to steal and improvise. Cleverness and adaptivity were imposed by the original situation, and the get-up-and-go of the early Venetian business men was typical of a self-made society. St. Mark's church is a (literally) shining example of this spirit of initiative, this gift for improvisation, for turning everything to account. It is made of bricks, like most Venetian churches, since brick was the easiest material to come by. Its external beauty comes from the thin marble veneers with which the brick surface is coated, just as though it were a piece of furniture. These marbles, for the most part, like the columns and facing inside, were the spoils of war, and they were put on almost haphazardly, green against gray, against red or rose or white with red veining, without any general principle of design beyond the immediate pleasure of the eye. On the Piazzetta side, this gives the effect of a gay abstract painting. Parvenu art, more like painting than architecture . . . , and yet it "worked." The marble veneers of St. Mark's sides, especially when washed by the rain so that they look like oiled silk, are among the most beautiful things in Venice. And it is their very thinness, the sense they give of being a mere lustrous coating, a film, that makes them beautiful. A palace of solid marble, rainwashed, simply looks bedraggled.

St. Mark's as a whole, unless seen from a distance or at twilight, is not beautiful. The modern mosaics (seventeenth century) are generally admitted to be extremely ugly, and I myself do not care for most of the Gothic statuary of the pinnacles. The horses, the colored marble veneers, the Byzantine Madonna of the front, the old mosaic on the left, the marble columns of the portal, the gold encrustations of the top, the five grey domes with their strange ornaments, like children's jacks—these are the details that captivate. As for the rest, it is better not to look too closely, or the whole will begin to seem tawdry, a hodge-podge, as so many critics have said. The whole is not beautiful, and yet again it is. It depends on the light and the time of day or on whether you narrow your eyes, to make it look flat, a painted surface. And it can take you unawares, looking beautiful or horribly ugly, at a time you least expect. Venice, Henry James said, is as changeable as a nervous woman, and this is particularly true of St. Mark's façade.

But why should it be beautiful at all? Why should Venice, aside from its situation, be a place of enchantment? One appears to be confronted with a paradox. A commercial people who lived solely for gain—how could they create a city of fantasy, lovely as a dream or a fairy-tale? This is the central puzzle of Venice, the stumbling-block that one keeps coming up against if one tries to *think* about her history, to put the facts of her history together with the visual fact that is there before one's eyes. It cannot be that Venice is a happy accident or a trick of light. I have thought about this a long time, but now it occurs to me that, as with most puzzles, the clue to the answer lies in the way the question is framed. "Lovely as a dream or a fairy tale. . . ."There is no contradiction, once you stop to think what images of beauty arise from fairy tales. They are images of money. Gold, caskets of gold, caskets of silver, the miller's daughter spinning gold all night long, thanks to Rumplestiltskin, the cave of Ali Baba stored with stolen gold and silver, the underground garden in which Aladdin found jewels growing on trees, so that be could gather them in his hands, rubies and diamonds and emeralds, the Queen's lovely daughter whose hair is black as ebony and lips are red as rubies, treasure buried in the forest, treasure guarded by dogs with eyes as big as carbuncles, treasure guarded by a Beast—this is the spirit of the enchantment under which Venice lies, pearly and roseate, like the Sleeping Beauty, changeless throughout the centuries, arrested, while the concrete forest of the modern world grows up around her.

A wholly materialist city is nothing but a dream incarnate. Venice is the world's   10 unconscious: a miser's glittering hoard, guarded by a Beast whose eyes are made of white agate, and by a saint who is really a prince who has just slain a dragon.

A list of the goods in which the early Venetian merchants trafficked arouses a sense of pure wonder: wine and grain from Apulia, gems and drugs from Asia, metal-work, silk, and cloth of gold from Byzantium and Greece. These are the gifts of the Magi, in the words of the English hymn: "Pearls from the ocean and gems from the mountain; myrrh from the forest and gold from the mine." During the Middle Ages, as a part of his rightful revenue, the doge had his share in the apples of Lombardy and the crayfish and cherries of Treviso—the Venetian mind, interested only in the immediate and the solid, leaves behind it, for our minds, clear, dawn-fresh images out of fairy tales.

Questions for Discussion and Writing

1. What details convey the materialistic nature of St. Mark's? What is the paradox to which McCarthy refers in the title?
2. How does the phrase the "robber's den" provide a metaphor with which to understand how the commercial and materialistic aspects of Venice strike the visitor?
3. How does McCarthy's depiction of Venice differ from the way it is usually represented in films and travel books? To what extent did McCarthy change your perception of what Venice is like?

LANCE MORROW

Lance Morrow was born in Philadelphia in 1939, received his B.A. from Harvard in 1963, and joined the staff of Time magazine shortly after graduation. As one of the magazine's regular contributors, he has written articles on a broad range of topics. Among his published works are The Chief: A Memoir of Fathers and Sons *(1985),* America: A Rediscovery *(1987),* Fishing in the Tiber *(1989), and* Safari: Experiencing the Wild *(with Neil Leifer, 1992), and* Heart: A Memoir *(1995). "Imprisoning Time in a Rectangle" first appeared in the special issue of* Time *(Fall 1989) devoted to photojournalism.*

Imprisoning Time in a Rectangle

Balzac[1] had a "vague dread" of being photographed. Like some primitive peoples, he thought the camera steals something of the soul—that, as he told a friend "every body in its natural state is made up of a series of ghostly images superimposed in layers to infinity, wrapped in infinitesimal films." Each time a photograph was made, he believed, another thin layer of the subject's being would be stripped off to become not life as before but a membrane of memory in a sort of translucent antiworld.

If that is what photography is up to, then the onion of the world is being peeled away, layer by layer—lenses like black holes gobbling up life's emanations. Mere images proliferate, while history pares down to a phosphorescence of itself.

The idea catches something of the superstition (sometimes justified, if you think about it) and the spooky metaphysics that go ghosting around photography. Taking pictures is a transaction that snatches instants away from time and imprisons them in rectangles. These rectangles become a collective public memory and an image-world that is located usually on the verge of tears, often on the edge of a moral mess.

It is possible to be entranced by photography and at the same time disquieted by its powerful capacity to bypass thought. Photography, as the critic Susan Sontag has pointed out, is an elegiac, nostalgic phenomenon. No one photographs the future. The instants that the photographer freezes are ever the past, ever receding. They have about them the brilliance or instancy of their moment but also the cello sound of loss that life makes when going irrecoverably away and lodging at last in the dreamworks.

The pictures made by photojournalists have the legitimacy of being news, fresh information. They slice along the hard edge of the present. Photojournalism is not self-conscious, since it first enters the room (the brain) as a battle report from the far-flung Now. It is only later that the artifacts of photojournalism sink into the textures of the civilization and tincture its memory: Jack Ruby shooting Lee Harvey Oswald,[2] an image so raw and shocking, subsides at last into the ecology of memory where we also find thousands of other oddments from the time—John John saluting at the funeral, Jack and Jackie on Cape Cod, who knows?—bright shards that stimulate old feelings (ghost pangs, ghost tendernesses, wistfulness) but not thought really. The shocks turn into dreams. The memory of such pictures,

5

---

[1] *Honoré de Balzac (born Honoré Balssa, 1799–1850):* French writer, best known for the novels and short stories of *La Comédie Humaine (The Human Comedy).*   [2] *Jack L. Ruby (1911–1967):* shot and killed Lee Harvey Oswald (1939–1963), the accused assassin of President John F. Kennedy, on November 24, 1963, two days after Kennedy was shot, in the Dallas County Jail, where Oswald was being held under arrest. A national television audience witnessed the event.

flipped through like a disordered Rolodex, makes at last a cultural tapestry, an inventory of the kind that brothers and sisters and distant cousins may rummage through at family reunions, except that the greatest photojournalism has given certain memories the emotional prestige of icons.

If journalism—the kind done with words—is the first draft of history, what is photojournalism? Is it the first impression of history, the first graphic flash? Yes, but it is also (and this is the disturbing thing) history's lasting visual impression. The service that the pictures perform is splendid, and so powerful as to seem preternatural. But sometimes the power they possess is more than they deserve.

Call up Eddie Adams's 1968 photo of General Nguyen Ngoc Loan, the police chief of Saigon, firing his snub-nosed revolver into the temple of a Viet Cong officer. Bright sunlight, Saigon: the scrawny police chief's arm, outstretched, goes by extension through the trigger finger into the V.C.'s brain. That photograph, and another in 1972 showing a naked young Vietnamese girl running in arms-outstretched terror up a road away from American napalm, outmanned the force of three U.S. Presidents and the most powerful Army in the world. The photographs were considered, quite ridiculously, to be a portrait of America's moral disgrace. Freudians spend years trying to call up the primal image-memories, turned to trauma, that distort a neurotic patient's psyche. Photographs sometimes have a way of installing the image and legitimizing the trauma: the very vividness of the image, the greatness of the photograph as journalism or even as art, forestalls examination.

Adams has always felt uncomfortable about his picture of Loan executing the Viet Cong officer. What the picture does not show is that a few moments earlier the Viet Cong had slaughtered the family of Loan's best friend in a house just up the road. All this occurred during the Tet offensive, a state of general mayhem all over South Vietnam. The Communists in similar circumstances would not have had qualms about summary execution.

But Loan shot the man; Adams took the picture. The image went firing around the world and lodged in the conscience. Photography is the very dream of the Heisenberg[3] uncertainty principle, which holds that the act of observing a physical event inevitably changes it. War is merciless, bloody, and by definition it occurs outside the orbit of due process. Loan's Viet Cong did not have a trial. He did have a photographer. The photographer's picture took on a life of its own and changed history.

All great photographs have lives of their own, but they can be as false as dreams.   10
Somehow the mind knows that and sorts out the matter, and permits itself to enjoy the pictures without getting sunk in the really mysterious business that they involve.

Still, a puritan conscience recoils a little from the sheer power of photographs. They have lingering about them the ghost of the golden calf—the bright object

----

[3] *Werner Heisenberg (1901–1976):* German physicist famous for formulating the quantum theory, which converted the laws of physics into statements about relative, instead of absolute, certainties. He received the 1932 Nobel Prize in physics.

too much admired, without God's abstract difficulties. Great photographs bring the mind alive. Photographs are magic things that traffic in mystery. They float on the surface, and they have a strange life in the depths of the mind. They bear watching.

General Nguyen Ngoc Loan, head of South Vietnam's police and intelligence, executing a prisoner. 1969 photograph by Eddie Adams.

Questions for Discussion and Writing

1. How, in Morrow's view, does photojournalism go beyond merely recording events in history to help create history itself?

2. How does Morrow use photos of Jack Ruby shooting Lee Harvey Oswald and a police chief of Saigon shooting a Viet Cong to illustrate the power of photojournalism to affect history? (See photo above of General Loan by Eddie Adams.)

3. Compare two newspapers or magazines to find two or more photographs of the same current event. In what ways do these two photos interpret the event in ways that are different from each other? Why would it be important to have a context within which to interpret the photos?

Fiction

JUNICHIRO TANIZAKI

Junichiro Tanizaki (1886–1965) was born in Tokyo, where his family owned a printing estab-
lishment and he studied Japanese literature at Tokyo Imperial University. His early novels were
strongly influenced by Poe, Baudelaire, and Oscar Wilde. After he moved to Kyoto in 1923, he   5
became absorbed in the Japanese past and abandoned his superficial westernization. Two of his
most important novels are Captain Shigemoto's Mother *(1949) and* The Key *(1956). The*
following story is from Seven Japanese Tales, *translated by Howard Hibbett (1963) .*

The Tattooer

It was an age when men honored the noble virtue of frivolity, when life was
not such a hush struggle as it is today. It was a leisurely age, an age when professional wits could make an excellent livelihood by keeping rich or wellborn young
gentlemen in a cloudless good humor and seeing to it that the laughter of Court
ladies and geisha was never stilled. In the illustrated romantic novels of the day, in
the Kabuki theater[1], where rough masculine heroes like Sadakuro and Jiraiya were
transformed into women—everywhere beauty and strength were one. People did
all they could to beautify themselves, some even having pigments injected into
their precious skins. Gaudy patterns of line and color danced over men's bodies.

Visitors to the Pleasure quarters of Edo[2] preferred to hire palanquin bearers
who were splendidly tattooed; courtesans of the Yoshiwara and the Tatsumi quarter
fell in love with tattooed men. Among those so adorned were not only gamblers,
firemen, and the like, but men of the merchant class and even samurai. Exhitions
were held from time to time; and the participants, stripped to show off their filigreed bodies, would pat themselves proudly, boast of their own novel designs, and
criticize each other's merits.

There was an exceptionally skillful young tattooer named Seikichi. He was
praised on all sides as a master the equal of Charibun or Yatsuhei, and the skins of
dozens of men had been offered as the silk for his brush. Much of the work admired at the tattoo exhibitions was his. Others might be more noted for their shading, or their use of cinnabar, but Seikichi was famous for the unrivaled boldness
and sensual charm of his art.

Seikichi had formerly earned his living as an ukiyoye painter of the school of
Toyokuni and Kunisada, a background which, in spite of his decline to the sum of a
tattooer, was evident from his artistic conscience and sensitivity. No one whose skin

---

[1] Popular drama of Japan characterized by elaborate costumes and highly stylized acting, music,
and dancing where male actors perform both male and female roles.   [2] Former name of Tokyo.

or whose physique failed to interest him could buy his services. The clients he did accept had to leave the design and cost entirely to his discretion—and to endure for one or even two months the excruciating pain of his needles.

Deep in his heart the young tattooer concealed a secret pleasure, and a secret desire. His pleasure lay in the agony men felt as he drove his needles into them, torturing their swollen, blood-red flesh; and the louder they groaned, the keener was Seikichi's strange delight. Shading and vermilioning—these are said to be especially painful—were the techniques he most enjoyed.

When a man had been pricked five or six hundred times in the course of an average day's treatment and had then soaked himself in a hot bath to bring out the colors, be would collapse at Seikichi's feet half dead. But Seikichi would look down at him coolly. "I dare say that hurts," he would remark with an air of satisfaction.

Whenever a spineless man howled in torment or clenched his teeth and twisted his mouth as if he were dying, Seikichi told him: "Don't act like a child. Pull yourself together—you have hardly begun to feel my needles!" And he would go on tattooing, as unperturbed as ever, with an occasional sidelong glance at the man's tearful face.

But sometimes a man of immense fortitude set his jaw and bore up stoically, not even allowing himself to frown. Then Seikichi would smile and say: "Ah, you are a stubborn one! But wait. Soon your body will begin to throb with pain. I doubt if you will be able to stand it. . . ."

For a long time Seikichi had cherished the desire to create a masterpiece on the skin of a beautiful woman. Such a woman had to meet various qualifications of character as well as appearance. A lovely face and a fine body were not enough to satisfy him. Though he inspected all the reigning beauties of the Edo gay quarters he found none who met his exacting demands. Several years had passed without success, and yet the face and figure of the perfect woman continued to obsess his thoughts. He refused to abandon hope.

One summer evening during the fourth year of his search Seikichi happened to be passing the Hirasei Restaurant in the Fukagawa district of Edo, not far from his own house, when he noticed a woman's bare milk white foot peeping out beneath the curtains of a departing palanquin. To his sharp eye, a human foot was as expressive as a face. This one was sheer perfection. Exquisitely chiseled toes, nails like the iridescent shells along the shore at Enoshima, a pearl-like rounded heel, skin so lustrous that it seemed bathed in the limpid waters of a mountain spring— this, indeed, was a foot to be nourished by men's blood, a foot to trample on their bodies. Surely this was the foot of the unique woman who had so long eluded him. Eager to catch a glimpse of her face, Seikichi began to follow the palanquin. But after pursuing it down several lanes and alleys he lost sight of it altogether.

Seikichi's long-held desire turned into passionate love. One morning late the next spring he was standing on the bamboo-floored veranda of his home in Fukagawa, gazing at a pot of *omoto* lilies, when he heard someone at the garden gate. Around the comer of the inner fence appeared a young girl. She had come on an errand for a friend of his, a geisha of the nearby Tatsumi quarter.

"My mistress asked me to deliver this cloak, and she wondered if you would be so good as to decorate its lining," the girl said. She untied a saffron-colored cloth parcel and took out a woman's silk cloak (wrapped in a sheet of thick paper bearing a portrait of the actor Tojaku) and a letter.

The letter repeated his friend's request and went on to say that its bearer would soon begin a career as a geisha under her protection. She hoped that, while not forgetting old ties, he would also extend his patronage to this girl.

"I thought I had never seen you before," said Seikichi, scrutinizing her intently. She seemed only fifteen or sixteen, but her face had a strangely ripe beauty, a look of experience, as if she had already spent years in the gay quarter and had fascinated innumerable men. Her beauty mirrored the dreams of the generations of glamorous men and women who had lived and died in this vast capital, where the nation's sins and wealth were concentrated.

Seikichi had her sit on the veranda, and he studied her delicate feet, which were bare except for elegant straw sandals. "You left the Hirasei by palanquin one night last July, did you not?" he inquired.   15

"I suppose so," she replied, smiling at the odd question. "My father was still alive then, and he often took me there."

"I have waited five years for you. This is the first time I have seen your face, but I remember your foot. . . . Come in for a moment, I have something to show you."

She had risen to leave, but he took her by the hand and led her upstairs to his studio overlooking the broad river. Then he brought out two picture scrolls and unrolled one of them before her.

It was a painting of a Chinese princess, the favorite of the cruel Emperor Chou of the Shang Dynasty. She was leaning on a balustrade in a languorous pose, the long skirt of her figured brocade robe trailing halfway down a flight of stairs, her slender body barely able to support the weight of her gold crown studded with coral and lapis lazuli. In her right hand she held a large wine cup, tilting it to her lips as she gazed down at a man who was about to be tortured in the garden below. He was chained hand and foot to a hollow copper pillar in which a fire would be lighted. Both the princess and her victim—his head bowed before her, his eyes closed, ready to meet his fate—were portrayed with terrifying vividness.

As the girl stared at this bizarre picture her lips trembled and her eyes began   20
to sparkle. Gradually her face took on a curious resemblance to that of the princess. In the picture she discovered her secret self.

"Your own feelings are revealed here," Seikichi told her with pleasure as he watched her face.

"Why are you showing me this horrible thing?" the girl asked, looking up at him. She had turned pale.

"The woman is yourself. Her blood flows in your veins." Then he spread out the other scroll.

This was a painting called "The Victims." In the middle of it a young woman stood leaning against the trunk of a cherry tree: she was gloating over a heap of men's corpses lying at her feet. Little birds fluttered about her, singing in triumph; her eyes radiated pride and joy. Was it a battlefield or a garden in spring? In this picture the girl felt that she had found something long hidden in the darkness of her own heart.

"This painting shows your future," Seikichi said, pointing to the woman   25 under the cherry tree—the very image of the young girl. "All these men will ruin their lives for you."

"Please, I beg of you to put it away!" She turned her back as if to escape its tantalizing lure and prostrated herself before him, trembling. At last she spoke again. "Yes, I admit that you are right about me—I *am* like that woman. . . . So please, please take it away."

"Don't talk like a coward," Seikichi told her, with his malicious smile. "Look at it more closely. You won't be squeamish long."

But the girl refused to lift her head. Still prostrate, her face buried in her sleeves, she repeated over and over that she was afraid and wanted to leave.

"No, you must stay—I will make you a real beauty," he said, moving closer to her. Under his kimono was a vial of anesthetic which he had obtained some time ago from a Dutch physician.

The morning sun glittered on the river, setting the eight-mat studio ablaze   30 with light. Rays reflected from the water sketched rippling golden waves on the paper sliding screens and on the face of the girl, who was fast asleep. Seikichi had closed the doors and taken up his tattooing instruments, but for a while he only sat there entranced, savoring to the full her uncanny beauty. He thought that he would never tire of contemplating her serene masklike face. Just as the ancient Egyptians had embellished their magnificent land with pyramids and sphinxes, he was about to embellish the pure skin of this girl.

Presently he raised the brush which was gripped between the thumb and last two fingers of his left hand, applied its tip to the girl's back, and, with the needle which he held in his right hand, began pricking out a design. He felt his spirit dissolve into the charcoal-black ink that stained her skin. Each drop of Ryukyu cinnabar that he mixed with alcohol and thrust in was a drop of his lifeblood. He saw in his pigments the hues of his own passions.

Soon it was afternoon, and then the tranquil spring day drew toward its close. But Seikichi never paused in his work, nor was the girl's sleep broken. When a servant came from the geisha house to inquire about her, Seikichi turned him away, saying that she had left long ago. And hours later, when the moon hung over the mansion across the river, bathing the houses along the bank in a dream like radiance, the tattoo was not yet half done. Seikichi worked on by candlelight.

Even to insert a single drop of color was no easy task. At every thrust of his needle Seikichi gave a heavy sigh and felt as if he had stabbed his own heart. Little by little the tattoo marks began to take on the form of a huge black-widow spider; and by the time the night sky was paling into dawn this weird, malevolent creature had stretched its eight legs to embrace the whole of the girl's back.

In the full light of the spring dawn boats were being rowed up and down the river, their oars creaking in the morning quiet; roof tiles glistened in the sun, and the haze began to thin out over white sails swelling in the early breeze. Finally Seikichi put down his brush and looked at the tattooed spider. This work of art had been the supreme effort of his life. Now that he had finished it his heart was drained of emotion.

The two figures remained still for some time. Then Seikichi's low, hoarse voice echoed quaveringly from the walls of the room: 35

"To make you truly beautiful I have poured my soul into this tattoo. Today there is no woman in Japan to compare with you. Your old fears are gone. All men will be your victims."

As if in response to these words a faint moan came from the girl's lips. Slowly she began to recover her senses. With each shuddering breath, the spider's legs stirred as if they were alive.

"You must be suffering. The spider has you in its clutches."

At this she opened her eyes slightly, in a dull stare. Her gaze steadily brightened, as the moon brightens in the evening, until it shone dazzlingly into his face.

"Let me see the tattoo," she said, speaking as if in a dream but with an   40
edge of authority to her voice. "Giving me your soul must have made me very beautiful."

"First you must bathe to bring out the colors," whispered Seikichi compassionately. "I am afraid it will hurt, but be brave a little longer."

"I can bear anything for the sake of beauty." Despite the pain that was coursing through her body, she smiled.

"How the water stings! . . . Leave me alone—wait in the other room! I hate to have a man see me suffer like this!"

As she left the tub, too weak to dry herself, the girl pushed aside the sympathetic hand Seikichi offered her, and sank to the floor in agony, moaning as if in a nightmare. Her disheveled hair hung over her face in a wild tangle. The white soles of her feet were reflected in the mirror behind her.

Seikichi was amazed at the change that had come over the timid, yielding girl   45
of yesterday, but he did as he was told and went to wait in his studio. About an hour later she came back, carefully dressed, her damp, sleekly combed hair hanging down over her shoulders. Leaning on the veranda rail, she looked up into the faintly hazy sky. Her eyes were brilliant; there was not a trace of pain in them.

"I wish to give you these pictures too," said Seikichi placing the scrolls before her. "Take them and go."

"All my old fears have been swept away—and you are my first victim!" She darted a glance at him as bright as a sword. A song of triumph was ringing in her ears.

"Let me see your tattoo once more," Seikichi begged.

Silently the girl nodded and slipped the kimono off her shoulders. Just then her resplendently tattooed back caught a ray of sunlight and the spider was wreathed in flames.

Questions for Discussion and Writing

1. What aspects of "The Tattooer" dramatize the secret affinity between love and cruelty?
2. In what way is the beautiful girl transformed psychologically by receiving the elaborate tattoo?
3. The *femme fatale* is a recurring archetype in literature and film throughout the world. What is the Western equivalent of the decadent glamour depicted in Tanizaki's story?

ANNE BRADSTREET

Anne Bradstreet (1612?–1672) was born in England and received a far fuller education than was usual for a young woman at that time. At the age of sixteen she married Simon Bradstreet and in 1630 the couple sailed to America with the first group of Massachusetts Bay settlers. Both her father and her husband later became governors of the colony. Despite the heavy demands placed on her as a housewife, mother of eight, and hostess at state affairs, Bradstreet wrote poems that her brother-in-law published in London (without her knowledge) in 1650. This volume, The Tenth Muse Lately Sprung Up in America, *presents Bradstreet as an ironic addition to the traditional nine muses of Greek mythology and was the first book of poetry published by a woman writer in colonial America. The following poem was composed in anticipation of a second edition of this volume (which appeared six years after her death).*

The Author to Her Book

Thou ill-formed offspring of my feeble brain,
Who after birth did'st by my side remain,
Till snatched from thence by friends, less wise than true,
Who thee abroad exposed to public view;
Made thee in rags, halting, to the press to trudge,   5
Where errors were not lessened, all my judge.
At they return my blushing was not small,
My rambling brat[1] (in print) should mother call;
I cast thee by as one unfit for light,
Thy visage was so irksome in my sight;   10
Yet being mine own, at length affection would
Thy blemishes amend, if so I could:
I washed thy face, but more defects I saw,
And rubbing off a spot, still made a flaw.
I stretched thy joints to make thee even feet,[2]   15
Yet still thou run'st more hobbling than is meet;

---

[1] *brat:* the word here emphasizes the insignificance rather than the unpleasant aspects of a child.
[2] Bradstreet is referring to her revision of the original poem to make the number of feet in each line match.

In better dress to trim thee was my mind,
But nought save homespun cloth, in the house I find.
In this array, 'mongst vulgars may'st thou roam;
In the critics' hands beware thou dost not come;   20
And take thy way where yet thou art not known.
If for thy Father asked, say thou had'st none;
And for thy Mother, she alas is poor,
Which caused her thus to send thee out of door.

Questions for Discussion and Writing

1. What is Bradstreet's attitude toward her "child," that is, her book of poetry, and to its initial publication without her consent?
2. What inferences can you draw about her everyday life from the homespun metaphors she applies to her writing?
3. Bradstreet refers to her work as if it were a child. In what sense do writers often think of their work as a kind of creation?

EMILY DICKINSON

Emily Dickinson (1830–1886) was born in Amherst, Massachusetts, and spent her entire life there. She attended the Mount Holyoke Female Seminary, where she quarreled frequently with the school's headmistress, who wanted her to accept Calvinist views. Dickinson became more reclusive in her mid-twenties, retired to the seclusion of her family, and in 1861 began writing poetry that was strongly influenced by the ideas of Ralph Waldo Emerson. She maintained a correspondence with Thomas Wentworth Higginson, an abolitionist editor who encouraged her to write poetry. During her life, she published only seven of the nearly eighteen hundred poems that she wrote. After her death, a selection of her work aroused public interest, and her stature as one of the great American poets is now unquestioned. "Tell All the Truth but Tell It Slant" expresses her artistic credo.

Tell All the Truth but Tell It Slant

Tell all the Truth but tell it slant—
Success in Circuit lies
Too bright for our infirm Delight
The Truth's superb surprise
As Lightning to the Children eased   5
With explanation kind
The Truth must dazzle gradually
Or every man be blind—

Questions for Discussion and Writing

1. How might the quality of Dickinson's personal reticence lead some readers to perceive her poetry as obscure?
2. How does the metaphor that Dickinson uses to explain her reasons for telling the truth indirectly illuminate her choice?
3. In your experiences, have there been circumstances in which the truth was too strong and could be approached only indirectly? Describe these circumstances.

LAWRENCE FERLINGHETTI

Lawrence Ferlinghetti was born in 1919 in Yonkers, New York, of immigrant Italian parents and was orphaned at an early age. With the help of a distant relative, he was able to attend the University of North Carolina. After he graduated, he served in the navy. During World War II, he was assigned to the Norwegian underground. After the war, he worked for Time *magazine and received an M.A. from Columbia University in 1948 and a Ph.D. from the Sorbonne in 1951. Ferlinghetti played a major role in the emergence of antiestablishment beat poetry and co-founded, with Peter D. Martin, City Lights Publishing House (the first all-paperback bookstore in the country) in San Francisco in 1952. His poetry, which is strongly political, is written in language and speech rhythms that ordinary people use. An influential collection of his beat poetry is* A Coney Island of the Mind *(1958). His most recent works are* A Far Rockaway of the Heart *(1997) and* How to Paint Sunlight: Lyric Poems and Others *(1997–2000) (2001). In the following poem, Ferlinghetti returns to the tyrannical repression of Spanish citizens that Goya[1] depicted in his series of etchings* Disasters of War *(Desastres de la Guerra) and his monumental painting* The Third of May, 1808.

In Goya's Greatest Scenes We Seem to See (1958)

In Goya's greatest scenes we seem to see
                                                   the people of the world
        exactly at the moment when
                they first attained the title of
                                           "suffering humanity"   5
        They writhe upon the page
                        in a veritable rage
                                of adversity

---

[1] *Francisco Goya (1746–1828):* eminent Spanish graphic artist and painter.

Heaped up
            groaning with babies and bayonets   10
                        under cement skies
    in an abstract landscape of blasted trees
        bent statues bats wings and beaks
            slippery gibbets
    cadavers and carnivorous cocks   15
    and all the final hollering monsters
            of the
                "imagination of disaster"
    they are so bloody real
                it is as if they really still existed   20

And they do
    Only the landscape is changed
They still are ranged along the roads
        plagued by legionnaires
                        false windmills and demented roosters   25
They are the same people
                only further from home
    on freeways fifty lanes wide
                on a concrete continent
                        spaced with bland billboards   30
                illustrating imbecile illusions of happiness
The scene shows fewer tumbrils
            but more maimed citizens
                        in painted cars
    and they have strange license plates   35
    and engines
            that devour America

Questions for Discussion and Writing

1. What images in the poem evoke the savagery, violence, and repression depicted in Goya's intense painting?
2. How does Ferlinghetti communicate a sense of the nameless victims' despair
   as they are exterminated?
3. In what ways can art, whether poetry or painting, serve as a vehicle of social
   criticism? What effect does Ferlinghetti achieve by transposing elements of
   the original scene into contemporary American society? What criticism of
   modern life is Ferlinghetti making?

Francisco Goya—The Third of May, 1808
Francisco Goya (1746–1828), the Spanish painter and etcher, did his early work in Madrid. In his work, we can see the arrival of romanticism. Goya became a libertarian in the late 1780s and later sympathized with the French Revolution, although he was appointed court painter to the king of Spain in 1799. When Napoleon's army occupied Spain in 1808, Goya initially hoped for liberal reforms, but his hopes were soon crushed by the unexpected savagery of the French troops. Many of his works between 1810 and 1815 reflect this bitter experience. Of these, one of the most impressive is The Third of May, *1808, commemorating the execution of a group of Madrid citizens. Goya's evocation of citizens as martyrs dying for the sake of liberty creates an indelible image that is timeless in its impact.*

Connections for Chapter 10:
The Artistic Impulse

1. **Kurt Vonnegut, Jr.,** *How to Write with Style*
   Compare the reasons why both Vonnegut and Alice Munro believe that writers should stick to what they know and keep it simple.

2. **Anne Tyler,** *Still Just Writing*

   In what way does Tyler's approach to writing, seeing the world through a "mist of irony," correspond to Emily Dickinson's desire to "tell it slant"?

   In your opinion, why does society place such different values on being a writer and being a rock star, such as Mick Jagger, as portrayed by Sheila Whiteley?

3. **Alice Munro,** *What Is Real?*

   Compare how Munro and Anne Tyler draw on real-life experiences for their fiction.

   In what sense is the idea of Niagara Falls as much a social construct (see William Zinsser's "Niagara Falls" in Chapter 2) as the illusions artists create?

4. **Wilson Bryan Key,** The Exorcist *Massage Parlor*

   Compare the archetypal significance of pigs in *The Exorcist* as discussed by Key and their religious meanings, as analyzed by Dinitia Smith in Chapter 11.

   What role does the demonic play in *The Exorcist* and in W. B. Yeats's poem "The Second Coming" (in Chapter 11)?

5. **Sheila Whiteley,** *Mick Jagger, Sexuality, Style, and Image*

   Discuss how Mick Jagger appropriated elements of the same devil archetype that pervades *The Exorcist,* according to Wilson Bryan Key.

   What role do pornographic and voyeuristic elements (see Margaret Atwood's "Pornography" in Chapter 4) play in Mick Jagger's performances?

6. **Mary McCarthy,** *The Paradox of St. Mark's*

   In what way does McCarthy's analysis point out the materialistic aspects of Venice that link it with America's consumer culture, as depicted by Juliet B. Schor in "The Culture of Consumerism" in Chapter 5?

7. **Lance Morrow,** *Imprisoning Time in a Rectangle*

   How do the Vietnam-era photographs described by Morrow help explain Tim O'Brien's ambivalence about serving in this war, as he describes it in "If I Die in a Combat Zone" in Chapter 11?

8. **Junichiro Tanizaki,** *The Tattooer*

   Compare the transformation of the girl in Tanizaki's story with the *personas* adopted by Mick Jagger, as described by Sheila Whiteley.

   In what way do Tanizaki and Douchan Gersi (see "Initiated into an Iban Tribe of Headhunters," Chapter 1) describe rites of passage that transform those who undergo them?

9. **Anne Bradstreet,** *The Author to Her Book*

   In what respects does Bradstreet's self-deprecating tone correspond to Anne Tyler's attitude toward her own writing?

10. **Emily Dickinson,** *Tell the Truth but Tell It Slant*

    Compare what Dickinson and Kurt Vonnegut say about the virtues of being concise.

    In what sense do Dickinson and Wilson Bryan Key (in "*The Exorcist* Massage Parlor") espouse the advantages of less-than-obvious methods of reaching audiences?

11. **Lawrence Ferlinghetti,** *In Goya's Greatest Scenes We Seem to See* (1958)
    From Ferlinghetti's perspective, a tragic undertone reminiscent of Goya's
    works can be discerned even in the most ordinary circumstances of Ameri-
    can life. What corresponding perceptions can you discover in Alice Munro's
    essay?

11

MATTERS OF ETHICS, PHILOSOPHY, AND RELIGION

Essays in this chapter offer a vivid and extensive range of responses to universal questions of good and evil and life and death. Clarence Darrow investigates the assumptions underlying the belief in immortality. Dinitia Smith examines the particular cultural settings in which pork became a sign of differentiation between religions. A selection by Garrett Hardin investigates the moral and ethical criteria by which actions are judged to be right or wrong and the trade-offs that must be accepted in some situations. As the writers in this chapter make clear, ethics become even more important as society becomes more complex and technological, and as people lose sight of important values.

Because ethical dilemmas involve choices, hypothetical scenarios are invaluable in dramatizing the consequences of these choices. Stephen Chapman compares Eastern and Western methods of punishment to discover which is more humane and just. Hans Ruesch offers insight into the ongoing ethical issue of vivisection.

Tim O'Brien confronts the dilemma of whether or not to serve in the U.S. Army during the Vietnam War, and Langston Hughes recalls a moment of personal choice when he confronted the issue of hypocrisy and religious faith.

Plato's "Allegory of the Cave" and parables drawn from the New Testament and from Buddhist and Islamic traditions are designed to convey a truth or a moral lesson. These works use distinctive comparisons, analogies, and storytelling techniques to transform philosophical issues into tangible, accessible, and relevant anecdotes.

The fiction of H. G. Wells and Joyce Carol Oates dramatizes various moral and ethical dilemmas by creating confrontations that require the main characters to make important choices.

The poems in this chapter dramatize life choices that we all confront: Robert Frost frames the issue in his classic poem, Lisel Mueller recaptures a lost optimism, and Dylan Thomas shares his deeply felt response to his father's mortality. Lastly, W. B. Yeats creates a moment of prophetic insight into evil that assumes the form of an awakened "rough beast."

Nonfiction

CLARENCE DARROW

Clarence Darrow (1857–1938) was one of the most colorful and controversial figures of his time. In 1925 he defended the biology teacher John T. Scopes in the infamous "monkey trial" concerning the teaching of evolution in Dayton, Tennessee. His best-known books are Crime, Its Cause and Treatment *(1925) and* The Story of My Life *(1932). The following article originally appeared under the title "The Myth of the Soul" in* The Forum *(October 1928) and contains Darrow's defense of agnosticism.*

The Myth of Immortality

There is, perhaps, no more striking example of the credulity of man than the widespread belief in immortality. This idea includes not only the belief that death is not the end of what we call life, but that personal identity involving memory persists beyond the grave. So determined is the ordinary individual to hold fast to this belief that, as a rule, he refuses to read or to think upon the subject lest it cast doubt upon his cherished dream. Of those who may chance to look at this contribution, many will do so with the determination not to be convinced, and will refuse even to consider the manifold reasons that might weaken their faith. I know that this is true, for I know the reluctance with which I long approached the subject and my firm determination not to give up my hope. Thus the myth will stand in the way of a sensible adjustment to facts.

Even many of those who claim to believe in immortality still tell themselves and others that neither side of the question is susceptible of proof. Just what can these hopeful ones believe that the word "proof" involves? The evidence against the persistence of personal consciousness is as strong as the evidence of gravitation, and much more obvious. It is as convincing and unassailable as the proof of the destruction of wood or coal by fire. If it is not certain that death ends personal identity and memory, then almost nothing that man accepts as true is susceptible of proof. . . .

It is customary to speak of a "belief in immortality." First, then, let us see what is meant by the word "belief." If I take a train in Chicago at noon, bound for New York, I believe I will reach that city the next morning. I believe it because I have been to New York. I have read about the city, I have known many other people who have been there, and their stories are not inconsistent with any known facts in my own experience. I have even examined the timetables, and I know just how I will go and how long the trip will take. In other words, when I board the train for New York, I believe I will reach that city because I have *reason* to believe it.

But if I am told that next week I shall start on a trip to Goofville; that I shall not take my body with me; that I shall stay for all eternity: can I find a single fact connected with my journey—the way I shall go, the part of me that is to go, the time of the journey, the country I shall reach, its location in space, the way I shall live there—or anything that would lead to a rational belief that I shall really make the trip? Have I ever known anyone who has made the journey and returned? If I am really to believe, I must try to get some information about all these important facts.

But people hesitate to ask questions about life after death. They do not ask, for they know that only silence comes out of the eternal darkness of endless space. If people really believed in a beautiful, happy, glorious land waiting to receive them when they died; if they believed that their friends would be waiting to meet them; if they believed that all pain and suffering would be left behind: why should they live through weeks, months, and even years of pain and torture while a cancer eats its way to the vital parts of the body? Why should one fight off death? Because he does *not* believe in any real sense: he only hopes. Everyone knows that there is no real evidence of any such state of bliss; so we are told not to search for proof. We are to accept through faith alone. But every thinking person knows that faith can only come through belief. Belief implies a condition of mind that accepts a certain idea. This condition can be brought about only by evidence. True, the evidence may be simply the unsupported statement of your grandmother; it may be wholly insufficient for reasoning men; but, good or bad, it must be enough for the believer or he could not believe.

Upon what evidence, then, are we asked to believe in immortality? There is no evidence. One is told to rely on faith, and no doubt this serves the purpose so long as one can believe blindly whatever he is told. But if there is no evidence upon which to build a positive belief in immortality, let us examine the other side of the question. Perhaps evidence can be found to support a positive conviction that immortality is a delusion.

THE SOUL

The belief in immortality expresses itself in two different forms. On the one hand, there is a belief in the immortality of the "soul." This is sometimes interpreted to mean simply that the identity, the consciousness, the memory of the individual persists after death. On the other hand, many religious creeds have formulated a belief in "the resurrection of the body"—which is something else again. It will be necessary to examine both forms of this belief in turn.

The idea of continued life after death is very old. It doubtless had its roots back in the childhood of the race. In view of the limited knowledge of primitive man, it was not unreasonable. His dead friends and relatives visited him in dreams and visions and were present in his feeling and imagination until they were forgotten. Therefore the lifeless body did not raise the question of dissolution, but rather of duality. It was thought that man was a dual being possessing a body and a soul as separate entities, and that when a man died, his soul was released from his body to continue its life apart. Consequently, food and drink were placed upon the graves of the dead to be used in the long journey into the unknown. In modified forms, this belief in the duality of man persists to the present day.

But primitive man had no conception of life as having a beginning and an end. In this he was like the rest of the animals. Today, everyone of ordinary intelligence knows how life begins, and to examine the beginnings of life leads to inevitable conclusions about the way life ends. If a man has a soul, it must creep in somewhere during the period of gestation and growth.

All the higher forms of animal life grow from a single cell. Before the individual life can begin its development, it must be fertilized by union with another cell; then the cell divides and multiplies until it takes the form and pattern of its kind. At a certain regular time the being emerges into the world. During its term of life millions of cells in its body are born, die, and are replaced until, through age, disease, or some catastrophe, the cells fall apart and the individual life is ended.

It is obvious that but for the fertilization of the cell under right conditions, the being would not have lived. It is idle to say that the initial cell has a soul. In one sense it has life; but even that is precarious and depends for its continued life upon union with another cell of the proper kind. The human mother is the bearer of probably ten thousand of one kind of cell, and the human father of countless billions of the other kind. Only a very small fraction of these result in human life. If the unfertilized cells of the female and the unused cells of the male are human beings possessed of souls, then the population of the world is infinitely greater than has ever been dreamed. Of course no such idea as belief in the immortality of the germ cells could satisfy the yearnings of the individual for a survival of life after death.

If that which is called a "soul" is a separate entity apart from the body, when, then, and where and how was this soul placed in the human structure? The individual began with the union of two cells, neither of which had a soul. How could these two soulless cells produce a soul? I must leave this search to the metaphysicians. When they have found the answer, I hope they will tell me, for I should really like to know.

We know that a baby may live and fully develop in its mother's womb and then, through some shock at birth, may be born without life. In the past, these babies were promptly buried. But now we know that in many cases, where the bodily structure is complete, the machine may be set to work by artificial respiration or electricity. Then it will run like any other human body through its allotted term of years. We also know that in many cases of drowning, or when some mishap virtually destroys life without hopelessly impairing the body, artificial means may set it in motion once more, so that it will complete its term of existence until the final catastrophe comes. Are we to believe that somewhere around the stillborn child and somewhere in the vicinity of the drowned man there hovers a detached soul waiting to be summoned back into the body by a pulmotor? This, too, must be left to the metaphysicians.

The beginnings of life yield no evidence of the beginnings of a soul. It is idle to say that the something in the human being which we call "life" is the soul itself, for the soul is generally taken to distinguish human beings from other forms of life. There is life in all animals and plants, and at least potential life in inorganic matter. This potential life is simply unreleased force and matter—the great storehouse from which all forms of life emerge and are constantly replenished. It is impossible to draw the line between inorganic matter and the simpler forms of plant life, and equally impossible to draw the line between plant life and animal life, or between other forms of animal life and what we human beings are pleased to call the highest form. If the thing which we call "life" is itself the soul, then cows have souls; and, in the very nature of things, we must allow souls to all forms of life and to inorganic matter as well.

Life itself is something very real, as distinguished from the soul. Every man knows that his life had a beginning. Can one imagine an organism that has a beginning and no end? If I did not exist in the infinite past, why should I, or could I, exist in the infinite future? "But," say some, "your consciousness, your memory may exist even after you are dead. This is what we mean by the soul." Let us examine this point a little.

15

I have no remembrance of the months that I lay in my mother's womb. I cannot recall the day of my birth nor the time when I first opened my eyes to the light of the sun. I cannot remember when I was an infant, or when I began to creep on the floor, or when I was taught to walk, or anything before I was five or six years old. Still, all of these events were important, wonderful, and strange in a new life. What I call my "consciousness," for lack of a better word and a better understanding, developed with my growth and the crowding experiences I met at every turn. I have a hazy recollection of the burial of a boy soldier who was shot toward the end of the Civil War. He was buried near the schoolhouse when I was seven years old. But I have no remembrance of the assassination of Abraham Lincoln, although I must then have been eight years old. I must have known about it at the time, for my family and my community idolized Lincoln, and all America was in mourning at his death. Why do I remember the dead boy soldier who was buried a year before? Perhaps because I knew him well. Perhaps because his family was close to my childish life. Possibly because it came to me as my first knowledge of death. At all events, it made so deep an impression that I recall it now.

"Ah, yes," say the believers in the soul, "what you say confirms our own belief. You certainly existed when these early experiences took place. You were conscious of them at the time, even though you are not aware of it now. In the same way, may not your consciousness persist after you die, even though you are not aware of the fact?"

On the contrary, my fading memory of the events that filled the early years of my life lead me to the opposite conclusion. So far as these incidents are concerned, the mind and consciousness of the boy are already dead. Even now, am I fully alive? I am seventy-one years old. I often fail to recollect the names of some of those I knew full well. Many events do not make the lasting impression that they once did. I know that it will be only a few years, even if my body still survives decay, when few important matters will even register in my mind. I know how it is with the old. I know that physical life can persist beyond the time when the mind can fully function. I know that if I live to an extreme old age, my mind will fail. I shall eat and drink and go to my bed in an automatic way. Memory—which is all that binds me to the past—will already be dead. All that will remain will be a vegetative existence; I shall sit and doze in the chimney corner, and my body will function in a measure even though the ego will already be practically dead. I am sure that if I die of what is called "old age," my consciousness will gradually slip away with my failing emotions; I shall no more be aware of the near approach of final dissolution than is the dying tree.

In primitive times, before men knew anything about the human body or the universe of which it is a part, it was not unreasonable to believe in spirits, ghosts, and the duality of man. For one thing, celestial geography was much simpler then. Just above the earth was a firmament in which the stars were set, and above the firmament was heaven. The place was easy of access, and in dreams the angels were seen going up and coming down on a ladder. But now we have a slightly more adequate conception of space and the infinite universe of which we are so small a part. Our great telescopes reveal countless worlds and planetary systems which make our own sink into utter insignificance in comparison. We have every reason to think that beyond our sight there is endless space filled with still more planets, so infinite in size and number that no brain has the smallest conception of their extent. Is there any reason to think that in this universe, with its myriads of worlds, there is no other life so important as our own? Is it possible that the inhabitants of the earth have been singled out for special favor and endowed with souls and immortal life? Is it at all reasonable to suppose that any special account is taken of the human atoms that forever come and go upon this planet?

If man has a soul that persists after death, that goes to a heaven of the blessed or to a hell of the damned, where are these places? It is not so easily imagined as it once was. How does the soul make its journey? What does immortal man find when he gets there, and how will he live after he reaches the end of endless space? We know that the atmosphere will be absent; that there will be no light, no heat—only the infinite reaches of darkness and frigidity. In view of modern knowledge, can anyone *really believe* in the persistence of individual life and memory?

20

THE RESURRECTION OF THE BODY

There are those who base their hope of a future life upon the resurrection of the body. This is a purely religious doctrine. It is safe to say that few intelligent men who are willing to look obvious facts in the face hold any such belief. Yet we are seriously told that Elijah was carried bodily to heaven in a chariot of fire, and that Jesus arose from the dead and ascended into heaven. The New Testament abounds in passages that support this doctrine. St. Paul states the tenet over and over again. In the fifteenth chapter of First Corinthians he says: "If Christ be preached that he arose from the dead, how say some among you that there is no resurrection of the dead? . . . And if Christ be not risen, then is our preaching vain. . . . For if the dead rise not, then is not Christ raised." The Apostles' Creed says: "I believe in the resurrection of the body." This has been carried into substantially all the orthodox creeds; and while it is more or less minimized by neglect and omission, it is still a cardinal doctrine of the orthodox churches.

Two thousand years ago, in Palestine, little was known of man, of the earth, or of the universe. It was then currently believed that the earth was only four thousand years old, that life had begun anew after the deluge about two thousand years before, and that the entire earth was soon to be destroyed. Today it is fairly well established that man has been upon the earth for a million years. During that long stretch of time the world has changed many times; it is changing every moment. At least three or four ice ages have swept across continents, driving death before them, carrying human beings into the sea or burying them deep in the earth. Animals have fed on man and on each other. Every dead body, no matter whether consumed by fire or buried in the earth, has been resolved into its elements, so that the matter and energy that once formed human beings has fed animals and plants and other men. As the great naturalist, Fabre[1] has said: "At the banquet of life each is in turn a guest and a dish." Thus the body of every man now living is in part made from the bodies of those who have been dead for ages.

Yet we are still asked to believe in the resurrection of the body. By what alchemy, then, are the individual bodies that have successfully fed the generations of men to be separated and restored to their former identities? And if I am to be resurrected, what particular *I* shall be called from the grave, from the animals and plants and the bodies of other men who shall inherit this body I now call my own? My body has been made over and over, piece by piece, as the days went by, and will continue to be so made until the end. It has changed so slowly that each new cell is fitted into the living part, and will go on changing until the final crisis comes. Is it the child in the mother's womb or the tottering frame of the old man that shall be brought back? The mere thought of such a resurrection beggars reason, ignores facts, and enthrones blind faith, wild dreams, hopeless hopes, and cowardly fears as sovereign of the human mind.

THE INDESTRUCTIBILITY OF MATTER AND FORCE

Some of those who profess to believe in the immortality of man—whether it be of his soul or of his body—have drawn what comfort they could from the modern scientific doctrine of the indestructibility of matter and force. This doctrine, they say, only confirms in scientific language what they have always believed. This, however, is pure sophistry. It is probably true that no matter or force has even been or ever can be destroyed. But it is likewise true that there is no connection whatever between the notion that personal consciousness and memory persist after death and the scientific theory that matter and force are indestructible. For the scientific theory carries with it a corollary, that the forms of matter and energy are constantly changing through an endless cycle of new combinations. Of what possible use would it be, then, to have a consciousness that was immortal, but which, from the moment of death, was dispersed into new combinations so that no two parts of the original identity could ever be reunited again?

These natural processes of change, which in the human being take the forms 25 of growth, disease, senility, death, and decay, are essentially the same as the processes

---

[1] *Jean H. C. Fabre (1823–1915):* a French biologist, renowned for his observations and experiments on insects, spiders, and scorpions.

by which a lump of coal is disintegrated in burning. One may watch the lump of coal burning in the grate until nothing but ashes remains. Part of the coal goes up the chimney in the form of smoke; part of it radiates through the house as heat; the residue lies in the ashes on the hearth. So it is with human life. In all forms of life nature is engaged in combining, breaking down, and recombining her store of energy and matter into new forms. The thing we call "life" is nothing other than a state of equilibrium which endures for a short span of years between the two opposing tendencies of nature—the one that builds up, and the one that tears down. In old age, the tearing-down process has already gained the ascendency, and when death intervenes, the equilibrium is finally upset by the complete stoppage of the building-up process, so that nothing remains but complete disintegration. The energy thus released may be converted into grass or trees or animal life; or it may lie dormant until caught up again in the crucible of nature's laboratory. But whatever happens, the man—the *You* and the *I*—like the lump of coal that has been burned, is gone, irrevocably dispersed. All the King's horses and all the King's men cannot restore it to its former unity.

The idea that man is a being set apart, distinct from all the rest of nature, is born of man's emotions, of his loves and hates, of his hopes and fears, and of the primitive conceptions of undeveloped minds. The *You* or the *I* which is known to our friends does not consist of an immaterial something called a "soul" which cannot be conceived. We know perfectly well what we mean when we talk about this *You* and this *Me*; and it is equally plain that the whole fabric that makes up our separate personalities is destroyed, dispersed, disintegrated beyond repair by what we call "death."

THE DESIRE FOR ANOTHER LIFE

Those who refuse to give up the idea of immortality declare that nature never creates a desire without providing the means for its satisfaction. They likewise insist that all people, from the rudest to the most civilized, yearn for another life. As a matter of fact, nature creates many desires which she does not satisfy; most of the wishes of men meet no fruition, But nature does not create any emotion demanding a future life. The only yearning that the individual has is to keep on living—which is a very different thing. This urge is found in every animal, in every plant. It is simply the momentum of a living structure: or, as Schopenhauer[2] put it, "the will to live." What we long for is a continuation of our present state of existence, not an uncertain reincarnation in a mysterious world of which we know nothing.

THE BELIEVER'S LAST RESORT

All men recognize the hopelessness of finding any evidence that the individual will persist beyond the grave. As a last resort, we are told that it is better that the doctrine be believed even if it is not true. We are assured that without this

---

[2] *Arthur Schopenhauer (1788–1860):* German philosopher who believed in the primacy of the will.

faith, life is only desolation and despair. However that may be, it remains that many of the conclusions of logic are not pleasant to contemplate; still, so long as men think and feel, at least some of them will use their faculties as best they can. For if we are to believe things that are not true, who is to write our creed? Is it safe to leave it to any man or organization to pick out the errors that we must accept? The whole history of the world has answered this question in a way that cannot be mistaken.

And after all, is the belief in immortality necessary or even desirable for man? Millions of men and women have no such faith; they go on with their daily tasks and feel joy and sorrow without the lure of immortal life. The things that really affect the happiness of the individual are the matters of daily living. They are the companionship of friends, the games and contemplations. They are misunderstandings and cruel judgments, false friends and debts, poverty and disease. They are our joys in our living companions and our sorrows over those who die. Whatever our faith, we mainly live in the present—in the here and now. Those who hold the view that man is mortal are never troubled by metaphysical problems. At the end of the day's labor we are glad to lose our consciousness in sleep; and intellectually, at least, we look forward to the long rest from the stresses and storms that are always incidental to existence.

When we fully understand the brevity of life, its fleeting joys and unavoidable   30
pains; when we accept the fact that all men and women are approaching an inevitable doom: the consciousness of it should make us more kindly and considerate of each other. This feeling should make men and women use their best efforts to help their fellow travellers on the road, to make the path brighter and easier as we journey on. It should bring a closer kinship, a better understanding, and a deeper sympathy for the wayfarers who must live a common life and die a common death.

Questions for Discussion and Writing

1. What baseless assumptions, in Darrow's view, are responsible for the widespread belief in immortality?
2. According to Darrow, what are the real questions people should ask? Do you agree with him? Why or why not?
3. Since Darrow was seventy-one when he wrote this, he might have been expected to become more religious as he reached the end of his life. Is this a phenomenon that you have observed? Are Darrow's viewpoints uncommon? Do you know anyone like him? In a short essay, write a rebuttal to Darrow or support his argument with additional points.

DINITIA SMITH

Dinitia Smith (b. 1945) is an accomplished journalist who has won an Emmy Award, a Broadcast Media Award, and a Golden Gate Award. Her published works include Hard Rain *(1980),* Remember This *(1989), and* Illusionist: A Novel *(1997), in addition to stories for the* Hudson Review *and* Cosmopolitan. *In the following article, which first appeared in* The New York Times *(1998), Smith explores why various religions down through the ages have invested such significance in the consumption or avoidance of pork.*

Did a Barnyard Schism Lead to a Religious One?

Throughout history, the pig has been an animal with a deeply fraught significance for Christians and Jews as well as Muslims. Why, for example, are Jews forbidden to eat pig meat at the same time Christians happily serve up ham for Easter?

The answer may involve more than simply the biblical prohibition against Jews eating pork. If you understand the pig's symbolism, you can understand the complex and often tortured relationship between Jews and Christians, says the French cultural anthropologist, Claudine Fabre-Vassas. In her book *The Singular Beast: Jews, Christians and the Pig* (Columbia University Press, 1997), Ms. Fabre-Vassas depicts the pig not only as a beloved figure in medieval and modern Christian households, prized as both a pet in peasant cultures and a source of delicious food, but also as a symbol of a hated figure, the Jew, of the very group that scorns it as unclean. Ms. Fabre-Vassas argues that the cultural tension between those who did and those who did not eat pork helps set the stage for a murderous anti-Semitism.

The Jewish interdiction against the pig is first mentioned in the Old Testament. In Leviticus 11:27, God forbids Moses and his followers to eat swine "because it parts the hoof but does not chew the cud." Furthermore, the prohibition goes, "Of their flesh you shall not eat, and their carcasses you shall not touch; they are unclean to you." That message is later reinforced in Deuteronomy. Muslims, who follow Mosaic law inherited the prohibition.

Over the years, various explanations have been offered for the Old Testament commandment. The 12th-century rabbi Moses Maimonides, court physician to the Muslim sultan and warrior Saladin, said the prohibition against eating pig meat was for health reasons as it had a "bad and damaging effect" upon the body.

Beginning in the 19th century, scholars offered a different explanation. In *The Golden Bough,* Sir James Frazer wrote that pig meat was forbidden because it had originally been used for sacrifice. "All so-called unclean animals were originally sacred," Sir James wrote. "The reason for not eating them is that many were originally divine."   5

The British anthropologist Mary Douglas, in her 1966 book *Purity and Danger: An Analysis of Concepts of Pollution and Taboo,* explains the prohibition as a problem of taxonomy: the pig did not fit conveniently into the Israelites' definitions of what a domestic animal should be (the cloven hooves, the failure to chew their cuds like cows). Animals like pigs that cross over definitions, Ms. Douglas argues, that crawl instead of walk or swarm instead of fly, defied the tribal need to create an intellectual ordering of the world. Disorder of any kind, Ms. Douglas writes, provided a frightening glimpse into the chaos inherent in the universe.

Later, another anthropologist, Marvin Harris, gave a decidedly utilitarian explanation for the taboo against pork, arguing in his 1974 book *Cows, Pigs, Wars and*

Witches: The Riddles of Culture that the prohibition was a response to the realities of nomadic life in the arid stretches of Palestine.

Mr. Harris points out that the pig does indeed wallow in its own filth, and eats its own feces, but usually only under conditions of severe drought. Cows and sheep will also eat their own feces under extremely dry conditions, he adds.

But pigs require larger amounts of moisture than cows or sheep, he says, and are therefore difficult to raise in hot, dry climates: it was easier, in the end, to forbid people to eat something that they might long for. "Better then, to interdict the consumption of pork entirely," Mr. Harris writes, "and to concentrate on raising goats, sheep and cattle. Pigs tasted good, but it was too expensive to feed them and keep them cool."

Whatever the reason, the prohibition against eating pig meat became an iden-   10
tifying feature, a defining characteristic of Jewishness. And that, says Alan Dundes, professor of anthropology and folklore at the University of California, Berkeley, is precisely the reason that Christians not only eat pork, but even celebrate it by eating it on holidays. "You distinguish yourself by not doing what others do," Mr. Dundes writes.

It was in the early Christian period, in the first century, that the great divide opened up between those who ate pork and those who didn't. Early Christians, then simply a sect among the Jews, were faced with the problem of distinguishing themselves. They did not circumcise their children. And they ate pork, the very animal that their fellow Jews avoid. What's more, where Jews, under biblical command, drained the blood of meat before they ate it, Christians symbolically drank the blood of Christ and ate His body through the sacrament of the Eucharist.

"It is in the most intimate things, the things people sometimes take for granted that people define themselves," said Gilliar Feeley-Harnik, a professor of anthropology at John Hopkins University and the author of *The Lord's Table: The Meaning of Food in Early Judaism and Christianity* (Smithsonian Institution Press, 1994). "There is virtually no religion that we know of that doesn't define itself with food."

It is a tragic irony, Ms. Fabre-Vassas writes in her book, that as anti-Semitism took on its shape in medieval Europe, the pig—and his blood—became a symbol for the Jew himself.

Taking her cue from the French anthropologist Claude Lévi-Strauss, Ms. Fabre-Vassas studied the culinary habits of southern France, and the way in which the pig began to be associated with the Jew in the anti-Semitic imaginings of peasant culture, and by implication the rest of Europe. Ms. Fabre-Vassas shows how the pig become the food of choice for many Christian religious feasts.

"In my research in the mountains, she said recently, through a translator, "I re-   15
alized that the pig was the most important animal in the village culinary tradition. A whole ceremony is attached to its death and cooking. It unites members of the community around a party." Ms. Fabre-Vassas studied methods of breeding pigs, feeding them, circumcising them, detecting disease in them and slaughtering them, up until the 20th century.

But according to Ms. Fabre-Vassas, Christians were faced with the problem. They had defined themselves as being "not Jews," in other words pig eaters and, symbolically, blood drinkers. Yet at the same time, Christians acknowledge the Hebrew Bible, the Old Testament, as part of their Scripture. Ms. Fabre-Vassas writes that Christians were faced with the spiritual problem of how to separate themselves from their Jewish heritage while acknowledging their common Old Testament roots.

Therefore, she writes, rituals grew up around the pig that drew on both traditions. For instance, frequently the blood was drained from the pig before it was cooked and eaten, as Jewish law decrees, in the eating of all meats.

Above all, Christians had to explain away the Jewish prohibition against eating the pig, a central tenet of Old Testament Law. "The duality of the pig's image is fascinating," she said, "It is seen as evil, wild, diabolical on one side, and on the other it is a symbol of the wealth and pride in the house." More than any other barnyard animal, pigs were adaptable as household pets, often living in close proximity to children. There had to be a justification for the eventual killing of these pets for meat, she said. It was amid these seemingly insoluble problems that the pig began to be seen as a symbol for Jews.

In the anti-Semitic lore that sprang up, it was said that Christ had turned Jewish children into pigs to show His power, and that Jews didn't eat pigs because they were their own children. Another result of these crude imaginings was the explanation that Jews actually originated from pigs, that they didn't eat pig meat because it would be like eating themselves. "Since they deprived themselves of this meat," Ms. Fabre-Vassas wrote, "they were constantly seeking the closest human substitute, the flesh and blood of Christian children." Myths like these spread through the folklore of Poland and the Ukraine, areas that were to become the killing grounds of the Holocaust.

Ms. Fabre-Vassas's book includes illustrations of anti-Semitic woodcuts that show Jews suckling pigs. Later, during the 1930's, it was vicious, primitive images like these that found their way into the anti-Semitic writings of Julius Streicher's newspaper *Stürmer,* which has been called the mass circulation gazette of genocide. [20]

Through a complex, subrational process, Ms. Fabre-Vassas writes, it was as if a tragic variation of the old folkloric belief had taken place: in the end, Jews had become what they did not eat.

Questions for Discussion and Writing

1. The emotionally charged meanings attached to the eating of pork provide a fascinating glimpse into how religions differentiate themselves from other religions by using food taboos. According to Smith, how does this differentiation work?

2. Smith cites a number of anthropologists as sources for a variety of conjectures on the history of pig symbolism. How would theologians view the same phenomenon in a very different way from the anthropologists?

3. Do you observe any food taboos based on religious or ethical beliefs? If so, discuss their significance and investigate their origins.

HANS RUESCH

*Hans Ruesch (b. 1913) is a modern-day Renaissance man who not only is a scholar of the history of medicine but has also written best-selling novels—*The Racer *(1953),* Savage Innocents *(1960), and* Back to the Top of the World *(1973)—and many short stories that have appeared in* The Saturday Evening Post, Esquire, *and* Redbook. *This Swiss author is best known for his brilliant exposés of the animal experimentation industry, catalogued in such books as* Naked Empress: The Great Medical Fraud *(1982) and* Slaughter of the Innocent *(1983), from which the following chapter is reprinted. He currently lives in Milan, Italy, and is the founder and director of Civis: The International Foundation Report Dedicated to the Abolition of Vivisection.*

Slaughter of the Innocent

SCIENCE OR MADNESS

A dog is crucified in order to study the duration of the agony of Christ. A pregnant bitch is disemboweled to observe the maternal instinct in the throes of pain. Experimenters in an American university cause convulsions in dogs and cats, to study their brain waves during the seizures, which gradually become more frequent and severe until the animals are in a state of continual seizure that leads to their death in 3 to 5 hours; the experimenters then supply several charts of the brain waves in question, but no idea how they could be put to any practical use.

Another team of "scientists" submits to fatal scaldings 15,000 animals of various species, then administer to half of them a liver extract that is already known to be useful in case of shock: As expected, the treated animals agonize longer than the others.

Beagles, well-known for their mild and affectionate natures, are tortured until they start attacking each other. The "scientists" responsible for this announce that they were "conducting a study on juvenile delinquency."

Exceptions? Borderline cases? I wish they were.

Every day of the year, at the hands of white-robed individuals recognized as   5
medical authorities, or bent on getting such recognition, or a degree, or at least a lucrative job, millions of animals—mainly mice, rats, guinea-pigs, hamsters, dogs, cats, rabbits, monkeys, pigs, turtles; but also horses, donkeys, goats, birds and fishes—are slowly blinded by acids, submitted to repeated shocks or intermittent submersion, poisoned, inoculated with deadly diseases, disemboweled, frozen to be revived and refrozen, starved or left to die of thirst, in many cases after various glands have been entirely or partially extirpated or the spinal cord has been cut.

The victims' reactions are then meticulously recorded, except during the long weekends, when the animals are left unattended to meditate about their sufferings; which may last weeks, months, years, before death puts an end to their ordeal—death being the only effective anesthesia most of the victims get to know.

But often they are not left in peace even then: Brought back to life—miracle of modern science—they are subjected to ever new series of tortures. Pain-crazed dogs have been seen devouring their own paws, convulsions have thrown cats against the walls of their cages until the creatures collapsed, monkeys have clawed and gnawed at their own bodies or killed their cage mates.

This and much more has been reported by the experimenters themselves in leading medical journals such as Britain's *Lancet* and its American, French, German and Swiss counterparts, from which most of the evidence here presented derives.

But don't stop reading just yet—because the purpose of this book is to show you how you can, and why you should, put a stop to all that.

THE REFINEMENTS

Each new experiment inspires legions of "researchers" to repeat it, in the hope of confirming or debunking it; to procure the required tools or to devise new, "better" ones. Apart from a long series of "restraining devices," derived from the "Czermak Table," the "Pavlov Stock" and other classic apparatuses which decorate those pseudoscientific laboratories the world over, there exist some particularly ingenious instruments, usually named after their inventors.

One is the *Noble-Collip Drum,* a household word among physiologists since 1942, when it was devised by two Toronto doctors, R. L. Noble and J. B. Collip, who described it in *The Quarterly Journal of Experimental Physiology* (Vol. 31, No. 3, 1942, p. 187) under the telltale title "A Quantitative Method for the Production of Experimental Traumatic Shock without Haemorrhage in Unanesthetized Animals": "The underlying principle of the method is to traumatize the animal by placing it in a revolving drum in which are projections or bumps . . . The number of animals dying showed a curve in proportion to the number of revolutions . . . When animals were run without having their paws taped they were found to give irregular results, since some would at first jump over the bumps until fatigued, and so protect themselves . . ."

There is the *Ziegler Chair,* an ingenious metal seat described in *Journal of Laboratory and Clinical Medicine* (Sept. 1952), invented by Lt. James E. Ziegler of the Medical Corps, U.S. Navy, Johnsville, Pa. One of the advantages claimed in the descriptive article for the apparatus is that "the head and large areas of the monkey's body are exposed and thus accessible for various manipulations." The uses of the chair include perforation of the skull with stimulation of the exposed cortex, implantation of cranial windows, general restraint for dressings, and as a seat for the monkey in various positions on the large experimental centrifuge for periods that may last uninterruptedly for years, until death.

There is the *Blalock Press,* so named after Dr. Alfred Blalock of the famed Johns Hopkins Institute in Baltimore, Md. Constructed of heavy steel, it resembles an ancient printing press. But the plates are provided with steel ridges that mesh together when the top plate is forced against the bottom plate. Pressure of up to 5,000 pounds is exerted by a heavy automobile spring compressed by tightening four nuts. The purpose is to crush the muscular tissue in a dog's legs without crushing the bone.

There is the *Collison Cannula,* designed to be implanted into the head of various animals to facilitate the repeated passage of hypodermic needles, electrodes,

10

pressure gauges, etc., into the cranial cavity of the fully conscious animal—mostly cats and monkeys. The cannula is permanently fixed to the bone with acrylic cement anchored by four stainless-steel screws screwed into the skull. After undergoing this severe traumatic experience, the animal must be given at least a week to recover before the experiments proper can begin—as described in *Journal of Physiology,* October 1972. (In time, in an unsuccessful attempt to reject it, a purse of pus grows around the firmly anchored cannula and seeps into the victims' eyes and sinuses, eventually leading to blindness and death—sometimes one or two years later.)

There is the *Horsley-Clarke Stereotaxic Device,* so named after the two doctors   15
who designed it to immobilize small animals during the implantation of the aforementioned cannula, for the traditional brain "experiments" that have never led to any other practical result than procuring the Nobel Prize for Prof. Walter R. Hess of Zurich University in 1949, and fat subsidies for various colleagues all over the world.

It may as well be pointed out right now that Nobel prizes in biology, physiology and medicine—as well as the various grants for "medical research"—are conferred on the recommendations of committees of biologists, physiologists and doctors, who have either been similarly favored by the colleagues they recommend, or who hope to be repaid in kind.

WHAT IS VIVISECTION?

The term vivisection "is now used to apply to all types of experiments on living animals, whether or not cutting is done." So states the *Encyclopedia Americana* (International Edition, 1974). And the large *Merriam-Webster* (1963): ". . . broadly, any form of animal experimentation, especially if considered to cause distress to the subject." Thus the term also applies to experiments done with the administration of noxious substances, bums, electric or traumatic shocks, drawn-out deprivations of food and drink, psychological tortures leading to mental imbalance, and so forth. The term was employed in that sense by the physiologists of the last century who started this kind of "medical research," and so it will be used by me. By "vivisectionist" is usually meant every upholder of this method; by "vivisector" someone who performs such experiments or participates in them.

The "scientific" euphemism for vivisection is "basic research" or "research on models"—"model" being the euphemism for laboratory animal.

Though the majority of practicing physicians defend vivisection, most of them don't know what they are defending, having never set foot in a vivisection laboratory. Conversely, the great majority of vivisectors have never spent five minutes at a sick man's bedside, for the good reason that most of them decide to dedicate themselves to laboratory animals when they fail that most important medical examination, the one that would allow them to practice medicine. And many more take up "research" because that requires no formal studying. Any dunce can cut up live animals and report what he sees.

The number of animals dying of tortures through the practice of vivisection   20
is estimated at around 400,000 a day worldwide at the time of this writing, and is

growing at an annual rate of about 5 percent. Those experiments are performed in tens of thousands of clinical, industrial and university laboratories. All of them, without exception, deny access to channels of independent information. Occasionally, they take a journalist, guaranteed "tame," on a guided tour of a laboratory as carefully groomed as one of Potemkin's villages.

Today we no longer torture in the name of the Lord, but in the name of a new, despotic divinity—a so-called Medical Science which, although amply demonstrated to be false, successfully uses through its priests and ministers the tactics of terrorism: "If you don't give us plenty of money and a free hand with animals, you and your children will die of cancer"—well knowing that modern man does not fear God, but fears Cancer, and has never been told that most cancers, and maybe all, are fabricated through incompetence in the vivisection laboratories.

In the past, humanity was trained to tolerate cruelty to human beings on the grounds of a widespread superstition. Today humanity has been trained to tolerate cruelty to animals on the grounds of another superstition, equally widespread. There is a chilling analogy between the Holy Inquisitors[1] who extracted confessions by torture from those suspected of witchcraft, and the priests of modern science who employ torture trying to force information and answers from animals. Meanwhile, the indifferent majority prefers to ignore what is going on around them, so long as they are left alone.

Vivisectors indignantly reject charges that their driving motive is avarice, ambition, or sadism disguised as scientific curiosity. On the contrary, they present themselves as altruists, entirely dedicated to the welfare of mankind. But intelligent people of great humanity—from Leonardo da Vinci to Voltaire to Goethe to Schweitzer[2]—have passionately declared that a species willing to be "saved" through such means would not be worth saving. And furthermore there exists by now a crushing documentation that vivisection is not only an inhuman and dehumanizing practice, but a continuing source of errors that have grievously damaged true science and the health of humanity at large.

If such a sordid approach to medical knowledge were as useful as advertised, the nation with the highest life expectancy should be the United States, where expenditures for vivisection are a multiple of those in any other country, where more "life-saving" operations are performed, and whose medical profession considers itself to be the world's finest, besides being the most expensive. In fact, "Among the nations that measure average life expectancy, America ranks a relatively low 17th—behind most of Western Europe, Japan, Greece, and even Bulgaria," reported *Time*

---

[1] Refers to the Inquisition in Spain during the fifteenth century, in which a special tribunal was established to combat and punish heresy in the Roman Catholic Church.   [2] *Leonardo da Vinci (1452–1519):* Italian painter, sculptor, architect, and mathematician; *Voltaire (1694–1778):* pen name of Francois Marie Arouet, French philosopher, historian, dramatist, and essayist; *Johann Wolfgang von Goethe (1749–1832)* German poet, dramatist, and novelist; *Albert Schweitzer (1875–1965):* Alsatian missionary, doctor, and musician in Africa who received the Nobel Peace Prize in 1952.

Magazine, July 21, 1975, after having reported on December 17, 1973, that "The U.S. has twice as many surgeons in proportion to population as Great Britain—and Americans undergo twice as many operations as Britons. Yet, on the average, they die younger."

All this in spite of Medicare and Medicaid and the formidable therapeutic ar-   25
senal at the disposal of American doctors and patients.

MAN AND ANIMALS

Many of the medical men who have denounced the practice of vivisection as inhuman, fallacious and dangerous have been among the most distinguished in their profession. Rather than a minority, they ought to be called an élite. And in fact, opinions should not only be counted—they should also be weighed.

The first great medical man who indicated that vivisection is not just inhuman and unscientific, but that it is unscientific *because* it is inhuman was Sir Charles Bell (1774–1824), the Scottish physician, surgeon, anatomist and physiologist to whom medical science owes "Bell's law" on motor and sensory nerves. At the time the aberration of vivisection began to take root in its modern form, he declared that it could only be practiced by callous individuals, who couldn't be expected to penetrate the mysteries of life. Such individuals, he maintained, lack real intelligence—sensibility being a component, and certainly not the least, of human intelligence.

Those who hope to find remedies for human ills by inflicting deliberate sufferings on animals commit two fundamental errors in understanding. The first is the assumption that results obtained on animals are appropriate to man. The second, which concerns the inevitable fallacy of experimental science in respect to the field of organic life, will be analyzed in the next chapter. Let us examine the first error now. Already the Pharaohs knew that to find out whether their food was poisoned they had to try it on the cook, not on the cat.

Since animals react differently from man, every new product or method tried out on animals must be tried out again on man, through careful clinical tests, before it can be considered safe. *This rule knows no exceptions.* Therefore, tests on animals are not only dangerous because they may lead to wrong conclusions, but they also retard clinical investigation, which is the only valid kind.

René Dubos, Pulitzer Prize-winner and professor of microbiology at the   30
Rockefeller Institute of New York, wrote in *Man, Medicine and Environment* (Praeger, New York, 1968, p. 107): "Experimentation on man is usually an indispensable step in the discovery of new therapeutic procedures or drugs . . . The first surgeons who operated on the lungs, the heart, the brain were by necessity experimenting on man, since knowledge deriving from animal experimentation is never entirely applicable to the human species."

In spite of this universally recognized fact, not only, the vivisectors, but also health authorities everywhere, having been trained in the vivisectionist mentality, which is a throwback to the last century, allow or prescribe animal tests, thus washing their hands of any responsibility if something goes wrong, as it usually does.

This explains the long list of products developed in laboratories, *and* presumed safe after extensive animal tests, which eventually prove deleterious for man:

Due to a "safe" painkiller named Paracetamol, 1,500 people had to be hospitalized in Great Britain in 1971. In the United States, Orabilex caused kidney damages with fatal outcome, MEL/29 caused cataracts, Metaqualone caused psychic disturbances leading to at least 366 deaths. Worldwide Thalidomide caused more than 10,000 deformed children. Chloramphenicol (Chloromycetin) caused leukemia; Stilbestrol cancer in young women. In the sixties a mysterious epidemic killed so many thousands of asthma sufferers in various countries that Dr. Paul D. Stolley of Johns Hopkins Hospital—who in July 1972 finally found the killer in Isoproterenol, packaged in England as an aerosol spray—spoke of the "worst therapeutic drug disaster on record." In the fall of 1975, Italy's health authorities seized the anti-allergic Trilergan, responsible for viral hepatitis. In early 1976 the laboratories Salvoxyl-Wander, belonging to Switzerland's gigantic Sandoz enterprise, withdrew their Flamanil, created to fight rheumatisms, but capable of causing loss of consciousness in its consumers—certainly one effective way to free them of all pains. A few months later, Great Britain's chemical giant, ICI (Imperial Chemical Industries), announced that it had started paying compensations to the victims (or their survivors) of its cardiotonic Eraldin, introduced on the market after 7 years of "very intensive" tests; but hundreds of consumers had then suffered serious damages to the eyesight or the digestive tract, and 18 had died.

The Great Drug Deception by Dr. Ralph Adam Fine (Stein and Day, New York, 1972) is just one of the many books published in the last decade on the subject of dangerous and often lethal drugs, but it achieved no practical results. Health authorities, as well as the public stubbornly refused to take cognizance of the fact that all those drugs had been okayed and marketed after having been proved safe for animals. Actually it is unfair to single out just a few dangerous drugs, since there are thousands of them.

Of course the fallacy works both ways, precluding the acceptance of useful drugs. There is the great example of penicillin—if we want to consider this a useful drug. Its discoverers said they were fortunate. No guinea pigs were available for the toxicity tests, so they used mice instead. Penicillin kills guinea pigs. But the same guinea pigs can safely eat strychnine, one of the deadliest poisons for humans—but not for monkeys.

Certain wild berries are deadly for human beings, but birds thrive on them. A dose of belladonna that would kill a man is harmless for rabbits and goats. Calomelan doesn't influence the secretion of bile in dogs, but can treble it in man. The use of digitalis—the main remedy for cardiac patients and the savior of countless lives the world over—was retarded for a long time because it was first tested on dogs, in which it dangerously raises blood pressure. And chloroform is so toxic to dogs that for many years this valuable anesthetic was not employed on patients. On the other hand a dose of opium that would kill a man is harmless to dogs and chickens.

Datura and henbane are poison for man, but food for the snail. The mushroom *amanita phalloides,* a small dose of which can wipe out a whole human family is consumed without ill effects by the rabbit, one of the most common laboratory animals. A porcupine can *eat* in one lump without discomfort as much opium as a human addict *smokes* in two weeks, and wash it down with enough prussic acid to poison a regiment of soldiers.

The sheep can swallow enormous quantities of arsenic, once the murderers' favorite poison.

Potassium cyanide, deadly for us, is harmless for the owl, but one of our common field pumpkins can put a horse into a serious state of agitation. Morphine, which calms and anesthetizes man, causes maniacal excitement in cats and mice, but dogs can stand doses up to twenty times higher than man. On the other hand, our sweet almonds can kill foxes and chickens, and our common parsley is poison to parrots.

Robert Koch's Tuberkulin, once hailed as a vaccine against tuberculosis be-   40
cause it cured TB in guinea pigs, was found later on to *cause* TB in man[3].

There are enough such instances to fill a book—all proving that it would be difficult to find a more absurd and less scientific method of medical research.

Moreover, the anguish and sufferings of the animals, deprived of their natural habitat or habitual surroundings, terrorized by what they see in the laboratories and the brutalities they are subjected to, alter their mental balance and organic re-actions to such an extent that *any* result is a priori valueless. The laboratory animal is a monster, made so by the experimenters. Physically and mentally it has very lit-tle in common with a normal animals and much less with man.

As even Claude Bernard (1813–1878), founder of the modern vivisectionist method, wrote in his *Physiologie opératoire* (p. 152): "The experimental animal is never in a normal state. The normal state is merely a supposition, an assumption." (*Une pure conception de l'esprit.*)

Not only do all animals react differently—even kindred species like rat and mouse, or like the white rat and brown rat—not even two animals of the identical strain react identically; furthermore, they may be suffering from different diseases.

To counter this disadvantage, somebody launched the idea of breeding strains   45
of bacteriologically sterile laboratory animals—mass-born by Caesarean section in sterile operating rooms, raised in sterile surroundings and fed with sterile foods—to provide what the researchers called a "uniform biological material," free of diseases.

One delusion spawned another. Consistent failures made certain of those misguided scientists realize—some haven't realized it yet—that organic "material" raised under such abnormal conditions differs more than ever from normal or-ganisms. Animals so raised never develop the natural defense mechanism, the so-called immunological reaction, which is a salient characteristic of every living organism. So it would be difficult to devise a less reliable experimental material. Besides, animals are by nature immune to most human infections—diphtheria, ty-phus, scarlet fever, German measles, smallpox, cholera, yellow fever, leprosy, and

---

[3] *Robert Koch (1843–1910):* German bacteriologist and physician who won the Nobel Prize in 1905.

bubonic plague, while other infections, such as TB and various septicemias, take up different forms in animals. So the claim that through animals we can learn to control human diseases could seem a sign of madness if we didn't know that it is just a pretext for carrying on "experiments" which, however dangerously misleading for medical science, are either intimately satisfying for those who execute them, or highly lucrative.

The Swiss nation illustrates well to what extent the profit motive promotes vivisection: With a population of less than 6 million, Switzerland uses up annually many times as many laboratory animals as does all of Soviet Russia with its 250 million inhabitants, but where there is no money in the making of medicines.

EXPERIMENTAL RESEARCH

Experimental research has brought about all human inventions and most discoveries—except in medicine.

When speaking of modern invention, the first name that comes to mind is Thomas Edison[4]. His case is particularly interesting because Edison attended school for only three months, whereafter he had to start making a living. Thus Edison was not a well-educated man. But it was just this lack of formal education—the lack of notions blindly accepted by most educated people, including the scientists, inculcated into them at an early stage by rote—that enabled Edison to accomplish the extraordinary series of inventions that altered man's way of life.

For instance, in trying to perfect the first electric light bulb Edison wanted a wire that would remain incandescent for a reasonable length of time. No university professor, no metallurgical expert was able to help him. So Edison resorted to pure empiricism. He started trying out *every type of wire* he could think of—including the least likely ones, such as, say, a thread of charred cotton. Over a period of years, Edison spent $40,000 having his assistants trying out one material after another. Until he found a wire that remained incandescent for 40 consecutive hours. It was a charred cotton thread . . .

However, experimental science had started modifying the face of the earth two and a half centuries before Edison went about lighting up the nights. The beginning took place in 1637 with the publication of that *Discourse on Method* by Descartes[5] which taught man a new way of thinking, and led to modern technology. But, who could foresee in this New World being born in the midst of widespread enthusiasm the danger of an exclusively mechanistic knowledge? Hardly Descartes, who was himself a negation of the arts and all human sentiments—his private life was a failure—and who believed in a mechanistic biology, establishing the basis for what may well be mankind's greatest error.

In his thirst for knowledge through experimentation, Descartes also practiced vivisection, making it a symbol of "progress" to succeeding mechanists. Descartes

50

---

[4] *Thomas Alva Edison (1847–1931):* U.S. inventor of the electric light, phonograph, and other devices. [5] *René Descartes (1596–1650):* French philosopher and mathematician.

himself, of course, had learned nothing from this practice, as demonstrated by his statement that animals don't suffer, and that their cries mean nothing more than the creaking of a wheel. Then why not whip the cart instead of the horse? Descartes never troubled to explain that. But he gave as "proof" of his theory the fact that the harder one beats a dog, the louder it howls. Through him a new science was born, deprived of wisdom and humanity, thus containing the seed of defeat at birth.

Rid at last of the yoke of medieval obscurantism, man went all out for experimentation. The sensational conquests of technology led some doctors of limited mental power to believe that experimental science would bring about equally sensational results in their own field; that living organisms react like inanimate matter, enabling medical science to establish absolute, mathematical rules. And today's vivisectionists still cling to that belief, no matter how often it has proved tragically wrong.

The experiment Galileo[6] made from Pisa's leaning tower, demonstrating that a light stone and a heavy stone fall at one and the same speed, established an absolute rule because it dealt with inanimate matter. But when we deal with living organisms, an infinity of different factors intervene, mostly unknown and not entirely identifiable, having to do with the mystery of life itself. It is difficult to disagree with Charles Bell that callous, dehumanized individuals are the least likely ever to penetrate these mysteries.

In his book *La sperimentazione sugli animali* (2nd ed., 1956), Gennaro Ciaburri, one of Italy's antivisectionist doctors, provides among many others the following insight: "Normally, pressure on one or both eyeballs will slow down the pulse . . . This symptom has opened up a vast field for vivisection. Experimenters squashed the eyes of dogs to study this reflex, to the point of discovering that the heartbeat was slowing down—owing to the death of the animal . . ." 55

That such vivisectionist divertissements achieve nothing more than to provide a measure of human stupidity, has been declared repeatedly. The famed German doctor Erwin Liek—of whom the major German encyclopedia, *Der Grosse Brockhaus,* says, "he advocated a medical art of high ethical level, which takes into consideration the patient's psyche"—gives us the following information:

"Here is another example that animal experimentation sometimes can't answer even the simplest questions.

I know personally two of Germany's most authoritative researchers, Friedberger of the Kaiser Wilhelm Institute for Nutritional Research and Prof. Scheunert of the Institute of Animal Physiology at Leipzig. Both wanted to investigate the simple question as to whether a diet of hardboiled eggs or of raw eggs is more beneficial. They employed the same animals: 28-day-old rats. Result: over an observation period of three months, Friedberger's animals prospered on a diet of raw eggs, while the control animals which got hardboiled eggs pined, lost their hair, developed eye troubles; several died after much suffering. At Scheunert's I witnessed the identical

---

[6] *Galileo Galile (1564–1642):* Italian physicist and astronomer.

experiments, with exactly opposite results." (From *Gedanken eines Arztes*, Oswald Arnold, Berlin, 1949.)

Of course any disease deliberately provoked is unlike any disease that arises spontaneously.

Let's take the case of arthritis, a degenerative disease causing painful inflam-   60
mation of the joints, and bringing about lesions or destruction of the cartilage. Overeating is one of its causes, regular exercise at an early stage of the malady is the only reliable cure we know to date. And yet the drug firms keep turning out "miracle" remedies based on animal tortures: mere palliatives that mask the symptoms, reducing the pain for a while but in the meantime ruining the liver or the kidneys or both, thus causing much more serious damage than the malady they pretend to cure—and eventually aggravating the malady.

While no solution to any medical problem has ever been found through animal experimentation, so on the other hand one can prove practically anything one sets out to prove using animals, as in the following case reported in the monthly *Canadian Hospital* (Dec. 1971): In the Montreal Heart Institute are thousands of cages full of rats used to determine the effects of specific diets on animals. One of the "researchers" in charge, Dr. Serge Renaud, "took one of the animals from its cage; its hair had fallen out; its arteries had hardened and it was ripe for a heart attack. This rat, with a normal life span of two years, was old at two months. 'We kill them with pure butter,' said Dr. Renaud."

So butter is poison! Science or idiocy?

Sometimes it is neither one nor the other, but a highly profitable business gimmick, as the cyclamate and the saccharin cases demonstrate. In the mid-sixties the new artificial sweeteners known as cyclamates had become a huge commercial success because they cost 5 times less than sugar and had 30 times the sweetening power, besides being non-fattening. So the American Sugar Manufacturers Association set about financing "research" on cyclamates, as did the sugar industries in some other countries. To "prove scientifically" what the sugar industry was determined to prove from the start—that cyclamates should be outlawed—hundreds of thousands of animals had to die painfully.

They were force-fed such massive, concentrated doses of the product that they were bound to become seriously sick, developing all sorts of diseases, including cancer. To consume the equivalent amount of artificial sweetener a human would have to drink more than 800 cans of diet soda every day of his life. In 1967 the British Sugar Bureau, a public relations organization set up by the sugar industry, was pressuring members of Parliament about the deadly dangers of cyclamates. The same was happening in the United States—the sugar lobby besieging the politicians. I am not saying that money changed hands, because I don't know. All I know is that in 1969 both the American and British Governments banned the sale of cyclamates. It wasn't banned in Switzerland, however, where there is no powerful sugar lobby, but a powerful chemical lobby instead. In Switzerland, cyclamates are still on sale, 8 years after they were taken off the shelves in America and Britain.

Then there was a repeat performance of the whole three-ring scientific circus   65
in 1976 in regard to saccharin—and once more uncounted thousands of innocent animals were caught in the crossfire of embattled industrial giants.

Financed by a grant of $641,224 for 1971–72, researchers at the Center for Prevention and Treatment of Arteriosclerosis at Albany Medical College experimented with an initial group of 44 pigs. One by one these animals were made to die of induced heart disease resulting from arteriosclerosis. Using an extreme form of diet known to be injurious to the vascular system, the process was further speeded up by X rays that damage the coronary arteries. Personnel were always on hand when an animal dropped dead; they hoped to pinpoint precisely what happens to the heart of a pig at this critical moment. Such, in essence, was a report in the *Times Union* of Buffalo, New York, Oct. 24, 1971.

Except for the money angle, the whole thing appears sophomoric. Yet similar programs utilizing various experimental animals were in progress at the same time at 12 other medical institutions all over the U.S. All of them proved adept at creating a wide range of diseases in animals, but were notable failures at coming up with a solution. Research of this nature has been practiced for decades, and millions of animals have died in the process, while the cures are still pies in the sky.

Today's pseudoscience proceeds similarly on all fronts. In the "fight against epilepsy," monkeys are submitted to a series of electroshocks that throw them into convulsions, until they become insane and manifest symptoms that may outwardly resemble epileptic fits in man—frothing at the mouth, convulsive movements, loss of consciousness, and such. Obviously the monkeys' fits have nothing to do with human epilepsy, as they are artificially induced, whereas man's epilepsy arises inside from reasons deeply rooted in the individual's organism or psyche, and not from a series of electroshocks. And by trying out on these insane monkeys a variety of "new" drugs—always the same ones, in different combinations—vivisectionists promise to come up with "a remedy against epilepsy" some time soon, provided the grants keep coming. And such methods sail today under the flag of science—which is an insult to true science, as well as to human intelligence. Small wonder that epilepsy is another disease whose incidence is constantly increasing.

One of the latest shifts devised by medical research to make quick money is the invention of drugs that promise to prevent brain hemorrhages. How is it done? Easy. By now any attentive reader can do it. Take rats, dogs, rabbits, monkeys, and cats, and severely injure their brains. How? Our laboratory "Researchers" brilliantly solve that problem with hammer blows. Under the broken skulls, the animals' brains will form blood clots, whereafter various drugs are administered to the traumatized victim. As if blood clots due to hammer blows were the equivalent of circulation troubles which have gradually been building up in a human brain that is approaching the natural end of its vital arch, or has grown sclerotic through excessive intake of alcohol, food, tobacco, or from want of exercise, of fresh air, or mental activity. Everybody knows what to do to keep physically and mentally fit. But it is less fatiguing to swallow, before each rich meal, a couple of pills, and hope for the best.

Anybody suggesting that these pills are of no use would be in bad faith. They 70 *are* useful: They help increase the profits of the world's most lucrative industry—and further ruin the organism, thus creating the necessity for still more "miracle" drugs.

THE SOLID GOLD SOURCE

The cancer bogy has become the vivisectionists' most powerful weapon. Dr. Howard M. Temin, a well-known scientist, said in a recent address at the University of Wisconsin that scientists are also interested in money, power, publicity and prestige, and that "some promise quick cures for human diseases, provided they are given more power and more money." He added that there is a tremendous advantage in the assertion that "If I am given 500 million dollars for the next five years, I can cure cancer," pointing out that if a rainmaker puts the time far enough in the future, no one can prove him wrong.

But so far as cancer is concerned, the rain may not come in our lifetime. It is obvious to anybody who has not been brainwashed in the western hemisphere's medical schools that an experimental cancer, one caused by grafting cancerous cells into an animal, or in other arbitrary ways, is entirely different from cancer that develops on its own and, furthermore, in a human being. A spontaneous cancer has an intimate relationship to the organism that developed it, and probably to the mind of that organism as well, whereas cancerous cells implanted into another organism have no "natural" relationship whatsoever to that organism, which merely acts as a soil for the culture of those cells.

However, the ably exploited fear of this dread disease has become an inexhaustible source of income for the researchers. In the course of our century, experimental cancer has become a source of solid gold without precedent.

Questions for Discussion and Writing

1. What features of this analysis are designed to show that animal experimentation in medical research is not only sadistic but unreliable, misleading, and even dangerous when the results are used as models for humans?

2. The assumptions on which animal research is based are so commonly accepted that Ruesch's counterargument may strike some readers as unwarranted. What means does Ruesch take to forestall criticism and better support his argument?

3. Do some research into the guidelines that govern animal research at your college or university. Based on your findings, write a rebuttal to Ruesch or identify additional instances that support his thesis.

GARRETT HARDIN

Garrett Hardin was born in 1915 in Dallas, Texas. He graduated from the University of Chicago in 1936 and received a Ph.D. from Stanford University in 1941. A biologist, he was a professor of human ecology at the University of California at Santa Barbara until 1978. He is the author of many books and over two hundred articles, including Nature and Man's Fate *(1959), "The Tragedy of the Commons" in* Science *(December 1968), and* Exploring New Ethics for Survival *(1972). His latest works are* Stalking the Wild Taboo *(1996) and* The

Ostrich Factor: Our Population Myopia *(1998).* "Lifeboat Ethics: The Case against Helping the Poor" first appeared in the September 1974 issue of Psychology Today. In this article,
Hardin compares a country that is well off to a lifeboat that is already almost full of people. Outside the lifeboat are the poor and needy, who desperately wish to get in. Hardin claims that an
ill-considered ethic of sharing will lead to the swamping of the lifeboat unless its occupants maintain a margin of safety by keeping people out.

Lifeboat Ethics: The Case against Helping the Poor

Environmentalists use the metaphor of the earth as a "spaceship" in trying to
persuade countries, industries and people to stop wasting and polluting our natural
resources. Since we all share life on this planet, they argue, no single person or institution has the right to destroy, waste or use more than a fair share of its resources.

But does everyone on earth have an equal right to an equal share of its resources? The spaceship metaphor can be dangerous when used by misguided idealists to justify suicidal policies for sharing our resources through uncontrolled
immigration and foreign aid. In their enthusiastic but unrealistic generosity, they
confuse the ethics of a spaceship with those of a lifeboat.

A true spaceship would have to be under the control of a captain, since no
ship could possibly survive if its course were determined by committee. Spaceship
Earth certainly has no captain; the United Nations is merely a toothless tiger, with
little power to enforce any policy upon its bickering members.

If we divide the world crudely into rich nations and poor nations, two thirds
of them are desperately poor, and only one third comparatively rich, with the
United States the wealthiest of all. Metaphorically each nation can be seen as a
lifeboat full of comparatively rich people. In the ocean outside each lifeboat swim
the poor of the world, who would like to get in, or at least to share some of the
wealth. What should the lifeboat passengers do?

First, we must recognize the limited capacity of any lifeboat. For example, a   5
nation's land has a limited capacity to support a population and as the current energy crisis has shown us, in some ways we have already exceeded the carrying capacity of our land.

ADRIFT IN A MORAL SEA

So here we sit, say fifty people in our lifeboat. To be generous, let us assume it
has room for ten more, making a total capacity of sixty. Suppose the fifty of us in
the lifeboat see 100 others swimming in the water outside, begging for admission
to our boat or for handouts. We have several options: We may be tempted to try to
live by the Christian ideal of being "our brother's keeper," or by the Marxist ideal
of "to each according to his needs." Since the needs of all in the water are the same,
and since they can all be seen as "our brothers," we could take them all into our
boat, making a total of 150 in a boat designed for sixty. The boat swamps, everyone
drowns. Complete justice, complete catastrophe.

Since the boat has an unused excess capacity of ten more passengers, we
could admit just ten more to it. But which ten do we let in? How do we choose?

Do we pick the best ten, the neediest ten, "first come, first served"? And what do we say to the ninety we exclude? If we do let an extra ten into our lifeboat, we will have lost our "safety factor," an engineering principle of critical importance. For example, if we don't leave room for excess capacity as a safety factor in our country's agriculture, a new plant disease or a bad change in the weather could have disastrous consequences.

Suppose we decide to preserve our small safety factor and admit no more to the lifeboat. Our survival is then possible, although we shall have to be constantly on guard against boarding parties.

While this last solution clearly offers the only means of our survival, it is morally abhorrent to many people. Some say they feel guilty about their good luck. My reply is simple: "Get out and yield your place to others." This may solve the problem of the guilt-ridden person's conscience, but it does not change the ethics of the lifeboat. The needy person to whom the guilt-ridden person yields his place will not himself feel guilty about his good luck. If he did, he would not climb aboard. The net result of conscience-stricken people giving up their unjustly held seats is the elimination of that sort of conscience from the lifeboat.

This is the basic metaphor within which we must work out our solutions. Let   10 us now enrich the image, step by step, with substantive additions from the real world, a world that must solve real and pressing problems of overpopulation and hunger.

The harsh ethics of the lifeboat become even harsher when we consider the reproductive differences between the rich nations and the poor nations. The people inside the lifeboats are doubling in numbers every eighty-seven years; those swimming around outside are doubling, on the average, every thirty-five years, more than twice as fast as the rich. And since the world's resources are dwindling, the difference in prosperity between the rich and the poor can only increase.

As of 1973, the U.S had a population of 210 million people, who were increasing by 0.8 percent per year. Outside our lifeboat, let us imagine another 210 million people (say the combined populations of Colombia, Ecuador, Venezuela, Morocco, Pakistan, Thailand and the Philippines), who are increasing at a rate of 3.3 percent per year. Put differently, the doubling time for this aggregate population is twenty-one years, compared to eighty-seven years for the U.S.

MULTIPLYING THE RICH AND THE POOR

Now suppose the U.S. agreed to pool its resources with those seven countries, with everyone receiving an equal share. Initially the ratio of Americans to non-Americans in this model would be one-to-one. But consider what the ratio would be after eighty-seven years, by which time the Americans would have doubled to a population of 420 million. By then, doubling every twenty-one years, the other group would have swollen to 354 billion. Each American would have to share the available resources with more than eight people.

But, one could argue, this discussion assumes that current population trends will continue, and they may not. Quite so. Most likely the rate of population increase will decline much faster in the U.S. than it will in the other countries, and

there does not seem to be much we can do about it. In sharing with "each according to his needs," we must recognize that needs are determined by population size,
which is determined by the rate of reproduction, which at present is regarded as a
sovereign right of every nation, poor or not. This being so, the philanthropic load
created by the sharing ethic of the spaceship can only increase.

THE TRAGEDY OF THE COMMONS

The fundamental error of spaceship ethics, and the sharing it requires, is that   15
it leads to what I call "the tragedy of the commons." Under a system of private
property, the men who own property recognize their responsibility to care for it,
for if they don't they will eventually suffer. A farmer, for instance, will allow no
more cattle in a pasture than its carrying capacity justifies. If he overloads it, erosion
sets in, weeds take over, and he loses the use of the pasture.

If a pasture becomes a commons open to all, the right of each to use it may
not be matched by a corresponding responsibility to protect it. Asking everyone to
use it with discretion will hardly do, for the considerate herdsman who refrains
from overloading the commons suffers more than a selfish one who says his needs
are greater. If everyone would restrain himself, all would be well; but it takes only
one less than everyone to ruin a system of voluntary restraint. In a crowded world
of less than perfect human beings, mutual ruin is inevitable if there are no controls.
This is the tragedy of the commons.

One of the major tasks of education today should be the creation of such an
acute awareness of the dangers of the commons that people will recognize its many
varieties. For example, the air and water have become polluted because they are
treated as commons. Further growth in the population or per-capita conversion of
natural resources into pollutants will only make the problem worse. The same holds
true for the fish of the oceans. Fishing fleets have nearly disappeared in many parts
of the world, technological improvements in the art of fishing are hastening the day
of complete ruin. Only the replacement of the system of the commons with a responsible system of control will save the land, air, water and oceanic fisheries.

THE WORLD FOOD BANK

In recent years there has been a push to create a new commons called a
World Food Bank, an international depository of food reserves to which nations
would contribute according to their abilities and from which they would draw according to their needs. This humanitarian proposal has received support from
many liberal international groups, and from such prominent citizens as Margaret
Mead, U.N. Secretary General Kurt Waldheim, and Senators Edward Kennedy and
George McGovern.

A world food bank appeals powerfully to our humanitarian impulses. But before we rush ahead with such a plan, let us recognize where the greatest political
push comes from, lest we be disillusioned later. Our experience with the "Food for

Peace program," or Public Law 480, gives us the answer. This program moved billions of dollars' worth of U.S. surplus grain to food-short, population-long countries during the past two decades. But when P.L. 480 first became law, a headline in the business magazine *Forbes* revealed the real power behind it: "Feeding the World's Hungry Millions: How It Will Mean Billions for U.S. Business."

And indeed it did. In the years 1960 to 1970, U.S. taxpayers spent a total of   20
$7.9 billion on the Food for Peace program. Between 1948 and 1970, they also paid an additional $50 billion for other economic-aid programs, some of which went for food and food-producing machinery and technology. Though all U.S. taxpayers were forced to contribute to the cost of P.L. 480, certain special interest groups gained handsomely under the program. Farmers did not have to contribute the grain; the Government, or rather the taxpayers, bought it from them at full market prices. The increased demand raised prices of farm products generally. The manufacturers of farm machinery, fertilizers and pesticides benefited by the farmers' extra efforts to grow more food. Grain elevators profited from storing the surplus until it could be shipped. Railroads made money hauling it to ports, and shipping lines profited from carrying it overseas. The implementation of P.L. 480 required the creation of a vast Government bureaucracy, which then acquired its own vested interest in continuing the program regardless of its merits.

EXTRACTING DOLLARS

Those who proposed and defended the Food for Peace program in public rarely mentioned its importance to any of these special interests. The public emphasis was always on its humanitarian effects. The combination of silent selfish interests and highly vocal humanitarian apologists made a powerful and successful lobby for extracting money from taxpayers. We can expect the same lobby to push now for the creation of a World Food Bank.

However great the potential benefit to selfish interests, it should not be a decisive argument against a truly humanitarian program. We must ask if such a program would actually do more good than harm, not only momentarily but also in the long run. Those who propose the food bank usually refer to a current "emergency" or "crisis" in terms of world food supply. But what is an emergency? Although they may be infrequent and sudden, everyone knows that emergencies will occur from time to time. A well-run family, company, organization or country prepares for the likelihood of accidents and emergencies. It expects them, it budgets for them, it saves for them.

LEARNING THE HARD WAY

What happens if some organizations or countries budget for accidents and others do not? If each country is solely responsible for its own well-being, poorly managed ones will suffer. But they can learn from experience. They may mend their ways, and learn to budget for infrequent but certain emergencies. For example, the weather varies from year to year, and periodic crop failures are certain. A wise and competent government saves out of the production of the good years in anticipation of bad years to come. Joseph taught this policy to Pharaoh in Egypt more than 2,000 years ago. Yet the great majority of the governments in the world today do not follow such a policy. They lack either the wisdom or the competence, or both. Should those nations that do manage to put something aside be forced to come to the rescue each time an emergency occurs among the poor nations?

"But it isn't their fault!" some kindhearted liberals argue. "How can we blame the poor people who are caught in an emergency? Why must they suffer for the sins of their governments?" The concept of blame is simply not relevant here. The real question is, what are the operational consequences of establishing a world food bank? If it is open to every country every time a need develops, slovenly rulers will not be motivated to take Joseph's advice. Someone will always come to their aid. Some countries will deposit food in the world food bank, and others will withdraw it. There will be almost no overlap. As a result of such solutions to food shortage emergencies, the poor countries will not learn to mend their ways, and will suffer progressively greater emergencies as their populations grow.

POPULATION CONTROL THE CRUDE WAY

On the average, poor countries undergo a 2.5 percent increase in population each year; rich countries, about 0.8 percent. Only rich countries have anything in the way of food reserves set aside, and even they do not have as much as they should. Poor countries have none. If poor countries received no food from the outside, the rate of their population growth would be periodically checked by crop failures and famines. But if they can always draw on a world food bank in time of need, their populations can grow unchecked, and so will the "need" for aid. In the short run, a world food bank may diminish that need, but in the long run it actually increases the need without limit.

Without some system of worldwide food sharing, the proportion of people in the rich and poor nations might eventually stabilize. The overpopulated poor countries would decrease in numbers, while the rich countries that had room for more people would increase. But with a well-meaning system of sharing, such as a world food bank, the growth differential between the rich and the poor countries will not only persist, it will increase. Because of the higher rate of population growth in the poor countries of the world, 88 percent of today's children are born poor, and only 12 percent rich. Year by year the ratio becomes worse, as the fast-reproducing poor outnumber the slow-reproducing rich.

A world food bank is thus a commons in disguise. People will have more motivation to draw from it than to add to any common store. The less provident and less able will multiply at the expense of the abler and more provident, bringing eventual ruin upon all who share in the commons. Besides, any system of "sharing" that amounts to foreign aid from the rich nations to the poor nations will carry the taint of charity, which will contribute little to the world peace so devoutly desired by those who support the idea of a world food bank.

As past U.S. foreign-aid programs have amply and depressingly demonstrated, international charity frequently inspires mistrust and antagonism rather than gratitude on the part of the recipient nation.

CHINESE FISH AND MIRACLE RICE

The modern approach to foreign aid stresses the export of technology and advice, rather than money and food. As an ancient Chinese proverb goes: "Give a man a fish and he will eat for a day; teach him how to fish and he will eat for the rest of his days." Acting on this advice, the Rockefeller and Ford Foundations have financed a number of programs for improving agriculture in the hungry nations. Known as the "Green Revolution," these programs have led to the development of "miracle rice" and "miracle wheat," new strains that offer bigger harvests and greater resistance to crop damage. Norman Borlaug, the Nobel Prize–winning agronomist who, supported by the Rockefeller Foundation, developed "miracle wheat," is one of the most prominent advocates of a world food bank.

Whether or not the Green Revolution can increase food production as much   30
as its champions claim is a debatable but possibly irrelevant point. Those who support this well-intended humanitarian effort should first consider some of the fundamentals of human ecology. Ironically, one man who did was the late Alan Gregg, a vice president of the Rockefeller Foundation. Two decades ago he expressed strong doubts about the wisdom of such attempts to increase food production. He likened the growth and spread of humanity over the surface of the earth to the spread of cancer in the human body, remarking that "cancerous growths demand food; but, as far as I know, they have never been cured by getting it."

OVERLOADING THE ENVIRONMENT

Every human born constitutes a draft on all aspects of the environment: food, air, water, forests, beaches, wildlife, scenery and solitude. Food can, perhaps, be significantly increased to meet a growing demand. But what about clean beaches, unspoiled forests and solitude? If we satisfy a growing population's need for food, we necessarily decrease its per-capita supply of the other resources needed by men.

India, for example, now has a population of 600 million, which increases by 15 million each year. This population already puts a huge load on a relatively impoverished environment. The country's forests are now only a small fraction of what they were three centuries ago, and floods and erosion continually destroy the insufficient farmland that remains. Every one of the 15 million new lives added to India's population puts an additional burden on the environment, and increases the economic and social costs of crowding. However humanitarian our intent, every Indian life saved through medical or nutritional assistance from abroad diminishes the quality of life for those who remain, and for subsequent generations. If rich countries make it possible, through foreign aid, for 600 million Indians to swell to 1.2 billion in a mere twenty-eight years, as their current growth rate threatens, will future generations of Indians thank us for hastening the destruction of their environment? Will our good intentions be sufficient excuse for the consequences of our actions?

My final example of a commons in action is one for which the public has the least desire for rational discussion—immigration. Anyone who publicly questions the wisdom of current U.S. immigration policy is promptly charged with bigotry,

prejudice, ethnocentrism, chauvinism, isolationism or selfishness. Rather than encounter such accusations, one would rather talk about other matters, leaving immigration policy to wallow in the crosscurrents of special interests that take no
account of the good of the whole, or the interest of posterity.

Perhaps we still feel guilty about things we said in the past. Two generations
ago the popular press frequently referred to Dagos, Wops, Polacks, Chinks and
Krauts, in articles about how America was being "overrun" by foreigners of supposedly inferior genetic stock. But because the implied inferiority of foreigners
was used then as justification for keeping them out, people now assume that restrictive policies could only be based on such misguided notions. There are no
other grounds.

A NATION OF IMMIGRANTS

Just consider the numbers involved. Our Government acknowledges a net in-   35
flow of 400,000 immigrants a year. While we have no hard data on the extent of illegal entries, educated guesses put the figure at about 600,000 a year. Since the
natural increase (excess of births over deaths) of the resident population now runs
about 1.7 million per year, the yearly gain from immigration amounts to at least 19
percent of the total annual increase, and may be as much as 37 percent if we include the estimate for illegal immigrants. Considering the growing use of birth-
control devices, the potential effect of educational campaigns by such organizations
as Planned Parenthood Federation of America and Zero Population Growth, and
the influence of inflation and the housing shortage, the fertility rate of American
women may decline so much that immigration could account for all the yearly increase in population. Should we not at least ask if that is what we want?

For the sake of those who worry about whether the "quality" of the average
immigrant compares favorably with the quality of the average resident, let us assume that immigrants and native born citizens are of exactly equal quality, however
one defines that term. We will focus here only on quantity; and since our conclusions will depend on nothing else, all charges of bigotry and chauvinism become
irrelevant.

IMMIGRATION VS. FOOD SUPPLY

World food banks *move food to the people,* hastening the exhaustion of the environment of the poor countries. Unrestricted immigration, on the other hand,
moves people to the food, thus speeding up the destruction of the environment of the
rich countries. We can easily understand why poor people should want to make
this latter transfer, but why should rich hosts encourage it?

As in the case of foreign-aid programs, immigration receives support from
selfish interests and humanitarian impulses. The primary selfish interest in unim-
peded immigration is the desire of employers for cheap labor, particularly in industries and trades that offer degrading work. In the past, one wave of foreigners after
another was brought into the U.S. to work at wretched jobs for wretched wages. In
recent years, the Cubans, Puerto Ricans and Mexicans have had this dubious

honor. The interests of the employers of cheap labor mesh well with the guilty silence of the country's liberal intelligentsia. White Anglo-Saxon Protestants are particularly reluctant to call for a closing of the doors to immigration for fear of being called bigots.

But not all countries have such reluctant leadership. Most educated Hawaiians, for example, are keenly aware of the limits of their environment, particularly in terms of population growth. There is only so much room on the islands, and the islanders know it. To Hawaiians, immigrants from the other forty-nine states present as great a threat as those from other nations. At a recent meeting of Hawaiian government officials in Honolulu, I had the ironic delight of hearing a speaker, who like most of his audience was of Japanese ancestry, ask how the country might practically and constitutionally close its doors to further immigration. One member of the audience countered: "How can we shut the doors now? We have many friends and relatives in Japan that we'd like to bring here some day so that they can enjoy Hawaii too." The Japanese-American speaker smiled sympathetically and answered: "Yes, but we have children now, and someday we'll have grandchildren too. We can bring more people here from Japan only by giving away some of the land that we hope to pass on to our grandchildren some day. What right do we have to do that?"

At this point, I can hear U.S. liberals asking: "How can you justify slamming   40
the door once you're inside? You say that immigrants should be kept out. But aren't we all immigrants, or the descendants of immigrants? If we insist on staying, must we not admit all others?" Our craving for intellectual order leads us to seek and prefer symmetrical rules and morals: a single rule for me and everybody else; the same rule yesterday, today, and tomorrow. Justice, we feel, should not change with time and place.

We Americans of non-Indian ancestry can look upon ourselves as the descendants of thieves who are guilty morally, if not legally, of stealing this land from its Indian owners. Should we then give back the land to the now living American descendants of those Indians? However morally or logically sound this proposal may be, I, for one, am unwilling to live by it and I know no one else who is. Besides, the logical consequence would be absurd. Suppose that, intoxicated with a sense of pure justice, we should decide to turn our land over to the Indians. Since all our wealth has also been derived from the land, wouldn't we be morally obliged to give that back to the Indians too?

PURE JUSTICE VS. REALITY

Clearly, the concept of pure justice produces an infinite regression to absurdity. Centuries ago, wise men invented statutes of limitations to justify the rejection of such pure justice, in the interest of preventing continual disorder. The law zealously defends property rights, but only relatively recent property rights. Drawing a line after an arbitrary time has elapsed may be unjust, but the alternatives are worse.

We are all descendants of thieves, and the world's resources are inequitably distributed. But we must begin the journey to tomorrow from the point where we are today. We cannot remake the past. We cannot safely divide the wealth equitably among all peoples so long as people reproduce at different rates. To do so would guarantee that our grandchildren, and everyone else's grandchildren, would have only a ruined world to inhabit.

To be generous with one's own possessions is quite different from being generous with those of posterity. We should call this point to the attention of those who, from a commendable love of justice and equality, would institute a system of the commons, either in the form of a world food bank, or of unrestricted immigration. We must convince them if we wish to save at least some parts of the world from environmental ruin.

Without a true world government to control reproduction and the use of available resources, the sharing ethic of the spaceship is impossible. For the foreseeable future, our survival demands that we govern our actions by the ethics of a lifeboat, harsh though they may be. Posterity will be satisfied with nothing less. 45

Questions for Discussion and Writing

1. What does Hardin mean by the expression "the tragedy of the commons"? How does the idea underlying this phrase rest on the assumption that human beings are not capable of responsible, voluntary restraint in using resources?

2. How does the analogy of the lifeboat support Hardin's contention that affluent nations have no obligation to share their food and resources with the world's starving masses? Evaluate Hardin's argument that our obligation to future generations should override our desire to help starving masses in the present.

3. To put Hardin's scenario in terms of personal moral choice, consider the following dilemmas and write a short essay on either (a) or (b) or both, and discuss the reasons for your answer(s):

    a. Would you be willing to add five years to your life even though it would mean taking five years away from the life of someone else you do not know? Would your decision be changed if you knew who the person was?

    b. If you had a child who was dying and the only thing that could save him or her was the bone marrow of a sibling, would you consider having another baby in order to facilitate what was almost sure to be a positive bone marrow transplant?

STEPHEN CHAPMAN

Stephen Chapman (b. 1954) has served as the associate editor of the New Republic *and as a columnist with the* Chicago Tribune. *In "The Prisoner's Dilemma" (which first appeared in the* New Republic *of March 8, 1980), Chapman calls into question the widely held assumption that the system of imprisonment as punishment employed in the West is more humane and less barbaric than the methods of punishment (including flogging, stoning, amputation) practiced in Eastern Islamic cultures.*

> *If the punitive laws of Islam were applied for only one year, all the devastating injustices would be uprooted. Misdeeds must be punished by the law of retaliation: cut off the hands of the thief; kill the murderers; flog the adulterous woman or man. Your concerns, your "humanitarian" scruples are more childish than reasonable. Under the terms of Koranic law, any judge fulfilling the seven requirements (that he have reached puberty, be a believer, know the Koranic laws perfectly, be just, and not be affected by amnesia, or be a bastard, or be of the female sex) is qualified to be a judge in any type of case. He can thus judge and dispose of twenty trials in a single day, whereas the Occidental justice may take years to argue them out.*
> —from Sayings of the Ayatollah Khomeini (Bantam Books)

The Prisoner's Dilemma

One of the amusements of life in the modern West is the opportunity to observe the barbaric rituals of countries that are attached to the customs of the dark ages. Take Pakistan, for example, our newest ally and client state in Asia. Last October President Zia, in harmony with the Islamic fervor that is sweeping his part of the world, revived the traditional Moslem practice of flogging lawbreakers in public. In Pakistan, this qualified as mass entertainment, and no fewer than 10,000 law-abiding Pakistanis turned out to see justice done to 26 convicts. To Western sensibilities the spectacle seemed barbaric—both in the sense of cruel and in the sense of pre-civilized. In keeping with Islamic custom each of the unfortunates—who had been caught in prostitution raids the previous night and summarily convicted and sentenced—was stripped down to a pair of white shorts, which were painted with a red stripe across the buttocks (the target). Then he was shackled against an easel, with pads thoughtfully placed over the kidneys to prevent injury. The floggers were muscular, fierce-looking sorts—convicted murderers, as it happens—who paraded around the flogging platform in colorful loincloths. When the time for the ceremony began, one of the floggers took a running start and brought a five-foot stave down across the first victim's buttocks, eliciting screams from the convict and murmurs from the audience. Each of the 26 received from five to 15 lashes. One had to be carried from the stage unconscious.

Flogging is one of the punishments stipulated by Koranic law, which has made it a popular penological device in several Moslem countries, including Pakistan, Saudi Arabia, and, most recently, the ayatollah's Iran. Flogging, or *Ta'zir,* is the general punishment prescribed for offenses that don't carry an explicit Koranic penalty. Some crimes carry automatic *hadd* punishments—stoning or scourging (a severe whipping) for illicit sex, scourging for drinking alcoholic beverages, amputation of the hands for theft. Other crimes—as varied as murder and abandoning Islam—carry the death penalty (usually carried out in public). Colorful practices like these have given the Islamic world an image in the West, as described by historian G. H. Jansen, "of blood dripping from the stumps of amputated hands and from the striped backs of malefactors, and piles of stones barely concealing the battered bodies of adulterous couples." Jansen, whose book *Militant Islam* is generally effusive in its praise of Islamic practices, grows squeamish when considering devices like flogging, amputation, and stoning. But they are given enthusiastic endorsement by the Koran itself.

Such traditions, we all must agree, are no sign of an advanced civilization. In the West, we have replaced these various punishments (including the death penalty in most cases) with a single device. Our custom is to confine criminals in prison for varying lengths of time. In Illinois, a reasonably typical state, grand theft carries a punishment of three to five years; armed robbery can get you from six to 30. The lowest form of felony theft is punishable by one to three years in prison. Most states impose longer sentences on habitual offenders. In Kentucky, for example, habitual offenders can be sentenced to life in prison. Other states are less brazen, preferring the more genteel sounding "indeterminate sentence," which allows parole boards to keep inmates locked up for as long as life. It was under an indeterminate sentence of one to 14 years that George Jackson served 12 years in California prisons for committing a $70 armed robbery. Under a Texas law imposing an automatic life sentence for a third felony conviction, a man was sent to jail for life last year because of three thefts adding up to less than $300 in property value. Texas also is famous for occasionally imposing extravagantly long sentences, often running into hundreds or thousands of years. This gives Texas a leg up on Maryland, which used to sentence some criminals to life plus a day—a distinctive if superfluous flourish.

The punishment *intended* by Western societies in sending their criminals to prison is the loss of freedom. But, as everyone knows, the actual punishment in most American prisons is of a wholly different order. The February 2 riot at New Mexico's state prison in Santa Fe, one of several bloody prison riots in the nine years since the Attica bloodbath, once again dramatized the conditions of life in an American prison. Four hundred prisoners seized control of the prison before dawn. By sunset the next day 33 inmates had died at the hands of other convicts and another 40 people (including five guards) had been seriously hurt. Macabre stories came out of prisoners being hanged, murdered with blowtorches, decapitated, tortured, and mutilated in a variety of gruesome ways by drug-crazed rioters.

The Santa Fe penitentiary was typical of most maximum-security facilities, with prisoners subject to overcrowding, filthy conditions, and routine violence. It also housed first-time, non-violent offenders, like check forgers and drug dealers, with murderers serving life sentences. In a recent lawsuit, the American Civil Liberties Union called the prison "totally unfit for human habitation." But the ACLU says New Mexico's penitentiary is far from the nation's worst.

That American prisons are a disgrace is taken for granted by experts of every ideological stripe. Conservative James Q. Wilson has criticized our "crowded, antiquated prisons that require men and women to live in fear of one another and to suffer not only deprivation of liberty but a brutalizing regimen." Leftist Jessica Mitford has called our prisons "the ultimate expression of injustice and inhumanity." In 1973 a national commission concluded that "the American correctional system today appears to offer minimum protection to the public and maximum harm to the offender." Federal courts have ruled that confinement in prisons in 16 different states violates the constitutional ban on "cruel and unusual punishment."

What are the advantages of being a convicted criminal in an advanced culture? First there is the overcrowding in prisons. One Tennessee prison, for example, has a capacity of 806, according to accepted space standards, but it houses 2300 inmates. One Louisiana facility has confined four and five prisoners in a single six-foot-by-six-foot cell. Then there is the disease caused by overcrowding, unsanitary conditions, and poor or inadequate medical care. A federal appeals court noted that the Tennessee prison had suffered frequent outbreaks of infectious diseases like hepatitis and tuberculosis. But the most distinctive element of American prison life is its constant violence. In his book *Criminal Violence, Criminal Justice,* Charles Silberman noted that in one Louisiana prison, there were 211 stabbings in only three years, 11 of them fatal. There were 15 slayings in a prison in Massachusetts between 1972 and 1975. According to a federal court, in Alabama's penitentiaries (as in many others), "robbery, rape, extortion, theft and assault are everyday occurrences."

At least in regard to cruelty, it's not at all clear that the system of punishment that has evolved in the West is less barbaric than the grotesque practices of Islam. Skeptical? Ask yourself: would you rather be subjected to a few minutes of intense pain and considerable public humiliation, or to be locked away for two or three years in a prison cell crowded with ill-tempered sociopaths? Would you rather lose a hand or spend 10 years or more in a typical state prison? I have taken my own survey on this matter. I have found no one who does not find the Islamic system hideous. And I have found no one who, given the choices mentioned above, would not prefer its penalties to our own.

The great divergence between Western and Islamic fashions in punishment is relatively recent. Until roughly the end of the 18th century, criminals in Western countries rarely were sent to prison. Instead they were subjected to an ingenious assortment of penalties. Many perpetrators of a variety of crimes simply were executed, usually by some imaginative and extremely unpleasant method involving prolonged torture, such as breaking on the wheel, burning at the stake, or drawing and quartering. Michel Foucault's book *Discipline and Punish: The Birth of the Prison* notes one form of capital punishment in which the condemned man's "belly was opened up, his entrails quickly ripped out, so that he had time to see them, with his own eyes, being thrown on the fire; in which he was finally decapitated and his body quartered." Some criminals were forced to serve on slave galleys. But in most cases various corporal measures such as pillorying, flogging, and branding sufficed.

In time, however, public sentiment recoiled against these measures. They were replaced by imprisonment, which was thought to have two advantages. First, it was considered to be more humane. Second, and more important, prison was supposed to hold out the possibility of rehabilitation—purging the criminal of his criminality—something that less civilized punishments did not even aspire to. An 1854 report by inspectors of the Pennsylvania prison system illustrates the hopes nurtured by humanitarian reformers: 10

> Depraved tendencies, characteristic of the convict, have been restrained by the ab-
> sence of vicious association, and in the mild teaching of Christianity, the unhappy
> criminal finds a solace for an involuntary exile from the comforts of social life. If hun-
> gry, he is fed; if naked, he is clothed; if destitute of the first rudiments of education,
> he is taught to read and write; and if he has never been blessed with a means of
> livelihood, he is schooled in a mechanical art, which in after life may be to him the
> source of profit and respectability. Employment is not his toil nor labor, weariness.
> He embraces them with alacrity, as contributing to his moral and mental elevation.

Imprisonment is now the universal method of punishing criminals in the
United States. It is thought to perform five functions, each of which has been
given a label by criminologists. First, there is simple *retribution:* punishing the law-
breaker to serve society's sense of justice and to satisfy the victims' desire for revenge. Second, there is *specific deterrence:* discouraging the offender from
misbehaving in the future. Third, *general deterrence:* using the offender as an example to discourage others from turning to crime. Fourth, *prevention:* at least during
the time he is kept off the streets, the criminal cannot victimize other members of
society. Finally, and most important, there is *rehabilitation:* reforming the criminal
so that when he returns to society he will be inclined to obey the laws and able to
make an honest living.

How satisfactorily do American prisons perform by these criteria? Well, of
course, they do punish. But on the other scores they don't do so well. Their effect
in discouraging future criminality by the prisoner or others is the subject of much
debate, but the soaring rates of the last 20 years suggest that prisons are not a dramatically effective deterrent to criminal behavior. Prisons do isolate convicted
criminals, but only to divert crime from ordinary citizens to prison guards and fellow inmates. Almost no one contends anymore that prisons rehabilitate their inmates. If anything, they probably impede rehabilitation by forcing inmates into
prolonged and almost exclusive association with other criminals. And prisons cost a
lot of money. Housing a typical prisoner in a typical prison costs far more than
a stint at a top university. This cost would be justified if prisons did the job they
were intended for. But it is clear to all that prisons fail on the very grounds—humanity and hope of rehabilitation—that caused them to replace earlier, cheaper
forms of punishment.

The universal acknowledgment that prisons do not rehabilitate criminals has
produced two responses. The first is to retain the hope of rehabilitation but do away
with imprisonment as much as possible and replace it with various forms of "alternative treatment," such as psychotherapy, supervised probation, and vocational
training. Psychiatrist Karl Menninger, one of the principal critics of American
penology, has suggested even more unconventional approaches, such as "a new job
opportunity or a vacation trip, a course of reducing exercises, a cosmetic surgical
operation or a herniotomy, some night school courses, a wedding in the family
(even one for the patient!), an inspiring sermon." The starry-eyed approach naturally has produced a backlash from critics on the right, who think that it's time to
abandon the goal of rehabilitation. They argue that prisons perform an important

service just by keeping criminals off the streets, and thus should be used with that purpose in mind.

So the debate continues to rage in all the same old ruts. No one, of course, would think of copying the medieval practices of Islamic nations and experimenting with punishments such as flogging and amputation. But let us consider them anyway. How do they compare with our American prison system in achieving the ostensible objectives of punishment? First, do they punish? Obviously they do, and in a uniquely painful and memorable way. Of course any sensible person, given the choice, would prefer suffering these punishments to years of incarceration in a typical American prison. But presumably no Western penologist would criticize Islamic punishments on the grounds that they are not barbaric enough. Do they deter crime? Yes, and probably more effectively than sending convicts off to prison. Now we read about a prison sentence in the newspaper, then think no more about the criminal's payment for his crimes until, perhaps, years later we read a small item reporting his release. By contrast, one can easily imagine the vivid impression it would leave to be wandering through a local shopping center and to stumble onto the scene of some poor wretch being lustily flogged. And the occasional sight of an habitual offender walking around with a bloody stump at the end of his arm no doubt also would serve as a forceful reminder that crime does not pay.

Do flogging and amputation discourage recidivism? No one knows whether   15
the scars on his back would dissuade a criminal from risking another crime, but it is hard to imagine that corporal measures could stimulate a higher rate of recidivism than already exists. Islamic forms of punishment do not serve the favorite new right goal of simply isolating criminals from the rest of society, but they may achieve the same purpose of making further crimes impossible. In the movie *Bonnie and Clyde*, Warren Beatty successfully robs a bank with his arm in a sling, but this must be dismissed as artistic license. It must be extraordinarily difficult, at the very least, to perform much violent crime with only one hand.

Do these medieval forms of punishment rehabilitate the criminal? Plainly not. But long prison terms do not rehabilitate either. And it is just as plain that typical Islamic punishments are no crueler to the convict than incarceration in the typical American state prison.

Of course there are other reasons besides its bizarre forms of punishment that the Islamic system of justice seems uncivilized to the Western mind. One is the absence of due process. Another is the long list of offenses—such as drinking, adultery, blasphemy, "profiteering," and so on—that can bring on conviction and punishment. A third is all the ritualistic mumbojumbo in pronouncements of Islamic law (like that talk about puberty and amnesia in the ayatollah's quotation at the beginning of this article). Even in these matters, however, a little cultural modesty is called for. The vast majority of American criminals are convicted and sentenced as a result of plea bargaining, in which due process plays almost no role. It has been only half a century since a wave of religious fundamentalism stirred this country to outlaw the consumption of alcoholic beverages. Most states also still have laws imposing austere constraints on sexual conduct. Only two weeks ago the *Washington Post* reported that the FBI had spent two and a half years and untold amounts of money to break up a nationwide pornography ring. Flogging the clients of prostitutes, as the Pakistanis did, does seem silly. But only a few months ago Mayor Koch of New York was proposing that clients caught in his own city have their names broadcast by radio stations. We are not so far advanced on such matters as we often like to think. Finally, my lawyer friends assure me that the rules of jurisdiction for American courts contain plenty of petty requirements and bizarre distinctions that would sound silly enough to foreign ears.

Perhaps it sounds barbaric to talk of flogging and amputation, and perhaps it is. But our system of punishment also is barbaric, and probably more so. Only cultural smugness about their system and willfull ignorance about our own make it easy to regard the one as cruel and the other as civilized. We inflict our cruelties away from public view, while nations like Pakistan stage them in front of 10,000 onlookers. Their outrages are visible; ours are not. Most Americans can live their lives for years without having their peace of mind disturbed by the knowledge of what goes on in our prisons. To choose imprisonment over flogging and amputation is not to choose human kindness over cruelty, but merely to prefer that our cruelties be kept out of sight, and out of mind.

Public flogging and amputation may be more barbaric forms of punishment than imprisonment, even if they are not more cruel. Society may pay a higher price for them, even if the particular criminal does not. Revulsion against officially sanctioned violence and infliction of pain derives from something deeply ingrained in the Western conscience, and clearly it is something admirable. Grotesque displays of the sort that occur in Islamic countries probably breed a greater tolerance for physical cruelty, for example, which prisons do not do precisely because they conceal their cruelties. In fact it is our admirable intolerance for calculated violence that makes it necessary for us to conceal what we have not been able to do away with. In a way this is a good thing, since it holds out the hope that we may eventually find a way to do away with it. But in another way it is a bad thing, since it permits us to congratulate ourselves on our civilized humanitarianism while violating its norms in this one area of our national life.

Questions for Discussion and Writing

1. According to Chapman, what are the five objectives that imprisonment is supposed to achieve in Western culture? How satisfactorily do American prisons perform these functions?
2. How do practices of punishment in Eastern cultures differ from those in Western societies? What is Chapman's attitude toward these practices in comparison with Western methods of punishment? How does he use comparison and contrast to more clearly illustrate the differences between them?
3. Write an essay that answers Chapman's question, "Would you rather be subjected to a few minutes of intense pain and considerable public humiliation, or be locked away for two or three years in a prison cell crowded with ill-tempered sociopaths" (para. 8)?

TIM O'BRIEN

Tim O'Brien was born in 1946 in Austin, Minnesota, and was educated at Macalester College and Harvard University. Drafted into the army during the Vietnam War, he attained the rank of sergeant and received the Purple Heart. His first published work, If I Die in a Combat Zone, Box Me Up and Ship Me Home *(1973), relates his experiences in Vietnam. This book is an innovative mixture of alternating chapters of fiction and autobiography in which the following nonfiction account first appeared.*

O'Brien's novel Northern Lights *(1974) was followed by the acclaimed work* Going After Cacciato *(1978), which won the National Book Award. Other works include* The Nuclear Age *(1985), a collection of stories entitled* The Things They Carried *(1990), and most recently,* Tomcat in Love *(1998).*

If I Die in a Combat Zone

The summer of 1968, the summer I turned into a soldier, was a good time for talking about war and peace. Eugene McCarthy was bringing quiet thought to the subject. He was winning votes in the primaries. College students were listening to him, and some of us tried to help out. Lyndon Johnson was almost forgotten, no longer forbidding or feared; Robert Kennedy was dead but not quite forgotten; Richard Nixon looked like a loser. With all the tragedy and change that summer, it was fine weather for discussion.

And, with all of this, there was an induction notice tucked into a corner of my billfold.

So with friends and acquaintances and townspeople, I spent the summer in Fred's antiseptic cafe, drinking coffee and mapping out arguments on Fred's napkins. Or I sat in Chic's tavern, drinking beer with kids from the farms. I played some golf and tore up the pool table down at the bowling alley, keeping an eye open for likely-looking high school girls.

Late at night, the town deserted, two or three of us would drive a car around and around the town's lake, talking about the war, very seriously, moving with care from one argument to the next, trying to make it a dialogue and not a debate. We covered all the big questions: justice, tyranny, self-determination, conscience and the state, God and war and love.

College friends came to visit: "Too bad, I hear you're drafted. What will you do?"   5

I said I didn't know, that I'd let time decide. Maybe something would change, maybe the war would end. Then we'd turn to discuss the matter, talking long, trying out the questions, sleeping late in the mornings.

The summer conversations, spiked with plenty of references to the philosophers and academicians of war, were thoughtful and long and complex and careful. But, in the end, careful and precise argumentation hurt me. It was painful to tread deliberately over all the axioms and assumptions and corollaries when the people on the town's draft board were calling me to duty, smiling so nicely.

"It won't be bad at all," they said. "Stop in and see us when it's over."

So to bring the conversations to a focus and also to try out in real words my secret fears, I argued for running away.

I was persuaded then, and I remain persuaded now, that the war was wrong. And since it was wrong and since people were dying as a result of it, it was evil. Doubts, of course, hedged all this: I had neither the expertise nor the wisdom to synthesize answers; most of the facts were clouded, and there was no certainty as to the kind of government that would follow a North Vietnamese victory or, for that matter, an American victory, and the specifics of the conflict were hidden away— partly in men's minds, partly in the archives of government, and partly in buried, ir- retrievable history. The war, I thought, was wrongly conceived and poorly justified. But perhaps I was mistaken, and who really knew, anyway?

Piled on top of this was the town, my family, my teachers, a whole history of the prairie. Like magnets, these things pulled in one direction or the other, almost physical forces weighting the problem, so that, in the end, it was less reason and more gravity that was the final influence.

My family was careful that summer. The decision was mine and it was not talked about. The town lay there, spread out in the corn and watching me, the mouths of old women and Country Club men poised in a kind of eternal readiness to find fault. It was not a town, not a Minneapolis or New York, where the son of a father can sometimes escape scrutiny. More, I owed the prairie something. For twenty-one years I'd lived under its laws, accepted its education, eaten its food, wasted and guzzled its water, slept well at night, driven across its highways, dirtied and breathed its air, wallowed in its luxuries. I'd played on its Little League teams. I remembered Plato's *Crito,* when Socrates, facing certain death—execution, not war—had the chance to escape. But he reminded himself that he had seventy years in which he could have left the country, if he were not satisfied or felt the agree- ments he'd made with it were unfair. He had not chosen Sparta or Crete. And, I re- minded myself, I hadn't thought much about Canada until that summer.

The summer passed this way. Gold afternoons on the golf course, a comfort- ing feeling that the matter of war would never touch me, nights in the pool hall or drug store, talking with towns-folk, turning the questions over and over, being a philosopher.

Near the end of that summer the time came to go to the war. The family in- dulged in a cautious sort of Last Supper together, and afterward my father, who is brave, said it was time to report at the bus depot. I moped down to my bedroom and looked the place over, feeling quite stupid, thinking that my mother would come in there in a day or two and probably cry a little. I trudged back up to the kitchen and put my satchel down. Everyone gathered around, saying so long and good health and write and let us know if you want anything. My father took up the induction papers, checking on times and dates and all the last-minute things, and when I pecked my mother's face and grabbed the satchel for comfort, he told me to put it down, that I wasn't supposed to report until tomorrow.

After laughing about the mistake, after a flush of red color and a flood of rib- bing and a wave of relief had come and gone, I took a long drive around the lake, looking again at the place. Sunset Park, with its picnic table and little beach and a

10

15

brown wood shelter and some families swimming. The Crippled Children's School. Slater Park, more kids. A long string of split level houses, painted every color.

The war and my person seemed like twins as I went around the town's lake. Twins grafted together and forever together, as if a separation would kill them both.

The thought made me angry.

In the basement of my house I found some scraps of cardboard and paper. With devilish flair, I printed obscene words on them, declaring my intention to have no part of Vietnam. With delightful viciousness, a secret will, I declared the war evil, the draft board evil, the town evil in its lethargic acceptance of it all. For many minutes, making up the signs, making up my mind, I was outside the town. I was outside the law, all my old ties to my loves and family broken by the old crayon in my hand. I imagined strutting up and down the sidewalks outside the depot, the bus waiting and the driver blaring his horn, the *Daily Globe* photographer trying to push me into line with the other draftees, the frantic telephone calls, my head buzzing at the deed.

On the cardboard, my strokes of bright red were big and ferocious looking. The language was clear and certain and burned with a hard, defiant, criminal, blasphemous sound. I tried reading it aloud.

Later in the evening I tore the signs into pieces and put the shreds in the garbage can outside, clanging the gray cover down and trapping the messages inside. I went back into the basement. I slipped the crayons into their box, the same stubs of color I'd used a long time before to chalk in reds and greens on Roy Rogers' cowboy boots.

I'd never been a demonstrator, except in the loose sense. True, I'd taken a stand in the school newspaper on the war, trying to show why it seemed wrong. But, mostly, I'd just listened.

"No war is worth losing your life for," a college acquaintance used to argue. "The issue isn't a moral one. It's a matter of efficiency: what's the most efficient way to stay alive when your nation is at war? That's the issue."

But others argued that no war is worth losing your country for, and when asked about the case when a country fights a wrong war, those people just shrugged.

Most of my college friends found easy paths away from the problem, all to their credit. Deferments for this and that. Letters from doctors or chaplains. It was hard to find people who had to think much about the problem. Counsel came from two main quarters, pacifists and veterans of foreign wars.

But neither camp had much to offer. It wasn't a matter of peace, as the pacifists argued, but rather a matter of when and when not to join others in making war. And it wasn't a matter of listening to an ex-lieutenant colonel talk about serving in a right war, when the question was whether to serve in what seemed a wrong one.

On August 13, I went to the bus depot. A Worthington *Daily Globe* photographer took my picture standing by a rail fence with four other draftees.

20

25

Then the bus took us through corn fields, to little towns along the way—Lismore and Rushmore and Adrian—where other recruits came aboard. With some of the tough guys drinking beer and howling in the back seats, brandishing their empty cans and calling one another "scum" and "trainee" and "GI Joe," with all this noise and hearty farewelling, we went to Sioux Falls. We spent the night in a YMCA. I went out alone for a beer, drank it in a corner booth, then I bought a book and read it in my room.

By noon the next day our hands were in the air, even the tough guys. We recited the proper words, some of us loudly and daringly and others in bewilderment. It was a brightly lighted room, wood paneled. A flag gave the place the right colors, there was some smoke in the air. We said the words, and we were soldiers.

I'd never been much of a fighter. I was afraid of bullies. Their ripe muscles made me angry: a frustrated anger. Still, I deferred to no one. Positively lorded myself over inferiors. And on top of that was the matter of conscience and conviction, uncertain and surface-deep but pure nonetheless: I was a confirmed liberal, not a pacifist; but I would have cast my ballot to end the Vietnam war immediately, I would have voted for Eugene McCarthy, hoping he would make peace. I was not soldier material, that was certain.

But I submitted. All the personal history, all the midnight conversations and books and beliefs and learning, were crumpled by abstention, extinguished by forfeiture, for lack of oxygen, by a sort of sleepwalking default. It was no decision, no chain of ideas or reasons, that steered me into the war.   30

It was an intellectual and physical stand-off, and I did not have the energy to see it to an end. I did not want to be a soldier, not even an observer to war. But neither did I want to upset a peculiar balance between the order I knew, the people I knew, and my own private world. It was not that I valued that order. But I feared its opposite, inevitable chaos, censure, embarrassment, the end of everything that had happened in my life, the end of it all.

And the stand-off is still there. I would wish this book could take the form of a plea for everlasting peace, a plea from one who knows, from one who's been there and come back, an old soldier looking back at a dying war.

That would be good. It would be fine to integrate it all to persuade my younger brother and perhaps some others to say no to wars and other battles.

Or it would be fine to confirm the odd beliefs about war: it's horrible, but it's a crucible of men and events and, in the end, it makes more of a man out of you.

But, still, none of these notions seems right. Men are killed, dead human beings are heavy and awkward to carry, things smell different in Vietnam, soldiers are   35
afraid and often brave, drill sergeants are boors, some men think the war is proper and just and others don't and most don't care. Is that the stuff for a morality lesson, even for a theme?

Do dreams offer lessons? Do nightmares have themes, do we awaken and analyze them and live our lives and advise others as a result? Can the foot soldier teach anything important about war, merely for having been there? I think not. He can tell war stories.

Questions for Discussion and Writing

1. What conflicting sets of values weighed on O'Brien when he learned he was drafted? Of these, which was the most significant in determining his ultimate decision?
2. Which features of this account provide insight into a Tim O'Brien who was very different from the one townspeople knew?
3. What do you think you would have done if you were in the same situation as O'Brien?

LANGSTON HUGHES

Langston Hughes (1902–1967) was born in Joplin, Missouri, and started writing poetry as a student in Central High School in Cleveland. After graduation he worked his way through Africa and Europe on cargo ships. In 1925, while he was working as a busboy in Washington, D.C., he encountered the poet Vachel Lindsay, who after reading Hughes's poems helped him publish his works. After the publication of his first book, The Weary Blues *(1926), Hughes toured the country giving poetry readings and became a leading figure in the Harlem Renaissance. He graduated from Lincoln University in Pennsylvania in 1929, returned to Harlem, and provided invaluable guidance to young writers. In "Salvation," which first appeared in his autobiography,* The Big Sea *(1940), Hughes reveals his uncanny gift for dialogue and irony, as he re-creates a revival meeting that played a crucial role in his life.*

Salvation

I was saved from sin when I was going on thirteen. But not really saved. It happened like this. There was a big revival at my Auntie Reed's church. Every night for weeks there had been much preaching, singing, praying, and shouting, and some very hardened sinners had been brought to Christ, and the membership of the church had grown by leaps and bounds. Then just before the revival ended, they held a special meeting for children, "to bring the young lambs to the fold." My aunt spoke of it for days ahead. That night I was escorted to the front row and placed on the mourners' bench with all the other young sinners, who had not yet been brought to Jesus.

My aunt told me that when you were saved you saw a light, and something happened to you inside! And Jesus came into your life! And God was with you from then on! She said you could see and hear and feel Jesus in your soul. I believed her. I had heard a great many old people say that same thing and it seemed to me they ought to know. So I sat there calmly in the hot, crowded church, waiting for Jesus to come to me.

The preacher preached a wonderful rhythmical sermon, all moans and shouts and lonely cries and dire pictures of hell, and then he sang a song about the ninety and nine safe in the fold, but one little lamb was left out in the cold. Then he said:

"Won't you come? Won't you come to Jesus? Young lambs, won't you come?" And he held out his arms to all us young sinners there on the mourners' bench. And the little girls cried. And some of them jumped up and went to Jesus right away. But most of us just sat there.

A great many old people came and knelt around us and prayed, old women with jet-black faces and braided hair, old men with work-gnarled hands. And the church sang a song about the lower lights are burning, some poor sinners to be saved. And the whole building rocked with prayer and song.

Still I kept waiting to *see* Jesus.   5

Finally all the young people had gone to the altar and were saved, but one boy and me. He was a rounder's son named Westley. Westley and I were surrounded by sisters and deacons praying. It was very hot in the church, and getting late now. Finally Westley said to me in a whisper: "God damn! I'm tired o' sitting here. Let's get up and be saved." So he got up and was saved.

Then I was left all alone on the mourners' bench. My aunt came and knelt at my knees and cried, while prayers and song swirled all around me in the little church. The whole congregation prayed for me alone in a mighty wail of moans and voices. And I kept waiting serenely for Jesus, waiting, waiting—but he didn't come. I wanted to see him, but nothing happened to me. Nothing! I wanted something to happen to me, but nothing happened.

I heard the songs and the minister saying: "Why don't you come? My dear child, why don't you come to Jesus? Jesus is waiting for you. He wants you. Why don't you come? Sister Reed, what is this child's name?"

"Langston," my aunt sobbed.

"Langston, why don't you come? Why don't you come and be saved? Oh,   10
Lamb of God! Why don't you come?"

Now it was really getting late. I began to be ashamed of myself, holding everything up so long. I began to wonder what God thought about Westley, who certainly hadn't seen Jesus either, but who was now sitting proudly on the platform, swinging his knickerbockered legs and grinning down at me, surrounded by deacons and old women on their knees praying. God had not struck Westley dead for taking his name in vain or for lying in the temple. So I decided that maybe to save further trouble, I'd better lie, too, and say that Jesus had come, and get up and be saved.

So I got up.

Suddenly the whole room broke into a sea of shouting, as they saw me rise. Waves of rejoicing swept the place. Women leaped in the air. My aunt threw her arms around me. The minister took me by the hand and led me to the platform.

When things quieted down, in a hushed silence, punctuated by a few ecstatic "Amens," all the new young lambs were blessed in the name of God. Then joyous singing filled the room.

That night, for the last time in my life but one—for I was a big boy twelve   15
years old—I cried. I cried, in bed alone, and couldn't stop. I buried my head under the quilts, but my aunt heard me. She woke up and told my uncle I was crying because the Holy Ghost had come into my life, and because I had seen Jesus. But I

was really crying because I couldn't bear to tell her that I had lied, that I had deceived everybody in the church, that I hadn't seen Jesus, and that now I didn't believe there was a Jesus any more, since he didn't come to help me.

Questions for Discussion and Writing

1. Who are some of the people who have an interest in "saving" the young Langston Hughes? In each case, how would his salvation serve their interests?
2. What ultimately tips the balance and impels Hughes to declare himself saved? How does he use imagery and figurative language to intensify a sense of drama?
3. Have you ever been in a situation in which others tried to manipulate you into doing or saying something you would not have done otherwise? Describe the circumstances and what was at stake. How do you now feel in retrospect about that experience?

Fiction

H. G. WELLS

H.G. (Herbert George) Wells (1866–1946) is generally acknowledged to have originated the genre of literature we now call science fiction with his novel The Time Machine *(1895). Born into a poor family and afflicted with tuberculosis, Wells was a student of the biologist Thomas Henry Huxley (whose grandson Aldous Huxley wrote* Brave New World *in 1932) who opened his mind to Charles Darwin's theories and the concept that humanity is an evolving species. Wells joined the Fabian Society of Socialists in 1903 and was strongly influenced by their concept of a utopian political state. His brilliant novels include* The Island of Dr. Moreau *(1896),* The Invisible Man *(1897), and* The War of the Worlds *(1898), which was the basis of Orson Welles's famous 1938 radio play (which caused a panic throughout the United States). "The Country of the Blind" (1911) is perhaps Wells's finest short story and will evoke for many, Plato's "The Allegory of the Cave."*

The Country of the Blind

Three hundred miles and more from Chimborazo, one hundred from the snows of Cotopaxi, in the wildest wastes of Ecuador's Andes, there lies that mysterious mountain valley, cut off from the world of men, the Country of the Blind. Long years ago that valley lay so far open to the world that men might come at last through frightful gorges and over an icy pass into its equable meadows; and thither indeed men came, a family or so of Peruvian half-breeds fleeing from the lust and tyranny of an evil Spanish ruler. Then came the stupendous outbreak of Mindobamba, when it was night in Quito for seventeen days, and the water was boiling at Yaguachi and all the fish floating dying even as far as Guayaquil; everywhere along the Pacific slopes there were landslips and swift thawings and sudden floods, and one whole side of the Arauca crest slipped and came down in thunder, and cut off the Country of the Blind for ever from the exploring feet of men. But one of these early settlers had chanced to be on the hither side of the gorges when the world had so terribly shaken itself, and he perforce had to forget his wife and his child and all the friends and possessions he had left up there, and start life over again in the lower world. He started it again but ill, blindness overtook him, and he died of punishment in the mines; but the story he told begot a legend that lingers along the length of the Cordilleras of the Andes to this day.

He told of his reason for venturing back from that fastness, into which he had first been carried lashed to a llama, beside a vast bale of gear, when he was a child. The valley, he said, had in it all that the heart of man could desire—sweet water, pasture, and even climate, slopes of rich brown soil with tangles of a shrub that bore an excellent fruit, and on one side great hanging forests of pine that held the avalanches high. Far overhead, on three sides, vast cliffs of grey-green rock were capped by cliffs of ice; but the glacier stream came not to them but flowed away by the farther slopes, and only now and then huge ice masses fell on the valley side. In this valley it neither rained nor snowed, but the abundant springs gave a rich green pasture, that irrigation would spread over all the valley space. The settlers did well indeed there. Their beasts did well and multiplied, and but one thing marred their happiness. Yet it was enough to mar it greatly. A strange disease had come upon them, and had made all the children born to them there—and indeed, several older children also—blind. It was to seek some charm or antidote against this plague of blindness that he had with fatigue and danger and difficulty returned down the gorge. In those days, in such cases, men did not think of germs and infections but of sins; and it seemed to him that the reason of this affliction must lie in the negligence of these priestless immigrants to set up a shrine so soon as they entered the valley. He wanted a shrine—a handsome, cheap, effectual shrine—to be erected in the valley; he wanted relics and such-like potent things of faith, blessed objects and mysterious medals and prayers. In his wallet he had a bar of native silver for which he would not account; he insisted there was none in the valley with something of the insistence of an inexpert liar. They had all clubbed their money and ornaments together, having little need for such treasure up there, he said, to buy them holy help against their ill. I figure this dim-eyed young mountaineer, sunburnt, gaunt, and anxious, hat-brim clutched feverishly, a man all unused to the ways of the lower world, telling this story to some keen-eyed, attentive priest before the great convulsion; I can picture him presently seeking to return with pious and infallible remedies against that trouble, and the infinite dismay with which he must have faced the tumbled vastness where the gorge had once come out. But the rest of his story of mischances is lost to me, save that I know of his evil death after several years. Poor stray from that remoteness! The stream that had once made the gorge now bursts from the mouth of a rocky cave, and the legend his poor, ill-told story set going developed into the legend of a race of blind men somewhere "over there" one may still hear to-day.

And amidst the little population of that now isolated and forgotten valley the disease ran its course. The old became groping and purblind, the young saw but dimly, and the children that were born to them saw never at all. But life was very easy in that snow-rimmed basin, lost to all the world, with neither thorns nor briars, with no evil insects nor any beasts save the gentle breed of llamas they had lugged and thrust and followed up the beds of the shrunken rivers in the gorges up which they had come. The seeing had become purblind so gradually that they scarcely noted their loss. They guided the sightless youngsters hither and thither until they knew the whole valley marvellously, and when at last sight died out among them the race lived on. They had even time to adapt themselves to the blind control of fire, which they made carefully in stoves of stone. They were a simple strain of people at the first, unlettered, only slightly touched with the Spanish civilisation, but with something of a tradition of the arts of old Peru and of its lost philosophy. Generation followed generation. They forgot many things; they devised many things. Their tradition of the greater world they came from became mythical in colour and uncertain. In all things save sight they were strong and able; and presently the chance of birth and heredity sent one who had an original mind and who could talk and persuade among them, and then afterwards another. These two passed, leaving their effects, and the little community grew in numbers and in understanding, and met and settled social and economic problems that arose. Generation followed generation. Generation followed generation. There came a time when a child was born who was fifteen generations from that ancestor who went out of the valley with a bar of silver to seek God's aid, and who never returned. Thereabouts it chanced that a man came into this community from the outer world. And this is the story of that man.

He was a mountaineer from the country near Quito, a man who had been down to the sea and had seen the world, a reader of books in an original way, an acute and enterprising man, and he was taken on by a party of Englishmen who had come out to Ecuador to climb mountains, to replace one of their three Swiss guides who had fallen ill. He climbed here and he climbed there, and then came the attempt on Parascotopetl, the Matterhorn of the Andes, in which he was lost to the outer world. The story of the accident has been written a dozen times. Pointer's narrative is the best. He tells how the party worked their difficult and almost vertical way up to the very foot of the last and greatest precipice, and how they built a night shelter amidst the snow upon a little shelf of rock, and, with a touch of real dramatic power, how presently they found Nunez had gone from them. They shouted, and there was no reply, shouted and whistled, and for the rest of that night they slept no more.

As the morning broke they saw the traces of his fall. It seems impossible he could have uttered a sound. He had slipped eastward towards the unknown side of the mountain; far below he had struck a steep slope of snow, and ploughed his way down it in the midst of a snow avalanche. His track went straight to the edge of a frightful precipice, and beyond that everything was hidden. Far, far below, and hazy with distance, they could see trees rising out of a narrow, shut-in valley—the lost Country of the Blind. But they did not know it was the lost Country of the Blind, nor distinguish it in any way from any other narrow streak of upland valley. Unnerved by this disaster, they abandoned their attempt in the afternoon, and Pointer was called away to the war before he could make another attack. To this day Parascotopetl lifts an unconquered crest, and Pointer's shelter crumbles unvisited amidst the snows.

And the man who fell survived.

At the end of the slope he fell a thousand feet, and came down in the midst of a cloud of snow upon a snow slope even steeper than the one above. Down this he was whirled, stunned and insensible, but without a bone broken in his body; and then at last came to gentler slopes, and at last rolled out and lay still, buried amidst a softening heap of the white masses that had accompanied and saved him. He came to himself with a dim fancy that he was ill in bed; then realised his position with a mountaineer's intelligence, and worked himself loose and, after a rest or so, out until he saw the stars. He rested flat upon his chest for a space, wondering where he was and what had happened to him. He explored his limbs, and discovered that several of his buttons were gone and his coat turned over his head. His knife had gone from his pocket and his hat was lost, though he had tied it under his chin. He recalled that he had been looking for loose stones to raise his piece of the shelter wall. His ice-axe had disappeared.

He decided he must have fallen, and looked up to see, exaggerated by the ghastly light of the rising moon, the tremendous flight he had taken. For a while he lay, gazing blankly at that vast pale cliff towering above, rising moment by moment out of a subsiding tide of darkness. Its phantasmal, mysterious beauty held him for a space, and then he was seized with a paroxysm of sobbing laughter. . . .

After a great interval of time he became aware that he was near the lower edge of the snow. Below, down what was now a moonlit and practicable slope, he saw the dark and broken appearance of rock-strewn turf. He struggled to his feet, aching in every joint and limb, got down painfully from the heaped loose snow about him, went downward until he was on the turf, and there dropped rather than lay beside a boulder, drank deep from the flask in his inner pocket, and instantly fell asleep.

He was awakened by the singing of birds in the trees far below.

He sat up and perceived he was on a little alp at the foot of a vast precipice, that was grooved by the gully down which he and his snow had come. Over against him another wall of rock reared itself against the sky. The gorge between these precipices ran cast and west and was full of the morning sunlight, which lit to the westward the mass of fallen mountain that closed the descending gorge. Below him it seemed there was a precipice equally steep, but behind the snow in the gully he found a sort of chimney-cleft dripping with snow-water down which a desperate man might venture. He found it easier than it seemed, and came at last to another desolate alp, and then after a rock climb of no particular difficulty to a steep slope of trees. He took his bearings and turned his face up the gorge, for he saw it

10

opened out above upon green meadows, among which he now glimpsed quite distinctly a cluster of stone huts of unfamiliar fashion. At times his progress was like clambering along the face of a wall, and after a time the rising sun ceased to strike along the gorge, the voices of the singing birds died away, and the air grew cold and dark about him. But the distant valley with its houses was all the brighter for that. He came presently to talus, and among the rocks he noted—for he was an observant man—an unfamiliar fern that seemed to clutch out of the crevices with intense green hands. He picked a frond or so and gnawed its stalk and found it helpful.

About midday he came at last out of the throat of the gorge into the plain and the sunlight. He was stiff and weary; he sat down in the shadow of a rock, filled up his flask with water from a spring and drank it down, and remained for a time resting before he went on to the houses.

They were very strange to his eyes, and indeed the whole aspect of that valley became, as he regarded it, queerer and more unfamiliar. The greater part of its surface was lush green meadow, starred with many beautiful flowers, irrigated with extraordinary care, and bearing evidence of systematic cropping piece by piece. High up and ringing the valley about was a wall, and what appeared to be a circumferential water-channel, from which the little trickles of water that fed the meadow plants came, and on the higher slopes above this flocks of llamas cropped the scanty herbage. Sheds, apparently shelters or feeding-places for the llamas, stood against the boundary wall here and there. The irrigation streams ran together into a main channel down the centre of the valley, and this was enclosed on either side by a wall breast high. This gave a singularly urban quality to this secluded place, a quality that was greatly enhanced by the fact that a number of paths paved with black and white stones, and each with a curious little kerb at the side, ran hither and thither in an orderly manner. The houses of the central village were quite unlike the casual and higgledy-piggledy agglomeration of the mountain villages he knew; they stood in a continuous row on either side of a central street of astonishing cleanness; here and there their parti-coloured façade was pierced by a door, and not a solitary window broke their even frontage. They were parti-coloured with extraordinary irregularity; smeared with a sort of plaster that was sometimes grey, sometimes drab, sometimes slate-coloured or dark brown; and it was the sight of this wild plastering first brought the word "blind" into the thoughts of the explorer. "The good man who did that," he thought, "must have been as blind as a bat."

He descended a steep place, and so came to the wall and channel that ran about the valley, near where the latter spouted out its surplus contents into the deeps of the gorge in a thin and wavering thread of cascade. He could now see a number of men and women resting on piled heaps of grass, as if taking a siesta, in the remoter part of the meadow, and nearer the village a number of recumbent children, and then nearer at hand three men carrying pails on yokes along a little path that ran from the encircling wall towards the houses. These latter were clad in garments of llama cloth and boots and belts of leather, and they wore caps of cloth with back and ear flaps. They followed one another in single file, walking slowly and yawning as they walked, like men who have been up all night. There was something so reassuringly prosperous and respectable in their bearing that after a moment's hesitation Nunez stood forward as conspicuously as possible upon his rock, and gave vent to a mighty shout that echoed round the valley.

The three men stopped, and moved their heads as though they were looking 15
about them. They turned their faces this way and that, and Nunez gesticulated with freedom. But they did not appear to see him for all his gestures, and after a time, directing themselves towards the mountains far away to the right, they shouted as if in answer. Nunez bawled again, and then once more, and as he gestured ineffectually the word "blind" came up to the top of his thoughts. "The fools must be blind," he said.

When at last, after much shouting and wrath, Nunez crossed the stream by a little bridge, came through a gate in the wall, and approached them, he was sure that they were blind. He was sure that this was the Country of the Blind of which the legends told. Conviction had sprung upon him, and a sense of great and rather enviable adventure. The three stood side by side, not looking at him, but with their ears directed towards him, judging him by his unfamiliar steps. They stood close together like men a little afraid, and he could see their eyelids closed and sunken, as though the very balls beneath had shrunk away. There was an expression near awe on their faces.

"A man," one said, in hardly recognisable Spanish—"a man it is—a man or a spirit—coming down from the rocks."

But Nunez advanced with the confident steps of a youth who enters upon life. All the old stories of the lost valley and the Country of the Blind had come back to his mind, and through his thoughts ran this old proverb, as if it were a refrain—

"In the Country of the Blind the One-eyed Man is King.

"In the Country of the Blind the One-eyed Man is King." 20

And very civilly he gave them greeting. He talked to them and used his eyes.

"Where does he come from, brother Pedro? asked one.

"Down out of the rocks."

"Over the mountains I come," said Nunez, "out of the country beyond there—where men can see. From near Bogotá,[1] where there are a hundred thousands of people, and where the city passes out of sight."

"Sight?" muttered Pedro. "Sight?" 25

"He comes," said the second blind man, "out of the rocks."

The cloth of their coats Nunez saw was curiously fashioned, each with a different sort of stitching.

They startled him by a simultaneous movement towards him, each with a hand outstretched. He stepped back from the advance of these spread fingers.

"Come hither," said the third blind man, following his motion and clutching him neatly.

---

[1] *Bogotá:* the capital of Colombia.

And they held Nunez and felt him over, saying no word further until they had   30
done so.

"Carefully," he cried, with a finger in his eye, and found they thought that
organ, with its fluttering lids, a queer thing in him. They went over it again.

"A strange creature, Correa," said the one called Pedro. "Feel the coarseness of
his hair. Like a llama's hair."

"Rough he is as the rocks that begot him," said Correa, investigating Nunez's
unshaven chin with a soft and slightly moist hand. "Perhaps he will grow finer."
Nunez struggled a little under their examination, but they gripped him firm.

"Carefully," he said again.

"He speaks," said the third man. "Certainly he is a man."   35

"Ugh!" said Pedro, at the roughness of his coat.

"And you have come into the world?" asked Pedro.

"Out of the world. Over mountains and glaciers; right over above there, halfway to the sun. Out of the great big world that goes down, twelve days' journey to
the sea."

They scarcely seemed to heed him. "Our fathers have told us men may be
made by the forces of Nature," said Correa. "It is the warmth of things and moisture, and rottenness—rottenness."

"Let us lead him to the elders," said Pedro.   40

"Shout first," said Correa, "lest the children be afraid. This is a marvelous
occasion."

So they shouted, and Pedro went first and took Nunez by the hand to lead
him to the houses.

He drew his hand away. "I can see," he said.

"See?" said Correa.

"Yes, see," said Nunez, turning towards him, and stumbled against Pedro's pail.   45

"His senses are still imperfect," said the third blind man. "He stumbles, and
talks unmeaning words. Lead him by the hand."

"As you will," said Nunez, and was led along, laughing.

It seemed they knew nothing of sight.

Well, all in good time, he would teach them.

He heard people shouting, and saw a number of figures gathering together in   50
the middle roadway of the village.

He found it taxed his nerve and patience more than he had anticipated, that
first encounter with the population of the Country of the Blind. The place seemed
larger as he drew near to it, and the smeared plasterings queerer, and a crowd of
children and men and women (the women and girls, he was pleased to note, had
some of them quite sweet faces, for all that their eyes were shut and sunken) came
about him, holding on to him, touching him with soft, sensitive hands, smelling at
him, and listening at every word he spoke. Some of the maidens and children, however, kept aloof as if afraid, and indeed his voice seemed coarse and rude beside
their softer notes. They mobbed him. His three guides kept close to him with an
effect of proprietorship, and said again and again, "A wild man out of the rocks."

"Bogotá," he said. "Bogotá. Over the mountain crests."

"A wild man—using wild words," said Pedro. "Did you hear that—*Bogotá?* His mind is hardly formed yet. He has only the beginnings of speech."

A little boy nipped his hand. "Bogotá!" he said mockingly.

"Ay! A city to your village. I come from the great world—where men have eyes and see." 55

"His name's Bogotá," they said.

"He stumbled," said Correa, "stumbled twice as we came hither."

"Bring him to the elders."

And they thrust him suddenly through a doorway into a room as black as pitch, save at the end there faintly glowed a fire. The crowd closed in behind him and shut out all but the faintest glimmer of day, and before he could arrest himself he had fallen headlong over the feet of a seated man. His arm, outflung, struck the face of someone else as he went down; he felt the soft impact of features and heard a cry of anger, and for a moment he struggled against a number of hands that clutched him. It was a one-sided fight. An inkling of the situation came to him, and he lay quiet.

"I fell down," he said; "I couldn't see in this pitchy darkness." 60

There was a pause as if the unseen persons about him tried to understand his words. Then the voice of Correa said: "He is but newly formed. He stumbles as he walks and mingles words that mean nothing with his speech."

Others also said things about him that he heard or understood imperfectly.

"May I sit up?" he asked, in a pause. "I will not struggle against you again."

They consulted and let him rise.

The voice of an older man began to question him, and Nunez found himself 65 trying to explain the great world out of which he had fallen, and the sky and mountains and sight and such-like marvels, to these elders who sat in darkness in the Country of the Blind. And they would believe and understand nothing whatever he told them, a thing quite outside his expectation. They would not even understand many of his words. For fourteen generations these people had been blind and cut off from all the seeing world; the names for all the things of sight had faded and changed; the story of the outer world was faded and changed to a child's story; and they had ceased to concern themselves with anything beyond the rocky slopes above their circling wall. Blind men of genius had arisen among them and questioned the shreds of belief and tradition they had brought with them from their seeing days, and had dismissed all these things as idle fancies, and replaced them with new and saner explanations. Much of their imagination had shrivelled with their eyes, and they had made for themselves new imaginations with their ever more sensitive ears and finger-tips. Slowly Nunez realised this; that his expectation of wonder and reverence at his origin and his gifts was not to be borne out; and after his poor attempt to explain sight to them had been set aside as the confused version of a new-made being describing the marvels of his incoherent sensations, he subsided, a little dashed, into listening to their instruction. And the eldest of the blind men explained to him life and philosophy and religion, how that the world (meaning their valley) had been first an empty hollow in the rocks, and then had come, first, inanimate things without the gift of touch, and llamas and a few other creatures that had little sense, and then men, and at last angels, whom one could hear singing and making fluttering sounds, but whom no one could touch at all, which puzzled Nunez greatly until he thought of the birds.

He went on to tell Nunez how this time had been divided into the warm and the cold, which are the blind equivalents of day and night, and how it was good to sleep in the warm and work during the cold, so that now, but for his advent, the whole town of the blind would have been asleep. He said Nunez must have been specially created to learn and serve the wisdom they had acquired, and for that all his mental incoherency and stumbling behavior he must have courage, and do his best to learn, and at that all the people in the doorway murmured encouragingly. He said the night—for the blind call their day night—was now far gone, and it behooved every one to go back to sleep. He asked Nunez if he knew how to sleep, and Nunez said he did, but that before sleep he wanted food.

They brought him food—llama's milk in a bowl, and rough salted bread—and led him into a lonely place to eat out of their hearing, and afterwards to slumber until the chill of the mountain evening roused them to begin their day again. But Nunez slumbered not at all.

Instead, he sat up in the place where they had left him, resting his limbs and turning the unanticipated circumstances of his arrival over and over in his mind.

Every now and then he laughed, sometimes with amusement, and sometimes with indignation.

"Unformed mind!" he said. "Got no senses yet! They little know they've been insulting their heaven-sent king and master. I see I must bring them to reason. Let me think—let me think." 70

He was still thinking when the sun set.

Nunez had an eye for all beautiful things, and it seemed to him that the glow upon the snowfields and glaciers that rose about the valley on every side was the most beautiful thing he had ever seen. His eyes went from that inaccessible glory to the village and irrigated fields, fast sinking into the twilight, and suddenly a wave of emotion took him, and he thanked God from the bottom of his heart that the power of sight had been given him.

He heard a voice calling to him from out of the village.

"Ya ho there, Bogotá! Come hither!"

At that he stood up smiling. He would show these people once and for all what sight would do for a man. They would seek him, but not find him. 75

"You move not, Bogotá," said the voice.

He laughed noiselessly, and made two stealthy steps aside from the path.

"Trample not on the grass, Bogotá; that is not allowed."

Nunez had scarcely heard the sound he made himself. He stopped amazed.

The owner of the voice came running up the piebald path towards him. 80

He stepped back into the pathway. "Here I am," he said.

"Why did you not come when I called you?" said the blind man. "Must you be led like a child? Cannot you hear the path as you walk?"

Nunez laughed. "I can see it," he said.

"There is no such word as *see*," said the blind man, after a pause. "Cease this folly, and follow the sound of my feet."

Nunez followed, a little annoyed. 85

"My time will come," he said.

'You'll learn," the blind man answered. "There is much to learn in the world."

"Has no one told you, 'In the Country of the Blind the One-eyed Man is King'?"

"What is blind?" asked the blind man carelessly over his shoulder.

Four days passed, and the fifth found the King of the Blind still incognito, as a   90
clumsy and useless stranger among his subjects.

It was, he found, much more difficult to proclaim himself than he had supposed, and in the meantime, while he meditated his *coup d'état,* he did what he was told and learned the manners and customs of the Country of the Blind. He found working and going about at night a particularly irksome thing, and he decided that should be the first thing he would change.

They led a simple, laborious life, these people, with all the elements of virtue and happiness, as these things can be understood by men. They toiled, but not oppressively; they had food and clothing sufficient for their needs; they had days and seasons of rest; they made much of music and singing, and there was love among them, and little children.

It was marvellous with what confidence and precision they went about their ordered world. Everything, you see, had been made to fit their needs; each of the radiating paths of the valley area had a constant angle to the others, and was distinguished by a special notch upon its kerbing; all obstacles and irregularities of path or meadow had long since been cleared away; all their methods and procedure arose naturally from their special needs. Their senses had become marvellously acute; they could hear and judge the slightest gesture of a man a dozen paces away—could hear the very beating of his heart. Intonation had long replaced expression with them, and touches gesture, and their work with hoe and spade and fork was as free and confident as garden work can be. Their sense of smell was extraordinarily fine; they could distinguish individual differences as readily as a dog can, and they went about the tending of the llamas, who lived among the rocks above and came to the wall for food and shelter, with ease and confidence. It was only when at last Nunez sought to assert himself that he found how easy and confident their movements could be.

He rebelled only after he had tried persuasion.

He tried at first on several occasions to tell them of sight. "Look you here, you   95
people," he said. "There are things you do not understand in me."

Once or twice one or two of them attended to him; they sat with faces downcast and ears turned intelligently towards him, and he did his best to tell them what it was to see. Among his hearers was a girl, with eyelids less red and sunken than the others, so that one could almost fancy she was hiding eyes, whom especially he hoped to persuade. He spoke of the beauties of sight, of watching the mountains, of the sky and the sunrise, and they heard him with amused incredulity that presently became condemnatory. They told him there were indeed no mountains at all, but that the end of the rocks where the llamas grazed was indeed the end of the world; thence sprang a cavernous roof of the universe, from which the dew and the avalanches fell; and when he maintained stoutly the world had neither end nor roof such as they supposed, they said his thoughts were wicked. So far as he could describe sky and clouds and stars to them it seemed to them a hideous void, a terrible blankness in the place of the smooth roof to things in which they believed—it was an article of faith with them that the cavern roof was exquisitely smooth to the touch. He saw that in some manner he shocked them, and gave up that aspect of the matter altogether, and tried to show them the practical value of sight. One morning he saw Pedro in the path called Seventeen and coming towards the central houses, but still too far off for hearing or scent, and he told them as much. "In a little while," he prophesied, "Pedro will be here." An old man remarked that Pedro had no business on Path Seventeen, and then, as if in confirmation, that individual as he drew near turned and went transversely into Path Ten, and so back with nimble paces towards the outer wall. They mocked Nunez when Pedro did not arrive, and afterwards, when he asked Pedro questions to clear his character, Pedro denied and outfaced him, and was afterwards hostile to him.

Then he induced them to let him go a long way up the sloping meadows towards the wall with one complacent individual, and to him he promised to describe all that happened among the houses. He noted certain goings and comings, but the things that really seemed to signify to these people happened inside of or behind the windowless houses—the only things they took note of to test him by—and of these he could see or tell nothing; and it was after the failure of this attempt, and the ridicule they could not repress, that he resorted to force. He thought of seizing a spade and suddenly smiting one or two of them to earth, and so in fair combat showing the advantage of eyes. He went so far with that resolution as to seize his spade, and then he discovered a new thing about himself, and that was that it was impossible for him to hit a blind man in cold blood.

He hesitated, and found them all aware that he snatched up the spade. They stood alert, with their heads on one side, and bent ears towards him for what he would do next.

"Put that spade down," said one, and he felt a sort of helpless horror. He came near obedience.

Then he thrust one backwards against a house wall, and fled past him and out of the village. 100

He went athwart one of their meadows, leaving a track of trampled grass behind his feet, and presently sat down by the side of one of their ways. He felt something of the buoyancy that comes to all men in the beginning of a fight, but more perplexity. He began to realise that you cannot even fight happily with creatures who stand upon a different mental basis to yourself. Far away he saw a number of men carrying spades and sticks come out of the street of houses, and advance in a spreading line along the several paths towards him. They advanced slowly, speaking frequently to one another, and ever and again the whole cordon would halt and sniff the air and listen.

The first time they did this Nunez laughed. But afterwards he did not laugh.

One struck his trail in the meadow grass, and came stooping and feeling his way along it.

For five minutes he watched the slow extension of the cordon, and then his vague disposition to do something forthwith became frantic. He stood up, went a pace or so towards the circumferential wall, turned, and went back a little way. There they all stood in a crescent, still and listening.

He also stood still, gripping his spade very tightly in both hands. Should he   105
charge them?

The pulse in his ears ran into the rhythm of "In the Country of the Blind the One-eyed Man is King!"

Should he charge them?

He looked back at the high and unclimbable wall behind—unclimbable because of its smooth plastering, but withal pierced with many little doors, and at the approaching line of seekers. Behind these, others were now coming out of the street of houses.

Should he charge them?

"Bogotá!" called one. "Bogotá! where are you?"   110

He gripped his spade still tighter, and advanced down the meadows towards the place of habitations, and directly he moved they converged upon him. "I'll hit them if they touch me," he swore; "by Heaven, I will. I'll hit." He called aloud, "Look here, I'm going to do what I like in this valley. Do you hear? I'm going to do what I like and go where I like!"

They were moving in upon him quickly, groping, yet moving rapidly. It was like playing blind man's buff, with everyone blindfolded except one. "Get hold of him!" cried one. He found himself in the arc of a loose curve of pursuers. He felt suddenly he must be active and resolute.

"You don't understand," he cried in a voice that was meant to be great and resolute, and which broke. "You are blind, and I can see. Leave me alone!"

"Bogotá! Put down that spade, and come off the grass!"

The last order, grotesque in its urban familiarity, produced a gust of anger.   115

"I'll hurt you," he said, sobbing with emotion. "By Heaven, I'll hurt you. Leave me alone!"

He began to run, not knowing clearly where to run. He ran from the nearest blind man, because it was a horror to hit him. He stopped, and then made a dash to escape from their closing ranks. He made for where a gap was wide, and the men on either side, with a quick perception of the approach of his paces, rushed in on one another. He sprang forward, and then saw he must be caught, and *swish!* the spade had struck. He felt the soft thud of hand and arm, and the man was down with a yell of pain, and he was through.

Through! And then he was close to the street of houses again, and blind men, whirling spades and stakes, were running with a sort of reasoned swiftness hither and thither.

He heard steps behind him just in time, and found a tall man rushing forward and swiping at the sound of him. He lost his nerve, hurled his spade a yard wide at his antagonist, and whirled about and fled, fairly yelling as he dodged another.

He was panic-stricken. He ran furiously to and fro, dodging when there was   120
no need to dodge, and in his anxiety to see on every side of him at once, stumbling. For a moment he was down and they heard his fall. Far away in the circumferential

wall a little doorway looked like heaven, and he set off in a wild rush for it. He did not even look round at his pursuers until it was gained, and he had stumbled across the bridge, clambered a little way among the rocks, to the surprise and dismay of a young llama, who went leaping out of sight, and lay down sobbing for breath.

And so his *coup d'état* came to an end.

He stayed outside the wall of the valley of the Blind for two nights and days without food or shelter, and meditated upon the unexpected. During these meditations he repeated very frequently and always with a profounder note of derision the exploded proverb: "In the Country of the Blind the One-eyed Man is King." He thought chiefly of ways of fighting and conquering these people, and it grew clear that for him no practicable way was possible. He had no weapons, and now it would be hard to get one.

The canker of civilisation had got to him even in Bogotá, and he could not find it in himself to go down and assassinate a blind man. Of course, if be did that, he might then dictate terms on the threat of assassinating them all. But—sooner or later he must sleep! . . .

He tried also to find food among the pine trees, to be comfortable under pine boughs while the frost fell at night, and—with less confidence—to catch a llama by artifice in order to try to kill it—perhaps by hammering it with a stone—and so finally, perhaps, to eat some of it. But the llamas had a doubt of him and regarded him with distrustful brown eyes, and spat when he drew near. Fear came on him the second day and fits of shivering. Finally he crawled down to the wall of the Country of the Blind and tried to make terms. He crawled along by the stream, shouting, until two blind men came out to the gate and talked to him.

"I was mad," he said. "But I was only newly made."   125

They said that was better.

He told them he was wiser now, and repented of all he had done.

Then he wept without intention, for he was very weak and ill now, and they took that as a favourable sign.

They asked him if he still thought he could *"see."*

"No," he said. "That was folly. The word means nothing—less than nothing!"   130

They asked him what was overhead.

"About ten times ten the height of a man there is a roof above the world of—of rock—and very, very smooth." . . . He burst again into hysterical tears. "Before you ask me any more, give me some food or I shall die."

He expected dire punishments, but these blind people were capable of toleration. They regarded his rebellion as but one more proof of his general idiocy and inferiority; and after they had whipped him they appointed him to do the simplest and heaviest work they had for anyone to do, and he, seeing no other way of living, did submissively what he was told.

He was ill for some days, and they nursed him kindly. That refined his submission. But they insisted on his lying in the dark, and that was a great misery. And blind philosophers came and talked to him of the wicked levity of his mind, and reproved him so impressively for his doubts about the lid of rock that covered their cosmic casserole that he almost doubted whether indeed he was not the victim of hallucination in not seeing it overhead.

So Nunez became a citizen of the Country of the Blind, and these people   135
ceased to be a generalised people and became individualities and familiar to him,
while the world beyond the mountains became more and more remote and unreal.
There was Yacob, his master, a kindly man when not annoyed; there was Pedro,
Yacob's nephew; and there was Medina-saroté, who was the youngest daughter of
Yacob. She was little esteemed in the world of the blind, because she had a clear-
cut face, and lacked that satisfying, glossy smoothness that is the blind man's ideal of
feminine beauty; but Nunez thought her beautiful at first, and presently the most
beautiful thing in the whole creation. Her closed eyelids were not sunken and red
after the common way of the valley, but lay as though they might open again at any
moment; and she had long eyelashes, which were considered a grave disfigurement.
And her voice was strong, and did not satisfy the acute hearing of the valley swains.
So that she had no lover.

There came a time when Nunez thought that, could he win her, he would be
resigned to live in the valley for all the rest of his days.

He watched her; he sought opportunities of doing her little services, and
presently he found that she observed him. Once at a rest-day gathering they sat side
by side in the dim starlight, and the music was sweet. His hand came upon hers and
he dared to clasp it. Then very tenderly she returned his pressure. And one day, as
they were at their meal in the darkness, he felt her hand very softly seeking him, and
as it chanced the fire leaped then and he saw the tenderness of her face.

He sought to speak to her.

He went to her one day when she was sitting in the summer moonlight spinning. The light made her a thing of silver and mystery. He sat down at her feet and
told her he loved her, and told her how beautiful she seemed to him. He had a
lover's voice, he spoke with a tender reverence that came near to awe, and she had
never before been touched by adoration. She made him no definite answer, but it
was clear his words pleased her.

After that he talked to her whenever he could make an opportunity. The val-   140
ley became the world for him, and the world beyond the mountains where men
lived in sunlight seemed no more than a fairy tale he would some day pour into
her ears. Very tentatively and timidly he spoke to her of sight.

Sight seemed to her the most poetical of fancies, and she listened to his description of the stars and the mountains and her own sweet white-lit beauty as
though it was a guilty indulgence. She did not believe, she could only half understand, but she was mysteriously delighted, and it seemed to him that she completely
understood.

His love lost its awe and took courage. Presently he was for demanding her
of Yacob and the elders in marriage, but she became fearful and delayed. And it
was one of her elder sisters who first told Yacob that Median-saroté and Nunez
were in love.

There was from the first very great opposition to the marriage of Nunez and
Median-saroté; not so much because they valued her as because they held him as a
being apart, an idiot, an incompetent thing below the permissible level of a man.
Her sisters opposed it bitterly as bringing discredit on them all; and old Yacob,
though he had formed a sort of liking for his clumsy, obedient serf, shook his head

and said the thing could not be. The young men were all angry at the idea of corrupting the race, and one went so far as to revile and strike Nunez. He struck back. Then for the first time he found an advantage in seeing, even by twilight, and after that fight was over no one was disposed to raise a hand against him. But they still found his marriage impossible.

Old Yacob had a tenderness for his last little daughter, and was grieved to have her weep upon his shoulder.

"You see, my dear, he's an idiot. He has delusions; he can't do anything right." 145

"I know," wept Medina-saroté. "But he's better than he was. He's getting better. And he's strong, dear father, and kind—stronger and kinder than any other man in the world. And he loves me—and, father, I love him."

Old Yacob was greatly distressed to find her inconsolable, and, besides—what made it more distressing—he liked Nunez for many things. So he went and sat in the windowless council-chamber with the other elders and watched the trend of the talk, and said, at the proper time, "He's better than he was. Very likely, some day, we shall find him as sane as ourselves."

Then afterwards one of the elders, who thought deeply, had an idea. He was the great doctor among these people, their medicine-man, and he had a very philosophical and inventive mind, and the idea of curing Nunez of his peculiarities appealed to him. One day when Yacob was present he returned to the topic of Nunez.

"I have examined Bogotá," he said, "and the case is clearer to me. I think very probably he might be cured."

"That is what I have always hoped," said old Yacob. 150

"His brain is affected," said the blind doctor.

The elders murmured assent.

"Now, *what* affects it?"

"Ah!" said old Yacob.

"*This,*" said the doctor, answering his own question. "Those queer things that 155 are called the eyes, and which exist to make an agreeable soft depression in the face, are diseased, in the case of Bogotá, in such a way as to affect his brain. They are greatly distended, he has eyelashes, and his eyelids move, and consequently his brain is in a state of constant irritation and distraction."

"Yes?" said old Yacob. "Yes?"

"And I think I may say with reasonable certainty that, in order to cure him completely, all that we need do is a simple and easy surgical operation—namely, to remove these irritant bodies."

"And then he will be sane?"

"Then he will be perfectly sane, and a quite admirable citizen."

"Thank Heaven for science!" said old Yacob, and went forth at once to tell 160 Nunez of his happy hopes.

But Nunez's manner of receiving the good news struck him as being cold and disappointing.

"One might think," he said, "from the tone you take, that you did not care for my daughter."

It was Medina-saroté who persuaded Nunez to face the blind surgeons.

"*You* do not want me," he said, "to lose my gift of sight?"

She shook her head.   165

"My world is sight."

Her head drooped lower.

"There are the beautiful things, the beautiful little things—the flowers, the lichens among the rocks, the lightness and softness on a piece of fur, the far sky with its drifting down of clouds, the sunsets and the stars. And there is *you*. For you alone it is good to have sight, to see your sweet, serene face, your kindly lips, your dear, beautiful hands folded together. . . . It is these eyes of mine you won, these eyes that hold me to you, that these idiots seek. Instead, I must touch you, hear you, and never see you again. I must come under that roof of rock and stone and darkness, that horrible roof under which your imagination stoops. . . . No; you would not have me do that?"

A disagreeable doubt had risen in him. He stopped, and left the thing a question.

"I wish," she said, "sometimes—" She paused.   170

"Yes?" said he, a little apprehensively.

"I wish sometimes—you would not talk like that."

"Like what?"

"I know it's pretty—it's your imagination. I love it, but *now*—"

He felt cold. "*Now?*" he said faintly.   175

She sat quite still.

"You mean—you think—I should be better, better perhaps—"

He was realising things very swiftly. He felt anger, indeed, anger at the dull course of fate, but also sympathy for her lack of understanding—a sympathy near akin to pity.

"Dear," he said, and he could see by her whiteness how intensely her spirit pressed against the things she could not say. He put his arms about her, he kissed her ear, and they sat for a time in silence.

"If I were to consent to this?" he said at last, in a voice that was very gentle.   180

She flung her arms about him, weeping wildly. "Oh, if you would," she sobbed, "if only you would!"

For a week before the operation that was to raise him from the servitude and inferiority to the level of a blind citizen, Nunez knew nothing of sleep, and all through the warm sunlit hours, while the others slumbered happily, he sat brooding or wandered aimlessly, trying to bring his mind to bear on his dilemma. He had given his answer, he had given his consent, and still he was not sure. And at last work-time was over, the sun rose in splendour over the golden crests, and his last day of vision began for him. He had a few minutes with Medina-saroté before she went apart to sleep.

"To-morrow," he said, "I shall see no more."

"Dear heart!" she answered, and pressed his hands with all her strength.

"They will hurt you but little," she said; "and you are going through this   185
pain—you are going through it, dear lover, for *me*. . . . Dear, if a woman's heart and life can do it, I will repay you. My dearest one, my dearest with the tender voice, I will repay."

He was drenched in pity for himself and her.

He held her in his arms, and pressed his lips to hers, and looked on her sweet face for the last time. "Good-bye!" he whispered at that dear sight, "good-bye!"

And then in silence he turned away from her.

She could hear his slow retreating footsteps, and something in the rhythm of them threw her into a passion of weeping.

He had fully meant to go to a lonely place where the meadows were beauti- 190
ful with white narcissus, and there remain until the hour of his sacrifice should come, but as he went he lifted up his eyes and saw the morning, the morning like an angel in golden armour, marching down the steeps. . . .

It seemed to him that before this splendour he, and this blind world in the valley, and his love, and all, were no more than a pit of sin.

He did not turn aside as he had meant to do, but went on, and passed through the wall of the circumference and out upon the rocks, and his eyes were always upon the sunlit ice and snow.

He saw their infinite beauty, and his imagination soared over them to the things beyond he was now to resign for ever.

He thought of that great free world he was parted from, the world that was his own, and he had a vision of those further slopes, distance beyond distance, with Bogotá, a place of multitudinous stirring beauty, a glory by day, a luminous mystery by night, a place of palaces and fountains and statues and white houses, lying beautifully in the middle distance. He thought how for a day or so one might come down through passes, drawing ever nearer and nearer to its busy streets and ways. He thought of the river journey, day by day, from great Bogotá to the still vaster world beyond, through towns and villages, forest and desert places, the rushing river day by day, until its banks receded and the big steamers came splashing by, and one had reached the sea—the limitless sea, with its thousand islands, its thousands of islands, and its ships seen dimly far away in their incessant journeyings round and about that greater world. And there, unpent by mountains, one saw the sky—the sky, not such a disc as one saw it here, but an arch of immeasurable blue, a deep of deeps in which the circling stars were floating. . . .

His eyes scrutinised the great curtain of the mountains with a keener 195
inquiry.

For example, if one went so, up that gully and to that chimney there, then one might come out high among those stunted pines that ran round in a sort of shelf and rose still higher and higher as it passed above the gorge. And then? That talus might be managed. Thence perhaps a climb might be found to take him up to the precipice that came below the snow; and if that chimney failed, then another farther to the east might serve his purpose better. And then? Then one would be out upon the amber-lit snow there, and halfway up to the crest of those beautiful desolations.

He glanced back at the village, then turned right round and regarded it steadfastly.

He thought of Medina-saroté, and she had become small and remote.

He turned again towards the mountain wall, down which the day had come to him.

Then very circumspectly he began to climb.   200

When sunset came he was no longer climbing, but he was far and high. He had been higher, but he was still very high. His clothes were torn, his limbs were blood-stained, he was bruised in many places, but he lay as if he were at his ease, and there was a smile on his face.

From where he rested the valley seemed as if it were in a pit and nearly a mile below. Already it was dim with haze and shadow, though the mountain summits around him were things of light and fire. The little details of the rocks near at hand were drenched with subtle beauty—a vein of green mineral piercing the grey, the flash of crystal faces here and there, a minute, minutely beautiful orange lichen close beside his face. There were deep mysterious shadows in the gorge, blue deepening into purple, and purple into a luminous darkness, and overhead was the illimitable vastness of the sky. But he heeded these things no longer, but lay quite inactive there, smiling as if he were satisfied merely to have escaped from the valley of the Blind in which he had thought to be King.

The glow of the sunset passed, and the night came, and still he lay peacefully contented under the cold stars.

Questions for Discussion and Writing

1. Why does Nunez expect to become the ruler of the community of people who are born blind? How, in turn, do they view Nunez?
2. In which specific details can you observe Wells's ingenuity in not only imagining the physical terrain, but in creating the coherent value system of the inhabitants in the Country of the Blind?
3. What is at stake for Nunez in the ultimate choice he faces? If you had a choice such as this, which of your senses, if any, would you be willing to relinquish in order to be with the one you loved?

Joyce Carol Oates

Joyce Carol Oates was born in Lockport, New York, in 1938 and was raised on her grandparents' farm in Erie County, New York. She graduated from Syracuse University in 1960 and earned an M.A. at the University of Wisconsin. She has taught writing and literature at Princeton University since 1978. Oates received the O. Henry Special Award for Continuing Achievement and the National Book Award in 1970 for her novel them. *Perhaps the most productive American author, she has published on average two books a year and has written countless essays and reviews. Her work covers the spectrum from novels and short fiction, poetry, plays, and criticism to nonfiction works on topics ranging from the poetry of D. H. Lawrence to boxing. A recent collection of stories is* Faithless: Tales of Transgression *(2001). Her latest novels include* We Were the Mulvaneys *(1991) and* Middle Age: A Romance *(2001). "Where Are You Going, Where Have You Been?" first appeared in* The Wheel of Love *(1965).*

Where Are You Going, Where Have You Been?

For Bob Dylan

Her name was Connie. She was fifteen and she had a quick nervous giggling habit of craning her neck to glance into mirrors, or checking other people's faces to make sure her own was all right. Her mother, who noticed everything and knew everything and who hadn't much reason any longer to look at her own face, always scolded Connie about it. "Stop gawking at yourself, who are you? You think you're so pretty?" she would say. Connie would raise her eyebrows at these familiar complaints and look right through her mother, into a shadowy vision of herself as she was right at that moment: she knew she was pretty and that was everything. Her mother had been pretty once too, if you could believe those old snapshots in the album, but now her looks were gone and that was why she was always after Connie.

"Why don't you keep your room clean like your sister? How've you got your hair fixed—what the hell stinks? Hair spray? You don't see your sister using that junk."

Her sister June was twenty-four and still lived at home. She was a secretary in the high school Connie attended, and if that wasn't bad enough—with her in the same building—she was so plain and chunky and steady that Connie had to hear her praised all the time by her mother and her mother's sisters. June did this, June did that, she saved money and helped clean the house and cooked and Connie couldn't do a thing, her mind was all filled with trashy daydreams. Their father was away at work most of the time and when he came home he wanted supper and he read the newspaper at supper and after supper he went to bed. He didn't bother talking much to them, but around his bent head Connie's mother kept picking at her until Connie wished her mother was dead and she herself was dead and it was all over. "She makes me want to throw up sometimes," she complained to her friends. She had a high, breathless, amused voice which made everything she said a little forced, whether it was sincere or not.

There was one good thing: June went places with girl friends of hers, girls who were just as plain and steady as she, and so when Connie wanted to do that her mother had no objections. The father of Connie's best girl friend drove the girls the three miles to town and left them off at a shopping plaza, so that they could walk through the stores or go to a movie, and when he came to pick them up again at eleven he never bothered to ask what they had done.

They must have been familiar sights, walking around that shopping plaza in their shorts and flat ballerina slippers that always scuffed the sidewalk, with charm bracelets jingling on their thin wrists; they would lean together to whisper and laugh secretly if someone passed by who amused or interested them. Connie had long dark blond hair that drew anyone's eye to it, and she wore part of it pulled up on her head and puffed out and the rest of it she let fall down her back. She wore a pullover jersey blouse that looked one way when she was at home and another way when she was away from home. Everything about her had two sides to it, one

5

for home and one for anywhere that was not home: her walk that could be child-like and bobbing, or languid enough to make anyone think she was hearing music in her head, her mouth which was pale and smirking most of the time, but bright and pink on these evenings out, her laugh which was cynical and drawling at home—"Ha, ha, very funny"—but high-pitched and nervous anywhere else, like the jingling of the charms on her bracelet.

Sometimes they did go shopping or to a movie, but sometimes they went across the highway, ducking fast across the busy road, to a drive-in restaurant where older kids hung out. The restaurant was shaped like a big bottle, though squatter than a real bottle, and on its cap was a revolving figure of a grinning boy who held a hamburger aloft. One night in midsummer they ran across, breathless with dar-ing, and right away someone leaned out a car window and invited them over, but it was just a boy from high school they didn't like. It made them feel good to be able to ignore him. They went up through the maze of parked and cruising cars to the bright-lit, fly-infested restaurant, their faces pleased and expectant as if they were entering a sacred building that loomed out of the night to give them what haven and what blessing they yearned for. They sat at the counter and crossed their legs at the ankles, their thin shoulders rigid with excitement and listened to the music that made everything so good: the music was always in the background like music at a church service, it was something to depend upon.

A boy named Eddie came in to talk with them. He sat backwards on his stool, turning himself jerkily around in semi-circles and then stopping and turning again, and after a while he asked Connie if she would like something to eat. She said she did and so she tapped her friend's arm on her way out—her friend pulled her face up into a brave droll look—and Connie said she would meet her at eleven, across the way. "I just hate to leave her like that," Connie said earnestly, but the boy said that she wouldn't be alone for long. So they went out to his car and on the way Connie couldn't help but let her eyes wander over the windshields and faces all around her, her face gleaming with the joy that had nothing to do with Eddie or even this place; it might have been the music. She drew her shoulders up and sucked in her breath with the pure pleasure of being alive, and just at that moment she happened to glance at a face just a few feet from hers. It was a boy with shaggy black hair, in a convertible jalopy painted gold. He stared at her and then his lips widened into a grin. Connie slit her eyes at him and turned away, but she couldn't help glancing back and there he was still watching her. He wagged a finger and laughed and said, "Gonna get you, baby," and Connie turned away again without Eddie noticing anything.

She spent three hours with him, at the restaurant where they ate hamburgers and drank Cokes in wax cups that were always sweating, and then down an alley a mile or so away, and when he left her off at five to eleven only the movie house was still open at the plaza. Her girl friend was there, talking with a boy. When Connie came up the two girls smiled at each other and Connie said, "How was the movie?" and the girl said, "*You* should know." They rode off with the girl's father, sleepy and pleased, and Connie couldn't help but look at the darkened shopping plaza with its big empty parking lot and its signs that were faded and ghostly now, and over at the drive-in restaurant where cars were still circling tirelessly. She couldn't hear the music at this distance.

Next morning June asked her how the movie was and Connie said, "So-so."

She and that girl and occasionally another girl went out several times a week that way, and the rest of the time Connie spent around the house—it was summer vacation—getting in her mother's way and thinking, dreaming, about the boys she met. But all the boys fell back and dissolved into a single face that was not even a face, but an idea, a feeling, mixed up with the urgent insistent pounding of the music and the humid night air of July. Connie's mother kept dragging her back to the daylight by finding things for her to do or saying suddenly, "What's this about the Pettinger girl?"

And Connie would say nervously, "Oh, her. That dope." She always drew thick clear lines between herself and such girls, and her mother was simple and kindly enough to believe her. Her mother was so simple, Connie thought, that it was maybe cruel to fool her so much. Her mother went scuffling around the house in old bedroom slippers and complained over the telephone to one sister about the other, then the other called up and the two of them complained about the third one. If June's name was mentioned her mother's tone was approving, and if Connie's name was mentioned it was disapproving. This did not really mean she disliked Connie and actually Connie thought that her mother preferred her to June because she was prettier, but the two of them kept up a pretense of exasperation, a sense that they were tugging and struggling over something of little value to either of them. Sometimes, over coffee, they were almost friends, but something would come up—some vexation that was like a fly buzzing suddenly around their heads—and their faces went hard with contempt.

One Sunday Connie got up at eleven—none of them bothered with church —and washed her hair so that it could dry all day long, in the sun. Her parents and sister were going to a barbecue at an aunt's house and Connie said no, she wasn't interested, rolling her eyes, to let mother know just what she thought of it. "Stay home alone then," her mother said sharply. Connie sat out back in a lawn chair and watched them drive away, her father quiet and bald, hunched around so that he could back the car out, her mother with a look that was still angry and not at all softened through the windshield, and in the back seat poor old June all dressed up as if she didn't know what a barbecue was, with all the running yelling kids and the flies. Connie sat with her eyes closed in the sun, dreaming and dazed with the warmth about her as if this were a kind of love, the caresses of love, and her mind slipped over onto thoughts of the boy she had been with the night before and how nice he had been, how sweet it always was, not the way someone like June would suppose but sweet, gentle, the way it was in movies and promised in songs; and when she opened her eyes she hardly knew where she was, the back yard ran off into weeds and a fenceline of trees and behind it the sky was perfectly blue and still. The asbestos "ranch house" that was now three years old startled her—it looked small. She shook her head as if to get awake.

It was too hot. She went inside the house and turned on the radio to drown out the quiet. She sat on the edge of her bed, barefoot, and listened for an hour and a half to a program called XYZ Sunday Jamboree, record after record of hard, fast, shrieking songs she sang along with, interspersed by exclamations from "Bobby King": "An' look here you girls at Napoleon's—Son and Charley want you to pay real close attention to this song coming up!"

And Connie paid close attention herself, bathed in a glow of slow-pulsed joy that seemed to rise mysteriously out of the music itself and lay languidly about the airless little room, breathed in and breathed out with each gentle rise and fall of her chest.

After a while she heard a car coming up the drive. She sat up at once, startled, 15 because it couldn't be her father so soon. The gravel kept crunching all the way in from the road—the driveway was long—and Connie ran to the window. It was a car she didn't know. It was an open jalopy, painted a bright gold that caught the sun opaquely. Her heart began to pound and her fingers snatched at her hair, checking it, and she whispered "Christ. Christ," wondering how bad she looked. The car came to a stop at the side door and the horn sounded four short taps as if this were a signal Connie knew.

She went into the kitchen and approaching the door slowly, then hung out the screen door, her bare toes curling down off the step. There were two boys in the car and now she recognized the driver: he had shaggy, shabby black hair that looked crazy as a wig and he was grinning at her.

"I ain't late, am I?" he said.

"Who the hell do you think you are?" Connie said.

"Toldja I'd be out, didn't I?"

"I don't even know who you are."   20

She spoke sullenly, careful to show no interest or pleasure, and he spoke in a fast bright monotone. Connie looked past him to the other boy, taking her time. He had fair brown hair, with a lock that fell onto his forehead. His sideburns gave him a fierce, embarrassed look, but so far he hadn't even bothered to glance at her. Both boys wore sunglasses. The driver's glasses were metallic and mirrored everything in miniature.

"You wanta come for a ride?" he said.

Connie smirked and let her hair fall loose over one shoulder.

"Don'tcha like my car? New paint job," he said. "Hey."

"What?"   25

"You're cute."

She pretended to fidget, chasing flies away from the door.

"Don'tcha believe me, or what?" he said.

"Look, I don't even know who you are," Connie said in disgust.

"Hey, Ellie's got a radio, see. Mine's broke down." He lifted his friend's arm   30
and showed her the little transistor the boy was holding, and now Connie began to hear the music. It was the same program that was playing inside the house.

"Bobby King?" she said.

"I listen to him all the time. I think he's great."

"He's kind of great," Connie said reluctantly.

"Listen, that guy's *great*. He knows where the action is."

Connie blushed a little, because the glasses made it impossible for her to see   35
just what this boy was looking at. She couldn't decide if she liked him or if he was
just a jerk, and so she dawdled in the doorway and wouldn't come down or go
back inside. She said, "What's all that stuff painted on your car?"

"Can'tcha read it?" He opened the door very carefully, as if he was afraid it
might fall off. He slid out just as carefully, planting his feet firmly on the ground,
the tiny metallic world in his glasses slowing down like gelatine hardening and in
the midst of it Connie's bright green blouse. "This here is my name, to begin with,"
he said. ARNOLD FRIEND was written in tar-like black letters on the side, with
a drawing of a round grinning face that reminded Connie of a pumpkin, except it
wore sunglasses. "I wanta introduce myself, I'm Arnold Friend and that's my real
name and I'm gonna be your friend, honey, and inside the car's Ellie Oscar, he's
kinda shy." Ellie brought his transistor up to his shoulder and balanced it there.
"Now these numbers are a secret code, honey," Arnold Friend explained. He read
off the numbers 33, 19, 17 and raised his eyebrows at her to see what she thought
of that, but she didn't think much of it. The left rear fender had been smashed and
around it was written, on the gleaming gold background: DONE BY CRAZY
WOMAN DRIVER. Connie had to laugh at that. Arnold Friend was pleased at
her laughter and looked up at her. "Around the other side's a lot more—you wanta
come and see them?"

"No."

"Why not?"

"Why should I?"

"Don'tcha wanta see what's on the car? Don'tcha wanta go for a ride?"   40

"I don't know."

"Why not?"

"I got things to do."

"Like what?"

"Things."   45

He laughed as if she had said something funny. He slapped his thighs. He was
standing in a strange way, leaning back against the car as if he were balancing himself. He wasn't tall, only an inch or so taller than she would be if she came down
to him. Connie liked the way he was dressed, which was the way all of them
dressed: tight faded jeans stuffed into black, scuffed boots, a belt that pulled his waist
in and showed how lean he was, and a white pull-over shirt that was a little soiled
and showed the hard small muscles of his arms and shoulders. He looked as if he
probably did hard work, lifting and carrying things. Even his neck looked muscular. And his face was a familiar face, somehow: the jaw and chin and cheeks slightly
darkened, because he hadn't shaved for a day or two, and the nose long and hawk-
like, sniffing as if she were a treat he was going to gobble up and it was all a joke.

"Connie, you ain't telling the truth. This is your day set aside for a ride with
me and you know it," he said, still laughing. The way he straightened and recovered
from his fit of laughing showed that it had been all fake.

"How do you know what my name is?" she said suspiciously.

"It's Connie."

"Maybe and maybe not."   50

"I know my Connie," he said, wagging his finger. Now she remembered him even better, back at the restaurant, and her cheeks warmed at the thought of how she sucked in her breath just at the moment she passed him—how she must have looked to him. And he had remembered her. "Ellie and I come out here especially for you," he said. "Ellie can sit in back. How about it?"

"Where?"

"Where what?"

"Where're we going?"

He looked at her. He took off the sunglasses and she saw how pale the skin   55 around his eyes was, like holes that were not in shadow but instead in light. His eyes were like chips of broken glass that catch the light in an amiable way. He smiled. It was as if the idea of going for a ride somewhere, to some place, was a new idea to him.

"Just for a ride, Connie sweetheart."

"I never said my name was Connie," she said.

"But I know what it is. I know your name and all about you, lots of things," Arnold Friend said. He had not moved yet but stood still leaning back against the side of his jalopy. "I took a special interest in you, such a pretty girl, and found out all about you like I know your parents and sister are gone somewheres and I know where and how long they're going to be gone, and I know who you were with last night, and your best friend's name is Betty. Right?"

He spoke in a simple lilting voice, exactly as if he were reciting the words to a song. His smile assured her that everything was fine. In the car Ellie turned up the volume on his radio and did not bother to look around at them.

"Ellie can sit in the back seat," Arnold Friend said. He indicated his friend   60 with a casual jerk of his chin, as if Ellie did not count and she could not bother with him.

"How'd you find out all that stuff?" Connie said.

"Listen? Betty Schultz and Tony Fitch and Jimmy Pettinger and Nancy Pettinger," he said, in a chant. "Raymond Stanley and Bob Hutter—"

"Do you know all those kids?"

"I know everybody."

"Look, you're kidding. You're not from around here."   65

"Sure."

"But—how come we never saw you before?"

"Sure you saw me before," he said. He looked down at his boots, as if he were a little offended. "You just don't remember."

"I guess I'd remember you," Connie said.

"Yeah?" He looked up at this, beaming. He was pleased. He began to mark   70 time with the music from Ellie's radio, tapping his fists lightly together. Connie looked away from his smile to the car, which was painted so bright it almost hurt her eyes to look at it. She looked at that name, ARNOLD FRIEND. And up at the front fender was an expression that was familiar—MAN THE FLYING SAUCERS. It was an expression kids had used the year before, but didn't use this year. She looked at it for a while as if the words meant something to her that she did not yet know.

"What're you thinking about? Huh?" Arnold Friend demanded. "Not worried about your hair blowing around in the car, are you?"

"No."

"Think I maybe can't drive good?"

"How do I know?"

"You're a hard girl to handle. How come?" he said. "Don't you know I'm your friend? Didn't you see me put my sign in the air when you walked by?" 75

"What sign?"

"My sign." And he drew an X in the air, leaning out toward her. They were maybe ten feet apart. After his hand fell back to his side the X was still in the air, almost visible. Connie let the screen door close and stood perfectly still inside it, listening to the music from her radio and the boy's blend together. She stared at Arnold Friend. He stood there so stiffly relaxed, pretending to be relaxed, with one hand idly on the door handle as if he were keeping himself up that way and had no intention of ever moving again. She recognized most things about him, the tight jeans that showed his thighs and buttocks and the greasy leather boots and the tight shirt, and even that slippery friendly smile of his, that sleepy dreamy smile that all the boys used to get across ideas they didn't want to put into words. She recognized all this and also the singsong way he talked, slightly mocking, kidding, but serious and a little melancholy, and she recognized the way he tapped one fist against the other in homage to the perpetual music behind him. But all these things did not come together.

She said suddenly, "Hey, how old are you?"

His smile faded. She could see then that he wasn't a kid, he was much older—thirty, maybe more. At this knowledge her heart began to pound faster.

"That's a crazy thing to ask. Can'tcha see I'm your own age?" 80

"Like hell you are."

"Or maybe a coupla years older, I'm eighteen."

"Eighteen?" she said doubtfully.

He grinned to reassure her and lines appeared at the corners of his mouth. His teeth were big and white. He grinned so broadly his eyes became slits and she saw how thick the lashes were, thick and black as if painted with a black tar-like material. Then he seemed to become embarrassed, abruptly, and looked over his shoulder at Ellie. "*Him,* he's crazy," he said. "Ain't he a riot, he's a nut, a real character." Ellie was still listening to the music. His sunglasses told nothing about what he was thinking. He wore a bright orange shirt unbuttoned halfway to show his chest, which was a pale, bluish chest and not muscular like Arnold Friend's. His shirt collar was turned up all around and the very tips of the collar pointed out past his chin as if they were protecting him. He was pressing the transistor radio up against his ear and sat there in a kind of daze, right in the sun.

"He's kinda strange," Connie said. 85

"Hey, she says you're kinda strange! Kinda strange!" Arnold Friend cried. He pounded on the car to get Ellie's attention. Ellie turned for the first time and

Connie saw with shock that he wasn't a kid either—he had a fair, hairless face, cheeks reddened slightly as if the veins grew too close to the surface of his skin, the face of a forty-year-old baby. Connie felt a wave of dizziness rise in her at this sight and she stared at him as if waiting for something to change the shock of the moment, make it all right again. Ellie's lips kept shaping words, mumbling along with the words blasting his ear.

"Maybe you two better go away," Connie said faintly.

"What? How come?" Arnold Friend cried. "We come out here to take you for a ride. It's Sunday." He had the voice of the man on the radio now. It was the same voice, Connie thought. "Don'tcha know it's Sunday all day and honey, no matter who you were with last night today you're with Arnold Friend and don't you forget it!—Maybe you better step out here," he said, and this last was in a different voice. It was a little flatter, as if the heat was finally getting to him.

"No. I got things to do."

"Hey."   90

"You two better leave."

"We ain't leaving until you come with us."

"Like hell I am—"

"Connie, don't fool around with me. I mean, I mean, don't fool *around*," he said, shaking his head. He laughed incredulously. He placed his sunglasses on top of his head, carefully, as if he were indeed wearing a wig, and brought the stems down behind his ears. Connie stared at him, another wave of dizziness and fear rising in her so that for a moment he wasn't even in focus but was just a blur, standing there against his gold car, and she had the idea that he had driven up the driveway all right but had come from nowhere before that and belonged nowhere and that everything about him and even the music that was so familiar to her was only half real.

"If my father comes and sees you—"   95

"He ain't coming. He's at a barbecue."

"How do you know that?"

"Aunt Tillie's. Right now they're—uh—they're drinking. Sitting around," he said vaguely, squinting as if he were staring all the way to town and over to Aunt Tillie's back yard. Then the vision seemed to clear and he nodded energetically. "Yeah. Sitting around. There's your sister in a blue dress, huh? And high heels, the poor sad bitch—nothing like you, sweetheart! And your mother's helping some fat woman with the corn, they're cleaning the corn—husking the corn—"

"What fat woman?" Connie cried.

"How do I know what fat woman. I don't know every goddamn fat woman   100 in the world!" Arnold Friend laughed.

"Oh, that's Mrs. Hornby. . . . Who invited her?" Connie said. She felt a little light-headed. Her breath was coming quickly.

"She's too fat. I don't like them fat. I like them the way you are, honey," he said, smiling sleepily at her. They stared at each other for a while, through the screen door. He said softly, "Now what you're going to do is this: you're going to come out that door. You're going to sit up front with me and Ellie's going to sit in the back, the hell with Ellie, right? This isn't Ellie's date. You're my date. I'm your lover, honey."

"What? You're crazy—"

"Yes, I'm your lover. You don't know what that is but you will," he said. "I know that too. I know all about you. But look: it's real nice and you couldn't ask for nobody better than me, or more polite. I always keep my word. I'll tell you how it is, I'm always nice at first, the first time. I'll hold you so tight you won't think you have to try to get away or pretend anything because you'll know you can't. And I'll come inside you where it's all secret and you'll give in to me and you'll love me—"

"Shut up! You're crazy!" Connie said. She backed away from the door. She put   105
her hands against her ears as if she'd heard something terrible, something not meant for her. "People don't talk like that, you're crazy," she muttered. Her heart was al-most too big now for her chest and its pumping made sweat break out all over her. She looked out to see Arnold Friend pause and then take a step toward the porch lurching. He almost fell. But, like a clever drunken man, he managed to catch his balance. He wobbled in his high boots and grabbed hold of one of the porch posts.

"Honey?" he said. "You still listening?"

"Get the hell out of here!"

"Be nice, honey. Listen."

"I'm going to call the police—"

He wobbled again and out of the side of his mouth came a fast spat curse, an   110
aside not meant for her to hear. But even this "Christ!" sounded forced. Then he began to smile again. She watched this smile come, awkward as if he were smiling from inside a mask. His whole face was a mask, she thought wildly, tanned down onto his throat but then running out as if he had plastered make-up on his face but had forgotten about his throat.

"Honey—? Listen, here's how it is. I always tell the truth and I promise you this: I ain't coming in that house after you."

"You better not! I'm going to call the police if you—if you don't—"

"Honey," he said, talking right through her voice, "honey, I'm not coming in there but you are coming out here. You know why?"

She was panting. The kitchen looked like a place she had never seen before, some room she had run inside but which wasn't good enough, wasn't going to help her. The kitchen window had never had a curtain, after three years, and there were dishes in the sink for her to do—probably—and if you ran your hand across the table you'd probably feel something sticky there.

"You listening, honey? Hey?"   115

"—going to call the police—"

"Soon as you touch the phone I don't need to keep my promise and can come inside. You won't want that."

She rushed forward and tried to lock the door. Her fingers were shaking. "But why lock it," Arnold Friend said gently, talking right into her face. "It's just a screen door. It's just nothing." One of his boots was at a strange angle, as if his foot wasn't in it. It pointed out to the left, bent at the ankle. "I mean, anybody can break through a screen door and glass and wood and iron or anything else if he needs to, anybody at all and specially Arnold Friend. If the place got lit up with a fire, honey, you'd come running out into my arms, right into my arms and safe at home—like you knew I was your lover and'd stopped fooling around, I don't mind a nice shy girl but I don't like no fooling around." Part of those words were spoken with a slightly rhythmic lilt, and Connie somehow recognized them—the echo of a song from last year, about a girl rushing into her boy friend's arms and coming home again—

Connie stood barefoot on the linoleum floor, staring at him. "What do you want?" she whispered.

"I want you," he said.   120

"What?"

"Seen you that night and thought, that's the one, yes sir. I never needed to look any more."

"But my father's coming back. He's coming to get me. I had to wash my hair first—" She spoke in a dry, rapid voice, hardly raising it for him to hear.

"No, your daddy is not coming and yes, you had to wash your hair and you washed it for me. It's nice and shining and all for me, I thank you, sweetheart," he said, with a mock bow, but again he almost lost his balance. He had to bend and adjust his boots. Evidently his feet did not go all the way down; the boots must have been stuffed with something so that he would seem taller. Connie stared out at him and behind him Ellie in the car, who seemed to be looking off toward Connie's right, into nothing. This Ellie said, pulling the words out of the air one after another as if he were just discovering them, "You want me to pull out the phone?"

"Shut your mouth and keep it shut," Arnold Friend said, his face red from   125
bending over or maybe from embarrassment because Connie had seen his boots. "This ain't none of your business."

"What—what are you doing? What do you want?" Connie said. "If I call the police they'll get you, they'll arrest you—"

"Promise was not to come in unless you touch that phone, and I'll keep that promise," he said. He resumed his erect position and tried to force his shoulders back. He sounded like a hero in a movie, declaring something important. He spoke too loudly and it was as if he were speaking to someone behind Connie. "I ain't made plans for coming in that house where I don't belong but just for you to come out to me, the way you should. Don't you know who I am?"

"You're crazy," she whispered. She backed away from the door but did not want to go into another part of the house, as if this would give him permission to come through the door. "What do you. . . . You're crazy, you. . . ."

"Huh? What're you saying, honey?"

Her eyes darted everywhere in the kitchen. She could not remember what it   130
was, this room.

"This is how it is, honey: you come out and we'll drive away, have a nice ride. But if you don't come out we're gonna wait till your people come home and then they're all going to get it."

"You want that telephone pulled out?" Ellie said. He held the radio away from his ear and grimaced, as if without the radio the air was too much for him.

"I toldja shut up, Ellie." Arnold Friend said, "You're deaf, get a hearing aid, right? Fix yourself up. This little girl's no trouble and's gonna be nice to me, so Ellie keep to yourself, this ain't your date—right? Don't hem in on me. Don't hog. Don't crush. Don't bird dog. Don't trail me," he said in a rapid meaningless voice, as if he were running through all the expressions he'd learned but was no longer sure which one of them was in style, then rushing on to new ones, making them up with his eyes closed, "Don't crawl under my fence, don't squeeze in my chipmunk hole, don't sniff my glue, suck my popsicle, keep your own greasy fingers on yourself!" He shaded his eyes and peered in at Connie, who was backed against the kitchen table. "Don't mind him, honey, he's just a creep. He's a dope. Right? I'm the boy for you and like I said you come out here nice like a lady and give me your hand, and nobody else gets hurt, I mean, your nice old bald-headed daddy and your mummy and your sister in her high heels. Because listen: why bring them in this?"

"Leave me alone," Connie whispered.

"Hey, you know that old woman down the road, the one with the chickens and stuff—you know her?" 135

"She's dead!"

"Dead? What? You know her?" Arnold Friend said.

"She's dead—"

"Don't you like her?"

"She's dead—she's—she isn't here any more—" 140

"But don't you like her, I mean, you got something against her? Some grudge or something?" Then his voice dipped as if he were conscious of rudeness. He touched the sunglasses on top of his head as if to make sure they were still there. "Now you be a good girl."

"What are you going to do?"

"Just two things, or maybe three," Arnold Friend said. "But I promise it won't last long and you'll like me that way you get to like people you're close to. You will. It's all over for you here, so come on out. You don't want your people in any trouble, do you?"

She turned and bumped against a chair or something, hurting her leg, but she ran into the back room and picked up the telephone. Something roared in her ear, a tiny roaring, and she was so sick with fear that she could do nothing but listen to it—the telephone was clammy and very heavy and her fingers groped down to the dial but were too weak to touch it. She began to scream into the phone, into the roaring. She cried out, she cried for her mother, she felt her breath start jerking back and forth in her lungs as if it were something Arnold Friend were stabbing her with again and again with no tenderness. A noisy sorrowful wailing rose all about her and she was locked inside it the way she was locked inside this house.

After a while she could hear again. She was sitting on the floor, with her wet back against the wall. 145

Arnold Friend was saying from the door, "That's a good girl. Put the phone back."

She kicked the phone away from her.

"No, honey. Pick it up. Put it back right."

She picked it up and put it back. The dial tone stopped.

"That's a good girl. Now you come outside."   150

She was hollow with what had been fear, but what was now just an empti-ness. All that screaming had blasted it out of her. She sat, one leg cramped under her, and deep inside her brain was something like a pinpoint of light that kept going and would not let her relax. She thought, I'm not going to see my mother again. She thought, I'm not going to sleep in my bed again. Her bright green blouse was all wet.

Arnold Friend said, in a gentle-loud voice that was like a stage voice. "The place where you came from ain't there any more, and where you had in mind to go is cancelled out. This place you are now—inside your daddy's house—is nothing but a cardboard box I can knock down any time. You know that and always did know it. You hear me?"

She thought, I have got to think. I have to know what to do.

"We'll go out to a nice field, out in the country here where it smells so nice and it's sunny," Arnold Friend said. "I'll have my arms tight around you so you won't need to try to get away and I'll show you what love is like, what it does. The hell with this house! It looks solid all right," he said. He ran a fingernail down the screen and the noise did not make Connie shiver, as it would have the day before. "Now put your hand on your heart, honey. Feel that? That feels solid too but we know better, be nice to me, be sweet like you can because what else is there for a girl like you but to be sweet and pretty and give in?—and get away before her people come back?"

She felt her pounding heart. Her hands seemed to enclose it. She thought for   155 the first time in her life that it was nothing that was hers, that belonged to her, but just a pounding, living thing inside this body that wasn't hers either.

"You don't want them to get hurt," Arnold Friend went on. "Now get up, honey. Get up all by yourself."

She stood.

"Now turn this way. That's right. Come over to me—Ellie, put that away, didn't I tell you? You dope. You miserable creep dope," Arnold Friend said. His words were not angry but only part of an incantation. The incantation was kindly. "Now come out through the kitchen to me honey and let's see a smile, try it, you're a brave sweet little girl and now they're eating corn and hotdogs cooked to bursting over an outdoor fire, and they don't know one thing about you and never did and honey you're better than them because not one of them would have done this for you."

Connie felt the linoleum under her feet; it was cool. She brushed her hair back out of her eyes. Arnold Friend let go of the post tentatively and opened his arms for her, his elbows pointing up toward each other and his wrist limp, to show that this was an embarrassed embrace and a little mocking, he didn't want to make her self-conscious.

She put out her hand against the screen. She watched herself push the door   160
slowly open as if she were safe back somewhere in the other doorway, watching
this body and this head of long hair moving out into the sunlight where Arnold
Friend waited.

"My sweet little blue-eyed girl," he said, in a half-sung sigh that had nothing
to do with her brown eyes but was taken up just the same by the vast sunlit reaches
of the land behind him and on all sides of him, so much land that Connie had ever
seen before and did not recognize except to know that she was going to it.

Questions for Discussion and Writing

1. Why is it significant that everything about Connie "had two sides to it"?
   How does Connie see herself as being different from both her mother and
   her sister?

2. How does the description of Arnold Friend—his unusual hair, pale skin,
   awkward way of walking in his boots, out-of-date expressions, and car—suggest he is not what he appears to be? Who do you think he really is, or what
   do you think he represents?

3. What do you think Friend means when he says at the end, "Not a one of
   them would have done this for you"? In your opinion, does Connie really
   have a choice, and if so, what is it?

Parables

PLATO

*Plato (428–347 B.C.), the philosopher who was a pupil of Socrates and the teacher of Aristotle,
went into exile after the death of Socrates in 399 B.C. Plato returned to Athens in 380 B.C. to
establish his school, known as the Academy, where he taught for the next forty years. Most of
Plato's works are cast in the form of dialogues between Socrates and his students. The earliest of
these, the* Ion, Euthyphro, Protagoras, *and* Gorgias, *illustrate the so-called Socratic method,
in which questions are asked until contradictions in the answers disclose the truth. Later in his
life, Plato also wrote* Crito, Apology, Phaedo, Symposium, *and* Timaeus, *among other dialogues, as well as his influential treatises* The Republic *and* The Laws. *Plato's formative influence on Western thought can be traced to his belief that the soul and body have distinct and
separate existences and that beyond the world of the senses exists an eternal order of ideal Forms.
In "The Allegory of the Cave," from* The Republic, *Plato creates an extended analogy to
dramatize the importance of recognizing that the "unreal" world of the senses and physical phenomena are merely shadows cast by the immortal life of the "real" world of ideal Forms.*

The Allegory of the Cave

Socrates: And now, I said, let me show in a figure[1] how far our nature is enlightened or unenlightened:—Behold! human beings living in an underground den, which has a mouth open towards the light and reaching all along the den: here they have been from their childhood, and have their legs and necks chained so that they cannot move, and can only see before them, being prevented by the chains from turning round their heads. Above and behind them a fire is blazing at a distance, and between the fire and the prisoners there is a raised way; and you will see, if you look, a low wall built along the way, like the screen which marionette players have in front of them, over which they show the puppets.

Glaucon: I see.

And do you see, I said, men passing along the wall carrying all sorts of vessels, and statues and figures of animals made of wood and stone and various materials, which appear over the wall? Some of them are talking, others silent.

The den, the prisoners: the light at a distance;

You have shown me a strange image, and they are strange prisoners.

Like ourselves, I replied; and they see only their own shadows, or the shadows of one another, which the fire throws on the opposite wall of cave?

The low wall, and the moving figures of which the shadows are seen on the opposite wall of the den.   5

True, he said; how could they see anything but the shadows if they were never allowed to move their heads?

And of the objects which are being carried in like manner they would only see the shadows?

Yes, he said.

And if they were able to converse with one another, would they not suppose that they were naming what was actually before them?

Very true.   10

And suppose further that the prison had an echo which came from the other side, would they not be sure to fancy when one of the passers-by spoke that the voice which they heard came from the passing shadow?

The prisoners would mistake the shadows for realities.

No question, he replied.

---

[1] *Figure:* a picture or image.

To them, I said, the truth would be literally nothing but the shadows of the images.

That is certain.

And now look again, and see what will naturally follow if the prisoners are released and disabused of their error. At first, when any of them is liberated and compelled suddenly to stand up and turn his neck round and walk and look towards the light, he will suffer sharp pains; the glare will distress him, and he will be unable to see the realities of which in his former state he had seen the shadows; and then conceive some one saying to him, that what he saw before was an illusion, but that now, when he is approaching nearer to being and his eye is turned towards more real existence, he has a clearer vision,—what will be his reply? And you may further imagine that his instructor is pointing to the objects as they pass and requiring him to name them,—will he not be perplexed? Will he not fancy that the shadows which he formerly saw are truer than the objects which are now shown to him?

And when released, they would still persist in maintaining the superior truth of the shadows.

15

Far truer.

And if he is compelled to look straight at the light, will he not have a pain in his eyes which will make him turn away to take refuge in the objects of vision which he can see, and which he will conceive to be in reality clearer than the things which are now being shown to him?

True, he said.

And suppose once more, that he is reluctantly dragged up a steep and rugged ascent, and held fast until he is forced into the presence of the sun himself, is he not likely to be pained and irritated. When he approaches the light his eyes will be dazzled, and he will not be able to see anything at all of what are now called realities.

When dragged upwards, they would be dazzled by excess of light.

Not all in a moment, he said.

20

He will require to grow accustomed to the sight of the upper world. And first he will see the shadows best, next the reflections of men and other objects in the water, and then the objects themselves; then he will gaze upon the light of the moon and the stars and the spangled heaven; and he will see the sky and the stars by night better than the sun or the light of the sun by day?

Certainly.

Last of all he will be able to see the sun, and not mere reflections of him in the water, but he will see him in his own proper place, and not in another; and he will contemplate him as he is.

At length they will see the sun and understand his nature.

Certainly.

He will then proceed to argue that this is he who gives the season and the years, and is the guardian of all that is in the visible world, and in a certain way the cause of all things which he and his fellows have been accustomed to behold?

Clearly, he said, he would first see the sun and then reason about him.

And when he remembered his old habitation, and the wisdom of the den and his fellow-prisoners, do you not suppose that he would felicitate himself on the change, and pity them?

They would then pity their old companions of the den.

Certainly, he would.

And if they were in the habit of conferring honours among themselves on those who were quickest to observe the passing shadows and to remark which of them went before, and which followed after, and which were together; and who were therefore best able to draw conclusions as to the future, do you think that he would care for such honours and glories, or envy the possessors of them? Would he not say with Homer, "Better to be the poor servant of a poor master," and to endure anything, rather than think as they do and live after their manner?

Yes, he said, I think that he would rather suffer anything than entertain those false notions and live in this miserable manner.

Imagine once more, I said, such an one coming suddenly out of the sun to be replaced in his old situation; would he not be certain to have his eyes full of darkness?

To be sure, he said.

And if there were a contest, and he had to compete in measuring the shadows with the prisoners who had never moved out of the den, while his sight was still weak, and before his eyes had become steady (and the time which would be needed to acquire this new habit of sight might be very considerable), would he not be ridiculous? Men would say of him that up he went and down he came without his eyes; and that it was better not even to think of ascending; and if any one tried to loose another and lead him up to the light, let them only catch the offender, and they would put him to death.

But when they returned to the den they would see much worse than those who had never left it.

No question, he said.

This entire allegory, I said, you may not append, dear Glaucon, to the previous argument; the prison-house is the world of sight, the light of the fire is the sun, and you

The prison is the world of sight, the light of the fire is the sun.

25

30

35

will not misapprehend me if you interpret the journey
upwards to be the ascent of the soul into the intellectual
world according to my poor belief, which, at your desire, I
have expressed—whether rightly or wrongly God knows.
But, whether true or false, my opinion is that in the world
of knowledge the idea of good appears last of all, and is
seen only with an effort; and when seen, is also inferred to
be the universal author of all things beautiful and right,
parent of light and of the lord of light in this visible world,
and the immediate source of reason and truth in the intellectual; and that this is the power upon which he who
would act rationally either in public or private life must
have his eye fixed.

I agree, he said, as far as I am able to understand you.

Questions for Discussion and Writing

1. Why do the prisoners in the cave believe the shadows on the wall are real?
   Why would a prisoner who was released and allowed to leave the cave be
   unwilling to believe that what he is seeing is real? After his eyes adjust to the
   light, what will he think about his former life inside the cave?

2. If the prisoner returns to the cave and is unable to see in the dark as well as
   the others, how would they respond to his report of a greater light outside?
   Why would they be unwilling to allow other prisoners to follow him
   outside?

3. Plato used this allegory as a teaching tool. If you were one of his philosophy
   students, what would the allegorical equivalence or meaning of the cave, the
   prisoners, the fire, the shadow, and the sun make you realize about the human
   condition? What do you think Plato means when he says that the sun is like
   the "idea of good" that "appears last of all, and is seen only with an effort"?

MATTHEW

In the Gospels—that is, in the four biographies of Jesus in The New Testament *that are attributed to Matthew, Mark, Luke, and John—parables are short illustrative narratives and figurative statements. The teaching that Christ gives in* The New Testament *takes different forms.
The form in which the language of parables is cast is designed to create a bridge between the part
of the mind that responds to the literal and the normally undeveloped capacities for spiritual reflection. The fact that the language in parables can be taken in two ways is meant to stimulate an
awareness of this higher dimension. In the thirteenth chapter of Matthew, Christ begins to speak*

in parables to the multitude[1]. His disciples ask why he suddenly has begun to use parables, and he responds that it is because he is speaking about the kingdom of heaven—that is, about a spiritual reality that would be impossible to grasp otherwise. The Parable of the Sower and the Seed is the starting point of Christ's teaching about the kingdom of heaven. Not surprisingly, this master parable is about the way people differ in their capacity to understand this teaching. Differences in receptivity are presented in the parable by analogy as differences in the kinds of ground or earth into which the seed is sown: the wayside, stony places, ground where the seed does not take root, seed planted among thorns, and varying quantities of harvest grown from the seed. From this analysis of capacity for receiving the teachings, there follow parables about the Grain of Mustard Seed, the Woman and the Leaven, the Wheat and the Tares, the Net, the Pearl of Great Price, and the Net Cast into the Sea. Each in its own way deals with the kingdom of heaven and the teaching concerning it. The twentieth chapter of Matthew, in the Parable of the Laborers in the Vineyard, presents a seemingly paradoxical idea that challenges conventional concepts of what is just and what is unjust. Laborers who have spent a whole day in the scorching heat of the fields are aghast that those who have simply labored one hour are paid the same. The parable teaches that the kingdom of heaven cannot be thought of in terms of conventional rewards. The seeming injustice of the parable—that those who work longer do not gain a greater reward— hints that the kingdom of heaven has to do with eternity. The context in which the parable is given suggests that it is meant as an answer to the disciples who have abandoned all they had to follow Jesus and now want a reward in the conventional sense.

Parables in The New Testament

CHAPTER 13

The same day went Jesus out of the house, and sat by the sea side.

2 And great multitudes were gathered together unto him, so that he went into a ship, and sat; and the whole multitude stood on the shore.

3 And he spake many things unto them in parables, saying, Behold, a sower went forth to sow:

4 And when he sowed, some seeds fell by the way side, and the fowls came and devoured them up.

5 Some fell upon stony places, where they had not much earth: and forthwith they sprung up, because they had no deepness of earth.

6 And when the sun was up, they were scorched; and because they had no root, they withered away.

7 And some fell among thorns; and the thorns sprung up, and choked them;

8 But other fell into good ground, and brought forth fruit, some an hundredfold, some sixtyfold, some thirtyfold.

9 Who hath ears to hear, let him hear.

---

[1] The Gospel According to St. Matthew is one of the first four books of *The New Testament*, a collection of documents from the early Christian community written in the first two centuries after Jesus. The Gospel of St. Matthew, believed to have been written between A.D. 80 and 95, stresses the ways in which Jesus fulfills the prophecies of *The Old Testament*. This Gospel also contains the Sermon on the Mount.

10 And the disciples came, and said unto him, Why speakest thou unto them in parables?

11 He answered and said unto them: Because it is given unto you to know the mysteries of the kingdom of heaven, but to them it is not given.

12 For whosoever hath, to him shall be given, and he shall have more abundance, but whosoever hath not, from him shall be taken away even that he hath.

13 Therefore speak I to them in parables: because they seeing see not; and hearing they hear not, neither do they understand.

14 And in them is fulfilled the prophecy of Esaias[2] which saith: By hearing ye shall hear, and shall not understand; and seeing ye shall see, and shall not perceive.

15 For this people's heart is waxed gross, and their ears are dull of hearing, and their eyes they have closed; lest at any time they should see with their eyes, and hear with their ears, and should understand with their heart, and should be converted, and I should heal them.

16 But blessed are your eyes, for they see; and your ears, for they hear.

17 For verily I say unto you, That many prophets and righteous men have desired to see those things which ye see, and have not seen them; and to hear those things which ye hear, and have not heard them.

18 Hear ye therefore the parable of the sower.

19 When any one heareth the word of the kingdom, and understandeth it not, then cometh the wicked one, and catcheth away that which was sown in his heart. This is he which received seed by the way side.

20 But he that received the seed into stony places, the same is he that heareth the word, and anon with joy receiveth it;

21 Yet hath he not root in himself, but dureth for a while: for when tribulation or persecution ariseth because of the word, by and by he is offended.[3]

22 He also that received seed among the thorns is he that heareth the word; and the care of this world, and the deceitfulness of riches, choke the word, and he becometh unfruitful.

23 But he that received seed into the good ground is he that heareth the word, and understandeth it; which also beareth fruit, and bringeth forth, some an hundredfold, some sixty, some thirty.

24 Another parable put he forth unto them, saying, The kingdom of heaven is likened unto a man which sowed good seed in his field.

25 But while men slept, his enemy came and sowed tares among the wheat, and went his way.[4]

26 But when the blade was sprung up, and brought forth fruit, then appeared the tares also.

---

[2] *Esaias:* Isaiah 5:9–10.   [3] *Offended:* falls away.   [4] *Tares:* a noxious weed, probably the darnel.

27 So the servants of the householder came and said unto him, Sir, didst not thou sow good seed in thy field? from whence then hath it tares?

28 He said unto them, An enemy hath done this. The servants said unto him, Wilt thou then that we go and gather them up?

29 But he said, Nay; lest while ye gather up the tares, ye root up also the wheat with them.

30 Let both grow together until the harvest; and in the time of harvest I will say to the reapers, Gather ye together first the tares, and bind them in bundles to burn them: but gather the wheat into my barn.

31 Another parable put he forth unto them, saying, The kingdom of heaven is like to a grain of mustard seed, which a man took, and sowed in his field:

32 Which indeed is the least of all seeds: but when it is grown, it is the greatest among herbs, and becometh a tree, so that the birds of the air come and lodge in the branches thereof.

33 Another parable spake he unto them: The kingdom of heaven is like unto leaven, which a woman took, and hid in three measures of meal, till the whole was leavened.

34 All these things spake Jesus unto the multitude in parables; and without a parable spake he not unto them,

35 That it might be fulfilled which was spoken by the prophet, saying, I will open my mouth in parables; I will utter things which have been kept secret from the foundation of the world.

36 Then Jesus sent the multitude away, and went into the house: and his disciples came unto him, saying, Declare unto us the parable of the tares of the field.

37 He answered and said unto them; He that soweth the good seed is the Son of man;

38 The field is the world; the good seed are the children of the kingdom; but the tares are the children of the wicked one.

39 The enemy that sowed them is the devil; the harvest is the end of the world; and the reapers are the angels.

40 As therefore the tares are gathered and burned in the fire; so shall it be in the end of this world.

41 The Son of man shall send forth his angels, and they shall gather out of his kingdom all things that offend, and them which do iniquity;

42 And shall cast them into a furnace of fire: there shall be wailing and gnashing of teeth.

43 Then shall the righteous shine forth as the sun in the kingdom of their Father. Who hath ears to hear, let him hear.

44 Again, the kingdom of heaven is like unto treasure hid in a field; the which when a man hath found, he hideth, and for joy thereof goeth and selleth all that he hath, and buyeth that field.

45 Again, the kingdom of heaven is like unto a merchant man, seeking goodly pearls:

46 Who, when he had found one pearl of great price, went and sold all that he had, and bought it.

47 Again, the kingdom of heaven is like unto a net, that was cast into the sea, and gathered of every kind:

48 Which, when it was full, they drew to shore, and sat down, and gathered the good into vessels, but cast the bad away.

49 So shall it be at the end of the world: the angels shall come forth, and sever the wicked from among the just,

50 And shall cast them into the furnace of fire: there shall be wailing and gnashing of teeth.

51 Jesus saith unto them, Have ye understood all these things? They say unto him, Yea, Lord.

52 Then said he unto them, Therefore every scribe which is instructed unto the kingdom of heaven is like unto a man that is an householder, which bringeth forth out of his treasure things new and old.

53 And it came to pass, that when Jesus had finished these parables, he departed thence.

54 And when he was come into his own country, he taught them in their synagogue, insomuch that they were astonished, and said, Whence hath this man this wisdom, and these mighty works?

55 Is not this the carpenter's son? is not his mother called Mary? and his brethren, James, and Joses, and Simon, and Judas?

56 And his sisters, are they not all with us? Whence then hath this man all these things?

57 And they were offended in him. But Jesus said unto them, A prophet is not without honour, save in his own country, and in his own house.

58 And he did not many mighty works there because of their unbelief.

CHAPTER 20

For the kingdom of heaven is like unto a man that is an householder, which went out early in the morning to hire labourers into his vineyard.

2 And when he had agreed with the labourers for a penny a day, he sent them into his vineyard.

3 And he went out about the third hour, and saw others standing idle in the marketplace,

4 And said unto them; Go ye also into the vineyard, and whatsoever is right I will give you. And they went their way.

5 Again he went out about the sixth and ninth hour, and did likewise.

6 And about the eleventh hour he went out, and found others standing idle, and saith unto them, Why stand ye here all the day idle?

7 They say unto him, Because no man hath hired us. He saith unto them, Go ye also into the vineyard; and whatsoever is right, that shall ye receive.

8 So when even was come, the lord of the vineyard saith unto his steward, Call the labourers, and give them their hire, beginning from the last unto the first.

9 And when they came that were hired about the eleventh hour, they received every man a penny.

10 But when the first came, they supposed that they should have received more; and they likewise received every man a penny.

11 And when they had received it, they murmured against the goodman of the house,

12 Saying, These last have wrought but one hour, and thou hast made them equal unto us, which have borne the burden and heat of the day.

13 But he answered one of them, and said, Friend, I do thee no wrong: didst not thou agree with me for a penny?

14 Take that thine is, and go thy way: I will give unto this last, even as unto thee.

15 Is it not lawful for me to do what I will with mine own? Is thine eye evil, because I am good?

16 So the last shall be first, and the first last: for many be called, but few chosen.

Questions for Discussion and Writing

1. What differences can you discover between the four kinds of ground described in the Parable of the Sower and the Seed and the response to Christ's teaching that is implied by each of these categories? Why would this master parable be an important starting point for an attempt to understand the other parables?

2. How does the Parable of the Laborers in the Vineyard contradict conventional ideas about justice and injustice?

3. Pick any of the parables in the preceding selection or any other in *The New Testament,* and write an essay exploring how the language of the parable functions as a bridge between literal and spiritual meanings.

THE BUDDHA

The Buddha is the title given to the founder of Buddhism, Siddhartha Gautama (563–483 B.C.), who was born into a family of great wealth and power in southern Nepal. Although reared in great luxury, Siddhartha renounced this life of privilege at the age of twenty-nine to become a wandering ascetic and to seek an answer to the problems of death and human suffering. After six years of intense spiritual discipline, he achieved enlightenment while meditating under a pipal tree at Bodh Gaya. He spent the remainder of his life teaching, and he established a community of monks to carry on his work. In the Buddha's view, bondage to the repeating cycles of birth and death and the consequent suffering are caused by desire. The method of breaking this cycle is the eightfold noble path that encompasses right views, right resolve, right speech, right action, right livelihood, right effort, right mindfulness, and right concentration. Buddhist parables are well suited to communicate important lessons or moral truths.

"Buddha-nature" and "The Way of Purification"

BUDDHA-NATURE

Once upon a time a king gathered some blind men about an elephant and asked them to tell him what an elephant was like. The first man felt a tusk and said an elephant was like a giant carrot; another happened to touch an ear and said it was like a big fan; another touched its trunk and said it was like a pestle; still another, who happened to feel its leg, said it was like a mortar; and another, who grasped its tail said it was like a rope. Not one of them was able to tell the king the elephant's real form.

In like manner, one might partially describe the nature of man but would not be able to describe the true nature of a human being, the Buddha-nature.

There is only one possible way by which the everlasting nature of man, his Buddha-nature, that can not be disturbed by worldly desires or destroyed by death, can be realized, and that is by the Buddha and the Buddha's noble teaching.

THE WAY OF PURIFICATION

At one time there lived in the Himalayas a bird with one body and two heads. Once one of the heads noticed the other head eating some sweet fruit and felt jealous and said to itself: "I will then eat poison fruit." So it ate poison and the whole bird died.

Questions for Discussion and Writing

1. How do the many different conclusions the blind men reach about the nature of the elephant reveal the partial, limited, and contradictory perceptions that are the result of their being unable to see the whole elephant? In this case, what might being blind mean in relation to the Buddha-nature of humans?
2. What aspect of human nature is illustrated in the story of the bird with one body and two heads?
3. Have you ever had an experience whose meaning could be understood more clearly in light of either of these parables? Describe this experience and what you learned about yourself from it.

Nasreddin Hodja

Nasreddin Hodja was born in Sivrihisar, Turkey, in the early thirteenth century and died in 1284 near present-day Kenya. His father was the religious leader, the imam, of his village, and Hodja, too, served as imam. Later he traveled to Aksehir, where he became a dervish and was associated with a famous Islamic mystical sect. He also served as a judge and university professor. The stories that have made Hodja immortal blend wit, common sense, ingenuousness, and ridicule to reveal certain aspects of human psychology. Today, Hodja's stories are widely known throughout Turkey, Hungary, Siberia, North Africa, and the Middle East. They are told in teahouses, schools, and caravansaries and are even broadcast on the radio. Each tale is a certain kind of joke, a joke with a moral that has long been associated with the Sufi tradition of Islamic teaching. Unlike the philosophical allegories of Plato or the spiritual parables recorded in The New Testament, *Hodja's stories use humor to surreptitiously bypass habitual patterns of thought in order to reveal a central truth about the human condition. Hodja very frequently uses the dervish technique of playing the fool. At other times, he is the embodiment of wisdom. All his stories are designed to sharpen our perceptions.*

Islamic Folk Stories

WE ARE EVEN

One day, Hodja went to a Turkish bath but nobody paid him much attention. They gave him an old bath robe and a towel. Hodja said nothing and on his way out he left a big tip. A week later, when he went back to the same bath, he was very well received. Everybody tried to help him and offered him extra services. On his way out, he left a very small tip.

"But, Hodja," they said, "Is it fair to leave such a small tip for all the attention and extra services you received?"

Hodja answered,

"Today's tip is for last week's services and last week's tip was for today's services. Now we are even."

Do As You Please

Hodja and his son were going to another village. His son was riding the donkey and Hodja was walking along. A few people were coming down the road. They stopped and pointing at his son they muttered, "Look at that! The poor old man is walking and the young boy is riding the donkey. The youth of today has no consideration!" Hodja was irritated. He told his son to come down, and he began to ride the donkey himself. Then, they saw another group of people, who remarked, "Look at that man! On a hot day like this, he is riding the donkey and the poor boy is walking."

So, Hodja pulled his son on the donkey, too. After awhile, they saw a few more people coming down the road.

"Poor animal! Both of them are riding on it and it is about to pass out."

Hodja was fed up. He and his son got down and started walking behind the donkey. Soon, they heard a few people say,

5

"Look at those stupid people. They have a donkey but won't ride it."

Finally, Hodja lost his patience. He turned to his son and said, "You see, you   10
can never please people and everybody says something behind your back. So, always do as you please."

You Believed That It Gave Birth

Hodja had borrowed his neighbour's cauldron. A few days later, he put a bowl in it and returned it. When his neighbour saw the bowl, he asked,

"What is this?"

Hodja answered,

"Your cauldron gave birth!"

His neighbour was very happy. He thanked Hodja and took the cauldron and   15
the bowl.

A few weeks later, Hodja borrowed the cauldron again but this time he didn't return it. When his neighbour came to ask for it, Hodja said,

"Your cauldron died. I am sorry."

The man was surprised.

"Oh, come on!" he said, "Cauldrons don't die."

Hodja snapped back, "Well, you believed that it gave birth, then why don't   20
you believe that it died?"

Questions for Discussion and Writing

1. How does the story "We Are Even" suggest that we should not be concerned about how others view our actions so long as we are aware of what we are doing and why we are doing it?

2. What do the experiences of Hodja and his son in "Do As You Please" tell us about human nature? Have you ever had a similar experience that led you to the same conclusion? Describe the circumstances.

3. In your view, what is the point of "You Believed That It Gave Birth"? Discuss your interpretation in a short essay. How is this or any of Hodja's stories designed to awaken people from the bonds of conditioning?

Poetry

Robert Frost

Robert Frost (1874–1963) was born in San Francisco and lived there until the age of eleven, although most people think of him as having grown up in New England. He spent his high school years in a Massachusetts mill town and studied at Harvard for two years. He worked a farm in New Hampshire that he had acquired in 1900, took a teaching job at the Pinkerton Academy, and wrote poetry that he had no luck in getting published. In 1912 he moved with his wife and five children to England, rented a farm, and met with success in publishing A Boy's Will *(1913) and* North of Boston *(1914). After the outbreak of World War I, he returned to the United States, where he was increasingly accorded recognition. He taught at Amherst College sporadically for many years. Frost won the Pulitzer Prize for poetry four times. He was a friend of John F. Kennedy, who invited him to read a poem at the presidential inauguration in 1961. Many of the qualities that made Frost's poetry so popular can be seen in "The Road Not Taken" (1916).*

The Road Not Taken

Two roads diverged in a yellow wood,
And sorry I could not travel both
And be one traveler, long I stood
And looked down one as far as I could
To where it bent in the undergrowth;   5

Then took the other, as just as fair,
And having perhaps the better claim,
Because it was grassy and wanted wear;
Though as for that the passing there
Had worn them really about the same,   10

And both that morning equally lay
In leaves no step had trodden black.
Oh, I kept the first for another day!
Yet knowing how way leads on to way,
I doubted if I should ever come back.   15

I shall be telling this with a sigh
Somewhere ages and ages hence:
Two roads diverged in a wood, and I—
I took the one less traveled by,
And that has made all the difference.   20

Questions for Discussion and Writing

1. How does Frost use a simple subject as a springboard to express a profound insight?
2. What prevents the speaker from berating himself for not having chosen a different, possibly easier, road?
3. In what way is it implied that the psychological sensibility of the speaker is more sophisticated than the anecdotal manner in which the poem is written?

DYLAN THOMAS

Dylan Thomas (1914–1953) was born in Swansea, Wales, a place that provided the setting for much of his work. He grew up hearing his father read Shakespeare, other poets, and the Bible, which began his fascination with the sound of words. He left school at fifteen, spent a brief time as a newspaper reporter, and published his first volume of poetry when he was twenty. He went on to live in London that year; married Caitlin Macnamara, with whom he had a turbulent relationship; and began publishing well-received books of poetry and short fiction. A collection of stories of his childhood, Portrait of the Artist as a Young Dog, *appeared in 1940. Thomas also wrote a number of radio plays, the most successful of which was* Under Milkwood *(published posthumously in 1954), which depicts the residents of a small Welsh town over the period of one day. Thomas's poetry, especially the volume* Deaths and Entrances *(1946), moves from the obscurity of his early verse to a simple, direct, and passionate statement about all living things moving through cycles of death and birth. "Do Not Go Gentle into That Good Night" (1952) was written at a time when Thomas's father was gravely ill and would live for only a short time.*

Do Not Go Gentle into That Good Night[1]

Do not go gentle into that good night,
Old age should burn and rave at close of day;
Rage, rage against the dying of the light.

Though wise men at their end know dark is right,
Because their words had forked no lightning they   5
Do not go gentle into that good night.

Good men, the last wave by, crying how bright
Their frail deeds might have danced in a green bay,
Rage, rage against the dying of the light.

Wild men who caught and sang the sun in flight,   10
And learn, too late, they grieved it on its way,
Do not go gentle into that good night.

Grave men, near death, who see with blinding sight
Blind eyes could blaze like meteors and be gay,
Rage, rage against the dying of the light.   15

And you, my father, there on the sad height,
Curse, bless, me now with your fierce tears, I pray.
Do not go gentle into that good night.
Rage, rage against the dying of the light.

---

[1] This poem is in the form of a villanelle, a form consisting of nineteen lines written in five tercets and a final quatrain, rhyming aba aba aba aba aba abaa. Because of the limitaions imposed by the form, many words of the poem carry a double meaning.

Questions for Discussion and Writing

1. According to the speaker, how should death be met? Why does he think it is important to have this attitude?
2. How does each of the four types of men ("wise men," "good men," "wild men," and "grave men") react to death? What motivates each in reacting the way they do?
3. How does the refrain "do not go gentle" change in meaning as this phrase is repeated throughout the course of the poem?

LISEL MUELLER

Lisel Mueller (b. 1924) came to the United States from Germany in 1939. She studied at the University of Indiana and has taught at Goddard College in Vermont. Volumes of her poems include Dependencies *(1965; reissued 1998) and* Alive Together: New and Selected Poems *(1996), which won the Pulitzer Prize and in which "Hope" first appeared. Her honors include the Carl Sandburg Award and a National Endowment for the Arts fellowship.*

Hope

It hovers in dark corners
before the lights are turned on,
   it shakes sleep from its eyes
   and drops from mushroom gills,
      it explodes in the starry heads   5
      of dandelions turned sages,
         it sticks to the wings of green angels
         that sail from the tops of maples.

It sprouts in each occluded eye
of the many-eyed potato,   10
   it lives in each earthworm segment
   surviving cruelty,

      it is the motion that runs
      from the eyes to the tail of a dog,
         it is the mouth that inflates the lungs   15
         of the child that has just been born.

It is the singular gift
We cannot destroy in ourselves,
The argument that refutes death,
The genius that invents the future,   20
All we know of God.

It is the serum which makes us swear
Not to betray one another;
It is in this poem, trying to speak.

Questions for Discussion and Writing

1. Hope is usually thought of in the abstract, but Mueller reveals its presence in a multitude of ordinary circumstances. What are some of these? Do you find her choices compelling? Why or why not?

2. Mueller makes a number of statements that would seem to require further exploration. Select one of these (for example, hope is a "serum which makes us swear/Not to betray one another"), and elaborate on her idea.

3. Discuss a few additional locations where "hope" may be found.

W. B. YEATS

William Butler Yeats (1865–1939), an Irish poet and playwright, was the son of the artist John Yeats. William initially studied painting and lived in London and in Sligo, where many of his poems are set. Fascinated by Irish legend and the occult, he became a leader of the Irish Literary Renaissance. The long poems in his early book, The Wanderings of Oisin *(1889), show an intense nationalism, a feeling strengthened by his hopeless passion for the Irish patriot Maude Gonne. In 1898 he helped to found the Irish Literary Theatre and later the Abbey Theatre. As he grew older, Yeats's poetry moved from transcendentalism to a more physical realism, and polarities between the physical and the spiritual are central in poems like "Sailing to Byzantium" and the "Crazy Jane" sequence. Some of his best work came late, in* The Tower *(1928) and Last* Poems *(1940). Yeats received the Nobel Prize for literature in 1923 and is widely considered the greatest poet of the twentieth century. The extraordinary vibrancy of Yeats's later poetry can be seen in "The Second Coming" (1919), widely acknowledged to be his signature poem.*[1]

The Second Coming

Turning and turning in the widening gyre
The falcon cannot hear the falconer;
Things fall apart; the centre cannot hold;
Mere anarchy is loosed upon the world,
The blood-dimmed tide is loosed, and everywhere   5
The ceremony of innocence is drowned;

---

[1] The return ("second coming") of Christ is prophesied in the New Testament (Matthew 24). Here the return is not of Jesus but of a terrifying inhuman embodiment of pre-Christian and pre-Grecian barbarism. The poem is a sharply prophetic response to the turmoil of Europe following World War I.

The best lack all conviction, while the worst
Are full of passionate intensity.
Surely some revelation is at hand;
Surely the Second Coming is at hand.   10
The Second Coming! Hardly are those words out
When a vast image out of *Spiritus Mundi*[2]
Troubles my sight: somewhere in sands of the desert
A shape with lion body and the head of a man,

A gaze blank and pitiless as the sun,   15
Is moving its slow thighs, while all about it
Reel shadows of the indignant desert birds.
The darkness drops again; but now I know
That twenty centuries of stony sleep
Were vexed to nightmare by a rocking cradle,   20
And what rough beast, its hour come round at last,
Slouches towards Bethlehem to be born?

Questions for Discussion and Writing

1. How do the images with which the poem begins suggest to the speaker that
   the conditions prophesied in the New Testament (Matthew 24) signify the
   second coming of Christ? How does the vision that suddenly appears refute
   this expectation?
2. What is the relationship between the birth of Christ 2,000 years before and the
   risen Sphinx "slouching" over the desert? How would you characterize the
   shift in the emotional state of the speaker throughout the course of the poem?
3. What aspects of this "rough beast" suggest to the speaker that a new age of
   barbarism is about to begin with the twentieth century?

Connections for Chapter 11:
Matters of Ethics, Philosophy
and Religion

1. **Clarence Darrow,** *The Myth of Immortality*
   Darrow is skeptical about the existence of a soul that survives death, although
   he acknowledges the powerful emotional need such a belief fulfills. Compare

---

[2] *Spiritus Mundi (Latin):* Spirits of the World, that is, archetypal images in the "Great Memory" of
the human psyche.

his arguments in "The Myth of Immortality" with the teachings presented in the parables of *The New Testament*. Which do you find more compelling, and why?

2. **Dinitia Smith,** *Did a Barnyard Schism Lead to a Religious One?*
   In what respects do both Smith and Hans Ruesch (in "Slaughter of the Innocent") argue for a fundamental reassessment of the value of animals (used for sacramental or scientific purposes)? In what sense do both authors demythologize the belief systems of organized religions and experimental science in regard to animals?

3. **Hans Ruesch,** *Slaughter of the Innocent*
   In "Slaughter of the Innocent," Ruesch condemns vivisectionists as sadists who are untroubled by ethical issues raised by animal experimentation. In what respects might his beliefs be compatible with those of Buddhists (see "Parables of Buddha")?
   In what respects does Carol Grunewald's argument against the genetic engineering of animals (in "Monsters of the Brave New World" Chapter 9) explore the moral issues that Ruesch raises in connection with vivisection?

4. **Garrett Hardin,** *Lifeboat Ethics: The Case against Helping the Poor*
   To what extent does the conflict between enlightened self-interest and consideration of others that Hardin sees as the crux of the lifeboat dilemma enter into H. G. Wells's story?

5. **Stephen Chapman,** *The Prisoner's Dilemma*
   In what way is Tim O'Brien's likely future—lifelong exile or a short, but possibly fatal, tour in Vietnam—comparable to the prisoner's dilemma?

6. **Tim O'Brien,** *If I Die in a Combat Zone*
   In what respects do O'Brien and Daru in Albert Camus's story "The Guest" (Chapter 8) confront similiar choices as to the allegiance that they owe the state?

7. **Langston Hughes,** *Salvation*
   In what sense is Hughes's situation analogous to Tim O'Brien's in terms of the expectations of his family and society?
   Gayle Pemberton's grandmother (see "Antidisestablishmentarianism" in Chapter 2) and Hughes's aunt greatly influenced each of the authors. Compare the lessons each child learned from the adults.

8. **H. G. Wells,** *The Country of the Blind*
   Analyze some of the ways in which Plato's "The Allegory of the Cave" can be considered a model for this story. How is Nunez's predicament similar to that of the prisoners in the cave?
   How does Wells's story illustrate the nature of choice depicted in Robert Frost's poem "The Road Not Taken"?

9. **Joyce Carol Oates,** *Where Are You Going, Where Have You Been?*
   How does Oates's characterization of Connie underscore her longing for the "road not taken," as in Robert Frost's poem?
   In what sense has Connie evoked her own version of the "rough beast" portrayed by W. B. Yeats in "The Second Coming"?

Although not religious in a conventional sense, Connie acts selflessly. Compare her motivations with those of Langston Hughes in "Salvation."

10. **Plato,** *The Allegory of the Cave*
    Compare Plato's allegory (as a method for teaching about the nature of absolute good) with the parables in the New Testament about the nature of the kingdom of heaven. How do both works convey subtle concepts that are hard to grasp?

11. ***Matthew*** *Parables in The New Testament*
    What similarities can you discover between any of the parables and Anna Kamieńska's depiction of the human condition in her poem "Funny" (in Chapter 1)?

12. **The Buddha,** *"Buddha-nature" and "The Way of Purification"*
    Compare the lessons about human nature communicated in Buddha's parables with those conveyed by Nasreddin Hodja's stories.
    How does Buddha's parable about the elephant illuminate Raymond Carver's story "What We Talk About When We Talk About Love" in Chapter 4?
    What lessons about the effects of jealousy are related in Buddha's second parable, compared with Jerzy Kosinski's short work of fiction "The Miller's Tale" in Chapter 1?

13. **Nasreddin Hodja,** *Islamic Folk Stories*
    What similarities can you discover between Hodja's teaching methods and those of George Gurdjieff as described by Fritz Peters in "Boyhood with Gurdjieff" (Chapter 1)?
    Hodja as a teaching figure is a homespun, down-to-earth "wise fool" who strongly contrasts with the elevated figures of Christ and Buddha. Discuss the personalities of these three figures in terms of their messages to humanity.

14. **Robert Frost,** *The Road Not Taken*
    How does Václav Havel's play *Protest* (in Chapter 8) dramatize the nature of the choice depicted in Frost's poem?

15. **Lisel Mueller,** *Hope*
    In what sense is Joyce Carol Oates's story about "hope"—in the sense that Mueller means it in her poem?
    What different strategies do Mueller and Anna Kamieńska (see "Funny" in Chapter 1) use in their poems to characterize the human condition?

15. **Dylan Thomas,** *Do Not Go Gentle into That Good Night*
    What similarities and differences in attitudes toward mortality are conveyed in this poem and in Guy de Maupassant's story "An Old Man" in Chapter 5?

16. **W. B. Yeats,** *The Second Coming*
    In what ways do both Yeats and Joyce Carol Oates (in her story "Where Are You Going, Where Have You Been?") use misdirection to create suspense? What role does religious symbolism play in both works?

CREDITS

Golda Meir, "We Have Our State" from *My Life.* Copyright © 1975 by Golda Meir. Reprinted with the permission of The Putnam Publishing Group, Inc.

Fatima Mernissi, "Moonlit Nights of Laughter" from *Dreams of Trespass: Tales of a Harem Girlhood.* Copyright © 1994 by Fatima Mernissi. Reprinted with the permission of Perseus Books Publishers, a member of Perseus Books L.L.C.

Lance Morrow, "Advertisements for Oneself" from *Fishing in the Tiber.* Copyright © 1988 by Lance Morrow. Reprinted with the permission of Henry Holt and Company, Inc.

Lisel Mueller, "Hope" from *Alive Together: New and Selected Poems.* Copyright © 1996 by Lisel Mueller. Reprinted with the permission of Louisiana State University Press.

Alice Munro, "What Is Real?" from *Making It New: Contemporary Canadian Stories,* edited by John Metcalf (London: Methuen, 1982). Copyright © 1982 by Alice Munro. Reprinted with the permission of Virginia Barber Literary Agency, Inc.

Jill Nelson, "Number One!" from *Volunteer Slavery.* Copyright © 1993 by Jill Nelson. Reprinted with the permission of the Faith Childs Literary Agency.

Joyce Carol Oates, "Where Are You Going, Where Have You Been?" from *The Wheel of Love and Other Stories.* Copyright © 1970 by Joyce Carol Oates. Reprinted with the permission of John Hawkins & Associates, Inc.

Tim O'Brien, "If I Die in a Combat Zone" from *If I Die in a Combat Zone: Box Me Up And Ship Me Home.* Copyright © 1973 by Tim O'Brien. Reprinted with the permission of Dell Publishing, a division of Random House, Inc.

Mary Oliver, "Sleeping in the Forest" from *Twelve Moons.* Originally published in The Ohio Review. Copyright © 1978 by Mary Oliver. Reprinted with the permission of Little, Brown & Company.

P. J. O'Rourke, "The Greenhouse Affect" from Rolling Stone (June 28, 1990). Copyright © 1990 by P. J. O'Rourke. Reprinted with the permission of P. J. O'Rourke.

P. D. Ouspensky, "The Taj Mahal" (editors' title, originally titled "The Soul of the Empress Mumtaz-I-Mahal") from *A New Model of the Universe.* Copyright © 1971 by P. D. Ouspensky. Reprinted with the permission of Random House, Inc.

Gayle Pemberton, "Antidisestablishmentarianism" from *The Hottest Water in Chicago* (Boston: Faber and Faber, 1992). Copyright © 1992 by Gayle Pemberton. Reprinted with the permission of the author.

Fritz Peters, "Boyhood with Gurdjieff" from *My Journey With a Mystic.* Copyright © 1964 by Fritz Peters. Reprinted with the permission of Tale Weaver Publishing

Marge Piercy, "Barbie Doll" from *Circles on the Water.* Copyright © 1982 by Marge Piercy. Reprinted with the permission of Alfred A. Knopf, a division of Random House, Inc.

Neil Postman and Steve Powers, "TV News As Entertainment" from *How to Watch TV News.* Copyright © 1992 by Neil Postman and Steve Powers. Reprinted with the permission of Viking Penguin, a division of Penguin Putnam Inc.

Hans Reusch, "Slaughter of the Innocent" from *Slaughter of the Innocent.* Copyright © 1978 by Bantam Books, Inc. Reprinted with the permission of Bantam Books, a division of Random House, Inc.

Richard Rodriguez, "On Becoming a Chicano." Copyright © 1975 by Richard Rodriguez. Reprinted with the permission of Georges Borchardt, Inc. on behalf of the author.

David Rothenberg, "How the Web Destroys the Quality of Students' Research Papers" from The Chronicle of Higher Education (August 15, 1997). Copyright © 1997 by David A. Rothenberg. Reprinted with the permission of the author.

Juliet B. Schor, "The Culture of Consumerism" from *The Overspent American: Upscaling, Downshifting, and the New Consumer.* Copyright © 1998 by Juliet B. Schor. Reprinted with the permission of Basic Books, a member of Perseus Books, L.L.C.

Peggy Seeger, "I'm Gonna Be An Engineer." Copyright © 1976 by STORMKING MUSIC, Inc. Reprinted by permission. All rights reserved.

Luis Sepulveda, excerpt from *Full Circle: A South American Journey,* translated by Chris Andrews. Copyright © 1996. Reprinted with the permission of Lonely Planet Publications.

Linda Simon, "The Naked Source" from "Inquiry," Michigan Quarterly Review, Vol. XXVII, No. 3 (Summer 1988). Reprinted with the permission of the author.

Joseph K. Skinner, "Big Mac and the Tropical Forests," Monthly Review (1985). Copyright © 1985 by Monthly Review Press. Reprinted with the permission of Monthly Review Foundation.

Philip Slater, "Want-Creation Fuels American's Addictiveness" from Newsday (September 2, 1984). Copyright © 1984 by Philip Slater. Reprinted with the permission of the author.

David R. Slavitt, "Titanic" from *Big Nose.* Copyright © 1981 by David R. Slavitt. Reprinted with the permission of Louisiana State University Press.

INDEX